BRIAN G. JACKSON
17 SAW MILL DR
SOMERSET, NJ 08873

Win32 Programming

Addison-Wesley Advanced Windows Series

Alan Feuer, Series Editor

The **Addison-Wesley Advanced Windows Series** focuses on programming for the 32-bit Windows Operating Systems. The series provides experienced programmers with practical books that are technically sophisticated. Each book covers in detail a specific aspect of Windows programming and contains interesting sample programs that can be used as a springboard for writing other applications. A CD-ROM accompanies many texts, containing the source code described in the text, pertinent reference material, useful tools, and links to related sites on the Internet.

Titles in the series:

Brent E. Rector, *Component Development with ATL*, 0-201-69589-8

Alan Feuer, *MFC Programming*, 0-201-63358-2

Brent E. Rector and Joseph M. Newcomer, *Win32 Programming*, 0-201-63492-9

Johnson M. Hart, *Win32 System Programming*, 0-201-63465-1

Chris Sells, *Win32 Telephony Programming: A Developer's Guide to TAPI*, 0-201-63450-3

Bob Quinn and Dave Shute, *Windows™ Sockets Network Programming*, 0-201-63372-8

Please see our web site (http://www.awl.com/cseng/series/advwinser) for more information on these titles.

Win32 Programming

Brent E. Rector
and
Joseph M. Newcomer

ADDISON-WESLEY

An imprint of Addison Wesley Longman, Inc.

Reading, Massachusetts • Harlow, England • Menlo Park, California
Berkeley, California • Don Mills, Ontario • Sydney
Bonn • Amsterdam • Tokyo • Mexico City

The publisher offers discounts on this book when ordered in quantity for special sales.

For more information, please contact:

Corporate & Professional Publishing Group
Addison Wesley Longman, Inc.
One Jacob Way
Reading, Massachusetts 01867

ISBN 0-201-63492-9

4 5 6 7 8 9 CRW 01009998

4th printing, December 1998

Contents

4 Displaying Text in a Window   153

5 Examining a Device Context in Depth   219

Figures

Tables

Listings

Preface

How do you write a book this long? Simple. One page at a time.

I wish I'd understood that better when I started.

Addison Wesley Longman approached me over a year ago, asking if I'd be interested in helping revise a book on Windows programming. I had met the original author, Brent Rector, in a course taught by Technology Exchange Company, for whom Brent and I are both instructors; I was taking his OLE Automation course preparatory to teaching it. Brent and I share a lot of strong opinions on the "right" way to write Windows code. Mike Hendrickson, our editor at AWL, didn't know that we knew each other when he approached me.

Brent's original book was interesting. I wish I'd had it when I started programming Windows. His insight into what makes a real Windows program is something that stands out. So when I started the revisions, I started with what was in my opinion an excellent basis for the new 32-bit edition.

Organizationally and philosophically, I was right. I've adopted Brent's style of writing, which is much more straightforward and less formal than mine and I think much more readable (the remnants of passive voice you find are my reverting to type–I'm an ex-academic). But Win32, compared to Win16, is bigger and more interesting, in some cases much easier to explain, while in others much harder. I didn't know what I was getting into! At the detail level, I had to examine every sentence for correctness in the Win32 environment. If you own one of Brent's Win16 editions, you'll see that there is tremendous similarity in many sections between this edition and the earlier ones. But it still took a lot of work. I wanted this book to have the same strength in Win32 that his earlier editions brought to the GUI in general and Win16 in particular. That was a hard standard to meet. I hope I've succeeded.

For someone who has been programming Windows since the release of 3.0, I thought I understood much of the GUI. Surprise! When I found I had to write about it, I had to get everything *right*. You, the reader, are depending on me to do that. And there was *so much* new stuff to write about! I started writing little programs to test various features. Being a lazy programmer, I wrote them so that they were easily extended and configured for new tests. For the same reason, I wrote them largely in C++/MFC. After I'd written about 30,000 lines of code or so, it occurred to me that if I found these programs useful and informative, *you* probably would also. Hence the idea of the Explorers. These are the programs I used to check out the features so that I could write about them competently. The result is over 150,000 lines of code for you to play with. The sheer volume of code required is the main reason they're in C++. While programming Windows in C is what this book is about, we don't actually advocate that you do this. Brent, Alan Feuer (the series editor, who is writing a book on C++/MFC), and I all use C++/MFC by preference. It makes us so much more productive. No, it is not the Universal Solution To Everything, and in fact for some applications, it is simply the wrong tool entirely. But for the bulk of what you want to do, you should learn C++ and MFC.

So why do you need a book on plain C programming, when even the authors don't want to use it? Because underlying that lovely C++/MFC facade is the real nitty-gritty of the Windows API. As you read the source code for the Explorers, you will even see places where I've had to use subterfuge to fool MFC into cooperating with me, and this subterfuge is in C. And there's another reason: MFC is a *big* system. A book on how to program using MFC is going to be quite large, and it will hardly touch on any of the topics we cover here.

Learning GDI in detail, really understanding window subclassing (MFC does the subclassing for you, mostly correctly, but oh, when it fails . . .), the details of font creation, covering all the events for the controls–you won't find that in most MFC books. In fact, Alan Feuer did his book knowing he could reference ours when you need all the details. The syntax and some superficial details change a bit when you move to MFC, but the basic concepts we describe here are at a level of detail you won't find in many other places.

And, for a number of applications, or special cases of general MFC applications, MFC is not the right tool. For example, NT System Services are usually best coded in C because you have better control over such details as storage fragmentation, which can ultimately kill a service. For certain high-performance tasks, where efficiency *really* matters, MFC puts too much overhead in the path of some operations. If this is the overhead that matters to you, you may want to either use plain C or code that part of your MFC application in plain C. And that's where you need this book.

Doing a book like this is an adventure. Remember adventure: that which happens to other people, far away. Ask those other people what "adventure" is like. Well, there's a lot of mud, and mosquitoes, and carnivorous native fauna that either objects to what they're doing or sees them as an exotic new food source. Testing everything under three different operating systems (Windows NT 3.51, Windows NT 4.0 and Windows 95) was by itself an effort more massive than I anticipated. Getting all the illustrations to work, doing the final layout (in a system prone to crash when you need a floating text frame), and getting an install program that makes your installation of the CD-ROM software go smoothly were all at the mud-and-mosquitoes level. But the result, I hope, is that you now know the Source of the Nile (or at least can read the source of the Nile . . . sorry, I couldn't resist that . . .) and don't have to go through the mud yourself to see it.

There are a lot of people to thank for this book. Mike Hendrickson, at Addison Wesley Longman, for his infinite patience in what became a months-longer-than-ever-imagined task. Alan Feuer, series editor, who read and commented on drafts of many of the chapters. Jake Callery helped convert some of the chapters from Microsoft Word to Adobe FrameMaker (a non-trivial effort that ultimately took months), and helped in the preparation of the CD-ROM installation software. Laura Michaels, our copy editor, whose excellent work made the whole book more coherent. Avanda Peters, production coordinator at AWL, who kept me on schedule at the end. And of course my co-author, Brent Rector, whose massive initial investment of time in the first two 16-bit editions of this book made this edition possible, and who read and commented on many of the chapters. I hate to think of how hard this would have been to do from scratch without his excellent material as the core. (He also completely rewrote Chapter 2 and the Skeleton, Template, Keyboard Explorer, Towers of Hanoi, Menu, Registry, ToolBar, and Version programs for this edition.)

This is where most authors thank their cat. I especially thank The Little Gray Cat (a.k.a. Bernadette Callery) for her patience and tolerance during the last several months. A relationship that can withstand the trials and tribulations of writing a book, even after thirty years together, is True Love indeed.

So in spite of the mud and mosquitoes, the adventure was fun. It's a lot more fun to look back on from the comfort of home. You're about to embark on your own adventures of Windows programming. I hope the maps we give in this atlas keep you on the path to your goal. We've even tried to tell you where the quicksand is. But there's more than enough out there for more adventures. Have fun.

In memory of Jim Miller and Steve Hoffman. Genuinely good people who contributed directly to my ability to do this book. They each died too young, and for the wrong reasons.

Joseph M. Newcomer
Pittsburgh, PA
October, 1996
newcomer@flounder.com

To my wife, Lisa, who both encourages and prods me when necessary during the seeming eternity required for me to complete a book. We are, as always, a team. To my daughter, Carly, and son, Sean, who tried very hard not to interfere too much while I was working. You failed miserably on occasion, but I love you all the more for it.

Brent E. Rector
San Diego, CA
October, 1996
brent@wiseowl.com

Welcome

Welcome to our book. This book is aimed at three audiences, and we have tried to orient it that way:

- The experienced C programmer who is new to Windows.

- The experienced Windows 16-bit programmer who wants to learn Win32.

- The experienced Win32 programmer who wants to know more.

We didn't want to do a book that was useful in your first month of programming and then would sit on the shelf. We wanted a book that would continue to be a useful reference for you for years. To accomplish this, we have gone into depth in a number of selected areas, and provided example code for you to either directly experiment with or use as the basis of your own code. As you move from "pure C" programming to C++, you will find many useful classes lurking in our C++ application code.

C++ code in a book on C programming? Yes. Go read the introductory remarks on page xxxv as to why this makes sense. But sooner or later you will end up programming in C++, so we've provided plenty of example code for you.

We also wanted programs that had depth as well as flash, and that themselves would continue to be useful to you. This collection of programs, the Explorers, allows you to poke and prod at real, live Windows objects, sending them messages and seeing what effects you get or what results are returned. It is often easier to conduct a "quick experiment" in an Explorer than try to debug a very complex interaction in the context of your own program. Since I (*jmn*) wrote the Explorers, I've used them myself to test out sequences in code that I'm writing for other purposes than this book, and I've found them quite useful.

Because of the depth and breadth of information we give on topics like controls and the GDI, we hope that this book will continue to be a valuable reference.

Tools Required

You can't do anything without the right tools. If you're new to Windows programming, here's a list of *some* of the tooling that will make your life easier:

- A C and/or C++ development environment. All our examples were done under the Microsoft product environments, our environment of choice, but there are many options out there and you should choose one that you like.

- The Microsoft Development Network (MSDN) CD-ROMs. These CD-ROMs were invaluable in writing this book, as they go well beyond the printed Windows documentation you can buy from Microsoft (they contain nearly all of the printed documentation as a subset). They are full of articles and sample code, and even contain bug reports. In our opinion, this is the single most important tool (beyond the compiler) a Windows programmer can own. Microsoft has offered this in a variety of configurations, from a once-only low-priced version to an extensive annual subscription encompassing their entire product line. The precise offerings available will depend upon what packaging their marketing department chooses to offer, and has changed often enough that we won't even list the current options here. Which level you choose will depend on what is available, at what price, and what you need. But *not* having it is almost like trying to program with a broken keyboard and a red-letters-on-blue-background color scheme. (While our book is clearly thick, the lowest level MSDN gives you something equivalent to about six feet of documentation. But we can also attest to the fact that, having used it to write this book, some of it is quite hard to understand–my favorite description is "all of the facts and none of the truth"–and that's what we've distilled here for you).

- Extended debuggers. There are several of these, but the one we use extensively and rely upon is a program called Bounds Checker for Windows, from Nu-Mega Technologies. This particular product integrates into Microsoft's development environment and provides diagnostics and analysis information that goes beyond what an ordinary debugger can give.

- A lint program. While the purpose of the original lint program was to provide cross-module type checking of parameters in the days before ANSI function prototypes, the new lint programs are extremely sophisticated diagnostic tools. My *(jmn)* favorite is Gimpel's C++ lint. It is an excellent Quality Assurance QA tool.

- Test driver software. Microsoft Test is a product that allows you to build test scripts so you don't have to keep testing the same sequences "by hand" each time, and makes it possible to do serious QA regression tests on product releases.

There are even some serious luxuries that the hard-core developer might desire:

- Dual displays. This makes it possible to debug your application on one display while watching the debugger on another display. A number of hardware vendors sell display cards that can be configured to support multiple display cards in a single computer. These are currently supported only under Windows NT, but the availability of Windows 95 support will be determined by the market and technical issues.

- A second computer. A somewhat more expensive solution than the dual displays, this allows you to run the debugger on one machine while running the application on another machine. The debugger is network-aware and can run over your LAN or over two machines connected via their serial ports.

There are many other optional tools you will discover; the market is large enough that new vendors regularly produce interesting and useful utilities and debugging aids for developers. Depending upon what you do, these packages range from uninteresting to invaluable, and only you can determine where any particular product lies within this range. The specific products we've suggested above have a more universal appeal, and we feel they are important to any developer. The tools we've mentioned are those we have actively used; there are so many good tools out there that we cannot possibly identify and test each one.

Typeface Conventions

The following typeface conventions will be used throughout the book.

Example	Explanation
`Symbol font`	This font is used for all API symbols, C source code references, and the like.
Menu font	This font is used to indicate selections from a menu, or a control caption, typically for a pushbutton, check box, or the like.
Key font	This font is used to indicate a key on the keyboard. When two keys must be pressed, the + sign is used; for example, **Ctrl+N** or **Alt+A**.
filename.font	This font is used for file names.
`lowerCaseName`	Names that we defined in programs almost always (except when constrained by the rules of Windows or certain stylistic conventions we don't want to violate) start with a lower case letter. So if you see a function name starting with a lower case letter, but which contains upper case letters, it is not a Windows API function; you'll find it somewhere in our source code.

Icons for Insertions

We have done a number of text insets. These elaborate on points that have specific audiences, and rather than put everything inline in the text, we have pulled some discussions out into these sidebar-like annotations. To clue you as to their relevance, we have a series of icons that we use to indicate the contents.

This indicates a potential bug. Sometimes it is a bug in the documentation, sometimes it is a bug in a particular release of the operating system.

This indicates some informational aside. The information may be useful to you, but it is not as important as the main-line text.

This indicates a potential pitfall. Often it is a compatibility issue, such as a Win16/Win32 difference that is otherwise undocumented, or obscurely documented, or a difference between two Win32 versions. Occasionally, we use it to indicate other possible failures that would otherwise be hard to discover. These failures include obscure or undocumented limitations, or places where you are likely to get into trouble In some cases, the behavior of a Windows operation is not "intuitively obvious", and if you do what you think is "right", it won't work as expected.

 This indicates that there is a potential hazard. You should take note of this when using the related material.

 This indicates something that a Win16 programmer should take note of. Generally, it indicates a situation in which the behavior of Win32 is sufficiently different from the behavior of Win16 that, if you are accustomed to thinking in Win16 terms, you will have either an unpleasant surprise or at least a disconcerting experience.

 This indicates something that is an interesting feature of Win32. It is very similar to the signal about Win16, but the Win16 notes explain the problem primarily from the viewpoint of a Win16 programmer in Win16 terms and this tends to explain the difference in terms of Win32.

 This indicates a situation in which the behavior of the Win32s subsystem that runs on Win16 is different from the behavior of a "native" Win32 operating environment. If you plan to run your application on Win32s, you should take note of whatever is discussed.

 This represents a feature that is different in Windows 95 when compared to either Windows NT 3.5*x* or Windows NT 4.*x*. It often indicates compatibility problems between the two systems that would otherwise not be evident, or that we wish to emphasize.

 This indicates that the feature discussion is pointing out something specific to Windows NT, compared to Windows 95 or Win32s.

 This indicates a feature which is unique to Windows NT and is not defined in Windows 95 or Win32s.

1 Introduction to Windows Concepts

What Is Windows?

Microsoft Windows is a graphical environment. The early versions of Windows, those prior to 3.1, ran on an Intel 8088, 8086, 80286, 80386, or 80486 processor with at least 640K of conventional memory and as little as 2MB of total memory. Windows 3.1 required at least an 80286 processor and 4MB of total memory. Windows 95 in its initial release requires an 80386 or higher processor with at least 4MB of memory. The earlier versions of Windows ran on MS-DOS or PC-DOS version 3.1 or

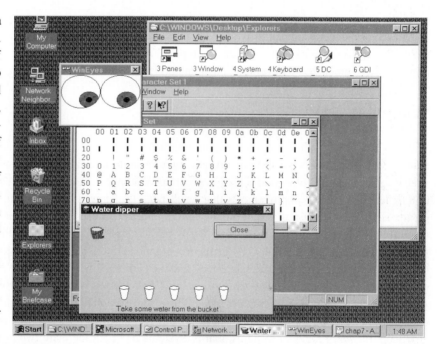

Figure 1.1: A view of the Windows desktop

later; Windows 95 contains its own underlying support and will not run on any other version of DOS. Windows NT is a complete operating system without any underlying DOS (although it emulates a significant fraction of DOS, there is no actual DOS present) and requires an 80386 or higher processor with at least 16MB of memory. Both Windows 95 and Windows NT represent a new and significant improvement over the older versions of Windows (3.1 and Windows for Workgroups 3.11) in that they support programs that use the native 32-bit instruction set of the computers. This makes programming simpler and programs run faster.

Windows provides a multitasking graphical windowing environment that runs multiple applications simultaneously. Each application displays all output in a rectangular area of the computer screen called a *window*. The entire computer screen is referred to as the *desktop*. A user can arrange windows on the desktop in a manner similar to placing pieces of paper on an actual desk. For example, you can run two programs in adjacent windows while other programs are temporarily set aside, as shown in Figure 1.1. All the programs in the figure are running, even those set aside as icons. Although most applications are idle when the user isn't interacting with them, some applications may be working even when iconic. For example, a spreadsheet application might continue to recalculate the values of a spreadsheet while iconic. A communications program, email reader, or other type of communication program may continue to read modem or network messages and process them even when it is iconic.

For you, the programmer, Windows provides a rich programming environment that supplies extensive support for developing easy-to-use and consistent user interfaces. Menus, dialog boxes, list boxes, scroll bars, push buttons, and other components of a user interface are supplied to the developer by Windows. Windows provides device-independent graphics, thereby allowing you to write programs without having detailed knowledge of the hardware platform on which they will eventually run. This device independence extends to the basic hardware devices on a personal computer. A programmer also can access the keyboard, mouse, printer, system timer, and serial communication ports in a device-independent manner.

What Is Win32?

Win32 is a *family* of Windows programming interfaces. It is the standard programming interface for Windows 95 and Windows NT. The Win32 Application Program Interface (API) is specified in terms of 32-bit values, rather than the 16-bit values used to program Windows 3.*x* and earlier versions of Windows. In addition to the performance improvements that result from the larger integer size, the use of 32-bit addresses greatly simplifies that task of programming. Programmers work in a "flat" 32-bit address space, instead of the 16-bit "segmented" addresses of the older Windows versions. The Win32 API also includes many new functions. For example, the Win95 API supports graphical operations such as Bézier curves and the use of (restricted) graphical transformation matrices, and the kernel allows you to create powerful and flexible programs by using a capability called *multithreading*. The Windows NT API supports everything in the Win95 API as well as more powerful graphics capabilities (for example, graphics coordinates greater than 65,536 units and fully general transformation matrices) and sophisticated file protection and sharing. Windows NT also supports *multiprocessor* systems, that is, systems in which there are two or more processors (CPUs) sharing the same physical memory.

Both the Win95 and Windows NT APIs support powerful controls, such as the Rich Text Control, that allow you to construct much nicer user interfaces quickly. Like the "common dialogs" introduced so successfully into Windows 3.1, the Win32 "common controls" make it easy to standardize the "look and feel" of your applications.

Win32 also supports a style of control called the "OCX" control. OCX controls are implemented using OLE Automation. Unlike VBX controls, which could operate only under Win16, you can build OCX controls in both 16- and 32-bit versions. Using OCX controls allows you to readily integrate new kinds of controls into your application.

There is even a version of Win32, called Win32s, which allows you to deliver 32-bit programs that run on Windows 3.1 or Windows for Workgroups 3.11, although the interest in these platforms is diminishing rapidly.

While a full comparison of Windows 95, Windows NT, and Win32s is outside the scope of this book, we will point out significant and important differences in these APIs throughout the book.

An Historical Perspective on User Interfaces

Early "personal" computing was often characterized by computers that had toggle switches and lights.[1] To load a program into a computer, a user set a number of toggle switches in a proper pattern, then pressed a button to load one character, byte, or word into the computer's memory. Needless to say, this method was very slow and extremely error-prone. Output from the computer was often displayed in binary on a panel of lights.

A major improvement came about with the introduction of punched paper tape, punched cards, and line printers. After the tape or card was punched correctly, programs could at least be loaded more accurately and output produced in a readable form. Barring events such as a dropped deck of punched cards or paper jams in the printer, interacting with a computer became much less tedious and error-prone.

Still, interacting with the computer was often difficult. Card decks of programs often were saved until enough work had accumulated to run them in batches. Having a particular job run through the computer more than once a day was an event worth celebrating. The introduction of Teletypes (TTYs) and, later, CRT ("Cathode Ray Tube") or VDT ("Video Display Terminals") terminals (called "glass TTYs" at the time) enabled a user to interact directly with a computer, often for the first time. Such access was pioneered in the 1960s by such systems as MIT's CTSS ("Compatible *Time-Sharing System*") and MULTICS (*MULTI*plexed *Computer System*), among many others. Video terminals came into common usage in the late 1970s, and graphical displays, dating back to the mid-1960s, became economically feasible for widespread usage in the early 1980s.[2]

Initially, display terminals were treated as nothing more than printing terminals at which you could see only the last 24 lines or so of what had been printed. In fact, the DOS operating system on IBM personal computers or compatible machines still treats the display in this fashion. Often when you ask for a directory listing, it will flash right on by. You get to see only the last few lines of a long directory listing.

---

[1] The Digital Equipment Corporation PDP-8 was one of the first "personal" computers–a computer that could actually be afforded by, and dedicated to, a single human being. You had to key in the bootstrap loader through the switches, and early PDP-8 programmers can still, today, recite the boot load toggle switch sequence.

[2] For an overview of the early history of the personal workstation, you may want to look at the *Proceedings of the ACM Conference on the History of Personal Workstations*, cited in the "Further Reading" section.

As part of the continuing quest for better user interfaces, the computer display was used as a randomly accessible device rather than as a sequential line-by-line device such as a printing terminal. Programs started displaying forms on the screen and accepting input from input fields. Programmers were still limited in a number of ways, however. It was commonly assumed that a display consisted of 24 lines by 80 columns. The effects of such assumptions are still with us today. The text display of the first IBM personal computer was a 25-line by 80-column display. Programs that were designed for a 24-line by 80-column display were expected to easily be converted to run on the personal computer. As a bonus, that twenty-fifth line was available for PC-specific versions of the programs. Displays such as the Color Graphics Adapter (CGA), Enhanced Graphics Adapter (EGA), Video Graphics Array (VGA), super VGA, and 8514 adapters can display graphics as well as text with varying numbers of lines and columns. Some older programs work oddly with such displays, often using only the first 25 lines and the left-most 80 columns. Using the graphics modes of such displays was even more difficult for a programmer to deal with. Built-in support for graphics was practically nonexistent, so each programmer had to reinvent the graphical wheel. And after a program was working correctly on a particular graphical display, a new wheel had to be painstakingly carved from stone to get the program running on a different display. This process was not aided by the fact that many display cards that claimed they were "compatible" with the "standard" were not, nor were they compatible with each other.

Microsoft Windows was announced in November 1983 as a solution to these problems. It was released in November 1985 as Windows version 1.01. A number of small revisions to Windows were released over the next two years. During this time, several other software manufacturers released software products that ran programs in graphical or windowing environments. Most of these are now history.

With the introduction of Windows 2.0 in November 1987, Windows applications switched from the "tiled" windows of the 1.*x* versions to the "overlapped" windows used by all later versions of Windows. This and other changes in the appearance and interaction of the user interface for Windows 2.0 were made to be consistent with the user interface of the OS/2 Presentation Manager.

Windows 3.0 was introduced in May 1990 and brought many significant additions to the windowing environment, both for the user and for the developer. From the first look at the display, the user noticed a distinct improvement in the appearance of the desktop over the earlier versions. Many of the icons and buttons had a "three-dimensional" look. Proportionally spaced type was used in the menus and dialog boxes. Windows 3.0 was no longer limited by the 640K boundary and could use *extended memory.* This is the memory above the one-megabyte boundary available on Intel 80286 and more powerful processors. Multiple, complex applications could now run simultaneously side-by-side on a color graphical display. User interfaces had come a long way.

Windows 3.1 was introduced in April 1992 and further improved the Microsoft Windows environment. Windows 3.1 was easier for a user to install and configure. It included a tutorial that taught new users how to use Windows productively from the beginning. From a programming viewpoint, many of the detailed concepts of memory management that made Windows programming so difficult in 3.0 and earlier became nearly obsolete; programmers could and did write programs that could consider allocating a megabyte bitmap.

Windows 3.1 introduced such concepts as the Common Dialog Boxes. Common Dialog Boxes, such as Open, SaveAs, Font selection, Color Selection, Communications, Print Setup and Print, now look the same throughout the system. You can use these same common dialogs in your own Windows applications. When you use the common dialogs for common functions, you make your application familiar to a new user. A user finds that your application performs the same function as another application (saving a file, printing a document, etc.) using the same user interface.

The Windows 3.1 File Manager was much faster than all previous versions and allowed the user to drag files from the File Manager and drop them onto other applications. This concept, difficult to program in Windows 3.1, is pervasive and easy to program in Win32. You can make your Win32 application drag-and-drop aware so that a user can drop files on it, if appropriate.

Windows 3.1 introduced TrueType scalable fonts. Using TrueType fonts allows your application to display good-looking output on your screen and print to any type of printer using the best resolution the printer is capable of. TrueType fonts are *scalable*, which means you or the user can choose any font size without the user's having to store separate bitmap files for every size of every font. TrueType is supported in all Win32 interfaces.

Windows 3.1 also introduced a new subsystem, Win32s, a 32-bit operating environment that runs on the 16-bit Windows 3.1 platform. Win32s is a subset of Windows 95, and suffers from many of the limitations of the underlying 16-bit platform, including the critical resource limitations in the "User" and "GDI" modules. The lack of adequate development tools, and serious bugs in the early versions, limited the usefulness of Win32s. However, significant new releases of Win32s have enabled developers with 32-bit compilers to develop 32-bit applications that run on the 16-bit platform. However, some important applications such as the Office95 Suite and the Visual C++ environment will not run on Win32s. Writing a program that runs on Win32s requires great care and awareness of the 16-bit limitations.

Windows for Workgroups version 3.1 was introduced in November of 1992. Basically identical to Windows 3.1, it added network support. Most of the differences between the two are in the modules that provide the network interfacing and the file and printer sharing capabilities. Windows for Workgroups 3.11, a revision, was introduced in December 1993.

Windows NT version 3.1 was introduced in August 1993. Windows NT is a complete operating system written from the ground up. It supports *preemptive* multitasking, which means that if one program hangs you do not have to reboot the entire system. Nor are you locked out from using other applications while a long, complicated operation consumes hours of computer time. All earlier versions of Windows depended on *cooperative* multitasking, in which you, the programmer, had to explicitly release control during long computations. Much folklore surrounded the correct ways of doing this, particularly when it was discovered that the traditional ways of doing this interfered with laptop "power management" software. You no longer have to worry about releasing control; when appropriate, your control will be preempted by another task. A task in Windows NT also runs in a completely separate address space, making it impossible for it to damage any other running task, or the operating system itself, or to be damaged by an errant task.

Windows NT also introduced powerful new graphics capabilities, such as Bézier curves, paths, and transformation matrices, among other features. Further, it supports *security and protection*, thereby allowing you to grant or restrict permission to your files, and meets DoD C2 security requirements. Windows NT can run on *multiprocessor* systems, in which two or more processors share the same memory. It assumes the existence of a network and has built-in peer-to-peer and client/server networking. And it is portable. It is implemented on a variety of 32-bit platforms, including not only the traditional Intel platforms (386, 486, Pentium, and Pentium Pro), but also RISC-based platforms such as MIPS R4000, the Digital Alpha, and the PowerPC. Each of these platforms presents the same API. If you do not write platform-specific code in your application, it should compile and run on all of these platforms.

Windows NT Advanced Server was released in July 1993. A version of Windows NT, Windows NT Server was optimized to be a file server. It can support products such as the SQL Server for doing client/server database systems. It can also serve as a central file system, thereby enabling a tape backup program running on a Windows NT server to back up all the workstations on the network.

Windows NT Server 3.5 was introduced in September 1994. Windows NT Workstation 3.5 was introduced in October 1994. This was followed shortly by the release of Windows NT Workstation 3.51 in May 1995 and Windows NT Server 3.51 following in July 1995. From the API viewpoint, these represent minor enhancements and bug fixes to the original Windows NT API.

Windows NT did have one significant drawback: It required substantial resources to operate. While the 16-bit Windows 3.1 could operate on a low-end 386 processor with as little as 2MB of memory, the first release of Windows NT 3.1 required a *minimum* of 16MB of memory. The minimum requirement for Windows NT 3.5 and 3.51 is 12MB, but some applications require more. Programming environments such as Visual C++ recommend a minimum of 20MB of memory, with 32MB preferred. These requirements put Windows NT out of reach as a desktop environment for thousands of users who did not have the ability to upgrade to larger machines. Windows 95, code-named "Chicago" during its early development, was the response to this.

Windows 95, released in August 1995, is a hybrid of a 32-bit environment running on a largely 16-bit substrate. It implements a subset of the Win32 API. Although not portable–much of it is still written in assembly language–it is unlike Windows NT in that it runs in as little as 4MB of memory (although serious developers will want at least 16MB to run the 32-bit development environments). Windows 95 supports preemptive multitasking, multithreading, and separate address spaces for tasks, much like Windows NT, but there is only a moderate amount of protection between address spaces and virtually none on the file system. Windows 95 introduced new standard controls, which are also available on Windows NT, and a replacement for the old "Program Manager" interface; this new interface is also available for Windows NT. And like Windows NT, it is "network-aware" and absorbs all the functionality of Windows for Workgroups. Many of the advanced graphics features of Windows NT, such as paths and Bézier curves, also were implemented in Windows 95.

Windows 95 is not actually a subset of the Win32 interface of Windows NT 3.*x*; it is a subset of the "Level 4" Win32 interface. This interface contains significant new API functionality not available in Windows NT 3.*x*, but which is available in Windows NT 4.*x*. The lack of these functions in Windows NT 3.*x* can cause you problems; we try to point out the differences as often as we can.

Windows 95 also includes some capabilities not available on Windows NT 3.*x*, such as telephony and modem support via the Telephony API (TAPI).

Both Windows 95 and Windows NT will continue to evolve. Indeed, Windows 95 is an evolutionary step for most users, allowing them to run 32-bit applications on more modest hardware. Windows NT is recommended for heavy-duty enterprise computing, particularly where security of information is involved.

Windows NT Workstation 4.0 and Windows NT Server 4.0 were introduced in August 1996. These releases implement the full 4.*x* level API, thereby making the Windows 95 API a subset of the Windows NT 4.0 API. With only a moderate amount of care, you can write applications that run on both Windows 95 and Windows NT 4.*x*. They need only test for the proper execution of functions not implemented on Windows 95.

Shortly before the release of Windows 95, Microsoft announced that Windows NT 4.0 would require only 10MB of memory, while the next release of Windows 95 would be targeted for 8MB of memory. We are suspicious of these small numbers, since we have used Windows 95, Windows NT 3.51, and Windows NT 4.0. The changes in memory cost render most of these "small machine" arguments moot. As a developer, you should expect to require *at least* 32MB. Memory cost, once seen as the significant barrier to the adoption of Windows NT, is no longer a significant factor. Memory prices dropped by a factor of more than 25 between the introduction of Windows NT 3.1 and Windows NT 4.0.

Microsoft is heavily committed to the support and evolution of the Win32 API. As new application domains evolve, including so-called "palmtop" devices, "Personal Digital Assistants" (PDAs), and even embedded systems, Microsoft is looking at the Win32 API as the definitive interface to the underlying facilities on all these systems.

The subject of this book is developing 32-bit Windows applications. Windows applications can broadly be placed in four classes:

1. Those that must run under Win32s

2. Those that must run on either Windows 95 or Windows NT

3. Those that require Windows 95

4. Those that require Windows NT

You can also add additional limitations, such as requiring Windows NT 4.*x* instead of Windows NT 3.*x*. Some applications require Windows 95 or Windows NT 4.*x* and will not run on the 3.*x* level systems. Some that were hastily converted from 16-bit Windows still require 16-bit interface code that can run only on Windows 95. And others require device drivers that have not yet been converted to Windows NT but which still run on Windows 95.

Because Win32s is at best a stopgap measure during the transition to Windows 95 and Windows NT, we touch only briefly on a few of the constraints you must obey if you want your program to run under Win32s. We also only briefly discuss those differences between Windows 95 and Windows NT that affect the GUI; a complete discussion of multithreading or security is beyond what we can hope to cover in depth in this book. However, since this book is also intended for Windows 3.*x* programmers who want to start writing in Win32, as well as those coming to Windows programming for the first time, we point out significant differences between the Win16 and Win32 API, particularly as they affect porting existing 16-bit applications to Win32 or, even more important, porting your knowledge of 16-bit programming to Win32. This book teaches 32-bit Windows programming using techniques that work under Windows 95 and Windows NT. All example programs in this book run properly under both, with two qualifications. An example program that calls a Windows NT-specific function obviously won't work well under Windows 95, which doesn't have that function. Careful programming is required so that an application that relies on a Windows NT capability, such as transformation matrices or file security, will run without that capability under Windows 95. In fact, Microsoft *requires* this as part of its "logo certification" for 32-bit applications: The application must run on both Windows 95 and Windows NT, even if it can use Windows NT facilities not available on Windows 95.

Differences between a Windows Program and a Typical DOS or Unix Program

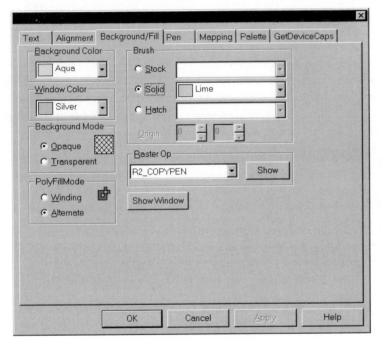

Figure 1.2: Some of the Windows input controls

There are a number of differences between a Windows program and a typical DOS program. Windows applications must share system resources; DOS applications generally don't need to share. Windows applications produce graphical output; DOS applications generally produce text displays. Windows applications also accept input and manage memory quite differently from DOS applications. Windows applications do not require detailed hardware knowledge, whereas DOS applications often work on only one type of device.

Resource Sharing

Windows applications are designed from the start to share the resources of the system on which they run. Resources such as main memory, the processor, the display, the keyboard, hard disks, and diskette drives are shared by all applications running under Windows. To accomplish this sharing, a Windows application must interact with the resources of the computer only through Windows' *Application Program Interface* (API). Accessing the resources only through the Windows API enables Windows to control those resources. This restriction enables multiple programs to run concurrently in the Windows environment.

By contrast, DOS applications typically expect all the resources of the system to be available to the application. A DOS application can allocate all available memory without concern for other applications. It can directly manipulate the serial and parallel ports. It can even intercept the keyboard interrupts and handle key down/key up transitions directly. DOS applications do not need to be designed to share system resources.

Unix programmers, on the other hand, will see nothing new about the Win32 operating environment in this regard. Like Unix, the Win32 memory environment is based on the notion of private address spaces.

Graphical User Interface

Windows applications typically run with a *graphical user interface* (GUI).[3] Because multiple applications may be running concurrently, each application is given access to the graphical display through a "window". It is through this window that an application interacts with the user. Windows applications are not restricted to one window per application. A Windows application may have more than one window on the graphical display simultaneously.

Windows also provides a rich set of input controls as part of the graphical user interface. A few of these controls are dialog boxes, combo boxes, all types of buttons, menus, and scroll bars. Figure 1.2 shows a dialog box containing tab controls, push buttons, radio buttons, up-down ("spin") controls, edit controls, standard combo boxes, combo boxes containing graphics (done as "owner-draw" controls), and three custom controls. Dialog boxes appear on the screen to display information to the user and to request input. In other words, they provide a method for a programmer to "package" a conversation or dialog with the user. Push buttons, check boxes, and radio buttons allow the user to select true/false, on/off, enabled/disabled types of program options without the traditional requirement of a question-and-answer conversation between the user and the application. Menus can be displayed as necessary to enable the user to direct program actions. Scroll bars enable a user to indicate to an application what portions of a file, document, or other output display should be displayed in the current window.

What about Unix, X, Motif, OS/2, or the Macintosh?

Many programmers approaching Win32 for the first time are coming from a background of Unix, X Windows, Motif, OS/2, or even the Macintosh. Those coming from a traditional Unix "shell" background may encounter the same problems in paradigm shift that DOS programmers do: Interaction is quite different. Those coming from an X Windows, Motif, or Macintosh background will find few surprises. Details of the style and some of the naming conventions are different, so you have to learn new names for old ideas. There also are differences in the API calls. Those coming from an OS/2 Presentation Manager background will likewise find a strong similarity. The OS/2 PM is quite similar, in some ways identical, to the Win32 API.

Input Facilities

User input is one of the greatest differences encountered by a programmer new to the Windows environment. Windows controls the input devices and distributes input from the devices among each of the multiple concurrent applications as required. A Windows application cannot read an input device such as the mouse or keyboard on demand. A Windows application is structured to *accept* input whenever it is produced by the user, rather than *demand* it when it is required by the application. If you come from a conventional DOS or Unix programming background, be aware that there is no `getch()` function.[4]

---

[3] There are special kinds of applications, such as *console applications* and *NT System Services*, that often run without a GUI. These applications generally do not interact with the user directly. We do not cover these applications in this book.

[4] For a clever use of the API to build a DOS or Unix-like shell, you might look at Schulman, Maxey and Pietrek's *Undocumented Windows*. See the "Further Reading" section in this chapter. However, this book applies only to Windows 3.1. There is a way to program "shell"-style applications and "filters" in a Unix-compatible or DOS-compatible style in Windows NT by using the "console" subsystem.

A Windows application is told whenever a user presses or releases a key. As the mouse cursor moves across an application's window, a stream of messages pours into the application, keeping it informed as to the mouse cursor's current location. When a mouse button is pressed or released, Windows notifies the application of the event and tells it where in the window the mouse cursor was pointing when the event occurred. While the user is selecting from a menu, checking a check box, pushing a push button, or scrolling a scroll bar, to name just a few examples, the application program receives a constant flow of messages updating it as to exactly what the user is doing.

This aspect of Windows applications is quite different from standard DOS or Unix shell applications. It requires a program that is structured quite differently from a standard DOS or Unix shell program. Windows applications are not necessarily more difficult to write than standard DOS or Unix shell programs. The structure is unfamiliar, and old habits and methods no longer work. However, after you master the new concepts involved in Windows programming, you will be able to write applications that are easier to use than many text-based DOS or Unix shell applications. The programming environments, particularly such rich libraries and tooling as the Microsoft Foundation Classes (MFC), in many ways make program construction *easier* than conventional DOS or Unix programming, simply because the tooling does the boring parts for you.

Memory Management

Memory is but another resource that all applications share in the Windows environment. Unlike a standard DOS program that often assumes that the entire computer's memory is available for its use, multiple Windows applications must share available memory. Instead of initially reserving all memory required by an application and holding it until the application terminates, a Windows application should allocate only the storage required at any given time and free it as soon as it is no longer needed.

Early versions of Windows required that you use elaborate memory management strategies designed to cope with the limitations of the 640K memory space of the 8088, and later with the segmented architecture of the 16-bit protected memory of the 286, 386, and higher Intel processors. Win32 programmers can generally use the familiar `malloc()` function of C or new of C++. There are a few exceptions that we point out where they occur.

Device-independent Graphics

Finally, Windows provides device-independent graphical operations. As soon as a Windows programmer can draw lines and circles on the graphical display, the same program will draw the figures correctly on all graphical displays supported by Windows. In fact, this device independence is not limited to displays. The same graphical operations that produce a pie chart on the display also will draw one on a dot-matrix printer, a laser printer, a plotter, or other output devices supported by Windows. And, unlike DOS, you need only *one* interface for printing. You almost never have to worry about whether the user has an FX-80 from the early days of PCs or a 600 dpi full-color laser printer.

The Windows Programming Model

Windows programming has the reputation of being difficult to learn. This reputation is partially due to the richness of the programming environment. The sheer number of Windows API functions can easily overwhelm you. There are two significant impediments to learning Windows programming:

1. Windows programs require a different conceptual model of the problem than is used by traditional DOS or Unix shell programs.

2. The tools used to write a program based on this conceptual model do not directly support the concepts used.

The Conceptual Model

Windows applications are programs that react to different forms of user input and provide sophisticated graphical output for the user. Any window displayed by an application must react to user actions. Menus must pop down and enable selections. Push buttons must depress and spring back when released. Check boxes must check and uncheck themselves. Objects in general in Windows must react when manipulated. This encourages a conceptual view of a Windows application as a collection of objects. This is exactly the view proposed by object-oriented programming.

The concept of object-oriented GUI programming originated in the mid-1970s at the Xerox Palo Alto Research Center (PARC) along with the concept of graphical programming environments. In object-oriented programming, a programmer creates abstract data types. These abstract data types are commonly called *objects* and consist of a data structure and associated functions, commonly called *methods*, that manipulate the data structure. Typically, the data structure of an object is completely unknown outside of the methods it provides to the outside world. This approach, called *data encapsulation*, enables the internal structure of the object to change at will. As long as the external interface provided by its methods remains unchanged, the rest of the program does not need to know what the object looks like internally or how it implements its functionality.

These concepts apply quite naturally to Windows applications. There are many objects in Windows, including these:

- *Pens*–objects that have a width, a color, and a dash style and are used to draw lines

- *Brushes*–objects that have a color and leave a certain pattern when used to paint areas

- *Menus* and *dialog boxes*

But the first and most fundamental object is called a "window".

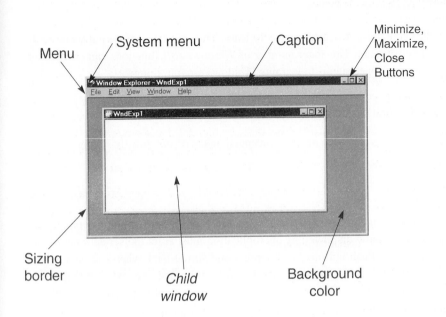

Figure 1.3: The main attributes of a window

Certainly a window displayed on the screen has data associated with it. After all, it has a background color, a title, possibly a menu, and numerous other attributes. Figure 1.3 shows the main attributes of a window. As it turns out, Windows hides the implementation of these attributes. The only way to change them is via the external interface provided by the window. What should happen when the user depresses a mouse button while the cursor is pointing somewhere within the window? An object-oriented viewpoint says, send the window a notification of the event and let it decide. Figure 1.3 also shows that a window can (recursively) contain another window. This *child window* also has all of the window properties (except a menu). If the mouse is clicked over the child window, the child window is notified. It may then choose to notify its parent window.

You may ask, "What about those neat facilities such as docking windows, those little tool palettes, and those windows that split?" Those are not part of the Windows API. They are implemented in application code, most commonly via the Microsoft Foundation Class (MFC) library. MFC is a collection of C++ classes and methods that give you a high-level programming interface to Windows. MFC is not covered in this book; you should see Alan Feuer's *MFC Programming* (see the "Further Reading" section). Some facilities, such as tool bars, were once implemented entirely in MFC, but are now provided as a separate facility using the *Common Control Library.* Other libraries have been added to Windows over its evolution, including the OLE libraries. If you were to be concentrating on programming OLE or ActiveX, you would think of these libraries as being an essential part of the "Win32 API". It is sometimes hard to tell where the "pure" Win32 API leaves off and the library-based extensions begin. This is not necessarily a Bad Thing.[5]

---

[5] We could claim that the "pure" Win32 API is that collection of API functions implemented in three key Windows libraries: Kernel, User, and GDI. But facilities such as the Common Dialogs and Common Controls are so important that their separation seems more an historical accident of how Windows evolved. This book will cover aspects of the three core libraries, common dialogs, and common controls, as well as occasional forays to other libraries where they are important.

Object-oriented programming also encourages *polymorphism*–the ability of an object to take on many different behaviors. In the example in Figure 1.3, one window may react in one manner to a depressed mouse button, whereas another window might react quite differently to the same action. It might even ignore the event completely.

Object-oriented programming also provides *inheritance*. It is often convenient in Windows programming to create a window "just like that window over there", except with additional (or reduced or slightly different) functionality. You could use existing windows as templates for designing new ones, rather than create a new window each time. Windows allows you to do just that. This is also important if you are modifying the behavior of the built-in controls, since otherwise you would have to program *all* of their functionality into your application. Instead, you program only the *changes* in functionality that you deem important.

The tools used to develop Windows applications do not directly support this kind of conceptual model. That is, you cannot directly map an object-based view of a system to a particular program statement or series of statements in C, Pascal, or assembler. For example, there is no statement in C to declare an object in the sense that "object" is used in object-oriented programming.

Because of the paradigm shift and the weakness of the tools, a Windows programmer must, in effect, jump two hurdles to reach the goal of a working Windows application:

1. As in all programming, you must take a particular problem and abstract it, moving from a specific case to the desired general behavior. The conceptual model used in Windows programming (the object-oriented approach) is initially unfamiliar to most programmers. Tried-and-true sequential, procedural approaches cannot be used in the Windows environment. Getting used to structuring a solution to a programming task in this new manner takes time.

2. After you jump the first hurdle, another is waiting just ahead to trip you up. C, the programming language used in the book, does not provide support for direct expression of these object-oriented concepts. Therefore you must, in effect, now write procedural code in a non–object-oriented language that correctly models an object-oriented design of a solution.

Note that this "object-oriented" approach is independent of whether you are programming in C or C++. In Windows, the basic "object" is a *window* and the "methods" are the messages you can send it. C++ introduces another view of objects. In fact, libraries from Microsoft, Borland, and others provide libraries that define C++ objects representing windows and all their variants such as scroll bars, edit controls, and the like. In this book, we touch briefly on some ways your paradigms may change slightly when you use a C++ library. However, discussing these libraries is well outside anything we could cover effectively here. We suggest Alan Feuer's book on the MFC libraries for an introduction to C++ and MFC (see the "Further Reading" section). The MFC library attempts to model the Windows object-oriented structure using an object-oriented language whose object model is not quite identical, and it actually succeeds in covering up most of the differences between the two object models.

It is also important to realize that these "object-oriented" Windows libraries are often a very thin veneer over the underlying API. While the capabilities you gain from having a language like C++ are important, the fundamental paradigms are remarkably similar whether you are programming in C or C++. In C++, the libraries hide some of the detail, but unless you understand the underlying Windows mechanisms and the capabilities of the API you will find that using the "object-oriented" C++ libraries is surprisingly difficult.

In many ways, writing a report program in FORTRAN rather than in Visual Basic is a similar problem. It can be done, but a significant amount of the effort in doing so is expended in phrasing the problem in a language not particularly suited for the problem. The reverse is also true, of course. You should not write a computationally intense program in Visual Basic when FORTRAN is available.

So how does Windows implement its side of this paradigm (the notification of the events), and how do we as programmers write a program that properly reacts to such notifications, constrained as we are by a language not particularly suited for this task? The answer lies in *windows*, their associated *window functions*, and *messages*.

Windows and Their Associated Window Functions

As mentioned earlier, when a program creates a window, that window has certain characteristics–its location on the screen, a title, a size, a menu, and so on. Think of these as its *physical* characteristics. But it also has other characteristics: how it reacts to the notifications of various events. These are its *behavioral* characteristics. All windows have an associated function, called the *window function*, that determines how the window reacts to the notification of an event. The notification itself is called a *message*. For example, buttons and scroll bar controls, themselves contained within a window, are also windows. So they too have an associated window function that controls how the button or scroll bar control reacts. A scroll bar "window" reacts to a mouse click by visually changing the appearance of the window and sending a message to its parent window, which notifies the parent of the request to scroll.

We've stated that Windows notifies a window when an event occurs that might affect the window. This is usually described differently. That is, a message is sent to the window or, depending on your point of view, the window receives a message notifying it of the event. In actuality, Windows calls the function associated with the window, passing information in the arguments of the call that describe the event that has occurred. Windows, their associated window functions, and the messages they receive are, therefore, interrelated. This is illustrated in Figure 1.4, where three windows are shown. Two windows are of the same kind, called a *window class*, and one is a different kind. The two "class A" windows have a single associated function that handles their messages, and the "class B" window has a similar function that handles its messages.

Where do messages come from? What kinds of messages are there? How do you get them? Messages originate from many different sources. Although most messages originate from the Windows operating environment, an application may send messages from one window to another. A window may even send itself a message. A Windows application uses messages to tell itself to do something in the future. Later, when the message arrives, the application performs the desired action. An application may send a message to a completely different application. Often a message received from Windows will result in a deluge of spawned messages. What kinds of messages are there? Most messages are *notifications* of some external event. Something has happened, such as a mouse click or a key press. Such notifications are sent to a selected window (*which* window is a topic we cover in some depth). This window may in turn send notifications to other windows. Windows are also sent messages that are requests for information from the window. A message may ask a window what its caption is, or its status, or if it is willing to be destroyed. Finally, there are messages that tell a window to do something, for example, to change its caption, or its color, or some other feature of its appearance. How do you get them? Because delivering messages in the proper sequence to the proper destination is the key to Windows operations, we will look at how this is done in detail.

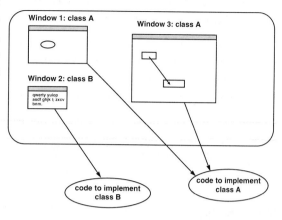

Windows Queues and the Message Loop

Many messages in Windows originate from devices. Depressing and releasing a key on the keyboard generates interrupts that are handled by the keyboard device driver. Moving the mouse and clicking the mouse buttons generate interrupts that are handled by the mouse device driver. These device drivers call Windows to translate the hardware event into a message. The resulting message is then placed into the Windows *system queue*.

Figure 1.4: Windows and window functions

There are two types of queues in Windows: *system* and *thread*. There is only one system queue. Hardware events that are converted into messages are placed into the system queue. Messages reside in the system queue only briefly. Each running Windows application has its own unique thread queue. (In Win32, each running application can have multiple threads of execution, and each thread that is processing messages has its own unique thread queue, but we haven't yet discussed multithreading in detail.) Windows transfers the messages in the system queue to the appropriate thread queue. Each of a program's thread queues holds all messages for all windows running in a particular thread. Consequently, within a thread all messages are processed in first-in-first-out (FIFO) order.

Programmers who know the Win16 architecture may remember that each application had its own private *application queue* and that there was a single *system queue*. However, this system queue was handled somewhat differently. The Win16 subsystem, running under Win32, simulates this system queue behavior with respect to interacting Win16 applications.

Windows implements the sharing of the shared resources (such as the mouse and the keyboard) by using the system queue. When an event occurs, a message is placed into the system queue. Windows then must, in effect, decide which thread queue should receive the message. How it does this can vary, depending on the event. Windows uses the concept of the *input focus* to decide which thread queue should receive the message. The input focus is an attribute possessed by only one window in the system at a time. The window with the input focus is the focal point for all keyboard input. Keyboard messages are moved from the system queue into the thread queue for the thread with a window that presently has the input focus. As the input focus moves from window to window, Windows moves keyboard messages from the system queue to the proper thread queue. This is performed on a message-by-message basis because certain keystrokes are requests to change the input focus from one window to another window. Subsequent keyboard messages in the system queue may then go to a different thread queue.

Mouse messages are handled a little differently. The mouse is another shared resource. Mouse messages usually are sent to the window that is underneath the mouse pointer. When multiple windows are overlapped, the one on the top–that is, the one being displayed–receives the mouse message. The one exception to this rule involves *capturing* the mouse. When a Windows application captures the mouse (which is done by making a Windows function call), Windows moves all subsequent mouse messages from the system queue to the capturing window's thread queue, no matter where the mouse is pointing on the screen. The application must eventually release the captured mouse to allow other applications to use it.

The hardware timer generates periodic interrupts that are handled by the timer device driver. Like the keyboard and mouse device drivers, the timer device driver calls Windows to translate the hardware event into a message. Unlike the keyboard and mouse messages, the resulting timer message is placed directly into a program's application queue. Because multiple programs might request that timer messages be periodically sent to one or more of their windows, a single timer interrupt may result in Windows placing timer messages in multiple application queues. In this way, Windows makes the single hardware timer a shareable device. Individual windows each think they have their own private timer.

Windows places other messages into a program's thread queue as a result of the program's calling certain Windows functions. For example, a program might call Windows to tell it that an area of a window is no longer up-to-date. Windows will place a message into the thread queue for that window that eventually results in the program's redrawing the out-of-date region of the window.

Now that as a program's thread queues are filling with messages, how does the program get the message from a thread queue and deliver it to the proper window function? You write a small piece of code called the *message loop*. The message loop retrieves input messages from the application queue and dispatches them to the appropriate window functions. The message loop continually retrieves and dispatches messages until it retrieves a special message that signals that the loop should terminate. One message loop is the main body of a Windows application. A Windows application initializes, repeatedly executes the message loop logic until instructed to stop, and then terminates.

A program calls the Windows GetMessage function to retrieve a message from its thread queue. Windows moves the message from the queue into a data area within the program.

Now the program has the message, but the message still needs to be sent to the proper window function. To do this, the program calls the Windows DispatchMessage function. You might wonder why you call Windows to send a message to a window function within your program. A program may create more than one window. Each window may have its own unique window function, or multiple windows may use the same window function, as shown in Figure 1.4. In addition, many of the window functions for window types provided by Windows are not in your program at all; they are inside Windows. The DispatchMessage function in Windows hides all this complexity by determining which of the program's window functions or Windows's built-in window functions gets the message. It then calls the proper window function directly. Figure 1.5 shows the path that keyboard input takes through the system.

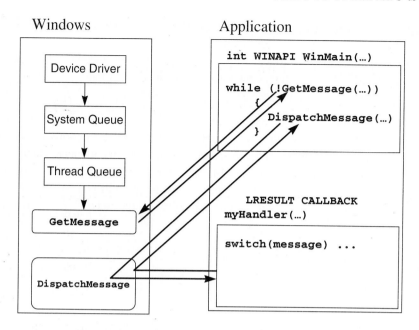

Figure 1.5: Keyboard input to a single Windows application

Windows Operating Modes

Windows 95 and Windows NT run on microprocessors of the Intel 80x86 family. Currently this family includes the 80386, 80486, and Pentium microprocessors and excludes the older 8086, 8088, 80186, 80188, and 80286 microprocessors. The 80386 and above microprocessors can run in *protected mode,* which is required by Windows 95 and Windows NT. The hardware capabilities of these various processors vary greatly from the low end of the spectrum to the high end. Windows is not limited to the capability of the least powerful microprocessor in the series. For example, Windows NT can run on 8-processor Pentium multiprocessor systems and take full advantage of all the processors. Windows 95 is currently limited to a single processor system. For most of this book, we assume you understand that Windows NT also runs on a variety of non-Intel platforms.

Windows 95 and Windows NT run in the so-called "386" *enhanced mode* on an 80386, 80486, or Pentium processor. Virtual memory capabilities enable Windows to use disk space as additional (but slower) main memory. This allows Windows applications to use more "memory" than is physically available. Windows applications running under Windows execute in the protected mode of the processor.

It is best to test an application in both Windows 95 and Windows NT. Microsoft requires this for its "logo certification" program. You need to test your code on both platforms because there are facilities of each environment that are not available in the other.

Program Memory Models

In Win16, the programmer had to be aware of "memory models" such as "medium" and "large", deal with the effects of the segmented addresses referencing blocks of memory larger than 64K ("huge" pointers), and deal with the differences between 16-bit ("near") pointers and 32-bit ("far") segmented pointers. All of this is irrelevant in Win32 programming. There is just one "memory model": a uniform 32-bit address space.

This is both good and bad. It greatly simplifies programming, removes size restrictions, and can significantly improve performance. (Pointer arithmetic in Win16's "huge" model required a runtime subroutine call to do the arithmetic!) It also removes restrictions that Win16 programmers had to live with, such as the 8,192-selector limit (if you are just starting as a Windows programmer, be grateful you don't have to know about this). But in Win16, if you allocated a segment and then addressed off the end of it, you were usually greeted with a General Protection Fault (GPF). In Win32, you might simply overwrite a piece of your own memory you never heard of. This can result in bizarre behavior. Those who programmed in DOS or in mainframe, mini, or workstation environments already know about this problem. However, if you became accustomed to Win16 trapping your bad writes, you must be aware that this capability is now gone. Fortunately, unlike as with DOS, you cannot overwrite the operating system when using Windows NT. It is challenging, but not impossible, to overwrite the operating system in Windows 95. (This means it is hard to do by accident.)

However, it was very satisfying to be able, in this book, to eliminate lengthy, tedious, and complex discussions of segmented memory and the various memory models.

Memory Models and Porting 16-bit Code

In Win16 programming, the programmer had to be aware of the details of the memory model. For technical reasons, the 16-bit environment could not support more than one copy of a program running if the "large" model was used, so programmers who wished to write applications with multiple instances used the "medium" model. Many programmers used the medium model even when there was no compelling reason to do so. In Win32, there is only one memory model, so all of these details seem to be irrelevant. But alas, they are not, if you are porting an older program. Programmers often played clever tricks knowing that pointers could be 16-bit values, such as putting two pointers in a single 32-bit word, or a pointer and a window handle in a single 32-bit word. But in Win32, both pointers and handles are 32-bit values. These Win16 tricks often make your life difficult if you are porting an existing Win16 application.

__cdecl and __stdcall Calling Sequences

Calling most Windows functions requires that you pass some number of parameters to the function. Parameters to a function are passed on the stack. Placing copies of the parameters on the stack is called *pushing* parameters on the stack. Removing them is called *popping* parameters from the stack. Parameters in a function call may be pushed on the stack from left to right (as they are listed in the C language function call) or from right to left. As it turns out, C functions normally use a right-to-left ordering when pushing parameters on the stack (that is, the first–that is, left-most–parameter is the last parameter pushed onto the stack) and expects the caller to remove the parameters from the stack. However, when running on Intel platforms,

Windows API calls expect to remove the parameters from the stack themselves. These cases are distinguished by the __cdecl (the default) and the __stdcall linkage types. All Win32 API functions running on Intel platforms expect parameters to be pushed in right-to-left ordering.

Programmers who know the Win16 API may be familiar with the __cdecl and __pascal linkage types. Windows API and callback functions in Win16 were FAR PASCAL. In Win32 they are __stdcall. Note also that the __pascal linkage type pushed parameters left-to-right and expected the caller to remove the parameters.

After a function has completed its job, the pushed parameters must be removed from the stack. That is, the correct number of parameters must be popped from the stack. The compiler generally does not know at compile time how many parameters a particular function might receive. In fact, a specific C function might receive a different number of parameters each time it is called. The printf function is the ultimate example of such usage. A called C function cannot clean up the parameters passed to it on the stack because the number of parameters might vary and is unknown until runtime. Responsibility, therefore, lies with the calling program. After the call returns from the function, the same number of parameters that were pushed onto the stack are removed from the stack.

As it turns out, there is a slightly more efficient calling sequence. By your restricting a function to a fixed number of arguments, parameters may be pushed in either order. Also, the compiler knows at compile time the number of parameters expected by a function. The compiler can then generate the code to remove the parameters from the stack at the end of the called function rather than after every call to the function. Generating this code once instead of multiple times saves space in the resulting program. In addition, the Intel and several other architectures provide hardware support for returning from a function while simultaneously removing parameters from the stack. The C language carefully does not specify if parameters should be pushed in left-to-right or right-to-left order. You should be very careful how you call API functions, and you should not make any assumptions about the order in which parameters are evaluated. This is because you might port your code to some non-Intel Windows platform whose compiler takes advantage of this freedom and evaluates the parameters in a different order. (In addition to the "official" NT platforms, such as the PowerPC, MIPS, and DEC Alpha, there is now a trend in the industry to adopt the Windows API for non-Windows platforms. For example, the Open Software Foundation (OSF) has a specification of a Windows API, and at least three vendors offer X-based or Motif-based versions of the Windows API, implemented as a set of libraries that run on stock Unix platforms.)

By default, the Microsoft C compiler generates calls to functions using the __cdecl calling sequence that supports a variable number of parameters. This supports the C language as defined. However, most Windows functions take a fixed number of parameters. So these functions use the __stdcall calling sequence to gain the additional efficiency. The Microsoft C compiler recognizes two keywords, __cdecl and __stdcall, that enable you to specify on a function-by-function basis which calling sequence to use. The __cdecl keyword tells the compiler that the next function uses the C calling sequence, and the __stdcall keyword tells the compiler that the next function uses the more efficient calling sequence. Windows functions are defined in the windows.h file, via a number of typedefs, to use the __stdcall calling sequence.

To make your program "platform-independent", you should not use these keywords in your code. Windows API functions are normally declared with a macro, `WINAPI`, and Windows callback functions are declared with a macro, `CALLBACK`. A given platform may define these differently than Microsoft C does. If you use the actual reserved words, your code may not port to a different compiler or hardware platform.

Static and Dynamic Linking

We've discussed how to use the correct calling sequence when calling the window function so that it can find the passed information. A couple of questions remain. *Where* is the window function? And *how* does the call in your application get connected with the function hiding somewhere inside Windows?

The linker connects a call in your application to its called function. When linking one or more object modules (.obj files) together to form an executable program (.exe file), the linker matches calls within the object modules to functions within either the same or another object module. After performing this step, if unresolved calls remain, the linker searches library files for the missing functions. The library files searched by the linker are those specified on the LINK command line (which you usually specify via your development environment) and those explicitly named within the object modules being linked. If, after searching all named libraries, the linker still cannot find the called function, the linker will produce an "unresolved external reference" message telling you that one or more of the functions called by your program could not be found. If the linker does find the function, its object code is copied from the library and inserted into the executable file. This is the usual form of linking and is called *static linking*. Static linking requires the linker to know at link time where a function will reside in memory and to have access to the object code comprising the function.

The linker, however, does not know at link time where a Windows function resides in memory. Windows is a cooperative environment. Multiple applications run simultaneously. It would be nice if a method could be devised by which all applications running concurrently could share a single copy of each Windows function. Such a method does exist and is called *dynamic linking*. Actually, a Windows function might appear in memory at a different address in each program that uses it, so even if the linker knew the location for one task, the function would not necessarily be at the same location when called by another task. The address will also change from one release to another of Windows and be different in Windows 95 and Windows NT.

This may surprise you. You would think that "the operating system" would always be in the same location. In fact, in any given release of Windows, the operating system *does* appear in the same locations in all the programs. But in Windows, much of what we think of as "the" operating system is actually distributed among dozens of dynamic link libraries (DLLs), so the common dialogs, common controls, OLE support, and the like are not actually part of the core operating system. Depending on which DLLs you require, and what order they are required in, you will find that they load into each task in a different location and may even load into your own application in different locations each time it is run. So dynamic linking has to deal with this.

Dynamic linking is a technique by which the linker defers full resolution of a function call until the program is executed. Rather than fix all calls at link time, the linker inserts additional information into the executable program, informing Windows of the unresolved functions. As Windows loads the program, the deferred calls are dynamically resolved to the proper function within Windows. The linker determines that an external reference should be dynamically linked through the use of an *import library*.

The linker searches import libraries for undefined external references present in the program being linked, just as it searches object code libraries. However, import libraries contain no code. Instead, they contain records that name the Windows module containing the external reference and the name or number of the entry point within the Windows module containing the function. This information is copied to the executable program, and the external reference is considered resolved by the linker. Later, when the program is executed, Windows uses this information to resolve the call.

There are several import libraries used for linking Windows programs. The most important are those that supply the interfaces for the key modules of Windows: kernel32.lib, user32.lib and gdi32.lib. These libraries contains no code. Instead, they contain import records for the key API Windows functions that can be called by a Windows application. A library also can contain the object modules for functions used in static linking as well as the import records used for dynamic linking.

Dynamic Link Libraries

The linker can produce either program modules or *dynamic link libraries* (DLLs). Program modules are executable (.exe) files that you can run. Dynamic link libraries are also executable (.dll) files but are never directly executed. The two are quite different from each other.

Programs run as tasks under Windows, and they receive messages. A task is an independent executing entity. For example, you can run two copies of the NotePad program concurrently. Windows creates two tasks, one running each copy of the NotePad program, but only one copy of the code for the NotePad program is in memory. Each task, however, has its own private data. Hence each task can be working on a different file.

DLLs are simply collections of routines that can be used by programs or by other DLLs. A DLL never runs as a task under Windows. A DLL function must be called, directly or indirectly, from a running program that is a task under Windows. A program calls a subroutine in a DLL through dynamic links as described earlier. The Windows functions your application calls are contained within dynamic link libraries. Windows itself consists of the following four main dynamic link libraries:

1. user32.dll manages the Windows environment in addition to managing all your application's windows. Menus, built-in controls, and the like are managed here.

2. kernel32.dll provides the system services of Windows. These services include multitasking, multithreading, memory management, and resource management.

3. gdi32.dll provides the Graphic Device Interface, which is what you use whenever you draw on a window. Operations for drawing lines and text, for example, are here.

4. *console subsystem* (in kernel32.dll) provides an interface for character-based applications. Since this book concentrates on the GUI aspects of programming Windows, we have little to say about this capability.

Programmers who know the Win16 system may be familiar with the module names `gdi.exe`, `kernel.exe`, and `user.exe`. In fact, if you look in the Windows system directory, you will find these modules. These are used to provide the interface between a running Win16 application and the Win32 environment.

DLLs are created much like a Windows program is. The linker links object module files together, thereby creating an executable file. As we mentioned, this executable file is not directly executed. When Windows loads a program containing external references that need to be dynamically linked, those references will name the DLL and the entry point within the DLL that resolves the reference. Windows then looks for a DLL by that name and loads it in addition to the original program. That DLL may, in turn, contain external references to another DLL that need resolving. This process continues until all references are resolved or a DLL cannot be found.

Using dynamic link libraries instead of static link libraries provides a number of benefits to you, the programmer. Multiple applications using a single library routine from a static link library each contain a separate copy of the routine. When multiple applications use a routine contained in a DLL, all the applications share a single copy of the routine. In addition, when a static link library function is changed, all applications that use the routine must be relinked to use the updated version. It is bad enough having to relink, but first you have to determine which programs use the changed function or else give up and relink everything "just in case". When a routine in a DLL is changed, the DLL is relinked and all applications that need it will use the updated version the next time they are executed. There is no need to update the application simply because a library routine has changed.

Of course, this method has its own set of pitfalls. For example, you must, if you are updating a DLL, make sure that it is still compatible with earlier versions, since a large code base may exist of which you have no knowledge and over which you have no control. You must provide a way for a program to find out which version of a DLL it is using. Also, if the program depends on features at a certain release level of the DLL, it should be able to detect and report an attempt to use an earlier version. Your "installer" must make sure that it doesn't overwrite a newer version of the DLL with an older version on its distribution disk. Nonetheless, the power and flexibility of using DLLs is so significant that they are the mechanism of choice in most cases.

Exports and Imports, or Who's Looking for Whom?

Dynamic link libraries provide functions that are called by programs or other DLLs. A dynamic link library must *export* a function in order for it to be used by another DLL or program. Exporting a function creates a record in the executable file. This record identifies the name and ordinal number of the entry point as well as the location of the function within the module.

A program must *import* functions that it calls using dynamic links. Importing a function notifies the linker that the reference is a dynamic link and will not be resolved until runtime. A function can be imported either by placing an explicit import statement in the application's module definition file (a file needed when linking the application) or by allowing the linker to find an import record for the called function in a library. Either way, the linker places a record in the program's executable file to notify Windows of the dynamic link. When Windows loads a program and finds an import record for a dynamic link, it resolves the call. The import record names the dynamic link library and the function name or ordinal number of the routine within the library that the program is calling. Windows loads the named DLL and looks for an export record for the same function name or ordinal number. The export record tells Windows where in the library the function resides. Windows now dynamically *binds* the call in the program to the function with the DLL.

Programmers who know Win16 are aware of the __export keyword used to mark callbacks and DLL entry points. In Win32, a callback is simply a __stdcall linkage and needs no special export declaration. A DLL entry point can be specified in the module-definition file, on the linker command line, or by adding the "storage class modifier" __declspec(dllexport) to the declaration of the entry point.

Windows Memory Management

Windows programs can consist of one or more code segments and one or more data segments. Dynamic-link libraries may have one or more code segments and one or more data segments. Multiple Windows programs can be running concurrently, and multiple instances of the same program also may run concurrently. In Win32, some number of these data segments (perhaps none) can be shared with all programs that are using the DLL.

Experienced Win16 DLL writers are painfully aware of the limitations of Win16 DLLs, namely, that there is at most one data segment and it is shared among all clients of the DLL. In Win32, you can have both private and shared data segments and a DLL can even allocate thread-specific storage.

The `windows.h` Header File

The next chapter has an example Windows program. It doesn't do much, but one of the first things you will notice about it is that many of the data types used by the program are not standard C data types. These data types are defined in an include file that must be included in every Windows module. All Windows programs should start with the following statement:

```
#include <windows.h>
```

A significant percentage of the Windows API is defined by the windows.h file. In earlier versions of Windows, this file included all of the basic definitions for the API calls, the symbolic constants associated with those calls, and the structures and typedefs that defined data values. As Windows evolved, several problems arose with this approach:

- The size of the file became unwieldy.

- The introduction of new symbols and interfaces could cause existing code to no longer compile in later Windows releases because of new symbols conflicting with existing symbols.

- The size of the file became a significant factor in the compilation time necessary to re-build a system. The (approximately) 5,300 source lines of this one file would often overwhelm the source file size of the application code, and it would be included in every compilation unit.

- Much of the compiler time and effort spent on this file was wasted because in a typical module, perhaps only a dozen or so of the several thousand symbols defined would be needed.

Microsoft addressed these problems in several ways. One was to modify their compilers to allow for "pre-compiled headers", a technique that eliminates the need to actually read and parse the header files. In fact, the files are saved in a semidigested form and only those pieces required are read in, in binary form, by the compiler. Other vendors offer similar strategies. The problems of potential symbol incompatibility were addressed by adopting more complex naming conventions and by putting new features in new header files. Starting with Windows 3.1, features such as the "shell extensions", "tool extensions", "3-D controls", and Object Linking and Embedding (OLE) were added as separate header files you had to explicitly include. Conditional compilation, which we will discuss later in this chapter, was used to allow you to drop features you did not need. Finally, in Win32, windows.h itself was split up into nearly 30 separate files. For compatibility, the same conditional compilation options of Windows 3.1 were retained, and there is a single windows.h file that selectively includes these separate files based on the conditional options you select.

In this book, it seemed overly pedantic to refer to symbols by their specific files, or discuss the details of the various header files included by windows.h in ordinary discussion. In particular, Microsoft has been rearranging these files internally for different releases. Therefore, in this book, we often refer to functions, symbols, and data types "defined in [or by] windows.h". By this we mean that if you include the windows.h header file without taking any special action (such as defining conditional compilation options), you will get the definition or definitions we refer to. But in fact, in Win32, the definitions are going to be in some other file that is (selectively) included by windows.h.

The files included via windows.h contain mainly three types of statements: `#define`, `typedef`, and function prototypes. windows.h and its components are ultimately quite large for an include file, and many Windows applications do not use much of the information present in windows.h. For this reason, many parts of windows.h can be conditionally excluded from processing. For example, all the example programs given in this book use the StdSDK.h file, which starts as follows:

```
#define STRICT
#include <windows.h>
```

The first statement is a preprocessor directive that defines the symbol STRICT. Although STRICT has no value, it is important to realize that it is defined as a symbol that has no replacement value. That is, all occurrences of the characters "STRICT" will be removed whenever they are found in the source code that follows them. However, this symbol is used by preprocessor directives in the windows.h header file.

When you define the symbol STRICT and then include the windows.h header file, many Windows program data types are specified differently than they are when the symbol is not defined. The symbol STRICT enables stricter type-checking and should always be used in newly written Windows source files. Older Windows programs usually need to be modified, sometimes significantly, before they will compile warning free with strict type-checking enabled. The existence of these warnings often indicates potentially incorrect code. Eliminating them from all Windows application code is always beneficial. Many porting errors that would make Win16 programs not run under Win32 can be caught by using STRICT type checking.

We prefer to let the C compiler do as much checking of the program as possible during compilation. Warning level 4 of the Microsoft C compiler can be used when compiling Windows applications to request extra-strict checking by the compiler. The compiler at warning level 4 will warn you about possible portability problems in your code. One item that generates such warnings is the use of bit fields in structures. The communications structures use bit fields. With warning level 4, you can eliminate these warnings by using the #define NOCOMM before including the windows.h header file as long as you are not using communications routines. The areas that may be excluded from processing by using #define statements are listed in Table 1.1.

In addition, you can force many of the warning messages to be actual compilation errors. This prevents the compiler from generating a .OBJ file and successfully linking a possibly incorrect program. The C language does not force many conditions to be errors. This would violate the "spirit" of the language and might possibly make it impossible to successfully compile existing code that relied upon the language's forgiving nature. But you can force the compiler to be much more conservative. In Microsoft C compilers, you do this by using the #pragma warning() declaration:

```
#pragma warning(error, 4002) // Too many actual parameters to macro
#pragma warning(error, 4003) // Too few actual parameters to macro
#pragma warning(error, 4020) // Too few actual parameters
#pragma warning(error, 4021) // Too many actual parameters
#pragma warning(error, 4024) // different types for formal and actual
```

However, this technique is specific to Microsoft C compilers. You must use it with care if you expect your code to be compiled under other compilers. An example of such a file is shown in Appendix D.

Table 1.1: Symbols used to exclude portions of `windows.h`

Symbol	What It Excludes
NOATOM	Atom function prototypes.
NOCLIPBOARD	CF_* clipboard message constants and clipboard function prototypes.
NOCOMM	DCB, COMSTAT structs, CE_*, IE_*, EV_*, CBR_*, CN_*, CSTF_*, and communication function prototypes.
NOCTLMGR	WC_DIALOG, DLGWINDOWEXTRA, DS_*, DM_*, DC_*, DLGPROC, DWL_*, DLGC_*, CTLCOLOR_*, WM_CTLCOLOR, WM_GETFONT, WM_SETFONT, and dialog and control function prototypes and the control styles SS_*, BS_*, ES_*, SBS_*, LBS_*, and CBS_*.
NOCOLOR	GetSysColor, SetSysColors, and COLOR_*.
NODEFERWINDOWPOS	HDWP, BeginDeferWindowPos, DeferWindowPos, and EndDeferWindowPos.

Table 1.1: Symbols used to exclude portions of `windows.h`

Symbol	What It Excludes
NODESKTOP	Desktop symbols and methods–DESKTOP_* and *Desktop.
NODRAWTEXT	DrawText and DT_*.
NOEXTAPI	"Extended" API functions unique to Win32. Use this if you don't need the extended capabilities and there are conflicts with existing code.
NOFONTSIG	Font signature structures, TCI_*.
NOGDI	All GDI defines and function prototypes.
NOGDICAPMASKS	Capabilities DT_*, CC_*, LC_*, PC_*, CP_*, TC_*, and RC_*.
NOHELP	WinHelp, HELP_*, MULTIKEYHELP, and HELPWININFO.
NOICONS	Standard Icon IDs–IDI_*.
NOIME	Input method manager: IME symbols–IMC_* and IMN_*.
NOIMM	Input method manager–Imm* methods and their associated structures, WM_IME_* messages, and IMC_*.
NOKANJI	Kanji support.
NOKERNEL	WinMain; All kernel defines and function prototypes.
NOKEYSTATES	Key state masks for mouse messages MK_*.
NOLANGUAGE	Language support–IsChar*.
NOMB	MessageBox, MessageBeep, and MB_*.
NOMCX	Modem interface structures and calls.
NOMEMMGR	GMEM_*, GHND, GPTR, LHND, and associated function prototypes.
NOMENUS	MENUITEMTEMPLATEHEADER, MENUITEMTEMPLATE, MF_*, TPM_*, WM_MENUSELECT, WM_MENUCHAR, and menu function prototypes.
NOMETAFILE	HMETAFILE, META_*, HANDLETABLE, METARECORD, METAFILEPICT, METAHEADER, MPENUMPROC, and metafile function prototypes.
NOMINMAX	Macros min and max.
NOMSG	MSG, PM_*, and message handling function prototypes.
NONCMESSAGES	Nonclient message constants–HT_* and SMTO_*.
NONLS	All NLS (National Language Support) defines and routines–MB_, WC_, CT_, C1_, C2_, C3_, NORM_, MAP_, LCMAP_, CTRY_, and LOCALE_.

Table 1.1: Symbols used to exclude portions of `windows.h`

Symbol	What It Excludes
NOOPENFILE	OpenFile, OFSTRUCT, OF_*, and temp file function prototypes.
NOPROFILER	Profiler function prototypes.
NORASTEROPS	Binary (R2_*), ternary, and quaternary raster operation codes.
NORESOURCE	RT_*.
NOSCROLL	WM_HSCROLL, WM_VSCROLL, SB_*, ESB_*, and scroll bar function prototypes.
NOSECURITY	All security operations.
NOSERVICE	All service controller routines, SERVICE_ symbols.
NOSHOWWINDOW	ShowWindow parameters SW_* and WM_SHOWWINDOW.
NOSOUND	S_* and sound function prototypes.
NOSYSCOMMANDS	System commands–SC_*.
NOSYSMETRICS	GetSystemMetrics and SM_*.
NOSYSPARAMS	System parameter information–GetSystemParametersInfo, SPI_*, SPIF_*, NONCLIENTMETRICS, ARW_*, MINIMIZEDMETRICS, ICONMETRICS, ANIMATION-INFO, SERIALKEYS, SERKF_*, HCF_*, CDS_*, DISP_*, ChangeDisplaySettings, and SystemParametersInfo.
NOTEXTMETRIC	GetTextMetrics, TEXTMETRIC, TMPF_*, NEWTEXTMETRIC, NTM_*, OUTLINE-TEXTMETRIC, GetOutlineTextMetrics, KERNINGPAIR, GetKerningPairs, FONTENUMPROC, EnumFonts, EnumFontFamilies, and *_FONTTYPE.
NOUSER	All user defines and function prototypes.
NOVIRTUALKEY-CODES	Virtual key codes–VK_*.
NOWH	WH_*, *HOOKSTRUCT, HHOOK, HOOKPROC, HC_*, HCBT_*, HSHELL_*, and hook function prototypes.
NOWINDOWSTATION	Window station support–WINSTA_*, *WindowStation
NOWINMESSAGES	Window messages–WM_*, EM_*, LB_*, and CB_* and symbols NF_*, NFR_*, PWR_*, and WMSZ_*.
NOWINOFFSETS	GWL_*, GCL_*, GWW_*, GCW_*, and window and class extra area access function prototypes.
NOWINSTYLES	Window styles–WS_*, CS_*, ES_*, LBS_*, SBS_*, and CBS_*.
OEMRESOURCE	OEM resources–OBM_*, OCR_*, and OIC_*.

We strongly urge you to study how to use "precompiled headers". Both Borland and Microsoft support these, as do some other compilers. A precompiled header is a collection of the information derived from a sequence of header files that is stored in a quickly loaded binary form. Use of precompiled headers can substantially reduce your compilation time.

There is one serious problem with using precompiled headers and using any of the symbols from Table 1.1. The file that controls the compilation of the precompiled header is the one that determines which symbols are included or excluded from the system. For example, if you want to include OEM resources, you might add the #define OEMRESOURCE as shown below:

```
#define OEMRESOURCE    // include OEM symbols
#include "StdSDK.h"
```

in the compilation of one of your programs. This doesn't work. The precompiled header, which doesn't have any of the symbols defined by including OEMRESOURCE, has already been compiled, and so you will get an undefined symbol error when you compile the program. If you were trying to exclude some symbols because of a name conflict, the name conflict would likewise remain. One solution to this is to add the OEMRESOURCE declaration to the file that defines the precompiled header and rebuild your entire source system. This will now get the correct symbols defined, or excluded, but this applies to *every* file in your compilation, since they share the same precompiled header. The other way is to disable precompiled headers for the one particular file that you need to have special symbol definitions for. Some environments, such as Microsoft's Visual C++, support this.

The actual split-up of the header files, as currently done, is shown in Table 1.2. Because the symbols excluded by the definitions of Table 1.1 do not quite follow the new file arrangement, there is conditional compilation within each file. However, some of the files given in Table 1.2 can be conditionally included or excluded in their entirety by defining the symbols shown. In the past, the actual arrangement of files and their contents has changed several times, and different releases of the compiler have had different setups. You should treat the information in Table 1.2 as suggestive, not definitive, because there may be changes in the future.

Table 1.2: Components of `windows.h`

File Name	Definitions
excpt.h	Structured exception handler API.
stdarg.h	ANSI variable-argument list.
windef.h	Base types: ULONG, NULL, TRUE, FALSE, BOOL, DWORD, RECT, POINT, etc.
winbase.h	Base API: file, security, exception symbols, COM port symbols, most other constants.
wingdi.h	GDI symbols: ROP codes, metafile codes, printer escapes, GDI API.
winuser.h	USER symbols: resource symbols and macros, wsprintf, control symbols, virtual key codes, hook symbols, keyboard layout, desktop, message API.
winnls.h	National Language Support constants and API.
wincon.h	CONSOLE interface.
winver.h	VERSIONINFO resource API.

Table 1.2: Components of `windows.h`

File Name	Definitions
winreg.h	Registry interface API.
winnetwk.h	Network API, WNet API calls, and symbols.

The following will be excluded if you define the symbol `WIN32_LEAN_AND_MEAN`.

File Name	Definitions
cderr.h	Common dialog error codes, CDERR_, FNERR_, PDERR_.
dde.h	DDE interface, WM_DDE messages.
ddeml.h	DDEML interface.
dlgs.h	Symbols for controls in common dialogs.
lzexpand.h	Data compression DLL API.
mmsystem.h	Multimedia system.
nb30.h	Portable NetBIOS 3.0 interface.
rpc.h	Remote Procedure Call interface. Includes rpcdce.h, rpcnsi.h, rpcnterr.h.
shellapi.h	Shell API: drag-and-drop, ShellExecute, ExtractIcon, etc.
winperf.h	Performance monitor API including registry interface.
winsock.h	Network sockets API.

The following will be excluded if you define `NOGDI`.

File Name	Definitions
commdlg.h	Common dialog API.
winspool.h	Printer API.

The following will be included if you define the symbol `INC_OLE1`.

File Name	Definitions
ole.h	Object linking and embedding (OLE) API.

The following will be included if you define the symbol `INC_OLE2`.

File Name	Definitions
ole2.h	Object linking and embedding 2.x (OLE) API; includes oleidl.h.

The following will be excluded if you define the symbol `NOSERVICE`.

File Name	Definitions
winsvc.h	Service control manager (SCM) API.

The following will be excluded if you define the symbol `NOMCX`.

File Name	Definitions
mcx.h	MCX (Modem Control Extension) API.

Table 1.2: Components of `windows.h`

File Name	Definitions
The following will be excluded if you define the symbol `NOIME`.	
imm.h	IMM (Input Method Manager) API.

Most `#define` statements in windows.h are used to provide symbolic names for numeric values. For example, a window frequently receives a `WM_COMMAND` message, which windows.h defines as

```
#define WM_COMMAND          0x0111
```

Table 1.3: Platform-independent keywords

Declaration	Win16	Win32
`#define FAR`	far	Obsolete, empty
`#define NEAR`	near	Obsolete, empty
`#define LONG`	long	long
`#define VOID`	void	void
`#define CDECL`	__cdecl	__cdecl
`#define PASCAL`	__pascal	__stdcall
`#define WINAPI`	_far __pascal	__stdcall
`#define APIPRIVATE`	No keyword	__stdcall
`#define WINAPIV`	No keyword	__cdecl
`#define CALLBACK`	_far __pascal	__stdcall

windows.h also contains #define statements for the nonstandard C keywords used for portable programming. These are primarily of interest to programmers who are porting Win16 applications to Win32. But they are also important for certain cross-platform compatibility in Windows NT. Consequently, it is important that you use these keywords, particularly if you plan to port your 32-bit application to the MIPS, Alpha, PowerPC, or future 32-bit Windows NT platforms.

You should use the uppercase forms of the keywords in Table 1.3 rather than their lowercase forms.

Should you ever need to convert to a different C compiler or implementation of the API, it is much easier to change the defined value of `WINAPI` one time in a header file rather than `__stdcall` throughout all your code. In fact, this is already done for you by the vendor of the platform. You can easily adapt your code by planning ahead and using the defined values instead of the built-in keywords.

You may encounter, particularly in older code (dating back to Windows 3.0), the use of explicit keywords `far`, `near` and `pascal`, that is, without the underscore. The Microsoft C compiler 6.0 and later versions introduced the underscore on nonstandard keywords to be compatible with the ANSI standard. However, the compilers continued to recognize the older forms of the keywords for compatibility. Then, in the next revision of the Draft ANSI standard, the convention was changed to using a double-underscore, so the compilers "officially" recognize names like `__far`, while still, for compatibility, recognizing `_far` and `far`. This is one of the many reasons the macro names are a better choice. Most of the 32-bit compilers for Intel platforms will issue warning messages if they encounter 16-bit keywords such as `far` or `__far`. Compilers for other platforms may simply refuse to parse these unknown keywords and give you compilation errors.

windows.h also defines the symbolic constant NULL. However, the Windows definition of NULL is sometimes different from the Microsoft C compiler definition or the ANSI specification. In Win32, compiling for C++, windows.h defines NULL as

```
#define NULL 0
```

The Microsoft C library header files, or windows.h when compiling for C (instead of C++), define NULL according to the recommended ANSI specification:

```
#define NULL ((void *)0)
```

For compatibility, you should assign NULL only to pointer variables (or handles). You should not assign NULL to a basic data type such as int, WORD, LONG, and so on. For those cases, you should explicitly assign a 0 constant. For example, the following code compiles without warnings no matter which definition of NULL is in effect:

```
LPSTR MenuName ;
    MenuName = NULL ;
```

However, the following code produces a warning with the C definition of NULL in effect and does not produce a warning with the C++ definition of NULL:

```
int i ;

    i = NULL ; /* This produces a warning */
```

Writing your code using a 0 constant where numeric 0 is meant and the symbol NULL when a null pointer to a data object is meant makes your code more portable and actually more correct. A null pointer in C actually is defined as a pointer value that is guaranteed not to point to any valid item. A null pointer in C does not have to be a bit pattern in which all bits are 0.[6] Assigning a constant literal 0 to a pointer in C could, on some architectures, validly set the pointer to a nonzero bit pattern. Setting **i** in the second line of the preceding example to a nonzero bit pattern probably is not what you intend. In addition, you are assigning a pointer to a nonpointer variable. For these reasons, the compiler produces a warning. This is why you should always test a null pointer by writing

```
LPSTR p;
  // ...
  if ( p == NULL)
```

and not by writing

```
LPSTR p;
  // ...
  if (!p)
```

The latter style is based on a property that the original rather simplistic code generator of the PDP-11 implementation of the C compiler (in the early 1970s) could produce ever-so-slightly-smaller code and the 64K

---

[6] "[The macro] NULL expands *to an implementation-defined null pointer constant*" (emphasis added). See *The Annotated ANSI C Standard,* §7.1.6. The full citation is given in the "Further Reading" section.

PDP-11 used 0 for a NULL pointer. On any modern machine with a modern compiler the first form, which is clearer and more correct, will be no more expensive to execute than the latter. You should never confuse pointer, integer, and Boolean operations.

That said, much currently written code freely assigns the symbolic constant NULL to pointers and nonpointers alike. This is largely because most Windows "handles" were declared as 16-bit integers, but NULL was supposed to represent a NULL handle, which was logically, if not actually, a pointer. Furthermore, the Microsoft documentation is riddled with inconsistencies; return values from some functions are given as type int but the value NULL is explicitly stated as a valid value, or as being pointers and the value 0 is explicitly stated as being a valid value. (This is the same documentation that states that –1 is a valid *unsigned* integer value that a function can return).

It is possible to avoid compiler warnings by ensuring that your program includes the windows.h header file before including any header files from the C runtime library that define NULL. For example:

```
#define STRICT
#include <windows.h>
#include <stddef.h> // a typical C library file
```

You will find that we pick a middle ground and when assigning a "null handle" tend to cast the NULL value to the type of the handle, for example,

```
wc.hIcon = (HICON)NULL ;
```

Just to add to the confusion, there is also the "null character" definition. This is also not NULL. The correct spelling of this character is "NUL", with one "L", because it is defined in ASCII as a control character, and all the control characters in ASCII have two- or three-letter names.[7] In Win32, this might be an 8-bit or 16-bit value because you might be using Unicode, a topic we discuss in Chapter 7 starting on page 427. Technically, it is *always* incorrect to set a character to the NUL value by an assignment such as

```
char string[40];
// ...
string[i] = NULL;  // make sure terminating character is there
```

because this is attempting to assign a pointer value to a character. Use the value 0, or more correctly '\0'. If you expect to support Unicode, you should declare and use the constant

```
#define NUL TEXT('\0')
```

which is discussed in more detail when we discuss Unicode.

---

[7] See page 17 in Hummel's book on data communication, cited in the "Further Reading" section. The first 32 ASCII characters, character codes 0 .. 31, are NUL, SOH, STX, ETX, EOT, ENQ, ACK, BEL, BS, HT, LF, VT, FF, CR, SO, SI, DLE, DC1, DC2, DC3, DC4, NAK, SYN, ETB, CAN, EM, SUB, ESC, FS, GS, RS, and US.

windows.h typedef **Declarations**

windows.h also uses many typedef declarations to permit a Windows program to be more independent of the actual architecture of the computer on which it is running. For example, a char variable on one system might be signed, but on another it might be unsigned. In fact, the Microsoft C compiler has the /J command line option, which changes the default type for char variables from signed to unsigned at compile time. While its use is uncommon (it was added so that older, pre-ANSI-standard unsigned-character-based C code could be compiled), it doesn't hurt to be precise about character specifications.

Other typedefs are used to declare types for which C does not have a native type. For example, C does not have a native Boolean type. Although a char or an int may be used as a Boolean, confusion arises when others read your code. Questions arise such as, "Is it significant that this variable has the value -1 as opposed to +1? After all, it is an integer variable." Defining and using an explicit Boolean type, BOOL, eliminates this potential confusion. Resist all temptations to confuse BOOL and integer types. If you declare a Boolean type, follow the style guidelines we suggest in Figure 1.6.

It is particularly important that you *never* test for a true Boolean by writing (var == TRUE). This is because many API calls that specify that they return a BOOL value in fact return 0 for FALSE and some other *nonzero* value for "true". Thus the test against the *literal* TRUE will fail. This is a source of many obscure bugs. In particular, Windows 95 often returns a nonzero value not equal to TRUE for many API functions for which Windows NT returns the literal value TRUE. The formal definition of the API function is that it returns type BOOL. This means that code that tests for equality to TRUE would function correctly on Windows NT but could (apparently inexplicably) fail when run on Windows 95.

Good Style	Bad Style
BOOL var;	int var, unsigned int var, char var, unsigned char var, short var, unsigned short var
var = TRUE;	var++, var = 1
var = FALSE;	var--, var = 0
if(var)	if(var != 0) if(var == TRUE)
if(!var)	if(var == 0) if(var == FALSE)

Figure 1.6: Good and bad style for BOOL **values**

Similarly, do not confuse integer and Boolean operations by testing for integer 0 with the Boolean not (!) operator. It is far clearer to write, read, and understand the test

```
int p;
  // ...
  if ( p == 0 )
```

than the rather dated, and obscure

```
int p;
  // ...
  if (!p)
```

It is best to use the typedefs declared by windows.h whenever possible. Some of the more common and basic types are listed in Table 1.4. windows.h uses the convention of prefixing a type with NP for a "near pointer", an irrelevant Win16 concept, to the type; LP for a far (long) pointer to the type and P for a pointer (unspecified as to near or far) to a type. In Win32, for compatibility with existing code, the NP and P prefixes are retained but are identical in all respects to the LP prefix. You should use only the LP prefix for new Win32 code. Why LP instead of just P? Well, for one thing, all of Microsoft's documentation explicitly specifies LP-style names. This suggests that they have not decommitted from the naming convention. In addition, with the future 64-bit platforms we may yet again get "near" (32-bit) and "far" (64-bit) pointers. Since most software companies will not publicly discuss future plans, we cannot tell what the future will hold in this regard. So we have chosen to follow Microsoft's current convention.

Table 1.4: Basic data types defined by `windows.h`

Desired Data Type	Type to Use	windows.h typedef
constant pointer to a Unicode string	LPCWSTR	const wchar_t *
pointer to a Unicode string	LPWSTR	wchar_t *wchar_t
constant pointer to an 8-bit string	LPCSTR	const char *
pointer to an 8-bit string	LPSTR	char *
constant pointer to a string	LPCTSTR	LPCWSTR or LPCSTR
pointer to a string	LPTSTR	LPWSTR or LPSTR
pointer to a byte	LPBYTE	BYTE *
pointer to an int	LPINT	int *
pointer to a 16-bit unsigned integer	LPWORD	WORD *
pointer to a 32-bit signed integer	LPLONG	long *
pointer to a 32-bit unsigned integer	LPDWORD	DWORD *
generic pointer	LPVOID	void *
The following are synonyms for the above:		
pointer to a byte	PBYTE	BYTE *
pointer to an int	PINT	int *
pointer to a 16-bit unsigned integer	PWORD	WORD *
pointer to a 32-bit signed integer	PLONG	long *
pointer to a 32-bit unsigned integer	PDWORD	DWORD *

Table 1.4: Basic data types defined by `windows.h`

Desired Data Type	Type to Use	windows.h typedef
generic pointer	PVOID	void *
The following are obsolete in Win32:		
near pointer to a byte	NPBYTE	BYTE NEAR *
near pointer to a signed integer	NPINT	int NEAR *
near pointer to a 16-bit unsigned integer	NPWORD	WORD NEAR *
near pointer to a 32-bit signed integer	NPLONG	long NEAR *
near pointer to a 32-bit unsigned integer	NPDWORD	DWORD NEAR *

The LP forms of the pointers are those that are specified by the API. The P forms are considered "more natural" by purists because the "large" model that required "far" (LP) pointers is now history. For consistency with the API documentation, we use LP-style definitions throughout this book.

The definition of the WORD typedef changed subtly in the Windows 3.1 version of the windows.h header file, and the older folklore often persists. The change in definition may also cause problems in porting code. Previously versions of the windows.h header file defined a WORD as an `unsigned int`. Beginning with Windows 3.1, a WORD is defined as an `unsigned short`. Both types are equivalent to a 16-bit unsigned value in programs compiled for a 16-bit version of Windows. However, the types are *not* equivalent in programs compiled for a 32-bit version of Windows.

If you are porting existing code from Win16 to Win32, one important place to check is for consistent and correct use of WORD. In particular, the use of WORD instead of UINT may give you portability problems. Also, watch out for window handlers that declare "WORD wParam" instead of "WPARAM wParam", the recommended practice starting with Windows 3.1. The declaration of wParam as a WORD will cause unexpected failures if you attempt to run the code in Win32.

An `int` in the C language is the "natural size" supported by the architecture. For a 16-bit processor, an integer's natural size is 16 bits. Similarly, for a 32-bit processor, an integer's natural size is 32 bits. A `short int` can be smaller than an `int` and is typically 16-bits wide. A `long` can be larger than an `int` and is typically 32 bits wide. (All three types could use the same size, and on some word-oriented architectures such as Digital Signal Processors (DSPs), there are C compilers that implement `int`, `short`, `long`, and even `char` as 32-bit values!) An `unsigned int` is a 16-bit value in 16-bit Windows applications and a 32-bit value in 32-bit Windows applications. An `unsigned short` is a 16-bit value in both environments. Basically a WORD is now defined to be a 16-bit unsigned value, always. The long-obsolete definition of WORD caused WORD variables to change size based on the compiler used.

The typedef UINT represents an unsigned `int` value, in other words, an unsigned integer that is the natural size used by the processor. You define a variable of type UINT when you want a "generic" unsigned value that is efficiently used by the processor but where a 16-bit value would suffice if that is what the processor best uses.

The new types LPWSTR represent pointers to *Unicode* strings. Unicode is a 16-bit character code that allows you to intermix a variety of international languages in your application. Unicode is currently supported only on Windows NT. In fact, all of Windows NT internally is implemented in terms of Unicode. A string may be either an 8-bit (ANSI/ISO) character string or a Unicode string, depending on whether the UNICODE symbol is defined at compile time. The definitions of LPTSTR and LPCTSTR change depending on whether this symbol is defined. If you are compiling for Unicode, they will be Unicode strings; otherwise, they will be ordinary 8-bit character strings. If you use LPTSTR and LPCTSTR in your code and follow some other conventions, a flip of a compiler switch will allow you to compile either a conventional 8-bit character set application for Windows 95 or Windows NT or a Unicode application for Windows NT. However, you must be careful how you define your strings and how you compute their lengths, which we do not go into here (but we discuss in great detail in Chapter 7). But most Win32 API calls that want strings specify LPTSTR and LPCTSTR parameters, so if you expect to eventually support Unicode, you should read the relevant documentation carefully and use these declarations. In Windows 95 and Windows NT 8-bit character mode, LPTSTR is exactly LPSTR and LPCTSTR is exactly LPCSTR. If you were to use the underlying wchar_t declaration, you would be committed to using Unicode. The definitions LPTSTR and LPCTSTR give you the flexibility of deferring this decision. All of our example code is Unicode-aware, and much of it has been compiled and tested using Unicode.

Getting a Handle on Handles

Another important data type defined by windows.h is that of a *handle*. A handle to a datum is used to reference the datum much like a pointer. Unlike a pointer, a handle may not be dereferenced. Additionally, a handle is not a "pointer to a pointer" as it is on other systems. A Windows handle basically is a claim check or token. At a theater or restaurant, you might give your coat or hat to a hat-check person. In return, you receive a claim check that you later use to retrieve your belongings. You have no idea what the information on the claim check means or how it relates to where your belongings are stored. You simply provide the claim check when required, and your belongings are returned.

Handles are used in the same way. For example, when you call the CreateWindow function, it returns a "window handle" that identifies the created window. You use this window handle whenever you ask Windows to perform some action on behalf of that window. In addition, whenever Windows sends your window function a message about a window, the window handle is included as part of the message to identify the window to which the message applies. You haven't the faintest idea what the internal representation of the handle means, but you don't need to know. You provide it when required, and Windows locates the data with which it is associated.

Handles are used throughout Windows. They provide a way to reference items that are managed by the operating system. Handles remain constant where pointers would be meaningless (because the operating system is in a separate address space) and could become invalid. Most Windows objects are identified by a handle. There are handles to windows; to resources such as strings, icons, menus, and cursors; to instances of a program; to graphical objects such as pens, fonts, brushes, and bitmaps; to device contexts; to regions; to color palettes; and even to dynamically allocated memory. Table 1.5 lists the various types of handles defined by windows.h.

 In Win16, a handle was always 16 bits; in Win32, a handle is always 32 bits. If you are porting code from Win16, beware of a tendency of programmers to pack two handles into a single long word or to combine a handle and some other 16-bit quantity into a 32-bit long word. There are other important implications of this change that result in incompatible messages between Win16 and Win32, which we point out as they occur.

Table 1.5: Types of handles defined by windows.h

`windows.h` typedef	Handle Type	`windows.h` typedef	Handle Type
HACCEL	Accelerator	HINSTANCE	Program instance
HBITMAP	Bitmap (GDI)	HKEY	Registry key
HBRUSH	Brush (GDI)	HLOCAL *(obsolete)*	Local memory
HCURSOR	Cursor	HMENU	Menu
HDC	Device context	HMETAFILE *(obsolete)*	Metafile
HDRVR	Device driver	HMODULE	Module
HDWP	Deferred window position	HPALETTE	Palette (GDI)
HENHMETAFILE	Enhanced metafile	HPEN	Pen (GDI)
HFONT	Font (GDI)	HRGN	Region (GDI)
HGDIOBJ	General GDI Object	HRSRC	Resource
HGLOBAL	Global memory	HSTR	String for OLE/DDE
HHOOK	Hook	HTASK	Task
HICON	Icon	HWND	Window

Using the Windows C Runtime Libraries and Header Files

Whenever you need to include both Windows header files and standard C library header files, you should include the Windows libraries first. This guarantees that certain symbols that must be defined specifically for Windows, such as NULL, are correctly defined. Microsoft has set its header files up in such a way that this will always work correctly. If you are using other header files or header files for third-party libraries, you should ensure these header files do not force symbols, such as NULL, to have definitions that conflict with the Windows definitions. While NULL is usually handled correctly in third-party software designed for Windows, the inclusion of other C runtime headers from third-party vendors occasionally causes problems if these headers are not "Windows-aware" and do not follow the correct conventions.

Using Strict Type Checking

You can take advantage of stricter type checking by defining the symbol STRICT this way before including the windows.h header file:

```
#define STRICT
```

When the symbol STRICT is defined, the windows.h header file defines many data types in a more precise way. This alternative definition of various data types causes the C compiler to differentiate data types that are considered identical when STRICT is not defined.

For example, when STRICT is not defined you can pass a handle to a device context (HDC) to a function expecting a handle to a window (HWND) without comment by the compiler. Both handles are typedefed as UINT types, so they do not actually differ in type. When STRICT is defined, the compiler will generate an error because windows.h defines each type as a pointer to different types of imaginary structures. (Structures of these types are never allocated. Only the type definition itself is used.)

This pointer very deliberately occupies the same space as an UINT variable, but the compiler can detect passing one type of pointer to a function expecting a different type. So parameter mismatches that previously were not detected will be when strict type checking is enabled.

However, when strict type checking is enabled, your code can no longer indiscriminately assign variables of different types to each other without the compiler's producing warnings and errors about such usage. A handle to a window (HWND) differs from a handle to a menu (HMENU). If you try to save one in a variable defined to be the other, the compiler will complain about it. Although it's a bit of work to write code to compile without warnings with strict type checking enabled, it's to your benefit to do so. Code that compiles without warnings with strict type checking enabled often contains fewer bugs and is far more portable between 16-bit and 32-bit Windows applications. Often, if you are porting a Win16 application to Win32, you might be well-served to insert the STRICT definition and recompile the Win16 application using a 16-bit compiler. STRICT may catch problems that would interfere with porting.

Naming Conventions

Microsoft suggests that you write Windows applications following its suggested naming conventions. Doing this, it believes, makes your applications easier to understand and to maintain. It recommends specific naming conventions for function names and variable names.

Function Names

Windows functions are named according to a verb-noun model that identifies what the function does (verb) and what the function operates on (noun). Function names begin with an uppercase letter, each word in a function name is individually capitalized, and all words are concatenated (no spaces or underscores separate the words). The example programs in this book use the same naming convention. Some examples of Windows function names include these:

- `RegisterClass`
- `CreateWindow`
- `PostMessage`

Parameter Names

Windows programmers typically use a naming convention for variables as well. Microsoft has decided that variables should be named in a way that identifies the data type of the variable. Variable names are given a lowercase prefix that indicates the general type of the variable, followed by one or more words describing the variable's contents. Multiple words in a variable name are individually capitalized and concatenated, as in function names. Table 1.6 lists standard prefixes used in Windows programming. When no lowercase prefix is used, a variable normally is a short integer whose name is descriptive.

 Somebody has to come out in public and try to restore sanity. I don't like the Hungarian Notation, consider it a grotesque aberration in the history of computing, and have found it to cause more problems than it claims to solve. One advantage of writing a book is that the authors get to express their opinions, and this is mine. It is based on 33 years in the profession, a Ph.D. in computer science, many years of experience in commercial software development, and a more-than-casual study of human cognition and reasoning. The few popular systems that incorporated type information into names that are still with us are FORTRAN and BASIC, and both of those abandoned this technique after a few years of evolution, and for compelling reasons. Hungarian notation originated in the pre-ANSI C compilers where there was no cross-module type checking. In that context, it may have made sense, but its usefulness today is problematic. *joseph m. newcomer.*

It is worth observing that this naming convention produces very strange problems. For example, you may have a procedure that returns a BOOL result and, following the convention, declare a name to hold its result, such as

`BOOL bResult;`

But then you discover that the result type must reflect, say, three values, so you change the name to

`int bResult;`

and instead of assigning TRUE and FALSE you assign RESULT_OK, RESULT_BAD, and RESULT_UNKNOWN. Those reading your code will be surprised to see a "b"-type name assigned non-Boolean values. So you have to change the variable name to something more appropriate, such as `fResult`.

Another example is that often in Win16, a variable was declared

`WORD wSize;`

or, more seriously, a name declared in an interface structure:

```
typedef struct {
     WORD wSize;
     WORD wCount;
```

```
WORD wBits;
int  nWidth } FunnyStructure;
```

Table 1.6: Standard prefixes for Windows variables

Prefix	Data type	Meaning
b	BYTE	8-bit unsigned integer.
ch	CHAR	Character (an 8-bit signed value).
d	double	Double-precision floating-point.
dw	DWORD	32-bit unsigned integer.
f	BOOL	Boolean (nonzero is true; zero is false).
f	WORD	Bit flags packed into a 16-bit integer.
gh	GLOBALHANDLE	Handle to global storage from GlobalAlloc.
h	HANDLE	32-bit unsigned integer handle to an object.
hwnd	HWND	Window handle.
l	LONG	32-bit signed integer.
lp	FAR *	32-bit far (long) pointer
n	short	16-bit signed integer (number)
np	FAR *	32-bit pointer
p	* (pointer)	32-bit pointer (inconsistently used)
pt	POINT	32-bit x- and y-coordinates packed in a struct
rgb	RGB	RGB color value packed in a DWORD
sz	CHAR array	NUL-terminated character array (string)
w	WORD	16-bit unsigned integer (except wPARAM)

when in fact, as you discover in porting, it should have been a UINT. If you change the declaration to a UINT, you have to change the name everywhere to uSize. If you fail to change the name, the whole purpose of the naming convention is defeated. The use of the "w" prefix will mislead you into thinking that you are dealing with a 16-bit quantity, when in fact you are dealing with a 32-bit quantity. Furthermore, if this name is part of a published interface, you may not have the option of changing the name. Thus the published public interface, although it has changed in structure, now has a misleading name. The ultimate absurdity of this naming convention is the wParam parameter, which you would expect from its prefix to be a 16-bit unsigned integer. In Win32, however, it is really a 32-bit unsigned integer and so would have to be named uParam. The "cultural compatibility" that calls for the first parameter to a message to be called "wParam" was more important to retain than was the meaning of the prefix.

Consider further the issue of porting or extension. In the move to a 32-bit platform, the value in the structure, such as wSize, may have to be changed to a 32-bit value. As we pointed out, this should necessitate a change in the name. To do otherwise is misleading and a potential source of major misunderstanding on the part of the user of the structure. But to change the name will make obsolete all existing code, thereby rendering it uncompilable. The complementary situation could be that the variable declared as int should have been

declared as a `short` in order to be compatible with earlier file structures. Again, this generates either a m
understanding or an incompatibility. By eliminating the type from the name, these problems go away. So
ware evolves. Be prepared for this. Nonetheless, Microsoft has adopted these naming conventio
extensively, and you must at least understand how to read them. In some cases, violating the tradition (su
as changing the name of the two message parameters from `wParam` and `lParam`) will render your code u
readable to experienced Windows programmers. These naming conventions should be used, when at all, ve
carefully.

Some examples of the names this style generates are as follows: `fSuccess`, `chAnswer`, `szFilenam`
`wParam`, `lParam`, `dwValue`, `hwndButton`, `xPos`, `yPos`.

In addition to the `wParam` problem, we have found numerous instances in which Microsoft does not adhe
to its own naming convention, thus leading to type mismatch errors that cause compilations to fail. There a
API functions that take structures with names that start with `dw` that are actually declared as `LPVOID`, ar
names that start with `lp` that are actually `DWORD`s. This naming convention is at best highly suspect, no matt
how much Microsoft believes in it and tries to promote it. With few exceptions, largely those of cultur
compatibility (most notably `wParam` and `lParam`, and the use of an occasional h-prefix for window handles
we avoid it entirely in our sample code.

Example Code

We have adopted a convention to help you distinguish our functions from Windows functions. We hav
started every function name in our code with a lowercase letter, except when constrained by the rules o
Windows and except for some other very specific exceptions, which we try to point out when appropriate
Nearly all Windows API functions start with uppercase letters. The purpose of this convention is to save yo
confusion in looking up a function in the Windows API. If a function name starts with a lowercase letter, it i
either a function we have defined or it is part of the "traditional" C runtime library. All of our functions con
tain at least one embedded uppercase letter. Since we assume you have a background in the C language, w
expect that you will recognize most of the C library names.

Diving Right In

Much of the information just presented may tend to scare you away from Windows programming. I
shouldn't. Windows programming seems complex because of the tremendous variety and depth in the Win
dows API. Quite a bit of the information may not soak in until you actually start writing Windows programs
But you'll be a beginner only once. As you get more experience with Windows programming, you can re
view this chapter and gain more from it than you might have on the first reading. The tables in this chapte
are intended to be comprehensive at the risk of including more information than has been presented and ex
plained at this point. We find comprehensive tables to have more long-term reference value than multiple
pieces of related information scattered throughout a book.

We've always found it impossible to learn how to program in a new environment by reading about it. So
without further ado, we show you in Chapter 2 how to create a skeletal Windows program that will be the ba
sic structure from which all Windows applications may be developed.

Further Reading

Feuer, Alan, *MFC Programming*, Addison-Wesley, 1996. ISBN 0-201-63358-2.

An excellent companion to our book, this book covers how to use the Microsoft Foundation Class library, concentrating on the MFC and C++ aspects. If you're going to program in MFC, you should have this book also.

Harbison, Samuel P. III, and Steele, Guy L Jr., *C: A Reference Manual, Fourth Edition*, Prentice-Hall, 1995. ISBN 0-13-326224-3.

See the review on page 941.

Hummel, Robert L., *Programmer's Technical Reference: Data and Fax Communication*, Ziff-Davis Press, 1993. ISBN 1-56276-077-7.

More information than you could ever possibly absorb on the low-level details of modem command strings. A thoroughly researched book that describes the overlapping and conflicting codes that are used. A readily-accessible reference to the ANSI character set standard.

Proceedings of the ACM Conference on the History of Personal Workstations, January 9–10, 1986, Association for Computing Machinery (ACM Inc.). ISBN 0-89791-176-8.

Schildt, Herman, *The Annotated ANSI C Standard*, Osborne/McGraw-Hill, 1990. ISBN 0-07-881952-0.

Essential reading for anyone who cares about the formal definition of C. The annotations offer insight into the purpose of a language construct, point out ambiguities, and generally make this book more readable than the raw ANSI/ISO standard.

Schulman, Andrew, Maxey, David, and Pietrek, Matt, *Undocumented Windows,* Addison-Wesley, 1992. ISBN 0-201-60834-0.

See the review on page 274.

2 A Skeletal Windows Application

This chapter describes a skeletal Microsoft Windows program called Skeleton. Even though Skeleton is a simple Windows program, it is not an absolutely minimal Windows program. Skeleton is a program from which you can learn the basic components of all Windows applications. It is designed to be easily extensible and can be used as the foundation for future Windows applications of much greater complexity. Thus it does a few things in a more roundabout manner than is absolutely necessary. Rather than present an overly simplistic "first" Windows program—one that you would have to modify significantly each time you reuse it—we take the approach of doing things the "right" way. We've done this at the risk of introducing concepts not yet presented, such as resources and dialogs. Don't worry about the details of these concepts. They will be covered in greater depth in later chapters dedicated to those topics.

 Once you understand the Windows components discussed in this book, you may wish to use an even more complete, easily extensible Windows application as the starting point for your own applications. Included with this book is the Template example program. Template contains implementations of many of the capabilities discussed in the book: for example, a system information **About...** dialog box, common resource strings, common menu items, and common command handlers.

Skeleton is designed to illustrate the following concepts:

- Using the WinMain function

- Initializing a Windows program

- Writing the message loop

- Writing a window function

- Writing an About dialog function

- Terminating the application

- Creating a resource definition file

- Creating a module definition file

- Building a Windows application

he program is used as the starting point for developing all example programs in this book.

he **Skeleton** Application Source Program

<eleton is a standard Windows application. It is similar in functionality to the Generic program in-uded on the Microsoft Windows SDK Sample Source Code disk. It is not similar in its use of system re->urces, its structure, or its basic design goals.

<eleton complies with the recommendations for user-interface style given in the *Windows Interface uidelines for Software Design*, a publication included as part of the Microsoft Developer's Network ⁄ISDN) documentation and also available from Microsoft Press (see "Further Reading" on page 100). The ·ogram has a main window that has a border, an application menu (including only a **Help** menu because of e simple nature of this program), a minimize box, and a maximize box. Selecting the **Help** menu displays pop-up menu containing one item, an **About...** command. Selecting the **About...** menu item displays a di-og box (called the About dialog box) describing the Skeleton program.

he Skeleton program consists primarily of seven source code files, their supporting header (include) es, plus a few miscellaneous files (bitmaps, icons, makefiles, etc.). The main source files are

- About.c,

- Initialization.c,

- MainFrame.c,

- Skeleton.rc,

- StdSDK.c,

- Utility.c, and

- WinMain.c.

\ll Skeleton application C source files begin by including the application-defined StdSDK.h header le. You place #include statements for any infrequently changed but frequently used header files into this le. It contains the following lines:

```
*if !defined (_StdSDK_H_)
:define _StdSDK_H_

*define STRICT              // Enable strict type-checking of Windows handles
#include <windows.h>        // Fundamental Windows header file
#include <windowsx.h>       // Useful Windows programming extensions
#include <commctrl.h>       // Common Controls declarations

#include "Extensions.h"     // windowsx.h extensions
#include "Utility.h"        // Application-independent
                            //   debugging and utility functions
#include "Skeleton.h"       // Application declarations
#endif           /* _StdSDK_H_ */
```

The first line is a #define statement defining the symbolic constant STRICT. The windows.h header file contains C language preprocessor directives that define Windows data types and function prototypes differently based on the presence or absence of a definition for the symbol STRICT. For example, old versions of windows.h (prior to Windows 3.1) define both the   HWND and HDC data types as equivalent to the WORD data type. Because an HWND variable and an HDC variable are both WORDs, a C compiler will silently allow you to assign a window handle variable to a device context (DC) variable. However, passing an HDC handle to a function that is expecting an HWND handle results in a program that doesn't work and contains a difficult-to-find error.

For compatibility with old source code, current versions of windows.h, for both Win16 and Win32, define these data types as WORDs (Win16) or PVOIDs (Win32) when STRICT is not defined. However, when strict type checking is enabled, windows.h declares the HWND data type to be a synonym for a pointer to a constant HWND structure. Similarly, it declares (typedefs, actually) the HDC data type to be a synonym for a pointer to a constant HDC structure. This provides a number of benefits.

Because these data types are now pointers, a C compiler will warn you when you attempt to assign a variable of one type to a variable of the other type. windows.h also declares the pointers as pointers to constant structures. This prevents you from accidentally attempting to dereference these pointers and altering random memory. The structures to which windows.h defines variables of these types to point don't actually exist. Pointers and UINTs occupy the same space in Win32. So this is really just a case in which it's convenient to define multiple data types differently in order to gain additional error checking but in a manner whereby all different definitions occupy the same amount of storage. The size and value of the handle hasn't changed at all. Only how the compiler interprets one data type's equivalence to other data types changes.

Strict type checking also causes windows.h to prototype some functions slightly differently. For example, windows.h prototypes the GlobalLock function as returning a char * value when you don't enable strict type checking and as returning a void * value when you enable strict type checking.

You should also ensure that the symbol _WINDOWS is defined before you include any C runtime library header files. You should define the symbol like this:

```
#define _WINDOWS
```

Visual C++, which we used to compile all the example programs in this book, automatically defines _WINDOWS when you specify that you're compiling a Windows application. So we don't define it. If you're using a different vendor's C compiler, one that doesn't automatically define the symbol _WINDOWS, you should add this definition to the source code. If you prefer, you can add these three lines to ensure that the symbol is always defined while simultaneously avoiding a duplicate definition:

```
#if !defined (_WINDOWS)
#define _WINDOWS
#endif
```

Defining the symbol _WINDOWS (no matter how it's defined) actually has no effect in any of the source files of the Skeleton program. The symbol _WINDOWS has an effect only when including standard C runtime library header files. When the symbol _WINDOWS is defined while including standard C runtime header files, the preprocessor includes only the statements and functions from the header files that are compatible with the Windows environment. Skeleton doesn't include any of the C runtime header files because it doesn't use any of the runtime library functions.

However, we feel it's best to get into the habit of always defining the symbol (which isn't difficult when the compiler does it automatically!). Often a file initially does not contain calls to the runtime library, but it does use it eventually. Habitually defining the symbol never hurts. It produces the extra diagnostics when required, and you have one less thing to remember when writing a Windows program.

The first #include statement is for the standard Windows header file: windows.h. Every Windows program must include windows.h, which defines the data types used by Windows programs as well as the Windows Application Program Interface (API) functions. As you'll see shortly, defining the entry point function for a Windows program requires the data types WINAPI, HINSTANCE, and LPSTR.

The second #include statement is for the standard Windows header file: windowsx.h. The Windows 3.1 SDK introduced this header file, but it always surprises us that few Windows programmers seem to know about it. It contains macro definitions for many useful macros. Specifically, it contains macro API definitions and Windows *message cracker* definitions. This file contains useful extended declarations and definitions not present in the original windows.h header file. It is summarized in Appendix C.

Macro API definitions are C preprocessor macros that you call just as you do a Windows API. For example, a DeletePen macro API is defined to call the DeleteObject function with one parameter that is expected to be a pen. While calling a macro API is useful, doing so is more dangerous than calling a prototyped Windows function API, for two reasons. First, a macro is implemented as simple text substitution done by the C preprocessor. It can produce unexpected side effects as a result. For example, you might pass the parameter i++ to a macro. The macro definition might use that parameter more than once. Looking at the expanded macro, you would see that i++ used multiple times in the resulting source code. This is a case in which you would expect i to be incremented once, but it may be incremented zero, once, or numerous times depending on the actual implementation of the macro. Passing i++ to a function always causes i to be incremented once. However, in our experience, the number of times this actually happens in practice is very small.[1]

Any macro that references one of its parameters more than once can cause side effects; for example, the GlobalFreePtr and SetDlgMsgResult macros. As an extreme example, the SetDlgMsgResult macro evaluates one of its parameters six times and another parameter twice.

---

[1] This is due at least partly to my (jmn) personal style. I strongly disagree with a philosophy that introduces gratuitous side effects into contexts such as parameter passing or if-tests. Consequently, I *never* use an assignment embedded in an if-statement or a parameter evaluation. I find that these contribute significantly to long-term maintenance costs and diminish code clarity. I never use the ++ or -- operators embedded in parameter-passing contexts, meaning that it doesn't matter if I'm calling a macro or a function; nor do I have to care. The mythology that encourages these practices is based partly on compromises that had to be made to generate decent code on the original PDP-11 C compilers that ran in, and compiled for, 64K 16-bit machines. And it is based partly on an illusion that programs are "better" if they are encoded with the fewest number of lexemes. Since modern optimizing compilers render the first consideration irrelevant and the second substantially increases long-term maintenance costs, I reject both styles. It is surprising how much simpler programming, debugging, and long-term maintenance become when these practices, permitted by the compiler, are treated as if they are violations of the language. A good lint program can be told to flag these constructs, and these are the default settings I use.

The second reason calling a macro API is more dangerous is that the macro APIs cast their parameters to their expected data types. These casts tell the compiler to interpret the parameter as the specified data type regardless of the parameter's actual data type. This means you could write the following statement without the compiler's complaining:

```
DeletePen (1) ;
```

The DeletePen function actually expects the argument to be of type HPEN, not an integer.

Given these considerations, we *still* recommend the use of the macro API, although its use should be with considerable care. Future releases of Windows can implement actual function-prototyped APIs with the same name as a macro API, the macro definition can be removed from windowsx.h, and your program can immediately gain the additional type checking provided by the function prototyping. In the meantime, using the macro APIs improves the readability of your source code considerably.

In addition, the macros give platform independence. The macro GetWindowInstance(hWnd) correctly retrieves the application instance handle associated with the specified window when used in Win16 and Win32 applications. The macro hides the fact that the underlying API call used to retrieve the instance handle differs for Win16 and Win32 applications.

The windowsx.h header file also contains the definition of a number of *message cracker* macros. You can use these macros to further isolate your 16-bit application from the 16-bit design of Windows and make it more portable to a 32-bit version of Windows. Unfortunately, at the time of this writing, the message cracker macros do not form a complete set. You also cannot use them when writing common dialog hook functions. However, they make the code much easier to read and structure it nicely so that if you decide to convert your application to C++ and use the Microsoft Foundation Classes (MFC), your job will be *very* much easier. If you have an application that must compile for both Win16 and Win32 from the same source, the use of the message cracker macros is virtually mandatory. But we simply do not write C code that decodes raw messages in the "traditional" Windows style.

The third #include statement is for the standard Windows header file commctrl.h. Windows 95, Win32s version 1.3 and later (running on Windows 3.1), and Windows NT 3.51 introduced a number of "new" common user-interface controls (such as tree views, progress bars, and up-down controls). This header file contains declarations and definitions associated with the common controls. Microsoft has departed from the practice of attempting to define every possible symbol in a single header file, windows.h, as was done in the earlier releases.

The remaining #include statements are for extensions.h, Utility.h, and Skeleton.h. The extensions.h header file contains declarations and definitions we believe should have been in windows.h, windowsx.h, and commctrl.h, but aren't. The contents of extensions.h are summarized in Appendix C. The Utility.h header file contains useful declarations and definitions used by the Skeleton application. The Skeleton.h header file contains definitions of symbolic constants used by the Skeleton application and function prototypes for all nonstatic functions.

Microsoft apparently views the `windowsx.h` file as being solely for the purpose of Win16-to-Win32 conversion compatibility. Thus it has failed to keep it up-to-date with the Win32 API functions and messages; messages that did not exist in Win16 have no support in `windowsx.h`. Because of the increased readability of C code written using these kinds of macros, we felt compelled to complete the set. In addition, *some* of the messages in `commctrl.h` have macro APIs defined in `commctrl.h`, and others, for reasons that seem totally inexplicable, do not. We have tried to correct this deficiency as well by adding many of the missing `commctrl.h` features into `extensions.h`.

The `WinMain` Function

Just as every standard C program begins executing at the function called `main`, every standard C Windows program begins executing at the function called `WinMain`. However, `WinMain` is not the first code executed by a Windows application, just as `main` is not the first code executed by a standard C program. In both cases, the linker inserts some start-up code that actually gets control from the operating system. This start-up code in turn calls the function you view as the entry point of the application.

`WinMain` is typically a short function that performs three critical actions.

- It performs all necessary initialization. This includes, but is not limited to, loading resources used by the program, registering window classes, and creating windows.

- It executes a message loop fetching messages for the application and dispatching to the appropriate message-handling functions.

- It terminates the application when the message loop detects a `WM_QUIT` message after freeing any resources possibly reserved by the initialization code.

The `WinMain` function is located in the winmain.c source file and is defined as follows:

```
int WINAPI
WinMain (HINSTANCE hInstance,        // Current instance
         HINSTANCE hPrevInstance,    // Previous instance (unused)
         LPSTR lpszCmdLine,          // Pointer to command line
         int nCmdShow)               // ShowWindow parameter
{
    /* Initialization, message loop and termination. */
}
```

The Parameters to `WinMain`

`WinMain` is defined as a function that takes four parameters, is called using the `WINAPI` calling sequence, and returns an integer on exit.

When an application is started, Windows passes four parameters (indirectly, via the start-up code) to the `WinMain` function. Unlike C functions, functions using the `__stdcall` calling sequence must explicitly list all parameters to the function whether or not the function uses all parameters. Recall from the discussion of calling sequences on page 18 that `__stdcall` functions are expected to remove the parameters they were given from the stack. A `__stdcall` function will remove the same number of parameters from the stack as are listed in its definition. If the definition lists a different number than this, the stack will be incorrectly adjusted and the program will not operate properly.

We've defined WinMain using the ANSI standard method for defining function parameters. Subtle and difficult-to-find errors can be introduced into C programs that mix old-style (K&R C) and ANSI function declarations and definitions. Even though errors are not introduced by defining WinMain using the old-style parameter definition, it's best to adopt good habits across the board. Windows itself uses the ANSI style of function parameter declarations throughout windows.h. You should never use the old-style function declarations in Windows programming; they will only lead to calamity.

The first two parameters to WinMain are a specific type of handle, an HINSTANCE handle. The two parameters are typically named hInstance and hPrevInstance. You can think of a handle as a code or token or integer that uniquely identifies an object to Windows. Win32 provides WinMain with one handle, hInstance, to an instance. The hPrevInstance parameter is used only in Win16 and is retained in Win32 only for source compatibility. It will always have the value (HINSTANCE)NULL in Win32. But what in the world is an instance?

In this case, an *instance* is a particular copy of a running program. Not only can you run more than one application at a time in Windows, but you can also run multiple copies of the same application concurrently. Each copy of the running program is an "instance" of the application. Windows distinguishes among the copies by their instance handles.

When Windows loads a second or subsequent copy of a currently running application, it doesn't make a completely separate copy of the code and data for the application. Instead, only a new copy of the data for the application is loaded. The original copy of the application's code is kept in memory and runs both instances of the application. An application's WinMain function may be running on behalf of many different copies of the application. Windows passes the hInstance parameter to WinMain to identify the instance of the application for which WinMain is running. You will need this instance handle many times as you write functions that interact with the Win32 operating system services. It is therefore typical to store this value in a global variable. This global variable is "logically" a const, since it is initialized once and never modified. But the C language wouldn't let you declare it as a const because it must be stored into once, dynamically. Use of such a global variable does not violate our principle that the use of global variables in Windows almost always is an error in the program design. (That is, except in a few rare cases in which the API itself forces the use of a global variable because of the need for backward compatibility with the more primitive existing Win16 API functions, many of which were designed before the principle was understood by Microsoft.)

In Win16, the hPrevInstance parameter was used to determine if there was a previously running instance. It was important in Win16 to not attempt to register window classes twice. In Win32, there is no similar resource constraint. So that code can be readily ported to Win32, Win32 always passes in a NULL handle for the hPrevInstance pointer, so existing code will work correctly. However, some actions that depend on hPrevInstance being non-NULL must be carefully examined if you are porting existing code.

You might prefer that an attempt by the user to run a second instance of a currently running application would cause the existing application to "wake up" and respond to the user's request. You can do that with the following code. (Don't worry about understanding exactly what this code does right now. You'll learn that soon enough!)

```
HWND hwnd;
HWND hwndPopup ;

    hwnd = FindWindow (ClassName, NULL) ;
    if (IsWindow (hwnd)) {
        hwndPopup = GetLastActivePopup (hwnd) ;
        if (IsWindow (hwndPopup))
            hwnd = hwndPopup ;
        SetForegroundWindow (hwnd) ;
        if (IsIconic (hwnd))
            ShowWindow (hwnd, SW_RESTORE) ;
    }
    return FALSE ;
```

 In Win16, the previous code often appears inside a test for a non-NULL hPrevInstance. Watch out for this when porting a Win16 application. The Windows Programming Techniques guide suggests alternatives such as creating a uniquely named pipe (not available in Windows 95), creating or testing a named semaphore, or broadcasting a unique system-wide message.

The third parameter to `WinMain` is `lpszCmdLine`. According to the parameter name prefixing conventions as a guide (which seems silly, because the parameter type, LPSTR, says exactly the same thing), this should be a pointer to a NUL-terminated string called a `CmdLine`, which sounds like "Command line". In fact, this is exactly what it is. When you run a Windows program by selecting the **Run...** option from the menu produced by clicking on the Desktop Taskbar's **Start** button, a dialog box appears in which you can enter a command line to run a program. The first word on the command line is the program name, and all subsequent words appear in the string to which `lpszCmdLine` points. For example, if you enter the following command line:

```
Skeleton appears in a window
```

then Windows runs the Skeleton program and `lpszCmdLine` points to an array of characters containing the string "appears in a window" immediately followed by a 0 byte, that is, a NUL-terminated string. When you run the program using simply the program name in the dialog box without any additional arguments or from the File Manager's directory list, `lpszCmdLine` points to an empty string. There are other situations, such as drag-and-drop-onto-application, drag-and-drop-onto-printer, and OLE activation, that will provide additional text in the command line. (Those topics require a set of books that in total would be much thicker than this one, so we won't even touch on those topics here!)

The specification of `WinMain` may come as a surprise to those moving to Windows programming from a more traditional C environment. Where are our old friends `argc` and `argv`? Do we really have to parse the command line "by hand"? Well, one answer is that in Windows the command line is vastly less useful than in traditional programming environments. Most options that are normally set by command line arguments in traditional C environments are set by menu items, dialogs, and other sources. For now, the only significant use of the command line is to support OLE and drag-and-drop, topics outside the scope of this book. The Visual C++ runtime provides equivalents to the `argc` and `argv` parameters to `main` as global variables set by the C runtime: `__argc` and `__argv`. These variables are defined in the stdlib.h header file.

The fourth parameter to the `WinMain` function is `nCmdShow`. The `nCmdShow` parameter is an integer that specifies how the application should display its main window. Normally your application should use this value as an argument to the `ShowWindow` function when calling that function to display the application's main window. The `ShowWindow` function must be called only once per program with the `nCmdShow` parameter from the `WinMain` function. Subsequent calls to `ShowWindow` must use one of the window state values described in Table 2.1.

Table 2.1: ShowWindow window states

Value	Meaning
SW_HIDE	Hides the window and activates another window.
SW_MAXIMIZE	Same as `SW_SHOWMAXIMIZED`, which is the preferred usage. The window is displayed maximized, that is, as filling the entire screen area. The `SW_MAXIMIZE` name is considered obsolete in Win32.
SW_MINIMIZE	Same as `SW_SHOWMINIMIZED`, which is the preferred usage. The window is displayed as an icon. The `SW_MINIMIZE` name is considered obsolete in Win32.
SW_NORMAL	Same as `SW_SHOWNORMAL`, which is the preferred usage. The window placement is neither maximized nor iconic. The name `SW_NORMAL` is considered obsolete in Win32.
SW_RESTORE	Same as `SW_SHOWNORMAL`, which is the preferred usage. The name `SW_RESTORE` is considered obsolete in Win32.
SW_SHOW	Activates a window and displays it in its current size and position.
SW_SHOWDEFAULT	Sets the show state based on the `SW_` flag specified in the `STARTUPINFO` structure passed to the **CreateProcess** function by the program that started the application.
SW_SHOWMAXIMIZED	Activates a window and displays it maximized.
SW_SHOWMINIMIZED	Activates a window and displays it as iconic.
SW_SHOWMINNOACTIVE	Displays a window as iconic without activating it.
SW_SHOWNA	Displays a window in its current state without activating it.
SW_SHOWNOACTIVATE	Displays a window in its most recent size and position without activating it.
SW_SHOWNORMAL	Activates and displays a window. If the window is minimized or maximized, Windows restores it to its original size and position.

The program that starts your application provides the value of the `nCmdShow` parameter. It may supply any of the values listed in Table 2.1. Generally, your program should display its main application window using the value supplied in `nCmdShow`. You can ignore the `nCmdShow` parameter and display the window in whichever way you wish. However, doing so results in a program that users perceive as not behaving correctly. Honoring the nCmdShow parameter becomes more important in the future when you start dealing with drag-and-drop and OLE, so it is not a bad idea to get into the habit of honoring it.

For example, assume you've written your application to show the application's main window as a maximized window. When Windows starts your program, the nCmdShow parameter is set to the value SW_SHOWNORMAL. However, your application displays a maximized window rather than displaying a normal-sized window, as it was requested. The difference is more apparent when a user starts the program by listing it in the load section of win.ini. Windows calls your application with the nCmdShow parameter set to SW_SHOWMINNOACTIVE. The user expects the program to start up as an icon, neatly tucked away for later use; instead, it takes over the whole screen. When you don't use the nCmdShow parameter when initially displaying an application's window, you are ignoring a user's request to display the window in a particular fashion.

WinMain Initialization

Win32 applications generally require a set of standard initializations be done before the program really "runs". Typically, these involve registering one or more window classes and creating one or more windows. Skeleton places all of this code in a function called initInstance that is called by the following code:

```
if (!initInstance (hInstance, IDR_MAINFRAME, nCmdShow)) {
        return FALSE ;
    }
```

The initInstance function is called to perform any initialization. initInstance returns a Boolean value indicating whether its initialization was successful. When initInstance cannot successfully initialize the application, WinMain returns the value FALSE back to Windows. FALSE is defined by windows.h as the value 0. Although WinMain specifies that it returns an integer as its return value, Windows itself currently does not use the value returned by the WinMain function. (If you write a program that runs another program, however, you can check the return value yourself. Interpretation of the return value is up to the initiator of the program, and Windows ignores it.) Returning from the WinMain function causes Windows to terminate the application. As when returning from main in C, you will find that there is additional code that is executed on your behalf after you return from WinMain. However, you don't have to worry about what it is.

In Win16, there were two kinds of initialization: *application* and *instance*. The *application* initialization was done only once in the first instance, a situation that was detected by looking for a NULL hPrevInstance. The *instance* initialization was done for every instance. In Win32, there is no distinction of instances. For portability and compatibility, the hPrevInstance is always NULL, so existing code will work correctly. For new code, there is no reason to distinguish the two kinds of initialization.

Initialization: initInstance

One of the first operations an initInstance function does is to register the window classes. A *window class* is not a window but a template that is used when creating individual windows that are members of the class.

A window class has the same relationship to a window as does a cookie cutter to a cookie. Although a cookie cutter defines the shape and size of a cookie that it cuts out, no one mistakes a cookie cutter for a cookie. Similarly, a window class defines certain attributes common to all windows that are created based on that class, but it must not be mistaken for a window of the class.

Attributes of a window such as the address of the window function that processes messages for the window, the shape of the window's cursor, the icon used to represent the window when it is minimized, and the color and pattern used for the window's background are all *class attributes* of a window. Before a window of a given class is created, the window class must be defined. Defining a window class and notifying Windows of the new class is called *registering* a window class.

You register a window class by filling in a WNDCLASS structure (defined by windows.h) with information about the class. A pointer to the structure is passed as a parameter to the RegisterClass function. Once a window class has been successfully registered with Windows, you can create windows of the class.

Skeleton's initInstance function returns FALSE if the attempt to register the application's main (and only) window class fails. It also returns FALSE if the attempt to create the first (and only) window fails. The initInstance function is in the Initialization.c source file shown in Listing 2.1.

Listing 2.1: The initInstance function   *Source file = INITILIZATION.C*

```c
BOOL initInstance (HINSTANCE hinst, UINT resPoolID, int nCmdShow)
{
    HWND    hwnd;
    TCHAR ClassName [MAX_RESOURCESTRING + 1] ;

    VERIFY (LoadString (hinst, resPoolID, ClassName, DIM(ClassName))) ;

    // Constrain this application to run single instance
    hwnd = FindWindow (ClassName, NULL) ;
    if (hwnd)
        { /* window created */

        // A previous instance of this application is running.

        // Activate the previous instance, tell it what the user
        // requested this instance to do, then abort initialization
        // of this instance.

        if (IsIconic (hwnd))
            ShowWindow (hwnd, SW_RESTORE) ;

        SetForegroundWindow (hwnd) ;

        // Send an application-defined message to the previous
        // instance (or use some other type of IPC mechanism)
        // to tell the previous instance what to do.

        // Determining what to do generally depends on how the
        // user started this instance.

        // ... <some application-specific code here>

        // Abort this instance's initialization
```

```
      return FALSE ;
   } /* window created */

// Register all application-specific window classes
if (!registerWindowClasses (hinst, resPoolID))
   return FALSE ;

// Initialize the Common Controls DLL
// You must call this function before using any Common Control
InitCommonControls () ;

// Create the application's main frame window
if (!createMainFrameWindow (hinst, nCmdShow))
   return FALSE ;

return TRUE ;
}
```
// continued on page 55. See Listing 2.2

initInstance takes the handle of the present program instance, a resource identifier, and WinMain's nCmdShow parameter as parameters and returns a Boolean value indicating its success or failure in performing the initialization. initInstance performs four main operations. When it finds a prior running instance of the application, it activates the prior instance and terminates. Otherwise, it registers all window classes needed by the application, initializes the common controls dynamic link library (DLL), and creates the main frame window.

initInstance begins by defining the local variables used by the function:

```
HWND   hwnd;
TCHAR ClassName [MAX_RESOURCESTRING + 1] ;
```

The variable hwnd holds the window handle of the application window. The variable ClassName is an array of characters that contains the name of the application's window class. Each window class that your application registers must be given a unique name. The class name is later used as a parameter to the CreateWindow function to identify the window class to use for the window being created.

initInstance uses the FindWindow API to locate another application that is using the same window class name for its application as does the Skeleton application. This technique obviously requires you to select as unique a name as possible. Because the user never sees the window class name, if you want the maximum likelihood that your window class name will be unique, you might want to use the GUIDGEN application and use the globally unique identifier it produces as your window class name. To do this, you locate the GUIDGEN program (which is part of the Win32 SDK and whose icon caption is "Class ID Generator") and click its icon. When it completes, it leaves a string on the Clipboard that is a "guaranteed" globally unique ID, encoded in two ways (see the next inset). You can simply paste this string wherever you want to put your class name (delete the second line of the Clipboard text after the paste is complete).

We've separated the remaining initialization into three helper functions: registerWindowClasses, internalRegisterClass, and createMainFrameWindow.

The creation of globally unique names is very important in OLE-based technologies, such as ActiveX controls. Microsoft has provided a program that is "guaranteed" to generate a globally unique name and which is represented by a 128-bit string. This string is always shown in a "canonical": text format. For example, by running GUIDGEN and pasting the result in here, we obtained the data on the clipboard:

0C618BF0-11DB-11D0-833A-00AA005C0507
```
DEFINE_GUID(varNameHere, 0x0C618BF0L, 0x11DB, 0x11D0, 0x83, 0x3A, 0x00, 0xAA, 0x00, 0x5C,
0x05, 0x07);
```

We can use the first line of this, which we've boldfaced, as a unique window name. The second line is a macro that is mostly of interest to OLE and ActiveX developers. This ID string *will* be globally unique across all Win32 platforms if you have a network card. This is because a network card contains a guaranteed unique 48-bit network address, which is administered in such a way as to guarantee that there will never be two network cards of the same address, anywhere in the world, ever. This basic network address is combined with a time stamp and other computations so that on any given machine, the entire 128-bit value is guaranteed unique. Further, because it incorporates the network address of that machine, it will be unique across all other Win32 platforms. If your machine does *not* have a network card, guaranteeing a unique name is a bit more problematic. The algorithm relies on doing bizarre site-sensitive computations that produce a "statistically unique" global identifier such that there is only a very, very small chance that two non-network machines could ever produce the same ID. While not offering the same guarantees as when a network card is present, it can be thought of as being globally unique.

Registering the Window Class(es)

One approach to registering the window classes of your application is to register all your classes in a single function, which we call `registerWindowClasses`. This works when the number of classes you use is fixed and small. You may also choose to implement your initialization by having each module that implements a window class (other than the main window class, which we traditionally declare in `registerWindow-Classes`) contain the code to register the class as well as the window function that handles the messages to windows of that class. In this case, we have only one window, the main window, so we have no other registrations to do. When you use C++, you would register the class during the module initialization for the C++ class that implements the window class. The code for `registerWindowClasses` is shown in Listing 2.2.

Listing 2.2: The `registerWindowClasses` function
```
static BOOL
registerWindowClasses (HINSTANCE hinst, UINT resPoolID)
{
    TCHAR       ClassName [MAX_RESOURCESTRING + 1] ;
    WNDCLASSEX  wcex ;

    VERIFY (LoadString (hinst, resPoolID, ClassName, DIM(ClassName))) ;

    // Fill in window class structure with parameters that describe
    // the main window.
    wcex.cbSize        = sizeof (WNDCLASSEX) ;
    wcex.style         = CS_HREDRAW | CS_VREDRAW | CS_DBLCLKS ;
    wcex.lpfnWndProc   = mainFrameWndProc ;
    wcex.cbClsExtra    = 0 ;
    wcex.cbWndExtra    = 0 ;
    wcex.hInstance     = hinst ;
    wcex.hIcon         = LoadIcon (hinst, MAKEINTRESOURCE (resPoolID)) ;
    wcex.hCursor       = LoadCursor (NULL, IDC_ARROW) ;
    wcex.hbrBackground = (HBRUSH) (COLOR_WINDOW+1) ;
```

```
wcex.lpszMenuName   = MAKEINTRESOURCE (resPoolID) ;
wcex.lpszClassName = ClassName ;
wcex.hIconSm        = LoadImage (hinst,
                                 MAKEINTRESOURCE (resPoolID),
                                 IMAGE_ICON,
                                 GetSystemMetrics (SM_CXSMICON),
                                 GetSystemMetrics (SM_CYSMICON),
                                 LR_SHARED) ;

    // Register the window class and return success/failure code.
    return internalRegisterClass (&wcex) ;
}
```

The variable wcex is a WNDCLASSEX structure containing all the information required to describe a window class. Win16 programmers may be familiar with the WNDCLASS structure. Win32 at API level 4 and higher has the WNDCLASSEX structure. This structure allows additional specification, such as the image of the small icon to be used in the task bar display.

Skeleton does not hard-code the character strings it uses into the program. Instead, they are dynamically loaded at runtime from a pool of *string resources*. String resources are discussed in depth in Chapter 12, "Menus, Accelerators, Icons, String Resources, and MessageTable Resources." The string representing the name of the Skeleton program's main window classes is fetched from the program's string resources by the following lines of code:

```
VERIFY (LoadString (hinst, resPoolID, ClassName, DIM(ClassName))) ;
```

LoadString fetches the character string identified by the integer resPoolID from the executable file associated with the Windows module instance hinst (in this case, Skeleton.exe) and copies the string into the character array ClassName without writing past the end of the character array. LoadString returns the number of characters copied into the buffer. The VERIFY macro checks the return value in debug versions of the application and ensures that the specified resource string exists. If a 0 value is returned, the VERIFY macro will cause an ASSERT statement to be executed. LoadString returns a value indicating the number of characters copied; if the string is not found, the return value is 0.

Even though this approach of loading strings from a separate resource pool is overkill for a program as simple as Skeleton, it provides a number of advantages that are beneficial in larger applications. The character string itself is not a part of the program and can be changed without recompiling or relinking the program. The string never uses any space in the program's data space. Because it is needed only when registering the window class and when creating a window of that class, it is brought into memory only at those times. Once Windows copies the string resource into your local buffer, the memory occupied by the resource is available for other uses. Windows keeps the resource around in case it might be needed shortly, but the resource is marked as discardable in case the memory is required for other purposes. Because window classes are typically registered during the program's initialization and windows are created infrequently after initialization, the character string occupies no memory during most of the life of the program. The slight additional overhead required to load the string is so small as to be irrelevant.

initInstance next fills out the WNDCLASSEX structure wcex in preparation for registering the window class. The WNDCLASSEX structure has 12 fields and is defined by windows.h as follows:

```
typedef struct tagWNDCLASSEX {
    UINT         cbSize;
    /* Win 3.x */
    UINT         style;
    WNDPROC      lpfnWndProc;
    int          cbClsExtra;
    int          cbWndExtra;
    HINSTANCE    hInstance;
    HICON        hIcon;
    HCURSOR      hCursor;
    HBRUSH       hbrBackground;
    LPCTSTR      lpszMenuName;
    LPCTSTR      lpszClassName;
    /* Win 4.0 */
    HICON        hIconSm;
} WNDCLASSEX, *PWNDCLASSEX, NEAR *NPWNDCLASSEX, FAR *LPWNDCLASSEX;
```

For every Win32 data structure that deals with characters, there are actually *three* definitions: the ANSI definition, the Unicode definition, and the published definition. We explore the details of ANSI/Unicode distinctions in Chapter 7, page 427. The ANSI definition is actually called WNDCLASSEXA, and the Unicode definition is called WNDCLASSEXW. These are what you will really find if you search the definition file (in the current release, these definitions are found in winuser.h). The "published" definition is the one that represents how you, the programmer, should view the structure if you are in a pure-ANSI or pure-Unicode application. You can build applications that are a blend of ANSI and Unicode. In those cases, you may need to use one of the "base" definitions to get compatibility across the two modes. We consistently use the "published" definition throughout this book when we are describing a data structure.

The first field is the size of the window class structure. You must initialize this field to the size of the structure you are providing to Windows. Should future versions of Windows add additional fields to this structure, Windows can distinguish the different versions by the specified size:

```
wcex.cbSize = sizeof (WNDCLASSEX) ;
```

The second field is the window class style. initInstance sets it to values commonly used by Windows applications:

```
wcex.style = CS_HREDRAW | CS_VREDRAW | CS_DBLCLKS ;
```

Commonly used values for the window class style are CS_HREDRAW and CS_VREDRAW. These and the other window class style symbolic constants are bit-encoded flags. Use these symbolic constants by combining them with the C bitwise OR operator and assigning the resulting value to the WNDCLASSEX style field. The full set of class flags is discussed in detail in Chapter 3 and is summarized in Table 3.2 on page 110.

The CS_HREDRAW flag tells Windows that all windows created as instances of this class must have the entire client area of the window redrawn whenever the horizontal size of the window is changed. The CS_VREDRAW flag notifies Windows that the same thing must be done whenever the vertical size changes. The CS_DBLCLKS flag notifies Windows to send mouse double-click messages to all windows of this class.

The third field of the WNDCLASSEX structure contains the address of the function that processes all messages for all windows that are created based on this window class. Skeleton sets it by

```
wcex.lpfnWndProc = (WNDPROC) mainFrameWndProc ;
```

The prefix of the field name says that this is a long pointer to a function. Inspection of the definition of this field tells us that the type of this field is WNDPROC. windows.h defines a WNDPROC type this way:

```
typedef LRESULT (CALLBACK* WNDPROC)(HWND, UINT, WPARAM, LPARAM) ;
```

This typedef is somewhat involved, so we'll look at it more closely. A WNDPROC-type variable is a pointer to a CALLBACK function. This function requires four parameters: an HWND, a UINT, a WPARAM, and an LPARAM. It returns an LRESULT value. windows.h defines the CALLBACK type this way:

```
#define CALLBACK __stdcall
```

The HWND parameter is a handle to a window. The WPARAM type is a synonym for a UINT, so it also changes size to match the target environment for the program (16 or 32 bits). The LPARAM type is a synonym for a LONG and is a 32-bit signed integer.

> The UINT type is a typedef for an unsigned int. UINT-type variables change in size from 16-bit to 32-bit systems. A UINT variable is a 16-bit unsigned integer in Win16 applications (Windows 3.x applications) and a 32-bit unsigned integer in Win32 applications. The LPARAM type is a synonym for LONG and is a 32-bit integer in Win16 and Win32 programs.

Porting

> The types of the parameters to a CALLBACK differ from those used by Windows version 3.0 and earlier programs. The second parameter used to be defined as having the unsigned type rather than UINT. The third parameter used to be defined as having the WORD type rather than WPARAM. The last parameter was defined as a LONG rather than a LPARAM.
>
> You should use the new definitions for these parameters rather the previous ones. The new types have the same sizes as the types used in versions of Windows earlier than 3.1 so you can mix old and new code in Win16 programs. However, Win32 programs use a WPARAM variable for the third parameter of a window function, not a WORD variable as the parameter was defined in Windows 3.0. As mentioned just above, a WPARAM variable is 16 bits in Win16 programs but 32 bits in Win32 programs. The WORD type remains 16 bits in both Win16 and Win32 programs. Basically, code that defines WNDPROC functions using a WORD type for the third parameter is not portable to Win32. Code that defines the third parameter as a WPARAM is portable.

The function prototype for mainFrameWndProc is

```
LRESULT CALLBACK
mainFrameWndProc(HWND hwnd, UINT message, WPARAM wParam, LPARAM lParam)
```

> In Win16, this declaration usually included the nonstandard keyword __export. This keyword is not legal in a 32-bit compiler and will generate a warning message. You may add a preprocessor declaration of this form:
>
> ```
> #ifdef WIN32
> #define __export
> #endif
> ```

The fourth field is cbClsExtra. Windows allocates memory to contain information about a registered class. This field tells Windows how many extra bytes (storage in addition to whatever Windows requires) should be allocated for the class structure. All windows of a given class share a single class structure, so memory reserved in the class structure via the cbClsExtra field is shared by all windows of that class. Skeleton uses no class extra bytes, so it sets this field to 0:

```
wcex.cbClsExtra = 0 ;
```

It is very rare to see any additional class extra bytes being allocated.

The fifth field is cbWndExtra. Windows, as it does for class structures, allocates a structure for each window that is created. The cbWndExtra field specifies how many extra bytes should be allocated for each window structure created for windows of this class. It provides a way for an application to store data that should be associated with individual windows as part of Windows's window structure. Unlike cbClsExtra, Windows programmers frequently use cbWndExtra space. Typically, you allocate sizeof(*pointer_type*) window extra space, and you store all of the window-specific information in a structure referenced by the pointer you store in this space. The most common alternative to the assignment of 0 bytes is one that reads like this:

```
wcex.cbWndExtra = sizeof(LPVOID) ;// Window extra data for one pointer
```

In Win16, it was always necessary to allocate this space if you needed some extra bytes. In Win32, *every* window class, including the built-in window classes for push buttons, list boxes, and the like, has a special GWL_USERDATA field that you can access via SetWindowLong and GetWindowLong. Thus the need to allocate window extra bytes is reduced.

The sixth field of the WNDCLASSEX structure is hInstance. A window class is owned by the module instance assigned to this field. Most applications set this field to the instance handle that was passed to the application as a parameter of WinMain:

```
wcex.hInstance = hinst ;
```

Beginning with Windows 95 and Windows NT 4.0 and later, an application can have two class icons: one large and one small. Windows displays a window's large class icon in the task-switch window that appears when the user presses **Alt+Tab** and in the large icon views of the task bar and Explorer. The small class icon appears in a window's title bar and in the small icon views of the task bar and Explorer.

To specify the icons for a window class, specify the handles of the large and small icons in the hIcon and hIconSm members, respectively, of the WNDCLASSEX structure. The icons you specify must have the appropriate dimensions for large and small class icons. For a large class icon, you can determine the required dimensions by calling the GetSystemMetrics function and specifying the SM_CXICON and SM_CYICON values. For a small class icon, specify the SM_CXSMICON and SM_CYSMICON values.

You can create your own custom icons using one of the many different icon editors that are available. Microsoft Visual C++ has an integrated resource editor that allows you to create and edit icons, bitmaps, and cursors. Windows also has five predefined icons. Skeleton uses the LoadIcon function to load the application icon resource specified by the integer resPoolID. The MAKEINTRESOURCE macro allows you to specify an integer identifier, rather than a string resource name, for the resource. LoadIcon returns a handle to the icon that was loaded (or NULL if the icon named was not found).

```
wcex.hIcon = LoadIcon (hinst, MAKEINTRESOURCE (resPoolID)) ;
wcex.hIconSm = LoadImage (hinst,                            // resource segment
                    MAKEINTRESOURCE (resPoolID),            // image ID
                    IMAGE_ICON,                             // image is ICON
                    GetSystemMetrics (SM_CXSMICON),         // desired width
```

```
                    GetSystemMetrics (SM_CYSMICON),    // desired height
                    LR_SHARED) ;                       // share copy
```

When you set the hIcon and hIconSm members of the WNDCLASSEX structure to NULL, the system uses the default application icon as the large and small class icons for the window class. When you specify a large class icon but not a small one, the system creates a small class icon based on the large one. The resulting image often does not look as nice as one you might draw, so you generally want to specify an explicit small class icon. When you specify a small class icon but not a large one, the system uses the default application icon as the large class icon and the specified icon as the small class icon.

If you are using the Microsoft development environment, you can create a small icon with the same resource ID as a large icon by requesting a 16 × 16 icon in the icon editor. You can switch between the two while editing. The two icons represent one resource with two encodings. LoadImage can be used to select which of the two encodings is actually used based on its size arguments (which is what we do here).

The eighth field is hCursor. A *cursor* is a small bit-mapped image that can be coupled to the mouse. A cursor is used to show the user where actions initiated by the mouse will take place. When you move the mouse cursor over a window, Windows changes the cursor being displayed to the cursor identified in the window's class structure. Two cursors with which you are probably familiar are the arrow (used to point at things) and the hourglass (used to indicate that an operation will take a noticeable amount of time). You can create your own custom cursors using the resource editor cursor creation and editing capabilities. Windows has 14 predefined cursors (see Table 7.15 on page 475). Skeleton uses the LoadCursor function to load the predefined cursor resource for the standard arrow cursor. LoadCursor returns a handle to the cursor:

```
wcex.hCursor = LoadCursor (NULL, IDC_ARROW) ;
```

Table 2.2: The stock brushes predefined by Windows

Symbolic Name	Brush Color	Equivalent Color
BLACK_BRUSH	Black	RGB(0, 0, 0)
DKGRAY_BRUSH	Dark gray	RGB(64, 64, 64)
GRAY_BRUSH	Gray	RGB(128, 128, 128)
HOLLOW_BRUSH	Hollow	–
LTGRAY_BRUSH	Light gray	RGB(192, 192, 192)
NULL_BRUSH	Null	–
WHITE_BRUSH	White	RGB(255, 255, 255)

The ninth field of the WNDCLASSEX structure is hbrBackground. The field is a handle to a *brush*. A brush in Windows is a small, colored bitmap pattern of pixels. Windows uses the brush indicated in this field to paint the background of the client area of all windows created that are based on this class. Windows has seven predefined, or "stock", brushes, which are listed in Table 2.2.

To use a stock brush for the background color and pattern of windows created based on this class, you must get a handle to the stock brush and assign it to this field:

```
wcex.hbrBackground = GetStockBrush (WHITE_BRUSH) ;
```

The GetStockBrush function is a macro API defined in the windowsx.h header file like this:

```
#define GetStockBrush(i)    ((HBRUSH)GetStockObject(i))
```

The GetStockBrush macro function is a convenient way to call the general GetStockObject API function to retrieve a stock brush. Using the macro rather than the general API makes the purpose of your code more understandable. It also correctly defines the return value of the call as an HBRUSH, thereby allowing the compiler to perform additional checking for type mismatches.

The previous GetStockBrush function call causes all windows created based on this class to have a white background because the stock object WHITE_BRUSH was used as the background brush. However, the user might have used the Control Panel utility to change the colors of various parts of the Windows desktop. Particularly, the user might want Windows applications to use a color other than white for their backgrounds.

To be compatible with such user requests, you shouldn't set the hbrBackground field to a brush at all. You should set it to a *system color index*. To use a system color as the background of the client area of windows based on this class, you must set the hbrBackground field to one of the system colors listed in Table 2.3, plus one. (The "plus one" is required solely to ensure that the value is not 0.)

Table 2.3: The system colors predefined by Windows

Symbolic Name	Meaning
COLOR_3DDKSHADOW	Dark shadow for 3D display elements.
COLOR_3DFACE	"Face" color (background color) for 3D display elements.
COLOR_3DHIGHLIGHT	Highlight color for 3D display elements (for edges facing the light source).
COLOR_3DHILIGHT	Synonym for COLOR_3DHIGHLIGHT.
COLOR_3DLIGHT	Light color for 3D display elements (for edges facing the light source).
COLOR_3DSHADOW	Shadow color for 3D display elements (for edges facing away from the light source).
COLOR_ACTIVEBORDER	The active window border color.
COLOR_ACTIVECAPTION	The active window caption color.
COLOR_APPWORKSPACE	Multiple Document Interface (MDI) client window background.
COLOR_BACKGROUND	The desktop color.
COLOR_BTNFACE	Synonym for COLOR_3DFACE.
COLOR_BTNHIGHLIGHT	Synonym for COLOR_3DHIGHLIGHT.
COLOR_BTNHILIGHT	Synonym for COLOR_3DHIGHLIGHT.

Table 2.3: The system colors predefined by Windows

Symbolic Name	Meaning
COLOR_BTNSHADOW	Synonym for COLOR_3DSHADOW.
COLOR_BTNTEXT	The text color on push buttons.
COLOR_CAPTIONTEXT	The text color in captions, size boxes, and scroll-bar arrow boxes.
COLOR_DESKTOP	Synonym for COLOR_BACKGROUND.
COLOR_GRAYTEXT	The text color for grayed (disabled) text.
COLOR_HIGHLIGHT	The color of items selected in a control.
COLOR_HIGHLIGHTTEXT	The color of the text of an item selected in a control.
COLOR_INACTIVEBORDER	The inactive window border color.
COLOR_INACTIVECAPTION	The inactive window caption color.
COLOR_INACTIVECAPTIONTEXT	The color of text in an inactive window caption (Windows 3.1 and later).
COLOR_INFOTEXT	Text color for tooltip controls.
COLOR_INFOBK	Background color for tooltip controls.
COLOR_MENU	The background color of a menu.
COLOR_MENUTEXT	The color of text in a menu.
COLOR_SCROLLBAR	The color of a scroll bar's "gray" (background) area.
COLOR_WINDOW	The window background color.
COLOR_WINDOWFRAME	The window frame color.
COLOR_WINDOWTEXT	The color of text in a window.

The system color for the user-selected window background color is called COLOR_WINDOW. The following statement defines the background color for windows of this class to be the system background color, whatever that might be:

```
wcex.hbrBackground = (HBRUSH) (COLOR_WINDOW + 1) ;
```

When you enable strict type checking, you must cast the integer value COLOR_WINDOW + 1 to an HBRUSH, a handle to a brush. The C compiler will complain about mismatched types if you don't.

The tenth field of the WNDCLASSEX structure is lpszMenuName. This is an LPCTSTR, a pointer to a NUL-terminated string. This string is the name of a menu resource that is the menu used for all windows created based

Why the "+1"? This is one of those odd quirks of history. Initially, Windows didn't have a Control Panel, so you had to supply a brush handle. When Windows got a Control Panel that let the user select the color scheme, the system color indices were assigned starting at 0. But a 0 value for a brush handle already meant a NULL handle, meaning there was no brush assigned. So it would be impossible to tell the difference between the selection of color index 0 and a NULL brush handle. Rather than making 0 an illegal system color index, Microsoft decided it was easier to force all programmers, forevermore, to remember to add 1 to the system color index when assigning it as a simulated brush. This seems, in retrospect, to have been an odd trade-off.

on the class. We could use the same approach used for the window class name string–that is, load it from a resource–because the argument we used previously for loading strings from resources applies here as well.

We could load this character string from the application's string resources. We could even take the simple approach and hard-code the character string right into the code. But there is a better way. Menus can be given an integer ID instead of a name. The MAKEINTRESOURCE macro is defined by windows.h and converts an integer ID, in this case the menu ID resPoolID, to a LPCTSTR that is assigned to this field. We show you later in this chapter where this menu is defined. You can assign NULL to this field when windows of this class have no menu:

```
wcex.lpszMenuName = MAKEINTRESOURCE (resPoolID) ;
```

Traditional books on Windows programming use a resource *name*, which is a character string. A resource can be named by either a string name or an integer. We avoid the use of string names simply because the Microsoft tooling *strongly* favors the use of integer names for resources. At least it provides you a suitable #define so that you can reference the resource with a symbolic name in your program. The Microsoft Foundation Classes (MFC) critically depend on the use of integer, rather than string, resource IDs. We use them here so that you will become accustomed to them. This will make your transition to using MFC much easier. The argument usually presented– that resources named by integer IDs can be found "faster" than resources named by string IDs–strikes us as specious. The overall change in performance is probably unmeasurable.

The eleventh field in the WNDCLASSEX structure is lpszClassName. This is also a pointer to a NUL-terminated string. The address of the first character of the string loaded by the LoadString function is stored in lpszClassName:

```
wcex.lpszClassName = ClassName ;
```

At last, the WNDCLASSEX structure is completely filled out! You can now register the class described by the structure by using the RegisterClassEx function as follows:

```
aWndClass = RegisterClassEx (&wc) ;
```

This function returns an ATOM that uniquely identifies the class being registered or 0 if an error occurred. You can also use this atom, instead of the string name of the class, when you create a new window with CreateWindow or CreateWindowEx.

Unfortunately, the RegisterClassEx function did not exist in versions of Windows prior to API level 4.0 (Windows 95 and Windows NT 4.0). This meant that attempting to run a program on Windows NT 3.*x* that called RegisterClassEx directly would fail because as the program was loaded, an attempt would be made to find the RegisterClassEx function and the resultant failure would terminate the loading process.

If you plan to operate only on API level 4 platforms, you can call RegisterClassEx just as we have shown. But we want the Skeleton example program to work on earlier versions of Win32. We accomplish this by esting, at runtime, for the presence of the `RegisterClassEx` API. When it is not present, we copy the `WNDCLASSEX` structure to a `WNDCLASS` structure and call the original Windows `RegisterClass` API. This API does not support specifying a small class icon; otherwise, it operates similarly to the `RegisterClassEx` function. But if `RegisterClassEx` is not defined, you are running on Windows NT 3.*x*, where the small icon is not supported, so no functionality is lost by dropping it. The `internalRegisterClass` function of the skeleton application encapsulates this difference in Windows versions. You don't really need to understand this now. We explain it in great detail in the upcoming section "A Diversion into Advanced Techniques: Locating API Level 4 Entry Points".

`RegisterClassEx`, or `RegisterClass`, returns 0 when an error occurs and a nonzero `ATOM` when the new class is successfully registered. You can use the `GetLastError` function to obtain information about why the function failed. We defined the `initInstance` function as returning a `Boolean` value. We convert the 0/`ATOM` result from the `RegisterClassEx` function to a 0/1 (FALSE/TRUE) `Boolean` value. When this value is nonzero, we return FALSE as the `Boolean` value as the result of the `initInstance` function:

```
return internalRegisterClass (&wcex) != (ATOM) 0 ;
```

You could keep track of the `ATOM` that identifies each window class that you create, but you rarely have a use for doing so. On an 8088-based machine with 640K of memory running Windows 1.0, the few extra bytes saved by using the `ATOM` may have mattered. It seems pointless on a Win32 machine.

We could have simply returned the `ATOM` value as the result value of the `registerWindowClasses` function. After all, an `ATOM` is nonzero (TRUE) when the `RegisterClassEx` function succeeds and 0 (FALSE) when the function fails. However, having a function that is documented to return a `BOOL` actually return an `ATOM` allows potential errors to creep into an application. The `initInstance` function might eventually be modified to rely on undocumented behavior, that is, that `registerWindowClasses` actually returns an `ATOM` although it claims to return a `BOOL`. Such dependencies make your application harder to maintain, although they have not stopped Microsoft from committing the same sins in Windows 95, as we point out in Chapter 1 (page 33).

Another feature that makes applications harder to maintain is a desire to minimize the number of lines of code written. Often when several window classes are being registered, after the first `RegisterClassEx` only the class name and `lpfnWndProc` values are changed. Then the new class is registered. The problem with this technique is that as you add each class, you start to generate "serial dependencies" in the initialization. For example, adding bits to the window styles or changing the cursor will affect all subsequent window registrations. Eventually, this results in "spaghetti code" in which you have to read every single preceding line to create and initialize a new class. This is wrong. It simply doesn't cost that much in space or time to reinitialize all the fields. The result means that any one registration is complete unto itself. When you finally have a dozen windows being registered and the code runs to several screens or pages, you don't need to keep scrolling back to see what was previously set. You also greatly reduce the chances of introducing an error if you modify one window class (such errors are often hard to find, particularly when style bits are involved).

A Diversion into Advanced Techniques: Locating API Level 4 Entry Points

If you're just learning Windows programming, you can skip this section and go immediately to "Creating the Main Window" on page 67.

We show the `internalRegisterClass` function in Listing 2.3. If this is your first reading about Windows programming, You Do Not Need To Understand This. You can treat it as magic that works. But the technique is sufficiently useful, particularly if you have to deal with running on a Windows NT 3.*x* platform, that we take time here to document it. You may find the technique useful for dealing with the requirement to support a program on Windows NT 3.*x* while taking advantage of Win32 API 4 level functions whenever they are available. When the need arises, you can refer back to Listing 2.3 and its accompanying description. This is Very Advanced Windows Magic. Note that this does *not* work if you are trying to support an application on Windows 95 and Windows NT 4.*x*. In this case, the entry points *are* defined in Windows 95, but they do nothing and they return an error code, thereby indicating that the function failed. You can use `GetLastError` to determine that the reason the function failed was specifically that it is not implemented on the platform.

Listing 2.3: The `internalRegisterClass` function

```
typedef ATOM (WINAPI* REGISTERCLASSEXPROC)(const LPWNDCLASSEX lpwcex) ;

ATOM
internalRegisterClass (const LPWNDCLASSEX lpwcex)
{
    WNDCLASS wc ;

    // Get the module handle of the 32-bit USER DLL
    HANDLE hModule = GetModuleHandle (_T("USER32")) ;
    if (NULL != hModule)
      { /* found module */
        // If we're running on a Win32 version supporting RegisterClassEx
        //   get the address of the function so we can call it

#if defined (UNICODE)
        REGISTERCLASSEXPROC proc =
          (REGISTERCLASSEXPROC) GetProcAddress (hModule, "RegisterClassExW") ;
#else
        REGISTERCLASSEXPROC proc =
          (REGISTERCLASSEXPROC) GetProcAddress (hModule, "RegisterClassExA") ;
#endif

        // If we found the address of RegisterClassEx, call it and return
        if (NULL != proc)
            return proc(lpwcex) ;
      } /* found module */

    // If we get here, the module handle was not found, or we did not find
    // the RegisterClassEx address
    // Convert the WNDCLASSEX structure to a WNDCLASS structure
    wc.style         = lpwcex->style ;
    wc.lpfnWndProc   = lpwcex->lpfnWndProc ;
    wc.cbClsExtra    = lpwcex->cbClsExtra ;
    wc.cbWndExtra    = lpwcex->cbWndExtra ;
    wc.hInstance     = lpwcex->hInstance ;
    wc.hIcon         = lpwcex->hIcon ;
    wc.hCursor       = lpwcex->hCursor ;
    wc.hbrBackground = lpwcex->hbrBackground ;
    wc.lpszMenuName  = lpwcex->lpszMenuName ;
    wc.lpszClassName = lpwcex->lpszClassName ;
    return RegisterClass (&wc) ;
}
```

Remember: You Do Not Have To Understand This. At least not until you need a similar capability for your own application. . . .

To reduce syntactic clutter, we define a convenient `typedef` that encapsulates the notion of a pointer to the function we wish to call:

```
typedef ATOM (WINAPI* REGISTERCLASSEXPROC)(const LPWNDCLASSEX lpwcex) ;
```

```
Microsoft (R) COFF Binary File Dumper Version 3.10.6038
Copyright (C) Microsoft Corp 1992-1996. All rights reserved.
Dump of file \winnt35\system32\user32.dll
File Type: DLL
        Section contains the following Exports for USER32.dll
                    0 characteristics
            2FBE491B time date stamp Sat May 20 15:55:07 1995
                 0.00 version
                    1 ordinal base
                  589 number of functions
                  589 number of names
          ordinal hint    name
                1    0    ActivateKeyboardLayout   (00020C36)
                2    1    AdjustWindowRect   (00004C40)
                3    2    AdjustWindowRectEx   (00004C18)
                4    3    AnyPopup   (0002AFEB)
                5    4    AppendMenuA   (0000A7F2)
                6    5    AppendMenuW   (00020F9B)
                ...
              427  1AA    RedrawWindow   (00010088)
              428  1AB    RegisterClassA   (0000AB9B)
              429  1AC    RegisterClassExA   (0002AC87)
              430  1AD    RegisterClassExW   (0002AC9F)
              431  1AE    RegisterClassW   (0000CBD2)
                ...
```

Figure 2.1: Locating an API name (`dumpbin` output)

To locate the address of the function you want to call, you have to know in which of the Windows implementation modules it resides. For some function names, you will be able, after a bit of experience, to make a pretty good guess as to which module the name might be found in. For example, since we are dealing with a GUI-oriented concept (the registration of a window class), we could guess that it might be found in the user32.dll module. But how can you find out, in general, where a function is located?

Microsoft supplies a program dumpbin.exe, part of the Windows SDK, that can reveal all kinds of useful information about an object, library, or executable file. We ran it against user32.dll and got the output (highly truncated) shown in Figure 2.1. We stored the output in a file and were able to use a text editor to search for the function name we wanted to find. If we hadn't found it, we would have then tried kernel32.dll or gdi32.dll. The command line we used specified that we wished to see the list of *exported* names. It was

```
d:\msdev\bin\dumpbin \winnt35\system32\user32.dll /exports > user32.lst
```

Having thus determined which module holds the function we want to call, we next must obtain a *module handle* to that module. This will let us query the module for the address of the function we want.

```
HMODULE hModule = GetModuleHandle (_T("USER32")) ;
```

If this succeeds, it returns a non-NULL value that is the handle. If it fails, we have to fall back to using RegisterClass.

Given the handle to the module, we can now inquire about the address of the function. This is done by calling the GetProcAddress function and passing to it the module handle for the module we are querying and the string name of the function we wish to locate. You might assume that the name of the function is RegisterClassEx, but in fact this is not the actual name.

Windows supports both 8-bit character applications (ANSI applications) and 16-bit wide character applications (Unicode applications). Any API that is sensitive to this difference is exported from the Win32 implementation in two forms: the ANSI form, which is the name with the letter "A" appended, and the Unicode form, which is the name with the letter "W" appended. If you have a Unicode application, you want the "W" form. When we discuss the Unicode/ANSI differences in more detail in Chapter 7, page 427, we give more detail about this. For now, however, you also need to know that the preprocessor symbol UNICODE is defined if the application is a Unicode application and undefined if it is an ANSI application. This now explains the following lines of code:

```
#if defined (UNICODE)
        REGISTERCLASSEXPROC proc =
          (REGISTERCLASSEXPROC) GetProcAddress (hModule, "RegisterClassExW") ;
#else
        REGISTERCLASSEXPROC proc =
          (REGISTERCLASSEXPROC) GetProcAddress (hModule, "RegisterClassExA") ;
#endif
```

Note that the name passed to GetProcAddress is an 8-bit character string, *even for the Unicode version.* (If you don't understand what this means now, don't worry. By the time you need to use this function, you will understand the issue.)

One of these lines of code will be compiled into the program. You will end up with either the address of RegisterClassExW, the Unicode version, or RegisterClassExA, the ANSI version, whichever one is the appropriate one for your application to call.

What about the name RegisterClassEx? That's an illusion. In the file that defines the API call (for this call, it is in the file winuser.h in the release of the Microsoft development environment we are using to write this book), it is defined as

```
#ifdef UNICODE
#define RegisterClassEx  RegisterClassExW
#else
#define RegisterClassEx  RegisterClassExA
#endif // !UNICODE
```

GetProcAddress returns either the address of the function whose name we supply or NULL. Once we have in hand the address of the function we wish to call, we can do so like this:

```
        if (NULL != proc)
            return proc(lpwcex) ;
```

We show you a similar technique when we talk about dynamically loaded DLLs of our own, in Chapter 16.

Creating the Main Window

Now that we have registered the window class, the next initialization task is the creation of an application's main window. initInstance does this by calling the createMainFrameWindow helper function, shown in Listing 2.4.

Listing 2.4: The createMainFrameWindow function

```
static HWND
createMainFrameWindow (HINSTANCE hinst, int nCmdShow)
{
    HWND  hwnd ;
    TCHAR ClassName [MAX_RESOURCESTRING + 1] ;
    TCHAR Title [MAX_RESOURCESTRING + 1] ;

    // Create the main frame window
    VERIFY (LoadString (hinst, IDR_MAINFRAME, ClassName, DIM(ClassName))) ;
    VERIFY (LoadString (hinst, IDS_APP_TITLE, Title, DIM(Title))) ;

    hwnd =
        CreateWindowEx (0,                       // Extended window styles
                        ClassName,               // Address of registered class name
                        Title,                   // Address of window name
                        WS_OVERLAPPEDWINDOW,     // Window style
                        CW_USEDEFAULT,           // Horizontal position of window
                        0,                       // Vertical position of window
                        CW_USEDEFAULT,           // Window width
                        0,                       // Window height
                        NULL,                    // Handle of parent or owner window
                        NULL,                    // Handle of menu or child-window id
                        hinst,                   // Handle of application instance
                        NULL) ;                  // Address of window-creation data

    ASSERT (NULL != hwnd) ;
    if (hwnd == NULL)
        return NULL ;

    ShowWindow (hwnd, nCmdShow) ;
    UpdateWindow (hwnd) ;

    return hwnd ;
}
```

createMainFrameWindow begins by defining the local variables it uses:

```
    HWND  hwnd ;
    TCHAR ClassName [MAX_RESOURCESTRING + 1] ;
    TCHAR Title [MAX_RESOURCESTRING + 1] ;
```

The variable ClassName is a local character array that contains the name of the window class on which we will base a window soon to be created. Note that we declare the variable as a TCHAR character array. The TCHAR data type is conditionally defined. For Unicode applications, a TCHAR is a "wide" character (16 bits, type wchar_t), but for non-Unicode (ANSI) applications, a TCHAR is equivalent to the char data type. The CreateWindow and CreateWindowEx API functions, as do many Win32 API functions, require a pointer to a wide-character array (Unicode character string) when called by a Unicode application but a char array when called by a non-Unicode application. The variable Title is also a TCHAR array that will hold the character string to be used as the title for the window we'll create.

The variable hwnd holds the window handle of the created main frame window. You may have noticed that there are many different types of handles in Windows. Previously you saw *instance handles*; hwnd is a *window handle*. When you create a window, Windows does not return a pointer to its internal window structure.

Instead you receive a window handle. You give the window handle back to Windows whenever you need to identify the window.

The values of the ClassName and Title variables are fetched from the program's string resource pool just as the name of the window class was during the window class registration.

We place the class name string in the program's string resource pool, although there is no specific reason for doing so other than a desire to keep all strings together. A window class name is never displayed to the user, so the string never needs to be localized. An equally valid and–to some people–better place to store a window class name is as a static global variable. Our dislike for global variables sometimes results in a long, although scenic, path:

```
VERIFY (LoadString (hinst, IDR_MAINFRAME, ClassName, DIM(ClassName))) ;
VERIFY (LoadString (hinst, IDS_APP_TITLE, Title, DIM(Title))) ;
```

Both strings should be present in the application's string resources; this can be checked in a debug build. We use the VERIFY macro once again to test the return value from the LoadString function call only during debug builds. The call should never fail unless the specified resource isn't present in the string resources.

Finally, we are ready to create our first (and in Skeleton, only) window. Although we specified 11 different characteristics when we defined the window class, the CreateWindowEx function call requires 11 more. Unlike the window class characteristics, which apply to all windows based on the class, the characteristics supplied in the CreateWindowEx call apply only to the individual window being created. Skeleton uses the following CreateWindowEx call:

```
hwnd =
    CreateWindowEx (0,                     // Extended window styles
                    ClassName,             // Address of registered class name
                    Title,                 // Address of window name
                    WS_OVERLAPPEDWINDOW,// Window style
                    CW_USEDEFAULT,         // Horizontal position of window
                    0,                     // Vertical position of window
                    CW_USEDEFAULT,         // Initial window width
                    0,                     // Initial window height
                    NULL,                  // Handle of parent or owner window
                    NULL,                  // Handle of menu or child-window id
                    hinst,                 // Handle of application instance
                    NULL) ;                // Address of window-creation data
```

The first parameter allows you to specify *extended* window styles, styles in addition to those you can specify in the fourth parameter. Basically 32 bits of styles turned out to be insufficient so, with the addition of the CreateWindowEx API, Microsoft added another 32 bits of style flags.

The second parameter, ClassName, is a pointer to a character string that is the name of the window class on which to base this newly created window. This parameter associates a created window with a previously registered window class. Skeleton uses the string identified by the symbolic constant IDR_MAINFRAME when registering a class and the same string when creating a window based on that class. Alternatively, you could specify the atom returned by the RegisterClassEx function if you stored it in a known place. You would in this case use the MAKEINTATOM call to convert the atom to a type that does not cause a compilation warning:

```
CreateWindowEx (0, MAKEINTATOM(classAtom),  //... other parameters as above
```

The third parameter, `Title`, is a pointer to a character string that is the window caption. In this particular case, this character string will appear in the window's caption in the title bar. The `CreateWindowEx` function prototype defines this parameter as a pointer.

The fourth parameter, `WS_OVERLAPPEDWINDOW`, indicates the style of the created window. The `WS_OVERLAPPEDWINDOW` "style" is a symbolic constant for several style flags combined with a bitwise OR operation:

```
#define WS_OVERLAPPEDWINDOW (WS_OVERLAPPED    | \
                             WS_CAPTION       | \
                             WS_SYSMENU       | \
                             WS_THICKFRAME    | \
                             WS_MINIMIZEBOX   | \
                             WS_MAXIMIZEBOX)
```

Skeleton creates an overlapped window that has a caption (`WS_CAPTION`), a system menu box to the left of the caption (`WS_SYSMENU`), both a minimize (`WS_MINIMIZE`) and a maximize (`WS_MAXIMIZE`) box to the right of the caption, and a thick frame (`WS_THICKFRAME`) around the perimeter of the window. The system menu allows the user to, among other things, close the window. The minimize box permits the user to shrink the window to an icon. The maximize box permits the user to expand the window to cover the entire screen. And, finally, the thick frame allows the user to use the mouse to pull on the window frame to stretch or squeeze the window to the size desired.

The fifth parameter is the horizontal position of the upper-left corner of the window. The sixth parameter is the vertical position of the upper-left corner of the window. These coordinates are relative to the upper-left corner of the screen. (This is true only for overlapped windows. Child and pop-up windows are slightly different. We discuss them in great detail in Chapter 3, "Exploring Variations on a Window").

Using `CW_USEDEFAULT` for the horizontal coordinate instructs Windows to select a default position for the window's upper-left corner. For overlapped windows where the horizontal position is `CW_USEDEFAULT`, the vertical position parameter can be one of the show-style parameters listed in Table 2.1. For creating the first overlapped window for the application, it can be the `nCmdShow` parameter Windows passed to the `WinMain` function.

Skeleton specifies `CW_USEDEFAULT` for the horizontal coordinate to request a default position for the window and 0 for the vertical coordinate, although the latter value isn't used. Skeleton passes the `nCmdShow` parameter to Windows with an explicit call to the `ShowWindow` function.

The seventh and eighth parameters, marked "Initial window width" and "Initial window height", specify the width and height of the window. Using `CW_USEDEFAULT` for the window's width instructs Windows to select both a default width and a default height for the window. The default height parameter is not used when the default width parameter is set to `CW_USEDEFAULT`. The default width of a window extends from the default horizontal position (parameter four) to the right edge of the screen. The default height of a window extends from the default vertical position (parameter five) to the top of the icon area.

The ninth parameter, marked "Handle of parent or owner window", is set to `NULL` because this window, being the first and only window for the Skeleton application, has no parent window.

The tenth parameter (menu handle or child window identifier) specifies the menu to be used with the window when you are creating an overlapped or pop-up window. Each individually created window may have its own unique menu. When this parameter is set to NULL, the menu, if any, specified in the definition of this window's window class is used.

The eleventh parameter (instance handle) is used to associate the created window with an instance of a running program.

The last parameter is a pointer to a programmer-defined area or structure. Windows does not use this pointer. It simply passes it to the window function associated with this window when it notifies the function that a new window is being created. You might use this pointer within the window function to access data specific to this particular window. Remember, one window function is called for all windows of a given class, but you can specify a different pointer during each CreateWindow or CreateWindowEx function call.

Windows provides this pointer to your window function when it sends the WM_CREATE message. When the message is received, its lParam contains a pointer to a CREATESTRUCT. The CREATESTRUCT contains, in *its* lParam member, the value of the last parameter to the CreateWindow or CreateWindowEx function. You can then use this value in your WM_CREATE handler for whatever purpose you wish. Skeleton does not take advantage of this capability and sets this parameter to the symbolic constant NULL. You should notice that although CreateWindow and CreateWindowEx specify the parameter as an LPVOID type (a pointer), the CREATESTRUCT specifies it as an LPARAM, which is an integer type (consistency of the interface is not one of Windows's virtues).

The CreateWindowEx function returns the window handle that identifies the window created. When the CreateWindowEx function call fails, it returns a 0. The helper function createMainFrameWindow returns NULL when it cannot create the frame window. The initInstance function returns FALSE in this case, so Skeleton terminates if it cannot create its main application window:

```
if (!createMainFrameWindow (hinst, nCmdShow))
        return FALSE ;
```

All right! Our very first window has now been created! But where is it? If you stopped Skeleton at this point by setting a breakpoint with a debugger, you would not see a window (from Skeleton). The window, although created, has not yet been made visible. You make the window visible by using the ShowWindow function. ShowWindow is passed two parameters: the window handle returned by the CreateWindow call (used to identify the window to show) and the nCmdShow parameter originally passed to WinMain (which specifies how the window should appear):

```
ShowWindow (hwnd, nCmdShow) ;
```

The ShowWindow function call displays the window on the screen. The window will be normal-sized, maximized, or iconic depending on the value of the nCmdShow parameter. When the window is either normally displayed or maximized (or, conversely, not iconic), the client area of the window will be erased by painting it with the background brush specified in the window class.

An equivalent, but far more obscure, way to achieve the same result is to do this. When calling the CreateWindowEx function, specify the WS_VISIBLE window style to create the window initially visible.

Specify the CW_USEDEFAULT value for the horizontal coordinate parameter and the nCmdShow parameter for the vertical coordinate parameter.

Normally the client area of a window is updated when Windows has nothing else to do. Windows operates under the premise that as long as there are more messages to give an application that is notifying it of events of possible interest, it should hold off asking for the window's client area to be redrawn. After all, why bother going to all the work of having the window function redraw the window when the very next message, which is already waiting to be processed, might cause the contents of the window to be changed. When no more messages await an application and the window needs to be redrawn, Windows sends the window function a message requesting that it update the client area of the window.

Sometimes you'd rather not wait for Windows to do this. The UpdateWindow function forces the client area to be updated immediately if it needs it. If no changes need to be made to the client area, it is not redrawn. Skeleton forces the client area of the window to be drawn because the user benefits from immediate feedback indicating that the program has begun executing. The following call forces the client area of Skeleton's main application window to be redrawn.

```
UpdateWindow (hwnd) ;          /* Sends a WM_PAINT message */
```

The Skeleton program does not process the resulting WM_PAINT message. Instead, it passes the message to Windows's default window function message-processing function. That function performs the default action for the WM_PAINT message, which is to paint the client area of the window with the background brush or system color. (You specified the brush when registering the window class.) The net result is that the Skeleton window is now displayed with the client area set to the background color.

The initInstance function has now successfully completed its only tasks–creating and displaying the application's main window–so it returns TRUE to WinMain:

```
return TRUE ;
```

WinMain's Message Loop

Skeleton now has a registered window class, and the window has been displayed on the screen. What's left? The main responsibility of all Windows applications. That is, all Windows applications must read messages from the application's message queue and dispatch them to the appropriate place. Most messages are sent to a window or, more correctly in one sense though less useful in others, to a *window function* associated with the window to which the message pertains. Others are sent to *callback* routines. The message loop reads messages from the application queue and dispatches them to the appropriate place. Skeleton's message loop is near the end of the WinMain function in the WinMain.c source file and looks like the following:

```
while (GetMessage (&msg, NULL, 0, 0)) {
    if (!TranslateAccelerator (msg.hwnd, haccel, &msg)) {
        TranslateMessage (&msg) ;
        DispatchMessage (&msg) ;
    }
}
```

The GetMessage function retrieves a message from the message queue.[1] The GetMessage function automatically yields control to other Windows applications when there are no messages in the queue. No messages in the queue means that there is nothing for the application to do; thus Windows can give control to another application. Because all other Windows applications have their own message loop, each containing a GetMessage call, every application gives up control of the CPU when it has nothing to do. In addition, Windows 95 and Windows NT both use *preemptive* schedulers. This means that when an application has used its allotted time, called a *time slice*, control is taken from it and granted to another application that has been idle. This preemption can occur at any time, even if there are messages in the queue and even when the program is not executing a GetMessage call. You, the programmer, have no control over when this will happen. When you issue a GetMessage call, if there is no message in the queue, control will be relinquished whether or not the time slice has been used. Otherwise, control can be taken away from your application without any warning and at any time.

Win16 programmers often took advantage of the fact that Win16 could not preempt the running application. For example, you knew that if you did an OpenClipboard operation, nobody else would even attempt to use the Clipboard until you finished because you did not do a GetMessage and therefore could not lose control. You also knew that if you opened the Clipboard, you would get it because nobody else (at least, no well-behaved somebody) would have the Clipboard open when they relinquished control. In Windows 95 and Windows NT, you can get control at any time and must be prepared to deal with failures that arise due to attempts to access shared resources (such as the Clipboard) that may already be locked. If you are an experienced Win16 programmer, many of your cherished assumptions about Windows and how control transfers among applications are now incorrect. If you ever took advantage of the cooperative multitasking in Win16, you will find that the tricks and techniques no longer work.

Because Win32s runs on Win16, it cannot take advantage of preemptive multitasking. This means that a Win32s program must obey all the strange restrictions and protocols of Win16 as far as relinquishing control during long periods of computation. A discussion of these methods is beyond the scope of this book. We recommend the extensive Win16 literature on the subject of PeekMessage.

When a message is in the queue at the time of the call to GetMessage, the GetMessage function copies the message into the MSG structure named msg, removes it from the queue, and returns. If the queue is empty, Windows will suspend the application.[2] When a message arrives in the empty queue for which GetMessage is waiting, the application will be able to run again; when it starts running, the GetMessage function completes its copying action and returns. As a programmer, you cannot tell if GetMessage has suspended or immediately returned.

The MSG structure looks like this:

---

[1] We're going to finesse some details here. There are several queues. One of them is the *thread queue*, which is where the message really comes from. But for right now, we simplify by referring to "the queue." It's a good enough approximation for now.

[2] Strictly speaking, it suspends the *thread*, but we're simplifying the exposition here.

```
typedef struct tagMSG
  {
    HWND        hwnd ;        // The message is for this window
    UINT        message ;     // This is the actual message number
    WPARAM      wParam ;      // parameter - additional info
    LPARAM      lParam ;      // parameter - additional info
    DWORD       time ;        // The time at which the message was posted
    POINT       pt ;          // The position of the cursor when the msg was posted
  } MSG ;
```

The second parameter to GetMessage specifies the handle of the window for which to retrieve a message. When this parameter is nonzero, only messages having a matching hwnd field value will be retrieved. When this parameter is NULL, as it usually is, GetMessage retrieves messages for any window that belongs to the application making the call. The GetMessage function will not retrieve a message for a window owned by a different application.

Windows identifies messages by an integer even though the messages are usually referred to by their symbolic names, such as WM_PAINT, WM_COMMAND, and WM_QUIT. Occasionally, you may wish to retrieve only certain types of messages. The third and fourth parameters specify the integer value of the lowest and highest message number to retrieve. For example, windows.h defines the symbolic constants WM_MOUSEFIRST and WM_MOUSELAST. You could use these constants as parameters three and four of a GetMessage function call to retrieve only those messages that apply to the mouse. When both the third and fourth parameters are 0, as they are in Skeleton, no message filtering is performed and GetMessage returns any available message. The message number is stored in the message field of an MSG structure.

Some messages–in particular, those about keyboard input–should be translated before sending them to the appropriate window function. When a user depresses a key on the keyboard while one of an application's windows has the input focus, a WM_KEYDOWN message is placed in the message queue. Sometime later, when the user releases the key, a WM_KEYUP message is also placed in the message queue. The Translate-Accelerator function translates a keyboard accelerator key press into a WM_COMMAND message as defined in the accelerator table. Windows provides the TranslateMessage function that matches the WM_KEYDOWN and WM_KEYUP messages and determines if a key with a ANSI code equivalent was pressed. The Translate-Message function looks for matching WM_KEYDOWN and WM_KEYUP messages and generates a corresponding WM_CHAR message. The WM_CHAR message contains the ANSI character code for the key that was depressed and released. In Windows NT, a Unicode-based application will receive the Unicode character code for the key that was depressed.

Once the message is translated (if it didn't need to be translated, there is no special action taken), the message loop calls the DispatchMessage function to instruct Windows to send the message directly to the appropriate window function. You should note that a Windows application never directly calls a window function. In fact, you *must not* call a window function directly. Windows calls a window function when the message loop calls the DispatchMessage function with a message destined for a window associated with the window function.

The *loop* part of the term *message loop* comes from the while statement that keeps repeating the Get-Message-TranslateMessage-DispatchMessage cycle as long as GetMessage returns a nonzero value. The GetMessage function returns a nonzero value if a message other than WM_QUIT is retrieved; it returns 0

In Win16, the `CallWindowProc` call was required because of the peculiar constraints of the Win16 addressing environment; for example, to guarantee data addressability. Much discussion of callbacks, including the need to export names, interactions with the linker, and so on, appear in the Win16 literature. Because none of the addressability problems of Win16 would be an issue in Win32, the natural question is, why *not* call the functions directly. It turns out that there are both long-term and short-term considerations involved. In the long term, addressability or other interface considerations could still be an issue on some platforms. Windows does not guarantee addressability, which is why the CALLBACK keyword is required. But more importantly, the short-term consideration is that certain transformations, such as Unicode-to-ANSI or ANSI-to-Unicode, will automatically take place if you pass string parameters to a window. For example, the calling function may be an ANSI language application, while the called window procedure could be in a Unicode application. To guarantee the correct behavior, you must use `CallWindowProc`.

when the `WM_QUIT` message is retrieved. Retrieving a `WM_QUIT` message is the signal for the application to stop retrieving messages and to terminate the message loop. If the message loop is the one in `WinMain`, the application will then terminate.

Typically, the window function for the application's main window places a `WM_QUIT` message in the message queue when destroying the main window. This signals the message loop that the application should be terminated. Calling the `PostQuitMessage` function places the `WM_QUIT` message in the message queue. This function allows the caller to specify a value that `WinMain` should return as the application's return status. This value is copied to the `wParam` parameter of the `WM_QUIT` message. `WinMain` returns this value to Windows with the following statement:

```
return exitInstance (&ms) ;
```

This code structure allows you to easily add additional termination code. As mentioned earlier in the chapter, Windows does not currently use the value returned by the `WinMain` function.

Windows applications should release their resources within each window function as each window is destroyed. You should not release resources after the message loop terminates and prior to returning from `WinMain`. When Windows itself terminates, it sends messages to each window function, destroying each window (doing this allows the window function to release resources); however, it never returns control to your message loop. Because the message loop never gets control again and never retrieves a `WM_QUIT` message, code placed after the message loop will never be executed. Windows will send each application a `WM_QUERYENDSESSION` message notifying it of the impending shutdown so that an application does get a chance to terminate cleanly.

The Window Function

General Structure

Once the message loop begins executing, Skeleton begins retrieving messages and dispatching them to the appropriate message function(s). So far, Skeleton requires only one message function. Back in the `registerWindowClasses` function, Skeleton registered a window class and one of the fields of the WND-CLASSEX structure was filled in as follows:

```
wc.lpfnWndProc = (WNDPROC) mainFrameWndProc ;
```

The `mainFrameWndProc` function is responsible for processing all messages for windows of this class. Window functions have been historically named `WndProc`s. Windows calls the `mainFrameWndProc` function directly every time `DispatchMessage` is called within `WinMain` with a message destined for a window of this class. All window functions *must* be defined as follows:

```
LRESULT CALLBACK
mainFrameWndProc (HWND hwnd, UINT message, WPARAM wParam, LPARAM lParam)
{
   // .. your own code here
   return DefWindowProc(hwnd, message, wParam, lParam);
}
```

A window function is one type of *callback function*. The symbol `CALLBACK` defines this function as a callback function; it was introduced in Windows 3.1. The windows.h header file defines the symbol `CALLBACK` to be `__stdcall`. Applications written for Windows versions 3.0 and earlier explicitly defined callback functions to be `FAR PASCAL` functions. `FAR` and `PASCAL` are themselves definitions for `__far` and `__pascal`. However, this was idiosyncratic to the Win16 environment and not portable to Win32, so the more general name was introduced. Different Win32 platforms may define callback functions to use a different calling sequence. Defining your application callback functions using the `CALLBACK` symbol, rather than the explicit `__stdcall`, makes your application more portable to various Win32 platforms.

The Microsoft C compiler versions 5.*x*, 6.*x*, and 7.0 have each introduced a new name for the `__far`, `__near`, `__pascal`, and similar keywords. Version 5 accepted only the keywords that didn't have an underscore prefix. Version 6 preferred keywords with a single underscore prefix but also accepted the nonprefixed form. Version 7 and later use the double-underscore prefix versions of the names, which are ANSI-compliant, implementation-defined names. This explains the idiosyncrasies you may find if you are porting an older Win16 application to Win32. The 32-bit compilers will complain about the use of obsolete reserved words if you use the keywords `__far`, `__near`, or `__pascal`.

A window function should return an `LRESULT` value. The actual value to be returned depends on the message received by the window function, but for most messages, the return value is not used. (It's those odd messages that catch you. When in doubt, always check the documentation for each message your window function processes to see whether it requires a specific return value. The examples in this book will use a few such messages.) The value returned by a window function is ultimately the value returned by the `DispatchMessage` function call that routed the message to the window function. When a message is sent to a window via the `SendMessage` function, the value returned becomes the result of that function.

The four parameters to a window function are the first four fields of the `MSG` structure. A window function may receive messages for any number of different windows. The `hwnd` parameter identifies the window to which this message applies. The `message` parameter identifies the specific message. You use this parameter, typically in a `switch` statement to determine which message it is and to process it properly. The `wParam` parameter is a `WPARAM` that contains additional information about the message. Likewise, the `lParam` parameter is a `LPARAM` that contains additional information about the message. The interpretation of the `wParam` and `lParam` parameters depends on the message received. The `time` and `pt` fields of the `MSG` structure are not passed to a window function as parameters of the call. A window function may retrieve the value of the `time` and `pt` fields by calling the `GetMessageTime` and `GetMessagePos` functions.

A window function receives many messages. In fact, many of these are often of absolutely no interest to the window function! A window function must pass all messages that it does not process back to Windows by calling the DefWindowProc function. DefWindowProc is the Windows *default window function*. It processes messages to give a window a *default behavior*. To accomplish this, the DefWindowProc function provides specific processing for some of the window messages. Any messages not defined as having a particular default action are ignored by DefWindowProc, and it returns 0. For all messages the window function passes to DefWindowProc, your window function should return the result of the DefWindowProc function.

Initially, it seems a bit strange for Windows to send a window function messages destined to be handed right back to Windows itself. But, at the cost of a little extra overhead, this design gives an application the ability to exert much greater control over the appearance and operation of a Windows program than would be possible otherwise.

For example, the Skeleton application does not process the WM_NCLBUTTONDOWN message that notifies a window that the user clicked the nonclient area of the window (basically, some portion of the window frame or caption). The application passes the WM_NCLBUTTONDOWN message to the DefWindowProc function. DefWindowProc processes the message by allowing the user to drag the window around the screen by the mouse when the click is in the caption bar.

If you fail to call DefWindowProc for this message, you will discover that the window does not provide the "expected" window behavior. Of course, you could always implement all the "expected" window behavior yourself. But remember: There are several hundred Windows messages. You would have to implement all of the correct behavior for every one of them; otherwise, your users would complain that your application did not obey Windows GUI standards. In addition, the "expected" behavior has changed in the multiple versions of Windows. It is much easier simply to let DefWindowProc handle any message you don't care about.

The message loop fetches messages from the application queue and sends them to the appropriate window function. However, the message loop isn't the only routine calling a window function. Windows sends window management messages directly to a window function. These messages do not go through the application queue or get dispatched by the message loop.

For example, calling the CreateWindowEx function in the initInstance function results in Windows's calling the mainFrameWndProc function four times. The ShowWindow function call results in 13 calls to the mainFrameWndProc function. The UpdateWindow function call results in one additional call to the mainFrameWndProc function. We list in Table 2.4 the messages sent to the mainFrameWndProc function during these function calls. What these messages do isn't as important right now as realizing that Windows has called a window function numerous times prior to an application's entering its message loop. It is also important to realize that Microsoft does not guarantee the order of messages; this table should be viewed as illustrative rather than definitive. There were significant changes in message order between Windows 2.*x* and 3.0 and between 3.0 and 3.1. There is no guarantee that Win32 will have the same message order on Windows 95 or Windows NT or even on two releases of the same platform.

Global data used by a window function may need to be initialized before you create a window of that class because the act of creating the window calls the window function. A window function may also need to be reentrant. For example, if, during the processing of a message in a window function, you invalidate a portion

Table 2.4: The messages sent as a result of the CreateWindowEx, ShowWindow and UpdateWindow function calls

Hexadecimal Message Number	Symbolic Name
The CreateWindow function call sends the following messages to the window:	
0024	WM_GETMINMAXINFO
0081	WM_NCCREATE
0083	WM_NCCALCSIZE
0001	WM_CREATE
The ShowWindow function call sends the following messages to the window:	
0018	WM_SHOWWINDOW
0046	WM_WINDOWPOSCHANGING
001C	WM_ACTIVATEAPP
0086	WM_NCACTIVATE
000D	WM_GETTEXT
0006	WM_ACTIVATE
0007	WM_SETFOCUS
0085	WM_NCPAINT
000D	WM_GETTEXT
0014	WM_ERASEBKGND
0047	WM_WINDOWPOSCHANGED
0005	WM_SIZE
0003	WM_MOVE
The UpdateWindow function call sends the following message:	
000F	WM_PAINT

of the window and call the UpdateWindow function to force the window to be repainted, the window function will be recursively called with a WM_PAINT message. Only after the message function returns from processing the WM_PAINT message will control return from the UpdateWindow function call. It is not at all uncommon to find yourself nested recursively three or four levels deep in your window function. You should always write your window function as if it will be applied to multiple concurrent windows, can be applied to any one of them at any time, and will be called recursively. Any shortcuts you take that compromise these goals will ultimately cause subtle bugs that will take a very long time to find and over time will mean that your application will be less robust. *Even if you think there is only ever going to be one window, apply these rules.* The number of times that applications have to be changed from single-window to multiple-window (usually Multiple Document Interface) applications is surprisingly high. Your basic assumption about single-windowness is often violated a year into the project. The single-window assumptions will have been long since forgotten, although the code critically depends on them for correct execution.

Skeleton's main application window uses the following window function:

```
LRESULT CALLBACK
mainFrameWndProc (HWND hwnd, UINT message, WPARAM wParam, LPARAM lParam)
{
  switch (message) {
    case WM_COMMAND:              // Notification from menu or control
      return HANDLE_WM_COMMAND (hwnd, wParam, lParam, mainFrame_OnCommand) ;
                                 // mainFrame_OnCommand is shown on page 83

    case WM_DESTROY:             // Window is being destroyed
      return HANDLE_WM_DESTROY (hwnd, wParam, lParam, mainFrame_OnDestroy) ;
                                 // mainFrame_OnDestroy is shown on page 79

    default:
      return DefWindowProc (hwnd, message, wParam, lParam) ;
  }
}
```

In the Skeleton, the hwnd parameter for this function will always equal the value returned by the CreateWindowEx function call in initInstance because Skeleton creates only one window of this class. When an application creates multiple windows of a given class, the hwnd parameter identifies the window to which the message applies. The message parameter identifies the specific message. The wParam and lParam parameters contain message-specific information.

This relatively simple window function does the following:

- Selects two specific messages for processing.

- Calls the appropriate application-specific message-handling function.

- Uses message-cracker macros to decode the message-specific meaning of the wParam and lParam message parameters.

- Returns the value, if any, of the called message-handler function.

All unprocessed messages are returned to Windows by calling the DefWindowProc function and passing it the same four parameters given to the window function. The DefWindowProc function performs any default processing for a message. The value returned by DefWindowProc is used as the return value for the window function:

```
return DefWindowProc (hwnd, msg, wParam, lParam) ;
```

Note: DefWindowProc is *guaranteed* to return 0 for any message it does not understand. We take advantage of this feature in later examples.

Message Handling: WM_DESTROY

We examine the WM_DESTROY message-handling first because it's the simplest.

```
static void
mainFrame_OnDestroy (HWND hwnd)
```

```
{
    PostQuitMessage (0) ;
}
```

Windows sends a WM_DESTROY message to a window *after* removing the window from the screen to inform it that the window *is being destroyed*. We use the HANDLE_WM_DESTROY message-cracker macro to call the application's mainFrame_OnDestroy function to process the message. The wParam and lParam parameters are not used in a WM_DESTROY message, a fact understood by the message-cracker macro and the reason why the mainFrame_OnDestroy function accepts only one parameter: a window handle. We discuss the various message-cracker macros in depth at the end of this chapter. A complete summary is given in Appendix B.

A window function should use the WM_DESTROY message as a signal to do any final processing necessary before the window is destroyed. Because Skeleton has only one window, and that window does not need to perform any termination processing, destroying it means that the application should terminate. However, a Windows application is not automatically terminated by Windows because it would be The Right Thing To Do When There Are No More Windows. Rather, it is the responsibility of the application to notify Windows that it wishes to quit at some time in the future. It does this by calling the PostQuitMessage function. This is not a design oversight on the part of the Windows designers; there is not a unique Right Thing To Do. An application may choose to briefly have no top-level window because it is in the process of creating a new one. So the absence of a window is a transient condition. It may be a Windows NT *system service*, which normally does not have a window, but which might create one for a brief user interaction. So its *normal* state is to have no window! Or the program may start up with a window, interact with the user briefly, and then "background" itself to provide a service (along the lines of an NT system service but not as a full-fledged NT service). It would destroy its only window because it interacts with the operating system via some other mechanism, such as a *pipe*. Rather than try to second-guess the programmer, Windows simply requires being kept informed of what is desired.

The PostQuitMessage function places a WM_QUIT message in the application queue and returns immediately to the window function. The parameter to the PostQuitMessage function call specifies the value to be returned in the wParam field of the MSG structure when the message is received. When you drop out of your message loop, you can examine this value. In the case of Skeleton, we use this value as the application's exit code.

The mainFrameWndProc function processes the WM_DESTROY message by notifying Windows that it wishes to terminate and that a 0 should be returned as the application's exit code. It does this as follows:

```
PostQuitMessage (0) ;
```

The argument to the PostQuitMessage is used as the wParam parameter to the WM_QUIT message that is placed in the application queue. Eventually, the message loop will retrieve the WM_QUIT message from the application queue, thus causing the message loop to exit. In Skeleton, the following statement

```
return msg.wParam
```

in exitInstance returns the value given as the parameter to the PostQuitMessage function call–in this case, a 0–to WinMain, which passes it back to Windows as the result value of WinMain. A common error is omitting the `PostQuitMessage` function call in the `WM_DESTROY` message-processing logic. The application window is still destroyed, so the application is not visible to the user who assumes the application is terminated. However, the application would still be running the message loop and still be present in memory! You should ensure that a Windows application calls `PostQuitMessage` at least once to terminate the message loop.

If you fail to post the `WM_QUIT` message, your process is still running, but is almost inaccessible. We often call this a "rogue process". In Win32, you can easily deal with this situation, once you realize what has happened, by using the `pview` program. The `pview` program is part of the Windows SDK and is the "process viewer". It will give you a list of all the running processes in the system. On Windows NT, *most* of those processes will not have windows! But you will see the name of your program listed there. You won't find it in the Task Manager (Windows NT 3.*x*) or on the Task Bar (Windows 95 and Windows NT 4.*x*), but its presence in the process list is a dead giveaway that you forgot to `PostQuitMessage`. One of the facilities `pview` has is the ability to kill any process. (Be careful! A misplaced mouse click that selects the wrong process could kill off some essential operating system service, and you will have to reboot the system!)

One good indication that you have a rogue process is that when you try to recompile your application, you will get an error message from the linker telling you it is unable to open the `.exe` file for output. This will be true any time you have a running version of the program anywhere on your system. But if you can't *find* a running version on the Task Manager or in the Task Bar, then you have a rogue process.

You must also be aware that not finding a running instance on your machine doesn't prove there isn't a running instance somewhere. For checking out our code for this book, I have four machines on the network: A Windows NT 3.51 machine (primary development), a Windows NT 4.*x* workstation, a Windows NT 4.*x* server, and a Windows 95 machine. Leaving a running copy of the executable on *any* of the networked machines keeps us from relinking the version on the main development machine. Fortunately, a keyboard/screen/mouse multiplexor lets me quickly switch to each machine in turn to discover on which one I left the instance running. – *jmn*

That's it! The `WM_DESTROY` message processing is complete. We return from the message handler, and the `WM_DESTROY` message-cracker macro provides a 0 value as the window function return value. Many messages do not require you to return any value as a result of processing the message. However, the function prototype of a window function requires that a message handler return some value regardless of whether such a value has any meaning. Conventionally, one returns a 0 value in this case. The message-cracker macros provide the 0 value for you.

When you call the `DispatchMessage` function to dispatch a message to a window function, the value returned by the window function as a result of processing the message becomes the return value of the `DispatchMessage` function call. In this situation, the return value of message processing doesn't matter because we have never seen *any* code that checks the value returned by the `DispatchMessage` function (although there's probably some strange person somewhere who has written such code). However, Windows delivers the majority of messages to a window function as a result of a call to the `SendMessage` function, and callers of `SendMessage` very frequently check the return value. In many cases, the whole purpose of sending the message is to obtain the result via storing the return value of `SendMessage`. The bottom line is that you should always return an appropriate value even if it might on occasion be ignored.

Notice in our example that the `DefWindowProc` function is never called when processing a `WM_DESTROY` message because the window function intercepts and processes the message.

There are several termination messages that you might receive. WM_CLOSE and WM_DESTROY should be carefully distinguished. WM_CLOSE is a *request* to close the window. You can choose to honor the request by passing the message on to DefWindowProc or directly calling DestroyWindow. Or you can choose to ignore the request by simply returning. WM_DESTROY informs you that the window *has been* destroyed. WM_NCDESTROY is finally, with Win32, officially documented to be the very last message a window will ever receive. WM_QUERYENDSESSION is sent when you are shutting down Windows. It asks each application if it is willing to be shut down. If your application refuses to shut down, Windows will not be shut down.

Message Handling: WM_COMMAND

Next we examine the WM_COMMAND message processing. Windows places a WM_COMMAND message into the application queue when the user selects an item from a menu, when a control passes a message to its parent window, or when an accelerator keystroke is translated. All these topics are addressed in detail in later chapters. For now, we concentrate on menu selections.

The main application window for the Skeleton program has a menu. Because no menu was specified when the window was created (the tenth parameter of the CreateWindowEx function call was 0), the window uses the default menu for the window class. Skeleton identified the default menu when registering the window class with the statement

wcex.lpszMenuName = MAKEINTRESOURCE (resPoolID) ;

The parameter resPoolID identifies the menu used by the window. Menus, as well as other resources, can be created at runtime or statically defined separately from the application program. Skeleton uses the latter approach, which we describe in this chapter in the section "Resource Definition Files" starting on page 89.

We defined a menu statically by creating a text file, called a *resource script*, that describes the menu. This text, part of what is in the Skeleton.rc file, is

```
IDR_MAINFRAME MENU DISCARDABLE
BEGIN
    POPUP "&File"
    BEGIN
        MENUITEM "E&xit",                    ID_APP_EXIT
    END
    POPUP "&Help"
    BEGIN
        MENUITEM "&About Skeleton...",        ID_APP_ABOUT
    END
END
```

Skeleton's menu has only two command items. The definition of the **Exit** menu item associates the symbolic constant ID_APP_EXIT with the menu item. When a user selects this menu item, Windows places a WM_COMMAND message in the message queue with the low-order 16 bits of the wParam parameter of the message set to the value ID_APP_EXIT and the lParam parameter set to 0 to indicate that the message is from a menu. The second menu item operates similarly in that when a user selects the **About Skeleton...** menu item, Windows places a WM_COMMAND message in the application queue with the low-order 16 bits of the wParam parameter of the message set to the value ID_APP_ABOUT.

When processing a WM_COMMAND message, mainFrameWndProc uses the WM_COMMAND message-cracker macro to extract the various parameters encoded in the wParam and lParam arguments and to call the WM_COMMAND message handler function with the parameters.

Those who know Win16 will note that the decoding of the WM_COMMAND message is not the same on Win32. In Win16, the wParam contained the control ID, the LOWORD(lParam) was the control handle, and the HIWORD(lParam) was the notification code. In Win32, the HIWORD(wParam) is the notification code, the LOWORD(wParam) is the control ID, and the lParam is the control handle. By using the message-cracker macros, you do not need to embed such platform-specific dependencies in your code. In addition, looking up each message while you're writing code is often a very tedious activity. The message-cracker macros not only give you platform independence; they also provide a cleaner, easier-to-understand interface to the messages.

```
static void
mainFrame_OnCommand (HWND hwnd, int id, HWND hwndCtl, UINT codeNotify)
{
  switch (id) {
    case ID_APP_ABOUT:
    {
     doAbout(hwnd);
    }
    return ;

    case ID_APP_EXIT:
      DestroyWindow (hwnd) ;
      return ;

    default:
      FORWARD_WM_COMMAND (hwnd, id, hwndCtl, codeNotify, DefWindowProc) ;
  }
}
```

The only WM_COMMAND messages processed by mainFrame_OnCommand are the ID_APP_ABOUT and ID_APP_EXIT menu item selection messages. All others are passed back to Windows by forwarding the WM_COMMAND message (using the message *un*cracker FORWARD_WM_COMMAND macro) to the DefWindowProc function (which, as it turns out, will ignore the messages; but, who knows, maybe one day it won't, and we'll be ready for that).

Here is an example where the user selects the **About Skeleton...** menu item from the window's **Help** menu. In this case, selecting the menu item indicates a request to display the application's About dialog box. A *dialog box* (strictly speaking, a *modal dialog box*) is a temporary window that displays information or requests information from the user. An About dialog box displays information about the application such as its name, author, and copyright information. The *Windows Interface Guidelines for Software Design* recommends that an About dialog box be included with every application. Skeleton includes an About dialog box so that it can be used as a complete skeletal application meeting these user interface guidelines. Doing this introduces a few concepts a bit early, but it makes for a more complete Windows program template. For a far more sophisticated About dialog box that displays the current operating system, current processor type, and other information, look at the Template example program.

Once Skeleton determines that the About dialog box should be displayed, the following code displays the box, waits for the user to respond to it (that is, it gives the user a chance to read the information in it), removes the box from the screen, and frees resources used in displaying the box. The doAbout function is found in the file About.c and is as follows:

```
static void
doAbout(HWND hwnd)
{
  HINSTANCE hinst = GetWindowInstance (hwnd) ;
  DialogBox (hinst, MAKEINTRESOURCE (IDD_ABOUTBOX), hwnd, (DLGPROC) aboutDlgProc) ;
}
```

Why not put those lines in the doAbout function in the WM_COMMAND handler instead of creating a function in the About.c file? We strongly believe that all code relevant to a dialog should be in a separate source file. We also believe that each dialog box should have its own unique source file. In this source file, you should encapsulate all of the information and code necessary to make the dialog box work and should use no global state elsewhere in the program to accomplish this (essentially, the source file for the dialog box uses no extern variables). To put those lines in the mainFrame_OnCommand handler means the handler *knows* how the dialog box is implemented; for example, that it is called by DialogBox, not DialogBoxParam, that it has a specific handler, and that the name of the handler is known to the caller. This is far too much knowledge to have the caller know about, and it violates modularity in too many ways for comfort. So we move *all* of the knowledge of how to activate the dialog box into the box's source file and export only an abstract interface specification, doAbout. It is surprising how much easier this makes life in the long run.

The GetWindowInstance function call is a macro API appearing in the windowsx.h header file. That header file defines the macro as a call to the GetWindowLong function that specifies the GWL_HINSTANCE parameter. The symbolic constant GWL_HINSTANCE specifies that the instance handle of the module (in this case, the Skeleton program itself) that owns the window hwnd be retrieved. This is a slightly roundabout method of retrieving the same handle as the one passed to WinMain as the hInstance parameter.

Win16 used GetWindowWord to retrieve the 16-bit handle; Win32 uses GetWindowLong to retrieve the 32-bit handle. One reason you should use the GetWindowInstance macro is that it does the right thing independent of on what platform it is running.

Many programmers prefer to save the hInstance parameter to WinMain in a global variable. The global variable can be used rather than retrieving the handle by using the GetWindowInstance function. A global variable is more efficient than the indirect method used here. However, the time saved by using a global variable is insignificant when compared to the time elapsed in displaying the dialog box, waiting for the user to read the information displayed, and removing the dialog box from the screen. Also, indiscriminate proliferation of global variables generally makes a program difficult to understand and to maintain. Because use of global variables should generally be avoided and the overhead incurred by not using a global variable is acceptable, Skeleton takes the indirect approach.

Windows calls the dialog function directly. There will be only one copy of the code for the dialog function in memory. Multiple instances of the program may, however, be present in memory. Typically only one of the instances will display the dialog box at a time, although this is completely up to the user and all instances could be executing the dialog function concurrently.

The DialogBox function call creates and displays the dialog box. It requires the current application's instance handle and an identification of a template it will use to create the dialog box. A dialog box template identifier can be either a character string, giving the name of the template, or an integer, depending on

Those familiar with Win16 may remember `MakeProcInstance` and `FreeProcInstance`. These were *effectively* obsolete in Windows 3.1; they are now *officially* obsolete. The complex issues of data addressability so critical to the success of a Win16 program simply don't exist in Win32.

whether the template is defined by name or number. Skeleton uses the integer symbolic constant `IDD_ABOUTBOX` (the IDD prefix stands for *ID D*ialog) to identify the proper dialog box template to be used. The `hwnd` parameter is the handle of the window that owns the dialog box.

The fourth parameter is the name (actually the address) of the dialog function associated with the dialog box to be displayed. A *dialog function* is very similar, though not identical, to a window function. You have seen that all windows have an associated window function and that Windows sends messages about a window to its associated window function. A dialog box is fundamentally a special kind of window. A dialog box must have an associated dialog function. Windows sends messages about a dialog box window to a `DIALOG` class *window function* that is internal to Windows itself. This window function is similar to the main frame window function we previously discussed, except the function is written for you and provided as part of Windows. The `DIALOG` class window function, in turn, passes the message to the *dialog function* associated with the dialog box window. However, there are a couple of complications in calling dialog functions.

The `DialogBox` function call does not return until the dialog function terminates. Typically, a dialog box provides a means for the user to close its window. When the dialog function receives the request to close its window, it terminates and the function that called `DialogBox` resumes.

If you don't provide code to close the dialog box, you will not be able to close the dialog box and will not be able to regain control of your application. You can force it to terminate, but you will not be able to get control of it. You can use the `pview` program (see the inset on page 81) to kill off such a program.

The About Dialog Function

Dialog functions are similar to window functions. For example, look at the definition of the `aboutDlgProc` dialog function used by Skeleton:

```
BOOL CALLBACK
aboutDlgProc (HWND hwnd, UINT message, WPARAM wParam, LPARAM lParam)
{
  switch (message) {
    case WM_COMMAND:                        // Notification from a control
      return HANDLE_WM_COMMAND (hwnd, wParam, lParam, aboutDlg_OnCommand) ;

    case WM_INITDIALOG:                     // Initialization of controls complete
      return HANDLE_WM_INITDIALOG (hwnd, wParam, lParam, aboutDlg_OnInitDialog) ;

  }
  return FALSE ;
}
```

Like window functions, dialog functions must be declared as CALLBACK functions. Dialog functions also take the same four parameters as window functions. The first difference is the function's return value. Dialog functions return a Boolean value, where a nonzero value means the function processed the message it was sent and a 0 value means it did not.

 Actually, this is a little bit misleading. There are special cases in which a dialog function will return other than these two values. There also is a special means by which you can return an arbitrary 32-bit value to a SendMessage that has called the dialog function. The WM_CTLCOLOR* messages–WM_COMPAREITEM, WM_VKEYTOITEM, WM_CHARTOITEM, and WM_QUERYDRAGICON–have special return values. See the windowsx.h macro SetDlg-MessageResult for returning values to SendMessage.

However, *dialog functions* are not *window functions*. Dialog functions must *not* call the DefWindowProc function to process unwanted messages as a window function does. A dialog box already has a window function. After all, it is a window. The DIALOG class window function for a dialog box resides within Windows itself. The message loop dispatches messages for the dialog box to this window function. The DIALOG class window function, in turn, calls the dialog function within your application.

The first message processed by the About dialog function is WM_INITDIALOG. The DIALOG class window function sends this message to the dialog function immediately before it displays the dialog box. This message gives the dialog box function a chance to load any values into the controls that you may want to initialize. Also, you can set the input focus to a specific control within the dialog box (normally, the first nonstatic, visible, enabled control will get the focus). Again, we use a message-cracker macro to separate the components of the wParam and lParam parameters to the WM_INITDIALOG message and to call the message handler.

This code completely handles the WM_INITDIALOG message:

```
static BOOL
aboutDlg_OnInitDialog (HWND hwnd, HWND hwndFocus, LPARAM lParam)
{
  return TRUE ;
}
```

The **About...** dialog box doesn't wish to set the input focus to a specific control, so it returns TRUE, thus telling Windows to set the input focus to the first control within the dialog box. We haven't discussed controls yet, but in this example, the input focus will be set to the **OK** default push button within the dialog box. We don't have any controls to load, so this function actually has nothing to do except return TRUE.

The only other message processed by the About dialog function is the WM_COMMAND message. It is processed as follows:

```
static
void aboutDlg_OnCommand (HWND hwnd, int id, HWND hwndCtl, UINT codeNotify)
{
  switch (id) {
    case IDOK:                      // OK pushbutton/Enter keypress
    case IDCANCEL:                  // Esc keypress
      EndDialog (hwnd, TRUE) ;      // Dismiss the about dialog box
      break ;
  }
}
```

Previously you saw a WM_COMMAND message sent as a result of the user's selecting a menu item. This case is slightly different. A WM_COMMAND message is also sent when the user changes the state of a control. In this example, when the user clicks the **OK** push button, presses the space bar when the **OK** push button has the input focus, or presses the **Enter** key on the keyboard, the push button control sends a WM_COMMAND message to its parent window, in this case, the dialog box window. The LOWORD(wParam) parameter of the WM_COMMAND message is set to the control ID of the control sending the message. The **OK** push button has the control ID of IDOK. When the user presses the **Esc** key, a WM_COMMAND message is sent with the LOWORD(wParam) parameter set to IDCANCEL. We use the HANDLE_WM_COMMAND message-cracker macro once again to extract the parameters to the WM_COMMAND message and to call its message handler, aboutDlg_OnCommand.

The message handler determines that the WM_COMMAND message was either from the **OK** push button or a result of an **Esc** key press and, in either case, calls the EndDialog function to terminate the dialog box identified by hwnd. The second parameter, TRUE in this example, is the value that will eventually be the return value of the call to the DialogBox function that created the dialog box.

The EndDialog function does not terminate the dialog box immediately. Instead, it sets a flag that directs the dialog-class window function to terminate the dialog box when the dialog function finishes processing the current message. The EndDialog function call then completes and returns to the dialog function. Next, the dialog function immediately returns TRUE to the DIALOG class window function, thus signifying that the WM_COMMAND message was processed. The DIALOG class window function, noticing that the completion flag is set, itself terminates, and control returns from the original call to the DialogBox function that started everything rolling.

No other messages, other than WM_COMMAND and WM_INITDIALOG, are processed by the Skeleton dialog function. For these other messages, the dialog function returns the value FALSE and notifies the DIALOG class window function that the message was not processed. The DIALOG class window function will provide default processing for certain messages that are not handled by a dialog function.

You may discover the DefDlgProc and think that it should be used like DefWindowProc, that is, at the end of a dialog function. If you use it in a dialog box function, you will get a stack overflow, as you will end up in a recursive loop. The DefDlgProc is for advanced use and is not covered in this book. DefDlgProc is actually called by the DIALOG class function.

The Components of the **Skeleton** Application

That's it! You've now seen all the code that comprises a skeletal Windows application. However, a few steps remain before you can run the application.

First, the code must be compiled. Windows applications typically consist of multiple source files (even Skeleton is partitioned into six source files, a resource file, and a number of header files). Skeleton uses a *makefile* to build the application properly. A makefile is a series of specifications that allow a tool, such as Microsoft's nmake, to perform a "minimum" compilation, that is, to compile as few files as possible to produce a consistent set of files for generating the executable file. The art of constructing a makefile is arcane; fortunately, the Microsoft development environment constructs these automatically for you. Other development environments provide similar tools and facilities, either as explicit control files or as part of a "project description file".

The CD-ROM that is supplied with this book provides project files for the Microsoft Visual C++ 4.*x* environment. You may ignore these project files and reconstruct them from the original source files, adapt them to some other environment that you are using, or create project files using your own favorite environment tools.

Building a simple Windows application consists of these steps:

1. Compile the source code using a C/C++ compiler, generating object files.

2. Compile the resource script using the Resource Compiler, generating an object file.

3. Link the object files (containing code and resources) into an executable program or DLL.

Somewhat obviously, we use the C compiler to compile all of our C source code into object files. However, our source code refers to a number of its resources by symbolic names. We refer to the menu and window class name by the symbol IDR_MAINFRAME. We refer to the About dialog box template by the symbol IDD_ABOUTBOX. The definitions of these resources do not appear anywhere in our C source code.

You define the resources used by a Windows program in another type of source file called a *resource definition file*. Resource definition files are compiled into binary files similarly to the way C source files are compiled into object files. Naturally, you don't use the C compiler to do this. You use rc, the Resource Compiler, to compile resource definition files.

Next, the linker assembles the object modules to make an executable program. Linking Windows applications can also utilize a file not needed when linking DOS programs. This linker source file is called a *module definition file*. A module definition file is usually optional for Windows.exe files, but you'll frequently need to use one when building a DLL.

In Win16, a module definition file was not optional. In Win32, it is optional because many of the specifications of the file are either obsolete or can be specified with linker switches.

In the Microsoft Visual C++ environment, this is all more or less done for you automatically. So automatically, in fact, that you may find yourself faced with a collection of files you have never heard of that are doing things you don't understand. So we take some time here to explain these files and what they do.

The Visual C++ environment is very rich, but in many ways it is strongly biased to programming in C++ using the Microsoft Foundation Classes (MFC), a topic well outside the scope of this book. However, it is still useful for writing, compiling, and debugging straight C code, and its resource editor is a very pleasant means of editing the resource files. Its clear C++ bias should not discourage you from exploiting its strengths for ordinary C programming. We use it for the examples.

The Skeleton application is divided into multiple files, as listed in Table 2.5.

Table 2.5: Layout of `Skeleton`'s source files and functions

Filename	Usage	Contents
about.c	Source file.	`aboutDlgProc` dialog function.
initialization.c	Source file.	Program initialization code. `initInstance`
Mainframe.c	Source file.	Program initialization code. `mainFrameWndProc`
Winmain.c	Source file.	Initial entry point of application. `WinMain`
Wndproc.c	Source file.	Application main window function. `mainFrameWndProc`
Skeleton.rc	Resource definition file.	Contains the menus, string table, and the About dialog box template.
resource.h	Source file: resource symbols.	Contains symbolic constants used in dialog box definitions, menus, string tables, etc.
Skeleton.h	Source file: external declarations.	Contains function prototypes for all global functions in Skeleton and symbolic constants used by all source files.
StdSdk.h	Include file	Includes all the standard header files for the application, those that apply to all modules.
The following files are specific to the Microsoft Visual C++ environment:		
Skeleton.mdp	Visual C++ project.	Visual C++ project workspace definition file.
Skeleton.mak	Compilation control.	Program build instructions.
Skeleton.aps	Resource editor: configuration.	Remembers the configuration information between runs of the resource editor.
Skeleton.def	Linker control.	The optional module definition file.

Resource Definition Files

The Skeleton application uses a few resources not defined in the source code, such as a menu, two strings, and a dialog box template. The resource.h header file generally contains only #define preprocessor directives, and Visual C++ generally maintains that file. The resource.h header file *is* used by your project, although Visual C++ does not list the file in its file list pane due to the NO_DEPENDENCIES directive in the file. You will have to open the file using the Visual C++ **FilelOpen** menu item if you wish to examine the file. We show part of the resource.h file in Listing 2.5. (Much of what is not shown is "overhead"–declarations used by the Visual C++ environment to manage the resources and which are never seen by your application).

Listing 2.5: Partial listing of Skeleton's `resource.h` header file

```
//{{NO_DEPENDENCIES}}
// Microsoft Visual C++ generated include file.
// Used by Skeleton.rc
//

#define IDS_APP_TITLE                   1
#define IDR_MAINFRAME                   2
#define IDD_ABOUTBOX                    3
#define ID_APP_ABOUT                    4
#define ID_APP_EXIT                     5

#define MAX_RESOURCESTRING              255

#define IDC_STATIC                      -1
....
```

Skeleton places its only dialog template (the About dialog template) in the Skeleton.rc file. This file can be constructed by the resource editor, but it can also be constructed by hand. If you don't do anything esoteric, you can easily import it into the resource editor of Visual C++. Following is a partial listing of Skeleton's Skeleton.rc file.

```
IDD_ABOUTBOX DIALOG DISCARDABLE  22, 17, 204, 83
STYLE DS_MODALFRAME | WS_POPUP | WS_VISIBLE | WS_CAPTION | WS_SYSMENU
CAPTION "About Skeleton"
FONT 10, "System"
BEGIN
    DEFPUSHBUTTON       "OK",IDOK,166,63,32,14,WS_GROUP
    ICON                IDR_MAINFRAME,IDC_STATIC,3,2,18,20
    LTEXT               "Skeleton Example Application",IDC_STATIC,
                        30,2,118,8
    TEXT                "1.0",IDC_STATIC,180,2,17,8
    LTEXT               "Copyright © 1996 Wise Owl Consulting, Inc.",
                        IDC_STATIC,30,10,168,8
    LTEXT               "Author: Brent Rector",IDC_STATIC,30,18,168,8
    CONTROL             "",IDC_STATIC,"Static",SS_BLACKRECT,2,31,200,1
    LTEXT               "Operating System Name Goes Here",IDC_STATIC,4,
                        34,196,8
    LTEXT               "Processor Type Goes Here",IDC_STATIC,4,
                        42,196,8
    CONTROL             "",IDC_STATIC,"Static",SS_BLACKRECT,2,52,200,1
    LTEXT               "I have no trademarks, legal or otherwise.",
                        IDC_STATIC,3,57,156,18
    LTEXT               "Version ",IDC_STATIC,152,2,28,8
END
```

The Skeleton.rc file contains a template for the About dialog box. The DIALOG statement is the first statement in a dialog template. This statement defines a template that can be referenced by the symbolic constant IDD_ABOUTBOX. The upper-left corner of the dialog box will be displayed at the point (22, 17) in it parent window's client area. The dialog box is 204 units wide by 83 units high. The caption "About Skele-ton" appears in the title bar of the dialog box (which is really just a particular type of window). The window styles mentioned in the STYLE statement, in addition to the default styles, create a framed window having a caption and a system menu. The BEGIN/END statement pair delimits the statements that describe the content of the dialog box.

The About dialog box has the following parts:

- A default push button containing an "**OK**" label.

- An icon.

- Four lines of left-justified text.

- A black rectangle shaped into a line.

- Two more lines of left-justified text.

- Another black rectangle shaped into a line.

- Two final lines of left-justified text.

Clicking the default push button sends a WM_COMMAND message with the control identifier parameter set to IDOK.

Skeleton also uses a menu and some character strings. These resources are defined in the resource script file Skeleton.rc as well. Menus and string resources are covered in depth in Chapter 12, "Menus, Accelerators, Icons, String Resources, and MessageTable Resources", but we briefly explain these simple definitions here. The MENU resource, which describes the menu used by the application, is shown in Listing 2.6.

Listing 2.6: Skeleton's Skeleton.rc resource definition file: the menu

```
IDR_MAINFRAME MENU DISCARDABLE
BEGIN
    POPUP "&File"
    BEGIN
        MENUITEM "E&xit",                   ID_APP_EXIT
    END
    POPUP "&Help"
    BEGIN
        MENUITEM "&About Skeleton",         ID_APP_ABOUT
    END
END
```

The MENU statement defines a menu having the symbolic ID IDR_MAINFRAME, which happens to have the arbitrary value of 2 (see Listing 2.5). The first item on this menu is a pop-up menu that has the label "**File**". An ampersand (&) character causes Windows to draw the character that follows it as underlined. It also signals that the following character is the mnemonic character for the menu; that is, in this example, an **Alt+F** key press should pop up the **File** menu.

We have indicated that the resource has "the symbolic ID IDR_MAINFRAME, which happens to have the arbitrary value of 2" (see Listing 2.5). *You can't tell this by looking at the resource file!* When a name appears with a resource, it is *either* a string name *or* an integer designator. The only way to tell is to examine the `resource.h` file (and any other header files you might include in your `.rc` file). If there is a definition of the symbol as an integer, then the resource has an integer ID and you will need to use the MAKEINTRESOURCE(*name*) macro to reference it from your program. If you don't find a definition, then it is a string name, and you should use the quoted string, _T("*name*"), to reference it. All of the early books on Windows programming used string names because they were easier to maintain and deal with in the absence of any automated tooling. But with the advent of integrated development environments like Visual C++ and many others, this tedious task is handled for you, and numeric resource IDs with their corresponding `resource.h` definitions are the more common practice.

When a mouse button is depressed while the cursor is over the "**File**" label, Windows displays a pop-up window containing the **Exit** menu item. Selecting the **Exit** menu item causes Windows to send a WM_COMMAND message to the window function associated with the window that contains this menu. The LOWORD(wParam) parameter of the WM_COMMAND message has the value ID_APP_EXIT because that is the value given on the MENUITEM "E&xit" statement:

```
STRINGTABLE DISCARDABLE
BEGIN
    IDS_APP_TITLE           "Skeleton Example Application"
    IDR_MAINFRAME           "Skeleton Application Frame Window Class"
END
```

The STRINGTABLE section of the resource definition file defines two character strings. You reference the "Skeleton Example Application" character string using the symbolic constant IDS_APP_TITLE and load the string by calling the LoadString API. You similarly reference all other strings in an application's string resource table.

You must remember to change these strings when you use Skeleton (or Template) as the basis of your new application. The code we show in Listing 2.1 (on page 53) shows how we keep more than one instance of the application from executing. We use the FindWindow function to search for any other application that has the same window class name registered. If you don't change the IDR_MAINFRAME string resource, then two completely different applications will have the same registered class name and only one of them will be able to run at a time! The use of globally unique names, described on page 55, can guarantee that there will never be a conflict.

If you import a "straight" resource file into the Visual C++ resource editor, two significant changes will occur: first, your comments will be discarded, and second, a large number of "decorations" will be added. These "decorations" include various compile-time conditionals, references to particular resource types, and the like that are used by the resource editor to manage your resource file. Generally, you should leave these alone. If they are absent, it will attempt to regenerate them. If you delete or otherwise modify one in a way that is incompatible with the resource editor, you most likely will be unable to use it to edit your resource file. In this book, we will tend to show the "undecorated" resource files, leaving the details of how Visual C++ works to Visual C++. The comments we add are for exposition in this book, but they will be deleted by the Visual C++ resource editor if you use that editor.

The Skeleton.h Header File

The Skeleton.h header file contains the function prototypes for the global functions in the Skeleton application and some symbolic constants used within the application's code (but ones unrelated to resources). Because Skeleton is so skeletal, there isn't much in Skeleton.h.

Most of our source code files (.c) will have an accompanying header file (.h). Generally, for any large project, the use of a single massive header file is almost always a bad idea. The problem is that if you change any one constant, you force your entire system to rebuild. Detailed studies of actual programs under actual change scenarios have shown that, even taking file open time into account, total compilation time is significantly reduced by having as many header files as possible, generally one per source file, and including in any one .c file *only* those header files that it requires.[1] A good lint program will tell you if you have any unneeded header files in a compilation.

The projects in this book use the *precompiled header file* option offered by Visual C++ in order to reduce compile time. We include frequently used but infrequently changed header files in the StdSDK.h header file. Visual C++ compiles these header files only when compiling the StdSDK.c source file and uses the precompiled versions of the header files when compiling all other source files.

You might suspect that the resource.h file would be a prime source of such system-wide rebuilds, since every change to a resource would generate a new resource.h file. However, resource.h is treated specially by being marked by a comment that says that changes to resource.h should be ignored by the rebuild dependency-check process. Recognizing this exclusion is handled by the Visual C++ system when it creates the dependency lists for each module. There is, however, one nasty side effect of this. *If you change the* resource.h *file "by hand" using an external text editor for any reason or use the resource editor to change the assignments of control IDs, string IDs, and the like, the only way you can be sure to be safe is to completely rebuild your system, from scratch.* You can ask the Microsoft development environment (or whichever one you are using) to rebuild your entire project (**Build|Rebuild All** is the Microsoft menu selection) or specify the –A option to nmake.

Notice that the structure of a Windows application separates the application resources from the source code of the application. This permits you to maintain and update the resources separately from the logic of the executable program. As a Windows application becomes more and more complex, a considerable portion of the resources used by the application can be maintained separately from the source code. This separate maintenance is, in itself, beneficial. In addition, Windows resources are loaded on demand; therefore, they occupy memory only when they are actually used, unlike data compiled into the program.

Finally, a point that is becoming more and more important: The use of resources makes *internationalization* much easier. If your program has no native-language strings anywhere in it and every string is stored as a resource, you can translate your application to French, or German, or Spanish, or any other language by using the resource editor to change the strings from your native language to another language. There are many third-party utility programs that will allow you to quickly internationalize your application. You simply give them a binary resource file or an executable and a set of translation rules (essentially, a list of resource strings and their identification and a matching set of target strings). Internationalization does require much more effort than this to get exactly right, but getting all of your national language-specific strings (essentially, every string not containing something like "%d" or other language-independent punctuation as its entire contents) into the resource file is a critical first step.

---

[1] See the citation for Ellen Borison's research in "Further Reading" at the end of this chapter.

A full discussion of internationalization is beyond the scope of this book. We will simply point out that time of day, date, punctuation for decimals and thousands, currency, currency symbols, and even subtle phrasings that dictate word order are all potential sources of incompatibility at the GUI level when you are interfacing to someone in another language. There is some support in the registration database file for internationalization, but you have to explicitly use it. We touch on more internationalization issues in Chapter 7 and 12.

Building and Running the `Skeleton` Program

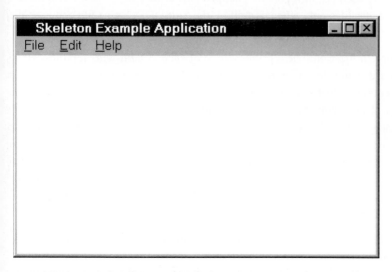

Figure 2.2: `Skeleton`'s main application window

Skeleton creates and displays its application window as shown in Figure 2.2. The window has a caption, thick frame, system menu, minimize and maximize boxes–all because you used the `WS_OVERLAPPEDWINDOW` window style when you created the window.

The system menu contains all default entries, as shown in Figure 2.3. To terminate the Skeleton program, either pull down the system menu and select the `Close` menu item or double-click the system menu box.

The only selection on the menu bar is the **Help** menu. It originates from the menu resource defined in Skeleton.rc. Pulling down the **Help** menu displays the "**About Skeleton...**" menu item as shown in Figure 2.4.

Finally, choosing the "**About Skeleton...**" menu item displays the **About...** dialog box, which gives information about the program, as shown in Figure 2.5.

Congratulations! That's it! You made it through a complete Windows program. Everything

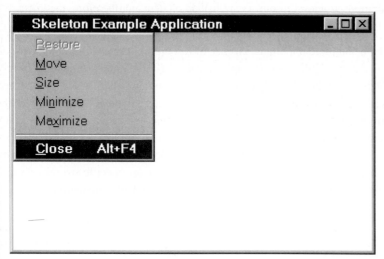

Figure 2.3: `Skeleton`'s default system menu

else is a bell or a whistle (or a push button or a dialog box) added to the above. Of course, there are man
bells and whistles in Microsoft Windows, so there's plenty left to learn (to get an idea, compare the thicknes
of this book on your left to the thickness of this book on your right!). But all Windows programs use the con
cepts illustrated in this one simple program. In fact, this book modifies Skeleton time and time again to il
lustrate each new point.

Now that you've seen a complete Windows program, it's time to examine individual features of Windows. Because Windows seems to be quite fond of windows–after all, a program can't do much of anything without one–that's the subject of the next chapter.

First, however, we have to present an important, and largely undocumented, feature of Windows–one we've been using throughout the Skeleton example program: message-cracker macros.

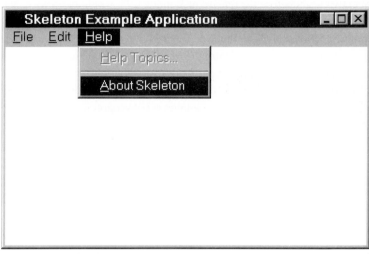

Figure 2.4: `Skeleton`'s **Help** menu

Message Crackers

We have written this largely in terms of the *message-cracker* macros. Many Windows programming texts illustrate message processing using the most basic techniques: extracting the LOWORD and HIWORD from the wParam and lParam parameters of the message in a large switch statement in a huge, monolithic window

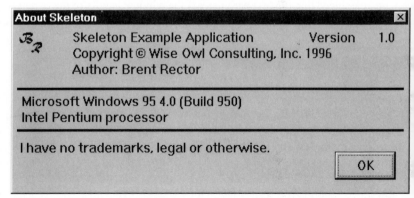

Figure 2.5: `Skeleton`'s **About...** dialog box

function. This approach, however, leads to some very unwieldy code in actual systems. The problem is tha
as you handle more and more messages, you grow the switch statement until it runs on for many screens
You can even hit built-in compiler limitations in extreme cases! If you have enabled global register alloca
tion, the complexity of the code makes the compiler run far more slowly and for actually very little gain in

performance. The apparent "visibility" of variables encourages highly error-prone techniques such as storing values in `static` variables between messages, one of the worst ideas to have ever emerged in the Windows programming literature.

A more significant problem arises if you are porting an application from Win16: The interpretation of the message parameters, `wParam` and `lParam`, has changed dramatically between the two systems. The best advice, two years before the release of Windows 95, would have been, "Don't write any new application without using the message-cracker macros". If you are porting a Win16 program and are requiring that it have a common source between Win16 and Win32, this is still important advice. In fact, the *first* thing you should do in porting a Win16 application to Win32–even if you have no intention of supporting it on Win16–is *rewrite* its entire message-handling mechanism using the message-cracker macros.[1] And if you plan to move to one of the object-oriented libraries, such as MFC (Microsoft) or OWL (Borland), you should use these macros today. They will greatly simplify a conversion in the future, and the models of construction of your program will be very similar.

The message-cracker macros come in two flavors: the 16-bit set and the 32-bit set. Both are in files of the same name: windowsx.h. Which is actually included depends on whether you are using the 16-bit compiler and its include directory or the 32-bit compiler and its include directory. The core macros are the same in both, although the 32-bit version has more message crackers to handle the new Win32 messages. But the implementations are quite different. The 16-bit HANDLE_WM_COMMAND message unpacks the `wParam` and `lParam` values quite differently than does the 32-bit HANDLE_WM_COMMAND. However, the *function signatures* of the procedures they call are *identical* in both implementations. Thus if you write a function, called a *message-handler function*, such as

```
void cls_OnCommand(HWND hwnd, int id, HWND ctl, UINT codenotify)
```

you are guaranteed that the first parameter is the window handle of the parent window, the second is the control ID, the third is the handle of the control, and the fourth is the notification code. But if we look at the WM_COMMAND parameters for the two systems, as shown in Figure 2.6, we see that the information arrives in quite different forms in the two systems.

	wParam		lParam	
Platform	LOWORD	HIWORD	LOWORD	HIWORD
Win16	Control/menu ID.		Control handle.	Notification code.
Win32	Control/menu ID.	Notification code.	Control handle.	

Figure 2.6: Comparison of Win16/Win32 WM_COMMAND

---

[1] There was only one time I did a port, my first port of a Win16 application to Win32, and I didn't do this. I lived to regret it profoundly. On all subsequent ports, I did the immediate rewrite (which takes a few days). Doing this not only made the port go more smoothly. It also allowed me to discover subtle 16-bit-to-32-bit bugs that otherwise would not have become evident, as well as find those really awful places where the original author had stored values in `static` variables, a technique absolutely doomed by the preemptive multitasking model of Win32. *–jmn*

There are also many very bad practices that the use of the message crackers tends to discourage. For example, we briefly mentioned the use of a `static` variable in the window function that preserves information across calls. This use is bad because if you ever have a second instance of the window, both windows share the same handler and hence the same static variable location. In the presence of Win32 multithreading and preemptive multitasking, the practice leads to particularly insidious bugs. And no, *don't* substitute a variable global to all the procedures to hold the same information! We'll show you later how to avoid such practices, which often lead to really obscure bugs.

Another pitfall that invites long-term disaster is the tendency to "share code" by using the `goto` instead of calling common procedures. A `goto` into the middle of a case of a nested `switch` is a guarantee of a long-term maintenance nightmare! Windows programs are complex enough without creating new opportunities for catastrophe by making the code so obscure that it cannot be modified without introducing more bugs than the change fixes! What makes Windows programs intellectually manageable is to write them very cleanly and elegantly so that they are readable and maintainable. The older criteria of "efficient code" and "small code size" are often so misleading as to be negative concepts. (We go to great lengths to actually justify our position on this. It is a paradigm shift from the days of programming 64K PDP-11's, where every bit and every instruction cycle counted!) Development time (read: time to market), development cost, and long-term maintenance effort have become dominant considerations in the modern era of fractional-year product release cycles. Saving 2 milliseconds on initiating an operation that is going to take a significant number of hundreds of milliseconds to complete is not worth the added cost of development and maintenance that seems to naturally follow.

There are two slightly different ways to use the message-cracker macros. The first and simplest is to use the `HANDLE_MSG` macro in an ordinary window procedure. This is done as shown in Listing 2.7. In this procedure, the `switch` statement is very straightforward; there is simply an enumeration of each message and its associated handler function. Each handler function is written according to its specification, which is given in windowsx.h, as well as in Appendix B. For the `HANDLE_MSG` macro to work correctly, the two parameters to the handler function *must* be named wParam and lParam. The macro is defined in windowsx.h as

```
#define HANDLE_MSG(hwnd, message, fn)      \
    case (message): return HANDLE_##message((hwnd), \
                            (wParam), (lParam), (fn))
```

This macro constructs the `case` clause to fit within a `switch` statement. It constructs a call to a macro whose name depends on the second parameter. A call such as

```
HANDLE_MSG(hwnd, WM_COMMAND, cls_OnCommand)
```

expands to the code

```
case WM_COMMAND: return HANDLE_WM_COMMAND((hwnd),
                        (wParam), (lParam), cls_OnCommand);
```

Listing 2.7: Message Cracker in a normal window procedure
```
LRESULT CALLBACK
myclassWndProc(HWND hWnd, UINT msg, WPARAM wParam, LPARAM lParam)
    {
      switch(msg)
```

```
    { /* msg */
      HANDLE_MSG(WM_COMMAND, myclass_OnCommand);
      HANDLE_MSG(WM_DESTROY, myclass_OnDestroy);
      HANDLE_MSG(WM_CLOSE,   myclass_OnClose);
      HANDLE_MSG(WM_HSCROLL, myclass_OnHScroll);
    } /* msg */
  return DefWindowProc(hWnd, msg, wParam, lParam);
}
```

This produces a window handler that is quite easy to read and gives you platform independence as well. It greatly enhances the readability of your code and ultimately produces programs that are easier to write and maintain over their lifetimes.

Using the message crackers in a dialog handler is a bit trickier. In this case, you have to deal with the fact that the dialog function itself expects you to return TRUE or FALSE. You can't use the HANDLE_MSG macro because it expects to return the value that was returned from the handler or 0 if the handler is a void function. But the difficulty, with only one exception we know of thus far, is only minor, as shown in Listing 2.8. You have to explicitly call each HANDLE_WM_*whatever* macro and then return TRUE or FALSE as appropriate, except for those calls that must return a specific type of result to the dialog procedure. All HANDLE_WM_ macros take exactly the same parameter list:

```
#define HANDLE_WM_whatever(hwnd, wParam, lParam, fn) \
```

Only the function signature changes, and for each HANDLE_WM_ macro there is an associated *handler function*. This is the same function that is specified in the more general HANDLE_MSG macro.

Listing 2.8: Using message crackers in dialog handlers

```
BOOL CALLBACK
mydialogWndProc(HWND hdlg, UINT msg, WPARAM wParam, LPARAM lParam)
    {
    switch(msg)
        { /* msg */
        case WM_INITDIALOG:
            return (BOOL)HANDLE_WM_INITDIALOG(hdlg, wParam, lParam,
                                               mydialog_OnInitDialog);
        case WM_COMMAND:
            HANDLE_WM_COMMAND(hdlg, wParam, lParam, mydialog_OnCommand);
            return TRUE;
        case WM_CLOSE:
            HANDLE_WM_CLOSE(hdlg, wParam, lParam, mydialog_OnClose);
            return TRUE;
        case WM_DESTROY:
            HANDLE_WM_DESTROY(hdlg, wParam, lParam, mydialog_OnDestroy);
            return TRUE;
        } /* msg */
    return FALSE;
    }
```

The one exception we have discovered in common usage is processing the WM_CHAR message in a dialog box. (You may find the same problem with other messages, but this is the only one we've been bothered by.) When you handle the character, you need to return TRUE; if you don't handle the character, you need to return FALSE. But the HANDLE_WM_CHAR macro is defined, as are most of the handlers, to call a void function.

Its definition is

```
#define HANDLE_WM_CHAR(hwnd, wParam, lParam, fn) \
  ( (fn)((hwnd), (TCHAR)(wParam), (int)(short)LOWORD(lParam)), 0)
```

(emphasis added). Note that the body is a parenthesized, comma-separated expression. The first expression is a function call passing in the parameters. The second expression is 0. This second expression becomes the value of the parenthesized expression, so the HANDLE_WM_CHAR macro always returns 0 (FALSE). You have to resort to some trickery to return a TRUE if you have handled the message. Of course, the simplest technique is simply to set a global variable to the result value for WM_CHAR messages in your OnChar handler and return that value. But again, remember, if you are in a multithreaded environment, this can get you into very deep trouble. Or you may have to rewrite the message cracker, an unfortunate side effect of Microsoft not having followed its own specification.

We have shown how to take the wParam and lParam of a message apart in a platform-independent fashion. But is there an inverse operation–putting the parameters back together into a wParam and lParam? Do we really need to do this? The answer is yes, there is a way to repack the parameters and yes, we need to do this.

Sometimes a message handler wishes to forward the message to a different handler for processing. The message-cracker macros have separated the wParam and lParam parameters into the appropriate components for the message. The message handler needs to repack the components to recreate the original message so that it can forward the message. Some messages have parameter packing that differs between platforms.

Consider a handler like WM_HSCROLL. It has a quite different parameter packing on Win16 than on Win32. We would also like to ignore how this packing is done, even if we are programming only in Win32, so we write a handler function according to the specifications. But now we need to send the message on to another handler. Possibly this is DefWindowProc, possibly it is SendMessage, or perhaps it is even the superclass handler for the control we have subclassed (we haven't discussed this yet, but we will). We need to package up the parameters to the procedure we are calling in a fashion that does not require that we know the message format.

This is done by the FORWARD_WM_* message "uncracker" macros. Examples of the use of FORWARD_WM_* macros are shown in Listing 2.9. These are intended to be code fragments, so computations that depend on how you have organized your data and windows are omitted.

Listing 2.9: FORWARD_WM_ macro usage
```
void myclass_OnHScroll(HWND hwnd, HWND ctl, UINT code, int pos)
    {
    // ...do some processing
    // If we wanted to send it to another window...
    HWND otherwnd = ...;    // get handle by appropriate means
    FORWARD_WM_HSCROLL(otherwnd, ctl, code, pos, SendMessage);

    // Alternatively, if we wanted to call DefWindowProc
    FORWARD_WM_HSCROLL(hwnd, ctl, code, pos, DefWindowProc);

    // Or another alternative: we want to call a
    // superclass handler
    FORWARD_WM_HSCROLL(hwnd, ctl, code, pos, myclass_callparent);
    }
```

```
// We need to indirect via a function to call the parent
LRESULT myclass_callparent(HWND hwnd, UINT msg, WPARAM wParam, LPARAM lParam)
    {
      WNDPROC proc = ... ; // get pointer to procedure
      return CallWindowProc(proc, hwnd, msg, wParam, lParam);
    }
```

The FORWARD_WM_* uncrackers take the same parameters as the handler defined for a message of that type and in the same order. Thus in our example, HANDLE_WM_HSCROLL takes a window handle, a control handle, a scroll type, and a scroll position, in that order, and FORWARD_WM_HSCROLL takes a window handle, a control handle, a scroll type, and a scroll position, in exactly the same order. It also takes, as an additional, final parameter, the name of a function to call; this function must have this signature:

LRESULT *name*(HWND hWnd, UINT msg, WPARAM wParam, LPARAM lParam)

Note, however, that you must *not* call the window handler function directly, even in Win32, where you would think that addressability would not be an issue (addressability is the prime reason for this prohibition in Win16). This is because there are other issues, such as Unicode translation, that become relevant.

Rather than force you to go to windowsx.h to look up the parameters to each message-cracker handler, we give you throughout the book the complete message-cracker handler signatures for each one we use. The format is as follows.

---

xxx **Message Cracker Handlers**

BOOL *cls*_OnXxx(HWND hwnd, int val);				
BOOL *cls*_OnYyy(HWND hwnd, int val);				
Result	TRUE if Windows did one thing; FALSE if it did another.			
	wParam		**lParam**		
Parameter	lo	hi	lo	hi	**Meaning**
hwnd					Window handle of the parent window.
val	■				Value that has some meaning for this message.
val32			■		Value that has some meaning for this message.

In this table, we give the prototype for the message cracker, describe its result (if not void), and describe the parameters. So that you may more readily correlate the parameters to the documentation of the message, we show by an encoding what parts of the wParam and lParam provide the information in Win32. A summary of the message crackers is given in Appendix B.

Further Reading

Borison, Ellen, *Program Changes and the Cost of Selective Recompilation*, Ph.D. dissertation, Carnegie Mellon University Department of Computer Science, 1989.

Microsoft Corporation, *The Windows Interface Guidelines for Software Design*, Microsoft Press, 1995. ISBN 1-55615-679-0.

> This book is not optional for a Windows programmer. If you are designing a GUI, you *must* read it. We review this book on page 151.

O'Donnell, Sandra Martin, *Programming for the World: A Guide to Internationalization*, Prentice-Hall, 1994.

> While this book focuses primarily on Unix-based systems, the issues it raises are platform-independent. Many of the proposed solutions are Unix simulations of fundamental Windows capabilities, such as simulations of `LoadString`. But the book also gives good insight into many of the subtle issues of internationalization.

3 Exploring Variations on a Window

In this chapter, we concentrate on describing the types of windows you can create in a Windows program. The rest of the book shows you the various things you can do with a window once you've created it. The first step, however, is to know which type of window you need and how it works in the Windows environment. This chapter covers the following topics:

- The window class styles. You can specify that all windows created based on a class appear and behave in a certain manner. You do this by specifying certain class styles when registering the window class.

- The window styles. You can also specify when you create the window that it have a certain appearance and behavior.

- The difference between overlapped, pop-up, and child windows. Selecting the correct window style is crucial to having the window operate as desired.

- The Panes example program. We give and explain an example program that creates a window of each of the main styles and shows you how the choice of styles affects the window's appearance and behavior.

- The Window Explorer. This program lets you create windows with your own selection of styles so that you can see how various combinations of styles work together.

When you create a window, you control every aspect of its behavior and appearance. A window's associated window function completely controls its behavior. Generally, this is the window function specified when you register the window's class, and all windows belonging to the same class behave similarly. Because one of a window function's responsibilities is to paint the window, controlling a window's behavior controls its appearance as well.

The WM_PAINT message requests the window function to draw the window's client area, and the WM_NCPAINT message requests the window function to draw the window's nonclient areas such as the title bar and the window border. By intercepting these, a window function can control the appearance of every pixel within the window. And by intercepting mouse messages and keyboard messages, the function can control every interaction a user has with the window. But this is a lot of work! You'd have to decide how your menus should work, how buttons should operate, and how to resize the window, as well as numerous other messy tasks. Windows doesn't require you to do this, although it permits you to if you wish to do it.

Generally, you shouldn't want to. Users have an expectation of how the GUI is going to behave. In many cases, you violate these expectations at the risk that your users will complain bitterly that you are not obeying the "Windows standard". This is not to say the standard way is perfect, or even complete. In many cases, what appears to be "standard" is simply a convention that many programmers follow, rather than something stated explicitly in Microsoft's design guides. In other cases, tasteful violation of the "standard" results in a far "friendlier" program. And in some cases, you will find that the default behavior actually makes the interface behave in what appears to be a completely unexpected fashion, even though it is doing exactly what it is supposed to. In this case, you intercept the messages and take your own actions to *preserve* what is the "expected" behavior.

This is part of what makes programming Windows challenging. Not only are technical issues involved, but you also must address issues of conforming or diverging from "standards", as well as bring artistic, aesthetic, and human factors skills to bear. A good book on the basic principles of cognitive psychology (which covers such issues as perception, motor skills, how users' mental models shape their world view and expectations, and the like) can be as important for a GUI designer as the API Reference. Two particularly good references on cognitive psychology are *Human Information Processing* and *The Design of Everyday Things*. For GUI design, we recommend *Designing the User Interface* and the Microsoft reference, *The Windows Interface Guidelines for Software Design*. (See the Further Reading section on page 151 for full citations.)

Default Behavior for a Window

Windows provides default behaviors for many aspects of a window's operation. These are invoked whenever you pass a message to the `DefWindowProc` function. For example, most window functions pass all the nonclient area messages to the `DefWindowProc` function. Windows then performs the appropriate default actions that should be carried out on the nonclient areas of the window. The client area of a window is generally your responsibility. However, if you specify a background brush when you register the window class, `DefWindowProc` will respond to the `WM_ERASEBKGND` message by setting invalid areas of the client area to the background color. Table 3.1 lists the messages that are processed by the `DefWindowProc` function and the action it takes for each. `DefWindowProc` has one other documented property that is important: For any message is does not understand, it is guaranteed to return a 0 value as a result. This is a defined behavior we can often take advantage of.

It is very important that you pass all unprocessed messages to `DefWindowProc`. If you fail to do so, your window will not behave properly. For example, you will not be able to resize a window, drag it around, activate it, close it, minimize it, maximize it, or do much of anything else that you would expect to do with it unless you yourself have written code to handle each of these cases. You don't really want to do this. These actions and many others are all handled by `DefWindowProc`. Occasionally, you will want to completely override this built-in behavior; more often, you will want to take note of the message, but otherwise let the default processing occur. We cover all of these cases.

Table 3.1: Messages processed by the `DefWindowProc` function

Message	Default Action
WM_ACTIVATE	Sets the input focus to the window if the window is not minimized and is being activated.
WM_CANCELMODE	Terminates internal processing of standard scroll-bar input. Terminates internal menu selection processing. Releases mouse capture.
WM_CHARTOITEM	Returns -1.
WM_CLOSE	Destroys the window.
WM_CTLCOLORBTN WM_CTLCOLORDLG WM_CTLCOLOREDIT WM_CTLCOLORLISTBOX WM_CTLCOLORMSGBOX WM_CTLCOLORSTATIC	For all controls except scroll-bar controls, sets the text color to COLOR_WINDOWTEXT, sets the background color to COLOR_WINDOW, and returns a handle to a brush used to paint the control's background.
WM_CTLCOLORSCROLLBAR	For scroll-bar controls, sets the text color to black, sets the background color to black, and returns a handle to a brush used to paint scroll-bar controls. The UnrealizeObject function has already been called on this brush.
WM_DRAWITEM	Performs the default drawing for owner draw list box items.
WM_ERASEBKGND	Fills the client area with the color and pattern specified by the class brush, if any.
WM_GETHOTKEY	Returns the virtual-key code of the hot key associated with the window.
WM_GETICON	Returns either a small icon (wParam == ICON_SMALL) or normal icon (wParam == ICON_BIG).
WM_GETTEXT	Copies the text associated with the window into the specified buffer. Returns the number of bytes copied. For edit and combo-box edit controls, the text copied is the content of the edit control. For list boxes, the text is the current selected item. For buttons, the text is the button's name. For other windows, the text is the caption.
WM_GETTEXTLENGTH	Returns the length (in characters) of the text associated with a window. DefWindowProc may return a value larger than the actual text to allow for a mix of Unicode and ANSI windows. However, the value returned will always be large enough so that if a number of *bytes* are allocated, there will be enough space for all the *characters*.

[3]Only at API level 3. Not supported at API level 4.
[4]Only at API level 4 and higher.

Table 3.1: Messages processed by the DefWindowProc function

Message	Default Action
WM_HELP	Passes the WM_HELP message to the parent window (if processed for a child window) or the owner of a top-level window.
WM_ICONERASEBKGND	Fills the icon background using the default brush (the class background brush) of the parent window.
WM_IME_CHAR	If the WM_IME_CHAR message contains double-byte characters, the message is converted to two WM_CHAR messages, each of which holds one of the two bytes.
WM_IME_COMPOSITION	Passes the message to the default IME window.
WM_IME_ENDCOMPOSITION	Passes the message to the default IME window.
WM_IME_KEYDOWN	Converts the message to a WM_KEYDOWN message.
WM_IME_KEYUP	Converts the message to a WM_KEYUP message.
WM_IME_SELECT	Passes the message to the default IME window.
WM_IME_STARTCOMPOSITION	Passes the message to the default IME window.
WM_INPUTLANGCHANGE	Passes the message to each of the direct child windows.
WM_INPUTLANGCHANGEREQUEST	Returns a nonzero value signifying acceptance of the language change. Activates the new input locale and sends WM_INPUTLANGCHANGE.
WM_KEYUP	Notifies the top-level active window via a WM_SYSCOMMAND message with the SC_KEYMENU code when the **F10** key or **Alt** key is pressed and released.
WM_MOUSEACTIVATE	Sends the message to the window's parent window. Halts WM_MOUSEACTIVATE message processing when the parent window returns a nonzero value. Otherwise, activates the window.
WM_NCACTIVATE	Activates and deactivates the window. When the window is visible, the caption is redrawn using the appropriate color– COLOR_ACTIVECAPTION or COLOR_INACTIVECAPTION. When the window is iconic, the icon title is redrawn.
WM_NCCALCSIZE	Calculates the size of the client area based on the window characteristics such as the presence of scroll bars, menus, and captions and on the type of border. May force a redraw if the window has CS_HREDRAW or CS_VREDRAW styles.

[3]Only at API level 3. Not supported at API level 4.
[4]Only at API level 4 and higher.

Table 3.1: Messages processed by the `DefWindowProc` function

Message	Default Action
WM_NCCREATE	Initializes the horizontal and vertical scroll bar, if any. Saves the window caption text. Returns TRUE.
WM_NCDESTROY	Frees the allocated memory associated with the window. Releases the memory containing the window text.
WM_NCHITTEST	Returns a value indicating the position of the cursor.
WM_NCLBUTTONDBLCLK	Tests the location of the cursor when the left button is double-clicked in the nonclient area of the window and, if appropriate, sends a WM_SYSCOMMAND message.
WM_NCLBUTTONDOWN	Tests the location of the cursor when the left button is pressed in the nonclient area of the window and, if appropriate, sends WM_SYSCOMMAND messages.
WM_NCLBUTTONUP	Tests the location of the cursor when the left button is released in the nonclient area of the window and, if appropriate, sends WM_SYSCOMMAND messages.
WM_NCMOUSEMOVE	Tests the location of the cursor when the mouse is moved in the nonclient area of the window and, if appropriate, sends WM_SYSCOMMAND messages.
WM_NCPAINT	Draws the nonclient areas of the window (i.e., the border, system menu icon, minimize and maximize icons, caption, menu, and horizontal and vertical scroll bars), as appropriate.
WM_NCRBUTTONDOWN[4]	Tests the location of the cursor when the right button is pressed in the nonclient area of the window and, if appropriate, sends WM_SYSCOMMAND messages.
WM_NCRBUTTONUP[4]	Generates a WM_CONTEXTMENU message.
WM_NOTIFYFORMAT	Responds with NFR_ANSI or NFR_UNICODE based on the type of window.
WM_PAINT	Validates the current update region but does not paint the client area. Effectively, the BeginPaint function is called and is immediately followed by a call to the EndPaint function. If any invalidated regions are to be erased, the normal BeginPaint action of sending a WM_ERASEBKGND will occur.
WM_PAINTICON[3]	Draws the window's class icon, if any.

[3]Only at API level 3. Not supported at API level 4.
[4]Only at API level 4 and higher.

Table 3.1: Messages processed by the `DefWindowProc` function

Message	Default Action
WM_PRINT	Depends on the printing option selected. If PRF_CHECKVISIBLE is specified and the window is not visible, it does nothing. If PRF_NONCLIENT is specified, it draws the nonclient area. If PRF_ERASEBKGND is specified, it sends the window a WM_ERASEBGND message. If PRF_PRINTCLIENT is specified, it sends a WM_PRINTCLIENT message to the window. If PRF_PRINTCHILDREN is specified, it sends a WM_PRINT message to each visible child window. If PRF_OWNED is specified, it sends a WM_PRINT message to each owned window.
WM_QUERYDRAGICON	Returns the handle to the class (default) cursor.
WM_QUERYENDSESSION	Returns TRUE.
WM_QUERYOPEN	Returns TRUE.
WM_RBUTTONUP[4]	Generates a WM_CONTEXTMENU message.
WM_SETCURSOR	Sends the message to the window's parent window. Halts WM_SETCURSOR message processing when the parent window returns TRUE. Otherwise, it sets the cursor to an arrow when in the nonclient area of the window or to the window's class cursor when in the client area.
WM_SETHOTKEY	Sets the hot key associated with this window to the specified virtual-key code and returns the status of the hot key change operation.
WM_SETICON	Sets the icon based on the value of wParam: ICON_BIG or ICON_SMALL. Returns the handle to the previously established large or small icon.
WM_SETREDRAW	Allows or prevents changes in the window from being redrawn.
WM_SETTEXT	Saves a copy of the string parameter to this function as the text associated with the window. When the window is visible and iconic, the icon title is redrawn. When the window is visible, noniconic, and has a caption, the caption is redrawn.
WM_SHOWWINDOW	Hides or shows the window as specified by the message.
WM_SYSCHAR	Restores a window when **Alt+Enter** is pressed. Translates an **Alt+*character*** keystroke into a WM_SYSCOMMAND message of type SC_KEYMENU. **Alt+Tab** and **Alt+Esc** are ignored by `DefWindowProc`. A WM_SYSCOMMAND message for an **Alt+space** character is sent only to the top-level windows. Beeps when an invalid system character is received.

---

[3]Only at API level 3. Not supported at API level 4.

[4]Only at API level 4 and higher.

Table 3.1: Messages processed by the `DefWindowProc` function

Message	Default Action
WM_SYSCOMMAND	Performs the requested System-menu command.
WM_SYSKEYDOWN	Examines the key and generates a WM_SYSCOMMAND message if the key is either **Tab** or **Enter**.
WM_SYSKEYUP	Notifies the top-level active window via a WM_SYSCOMMAND message with the SC_KEYMENU code when the **F10** key or **Alt** key is pressed and released. Monitors **F10** key presses, which come in as WM_SYSKEYDOWN messages.
WM_VKEYTOITEM	Returns `-1`.
WM_WINDOWPOSCHANGED	Sends WM_SIZE and WM_MOVE messages to the window.
WM_WINDOWPOSCHANGING	Sends a WM_GETMINMAXINFO message to the window if it has either the WS_OVERLAPPED or WS_THICKFRAME window style.

[3]Only at API level 3. Not supported at API level 4.
[4]Only at API level 4 and higher.

My, How Stylish You Look

Windows also provides a default appearance for many aspects of a window. When you call the `CreateWindow` function to create a window, you specify the type of window you'd like to have, along with any desired styles. For example, you might call the `CreateWindow` function and say:

> I'd like one standard overlapped window complete with a title bar. Include the optional minimize and maximize boxes and throw in a system menu to boot. Please wrap it all up with a standard window border.

The `DefWindowProc` function shoulders the burden of drawing the nonclient area of the window and responding to user actions in that area. The options that you can specify for a window are called *styles*. Styles affect both the appearance and the behavior of a window. Some styles simply request a specific appearance for the window (such as the window border appearance), whereas others have diverse, far-reaching effects such as controlling the window's relationship to other windows in the system and preventing the window from receiving any messages.

Windows provides several different styles that you may select when creating a window. Styles are partitioned into two groups–*class* and *window*. As you would expect from the name, a class style is specified when you register a window class. It applies to all windows created based on the class. A window style is specified when a window is created. It applies solely to that window. Two windows, based on a common window class, may look quite different depending on their individual window styles.

Class Styles

The class styles that may be specified when you register a class are listed in Table 3.2. Two or more of these styles can be combined by using the bitwise OR operator:

```
wc.style = CS_HREDRAW | CS_VREDRAW ;
```

Table 3.2: Window class styles

Style	Function
CS_BYTEALIGNCLIENT	Aligns the window's client area on a byte boundary (in the *x*-direction).
CS_BYTEALIGNWINDOW	Aligns the entire window (not simply the client area) on a byte boundary (in the *x*-direction).
CS_CLASSDC	Creates a single display context to be shared by all windows in the class.
CS_DBLCLKS	Permits double-click messages to be sent to the window function for windows of this class.
CS_GLOBALCLASS	Specifies that the class is an application global class. This class name is visible to other applications, so they may create windows based upon this class.
CS_HREDRAW	Requests that the client area of the window be redrawn whenever the width of the client area changes.
CS_NOCLOSE	Disables the close option on the window's System menu.
CS_OWNDC	Creates a unique display context for each window created based on this class.
CS_PARENTDC	Requests that the clipping region for a display context allocated to this window be the parent window's client area (See Chapter 5 for more about display contexts and this style, in particular read the section starting on page 225, especially the bug note).
CS_SAVEBITS	Requests that Windows save a bitmap image of the screen area overlaid by a window when the window is displayed. When the window is later destroyed or hidden, the underlying screen image is restored from the bitmap, if the underlying bitmap is still considered valid.
CS_VREDRAW	Requests that the client area of the window be redrawn whenever the height of the client area changes.

The CS_BYTEALIGNCLIENT style requests that Windows align the client area of the window to a byte boundary in the video display memory. The CS_BYTEALIGNWINDOW class style requests that Windows align the window itself to a byte boundary in the video display memory. An area that is aligned on a byte boundary can sometimes be updated more quickly than one that is not. A program that must update a window quickly, such as to draw animated graphics, might be able to use these styles to make the drawing more efficient. However, a user might not be able to position a window to an arbitrary pixel when using these styles. Most programs do not need to use them. With modern video accelerator cards and machines faster than the 8088—for which these styles were intended—their value is usually insignificant, particularly in light of the limitations their use places on the user.

The CS_CLASSDC and CS_OWNDC class styles request Windows to assign varying display contexts for a window. All programs draw on their window by using a display context (DC). These class styles and display contexts are discussed in depth in Chapter 5, page 225. Because it takes some amount of overhead to allocate and initialize a display context, it is sometimes possible to get slightly better performance in graphics-intensive applications by using these preallocated DCs. However, for most applications, using these styles carries no particular advantage.

The CS_PARENTDC class style establishes a DC whose clipping region is the parent window client area. This is not what most of the documentation says; this is a documentation error and is explained in detail on page 225.

The CS_DBLCLKS class style requests Windows to send mouse *double-click messages* to a window. Only a window whose window class has the CS_DBLCLKS style receives double-click messages. Windows generates a double-click message when the user presses, releases, and then presses a mouse button again within the system's double-click time and space limits. Double-clicking generates four messages: button down, button up, and button double-click, plus a second button up message. Double-clicking in a window lacking this class style also generates four messages, but the third message in the sequence is a button down message, not a button double-click message. See page 462.

The CS_GLOBALCLASS class style identifies this class as an application global class. You omit this class style to define a class as an application local class, the most commonly used type. Only in special circumstances will you need to use the CS_GLOBALCLASS style. An application global class is globally available to all applications within the system. The style is used by a dynamic link library when it creates window classes used by applications that call the library. Windows does not automatically destroy an application global class when the application (or, more likely, the library) that registered the class terminates. For this reason, all applications must explicitly unregister the class using the UnregisterClass function. This is done when the last application finishes using the class (typically by handling the DLL_PROCESS_DETACH event in the DLL and as a consequence of decrementing a shared counter to 0; we discuss this in Chapter 16). You must register this class in the DLL initialization code (on the DLL_PROCESS_ATTACH event) of a DLL that is specified in the registry under the following key:

HKEY_LOCAL_MACHINE\Software\Microsoft\Windows NT\CurrentVersion\Windows\APPINIT_DLLS

Whenever any process starts, the operating system loads the specified DLLs in the context of the newly started process before calling the main function in that process. The DLL must register the class during its initialization procedure and must specify the CS_GLOBALCLASS style. This means that *every* process will have access to this DLL (whether or not it wants it).

When an application creates a window, Windows searches for the specified class in the following sequence:

1. Search for an application local class with the specified name. If found, use the local class definition.

2. Search for an application global class with the specified name. If found, use the global class definition.

3. Search the system global class list. (These are the window classes created by Windows when it starts and are available for use by all applications, such as LISTBOX, BUTTON, and the like.)

This search order permits an application to override system global classes, such as edit control and push button control classes, without affecting other applications.

The CS_HREDRAW and CS_VREDRAW class styles indicate that a window based on a class with these styles must be informed whenever the user changes the size of its client area. Without these styles, when a user shrinks a window, Windows discards the excess client area and does not request the window function to redraw the client area. When the user increases a window's size, Windows requests the window function to draw only those newly exposed areas rather than the entire window. Typically, you omit these styles for a window that draws in its client area at a fixed scale, and more or less of the drawing can be seen as the window is resized.

There is a particular danger in using these styles that you should be aware of. If you include the WS_HSCROLL or WS_VSCROLL styles and optionally enable or disable the scroll bars using the SetScrollRange call, you can get into a nasty loop condition. Consider the CS_VREDRAW case. Suppose you have scrolled the window vertically so that a line longer than your client area is displayed at the bottom of the client area. You detect this condition and enable the horizontal scroll bar. But the horizontal scroll bar now "hides" the last line, so you detect that no lines are longer than the client area. You then disable the horizontal scroll bar. Doing this "exposes" the last line, so you detect the long line, and . . . needless to say, this can go on for a very long time. These styles should be used with caution.

For some windows, it's more appropriate to draw the entire contents of a window's client area scaled to the current size of the window. Many of the Explorer programs that are included on this CD-ROM use this technique to scale the drawing to the current window size.

A window may need to redraw its client area when the width or the height changes. The CS_HREDRAW class style requests Windows to cause a WM_PAINT message to be received by the window function whenever the horizontal size of the window changes. The CS_VREDRAW class style requests Windows to cause a WM_PAINT message to be received by the window function whenever the vertical size of the window changes. The WM_PAINT message indicates that the entire client area must be redrawn. Alternatively, you can ignore these styles and choose yourself to determine if a window should be redrawn on a resize operation by responding to the WM_SIZE message and generating your own redraw request.

The CS_NOCLOSE class style disables the **Close** option on the System menu of a window based on this class. This style does not request a system menu for a window; it requests only that its **Close** option be disabled. You request a system menu by using a combination of two window styles, as you'll see shortly.

A window based on a class with the CS_SAVEBITS class style saves the portion of the screen image that it overlays as a bitmap. When the window is destroyed or hidden, the bitmap is used to restore the screen contents and the previously obscured windows do not receive WM_PAINT messages. At least, that's how you hope things turn out. The bitmap is discardable so that Windows can throw it away and reclaim its memory in tight memory situations. Other actions–such as one of the obscured windows updating its client area while covered–can also invalidate the saved bitmap. In addition, windows with this class style display more slowly than those without due to the time involved in allocating and saving the bitmap. For example, a full-screen VGA-resolution low-color (640×480×16) bitmap requires 150K of memory just to store the pixels of the image, while a high-resolution "true-color" $1600×1200×2^{24}$ bitmap requires between 5.7 and 7.8 *mega*bytes, depending on how it stores the 24-bit color data! To minimize these effects, use this style only for small windows that are displayed for short periods and quickly removed. Like the byte alignment styles, this style was far more advantageous on an 8088 running a CGA than it is on any Win32-capable machine.

Class styles are somewhat indirectly specified for a window. All windows based on the same class have the same class styles. Often you'd like to create more individualistic, or stylistically unique, windows. You do this by specifying window styles when creating a window. You can specify a unique set of window styles for every window you create, even windows based on the same class.

Window Styles

Roughly 20 different basic window styles may be specified when creating a window. We say "roughly" because some styles are defined as combinations of others. Other styles use identical bit settings and must be distinguished by the context (not a display context but in the sense of their surroundings) in which they are used. In API level 4, there are nearly as many "extended" window styles available. The Window Explorer application lets you create windows with various combinations of styles and see the effects.

Some styles are more important than others; these approximately 20 styles can be further categorized as five major styles. More often, two of these five styles are combined with two others, leaving three major styles (overlapped, pop-up, and child, as listed in Table 3.3). Pop-up windows are a special case of overlapped windows, so you could say that there are two main styles of windows. All this is to give you the impression that there are many ways to present window styles.

Table 3.3: Three-style and five-style categories of windows

General Class	Variation	Typical Uses
Overlapped	Owned	
	Unowned	Top-level window
Pop-up	Owned	Dialogs
	Unowned	
Child	Child	Controls

We prefer an approach somewhere between the three and five major styles classification. Windows provides three main styles of windows–overlapped, pop-up, and child. Overlapped and pop-up windows can have an *owner*. Owned windows behave slightly differently from unowned windows. They aren't sufficiently different to justify equality with the three major styles but, then again, they are different enough to deserve independent consideration as a style. Therefore the rest of this section covers overlapped windows (owned and unowned), pop-up windows (owned and unowned), and child windows. Then we cover the other window styles that control the appearance of the window, options available on the window, and the behavior of multiple child windows.

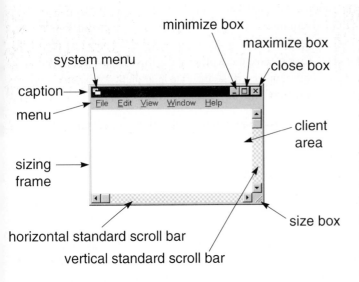

Figure 3.1: A window created with WS_OVERLAPPEDWINDOW | WS_HSCROLL | WS_VSCROLL

Overlapped Windows

Nearly every Windows application creates an *overlapped window* as the application's main window. (The exceptions are *console applications*, which typically don't have a window and are often written as either utility programs or as *NT System Services.* (See the Further Reading section on page 151). The window created by the Skeleton and Template example programs is an overlapped window. An overlapped window is a top-level window and, as such, does not have a parent window. An overlapped window, shown in Figure 3.1, almost always has a border around the window, a title bar called the *caption* at the top of the window, and a client area. An overlapped window can but isn't required to have a *system menu*, a *minimize box*, a *maximize box*, a *close box*, a *horizontal standard scroll bar,* a *vertical standard scroll bar,* and a *menu.* An overlapped window can be represented by an icon when the window is minimized by the user.

An overlapped window is called "overlapped" because as a top-level window (its typical use), it can overlap other applications' top-level windows. Originally the term distinguished such windows from the tiled windows used in Windows version 1.*x*. Tiled windows are no longer used, so an overlapped window, particularly an unowned overlapped window, is synonymous with "top-level window".

You use one of two window style names when creating overlapped windows: either the base style name, WS_OVERLAPPED, or the composite style name, WS_OVERLAPPEDWINDOW. These symbols are defined by windows.h as follows:

```
#define WS_OVERLAPPED       0x00000000L
#define WS_OVERLAPPEDWINDOW (WS_OVERLAPPED | WS_CAPTION | \
                            WS_SYSMENU | WS_THICKFRAME | \
                            WS_MINIMIZEBOX | WS_MAXIMIZEBOX)
```

Because WS_OVERLAPPED is defined as a long 0 value, passing a window style of 0 in a CreateWindow call is the same as specifying an overlapped window. In other words, if you don't specify any other kind of window (pop-up or child), you get an overlapped window. Figure 3.1 shows a window created with the WS_OVERLAPPEDWINDOW style and, in addition, the WS_HSCROLL and WS_VSCROLL styles.

A Window created with the WS_OVERLAPPED style always has a border, title bar, and client area. Using the WS_OVERLAPPEDWINDOW style creates a window with a thick-frame rather than a thin-frame border. The thick-frame border is sometimes called a *sizing border* because it permits the user to resize the window. Using WS_OVERLAPPEDWINDOW also creates a title bar, a system menu, a minimize box, and a maximize box.

When you create an overlapped window, the initial *x*- and *y*-position parameters of the CreateWindow function call are the coordinates of the upper-left corner of the window relative to the upper-left corner of the screen (that is, in screen coordinates). Likewise, the width and height parameters for an overlapped window are specified in screen coordinates. The Panes example program in this chapter creates its main application window using the WS_OVERLAPPEDWINDOW style.

An overlapped window can also be an *owned* window. Recall that an overlapped window is always a top-level window and has no parent window. You create an owned, overlapped window by specifying the window handle of its owner window as the hwndParent parameter of the CreateWindow function call. The owner window must itself be an overlapped window. Thus the "parent" parameter specifies an *owner* window when creating an overlapped window, *not* a parent window.

Windows manages owned windows slightly differently from unowned windows. Some operations on an owned window also affect all the windows it owns. These effects are as follows:

- An owned window is hidden when its owner is minimized. If the owned window is already minimized (i.e., iconic) when its owner is minimized, the owned window's icon is hidden.

- Destroying a window also destroys all windows it owns.

- Windows always displays owned windows on top of their owners. An owned window always obscures its owner when the owned window area overlaps the owner window area.

Pop-up Windows

Pop-up windows are a special kind of overlapped window. You generally create pop-up windows to display information that needs to remain on the screen a short period of time. Pop-up windows are typically small windows. For these reasons, the class style CS_SAVEBITS is most often used with pop-up window classes.

Pop-up windows are nearly identical to overlapped windows. The main exception is that an overlapped window always has a caption whereas for a pop-up window, a caption is optional. Two window styles can be used to create pop-up windows: WS_POPUP and WS_POPUPWINDOW. You can use one of two style names when creating a pop-up window. The symbols are defined by windows.h as follows:

```
#define WS_POPUP        0x80000000L
#define WS_POPUPWINDOW  (WS_POPUP | WS_BORDER | WS_SYSMENU)
```

The WS_POPUP window style creates a pop-up window. The WS_POPUPWINDOW window style creates a pop-up window with a border. The window will also have the WS_SYSMENU style, but the system menu will not be visible unless the window also has a title bar. Combining the WS_CAPTION window style with the WS_POPUPWINDOW window style produces a pop-up window with a border, a title bar, and a system menu.

Like overlapped windows, pop-up windows can be owned or unowned. The constraints applied to owned, overlapped windows apply equally to owned, pop-up windows. A pop-up window's initial *x*- and *y*-positions, width, and height are specified in screen coordinates, the same as for overlapped windows. As an example, dialog boxes are normally owned, pop-up windows. They always display "above" their owner. Also, when modeless (a concept we cover when discussing dialog boxes), they are hidden when the owner window is minimized and destroyed when the owner window is destroyed.

Child Windows

A *child window* is quite different from an overlapped window and pop-up window. Child windows are used more frequently than any other type of window. Whereas there might be only a few overlapped or pop-up windows created at any given time, there are most likely tens, if not hundreds, of child windows in existence. A child window can be difficult to recognize. What appears to be a completely blank area in the client area of a window might actually be divided into many child windows. The appearance of a child window can be completely controlled by your application. Windows provides many precoded child windows called *controls*. These include push buttons, scroll bars, check boxes, and static text.

You can use either the WS_CHILD window style or the WS_CHILDWINDOW window style to create a child window. They are defined by windows.h as follows:

```
#define WS_CHILD            0x40000000L
#define WS_CHILDWINDOW      (WS_CHILD)
```

The WS_CHILDWINDOW style is a synonym for WS_CHILD that follows the naming convention established for WS_OVERLAPPED and WS_OVERLAPPEDWINDOW and for WS_POPUP and WS_POPUPWINDOW. Unlike overlapped and pop-up windows, a child window typically has only a client area. Although you can request a border, a caption, a minimize box, a maximize box, and horizontal and vertical scroll bars for a child window, typically you wouldn't, except for "MDI windows", a topic we discuss in Chapter 17. An application generally draws its own custom features in child windows.

While an overlapped or a pop-up window can be a top-level window and stand alone, a child window must have a parent window. Actually, only a child window *can* have a parent window. Overlapped windows and pop-up windows have owners, not parents. They aren't synonymous, and you shouldn't mistakenly use one term for the other. It causes problems later on when you try to retrieve the parent and/or owner window handle. For example, the GetParent function always (correctly!) returns NULL when called about an overlapped window–even an overlapped window that has an owner–because an overlapped window does not have a parent. The parent window of a child window can be either an overlapped window, a pop-up window, or another child window. To correctly get the owner of an owned window, you must explicitly ask for it. This can be done by one of the functions shown in Table 3.4.

The parent-child window relationship does not imply any inheritance by the child window of any of its parent window's characteristics.[1] The relationship implies that boundaries of and operations performed on a

---

[1] Well, this is almost true. A child window that has the CS_PARENTDC class style inherits the clipping region of its parent.

parent window also affect all of that parent's child windows. In addition, a child window cannot be created without a parent window. Let's examine some of the interactions between parent and child windows in detail.

Table 3.4: Techniques for getting the owner of a window

GetWindow(hwnd, GW_OWNER)
GetWindowOwner(hwnd)[x]

[x]Defined in `windowsx.h`.

The parent window must turn over a portion of its client area to the child window. The child window displays in this portion of its parent window's client area and receives all input from this area. Input, such as mouse movements and button clicks, is normally sent to the window under the cursor. The child window *overlays* its parent window's client area and, therefore, is the window directly under the cursor. This input is sent directly to the child window; the parent window never sees it. A special case arises when the child window has been disabled by the EnableWindow function. A disabled window does not receive input, so the input is given to the next window down, in this example, the parent window. A child window created with the WS_EX_TRANSPARENT style (see page 129) will be transparent to mouse messages. Mouse messages sent to a child window will be sent directly to its parent window, which you can verify by using the Window Explorer and Spy++.

Because a child window is confined to its parent window's client area, the initial *x*- and *y*-position parameters to the CreateWindow function are interpreted differently when creating child windows. For a child window, these parameters specify the position of the upper-left corner of the child window relative to the upper-left corner of the parent window's client area.

When you create a child window, you give it an integer identifier. You do this by supplying it in place of a menu handle in the hmenu parameter of the CreateWindow function (since a child window cannot have a menu). Any 16-bit integer value may be used for a child window identifier. Multiple child windows belonging to the same parent can be given the same identifier, although this is not recommended with one exception. A child window should use this identifier as part of any messages it sends to its parent window. If multiple child windows are given the same identifier, the parent window will be unable to identify, using the identifier, the child window sending the message. (Often such messages also include the window handle of the sender. You can always distinguish windows by their handles). The one exception is for windows that will never be referenced by your program and never generate notifications to your program, such as static text used as labels.

A child window can be moved within its parent window's client area, either by giving the child window a caption so that the user can move the window using the mouse, or you can move it with the MoveWindow function. Either way, the child window is positioned relative to the upper-left corner of its parent window's client area. You can never display a child window outside its parent window's client area. When all or part of a child window extends outside the visible portion of its parent window's client area, the portion outside the client area is not displayed (it's clipped). Compare, for example, the child window shown in Figure 3.7 (page 129) with the same window, repositioned, shown in Figure 3.8 (page 149).

Here is a simple example of how a notification message can be implemented. You can create a (non-WS_EX_TRANSPARENT) child window that is a "push button" control. When the mouse cursor is over the push button, the mouse movement messages are sent to the push button (child window), not to the parent window of the push button. When you click the left mouse button while over the push button control, Windows sends the mouse click message to the push button. The push button sends a notification message to its parent window to inform the parent that the push button was pushed. If you position the push button so that part of it extends beyond the boundaries of its parent window's client area, only the part of the push button within the client area is visible. The push button, like all child windows, is clipped to its parent window's client area boundaries. The code to handle a button-down notification is something like this:

```
static LRESULT
myButtonWndProc(HWND hwnd, UINT message, WPARAM wParam, LPARAM lParam)
{
  switch(message)
      { /* message */
       HANDLE_MSG(hwnd, WM_LBUTTONDOWN, myButton_OnLButtonDown);
       HANDLE_MSG(hwnd, WM_LBUTTONDBLCLK, myButton_OnLButtonDown);
       // ... more handlers here
      } /* message */
   return DefWindowProc(hwnd, message, wParam, lParam);
}

static void myButton_OnLButtonDown(HWND hwnd, BOOL dblclk, int x, int y, UINT flags)
{
  FORWARD_WM_COMMAND(GetParent(hwnd), GetWindowLong(hwnd, GWL_ID), hwnd,
                       (dblclk ? MBN_DBLCLK : MBN_CLICKED), SendMessage);
}
```

You define MBN_CLICKED and MBN_DBLCLK to be nonzero values.

Some operations on a parent window also affect all its child windows, as follows:

- Showing the parent window shows the parent window and then the child window.

- Hiding the parent window hides the child window and then the parent window.

- Destroying the parent window destroys the child window and then the parent window.

- Moving the parent window moves the child window as part of the parent window's client area.

- Increasing the size of the parent window results in the child window receiving paint messages for any previously clipped, but now exposed, areas. Of particular note is that when a window is resized, Windows sends WM_SIZE messages only to that window, not to any of its child windows. When a child window should be resized when its parent window changes in size, the parent window must explicitly resize the child window.

Other Window Styles

Once you've decided whether a window should be an overlapped, pop-up, or child window, there are a number of remaining window styles that you can use in combination with one of the foregoing styles to fully specify a window's appearance. All the window styles listed in windows.h are shown in Table 3.5. Dialog styles that are used with dialog boxes are discussed in Chapter 11, "Dialog Boxes".

Table 3.5: Window styles

Symbolic Name	Overlapped	Pop-up	Child	Meaning
	Use With			
MDIS_ALLCHILDSTYLES				Used only when creating a MDI child window to specify that the window can be any combination of window styles. By default, an MDI child window has the WS_MINIMIZE, WS_MAXIMIZE, WS_HSCROLL, and WS_VSCROLL window styles.
WS_BORDER	✓	✓	✓	Creates a window with a border.
WS_CAPTION	✓	✓	✓	Creates a window with a title bar. Implies the WS_BORDER style. Precludes the WS_DLGFRAME style.
WS_CHILD			✓	Creates a child window. Precludes the WS_POPUP style.
WS_CHILDWINDOW			✓	Synonym for WS_CHILD.
WS_CLIPCHILDREN	✓	✓	✓	Prevents a parent window from drawing in client areas occupied by child windows. Used when creating the parent window.
WS_CLIPSIBLINGS			✓	Prevents a child window from drawing in portions of its client area that overlap other sibling windows' client areas.
WS_DISABLED	✓	✓	✓	Creates a window that is initially disabled. Newly created windows are enabled by default.
WS_DLGFRAME	✓	✓	✓	Creates a window with a dialog border but no title. Precludes the WS_CAPTION style.
WS_GROUP			✓	Specifies the first control in a group of controls. Used typically by controls in dialog boxes. Has the same value as the WS_MINIMIZEBOX style, so they cannot be distinguished except by context.
WS_HSCROLL	✓	✓	✓	Creates a window containing a horizontal scroll bar.
WS_ICONIC	✓			Synonym for WS_MINIMIZE.
WS_MAXIMIZE	✓			Creates a window of maximum size (i.e., a window that completely fills the screen).

Note: The check marks indicate that a window style is compatible with and may be specified when creating a window of the type given at the top of the column.

Table 3.5: Window styles

Symbolic Name	Overlapped	Pop-up	Child	Meaning
	Use With			
WS_MAXIMIZEBOX	✓	✓	✓	Creates a window containing a maximize box. Must be combined with WS_OVERLAPPED or WS_CAPTION to make the maximize box visible.
WS_MINIMIZE	✓			Creates a minimally sized window.
WS_MINIMIZEBOX	✓	✓	✓	Creates a window containing a minimize box. Must be combined with WS_OVERLAPPED or WS_CAPTION to make the minimize box visible.
WS_OVERLAPPED	✓			Creates an overlapped window containing a caption and a border.
WS_OVERLAPPEDWINDOW	✓			A synonym for a combination of the following styles: WS_OVERLAPPED, WS_CAPTION, WS_SYSMENU, WS_THICKFRAME, WS_MINIMIZEBOX, WS_MAXIMIZEBOX.
WS_POPUP		✓		Creates a pop-up window. Precludes the WS_CHILD style.
WS_POPUPWINDOW		✓		A synonym for a combination of the following styles: WS_POPUP, WS_BORDER, WS_SYSMENU. The system menu will not be visible unless this style is combined with the WS_CAPTION style.
WS_SYSMENU	✓	✓	✓	Creates a window containing a system menu.
WS_TABSTOP			✓	Indicates a control to which the user can move by using the **Tab** key. Used typically by child windows in a dialog box. Has the same value as the WS_MAXIMIZEBOX style, so they cannot be distinguished except by context.
WS_THICKFRAME	✓	✓	✓	Creates a window with a sizing border (thick frame) that the user can use to resize the window.
WS_VISIBLE	✓	✓	✓	Creates the window initially visible. Windows are created invisible by default and can be shown by the ShowWindow function. Overlapped windows created using this style and with the *x*-position parameter to the CreateWindow function set equal to CW_USEDEFAULT pass the *y*-position parameter as the nCmdShow parameter to the ShowWindow function when CreateWindow calls it.

Note: The check marks indicate that a window style is compatible with and may be specified when creating a window of the type given at the top of the column.

Table 3.5: Window styles

Symbolic Name	Overlapped	Pop-up	Child	Meaning
	Use With			
WS_VSCROLL	✓	✓	✓	Creates a window with a vertical scroll bar.
WS_TILED				A synonym for WS_OVERLAPPED (obsolete. Ancient, in fact).
WS_SIZEBOX				A synonym for WS_THICKFRAME (obsolete).
WS_TILEDWINDOW				A synonym for WS_OVERLAPPEDWINDOW (obsolete).

Note: The check marks indicate that a window style is compatible with and may be specified when creating a window of the type given at the top of the column.

Most of the window styles listed in Table 3.5 are self-explanatory and need no detailed discussion. A few of the styles could use a bit more explanation.

The WS_BORDER style requests that a window have a border. Only overlapped windows get a border by default. See Figure 3.2.

The WS_DLGFRAME style creates a window with a special border, a *dialog frame,* but no title. See Figure 3.2.

The WS_CAPTION style requests that a window have a border and a title bar (caption). See Figure 3.2. A title bar is the rectangle at the top of a window that provides space for the window's title. The title that is placed in the title bar is passed as the second parameter to the CreateWindow function. You can change a window's title at any time with the SetWindowText function. Creating a window with a title bar permits the user to move the window on the screen by dragging it by its title bar; otherwise, the user cannot move a window. A window can have window text without a title bar. Often child windows do not have title bars but do have window text. For example, push buttons, a particular kind of child window, use the window text as the button label.

The WS_BORDER, WS_DLGFRAME, and WS_CAPTION styles should not be used in combination with one another and should be considered mutually exclusive styles. Combining the WS_BORDER and

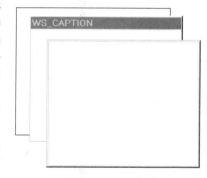

Figure 3.2: Frame styles (back to front): WS_BORDER, WS_CAPTION, and WS_DLGFRAME

WS_DLGFRAME styles creates a window with a caption and is equivalent to specifying only the WS_CAPTION style. This is surely not what is expected! The window has a border but only because a window with a caption always has a border. Combining WS_BORDER with WS_CAPTION results in a window with a caption and a border, but the WS_BORDER style is ignored. Again, captioned windows always have borders. Combining

WS_DLGFRAME and WS_CAPTION creates a window with a caption and a normal border, not a dialog frame; the WS_DLGFRAME style is ignored. (This restriction is corrected by the use of extended window styles, a subject covered later in this chapter in the section "Extended Window Styles" on page 124). Rather than your having to remember the interactions of these styles, view them as a set of three from which you can choose any one style.

The WS_SYSMENU, WS_MAXIMIZEBOX, and WS_MINIMIZEBOX styles request that a window have a system menu icon on the left end of the title bar, a maximize box icon towards the far right end of the title bar, and a minimize box icon next to the maximize box icon. The system menu contains system commands that permit the user to move, resize, and close a window. The maximize box permits the user to expand the window to occupy the entire screen. The minimize box permits the user to collapse a window into an icon. All three of these styles require that a window have a title bar, so they should always be used in combination with the WS_CAPTION style.

The WS_CLIPCHILDREN style is often used when creating a window that will be the parent window to one or more child windows. A parent window that does not have the WS_CLIPCHILDREN style can draw in its client area and overwrite child windows occupying the same area. When the WS_CLIPCHILDREN style is used, the portion of the parent window's client area that is occupied by child windows is clipped from the parent window's update region. In effect, the parent window can draw anywhere in its client area, but when the drawing enters a region occupied by a child window, the drawing will not be performed. In other words, the parent window cannot overwrite a child window. This style had more relevance on the older, slower machines because the algorithm to compute the clipping regions could be very slow, both to determine the clipping areas and to draw while obeying the clipping request. On modern Win32-capable machines, particularly those with graphics accelerator cards, the value of leaving this style off is debatable. So you should typically always include it in your window styles.

The WS_CLIPSIBLINGS style is quite similar. A parent window can have multiple child windows occupying its client area. Multiple child windows can even overlap one another. Normally, when child windows overlap, one child window can draw within its own client area and overwrite the client area of a neighboring but overlapping child window. When the WS_CLIPSIBLINGS style is used, a window can draw only in the portions of its client area that are not overlapped by its sibling windows. As with WS_CLIPCHILDREN, the virtue of omitting this style on modern machines is debatable. You should always include it.

The WS_CLIPCHILDREN and WS_CLIPSIBLINGS styles are often mistaken for one another. The WS_CLIPCHILDREN style is given to a parent window and prevents the parent from drawing in its child windows. The WS_CLIPSIBLINGS style is given to a child window and prevents the child window from drawing in its sibling windows. While using these styles results in a small loss of performance, you may discover that omitting them also produces very unexpected effects.

The WS_DISABLED style creates a window that is initially disabled. When a window is disabled, input such as mouse clicks and key presses are not sent to the window. A window can be explicitly enabled or disabled by the EnableWindow function.

The WS_HSCROLL style adds a horizontal scroll bar to a window, and the WS_VSCROLL style adds a vertical scroll bar to a window. These are bars on the bottom and right sides of a window, respectively, that let a user scroll the contents of the client area. The effects of using these styles are shown in Figure 3.3. Be forewarned that using these window styles does *not* give you a window in which the contents of the client area are automatically scrolled. Windows sends messages (such as WM_HSCROLL and WM_VSCROLL) to the window when the user manipulates a scroll bar. The window function must intercept and process these messages to scroll the window. Also, even though *controls* haven't been discussed yet in this book, don't mistake window scroll bars for *scroll-bar controls*. You create a window with scroll bars by using the WS_HSCROLL and WS_VSCROLL styles. You create a scroll-bar control as a specific class of child window.

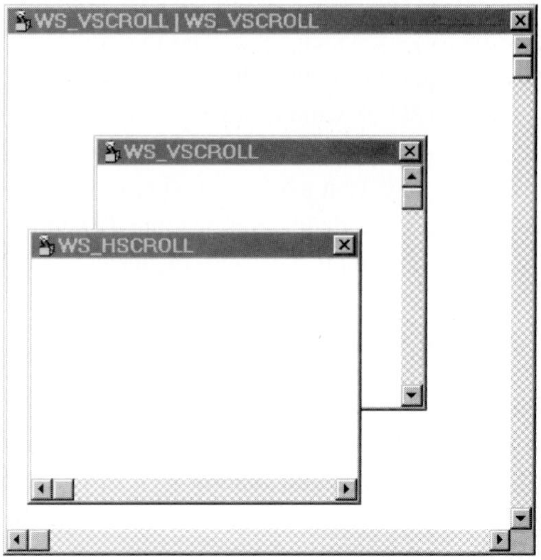

The WS_MAXIMIZE style creates a window that is initially full-screen; the WS_MINIMIZE style creates a window that is initially iconic. The WS_ICONIC style is a synonym for the WS_MINIMIZE style. These styles should be used only when you are creating overlapped windows.

Figure 3.3: Standard scroll bar styles

The WS_THICKFRAME style creates a window with a thicker than normal border. The user can drag on the sides and corners of the window with the mouse in order to resize the window. A window with a thick frame is shown in Figure 3.4.

The WS_VISIBLE style creates the window initially visible. If you don't give this style, windows are initially hidden when they are created and must be shown using the ShowWindow function. Using the WS_VISIBLE style creates a window that is initially displayed rather than hidden.When you create an overlapped window with the WS_VISIBLE style, you can specify the manner in which the window is initially displayed. When you set the *x*-position parameter of the CreateWindow function to CW_USEDEFAULT, the *y*-position parameter is passed to the ShowWindow function as its nCmdShow parameter when initially showing the window. The *y*-position parameter value can be any of the show-style values listed in Table 2.1 (page 51). For the first overlapped window created by the application, it can be the nCmdShow parameter that Windows passed to the WinMain function.

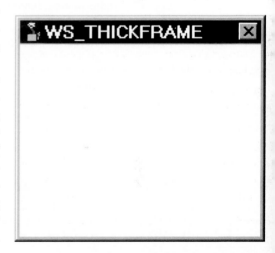

Figure 3.4: A window with WS_THICKFRAME, WS_CAPTION, and WS_SYSMENU styles

This leaves only the WS_GROUP and WS_TABSTOP window styles. A window created inside a dialog box uses these two styles, which we discuss in Chapter 11, "Dialog Boxes", along with dialog boxes in general. However, for now know that these two styles have the same numeric value as the WS_MINIMIZEBOX and WS_MAXIMIZEBOX window styles. Normally this isn't a problem because child windows of dialog boxes do not have either a minimize or a maximize box. Nevertheless, once you have a little experience with Windows, you may wish to create a window containing a minimize or maximize box and then use that window like a control in a dialog box. It's an odd and unusual thing to want to do, and it's made difficult, if not impossible, to accomplish because the meanings of the values of these two styles are overloaded.

Extended Window Styles

The original design of Windows set aside only 16 bits to hold a window's *window styles*. (Styles are stored in a DWORD [a 32-bit field], but the lower 16 bits are used by controls to hold *control styles*. Only the upper 16 bits are available to hold window styles). The styles just described require all 16 bits and leave no values that can be used to define new window styles. Another problem is that some window styles are defined in such a way that they preclude their use with another window style. Windows 3.0 added *extended window styles* to overcome these obstacles, and Win32 continues that practice.

You must call the CreateWindowEx function to create a window possessing any extended window styles. The CreateWindowEx function is identical to the CreateWindow function except that an additional parameter, the *extended window styles*, is passed to the function. In fact, the CreateWindow function passes all its parameters, along with a 0 for the extended window styles, to the CreateWindowEx function, which then does all the work. Here is the definition of the CreateWindowEx function:

```
CreateWindowEx(DWORD ExStyle, LPCTSTR Classname,
               LPCSTR WindowsName, DWORD Style,
               int X, int Y, int Width, int Height,
               HWND hParent, LPCTSTR hMenu,
               HINSTANCE hInstance, LPVOID Param);
```

The values for the ExStyle parameter to CreateWindowEx are listed in Table 3.6.

Table 3.6: Extended window styles

	Use With			
Symbolic Name	Overlapped	Pop-up	Child	**Meaning**
WS_EX_ACCEPTFILES	✓	✓	✓	Specifies that the window accepts drag-drop files.

The check marks indicate that a window style is compatible with a window of the type given at the top of the column and may be specified when creating such a window.

[3/4]Although the official documentation claims this is only available in API level 4, it appears to be functional in API level 3, or at least 3.51.

[4]Available only in API level 4 and higher.

Table 3.6: Extended window styles

| Symbolic Name | Use With | | | Meaning |
	Overlapped	Pop-up	Child	
WS_EX_APPWINDOW[4]	✓			A top-level window, when minimized, is forced onto the task bar.
WS_EX_CLIENTEDGE[4]	✓	✓	✓	The window has a border with a sunken edge.
WS_EX_CONTEXTHELP[3/4]	✓	✓		An icon with a question mark is included in the caption bar. Used for context-sensitive help. Cannot be used with WS_MINIMIZEBOX or WS_MAXIMIZEBOX styles.
WS_EX_CONTROLPARENT[4]	✓	✓		Allows the user to navigate among the child windows using the **Tab** key.
WS_EX_DLGMODALFRAME	✓	✓	✓	Creates a window with a double-border that may, optionally, be created with the WS_CAPTION style.
WS_EX_LEFT[4]	✓	✓	✓	The window has generic left-aligned properties (default).
WS_EX_LEFTSCROLLBAR[4]	✓	✓	✓	Applies only when the selected language is Hebrew or Arabic; the scroll bar, if present, is on the left side of the client area. For other languages, this style is ignored.
WS_EX_LTRREADING[4]	✓	✓	✓	The window uses left-to-right reading order (default).
WS_EX_MDICHILD[4]	✓	✓	✓	Specifies that the window is an MDI child window.
WS_EX_NOPARENTNOTIFY			✓	Instructs a child window to not send WM_PARENTNOTIFY messages to its parent window.
WS_EX_RIGHT[4]	✓	✓	✓	The window has generic right-aligned properties. The meaning of the properties is interpreted by the window class. For general windows, it has an effect only if the selected language is Hebrew or Arabic; otherwise, it's ignored.

The check marks indicate that a window style is compatible with a window of the type given at the top of the column and may be specified when creating such a window.

[3/4]Although the official documentation claims this is only available in API level 4, it appears to be functional in API level 3, or at least 3.51.

[4]Available only in API level 4 and higher.

Table 3.6: Extended window styles

Symbolic Name	Overlapped	Pop-up	Child	Meaning
WS_EX_RIGHTSCROLLBAR[4]	✓	✓	✓	The scroll bar, if present, is on the right side of the client area (default).
WS_EX_RTLREADING[4]	✓	✓	✓	The window text is displayed right to left. Applies only if the selected language is Hebrew, Arabic, or any other language that supports right-to-left display; otherwise, it's ignored.
WS_EX_STATICEDGE[4]	✓	✓	✓	Creates a window with a 3-D border style. Suggested for windows that do not accept user input.
WS_EX_TOOLWINDOW[4]	✓			Specifies that the window is a "tool window", a floating toolbar. Floating toolbars are dockable in the desktop window and do not appear on the task bar. Uses a short title bar and a small caption.
WS_EX_TOPMOST	✓	✓		Specifies the window should remain visible and displayed above all non-topmost windows, even when the window is deactivated. Can be added or removed by the SetWindowPos function.
WS_EX_TRANSPARENT	✓	✓	✓	Creates a transparent window. The window does not obscure other windows that are below it.
WS_EX_WINDOWEDGE[4]	✓	✓	✓	The window has a border with a raised edge.

The check marks indicate that a window style is compatible with a window of the type given at the top of the column and may be specified when creating such a window.

[3/4] Although the official documentation claims this is only available in API level 4, it appears to be functional in API level 3, or at least 3.51.

[4] Available only in API level 4 and higher.

The WS_EX_ACCEPTFILES extended window style specifies that the window accepts drag-drop files. You can add or remove this extended window style to or from a window by calling the DragAcceptFiles function.

The WS_EX_APPWINDOW style causes the window to be forced onto the task bar when it is minimized.

The WS_EX_CLIENTEDGE, WS_EX_WINDOWEDGE, and WS_EX_STATICEDGE styles change the appearance of a window. These are illustrated in Figure 3.5.

The WS_EX_DLGMODALFRAME extended window style creates a window with a "dialog" border, as shown in Figure 3.5. Unlike the WS_DLGFRAME window style, which also creates a window with a dialog border, the WS_EX_DLGMODALFRAME extended window style can be combined with the WS_CAPTION window style. When you want a window with a dialog border and a caption, you must use the WS_EX_DLGMODALFRAME extended window style and create the window by calling the CreateWindowEx function. The WS_EX_DLGMODALFRAME style is passed in the dwExStyle parameter, and the WS_CAPTION style is passed in the dwStyle parameter.

The WS_EX_CONTEXTHELP style produces a window with a context-sensitive-help indicator in the top and towards the right. This button, when selected, changes the cursor to the help cursor. A window created as a WS_POPUPWINDOW with WS_EX_CONTEXTHELP is shown in Figure 3.6. This window has a caption and a system menu and was constructed in the Window Explorer application.

Figure 3.5: Samples of window edges using extended styles

When the user has the help cursor, and a control in the window is clicked, Windows doesn't send a WM_COMMAND message to the parent. Instead, it sends the parent a WM_HELP message. You can then respond to this request by calling WinHelp. You must provide a table that gives the correspondence between a control ID and a help context identifier. The WinHelp function looks up the control ID and positions the Help file at the page with the corresponding context identifier. The table is an array of DWORD values, where the first value is the ID of a control and the second is the context ID[1] for the help topic. The last pair of values in the table must be 0, 0. Microsoft's suggested naming convention is that help context ID names start with the IDH_ prefix. You typically define your help context

Figure 3.6: A window with the WS_EX_CONTEXTHELP style

IDs in a separate file, which is included in your C source and is used to generate the appropriate input files for the Help Compiler hc. A sample table might look like:

```
static const DWORD ctlmap[] = {
  // Control ID          Context identifier
  // ------------------- -------------------
    IDC_CREATEWINDOWEX, IDH_CREATEWINDOWEX,
    IDC_X,              IDH_X,
```

---

[1] We won't talk about Help file construction in this book. There are some books (beyond the Microsoft documentation) suggested in the Further Reading section that cover both basic and advanced Help file construction. For now, just trust that the context ID is a number that you attach to a page in the Help file that lets you find the page.

```
    IDC_Y,              IDH_Y,
    ...
    IDC_PARENT,         IDH_PARENT,
    0,                  0 // end of table marker
};
```

The OnHelp message cracker is defined not in windowsx.h but in our extension file extensions.h. The HELPINFO structure contains useful information about the object selected by the help cursor and is defined as follows:

```
typedef struct tagHELPINFO{
    UINT    cbSize;      // structure size in bytes
    int     iContextType;
    int     iCtrlId;
    HANDLE  hItemHandle;
    DWORD   dwContextId;
    POINT   MousePos;
} HELPINFO, FAR * LPHELPINFO;
```

The call to WinHelp then looks like this:

```
WinHelp(helpinfo->hItemHandle, helpfilename, HELP_WM_HELP, ctlmap);
```

WM_HELP Message Cracker Handler

```
void cls_OnHelp(HWND hwnd, LPHELPINFO helpinfo);
```

| Parameter | wParam | | lParam | | Meaning |
	lo	hi	lo	hi	
hwnd					Window handle of a window.
helpinfo					A reference to a HELPINFO structure.

The WS_EX_CONTEXTHELP flag is not compatible with the use of the WS_MINIMIZEBOX or WS_MAXIMIZEBOX flag. If either or both of these flags are specified, the context Help button will not appear. The WS_EX_CONTEXTHELP flag also requires the WS_SYSMENU flag be present. See Knowledge Base article Q135787.

The WS_EX_NOPARENTNOTIFY extended window style is used with child windows. It specifies that the child window should not send WM_PARENTNOTIFY messages to its parent window. Normally, a child window sends such messages to its parent window when it is created or destroyed or when the user presses a mouse button while the cursor is over the child window.

The WS_EX_TOPMOST extended window style indicates that Windows should keep the window above all other non-topmost windows. The window remains above the other windows even when the window is deactivated. You can add or remove this extended window style to or from a window by calling the Set-

WindowPos function. To set it, use the HWND_TOPMOST value for the argument; to clear it, use the HWND_NOTOPMOST value, both as follows:

```
SetWindowPos(hwnd, HWND_TOPMOST, 0, 0, 0, 0, SWP_NOSIZE | SWP_NOMOVE);
SetWindowPos(hwnd, HWND_NOTOPMOST, 0, 0, 0, 0, SWP_NOSIZE | SWP_NOMOVE);
```

The WS_EX_TRANSPARENT extended window style specifies that the window is *transparent*. All windows that are beneath a window with this style are not obscured by the window. A window with this style receives its WM_PAINT messages only after all sibling windows beneath it have received their WM_PAINT message (and therefore have been updated). If the transparent window is also a child window, the mouse messages are sent directly to its parent window. You can see this using the Window Explorer and the Spy++ program.

The Panes Example Program

The Panes example program illustrates several of the window styles discussed in this chapter. The main application window is an unowned, overlapped window displayed with a default position and size, as are most main application windows. Panes also creates a second overlapped window that is owned by the first, two pop-up windows (one owned by the main application window and one with no owner) as well as a child window that has the main application window as its parent. Figure 3.7 shows the windows that are created by the Panes application.

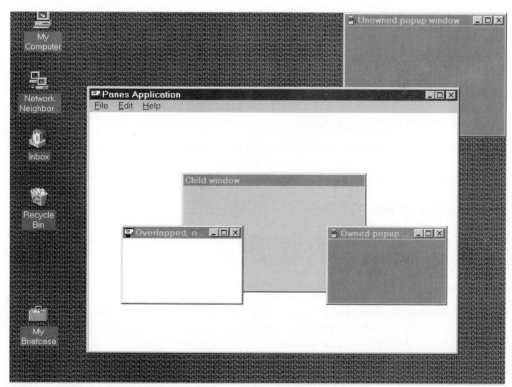

Figure 3.7: The windows created by the Panes example program

To see the external behavior, try these experiments:

- Drag the main window around by its caption bar. Note that the child window moves with it, but the owned overlapped window, owned pop-up, and unowned pop-up are not affected.

- Drag the owned pop-up around. Note that it is not clipped by its owner window, the main window of the Panes application.

- Drag the child window around. Note that it is clipped by its owner window.

- Click on the unowned pop-up. Note that it comes up on top of the other windows. It can be dragged around like any other window.

- Minimize the main window. Note that the unowned pop-up is not minimized, but the owned pop-up and the child window disappear because the main window is no longer able to show them.

- Minimize the unowned pop-up. Note that it now appears in the task bar.

- Minimize the owned pop-up. Note that it does not appear on the task bar, but its minimized representative appears on the desktop.

- Minimize the main window when the owned pop-up is minimized. Note that its minimized representative disappears from the desktop.

- Restore the main window. Note that the owned pop-up is also restored.

- Click the right mouse button over the child window to minimize it. Note that its minimized representative appears in its parent.

- Click the right mouse button over the child window to maximize it. Note that it fills the parent window.

- Use the system menu on the owned, overlapped window to close the window. Note that the application does not terminate; only the window closes, even though it has the same handler as the main window (as we explain shortly). We have to program this behavior.

The **Panes** Source Code

The Panes example program is nearly identical to the Template example program, so we show only those parts of the Panes code that differ (see Listings 3.1–3.3).

Listing 3.1: **Panes**: Excerpts from **initialization.c**

```
//
//  BOOL initInstance (HINSTANCE hinst, UINT resPoolID, int nCmdShow)
//

BOOL initInstance (HINSTANCE hinst, UINT resPoolID, int nCmdShow)
{
    HWND   hwnd;
    TCHAR  ClassName [MAX_RESOURCESTRING + 1] ;
```

```
    VERIFY (LoadString (hinst, resPoolID, ClassName, DIM(ClassName))) ;

    // Constrain this application to run single instance
    // ... as Template, dropped here for conciseness

    // Register all application-specific window classes
    if (!registerWindowClasses (hinst, resPoolID))
        return FALSE ;

    // Initialize the Common Controls DLL
    // You must call this function before using any Common Control
    InitCommonControls () ;

    // Create the application's main frame window
    hwnd = createMainFrameWindow (hinst, nCmdShow);

    if (hwnd == NULL)
        return FALSE ;

    // Create the owned, overlapped window

    if(createOverlappedWindow(hinst, hwnd, resPoolID) == NULL)
        return FALSE;

    // Create the sample popup window

    UnownedPopup = createPopupWindow(hinst, NULL, IDS_UNOWNEDPOPUPTITLE);
    if(UnownedPopup == NULL)
        return FALSE;

    if(createPopupWindow(hinst, hwnd, IDS_OWNEDPOPUPTITLE) == NULL)
        return FALSE;

    if(createChildWindow(hinst, hwnd) == NULL)
        return FALSE;

    return TRUE ;
}

//
//   BOOL registerWindowClasses (HINSTANCE hinst, UINT resPoolID)
//
static BOOL
registerWindowClasses (HINSTANCE hinst, UINT resPoolID)
{
    TCHAR       ClassName [MAX_RESOURCESTRING + 1] ;
    WNDCLASSEX  wcex ;

    VERIFY (LoadString (hinst, resPoolID, ClassName, DIM(ClassName))) ;

    // Fill in window class structure with parameters that describe
    // the main window.
    wcex.cbSize        = sizeof (WNDCLASSEX) ;
    wcex.style         = CS_HREDRAW | CS_VREDRAW | CS_DBLCLKS ;
    wcex.lpfnWndProc   = mainFrameWndProc ;
    wcex.cbClsExtra    = 0 ;
```

```
wcex.cbWndExtra     = 0 ;
wcex.hInstance      = hinst ;
wcex.hIcon          = LoadIcon (hinst, MAKEINTRESOURCE (resPoolID)) ;
wcex.hCursor        = LoadCursor (NULL, IDC_ARROW) ;
wcex.hbrBackground  = (HBRUSH) (COLOR_WINDOW+1) ;

wcex.lpszMenuName   = NULL;  // no class menu
wcex.lpszClassName  = ClassName ;
wcex.hIconSm        = LoadImage (hinst,
                                 MAKEINTRESOURCE (resPoolID),
                                 IMAGE_ICON,
                                 GetSystemMetrics (SM_CXSMICON),
                                 GetSystemMetrics (SM_CYSMICON),
                                 LR_SHARED) ;

// Register the window class and return success/failure code.
if(internalRegisterClass (&wcex) == 0)
    return FALSE;

VERIFY (LoadString (hinst, IDR_POPUP, ClassName, DIM(ClassName))) ;

wcex.style          = 0;
wcex.lpfnWndProc    = popupWndProc ;
wcex.cbClsExtra     = 0 ;
wcex.cbWndExtra     = 0 ;
wcex.hInstance      = hinst ;
wcex.hIcon          = LoadIcon (hinst, MAKEINTRESOURCE (IDR_POPUP)) ;
wcex.hCursor        = LoadCursor (NULL, IDC_ARROW) ;
wcex.hbrBackground  = GetStockBrush(GRAY_BRUSH);

wcex.lpszMenuName   = NULL;
wcex.lpszClassName  = ClassName ;
wcex.hIconSm        = LoadImage (hinst,
                                 MAKEINTRESOURCE (IDR_POPUP),
                                 IMAGE_ICON,
                                 GetSystemMetrics (SM_CXSMICON),
                                 GetSystemMetrics (SM_CYSMICON),
                                 LR_SHARED) ;

if(internalRegisterClass (&wcex) == 0)
    return FALSE;

VERIFY (LoadString (hinst, IDR_CHILD, ClassName, DIM(ClassName))) ;

wcex.style          = 0;
wcex.lpfnWndProc    = childWndProc ;
wcex.cbClsExtra     = 0 ;
wcex.cbWndExtra     = 0 ;
wcex.hInstance      = hinst ;
wcex.hIcon          = LoadIcon (hinst, MAKEINTRESOURCE (IDR_CHILD)) ;
wcex.hCursor        = LoadCursor (NULL, IDC_CROSS) ;
wcex.hbrBackground  = GetStockBrush(LTGRAY_BRUSH);

wcex.lpszMenuName   = (LPCTSTR)NULL;
wcex.lpszClassName  = ClassName ;
wcex.hIconSm        = LoadImage (hinst,
                                 MAKEINTRESOURCE (IDR_CHILD),
```

```
                                    IMAGE_ICON,
                                    GetSystemMetrics (SM_CXSMICON),
                                    GetSystemMetrics (SM_CYSMICON),
                                    LR_SHARED) ;

    if(internalRegisterClass (&wcex) == 0)
        return FALSE;
    return true;
}

//
//   HWND createMainFrameWindow (HINSTANCE hinst, int nCmdShow)
//

static HWND
createMainFrameWindow (HINSTANCE hinst, int nCmdShow)
{
    HWND  hwnd ;
    TCHAR ClassName [MAX_RESOURCESTRING + 1] ;
    TCHAR Title [MAX_RESOURCESTRING + 1] ;

    // Create the main frame window
    VERIFY (LoadString (hinst, IDR_MAINFRAME, ClassName, DIM (ClassName))) ;
    VERIFY (LoadString (hinst, IDS_APP_TITLE, Title, DIM (Title))) ;

    hwnd =
        CreateWindowEx (
                    0,                      // Extended window styles
                    ClassName,              // Address of registered class name
                    Title,                  // Address of window name
                    WS_OVERLAPPEDWINDOW,//  Window style
                    CW_USEDEFAULT,          // Horizontal position of window
                    0,                      // Vertical position of window
                    CW_USEDEFAULT,          // Window width
                    0,                      // Window height
                    NULL,                   // Handle of parent or owner window
                    LoadMenu(hinst, MAKEINTRESOURCE(IDR_MAINFRAME)),
                                            // Handle of menu or child-window identifier
                    hinst,                  // Handle of application instance
                    NULL) ;                 // Address of window-creation data

    ASSERT (NULL != hwnd) ;
    if (!hwnd)
        return NULL ;

    ShowWindow (hwnd, nCmdShow) ;
    UpdateWindow (hwnd) ;

    return hwnd ;
}
/****************************************************************************
*                         createOverlappedWindow
* Inputs:
*       HINSTANCE hinst: Instance handle
*       HWND hwnd: owner window, could be NULL
*       int resPoolID: ID of main window class
* Result: HWND
```

```
*       Window handle if successful, NULL if error
* Effect:
*       Creates an overlapped window which is owned by the main window
********************************************************************/

static HWND createOverlappedWindow(HINSTANCE hinst, HWND hwnd, int resPoolID)
    {
    HWND hwndOver;
    TCHAR ClassName [MAX_RESOURCESTRING + 1] ;
    TCHAR Title [MAX_RESOURCESTRING + 1] ;
    RECT r;
    int width;
    int height;
    POINT origin;

    GetClientRect(hwnd, &r);
    width = (r.right - r.left) / 3;
    height = (r.bottom - r.top) / 3;
    origin.x = r.left + (width / 3);
    origin.y = r.top + 3 * (height / 2);
    ClientToScreen(hwnd, &origin);

    VERIFY (LoadString (hinst, resPoolID, ClassName, DIM(ClassName))) ;
    VERIFY (LoadString (hinst, IDS_OVERLAPPED, Title, DIM(Title)));

    hwndOver = CreateWindow( ClassName,                          // Class name
                        Title,                           // Popup caption
                        WS_MINIMIZEBOX | WS_MAXIMIZEBOX |
                        WS_OVERLAPPEDWINDOW | WS_CAPTION,    // styles
                        origin.x,                           // origin
                        origin.y,                           // ...
                        width,                              // size
                        height,                             // ...
                        hwnd,                               // owner
                        (HMENU)NULL,                        // no menu
                        hinst,                          // Instance handle
                        NULL);                  // user-defined parameters
    if(hwndOver == NULL)
        return NULL;

    ShowWindow(hwndOver, SW_SHOWNOACTIVE);
    UpdateWindow(hwndOver);

    return hwndOver;
    }

/************************************************************************
*                           createPopupWindow
* Inputs:
*       HINSTANCE hinst: Instance handle
*       HWND hwnd: owner window, could be NULL
*       int titleid: ID of title
* Result: HWND
*       Window handle if successful, NULL if error
* Effect:
*       Creates a popup window which is owned by the main window
********************************************************************/
```

```
static HWND createPopupWindow(HINSTANCE hinst, HWND hwnd, int titleid)
    {
    HWND hwndPopup;
    TCHAR ClassName [MAX_RESOURCESTRING + 1] ;
    TCHAR Title [MAX_RESOURCESTRING + 1] ;
    RECT r;
    int width;
    int height;
    POINT origin;

    if(hwnd != NULL)
        { /* owned, window-relative */
        GetClientRect(hwnd, &r);
        width = (r.right - r.left) / 3;
        height = (r.bottom - r.top) / 3;
        origin.x = r.left + 2 * width;
        origin.y = r.top + 3 * (height / 2);
        ClientToScreen(hwnd, &origin);
        } /* owned, window-relative */
    else
        { /* unowned, screen-relative */
        SetRect(&r, 0, 0, GetSystemMetrics(SM_CXSCREEN),
                         GetSystemMetrics(SM_CYSCREEN));
        width = (r.right - r.left) / 3;
        height = (r.bottom - r.top) / 3;
        // Put in the top right corner of the screen
        origin.x = r.right - width;
        origin.y = 0;
        } /* unowned, screen-relative */

    VERIFY (LoadString (hinst, IDR_POPUP, ClassName, DIM(ClassName))) ;
    VERIFY (LoadString (hinst, titleid, Title, DIM(Title)));

    hwndPopup = CreateWindow( ClassName,                      // Class name
                        Title,                         // Popup caption
                        WS_MINIMIZEBOX | WS_MAXIMIZEBOX |
                        WS_POPUPWINDOW | WS_CAPTION,// window styles
                        origin.x,                            // origin
                        origin.y,                            // ...
                        width,                               // size
                        height,                              // ...
                        hwnd,                                // owner
                        (HMENU)NULL,                         // no menu
                        hinst,                       // Instance handle
                        NULL);          // user-defined parameters
    if(hwndPopup == NULL)
        return NULL;

    ShowWindow(hwndPopup, SW_SHOWNOACTIVATE);
    UpdateWindow(hwndPopup);

    return hwndPopup;
    }


/****************************************************************************
*                          createChildWindow
```

```
* Inputs:
*       HINSTANCE hinst: Instance handle
*       HWND hwnd: owner window, could be NULL
* Result: HWND
*       Window handle if successful, NULL if error
* Effect:
*       Creates a child window which is owned by the main window
*********************************************************************/

static HWND createChildWindow(HINSTANCE hinst, HWND hwnd)
    {
    HWND hwndChild;
    TCHAR ClassName [MAX_RESOURCESTRING + 1] ;
    TCHAR Title [MAX_RESOURCESTRING + 1] ;
    RECT r;
    int width;
    int height;
    POINT pt;

    GetClientRect(hwnd, &r);
    width = (r.right - r.left) / 2;
    height = (r.bottom - r.top) / 2;

    // We want the child window centered on the parent
    pt.x = (r.right - r.left) / 2 - width / 2;
    pt.y = (r.bottom - r.top) / 2 - height / 2;

    VERIFY (LoadString (hinst, IDR_CHILD, ClassName, DIM(ClassName))) ;
    VERIFY (LoadString (hinst, IDS_CHILDTITLE, Title, DIM(Title)));

    hwndChild = CreateWindowEx(
                    WS_EX_DLGMODALFRAME |
                    WS_EX_NOPARENTNOTIFY,
                    ClassName,                       // Class name
                    Title,                          // Child caption
                    WS_CHILDWINDOW | WS_CAPTION,    // window style
                    pt.x,                               // origin
                    pt.y,                               // ...
                    width,                             // size
                    height,                            // ...
                    hwnd,                              // owner
                    (HMENU)NULL,                       // no menu
                    hinst,                      // Instance handle
                    NULL);              // user-defined parameters
    if(hwndChild == NULL)
        return NULL;

    ShowWindow(hwndChild, SW_SHOWNOACTIVATE);
    UpdateWindow(hwndChild);

    return hwndChild;
    }

//
//  ATOM internalRegisterClass (const LPWNDCLASSEX lpwcex)
//

static ATOM
```

```
internalRegisterClass (const LPWNDCLASSEX lpwcex)
{
  //... as in Template application, no changes
}
```

Listing 3.2: Panes: Excerpts from `popup.c`

```
static void popup_OnDestroy(HWND hwnd)
{
    if (GetWindowOwner (hwnd) == (HWND)NULL)
      UnownedPopup = (HWND)NULL ;
}

LRESULT CALLBACK
popupWndProc (HWND hwnd, UINT msg, WPARAM wParam, LPARAM lParam)
{
    switch(msg)
        { /* msg */
          HANDLE_MSG(hwnd, WM_DESTROY, popup_OnDestroy);
        } /* msg */
    return DefWindowProc (hwnd, msg, wParam, lParam) ;
}
```

Listing 3.3: Panes: Excerpts from `child.c`

```
LRESULT CALLBACK
childWndProc (HWND hwnd, UINT message, WPARAM wParam, LPARAM lParam)
{
 switch(message)
    { /* message */
      HANDLE_MSG(hwnd, WM_CONTEXTMENU, child_OnContextMenu);
      HANDLE_MSG(hwnd, WM_COMMAND, child_OnCommand);
      HANDLE_MSG(hwnd, WM_INITMENUPOPUP, child_OnInitMenuPopup);
    } /* message */
 return DefWindowProc(hwnd, message, wParam, lParam);
}

static void
child_OnCommand(HWND hwnd, int id, HWND hctl, UINT codenotify)
{
 // We could have commands that are unique to this window, or general
 // commands.  If we recognize the command, do it, otherwise pass to
 // our parent

 switch(id)
    { /* id */
      case IDM_RESTORE:
              ShowWindow(hwnd, SW_RESTORE);
              return;
      case IDM_MINIMIZE:
              ShowWindow(hwnd, SW_MINIMIZE);
              return;
      case IDM_MAXIMIZE:
              ShowWindow(hwnd, SW_MAXIMIZE);
              return;
    } /* id */
 FORWARD_WM_COMMAND(GetParent(hwnd), id, hctl, codenotify, SendMessage);
}
```

```
//
// BOOL child_DisplayContextMenu HWND hwnd, POINT pt)
//

static BOOL
child_DisplayContextMenu (HWND hwnd, POINT pt)
{
    HMENU hmenu, hmenuPopup ;
    BOOL result;

    // Determine the appropriate context menu to display.
    // generally using the application state and mouse click coordinates.

    hmenu = LoadMenu(GetWindowInstance(hwnd), MAKEINTRESOURCE(IDR_CHILDCONTEXT));

    hmenuPopup = GetSubMenu (hmenu, 0) ;
    ASSERT (NULL != hmenuPopup) ;

    // Convert click location to screen coordinates
    ClientToScreen (hwnd, &pt) ;

    // Display the floating popup menu at the mouse click location
    // Track the right mouse as this function is called during
    // WM_CONTEXTMENU message processing.
    result = TrackPopupMenu (hmenuPopup,
                        TPM_LEFTALIGN | TPM_RIGHTBUTTON,
                        pt.x, pt.y, 0, hwnd, NULL) ;
    DestroyMenu(hmenu);
    return result;
}

/***************************************************************************
 *                          child_OnContextMenu
 *      Pops up a menu that allows the child to be maximized, minimized, or
 *      restored
 ***************************************************************************/

static BOOL child_OnContextMenu(HWND hwnd, HWND hwndctl, int x, int y)
{
    POINT pt = { x, y } ;    // location of mouse click
    RECT  rc ;               // client area of window

    // Get the bounding rectangle of the client area.
    GetClientRect (hwnd, &rc) ;

    // Convert the mouse position to client coordinates.
    ScreenToClient (hwnd, &pt) ;

    // If the mouse click was in the client area,
    // display the appropriate floating popup menu.
    if (PtInRect (&rc, pt))
        if (child_DisplayContextMenu (hwnd, pt))
            return TRUE ;

    // Otherwise forward the message for default processing
    return FORWARD_WM_CONTEXTMENU (hwnd, hwndctl, x, y, DefWindowProc) ;
}
```

```
/***********************************************************************
 *                      child_OnInitMenuPopup
 *        Enables appropriate menu items on the floating popup menu
 ***********************************************************************/

static void
child_OnInitMenuPopup(HWND hwnd, HMENU hmenu, UINT item, BOOL sysmenu)
{
EnableMenuItem(hmenu, IDM_RESTORE, IsZoomed(hwnd) || IsIconic(hwnd)
                            ? MF_BYCOMMAND | MF_ENABLED
                            : MF_BYCOMMAND | MF_GRAYED);
EnableMenuItem(hmenu, IDM_MINIMIZE, !IsIconic(hwnd)
                            ? MF_BYCOMMAND | MF_ENABLED
                            : MF_BYCOMMAND | MF_GRAYED);
EnableMenuItem(hmenu, IDM_MAXIMIZE, !IsZoomed(hwnd)
                            ? MF_BYCOMMAND | MF_ENABLED
                            : MF_BYCOMMAND | MF_GRAYED);
}
```

Class Registration in `Panes`

Nearly all the differences between the Panes code and the Template code reside in the initialization code in initialize.c, shown in Listing 3.1, so we examine initialize.c in detail. The `registerWindowClasses` function registers the application's window classes. The Panes program uses four window classes, one each for the main window, the overlapped windows, the pop-up windows, and the child window. This statement is slightly misleading because a window class does not determine whether a window is an overlapped, pop-up, or child window. That is specified when the window is actually created by the `CreateWindow` function. These window classes are used to make the various window styles visually distinct. The main window class is almost as we defined it for the Template program, but we do a slight variation here. We do not register a menu with the class; instead, we will attach the menu to the window during window creation. So we change the registration line to be as follows:

```
wcex.lpszMenuName  = (LPCTSTR)NULL;  // no class menu
```

We will create our main window from this class and attach to it a menu and a toolbar (which we will make invisible for the moment). We'll also create a second overlapped window from this class, which will have no menu or toolbar. The toolbar code, which is not shown here, is in MainFrameToolbar.c.

A slight problem arises because of some error checking we have done. In the main window handler, we call the function `toolbar_UpdateUI` to update the toolbar status. Because our second overlapped window will use this same handler, it will call `toolbar_UpdateUI` as well, but this second overlapped window has no toolbar. This will cause an assertion failure in the `toolbar_UpdateUI` handler. So we had to remove an ASSERT statement that makes this test and simply ignore the situation in which the toolbar does not exist. A cleaner solution might have been to subclass the main window class and override this message, but we haven't yet discussed how to do window subclassing (that's in the next chapter).

The second class, called the `PanesPopupClass`, is defined as follows:

```
VERIFY (LoadString (hinst, IDR_POPUP, ClassName, DIM(ClassName))) ;

wcex.style = 0 ;
wcex.lpfnWndProc = (WNDPROC) popupWndProc ;
```

```
wcex.cbClsExtra = 0 ;
wcex.cbWndExtra = 0 ;
wcex.hInstance = hinst ;
wcex.hIcon = LoadIcon(hinst, MAKEINTRESOURCE(IDR_POPUP)) ;
wcex.hCursor = LoadCursor (NULL, IDC_ARROW) ;
wcex.hbrBackground = GetStockBrush (GRAY_BRUSH) ;
wcex.lpszMenuName   = (LPCTSTR)NULL ;
wcex.lpszClassName = ClassName ;
wcex.hIconSm        = LoadImage (hinst,
                        MAKEINTRESOURCE (IDR_POPUP),
                        IMAGE_ICON,
                        GetSystemMetrics (SM_CXSMICON),
                        GetSystemMetrics (SM_CYSMICON),
                        LR_SHARED) ;
```

Note that we use the same symbol, IDR_POPUP, to designate the string name of the class and the icon. The numeric value or string name of a resource can be used to define a string resource, a menu resource, an accelerator resource, an icon resource, and so on, since the name has to be unique only within a resource type. So we have carefully chosen a name that has a value that is unique within all resource sets and that allows us to name both a string and an icon using the same name.

The decision whether a pop-up window can be minimized is yours. You can allow a system menu when you create the window or add a minimize box. If you do so (as we have done), you should define a class icon as follows:

```
wc.hIcon = LoadIcon(hinst, MAKEINTRESOURCE(IDR_POPUP)) ;
```

Here, the integer IDR_POPUP identifies the icon resource. Because it is an integer, and LoadIcon is expecting a string name as its second argument, we must use the MAKEINTRESOURCE macro to create a value that is acceptable to the compiler.

The cursor changes to the standard arrow cursor when it's over one of Panes' pop-up windows:

```
wcex.hCursor = LoadCursor (NULL, IDC_ARROW) ;
```

The pop-up windows also have a gray background:

```
wcex.hbrBackground = GetStockBrush (GRAY_BRUSH) ;
```

Finally, Panes registers the PanesChildClass window class. Panes creates its one child window based on the PanesChildClass. The class used for the child window has the same definition as the class used for the pop-up windows, except for some cosmetic differences. When the cursor enters the client area of the child window, it turns into a cross and the client area of the child window has a light gray background:

```
wcex.hCursor = LoadCursor (NULL, IDC_CROSS) ;
wcex.hbrBackground = GetStockBrush (LTGRAY_BRUSH) ;
```

Window Creation in **Panes**

After Panes registers its window classes, it creates several windows. The first is the main application window, which is the same as the main frame window for the Template example. The main application window has a menu. This is because one is specified in the CreateWindowEx function call.

```
hwnd =
    CreateWindowEx (
                    0,                        // Extended window styles
                    ClassName,                // Address of registered class name
                    Title,                    // Address of window name
                    WS_OVERLAPPEDWINDOW,// Window style
                    CW_USEDEFAULT,            // Horizontal position of window
                    0,                        // Vertical position of window
                    CW_USEDEFAULT,            // Window width
                    0,                        // Window height
                    NULL,                     // Handle of parent or owner window
                    LoadMenu(hinst, MAKEINTRESOURCE(IDR_MAINFRAME)),
                                              // Handle of menu
                    hinst,                    // Handle of application instance
                    NULL) ;                   // Address of window-creation data
```

When you specify the menu at the time of window creation, you cannot pass in the string name or numeric ID of a menu resource. Instead, you must pass in the handle to an actual menu. We get this handle by calling the LoadMenu function and specifying in it the resource ID. Because ID is numeric, we use MAKEINTRESOURCE to pass it in and avoid a compiler diagnostic about type mismatches.

Next, Panes creates a second overlapped window that has the main application window as its owner. We wanted the owned window to be one third the size of its owner window so that the initial relative sizes would imply their relationship. We choose a computation based on the client area of the parent window.

Calculating desired height and width is straightforward:

```
GetClientRect (hwndOverlapped, &rect) ;
height = (rect.bottom - rect.top) / 3 ;
width = (rect.right - rect.left) / 3 ;
```

We want to specify the origin in terms of the client area:

```
origin.x = r.left + (width / 3);
origin.y = r.top + 3 * (height / 2);
```

The only problem is that these coordinates are in *client coordinates*, that is, relative to the top left corner of the client area. But when we create an overlapped window, we have to specify *screen coordinates;* client coordinates are not useful here.

Screen coordinates take the origin (0, 0) as the upper-left corner of the Windows display screen. The y-axis increases downwardly (i.e., from the top of the screen to the bottom), and the x-axis increases from the left to the right. Screen coordinates are exactly what are needed when specifying where a window at creation should be positioned on the screen.

We wanted the owned window to be initially placed on top of its owner's window. The coordinates we chose place the window nicely relative to the soon-to-be created child window. We create each window so that it partially overlaps with the others. This visually demonstrates which window styles display "over" other styles. Don't let our desire to position one window relative to another mislead you as to what's occurring. The CreateWindow function sizes and positions an overlapped window relative to the screen origin, not relative to another window. Therefore we have to convert the client coordinate position we've just computed to screen coordinates:

```
ClientToScreen(hwnd, &origin);
```

Specifying the main application window handle as the hwndParent parameter to the CreateWindow function creates this window as an owned window, but the coordinates of this window are not used at all by CreateWindow. This is why we had to do the explicit coordinate conversion. The creation is accomplished by the following statement:

```
hwndOver = CreateWindow (
    ClassName,               /* Class of the window to create   */
    WindowTitle,             /* Window caption text             */
    WS_OVERLAPPEDWINDOW,     /* Window style(s)                 */
    origin.x,                /* Explicit horizontal position    */
    origin.y,                /* Explicit vertical position      */
    width,                   /* Explicit width                  */
    height,                  /* Explicit height                 */
    hwnd,                    /* Owner window                    */
    (HMENU)NULL,             /* Menu to be used for this window */
    hinst,                   /* Instance of module owning window */
    NULL) ;                  /* Ptr to user-defined parameters  */
```

Although the window has been successfully created, it isn't visible until it's shown. Panes shows the window but does not activate it by passing the SW_SHOWNOACTIVATE parameter to the ShowWindow function:

```
ShowWindow (hwndOver, SW_SHOWNOACTIVATE) ;
```

This makes the owned window visible but leaves the main application window active. All subsequent windows are shown after creation with the SW_SHOWNOACTIVATE parameter. For the Panes application, this results in the main application window's remaining the active window. Its title bar will remain highlighted to indicate that it is the active window.

Claiming that the window is now visible is a bit misleading. Windows knows that the window has been made visible but isn't completely displayed. There is an outstanding request for its client area to be painted. As soon as there is nothing much else going on, the window will receive a WM_PAINT message requesting it to paint its client area. Rather than wait for this to happen, you can call the UpdateWindow function, which immediately causes the window to receive a WM_PAINT message:

```
UpdateWindow (hwndOver) ;
```

When the UpdateWindow function returns, the window is displayed on the screen and its client area up-to-date. All the windows created by Panes are updated as soon as they are created, so the user sees the windows appear (and therefore the program running) as quickly as possible.

You might wonder why we go to all this trouble when none of the windows need to update their client area. The window functions don't even process the WM_PAINT message! But they do pass the message to the DefWindowProc function for default processing. The default processing for a WM_PAINT message calls the BeginPaint function, immediately followed by a call to the EndPaint function. While preparing the window to be painted, the BeginPaint function sends a WM_ERASEBKGND message to the window function requesting it to erase the background of the area to be updated.

The window function doesn't process the WM_ERASEBKGND message either. We call the DefWindowProc function to process a WM_ERASEBKGND message just as we do for WM_PAINT messages. The default processing for a WM_ERASEBKGND message sets the window's client area to the background color by using the class background brush. Effectively, the UpdateWindow function call displays the window and sets the client area to the class background color.

Next, Panes creates the two pop-up windows. The createPopupWindow function creates them. Both have the WS_POPUP, WS_BORDER, WS_SYSMENU, and WS_CAPTION styles. The first is unowned, and the second is owned by the main application window. Like an overlapped window, a pop-up window is positioned and sized in screen coordinates. Even though the two windows appear overlapping the main application window, their positions are specified relative to the screen origin. Their sizes and positions depend on whether the window is owned or unowned. The owned window is created relative to its owner, and the coordinates for its position are relative to the client area of its owner. The unowned pop-up is created in the top right corner of the screen, and its creation coordinates are screen relative. The code that does the computation is straightforward; the various size multipliers are just our choice of what makes a nice-looking example:

```
if(hwnd != NULL)
    { /* owned, window-relative */
    GetClientRect(hwnd, &r);
    width = (r.right - r.left) / 3;
    height = (r.bottom - r.top) / 3;
    origin.x = r.left + 2 * width;
    origin.y = r.top + 3 * (height / 2);
    ClientToScreen(hwnd, &origin);
    } /* owned, window-relative */
else
    { /* unowned, screen-relative */
    SetRect(&r, 0, 0, GetSystemMetrics(SM_CXSCREEN),
                    GetSystemMetrics(SM_CYSCREEN));
    width = (r.right - r.left) / 3;
    height = (r.bottom - r.top) / 3;
    // Put in the top right corner of the screen
    origin.x = r.right - width;
    origin.y = 0;
    } /* unowned, screen-relative */
```

Finally, Panes creates its only child window. Creating a child window is slightly different from creating overlapped and pop-up windows. A child window must have a parent window. Windows is a close-knit family and doesn't permit orphans. Also, Windows doesn't give a child window its own screen area in which to display itself. The parent window must provide part of its client area to the child window, and the child window displays in that area. Because a child window always displays in a portion of its parent window's client area, when you create it you make its position as a location relative to the upper-left corner of the parent window's client area, not to the upper-left corner of the parent window or the upper-left corner of the screen.

Panes creates the child window by calling the CreateWindowEx function to demonstrate the use of two extended window styles. You must use this function to create a window having both a dialog frame and a caption, as Panes does:

```
hwndChild = CreateWindowEx (
    WS_EX_DLGMODALFRAME |      /* Extended window styles     */
    WS_EX_NOPARENTNOTIFY,
    ClassName,                 /* Class of the window to create  */
```

```
  Title,                      /* Window caption text          */
  WS_CHILDWINDOW | WS_CAPTION,    /* Window style             */
  pt.x,                       /* Explicit horizontal position */
  pt.y,                       /* Explicit vertical position   */
  width,                      /* Explicit width               */
  height,                     /* Explicit height              */
  hwnd,                       /* Parent window                */
  (HMENU)NULL,                /* Menu to be used for this window */
  hinst,                      /* Instance of module owning window */
  NULL) ;                     /* Ptr to user-defined parameters*/
```

Message Handling in `Panes`

The OnCommand handler is likely the one that you will use most in your daily programming, so it is worth spending a bit more time discussing it. This handler receives four parameters:

1. The handle of the window that received the WM_COMMAND message

2. An integer ID that is either a control ID if the message came from a child control or a menu ID if the message came from a menu item or accelerator.

3. A control handle. If the message came from a child control, this is the handle of the child control. If the message came from a menu item, this value is 0.

4. A notification code that indicates the type of event that occurred. For a child control, this value depends on the nature of the child control. For example, a list box sends an LBN_ notification code, a combo box sends a CBN_ notification code, and an edit control sends an EN_ notification code. The notification code is 0 if the message came from a menu item and 1 if it came from an accelerator.

The Win32 *common controls*, however, do not send WM_COMMAND messages; they send a WM_NOTIFY message. So you will need to know whether you are using one of the built-in controls or one of the common controls and then write different handlers.

WM_COMMAND Message Cracker Handler

```
void cls_OnCommand(HWND hwnd, int id, HWND hctl, UINT codeNotify);
```

Parameter	wParam		lParam		Meaning
	lo	hi	lo	hi	
hwnd					The window handle of the parent window.
id	■				The control ID of a child control; the menu ID of a menu item.
hctl			■	■	The window handle of child control, or 0 if from a menu item or an accelerator.
codeNotify		■			Notification code from the child control; 0 if from a menu item and 1 if from an accelerator.

We use the OnDestroy handler to respond to WM_DESTROY messages. This handler takes only one parameter: the handle of the window.

WM_DESTROY **Message Cracker Handler**

`void cls_OnDestroy(HWND hwnd);`					
	wParam		**lParam**		
Parameter	**lo**	**hi**	**lo**	**hi**	**Meaning**
hwnd					The window handle of the window.

Handling the Pop-up Windows

The PanesPopupClass window differs slightly from the main window or the owned overlapped window. The pop-up windows created by Panes don't really do much. The user can move them and close them, but that behavior is provided by passing a message from the popupWndProc to the DefWindowProc function. The pop-up window class, which handles both the owned and unowned pop-ups, has to deal with only one case: the situation in which the unowned pop-up is destroyed. Because there is no owner, there is no way for the system to be notified that the unowned pop-up has been destroyed, so you need an OnDestroy handler. The file that handles this is shown nearly in its entirety in Listing 3.2.

The popupWndProc function monitors messages to both of the pop-up windows created by the Panes program. When the popupWndProc detects that the user has closed the top-level (unowned) pop-up window, it zeroes a global variable containing a handle to that window. When the user closes the Panes program's top-level overlapped window (which signifies the user is closing the application), the overlapped window function checks this global variable. If the unowned pop-up window has not been destroyed (as indicated by a nonzero handle in the global variable), the overlapped window function destroys the unowned pop-up window.

Windows does destroy existing top-level windows (and therefore the descendants of the windows) when an application terminates. However, it's better for your application not to rely on this behavior. In fact, the debug ("checked kernel") version of Windows issues warnings about an application when the application terminates without destroying all of its top-level windows, as do many third-party debugging aids. The Panes example program properly releases all resources and produces no complaint from the Windows debug version.

Handling the Child Window

A child window is most often used as a *control*, such as a button, a list box, or a check box. However, there is nothing that limits us to these built-in types; here we've created our own child window of our own class. This child window has a caption, but it doesn't have a minimize or maximize box. We've decided that we want to minimize and maximize the window anyway, so we need to provide a way to do this. We see this as an opportunity to demonstrate some more techniques for doing floating pop-up menus.

We need three handlers for this:

1.   The WM_CONTEXTMENU handler takes note of the fact that the right mouse button has been clicked and initiates the pop-up menu processing.

2.   The WM_INITMENUPOPUP handler makes sure the menu items are properly enabled or disabled before the menu is displayed.

3.   The WM_COMMAND handler handles any commands triggered by the menu.

The OnContextMenu handler for the child window is identical to the handler for the main frame. (With a little work, we could have used a single function for all of this, but we wanted to keep this simple.) However, the child_DisplayContextMenu function it calls differs somewhat from the Template handler.

We use a private menu for this purpose, one that is not already in existence. The menu is defined in the resource file like any other menu:

```
IDR_CHILDCONTEXT MENU DISCARDABLE
BEGIN
    POPUP "Popup"
    BEGIN
        MENUITEM "&Restore",              IDM_RESTORE
        MENUITEM "Mi&nimize",             IDM_MINIMIZE
        MENUITEM "Ma&ximize",             IDM_MAXIMIZE
        MENUITEM SEPARATOR
        MENUITEM "&Help Topics...",       ID_HELP_HELP_TOPICS
        MENUITEM SEPARATOR
        MENUITEM "&About Panes...",       ID_APP_ABOUT
    END
END
```

The last few items are just like the normal **Help** menu (and in fact were copied from it), but we've added three new items at the front of it: **Restore**, **Minimize**, and **Maximize**. These are the items that are specific to our child window. We wrap this pop-up menu inside another menu (a "top-level" menu, but we'll never use it that way) called IDR_CHILDCONTEXT. This menu has exactly one submenu: the pop-up menu we want to see on a right mouse click. We have to do this because the TrackPopupMenu function wants the handle to a pop-up menu; if it doesn't have one, it won't work right. The only way to create a pop-up menu in a resource file is to use the POPUP statement, but this only works inside a MENU statement. The menu title, "Popup", is a placeholder and is irrelevant; we just picked a nice, readable name. We could have just as easily called it "xyzzy".

We need to load this menu and extract the pop-up menu from it. We use the LoadMenu function to load the entire menu. Because of how we have created our menu, we know that the very first (and *only*) submenu in it, the one at position 0, is our desired pop-up menu. You should resist any temptation to "optimize" menus by bundling multiple pop-up menus into a single main menu. Unless you've got a very special case, this saves nothing and will cost you a lot in terms of increased maintenance costs over the lifetime of the program.

```
    HMENU hmenu, hmenuPopup ;
    BOOL result;
    hmenu = LoadMenu(GetWindowInstance(hwnd),
                        MAKEINTRESOURCE(IDR_CHILDCONTEXT));
    hmenuPopup = GetSubMenu (hmenu, 0) ;
    ASSERT (NULL != hmenuPopup) ;
```

The code that brings up the pop-up menu is the same that we used in the `mainFrame_OnContextMenu` handler:

```
// Convert click location to screen coordinates
ClientToScreen (hwnd, &pt) ;
result = TrackPopupMenu (hmenuPopup,
                        TPM_LEFTALIGN | TPM_RIGHTBUTTON,
                        pt.x, pt.y, O, hwnd, NULL) ;
```

However, the code is slightly different. Instead of directly returning the result of `TrackPopupMenu`, we have to store the result. This is because we must destroy the menu we loaded. Normally, a menu is associated with a window. When the window is destroyed, the menu associated with it is also destroyed. (This means you can't share the same instance of a menu between two windows without special care, although you can always make multiple menus from the same menu template.) But this pop-up menu is not associated with a window; once created, it will not be automatically destroyed until the program terminates. If you don't explicitly destroy the menu, you will get a new copy of the menu in memory each time you click the right mouse button! So you must call the `DestroyMenu` function to destroy the menu loaded by `LoadMenu`. This destroys the menu that was loaded and all its contained menus, including the submenu we used for the pop-up menu.

```
DestroyMenu(hmenu);
return result;
```

Before the menu comes up, we need to make sure that all of its items are properly enabled. In this case, we don't want to enable the menu selection for the current state of the window. We handle this in the `OnInitMenuPopup` handler.

```
static void
child_OnInitMenuPopup(HWND hwnd, HMENU hmenu, UINT item, BOOL sysmenu)
{
  EnableMenuItem(hmenu, IDM_RESTORE, IsZoomed(hwnd) || IsIconic(hwnd)
                            ? MF_BYCOMMAND | MF_ENABLED
                            : MF_BYCOMMAND | MF_GRAYED);
  EnableMenuItem(hmenu, IDM_MINIMIZE, !IsIconic(hwnd)
                            ? MF_BYCOMMAND | MF_ENABLED
                            : MF_BYCOMMAND | MF_GRAYED);
  EnableMenuItem(hmenu, IDM_MAXIMIZE, !IsZoomed(hwnd)
                            ? MF_BYCOMMAND | MF_ENABLED
                            : MF_BYCOMMAND | MF_GRAYED);
}
```

The `IsZoomed` function returns a nonzero value if the window is maximized, and the `IsIconic` function returns a nonzero value if the window is iconic.

When the user selects one of these menu items, the window receives a `WM_COMMAND` message. This message is routed to the `OnCommand` handler:

```
static void child_OnCommand(HWND hwnd, int id, HWND hctl, UINT codenotify)
{
// We could have commands that are unique to this window, or general
// commands. If we recognize the command, do it, otherwise pass to
// our parent

switch(id)
    { /* id */
```

```
    case IDM_RESTORE:
            ShowWindow(hwnd, SW_RESTORE);
            return;
    case IDM_MINIMIZE:
            ShowWindow(hwnd, SW_MINIMIZE);
            return;
    case IDM_MAXIMIZE:
            ShowWindow(hwnd, SW_MAXIMIZE);
            return;
    } /* id */
  FORWARD_WM_COMMAND(GetParent(hwnd), id, hctl, codenotify, SendMessage);
}
```

The three special menu items we've added are processed by calling the ShowWindow function with the appropriate SW_ code. Because we share menu items with the main window, which is our parent, any menu item message we don't handle we pass to our parent using FORWARD_WM_COMMAND.

Handling the Overlapped Windows

Panes lets Windows, via the DefWindowProc function, handle most of the work for these windows. All messages for all windows are passed back to Windows by calling DefWindowProc. The mainWndProc function--the window function for the overlapped windows–processes the WM_COMMAND and WM_DESTROY messages (as well as all the other messages that Template processes). The popupWndProc function–the window function for the pop-up windows–processes only the WM_DESTROY message. The childWndProc handles the WM_COMMAND, WM_INITMENUPOPUP, and WM_CONTEXTMENU messages. Generally, a window function processes a message the same for all windows of its class. That is, in general, you shouldn't process a message one way for window A and a different way for window B. The WM_DESTROY message is one typical exception to that rule.

You must process at least one WM_DESTROY message and post a WM_QUIT message to terminate the application. If you fail to call the PostQuitMessage function at least once, your application will never terminate. Removing the WM_DESTROY handling code in the mainWndProc function results in a program that appears to run and appears to terminate successfully. You can close all windows, and no evidence that the program is running is visible. However, if you examine the task list, such as by using the pview program supplied with the Microsoft Win32 SDK, you will see the Panes program still exists. It is running its message loop, but there is no window to receive the messages.

Placing a call to PostQuitMessage as the response to a WM_DESTROY message for an overlapped window has a side effect we don't want. Closing either of the two overlapped windows (via the **Close** option on the system menu) sends a WM_DESTROY message for the window. That means that closing either window would cause the PostQuitMessage call to be made and the application to terminate. It seems more sensible to terminate the application only when the overlapped window with the menu (i.e., the main application window) is closed. Closing the owned, overlapped window shouldn't really do much other than make it disappear. We use the following code to provide this behavior:

```
static void mainFrame_OnDestroy(HWND hwnd)
    {
    if (GetWindowOwner (hwnd) == NULL) {
```

```
          if (UnownedPopup != NULL)
               DestroyWindow (UnownedPopup) ;
          WinHelp (hwnd, getHelpFileName (), HELP_QUIT, (DWORD) 0) ;
          PostQuitMessage (0) ;
     }
}
```

The main application window does not have an owner, whereas the other overlapped window does. We obtain the window handle of the soon-to-be destroyed window's owner. We destroy the unowned pop-up window and post the WM_QUIT message only if the window being destroyed does not have an owner (it must therefore be the main application window).

Running the program gives you the best feel for the different behavior of each kind of window, but we'll point out a few things to notice. The windows appear in their location and stacking order as a result of their creation order.

Because the main application window and the unowned pop-up window are unowned, they are considered to be independent of each other. Windows places the active window on top of the inactive one. Activating the main application window (by clicking it) forces it "over" all other windows except those that it owns.

Unowned windows also appear in the Windows NT 3.*x* Task Manager's list of windows or the Windows 95 or Windows NT 4.*x* task bar just as if they were created by independent programs. You can switch to any unowned window–overlapped or pop-up–by using the **Switch To** command of the Win-

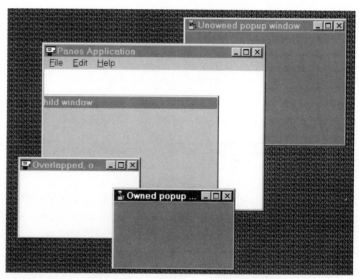

Figure 3.8: The stacking order of various windows of the Panes program

dows NT 3.*x* Task Manager or clicking the icon in the Windows 95 or Windows NT 4.*x* task bar. You can request Windows NT 3.*x* to display its Task Manager task list dialog box by either pressing **Ctrl+Esc**, double-clicking the right mouse button outside all windows (that is, on the Windows desktop), or running the taskman.exe program located in your Windows directory.

Owned windows always display above their owner window. Child windows display in their parent window's client area and always lie under windows owned by their parent window. Any portions of a child window extending outside the boundaries of its parent window's client area are clipped and are not displayed. Some artful rearrangement of the various windows demonstrates these points in Figure 3.8.

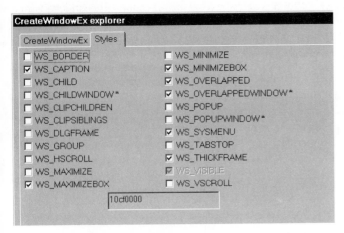

Figure 3.9: Window Explorer: Base style selection (secondary page)

You've read how to structure a Windows program and the various kinds of windows you can create. So far, however, there's been lots of talk and little action. Now we show you how to do something useful with a window. In the next chapter, you'll see how to display text in a window and scroll the window to see the text. We'll use this capability to display information about the Windows environment.

The Window Explorer

The Window Explorer application lets you create a window with any of the basic or extended styles. The window can be a top-level overlapped window, an owned overlapped window, an owned pop-up window, or a child window. It can have an optional menu. The two options pages of the Window Explorer are shown in Figure 3.9 and Figure 3.10. You can select the base

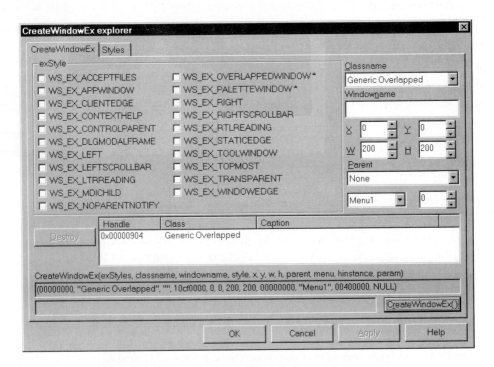

Figure 3.10: Window Explorer: Extended style selection (main page)

styles and the extended styles, a window class, a parent window, and a menu (for nonchild windows) or child ID (for child windows). You also can specify the position and size. When you click the `CreateWindowEx` button, a window will be created. You can click the right button over the window and get a pop-up menu that lets you destroy it. Most of the illustrations in this chapter were created with the Window Explorer.

Further Reading

Brain, Marshall, *Win32 System Services: The Heart of Windows NT*, PTR Prentice Hall, 1994. ISBN 0-13-097825-6.

> This book covers a lot of the techniques required for writing NT System Services, a topic well beyond the scope of our book.

Deaton, Mary and Zuback, Cheryl Lockett, *Designing Windows 95 Help: A Guide to Creating Online Documents*, Que Corporation, 1996. ISBN 0-7897-0362-9.

> This book covers in exquisite detail everything from the new Help Engine facilities, through the basics of help document design, to coverage of the more esoteric features of help macros and design guidelines for making useful, accessible, and effective online documents. I particularly like the points about indexing given on page 213 of this book. Most online help fails utterly because the content is inaccessible. This book explains how you must do the indexing to make it effective. (When applied in overkill, the result is often something more akin to the index of our book–massive is an understatement. But I wanted an index in our book like the indexes I wished all other Windows books had, and probably went too far!) But the number of useless online help files is so large that it is clear that the importance of topic access (of which indexing is only a part–hyperlinks, pop-up help, and topic lists are also critical design areas) is very plainly missed by most help authors. Remember: the person reading your help *doesn't know the answer* and it is your responsibility to help them find it. Deaton and Zuback understand this, and many other important issues about how to make effective help files. It isn't just the gadgetry; it is the philosophy. I consider this book a "must read".

Lindsay, Peter H. and Norman Donald A., *Human Information Processing, Second edition*, Academic Press, 1977 (now Harcourt Brace Jovanovich).

> This book covers such basic principles as pattern recognition, spatial perception, neural perception, the visual system, auditory perception, memory, language development, etc. It is a fundamental text on principles of cognitive psychology, but it actually says *nothing* about GUI design. But the principles gleaned from this can guide your GUI efforts. Such concepts as focus of attention, modality, reaction time, mental modeling, the human inference mechanism, and many related topics are treated in depth. The book is surprisingly readable and gives you insight into the "U" part of "GUI".

Microsoft Corporation, *The Windows Interface Guidelines for Software Design*, Microsoft Press, 1995. ISBN 1-55615-679-0.

> This book is required reading for all GUI designers. You may not always like Microsoft's choices; you may in fact disagree with them completely. But you need to know what they are so that you know that when you are deviating from the expected standard, you *are* deviating deliberately and

not accidentally. You will also read about some subtleties about the GUI specification you didn't know. This book is not optional.

Mischel, Jim, *The Developer's Guide to WINHELP.EXE: Harnessing the Windows Help Engine*, John Wiley & Sons, 1994. ISBN 0-471-30325-4.

This book comes in two editions: with and without an accompanying disk. Be sure you get the "with" edition! This book is based on the Windows 3.1 help engine, but most of the ideas carry across (the Win32 help engine is more powerful). It is a programmer-oriented approach, showing, for example, how to build extension DLLs for your Help file and showing how to use many undocumented features of the help engine.

Norman, Donald A., *The Design of Everyday Things* [formerly *The Psychology of Everyday Things*], Doubleday/Currency, 1990. ISBN 0-385-26774-6.

Norman, Donald A., *The Psychology of Everyday Things*, Basic Books, 1988. ISBN 0-465-06709-3. Reprinted as *The Design of Everyday Things* (see above citation).

Why are VCRs hard to program? What makes a good main entrance door? Why are some phones easy to use and others impossible to master? Why is the FrameMaker user interface so clumsy? Why is any interface that uses cursor keys and function keys hard for professional typists to use? Why are mice both highly effective and virtually unusable? What are the three basic design errors of the standard scroll bar? The basis for understanding how to ask these questions and how to avoid making GUI design errors that conflict with basic human perception and motor skills is discussed in this eminently readable book, no matter which title you read it under. This should be a Must Read for every GUI designer. If the designers of the current GUI systems had read this book, we would now have vastly better and far more usable interfaces.

Schneiderman, Ben, *Designing the User Interface: Strategies for Effective Human-Computer Interaction (2nd edition)*, Addison-Wesley, 1992. ISBN 0-201-57286-9.

ANTHONY G. DICKSON
President and Chief Executive Officer

NEW JERSEY MANUFACTURERS INSURANCE COMPANY

301 Sullivan Way, West Trenton, NJ 08628
609-883-1300 / www.NJM.com

Policy Number: F591333-0

Brian Jackson
17 Saw Mill Dr
Somerset NJ 08873
llll..l..l.l..l.l..lll..l..l.l..ll..l..ll..l.ll..ll..ll

Dear Mr. Jackson:

Enclosed is the renewal offer for your New Jersey Manufacturers Insurance Company personal auto policy. We thank you for your business and appreciate the stability that comes with long-term relationships with our customers.

Just as we hope to have a long-term relationship with you, all of our policyholders deserve to know that NJM is financially sound and remains dedicated to serving their needs for many years to come. Since several insurers have announced plans to leave New Jersey, concerns have been raised about the ability of the remaining auto insurers to handle a tremendous amount of customers who are newly shopping around. We want you to know that requests by new customers have increased recently, but our focus will continue to be serving you and our other existing policyholders first.

Thanks to our philosophy — operating exclusively for the benefit of policyholders — NJM is one of the strongest and most efficient property-casualty insurance companies in the nation. We are dedicated to providing quality service to New Jersey drivers, and we will work with State officials to assure that we can fulfill our commitment to you even as market conditions around us become difficult.

The renewal questionnaire presents the best opportunity for policyholders to tell us about how their insurance needs might have changed. Do you have a child about to obtain a learner's permit? Have you changed jobs, affecting the number of miles you travel? Letting us know how your driving habits might have changed is the best way to make sure you get the coverage you need at the fairest possible premium.

This is also the time to consider your levels of coverage. Perhaps your income has increased or you've purchased a new home or business. You might want to increase your liability limits. Or, perhaps you want greater Personal Injury Protection (PIP) to protect you or your family in case of an accident. Maybe you want to change your deductibles for Collision or Comprehensive coverage. Any of these changes have an effect on your premium.

Thank you for choosing NJM as your auto insurance provider. We are more than happy to address any questions you might have regarding your coverage. Please continue to drive safely.

Very truly yours,

Anthony G. Dickson

4 Displaying Text in a Window

In previous chapters, you read how to create various types of windows, but the windows haven't been terribly useful. The client area–all that empty space inside the window border–has been empty, a gaping void just waiting to be filled. In this chapter, you'll find out how to fill that void with text.

Once you decide to display some information in a window, questions immediately start popping up. How do you do it? What specifies where the text goes and how it appears? How much information can be displayed? How do you align columns of text? What do you do when the window isn't big enough to show everything at once? When should you display the information? The list goes on, but we think this gives you the sense that displaying information in a windowing environment is a bit more complicated than deciding in which row (out of 25) and in which column (out of 80) a field should be displayed.

Although all these concerns are valid, you shouldn't let them overwhelm you. We address each one in turn and, taken singly, each isn't difficult to solve.

In this chapter, you'll read about how to do the following:

- Obtain information about the system by calling the `GetSystemMetrics` function.

- Obtain information about the display device by calling the `GetDeviceCaps` function.

- Display text in a window using a display context.

- Scroll the contents of a window, when necessary, so that a user can view more information than can be displayed in the window.

- Use a technique called *subclassing* to separate the display and scrolling tasks. Subclassing allows you to write more modular and reusable code.

The Sysinfo example program presented later in the chapter shows you one way to use all these features. It creates a window class that can scroll the contents of a window. It also creates two additional window classes that display information about the system metrics and display device used to run the Sysinfo program. Each of these two window classes subclasses the scrolling window class to add the ability to scroll the text in their respective windows. The information itself is displayed in each window using the default proportional spaced font provided by Windows.

All output to a window in Microsoft Windows is displayed on the graphical display by calling the appropriate Graphics Device Interface (GDI) functions. The GDI functions used to retrieve text information, alter text alignment, alter text justification, and write text on a device or display surface are briefly described in Table 4.1.

Table 4.1: GDI functions for text information and display

Function Name	Description
DrawText	Draws formatted text into a specified rectangle.
DrawTextEx	Draws formatted text into a specified rectangle; allows additional specification of drawing parameters.
ExtTextOut	Writes a character string, within a rectangular region, using the currently selected font. The region can be opaque (filled with the current background color), and it can be a clipping region.
GetCharWidth	Retrieves the widths of consecutive characters in a range of consecutive characters in the current font.
GetCharABCWidths	Retrieves the "ABC" widths of consecutive characters in a specified range from the current TrueType font. We explain these in more detail in Chapter 15, page 1103.
GetCharABCWidthsFloat	Retrieves the "ABC" widths of consecutive characters in a specified range from the current TrueType font.
GetOutlineTextMetrics	Returns the metrics for the currently selected TrueType font.
GetTabbedTextExtent	Computes the height and width of a line of text possibly containing tab characters.
GetTextAlign	Returns the current text alignment flags. These flags determine how the TextOut and ExtTextOut functions align the text in relation to the given starting point.
GetTextCharacterExtra	Returns the current intercharacter spacing. This is also known as "track kerning," since it applies uniformly to all characters in the string, not to character pairs. We discuss this in great detail in Chapter 15, page 1107.
GetTextColor	Returns the current text color.
GetTextExtentPoint32	Computes the width and height of the specified text string and updates a SIZE structure.
GetTextFace	Returns the typeface name of the currently selected font.
GetTextMetrics	Returns the metrics for the currently selected font.

Table 4.1: GDI functions for text information and display

Function Name	Description
`GrayString`	Draws gray text at the specified location.
`SetTextAlign`	Sets the text alignment flags.
`SetTextCharacterExtra`	Sets the amount of intercharacter spacing.
`SetTextColor`	Sets the text color.
`SetTextJustification`	Sets the parameters used by GDI to justify a line of text.
`TabbedTextOut`	Writes a character string on the specified device, using the currently selected font, and expands tabs to the specified columns.
`TextOut`	Writes a character string on the specified device, using the currently selected font.

Device and Display Contexts

All GDI functions require a *device context* as a parameter. A device context is a link between your application, a device driver, and an associated output device, such as a printer or plotter. You make calls to GDI functions to request certain output operations. GDI forwards these requests (which are device-independent) to the particular device driver associated with the device. The device driver translates the device-independent request into one or more device-dependent operations.

You can obtain a *device* context for the system display device, but normally one isn't needed. A device context for the graphical display allows you to write anywhere on the device, even on top of another application's window. Instead, you generally use a *display* context when displaying in a window. A *display context* is simply a special device context. It treats each window as a separate display surface. An application using a display context for a window can write anything it wants in that window. It cannot, however, access or draw over any part of the system display that lies outside the window.

A display context can be viewed as a cache of drawing information for a window. Everything that GDI needs to know to properly output to a window is maintained in the display context. We examine display contexts in detail in Chapter 5, "Examining a Device Context in Depth". In this chapter, we only skim the surface of the display context pool.

When Do You Get a Display Context?

Each of the functions listed in Table 4.1 requires as a first parameter the handle to a device or display context. A display context handle is like all other handles in Windows. It is simply a token that Windows gives to you that represents an object, in this case, a display context. You give it back to Windows to specify the particular display context you're using.

So you need to obtain a display context handle before you can display anything. Display contexts generally should be allocated as needed and released as quickly as possible (we will ignore for the moment the CS_CLASSDC and CS_WINDOWDC options available under RegisterClass).

Display contexts were, in Win16, generally valuable and limited resources. You were not supposed to grab one and hoard it. Doing so could prevent other Windows applications, and even Windows itself, from obtaining a display context. Without one, the other Windows applications can't display anything. The end result is generally a system that appears to be frozen. This limitation is largely relaxed in Win32. However, you should be very careful not to keep allocating display contexts because, like any other memory allocation, you will eventually glut your memory with them. But the *real* reason you should obey the discipline of not hoarding a display context is that if your application runs using Win32s, it suffers from the same limitations of Win16. As a result, a program that operates perfectly well on Windows 95 or Windows NT will freeze the system on Win32s unless it is well-behaved with respect to display context allocation.

Therefore the question raised in this section's heading is easily answered. You should get a display context handle only when you are ready to display output, and you should release it as soon as the output is complete. This naturally leads into the next question: When exactly should a Windows program display its output? We're glad you asked!

Displaying Output upon Receipt of a WM_PAINT Message

The title says it all. You should structure your Windows application to perform output operations only when Windows notifies it that the client area of a window needs to be painted. Windows does this by sending a WM_PAINT message to the window.

This isn't to say that you can't draw at other times. You can. However, anything you draw in the client area will be erased the next time the window function receives a WM_PAINT message that affects that part of the client area. This is a result of the default message processing supplied by Windows.

Windows sends a WM_ERASEBKGND message to the window function when processing a WM_PAINT message. The DefWindowProc function processes the WM_ERASEBKGND message by filling the affected area using the class background brush. This erases any output you may have drawn previously.

Windows places a WM_PAINT message in an application's queue whenever the client area of the window needs to be repainted. A window can receive a WM_PAINT message whenever one of the following events occurs:

- A previously obscured area of the window becomes visible. This can happen when a user moves the window out from under another window or a covering window is moved or closed. Removing a dialog box or pop-up menu may also cause a window to receive a WM_PAINT message, even though Windows attempts to minimize the numbers of such occurrences. (See the discussion on the CS_SAVEBITS class style in Chapter 3, page 112 for more information.)

- The user resizes the window (only if the window class has either the CS_HREDRAW style or the CS_VREDRAW style or both).

- The contents of the client area of the window are explicitly invalidated via a call to either the InvalidateRect or InvalidateRgn functions.

- The contents of the client area of the window are scrolled via a call to the ScrollWindow function. The area uncovered then needs to be repainted.

Basically, this all means that the client area of a window can become invalid at any time because of forces beyond your control. Therefore your window function must be able to redraw its client area completely at any time. For some programs, redrawing the window is a simple task. Others may have to keep an extensive history of output to the window so that it can be used to redraw the window.

A well-designed Windows application concentrates all display output in the WM_PAINT message processing logic rather than sprinkling output statements throughout the program. When any part of your program (other than the WM_PAINT message processing code) wishes to redraw a portion of a window, it should simply notify Windows that the particular area of the window needs to be updated. As a result of this notification, Windows will eventually send a WM_PAINT message to the window function. The WM_PAINT message processing logic can then redraw the areas in need of update.

You notify Windows that an area of a window needs to be redrawn, or, in other words, is currently *invalid*, by calling either the InvalidateRect function or the InvalidateRgn function. These functions mark a rectangle or region of the client area of a window as invalid and in need of redrawing. All invalidated areas of a window—those that Windows adds and those that your application adds—are accumulated into an *update region*.

The term *region*, as used by Windows, denotes a special type of area. A region is an area that is a combination of rectangles, other polygons, and ellipses. For example, you can invalidate a rectangular area of the window, two elliptical areas, and a few polygonal areas and Windows will combine all these areas into the *region* that needs to be updated, the *update region*. A region cannot describe an arbitrarily shaped figure. That is, it cannot describe areas that cannot be decomposed into a combination of rectangles, polygons, and ellipses. However, Windows is good about building these combinations; you can even give the outline of text and Windows will construct enough rectangles, polygons, and ellipses to approximate the text outline.

An update region defines the part of the client area that needs to be repainted on the next WM_PAINT message. An update region saves some applications from having to paint the entire contents of the client area or from making many incremental changes to the client area. All changes to the client area are accumulated and delivered by one WM_PAINT message.

Doing this may at first seem like a roundabout way to get something done. However, it likely will soon become natural for you, and it can be quite efficient for many applications. If you are coming to Windows programming from the more traditional DOS or Unix styles, and have not seen this style of deferred painting before, be warned that this "paradigm shift" is one of the major hurdles in learning to "think Windows". You will have to master it. This method of maintaining the contents of the screen forms a deep and fundamental part of how Windows operates.

If you decide to update a specific part of the window before receiving a WM_PAINT message, you should call either the ValidateRect or ValidateRgn functions to remove a given rectangle or region from the update region. If there is no update region remaining, Windows will remove the WM_PAINT message from the queue.

Having stressed the importance of waiting until you receive a WM_PAINT message to draw in a window, we should mention that the wait can occasionally be longer than expected. Windows does not actually place a WM_PAINT message in your application's message queue. Instead, it sets a flag indicating that a WM_PAINT message needs to be sent to the appropriate window function. Messages can be posted to the message queue after Windows sets the WM_PAINT message pending flag. The GetMessage function will retrieve any messages waiting in the message queue. When there are none, the GetMessage function looks in the system queue for pending mouse and keyboard messages for the application. Finally, Windows checks to see if any timer event that requires a WM_TIMER message has occurred (see Chapter 7, page 504). Only if no message is found will the GetMessage function check the pending WM_PAINT message flag. When it finds the pending WM_PAINT message flag set, the GetMessage function synthesizes a WM_PAINT message and returns it. This means that WM_PAINT is the lowest-priority message in the system.

If you invalidate additional areas of a window after Windows sets the WM_PAINT message pending flag but before the WM_PAINT message is retrieved, Windows does not request that additional WM_PAINT messages be synthesized. Instead, it adds the newly invalidated areas to the previous area. When you retrieve a WM_PAINT message, the update region includes all changes up to the time when you retrieve the message.

Here's the reasoning behind this approach. Whereas the presence of a pending WM_PAINT message means the window needs to be redrawn to some extent, other messages in the queue are requests for the window function to perform some additional processing. This additional processing could cause areas of the window to need to be redrawn. If you painted the window and then processed the messages, you might find that something that was just drawn needs to be redrawn. Saving the WM_PAINT message until last lets you redraw all changes at once. This reduces wasted effort and annoying flickering of the display caused by rapid repainting of the screen.

How Do You Get a Display Context?

There are two ways to obtain a handle to a display context. In the first way, you use the GetDC function to retrieve a handle to a display context for the client area any time you need one other than when you're processing a WM_PAINT message. The following example shows how to use the GetDC function to do this and to use it to obtain metrics for the currently selected font:

```
HDC        hdc ;
HWND       hwnd ;
TEXTMETRIC tm ;

    .
    .
    .
hdc = GetDC (hwnd) ;
GetTextMetrics (hdc, &tm) ;
ReleaseDC (hwnd, hdc) ;
```

This example calls the GetDC function to retrieve a handle to the display context for the client area of the window identified by the hwnd parameter. It then calls the GetTextMetrics function, which copies metrics about the currently selected font into the TEXTMETRIC structure identified by the tm parameter. The display context is then released back to Windows via a call to the ReleaseDC function. You also use the GetDC function when you need to draw something as an immediate response to a user's action rather than wait for a WM_PAINT message. An example is drawing a rubber-band rectangle in response to mouse movements.

You may have noticed that we don't keep track of the font in the window. This is because the window itself can do it. If we want to change the font, we can use the WM_SETFONT message or the SetWindowFont macro API to set the window's font (we discuss fonts in Chapter 15). Once this is done, the DC will have the correct font established.

The second way to obtain a handle to the display context for the client area of a window is to call the BeginPaint function when processing a WM_PAINT message. You process a WM_PAINT message as shown in the following code fragment:

```
static void cls_OnPaint(HWND hwnd)
    {
    HDC hdc ;
    PAINTSTRUCT ps ;
    hdc = BeginPaint (hwnd, &ps) ;
    //... Output operations go here
    EndPaint (hwnd, &ps) ;
    }
```

This is normally called from your window procedure via the HANDLE_MSG call:

```
    HANDLE_MSG(hwnd, WM_PAINT, cls_OnPaint);
```

WM_PAINT Message Cracker Handler

void cls_OnPAINT(HWND hwnd);					
	wParam		lParam		
Parameter	lo	hi	lo	hi	Meaning
hwnd					A window handle of a window.

The BeginPaint function updates the PAINTSTRUCT structure, ps, with information about the paint request. It also returns a handle to a display context for the window. You use this handle as a parameter to all GDI output functions used to repaint the window. The EndPaint function ends the paint request and releases the display context back to Windows.

You cannot use the GetDC and ReleaseDC functions in place of the BeginPaint and EndPaint functions. BeginPaint and EndPaint perform special functions in addition to returning a handle to the display context. For example, the BeginPaint function sends the WM_ERASEBKGND message that causes the background of the invalid area to be erased, retrieves the update region (the part of the client area that needs to be redrawn), and validates the previously invalid areas of the window.

The invalid areas of a window are *not* validated by drawing in them. Calling the BeginPaint and EndPaint functions causes Windows to consider the window fully up-to-date (validated) whether or not you perform any drawing. If you use GetDC instead of BeginPaint, you can draw in the window, but you will not validate the invalid areas of the window. When you return from processing the WM_PAINT message, Windows will consider the window still in need of updating and will send you the same WM_PAINT message. Because the paint request will never be satisfied, Windows will keep sending you the same paint request over and over.

 In all versions of Windows, consuming all the available display contexts will give your program the appearance of having frozen up, but in Win32s you will not be able to do anything else because of the cooperative multi-tasking. Short of using **Ctrl+Alt+Del** to force the task to terminate, there is no recovery. In Windows 95 and Windows NT, you can actually do something else to another application while this is occurring. In particular, you can bring up the Task Manager in Windows NT 3.x, activate the task bar in Windows 95 and Windows NT 4.x, or bring up the pview (process status viewer) utility. You can even bring up the Spy program and watch the infinite number of WM_PAINT messages fly by.

The DefWindowProc function processes a WM_PAINT message by simply calling BeginPaint, followed immediately by a call to EndPaint. This action erases the invalid area and validates it, thus removing the WM_PAINT message from the queue.

Processing a WM_PAINT Message

You've already seen the first step of processing a WM_PAINT message. You retrieve a handle to the window's display context by calling the BeginPaint function. But the BeginPaint function also updates a PAINTSTRUCT structure. The structure looks like the following:

```
typedef struct tagPAINTSTRUCT
    {
    HDC     hdc;
    BOOL    fErase;
    RECT    rcPaint;
    BOOL    fRestore;
    BOOL    fIncUpdate;
    BYTE    rgbReserved[32];
    } PAINTSTRUCT;
```

The hdc field is the same display context handle as the one returned by the BeginPaint function. These values can be referenced interchangeably, but it takes less effort to use the value returned by the function call.

The fErase field is a Boolean value representing whether the background of the invalid area of the window has been erased. When the value is TRUE (nonzero), the BeginPaint function has sent a WM_ERASEBKGND message to the window function requesting it to erase the invalid area. Normally, a window function passes this message to the DefWindowProc function. This function erases the background of the invalid area by using the background brush that you specified when you registered the window's class. When the value is FALSE (zero), the background has not been erased.

Generally, this field is set to TRUE. However, as mentioned earlier in the chapter you can explicitly invalidate a portion of the client area of a window by calling the InvalidateRect or InvalidateRgn functions and specifying a rectangle or region, respectively, to be added to the window's update region. The third parameter to both functions specifies whether you want the background within the update area to be erased. If this parameter is FALSE, the background remains unchanged and the fErase field of the PAINTSTRUCT will be FALSE.

The rcPaint field is a RECTangle structure. Recall that a RECT structure looks like this:

```
typedef struct tagRECT
  {
   int    left;
   int    top;
   int    right;
   int    bottom;
  } RECT;
```

The rcPaint rectangle specifies the upper-left and lower-right corners of the rectangle that contains the *update region* in client coordinates. These are in units of pixels relative to the upper-left corner of the window's client area. If the entire client area of the window needs to be repainted, the rcPaint rectangle will be the same as a rectangle obtained by the GetClientRect function. Normally, much less than the entire client area of a window needs to be redrawn; the rcPaint field describes this area. Although it doesn't hurt anything (except performance) to repaint the entire window in response to a WM_PAINT message, you should use this rectangle to determine which items need to be redrawn and not display the others.

The invalid area of the window–the update region–may not be rectangular because regions may include polygonal and elliptical areas in addition to rectangular ones. The BeginPaint function, however, provides a rectangle (the rcPaint field of the PAINTSTRUCT structure) describing the update region. This rectangle actually describes the smallest bounding rectangle that completely surrounds the update region. When deciding what part of the window needs to be repainted, you'll find it's much easier to use a rectangular area rather than a possibly complex region. Even when your program uses the described rectangle, however, and redraws only those areas of the window that lie within that rectangle, only the areas that lie within the update region will be changed.

Windows selects the update region as the *clipping region* of the display context. When you issue a drawing request, GDI draws only those pixels that lie within the clipping region. All drawing that extends outside a clipping region is discarded. So even if you decide to redraw the entire window upon receipt of a WM_PAINT request, GDI will discard all output outside the update region. Sometimes it's best to go to the additional effort of determining what needs to be redrawn and to draw only those items.

The use of a rectangle to approximate the invalid area of the window provides a theoretical trade-off. Drawing in the invalid rectangle still can result in a bit more drawing than is absolutely necessary. This could still be faster, though, than determining exactly which portions of an update region need to be redrawn and then redrawing them. Generally, only rectangular areas are invalidated (pop-up menus disappear, dialog boxes close, rectangular windows are moved off a window). As a result, the invalid rectangle for a window is identical to the update region, and redrawing the rectangle involves exactly the minimum amount of work needed to update the window. If your application tends to invalidate small but widely separated areas and the cost of computing the update is very high, you may wish to actually look at the underlying region. The GetUpdateRgn call allows you to obtain the actual region description, which you can then use to determine exactly what parts of the screen you are going to redraw.

The remaining three fields of the PAINTSTRUCT structure–fRestore, fIncUpdate, and rbgReserved–are used internally by Windows and should not be modified.

Using `TextOut` to Display Text

We're finally ready to actually display something. Let's try "`Hello, world!`"–the old standby.

```
static void cls_OnPaint(HWND hwnd)
    {
    HDC              hdc ;
    PAINTSTRUCT      ps ;
    hdc = BeginPaint (hwnd, &ps) ;
    TextOut (hdc, 50, 50, "Hello, world!", 13) ;
    EndPaint (hwnd, &ps) ;
    }
```

The only difference from the previous example is the addition of a call to the `TextOut` function. The `TextOut` function has the following prototype in the windows.h header file:

```
BOOL WINAPI TextOut (HDC hdc, int x, int y, LPCTSTR lpString, int Count) ;
```

and is often used as follows:

```
TextOut (hdc, x, y, String, lstrlen(String)) ;
```

The first parameter is the handle to the display context to be used. In the previous example, this is the handle returned by the `BeginPaint` function.

A display context has many attributes. These are set to default values when the display context is created. A number of them affect the display of text. One such attribute is the *text color*, which is black by default. Another is the *background color*, which is white by default. A third is the *background mode*, which is "opaque" by default. When you display text using the `TextOut` (or any other text-drawing) function, Windows uses these attributes from the display context. Unless you change one of them, the text displays as black characters on a white background.

Figure 4.1:
Opaque
background

Figure 4.2:
Transparent
background

Windows always displays the character itself in the text color. Each character is contained within a *character cell*. When the background mode is *opaque*, the default, Windows fills the area around the character but within the character cell (the rectangle containing the pixels of the character) with the background color, as shown in Figure 4.1. When the background mode is *transparent*, Windows does not fill the area around the character; the area remains its current color(s), as shown in Figure 4.2. Frequently, this makes no difference, but when you have a colored background for the text, it can change entirely how the text looks.

It's important to realize that the background color from the display context isn't the same as the background brush specified in the window class. The background brush for the window class doesn't have to be a pure color, and it can have a pattern. Should you change the class background brush to a gray patterned brush and use the default display context attributes when displaying text, you'll see your text as black characters in white character cells, which are surrounded by the gray background of the window, an effect very much like we show in Figure 4.1. You can also see this effect in another context if you experiment with the CtlColor Explorer we describe in Chapter 17.

The second and third parameters to the `TextOut` function are the *x*- and *y*-coordinates that specify the point in the client area at which to start displaying the characters. The *x* parameter is the horizontal position in the client area, and the *y* parameter is the vertical position. Additional attributes of the display context affect the interpretation of the *x*- and *y*-values.

The fourth and fifth parameters to the `TextOut` function are a pointer to an array of characters and the number of characters from the array to display. Unlike most C runtime library functions, the `TextOut` function does not use a NUL-terminated string. The supplied count should not include the NUL character at the end of the string. If it does, the NUL byte will display as a solid block. The `TextOut` function does not interpret control characters such as backspaces, carriage returns, formfeeds, linefeeds, tabs, or vertical tabs. These are also displayed as solid blocks. Your program must provide any required cursor control. Rather than embed a carriage return and linefeed into the string, you'll have to display the two lines by making two separate calls to the TextOut function.

Logical Coordinates and Device Coordinates

All coordinates to GDI drawing functions, such as the `TextOut` function, are specified in *logical coordinates.* Drawing operations on a device require *device coordinates.* It's quite easy to use one coordinate system mistakenly when the other is required. Unfortunately, the default mode in which GDI operates permits you to make this mistake and get away with it. Programs containing such an error will work until you try to use "tried and true code" under other than the default conditions. It's important to understand the difference between the two coordinate systems from the start. We cover the basics here and go into depth on the available variations of logical coordinate systems in Chapter 5.

Within limits, you can define a logical coordinate system to be any coordinate system that is convenient for the application. You can specify the size of a unit in the logical coordinate system. You can specify the size in term of physical dimensions, pixels, or scaling factors. The size of a logical unit horizontally doesn't need to equal the size of a logical unit vertically. You can also specify the orientation of the axes of the logical coordinate system. The most common limitation encountered is Windows's use of 16-bit two's-complement integers as coordinate values. This limits the range of coordinate values from -32,768 to +32,767. Not until you get to Windows NT is this limitation relaxed.

Windows NT allows you to have full 32-bit coordinates. But you must be very careful. If you expect your Win32 application to run on both Windows 95 and Windows NT, you can't really take advantage of the 32-bit coordinate system. Windows 95 uses 32-bit integers to define coordinates, but it still limits their value to the range -32768..32767 (and in fact looks only at the low-order 16 bits of the 32-bit coordinate system!).

The ability to draw figures using logical coordinates is extremely helpful to a Windows programmer. You can establish a logical coordinate system that is appropriate to the task at hand and subsequently draw figures in terms familiar to the application rather than deal with issues particular to the actual display device. For example, it might be easier to write an application that displays text in different fonts if the text were written to the window using coordinates specified in points (a unit of character height measurement) vertically and average character width horizontally. You might wish to use the coordinate (10, 24) as meaning "the point that is displaced from the origin horizontally 10 times the width of an average character and vertically a distance equal to 24 points" (roughly $^{24}/_{72}$ inch).

An application intended for drawing building plans would naturally use a physical measurement coordinate system. You might like the application to use coordinates in feet because that may have been the original units used to describe a building. You can decide that a one millimeter long line on the display will represent one foot (one logical unit) and define such a logical coordinate system. In this logical coordinate system, the coordinate (10, 24) means "the point that is located 10 millimeters horizontally and 24 millimeters vertically from the origin".

We've rather blithely skipped over a couple of aspects of logical coordinate systems in the examples in the previous two paragraphs. For example, we made the statement "the point located x units horizontally", but we failed to mention in which direction. It's possible to establish a logical coordinate system in which increasing horizontal coordinates display from right to left rather than the more common left to right. Also, the origin of the logical coordinate system need not coincide with the origin of the device coordinate system.

Using a coordinate system that relates to the problem being solved makes an application easier to write and debug. It also relieves the application of many messy chores, the solution to which often requires that you understand implementation details of the display hardware. For example, on some displays pixels are not square. On an EGA display, for an historical example, the pixels had a 4:3 aspect ratio. Moving four pixels horizontally covers the same physical distance as moving three pixels vertically. If you drew a 100-pixels-by-100-pixels square on an EGA display, you would have seen a very nice rectangle. The same figure drawn on a VGA display appears square, as desired, because that display has a 1:1 aspect ratio. Nearly all modern displays have 1:1 aspect ratio.

Eventually, though, GDI must translate drawing requests specified in logical units and logical coordinates into drawing operations on a device. To draw on a device, GDI must convert the logical coordinates into device coordinates. Device coordinates aren't nearly as flexible as logical coordinates. The device coordinate system often depends on the actual device and sometimes even the operating mode of the device (for example, landscape and portrait modes of a laser printer typically use different device coordinate systems).

All display devices and most printers, however, use the following device coordinate system:

- The origin is located at the upper-left corner of the display (or page).

- Device units are equivalent to pixels. Increasing horizontal device coordinates proceed from left to right across the device surface.

- Increasing vertical device coordinates proceed from the top of the device surface to the bottom (downwards).

Notice that the vertical axis of a device coordinate system is inverted with respect to the commonly used Cartesian coordinate system. The screen coordinate system discussed in the previous chapter is a device coordinate system for the display device.

GDI translates (maps) logical coordinates into device coordinates by using the *mapping mode* attribute of a device context. Windows provides a number of mapping modes that you can use to specify how you want a logical coordinate to be mapped to its equivalent device coordinate. We cover these mapping modes thoroughly in the next chapter. For the purposes of this chapter, you need to understand only the default mappin mode of a device context: the MM_TEXT mapping mode.

The MM_TEXT Mapping Mode

GDI sets the mapping mode of a device context to the MM_TEXT mapping mode when it creates the devic context. This mapping mode specifies that moving one logical unit horizontally is equivalent to moving on pixel on the device horizontally. Also, the mode specifies that moving one logical unit vertically is equivalen to moving one pixel vertically. In addition, it specifies that the axes of the logical coordinate system have th same orientation as the respective axes in the device coordinate system. Finally, the mode specifies that th logical coordinate (0, 0) is coincident with the device coordinate (0, 0).

All these conditions result in a coordinate mapping such that every point in the logical coordinate system ha exactly the same coordinate value in the device coordinate system. In effect, there is no difference betwee logical coordinates and device coordinates.

The logical coordinate system in the MM_TEXT mapping mode has its origin at the upper-left corner of the de vice. Horizontal coordinates increase from left to right and vertical coordinates from top to bottom. The log ical coordinate (50, 30) specifies the pixel located 50 pixels to the right and 30 pixels down from the upper left corner of the display. The MM_TEXT mapping mode gets its name from the fact that the logical coordinate system used mimics the way we display and read text. We start at the upper-left corner of a page and read right to left from top to bottom. (Of course, those who read Arabic and Chinese may object to the ethnocen tric name. We hope not too much so).

Of critical importance is understanding that when you change to a different mapping mode, logical coordi nates are not necessarily the same as device coordinates. They happen to be identical when you use the de fault mapping mode for a device context. Should you switch to a different mapping mode, logical coordinates are completely different from device coordinates. Note also that a mapping mode is not a prop erty of a *window;* it is a changeable property of a *device context*. Thus you could lay down some text using MM_TEXT and then change to some other mapping mode and lay down a picture, quite arbitrarily and inter changeably. Those of you who have programmed DOS graphics likely know that once you chose a "display mode," that was *it*. You had 640×480 pixels, or 800×600, or whatever, and you couldn't change it. But in Windows, the *device* units are what are set up by the configuration of your display driver. The *logical* units are set up for each device context whenever it is created. You are free to change the mapping mode several times for drawing within the same DC. For example, in doing a selection, you may wish to highlight the se lected area in terms of device units but display the underlying drawing in logical units. You are not con strained to a single mapping mode even for successive drawing operations in the same DC.

Now, after this lengthy detour, we'll look once again at the TextOut function call that displays the "Hello, world!" character string:

```
TextOut (hdc, 50, 50, "Hello, world!", 13) ;
```

The coordinates (50, 50) are logical coordinates. In the code fragment given, no mention is made of chang ing the mapping mode of the device context specified by the hdc variable. Therefore the default MM_TEXT mapping mode is used, and the TextOut function displays the string at the equivalent device coordinate.

This is the pixel located 50 pixels to the right and 50 pixels down from the upper-left corner of the device surface. Typically, the device surface for a display context is a window. The string therefore displays 50 pixels to the right and 50 pixels down from the upper-left corner of the client area of the window.

You can change the mapping mode, and the same (50, 50) coordinates can be used to display the string anywhere in the window. In the rest of this chapter, we assume that the MM_TEXT mapping mode is used, and we won't dwell on the difference between logical coordinates and device coordinates. Chapter 5, "Examining a Device Context in Depth", examines other mapping modes and provides samples of their use.

When we describe the characters displayed by the TextOut function as beginning at the point (50, 50), we really haven't been specific enough. We've indicated that point within the client area but the displayed characters occupy quite a number of pixels. GDI needs to know the relationship between the given point and the rectangle that *bounds* the text. Each character is displayed within a character cell, and the adjacent character cells in the text string form the bounding rectangle for the text. By default, the given point specifies the position of the upper-left corner of the bounding rectangle for the text.

The relationship between the point specified and the bounding rectangle of the text is called the *text alignment mode*. The text alignment mode is also an attribute of the display context and can be changed by calling the SetTextAlign function. The prototype for this function looks like this:

```
UINT WINAPI SetTextAlign (HDC hdc, UINT mode) ;
```

The Windows documentation on the various GDI functions often describes the parameters to the functions in ways that have implicit assumptions as to the orientation of the logical coordinate system axes and the use of the MM_TEXT mapping mode. Some documentation (the LOGFONT structure definition, for example) further confuses the issue by occasionally using the terms "device unit" and "device coordinate" when it should state "logical unit" and "logical coordinate."

Further complicating the matter, some of the Windows functions (such as IntersectRect) have built-in assumptions that are violated in some mapping modes. For example, to calculate the intersection of two rectangles given points describing their corners, you must know the orientation of the axes of the coordinate system in order to decide which two pairs of coordinate values to compare. The IntersectRect function doesn't work properly when given points in a logical coordinate system that has the vertical axis increasing upwardly. Unfortunately, some of these functions are not documented as making mapping mode-dependent assumptions.

The first parameter is a device context handle and the second parameter is a combination of bit flags that specify the desired text alignment.

One set of flags allows you to specify the horizontal alignment of the text. You can specify that the point aligns to the left side, the right side, or the horizontal center of the bounding rectangle. A second set of flags allows you to specify the vertical alignment of the text. You can specify that the point aligns to the top or bottom of the bounding rectangle or to the baseline of the chosen font. A third set of flags allows you to specify whether the current position (another attribute of a device context, which we discuss in Chapter 5) should be updated after a call to the TextOut or ExtTextOut function.

You can select only one flag from each set. Table 4.2 lists the text alignment flags. You combine the selected flags using the logical OR operator. For example, the following statement explicitly selects the three default text alignment flags:

```
SetTextAlign (hdc, TA_LEFT | TA_TOP | TA_NOUPDATECP) ;
```

Table 4.2: The text alignment flags for the `SetTextAlign` function

Symbolic Name	Description
Group One: Horizontal Alignment	
TA_CENTER	Aligns the horizontal center of the bounding rectangle with the specified point.
TA_LEFT	Aligns the left side of the bounding rectangle with the specified point. (Default value).
TA_RIGHT	Aligns the right side of the bounding rectangle with the specified point.
Group Two: Vertical Alignment	
TA_TOP	Aligns the top of the bounding rectangle with the specified point. (Default value).
TA_BASELINE	Aligns the baseline of the chosen font with the specified point.
TA_BOTTOM	Aligns the bottom of the bounding rectangle with the specified point.
Group Three: Position Update	
TA_NOUPDATECP	Does not update the current position after each `TextOut` or `ExtTextOut` function call. (Default value.)
TA_UPDATECP	Updates the current position after each `TextOut` or `ExtTextOut` function call.

You can retrieve the current text alignment flags for a device context by calling the `GetTextAlign` function, as follows:

```
UINT Flags ;

Flags = GetTextAlign (hdc) ;
```

A comparison of the result of `GetTextAlign` to determine which flag is set is a bit more complicated than testing the result of most other functions. Some of the flags are not single-bit values. To test for a particular flag setting, you must use the following steps:

1. Use the bitwise OR operator to combine all flags in a group.

2. Use the bitwise AND operator to combine the result of step one with the flags returned by the `GetTextAlign` function.

3. Compare the desired flag value for equality with the result of step two.

The following code checks to see whether a device context is currently set to use right text alignment:

```
UINT    Flags;
UINT    HorzFlags ;

Flags = GetTextAlign (hdc) ;
HorzFlags = Flags & (TA_LEFT | TA_CENTER | TA_RIGHT) ;
```

```
if (HorzFlags == TA_RIGHT) {
    /* Device context is using right text alignment. */
}
```

Another function, `DrawText`, formats and draws text in the client area. It interprets these four characters as control characters: carriage return, linefeed, space, and tab. Also, it can justify text to the left, right, or center. Because of the additional processing, the `DrawText` function takes longer to execute than does the `TextOut` function.

What Do the Characters Look Like?

We've discussed how to display characters in the client area, but we ignored the fact that Windows applications can display characters in many different fonts. The font used to display characters is also an attribute of the display context. The default font for a display context is called the `SYSTEM_FONT`. This is the font you see Windows using in title bars (captions), menus, and dialog boxes.

The system font is a variable-pitch font. A *variable-pitch font* is a font whose character cells vary in size, depending on the actual width of the characters. Very early versions of Windows (pre-3.0) used a fixed-pitch font whose character cells remained fixed in size for all characters in the font. (The term "pitch" isn't used in the traditional sense in Windows. Traditionally, pitch refers to the number of characters from a font that will fit in a single inch. We use it in the Windows sense to be consistent with Windows documentation.)

Using a variable-pitch font often requires a little more work than a fixed-pitch font. For example, you can no longer line up columns of characters by spacing over to the next column. You can't count the number of characters displayed, multiply the count by the size of a character, and obtain the position where the next character should be displayed. The width of a string depends on the font used to display it and the actual characters in the string. You can use the `GetTextExtentPoint32` function to compute the width and height of a character string. This function uses the currently selected font in the specified device context and returns the width and height in logical units of the bounding rectangle that encloses the characters. Generally, if you really need to do full text manipulation using variable-pitch fonts, you should use one of the existing edit controls. This is because of the complexities of dealing with mouse hits, selection, highlighting, and the like. Note also that users not only have grown accustomed to the variable-pitch fonts; they also often prefer them over fixed-pitch fonts and view applications that use fixed-pitch fonts with disfavor.

You can obtain information about the dimensions of characters in a font by calling the `GetTextMetrics` function. The `GetTextMetrics` function returns information about the font currently selected into the specified device context. We previously showed you the following code fragment, which fetches information about the current font's character sizes:

```
HDC         hdc ;
HWND        hwnd ;
TEXTMETRIC  tm ;
    .
    .
    .
hdc = GetDC (hwnd) ;
GetTextMetrics (hdc, &tm) ;
ReleaseDC (hwnd, hdc) ;
```

Because the sizes of characters in a given font don't change in a single Windows session, you need to retrieve them only once. Often this code fragment is executed during the WM_CREATE message-processing logic of a window function. Values of interest from the TEXTMETRIC structure are saved for later use by the WM_PAINT message-processing logic. Saving these eliminates the overhead of retrieving needed values each time the window needs to be repainted, provided you are using the same font.

How to Use Text Metrics

The TEXTMETRIC structure provides more information than you generally need (or want) about the characters in a font. The example program in this chapter uses information from only three of the twenty fields in the TEXTMETRIC structure. The most commonly used fields give various width and height dimensions of characters in the font. Dimensions in the TEXTMETRIC structure are in logical units. These units change as the mapping mode of a device context is changed. You should get the metrics for a font after it has been selected into a device context and after setting the mapping mode. Next we look at the TEXTMETRIC structure and some of its fields.

```
typedef struct tagTEXTMETRIC {
    int         tmHeight ;
    int         tmAscent ;
    int         tmDescent ;
    int         tmInternalLeading ;
    int         tmExternalLeading ;
    int         tmAveCharWidth ;
    int         tmMaxCharWidth ;
    int         tmWeight ;
    BYTE        tmItalic ;
    BYTE        tmUnderlined ;
    BYTE        tmStruckOut ;
    BYTE        tmFirstChar ;
    BYTE        tmLastChar ;
    BYTE        tmDefaultChar ;
    BYTE        tmBreakChar ;
    BYTE        tmPitchAndFamily ;
    BYTE        tmCharSet ;
    int         tmOverhang ;
    int         tmDigitizedAspectX ;
    int         tmDigitizedAspectY ;
} TEXTMETRIC ;
```

Two fields provide information on the width of characters in the font. The tmAveCharWidth value specifies the average width of lowercase characters in the font. This is approximately the width of the lowercase letter *x*. The tmMaxCharWidth value specifies the width of the widest character in the font. All characters in a fixed-pitch font have the same width, so these two values are identical in fixed-pitch fonts. The width of a character in one fixed-pitch font, however, may not be the same as the width of a character in a different fixed-pitch font. In fact, it most likely isn't the same. Fixed-pitch fonts with the same name can have different character sizes depending on the monitor on which they are displayed. You shouldn't hard-code character size values into your programs. Instead, obtain the dimensions at runtime by calling the GetTextMetrics function.

Five fields provide information on the height of characters in the font, as shown in Figure 4.3.

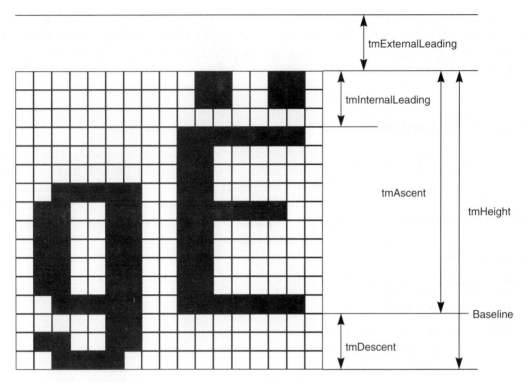

Figure 4.3: Two characters from the VGA system font

The Sysinfo example program uses the `tmHeight` and `tmExternalLeading` values. The `tmHeight` value is the actual height of the character cell. It is the sum of the `tmAscent` and `tmDescent` values. The `tmAscent` value includes the *internal leading* value specified by the `tmInternalLeading` field. Internal leading is the vertical distance reserved for marks such as accents, umlauts, and tildes above capital letters in non-English character sets. Internal leading can be set to 0 by the font designer. In that case, accented capital letters are compressed a little vertically so that they fit within the `tmAscent` height (which doesn't include any `tmInternalLeading` distance in this case because that value is 0).

External leading is the space you should leave between rows of text in a font. It is the space between the bottom of the character cell in one row of text and the top of the character cell in the adjacent row of text. The font designer specifies the amount of external leading that should be left between rows of text so that they are easily readable. External leading is considered optional, but if you don't use it, letters in adjacent rows of text can touch each other and be difficult to read. For example, using the VGA system font letters shown in Figure 4.3, the descender of the lowercase **g** will touch the umlaut over a capital **Ë** directly below it.

External leading is not accounted for in the text metrics for a font or by the `TextOut` function. You must account for it yourself when positioning text on the display. The Sysinfo example program in this chapter spaces lines of text `tmHeight` plus `tmExternalLeading` logical units apart–the recommended spacing between lines of text.

Historical note: the correct pronunciation of the word "leading" in the context of fonts with "bedding", not "weeding". This comes from the days when lead type was set by hand, one letter at a time. The intraline spacing was maintained by inserting very thin sheets of lead between each line of type. If you needed to "pad out" a column for vertical alignment or to fill the column, you just "increased the leading" by adding more, or slightly thicker, strips of lead between the lines.

Displaying Information about the Windows Environment

The example program in this chapter uses the concepts just discussed to display information about the Windows environment. There are two Windows functions that return information of particular interest: the GetSystemMetrics function and the GetDeviceCaps function.

You can call the GetSystemMetrics function to retrieve various metrics about Windows's components. For example, you can retrieve the width and height of the different types of window borders. You can retrieve the height of a window caption. You can retrieve the size of cursors and icons. You also can retrieve flags that indicate whether a mouse is installed on the system, whether the debugging version of Windows (now called the "checked kernel") is being used, and whether the left and right mouse buttons have been logically exchanged. (The latter can be done by using the Control Panel utility provided with Windows.)

The GetSystemMetrics function requires one parameter, an index that specifies which system metric to return; it returns the specified metric. All measurements are given in device units (pixels). Here is the function prototype for the function as well as a typical function call that retrieves the height of a caption bar:

```
int WINAPI GetSystemMetrics (int) ;
int        cyCaption ;

cyCaption = GetSystemMetrics (SM_CYCAPTION) ;
```

The symbolic names for the indices are defined in windows.h and are listed in Table 4.3. The Sysinfo example program in this chapter retrieves all these system metrics and displays their values using the TextOut function. We provide an example of its output (see Figure 4.7) later in this chapter after discussing the Sysinfo program.

Table 4.3: System metric indices

Win32s	Win32 3.x	Win32 4.x	Symbolic Name	Description
	✓		SM_ARRANGE	Flags specifying how the system arranges minimized windows.
				The following options are available to specify the starting position:
			ARW_BOTTOMLEFT	Start at the lower-left corner of the screen (default position).

Table 4.3: System metric indices

Win32s	Win32 3.x	Win32 4.x	Symbolic Name	Description	
				ARW_BOTTOMRIGHT	Start at the lower-right corner of the screen.
				ARW_HIDE	Hide minimized windows by moving them off the visible area of the screen.
				ARW_TOPLEFT	Start at the upper-left corner of the screen.
				ARW_TOPRIGHT	Start at the upper-right corner of the screen.
				The following options select the direction in which icons are arranged:	
				ARW_DOWN	Arrange vertically, top to bottom.
				ARW_LEFT	Arrange horizontally, left to right.
				ARW_RIGHT	Arrange horizontally, right to left.
				ARW_UP	Arrange vertically, bottom to top.
	✓		SM_CLEANBOOT	Value specifies how the system was started.	
				0	Normal boot.
				1	Fail-safe boot.
				2	Fail-safe with network boot.
	✓		SM_CMETRICS	Number of system metrics and flags.	
	✓		SM_CMOUSEBUTTONS	Number of buttons on the mouse.	
✓	✓	✓	SM_CXBORDER SM_CYBORDER	Dimensions of a window frame that cannot be sized, in pixels.	
✓	✓	✓	SM_CXCURSOR SM_CYCURSOR	Dimensions of a standard cursor bitmap, in pixels.	

Table 4.3: System metric indices

Win32s	Win32 3.x	Win32 4.x	Symbolic Name	Description
✓		✓	SM_CXDLGFRAME SM_CYDLGFRAME	Dimensions of a WS_DLGFRAME style window frame. *Obsolete in Win32 4.x.* Use SM_CYFIXEDFRAME or SM_CYFIXEDFRAME.
		✓	SM_CXDRAG SM_CYDRAG	Dimensions of a drag region. This represents a rectangle surrounding the mouse when a mouse click occurs. The mouse can be moved within this space without initiating a drag operation.
✓	✓	✓	SM_CXDOUBLECLK SM_CYDOUBLECLK	Dimensions of the double-click rectangle, in pixels.
		✓	SM_CXEDGE SM_CYEDGE	Dimensions of a 3D border. Similar to SM_CXBORDER and SM_CYBORDER.
	✓	✓	SM_CXFIXEDFRAME SM_CYFIXEDFRAME	Width of a window frame that cannot be sized.
✓		✓	SM_CXFRAME SM_CYFRAME	Width of a window frame that can be sized. *Obsolete. Use* SM_CXSIZEFRAME *and* SM_CYSIZEFRAME.
✓	✓	✓	SM_CXFULLSCREEN SM_CYFULLSCREEN	Dimensions of the client area of a maximized window.
✓	✓	✓	SM_CXHSCROLL SM_CYHSCROLL	Dimensions of the arrow bitmap on a horizontal scroll bar.
✓	✓	✓	SM_CXHTHUMB	Width of the scroll box on a horizontal scroll bar.
✓	✓	✓	SM_CXICON SM_CYICON	Dimensions of an icon, in pixels.
✓	✓	✓	SM_CXICONSPACING SM_CYICONSPACING	Dimensions of a grid cell for items in a large icon view, in pixels. SM_CXICONSPACING ≥ SM_CXICON; SM_CYICON-SPACING ≥ SM_CYICON
	✓		SM_CXMAXIMIZED SM_CYMAXIMIZED	Default dimensions of a maximized top-level window, in pixels.
	✓		SM_CXMAXTRACK SM_CYMAXTRACK	Default maximum dimensions of a window that has a caption and sizing border. The user cannot drag a window to a size larger than these dimensions unless over-ridden by WM_GETMINMAXINFO message processing.
	✓		SM_CXMENUCHECK SM_CYMENUCHECK	Dimensions of the default menu check-mark bitmap, in pixels.

Table 4.3: System metric indices

Win32s	Win32 3.x	Win32 4.x	Symbolic Name	Description
	✓		SM_CXMENUSIZE SM_CYMENUSIZE	Dimensions of menu bar buttons (for example, MDI child close), in pixels.
✓	✓	✓	SM_CXMIN SM_CYMIN	Minimum dimensions of a window.
	✓		SM_CXMINIMIZED SM_CYMINIMIZED	Dimensions of a normal minimized window, in pixels.
	✓		SM_CXMINSPACING SM_CYMINSPACING	Dimensions of a grid cell for minimized windows, in pixels. Always ≥ SM_CXMINIMIZED, SM_CYMINIMIZED.
✓	✓	✓	SM_CXMINTRACK SM_CYMINTRACK	Minimum tracking dimensions of a window. The user cannot drag the window to a size smaller than these dimensions unless overridden by WM_GETMINMAXINFO message processing.
✓	✓	✓	SM_CXSCREEN SM_CYSCREEN	Dimensions of the screen, in pixels.
✓	✓	✓	SM_CXSIZE SM_CYSIZE	Dimensions of the title bar bitmaps.
✓	✓	✓	SM_CXSIZEFRAME SM_CYSIZEFRAME	Dimensions of the frame for a window that can be sized.
	✓		SM_CXSMICON SM_CYSMICON	Recommended dimensions of a small icon, in pixels.
	✓		SM_CXSMSIZE SM_CYSMSIZE	Dimensions of small caption button, in pixels.
✓	✓	✓	SM_CXVSCROLL SM_CYVSCROLL	Dimensions of the arrow bitmap on a vertical scroll bar.
✓	✓	✓	SM_CYCAPTION	Height of a normal caption area.
✓	✓	✓	SM_CYKANJIWINDOW	Height of a Kanji window.
✓	✓	✓	SM_CYMENU	Height of a single line menu bar.
	✓		SM_CYSMCAPTION	Height of a small caption, in pixels.
✓	✓	✓	SM_CYVTHUMB	Height of the scroll box on a vertical scroll bar.
✓	✓	✓	SM_DBCSENABLED	Non-zero flag when Windows is using double-byte characters.

Table 4.3: System metric indices

Win32s	Win32 3.x	Win32 4.x	Symbolic Name	Description
✓	✓	✓	SM_DEBUG	Non-zero flag when running the Windows debugging version.
✓	✓	✓	SM_MENUDROPALIGNMENT	Pop-up menu alignment type flag.
	✓		SM_MIDEASTENABLED	Hebrew and Arabic support present.
✓	✓		SM_MOUSEPRESENT	Non-zero flag when a mouse is installed.
	✓		SM_NETWORK	The least significant bit is 1 when a network is present; 0 if no network present. The remaining bits are reserved for future use.
✓	✓	✓	SM_PENWINDOWS	Non-zero handle of Pen Windows DLL if Pen Windows installed.
	✓		SM_SECURE	TRUE if security is present; FALSE otherwise.
	✓		SM_SHOWSOUNDS	TRUE if user requires an application to present audible information in visual form.
	✓		SM_SLOWMACHINE	TRUE if the machine is determined to be a "low-end" (slow) processor.
✓	✓	✓	SM_SWAPBUTTON	Non-zero flag when left and right mouse buttons are swapped.

The GetDeviceCaps function returns device-specific information about the device associated with a specified device context. This information includes the horizontal and vertical resolution of the device, the number of colors the device supports, its aspect ratio, and its capabilities when drawing curves, lines, polygons, and text.

You call the GetDeviceCaps function much like you do the GetSystemMetrics function. You pass the GetDeviceCaps function a device context handle to identify the device and an index to identify which item the function should return. Here is the function prototype for the function:

```
int WINAPI GetDeviceCaps (HDC, int) ;
```

Here is a typical call that returns the number of adjacent bits per pixel used to represent the color of a pixel:

```
BitsPerPixel = GetDeviceCaps (hdc, BITSPIXEL) ;
```

There is no way in Win16 to determine the number of buttons on a mouse. The SM_CMOUSEBUTTONS code is not supported. If you are running under Win32s, you are limited by the underlying capabilities of Win16.

The symbolic names for the indices used in the GetDeviceCaps function are defined by including windows.h. Rather than list them here, we prefer to wait until we discuss device contexts in more depth, which we do in Chapter 5. You'll find the indices listed in that chapter in Table 5.4. The Sysinfo example program retrieves all the device capabilities for the system display and displays their values using the TextOut function. Once again, we provide an example of the device capabilities display (see Figure 4.8) later in this chapter after we discuss the Sysinfo program.

So far, you've seen how to call the TextOut function to display a character string. We've briefly discussed mapping modes (primarily the default MM_TEXT mapping mode) so that you have seen how the coordinate specified in a TextOut function call determines where in the window Windows displays the string. You've seen how to retrieve information about the size of characters in the system font. That lets you determine how far apart lines of text should be spaced. And finally, you saw how to retrieve quite a bit of information about the Windows environment as well as about the capabilities of a particular device. With all this, you're ready to display multiple lines of text in a window.

Here is one way to display (some of) the symbolic names of the various system metric indices in a window:

```
void cls_OnPaint(HWND hwnd)
  {
  HDC hdc ;
  int cyChar ;
  PAINTSTRUCT ps ;

  hdc = BeginPaint (hwnd, &ps) ;
  GetTextMetrics (hdc, &tm) ;
  cyChar = tm.tmHeight + tm.tmExternalLeading ;
  TextOut (hdc, 10, 1 * cyChar, _T("SM_CMETRICS"), 11) ;
  TextOut (hdc, 10, 2 * cyChar, _T("SM_CXBORDER"), 11) ;
  TextOut (hdc, 10, 3 * cyChar, _T("SM_CXCURSOR"), 11) ;
  TextOut (hdc, 10, 4 * cyChar, _T("SM_CXDLGFRAME"), 13) ;
  .
  .
  .
  EndPaint (hwnd, &ps) ;
  }
```

We leave a 10-pixel left margin and place the first line of text cyChar pixels down from the top of the window (which leaves a one-line top margin). Each subsequent TextOut function call displays the next line of text cyChar pixels farther down the window. Notice that there is no such thing as automatic carriage returns and line feeds when text is drawn on a window using the TextOut function. You have to explicitly place the lines of text at the proper position. Space them too closely together, and one line of text will be (at least partially) overwritten by the second line. This is quite different from text-based DOS or Unix programs in which there are distinct rows for text, and a character string can't be displayed halfway between two lines.

Introduction to Scroll Bars

One of the complications of displaying information in a window is that you have no control over the size of the window. (Actually, you can have absolute control over the size of the window–up to the maximum size permitted by the display–but you shouldn't exert it. The user should always be able to resize the window at will. Your application won't be seen as very usable if it insists on occupying a fixed amount of the screen.)

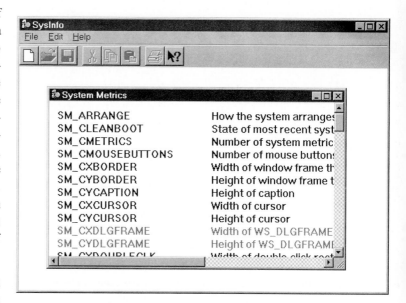

Figure 4.4: A window with horizontal and vertical scroll bars

So you should assume that you won't be able to fit into the window everything you want to display. You'll need to provide a mechanism to allow the user to scroll around in your display. The window is, in effect, a window into a portion of a larger display surface. Scrolling allows the user to see all your text, but only a portion of it at a time.

Fortunately, Windows provides standard scroll bars for exactly this purpose. A *standard scroll bar* is located along either the right edge of a window (for vertical scrolling) or the bottom edge of a window (for horizontal scrolling). It is part of the nonclient area of a window. A standard scroll bar always has a standard width and height. You can retrieve this width and height by fetching the SM_CXVSCROLL and SM_CYHSCROLL system metric values.

You also can create a scroll bar control. We discuss these in depth in Chapter 10, page 704, but for now, you should realize that there are two types of scroll bars: *standard* and *scroll-bar controls*. They operate very similarly but have subtle differences. Most of the following discussion applies to both kinds of scroll bars. We mention the few differences between the two when we discuss scroll-bar controls.

You can create a window that has standard scroll bars by including the WS_HSCROLL and WS_VSCROLL window styles. We added those styles to the WS_OVERLAPPEDWINDOW style in the CreateWindow function call in the Skeleton application to create the window shown in Figure 4.4.

The Parts of a Scroll Bar

There are five components to a scroll bar:

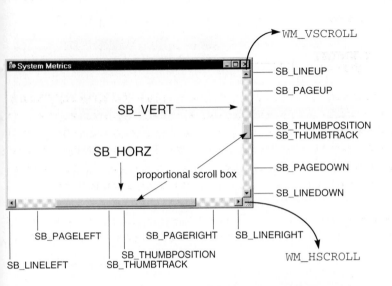

1 & 2: Two arrows (one on each end)

3: A scroll box (the box you see in the bar between the two arrows)

4 & 5: The two portions of the "bar" of the scroll bar (the portions between the scroll box and an arrow). When the scroll box is at the extreme ends, only one of these is visible.

You use the mouse to click the arrows to move the contents on the window a small amount, and click the body of the scroll bar between the scroll box and the endpoint arrow to move a larger amount. You can also position the cursor over the scroll box of a scroll bar, press

Figure 4.5: A window with two scroll bars showing the parts of a scroll bar and the associated messages and notification codes

and hold the left mouse button, and slide the scroll box up and down the scroll bar (called *dragging* the scroll box).

The length of the scroll bar represents the total length (for vertical scroll bars) or width (for horizontal scroll bars) of the information that can be displayed. The scroll boxes indicate the approximate position of the information that is visible in the window in relation to everything that can be displayed. The size of the scroll box shows the approximate ratio of the proportion of the information displayed to the total size of the information, subject to a minimum scroll box size. In Figure 4.4, the scroll boxes indicate that the window displays a portion of a document.

The *scroll box* was known in earlier versions of windows as the *thumb*. Hence the names of all the constants you will see are THUMB-based names, such as SB_THUMBPOSITION or SB_THUMBTRACK.

One thing that always seems to trip us up if we're not careful is the point of view of the window's messages with respect to scrolling. Scroll-bar terminology is in accordance with the user's view of a document. That is, scrolling *up* in a document means that earlier parts of the document come into view. You proceed toward the beginning of a document when scrolling up. Conversely, scrolling *down* brings later portions of the document into view. You move towards the end of a document when scrolling down.

The physical contents of the screen move in the opposite direction! To scroll up (toward the beginning of a document), you must move the contents of the client area *down* in the window, thereby making room for the earlier portions of the document to be displayed. To scroll down (toward the end of a document), you move the contents of the client area *up* in the window, thereby making room for the latter portions of the document to be displayed. You scroll the client area of a window in the opposite direction of that implied by the name of the scroll-bar messages.

Don't worry about accounting for the width and height of a scroll bar when retrieving the size of the client area. Windows takes care of that. The size of the client area always reflects the amount of displayable surface and does not include the size of any scroll bars that might be present. A window's scroll bars are not part of the client area, even though they look like they are. You generally don't need to worry about this dimension unless you are adding a horizontal scroll bar to a list box, a topic we discuss and show an example of in Chapter 9, page 619.

A scroll bar sends a scroll-bar message to the window function each time the user interacts with the scroll bar. A horizontal scroll bar sends a WM_HSCROLL message and a vertical scroll bar sends a WM_VSCROLL message. The code parameter of the message specifies the type of scrolling requested. The symbolic names for the values of the code field are defined by windows.h and begin with SB_ (for *Scroll Bar*). The possible messages are listed in Table 4.4 and illustrated in Figure 4.5. The hctl parameter is 0 for scroll-bar messages from the standard scroll bars. It contains the scroll control's window handle when sent by a scroll-bar control. The pos parameter is used only by the SB_THUMBPOSITION and SB_THUMBTRACK messages. In those messages, the pos parameter contains the current position of the scroll bar scroll box.

A standard scroll bar does not generate scroll-bar messages with the code parameter set to either SB_BOTTOM or SB_TOP. These messages indicate that the user has positioned the scroll bar to its maximum or minimum position, respectively, and are sent only by the keyboard interface to a scroll bar control.

A scroll bar generates an SB_LINEDOWN (or SB_LINERIGHT) message when the user clicks the bottom arrow on a vertical scroll bar or the right arrow on a horizontal scroll bar. It generates an SB_LINEUP (or SB_LINELEFT) message when the user clicks the top arrow on a vertical scroll bar or the left arrow on a horizontal scroll bar. A scroll bar generates an SB_PAGEDOWN (or SB_PAGERIGHT) message when the user clicks the body of the scroll bar between the scroll box and the bottom (or right) arrow. It generates an SB_PAGEUP (or SB_PAGELEFT) message when the user clicks the body of the scroll bar between the scroll box and the top (or left) arrow.

A scroll bar sends one of these four messages to your window function when the mouse button is initially pressed. If the user continues to hold the mouse button down while the cursor is positioned over the scroll bar, auto-repeat begins and the scroll bar will send the same message over and over. When the user releases the mouse button, the scroll bar sends the SB_ENDSCROLL message.

The user can also press the mouse button while over the scroll box of a scroll bar. Holding down the button and dragging the scroll box back and forth along the scroll bar produces a stream of SB_THUMBTRACK messages. The pos parameter of each SB_THUMBTRACK message call contains the current position of the scroll box. When the user releases the mouse button while dragging the scroll box, the scroll bar sends an

SB_THUMBPOSITION message. The pos parameter of the SB_THUMBPOSITION message contains the position of the scroll box when it was released.

	WM_HSCROLL, WM_VSCROLL **Message Cracker Handlers**

```
void cls_OnHScroll(HWND hwnd, HWND hctl, UINT code, int pos);
void cls_OnVScroll(HWND hwnd, HWND hctl, UINT code, int pos);
```

	wParam		lParam		
Parameter	**lo**	**hi**	**lo**	**hi**	**Meaning**
hwnd					Window handle of the parent window of the scroll bar (the window receiving the message).
hctl			▮		Window handle of the scroll bar control (0 for standard scroll bars).
code	▮				SB_ code.
pos		▮			Position for SB_THUMBTRACK and SB_THUMBPOSITION.

The pos parameter is only a 16-bit value and therefore reflects only the low-order 16 bits of the position! This was for compatibility with existing Windows 16 code and the lack of enough bits to pack a 32-bit handle, a 32-bit position, and a 16-bit code into 64 bits of message. For most applications, scroll positions in the 16-bit range are more than adequate. But if you need a larger range, you must explicitly request the full 32-bit position with the GetScrollInfo call. See Chapter 10, page 710.

You may be surprised to learn that scroll bars do nothing more than what we have described here. They only send messages in response to a user's manipulation of the scroll bar. They don't scroll anything! You must process the scroll-bar messages and perform all required scrolling yourself. Let's look a bit deeper into what's needed to do that.

Scrolling Text

The SB_LINEUP/SB_LINELEFT and SB_LINEDOWN/SB_LINERIGHT messages are relatively simple. You move the contents of the client area of the window one "line" down or up, respectively, to make room for one additional "line" of information. Remember, you scroll the contents of the client area in the opposite direction as that implied in the message. When processing these messages from a horizontal scroll bar, you would scroll the screen one column right or left, respectively. Because of the prevalence of variable-pitch fonts, the interpretation of "column" is often quite liberal, and it means "one horizontal unit". You get to define what this "unit" really is. For example, you could choose to use one "average character width" or some small multiple of "average character width". Or you could use "one device unit", that is, one pixel. You get to choose.

The SB_PAGEUP/SB_PAGELEFT and SB_PAGEDOWN/SB_PAGERIGHT are nearly the same. You move the contexts of the client area one "page" down or up, respectively. Or, in the case of a horizontal scroll bar, one "page" of columns to the right or left, respectively. You can most easily visualize this in terms of a text screen with a fixed pitch font. But you should interpret these messages in a way that makes sense for the application.

Determining the appropriate distance to scroll horizontally one character gets difficult when using a variable-pitch font because there is likely to be no specific columnar alignment of characters. When displaying graphics, you may find the best approach to be to scroll a fixed amount of the client area, say five or ten percent, for each "line" scroll. "Page" scrolls should likewise be interpreted in a reasonable way. For example, we prefer not to scroll an entire page when paging up and down. We compute the number of lines on the screen, and then scroll the screen one fewer lines than this value for each "page" scroll. This leaves the last or first line of the previous page on the screen (depending on the direction of the scroll), which places the newly visible material in context.

The SB_THUMBPOSITION and SB_THUMBTRACK messages are more difficult to process properly. A scroll bar sends a barrage of

Table 4.4: Scroll bar codes

Symbolic name	Interpretation
SB_BOTTOM	Scroll to bottom right.
SB_ENDSCROLL	Mouse button released; scroll request complete.
SB_LINEDOWN	Scroll one line down or one character right.
SB_LINEUP	Scroll one line up or one character left.
SB_LINELEFT	Scroll one horizontal unit left. Same code as SB_LINEUP.
SB_LINERIGHT	Scroll one horizontal unit right. Same code as SB_LINEDOWN.
SB_PAGEDOWN	Scroll one page down or one page right.
SB_PAGEUP	Scroll one page up or one page left.
SB_PAGELEFT	Scroll one page unit left. Same code as SB_PAGEUP.
SB_PAGERIGHT	Scroll one page unit right. Same code as SB_PAGEDOWN.
SB_THUMBPOSITION	Scroll to a specified position.
SB_THUMBTRACK	Current position of a moving scroll box.
SB_TOP	Scroll to upper left.

SB_THUMBTRACK messages to your window function when the user drags the scroll box. When you process this message, you should rewrite the client area to show the area of the document that begins at the position indicated by the current position of the scroll box drag message. However, a scroll bar often can send you messages more quickly than you can update the client area. When this happens, the user can drag the scroll box faster than the display updates. The user sees your application's response as slow and sluggish.

Another alternative is to ignore the SB_THUMBTRACK messages and to process the SB_THUMBPOSITION message. The user drags the scroll box back and forth; the display remains unchanged. When the user releases the mouse button, the client area displays the position in the document indicated by the current position of the scroll box drag message.

You should use the approach that makes the most sense for your application. Generally, if you can update the client area quickly enough, you should process the SB_THUMBTRACK message; otherwise, ignore it. You can also consider other alternatives. For example, you could have a small window pop up showing something useful about the position, such as a page number, record number, key record field, and the like. Or you could have the useful information display in a status line at the bottom of the client area.

While the user drags a scroll bar scroll box, the scroll box will be displayed at the *proposed* position of the scroll box. The user drags a simulated scroll box, not the actual scroll box. The SB_THUMBTRACK and SB_THUMBPOSITION messages report the position of this simulated scroll box. The actual scroll box is never repositioned by a scroll bar. You must use the SetScrollInfo function to move the scroll box to the new position (typically when the user stops dragging the scroll box).

Scroll bar status is manipulated and read by the SetScrollInfo and GetScrollInfo functions. The SetScrollInfo and GetScrollInfo functions pass a reference to a SCROLLINFO data structure. The SCROLLINFO data structure contains several variables and a set of flags that determine the effect of the function. The SCROLLINFO structure is defined as follows:

```
typedef struct tagSCROLLINFO {
    UINT cbSize ;          // size of this structure, in bytes
    UINT fMask ;           // flags of what to set or get
    int  nMin ;            // minimum scrolling position
    int  nMax ;            // maximum scrolling position
    UINT nPage ;           // page size (scroll box size control)
    int  nPos ;            // current position of scroll box
    int  nTrackPos ;       // immediate position during drag
    } SCROLLINFO;
```

As with all modern API calls, you first must initialize the first four bytes of the structure to indicate the size of the structure in bytes. Here is the cbSize member:

```
SCROLLINFO si;
si.cbSize = sizeof(SCROLLINFO);
```

Next, you set the fMask field to indicate which values you wish to set or get. For the GetScrollInfo, the designated values will be copied from the scroll bar control to the structure, and for the SetScrollInfo, the designated values will be copied from the structure to the scroll bar. The mask values are given in Table 4.5.

The SetScrollInfo and GetScrollInfo calls replace the older SetScrollPos and GetScrollPos and SetScrollRange and GetScrollRange calls. These provide more flexibility as well as allow you to get the entire 32-bit scroll bar position and set the "proportional scroll box" size.

Table 4.5: SCROLLINFO **flag values**

Bit Mask Name	Meaning
SIF_ALL	SIF_PAGE	SIF_POS	SIF_RANGE	SIF_TRACKPOS
SIF_DISABLENOSCROLL	Only for SetScrollInfo. If the parameter values make the scroll bar unnecessary, disable the scroll bar instead of removing it.

Table 4.5: SCROLLINFO **flag values**

Bit Mask Name	Meaning
SIF_PAGE	The nPage member gets or sets the page size for the proportional scroll box.
SIF_POS	The nPos member contains the scroll box position.
SIF_RANGE	The nMin and nMax members contain the parameters defining the scroll range.
SIF_TRACKPOS	The nTrackpos member will contain the current 32-bit tracking position (ignored for SetScrollInfo).

You set the scroll position by using the SetScrollInfo function as follows:

```
SCROLLINFO si;
si.cbSize = sizeof(SCROLLINFO);
si.fMask = SIF_POS;
si.nPos = position ;
SetScrollInfo(hwnd, scrollbarid, &si, TRUE);
```

The SetScrollInfo function is defined as follows:

```
int WINAPI SetScrollInfo (HWND hwnd, int Bar, LPSCROLLINFO si, BOOL Redraw);
```

The hwnd parameter is the window handle of the window containing the scroll bar. (For scroll bar controls, it is the window handle of the control.) The Bar parameter specifies which scroll bar to set. It can be one of the following values:

- SB_CTL: Used to indicate that the hwnd parameter specifies a scroll bar control.

- SB_HORZ: Sets the specified window's horizontal scroll bar information.

- SB_VERT: Sets the specified window's vertical scroll bar information.

The si parameter specifies the structure that defines the new position for the scroll box. The new position must be within the scrolling range (discussed shortly in this chapter). The Redraw parameter specifies whether the scroll bar should be redrawn to display the new scroll box position. When this parameter is non-zero, the scroll bar is redrawn. When it is 0, the scroll bar is not redrawn. Typically you set this value to TRUE in order to force the immediate redrawing. You set it to FALSE only when you are going to make a subsequent call to a scroll bar function and give a TRUE parameter to redraw the scroll bar.

The GetScrollInfo function returns the existing values of the scroll bar, such as the previous position of the scroll bar's scroll box. You can retrieve the current position of a scroll bar's scroll box without altering it by calling the GetScrollInfo function. To do this, you must initialize the cbSize member of the structure as with SetScrollInfo. You must then set the fMask member to indicate which value(s) you wish to retrieve. When the function returns, only those fields requested by the fMask parameter will be changed. For example, the following statement retrieves the current position for the vertical scroll bar in the hwnd window:

```
SCROLLINFO si;
si.cbSize = sizeof(SCROLLINFO);
si.fMask = SIF_POS;
GetScrollInfo (hwnd, SB_VERT, &si) ;
```

A scroll box position is an integer value that is relative to the top end of a vertical scroll bar or to the left end of a horizontal scroll bar. A scroll bar has a range–a minimum value–and a maximum value, any of which you can change by calling the SetScrollInfo function and specifying the SIF_RANGE flag in the mask. Standard scroll bars initially have a range of 0 to 100. (The default range for a scroll bar *control* is empty– both the minimum and maximum values are 0). Dragging the scroll box to the top of a vertical scroll bar and releasing it produces an SB_THUMBPOSITION message that specifies a current position of 0. Dragging it to the bottom produces an SB_THUMBPOSITION message that specifies a current position of 100. The scroll bar is divided into equal increments, so dropping the scroll box exactly in the center produces a current position of 50.

Some versions of the Microsoft documentation state that the nPos and nPage members of the SCROLLINFO structure compare to the nMax and nMin members of the SCROLLINFO structure, and that if they are out of range, they are brought into range by setting the out-of-range value to one or the other of the limit values. This is not true, as simple experimentation will show. The nPage and nPos values *are* compared to the *current* maximum and minimum settings of the scroll bar and brought into limit if necessary, but the nMin and nMax members of the SCROLLINFO structure are not involved unless the SIF_RANGE flag is also set. Then it is apparent that first the range is set and *then* the nPos and nPage values are compared to the *new* current values of the control.

As we've already pointed out, there is a problem with the WM_HSCROLL and WM_VSCROLL messages: even in Win32, they contain only 16 bits of position information when responding with SB_THUMBTRACK and SB_THUMBPOSITION codes. This handles a number of common cases readily but may not be suitable for all applications. For example, if you were tracking pixel positions with the scroll bar and were using a 20-pixel-high font, you would be limited to just slightly over 1600 lines of text, which is probably unreasonably small. If you were working with records in a database, you would be limited to 32,768 records, a fairly small database by most standards. So there needs to be a way to obtain the actual 32-bit scroll box tracking position. This is done by the nTrackPos member of the SCROLLINFO structure. This value represents the position of the scroll bar in the 32-bit range. You obtain this by calling GetScrollInfo.

You can set the scroll range for the standard vertical scroll bar of a window to be 1,000 units in the range –500 to +500 by calling the SetScrollInfo function as follows:

```
SCROLLINFO si ;
si.cbSize = sizeof(SCROLLINFO) ;
si.fMask = SIF_RANGE ;
si.nMin = -500 ;
si.nMax =  500 ;
SetScrollInfo (hwnd, SB_VERT, &si, TRUE) ;
```

You can use the GetScrollInfo function to fetch the current minimum and maximum scroll bar positions for a specified scroll bar.

```
SCROLLINFO si ;
si.cbSize = sizeof(SCROLLINFO) ;
si.fMask = SIF_RANGE ;
GetScrollInfo (hwnd, SB_VERT, &si) ;
// The scroll range can be found in
```

```
// si.nMin
// si.nMax
```

You cannot get the full 32-bit scroll position from the position parameter of a scroll bar message handler; only 16 bits of position are delivered. However, you can use the `GetScrollInfo` function with the `SIF_TRACKPOS` flag to obtain the full 32-bit tracking position.

 In some of the older documentation on Win32 scroll bars, including that published by Microsoft, you may read that you *cannot* obtain the scroll position while in a handler. The `SIF_TRACKPOS` flag was added after this documentation was published. Beware of this older documentation; it may have other obsolete features.

You can disable and hide a standard scroll bar when it is not needed. For example, when the current size of the client area is sufficient to contain the entire display, a scroll bar is not needed. There are two ways to display and hide a standard scroll bar.

The `SetScrollInfo` function hides and disables a standard scroll bar whenever the minimum and maximum values are equal. Calling the function again with unequal minimum and maximum values shows and enables the scroll bar. You can also call the `ShowScrollBar` function to hide or show a scroll bar without changing the scroll bar's range. The following statement hides a window's horizontal scroll bar:

```
ShowScrollBar (hwnd, SB_HORZ, FALSE) ;
```

You can also show or hide both of a window's horizontal and vertical scroll bars with one function call using the `ShowScrollBar` function and the value `SB_BOTH`. However, if you find the effect of the scroll bar's disappearing and reappearing to be visually disturbing, you can use the `SetScrollInfo` function using the `SIF_DISABLENOSCROLL` mask option. This merely disables the scroll bars, and does not cause them to disappear, a visually less disturbing effect:

```
void setVerticalScrollRange(HWND hwnd, int low, int high)
    {
    SCROLLINFO si ;
    si.cbSize = sizeof(SCROLLINFO) ;
    si.fMask = SIF_RANGE | SIF_DISABLENOSCROLL;
    si.nMin = low ;
    si.nMax = high ;
    SetScrollInfo (hwnd, SB_VERT, &si, TRUE) ;
    }
```

This has the property that if `low` == `high`, the scroll bar will be disabled but not hidden.

You can enable or disable either one or both of the arrows on a scroll bar by calling the `EnableScrollBar` function. Its prototype is:

```
BOOL WINAPI EnableScrollBar(HWND hwnd, int SBFlags, UINT ArrowFlags)
```

The `hwnd` parameter is a handle to either a window or a scroll bar control. The `SBFlags` parameter specifies whether the `hwnd` parameter is a window handle or a scroll bar control handle. When the `SBFlags` parameter is set to `SB_CTL`, the `hwnd` parameter is the handle of a scroll bar control. Similarly, the `SB_HORZ` and `SB_VERT` flags indicate that the `hwnd` parameter is a window handle and that the horizontal or vertical window scroll bar, respectively, should be enabled or disabled. The SB_BOTH flag value specifies that the arrows of the horizontal and vertical window scroll bars should be enabled or disabled.

The ArrowFlags parameter specifies whether the appropriate scroll bar arrows are enabled or disabled and which arrows are enabled or disabled. This parameter can be one of the values from Table 4.6.

Table 4.6: EnableScrollBar values

Name	Meaning
ESB_ENABLE_BOTH	Enables both arrows of a scroll bar.
ESB_DISABLE_LTUP	Disables the left arrow of a horizontal scroll bar or the up arrow of a vertical scroll bar.
ESB_DISABLE_RTDN	Disables the right arrow of a horizontal scroll bar or the down arrow of a vertical scroll bar.
ESB_DISABLE_BOTH	Disables both arrows of a scroll bar.

The EnableScrollBar function returns a nonzero value when the arrows are enabled or disabled as specified. Otherwise, it returns zero, thereby indicating that the arrows are already in the requested state or that an error occurred.

Finally we're ready to show you *how* you actually scroll text in a window. So far, nothing you've seen actually scrolls the text. A scroll bar sends messages to a window function notifying the function that the user is requesting scrolling operations. You use these messages to update the scroll bar's scroll box position to acknowledge the scrolling request. You also use the scroll bar messages to determine how much the contents of the window should be scrolled.

We can't emphasize enough that a scroll bar doesn't scroll a window. It only notifies your application that the user wishes to scroll the window. Exactly how you implement the scroll request depends on the application. Here's an example.

The default values for a standard scroll bar's range are 0 and 100 percent. Zero percent means to start displaying information from the beginning of a file of text. One hundred percent means to display the end of the file so that the last line in the file displays at the bottom of the window. A number between 0 and 100 means to start displaying text from that location in the file. (Often the information doesn't come from a file, but the same idea still applies.)

The simplest implementation would seek the appropriate offset in the file and completely redraw the window. You display the first line of text from that offset in the file on the first "line" in the window, move down tmHeight plus tmExternalLeading pixels and display the next line from the file, and so on. But this is quite inefficient. Suppose the user wants to move one line toward the bottom of the file and accordingly clicks only the bottom arrow of a vertical scroll bar. If we could slide the display in the window up tmHeight plus tmExternalLeading pixels (effectively moving all lines of text in the window up one line), we would need to display only the one new line of text at the bottom of the window. We could do that much more quickly than redrawing the entire window. In addition, it would reduce an annoying "flicker". If you had to redraw the entire screen, you would first have to erase it. Doing this would be noticeable in that the screen would be seen to "flash" at the user on each scroll. But ScrollWindow simply moves the screen bitmap in the client area (and with many accelerator cards, it asks the card to move the bitmap, which is even faster), leaving only a (relatively) small area at the top, bottom, left, or right that needs to be redrawn. Hence the display is much less annoying to the user.

You can scroll a window up or down and left or right in a single operation by calling the ScrollWindow function, defined as:

```
BOOL ScrollWindow (HWND hwnd, int XPixels, int YPixels,
            CONST RECT * rcScroll,
            CONST RECT * rcClip) ;
```

The hwnd parameter identifies the window whose client area you wish to scroll. The Xpixels parameter specifies the amount and direction (in device units) to scroll horizontally. The Ypixels parameter specifies the amount and direction (in device units) to scroll vertically. The rcScroll parameter is a pointer to a RECT structure that specifies the portion of the client area to scroll. Normally this parameter is set to NULL to scroll the entire client area. The rcClip parameter is a pointer to a RECT structure that specifies the clipping rectangle to be scrolled. Only the pixels within this clipping rectangle are actually scrolled. You set this parameter to NULL to scroll the entire client window. When the last two parameters are set to NULL, scrolling is much faster.

Scrolling is very fast using the ScrollWindow function because the function simply copies pixels from one place on the screen to another, in effect block-transferring an entire rectangle in a single operation. This is efficient because it is handled entirely within the GDI. The GDI queries the capabilities of the driver and may request the driver to perform the operation, which it often does by converting the request to a request for the accelerator card to do the copy directly "in the hardware". Thus, by using ScrollWindow, you can take maximum advantage of the performance of whatever platform your application is running on.

Because the ScrollWindow function scrolls the window in the requested direction, all lines of text remaining in the window need not be redisplayed. But what about the area "uncovered" by the scroll? It needs to have the new lines of text display on it. Before it can have that, however, the area must be erased because it still has its previous contents. These contents are not erased as part of the scrolling operation. But we're in the middle of processing a scroll bar message and we've already discussed how you shouldn't draw on the client area of a window except from within the WM_PAINT message processing logic.

Windows resolves these issues very nicely. It adds the area uncovered by a ScrollWindow function call to the update region for a window. The window will eventually receive a WM_PAINT message, and the rcPaint RECT structure contained in the PAINTSTRUCT structure updated by the BeginPaint function call will, at the very least, specify the uncovered area. Basically, you scroll a window using the ScrollWindow function while processing a scroll bar message and paint the window while processing a WM_PAINT message.

The ScrollWindowEx function is also available. An extended version of the ScrollWindow function, it is defined as follows:

```
int WINAPI ScrollWindowEx(HWND hwnd, int dx, int dy,
                CONST RECT * ScrollRect,
                CONST RECT * ClipRect,
                HRGN UpdateRgn,
```

```
RECT * UpdateRect,
UINT Scroll)
```

The first five parameters of this function have the same meaning as those for the ScrollWindow function described previously. The UpdateRgn parameter may be NULL or must be the handle of a region that is modified to hold the region invalidated by scrolling. The UpdateRect parameter may be NULL or must point to a rectangle that is modified to hold the boundaries of the area invalidated by scrolling. The Scroll parameter specifies a flag that controls scrolling; this parameter can be one of the values from Table 4.7.

Table 4.7: ScrollWindowEx Codes

Code	Meaning
SW_ERASE	Invalidates the region identified by the UpdateRgn parameter and erases the newly invalidated region by sending a WM_ERASEBKGND message to the window.
SW_INVALIDATE	Invalidates the region identified by the UpdateRgn parameter and does not erase the newly invalidated region.
SW_SCROLLCHILDREN	Scrolls all child windows that intersect the scrolling rectangle (*ScrollRect) by the number of pixels specified in the dx and dy parameters. Windows sends a WM_MOVE message to all child windows that intersect ScrollRect, even if they do not move. (A child window does not move if it intersects the scrolling rectangle but does not intersect the clipping region.) The caret is repositioned when a child window is scrolled and the cursor rectangle intersects the scroll rectangle.

Typically you'll need to keep some way to pass information from the scroll bar message processing logic to the WM_PAINT message processing logic. The WM_PAINT processing uses this information when it scrolls the window using either the ScrollWindow or ScrollWindowEx function. In this proposed example, the window painting logic needs to know where in the file to begin reading to display text in its window. The location was last determined by the scroll bar message processing logic. In this example, we use a static variable, although generally you will want to attach the information to the window itself. We have not yet discussed doing this, but we give an example of one of the general techniques on page 192 (the SetProp method). Another alternative would be to have the WM_PAINT logic query the scroll bar using the GetScrollInfo function to determine where to start the display.

Subclassing a Window Class

What is Subclassing?

We're almost ready to describe the Sysinfo sample program that demonstrates text display in a window that scrolls. First, we have one more small diversion to explore. We wanted a program that created two windows. One window would display all the system metrics, and the other would display the device capabilities of the system display device.

The code for painting each window is slightly different. The difference is sufficient that we make each window an instance of two different window classes. Doing this allows each window to have its own window function. We then can write the window-painting code for one window without worrying about the effects of a change on the painting of the other window.

Both windows should scroll their contents when necessary. The straightforward way to provide for this is to duplicate the scrolling code in each window function, but this wastes effort. Plus, if we wanted to create a third scrolling text window, we'd have to duplicate the scrolling code again. Instead, we use a technique called *subclassing*. A subclassed window has its own window function, but that window function passes all messages that it doesn't process off to *another* window function, called the *superclass function*. In a sense, all the windows you create are subclassing a window–an abstract window–whose behavior is provided by the DefWindowProc function.

In the normal case, a window function passes all unprocessed messages to the DefWindowProc function. You could consider the behavior provided by Windows (via the DefWindowProc function) as one window class. When you register a window class, you in effect create a subclass of the standard Windows window class. Your new window class (more correctly, the window function) extends and modifies the behavior of a window in whatever way it requires and passes all unprocessed messages on to Windows whenever it wants the default actions.

You can extend this subclassing technique further. You register a window class whose window function passes unprocessed messages to another window function rather than to the DefWindowProc function. That secondary window function, in turn, processes the message itself and either passes it off to yet a third window function or gives it to the DefWindowProc function for standard processing. Each level of subclassing results in a window that has less general and more specific behavior.

In the Sysinfo program, we create a scrolling window class that processes scroll-bar messages and provides scrolling without knowledge of the contents of the window that it scrolls. This window class passes all unprocessed messages off to the DefWindowProc function for default handling.

We also create two more window classes: one for a window that displays the system metrics and one for a window that displays the display device capabilities. Both of these subclass the scrolling window class. That is, they pass all unprocessed messages to the scrolling window function rather than to the DefWindowProc function. Because neither the system metrics class nor the device capabilities class process scroll-bar messages, they give the messages to the scrolling window class's window function. That function then processes the messages and provides the window scrolling. All messages that are unprocessed by the scrolling window function are passed to the DefWindowProc function. The relative positions of these window functions are shown in the class hierarchy depicted in Figure 4.6.

Messages are retrieved from the thread message queue and delivered to the window function associated with the window. In the Sysinfo program, there is one system metrics window and one device capability window. So all messages enter this window class hierarchy at the bottom of the tree shown in Figure 4.6. Messages not processed at one level are passed upward until they reach the DefWindowProc function. What makes this hierarchy interesting is that there is no actual registered window class for ScrollingWindow; this class is an abstract class represented by a function.

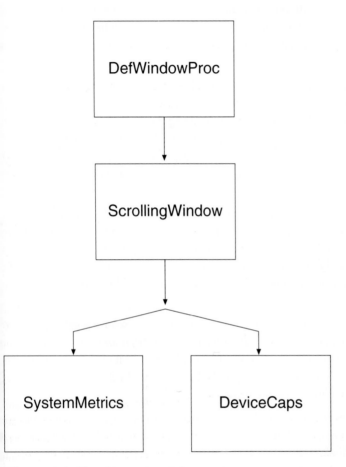

Figure 4.6: Class hierarchy of the Sysinfo program

A window function can generate additional messages while processing a message. It sends the additional messages to the window function by calling the SendMessage function. The Sysinfo program uses this feature to provide communication between the scrolling window function and the subclassing window functions. For example, the scrolling window function needs to get the range of the horizontal and vertical scroll bars. However, it has no knowledge of the contents of the window, let alone its size. It obtains the range by sending a message to the window. This message arrives in the appropriate window function (system metrics window function or the device capabilities window function), which replies with the size.

Subclassing Techniques

There are three ways to subclass a Windows class. Which one you choose depends on the circumstances. First is direct-call subclassing. This is the simplest way to subclass and occurs when you know the function name of the handler function for the superclass. The superclass handler may or may not have a registered window class; it may be, as we just discussed, an abstract class. Just as we call DefWindowProc (the abstract class handler for all Windows classes), we should be able to call our own class handler just by writing an ordinary C call to it. *This is not recommended.* It will work sometimes, but not always. In particular, it will not work when a mix of Unicode and non-Unicode functions are used. You should always call a handler by using the CallWindowProc function. This properly handles all Unicode translation issues.

Using the direct-call subclassing, your subclass handlers will look like this:

```
LRESULT CALLBACK
mySubclassHandler(HWND hwnd, UINT msg, WPARAM wParam, LPARAM lParam)
{
    switch(msg)
        { /* msg */
        case WM_whatever:
            // ... handlers look like this
```

```
        break;  // continue with default handler
    case WM_other:
        // ... handlers look like this
        return value;  // value as per message specification
    // ...
    } /* msg */
  return CallWindowProc(superClassHandler, hwnd, msg, wParam, lParam);
}
```

If we handle the message completely, we simply return the appropriate value (often just 0). If we want to intercept the message and do something before the superclass gets the message, we process it and then do break. If we don't handle it at all, or have done all we want with it, we fall into the CallWindowProc at the end of the function. This is the sort of subclassing we do in the Sysinfo program.

The second type of subclassing is superclass-driven subclassing. It is used when we construct a class that we want the user of the class to specialize using a user-defined handler. This is how dialogs are subclassed, as we explain in Chapter 11. In this model, the superclass receives the message, which it forwards to a subclass handler function. The handler function returns a simple value, such as a Boolean value, indicating whether it has processed the message. If the subclass handler has processed the message completely (usually indicated by returning TRUE), the superclass does no further processing. If the subclass handler wants the superclass handler to apply its normal processing, it returns a different code (usually FALSE) to indicate that the default processing should continue. This superclass-driven subclassing is not commonly done in programming in C but it is representative of how class libraries such as the Microsoft Foundation Classes (MFC) approach the subclassing problem.

The third type of subclassing is "classic" subclassing, the most commonly used in Windows. In this style you first create a window of the desired superclass and then replace its function pointer with one that points to your own subclass handler. If you handle the message in your subclass handler, you simply return the appropriate value. If you don't handle the message, or you want default handling, you simply call the superclass function. But how do you know what the superclass function is? For Windows controls, you can't find the name of it because it is buried deep in the binary executable of Windows.

To do classic subclassing, you first must get a copy of the superclass function pointer and save it somewhere. Although static variables have been the traditional place to store this information in, they can pose difficulties because of the preemptive multithreading of Win32. In fact, you can't successfully subclass certain controls, such as edit controls, using a single static variable because different styles of controls often use different handlers (Windows does subclassing internally!). So the *only* safe place to store the superclass function pointer is with the window you are subclassing.

There are several places you can store such a superclass function pointer that keep the saved value window specific. For example, you can use the GWL_USERDATA word if it is not being used otherwise. Or, since the GWL_USERDATA word is often used to hold subclass-specific information, such as a pointer to a struct, you can store the previous superclass function pointer in the struct that is referenced.

If you are controlling the class, you can register the class with an additional four bytes (the size of a pointer) as part of the cbWndExtra value in the WNDCLASS or WNDCLASSEX structure. You can then use SetWindowLong and GetWindowLong to set and retrieve the superclass function pointer. However, you can't always predict the availability of GWL_USERDATA, particularly in windows that are created by DLLs for which you may not have the source code. In these cases, and for all the built-in controls of Windows, you cannot change the number of extra bytes allocated for the class.

For general subclassing, we prefer the use of SetProp and GetProp. For example, here is a way to subclass a Windows control:

```
ATOM subclassname;

// in initialization:
subclassname = GlobalAddAtom(_T("myapplication.superclass"));

void subclassControl(HWND hctl, WNDPROC proc)
{
    WNDPROC old = (WNDPROC)GetWindowLong(hctl, GWL_WNDPROC);
    SetWindowLong(hctl, GWL_WNDPROC, (LONG)proc);
    SetProp(hctl, subclassname, (HANDLE)old);
} //¹
```

Our handler now has to look like this:

```
LRESULT CALLBACK
mySubclassHandler(HWND hwnd, UINT msg, WPARAM wParam, LPARAM lParam)
{
 WNDPROC oldproc = (WNDPROC) GetProp(hwnd, subclassname);

 switch(msg)
    { /* msg */
      case WM_DESTROY:
      HANDLE_WM_DESTROY(hwnd, wParam, lParam, mysubclass_OnDestroy);
          break;
      // ... other cases here
    } /* msg */
    return CallWindowProc(oldproc, hwnd, msg, wParam, lParam);
}
```

The OnDestroy handler is mandatory. It must do the following (besides any class-specific destruction actions your subclass actually requires):

```
static void
mysubclass_OnDestroy(HWND hwnd)
{
 SetWindowLong(hwnd, GWL_WNDPROC, (LONG)GetProp(hwnd, subclassname));
 RemoveProp(hwnd, subclassname);
}
```

You can attach as many properties as you wish (up to the maximum number of unique atoms, 16384) to a window, and the GetProp function will still be very fast. The only restriction is that you must remove the properties from the window before it is destroyed.

---

[1] This could be rewritten as a single line:
```
 SetProp(hctl, subclassname, (HANDLE)SetWindowLong(hctl, GWL_WNDPROC, (LONG)proc));
```
 but for exposition we tend to favor a simpler style that illustrates each detail.

During initialization, you register an *atom name* by giving a string that you hope is unique in your application (to guarantee this, you make it nice and long and therefore unlikely to generate a conflict with another atom of the same name). You then use the atom name to attach and retrieve properties. You use this name to name the "old class function" property, which you can use to call the superclass from your own handler.

One method that is not recommended is the use of the `GetClassInfo` function to obtain the pointer to the handler function defined by the class. Although this may appear safe, it works only if there has been no other subclassing of the window. Since you can't tell if there has been, you can't tell if the function pointer you get back in the class information structure is the function pointer that is *actually* being used in your window right now! For example, you might have a DLL that implements some sort of "fancy" edit control, say, a social-security-number input field that expects text in a certain form. The creator of this class may actually be using an edit control for most of the work, having subclassed it to handle the special needs of inputting a social security number. If you ask for the function used by `GetClassInfo`, you will get the function referenced by the original edit class when what you really want is the function referenced by the current window. If you do your superclassing by calling the function referenced by the `GetClassInfo` data, you will miss all the new functionality you thought you had. You should subclass only by looking at the `GWL_WNDPROC` value that is in the window *right now*.

Another argument you might make in favor of using `GetClassInfo` is that you *know* exactly what your program does and it doesn't do any other subclassing, so using `GetClassInfo` *must* be safe. We're going to disappoint you. There are special operations called "hook" operations that allow programs you never heard of to subclass your windows. These might be even be working as part of a third-party package you have purchased. We'll even show you how to write one of these in Chapter 16, page 1152. So `GetClassInfo` should not be considered a safe way to get a superclass function pointer.

The Sysinfo Program

The Sysinfo program defines four window classes. One is the main window class, which defines the outer frame window. The other three define child windows of the main frame. Windows of one class retrieve and display the system metrics by calling the `GetSystemMetrics` and `TextOut` functions. Windows of a second class retrieve and display the device capabilities for the system display device by calling the `GetDeviceCaps` and `TextOut` functions.

We never create windows based directly on the third window class. Instead, windows based on the previously described window classes are created as *subclassed* windows. Messages not processed by the window functions for the first two window classes are passed to the window function for this third window class. The third window class knows how to process scroll bar messages and uses them to make calls to the `ScrollWindow` function to scroll its associated window.

This design results in each text display window's gaining the ability to scroll its window when necessary without the need to explicitly include the scrolling logic in both text display window functions. All scrolling logic is isolated into a window function whose only tasks are to process scroll bar messages and scroll a window. Classes like this, for which there are never any actual window instances created, are called *abstract classes*. This is how we achieve, in pure C, the kind of subclassing that can be done in C++. In pure C, the messages are the equivalent of *method calls* in C++, the cases dispatched on message types represent the *methods*, window classes are the equivalent of classes in C++, and windows themselves are class instances.

The Source Code

Let's look at how all these concepts are implemented in an actual program. This program is based on the generic template program, so we include only those excerpts that illustrate the code specific to the SysInfo program. The complete source code is available on the CD-ROM that accompanies this book.

System metrics vary. Some apply to Windows NT 3.*x*, some to Windows 95, some to Win32s, and some to generic Win32. So we need to determine which type of system we are running on. This is shown in the header file systype.h in Listing 4.1 and in the corresponding code in systype.c shown in Listing 4.2.

Listing 4.1: Sysinfo: systype.h
```
WORD getSystemType();

// Returns one of the following bit values
#define SYSTYPE_API4 0x01          // feature supported in API4 only
#define SYSTYPE_API3 0x02          // feature supported in API3 only
#define SYSTYPE_W32s 0x04          // feature supported in Win32s

// The following codes can be entered in the table, but are not returned
// by getSystemType
#define SYSTYPE_W32 (SYSTYPE_API3 | SYSTYPE_API4 ) // feature in native Win32
#define SYSTYPE_ALL (SYSTYPE_W32 | SYSTYPE_W32s) // feature in all Win32
#define SYSTYPE_OBSOLETE4 0x10     // Name is obsolete in API4
```

Listing 4.2: Sysinfo: systype.c
```
#include "stdSDK.h"
#include "systype.h"

/**********************************************************************
*                          getSystemType
* Result: WORD
*       Contains a bit indicating which system type is being used, one of:
*               SYSTYPE_API3
*               SYSTYPE_API4
*               SYSTYPE_W32s
**********************************************************************/

WORD getSystemType()
    {
    OSVERSIONINFO osver;

    osver.dwOSVersionInfoSize = sizeof(OSVERSIONINFO);

    if(!GetVersionEx(&osver))
        return 0;  // should not be possible...

    switch(osver.dwPlatformId)
        { /* platform */
        case VER_PLATFORM_WIN32_NT:
                return (osver.dwMajorVersion < 4 ? SYSTYPE_API3
                                                : SYSTYPE_API4);
```

```
        case VER_PLATFORM_WIN32s:
                return SYSTYPE_W32s;
        case VER_PLATFORM_WIN32_WINDOWS:
                return SYSTYPE_API4;
        default:
                return 0;   // unknown
    } /* platform */

}
```

To register the classes, we create two separate functions in the modules that implement the classes and call them from `initInstance`. Because both child classes are nearly identical, we consolidate most of the code in the superclass from which both classes are derived. Note that we have to remove the `static` declaration from the `internalRegisterClass` function and place its definition in initialization.h to make it available to the caller. This change makes it possible to put the details of class registration in the modules that manage the class, instead of consolidating various distributed knowledge into initialization.c. For example, the registration of a child class is shown in Listing 4.3, with the support code shared among all the subclasses shown in Listing 4.4.

Listing 4.3: SysInfo: Sample child class registration

```
BOOL registerDevCaps(HINSTANCE hinst)
{
 return registerChildClass(hinst, IDS_DEVICECAPSCLASS, IDI_DEVCAPS,
                                    (WNDPROC)DeviceCapsWndProc);
}
```

Listing 4.4: SysInfo: Addition to scroll.c for class registration

```
BOOL registerChildClass(HINSTANCE hinst, UINT classid, UINT icon, WNDPROC proc)
    {
    TCHAR ClassName [MAX_RESOURCESTRING + 1] ;
    WNDCLASSEX wcex ;
    VERIFY (LoadString (hinst, classid, ClassName, DIM(ClassName))) ;
    wcex.cbSize        = sizeof (WNDCLASSEX) ;
    wcex.style         = CS_HREDRAW | CS_VREDRAW | CS_DBLCLKS ;
    wcex.lpfnWndProc   = proc ;
    wcex.cbClsExtra    = 0 ;
    wcex.cbWndExtra    = UGW_SWMAXUSED ;
    wcex.hInstance     = hinst ;
    wcex.hIcon         = LoadIcon (hinst, MAKEINTRESOURCE (icon)) ;
    wcex.hCursor       = LoadCursor (NULL, IDC_IBEAM) ;
    wcex.hbrBackground = (HBRUSH) (COLOR_WINDOW+1) ;
    wcex.lpszMenuName  = NULL;
    wcex.lpszClassName = ClassName ;
    wcex.hIconSm       = LoadImage (hinst,
                                   MAKEINTRESOURCE (icon),
                                   IMAGE_ICON,
                                   GetSystemMetrics (SM_CXSMICON),
                                   GetSystemMetrics (SM_CYSMICON),
                                   LR_SHARED) ;
    if(!internalRegisterClass (&wcex))
        return FALSE;
    return TRUE;
    }
```

The only modification we need to make to initInstance is shown in Listing 4.5. After we create our main frame window, we create our two child windows and force them to redraw. The painting code for the System Metrics subclass is shown in Listing 4.7.

Listing 4.5: SysInfo: Modifications to initInstance

```
    // Create the application's main frame window
    hwnd = createMainFrameWindow (hinst, nCmdShow);
    if (hwnd == NULL)
        return FALSE ;
    hwndChild = createSystemMetrics(hinst, hwnd);
    if(NULL == hwndChild)
        return FALSE;
    UpdateWindow(hwndChild);
    hwndChild = createDevCaps(hinst, hwnd);
    if(NULL == hwndChild)
        return FALSE;
    UpdateWindow(hwndChild);
    return TRUE ;
}
```

We need to make a number of modifications to mainframe.c to support our new application. These are shown in Listing 4.6. The messages we now handle, or handle differently, are indicated by an asterisk. Before we can talk about these, we need to show examples of how the rest of the windows actually work.

Listing 4.6: SysInfo: Additions to mainframe.c

```
//
//    LRESULT CALLBACK
//    mainFrameWndProc (HWND hwnd, UINT message, WPARAM wParam, LPARAM lParam)
//
//    hwnd            Handle of window to which this message applies
//    message         Message number
//    wParam          Message parameter
//    lParam          Message parameter
//
//    PURPOSE:  Processes messages for the main window.
//
//    MESSAGES:
//
//    *WM_ACTIVATEAPP    - notification that app is activated/deactivated
//    *WM_COMMAND        - notification from the menu or controls
//    WM_CONTEXTMENU     - request to display a context menu
//    WM_CREATE          - notification that a window is being created
//    WM_DESTROY         - window is being destroyed
//    WM_DISPLAYCHANGE   - display resolution change notification
//    *WM_INITMENUPOPUP  - set check marks in view menu
//    WM_NCRBUTTONUP     - right button release in nonclient area
//    WM_NOTIFY          - notification from a common control
//    WM_PAINT           - redraw all or part of the client area
//    WM_PRINTCLIENT     - request to draw all of client area into provided DC
//    WM_RBUTTONDOWN     - right button click in client area
//    WM_SETTINGCHANGE   - system parameter change notification
//    WM_SIZE            - window size has changed
//    WM_SYSCOLORCHANGE  - system color setting change notification
//    WM_USERCHANGED     - user log in/out notification
//
```

```
LRESULT CALLBACK
mainFrameWndProc (HWND hwnd, UINT message, WPARAM wParam, LPARAM lParam)
{

    switch (message) {
        case WM_ACTIVATE:
                return HANDLE_WM_ACTIVATE(hwnd, wParam, lParam, mainFrame_OnActivate);

        case WM_COMMAND:          // Notification from menu or control
            return HANDLE_WM_COMMAND (hwnd, wParam, lParam, mainFrame_OnCommand) ;

        // ...

        case WM_INITMENUPOPUP:  // Notification of menu activation
                return HANDLE_WM_INITMENUPOPUP(hwnd, wParam, lParam,
                                                mainFrame_OnInitMenuPopup);

        // ...

        default:
            return DefWindowProc (hwnd, message, wParam, lParam) ;
    }
}

//
// void mainFrame_OnActivate(HWND hwnd, UINT state, HWND hwndActDeact, BOOL fminized)
//
// hwnd: Window handle
// activate: TRUE if being activated
//           FALSE if being deactivated
// threadID: ignored
//

static HWND appfocus = NULL;

void mainFrame_OnActivate(HWND hwnd, UINT state, HWND hwndActDeact, BOOL fminized)
{
 switch(state)
    { /* state */
      case WA_INACTIVE:
            appfocus = GetFocus();
            break;
      case WA_ACTIVE:
      case WA_CLICKACTIVE:
            if(IsWindow(appfocus))
                SetFocus(appfocus);
    } /* state */
}

//
//  void mainFrame_OnCommand (HWND hwnd, int id, HWND hwndCtl, UINT codeNotify)
//
//  hwnd              Handle of window to which this message applies
//  id                Specifies the identifier of the menu item, control, or accelerator.
//  hwndCtl           Handle of the control sending the message if the message
//                    is from a control, otherwise, this parameter is NULL.
//  codeNotify        Specifies the notification code if the message is from a control.
//                    This parameter is 1 when the message is from an accelerator.
```

```
//                    This parameter is 0 when the message is from a menu.
//
//   PURPOSE:
//
//   COMMENTS:
//

static void
mainFrame_OnCommand (HWND hwnd, int id, HWND hwndCtl, UINT codeNotify)
{
    switch (id) {

        case ID_APP_ABOUT:
                {
                 HWND focus = GetFocus();
                 doAbout(hwnd);
                 SetFocus(focus);
                }
                return ;

        // ...

        case IDM_SYSMETRICS:
                // If the window does not exist, it is created
                // If it does exist, it is opened and brought to the top
                createSystemMetrics(GetWindowInstance(hwnd), hwnd);
                return;
        case IDM_DEVCAPS:
                // If the window does not exist, it is created
                // If it does exist, it is opened and brought to the top
                createDevCaps(GetWindowInstance(hwnd), hwnd);
                return;


        default:
            FORWARD_WM_COMMAND (hwnd, id, hwndCtl, codeNotify, DefWindowProc) ;
        }
}

//
//   BOOL mainFrame_OnInitMenuPopup (HWND hwnd, HMENU hmenu, UINT item, BOOL sysmenu)
//
//   hwnd        Handle of window to which this message applies
//   hmenu       Handle of popup menu being activated
//   item        Index of menu in menu bar (ignored)
//   sysmenu     TRUE if system menu (ignored)
//
//   PURPOSE:    Set the check marks in the View menu
//
//   COMMENTS:
//

static BOOL
mainFrame_OnInitMenuPopup (HWND hwnd, HMENU hmenu, UINT item, BOOL sysmenu)
{
 HWND focus = GetFocus();
```

```
CheckMenuItem(hmenu, IDM_SYSMETRICS, MF_UNCHECKED);
CheckMenuItem(hmenu, IDM_DEVCAPS,    MF_UNCHECKED);
if(focus != NULL && focus != hwnd)
    { /* has focus */
     int id = GetWindowLong(focus, GWL_ID);
     switch(id)
         { /* which id */
           case IDS_SYSTEMMETRICSCLASS:
                   CheckMenuItem(hmenu, IDM_SYSMETRICS, MF_CHECKED);
                   break;
           case IDS_DEVICECAPSCLASS:
                   CheckMenuItem(hmenu, IDM_DEVCAPS, MF_CHECKED);
                   break;
         } /* which id */
    } /* has focus */
 return TRUE;
}
```

Listing 4.7: SysInfo: **the** metrics_OnPaint **handler**

```
static void
metrics_OnPaint(HWND hwnd)
{
 HINSTANCE    hInstance;
 SIZE         TextExtent ;
 int          i;
 int          Count;
 int          value;
 int          LineFirst;
 int          LineLast ;
 LONG         lval ;
 PAINTSTRUCT  ps ;
 RECT         rectText;
 RECT         rectExplain;
 RECT         rect ;
 HDC          hdc;
 TCHAR        Buffer [MAX_RESOURCESTRING] ;
 int          cxLeftMargin ;
 int          cyTopMargin ;
 int          CurrHPos;
 int          CurrVPos ;
 WORD         SystemType ;
 int          SymExtent;
 int          DescExtent ;
 TEXTMETRIC   tm ;
 int          cxChar;
 int          cyChar;
 int          maxlen;

// Initialization

hdc = BeginPaint (hwnd, &ps) ;

GetTextMetrics (hdc, &tm) ;
cxChar = tm.tmMaxCharWidth ;
cyChar = tm.tmHeight + tm.tmExternalLeading ;

SystemType = getSystemType() ;
```

```
hInstance = GetWindowInstance (hwnd) ;
DescExtent = 0 ;
SymExtent = 0 ;

// Get the current margins
lval = SendMessage (hwnd, SM_GETMARGINS, 0, 0) ;
cxLeftMargin = LOWORD (lval) ;
cyTopMargin  = HIWORD (lval) ;

// Get the current position of the scroll bars.
// This uses our own defined message SM_GETSCROLLPOS
lval = SendMessage (hwnd, SM_GETSCROLLPOS, 0, 0L) ;
CurrHPos = LOWORD (lval) ;   // in pixels
CurrVPos = HIWORD (lval) ;   // in lines

/* Display the symbolic names */
rectText.left = cxLeftMargin - CurrHPos ;

// Compute the first and last lines that will be displayed

LineFirst = max (0, CurrVPos + ps.rcPaint.top / cyChar - 1) ;
LineLast  = min (DIM(SMtbl), CurrVPos + (ps.rcPaint.bottom + cyChar - 1) / cyChar) ;

for (i = 0; i < DIM(SMtbl); i++)
   { /* SMtbl names */
    // Show options not available in a dimmed color
    if ((SystemType & SMtbl[i].SystemType) == 0)
       SetTextColor(hdc, GetSysColor(COLOR_GRAYTEXT));
    else
       SetTextColor(hdc, GetSysColor(COLOR_WINDOWTEXT));

    // Get the SystemMetric's symbolic name.
    // Compute its maximum width so we know the overall max string size

    Count = LoadString (hInstance, SMtbl [i]. StringId,
                                           Buffer, DIM(Buffer)) ;
    GetTextExtentPoint32 (hdc, Buffer, Count, &TextExtent) ;
    SymExtent = max (SymExtent, TextExtent.cx) ;

    // If the line is off the screen, don't bother showing it.
    // But we've accounted for its width
    if (i < LineFirst || i >= LineLast)
        continue ;

    rectText.top = cyTopMargin + (i - CurrVPos) * cyChar ;
    rectText.right = rectText.left + TextExtent.cx;
    rectText.bottom = rectText.top + cyChar ;

    // Demonstrate optimization: only paint it if it is in the
    // invalidated rectangle
    if (IntersectRect (&rect, &rectText, &ps.rcPaint))
       TextOut (hdc, rectText.left, rectText.top,
                 Buffer, Count) ;

   } /* SMtbl names */

// Now that we've put out the first column, we know the widest string
```

```
// that has been displayed in that column

/* Display the descriptions */
rectText.left += (int) SymExtent + cxChar ;
for (i = 0; i < DIM(SMtbl); i++)
   { /* SMtbl descriptions */
   // Load the description and display it
   Count = LoadString (hInstance, SMtbl [i].StringId + 1,
                          Buffer, DIM(Buffer)) ;
   GetTextExtentPoint32 (hdc, Buffer, Count, &TextExtent) ;
   DescExtent = max (DescExtent, TextExtent.cx) ;

   if (i < LineFirst || i >= LineLast)
       continue ;

   if ((SystemType & SMtbl[i].SystemType) == 0)
      SetTextColor(hdc, GetSysColor(COLOR_GRAYTEXT));
   else
      SetTextColor(hdc, GetSysColor(COLOR_WINDOWTEXT));

   rectText.top = cyTopMargin + (i - CurrVPos) * cyChar ;
   rectText.right = rectText.left + TextExtent.cx;
   rectText.bottom = rectText.top + cyChar ;
   if (IntersectRect (&rect, &rectText, &ps.rcPaint))
           TextOut (hdc, rectText.left, rectText.top,
                          Buffer, Count) ;
   } /* SMtbl descriptions */

/* Display the values */
// We have to first compute the widest string.  To do this, we have a
// list of all the strings we use.  We compute the text extent based on this

LoadString(hInstance, IDS_VALUE, Buffer, DIM(Buffer));
GetTextExtentPoint32(hdc, Buffer, lstrlen(Buffer), &TextExtent);

rectText.left += (int) DescExtent + cxChar ;
rectText.right = rectText.left + TextExtent.cx;
for (i = LineFirst; i < LineLast; i++)
   { /* value */
   /* Get the SystemMetric's value. */
   if ((SystemType & SMtbl[i].SystemType) == 0)
      { /* not defined */
       SetTextColor(hdc, GetSysColor(COLOR_GRAYTEXT));
       lstrcpy(Buffer, _T("----"));
      } /* not defined */
   else
      { /* defined */
       SetTextColor(hdc, GetSysColor(COLOR_WINDOWTEXT));
       value = GetSystemMetrics (SMtbl [i].Index) ;
       wsprintf (Buffer, _T("%4d"), value) ;
      } /* defined */

   rectText.top = cyTopMargin + (i - CurrVPos) * cyChar ;
   rectText.bottom = rectText.top + cyChar ;

   SetTextAlign (hdc, TA_RIGHT) ;
   if (IntersectRect (&rect, &rectText, &ps.rcPaint))
```

```
        TextOut (hdc, rectText.right - 1, rectText.top, Buffer, lstrlen(Buffer));

    rectExplain = rectText;
    rectExplain.left = rectText.right + cxChar;
    // We will compute rectExplain.right as needed

    maxlen = rectText.right; // assume no explanations needed yet

    if(SMtbl[i].format != NULL && (SystemType & SMtbl[i].SystemType) != 0)
        { /* has explanation */
          SIZE tx;
          value = GetSystemMetrics (SMtbl [i].Index) ;
          SetTextAlign (hdc, TA_LEFT) ;
          SMtbl[i].format(hwnd, value, Buffer, DIM(Buffer));
          GetTextExtentPoint32(hdc, Buffer, lstrlen(Buffer), &tx);
          maxlen = max(maxlen, rectExplain.left + tx.cx);
          rectExplain.right = rectExplain.left + tx.cx;
          if(IntersectRect(&rect, &rectExplain, &ps.rcPaint))
              TextOut(hdc, rectExplain.left - 1, rectExplain.top,
                                            Buffer, lstrlen(Buffer));
        } /* has explanation */
    } /* value */

// Now set the horizontal and vertical scrolling limits

SendMessage(hwnd, SM_SETDOCSIZE, maxlen, DIM(SMtbl));
EndPaint (hwnd, &ps) ;
}
```

Listing 4.8: SysInfo: user-defined messages in scroll.h

```
/*****************************************/
/* Public section of the header file. */
/*****************************************/
// These definitions provide the external interface
// to the ScrollingWindow class.
//*********************************************************
// SM_GETMARGINS
// Inputs;
//     wParam: unused, 0
//     lParam:: unused, 0
// Result:
//     LOWORD: Left margin, in pixels
//     HIWORD: Top margin, in pixels
#define SM_GETMARGINS          (WM_USER+1)

//*********************************************************
// SM_GETDOCSIZE
// Inputs;
//     wParam: unused, 0
//     lParam:: unused, 0
// Result:
//     LOWORD: Number of horizontal pixels in document
//     HIWORD: Number of lines in document (not pixels)
#define SM_GETDOCSIZE          (WM_USER+2)

//*********************************************************
// SM_SETDOCSIZE
```

```
// Inputs:
//      wParam: Width, in pixels
//      lParam: Height, in lines
// Result:
//      0, always
// Effect:
//      Stores the current document size, in pixels
//      which is returned by SM_GETDOCSIZE
#define SM_SETDOCSIZE(WM_USER+3)

//****************************************************
// SM_GETSCROLLPOS
// Inputs;
//      wParam: unused, 0
//      lParam:: unused, 0
// Result:
//      LOWORD: Horizontal scrolling position, in pixels
//      HIWORD: Vertical scrolling position, in lines
#define SM_GETSCROLLPOS          (WM_USER+4)


LRESULT CALLBACK
scrollingWndProc (HWND hwnd, UINT msg, WPARAM wParam, LPARAM lParam);

HWND createChildWindow(HINSTANCE hinst, HWND hwnd, UINT classid, UINT titleid);
BOOL registerChildClass(HINSTANCE hinst, UINT classid, UINT icon, WNDPROC proc);


/****************************************/
/* Private section of the header file. */
/****************************************/
/* These definitions are used only by the ScrollingWindow class. */
/* These macros encapsulate the details of window extra area accesses      */
/* making it much easier to later rearrange the fields, if necessary.      */
/* They also provide the proper type casts for the data involved.          */
/* Window extra area field(s) */
#define UGWL_DOCSIZE              0
#define UGW_SWMAXUSED             (UGWL_DOCSIZE + sizeof(LONG))

#define getDocSize(w)      (GetWindowLong (w, UGWL_DOCSIZE))
#define setDocSize(wnd, w, h) (SetWindowLong (wnd, UGWL_DOCSIZE, MAKELONG(w,h)))
```

Sysinfo Initialization

The Sysinfo program registers two classes. The actual registration is done by common code, registerChildClass, in scroll.c. The classes have class styles to indicate that the window must be redrawn whenever the horizontal or vertical size of the window changes, plus an additional style to indicate that double-clicks will be reported:

```
wcex.style = CS_HREDRAW | CS_VREDRAW | CS_DBLCLKS;
```

The class registration function takes the address of a handler function as one of its parameters. It also requests that Windows allocate UGW_SWMAXUSED bytes of extra space in the window structure for each window of this type:

```
wc.lpfnWndProc = proc ;
wc.cbWndExtra = UGW_SWMAXUSED ;
```

The registration follows fairly closely the registration we defined for the main window class, except that it takes the string ID of the class, the icon ID of the class, and the procedure pointer as parameters. The scroll.c file also defines the `scrollingWndProc` function, which is used as the superclass handler for both classes.

Next, Sysinfo registers the `SystemMetricsClass` and the `DeviceCapsClass` window classes; however, both of these classes subclass the abstract `ScrollingWindowClass`. A message received by the `systemMetricsWndProc` window function is processed and forwarded to the `scrollingWndProc` window function.

Subclassing the System Metrics Window Class

The Sysinfo window classes are registered, and two windows have been created. Now the work really begins! Let's look in depth at the `SystemMetricsClass`. You'll see how it subclasses the `ScrollingWindowClass` and how it displays its text. The `DeviceCapsClass` is practically identical, and we're not going to discuss it. You can look at the listings and see its details.

The `systemMetricsWndProc` function processes messages for `SystemMetricsClass` windows. The first message it processes is the `WM_CREATE` message that signals the window creation. It is sent during the `CreateWindow` function call during the program initialization. We don't actually do anything in this handler, but it poses a particular danger that we point out in the next pitfall.

 Generally, the handlers for message crackers are defined as returning the same value that the message defines. The `OnCreate` handler, however, is a bizarre exception to this rule. Its response to a `WM_CREATE` message is either −1, indicating failure, or 0, indicating success. The `OnCreate` handler is expected to return `TRUE` for success and `FALSE` for failure, which means that forwarding to `DefWindowProc` in the expected fashion will do exactly the opposite. The result is that you will have window creation fail, returning `NULL` to `CreateWindow`, but `GetLastError` will return 0 because the error was not generated internally in Windows.

The way you might expect to call `DefWindowProc` is by a line of the following form:

```
static BOOL
scroll_OnCreate(HWND hwnd, LPCREATESTRUCT cs)
{
 // ...
 return FORWARD_WM_CREATE(hwnd, cs, DefWindowProc); // FAILS!!!! WRONG!!!
}
```

However, this fails, as we explain in the pitfall insert because `DefWindowProc` returns a "true" value for failure and a "false" value for success, the opposite of what the `HANDLE_WM_CREATE` macro expects! We have illustrated this by the following code:

```
static BOOL
scroll_OnCreate(HWND hwnd, LPCREATESTRUCT cs)
{
 // ... if there were initialization to do, we would do it here...
 return (-1 != FORWARD_WM_CREATE(hwnd, cs, DefWindowProc));
}
```

With this, the window function has nearly completed subclassing the `ScrollingWindowClass`. The only step remaining is to ensure that a message not completely handled within this window function is passed on to the base class's window function. This is done at the end of the `switch` statement by calling the `CallWindowProc` function:

```
return
    CallWindowProc (scrollingWndProc, hwnd, msg, wParam, lParam) ;
```

The `CallWindowProc` function calls the window function whose address is given by the first parameter. The other four parameters are the standard parameters to a window function. The value returned by the `CallWindowProc` function is the value returned by the window function that it calls. The `systemMetricsWndProc` function, in turn, passes the value back to the `DefWindowProc` function. You must call the subclassed window function by using the `CallWindowProc` function. You cannot call the window function indirectly via its address as follows:

```
return                  /* Don't do this! */
    scrollingWndProc(hwnd, msg, wParam, lParam) ;
```

This is equivalent to calling a window function directly; this also cannot be done. You can call a window function only via the `CallWindowProc` function. This is because a message may require additional processing as it is sent to a window procedure. It also accounts for the fact that only on some platforms, or under some conditions, there may be additional processing required to call a window procedure. In Win32, this may involve Unicode translations.

In Win16, you *had* to use `CallWindowProc` because of the peculiar requirements of maintaining addressability in the 16-bit segmented address space. In principle, you should be able to call a Win32 window procedure directly by name, instead of going through `CallWindowProc`. This would be true if it weren't for the additional requirements of Unicode translation. In addition, because the specification requires that this function be used, other platforms in the future may take advantage of this requirement.

Displaying the System Metrics

Several user-defined message are processed by the window function (although in this case the term *user* means you, the programmer). The user-defined application messages are defined in the scroll.h header file shown in Listing 4.8.

The `ScrollingWindowClass` uses these messages to request information from a subclassing window class. The scrolling window function sends the `SM_GETDOCSIZE` message to the window when it needs to know the size of the document it is scrolling. In response, the `systemMetricsWndProc` returns the width and height of the document:

```
case SM_GETDOCSIZE:
    return getDocSize(hwnd);
```

Note the careful documentation conventions we use for the messages. Since messages are logically methods of the class, they deserve the same level of detailed documentation any function deserves. It is often very difficult to remember–hours, weeks, or months after a user-defined message has been specified–exactly what this message was intended for, what its `wParam` and `lParam` meant, and what its result means. Short of your reading the code to decrypt its purpose, there is no way to tell what a message means. We urge you to try to document these messages carefully, as there is no compile-time type-checking that usually goes into sending one.

You should also adopt some naming conventions to make sure your messages are not confused with other messages in the system. For example, you should not name your messages with a "WM_" prefix. Typical conventions are prefixes such as "WMU_" or "UWM_" (to indicate *U*ser *W*indow *M*essages). Or, as has been done here, you could choose a prefix based on the window class to which the message can be sent. Techniques such as these greatly enhance the understandability of your code and reduce potential conflicts with future Windows releases.

Also, the simplicity of some of our handlers indicates that they likely could have been done as in-line code. We chose to split them into separate functions because although *this* version of the program has a simple computation, the next version may not. You will not be tempted to expand the code until you have a large, unwieldy case in the midst of the window function.

The window function really starts working when it receives a WM_PAINT message. First, the display context is retrieved along with the PAINTSTRUCT structure, which indicates the rectangle within the client area that needs repainting. Having retrieved the display context, we then paint the parts of the screen that need painting. Finally, we release the display context by calling EndPaint.

```
hdc = BeginPaint (hwnd, &ps) ;
```

All the character strings displayed by the Sysinfo program are located in *string resources;* they are not part of the code. Generally, a Windows application should store its character literals as string resources. You load resources, including string resources, into memory only when they are required, as we do in this example program. Resources can be discarded from memory when the space they occupy is needed for other purposes. Windows can discard resources because it can reload the resources from the executable file if they are needed again. It can't discard a program's data segment (which contains, among other things, string literals) as it can resources because the program may have changed the data in the segment since it was originally loaded. Resources are read-only, so they can be discarded and reloaded as necessary.

While the ability to reduce storage was considered critical in the memory-limited Win16, it is not nearly as critical in Win32. What has become more important in Win32 is the ability to change the text of the strings to support your application in multiple languages. We discuss internationalization issues further in Chapter 7 and Chapter 12. As a general policy, you should have no local-language strings anywhere in your program.

We have carefully arranged our string numbers so that the string at a specific string ID contains the code value, for example, "SM_CXICON", and the string ID exactly one position higher contains the explanation, for example, "Width of icon". We build a table that contains the index required to retrieve the value, the string ID of the code value, and a possible function pointer to get a textual explanation of the resulting value. The table also contains flags to indicate the platforms for which the index is meaningful (although it is not clear that the Microsoft documentation is accurate in all respects). A segment of the table is shown next.

```
static struct tagSMTbl {
    int         Index ;
    WORD        StringId ;
```

```
  WORD           SystemType ;
  void (*format)(HWND hwnd, int value, LPSTR Buffer, int size);
} SMtbl [] = {
  { SM_ARRANGE,       IDS_SM_ARRANGE,       SYSTYPE_API4, metrics_Arrange},
  { SM_CLEANBOOT,     IDS_SM_CLEANBOOT,     SYSTYPE_API4, metrics_CleanString},
  { SM_CMETRICS,      IDS_SM_CMETRICS,      SYSTYPE_API4, NULL },
  { SM_CMOUSEBUTTONS, IDS_SM_CMOUSEBUTTONS, SYSTYPE_API4, NULL },
  { SM_CXBORDER,      IDS_SM_CXBORDER,      SYSTYPE_ALL,  NULL },
  { SM_CYBORDER,      IDS_SM_CYBORDER,      SYSTYPE_ALL,  NULL },
  { SM_CYCAPTION,     IDS_SM_CYCAPTION,     SYSTYPE_ALL,  NULL },
  // ...
```

You need the instance handle of the module containing the resources in order to load them, so we fetch the handle from the window structure by calling the GetWindowInstance macro API function:

```
hInstance = GetWindowInstance (hwnd) ;
```

To display the text properly, you need to know what margins to use. To find out the margin settings for the current window, the systemMetricsWndProc function sends a message to the window it's going to paint to request the margins, as shown by the following statements:

```
lval = SendMessage (hwnd, SM_GETMARGINS, 0, 0) ;
cxLeftMargin = LOWORD (lval) ;
cyTopMargin  = HIWORD (lval) ;
```

Something a little unexpected is happening here. The SM_GETMARGINS message is sent to the window function for the window with the hwnd handle (that is, the systemMetricsWndProc function, the same function that is sending the message). This is effectively a recursive call. However, notice that the systemMetricsWndProc doesn't process an SM_GETMARGINS message. Rather, it passes it along to the window function for the base class. As you'll see later in the chapter, the scrollingWndProc function *does* process this message, and it returns a default margin size. This approach permits an individual window function either to establish its own unique margins or to do nothing at all and use the default margins supplied by the scrollingWndProc.

You can't simply start displaying the text from the beginning because the user may have scrolled down in the output. The systemMetricsWndProc function sends the SM_GETSCROLLPOS message to obtain the current position of the scroll boxes of the scroll bars. Like the previous message, this one also passes recursively through this window function, but in this case intercepting it never makes sense. Only the base class knows the current position of the scroll bars.

Now the text can be displayed, but you should try to display only the information contained within the invalid rectangle. As mentioned previously in the chapter, you can rewrite the entire screen, but Windows clips everything that is outside the invalid rectangle and is not written to the screen. Drawing outside the invalid rectangle simply wastes time. Trying to determine what to draw takes time as well, so there's a trade-off between the two.

We store the number of lines and the maximum width (in pixels) by sending the window an SM_SETDOCSIZE message containing the height and width. We can retrieve it later by sending an SM_GETDOCSIZE message, which returns the number of lines in its high-order 16 bits and the width in pixels in the low-order 16 bits.

It may be that not all of the lines of system information need to be displayed. We used the current vertical position of the scroll box (how far down in the list to start) and the location of the invalid rectangle to determine the first and last lines to repaint. We also used the margin settings and the current horizontal position of the scroll box (how far over in a line to start) to determine where to display each line horizontally:

```
rectText.left = cxLeftMargin - CurrHPos * cxChar ;
LineFirst = max (0, CurrVPos + ps.rcPaint.top / cyChar - 1) ;
LineLast  = min (DIM(SMtbl),
                 CurrVPos + (ps.rcPaint.bottom + cyChar - 1) / cyChar) ;
```

Even though we know the first and last lines of text that need to be repainted, we still must loop through each line. We want to produce a display containing three columns of text, one each for the symbolic name of each metric, the description of the metric, and the value of the metric on this system. However, we don't know how far apart they should be spaced. We could determine the maximum length of the character strings in each column, but we don't know how wide each character is. When a variable-pitch font is selected–and it normally is–each character can be a different width. Some devices perform *kerning* as well. On such devices, the width of a character string may not equal the sum of the widths of the individual characters. (*Kerning* is the term for changing the intercharacter spacing, typically by placing one character up under the overhang of another. For example, a lowercase **i** following an uppercase **W** might be placed under the overhang of the **W**. We talk more about this in Chapter 15.)

You can't determine the width of a character until a program executes and the current font is known. So we load the character string for every line from the resource file using the LoadString function and calculate its width in the current font using the GetTextExtentPoint32 function.

Programmers who know the Win16 API may remember the GetTextExtent API call. This call is obsolete and is not supported in Win32. It returned two 16-bit coordinates packed into a single DWORD. In Win32, we have a 32-bit coordinate space and therefore must have a reference to a POINT structure into which two 32-bit values can be placed.

Although we are working in a 32-bit coordinate space, remember that Windows 95 has a limitation that only the low-order 16 bits of a graphic coordinate are used. Therefore the GetTextExtentPoint32 returns two 16-bit values in the 32-bit integer fields of the POINT structure; the high-order 16 bits of each integer are all 0.

We save the width of the longest character string in the first column of text. We use this maximum width plus the width of a character as the starting horizontal position of the second column of text. This is done by the following code:

```
int SymExtent = 0;

for (i = 0; i < DIM(SMtbl); i++) {

    Count = LoadString (hInstance, SMtbl [i]. StringId, Buffer, DIM(Buffer)) ;

    GetTextExtentPoint32 (hdc, Buffer, Count, &TextExtent) ;
    SymExtent = max (SymExtent, TextExtent.cx) ;
```

A similar computation is performed a little later on the second column of text. We draw each string in each column individually. We draw first the left column of text from top to bottom, then the center column, and finally the right column.

One of the very nice features of Windows is that whether it is the screen or the printer you are drawing to, you do *not* need to draw the text one line at a time, top to bottom. The device context is a completely randomly addressable slate to which you can write anything anywhere. The screen output appears immediately. The printer output "appears" when a page is closed. (Of course, it actually appears after the document is closed, the Print Manager processes it, and the printer finally renders it, but you get the idea.)

Actually displaying the text takes a relatively long time as compared to simply computing whether it needs to be displayed. So once we've determined the length of the string, we don't do anything more with the string if it isn't on a line within the limits established from the invalid rectangle. In this way, we don't waste time displaying lines that are still on the screen.

The issue of the trade-off between displaying information unconditionally vs. doing the computations to avoid calling the GDI that we show here is not as simple as it might first appear. In the case we have, it is a very simple computation, which we can do quickly in our own code. But if you are doing general graphics drawing, you have to be able to answer questions like "does a straight line between these two points cross any invalidated area of the window?" or "does any part of this filled complex polygon intersect any invalidated area of the window?", which are hard questions to answer efficiently. Unless you are a Serious Graphics Wizard, you then haul out your books on graphics algorithms, attempt to write the code, and debug it. After all this work, you may be dismayed to learn that your code may actually be *slower* than simply drawing everything and letting GDI do the clipping! This is because the GDI algorithms are highly tuned (much of GDI is written in pure assembler for raw speed, using every sneaky trick that serious assembly programmers know) and, in cooperation with the device driver, will try to drop as much unnecessary computation at the highest level possible. Objects that lie outside all invalidated areas don't make it to the low-level driver at all. Filled polygons might be handled by passing the *display card* a clipping area and a polygon specification and telling the card to "fill this polygon subject to the clipping region", removing all complex GDI computations entirely. You can't hope to compete with these algorithms in simple cases, so it is often not worth the effort to do so. But if you have serious performance constraints (real-time animation, for example, or drawing thousands of objects on a screen), then you just *might* be able to beat the GDI performance. Much of the folklore of graphics optimization under Windows predates modern accelerator cards and Windows drivers, and was more relevant on an 8088 running a CGA or an 80286 running an EGA than a modern processor chip with an even moderately priced graphics accelerator card and a decent driver. Don't assume you can beat GDI performance. And don't assume you can't.

However, a string may not need repainting simply because it's on a line that needs repainting. For example, the left-most column of text may not be visible because the user has horizontally scrolled the window. In that case, we draw only the center and right columns of text because they are the only ones visible. We calculate the bounding rectangle for the string on each line that needs to be repainted:

```
rectText.top = cyTopMargin + (i - CurrVPos) * cyChar ;
rectText.right = rectText.left + (int) TextExtent.cx ;
rectText.bottom = rectText.top + cyChar ;
```

The `IntersectRect` function returns nonzero when the intersection of the bounding rectangle for the text and the invalid rectangle is not empty. A nonempty intersection means that part of a string lies in the invalid portion of the client area and needs to be repainted. The `TextOut` function displays the text string:

```
if (IntersectRect (&rect, &rectText, &ps.rcPaint))
    TextOut (hdc, rectText.left, rectText.top,
             Buffer, Count) ;
}
```

Nearly the same steps are performed for the second and third columns of text. One thing that deserves more attention is the output of the numeric values in the third column. Numerals are usually right-aligned rather than left-aligned, as are text strings. The usual approach of space-padding a numeric field to right-align the value does not work when you're using a variable-pitch font. Even though all numerals have equal widths, the width of a space character is less than the width of a numeral. The effect is that one space character does not space over as far as one numeral.

Rather than space-padding, you need to specify that the TextOut function should right-align the string. You call the SetTextAlign function to change the text alignment:

```
SetTextAlign (hdc, TA_RIGHT) ;
```

When you receive a common display context (which is the type Sysinfo uses), all attributes are set to default values each time the display context is retrieved. The BeginPaint function returns a display context that has the text alignment attribute set to the default value, left-aligned. We change the attribute to right-aligned before displaying the last column of text. When the next WM_PAINT message arrives, the display context will once again contain all default values.

Once you change to right-aligned output, you must pass the coordinates of the upper-right corner of the bounding rectangle of the string—not the coordinates of the upper-left corner—to the TextOut function. Because all numerals have equal widths, the coordinate of the right side of the bounding rectangle is the sum of the left side coordinate plus the length of any digit string (in most variable-pitch fonts the digits are all the same width, so that columns of digits will line up properly). We use the string resource IDS_VALUE (which holds a sequence of digits) to get our "prototype" value:

```
LoadString(hInstance, IDS_VALUE, Buffer, DIM(Buffer));
GetTextExtentPoint32 (hdc, Buffer, lstrlen(Buffer), &TextExtent)
rectText.right = rectText.left + TextExtent.cx;
```

Because some of the values are best expressed with a textual explanation, we allow a means for the program to pass the value to an interpretation routine and get back a string, which it then displays to the right of the numeric value. The normal "right end" of the text is the right side of where the digits are displayed, but if we add an explanation, we add its length to the length of the line. Ultimately, when we have written all the lines, we have a known horizontal distance and a known number of lines. We store this for future reference and also compute the settings for the scroll bars:

```
SendMessage(hwnd, SM_SETDOCSIZE, maxlen, DIM(SMtbl));
```

When you have displayed all necessary information, you must release the display context. Not doing so will cause Windows to eventually run out of display contexts and be unable to display anything. The system then will appear to hang. You release the display context by calling the EndPaint function:

```
EndPaint (hwnd, &ps) ;
return 0 ;
```

The WM_PAINT message processing is now complete. There is no additional processing required from any of the subclassed window functions, so we return a 0 value rather than allow the message to be passed on to the ScrollingWindowClass window function.

Scrolling the Window

You may have noticed how little the window function that displays the system metrics needs to know about scrolling. It must provide the document size to the scrolling function and retrieve the current position of the scroll bars from the scrolling function. Both of these actions are implemented by a standard Windows methodology called message passing. You've seen how messages sent to the text display window function end up passed on to the subclassed window function. Now it's time to look at what happens when they arrive.

The `scrollingWndProc` function in the scroll.c source file is the window function for the `ScrollingWindowClass`. The `SystemMetricsClass` examines all messages, processes them as necessary, and then passes them on to the `scrollingWndProc` for examination. The only exception is the `WM_PAINT` message. It is handled completely within the `systemMetricsWndProc`. Although it could be harmlessly passed on, doing so isn't necessary and passing on a completely processed message is less efficient.

If we were to pass the `WM_PAINT` message to the `scrollingWndProc` function, it would pass the message to the `DefWindowProc` function. The `DefWindowProc` function responds to a `WM_PAINT` message by calling the `BeginPaint` function and the `EndPaint` function. These function calls do absolutely nothing because the update region for the window was set to an empty region by the original call to the `BeginPaint` function in the `SystemMetricWndProc` function. This accomplishes nothing, so we avoid all this wasted effort by not passing the `WM_PAINT` message to the `scrollingWndProc` function.

The `scrollingWndProc` function initializes the horizontal and vertical scroll position for the window to 0. These positions can't be kept in either a static or a global variable. Each scrolling window must maintain an individual record of its own scroll-bar positions; however, a single window function is called on behalf of all windows of its class. In particular, Sysinfo creates two scrolling windows, and each one can be scrolled to a different position in its respective display.

Scrolling windows store the current horizontal and vertical scroll-bar positions in the *window extra* area. This provides a per-window storage area for the positions. (The *class extra* and the *window extra* areas are limited resources. When you need to store more than a few bytes–8 to 16 is a reasonable limit–you should allocate memory to hold the data and store the pointer to the memory [a 4-byte value] in the extra area.) You allocate this space by setting the `cbWndExtra` or `cbClassExtra` values to something other than 0 when registering the class (see what we did on page 204). All windows of the same class share one class extra area. Using the class extra area is uncommon, so we describe only the window extra area.

The scrolling window function processes the `SM_GETMARGINS` message by returning the number of pixels–horizontally and vertically–in an eighth of an inch. The number of pixels per inch can be obtained by calling the `GetDeviceCaps` function and inquiring for the `LOGPIXELSX` and `LOGPIXELSY` values as follows:

```
static LRESULT
scroll_GetMargins(HWND hwnd)
    {
    LONG result;
    hdc = GetDC (hwnd) ;
    result = MAKELONG ((GetDeviceCaps (hdc, LOGPIXELSX) / 8),
                       (GetDeviceCaps (hdc, LOGPIXELSY) / 8)) ;
    ReleaseDC (hwnd, hdc) ;
    return result ;
```

This code supplies default horizontal and vertical margins and ensures that this message will always receive a response even when subclassing functions don't override it. Subclassing functions can override this default value by processing this message and not passing it on to the base class.

The SM_GETSCROLLPOS message is used to respond to outside requests for the scroll bars' current scroll positions. The values are fetched from the scroll bars using the GetScrollInfo function and returned.

```
static LRESULT
scroll_OnGetScrollPos(HWND hwnd)
    {
      SCROLLINFO si;
      LONG h;
      LONG v;
      si.cbSize = sizeof(SCROLLINFO) ;
      si.fMask = SIF_POS;
      if(!GetScrollInfo(hwnd, SB_VERT, &si))
         v = 0;
      else
         v = si.nPos;
      if(!GetScrollInfo(hwnd, SB_HORZ, &si))
         h = 0;
      else
         h = si.nPos;
      return MAKELONG (LOWORD (h), LOWORD (v)) ;

    }
```

Note that we test the result of GetScrollInfo. This is because if there is no scroll bar actually being shown in the window, GetScrollInfo returns FALSE and does not change anything in the SCROLLINFO structure.

Quite a bit more occurs when the window changes in size. This is signaled by a WM_SIZE message. When a window changes size, the window function must calculate new values for the current position of a scroll bar's scroll box and the maximum value for the scroll bar's range. Because the size can change both horizontally and vertically, the window function must compute both values for both scroll bars.

WM_SIZE **Message Cracker Handler**

void cls_OnSize(HWND hwnd, UINT state, int cx, int cy);					
	wParam		**lParam**		
Parameter	**lo**	**hi**	**lo**	**hi**	**Meaning**
hwnd					Window handle of the window.
state	■				SIZE_ value indicating the type of resizing requested.
cx			■		New width of the client area, in logical units.
cy				■	New height of the client area, in logical units.

To compute these values, you must decide how the window should scroll. We use the vertical dimension as an example because that's the direction in which most people are used to viewing scrolling. But the example also applies to horizontal scrolling.

The document consists of a top margin, some number of text lines, and a bottom margin. When the scroll box is at the top of the vertical scroll bar (at position 0), the top margin of the document, followed by the beginning of the text, should be visible at the top of the window. When the scroll box is at the bottom of the vertical scroll bar, the bottom margin of the document should be visible at the bottom of the window. This approach is more usable than scrolling until one line (the last one) is displayed at the top of a window. We have to be careful, though, to not exceed the 16-bit limit. If our font is 20 pixels high, we hit this limit with only 1,638 lines, which is rather small by some measures.

What about those 32-bit graphics coordinates that Win32 uses? We should not be subject to a 16-bit limitation in Win32! But in fact we are. Both Win32s and Windows 95 run on a 16-bit substrate and inherit all the limitations of that 16-bit substrate. If you really need 32-bit coordinates, you are limited to running only on Windows NT. Of course, you could detect which version of Windows you are running on and adjust your program's behavior accordingly. But be aware that Windows 95 supports 32-bit coordinate *values*, but only looks at the low-order 16 bits. If you use a value that exceeds the 16-bit range, you will get no warning; you will just get strange behavior. And note that since we assume the 16-bit limitation will not be a problem for this application, we actually pack two 16-bit coordinates into a single 32-bit value. If you want full 32-bit coordinates, you will have to go through some extra work to get them.

The maximum vertical scroll-bar position must be greater than or equal to 0 and less than or equal to the number of lines in the document, minus the number of lines that can be displayed in the window. This difference can be less than 0 when the window is large enough to display all lines of output. In this case, the maximum range value is set to 0, the same as the minimum range value. Setting the minimum and maximum values of the scroll-bar range to the same values hides the scroll bar. Effectively, when the window becomes large enough to hold the entire display, the scroll bar disappears because it's not required. When the window is reduced in size to the point that scrolling is required, the maximum range value becomes greater than 0 and is no longer equal to its minimum range value. At this point, the scroll bar reappears.

```
static void
scroll_RecomputeVScroll(HWND hwnd)
    {
    SCROLLINFO si;
    int   MaxVPos ;
    int   CurrVPos ;
    int   cyChar;
    int   cyMargin ;
    int   LinesVisible;
    int   cy;
    // Get the size of a character in the current font (in pixels).
    {
    HDC   hdc;
    TEXTMETRIC tm;
    hdc = GetDC (hwnd) ;
    GetTextMetrics (hdc, &tm) ;
    ReleaseDC (hwnd, hdc);
    cyChar      = tm.tmHeight + tm.tmExternalLeading ;
    }
    // Get the present postion of the scroll bars.
    si.cbSize = sizeof(SCROLLINFO) ;
    si.fMask = SIF_POS;
    GetScrollInfo(hwnd, SB_VERT, &si);
```

```
CurrVPos   = si.nPos;
// Get the size of the document text.
{
 LONG tmp = SendMessage (hwnd, SM_GETDOCSIZE, 0, 0L) ;
 MaxVPos   = HIWORD (tmp) ; // vertical size, in lines
 // Get the size of the margins (in pixels).
 tmp = SendMessage (hwnd, SM_GETMARGINS, 0, 0L) ;
 cyMargin  = HIWORD (tmp) ;
}
// Get the size of the screen
{
 RECT r;
 GetClientRect(hwnd, &r);
 cy = r.bottom;
}
// Compute the number of lines visible on the screen
LinesVisible = (cy - 2 * cyMargin) / cyChar;
if(LinesVisible > MaxVPos) // Unlikely...
    CurrVPos = MaxVPos = 0;  // but if it happens, suppress the scroll bar
// Set the parameters of min, max, and page size
si.nMin = 0 ;
si.nMax = MaxVPos ;
si.nPos = CurrVPos;
si.nPage = LinesVisible;
si.fMask = SIF_POS | SIF_RANGE | SIF_PAGE ;
SetScrollInfo (hwnd, SB_VERT, &si, TRUE) ;
```

The TRUE parameter to the SetScrollInfo function specifies that the scroll bar should be redrawn.

Finally, we look at the actual scroll request message sent by a vertical scroll bar: the WM_VSCROLL message.

```
static void
scroll_OnVScroll(HWND hwnd, HWND hctl, UINT sbcode, int pos)
    {
    // ... declarations
    { /* get char height */
     TEXTMETRIC tm;
     HDC dc;
     dc = GetDC (hwnd) ;
     GetTextMetrics (dc, &tm) ;
     ReleaseDC (hwnd, dc);
     cyChar = tm.tmHeight + tm.tmExternalLeading ;
    } /* get char height */

    { /* get page size */
     RECT r;
     LONG l = SendMessage (hwnd, SM_GETMARGINS, 0, 0L) ;
     int cyMargin    = HIWORD (l) ;
     GetClientRect(hwnd, &r);
     pagesize = (r.bottom - r.top) / cyChar;
    } /* get page size */

    si.cbSize = sizeof(SCROLLINFO);
    si.fMask = SIF_POS | SIF_RANGE;
    GetScrollInfo(hwnd, SB_VERT, &si);
    CurrVPos = si.nPos;
    MaxVPos = si.nMax;
```

The height of a line of text is calculated based on the current font for the window. This height isn't stored because the font could be changed by a subclassing window function. We then compute the page size, that is, the maximum number of lines that can be on the page. This value will be used to compute the correct size for the proportional thumb control and how much to scroll when we scroll a "page". We then retrieve the current position and range so that we have the current values (we don't need to check for failure because we're in the OnVScroll handler, and we couldn't get here if the scroll bar were not visible).

The sbcode parameter of the OnVScroll handler specifies the type of scroll request, one of the SB_ symbols. In each case, the scrollingWndProc function calculates the number of lines to scroll relative to the current position. For the SB_BOTTOM message, this value is the number of lines between the current position and the maximum scroll range value:

```
delta = MaxVPos - CurrVPos ;
```

For the SB_TOP message, this means backing up from the current position to the 0 position. This is -CurrVPos lines:

```
delta = -CurrVPos ;
```

For the SB_LINEUP message, we need to scroll backwards one line so that delta is set to -1. For the SB_LINEDOWN message, we need to scroll forward one line so that delta is set to 1.

We've made the SB_PAGEUP and SB_PAGEDOWN messages scroll the window by the pagesize number of lines:

```
case SB_PAGEUP:
    delta = -pagesize;
    break ;

case SB_PAGEDOWN:
    delta = pagesize;
    break ;
```

We respond to both the SB_THUMBPOSITION and SB_THUMBTRACK messages by redisplaying the text starting at the line represented by the scroll box's position:

```
case SB_THUMBPOSITION:
case SB_THUMBTRACK:
    delta = pos - CurrVPos ;
    break ;
```

You can generally drag the scroll box more quickly than a fast computer can scroll and redraw the window. If you find processing SB_THUMBTRACK messages too sluggish, you can remove the case statement for it and update the display only when the scroll box is released. Note that because we know we have less than 32,768 lines, we do not need to use the 32-bit scroll position; a 16-bit scroll position is quite adequate.

Once we know how far the user has requested the window to be scrolled, it's time to calculate how far it is possible to scroll. You can't scroll forward more than the number of lines between the current position and the maximum scroll position, and you can't scroll backward more than the number of lines between the current position and the first position:

```
if (delta != 0)
    {
        int newpos;
        // Make sure we haven't exceeded limits
        newpos = CurrVPos + delta ;
        newpos = max(0, min(newpos, MaxVPos));
```

Finally, we put the scroll box of the scroll bar at the new current position and force an immediate repaint of the client area of the window:

```
        // Now set the new scroll position
        si.cbSize = sizeof(SCROLLINFO) ;
        si.fMask = SIF_POS ;
        si.nPos = newpos ;
        SetScrollInfo (hwnd, SB_VERT, &si, TRUE) ;
```

Having set the scroll box position, we scroll the window and force it to update the section that has been uncovered:

```
        // Scroll the window.  Convert line distance to pixel distance
        ScrollWindow (hwnd, 0, -cyChar * (newpos - CurrVPos), NULL, NULL) ;
        UpdateWindow (hwnd) ;
    }
```

That completes the handling of the vertical scroll-bar messages. Similar logic scrolls the window horizontally. The horizontal scroll arbitrarily scrolls left and right in units of the width of the maximum character in the font.

All other messages are passed along unprocessed to the `DefWindowProc` function.

When you put all the pieces together and run the program, the system metrics are displayed in one window and the device capabilities in another. We ran the Sysinfo program on a Windows 95 system with a VGA display, which produced the windows in Figure 4.7 and Figure 4.8.

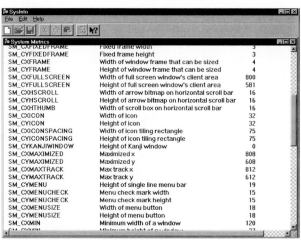

**Figure 4.7: Some system metrics for a system with a
super VGA display (800 × 600)**

Coming Attractions

You've read about the fundamentals of displaying text in a window and scrolling a window's contents. By now, you likely understand how to write text to a window. The step to writing text in multiple fonts isn't nearly as large. Nearly everything you've read about standard scroll bars applies equally well to scroll-bar controls, so you're in fine shape there, too. And now that you've seen an example of subclassing a window, you'll probably see many uses for the technique when we discuss Windows's standard controls. For example, you might want to subclass an input field control (called an *edit control*) to provide input validation.

Before we get to that, we'll complete our discussion of drawing in a window. This time, the emphasis is on drawing graphics, not text. To draw graphics, you need to understand Windows's mapping modes. And when we talk about mapping modes, we're talking about device contexts. You've seen a little about device contexts, and we've used a special one, a display context, frequently throughout this chapter. Chapter 5 delves deeply into the subject of device contexts and display context pools. Initially, it may feel like a extremely cold shower. But once you've warmed up to the subject (and appreciate the device independence provided by a device context), it will seem more like a warm, relaxing sauna that removes many worries from you as well as from your code.

Device Capabilities	
DRIVERVERSION	0x00000400
TECHNOLOGY	1
HORZSIZE	211
VERTSIZE	158
HORZRES	800
VERTRES	600
LOGPIXELSX	96
LOGPIXELSY	96
BITSPIXEL	8
PLANES	1
NUMBRUSHES	-1
NUMPENS	16
NUMFONTS	0
NUMCOLORS	20
ASPECTX	36
ASPECTY	36
ASPECTXY	51
PDEVICESIZE	1112
CLIPCAPS	1

Figure 4.8: Device capabilities for a super VGA display

5 Examining a Device Context in Depth

The Windows Graphics Device Interface (GDI) functions provide device-independent methods of generating a variety of text and graphics output on many different output devices. All the GDI output functions require a device context as a parameter. A device context links your Windows application with the device driver for the output device.

You specify an output request in device-independent terms. GDI passes the request, as modified by attributes of the device context, to the device driver, which then executes (translates) the request into device-dependent operations on the output device.

In this chapter, we discuss the following topics:

- Device and display contexts

- The four types of display context: common, class, private, and window

- How to create a device context, an information context, a memory device context, and a metafile device context

- The capabilities of a device as reported by the GetDeviceCaps function

- Each attribute of a device context

What Is a Device Context?

In the simplest view, a *device context* (sometimes DC) is a block of memory managed by the GDI. It is a data structure that contains information that GDI uses to determine how to perform a drawing request.[1] When a device context is for the display device, it is often called a *display context*. A display context is a specific kind of device context. Generally, a device context allows you access to the entire device, whereas a display context restricts your output to the area of its associated window. We used display contexts in Chapter 4

---

[1] The details of a Win16 GDI, if you're curious, are documented in Matt Pietrek's *Windows Internals* and Schulman, Maxey, and Pietrek's *Undocumented Windows* (see "Further Reading" at the end of this chapter). The Windows 95 and Windows NT structures will be richer than these.

when we displayed text output in a window. The Windows documentation does not always use the terms *display context* and *device context* appropriately. Often the documentation uses *display context* when the more general *device context* should be used. The functions that deliver a device context are listed in Table 5.1.

Table 5.1: Operations to obtain or release DCs

Operation	Purpose
BeginPaint	Obtains a client area DC in a WM_PAINT handler.
CloseEnhMetaFile	Releases a DC obtained by CreateEnhMetaFile.
CreateCompatibleDC	Creates a memory DC that is compatible with a given device.
CreateDC	Obtains a device context for a named device driver.
CreateEnhMetaFile	Creates a metafile DC associated with either a disk file or memory.
CreateIC	Creates an information context (a restricted form of DC) for a named device driver.
DeleteDC	Releases a DC obtained via CreateDC, CreateIC, or CreateCompatibleDC.
EndPaint	Releases a DC obtained by BeginPaint.
GetDC	Obtains a client area DC other than in a WM_PAINT handler.
GetDCEx	Obtains a DC. Is like GetDC, except it can also specify a clipping region and some special flags.
GetWindowDC	Obtains a display context for the entire window area.
PrintDlg	Enters a standard Print dialog and returns a DC for the selected printer.
ReleaseDC	Releases a DC obtained by GetDC, GetDCEx, or GetWindowDC.

GDI examines the attributes of the provided device context to determine how to perform a drawing operation. A few of the these attributes describe what kind of drawing object to use, such as a black pen or a blue hatched brush.

For example, line drawing requests use the pen identified by the appropriate device context attribute. The pen itself has attributes, such as the line width, line style, and pen color. This allows you to change the pen attribute of a device context only once but to draw many different lines, all with the indicated pen. GDI output functions would be cumbersome to use if every output request had to be accompanied by a full specification of the minutiae required to actually perform the request. Table 5.5 lists over two dozen attributes of a device context that could affect a drawing operation.

You must obtain a device context before you can issue any GDI output functions. There are two sources of device contexts–device contexts that you explicitly create, often by using the GetDC function, and device contexts that Windows creates and provides to you. The latter device contexts are always display contexts. Because display contexts are used so often, let's see how you get one, where they come from, and when they should be returned to Windows.

Display Contexts: A Specific Type of Device Context

A display context has one of these general forms (from the most frequently to the least frequently used):

- A display context for the client area of the window

- A display context for a window (which includes the nonclient areas, such as the title bar and frame)

- A display context for the desktop window (the display surface of the display device)

Display contexts for window client areas are the most commonly used; you can't draw a single pixel in the client area of a window without one. To support a rich variety of options to maximize programmer convenience or performance, Windows supports four types of display contexts: common, class, private, and window. The "parent DC" class is a special variant of the common display context.

You select which type of display context to use based on the drawing needs of a window. You use a common, class, or private display context when drawing in the client area of a window. You use a window display context when drawing anywhere in the window, including the nonclient areas of the window. You specify the type of display context for a window's client area by including the appropriate class style when you register the window class. When you create a window of that class, Windows assigns it the type of display context that was specified in the window's class style. The specific flags are shown in Table 5.2.

Table 5.2: Class flags for display contexts

Flag	Meaning	`GetDC/BeginPaint` Action
(none)	A common DC will be used.	A new DC is created each time. Initialized to default values (see Table 5.3).
CS_CLASSDC	A single DC is shared among all windows of the class.	A handle referencing the single class DC is returned. Changes are retained and visible to all windows.
CS_OWNDC	A private DC is allocated to the window on its creation and will be used for all subsequent operations.	A handle referencing the private DC is returned. Changes are retained.
CS_PARENTDC	A common DC will be used.	A new DC is created each time. Initialized to the default values (see Table 5.3) except for the clipping region, which is the clipping region of the parent window.

The Common Display Context

The common display context is the default type of display context given to a window. If you don't specify a different display context type in a window's class style parameter (see Table 5.2), Windows assigns a common display context to the window. This is the easiest way to get a display context for a window.

Win16 optimized performance by keeping a cache of common DCs available. There were only five common DCs system-wide shared among all applications and Windows itself. If you failed to release a DC after obtaining one via GetDC, eventually Windows came to a sad end. In Win32, the number of DCs is "limited by available memory". For Windows NT, this means there is a very, very large number available. For Windows 95, the number is limited but extremely large. For Win32s, the number is–that's right–five. Nonetheless, it is always a good idea to release a DC when you are done with it because otherwise your program will consume more and more resources, thus resulting in increasingly poor performance. Ultimately, you could even use up all the available DCs, even in Windows NT.

A common display context is the most frequently used form of display context. If the window class did not specify an explicit display context option, this is what Windows delivers when you request a display context for a window's client area by calling the GetDC function or the BeginPaint function.

It's best to test all Windows applications using the debugging version of Windows or a third-party product such as Bounds Checker for Windows. The debugging version of Windows, called the "checked version" in Windows NT, is included as part of the Microsoft Developer Network subscription. It detects many runtime errors commonly made in Windows applications, including failure to release resources such as Display Contexts.

Another consideration when using a common display context is that Windows resets all the attributes of a common display context to default values each time it retrieves a common display context. However, this requires you to explicitly set each attribute of a common display context that you want to a nondefault value each time you retrieve the display context. Table 5.3 lists the default settings for the attributes of a common display context. The meaning of each attribute is discussed later in this chapter.

Table 5.3: Default attributes for a common display context

Attribute	Default Value
Background color	RGB(255, 255, 255) *(White)*
Background mode	OPAQUE
Bitmap	No default value. Applies only to memory DCs.
Brush	WHITE_BRUSH
Brush origin	(0, 0)
Clipping region	Windows sets the clipping region to the entire client area. The update region is clipped if necessary. Child and pop-up windows overlaying the client area may also be clipped.
Color palette	DEFAULT_PALETTE
Current pen position	(0, 0)
Device origin	Upper-left corner of the client area.
Drawing mode	R2_COPYPEN
Font	SYSTEM_FONT

Table 5.3: Default attributes for a common display context

Attribute	Default Value
Graphics mode	GM_COMPATIBLE
Intercharacter spacing	0
Mapping mode	MM_TEXT
Miter limit	10.0
Pen	BLACK_PEN
Polygon filling mode	ALTERNATE
Relative-absolute flag	ABSOLUTE
Stretching mode	STRETCH_ANDSCANS (BLACKONWHITE [3])
Text color	RGB(0, 0, 0) *(Black)*
Text alignment	TA_TOP | TA_LEFT | TA_NOUPDATECP
Transformation matrix	$\begin{bmatrix} 1.0f & 0.0f \\ 0.0f & 1.0f \\ 0.0f & 0.0f \end{bmatrix}$ *identity*
Viewport extent	(1, 1)
Viewport origin	(0, 0)
Window extent	(1, 1)
Window origin	(0, 0)

[3] API level 3 name, now considered obsolete.

The Class Display Context

You can indicate that a window uses a class display context by specifying the CS_CLASSDC class style when you register the window class. Windows creates a class display context, initialized to the default values shown in Table 5.3, when you create the first window of the class. All subsequently created windows of the same class use the display context that you created for the first window.

A class display context is not created fresh each time. It is allocated and initialized precisely once for use by all windows of the class. Because a class display context is not a common display context, the requirement to release the display context after using it does not apply to a class display context.

You must *retrieve* a class display context before using it. A class display context is retrieved by using the GetDC or BeginPaint function. Once retrieved, you do not need to release it, but you should. The

`ReleaseDC` and `EndPaint` functions do nothing when called on a class display context. You can omit the matching call to release the class display context, and your program will work correctly. But it will work correctly only as long as you continue to use a class display context! It takes only a small change in a different part of the program (e.g., omitting the `CS_CLASSDC` style when registering the class) to cause the program to use a common display context that should be released. What is a shortcut in one situation leads to the failure of the program in another. Good software engineering methodology minimizes dependencies (documented or not) between disparate portions of the program. We always pair every retrieval of a display context with a matching release whether or not the release is absolutely required.

You may wonder whether you need to retrieve a class display context each time it's used. After all, if you don't need to release it (even though you should), maybe you don't need to retrieve it after you've obtained it the first time. The answer is to this question is a resounding "maybe".

Retrieving a class display context sets the device origin and clipping attributes of the display context to the appropriate values for the window that retrieves it. Basically, the act of retrieving the class display context associates it with the window. These attributes remain unchanged as long as no other window of the same class retrieves the display context.

When a second window of the class retrieves the class display context, the device origin and clipping attributes are changed to the appropriate values for the second window. The original window will need to retrieve the class display context once more before using it again in order to switch the device origin and clipping attributes back to the proper values for that window.

You don't need to retrieve a class display context each time it's used if you can guarantee that no other window of the same class has retrieved the display context since the first window retrieved it. Most of the time, this assurance is possible when only one window of the class exists. We recommend that you adopt a coding style that always retrieves a display context before using it–even when not absolutely necessary. This is, again, good defensive software engineering.

Windows gives a class display context the same default attributes it does a common display context when the class display context is originally created (see Table 5.3). Windows changes only the device origin and clipping region when you retrieve a class display context. As already mentioned, these attributes are set to the appropriate values for the window that is retrieving the display context. All other attributes keep the value to which they were last set no matter which window of the class retrieves the class display context or which window of the class sets the attribute. A change made to the class display context by one window affects all other windows that subsequently use that display context.

It is particularly important to be aware of this given the possibility of multithreading. A program that operated successfully in Win16, with cooperative multitasking, could be guaranteed that a class DC, once obtained, could not be modified by any other instance of the class. This was because no other instance could gain control until the program allowed this to happen. In Win32, you have no such guarantees. And in the presence of preemptive multithreading, there is a likelihood that another thread that wishes to update a window of the same class could gain control and modify the DC in ways that you are not aware of. When control returned to the original thread, you would continue doing your update with a modified DC. In general, you need to protect shared resources in a multithreading system, a topic covered in Chapter 18. If you need many of the features of a class DC, including performance, you may want to use a private display context.

(The significant advantage of a class DC under Win16 was the conservation of the extremely limited memory resources on an 8088, a consideration of little importance in Win32.)

The Private Display Context

A private display context is a display context permanently associated with only one window. You can indicate that a window use a private display context by specifying the CS_OWNDC class style when you register the window class. Based on the class, Windows creates a separate private display context for each window that you create when the window class specifies the CS_OWNDC class style.

Because each window has its own separate display context, you need to retrieve a private display context only once. Windows automatically updates the device origin and clipping region attributes of the context any time the window is moved or resized.

You can retrieve a private display context by using the GetDC or BeginPaint function. Once retrieved, you do not need to release it, but you should do so for exactly the same reasons we gave for releasing a class display context. The ReleaseDC and EndPaint functions have no effect on a private display context. You can omit the matching call to release the private display context and your program will work correctly.

Unlike a class display context, you need never retrieve a private display context after you've retrieved it once. A private display context is given the same default values when it is originally created as are given to a common display context (see Table 5.3). Subsequent changes to a private display context are preserved until you explicitly change them. Doing this often optimizes performance because a large set of attributes that may not be the defaults for a common display context, but which may be the defaults for your display context, can be retained and need not be set each time.

Again, the presence of multithreading can introduce complications. Ideally, a window should be managed by no more than one thread. This means that even if your thread is preempted and operates on another window of the same class, your DC will remain as you set it until control returns to you. But if you allow more than one thread to manage a single window, you're back in the same fix as if you used a class DC. That is, the integrity of your DC cannot be maintained in any guaranteed fashion unless you take explicit steps to synchronize the access. Therefore, if you limit yourself to no more than one thread per window, you will not need to synchronize your private display context access.

The Parent Display Context

You can specify the CS_PARENTDC class style when you register the window class. When you retrieve a display context for a child window with this style, Windows creates a common display context as if there was no special DC selected. Then it sets the clipping region for the DC to be the clipping region of the parent. This allows the child to draw on the parent's client area.

This is often desirable because there may be slight roundoff errors in computing sizes. Typical examples include the layout of controls in a dialog, where the measure is in *dialog box units* (we talk about these when we get to Chapter 11). It is possible to get the edges of the contents of the control clipped. In the case of fonts, the right edges of curved lines (such as the right edge of a "D") may "bulge" slightly from the nominal size if scaling is being used in the DC. So the bounding box computations (which are based on the original font size) may be inaccurate, thereby resulting in the right-most letter's being clipped in an ugly fashion. Also, GDI runs faster if it can quickly determine that no clipping is required at all. Controls in dialog boxes are normally created with the CS_PARENTDC style.

 All of Microsoft's documentation, and much of the material based on it, incorrectly claims that the CS_PARENTDC style causes the child window to inherit the DC of its parent. This has implications if the parent has a private display context or a class display context. In fact, the true situation is as we have just described. This documentation error is corrected in the Knowledge Base article Q111005, "DOCERR: CS_PARENTDC Class Style Description Incorrect".

This feature is not always as useful as you might think. It works only if the drawing in the child control is basically a static image. If it will be redrawn differently, then only the portion in the child window will be erased. The part that falls slightly outside the child window will remain, leaving an ugly blot of some sort just outside the window border. We discovered this in writing the Font Explorer, which suffers the roundoff problem just described; as the font changed, little chunks of the character as rendered in the previous font were left on the far right. We ended up having to defeat the CS_PARENTDC style that the dialog gave us by explicitly creating a clipping region equal to the child window size!

The Window Display Context

A window display context allows you to draw anywhere in the window. This includes the client area, title bar, menus, and scroll bars. A window display context has its origin at the upper-left corner of the window–not the upper-left corner of the client area, as do the other display contexts. You retrieve a window display context by calling the GetWindowDC function.

Windows retrieves a window display context in the same way as it does for a common display context. As with a common display context, you must release a window display context when you're done drawing with it by calling the ReleaseDC function.

The attributes of a window display context are set to the default values listed in Table 5.3 each time you retrieve it. The GetWindowDC function ignores the class styles of the window. The CS_OWNDC and CS_CLASSDC class styles apply only to display contexts for the client area of a window.

Other Types of Device Contexts

Up to now, you've looked only at device contexts that were created by Windows and provided to you on request. You can also create your own device context. You can create four types of device contexts, as follows:

- A *device context* for a physical device

- An *information context*, which can be used only to obtain information about a device

- A *memory device context*, which uses a block of memory (bitmap) as its drawing surface

- A *metafile device context*, which you can use to record drawing operations and "play" them back later

Creating a Device Context

The most common device context you will need to create is one for the printer. In Win32, the best way to accomplish this is by using the `PrintDlg` API call, which presents the user with all the necessary options for selecting a printer. A side effect of `PrintDlg` is that it can return a DC for the printer that the user selects. This is so simple that it would be extremely unusual that anyone would ever create a DC for a printer by any other means. The techniques for this are covered in great detail in Chapter 13.

If you are porting a Win16 program to Win32, you may find code that looks extremely complicated, reads values from the `WIN.INI` file using `GetProfileString`, and generally looks incomprehensible. We suggest that you replace this code whenever possible by code that uses `PrintDlg`.

The use of `PrintDlg` does not require that you actually interact with the user; a special flag, `PD_RETURNDEFAULT`, can be used to obtain the default printer selected by the Control Panel printer applet. When this is used together with the `PD_RETURNDC` flag, you will get a DC for the default printer without any user interaction at all. This is sometimes useful if you are writing daemon processes (called *services* in Windows NT) or if you are writing applications in which you do not expect to have even mildly experienced users who would know what to do with a print dialog if one were presented to them.

You create a device context for a device by specifying the device driver, the device name, and the physical output medium (file or hardware port) on the call to the `CreateDC` function:

```
hdc = CreateDC (DriverName, DeviceName, Output, lpInitData) ;
```

The details of how to get these strings for the default printer is covered in Chapter 13.

One other display context that is useful to have occasionally (the most common use is writing your own screen saver) is a context for the entire display. You can create this type of device context with the following statement:

```
hdc = CreateDC (_T("DISPLAY"), NULL, NULL, NULL) ;
```

However, it is generally considered easier to get a DC for the window handle returned by `GetDeskTopWindow`, as follows:

```
HWND hwnd = GetDeskTopWindow();
HDC hdc = GetDC(hwnd);
```

When you are finished with a device context, you must delete it by calling the `DeleteDC` function as follows:

```
DeleteDC (hdc) ;
```

The Information Context

Another specialized type of device context is the information context. An *information context* is a restricted type of device context; it cannot be used to draw on the device. An information context requires less memory than does a device context. This was once important on small machines under Win16. You can use an information context rather than a device context any time you want to retrieve information about a device rather than draw on it.

You create an information context by calling the `CreateIC` function and passing to it the same parameters used for the `CreateDC` function. Once you have the handle to the desired information context, you can specify the handle when calling the `GetDeviceCaps` function (which works for either a device context or an information context) to determine the device's capabilities. You must delete an information context when you have finished using it. You delete an information context the same way you delete a device context, by using the `DeleteDC` function:

```
DeleteDC (hInfoDC) ;
```

The most common information context you'll need is one for a printer. Obtaining one for the default printer is very trivial and can be done with the following code:

```
HDC getDefaultPrinterIC()

  {
  PRINTDLG pdsetup;

  memset(&pdsetup, 0, sizeof(PRINTDLG));
  pdsetup.lStructSize = sizeof(PRINTDLG);
  pdsetup.Flags = PD_RETURNDEFAULT | PD_RETURNIC ;

  if (PrintDlg(&pdsetup))
      return pdsetup.hDC;
  else
      return NULL;
  }
```

The Memory Device Context

You can also create a memory device context. A *memory device context* is another special type of device context. Its "display surface" is a bitmap that is compatible with a previously created device context. "Compatible," as used here, means the bits in the bitmap have the same bits per pixel, bit planes, and color values that are used by the device. Anything drawn on the memory device context is drawn in the bitmap. Once you've drawn the image in memory, you can copy it to the actual display surface of the compatible device. You can also retrieve the bits and save them to a file, send them out on a network connection, or otherwise manipulate them directly.

Occasionally you'll want to draw into a memory device context and then copy the resulting bitmap from the memory device context to an actual device context rather than draw directly on the destination device. For example, when you perform a series of incremental changes to a display, you can see the display "flicker". Although the changes may be made very quickly, the user–especially on a slow system–can often see a blur as the image changes from the initial display through all the incremental changes to the final image. You can prevent this flicker by drawing all the incremental changes in an off-screen bitmap (memory device context) and drawing only the final result on the screen (by copying bits from the memory device context to the actual device context). The user sees the image change directly from the initial display to the final image. This is one of the common techniques for producing low-flicker animations.

You create a memory device context by calling the `CreateCompatibleDC` function and passing it the handle of a device context:

```
hMemoryDC = CreateCompatibleDC (hdc) ;
```

When the `hdc` parameter is 0, the `CreateCompatibleDC` function creates a memory device context that is compatible with the system display.

The attributes of a newly created memory device context are all set to the normal default values for a device context (Table 5.5 on page 241). You can change the attributes, inquire as to the current state of an attribute, and draw into the device context just as if it were the compatible device. But you can't draw very much, at least not at first. GDI selects a 1 × 1 monochrome bitmap into a memory device context when it creates it. Because toggling a single bit on and off isn't terribly interesting, you'll probably want to change to a larger display surface. You do this by creating a bitmap of the desired size and selecting it into the memory device context.

Although you can use various functions to create a bitmap, you frequently will want to use the `CreateCompatibleBitmap` function. This function creates a bitmap that is compatible with the device indicated by its first parameter and that is of the size (in pixels, not bits!) specified by the second and third parameters:

```
hBitmap = CreateCompatibleBitmap (hdc, Width, Height) ;
```

The created bitmap has the same number of color planes and bits per pixel as the device indicated by the `hdc` parameter. This bitmap may be selected into any memory device context that is compatible with the specified device. However, it can be selected into only *one* device context at a time and can be selected into only a *memory device context*. You cannot select a bitmap into a normal device context or an information context.

You possibly will receive unexpected results when you pass the handle to a memory device context, rather than a regular device context, as the first parameter to the `CreateCompatibleBitmap` function. When `hdc` is a memory device context, the created bitmap has the same format as the bitmap that is presently selected into the memory device context. This could be either a color bitmap or a monochrome bitmap. That is not necessarily the same format as the format of the compatible device.

For example, the following lines of code create a monochrome `Width`-by-`Height` bitmap even when the display device has color capabilities. This is because a memory device context contains a selected monochrome bitmap when it is initially created.

```
hdc = GetDC (hwnd) ;
hMemoryDC = CreateCompatibleDC (hdc) ;
hBitmap = CreateCompatibleBitmap (hMemoryDC, Width, Height) ;
hOldBitmap = SelectObject (hMemoryDC, hBitmap) ;
```

To ensure that a color bitmap is created when using a color display device, you should change the parameter to the `CreateCompatibleBitmap` function from `hMemoryDC` to `hdc`. This creates a bitmap in the format of the display device rather than in the format of the bitmap selected into the memory device context.

```
hdc = GetDC (hwnd) ;
hMemoryDC = CreateCompatibleDC (hdc) ;
```

```
hBitmap = CreateCompatibleBitmap (hdc, Width, Height) ;
hOldBitmap = SelectObject (hMemoryDC, hBitmap) ;
DeleteDC (hdc) ;
```

The GetDC function returns a device context for the client area of the window identified by the hwnd parameter. The CreateCompatibleDC function returns a memory device context that has selected into it a monochrome 1 × 1 pixel bitmap. Next the CreateCompatibleBitmap function returns a Width-by-Height pixel bitmap that has the same number of color planes and bits per pixel as the display device. The SelectObject function selects the newly created bitmap into the memory device context and returns the handle to the previously selected bitmap–in this example, the default 1 × 1 pixel bitmap. The DeleteDC function releases the retrieved display context because it might be a common display context.

Of course, you must release or delete all these device contexts and bitmaps when you have finished using them. However, you must not delete a bitmap while it is currently selected into a device context. So, reselect the original default bitmap into the memory device context before deleting the compatible bitmap:

```
SelectObject (hMemoryDC, hOldBitmap) ;
DeleteObject (hBitmap) ;
```

You can combine these two statements into a single statement by taking advantage of the fact that the SelectObject function returns the handle of the previously selected object:

```
DeleteObject (SelectObject (hMemoryDC, hOldBitmap)) ;
```

Once you no longer need the memory device context, delete it by calling the DeleteDC function:

```
DeleteDC (hMemoryDC) ;
```

It's extremely important to ensure that you always delete a device context and a bitmap when you finish using them. Failure to delete GDI objects after using them is a common error that results in a "memory leak". The result is that in Windows NT, your program begins to take up more and more virtual memory until eventually you can consume all of the virtual memory in the system. While this is happening, your overall system performance degrades substantially. In Windows 95, you can consume the memory that supports the GDI in the 16-bit substrate. Although this memory pool is large, it is not nearly as large as the Windows NT memory pool. Once it is consumed, you can begin to see very strange failure modes. A program that has a severe memory leak but which apparently runs fine on Windows NT may fail in strange ways under Windows 95.

 When a 16-bit Windows application terminates, Windows frees the system resources that are owned by the application. However, device contexts and bitmaps (as well as pens, brushes, fonts, regions, palettes, and metafiles) are actually owned by the Win16 GDI module. They are not owned by an application. If your program terminates without deleting a device context or a bitmap, Windows does not automatically free the memory used to store the object. The memory remains unavailable for future use until the user terminates and restarts Windows. This restriction applies to Win32 programs running under Win32s.

The Metafile Device Context

There is one more type of device context: a *metafile device context*. A metafile is a file that records the GDI commands issued to a metafile device context. These GDI commands are stored in the file in a binary form and can be used to recreate the text or graphical image as required. Once these are stored, the text or graphical image created by them can be recreated by "replaying" the commands in the metafile.

Metafiles are device-independent. A metafile can be replayed onto a variety of output devices, and the image will be properly drawn on each device. For example, much "clip art" is distributed as metafiles, commonly with the .wmf (*Windows MetaFile*) extension (and a special header, as described in Figure 5.1). A metafile can also be used to pass a graphical image to a different application.

Programmers who knew the Win16 API may notice that the familiar metafile calls now have the phrase "Enh" attached. This is because the original Windows metafile design had several major defects, which were corrected by implementing a new metafile API for "enhanced" metafiles. Although the older API calls are retained for compatibility, they are deemed obsolete, so we do not discuss them.

A metafile that is *insertable*, for example, into a word processor document, consists of an ordinary metafile with a header attached. This header is not specified as part of the Windows specification but is a standard established by third-party vendors (it is sometimes referred to as the "Aldus placeable header"). You must prepend the information shown in the Win32 structure described here to the contents of the metafile after the metafile has been written. Note that this is slightly different from the specifications you might have seen for a metafile header. Previous specifications were written for Win16 and do not port directly to Win32 because several of the data types become 32-bit data types in Win32. The `#pragma pack` is essential for correct physical layout of the structure by the compiler.

```
#pragma pack(2)
typedef struct {
    DWORD       key;
    WORD        hmf;            // Unused "HANDLE" in Win16 is 16/ bit value
    SMALL_RECT  bbox;           // must NOT be RECT; must be 16-bit
    WORD        inch;
    DWORD       reserved;
    WORD        checksum;
} METAFILEHEADER;
#pragma pack()
```

Field	Explanation
DWORD key	0x9AC6CDD7. The special value that allows this file to be recognized as a placeable metafile.
WORD hmf	16-bit handle value; unused; must be 0.
SMALL_RECT bbox	A rectangle expressed in 16-bit coordinates. SMALL_RECT is defined in windows.h.
WORD inch	The number of metafile units per inch; should be less than 1440 to avoid integer overflow on 16-bit platforms.
DWORD reserved	32-bit value; unused; must be 0.
WORD checksum	XOR checksum of the first 10 words of the structure.

Figure 5.1: Insertable metafile header

You create a metafile device context by calling the `CreateEnhMetaFile` function:

```
hMetafileDC = CreateEnhMetaFile (hdcRef, FileName, rect, lpszDesc) ;
```

The first parameter is a "reference DC" and is used to record information about the device on which the image is first rendered. If you make this NULL, it will use the parameters of the current display device. You pass a filename to the CreateEnhMetaFile function to store the metafile in a disk file. You can store the metafile in memory by passing NULL as the filename parameter. The rect parameter points to a RECT structure that defines a bounding rectangle. If you pass a NULL argument, a bounding rectangle just large enough to encompass the drawn image is computed. The description string is optional and may be NULL. If it is not NULL, it must point to a pair of adjacent NUL-terminated strings. These strings are supposed to be the application name and a picture description. They are added as text to the enhanced metafile header. The second string must be terminated with two NUL characters. For example, in Windows 95 or Windows NT in 8-bit (not Unicode) mode, the string might be

```
char Desc[] = "My Application\0PrettyPicture\0";
```

Note that because C (or C++) automatically provides a terminating "\0" at the end of a string constant, the above string ends as "\0\0". If you are creating the string yourself in a buffer, you must make certain to put two "\0" characters at the end of the string. Remember that in Unicode (under Windows NT only), you are dealing with 16-bit characters.

You can draw into a metafile device context using a subset of the drawing functions that can be used on an actual device. Once you finish drawing into the metafile, you close the metafile.

```
hMF = CloseEnhMetaFile (hMetafileDC) ;
```

After you close the metafile, the handle to the metafile device context becomes invalid and must not be used. The CloseEnhMetaFile function returns a handle to the metafile (*not* to be confused with a handle to the metafile DC). You can initially create a memory metafile and later save it to a disk file by calling the CopyEnhMetaFile function. This function takes a handle to the memory metafile and the filename that specifies the file to which the metafile should be saved:

```
hDiskMF = CopyEnhMetaFile (hMF, Filename) ;
```

You can also use the CopyEnhMetaFile to make a clone of an existing memory metafile by passing NULL as the filename parameter:

```
hMemoryMF = CopyEnhMetaFile (hMF, NULL) ;
```

The PlayEnhMetaFile function uses a handle to a metafile and replays the recording into the specified device context:

```
PlayEnhMetaFile (hdc, hMF, rect) ;
```

As always, you must delete all resources once you are finished using them. Delete a metafile by calling the DeleteEnhMetaFile function and passing it the handle to the metafile:

```
DeleteEnhMetaFile (hMF) ;
```

The DeleteEnhMetaFile function frees the system resources associated with that metafile. It's extremely important to ensure that you always delete a metafile when you are finished using it. When a Windows application terminates, Windows frees the system resources owned by the application. However, like the bitmaps and device contexts described earlier in this section, metafiles are actually owned by the Windows GDI module, not by the creating application.

Deleting a memory metafile deletes the GDI storage containing the metafile, so the recording is lost. However, deleting a disk metafile does not delete the recording itself that is stored in the disk file. It deletes only the resources owned by the GDI module. Deleting a metafile invalidates the handle to the metafile. You can create a new handle to a previously created disk metafile by calling the `GetEnhMetaFile` function and passing the filename:

```
hMF = GetEnhMetaFile (Filename) ;

/* Do something with the metafile. */

DeleteEnhMetaFile (hMF) ;
```

When you no longer need the disk metafile, you simply delete it from the disk using the API call `DeleteFile`:

```
result = DeleteFile (Filename) ;
```

The `result` value can be tested to see if the deletion was successful.

The Capabilities of a Device

As you saw in Chapter 4, you can use the `GetDeviceCaps` function to retrieve device-specific information about the device associated with a device context. The `GetDeviceCaps` function returns the information specified by the `Index` parameter for the device associated with the `hdc` device context:

```
Capability = GetDeviceCaps (hdc, Index) ;
```

You'll often need to find out about the capabilities of a device before displaying graphics. For example, you might want to know the horizontal and vertical resolution of the display in pixels. You also might need to know whether the device can display in color, how many colors it supports, and whether the device supports a color palette. All this and more is available via the `GetDeviceCaps` function.

The `GetDeviceCaps` function also returns detailed information about the capabilities of the device driver. You'll rarely be interested in this information, but Windows uses it. GDI interrogates the device driver to determine its ability to complete complicated drawing requests on its own. When the device driver knows how to perform a complex drawing operation, GDI lets it. When the device driver doesn't know how to draw a certain type of figure, GDI draws the figure as a composite of simpler figures that the device driver does know how to draw.

For example, if a device driver responds that it knows how to draw an ellipse, GDI will pass a request to draw an ellipse directly to the device driver. The device driver then must draw the requested ellipse, possibly using hardware features of the device for rapid drawing. When a device driver responds that it hasn't the faintest idea what an ellipse is, let alone how to draw one, GDI takes over and draws the ellipse itself. It does this by converting your request to draw an ellipse into multiple, more primitive drawing commands to the device. In the extreme case, GDI can repeatedly tell the driver to "go here and draw a pixel".

The index values you use to obtain device-specific information from the `GetDeviceCaps` function as well as the returned values are listed in Table 5.4. An example of values is shown in Figure 5.14, which is a screen snapshot of the DC Explorer application running on Windows 95.

Table 5.4: Device capabilities

Index	Returns
ASPECTX	Relative width of a pixel.
ASPECTY	Relative height of a pixel.
ASPECTXY	Relative diagonal length of a pixel.
BITSPIXEL	Number of adjacent bits comprising the color of a pixel.
CLIPCAPS	Clipping capabilities of the device. It can be one of the following:

Name	Meaning
CP_NONE	Output is not clipped.
CP_RECTANGLE	Output is clipped to rectangles.
CP_REGION	Output is clipped to regions.

Index	Returns
COLORRES	The actual color resolution of the device in bits per pixel. This value is valid only for a palette-based device using a device driver version of 3.0 or later. You can determine whether the device is palette-based by retrieving the RASTERCAPS capabilities.
CURVECAPS	A bit mask that specifies the curve-drawing capabilities of the device. The following symbolic names are defined by windows.h for the bits:

Name	Meaning
CC_CIRCLES	Device can draw circles.
CC_CHORD	Device can draw chord arcs.
CC_ELLIPSES	Device can draw ellipses.
CC_INTERIORS	Device can draw interiors.
CC_NONE	Device cannot draw curves.
CC_PIE	Device can draw pie wedges.
CC_ROUNDRECT	Device can draw rectangles with rounded corners.
CC_STYLED	Device can draw styled borders.
CC_WIDE	Device can draw wide borders.

Table 5.4: Device capabilities

Index	Returns
	CC_WIDESTYLED Device can draw wide-styled borders.
DRIVERVERSION	The version number of the device driver. 0x300 (300 hexadecimal) means version 3.0. Windows 3.10 device drivers return 0x30a. You may encounter these in Windows 95 as well because it supports older drivers. Windows NT drivers are 0x350 and 0x351; new Windows NT and Windows 95 drivers are 0x0400 or higher.
HORZRES	The width of the display surface in pixels. For printers, this is the printable width and does not include any unprintable left and right margins.
HORZSIZE	The standard width of this type of display (in millimeters).
LINECAPS	A bit mask that specifies the line-drawing capabilities of the device. The following symbolic names are defined by windows.h for the bits:

Name	Meaning
LC_INTERIORS	Device can draw interiors.
LC_MARKER	Device can draw markers.
LC_NONE	Device cannot draw lines.
LC_POLYLINE	Device can draw polylines.
LC_POLYMARKER	Device can draw polymarkers.
LC_STYLED	Device can draw styled lines.
LC_WIDE	Device can draw wide lines.
LC_WIDESTYLED	Device can draw wide-styled lines.

Index	Returns
LOGPIXELSX	The number of pixels per logical inch horizontally.
LOGPIXELSY	The number of pixels per logical inch vertically.
NUMBRUSHES	The number of device-specific brushes.
NUMCOLORS	The number of colors reserved by Windows in the device's color palette if it has one. The number of colored pens for a plotter. The number of pure colors the device can display. A monochrome device returns the value 2. A device with more than 8 bits per pixel returns the value -1.
NUMFONTS	The number of device-specific fonts.
NUMMARKERS	The number of device-specific markers.
NUMPENS	The number of device-specific pens.

Table 5.4: Device capabilities

Index	Returns
NUMRESERVED	The number of reserved entries in the system palette. This value is valid only for a palette-based device using a device driver version of 3.0 or later. You can determine whether the device is palette-based by retrieving the RASTERCAPS capabilities.
PDEVICESIZE	The size of the PDEVICE internal data structure.
PLANES	The number of color planes.
POLYGONALCAPS	A bit mask that specifies the polygonal drawing capabilities of the device. The following symbolic names are defined by windows.h for the bits:

Name	Meaning
PC_INTERIORS	Device can draw interiors.
PC_NONE	Device cannot draw polygonal figures.
PC_PATHS	Device can draw paths.
PC_POLYGON	Device can draw polygons.
PC_POLYPOLYGON	Device can draw polypolygons.
PC_RECTANGLE	Device can draw rectangles.
PC_SCANLINE	Device can draw scanlines.
PC_STYLED	Device can draw styled borders.
PC_TRAPEZOID	Device can draw trapezoids. *Note: This is the same value as* PC_WINDPOLYGON.
PC_WIDE	Device can draw wide borders.
PC_WIDESTYLED	Device can draw wide-styled borders.
PC_WINDPOLYGON	Device can draw winding polygons. *Note: This is the same value as* PC_TRAPEZOID.

Index	Returns
RASTERCAPS	A bit mask that specifies the raster drawing capabilities of the device. The following symbolic names are defined by windows.h for the bits:

Name	Meaning
RC_BANDING	Device requires banding support. GDI must display on the device in bands (a number of small segments of output collectively making up a page).
RC_BIGFONT	Device supports fonts larger than 64K.

Table 5.4: Device capabilities

Index	Returns	
	RC_BITBLT	Device can transfer bitmaps.
	RC_BITMAP64	Device supports bitmaps larger than 64K.
	RC_DEVBITS	Device supports device bitmaps.
	RC_DI_BITMAP	Device supports the SetDIBits function and the GetDIBits function.
	RC_DIBTODEV	Device supports the SetDIBitsToDevice function.
	RC_FLOODFILL	Device can perform flood fills.
	RC_GDI20_OUTPUT	Device supports Windows version 2.0 features.
	RC_GDI20_STATE	Device includes a state block in the device context.
	RC_NONE	Device supports no raster operations.
	RC_OP_DX_OUTPUT	Device supports device opaque and DX array.
	RC_PALETTE	Device is a palette-based device.
	RC_SAVEBITMAP	Device saves bitmaps locally.
	RC_SCALING	Device can scale.
	RC_STRETCHBLT	Device supports the StretchBlt function.
	RC_STRETCHDIB	Device supports the StretchDIBits function.
SIZEPALETTE	The number of entries in the device's system palette. This value is valid only for a palette-based device using a device driver version of 3.0 or later. You can determine whether the device is palette-based by retrieving the RASTERCAPS capabilities.	
TECHNOLOGY	The type of the device, otherwise known as the device technology. It can be one of the following values:	

Name	Meaning
DT_CHARSTREAM	Character stream.
DT_DISPFILE	Display file.
DT_METAFILE	Metafile.
DT_PLOTTER	Vector plotter.
DT_RASDISPLAY	Raster display.

Table 5.4: Device capabilities

Index	Returns	
	DT_RASPRINTER	Raster printer.
	DT_RASCAMERA	Raster camera.
TEXTCAPS	A bit mask that specifies the text-drawing capabilities of the device. The following symbolic names are defined by windows.h for the bits:	

Name	Meaning
TC_OP_CHARACTER	Device supports character output precision. That is, the device can place device fonts at any pixel location. This is required for any device with device fonts.
TC_OP_STROKE	Device supports stroke output precision. That is, the device can omit any stroke of a device font.
TC_CP_STROKE	Device supports stroke clip precision. That is, the device can clip device fonts to a pixel boundary.
TC_CR_90	Device supports character rotation only in 90-degree increments.
TC_CR_ANY	Device supports character rotation to any angle.
TC_SF_X_YINDEP	Device can scale device fonts separately along the horizontal and vertical axes.
TC_SA_DOUBLE	Device can double the size of device fonts.
TC_SA_INTEGER	Device can scale device fonts by any integer multiple.
TC_SA_CONTIN	Device supports arbitrary scaling of device fonts and preserves the horizontal and vertical ratios.
TC_EA_DOUBLE	Device can make device fonts bold (double-weight characters).
TC_IA_ABLE	Device can make device fonts italic.
TC_UA_ABLE	Device can underline device fonts.
TC_SO_ABLE	Device can strike out device fonts.
TC_RA_ABLE	Device supports raster fonts. That is, GDI should enumerate any raster or TrueType fonts available for this device in response to a call to the EnumFonts or EnumFontFamilies function. If this bit is not set, GDI-supplied raster or TrueType fonts are not enumerated when these functions are called.

Table 5.4: Device capabilities

Index	Returns	
	TC_VA_ABLE	Device supports vector fonts. That is, the GDI should enumerate any vector fonts available for this device in response to a call to the EnumFonts or EnumFontFamilies function. This is significant for vector devices only (plotters). Display drivers must be able to use raster fonts. Raster printer drivers always enumerate vector fonts because GDI rasterizes vector fonts before sending them to the driver.
	TC_RESERVED	Currently this bit is not used.
VERTRES		The height of the display in pixels. For printers, this is the printable height and does not include any unprintable top and bottom margins.
VERTSIZE		The standard height of this type of display (in millimeters).

A few of these items deserve additional explanation. The ASPECTX, ASPECTY, and ASPECTXY indices return the relative size of a pixel–horizontally, vertically, and diagonally, respectively. These values give you the aspect ratio of a pixel on the device. For devices with "square" pixels, the first two values will be the same.

The BITSPIXEL index returns the number of adjacent bits comprising a pixel on the device. This is a common way to store the color value of a pixel. Raising 2 to the power of this value gives you the number of colors a pixel can represent.

The PLANES index returns the number of color planes for a device. A device can use color planes as an alternative way to store the color of a pixel. When a device uses color planes, each bit in a plane represents a different pixel on the device. Adjacent bits within a single plane are used for different pixels. This is unlike a device architecture that uses multiple bits per pixel.

Picture a series of planes aligned with each other horizontally and vertically (because they are only finite approximations to a "real" plane) and stacked parallel, one on top of the other. A vector normal to the planes intersects a collection of points (bits) that represent the color value for a pixel. Another way to look at it is that the bit at location (x_1, y_1) in plane 0 might represent bit 0 of the color value for the pixel at location (x_1, y_1). The bit at location (x_1, y_1) in plane 1 might represent bit 1 of the color value for the pixel at location (x_1, y_1). This one-to-one relationship continues. If the device has eight color planes, then 8 bits (one from each plane) will be used to represent a pixel's color so that each pixel can have one of 256 colors.

Most color devices use one representation or another. When a device uses more than 1 bit per pixel, it will report a PLANES value of one color plane. When a device uses multiple color planes, it will report a BITSPIXEL value of 1 (1 bit per pixel per plane). The number of colors the device can represent is 2 to the power of the number of planes or 2 to the power of the number of adjacent bits per pixel. You can use the knowledge that one of these values will be 1 and that left-shifting the value 1 is equivalent to taking 2 to an integral power (the shift count). With it, you can calculate the number of colors that can be simultaneously displayed on a video device as follows:

```
BitsPerPixel = GetDeviceCaps (hdc, BITSPIXEL) ;
Planes = GetDeviceCaps (hdc, PLANES) ;
SimulColors = 1 << (BitsPerPixel * Planes) ;
```

Further complicating the situation is the fact that the calculated number of colors that may be simultaneously displayed by the device might not agree with the value returned by the NUMCOLORS inquiry. The NUMCOLORS inquiry returns the number of pure colors the device supports without additional work.

For example, a device using a loadable display palette (such as the IBM 8514/A adapter) can simultaneously display as many colors as it has palette entries. For the 8514/A, that is 256 colors. However, what should these 256 colors be? All red? All blue? Or, more directly, which 256 of the 16,777,216 possible colors do you want to use? To resolve this problem, Windows reserves a fixed number of color entries in a loadable display palette, sets those entries to known colors, and returns the number of reserved, known colors as the result of a NUMCOLORS inquiry. In this way, a loadable display palette device always has a basic set of colors available for Windows's own use as well as your application's use. For the 8514/A and several other display types, this inquiry returns 20. If you want to use the other 236 colors, you must set them yourself.

Plotters are slightly unusual as well. They have only one plane–the sheet of paper–and they have only 1 bit per pixel–the pen is either up or down. But a plotter might have multiple pens! The NUMCOLORS inquiry returns the number of pens that a plotter can use.

However, when you're using a palette-based device, none of these approaches gives you the actual color resolution of the device. The bits per pixel and color plane values determine only how many palette entries there are. It is the size of the palette entry itself that determines the color resolution of the device. You use the COLORRES inquiry to retrieve the actual color resolution of a palette-based device in terms of the number of bits needed to describe a color. For example, a palette-based device containing palette entries using 8 bits for red, 8 bits for blue, and 8 bits for green returns 24 to a COLORRES inquiry.

The LOGPIXELSX and LOGPIXELSY indices return the number of pixels per logical inch horizontally and vertically, respectively. A logical inch isn't always equivalent to a physical inch (that is, an inch measured by a ruler). On a display device, a physical inch is often much too small to display readable versions of commonly used text fonts. For example, on a VGA display with standard dimensions, there are only approximately 6.5 pixels available per character in a horizontal physical inch when using a 12-point font. Characters formed from that few pixels wouldn't be readable. A logical inch is longer than a physical inch, so it contains more pixels, thereby allowing larger and more readable characters to be displayed when using normally sized fonts. This inflation of an inch occurs only on video display devices. For other devices, such as a laser printer, the values returned by the LOGPIXELSX and LOGPIXELSY are equivalent to a physical inch.

The Attributes of a Device Context

We've mentioned the attributes of a device context a number of times. Windows uses these attributes when you draw on an output device using the device context. These attributes describe the following:

- Proper drawing object to use (pen and brushes)

- The proper font in which to display text

- The foreground and background color of the text

- The orientation and scaling of the coordinate system used to specify an object's position and size

- The area on the output device to which drawing is permitted (the clipping region)

- The color palette to use

- A few more miscellaneous, but important, items

In Table 5.3, we listed the default attributes for a display context. Table 5.5 lists the default attributes for a device context and the Windows functions you use to get and set the attributes value.

Table 5.5: Default device context attributes and associated functions

Attribute	Default Value	Retrieve Value With:	Change Value With:
Background color	RGB(255,255,255)	GetBkColor	SetBkColor
Background mode	OPAQUE	GetBkMode	SetBkMode
Bitmap	None	SelectObject	SelectBitmap SelectObject
Brush	WHITE_BRUSH	SelectObject GetCurrentObject	SelectBrush SelectObject
Brush origin	(0, 0)	GetBrushOrgEx	SetBrushOrgEx
Clipping region	Display surface	SelectObject GetClipBox	SelectObject ExcludeClipRect ExcludeUpdateRgn IntersectClipRect OffsetClipRgn SelectClipRgn
Color palette	DEFAULT_PALETTE	SelectPalette GetCurrentObject	SelectPalette
Current pen position	(0, 0)	GetCurrentPositionEx	MoveToEx LineTo
Drawing mode	R2_COPYPEN	GetROP2	SetROP2
Font	SYSTEM_FONT	SelectObject GetCurrentObject	SelectFont SelectObject
Graphics mode	GM_COMPATIBLE	GetGraphicsMode	SetGraphicsMode
Intercharacter spacing (track kerning)	0	GetTextCharacterExtra	SetTextCharacterExtra
Mapping mode	MM_TEXT	GetMapMode	SetMapMode

Table 5.5: Default device context attributes and associated functions

Attribute	Default Value	Retrieve Value With:	Change Value With:
Miter limit	10.0	GetMiterLimit	SetMiterLimit
Pen	BLACK_PEN	SelectObject GetCurrentObject	SelectPen SelectObject
Polygon filling mode	ALTERNATE	GetPolyFillMode	SetPolyFillMode
Relative-absolute flag	ABSOLUTE		
Stretching mode	STRETCH_ANDSCANS BLACKONWHITE	GetStretchBltMode	SetStretchBltMode
Text color	RGB(0, 0, 0)	GetTextColor	SetTextColor
Text alignment	TA_TOP | TA_LEFT | TA_NOUPDATECP	GetTextAlign	SetTextAlign
Transformation matrix	$\begin{bmatrix} 1.0f & 0.0f \\ 0.0f & 1.0f \\ 0.0f & 0.0f \end{bmatrix}$	GetWorldTransform	SetWorldTransform ModifyWorldTransform
Viewport extent	(1, 1)	GetViewportExtEx	SetViewportExtEx ScaleViewportExtEx
Viewport origin	(0, 0)	GetViewportOrgEx	SetViewportOrgEx OffsetViewportOrgEx
Window extent	(1, 1)	GetWindowExtEx	SetWindowExtEx ScaleWindowExtEx
Window origin	(0, 0)	GetWindowOrgEx	SetWindowOrgEx OffsetWindowOrgEx

Windows initializes the attributes of a device context to the default values when the device context is first created. Additionally, Windows resets all attributes of a common display context to the default values each time it is retrieved by the GetDC or BeginPaint function.

You can change an attribute's value. The new value remains in effect until you either change the attribute's value once more, delete the device context, or release a common display context by calling ReleaseDC or EndPaint.

Color Attributes

GDI uses the background color attribute as the color used to fill the empty space around text in character cells, between the dots and dashes of styled lines, and between the lines in hatched brushes. Basically, the background color is used as filler between and around "things" you draw. Like all attributes, you can change the background color. GDI uses the new color whenever you draw lines, paint with a brush, and display text.

One often overlooked distinction is that the background color attribute of a device context is separate and has nothing to do with the "background color" of a window. You specify the background color of a window when you register the window's associated window class by specifying a color value, as follows:

```
wc.hbrBackground = (HBRUSH) (COLOR_WINDOW + 1) ;
```

or by specifying the handle to the physical brush to be used for painting the background, as follows:

```
wc.hbrBackground = GetStockBrush (WHITE_BRUSH) ;
```

The background color of a window is more properly called the *class background brush* for a window. Windows uses the class background brush when erasing the invalid area of a window. It uses the background color attribute of a device context when drawing with styled lines and hatched brushes and displaying text when the background mode is set to OPAQUE.

You can retrieve the current background color of a device context with the GetBkColor function and change it using the SetBkColor function. It's possible to set the background color to a value and subsequently retrieve a slightly different color value. The SetBkColor function attempts to set the background color to the specified RGB color value. However, if the device cannot represent that RGB color value, the SetBkColor function sets the background color to the nearest device color.

This means that you can specify the same RGB color value for the background brush color and the background color but end up using two different colors. GDI will dither the background brush color, if necessary, to draw in the color you specify. However, the background color is not dithered (see page 245). The device will use the nearest pure color that is available on the device.

A related attribute is the background mode. The background mode of a device context can be either OPAQUE or TRANSPARENT. When the background mode is OPAQUE, GDI uses the background color to fill the empty space around text characters in a character cell, between the dots and dashes of styled lines, and between the hatches of a hatched brush. When the background mode is TRANSPARENT, the existing background colors on the device are left as is when drawing text, styled lines, and hatched brushes. You can change the background mode from the default (opaque) value to transparent with the following statement:

```
SetBkMode (hdc, TRANSPARENT) ;
```

Setting the foreground color of an object isn't quite so straightforward. First, you have to know what the object is. To set the color of each character written by the DrawText, TextOut, and ExtTextOut functions, you call the SetTextColor function. GDI also uses the background color and the text color when converting a bitmap from color to monochrome and from monochrome to color.

However, the foreground color of a line drawn with a pen is determined by the pen's color, not the text color attribute. Similarly, the foreground color for an area painted with a brush is determined by the brush's color, not the text color attribute. We show you how to create pens and brushes of various styles, patterns, and colors in Chapter 6, "Graphical Output: Pixels, Lines, and Polygons".

Defining a Color

You specify a COLORREF value to describe a desired color to GDI functions that require a color. For example, both the SetBkColor and SetTextColor functions require a COLORREF value. You can describe a color in three ways to produce a COLORREF value:

- As an explicit RGB value

- As an index to the appropriate logical palette entry

- As a palette-relative RGB value

These values and their physical layouts are summarized in Figure 5.2.

COLORREF Layout

Macro	31	24	23	16	15	8	7	0
RGB(r, g, b)		0		b		g		r
PALETTEINDEX(n)		1		0			n	
PALETTERGB(r, g, b)		2		b		g		r

Figure 5.2: Layout of COLORREF **values**

Explicit RGB Color Values

An explicit RGB value is a COLORREF with the high-order byte set to 0, the next lower byte set to the blue intensity, the next lower byte set to the green intensity, and the lowest-order byte of the COLORREF set to the red intensity. Because each intensity occupies 1 byte, intensity can vary from 0 to 255. Therefore the hexadecimal value 0x00FF0000 specifies an explicit RGB value of blue at its maximum intensity, with no green and no red (i.e., pure blue). Rather than create the COLORREF manually each time (and therefore make it more prone to errors), you should use the RGB macro defined by windows.h. It looks like the following:

```
#define RGB(r, g, b) \
           ((COLORREF)(((BYTE)(r)|((WORD)(g)<<8))|(((DWORD)(BYTE)(b))<<16)))
```

You could set the color of text to maximum intensity blue with the following code:

```
COLORREF crColor ;

crColor = RGB (0,0,255) ;
SetTextColor (hdc, crColor) ;
```

Here's a simpler way to do the same thing:

```
SetTextColor (hdc, RGB (0,0,255)) ;
```

Using the RGB macro to define an explicit RGB color is preferable to shifting and bitwise ORing the individual values together. In particular, the high-order byte of a COLORREF value isn't ignored. Even though the high-order byte is 0 in this particular example, it isn't always that way. The high-order byte is used to encode the type of color the COLORREF represents. In this case, a 0 in the high-order byte indicates that this is an explicit RGB color value. Other macros are defined to create the other forms of a COLORREF value, so you don't need to know COLORREF's internal structure. The GetRValue, GetGValue, and GetBValue macros extract the red, green, or blue intensity value, respectively, from a supplied RGB color value.

The SetTextColor function and the SetBkColor function pass an explicit RGB value directly to the device driver for the device associated with the specified device context. The device driver actually uses the nearest available color on the device; it might not be exactly what you requested. When you need to know what is the nearest color to an explicit RGB value that a device can represent, you use the GetNearestColor function. It returns an RGB color value identifying the device's solid color that is closest to the specified color. The following statement retrieves the RGB color value for the solid color on the device that is closest to the color with a red intensity of 128, a green intensity of 64, and a blue intensity of 192.

```
crColor = GetNearestColor (hdc, RGB (128, 64, 192)) ;
```

The GetNearestColor function returns a solid color. Use a solid color when matching to a pen on a plotter and when drawing with a pen on a device using color raster technology. (That is, the GetDeviceCaps (hdc, TECHNOLOGY) function call returns either DT_RASDISPLAY, DT_RASPRINTER, or DT_RASCAMERA, and the device supports color.) When the RGB value is associated with a brush and the brush is used to draw on a color raster technology device, the device driver will approximate the explicit RGB color by mixing pixels of different colors from those the device can display. Mixing pixels of different colors to approximate another color is called *dithering*.

The device driver for a monochrome device approximates the explicit RGB value for a brush with either black, white, or a shade of gray. When the red, green, and blue intensity values are all 0, it uses a black brush. When all three intensity values are set to the maximum value of 255, it uses a white brush. The driver dithers white and black pixels to approximate various shades of gray for the other possible RGB values.

Palette-Index Color Values

You can also specify a color by indicating which entry in a palette of colors contains the color to be used. Many devices can display a large number of colors. Typical maximum values are 262,144 or 16,777,216. However, only a relatively small set of the colors can be displayed simultaneously–256 colors at one time is a frequent limit. You create a logical color palette that lists the colors you want to use chosen from the colors available on the device. Then, rather than specify an explicit RGB value for a color, you supply the number of the palette entry that contains the color to use. Palette table entries are numbered beginning at 0. Therefore the number of a palette table entry is called a *palette index* because it is used to index into the table of colors.

One advantage of using palette-index color values is that a color isn't hard-coded into your application as it might be if you use explicit RGB macros everywhere. Of course, you can avoid hard-coding color values into your application by defining each color you use as a separate macro that is specified in terms of the RGB macro. With palette-index colors, the color at entry 3 could be, by convention, your error message color. What color is actually used depends on what's currently in the palette. You can rapidly change the entry in a logical palette (palette animation), and the color on the display will change to match. Color palette animation is a common method used to get "flicker-free" animation effects for certain restricted cases of animation.

The following PALETTEINDEX macro produces a palette-index color value when given a palette index.

```
#define PALETTEINDEX(i) \
                ((COLORREF)(0x01000000 | (DWORD)(WORD)(i)))
```

Notice that the PALETTEINDEX macro returns a COLORREF value like the RGB macro does; however, the internal contents of the COLORREF value differ. The high-order byte contains a 1, which indicates the palette-index color value (see Figure 5.2). The low-order word of the COLORREF value contains the index into the logical palette. Therefore the GetRValue, GetGValue, and GetBValue macros cannot be used to extract the individual color intensities from a palette-index color value. They expect the red, green, and blue intensity values to be encoded into the low-order bytes of the COLORREF value.

Palette-Relative Color Values

Finally, you can specify a color as a palette-relative RGB value. You specify a palette-relative RGB value by supplying the red, green, and blue intensities of the color as you do for explicit RGB values. The PALETTERGB macro assembles these intensities into the same format as an explicit RGB color value but encodes the high-order byte as a 2:

```
#define PALETTERGB(r, g, b)   (0x02000000 | RGB(r, g, b))
```

Therefore the GetRValue, GetGValue, and GetBValue macros can be used to extract the individual color intensities from a palette-relative color value.

A palette-relative color value, which is quite handy, is a cross between an explicit RGB color value and a palette-index color value. When the device on which you're drawing supports a logical palette, GDI matches a palette-relative RGB color value to the nearest color in the logical palette. Specifying a palette-relative color value, however, is not completely equivalent to specifying the palette-index color value to which it is nearest in color. The entries in a logical palette can be changed. A recently added palette entry might more closely match the color specified in a previously used palette-relative color value. GDI matches a palette-relative color value against the (possibly changing) colors in the logical palette. When the device on which you're drawing doesn't support a logical palette, GDI uses a palette-relative RGB value as if it were an explicit RGB color value. The device uses the nearest solid color (or, for a brush, a dithered color) to approximate the color.

The Color Palette Attribute

When you use a palette-index color value or a palette-relative color value, GDI uses the palette attribute of the specified device context to determine the palette in which to look up the color. You use the SelectPalette function to change the palette attribute of a device context. When the attribute being changed refers to one of the GDI objects (bitmaps, brushes, fonts, pens, regions, and palettes), "changing the ____ attribute" is more commonly referred to as "selecting a new ____ into the device context".

You'll have to make a mental note that selecting a palette into a device context must be done differently from selecting all other GDI objects into a device context. You select all other GDI objects (bitmaps, brushes, fonts, pens, and regions) into a device context by calling the SelectObject function. A palette must be selected into a device context with the `SelectPalette` function. You can select a new logical palette into device context with the following code:

```
LOGPALETTE LogPalette ;
HPALETTE    hpalNew, hpalOld ;

hpalNew = CreatePalette (&LogPalette) ;

/* Fill out the palette. */

hpalOld = SelectPalette (hdc, hpalNew, FALSE) ;

/* Eventually... */

SelectPalette (hdc, hpalOld, FALSE) ;
DeletePalette (hpalNew) ;
```

The `SelectPalette` function returns the handle to the logical palette being replaced. If you need to get the handle to the current palette, you can use the `GetCurrentObject` function:

```
HPALETTE = (HPALETTE)GetCurrentObject(hdc, OBJ_PAL);
```

Another oddity of logical palettes is that although there is a special function to select a palette into a device context, you use the standard `DeleteObject` function to delete a logical palette when you're finished using it. We prefer to use the more meaningful `DeletePalette` macro API defined in the windowsx.h header file, as it makes our code more understandable. This macro is defined in this way:

```
#define DeletePalette(hpal) \
            DeleteObject((HGDIOBJ)(HPALETTE)(hpal))
```

The Bitmap, Brush, Font, Pen, and Region Attributes and Objects

There are five remaining device context attributes that represent selected GDI objects: *bitmap, brush, font, pen*, and *region*. All of these GDI objects have a number of similarities. You select them into a device context by calling the `SelectObject` function and passing it a handle to the new object. The `SelectObject` function replaces the object in the device context that has the same type as the new object.

Windows defines macro API equivalent functions (`SelectBitmap`, `SelectBrush`, `SelectFont`, and `SelectPen`) to select a bitmap, brush, font, and pen, respectively, into a device context. These macros are defined in the windowsx.h header file. They are defined in terms of a call to the `SelectObject` function, but the return value is cast to the proper type. These macros are defined as:

```
#define SelectBitmap(hdc, hbm) \
        ((HBITMAP)SelectObject((hdc), (HGDIOBJ)(HBITMAP)(hbm)))

#define SelectBrush(hdc, hbr)  \
        ((HBRUSH)SelectObject((hdc), (HGDIOBJ)(HBRUSH)(hbr)))

#define SelectFont(hdc, hfont) \
        ((HFONT)SelectObject((hdc), (HGDIOBJ)(HFONT)(hfont)))

#define SelectPen(hdc, hpen)   \
        ((HPEN)SelectObject((hdc), (HGDIOBJ)(HPEN)(hpen)))
```

There is no need for a macro API to select a palette into a device context, since the `SelectPalette` function already exists. There is no macro API for selecting a region into a device context because there is an explicit `SelectClipRgn` function. (You may have noticed that a consistent naming convention is not one of the strengths of Windows.)

Table 5.6: GetCurrentObject codes and results

objtype parameter	Result Returned
OBJ_BITMAP	HBITMAP
OBJ_BRUSH	HBRUSH
OBJ_FONT	HFONT
OBJ_PAL	HPALETTE
OBJ_PEN	HPEN

Therefore, when you call the `SelectBrush` function, passing it the handle to a new brush ("selecting a new brush into the device context"), the previous brush is replaced and `SelectBrush` returns the handle of that previous brush. Because selecting an object into a device context replaces the previous object, no more than one object of a given type can ever be selected into a device context at one time.

You can retrieve the current object in a DC by calling

```
GetCurrentObject(hdc, objtype);
```

and casting the value from the returned HGDIOBJ to the specific object type. The codes for `GetCurrentObject` and their types are shown in Table 5.6.

You should delete all GDI objects before your program terminates. When a Win16 GDI object is created, Windows allocates storage for the object that is owned by GDI. Because GDI owns the storage, the storage isn't released automatically when your program terminates. If you forget to delete an object that you've created, the storage occupied by the object is unavailable until Windows terminates. If you repeatedly create an object and forget to delete it, Windows will eventually run out of storage and fail. In Win32 this error will just cause your program to degrade in performance. But in Win32s, it will eventually cause Windows to malfunction unrecoverably. If you use a diagnostic tool that reports resource leakage, like Bounds Checker for Windows, you will likely want to know that all leakage reported is genuine and not the result of your assumption that all resources will be freed when the program terminates.

Deleting objects

All six GDI objects (the five mentioned in the previous section plus logical palettes) are deleted by calling the `DeleteObject` function and passing it the handle of the object. You must not delete a GDI object while it is selected into a device context. Doing this frees all system storage associated with the object and invalidates the handle. If the object is deleted while selected into a device context, GDI might try to use the now-invalid handle.

Windows defines macro API functions (`DeleteBitmap`, `DeleteBrush`, `DeleteFont`, `DeletePalette`, `DeletePen`, and `DeleteRgn`) to delete a previously created bitmap, brush, font, palette, pen, or region, respectively. They are defined in terms of a call to the `DeleteObject` function. These macros are defined like this:

```
#define DeleteBitmap(hbm)   \
            DeleteObject((HGDIOBJ)(HBITMAP)(hbm))

#define DeleteBrush(hbr)   \
            DeleteObject((HGDIOBJ)(HBRUSH)(hbr))

#define DeleteFont(hfont)   \
            DeleteObject((HGDIOBJ)(HFONT)(hfont))
```

```
#define DeletePen(hpen)        \
                DeleteObject((HGDIOBJ)(HPEN)(hpen))

#define DeletePalette(hpal) \
                DeleteObject((HGDIOBJ)(HPALETTE)(hpal))

#define DeleteRgn(hrgn)        \
                DeleteObject((HGDIOBJ)(HRGN)(hrgn))
```

A device context has a Windows stock object as the initially selected value for the bitmap (memory device contexts only), brush, font, palette, and pen. For example, the default palette is the stock object DEFAULT_PALETTE. The default pen is the stock object BLACK_PEN. An application can call DeleteObject on a stock object; the call will have no effect. (You may encounter "conventional wisdom" that states that you must not delete stock objects. This was the consequence of an antique bug fixed with the release of Windows 3.1, but the mythology persists into Win32.)

In general, it is *not* safe to assume that if you have released a DC that the objects in it will be no longer selected. If you have a class DC or a private DC, ReleaseDC has no effect, and in particular, the objects remain selected in the DC! Therefore attempting to delete the objects after a ReleaseDC is no guarantee that the operation will not corrupt your application. It is safest to select the original objects back, either with an explicit SelectObject (or SelectBrush, SelectPen, or one of the other macros that "wraps" the SelectObject call) or by doing a RestoreDC.

Another way, often simpler and frequently more efficient, to ensure that the objects you have created are not in the DC is to use the SaveDC and RestoreDC calls. We discuss these in more detail on page 272, but a simple example is shown next:

```
int save = SaveDC(hdc);
    HPEN redpen = CreatePen(PS_SOLID, 1, RGB(255, 0, 0));
    HBRUSH redbrush = CreateSolidBrush(RGB(255,0,0));
    SelectPen(hdc, redpen);
    SelectBrush(hdc, redbrush);
    // ... do drawing
RestoreDC(hdc, save);
DeleteObject(redpen);
DeleteObject(redbrush);
```

The RestoreDC restores the previous state of the DC saved by SaveDC. All objects selected into the DC since the SaveDC will be deselected.

Special Considerations on Object Selection

When you change the GDI objects that are selected into a device context, you need to keep a few things in mind in addition to the general comments just made.

Bitmaps

A bitmap can be selected *only* into a memory device context. Even though different bitmaps can be selected into different memory device contexts simultaneously, a particular bitmap cannot be selected into more than one memory device context at one time. Device contexts other than memory device contexts have no default-selected bitmap because they can't have a bitmap selected into them. A memory device context has a default 1 × 1 monochrome stock bitmap selected into it when it is created.

You can, however, select a pattern brush (which is defined using a bitmap) into any device context. When you delete the pattern brush, the bitmap associated with the brush is not deleted. You must make a separate call to delete the bitmap.

Fonts

A call to the GetTextMetrics function returns metrics based on the font currently selected into the device context. All sizes in the TEXTMETRIC structure are given in logical units that depend on the current mapping mode of the device context. You must, therefore, select a desired font into a device context before you retrieve its metrics. You must also establish the desired mapping mode, if necessary, so that the returned metrics are in the proper units.

Pens

Pens are straightforward. Just remember that you should delete any nonstock pens before you terminate the application. As always, this means selecting some other pen into the device context before you delete it. And as with a brush, you can select a stock pen into the device context to replace the custom pen in the context so that the custom pen can be deleted. This is done as follows:

```
DeletePen (SelectPen (hdc, GetStockPen (BLACK_PEN))) ;
```

When a pen is geometric and has a mitered line join, the *miter limit* determines when the attempt to create a well-defined sharp angle is abandoned. This is discussed in much more detail on page 306.

Regions

Regions are more complex than pens. You can change the clipping region attribute of a device context in a number of ways. You can select a new clipping region into a device context with the old standby SelectObject:

```
HRGN hrgn ;
```

```
SelectObject (hdc, hrgn) ;
```

You also can select a new clipping region into a device context with a special function, SelectClipRgn:

```
SelectClipRgn (hdc, hrgn) ;
```

Both the SelectObject function (when selecting a region) and the SelectClipRgn function return a value that specifies the region's type. These functions do not return the previously selected region. After these calls, unlike other objects that are selected into a device context, the region may be deleted as it is copied into the device context, rather than referenced. One of the side effects of the BeginPaint API call is to select the invalidated region as being the clipping region.

You can exclude a rectangular area from the clipping region by specifying the upper-left and lower-right corners of the rectangle when calling the ExcludeClipRect function:

```
ExcludeClipRect (hdc, xUL, yUL, xLR, yLR) ;
```

Similarly, you can exclude the update region of a window (the area in need of redrawing) from the clipping region of a device context by specifying the window when calling the `ExcludeUpdateRgn` function.

```
ExcludeUpdateRgn (hdc, hwnd) ;
```

This isn't very useful unless the device context is a window display context.

You can move (offset) the clipping region of a device context an arbitrary number of logical units along both the horizontal and vertical axes by using the `OffsetClipRgn` function. You specify the number of logical units to move horizontally and vertically:

```
OffsetClipRgn (hdc, xLogUnits, yLogUnits) ;
```

Because the units are logical units, positive values don't necessarily move the clipping region right (for the horizontal axis) and down (for the vertical axis). The direction depends on the current mapping mode.

You can create a new clipping region consisting of the area in common between the current clipping region and a rectangle specified by its upper-left and lower-right corners by calling the `IntersectClipRect` function:

```
IntersectClipRect (hdc, xUL, yUL, xLR, yLR) ;
```

Finally, you can retrieve the dimensions of the smallest bounding rectangle for the current clipping region of a device context by calling the `GetClipBox` function:

```
GetClipBox (hdc, &rect) ;
```

The Brush Origin Attribute

A brush is actually a bitmap pattern. In Windows 95, this bitmap is limited to being 8×8 pixels; in Windows NT, it can be any size. Windows paints an area with a brush by repeating the bitmap both horizontally and vertically until the entire area is covered. However, it isn't restricted to aligning the upper-left corner of the bitmap with the upper-left corner of the device context in which you wish to paint. The starting alignment of the bitmap with respect to the area to be painted is determined by two factors. The first is the brush origin attribute of a device context. The *brush origin* specifies the pixel within the brush bitmap that Windows aligns with the origin of the device context and can be any one of the pixels in the bitmap. The second factor is the relative position (in device coordinates) of the area to be painted with respect to the origin of the device context.

The brush origin can range from 0 to the width of the bitmap minus 1 for the horizontal coordinate and from 0 to the height of the bitmap minus 1 for the vertical coordinate. It is set by calling the `SetBrushOrgEx` function:

```
SetBrushOrgEx (HDC hdc, int xOrg, int yOrg, LPPOINT pt) ;
```

The `SetBrushOrgEx` function returns the previous origin of the brush via the `pt` parameter. If you don't need the previous origin, you can use the value NULL for this parameter. The `SetBrushOrgEx` does not actually change the origin of the currently selected brush. Instead it establishes the origin of the next brush that you select into the device context.

You can retrieve the current brush origin of a device context without changing it by calling the GetBrushOrgEx function:

```
POINT      Value ;
UINT       xOrigOrg;
UINT       yOrigOrg ;

GetBrushOrgEx (hdc, &Value) ;
xOrigOrg = Value.x ;
yOrigOrg = Value.y ;
```

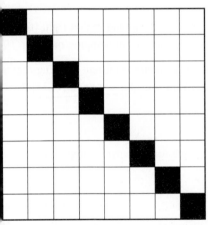

Figure 5.3: Hatched brush bitmap

Take, for example, a diagonally hatched brush. The bitmap is shown in Figure 5.3. The default brush origin for a device context is at the coordinate (0, 0) in device units–not logical units–for the device context. So, by default, the upper-left corner of the bitmap is aligned with the origin of the device context. For the client area of a window, the default origin of the device context is the upper-left corner of the client area of the window. When creating the window shown in Figure 5.4, we requested a class background hatched brush and specified the HS_FDIAGONAL hatch style for the brush. You can see that the downward diagonal line of the brush pattern exactly intersects the upper-left corner of the client area of the window.

Of secondary interest, the HS_FDIAGONAL hatch style is defined to produce a "45-degree upward hatch (left to right)". Instead it produces a downward hatch (left to right)–at least on our VGA system. The complementary HS_BDIAGONAL hatch style is defined to produce a "45-degree downward hatch (left to right)". Instead it produces a pattern sloping upward from left to right. Apparently the symbolic names have been exchanged in the header file.

The brush alignment is with respect to the origin of the device context, not the upper-left corner of the polygon in which the brush is being used. This means that the diagonally hatched brush, as used previously, will not necessarily intersect the upper-left corner of an arbitrary rectangle drawn in the device context. The diagonal intersects the upper-left corner of the window in Figure 5.4 not because it's the upper-left corner of the filled rectangle. Rather it does so because that corner is the origin of the device context and the brush origin defaults to (0, 0). If you visualize a rectangle and overlay it on the hatch-filled window, you can see that you can slide the rectangle horizontally and vertically while the pattern remains motionless. There are 64 different starting positions for the 8×8 hatched pattern with respect to a corner of the rectangle (all the stock hatch patterns are 8×8). If you then visualize a second rectangle positioned adjacent to the first, you'll see that even though the hatched pattern may start in a different position with respect to the same corner of the second rectangle, the pattern flows seamlessly from the first rectangle to the second.

Occasionally, you may prefer that the patterns in adjacent rectangles not align, for example, when drawing adjacent rectangles in a bar chart. When the pattern in each rectangular bar aligns with the pattern in an adjacent bar, the separate bars become hard to distinguish from one another. By changing the brush origin, you can offset the pattern slightly, thereby causing a noticeable discrepancy in the pattern and making the demarcation between the rectangles more apparent. Changing the brush origin as described in the preceding example is done with the following statement:

```
SetBrushOrgEx (hdc, 4, 0, NULL) ;
```

It shifts the diagonal line that previously intersected the upper-left corner 4 pixels to the left so that the line no longer intersects the corner. A better way to look at it is that pixel (4, 0) of the brush is now aligned with the origin of the device context rather than with the default pixel (0, 0). The changed brush origin will be used when the next brush is selected into the device context and is not used until the next object that uses a brush is drawn.

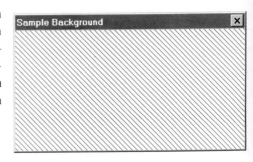

Figure 5.4: Brush alignment of an HS_FDIAGONAL hatch brush with the default (0, 0) brush origin

Only two steps are required to change the brush origin:

1. Call the SetBrushOrgEx function to change the brush origin.

2. Call the SelectBrush macro API to select the brush into the device context.

So, to change the brush origin as discussed here, you first need to ensure that the brush isn't currently selected into any device context. This usually isn't a problem when using a common display context because Windows gives the context to you with a stock brush already selected. Then you can change the brush origin with code similar to the following:

```
HBRUSH      hbrushPattern ;
HBRUSH      hbrushOld ;
HDC         hdc ;

hdc = BeginPaint (hwnd) ;
hbrushPattern = CreateHatchBrush (HS_FDIAGONAL, RGB (0,0,0)) ;
SetBrushOrgEx (hdc, 4, 0, NULL) ;
hbrushOld = SelectBrush (hdc, hbrushPattern) ;

/* Do something visible to justify this effort. */

SelectBrush (hdc, hbrushOld) ;
DeleteBrush (hbrushPattern) ;
ReleaseDC (hwnd, hdc) ;
```

The Mapping Mode, Window Origin and Extent, and Viewport Origin and Extent

The *mapping mode* attribute of a device context affects nearly all drawing operations performed on the device context. Four other attributes are used when certain mapping modes are selected: the *window* and *viewport origin* and the *window* and *viewport extent*.

GDI drawing functions typically require one or more coordinates or sizes. For example, you've seen the TextOut function, which requires the horizontal and vertical coordinates of the position at which to draw the text string:

```
TextOut (hdc, xLoc, yLoc, Buffer, lstrlen (Buffer)) ;
```

The TextOut function, as well as most (although not all) GDI functions, interprets coordinates and sizes in terms of logical coordinates and logical units. Windows translates these logical coordinates into device coordinates and the logical units into device units. This translation is controlled by the current mapping mode, the window and viewport origins, and the window and viewport extents.

Many of the possible mapping modes imply the position of the origin of the logical coordinate system as well as the orientation of the horizontal and vertical axes. For example, most mapping modes imply that values on the horizontal axis increase as you move toward the right side of the display and values on the vertical axis increase as you move toward the top of the display. However, the default mapping mode of MM_TEXT specifies that values on the vertical axis increase as you move toward the bottom of the display. Other mapping modes allow you to completely specify the size of a logical unit and the orientation of both axes.

Windows supports eight mapping modes, as given in Table 5.7.

Table 5.7: Mapping modes

Mapping Mode	Size of a Logical Unit	Direction of Increasing Values	
		Horizontal	**Vertical**
MM_ANISOTROPIC	Arbitrary ($x \neq y$)	Selectable $\Leftrightarrow$	Selectable $\Updownarrow$
MM_HIENGLISH	0.001 inch	Right $\Rightarrow$	Up $\Uparrow$
MM_HIMETRIC	0.01 mm	Right $\Rightarrow$	Up $\Uparrow$
MM_ISOTROPIC	Arbitrary ($x = y$)	Selectable $\Leftrightarrow$	Selectable $\Updownarrow$
MM_LOENGLISH	0.01 inch	Right $\Rightarrow$	Up $\Uparrow$
MM_LOMETRIC	0.1 mm	Right $\Rightarrow$	Up $\Uparrow$
MM_TEXT	1 pixel	Right $\Rightarrow$	Down $\Downarrow$
MM_TWIPS	$1/1440$ inch	Right $\Rightarrow$	Up $\Uparrow$

When you create a device context or retrieve a display context from the common display context pool, the device context initially has the MM_TEXT mapping mode. You can change the mapping mode by calling the SetMapMode function and specifying the symbolic name of the desired mapping mode as the MapMode parameter:

```
SetMapMode (hdc, MapMode) ;
```

You can retrieve the current mapping mode of a device context by calling the GetMapMode function:

```
MapMode = GetMapMode (hdc) ;
```

The default mapping mode of MM_TEXT maps one logical unit to one device unit (pixel). Windows interprets all dimensions as the number of device units and all coordinates as device coordinates. A call to the Rectangle function that looks like this:

```
Rectangle (hdc, 50, 50, 10, 20) ;
```

draws a rectangle whose upper-left corner is 50 pixels to the right of the origin and 50 pixels down from the origin and that extends 10 pixels to the right and 20 pixels down. The exact physical size of the rectangle is indeterminate. It depends on the size of a pixel, both horizontally and vertically.

If you change the mapping mode to MM_LOMETRIC, then logical units are interpreted in terms of tenths of a millimeter:

```
SetMapMode (hdc, MM_LOMETRIC) ;
```

The same call to the Rectangle function now produces a rectangle located 5 mm to the right of the origin and 5 mm up from the origin and that extends 1 mm to the right and 2 mm up.

You actually don't ever need to use any mapping mode other than the default MM_TEXT mapping mode. You can perform all required scaling yourself. Say you want to duplicate the effect of the MM_LOMETRIC mapping mode example just discussed. To do so, you retrieve the device capabilities for the device context (in particular, the width and height of the display in millimeters and the width and height of the display in pixels) with four calls to the GetDeviceCaps functions. Then you use the information to calculate the required scaling. Of course, using the mapping modes to do the work for you is much easier (not to mention the fact that you are less prone to make an error if you let GDI do the mapping for you).

You shouldn't get carried away and create logical coordinate systems with huge positions and extents. To be reasonably fast on unreasonably slow computers, Windows 95 uses 16-bit signed short integers for logical units and coordinates. Doing this limits the range of coordinates to -32,768..32,767. Windows functions that use a pair of points to specify the starting and ending points of a rectangle also limit the rectangle's height and width to 32,767 or less. Although you can use 32-bit coordinates in Windows NT, you cannot do so if you expect the program will also be run under Windows 95, which suffers from its 16-bit substrate. A program that works perfectly well on Windows NT could experience problems running on Windows 95 if it ever generated a coordinate value outside the range supported by 16 bits. Windows 95 simply ignores the high-order 16 bits of all 32-bit coordinates passed to the GDI. The same problems apply to Win32s.

All this is to caution you to be careful when you establish a logical coordinate system. You can actually create one in which portions of the device surface cannot be addressed because reaching it would exceed the range of a short signed integer.

Various Windows Coordinate Systems

Windows uses various coordinate systems under different circumstances. The basic coordinate system is the device coordinate system. This system uses units of pixels. That is, the terms *device unit* and *pixel* are synonymous. In this system, horizontal values increase from left to right and vertical values increase from top to bottom. The origin is the upper-left corner of the device surface. All non-GDI functions and all messages (such as WM_MOVE, WM_SIZE, and WM_MOUSEMOVE) return positions and sizes in terms of device coordinates. A few GDI functions use device coordinates as well.

The screen coordinate system is the device coordinate system that pertains to the entire display device. Screen coordinates are specified in terms of pixels, as are all device coordinate systems. After all, the display device is just another device. Screen coordinates are used when the entire screen must be addressed. For example, when you create a window, you specify its size and position in terms of screen coordinates. The CreateWindow, CreateWindowEx, and MoveWindow functions (when used for windows other than child windows) use screen coordinates. Other functions that use screen coordinates are GetCursorPos, GetMessagePos, GetWindowRect, SetCursorPos, and WindowFromPoint. All these functions use coordinates that indicate the position of an object (cursor or window) with respect to the upper-left corner of the screen.

Client area coordinates are also device coordinates; however, client area coordinates are not screen coordinates. The difference is the location of the origin of the coordinate system. Screen coordinates are relative to the upper-left corner of the display device. Client area coordinates are relative to the upper-left corner of the client area. Client area coordinates are given in device units (pixels) just as screen coordinates are. You can convert client area coordinates to screen coordinates very easily using the ClientToScreen function for just this purpose. The ScreenToClient function performs the opposite translation.

Window coordinates are nearly the same as client area coordinates. Window coordinates are relative to the upper-left corner of the window, not the upper-left corner of the window's client area. Generally, you need to use window coordinates only when you want to draw in the nonclient area portions of the window such as the title bar or window frame.

Only GDI functions (and not all of them) use logical coordinates. A logical coordinate system is not a form of device coordinate system. A logical coordinate system is always mapped to a device coordinate system. It is one you create (or one given to you by default in the case of the MM_TEXT mapping mode) because it's more convenient to use than a device coordinate system. For example, you can create a quadrant one Cartesian axes coordinate system in which the abscissa and the ordinate range from 0 to 1,000 and the full extents of the system are mapped to the current size of the client area of a window. This is a nice, simple, straightforward system. GDI maps (translates) all logical coordinates and logical units from this simple coordinate system to the appropriate device coordinate system.

Logical coordinates are mapped to the client area device coordinate system when the device context refers to the client area of a window. That is, the device context referenced in the GDI drawing function refers to a display context for a window's client area–one returned by the GetDC or BeginPaint functions. Logical coordinates are mapped to window coordinates when the device context is a window display context (i.e., a display context returned by the GetWindowDC function). Logical coordinates are mapped to screen coordinates when the device context refers to the entire screen (i.e., a device context returned by the CreateDC function with a parameter of "DISPLAY").

Windows provides the LPtoDP and DPtoLP functions to translate the coordinates of one or more points from/to a logical coordinate system to/from a device coordinate system. Both functions require a handle to a device context, the address of an array of POINT structures, and the number of points in the array to convert. The following statements convert a point in logical coordinates to device coordinates:

```
POINT pt ;

pt.x = 100 ;
pt.y = 250 ;
LPtoDP (hdc, &pt, 1) ;
```

The GetClientRect function returns the size of the client area in device units. Sometimes it's useful to have this information in logical coordinates. You can translate this information from device coordinates to logical coordinates with the following statements:

```
RECT rect ;

GetClientRect (hwnd, &rect) ;
DPtoLP (hdc, (LPPOINT) &rect, 2) ;
```

The device context parameter to the DPtoLP and LPtoDP functions identifies the logical coordinate system and the device coordinate system to use in the translation.

As mentioned earlier in the chapter, you can translate a point in client coordinates to its equivalent value in screen coordinates, and vice versa, using the ClientToScreen and ScreenToClient functions. The position and size of the window in screen coordinates, which establish the window coordinate system, are returned by the GetWindowRect function. When you're processing messages in screen and client area device coordinates and drawing figures using logical coordinates, keeping track of the coordinate currently in use becomes very important. These Windows functions allow you to easily convert from any coordinate system to any other–although not necessarily in one step.

The Viewport and the Window

How do you go about defining the coordinate system you want to use? First, you choose the proper device context mapping mode.

The mapping mode tells GDI how to map logical coordinates and dimensions supplied on calls to GDI output functions to the device coordinate system implied by the device context. GDI maps a "window" (logical coordinates) to a "viewport" (device coordinates). The terms *window* and *viewport* are used here in a sense unique to this discussion of GDI and mapping modes. The term *viewport* refers to a rectangular area of the device coordinate system defined by a device context. This will be a rectangular area of a client area coordinate system, a window coordinate system, or a screen coordinate system, depending on the type of device context. The term *window* in this context does not refer to a window on the display screen, which is the way we've been using it so far. When used to refer to GDI mapping modes, *window* refers to a rectangular area of the logical coordinate system defined by a device context. This is often the same area as a window on the screen, so confusion can easily arise.

For example, when the default MM_TEXT mapping mode is in effect, the "window" happens to be the rectangular area defined by the logical coordinate (0, 0) and the logical coordinate (client area width, client area height). Because the MM_TEXT mapping mode defines one logical unit as equal to one device unit, the origins of the two coordinate systems coincide and the orientation of the two axes is the same. The two coordinate systems completely overlay each other, and there is a one-to-one mapping. Because the default setup of the logical coordinate system makes it identical to the device coordinate system, they're often mistaken for each other.

You can, however, establish a radically different mapping. Take the earlier example of a quadrant one Cartesian axes coordinate system with positive extents of 1,000 units. You could define a "window" into this logical coordinate system starting at the point (100, 250) and extending 500 units in +x and 250 units in +y. This describes a rectangular area of the logical coordinate system. This "window" into the logical coordinate system is mapped to a "viewport" on the device coordinate system. The "viewport" itself is another rectangular area of the device coordinate system. The ratio of the horizontal and vertical extents of the "window" to the horizontal and vertical extents of the "viewport" (or the inverse), respectively, determine the scaling factors to use when translating coordinates. The "window" origin and "viewport" origin determine the offset needed when you translate coordinates.

We need to digress here to clarify another point. Even though you select a rectangular area of a logical coordinate system (the "window") and another rectangular area of a device coordinate system (the "viewport") and specify the two rectangular areas as the information needed to translate a coordinate in one system to the other system, coordinates are not restricted to lying in either the "window" or the "viewport" (which is the same thing, if you think about it).

In this quadrant-one coordinate system, the "window" was defined as extending from the point (100, 250) to the point (600, 500). The point (0, 0), although not in the "window" area, exists and will be mapped to a point in the device coordinate system based on the scaling and offset parameters determined by comparing the specified "window" and "viewport" areas. Then, as a completely separate issue, whether something is visible when displayed at logical point (0, 0) depends on whether the equivalent point in device coordinates is inside or outside the clipping region.

The general formulae for converting a "window" (logical) coordinate to a "viewport" (device) coordinate are as follows:

$$xViewPort = (xWindow - xWindowOrg) \times \frac{xViewportExt}{xWindowExt} + xViewportOrg$$

$$yViewPort = (yWindow - yWindowOrg) \times \frac{yViewportExt}{yWindowExt} + yViewportOrg$$

Here, the point ($xWindow$, $yWindow$) is a point in logical coordinates to be translated and the point ($xViewport$, $yViewport$) is the translated point in device coordinates.

The points ($xWindowOrg$, $yWindowOrg$) and ($xViewportOrg$, $yViewportOrg$) are the origins of the "window" and "viewport" rectangular areas. Both of these points are initially set to (0, 0) in a default device context. To map one coordinate system to another, you must specify a point in one coordinate system and the equivalent point in the other coordinate system. From the formulae above, you can see that the point ($xWindowOrg$, $yWindowOrg$) is always mapped to the point ($xViewportOrg$, $yViewportOrg$).

These formulae also use two "points" that specify the extents of an area in the logical coordinate system: (*xWindowExt*, *yWindowExt*). The points also specify the extents of an area in the device coordinate system: (*xViewportExt*, *yViewportExt*). It doesn't mean anything to say simply "the window extent is *xWindowExt* units long horizontally and *yWindowExt* units high vertically". Neither does the statement "the viewport extent is *xViewportExt* units long horizontally and *yViewportExt* units high vertically" convey any information. However, the ratio of the viewport extent to the window extent produces a scaling factor for translating logical units to device units. Basically, the extents say that "moving *xWindowExt* units horizontally in the logical coordinate system is the same as moving *xViewportExt* units horizontally in the device coordinate system" and equivalently for the vertical extents. You travel the same distance in each case.

The same cannot be said for direction. One or both extents can be negative; therefore the ratio of the two extents can be either positive or negative. When the ratio is positive, increasing values in logical units horizontally move to the right in device coordinates and increasing values in logical units vertically move down in device coordinates. When the ratio is negative, increasing values in logical units horizontally move left in device coordinates and increasing values in logical units vertically move up in device coordinates. Basically, an axis in logical coordinates has the opposite orientation from the axis in device coordinates when the scaling ratio is negative.

The translation formulae for mapping from viewport (device) coordinates to window (logical) coordinates are similar:

$$xWindow = (xViewport - xViewportOrg) \times \frac{xWindowExt}{xViewportExt} + xWindowOrg$$

$$yWindow = (yViewport - yViewportOrg) \times \frac{yWindowExt}{yViewportExt} + yWindowOrg$$

The MM_TEXT *Mapping Mode*

The default attributes of a device context that pertain to coordinate translation are as follows:

- Mapping mode: MM_TEXT

- Window origin: (0, 0)

- Viewport origin: (0, 0)

- Window extent: (1, 1)

- Viewport extent: (1, 1)

The MM_TEXT mapping mode is the default mapping mode. Because this is the mode used most frequently, we examine the effect these attribute settings have on the logical coordinate-to-device coordinate translation formulae previously described. Substituting the default values for the window origin, viewport origin, window extent, and viewport extent results in the following:

$$xViewport = xWindow$$

$$yViewPort = yWindow$$

This pair of equations makes it easy to see why logical coordinates and device coordinates are often mistaken for one another. In the default case, they are exactly the same!

You're not allowed to change the window extent or the viewport extent in the MM_TEXT mapping mode. The ratio of one extent to the other is always 1 in the MM_TEXT mapping mode. Therefore no scaling is performed and one logical unit is equal to one device unit.

The window origin and viewport origin can be changed in the MM_TEXT mapping mode. The logical coordinate-to-device coordinate translation formulae can be simplified to the following when you allow variable origins but fixed and equal extents:

$$xViewPort = xWindow - xWindowOrigin + xViewportOrigin$$

$$yViewPort = yWindow - yWindowOrigin + yViewportOrigin$$

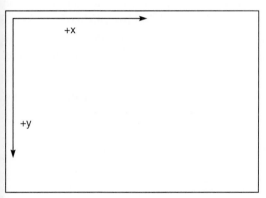

Figure 5.5: Orientation of the logical and device coordinate systems

These formulae show that ascending logical coordinate values of x and y produce ascending device coordinate values for x and y. In other words, the orientation of the logical coordinate system axes is identical to that of the device coordinate system axes. The result is the coordinate system shown in Figure 5.5. Horizontal coordinate values increase from left to right, whereas vertical coordinate values increase from top to bottom.

The origin of the logical coordinate system is mapped to the origin of the device coordinate system because the default window origin and viewport origin coordinates are equal. The device coordinate system origin is always the upper-left corner of the device display surface, no matter how you set window and viewport origins. Because logical coordinate (0, 0), or the window origin, maps to device coordinate (0, 0), or the viewport origin, the origin of the logical coordinate system is the upper-left corner of the device context display surface. Remember that for the system display, this could be the upper-left corner of the client area, the window, or the screen, depending on the type of device context.

You can change both the window origin and the viewport origin attributes using the SetWindowOrgEx and SetViewportOrgEx functions. The window origin is always mapped to the viewport origin. Therefore you use these functions to specify the point in the logical coordinate system and the point in the device coordinate system that you want coincident. These functions shift the origin and can be used to place the origin of the logical coordinate system at any location in the device coordinate system. You aren't stuck using the upper-left corner.

There are three ways to view the shifting of the origin of the logical coordinate system with respect to the origin of the device coordinate system:

1. Map logical point (0, 0) to device point *(xViewportOrigin, yViewportOrigin)*

2. Map logical point *(xWindowOrigin, yWindowOrigin)* to device point (0, 0)

3. Map logical point *(xWindowOrigin, yWindowOrigin)* to device point
   (xViewportOrigin, yViewportOrigin)

Any one of the three viewpoints can be used to establish the coordinate mapping; you should use the on
most suited to the problem you are trying to solve. For example, when you want to place the center of th
area you're drawing at the center of the client area of a window, you should use the first approach becaus
the information at hand is already in the proper form. The `GetClientRect` function returns the size of th
client area in device units. When the client area is `cxClient` device units (pixels) wide and `cyClient` devic
units high, the point of interest in the device coordinate system is (`cxClient`/2, `cyClient`/2). It's generall
easiest to draw around the origin if possible. Assuming that you're drawing around the origin (which is in th
logical coordinate system), you can establish this mapping with the following statement:

```
SetViewportOrgEx (hdc, cxClient / 2, cyClient / 2, NULL) ;
```

The `SetViewportOrgEx` function requires device coordinates and maps the point (`cxClient` / 2,
`cyClient`/2) to the logical coordinate (0, 0). The
logical coordinate (0, 0) is the initial default value for
the device context window origin attribute. The origin of the logical coordinate system has now been
shifted to the center of the client area. The axes still
have their original orientation, that is, *x*-values increase to the right and *y*-values increase downward,
as shown in Figure 5.6.

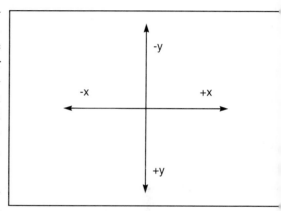

Maybe you'd like to place a known point in your
drawing space (logical coordinate system) in the
upper-left corner of the client area of a window. In

Figure 5.6: Orientation after using
`SetViewportOrgEx`

this situation, the logical coordinate (`xWindow`
`Origin, yWindowOrigin`) is known and you want to
place it at the device point (0, 0). This situation is equivalent to the second method of viewing GDI coordinate mapping. This `SetWindowOrgEx` function requires logical coordinates and maps the point in logical coordinates to the default viewport origin (0, 0):

```
SetWindowOrgEx (hdc, xWindowOrigin, yWindowOrigin, NULL) ;
```

The following code attempts to shift the axes to the center of the client area, as was done in the preceding
`SetViewportOrgEx` example. However, this code doesn't work in all cases whereas the previous example
does. Obviously, you should get into the habit of using the previous form, not this one. Consider this a simple test! By now, you should be able to tell why it's wrong and why it works anyway (sometimes):

```
HDC    hdc ;
RECT   rect ;

hdc = GetDC (hwnd) ;   /* Not the preferred method! */
GetClientRect (hwnd, &rect) ;
SetWindowOrgEx (hdc, rect.right / 2, rect.bottom / 2, NULL) ;
```

Dividing the right and bottom values from the RECT structure does give you the coordinates for the point at the center of the client area. But the coordinates are device coordinates, not logical coordinates; the SetWindowOrgEx function expects logical coordinates. This function call works only because the two coordinates are the same when the mapping mode is MM_TEXT. Because the SetViewportOrgEx function expects device coordinates, the example using it works in all mapping modes.

If you prefer this method, you should translate the device coordinate to a logical coordinate before using it in a call to the SetWindowOrgEx function. The following example does this and works in all mapping modes:

```
HDC      hdc ;
POINT    pt ;
RECT     rect ;

hdc = GetDC (hwnd) ;
GetClientRect (hwnd, &rect) ;
pt.x = rect.rect / 2 ;
pt.y = rect.bottom / 2 ;
DPtoLP (hdc, &pt, 1) ;
SetWindowOrgEx (hdc, pt.x, pt.y, NULL) ;
```

The third way to shift the axes is to make an arbitrary point in the logical coordinate system coincide with an arbitrary point in the device coordinate system. This is really what we've been doing all along. In the previous cases, one of the "arbitrary" points wasn't so arbitrary. It was the origin of either the device coordinate system or of the logical coordinate system. It was also the default value for the device context, so it didn't need to be changed.

Because both the window and viewport origins are arbitrary, you need to use both the SetWindowOrgEx and SetViewportOrgEx functions to change the respective device context attributes. The following example maps the origin of the logical coordinate system to the lower-right corner of the client area of a window. It works correctly only in the MM_TEXT mapping mode because client coordinates are being passed as logical coordinates to the SetWindowOrgEx function:

```
SetViewportOrgEx (hdc, cxClient / 2, cyClient / 2, NULL) ;
SetWindowOrgEx (hdc, -cxClient / 2, -cyClient / 2, NULL) ;
```

You can retrieve the current window and viewport origins from a device context by calling the GetWindowOrgEx and GetViewportOrgEx functions as shown by the following code:

```
POINT   vporg ;   // Viewport origin
POINT   worg ;    // Window origin

GetViewportOrgEx (hdc, &vporg) ;
GetWindowOrgEx (hdc, &worg) ;
```

The Physical Measurement Mapping Modes

The MM_TEXT mapping mode is handy for text output, but it isn't well suited for some graphical output. First, the vertical axis of the logical coordinate system is inverted with respect to a "normal" Cartesian coordinate system. Second, and probably more significant, the MM_TEXT mapping mode does not always produce a mapping in which logical coordinates on the horizontal axis and the vertical axis are equal in physical measurement. Whether it does depends on the type of display device. A VGA display has square pixels, so a line 100 pixels long horizontally is physically the same length as one that is 100 pixels long vertically. However, to show an historical example, the pixels on an EGA display were one third taller than they were wide. You had to draw a horizontal line 133 pixels long for it to have the same physical length as a 100-pixel-long vertical line. Such displays were referred to as having "rectangular pixels", while displays that have the same pixel spacing horizontally and vertically are referred to as having "square pixels".[1] While nearly all displays we know of have square pixels, this may not always be so. Many printers do not have the same resolution in the vertical and horizontal axes; for example, a resolution of 300×600 is not uncommon.

The physical mapping modes map equal distances in logical units in the horizontal axis and the vertical axis to equal distances on the device horizontally and vertically. You can use these modes to draw round circles and square squares without compensating for the aspect ratio of pixels on the device. Windows supplies any required compensation.

Two physical measurement mapping modes use metric units, two use English units, and the last uses twips. *Twip* is a fabricated word that stands for "twentieth of a point". A point is a unit of measurement used in typesetting. It is approximately $^1/_{72}$ inch, but GDI considers it to be exactly $^1/_{72}$ inch. Therefore a twip, or a *twentieth* of a *point*, is $^1/_{1440}$ inch.

The two English mapping modes are MM_LOENGLISH, which uses 0.01-inch logical units, and MM_HIENGLISH, which uses 0.001-inch logical units. The "LO" and "HI" refer to the resolution of the logical units. The MM_LOENGLISH mapping mode has a lower resolution than the MM_HIENGLISH mapping mode.

The two metric mapping modes are MM_LOMETRIC, which uses 0.1-mm logical units, and the MM_HIMETRIC, which uses 0.01-mm logical units. The MM_LOMETRIC mapping mode has a lower resolution than the MM_HIMETRIC mapping mode.

The last physical measurement mapping mode is called the MM_TWIPS mapping mode, which uses $^1/_{1440}$-inch logical units. This mode was chosen to allow you to internally represent variable-pitch text at a resolution higher than the pixels of MM_TEXT mode allow. It was decided that $^1/_{20}$th of a printer's point (approximately $^1/_{72}$ of an inch) was a satisfactory compromise between precision of layout and the 16-bit coordinate limitation. Ranked in order of increasing resolution, the mapping modes are MM_LOENGLISH, MM_LOMETRIC, MM_HIENGLISH, MM_TWIPS, and MM_HIMETRIC.

A figure drawn using the physical measurement mapping modes won't always be exactly the size at which it was drawn. Windows, after all, has no way to determine the physical size of the actual display device. It uses the device capabilities information to determine the physical size of the display device. The GetDeviceCaps function queries the device driver, which returns the physical size of the standard display for the device type. So, although a 100-mm line won't necessarily be 100 mm long on the display device, it will be the same physical length when drawn horizontally and vertically.

---

[1] These designations have nothing to do with what the pixels look like if you use a magnifying glass. Usually, the pixels are round in both cases because of the color screen technology used. The terms refer to the aspect ratio of the pixels.

The default window origin and extent and the viewport origin and extent for the physical measurement mapping modes are as follows:

- Window origin: (0, 0)

- Viewport origin: (0, 0)

- Window extent: (device dependent, device dependent)

- Viewport extent: (device dependent, device dependent)

Windows sets the window extent and viewport extent to compensate for the aspect ratio of the device. Remember, the actual values for *xWindowExtent, yWindowExtent, xViewportExtent,* and *yViewportExtent* aren't significant. But various ratios of the values are. Let's look at an example.

Suppose you want to draw a line 10 mm long horizontally, and you're using the MM_LOMETRIC mapping mode. The line is therefore 100 logical units long because each logical unit is 0.1 mm. You need to map 100 logical units to some unknown number of device units. Referring back to the coordinate translation formulae, you can see that the ratio used to determine the number of device units is the following:

$$xpixels \ = \ 100 \times \frac{xViewportExtent}{xWindowExtent}$$

The same line vertically uses the corresponding vertical ratio with a minor variation:

$$ypixels \ = \ 100 \times - \ \frac{yViewportExtent}{yWindowExtent}$$

The y-axis ratio is negated. All the physical measurement mapping modes use a logical coordinate system, in which the vertical axis values increase as you move upward. However, a device coordinate system always uses device coordinates, in which the vertical axis values increase as you move downward. The negative sign causes positive logical values of *y* (which are expected to be upward from the origin location) to be converted to negative device values of *y* (which are upward from the origin location).

You shouldn't get too carried away and expect that changing the DC to use a physical measurement mapping mode is all that's needed to work in a more "normal" coordinate system. Yes, the axes are now oriented in the more familiar Cartesian style. Yes, moving a given distance in logical units moves the same physical distance no matter which axis is used. But look at the default window origin and the viewport origin.

The default window and viewport origins are both (0, 0). This means the logical point (0, 0) is mapped to the device point (0, 0), which is the upper-left corner of the display surface. All physical measurement mapping modes, by default, use a coordinate system in which, in Cartesian terms, all visible output is produced in quadrant four. The axes in the client area of a window are mapped as shown in Figure 5.7.

You can switch to a more "normal" four-quadrant Cartesian system that has equally scaled axes with the following statement:

```
SetViewportOrgEx (hdc, cxClient / 2, cyClient / 2, NULL) ;
```

This call moves the origin of the coordinate system to the center of the client area. Or, maybe you'd prefer a first-quadrant-only Cartesian coordinate system. You get that by moving the origin of the coordinate system to the lower-left corner of the client area. That's the device point (0, cyClient - 1), so make the following function call instead:

```
SetViewportOrgEx (hdc, 0, cyClient-1,
NULL) ;
```

The MM_ANISOTROPIC and MM_ISOTROPIC Mapping Modes

All the previous mapping modes have been constrained mapping modes. You cannot change the physical unit to which a logical unit is mapped in a constrained mapping mode. They are *constrained* because the scaling factor for a given mapping mode is fixed. The MM_TEXT mode scales one logical unit to one pixel. The MM_LOMETRIC mapping mode scales one logical unit to 0.1 mm.

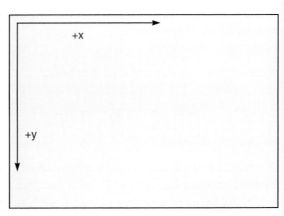

Figure 5.7: Orientation of the physical coordinate system

The MM_ANISOTROPIC mode is an *unconstrained* mapping mode, and the MM_ISOTROPIC mode is a *partially constrained* mapping mode. Both mapping modes allow you to specify the scaling factor for each axis. When you use the MM_ISOTROPIC mapping mode, Windows adjusts one of the scaling factors so that one logical unit maps to an identical distance on both axes. It is partially constrained because, although you can specify the scaling factors for both axes, Windows will change one of them so that a logical unit horizontally covers the same physical distance as a logical unit vertically. The MM_ANISOTROPIC mapping mode is similar to the physical measurement mapping modes except that you can choose the unit of measure and the orientation of the axes.

The MM_ANISOTROPIC mapping mode allows you to specify separate scaling factors for each axis. When you use the MM_ANISOTROPIC mapping mode, one logical unit along the horizontal axis doesn't necessarily travel the same physical distance as one logical unit along the vertical axis. Because Windows doesn't adjust any of the scaling factors you specify, this mode is *unconstrained*. These scaling factors are derived from two rectangular regions that you specify–the window and the viewport.

Previously we used only the window and viewport origins to shift the alignment of the logical and device coordinate system origins. But you'll recall that the window and viewport are defined as rectangular regions. The window resides in the logical coordinate space, and the viewport resides in the device coordinate space. Not only do they each have an origin, they also have a horizontal extent and a vertical extent. The window and viewport extents of the MM_TEXT mapping mode were fixed at (1, 1). The window and viewport extents of the physical measurement mapping modes were fixed to values determined by Windows.

You specify the window and viewport extents when using the MM_ANISOTROPIC and MM_ISOTROPIC mapping modes to scale a logical unit to any desired physical unit. The *horizontal extent* of the window and the viewport is the horizontal distance from any one corner to the opposing corner. The *vertical extent* of the window and the viewport is the vertical distance from any one corner to the opposing corner. You change the window extent by calling the SetWindowExtEx function and passing the horizontal and vertical extents in logical units. You change the viewport extent by calling the `SetViewportExtEx` function and passing the horizontal and vertical extents in device units. Windows calculates the horizontal scaling factor by dividing the viewport extent by the window extent. A similar calculation derives the vertical scaling factor.

Notice that two separate scaling factors are calculated. This means that one logical unit along the horizontal axis might not map to the same physical distance as one logical unit along the vertical axis. In fact, that is exactly the case for the `MM_ANISOTROPIC` mapping mode. This mode is well named because *anisotropic* means "of unequal physical properties along different axes". *Isotropic* means exactly the opposite: "of equal physical properties along all axes".

One typical example of a case in which you would use the `MM_ANISOTROPIC` mapping mode is when you want to draw an entire image scaled to fit exactly into the current size of a window. When you use this mapping mode, the user can change the size of the window. When the image is redrawn, Windows appropriately shrinks or enlarges it as necessary. The entire image remains visible, although possibly distorted, as the window changes size. The other mapping modes draw in fixed physical dimensions. As a result, changing the size of a window can result in portions of the image being drawn outside the boundaries of the window so that they are not visible.

You use the `MM_ISOTROPIC` mapping mode when you wish to create output with equally scaled axes. Because Windows scales a logical unit to a fixed physical unit regardless of the aspect ratio of the device, symmetrical figures drawn in the logical coordinate space remain symmetrical in the device or physical coordinate space. In other words, you use the `MM_ISOTROPIC` mapping mode when you want a logical unit to be mapped to a physical unit not available in one of the other mapping modes and when a square should look like a square when drawn on a device with an aspect ratio other than 1:1.

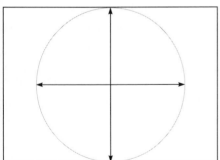

Figure 5.8: A window with a horizontal extent greater than 32,766 logical units

The `MM_ISOTROPIC` mapping mode is also often used when you want to draw an entire image appropriately scaled to fill the current size of a window just as we described for the `MM_ANISOTROPIC` mapping mode. The difference between using this mapping mode and the one in the previous example is that the `MM_ISOTROPIC` mapping mode results in Windows scaling the size of the image so that it is not distorted. Windows compensates for the aspect ratio of the device when using the `MM_ISOTROPIC` mapping mode by shrinking one of the viewport extents.

This all sounds rather theoretical, so here's an example. Suppose you want a "normal" four-quadrant Cartesian coordinate system. The horizontal and vertical axes should be equally scaled in physical units, the logical coordinates should range from −16,383 to 16,383 on both axes, and the origin should be at the center of the window.

The condition that logical units map to arbitrary, but equally scaled, physical units results in the mapping mode `MM_ISOTROPIC` being selected. The scaling and orientation of the axes is performed by the `SetWindowExtEx` and `SetViewportExtEx` functions. The `SetViewportOrgEx` function moves the origin of the logical coordinate system to the center of the client area of the window. You do everything mentioned here with the following statements:

```
SetMapMode (hdc, MM_ISOTROPIC) ;
SetWindowExtEx (hdc, 32766, 32766, NULL) ;
SetViewportExtEx (hdc, cxClient, -cyClient, NULL) ;
SetViewportOrgEx (hdc, cxClient / 2, cyClient / 2, NULL) ;
```

When using the MM_ISOTROPIC mapping mode, you must call the SetWindowExtEx function before calling the SetViewportExtEx function. Windows will change the viewport extents as necessary so that logical units map to equal physical units on both axes. Therefore the values returned by calling GetViewportExtEx may not equal the extents to which the viewport was set. The logical coordinate system just established appears as shown in Figure 5.8 when the client area is wider than it is high. When the window is taller than it is wide, then the logical coordinate system appears as shown in Figure 5.9.

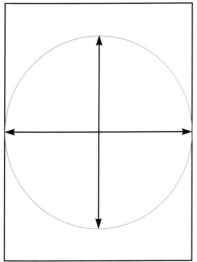

Figure 5.9: A window with a vertical extent greater than 32,766 logical units

Setting a window or viewport extent does not restrict the coordinates you use to those within the extent. Figures 5.8 and 5.9 demonstrate the mapping of the window extents to the client area. Whenever the window isn't physically square, one axis is longer than 32,766 logical units. Coordinates greater than the window extents can be used to draw within the area outside the illustrated axes. For example, you could draw a line starting at the logical coordinate (20000, 25000). The line will be clipped to the window, however, so part of it may not be visible if the logical coordinates map to a location outside the clipping region.

When using the MM_ANISOTROPIC mode, Windows does not adjust the viewport extents to compensate for the device's aspect ratio. Because the viewport extents remain arbitrary, one logical unit will, in general, map to a different physical distance on one axis as compared to the other. This has the effect of stretching or squeezing the logical coordinate space of the window as necessary to fit within the device coordinate space of the viewport.

Now we use the same coordinate system but change to the MM_ANISOTROPIC mapping mode:

```
SetMapMode (hdc, MM_ANISOTROPIC) ;
SetWindowExtEx (hdc, 32766, 32766, NULL) ;
SetViewportExtEx (hdc, cxClient, -cyClient, NULL) ;
SetViewportOrgEx (hdc, cxClient / 2, cyClient / 2, NULL) ;
```

When the window is as wide as it is high, the coordinate system appears as shown in Figure 5.10. Because Windows does not adjust the extents, each axis is 32,766 logical units long and extends the full width and height of the client area. Any point with a logical coordinate value on either axis that is less than −16,383 or greater than 16,383 is outside the clipping region of the window and will not be visible. Squares drawn in this coordinate system will, in general, be rectangular and circles will be elliptical because one logical unit horizontally will only by chance be equal in physical distance to one logical unit vertically.

You sometimes may find it handy to use the MM_ANISOTROPIC mapping mode when one of the other mapping modes is almost, but not quite, suitable. For example, you really would like to use the MM_TEXT mapping mode and work in units of pixels, but you'd prefer values on the vertical axis to increase upward rather than downward. You can't invert the axis by negating one of the extents because you can't change either extent in the MM_TEXT mapping mode.

When you change the mapping mode to MM_ANISOTROPIC, however, the extent attributes of the device context are not changed, so inverting an axis is quite simple. You set the mapping mode you want, change the mapping mode to MM_ANISOTROPIC, and retrieve the current extents from the device context. Then you negate the extent for the axis you wish to invert and change to the extent to the new value. The following code establishes an MM_TEXT mapping mode-like coordinate system except that the vertical axis is inverted:

```
HDC     hdc ;
HWND    hwnd ;
SIZE    size ;

hdc = GetDC (hwnd) ;
SetMapMode (hdc, MM_ANISOTROPIC) ;

GetViewportExtEx (hdc, &size) ;
SetViewportExtEx (hdc, size.cx, -size.cy, &size) ;

/* Do something worthwhile here... */

ReleaseDC (hwnd, hdc) ;
```

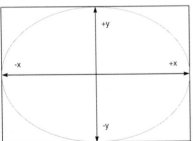

Figure 5.10: Both these axes are exactly 32,766 logical units long

Of course, you really don't have to go to all that trouble. The default viewport extent for the MM_TEXT mapping mode is (1, 1). Therefore you do not need to retrieve the viewport extents and instead you change them by simply calling the SetViewportExtEx function with the last parameter set to NULL:

```
SetViewportExtEx (hdc, 1, -1, NULL) ;
```

The retrieval of the current viewport extents is necessary when you want to use a physical measurement mapping mode but prefer an inverted axis. The viewport extents of the physical measurement mapping modes have no defined default values. Windows sets them based on the aspect ratio of the device and the default physical size of the display. You must first change the mapping mode to the desired physical measurement mapping mode. That causes Windows to change the viewport extents from the default (1, 1) value to the proper values for the device. You then change the mapping mode to MM_ANISOTROPIC so that Windows will permit you to change the viewport extents. Finally, retrieve the proper values, negate the value(s) for the axis or axes desired, and update the device context with the new values:

```
HDC    hdc ;
HWND   hwnd ;
SIZE   size ;
```

```
hdc = GetDC (hwnd) ;
SetMapMode (hdc, MM_ANISOTROPIC) ;

GetViewportExtEx (hdc, &size) ;
SetViewportExtEx (hdc, size.cx, -size.cy) ;

/* Do something worthwhile here... */

ReleaseDC (hwnd, hdc) ;
```

In case you're curious, we had four reasons for not choosing −32,768 to 32,767 as our range. First, having an equal distance on each side of 0 produces a center point that is exactly addressable. This is done by making the minimum value equal to the negation of the maximum value. Second, because the Windows 95 environment currently runs on a 16-bit two's-complement substrate, you can't negate a −32,768 minimum range value and obtain the corresponding maximum range value. Third, −32,768 is a value not available on one's-complement 16-bit architectures. Now, we don't know of any one's-complement 16-bit computer systems, but why build in architecture dependencies when you don't have to? The fourth and strongest reason for not choosing that range is that such a mapping is impossible to specify.

The range −32,767 to 32,767 would be nice. You do get more precision–twice as much, as a matter of fact. Also, logical coordinates in Windows can address every point in the range. These things being true, why don't we use this range? The problem is that many GDI functions require the extent of the figure. The extent itself is given as a signed 16-bit number and can't represent a value greater than 32,767. A line across the full extent of this range would be twice as long as the maximum representable extent. In fact, because the `SetWindowExtEx` function itself is limited, in Windows 95, to using only the low-order 16 bits of its parameters as the logical extent, you can't even request Windows 95 to set up such a mapping.

The Remaining Device Context Attributes

The remaining device context attributes we are going to discuss here are

- the drawing mode,

- the intercharacter spacing,

- the polygon-filling mode,

- the current pen position, and

- the stretching mode.

We discuss the miter limit and the transformation matrix in Chapter 6.

The *drawing mode attribute* specifies the appearance of a line drawn on the device context. Windows is not limited to drawing a line solely in the color of the pen. The color of a line can be dependent on both the pen color and the color of the surface on which it's writing. We discuss the drawing mode attribute in detail in Chapter 6, "Graphical Output: Pixels, Lines, and Polygons". For now, we'll just say that the device drawing mode for a device context is set to the symbolic value `R2_COPYPEN`. This value specifies that the pen color should be transferred to the writing surface without regard for the color of the surface. You can retrieve the current drawing mode with the `GetROP2` function and change it by calling the `SetROP2` function.

The *intercharacter spacing attribute* of a device context is set to 0 initially. GDI adds the specified amount of intercharacter spacing, which is given in logical units, to each character in a line of text written to the device context. Effectively, each character is separated from an adjacent character by an additional amount that is the intercharacter spacing value. The intercharacter spacing value cannot be negative, so you can't use this attribute to cause characters to be written more closely to each other. You can only separate them more than normal.

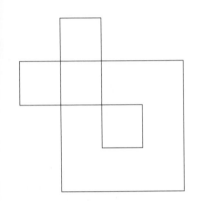

Figure 5.11: The perimeter of a complex, overlapping polygon

You can set the amount of intercharacter spacing by calling the SetTextCharacterExtra function. When the mapping mode isn't MM_TEXT, this function converts the specified number of logical units to pixels by rounding. You can retrieve the current intercharacter spacing by calling the GetTextCharacterExtra function. It converts the current intercharacter spacing in pixels to the nearest logical unit and returns the result. The amount of intercharacter spacing is called "kerning". Usually this term applies to the relationship between two characters, such as tucking a short glyph under a preceding overhanging glyph: for example, tucking the letter "o" under a preceding "W". This technique is called "pair kerning". When the amount of space added between letters is constant, as controlled by SetTextCharacterExtra, it is called "track kerning". You can experiment with these effects using the Kerning Explorer component of the Font Explorer application, which is included on the CD-ROM.

GDI uses the *polygon-filling mode* to determine how to fill a complex, overlapping polygon. There are two polygon-filling modes, which are set by the SetPolyFillMode call: WINDING and ALTERNATE. The WINDING mode causes GDI to calculate the border that is the perimeter of the complex polygon. All points within the perimeter that are within the polygon are filled. When using the ALTERNATE mode, GDI looks at each scan line of the polygon. The area between odd-numbered and even-numbered polygon sides is filled; the area between even-numbered and odd-numbered polygon sides is not. For example, given the complex polygon shown in Figure 5.11, the ALTERNATE and WINDING modes fill it in differently, as shown in Figure 5.12 and Figure 5.13, respectively.

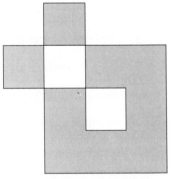

Figure 5.12: A filled complex, overlapping polygon using the ALTERNATE polygon-filling mode

The *current pen position attribute* specifies, in logical coordinates, the current position of the pen selected into the device context. This attribute can be changed by calling the MoveToEx and LineTo functions. The MoveToEx function changes the pen position attribute to the point specified by its X and Y parameters. It also returns the x- and y-coordinates of the previous position as the contents of a POINT structure, unless the reference is a NULL pointer. When you want to retrieve the current pen position without changing it, you call the GetCurrentPositionEx function.

When you call the `LineTo` function, a line is drawn from the current pen position up to, but not including, the point specified by the X and Y parameters of the `LineTo` function call. When the drawing completes successfully, GDI changes the pen position attribute to the point specified in the `LineTo` function call.

The *stretching mode attribute* is used when the `StretchBlt` function copies a bitmap from a source rectangle in the source device context to a destination rectangle in the destination device context. When the source bitmap must be compressed to fit in the destination rectangle, Windows uses the stretching mode attribute of the destination device context to determine how to compress the bitmap. It defines the rows and/or columns of pixels that are dropped from the source bitmap.

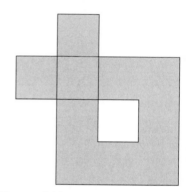

You set the stretching mode attribute by calling the `SetStretchBltMode` function:

`SetStretchBltMode (hdc, BltMode) ;`

and retrieve the current stretching mode by calling the `GetStretchBltMode` function:

`BltMode = GetStretchBltMode (hdc) ;`

Figure 5.13: A filled complex, overlapping polygon using the WINDING polygon-filling mode

The stretching modes for `StretchBlt` are described in Table 5.8.

Table 5.8: `StretchBlt` Modes

Stretch Type	Meaning
STRETCH_ANDSCANS BLACKONWHITE [3]	This is the default mode. `StretchBlt` combines two or more pixels into a single pixel by performing a logical AND operation on the pixels. The replacement pixel is black if *any* of the original pixels are black and white only if *all* the original pixels are white. Black pixels are preserved at a cost of losing white pixels.
STRETCH_ORSCANS WHITEONBLACK [3]	`StretchBlt` combines two or more pixels into a single pixel by performing a logical OR operation on the pixels. The replacement pixel is white if *any* of the original pixels are white and black only if *all* the original pixels are black. White pixels are preserved at a cost of losing black pixels.
STRETCH_DELETESCANS COLORONCOLOR [3]	`StretchBlt` eliminates rows or columns of pixels, or both. This is often the best selection for stretching or compressing color bitmaps. Losing rows and columns is preferable to contending with a color adjustment in the retained pixels that is caused by the eliminated pixels.
STRETCH_HALFTONE HALFTONE [3]	Maps pixels from the source into blocks of pixels, averaging the color over the destination block, so that visually the new pixels approximate the color of the source pixels.

[3]Name used in API level 3, now considered an obsolete name. The use of STRETCH_-prefix names is preferred.

Saving and Restoring the State of a Device Context

Occasionally, you might want to change some of the attributes of a device context temporarily. Once all desired attributes are changed, you could perform some drawing and, finally, restore each of the changed attributes to its previous value. As you've seen, you can retrieve the current value for each attribute individually, so restoring them is simple, although possibly tedious. There is, however, a better method.

Whenever you need to save and restore a number of device context attributes simultaneously, you can save *all* the attributes of a device context in a single operation by calling the SaveDC function:

```
SavedDC = SaveDC (hdc) ;
```

The SaveDC function copies attributes of the device context to a context stack and returns a value that specifies the saved device context. The attributes of a device context can later be restored to their states at the time of a particular save by calling the RestoreDC function and passing it the value returned by the SaveDC function call:

```
RestoreDC (hdc, SavedDC) ;
```

The SaveDC function can be called any number of times before calling the RestoreDC function. Therefore the saved context stack can hold the attributes for several device contexts. When the context specified by the SavedDC parameter to the RestoreDC function is not at the top of the saved context stack, the RestoreDC function deletes all saved contexts between the context specified by the SavedDC parameter and the top of the stack. You cannot restore a saved context once it has been deleted.

You can also restore a device context to its last saved state, rather than to a specific saved state. Calling the RestoreDC function and passing –1 as the SavedDC parameter restores the most recently saved device context:

```
RestoreDC (hdc, -1) ;
```

The DC Explorer

An application included on the CD-ROM that accompanies this book is the DC Explorer. This program allows you to set each attribute of a display context and see the effect of these settings on sample graphics. In addition, the DC Explorer has a page that allows you to see the device capabilities of your display. This is shown in Figure 5.14. The screen snapshot shown was run on Windows 95 on a display with 1024×768 resolution (as you can see from the HORZRES and VERTRES values shown).

This completes our in-depth look at the attributes of a device context. The attributes of a device context control practically every aspect of drawing using the Graphics Device Interface. Now that you know how to set up a device context in preparation for drawing, it's time to put all this knowledge to use. In the next chapter, we look at the graphical output commands and start drawing!

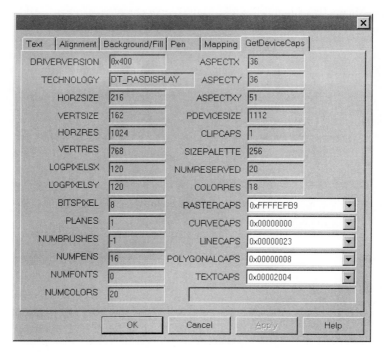

Figure 5.14: DC Explorer device capabilities page

Further Reading

Reviews by Joseph M. Newcomer.

Pietrek, Matt, *Windows 95 System Programming Secrets*, IDG Books, 1995. ISBN 1-56884-318-6.

This excellent book tells you more than you could ever hope to absorb about the internals of Windows 95. I've not had a chance to see how relevant some of this fine detail is to Windows NT, but there must be some similarities. If you see your Win32 platform of choice being Windows 95 this book is full of interesting information. It covers the internals of threads, memory, GDI, the 16-bit kernel, VxDs, and many other details. It also covers the Common Object File Format (COFF) and Portable Executable (PE) file format, topics which apply equally to Windows 95 and Windows NT.

Pietrek, Matt, *Windows Internals*, Addison-Wesley, 1993. ISBN 0-201-62217-3.

The classic work on the guts of Windows 3.1. Like *Undocumented Windows*, its relevance is marginal, and has been largely superseded by *Windows 95 System Programming Secrets*. This book has little relevance to much of Win32, except for some descriptions of objects like DCs, which are approximately like those of Win32 (except for 16/32 bit differences).

Schulman, Andrew, Maxey, David, and Pietrek, Matt, *Undocumented Windows*, Addison-Wesley, 1992. ISBN 0-201-60834-0.

> More than you ever wanted to know about Win16 internals, well beyond *Windows Internals*. Suprisingly, this book still has some relevance for Win32 programming because Windows 95 is built on the Win16 substrate (and in fact uses DOS 7 as its underlying operating system). You can see details of what makes a DC, for example, even though a Win32 DC is a much richer structure. But this is only for the hard-core fanatics, and the morbidly curious.

Schulman, Andrew, *Unauthorized Windows 95*, IDG Books Worldwide, 1994. ISBN 1-56844-305-4.

> The book that allegedly got Andrew bumped from the Windows 95 beta! Read the intimate details of Windows 95. Discover how much of Windows 95 is really DOS 7. More than most people care about the internals of Windows 95, it nonetheless is a compendium of incredible detail about how Windows 95 works internally. If you are curious, and use Windows 95, this can be an interesting book.

6 Graphical Output: Pixels, Lines, and Polygons

There are three types of graphical figures that can be produced by a Windows program. They are, from the simplest to the most complex: points, lines, and closed (bounded) areas. Points (or pixels) can be used to construct any of the more complex figures. A series of lines can be used to construct polygons. A Windows program is most efficient, however, when you use the most appropriate drawing command for the task. In Windows, this means that you should use the command that most closely generates the object you wish to draw instead of drawing the figure as a series of more primitive requests.

When you issue a complex drawing request (for example, drawing a filled area), GDI cooperates with the device driver to carry out your request. If the device driver supports the drawing request directly, GDI passes it unchanged to the driver. The driver itself may have highly optimized code to perform the drawing request or, as graphics processors become more common on video display adapters, the video hardware itself may actually execute the request. When GDI determines that the device driver cannot support the drawing request as issued, GDI itself breaks the operation into a series of simpler requests that the device driver can process.

You take maximum advantage of Windows graphical device hardware when you allow it to worry about the complexities of actually performing the drawing. That said, let's look at the drawing functions provided by Windows from the simplest to the most complex. This chapter covers the following topics:

- Drawing a single pixel

- Drawing lines with stock pens

- Creating custom pens for line drawing

- Changing the drawing mode for a line

- Drawing ellipses and polygons and filling their interiors with a stock brush

- Creating custom brushes for painting areas, including the interiors of ellipses and polygons

- Creating and using bitmaps. We describe how to use a bitmap as a pattern for a brush and how a bitmap can be used as a drawing surface.

- Using miscellaneous GDI drawing functions that don't fit in one of the previously listed categories

- Using regions to describe areas to paint or clip

- Using general paths to describe areas to outline, paint, or clip with

- Using transformation matrices

There are two graphics modes that we will discuss later in this chapter: GM_COMPATIBLE and GM_ADVANCED. The GM_COMPATIBLE mode is the only mode available on Windows 95 and Win32s. It is required (and is the default mode) on Windows NT so that Windows graphical operations are compatible with the old Windows 3.x style of graphics. The GM_ADVANCED mode enables the transformation matrix capabilities of the DC. We will discuss this more starting on page 370. A comparison of the details of GM_COMPATIBLE and GM_ADVANCED modes is given in Table 6.21 on page 376.

We'll start with two functions almost never used in a Windows application–getting and setting the color of a single pixel.

Getting and Setting the Color of a Pixel

The GetPixel function returns a COLORREF containing the RGB color value of the pixel identified by the logical coordinates specified by the X and Y parameters:

```
COLORREF   rgbColor ;
HDC        hdc ;
int        X, Y ;
.
.
rgbColor = GetPixel (hdc, X, Y) ;
```

You can retrieve the color value of a pixel only when the logical coordinates identify a point within the current clipping region. The GetPixel function returns -1 when the point is outside the current clipping region.

You can set the color of a particular pixel by calling the SetPixel function:

```
COLORREF SetPixel(HDC hdc, int x, int y, COLORREF color);
```

This function sets the pixel at the point identified by the logical coordinates X and Y to the nearest approximation to the specified color. The color that is actually used to paint the pixel is returned by the SetPixel function as an RGB color value. When the specified point is outside the current clipping region, the function call is ignored and the function returns -1. Even though multiple pixels can have the same logical coordinate (depending on the mapping mode), the SetPixel function changes only one pixel.

```
COLORREF   rgbActualColor, rgbDesiredColor ;
HDC        hdc ;
int        X, Y ;
```

```
rgbActualColor = SetPixel (hdc, X, Y, rgbDesiredColor) ;
```

For faster pixel setting, you can use the `SetPixelV` function. This takes the same arguments as the `SetPixel` function but has a different result type:

```
BOOL SetPixelV(HDC hdc, int x, int y, COLORREF color);
```

This function returns a Boolean value describing whether it succeeded or failed; if it failed, you can get more information by calling `GetLastError`. Generally it will fail because the pixel is outside the clipping region. Because it does not need to return the actual color value used, it is generally faster.

Lines, Pens, and Drawing Modes

Drawing lines is somewhat more interesting than drawing pixels. You can draw straight lines and curved lines. You can draw lines that are solid and lines that are broken. A line can be one pixel wide or as wide as you like. You can specify the color of the line as well as the color of the gaps in a broken line. You also can specify what should happen as the line draws over existing information on the display.

To draw a line, you must specify two sets of information about the line: its location and its appearance. You specify the location of a line as the parameters to one of the line-drawing functions. There are 11 functions that draw a line:

- `LineTo`, which draws a straight line

- `Polyline` and `PolyLineTo`, which draw a series of connected line segments

- `PolyPolyLine`, which draws one or more disjoint sets of connected line segments

- `AngleArc`, `Arc`, and `ArcTo`, which draw an elliptical line

- `PolyBezier` and `PolyBezierTo`, which draw cubic Bézier splines

- `PolyDraw`, which draws a sequence of lines and Bézier curves

- `StrokePath`, which draws a line along an arbitrary path

The appearance of a line is determined by four attributes of the device context: the selected pen, the background mode (for broken lines), the background color (when the background mode is OPAQUE), and the drawing mode. The selected pen determines the style of the line (solid or broken), the width of the line, and the color of the line. You have the ability to specify, with a pen, the way in which lines join, what the end caps look like, and either one of a selected set of broken lines or your own pattern of dots and dashes. GDI fills in the gaps of a broken line with the background color when the background mode is OPAQUE or leaves the underlying color in the gaps when the background mode is TRANSPARENT. The drawing mode specifies how to combine the color of the pen with the color(s) being overwritten by the line. We look first at how to specify the location of a line, and then we explain how to change its appearance.

The GDI Queue

In Windows NT 3.*x*, the GDI runs in its own thread. To enhance performance, GDI commands are "batched" into a queue. When the queue is filled, the commands to draw lines, fill figures, and the like are flushed from the queue and the requested graphics are actually drawn. This means that the return codes from GDI operations such as `LineTo` and `MoveToEx` do not indicate the success of the drawing, but only that the command has been successfully queued. This also means that normally you don't know when commands are being executed. However, any GDI call that does *not* return a `BOOL` result will force the queue to be flushed first. In addition, you can explicitly force the queue to be flushed by calling the `GdiFlush` function. This function will return `TRUE` if every queued command executed successfully and `FALSE` if any command failed. This is discussed in more detail on page 362. In Windows 95 there is no GDI queue.

Drawing Lines

Many of the line drawing functions utilize or modify the *current pen position*, an attribute of the DC. The current position is a point in the logical coordinate space. You can explicitly set or read this value. The collection of functions that draw lines are given in Table 6.1. This table also shows if a line drawing function changes or utilizes the current pen position.

Not all of these are available in all versions of Win32. We indicate their availability in the table. Note that Win32s has only the basic Win16-equivalent drawing functions. Therefore you must be prepared to deal with the fact that not all versions of Win32 have the full suite of functions available. If you expect your program to run on *all* versions of Win32, you can use only the common subset of line drawing functions. You can also, with careful programming, take advantage of as many features as are available; for example, by falling back to simpler functions if you find yourself running on Win32s, but using full functionality if you find yourself running on Windows NT.

Table 6.1: Line drawing and pen creation functions

Win32s	Win32 API 3	Win32 API 4	Batch	Function Name	Pen Position: Used	Pen Position: Modified	Description
		✓	Y	`AngleArc`	✓	✓	Draws a line segment and an arc, starting at the current pen position.
✓	✓	✓	Y	`Arc`			Draws a segment of an ellipse.
		✓	Y	`ArcTo`	✓	✓	Draws a segment of an ellipse.
✓	✓	✓		`CreatePen`			Creates a pen for line drawing, given the pen parameters. Implies round end caps and round joins.

Table 6.1: Line drawing and pen creation functions

| Win32s | Win32 API 3 | Win32 API 4 | Batch | Function Name | Pen Position | | Description |
					Used	Modified	
✓	✓	✓		CreatePenIndirect			Creates a pen for line drawing, given a reference to the pen parameters. Implies round end caps and round joins.
	✓	✓		ExtCreatePen			Creates a pen for line drawing. Allows specification of end caps and joins.
	✓	✓		GetArcDirection			Obtains the last value set by DC creation or the SetArcDirection call.
✓	✓	✓		GetCurrentPositionEx	✓		Returns the current pen position.
✓	✓	✓	Y	LineTo	✓	✓	Draws a line from the current pen position to the specified coordinate.
✓	✓	✓	Y	MoveToEx	✓	✓	Moves the pen to a specified coordinate; optionally returns the previous pen position.
	✓	✓	Y	PolyBezier	✓		Draws one or more Bézier curves; leaves the pen at the starting point.
	✓	✓	Y	PolyBezierTo	✓	✓	Draws one or more Bézier curves; moves the pen to the endpoint of the last curve drawn.
	‡	✓	Y	PolyDraw	✓	✓	Draws a set of line segments and Bézier curves.
✓	✓	✓	Y	Polyline			Draws a series of line segments.
	✓	✓	Y	PolylineTo	✓	✓	Draws a series of line segments starting at the current pen position; moves the current pen position to the endpoint of the last segment drawn.
	✓	✓	Y	PolyPolyLine			Draws multiple series of connected lines.

‡ Although PolyDraw is not available as a Windows 95 API call, a function PolyDraw95 that simulates PolyDraw is described, with its complete source code, in the Microsoft Knowledge Base article Q135059.

Table 6.1: Line drawing and pen creation functions

Win32s	Win32 API 3	Win32 API 4	Batch	Function Name	Pen Position		Description
					Used	Modified	
	✓	✓	N	SetArcDirection			Sets the drawing direction for arc and rectangle functions.
							AD_COUNTERCLOCKWISE Figure drawn counter-clockwise. AD_CLOCKWISE Figure drawn clock-wise.
✓	✓	✓	N	SetBkColor			Sets the background color used to fill in the gaps in dashed or dotted lines. See SetBkMode.
✓	✓	✓	N	SetBkMode			Sets the background mode. This determines what happens to the color in the gaps of dashed or dotted lines. OPAQUE The color set via SetBkColor is used to fill in the gaps. TRANSPARENT The existing color that is drawn over remains in the gaps.
	✓	✓	Y	StrokePath			Draws a line along an arbitrary path.

The simplest line-drawing function is the LineTo function. This function draws a line from the logical coordinate specified by the current pen position attribute of the specified device context up to, but not including, the logical coordinate specified by the parameters of the LineTo function. A typical call looks like the following:

```
BOOL Status ;
Status = LineTo (hdc, xEnd, yEnd) ;
```

The initial default setting for the current pen position attribute of a device context is the logical coordinate (0, 0). The preceding statement, issued on a device context with default values for its attributes, draws a line using the currently selected pen from the logical coordinate (0, 0) up to, but not including, the point (xEnd, yEnd). When all default settings for a device context (mapping mode, window, and viewport origin) are used, the line begins in the upper-left corner of the display surface (client area, window, screen, or device, depending on the type of device context). The LineTo function returns a nonzero value when the line is drawn and zero otherwise. After the line is drawn, the current pen position attribute of the device context is changed to the position (xEnd, yEnd).

Often you will want to start a line not at (0, 0) but at general coordinates such as (xBegin, yBegin). The MoveToEx function changes the current pen position attribute of a device context without drawing anything. The MoveToEx function returns the previous pen position in the specified POINT structure, if you provide one (if you don't need the previous value, just provide NULL as the parameter). The MoveToEx function returns a BOOL value that indicates the success or failure of the function call.

Therefore, to draw a line from the logical coordinates (xBegin, yBegin) up to, but not including, the logical coordinates (xEnd, yEnd), do the following:

```
POINT pt ;

MoveToEx (hdc, xBegin, yBegin, &pt) ;
LineTo (hdc, xEnd, yEnd) ;
```

The MoveToEx function returns a BOOL value that indicates the success or failure of the function call.

The AngleArc, ArcTo, LineTo, PolyBezier, PolyBezierTo, PolyDraw, and PolyLineTo functions are the only line drawing functions that use the current pen position attribute, as indicated in Table 6.1 (MoveToEx "uses" the pen position to return the previous value). The AngleArc, ArcTo, LineTo, MoveToEx, PolyBezierTo, PolyDraw, and PolyLineTo functions are the only line drawing functions that *change* the current pen position attribute of a device context. You can retrieve the current pen position without changing it by calling the GetCurrentPositionEx function:

```
POINT pt ;

GetCurrentPositionEx (hdc, &pt) ;
```

The GetCurrentPositionEx function returns the previous pen position in the specified POINT structure.

The separate functions for specifying the beginning and ending coordinates for a line are convenient when you are drawing a series of connected line segments. You call the MoveToEx function once to establish the beginning of the series of line segments, and then you call the LineTo function to draw each connected segment. This method is best when you don't know the coordinates of all the points ahead of time. As you determine the next point, all you need to do is use the LineTo function to draw to it. However, when you know all the points, there is an alternative way to draw a series of connected line segments.

The Polyline function draws a series of connected line segments. You pass it the address of an array of POINT structures and the number of points in the array (as well as the obligatory device context). It draws a line from the first point in the array through subsequent points in the array up to, but not including, the last point in the array. The `Polyline` function produces exactly the same output that would be produced by using the `MoveToEx` and `LineTo` functions to move to each point in the array and then drawing a line to the next point in the array when you use an ordinary (called "cosmetic") pen. The `Polyline` function, however, does not use or update the current pen position attribute of the device context. Since you know what the last pen position will be, namely, the last pair of coordinates, you can explicitly `MoveToEx` to that point if you need to. Alternatively, you can use the `PolyLineTo` function, which does update the current pen position. But unlike the `Polyline` function, in which the first point of the array is the first point of the polyline, `PolylineTo` specifies in the array the second point of the polyline; the first point is the current pen position.

If you are using a "geometric pen", however, the behavior of `PolyLine` and `PolyLineTo` are somewhat different. In Windows NT, the end cap and line join characteristics of the geometric pen come into play, and you will get lines with the selected style. In Windows 95, geometric pens are supported only when *stroking* a path, a topic we discuss starting on page 383. If you want geometric pen support on both platforms, you need to use `PolyLine` or `PolyLineTo` to establish a path and then stroke that path.

`PolyDraw` allows you to draw a complex figure composed of `MoveToEx`, `LineTo`, `PolyBezierTo` and `CloseFigure` operations, all in one function call. We will discuss it in detail in the section on paths, because we need to see how it relates to a path.

`PolyLine`, `Polygon`, `PolyPolygon`, and `PolyDraw` have one major advantage over drawing the individual lines to form the shape: If you draw the individual lines with `LineTo`, each line ends with a shape called an *end cap*, for example, a rounded end, which is the default. But if you are drawing thick lines, you may want the shapes to be smoothly joined. You will see how to control this when we talk about the Win32 pens in detail, in particular the `ExtCreatePen` function. But for now, be aware that these composite drawing functions really do have a potentially different effect than using the individual line drawing functions on the same set of point coordinates.

The following code draws a 10 × 10 logical unit square centered around the origin. Of course, unless the origin is moved, only a quarter of the square is visible. Not all the braces are absolutely required. We put them in to make the association of the coordinates more apparent:

```
POINT apt [] = { {-5, -5},
                 { 5, -5},
                 { 5,  5},
                 {-5,  5},
                 {-5, -5} } ;

Polyline (hdc, apt, DIM(apt)) ;
```

You should note that both the `LineTo`, `PolylineTo`, `Polyline`, and the `PolyDraw` functions draw up to, but not including, the terminal point. Because they do draw the starting point, you can connect line segments without writing any point on the line more than once. This becomes quite important when using some drawing modes in which the result of drawing a line depends partially on the contents of the display before drawing the line. Drawing modes are discussed in depth beginning on page 293.

The next line-drawing function is the Arc function, one of the several functions that draw curved lines. The Arc function draws a line from a portion of the perimeter of an ellipse. The general form of a call to the function looks like this:

```
Arc (hdc, xUL, yUL, xLR, yLR, xBegin, yBegin, xEnd, yEnd) ;
```

The two points (xUL, yUL) and (xLR, yLR) specify the upper-left and lower-right corners of a bounding rectangle. GDI draws the arc within the bounding rectangle. It uses the convention that a bounding rectangle specifies an area that includes the upper and left coordinates of the rectangle but excludes the lower and right coordinates of the rectangle. It is important to keep this in mind to avoid being off by one unit.

One and only one ellipse can be inscribed in a given rectangle, so specifying a bounding rectangle uniquely determines an ellipse. When the rectangle is a square, the ellipse is a circle. After you've specified the location and size of the ellipse, all that remains is to specify where on the perimeter of the ellipse the line segment should begin and end.

Windows, however, does not require you to calculate the exact coordinates of the beginning and ending points on the perimeter of the ellipse. The logical coordinates (xBegin, yBegin) are used as one end of an imaginary line to the point at the logical coordinates ((xUL+xLR)/2, (yUL+yLR)/2), which is the center of the rectangle and, therefore, the center of the ellipse. Windows uses the point of intersection of this imaginary line and the perimeter of the ellipse as the actual starting point for the line segment. Another imaginary line from the logical coordinate (xEnd, yEnd) to the center of the ellipse is similarly used to determine the actual ending point for the line segment.

The net effect is that the beginning and ending points passed to the Arc function need only be near where you want the line segment to begin and end. They do not need to be exactly on the perimeter of the ellipse. Windows draws the arc from the beginning point to the ending point in a counterclockwise direction around the perimeter of the ellipse. Figure 6.1 shows a line drawn with the Arc function. We've drawn the bounding rectangle, the ellipse the arc is based on, and the imaginary lines using a dotted pen. We drew the arc itself using a wider, solid pen.

Another arc-drawing function, ArcTo, is available in Windows NT but not in Windows 95 or Win32s. This works just like the Arc function, except that it also uses the current pen position. It draws a straight line segment between the current position and the specified starting point of the arc and updates the current pen position to be the endpoint of the elliptical segment. This effect can be seen also in Figure 6.2.

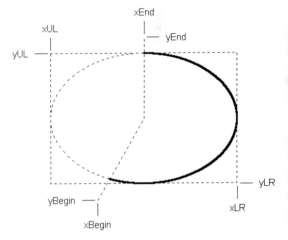

Figure 6.1: Lines drawn by the Arc function

The `AngleArc` function draws both a line segment and an arc. It draws the line segment from the current pen position to the beginning of the arc. The arc itself is drawn along the perimeter of a circle (unlike the `Arc` and `ArcTo` functions, which can draw along an ellipse). The center of the circle and its radius are specified as input parameters to the function. Two angles are specified: the angle at which the arc starts and the *sweep angle*, the number of degrees counterclockwise that the arc traverses. Note that these latter two values, unlike most angle functions found in the C math library, are specified in *degrees*, not *radians*. The following call will draw an arc 50 logical units in radius, starting at the current point and rotating for 30 degrees clockwise starting at the horizontal positive axis:

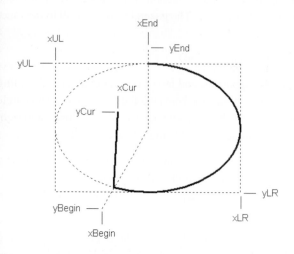

Figure 6.2: Lines drawn by the ArcTo function

```
POINT pt;

GetCurrentPointEx(hdc, &pt);
AngleArc(hdc, pt.x - 50, pt.y, 50, 0.0, -30.0);
```

The results are shown in Figure 6.3.

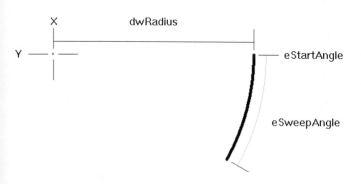

Figure 6.3: A line drawn by the AngleArc function

Win32 can draw compound curves using the `PolyBezier` and `PolyBezierTo` functions. These are not available in Win32s. They allow you to draw a complex curve by using a method known as a *cubic Bézier spline*. A Bézier spline, named after the person who first described and studied them,[1] is a curve that is specified by four control points, which we can call *p1, p2, p3,* and *p4*. The curve starts at the *x,y* position defined by p1 and ends at the *x,y* position defined by p4. The `PolyBezier` and `PolyBezierTo` take the first control point, *p1*, as the current position of the pen. Therefore, for a simple spline, you need to define only three control points: the points *p2, p3,* and *p4*. The "`Poly`" part of the name comes from the property that allows you to specify more than one group of three

---

[1] According to Charles Petzold, in the article "GDI Comes of Age: Exploring the 32-bit Graphics of Windows NT" (*Microsoft Systems Journal*, 1992, #5, September), Pierre Bézier did this in the 1960s while working for Renault. He needed a way to model complex curved surfaces in the then-new CAD workstations that Renault was developing.

control points. For example, given that *p1* is already specified, you can specify *p2, p3,* and *p4* to get a single Bézier curve. But if you specify three additional points, *p5, p6,* and *p7,* then the function will draw a second spline, starting at *p4* and using the additional points to define the endpoint (*p7*) and control points (*p5, p6*). You can specify as many triples of points as you wish. The `PolyBezier` function draws the curve(s) based on the specified points but leaves the current pen position unchanged. The `PolyBezierTo` function draws the curves exactly as `PolyBezier` but moves the pen to the endpoint of the last Bézier curve drawn.

A Bézier cubic spline is controlled by the two internal points. The curve starts from the first point specified, *p1,* and is drawn tangent to a line drawn between *p1*

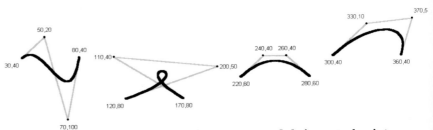

Figure 6.4: Some Bézier curves and their control points

and *p2.* The curve ends at the point *p4* and is tangent to a line drawn between *p3* and *p4.* Some examples are shown in Figure 6.4. The `WM_PAINT` handler that drew them is shown in Listing 6.1.

Listing 6.1: The `WM_PAINT` handler for the Bézier example

```
typedef struct {
                int caption;   // string id of caption
                BYTE style[4]; // coordinate style
                POINT pt[4];
                } bezier;

bezier b1 = { IDS_BEZIER_DOUBLE_CURVE,
                { DT_RIGHT | DT_TOP,
                  DT_CENTER | DT_BOTTOM,
                  DT_CENTER | DT_TOP,
                  DT_CENTER | DT_BOTTOM},
                { 30,   40,
                  50,   20,
                  70,  100,
                  80,   40}
            };
bezier b2 = { IDS_BEZIER_CROSSOVER,
                {DT_RIGHT | DT_TOP,
                 DT_LEFT | DT_VCENTER,
                 DT_RIGHT | DT_VCENTER,
                 DT_CENTER | DT_TOP},
                {120, 80,
                 200, 50,
                 110, 40,
                 170, 80}
            };

bezier b3 = { IDS_BEZIER_SIMPLE_CURVE,
                {DT_CENTER | DT_TOP,
                 DT_CENTER | DT_BOTTOM,
```

```
                    DT_CENTER | DT_BOTTOM,
                    DT_CENTER | DT_TOP},
                 {220, 60,
                  240, 40,
                  260, 40,
                  280, 60}
               };

bezier b4 = { IDS_BEZIER_COMPLEX_CURVE,
                {DT_CENTER | DT_TOP,
                 DT_RIGHT | DT_BOTTOM,
                 DT_LEFT | DT_BOTTOM,
                 DT_CENTER | DT_TOP},
                {300, 40,
                 330, 10,
                 370,  5,
                 360, 40}
               };

/*******************************************************************
*                            drawDot
* Inputs:
*       HDC hdc: display context
*       LPPOINT pt: Point at which to draw dot
*       BYTE style: Style control
*       LPSTR label: Optional label, or NULL
* Result: void
*
* Effect:
*       Draws the dot and labels it according to the given text
*******************************************************************/

static void drawDot(HDC hdc, LPPOINT pt, BYTE style, LPSTR label)
     {
      RECT r;
      HFONT f;
      SIZE size;
      SIZE space;
      TEXTMETRIC tm;
      int height;

#define DOTSIZE 1
      Ellipse(hdc, pt->x - DOTSIZE,
                   pt->y - DOTSIZE,
                   pt->x + DOTSIZE,
                   pt->y + DOTSIZE);

      if(label != NULL)
        { /* has text */
         // Create a nice small font

         f = createCaptionFont(-5, _T("Arial"));

         SelectFont(hdc, f);

         // Determine where to place our text
         GetTextExtentPoint32(hdc, _T(" "), 1, &space);
         GetTextExtentPoint32(hdc, label, lstrlen(label), &size);
```

```
        GetTextMetrics(hdc, &tm);
        height = tm.tmHeight + tm.tmInternalLeading;

        r.left = pt->x;
        r.top  = pt->y;

        if(style & DT_LEFT)
            r.left = pt->x + space.cx;
        else
        if(style & DT_CENTER)
            r.left = pt->x - size.cx / 2 - space.cx;
        else
        if(style & DT_RIGHT)
            r.left = pt->x - size.cx - 2 * space.cx;

        if(style & DT_TOP)
            r.top = pt->y + 16 * DOTSIZE;
        else
        if(style & DT_VCENTER)
            r.top = pt->y - height;
        else
        if(style & DT_BOTTOM)
            r.top = pt->y - 2 * height;

        r.bottom = r.top + 2 * height;
        r.right = r.left + size.cx + 2 * space.cx;

        // FrameRect(hdc, &r, GetStockBrush(BLACK_BRUSH));

        DrawText(hdc, label, -1, &r,
                 DT_CENTER | DT_VCENTER | DT_SINGLELINE);

        DeleteFont(f);
        } /* has text */
    }
/******************************************************************
 *                         drawBezierDot
 * Inputs:
 *       HDC hdc: display context
 *       bezier * b: Bezier descriptor
 *       int i: Index of bezier point to describe
 * Result: void
 *
 * Effect:
 *       Draws an illustrative dot using the currently selected
 *       pen and brush.  Draws the pen coordinates using the style
 *       parameters
 ******************************************************************/

static void drawBezierDot(HDC hdc, bezier * b, int i)
    {
    TCHAR coords[30];
    wsprintf(coords,_T("%d,%d"), b->pt[i].x, b->pt[i].y);

    drawDot(hdc, &b->pt[i], b->style[i], coords);

    }
```

```
/****************************************************************
*                           drawBezier
* Inputs:
*       HDC hdc: DC to draw in
*       bezier * b: Bezier point description
* Result: void
*
* Effect:
*       Draws a bezier curve, showing all the control points
****************************************************************/

static void drawBezier(HDC hdc, HWND hwnd, bezier * b)
    {
    HPEN showpen = CreatePen(PS_SOLID, 1, RGB(192,192,192)); example
    HPEN curvepen = CreatePen(PS_SOLID, 2, RGB(0,0,0));

    SelectPen(hdc, showpen);SelectPen
    Polyline(hdc, &b->pt[0], 4);

    SelectPen(hdc, curvepen);
    if(!PolyBezier(hdc, &b->pt[0], 4))
        { /* no beziers */
         PostMessage(hwnd, UWM_ERROR, IDS_BEZIER_FAILED,
                                 IDS_NOT_SUPPORTED);
        } /* no beziers */
    else
        { /* finish drawing */
         SelectPen(hdc, GetStockPen(BLACK_PEN));
         SelectBrush(hdc, GetStockBrush(BLACK_BRUSH));
         drawBezierDot(hdc, b, 0);
         drawBezierDot(hdc, b, 1);
         drawBezierDot(hdc, b, 2);
         drawBezierDot(hdc, b, 3);
        } /* finish drawing */

    DeletePen(showpen);
    DeletePen(curvepen);
    }
/****************************************************************
*                           scaleToWindow
* Inputs:
*       HDC hdc: Display context
*       HWND hwnd: Window handle
*       int width: Width to scale
*       int height: Height to scale
* Result: void
*
* Effect:
*       Scales the window.  Maintains isotropic scaling so the
*       entire image, whose dimensions are given as input
*       parameters, will fit in the resulting window.
*              min(hwnd.width()/width, hwnd.height/height)
****************************************************************/

void scaleToWindow(HDC hdc, HWND hwnd, int width, int height)
    {
    RECT r;
```

```
    GetClientRect(hwnd, &r);

    float dx = (float)r.right / (float)width;
    float dy = (float)r.bottom / (float) height;

    float scale = min(dx, dy);

    SetMapMode(hdc, MM_ISOTROPIC);
    SetWindowExtEx(hdc, 1000, 1000, NULL);
    SetViewportExtEx(hdc, (int)(1000.0f * scale),
                          (int)(1000.0f * scale),
                                         NULL);
}
/****************************************************************
*                        bezier_OnPaint
****************************************************************/

static void bezier_OnPaint(HWND hwnd)
    {
    PAINTSTRUCT ps;
    HDC hdc = BeginPaint(hwnd, &ps);
    int restore = SaveDC(hdc);

    SetGraphicsMode(hdc, GM_ADVANCED);
    translate(hdc, 0.0f, 20.0f);
    scaleToWindow(hdc, hwnd, 400, 120);
    drawBezier(hdc, hwnd, &b1);
    drawBezier(hdc, hwnd, &b2);
    drawBezier(hdc, hwnd, &b3);
    drawBezier(hdc, hwnd, &b4);

    RestoreDC(hdc, restore);
    EndPaint(hwnd, &ps);
    }
```

Creating Pens

As mentioned previously in the chapter, the appearance of a line is determined by the pen you use when drawing the line. Windows draws a line using the pen that is currently selected into the device context when you call the LineTo, Polyline, Arc, ArcTo, and the other drawing functions shown in Table 6.1. The default pen is a Windows stock object called BLACK_PEN. This pen draws a black line that is 1 pixel wide regardless of the current mapping mode. Windows has two more stock pens: WHITE_PEN and NULL_PEN. A WHITE_PEN draws a white line that is 1 pixel wide regardless of the current mapping mode. A NULL_PEN has no ink and does not leave a mark when you draw with it. (You occasionally use a NULL_PEN when drawing a filled polygon such as a rectangle. Using a NULL_PEN results in a rectangle with its interior filled by a brush but with no surrounding border.)

You call the GetStockPen macro API function (defined in windowsx.h as a call to the GetStockObject function) to get a handle to one of the stock pens. After you have the handle to the pen, you can select it into a device context by calling the SelectPen macro API function (defined in windowsx.h as a call to the

`SelectObject` function). For example, to use a white stock pen rather than the default black stock pen, you can do the following:

```
HPEN hpen ;

hpen = GetStockPen (WHITE_PEN) ;
SelectPen (hdc, hpen) ;
```

All lines drawn after selecting the white pen into the device context will be drawn in white. As long as you need only a 1-pixel-wide pen that can write in black, white, or invisible ink, you can stick with Windows's stock pens. Generally, though, you will want a little more variety in pens. To get it, you must abandon the stock pens and create your own.

Creating, using, and deleting your own pen is a five-step process:

1. Create a logical pen using the `CreatePen`, the `CreatePenIndirect`, or the `ExtCreatePen` function.

2. Select the logical pen into a device context by calling the `SelectPen` function.

3. Draw the lines using this pen by calling any of the line drawing functions, such as `LineTo`, `Polyline`, or `Arc`.

4. Select either the original pen or a stock pen into the device context by calling the `SelectPen` function or by using `RestoreDC` specifying a context that was saved before you did the `SelectPen` operation. This replaces your created pen.

5. Delete the logical pen by calling the `DeletePen` macro API function (defined in windowsx.h as a call to the `DeleteObject` function). You must not delete a pen while it is selected into a device context.

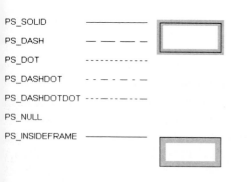

Figure 6.5: Lines in each of the seven pen styles

The easiest way to create a custom pen is to call the `CreatePen` function or the `CreatePenIndirect` function. You pass the style, width, and color of the pen as parameters, and it returns a handle of type `HPEN` to a logical pen. The call looks like the following:

```
HPEN hpen ;

hpen = CreatePen (PenStyle, Width, Color) ;
```

The `PenStyle` parameter specifies whether a line drawn with the created pen will be solid, broken, or invisible. The windows.h header file defines seven symbolic names for pen styles: two for solid lines, four for broken lines, and one for invisible lines. Figure 6.5 shows each symbolic name and the pattern produced by each style. The line samples in Figure 6.5 are all 1 pixel wide. The `PS_SOLID` and `PS_INSIDEFRAME` styles are also shown with a rectangle drawn with the pen selected and then overlaid with the same rectangle drawn with the stock black pen to show how the two pens relate to a rectangle. You can study all these effects using the DC Explorer application of Chapter 5.

The Width parameter normally specifies the width of the pen in *logical units*. When this parameter is 0, GDI draws a line that is one *device*-unit wide (1 pixel wide). When this parameter is 1 or greater, GDI draws a line that is Width-*logical*-unit-wide with half the width on each side of the line. The actual width of the line in device units depends on the mapping mode that's in effect. GDI converts the width of a pen from logical units to device units using the *x*-axis scaling factor as determined by the mapping mode.

The Width parameter also can affect the style of the drawn line. GDI cannot draw dotted or dashed lines with a pen created from CreatePen or CreatePenIndirect unless the pen is 1 pixel wide. When the Width parameter specifies a logical width that translates to physical width greater than 1, GDI draws with a solid pen of that width even when you request a dotted or dashed pen style. You always get a null pen when you request one, regardless of the physical width of the pen. You cannot create a pen to draw dashed or dotted lines wider than 1 pixel using CreatePen; you must use ExtCreatePen to get these.

GDI also handles the width slightly differently in some situations when the pen style is PS_INSIDEFRAME. The PS_INSIDEFRAME style specifies that the mark left by a wide pen should be positioned differently than usual when drawing an arc, a chord, an ellipse, a rectangle, or a rounded rectangle. All these are figures that are drawn relative to a specified bounding rectangle. PS_INSIDEFRAME will not apply to path stroking or region outlining, topics we have not yet discussed (we do so starting on page 383).

Normally, wide pens distribute the mark equally on each side of the line. This causes part of the line to extend outside the bounding rectangle. When you use the PS_INSIDEFRAME style, GDI does *not* center the width around the line but offsets the pen and draws the line entirely inside the bounding rectangle. This is shown in Figure 6.5. The rectangles are drawn in a thick gray pen, and then another rectangle with identical coordinates is drawn with a 1-pixel pen. Note that for PS_SOLID, the thick pen surrounds the rectangle border, but for PS_INSIDEFRAME the thick pen is entirely within the rectangle border. A PS_INSIDEFRAME pen will also draw using dithered colors if necessary; all other pens will be rendered to the nearest pure color that is found in the current palette. If you need dithered colors, use ExtCreatePen.

The third parameter is a COLORREF value specifying the *desired* color of the logical pen; GDI can use a different *actual* color. When you select a logical pen into a device context and the pen style is not PS_INSIDEFRAME, GDI uses the nearest pure color that the device can represent for the pen. GDI will use a dithered color only for PS_INSIDEFRAME-style pens that have a physical width greater than 1.

The CreatePenIndirect function can also be used to create a logical pen. This function requires the same style, width, and color information as the CreatePen function; however, the information is passed to Windows a little differently. Instead of passing each item as a separate parameter, you fill in a LOGPEN structure and pass the address of the structure as the only parameter to the CreatePenIndirect function. The LOGPEN structure looks like the following:

```
typedef struct tagLOGPEN {
    UINT      lopnStyle ;
    POINT     lopnWidth ;
    COLORREF  lopnColor ;
} LOGPEN ;
```

The lopnStyle field holds the pen styles, which can be any one of the values listed in Figure 6.5. The lopnWidth field is a POINT structure. You must store the width of the pen in the *x*-coordinate field of the point. The *y*-coordinate value in the POINT structure is not used. The lopnColor field holds the desired color for the pen.

For example, a call to the CreatePenIndirect function to create a palette-relative, red, dashed, logical pen looks like the following:

```
HPEN   hpen ;
LOGPEN logpen ;

logpen.lopnStyle    = PS_DASH;
logpen.lopnWidth.x = 0 ;
logpen.lopnColor    = PALETTERGB (255, 0, 0) ;

hpen = CreatePenIndirect (&logpen) ;
```

You also can ask Windows to copy information about an existing pen into a LOGPEN structure. The GetObject function can return information about an existing pen, brush, font, bitmap, or palette. The following code retrieves information about a pen given the handle to the pen:

```
LOGPEN logpen ;

GetObject ((HGDIOBJ) hpen, sizeof (logpen), (LPVOID) &logpen) ;
```

You may have noticed that we've been careful to call these pens *logical* pens. Like logical coordinates and logical units, a logical pen is a distinct entity from the *physical* pen used to draw into a device context. When you select a logical pen into a device context, only then are the physical width, style, and color actually determined. The same logical pen can produce differing results when used in two different device contexts.

It's worth repeating that pens (as well as brushes, bitmaps, regions, fonts, and palettes) are GDI objects. GDI objects are actually owned by the GDI, and their space is managed by the GDI. A Windows program should explicitly delete all GDI objects it creates before terminating. It should also release each GDI object as soon as it is done with it. Failure to do so can cause a "resource leak". In Windows NT, this space is private to each running application and will only result in your application's becoming bulkier and bulkier as more GDI resources are unreclaimed. In Windows 95, the resources will be also be reclaimed when your program terminates, but while it is running, these resources consume shared GDI space. Although this space is very large, it is not unlimited. You can eventually fill it up, thereby causing Windows 95 to exhibit strange behavior. And in Win32s, you can lock up all of Windows when the very limited (64K) GDI space becomes glutted with objects.

Another good reason for having a good GDI-resource-deletion strategy deals with a number of third-party development tools that track resource allocation and deallocation. These tools will give you a post mortem analysis of which resources you have allocated and failed to release. A not-uncommon scenario is that you allocate, say, 20 GDI objects at initialization and don't bother to delete them because you know they will be deleted anyway when the program terminates. When you examine the post mortem resource analysis, you see a large number of pens not deleted, so you ignore this part, knowing they were the initial pens. It turns out you have a resource leak, which "leaks" one pen every time a certain operation is done. In your testing, you do that operation once. The difference between 20 and 21 unreleased pens is not easy to see and therefore might be missed. However, under actual operating conditions, this operation might be done hundreds of times, thus leaving hundreds of pens glutting up the GDI space. If you arrange that all of your pens *should* be deleted, then *any* undeleted pen tells you immediately that you have a resource leak, which you can find and fix before the program goes into general use.

But you can't simply delete every pen you use. You must not delete a custom pen that is currently selected into a device context. You must take care to assure that each created pen is destroyed only *after* you're done using it. It is *not* sufficient to assume that because you have released a DC that the DC no longer exists and therefore the objects can be deleted. This is because you might have class-based or window-based DCs that continue to exist, as specified by the CS_CLASSDC or CS_OWNDC flags we discussed in Chapter 5.

You can create a pen of any style, width, and color you desire. Of course, the pen you're given by GDI occasionally will look a bit different than the one you expected. We already mentioned most of the caveats. Being aware of those caveats will enable you to actually create a pen that draws exactly the way you expect–with three additions in the case of CreatePen.

You cannot specify the style of the end caps for a line written with a "fat pen" (a pen of width greater than 0) created by CreatePen or CreatePenIndirect. The end caps are always circles with a diameter equal to the pen width. Use ExtCreatePen if you need to control the end caps. The only way to get a flat side on the end of a fat line in Win32s is to adjust the clipping region so that the end of the line is clipped.

The color of the gaps in the line drawn by a dashed or a dotted pen isn't specified by the pen but by two other attributes of the device context in which the pen is selected: the *background mode* and the *background color*. When the background mode established by SetBkMode is TRANSPARENT, the gaps in a line are not filled in. The original background is left untouched. When the background mode is OPAQUE, the gaps in a line are filled with the color indicated by the background color attribute of the device context as established by the SetBkColor function.

Now that you have completely specified what the mark left by a pen looks like, there comes the process of transferring the "ink" to the drawing surface. Windows supports the obvious need to draw on a display, overwriting anything already there, but there are 15 other ways of copying the "ink" to the drawing surface. These are called the *drawing modes*.

Drawing Modes

Windows uses the *drawing mode attribute* of a device context to determine how to copy the "ink" from a pen onto the drawing surface of the device context. When you draw with a pen, the pixel values of the "ink" of the pen actually are combined with the pixel values of the display surface in a bitwise Boolean operation. The drawing mode specifies the particular Boolean operation to use.

The SetROP2 function changes the drawing mode of a device context:

```
int SetROP2 (HDC hdc, int DrawMode) ;
```

You can retrieve the current drawing mode by calling the GetROP2 function, as follows:

```
int DrawMode ;
```

```
DrawMode = GetROP2 (hdc) ;
```

The "ROP" stands for *Raster OPeration*, the term used to describe a bitwise Boolean operation on the pixels of a raster display device. The "2" in "ROP2" derives from the two operands: the pixels written by the pen and the pixels on the display surface. These are binary raster operations because two operands are used. Later you'll see ternary raster operations in which a third operand is involved and quaternary raster operations that involve four operands.

There are 16 ROP2 codes. This number is derived from the 16 possible outcomes of combining a pen and a monochrome display surface. The pen can be either black or white. Likewise, the display surface pixel can be either black or white. There are four possible combinations of the pen and the display surface: a white pen on a white surface, a white pen on a black surface, a black pen on a white surface, and a black pen on a black surface. You must describe to GDI what the destination pixel's value should be for each of the four combinations of pen and destination. There are 16 such descriptions. One possible description would be as follows:

> When the pen and the destination have the same color (that is, white and white or black and black), set the destination pixel to black. But when the pen is white and the destination is black, or vice versa, set the destination pixel to white. This is called the R2_XORPEN drawing mode.

The symbolic names defined in windows.h for the raster operation codes are not assigned arbitrary values. Instead, each symbolic name is assigned the decimal result value listed in Table 6.2, plus 1. This result value is produced by performing the Boolean operation listed in the right-most column on all four possible combinations of pen color and destination color. These symbolic names and their associated Boolean operations are listed in Table 6.2.

All possible combinations are represented in this table, but some are less useful than others. For example, R2_NOP derives its name from the fact that no matter what color of pen you use, the destination remains unchanged. The drawing operation performs no operation. The R2_BLACK and R2_WHITE raster operations always write black pixels and white pixels, respectively, to the destination no matter what the pen color or original color of the destination. One useful drawing mode is R2_NOT. This mode inverts the color of the destination pixels written by the pen. The pen color isn't used by the operation. Because the line is written in the inverse color of the destination, it is generally visible no matter what the destination color.

The default drawing mode for a device context is the R2_COPYPEN mode. As you can see in Table 6.2, the result of the Boolean operation on the pen and destination pixel is always the color of the pen, no matter what the destination color is. This copies the pen color to the destination surface. Basically, the pen overwrites anything already present. In the table, black is represented by a 0, and white by a 1.

Table 6.2: Binary raster operation codes

Drawing Mode	Pen(P)	1	1	0	0	Decimal Result	Boolean Operation
	Dest(D)	1	0	1	0		
R2_BLACK		0	0	0	0	0	0
R2_NOTMERGEPEN		0	0	0	1	1	~(P | D)
R2_MASKNOTPEN		0	0	1	0	2	~P & D

Table 6.2: Binary raster operation codes

Drawing Mode	Pen(P) → Dest(D)	1 1	1 0	0 1	0 0	Decimal Result	Boolean Operation
R2_NOTCOPYPEN		0	0	1	1	3	~P
R2_MASKPENNOT		0	1	0	0	4	P & ~D
R2_NOT		0	1	0	1	5	~D
R2_XORPEN		0	1	1	0	6	P ∧ D
R2_NOTMASKPEN		0	1	1	1	7	~(P & D)
R2_MASKPEN		1	0	0	0	8	P & D
R2_NOTXORPEN		1	0	0	1	9	~(P ∧ D)
R2_NOPR2_NOP		1	0	1	0	10	D
R2_MERGENOTPEN		1	0	1	1	11	~P | D
R2_COPYPEN		1	1	0	0	12	P *(default)*
R2_MERGEPENNOT		1	1	0	1	13	P | ~D
R2_MERGEPEN		1	1	1	0	14	P | D
R2_WHITE		1	1	1	1	15	1

A similar procedure handles color pens writing on a color surface. Rather than use ones and zeros as you do for a monochrome system, GDI uses RGB values to represent the colors of the pen and the destination. An RGB color value is a long integer containing red, green, and blue color fields, each 1 byte wide, representing the intensity from 0 to 255. The bitwise Boolean operation is performed on the two RGB color values. Here's an example in which a red pen is writing on a white destination surface using the R2_NOTMASKPEN operation. This operation sets the destination to the result of negating the logical AND of the pen color and the original destination color. The pen is red (0xFF0000), the destination is originally white (0xFFFFFF), and the result is (0x00FFFF), or full-intensity green and blue (cyan).

Some color devices, especially those with color palettes, don't assign the same meaning to the bits of a pixel's color value. You can calculate what the result of a raster operation will be, but the color corresponding to that bit pattern may not be defined.

GDI uses the raster operation code when a color value is a palette index (see Chapter 5) just like it does with a RGB color value; however, the result is less meaningful. Assume you perform the R2_NOTMASKPEN operation and have a pen using the color with palette-index 1 (a PALETTEINDEX (1) COLORREF value). This has the value 0x01000001. The destination is white, which is typically palette-index 255 (a PALETTEINDEX (255) COLORREF value). This has the value 0x010000FF. Logically ANDing the palette-indices 0x01 and 0xFF produces 0x01, and complementing that produces 0xFE. The color in palette-index 254 is the resulting color–whatever that color may be.

We wrote a set of Windows functions that draw the figure pictured in Figure 6.1. In that figure, we used the MM_ISOTROPIC mapping mode to draw dotted and solid lines using the MoveToEx, LineTo, and Arc line drawing functions and labeled the graph using the TextOut function. The graph automatically scales to the size of the window when the window is resized. All in all, it uses quite a number of the GDI functions that we have discussed so far in this chapter and in Chapter 5. You will find code very similar to this in the GDI Explorer. However, this code is somewhat simplified, since we use the same function in the Explorer to draw several of the other figures.

Listing 6.2: WM_PAINT handler for Arc-drawing example

```
#define MARKLENG 50
#define MARKGAP  10

static TCHAR xULLabel []     = _T("xUL") ;
static TCHAR yULLabel []     = _T("yUL") ;
static TCHAR xLRLabel []     = _T("xLR") ;
static TCHAR yLRLabel []     = _T("yLR") ;
static TCHAR xBeginLabel [] = _T("xBegin") ;
static TCHAR yBeginLabel [] = _T("yBegin") ;
static TCHAR xEndLabel []    = _T("xEnd") ;
static TCHAR yEndLabel []    = _T("yEnd") ;

static void
lines_OnPaint(HWND hwnd)
{
    HDC         hdc ;
    HPEN        hpenDot;
    HPEN        hpenThin;
    HPEN        hpenThick;
    HPEN        hpenOrig ;
    int         cxClient;
    int         cyClient ;
    int         xUL;
    int         yUL;
    int         xLR;
    int         yLR;
    int         xBegin;
    int         yBegin ;
    int         xEnd;
    int         yEnd ;
    PAINTSTRUCT ps ;
    RECT        rect ;
    SIZE        size ;


    /* Set the coordinates of the points */
    /* used by the Arc function.         */

    xUL    = -300 ; yUL    =  200 ;
    xLR    =  300 ; yLR    = -200 ;
```

```
xBegin = -150 ; yBegin = -250 ;
xEnd   =    0 ; yEnd   =  250 ;

/* Get the present size of the client area. */

GetClientRect (hwnd, &rect) ;
cxClient = rect.right ;
cyClient = rect.bottom ;

/* Get the device context and        */
/* establish the coordinate mapping. */

hdc = BeginPaint (hwnd, &ps) ;
SetMapMode (hdc, MM_ISOTROPIC) ;Mapping mode:
SetViewportOrgEx (hdc, cxClient / 2, cyClient / 2, NULL) ;
SetWindowExtEx (hdc, 1000, 1000, NULL) ;
SetViewportExtEx (hdc, cxClient, -cyClient, NULL) ;

/* Create the drawing tools. */

hpenDot = CreatePen (PS_DOT, 0, RGB (0,0,0)) ;
hpenThin = CreatePen (PS_SOLID, 0, RGB (0,0,0)) ;
hpenThick = CreatePen (PS_SOLID, 5, RGB (0,0,0)) ;

/* Use a dotted pen to ... */

hpenOrig = SelectPen (hdc, hpenDot) ;

/* ...draw the rectangle and inscribed ellipse. */

Rectangle (hdc, xUL, yUL, xLR, yLR) ;
Ellipse   (hdc, xUL, yUL, xLR, yLR) ;

/* Draw the imaginary lines from the begin and */
/* end points to the center of the rectangle. */

LineTo    (hdc, xBegin, yBegin) ;
MoveToEx  (hdc, 0, 0, NULL) ;
LineTo    (hdc, xEnd, yEnd) ;

/* Use a solid thin pen to ... */

SelectPen (hdc, hpenThin) ;

/* Draw the point markers. */

MoveToEx (hdc, xUL - MARKGAP,     yUL, NULL) ;
LineTo   (hdc, xUL - MARKLENG,    yUL) ;
MoveToEx (hdc, xUL,               yUL + MARKGAP, NULL) ;
LineTo   (hdc, xUL,               yUL + MARKLENG) ;

MoveToEx (hdc, xLR + MARKGAP,     yLR, NULL) ;
LineTo   (hdc, xLR + MARKLENG,    yLR) ;
MoveToEx (hdc, xLR,               yLR - MARKGAP, NULL) ;
LineTo   (hdc, xLR,               yLR - MARKLENG) ;

MoveToEx (hdc, xBegin - MARKGAP,  yBegin, NULL) ;
LineTo   (hdc, xBegin - MARKLENG, yBegin) ;
```

```
MoveToEx (hdc, xBegin,              yBegin - MARKGAP, NULL) ;
LineTo   (hdc, xBegin,              yBegin - MARKLENG) ;

MoveToEx (hdc, xEnd + MARKGAP,      yEnd, NULL) ;
LineTo   (hdc, xEnd + MARKLENG,     yEnd) ;
MoveToEx (hdc, xEnd,                yEnd + MARKGAP, NULL) ;
LineTo   (hdc, xEnd,                yEnd + MARKLENG) ;

/* Place labels by the markers. */
/* Draw the xUL label.          */

GetTextExtentPoint32 (hdc, yULLabel,
                               lstrlen (yULLabel), &size) ;

TextOut (hdc,
         xUL - 2 * MARKGAP - MARKLENG - size.cx,
         yUL + size.cy / 2,
         yULLabel, lstrlen (yULLabel)) ;

/* Draw the xUL label. */

GetTextExtentPoint32 (hdc, xULLabel,
                               lstrlen (xULLabel), &size) ;

TextOut (hdc,
         xUL - size.cx / 2,
         yUL + MARKGAP + MARKLENG + size.cy,
         xULLabel, lstrlen (xULLabel)) ;

/* Draw the yLR label. */

GetTextExtentPoint32 (hdc, yLRLabel,
                               lstrlen (yLRLabel), &size) ;

TextOut (hdc,
         xLR + 2 * MARKGAP + MARKLENG,
         yLR + size.cy / 2,
         yLRLabel, lstrlen (yxLRLabel)) ;

/* Draw the xLR label. */

GetTextExtentPoint32 (hdc, xLRLabel,
                               lstrlen (xLRLabel), &size) ;

TextOut (hdc,
         xLR - size.cx / 2,
         yLR - MARKGAP - MARKLENG,
         xLRLabel, lstrlen (xLRLabel)) ;

/* Draw the yBegin label. */

GetTextExtentPoint32 (hdc, yBeginLabel,
                               lstrlen (yBeginLabel), &size) ;

TextOut (hdc,
         xBegin - 2 * MARKGAP - MARKLENG - size.cx,
         yBegin + size.cy / 2,
         yBeginLabel, lstrlen (yBeginLabel)) ;
```

```
/* Draw the xBegin label. */

GetTextExtentPoint32 (hdc, xBeginLabel,
                          lstrlen (xBeginLabel), &size) ;

TextOut (hdc,
         xBegin - size.cx / 2,
         yBegin - MARKGAP - MARKLENG,
         xBeginLabel, lstrlen (xBeginLabel)) ;

/* Draw the yEnd label. */

GetTextExtentPoint32 (hdc, yEndLabel,
                          lstrlen (yEndLabel), &size) ;
TextOut (hdc,
         xEnd + 2 * MARKGAP + MARKLENG,
         yEnd + size.cy / 2,
         yEndLabel, lstrlen (yEndLabel)) ;

/* Draw the xEnd label. */

GetTextExtentPoint32 (hdc, xEndLabel,
                          lstrlen (xEndLabel), &size) ;

TextOut (hdc,
         xEnd - size.cx / 2,
         yEnd + MARKGAP + MARKLENG + size.cy,
         xEndLabel, lstrlen (xEndLabel)) ;

/* Use a solid thick pen to ... */

SelectPen (hdc, hpenThick) ;
Arc (hdc, xUL,     yUL,     xLR, yLR,
          xBegin, yBegin, xEnd, yEnd) ;

SelectPen (hdc, hpenOrig) ;
DeletePen (hpenDot) ;
DeletePen (hpenThin) ;
DeletePen (hpenThick) ;
EndPaint (hwnd, &ps) ;
}
```

More-complex Lines

The original GDI was specified when the dominant display devices were the Color Graphics Adapter (CGA, 320 pixels × 200 pixels × 2 bits color) and the Hercules (monochrome!) Graphics Adapter (720 pixels × 350 pixels × 1 bit color). These devices were limited to rather low resolution by modern standards. When Windows 95 was released, it was possible to get a 21-inch display and an adapter card that would run it at 1200 pixels × 1600 pixels × 24 bit color resolution . . . rather a lot better. One consequence of the higher resolution was that you really don't want to draw a 1-pixel line as a separator–it is almost too fine to see. So the recommended practice for drawing a line is to use an internal value Windows uses to determine the "best" visual resolution for a simple line. You normally should create your pen not as a 1-pixel pen, but by using the following value:

```
Width = GetSystemMetrics(SM_CXBORDER);
```

The value returned is the value Windows uses for drawing "window borders" and is adjusted by the display driver to be a value that produces a "satisfactory" line for a horizontal border. There is also a value SM_CYBORDER, which is the recommended width for a vertical border. If you want to be strictly precise, you should use the border width based on the desired orientation of your line. However, in the modern world the aspect ratio of most displays is 1:1 ("square" pixels), so the two are usually interchangeable. Since this line is often for visual marking, then even if the values are different either one would probably suffice. However, in a given mapping mode the actual size of a logical pen that displays this "standard line" will vary. Once having obtained the "best" size for a thin pen in device units, you must also use DPtoLP on the current DC to determine the number of logical pixels you must use for your pen. Remember that if you are using the aniso-tropic mapping mode, the "logical units" may no longer be "square", so you may even have to compute pen widths for different angles if you want lines of equal visual thickness!

If you change mapping modes, you will have to create a new pen:

```
HPEN getThinPen(HDC hdc)
    {
      POINT Width;
      Width.x = GetSystemMetrics(SM_CXBORDER);
      Width.y = 0;  // unused, set to 0
      DPtoLP(hdc, &Width, 1);
      HPEN thinpen = CreatePen(PS_SOLID, Width.x, RGB(0,0,0));
      return thinpen;
    }
```

But this leads to a new and different problem: Such attributes as dotted and dashed lines are specified to work only for 1-pixel lines! This is one of the many limitations of normal Windows pens. Furthermore, addi-tional line capabilities were needed, such as being able to control the shape of the end caps of lines, to get joined lines in a PolyLine to match nicely, and to specify application-specific dotted or dashed lines (the de-fault dots and dashes were often insufficient for many applications, thus leading to "hand-drawn" dashed lines drawn as a series of individual LineTo operations, which are very inefficient to draw). And, while in the days of the 8-bit 8088 and the CGA the cost of computing all of these fancy features was prohibitive, to-day a graphics accelerator card often has all of these facilities "in the hardware". This removes the burden of doing it entirely from Windows.[2] Finally, there is the limitation in a pen created by CreatePen and CreatePenIndirect that such a pen is rendered to the nearest "pure" color except for PS_INSIDEFRAME. Again, the increase in computational power and graphics displays makes this limitation seem irrelevant. Many people run cards supporting full 24-bit graphics whose *video memory* is larger than the entire main memory of a 286 running Windows 3.0! Thus the early engineering trade-offs made in the Windows design seem inappropriate for a modern Win32 platform.

All of this leads up to the much more sophisticated graphics interface supported by Win32. We cover many of the features in this chapter. The first we cover is the ExtCreatePen interface, which allows us to create very fancy pens that give us control over the patterns, joins, and end caps. These newer pens are distin-

---

[2] It would be surprising to find a modern processor less than 200 times faster than the 8088, so even if it had to compute all the pixels it is now realistic to do so.

guished from the older Win16-compatible pens by calling them *geometric pens* and calling the older pens *cosmetic pens*. A cosmetic pen is currently always 1 pixel wide and can be created by calling CreatePen or CreatePenIndirect specifying a width of 0 or by specifying PS_COSMETIC to ExtCreatePen and specifying a width of 1. The stock pens, obtained from GetStockObject, are all cosmetic pens. Note that cosmetic pens created by ExtCreatePen and which are not solid do not support OPAQUE background mode.

Cosmetic pens are more efficient for the GDI to draw than are geometric pens. They also are independent of any scaling factors that may apply. Hence, as the image is scaled the cosmetic pens always draw as 1-pixel-wide pens. This is not always right, and you have to decide what makes sense for your application. For example, as we pointed out, a 1-pixel-wide pen on a very high resolution display may be virtually impossible to see.

The ExtCreatePen call takes a pen style that is made up of four components. Each of these is specified by choosing an element from the appropriate category and using the bitwise OR operation to combine them into a single 32-bit style value. The values available are given in Table 6.3.

Table 6.3: ExtCreatePen style parameters

Style Code	Meaning
Group 1: Pen Type	
PS_GEOMETRIC	A geometric pen.
PS_COSMETIC	A cosmetic pen (the same as CreatePen/CreatePenIndirect with a width of 0. For ExtCreatePen, you must specify a width of 1 for a cosmetic pen).
Group 2: Pen Style	
PS_ALTERNATE	Pen sets every other pixel (PS_COSMETIC pens only).
PS_SOLID	Pen is solid.
PS_DASH	Pen is dashed. Not supported in Windows 95 for PS_GEOMETRIC pens.
PS_DOT	Pen is dotted. Not supported in Windows 95 for PS_GEOMETRIC pens.
PS_DASHDOT	Pen has alternating dashes and dots. Not supported in Windows 95 for PS_GEOMETRIC pens.
PS_DASHDOTDOT	Pen has alternating dashes and double dots. Not supported in Windows 95 for PS_GEOMETRIC pens.
PS_NULL	Pen is invisible.
PS_USERSTYLE	Pen uses a styling array supplied by the user. Not supported in Windows 95.
PS_INSIDEFRAME	Pen is solid. When this pen is used for any object that uses a bounding box, such as a rectangle or ellipse, the dimensions are adjusted so that the pen fits entirely within the bounding box. This style is only for geometric pens.

Table 6.3: ExtCreatePen style parameters

Style Code	Meaning
Group 3: End Cap Style (PS_GEOMETRIC only) *Not supported in Windows 95 except when stroking paths.*	
PS_ENDCAP_ROUND	End caps are round.
PS_ENDCAP_SQUARE	End caps are square.
PS_ENDCAP_FLAT	End caps are flat.
Group 4: Line Join Styles (PS_GEOMETRIC only) *Not supported in Windows 95 except when stroking paths.*	
PS_JOIN_BEVEL	Line joins are beveled.
PS_JOIN_MITER	Line joins are mitered. See also SetMiterLimit.
PS_JOIN_ROUND	Line joins are rounded.

The *end cap* style determines the relationship of the end of the ink to the end of the logical line. This is shown in Figure 6.6. The white line in each drawing represents the actual coordinates used to draw the line. This line is drawn on top of the thick lines using a 1-pixel-wide pen. The thick black or gray line shows the line drawn by the pen, given a LineTo operation that uses the same coordinates as the thin white pen but draws with the thicker pen. In each example, the two lines are drawn independently using LineTo. Note that the square endcaps and the flat endcaps, although superficially the same, bear different relationships to the coordinates to which the line is drawn.

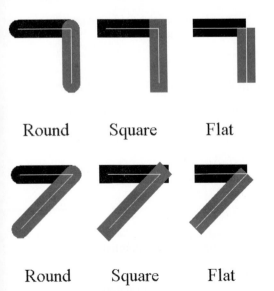

Round   Square   Flat

Round   Square   Flat

Figure 6.6: End cap styles from ExtCreatePen

The WM_PAINT handler for Figure 6.6 is shown in Listing 6.3.

Listing 6.3: WM_PAINT handler for end caps example

```
#define WIDTH 20

static void
drawPenExample(HWND hwnd, HDC hdc,
               LPRECT r, HPEN horz,
               HPEN vert, int caption,
               BOOL angle)
    {
    HPEN whitepen =
         GetStockPen(WHITE_PEN);
    TEXTMETRIC tm;
    RECT trect;
    TCHAR text[50];

    LoadString(GetWindowInstance(hwnd),
               caption,
               text, DIM(text));
```

```
    BeginPath(hdc);   // in case Windows 95

    // Draw the top line in the horizontal pen
    SelectPen(hdc, horz);
    MoveToEx(hdc, r->left, r->top, NULL);
    LineTo(hdc, r->right, r->top);

    // Draw the downward line either vertical or at an
    // angle depending on the 'angle' option

    SelectPen(hdc, vert);
    LineTo(hdc, (angle ? r->left : r->right), r->bottom);

    // Draw the thin white pen to show the actual LineTo
    // coordinates

    SelectPen(hdc, whitepen);
    MoveToEx(hdc, r->left, r->top, NULL);
    LineTo(hdc, r->right, r->top);
    LineTo(hdc, (angle ? r->left : r->right), r->bottom);

    EndPath(hdc);
    StrokePath(hdc);

    // define a rectangle for the text
    trect.left = r->left;
    trect.right = r->right;
    trect.top = r->bottom + 2 * WIDTH;
    GetTextMetrics(hdc, &tm);
    trect.bottom = trect.top +
                   2 * (tm.tmHeight + tm.tmExternalLeading);
    DrawText(hdc, text, -1, &trect, DT_CENTER | DT_VCENTER);
    }
static void
endcaps_OnPaint(HWND hwnd)
    {
    // Define some parameters for the line drawing
    #define X1 (1 * WIDTH)
    #define Y1 (2 * WIDTH)
    #define Y2 (6 * WIDTH)
    #define R  (3 * WIDTH)
    #define Dx (5 * WIDTH)
    #define Dy (8 * WIDTH)

    // Define the bounding rectangles for the six
    // illustrations
    RECT r1 = {X1,          Y1,      X1 + R,          Y1 + R};
    RECT r2 = {X1 + Dx,     Y1,      X1 + R + Dx,     Y1 + R};
    RECT r3 = {X1 + 2 * Dx, Y1,      X1 + R + 2 * Dx, Y1 + R};
    RECT r4 = {X1,          Y1 + Dy, X1 + R,          Y1 + Dy + R};
    RECT r5 = {X1 + Dx,     Y1 + Dy, X1 + R + Dx,     Y1 + Dy + R};
    RECT r6 = {X1 + 2 * Dx, Y1 + Dy, X1 + R + 2 * Dx, Y1 + Dy + R};

    // Define the brushes used by ExtCreatePen used for the
    // filling
    LOGBRUSH blackbrush = {BS_SOLID, RGB(0,0,0),       0 };
    LOGBRUSH graybrush  = {BS_SOLID, RGB(128,128,128), 0 };
```

```
// The pens we are going to use
HPEN roundblack =
      ExtCreatePen(PS_GEOMETRIC | PS_ENDCAP_ROUND,
                   WIDTH, &blackbrush, 0, NULL);
HPEN squareblack =
      ExtCreatePen(PS_GEOMETRIC | PS_ENDCAP_SQUARE,
                   WIDTH, &blackbrush, 0, NULL);
HPEN flatblack =
      ExtCreatePen(PS_GEOMETRIC | PS_ENDCAP_FLAT,
                   WIDTH, &blackbrush, 0, NULL);
HPEN roundgray =
      ExtCreatePen(PS_GEOMETRIC | PS_ENDCAP_ROUND,
                   WIDTH, &graybrush, 0, NULL);
HPEN squaregray =
      ExtCreatePen(PS_GEOMETRIC | PS_ENDCAP_SQUARE,
                   WIDTH, &graybrush, 0, NULL);
HPEN flatgray =
      ExtCreatePen(PS_GEOMETRIC | PS_ENDCAP_FLAT,
                   WIDTH, &graybrush, 0, NULL);

// Define a font to be used for the captions
HFONT font = createCaptionFont(-20, TimesFont) ;

PAINTSTRUCT ps;
HDC hdc;
int restore;

hdc = BeginPaint(hwnd, &ps);

if(roundblack == NULL)
   { /* no ExtCreatePen */
   // We are probably running under Windows 95
   PostMessage(hwnd, UWM_ERROR, IDS_EXTCREATEPEN_FAILED,
                               IDS_NOT_SUPPORTED);
   EndPaint(hwnd, &ps);
   DeleteFont(font);
   return;
   } /* no ExtCreatePen */

restore = SaveDC(hdc);
SelectFont(hdc, font);

drawPenExample(hwnd, hdc, &r1, roundblack, roundgray,
                                  IDS_ROUND, FALSE);
drawPenExample(hwnd, hdc, &r2, squareblack, squaregray,
                                  IDS_SQUARE, FALSE);
drawPenExample(hwnd, hdc, &r3, flatblack, flatgray,
                                  IDS_FLAT, FALSE);

drawPenExample(hwnd, hdc, &r4, roundblack, roundgray,
                                  IDS_ROUND, TRUE);
drawPenExample(hwnd, hdc, &r5, squareblack, squaregray,
                                  IDS_SQUARE, TRUE);
drawPenExample(hwnd, hdc, &r6, flatblack, flatgray,
                                  IDS_FLAT, TRUE);

RestoreDC(hdc, restore);
```

```
EndPaint(hwnd, &ps);

// Now that we know all our objects are deselected,
// we can safely delete them
DeletePen(roundblack);
DeletePen(squareblack);
DeletePen(flatblack);
DeletePen(roundgray);
DeletePen(squaregray);
DeletePen(flatgray);
DeleteFont(font);
}
```

In this example, three pens are created in each color, representing each of the kinds of end caps possible. With each pen, two drawings are made: one with the lines at right angles and one with the lines at a 45° angle. The six drawings are specified by providing the function drawPenExample with a pair of pens (one for the horizontal line, one for the downward line), a rectangle whose corners are used to determine the endpoints of the lines, a caption to be placed, and an option indicating whether the second line is to be drawn vertically or at an angle.

Note that because we have selected a font and a pen, rather than saving individual objects returned by SelectObject and then restoring them individually at the end of the function, we used the SaveDC and RestoreDC functions to reset the entire DC to its initial state. We use RestoreDC rather than depending on ReleaseDC to implicitly deselect our objects because in the presence of a class DC or private DC, the ReleaseDC would have no effect, and we want our code to work reliably independent of such considerations.

You may ignore the BeginPath, EndPath, and StrokePath functions for the moment. On Windows NT, these are actually unnecessary. But on Windows 95, geometric pens have no effect except when these operations are used. We discuss paths more fully starting on page 383. We had to include them so that this code will work correctly on Windows 95.[3]

You may notice in Figure 6.6 that lines that meet with other than round end caps do not create a particularly good-looking result. This is why the default for lines from CreatePen (which was the only way to create a pen in Windows 3.1 and earlier versions) is round end caps. However, you may want to have a line that ends with square or flat end caps, but which in fact has several internal segments. This is why there are functions like PolyLine, PolyLineTo, PolyDraw, and the like. You can therefore specify a pen property of how two lines drawn with a single line drawing function are joined. In Windows 3.1, this made no difference: All lines ended with round end caps, and a multiline drawing was identical to a sequence of LineTo function calls. But round line joins are not the only possible style. Two others can be specified with a pen: *miter* and *bevel*.

A *bevel join*, shown in Figure 6.7, clips off the corners of the lines that would protrude and flattens the end. Compare the bevel join to the effect of simply drawing two lines with flat or square end caps at an angle, as shown in Figure 6.6. Note that the join style is independent of the end cap style. You can have round end caps and a bevel join. The bevel join works well at any angle.

---

[3] You may notice, if you read the code for the GDI Explorer, that the code we use is slightly more complex than is shown here. The details are not important for this discussion and deal with producing nice illustrations rather than base functionality, so we omitted them from these examples.

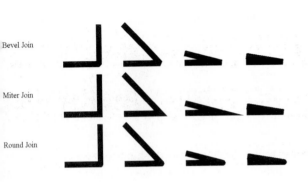

Bevel Join

Miter Join

Round Join

Figure 6.7: Line join styles

The *round join* is no different in appearance from the result of drawing two independent lines with round end caps. But since the join style is independent of the end cap style, with an `ExtCreatePen` pen you can have a line with square end caps and a round join, which is not possible with ordinary pens created with `CreatePen`. With an ordinary pen, although drawing two lines would look as if they had a round join, it would also draw lines with round end caps, because that is the only end cap style `CreatePen` supports. (These all presuppose that the drawing mode is something like `R2_COPYPEN`. It gets even more difficult to explain, or even accomplish, in other drawing modes.)

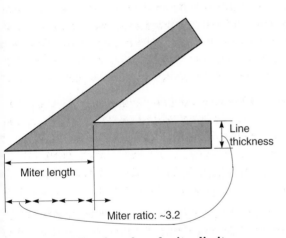

Line thickness

Miter length

Miter ratio: ~3.2

Figure 6.8: Miter length and miter limit

The *miter join*, also shown in Figure 6.7, has some very special properties. Note that it produces the effect of projecting the outer edges of the lines forming the angle until they meet. This produces a nice, sharp edge but doesn't work well for very small angles (and if you should happen to draw a pair of lines that started and ended at the same coordinate, that is, that overlapped, the projection would be parallel and could be extended to infinity!). So notice in Figure 6.7 that as we decrease the angle, the endpoint projects farther and farther out from the point where the two lines intersect. But if you follow the drawing horizontally, you see that the last example of the miter join looks remarkably like the bevel join. That is because the distance the miter would project exceeds the *miter limit*. The miter *length* is defined as the distance from the intersection of the "inner wall" of the line to the intersection of the "outer wall" of the line. The *miter limit* is the maximum allowed *ratio* of the miter length to the line width. These are illustrated in Figure 6.8. If your line exceeds the miter limit, the join style is changed to a bevel join. You can change the miter limit using the `SetMiterLimit` function. The previous setting of the miter limit can be obtained either by the `GetMiterLimit` function or by providing a non-NULL third parameter to the `SetMiterLimit` function:

```
FLOAT oldlimit;

SetMiterLimit(hdc, 8.0, &oldlimit);
```

is the same as

```
FLOAT oldlimit;

GetMiterLimit(hdc, &oldlimit);
SetMiterLimit(hdc, 8.0, NULL);
```

Like most Win32 GDI functions, both of these return a BOOL result: TRUE if they succeeded and FALSE if they failed. If you know the Windows 3.1 GDI, you will also note that this function takes a FLOAT value. We show other functions that take FLOAT values later in this chapter. Windows was originally designed for the 8088, which was a *slow* machine. A modern processor can perform a 32-bit floating point multiply in less time than an 8088 required for a 16-bit integer add, so Win32 is less reticent about using floating point values.

The program that created the line join illustration of Figure 6.7 is shown in Listing 6.4.

Listing 6.4: WM_PAINT handler for showing line joins

```
#define JOIN_PEN_WIDTH 15
#define JOIN_SAMPLE_SIZE 100
#define JOIN_WIDTH  (JOIN_SAMPLE_SIZE + 2 * JOIN_SAMPLE_SIZE/3)
#define JOIN_HEIGHT (JOIN_SAMPLE_SIZE + JOIN_SAMPLE_SIZE/4)

static void polyLineInRect(HDC hdc, LPRECT r, int adjust)
    {
     POINT pts[3];

     pts[0].x = r->left;
     pts[0].y = r->bottom;
     pts[1].x = r->right;
     pts[1].y = r->bottom;
     pts[2].x = r->right;
     pts[2].y = r->top - adjust;
     Polyline(hdc, pts, DIM(pts));

    }

static void
drawJoin(HWND hwnd, HDC hdc, int y, DWORD style, int caption)
    {
     LOGBRUSH blackbrush = {BS_SOLID, RGB(0,0,0), 0 };
     HPEN pen = ExtCreatePen(PS_GEOMETRIC | PS_ENDCAP_FLAT |
                     style, JOIN_PEN_WIDTH, &blackbrush,
                     0, NULL);
     int restore;
     RECT r;
     HFONT font = createCaptionFont(-20, TimesFont);
     TCHAR text[50];

     LoadString(GetWindowInstance(hwnd), caption,
                     text, DIM(text));

     restore = SaveDC(hdc);

       BeginPath(hdc);

     SelectFont(hdc, font);
```

```
        r.top = y;
        r.bottom = r.top + JOIN_SAMPLE_SIZE;
        r.left = 0;
        r.right = r.left + JOIN_WIDTH;

        DrawText(hdc, text, -1, &r,
                        DT_LEFT | DT_VCENTER | DT_SINGLELINE);

        SelectPen(hdc, pen);

        r.right = r.left + JOIN_SAMPLE_SIZE;

        OffsetRect(&r, JOIN_WIDTH, 0);
        polyLineInRect(hdc, &r, 0);

        OffsetRect(&r, JOIN_WIDTH, 0);
        polyLineInRect(hdc, &r, 0);

        OffsetRect(&r, JOIN_WIDTH, 0);
        polyLineInRect(hdc, &r, JOIN_SAMPLE_SIZE / 4 );

        OffsetRect(&r, JOIN_WIDTH, 0);
        polyLineInRect(hdc, &r, JOIN_SAMPLE_SIZE / 6 );

        EndPath(hdc);
        StrokePath(hdc);

        RestoreDC(hdc, restore);

        DeletePen(pen);
        DeleteFont(font);
        }
static void
join_OnPaint(HWND hwnd)
        {
#define START 20
        HDC hdc;
        PAINTSTRUCT ps;

        hdc = BeginPaint(hwnd, &ps);

        drawJoin(hwnd, hdc, START +                 0, PS_JOIN_BEVEL,
                                                IDS_BEVEL_JOIN);

        drawJoin(hwnd, hdc, START +     JOIN_HEIGHT, PS_JOIN_MITER,
                                                IDS_MITER_JOIN);

        drawJoin(hwnd, hdc, START + 2 * JOIN_HEIGHT, PS_JOIN_ROUND,
                                                IDS_ROUND_JOIN);

        EndPaint(hwnd, &ps);
        }
```

As with Listing 6.3, you can for the moment ignore the use of the BeginPath, EndPath, and StrokePath functions, which are necessary to make this work in Windows 95. Or you can jump ahead to page 383.

Geometric pens support additional capability beyond ordinary `CreatePen`/`CreatePenIndirect` style pens. For example, you can specify that a bitmap be used for the pen. This is because the "color" of the pen is actually specified by giving a `LOGBRUSH` structure, which can take a bitmap to define the brush. You can create a pen that is halftoned or plaid or that even contains an image. Those of you who programmed Windows 3.*x* may remember that patterned brushes were limited to bitmaps of 8 × 8 pixels. This limitation is removed in Windows NT. Unfortunately, it is still in Windows 95.

Drawing Filled Areas

Until now we've limited our drawing to text and lines. Windows also has functions to draw filled areas. In general, a filled area has a *perimeter* and an *interior*. Windows has functions to draw the following types of filled areas:

- Ellipses

- Polygons having an arbitrary number of sides

- The area bounded by the intersection of an ellipse and a line segment. (Windows incorrectly calls this area a *chord*. The chord is actually the line segment connecting the two points on the ellipse.)

- The pie-shaped wedge formed by drawing lines from the endpoints of an elliptical arc to the center of the arc

- Areas bounded by complex lines, including Bézier curves, polygons, and text outlines

Windows draws the perimeter of a filled area with the pen currently selected into the device context and fills the interior of the area by painting it with the brush currently selected into the device context. The functions that draw filled areas are listed in Table 6.4. When we discuss paths, you will see that *any* collection of line segments can form a path and any path can be filled using either the `FillPath` or `StrokeAndFillPath` functions.

Table 6.4: Filled-area drawing functions

Function	Description
`Chord`	Draws an arc on the perimeter of an ellipse and connects the endpoints of the arc with a chord (line segment).
`DrawFocusRect`	Draws a rectangle in the style that indicates the object has the focus.
`Ellipse`	Draws an ellipse.
`FillPath`	Fills a path with the currently selected brush.

Note: With rectangles, the sides of the rectangle are always parallel to the axes. Rotational and shearing transformations (which we have not discussed yet) in effect change the angles of the axes.
All of the above functions have `BOOL` results (and are batched in Windows NT 3.*x*).

Table 6.4: Filled-area drawing functions

Function	Description
FillRect	Fills the interior of a rectangle with a brush.
FillRgn	Fills a region with the indicated brush.
FrameRect	Draws a frame around a rectangle.
InvertRect	Inverts the contents of a rectangle.
Pie	Draws an arc on the perimeter of an ellipse and connects the endpoints of the arc to the center of the arc. This draws a pie-shaped wedge.
Polygon	Draws a closed polygon.
PolyPolygon	Draws a series of possibly open polygons.
Rectangle	Draws a rectangle.
RoundRect	Draws a rectangle with rounded corners.
StrokeAndFillPath	Fills the area marked off by a path with the current brush and draws its outline with the currently selected pen.

Note: With rectangles, the sides of the rectangle are always parallel to the axes. Rotational and shearing transformations (which we have not discussed yet) in effect change the angles of the axes.
All of the above functions have BOOL results (and are batched in Windows NT 3.x).

GDI draws the perimeter of a filled area with the pen that is selected into the device context. Everything that applies to drawing lines works the same when you are drawing the border of a filled area. This enables you to control the width of the perimeter of a filled area, its color, and its line style. In fact, you can draw the filled area without a border. Just select the NULL_PEN into the device context before drawing the filled area. You might be tempted to use the R2_NOP style, but this affects the brush as well as the pen. (For paths, you can selectively decide to draw the outline by using StrokePath, fill the interior by using FillPath, or do both by using StrokeAndFillPath. We discuss this in detail when we cover paths starting on page 383.)

GDI paints the interior of the filled area with the brush that is selected into the device context. A brush determines the color of the filled area the way a pen determines the color of a line. However, unlike most pens (except those created with PS_INSIDEFRAME or using ExtCreatePen), Windows isn't limited to using pure colors for brushes. When you request a brush color that isn't available on a raster device, GDI attempts to approximate the desired color by producing a *dithered* color. Dithering is the equivalent of "halftoning". In halftone printing, the size of the black dots is changed to fool the eye into perceiving shades of gray when, in fact, there are only two colors, black and white. Dithering is an effect wherein two colors are "mixed" to fool the viewer into thinking that another color is present. Often this is done by mixing either black pixels or white pixels with a pure color. The brain, when it sees a red area with a heavy sprinkling of black pixels, interprets this as "dark red", and with a heavy sprinkling of white pixels, interprets this as "light red". But in fact only two pure colors are present: red and black or red and white. If you do not have a color in the display's color palette that gives you a "solid" color, the GDI will use dithering to approximate it visually.

Brushes also can apply patterns when they're used. First, we show you how to draw a figure and then how to create different brushes to color it.

Drawing Rectangles and Ellipses

The Chord, DrawFocusRect, Ellipse, Pie, Rectangle, and RoundRect functions are quite similar to the Arc function discussed earlier in the chapter. All these functions require a bounding rectangle that specifies the position, shape, and size of their corresponding figure. The simplest object is the rectangle. The function call looks like the following:

```
BOOL Rectangle (HDC hdc, int xUL, int yUL, int xLR, int yLR) ;
```

The logical coordinates (xUL, yUL) and (xLR, yLR) specify the upper-left and lower-right corners, respectively, of the bounding rectangle that surrounds the desired rectangle. Because they are logical coordinates, the value of xUL isn't necessarily less than xLR. Similarly, yUL is not necessarily less than yLR. Do not rely on assumptions that are true when using the MM_TEXT mapping mode but may not be true when using other mapping modes. In addition, remember that the point (xLR, yLR) isn't on the perimeter of the drawn rectangle. In the default graphics mode (GM_COMPATIBLE), GDI draws up to, but not including, the right and bottom sides of the bounding rectangle. Figure 6.9 shows a rectangle drawn with the Rectangle function.

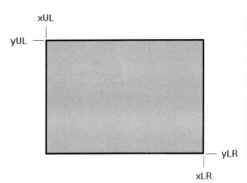

Figure 6.9: A rectangle drawn by the Rectangle function

The exterior is drawn with the selected pen (the default BLACK_PEN, in this case) and the interior is filled with the selected brush (a stock LTGRAY_BRUSH). In the extended graphics mode (GM_ADVANCED), GDI draws up to and including the right and bottom sides of the bounding rectangle. GM_ADVANCED mode is not available on Windows 95.

Exactly the same parameters are required by the Ellipse function to draw an ellipse. Figure 6.10 shows an ellipse drawn within the same bounding rectangle that was used for drawing the rectangle in Figure 6.9.

The Chord and Pie functions take exactly the same parameters as the Arc function:

```
Arc (HDC hdc,
          int xUL,    int yUL,
          int xLR,    int yLR,
          int xBegin, int yBegin,
          int xEnd,   int yEnd) ;
```

```
Chord (HDC hdc,
          int xUL,    int yUL,
          int xLR,    int yLR,
```

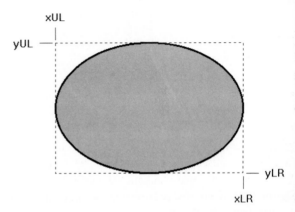

Figure 6.10: An ellipse drawn by the Ellipse function

```
        int xBegin, int yBegin,
        int xEnd, int yEnd) ;

Pie (HDC hdc, int xUL,     int yUL,     int xLR,   int yLR,
              int xBegin, int yBegin, int xEnd, int yEnd) ;
```

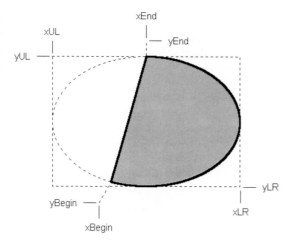

All three functions draw the same arc. The Arc function draws the specified arc and leaves the endpoints of the arc unconnected. The Arc function draws a curved line, not a filled area. The Chord function draws the specified arc and the chord connecting the two endpoints of the arc. It then paints the interior of the area with a brush. The Pie function draws the specified arc and a line from each of the endpoints of the arc to the center of the ellipse. It then paints the interior of the pie-shaped wedge with a brush.

Figure 6.11: A chord drawn by the Chord function

We drew the chord in Figure 6.11 and the pie in Figure 6.12 by changing the Arc function call in Listing 6.2 to Chord and Pie. The pie wedge in Figure 6.12 looks a bit strange because the pie isn't circular. There are no additional Windows functions for drawing circles and squares because they are special cases of ellipses and rectangles. To draw a circle or a square, the physical distance between the horizontal coordinates of the bounding rectangle must be equal to the physical distance between the vertical coordinates.

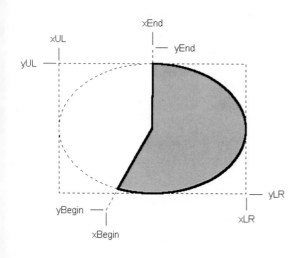

Figure 6.12: A pie wedge from a somewhat squashed pie drawn by the Pie function

All physical measurement mapping modes and the MM_ISOTROPIC mapping modes ensure that a logical unit maps to the same physical distance on each axis. When using one of these mapping modes, you need to ensure only that $|xUL - xLR|$ equals $|yUL - yLR|$. When using the MM_TEXT and MM_ANISOTROPIC mapping modes, you must adjust the logical coordinates to account for the aspect ratio of the device pixels. (The obsolete EGA did not have "square" pixels. In fact, it had a 4:3 ratio on pixel dimensions. This meant that if you drew a "square", that is, a figure *n* units wide and *n* units high, it would be distorted. While most modern display units have square pixels, not all printers do. Some common inkjet printers offer 600×300 resolution, for example). When using the MM_ANISOTROPIC mapping mode, you also must compensate for the scaling of the window to the viewport.

If you use a display or printer with nonsquare pixels, you must take extra care when drawing circles and squares to do it correctly. Pixels on a VGA have an aspect ratio of 1:1; that is, they are square. The following statement, drawing into a default common display context, draws what looks like a square on a VGA but might be a rectangle on other output devices:

```
Rectangle (hdc, 50, 50, 100, 100) ;
```

This is because of the implicit use of the MM_TEXT mapping mode in which logical units are equal to device units (or pixels). On a VGA with square pixels, everything looks correct, but on a display with rectangular pixels, a rectangle is drawn.

You can draw a rectangle with rounded corners with the RoundRect function. In many ways, this function is a cross between the Rectangle function and the Ellipse function. Like these, it draws a rectangle within a bounding rectangle. However, it rounds the corners of the rectangle to match one of the four quadrants of an ellipse that you also specify. The RoundRect function is defined as

```
BOOL RoundRect (HDC hdc, int xUL, int yUL, int xLR, int yLR,
                int Width, int Height) ;
```

The Width and Height parameters specify the width and height in logical units of the ellipse used to draw the rounded corners. By varying the width and height parameters, you can generate a rectangle with no rounding at the corners (width and height equal to 0) or, at the other extreme, produce a rectangle with so much rounding at the corners that it actually becomes an ellipse (width equal to $|xUL - xLR|$ and height equal to $|yUL - yLR|$). Figure 6.13 shows a rounded rectangle with the corner ellipse dimensions equal to one third of the corresponding rectangle sides.

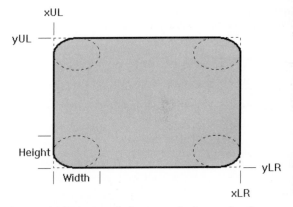

Figure 6.13: A rounded rectangle drawn by the RoundRect function

Finally, four rectangle drawing functions require a pointer to a RECT structure. The first is the DrawFocusRect function. This function draws a rectangle in the style used to indicate that an object has the focus. This rather strange function doesn't work the way the others do. A call to the function is defined as

```
BOOL DrawFocusRect(HDC hdc, CONST RECT * rect);
```

and can be called as

```
RECT rect = { xUL, yUL, xLR, yLR };

DrawFocusRect (hdc, &rect) ;
```

The first difference is that the upper-left and lower-right corners of the bounding rectangle aren't specified by separate parameters to the DrawFocusRect function. Instead, you must pass a pointer to a RECT structure containing the coordinates. This actually is a better way to pass the parameters. The other functions should have been designed to accept a RECT structure. But because they weren't, changing in midstream leaves this call as the oddball.

The second difference is that neither the currently selected pen nor the currently selected brush are used to draw the focus rectangle. The DrawFocusRect function draws the border of the rectangle using a dotted pen and doesn't fill the interior of the rectangle.

The third difference is that the DrawFocusRect function assumes that the mapping mode is MM_TEXT and fails to work properly when other mapping modes are in effect. The Windows documentation, unfortunately, fails to mention this assumption. To use this function when you use other mapping modes, you must convert the logical coordinates of the bounding rectangle to device coordinates. You also must change the mapping mode back to MM_TEXT, reset, if necessary, the window and viewport origin back to (0, 0), and call the DrawFocusRect function. We used a slight modification of the code in Listing 6.2 to draw Figure 6.14. The following lines of code generated the focus rectangle in Figure 6.14:

```
int saved = SaveDC(hdc);
SetRect (&rect, xUL, yUL, xLR, yLR) ;
LPtoDP (hdc, (LPPOINT) &rect, 2) ;
SetMapMode (hdc, MM_TEXT) ;
SetViewportOrgEx (hdc, 0, 0, NULL) ;
DrawFocusRect    (hdc, &rect) ;
RestoreDC(hdc, saved);
```

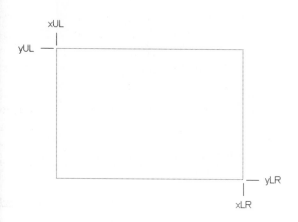

Figure 6.14: A rectangle drawn in the style used to indicate focus

Another big difference is that DrawFocusRect draws using the R2_XORPEN raster operation. Calling this function a second time with the same bounding rectangle erases the rectangle from the display without disturbing the underlying image. The functions we've seen previously can do almost the same thing, but you would need to select a dotted pen, select a null brush, change the drawing mode to R2_XORPEN, draw the rectangle, and finally, remember to delete the dotted pen. Even then, this only approximates the appearance of a focus rectangle. A dotted pen draws dots that are spaced farther apart than the dots in a focus rectangle. You can use ExtCreatePen to create a PS_ALTERNATE-style geometric pen to get this effect.

You cannot scroll an area of the display that contains a rectangle drawn by this function. When you want to scroll the area containing a rectangle drawn by the DrawFocusRect function, you must draw the focus rectangle a second time (which removes it from the display), scroll the area, and then draw the focus rectangle once more at the new location.

The three other rectangle drawing functions are as follows:

```
BOOL FillRect (HDC hdc, LPRECT rect, HBRUSH brush) ;
BOOL FrameRect (HDC hdc, LPRECT rect, HBRUSH brush) ;
BOOL InvertRect (HDC hdc, LPRECT rect) ;
```

The FillRect function uses the specified brush, rather than the brush currently selected in the device context, to fill the rectangle specified by the logical coordinates in the RECT structure. It fills the top and left borders of the rectangle and up to, but not including, the right and bottom borders. It also assumes that the axes in the logical coordinate system have the default orientation. That is, it requires that the bottom field of the RECT structure be greater than the top and that right be greater than left. When you invert an axis, such as switching to a Cartesian-style vertical axis, these assumptions are no longer true, and the FillRect function won't draw the rectangle.

```
BOOL fillCartesianRect(HDC hdc, LPRECT rect, HBRUSH brush)
    {
    RECT r = *rect; // make copy
    int saved = SaveDC(hdc);
    BOOL result;

    LPtoDP(hdc, (LPPOINT)&r, 2);
    SetMapMode(hdc, MM_TEXT);
    SetViewportOrgEx (hdc, 0, 0, NULL) ;
    result = FillRect(hdc, &r, brush);
    RestoreDC(hdc, saved);

    return result;
    }
```

The FrameRect function uses the specified brush to draw a border around the rectangle specified by the logical coordinates in the RECT structure. The border is one logical unit wide and high. All the functions described previously use the current pen to draw the border. Because a brush is used, the border does not have to be a pure color. When a logical unit is greater than a device unit, the border is drawn using dithered colors. The FrameRect function will not draw the border when the axes do not have the default orientation.

The InvertRect function inverts the contents of the specified rectangle. This changes all black pixels to white and all white pixels to black. Other colored pixels are changed to their respective inverse colors. A given color may have different inverse colors on different displays. Inverting the rectangle a second time restores the pixels to their original values. The InvertRect makes the same assumptions about the orientation of the axes as do the FillRect and FrameRect functions.

We discuss the FillRgn, FillPath, and StrokeAndFillPath functions when we discuss regions and paths. They are included in this list for completeness.

Many of the functions listed here work properly only if the axes have the default orientation. That is, *y*-values increase downward and *x*-values increase rightward. Be careful if you are using one of the mapping modes that allows you to change axis orientation.

A number of functions ease the effort of working with rectangles. Unfortunately, some of them also assume that horizontal axis values increase to the right and that vertical axis values increase downward. They don't work correctly when you use logical coordinates in the physical measurement mapping modes. The functions may or may not work using logical coordinates in the MM_ISOTROPIC or MM_ANISOTROPIC mapping modes. It depends on the orientation of the axes.

```
BOOL CopyRect (LPRECT rectDest, CONST RECT * rectSrc) ;
```

The CopyRect function makes one rectangle equal to another rectangle. You can do this just as easily with a structure assignment statement. This does the same thing with inline code rather than a function call to Windows:

```
rectDest = rectSrc ;
```

The InflateRect function adds the xDelta value to the right and the yDelta value to the bottom of a rectangle, and subtracts the xDelta value from the left and the yDelta value from the top. Positive values increase the size of the rectangle, and negative values shrink the rectangle. Note that this approach assumes that positive horizontal coordinates increase to the right and positive vertical coordinates increase downward. Here is a typical call to the InflateRect function:

```
BOOL InflateRect (LPRECT rect, int xDelta, int yDelta) ;
```

The IntersectRect function sets the Dest structure to the largest rectangle contained in both Src1 and Src2. It doesn't work properly unless the axes have the default orientation:

```
BOOL IntersectRect (LPRECT Dest, CONST RECT * Src1,
                    CONST RECT * Src2) ;
```

The OffsetRect function shifts the rectangle xOffset units horizontally and yOffset units vertically. The xOffset and yOffset parameters can be positive or negative, thus enabling you to shift the rectangle in any direction:

```
BOOL OffsetRect (LPRECT rect, int xOffset, int yOffset) ;
```

The SetRect function initializes the four fields of a RECT structure to the provided values:

```
BOOL SetRect (LPRECT rect, int xUL, int yUL, int xLR, int yLR) ;
```

The above statement is equivalent to the following:

```
rect.left   = xUL ;
rect.top    = yUL ;
rect.right  = xLR ;
rect.bottom = yLR ;
```

The SetRectEmpty function sets all fields in a RECT structure to 0:

```
BOOL SetRectEmpty (LPRECT rect) ;
```

The UnionRect function creates the union of the Src1 and Src2 rectangles. It sets the Dest rectangle to the smallest rectangle that can enclose the two source rectangles, that is, the bounding box that encloses the two source rectangles. It requires that the default coordinate orientation be used:

```
BOOL UnionRect (LPRECT Dest, CONST RECT * Src1,
                CONST RECT * Src2) ;
```

The `IsRectEmpty` function returns a nonzero value when the `rect` parameter is an empty rectangle. An empty rectangle is a rectangle with either top equal to bottom (zero height) or left equal to right (zero width), or both:

```
BOOL IsRectEmpty (LPRECT rect) ;
```

The `PtInRect` function returns a nonzero value when the point specified by the `pt` parameter is in the rectangle. A point is in a rectangle when it is within the four sides or on the left or top side. A point is not in a rectangle when it lies on the right or bottom side of the rectangle:

```
BOOL PtInRect (LPRECT rect, LPPOINT pt) ;
```

Drawing Polygons

Two functions for drawing filled areas with a border are the `Polygon` and `PolyPolygon` functions. The `Polygon` function takes the same arguments as does the `Polyline` function: a handle to a device context, a pointer to an array of `POINT` structures containing the logical coordinates of the vertices of the polygon, and the number of points in the array:

```
BOOL Polygon (HDC hdc, LPPOINT Points, int Count) ;
```

Unlike the `Polyline` function (which draws up to, but not including, the last point in the array), the `Polygon` function closes the polygon, if necessary, by drawing a line from the last vertex to the first. This is called "closing the figure", and you will see a generalization of it when we discuss paths (page 383). GDI draws the perimeter of the polygon with the selected pen and fills the interior of the polygon using the selected brush.

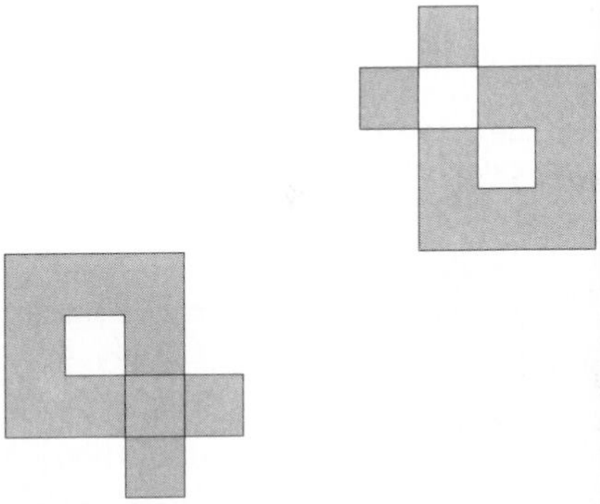

Unlike the simple rectangle and ellipse, a polygon can be a complex, overlapping figure. When a polygon is complex, the *polygon-filling mode* controls how GDI determines which points are interior points and therefore get filled. You get the polygon-filling mode with the `GetPolyFillMode` function and set it with the `SetPolyFillMode` function:

Figure 6.15: Example of the polygon-filling modes: WINDING (left) and ALTERNATE (right)

```
int PolyFillMode = GetPolyFillMode (hdc) ;
int PrevFillMode = SetPolyFillMode (hdc, PolyFillMode) ;
```

There are two polygon-filling modes: `ALTERNATE` (the default) and `WINDING`. When the polygon-filling mode is `ALTERNATE`, GDI fills every other enclosed area that is within the boundaries of the polygon. When the polygon-filling mode is `WINDING`, GDI computes a perimeter that encloses the polygon but does not overlap. This is the perimeter of the polygon drawn. The polygon itself can completely surround areas that aren't within the boundaries of the polygon. Those surrounded areas are not filled in either polygon-filling mode. In Figure 6.15, the left polygon was drawn with the `WINDING` polygon-filling mode. The right polygon was drawn with the `ALTERNATE` polygon-filling mode.

Listing 6.5 shows the WM_PAINT logic we used to draw the polygons in Figure 6.15. Notice that the same polygon is drawn twice. We inverted the orientation of both axes and changed from the default polygon-filling mode (ALTERNATE) to the WINDING polygon-filling mode before drawing the polygon the second time.

Listing 6.5: WM_PAINT logic for drawing Figure 6.15

```
POINT Points [] = {
          { 200, 400 },
          { 200,   0 },
          { 500,   0 },
          { 500, 300 },
          { 100, 300 },
          { 100, 200 },
          { 400, 200 },
          { 400, 100 },
          { 300, 100 },
          { 300, 400 }
} ;

static void
poly_OnPaint(HWND hwnd)
{
 RECT rect;
 int cxClient:
 int cyClient;
 HDC hdc;
 PAINTSTRUCT ps;
 HBRUSH hbr;
    /* Get the present size of the client area. */
    GetClientRect (hwnd, &rect) ;
    cxClient = rect.right ;
    cyClient = rect.bottom ;

    /* Get the device context and        */
    /* establish the coordinate mapping. */
    hdc = BeginPaint (hwnd, &ps) ;
    SetMapMode (hdc, MM_ISOTROPIC) ;
    SetViewportOrgEx (hdc, cxClient / 2, cyClient / 2, NULL) ;
    SetWindowExtEx (hdc, 1000, 1000, NULL) ;
    SetViewportExtEx (hdc, cxClient, -cyClient, NULL) ;
    hbr = GetStockBrush (LTGRAY_BRUSH) ;
    SelectBrush (hdc, hbr) ;

    /* Draw the right polygon. */
    Polygon (hdc, Points, DIM(Points)) ;

    /* Invert the coordinate system axes. */
    SetViewportExtEx (hdc, -cxClient, cyClient, NULL) ;

    /* Change the polygon-filling mode. */
    SetPolyFillMode (hdc, WINDING) ;

    /* Draw the left polygon. */
    Polygon (hdc, Points, DIM(Points)) ;
    EndPaint (hwnd, &ps) ;
}
```

The `PolyPolygon` function draws a series of polygons. Unlike the `Polygon` function, polygons drawn by the `PolyPolygon` function are not automatically closed. That is, the `PolyPolygon` function does not draw a line from the last vertex to the first. GDI draws the perimeter of the polygon with the selected pen and fills the interior of the polygon using the selected brush. The interior of the polygon is filled in accordance with the polygon-filling mode, as is done for the `Polygon` function. Figure 6.16 shows the drawn polygons. In this case, we use the same points that would have drawn the two polygons shown in Figure 6.15, but we divide the points differently. You can use the GDI Explorer application to see all the variants of this. Select the `PolyPolygon` display and then use the right mouse button to change the prop-

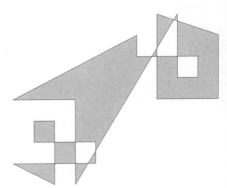

Figure 6.16: Bizarre polygons drawn using the `PolyPolygon` function

erties of the drawing by selecting a different set of vertices. Selecting the 0th, 4th, and 13th vertices will generate the image shown in Figure 6.16. When the polygons are disjoint, they are drawn as if each is filled separately.

Listing 6.6 gives the `WM_PAINT` logic for drawing the polygons shown in Figure 6.16. Note that the same coordinates are used as for Figure 6.15, but the splits between the two points are different.

Listing 6.6: Code to draw the bizarre polygons of Figure 6.16

```
POINT Points [] = {
            { 200, 400 },          /* Right polygon */
            { 200,   0 },
            { 500,   0 },
            { 500, 300 },
            { 100, 300 },
            { 100, 200 },
            { 400, 200 },
            { 400, 100 },
            { 300, 100 },
            { 300, 400 },

            { -200, -400 },        /* Left polygon */
            { -200,   0 },
            { -500,   0 },
            { -500, -300 },
            { -100, -300 },
            { -100, -200 },
            { -400, -200 },
            { -400, -100 },
            { -300, -100 },
            { -300, -400 }
} ;

int PolyCounts [] = { 4, 9, 8 } ;

static void
```

```
polypoly_OnPaint(HWND hwnd)
{
  RECT rect;
  HDC hdc;
  PAINTSTRUCT ps;
  HBRUSH hbr;
  int cxClient;
  int cyClient;

      /* Get the present size of the client area. */

      GetClientRect (hwnd, &rect) ;
      cxClient = rect.right ;
      cyClient = rect.bottom ;

      /* Get the device context and        */
      /* establish the coordinate mapping. */
      hdc = BeginPaint (hwnd, &ps) ;
      SetMapMode (hdc, MM_ISOTROPIC) ;
      SetViewportOrgEx (hdc, cxClient / 2, cyClient / 2, NULL) ;
      SetWindowExtEx (hdc, 1000, 1000, NULL) ;
      SetViewportExtEx (hdc, cxClient, -cyClient, NULL) ;

      hbr = GetStockBrush (LTGRAY_BRUSH) ;

      SelectBrush (hdc, hbr) ;

      /* Change the polygon-filling mode. */
      SetPolyFillMode (hdc, ALTERNATE) ;

      /* Draw the polygon. */
      PolyPolygon (hdc, Points, PolyCounts, DIM(PolyCounts)) ;
      EndPaint (hwnd, &ps) ;
      return 0 ;
```

All polygons drawn by the PolyPolygon function use the polygon-filling mode in effect at the time of the call. You can't draw multiple polygons using different polygon-filling modes with a single function call. Figure 6.16, drawn by the algorithm in Listing 6.6, is drawn using the ALTERNATE polygon-filling mode. You can use the GDI Explorer to change the polygon fill mode using the right mouse button in the PolyPolygon display.

Creating and Using Stock and Custom Brushes

Until now, most of the filled figures have been filled using the default WHITE_BRUSH. Like the rest of the attributes of a device context, however, you can change the selected brush so that the interiors of filled figures can have whatever color and pattern you want. In Chapter 5, "Examining a Device Context in Depth", we covered brushes and how changing the brush origin affects how the pattern is applied to the interior of a figure. Now we show you how to use and create a brush. These functions are summarized in Table 6.5.

You use a brush exactly the same as you do a pen. You select a brush into a device context by calling the SelectBrush macro API function. Windows defines the SelectBrush macro in windowsx.h as a call to the SelectObject function. It is defined as

Table 6.5: Functions that create brushes

Function	Explanation	
CreateSolidBrush	Creates a solid brush in a single color.	
CreateHatchBrush	Creates a brush using a predefined hatch pattern.	
CreatePatternBrush	Creates a brush using a bitmap pattern.	
CreateDIBPatternBrush	Creates a brush using a handle to a device-independent bitmap pattern. The interpretations of the colors are as follows:	
	DIB_PAL_COLORS	The color table is an array of 16-bit indices into the logical palette.
	DIB_RGB_COLORS	The color table is an array of literal COLORREF RGB colors.
	DIB_PAL_INDICES	No color table is provided; the bitmap gives indices into the logical palette in the DC.
CreateDIBPatternBrushPt	Creates a brush using a pointer to a device-independent bitmap pattern. The interpretations of the colors are as follows:	
	DIB_PAL_COLORS	The color table is an array of 16-bit indices into the logical palette.
	DIB_RGB_COLORS	The color table is an array of literal COLORREF RGB colors.
	DIB_PAL_INDICES	No color table is provided; the bitmap gives indices into the logical palette in the DC.
CreateBrushIndirect	Creates a brush from a LOGBRUSH specification.	

```
#define SelectBrush(hdc, hbr)
         ((HBRUSH)SelectObject((hdc), (HGDIOBJ)(HBRUSH)(hbr)))
```

You should use the SelectBrush macro API rather than a call to the SelectObject function. The macro is more descriptive. You use it like this:

```
HBRUSH hbrush;
HBRUSH hbrPrevious ;

hbrPrevious = SelectBrush (hdc, hbrush) ;
```

The SelectBrush function returns the previously selected object. In the immediately preceding example, the SelectBrush function returns the previously selected brush. You must delete all the brushes you create. You need not be concerned about accidentally deleting stock objects; DeleteObject applied to a stock brush does nothing. A brush must not be selected into a device context when it is deleted, so you must select a different brush into the device context and then delete the created brush.

Windows provides the DeleteBrush macro to delete a brush. It is defined in windowsx.h as a call to the DeleteObject function. It looks like this:

```
#define DeleteBrush(hbr)  DeleteObject((HGDIOBJ)(HBRUSH)(hbr))
```

Reselecting the previously selected brush always works, provided the previously selected brush was not also the current brush:

```
hbr = SelectBrush (hdc, hbrPrevious) ;
DeleteBrush (hbr) ;
```

Generally, you are selecting a previous brush that was replaced by a brush you have newly created. So you know that the previous brush cannot be the current brush, since the current brush is local to your procedure. But beware of this trap in the fully general case.

Stock Brushes

The easiest brushes to use are the *stock brushes*. The default brush in a device context is the stock object WHITE_BRUSH. Therefore, the following code is equivalent to that just preceding:

```
DeleteBrush (SelectBrush (hdc, GetStockBrush (WHITE_BRUSH))) ;
```

Windows provides six different monochrome stock brushes, as listed in Table 6.6. Note that there are, for historical reasons, seven names for the six stock brushes.

You retrieve the handle to a stock brush as you do for all stock objects: call the GetStockBrush function and pass the symbolic name of the desired stock brush. The Windows SDK defines the GetStockBrush macro API in windows.h. It looks like this:

```
#define GetStockBrush(i) ((HBRUSH)GetStockObject(i))
```

You can use the macro by writing something like this:

```
HBRUSH hbrush ;

hbrush = GetStockBrush (LTGRAY_BRUSH) ;
```

Custom Brushes

Creating a custom brush is a lot like creating a custom pen. A custom brush is a logical brush, just as a custom pen is a logical pen. So the appearance is not fully determined until the brush is selected into a device context. What happens when you select a logical brush into a device context depends on whether the brush is a solid brush or a brush that leaves a pattern. There are five functions you can use to create a custom brush: one to create a solid brush, three to create patterned brushes, and one that can create either type of brush.

Solid Brushes

The CreateSolidBrush function creates a logical brush that has the specified solid color:

```
HBRUSH CreateSolidBrush
              (COLORREF Color) ;
```

The Color parameter is a COLORREF value that specifies the color of the brush. As such, it can be an RGB, a PALETTEINDEX, or a PALETTERGB color value. When you select a solid brush into a device context, GDI attempts to produce a color as close as possible to your specified logical color. When the device supports a pure color identical to your requested color, you get that color. However, when the device doesn't support your logical color exactly, GDI will approximate the color by creating an 8×8 bitmap containing dithered pure colors. GDI then will use that bitmap for the brush. This is unlike ordinary ("cosmetic") pens in which GDI converts the specified color into the nearest pure color supported by the device.

Table 6.6: The stock brushes provided by Windows

Brush Name	Color
BLACK_BRUSH	Solid black brush.
DKGRAY_BRUSH	Dark gray brush.
GRAY_BRUSH	Gray brush.
HOLLOW_BRUSH	None (synonym for NULL_BRUSH).
LTGRAY_BRUSH	Light gray brush.
NULL_BRUSH	None (doesn't overwrite the interior).
WHITE_BRUSH	White brush (default brush for a device context).

Hatched Brushes

The CreateHatchBrush function creates a logical brush with a specified hatched pattern and color. The hatched pattern is produced by *hatch marks*–horizontal, vertical, and diagonal lines used to produce a "texture" to an area drawn by a brush. The CreateHatchBrush function call requires two parameters: the predefined hatch style name of the desired hatch style and a COLORREF value that specifies the color of the hatch marks. You create a hatched brush as follows:

```
hbrush = CreateHatchBrush(HatchStyle, Color);
```

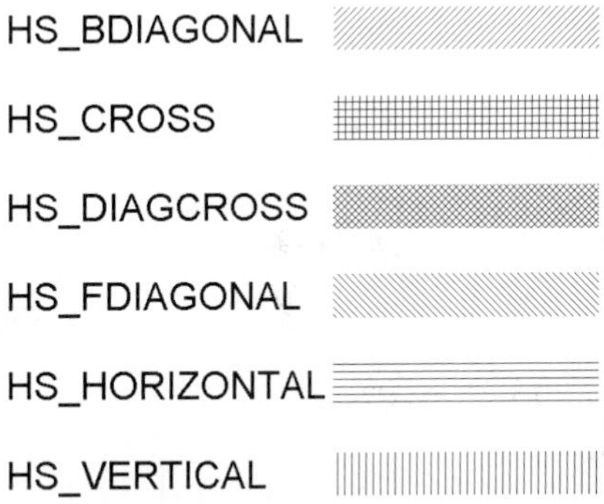

The HatchStyle parameter can be one of the symbolic values shown in Figure 6.17. The color specified in the call to the

HS_BDIAGONAL

HS_CROSS

HS_DIAGCROSS

HS_FDIAGONAL

HS_HORIZONTAL

HS_VERTICAL

Figure 6.17: The six styles used by the CreateHatchBrush function.

CreateHatchBrush function is the color of the hatch lines. GDI converts the specified color to the nearest pure color supported by the device. This differs from a solid brush, where dithered colors can be used. The color of the areas between the hatch lines is determined by the background mode attribute of the device context.

When the background mode is TRANSPARENT, GDI draws the hatch lines without changing the areas in between the lines. When the background mode is OPAQUE, GDI uses the background color (after converting it to a pure color) to fill in the areas between the hatches.

Bitmap Brushes

You aren't limited to using one of the six predefined hatch brushes. The CreatePatternBrush function creates a logical brush that has the pattern specified by the hBitmap parameter. A call to the function looks like the following:

```
hbrush = CreatePatternBrush (hbitmap) ;
```

When you create a brush based on a monochrome bitmap, the brush uses the current text and background colors. These are not necessarily black and white. Pixels represented in the bitmap by a 0 bit are drawn with the current text color, and pixels represented in the bitmap by a 1 bit are drawn with the current background color.

Because creating the bitmap can be a chore in itself, we will finish our examination of brush creation before we look at bitmaps.

 Programmers who know the Win16 API may remember that the `CreatePatternBrush` API call created a brush that was only 8 × 8, and in fact, used only the top-most, left-most 8 rows and columns no matter how large the bitmap was. A program that relied on this behavior in Win16 will probably create unexpected results in Win32. This is because there is no such restriction in Win32; the entire bitmap will be used.

An example of a pie chart created with a bitmap (in fact, our bitmap is the classic marble.bmp bitmap that comes with Windows) is shown in Figure 6.18. The accompanying code is in Listing 6.7, although the details of how a bitmap is created may not be apparent because we have not yet discussed that topic.

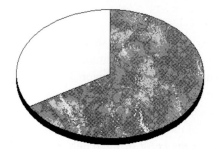

Our Share of the Marble Puff-Pastry Slab Market

Figure 6.18: Figure filled with bitmap brush

Listing 6.7: Code to fill using a bitmap
```
static BOOL
ids_GetTextExtentPoint32(HINSTANCE hinst, HDC hdc, int ids, LPSIZE size)
    {
     TCHAR text[256];
     LoadString(hinst, ids, text, DIM(text));

     return GetTextExtentPoint32 (hdc, text,
                                      lstrlen(text), size);
    }

static void
bmpbrush_OnPaint(HWND hwnd)
    {
     PAINTSTRUCT ps;
```

```
        HDC hdc     = BeginPaint(hwnd, &ps);
        int xUL     = -300;
        int yUL     =  200;
        int xLR     =  300;
        int yLR     = -200;
        int xBegin  = -250;
        int yBegin  = -100;
        int xEnd    = 0;
        int yEnd    = 250;
        RECT rect;
        RECT r;
#define BMP_CAPTION_OFFSET (-80)
        HFONT font = createCaptionFont(-(abs(BMP_CAPTION_OFFSET)),
                                        TimesFont);

        HBRUSH brush;
        HBITMAP bmp;
        int save = SaveDC(hdc);
        SIZE size;

        // Get the device context
        // and establish the coordinate mapping

        GetClientRect(hwnd, &rect);
        SetMapMode(hdc, MM_ISOTROPIC);
        SetViewportOrgEx(hdc, rect.right / 2,
                              rect.bottom / 2, NULL);
        SetWindowExtEx(hdc, 1000, 1000, NULL);
        SetViewportExtEx(hdc, rect.right, - rect.bottom, NULL);

        bmp = LoadBitmap(GetWindowInstance(hwnd),
                              MAKEINTRESOURCE(IDB_MARBLE));
        brush = CreatePatternBrush(bmp);

        // Do a drop-shadow 3-D effect here
#define BMP_SHADOW (-20)
        SelectBrush(hdc, GetStockObject(BLACK_BRUSH));
        Ellipse(hdc, xUL, yUL + BMP_SHADOW, xLR, yLR + BMP_SHADOW);

        SelectBrush(hdc, GetStockObject(WHITE_BRUSH));
        Ellipse(hdc, xUL, yUL, xLR, yLR);


        SelectBrush(hdc, brush);
        Pie(hdc, xUL, yUL, xLR, yLR, xBegin, yBegin, xEnd, yEnd);

        r = rect;
        DPtoLP(hdc, (LPPOINT)&r, 2);
        r.top = yLR + BMP_CAPTION_OFFSET;
        r.bottom = yLR + 2 * BMP_CAPTION_OFFSET;
        SelectFont(hdc, font);


        ids_GetTextExtentPoint32(GetWindowInstance(hwnd), hdc,
                              IDS_BMPBRUSH, &size);
        r.bottom = r.top - size.cy;

        ids_DrawText(GetWindowInstance(hwnd), hdc, IDS_BMPBRUSH, &r,
                      DT_CENTER);
```

```
    RestoreDC(hdc, save);

    DeleteObject(font);
    DeleteObject(brush);
    DeleteObject(bmp);
    EndPaint(hwnd, &ps);
}
```

The helper function `ids_GetTextExtentPoint32` simulates the effect of `GetTextExtentPoint32`, but it is passed an instance handle and a string ID instead of a string. The painting code first computes a scaled coordinate system with 0, 0 in the center of the client area. It loads a bitmap using `LoadBitMap`, which loads the "marble" bitmap we copied into our project and put into the resource file. The `createCaptionFont` helper function creates a font of a given size, which must be negative to indicate a desired point size. To ensure that the font value is always negative whether we place the caption above or below the pie chart, we pass in the negative of the absolute value of its separation. We use this value so that the font will always appear to be one "line" above or below the pie chart. After we draw a black ellipse slightly offset below a white ellipse (giving us a sort-of-3D effect), we draw our pie chart using the `Pie` function. To properly center the caption, we define a rectangle that is as wide as the window and use `DPtoLP` to convert the client coordinates we obtained from `GetClientRect` to logical coordinates in our new mapping. We then use the `ids_GetTextExtentPoint32` function to compute the height so that we have a rectangle we can use for `DrawText`.

The `CreateDIBPatternBrush` and `CreateDIBPatternBrushPt` functions create a logical brush that has the pattern specified by a device-independent bitmap (DIB). Normally, color bitmaps are device-specific. They contain assumptions about the representation of a color on the device (for example, the number of color planes or adjacent pixels), as well as which pixel value represents which color. A device-independent bitmap specification is a device-independent recipe for describing the colors and image in a color bitmap.

A logical brush created by the `CreateDIBPatternBrush` or `CreateDIBPatternBrushPt` functions can be subsequently selected into a device context for any device that supports raster operations. The DIB specification is translated into the device-specific bitmap that is actually used on the device. You create a pattern brush with this function as follows:

```
hbrush = CreateDIBPatternBrush (hPackedDIB, Usage) ;
```

```
hbrush = CreateDIBPatternBrushPt (lpPackedDIB, Usage) ;
```

The `hPackedDIB` parameter to `CreateDIBPatternBrush` specifies a handle to a global memory block containing a packed DIB. Global memory is largely a vestige of the old Windows memory management methods. More modern usage will tend to use ordinary memory pointers, and you are more likely, in Win32, to use the `CreateDIBPatternBrushPt` function, which takes an ordinary memory pointer to a packed DIB. The `Usage` parameter specifies whether the `bmiColors[]` array of the `BITMAPINFO` structure of the bitmap contains explicit RGB values or indices into the currently realized logical palette. Device-independent bitmaps will be covered in greater depth in the following section, "Creating and Using Bitmaps".

The final function that can be used to create a brush is the `CreateBrushIndirect` function. It works very much like the `CreatePenIndirect` function. You pass a pointer to a structure, and the function creates the type of brush indicated by information in the structure. You can create any of the previously mentioned custom brushes with the `CreateBrushIndirect` function. The only parameter to the function is a far pointer to a LOGBRUSH (logical brush) structure. A typical function call is as follows:

```
HBRUSH   hbrush ;
LOGBRUSH logbrush ;

/* Fill in LOGBRUSH structure. */
hbrush = CreateBrushIndirect (&logbrush) ;
```

The LOGBRUSH structure has three fields and defines the style, color, and hatch style of the logical brush to create. It has three corresponding fields and is defined as follows:

```
typedef struct tagLOGBRUSH {
    UINT       lbStyle ;
    COLORREF   lbColor ;
    int        lbHatch ;
} LOGBRUSH ;
```

You set the `lbStyle` field to indicate the type of brush you want the `CreateBrushIndirect` function to create. The possible values are listed in Table 6.7.

Table 6.7: Logical brush types for the `CreateBrushIndirect` function

lbStyle	lbColor	lbHatch
BS_DIBPATTERN	LOWORD (lbColor) contains either DIB_PAL_COLORS or DIB_RGB_COLORS	Handle to global memory containing a packed device-independent bitmap (DIB). Cast to a HANDLE before using in a handle context; cast to an `int` to store it.
BS_DIBPATTERNPT	LOWORD (lbColor) contains either DIB_PAL_COLORS or DIB_RGB_COLORS	Pointer to memory containing a packed device-independent bitmap (DIB). Cast to a pointer before using in a pointer context; cast to an `int` to store it.
BS_HATCHED	Color of hatches.	Hatch style as shown in Figure 6.17.
BS_HOLLOW	Ignored.	Ignored.
BS_PATTERN	Ignored.	Handle to a bitmap.
BS_SOLID	Color of brush.	Ignored.

The `GetObject` function works on brushes just as it does on pens. When you call the `GetObject` function and pass the handle to a logical brush as its parameter, it retrieves a LOGBRUSH structure that describes the brush. A typical call to `GetObject` for a logical brush is

```
LOGBRUSH logbrush ;

GetObject (hbrush, sizeof (logbrush), (LPSTR) &logbrush) ;
```

Note that how you interpret the lbHatch field depends on the value in the lbStyle field. You must explicitly cast the int value to a handle (for BS_SOLID or BS_DIBPATTERN styles) or a pointer (for the BS_PATTERN style) to use it to access the bitmap.

Now that you've seen how to create and use a brush, we need to fill a gap: how to create the bitmap that describes a custom brush's color and pattern. Any bitmap can be used when creating a brush. So we don't restrict the following discussion to bitmaps used only to create a brush; we look at bitmaps in general.

Creating and Using Bitmaps

There are two fundamental types of bitmaps in Windows: *device-specific bitmaps* and *device-independent bitmaps* (DIBs). A device-specific bitmap is a pattern of bits stored in memory. The bits for a pixel are organized in the same fashion as those on a particular output device. A bitmap for an output device that uses a different organization of bits for a pixel cannot be used on the first output device. Basically, the bits do not line up properly.

A DIB is also a pattern of bits stored in memory. However, the bits for a pixel in a DIB are not necessarily organized in the same manner as bits for a pixel on the eventual output device. They could be organized in the same fashion, but they do not need to be. Instead, the bitmap is organized in a fashion that best describes the encoded image. Doing this takes into account the number of colors used in the bitmap, the actual colors used, and the data redundancy in the bitmap (used when selecting a compressed bitmap format).

The format of a device-specific bitmap is known (by implication) from the device on which it is used. The format of a DIB is specified by an accompanying DIB specification. A DIB specification describes the following:

- The width and height of the bitmap

- The number of color planes

- The number of pixels

- The type of data compression used for a compressed bitmap

- The horizontal and vertical resolution of the target device for which the bitmap was designed

- The number of colors actually used by the bitmap

- The number of colors considered important for displaying the bitmap

To use a DIB on a device, the DIB first must be converted into a device-specific bitmap. GDI uses the DIB specification and the device capabilities to properly map pixel values in the DIB to the proper values in the device-specific bitmap.

Either type of bitmap can be used for either monochrome or color bitmaps for any device. There are trade-offs, however, that make one type or the other a better choice in differing situations. Monochrome bitmaps are, by their very nature, device-independent. Because they always have a known color format, it's easiest to use the device-specific bitmap functions when creating a monochrome bitmap. In that way, you don't have to create a DIB specification that describes the monochrome bitmap.

Color bitmaps are harder to create. If you're creating a color bitmap for a known device (such as a stock VGA), you can determine the color format of the device and create the bitmap accordingly. However, the bitmap won't take advantage of additional colors available on other devices, such as those supporting 24-bit color. So alternatively, you could create a blank bitmap for a specific device and draw the desired figure in it. This lets GDI worry about the details of the organization of the colors and bits. Often, though, you may want to create a bitmap ahead of time, and you would like it to look as good as possible on whatever display device Windows supports. This is a time to use a DIB.

DIBs are quite important if you want portability. While for a long time the "stock VGA" was the most popular display card, today there are a variety of display interfaces. These are operating at resolutions anywhere from the traditional VGA resolution of 640×480 to higher resolutions such as 1600×1200 and in any mode from "16-color" to 24-bit (RGB), to 30-bit (10 R, 10 G, 10 B), to 32-bit (CMYK) color. The device-specific layouts are numerous. You should think of working in DIBs as much as possible, saving the device-specific bitmaps only for when you can get Windows to handle the device-dependent details for you.

Copying a bitmap between two disparate devices requires the use of a DIB. You can copy a device-specific bitmap to a DIB, which encodes the image in a device-independent manner as described by the DIB specification. After you have the image in a DIB, you can copy it back to a different device, one that doesn't necessarily use the same pixel format as the original device's. DIBs are more efficient in many cases because the bitmap can be stored in a compressed format. For example, it may take longer to read an uncompressed bitmap from the disk than it does to read a compressed bitmap and uncompress it, depending on the speed of your processor and disk.

We first look at the functions that operate on bitmaps. Then we look at creating various device-specific bitmaps. Next, we discuss the functions that use DIBs. Finally, we cover a few functions that do not fit anywhere else.

Bitmap Functions

Table 6.8 lists the functions that create bitmaps as well as a few GDI drawing functions that haven't been presented. Once you've created a bitmap that is compatible with a specific device, you can select that bitmap into a memory device context for the device. You can then draw on the bitmap the same way you can draw on a device, by calling GDI drawing functions and specifying the device context.

For example, the LineTo and Polygon functions will draw a line and a polygon on a bitmap when you specify a memory device context. Other functions listed in Table 6.8 are often used to draw into a bitmap. The BitBlt function copies a rectangular area from one device context to another. When the device contexts are memory device contexts, this function copies part of one bitmap to another. You can also use it to copy part of a device's display surface, such as the pixels in a window, to a memory device context and thus to the pixels of a bitmap. The StretchBlt function works similarly to the BitBlt function but can also stretch or compress the copied bitmap. We look at some of the other "Blt" functions in more detail (see, for example, the description of the PatBlt function on page 339, the StretchBlt function on page 350, the PlgBlt function on page 352, and the MaskBlt function on 356). You also can use the "BLT Explorer" to see how these functions operate. This Explorer is a component of the GDI Explorer that is included on the CD-ROM that accompanies this book.

Table 6.8: Functions that operate on bitmaps

Function	Description
BitBlt	Copies a rectangular area from a source device context to a destination device context.
CreateBitmap	Creates a device-specific memory bitmap. This function is similar to CreateDIBitmap.
CreateBitmapIndirect	Creates a device-specific memory bitmap from a description in a data structure.
CreateCompatibleBitmap	Creates a device-specific memory bitmap that is compatible with a specified device and that may be selected into a memory device context associated with the device.
CreateDIBitmap	Creates a device-specific memory bitmap from a device-independent bitmap (DIB) specification. The pixels in the bitmap can be initialized when created, if desired. This function is similar to CreateBitmap.
CreateDIBSection	Creates a device-independent bitmap that applications can write to directly.
CreateDiscardableBitmap	Creates a discardable device-specific memory bitmap that is compatible with a specified device and that may be selected into a memory device context associated with the device.
ExtFloodFill	Fills an area of a display surface with the current brush. It can fill to a specified color boundary or fill an area that is a specified color.
FloodFill	Fills an area of a display surface with the current brush. It fills only to a specified color boundary.
GetBitmapBits	Retrieves the pixels from a specified bitmap. This function is similar to GetDIBits. It is present in Win32 for compatibility with older Win16 that is being ported, but it is considered obsolete. You shouldn't use it for any new code.
GetBitmapDimensionEx	Retrieves the height and width of a bitmap by updating a SIZE structure.
GetDIBits	Retrieves the pixels from a specified bitmap. This function is similar to GetBitmapBits, which it replaces in Win32 applications. It can also be used to retrieve bitmap dimensions.
GetPixel	Gets the RGB color value for a pixel.

Table 6.8: Functions that operate on bitmaps

Function	Description
LoadBitmap	Loads a bitmap from a resource file.
PatBlt	Sets the pixels of a bitmap to a pattern.
MaskBlt	Combines the color data for the source and destination using a bitmap mask and a pair of raster operations.
PlgBlt	Transfers a block of bits, optionally masking color bits, to a region delimited by a parallelogram. The mask is specified by a monochrome bitmap.
SetBitmapBits	Sets the pixels of a memory bitmap. This function is similar to SetDIBits. It is present in Win32 for compatibility with older Win16 code that is being ported, but it is considered obsolete.
SetBitmapDimensionEx	Sets the height and width of a bitmap and, optionally, updates a SIZE structure with the previous height and width.
SetDIBits	Sets the pixels of a memory bitmap directly from a DIB.
SetDIBitsToDevice	Draws on a device surface directly from a DIB.
SetPixel	Sets a pixel to the specified COLORREF color or to the nearest matching color. Returns the actual color.
SetPixelV	Sets a pixel to the specified COLORREF color or to the nearest matching color.
StretchBlt	Copies a rectangular area from a source device context to a destination device context. The source bitmap is stretched or compressed, if necessary.
StretchDIBits	Copies a rectangular area of a DIB to a different rectangular area on the device associated with the destination device context. The source bitmap is stretched or compressed, if necessary.

Creating a Bitmap

You create a bitmap by specifying the bitmap's width, height, and color format and, optionally, the initial value of the pixels. The phrase "create a bitmap" actually means "create a device-specific bitmap." The device-specific bitmap can be created from either device-dependent data or device-independent data.

When you create a device-specific bitmap, GDI actually allocates space for the bitmap and, if the bitmap is initialized, copies the initial values for the pixels to the bitmap. You receive a handle to the bitmap of type HBITMAP. You do not have direct access to the memory containing the pixels of the bitmap. A device-specific bitmap is a GDI object. GDI objects are automatically released when an application terminates. But it is generally cleaner to delete all bitmaps you create. In particular, because bitmaps can be quite large, if you fail to release them early your application will gradually consume more and more memory and bog down the system. As always, you must not delete a bitmap while it is currently selected into a memory device context.

There are several ways to create a bitmap:

1. Use external bitmap files. These files are created by a program such as the Paint application included with Microsoft Windows or by a tool such as the bitmap resource editor, which is part of most development environments (such as the Visual C++ Workbench).

    *   You can add these external bitmap files to your program's resources by including them in your resource script (.rc file) and the *resource compiler* will copy them into your resource segment. You can then use the LoadBitmap or LoadImage function to load the bitmap resource and obtain a handle to it.

    *   You can open the bitmap file directly, read its bits into memory, and copy them to a blank bitmap (see the next section).

2. Create a blank bitmap and draw the appropriate pattern on it using any GDI drawing functions such as TextOut, LineTo, and Polygon.

3. Create a blank bitmap and initialize its pixels to the image given by an array of bits.

4. Create a blank bitmap and initialize its pixels by copying the image from a DIB. A device-independent bitmap is a DIB specification with an accompanying array of pixel values specifying the bitmap image. This can be a collection of bits you read in from a file.

Each of these ways to create a bitmap are discussed next.

Creating a Bitmap Resource from a Bitmap File

The easiest way to create a bitmap file is to use a program such as the Windows Paint program. The Paint program can produce either monochrome or color DIB (.bmp) files. Many development environments, such as Microsoft's Visual C++ environment, have bitmap editors as well, and you can use any commercial program, including photo processing programs, that can produce a DIB file.

You also can create your own bitmap file. A bitmap file is a file containing binary data that consists of three sections. The file begins with a BITMAPFILEHEADER structure, which looks like the following:

```
typedef struct tagBITMAPFILEHEADER {
        WORD    bfType;
        DWORD   bfSize;
        WORD    bfReserved1;
        WORD    bfReserved2;
        DWORD   bfOffBits;
} BITMAPFILEHEADER;
```

The bfType field identifies the file as a DIB file. It must have the value "BM" (for *BitMap*, of course). Remember that multibyte integer values are stored in byte-swapped order on Intel processors. You must swap the bytes in an assignment so that they will be in the correct order in memory:

```
BITMAPFILEHEADER bmfh ;

bmfh.bfType = 0x4D42 ;    /* "MB" is swapped to "BM" in memory. */
```

The bfSize field specifies the size of the file in DWORDs. Both the bfReserved1 and bfReserved2 fields are reserved and must be set to 0. The bfOffBits field specifies the offset (in bytes) from the BITMAPFILEHEADER to the actual bitmap in the file.

Either a BITMAPINFO structure or a BITMAPCOREINFO structure must immediately follow the BITMAPFILEHEADER structure in the DIB file.

 A BITMAPCOREINFO structure defines the dimensions of the bitmap and the colors used in an OS/2 Presentation Manager version 1.x DIB. If you are running in an environment in which OS/2 is used or in which you might be importing OS/2 files, you need to be prepared to handle one of these. Windows can use either Windows DIBs or Presentation Manager DIBs. You can tell the difference between the two by the value of the first field in each structure. Because we're talking about Windows, we discuss only the Windows BITMAPINFO structure.

A BITMAPINFO structure defines the dimensions and color of a Windows DIB. It has the following definition:

```
typedef struct tagBITMAPINFO {
    BITMAPINFOHEADER bmiHeader;
    RGBQUAD          bmiColors[1];
} BITMAPINFO;
```

The bmiHeader field specifies a BITMAPINFOHEADER structure that contains information about the dimensions and color format of a DIB. The bmiColors field specifies an array of RGBQUAD data structures that define the colors in the bitmap. A BITMAPINFOHEADER has the following fields:

```
typedef struct tagBITMAPINFOHEADER{
    DWORD  biSize;
    LONG   biWidth;
    LONG   biHeight;
    WORD   biPlanes;
    WORD   biBitCount;
    DWORD  biCompression;
    DWORD  biSizeImage;
    LONG   biXPelsPerMeter;
    LONG   biYPelsPerMeter;
    DWORD  biClrUsed;
    DWORD  biClrImportant;
} BITMAPINFOHEADER;
```

The fields of a BITMAPINFOHEADER are described in Table 6.9.

Table 6.9: The fields of a BITMAPINFOHEADER structure

Field	Description
biSize	Size of a BITMAPINFOHEADER structure, in bytes.
biWidth	Width of the bitmap, in pixels.
biHeight	Height of the bitmap, in pixels.
biPlanes	Number of planes for the target device. Must be 1.
biBitCount	Number of bits per pixel. Must be 1, 4, 8, or 24.

Table 6.9: The fields of a BITMAPINFOHEADER structure

Field	Description	
biCompression	Type of compression for a compressed bitmap. It can be one of the following values:	
	BI_RGB	Bitmap is not compressed.
	BI_RLE8	Bitmap is run-length encoded and has 8 bits per pixel.
	BI_RLE4	Bitmap is run-length encoded and has 4 bits per pixel.
biSizeImage	Size of the image in bytes.	
biXPelsPerMeter	Horizontal resolution in pixels per meter of the target device for the bitmap. This is a suggested figure. You can use this number to locate a bitmap that best matches the device on which it will be used.	
biYPelsPerMeter	Vertical resolution in pixels per meter of the target device for the bitmap. This is a suggested figure. You can use this number to locate a bitmap that best matches the device on which it will be used.	
biClrUsed	Number of color indices in the color table actually used by the bitmap. When 0, the bitmap uses all the possible 2biBitCount color indices.	
biClrImportant	Number of color indices in the color table that hold colors important when displaying the bitmap. When 0, all colors are important.	

The biSizeImage, biXPelsPerMeter, and biYPelsPerMeter are advisory. Many applications, for example, set all three fields to 0 and may even also set biClrUsed and biClrImportant to 0.

The bmiColors field, which is an array of RGBQUAD structures, immediately follows the BITMAPINFOHEADER structure. Each element of the bmiColors array defines the color of a pixel whose value equals the index of the element. That is, the element bmiColors[0] contains the color for pixel values of 0, bmiColors[1] contains the color for pixel values of 1, and so on. You should arrange colors in the array in descending order of importance. When a DIB is converted to a device-specific bitmap for a device that supports fewer colors than are used in the DIB, Windows uses the colors listed at the beginning of the array. Pixels using later, unsupported colors are displayed in the nearest matching color.

The bmiColors array is defined to have one entry in order to establish the location of the beginning of the array. You must, however, provide room for one entry for each possible color. When the biBitCount field of the BITMAPINFOHEADER structure is set to 1, the bitmap is a monochrome bitmap, so the bmiColors field must contain two entries. (Have you ever noticed that monochrome really should be called bichrome?) Each bit in the bitmap represents a pixel and may be clear (0) or set (1). When the bit is clear, the pixel has the color of the first entry in the bmiColors array; when the bit is set, the pixel has the color of the second entry in the bmiColors array. Notice that a monochrome bitmap is not restricted to simply black and white, but can have any two colors: the color in bmiColors[0] and the color in bmiColors[1].

When the `biBitCount` field of the `BITMAPINFOHEADER` structure is set to 4, the bitmap contains pixels, each of which can have one of 16 colors. Therefore, the `bmiColors` field can contain up to 16 entries. You need to allocate room only for the number of entries used by pixel values in the bitmap. For example, when you use only 12 different pixel values, set the `biClrUsed` parameter to 12 and allocate only 12 entries in the `bmiColors` array.

When the `biBitCount` field of the `BITMAPINFOHEADER` structure is set to 8, the bitmap contains pixels, each of which can have one of 256 colors. Therefore, the `bmiColors` field can contain up to 256 entries. As before, you need to allocate space only for the entries actually used.

When the `biBitCount` field of the `BITMAPINFOHEADER` structure is set to 24, the bitmap contains pixels, each of which can have one of 16,777,216 colors. In this case, the `bmiColors` field is not used. The 24 bits for each pixel directly encode the red, green, and blue intensities.

Normally, you specify the colors in the `bmiColors` array as red, green, and blue intensities, each ranging from 0 to 255. Each `RGBQUAD` array element looks like the following. The `rgbReserved` field must be set to 0.

```
typedef struct tagRGBQUAD {
    BYTE     rgbBlue;
    BYTE     rgbGreen;
    BYTE     rgbRed;
    BYTE     rgbReserved;
} RGBQUAD;
```

A DIB uses a different coordinate system than a device-specific bitmap. A DIB uses a Cartesian first-quadrant coordinate system. The origin of the bitmap is the lower-left corner of the bitmap. Horizontal pixel coordinates increase from left to right and vertical pixel coordinates increase from bottom to top.

A device-specific bitmap uses device coordinates. So its origin is the upper-left corner of the bitmap. Horizontal coordinates increase the same direction as a DIB (left to right), but vertical coordinates increase in the opposite direction (top to bottom rather than bottom to top).

However, you also can allocate the `bmiColors` array as an array of `WORD`s rather than `RGBQUAD` structures. Each `WORD` entry represents an index into the currently selected and realized logical palette. When you use this format to specify the colors for a DIB, you must call the DIB functions with the `Usage` parameter set to `DIB_PAL_COLORS`. Typically, you don't use this format for a DIB stored in a file because the color palette may not have the proper colors when the DIB is next used.

The actual bitmap follows the `BITMAPINFO` structure. It does not have to be immediately contiguous because the location of the bitmap is specified by the `bfOffBits` parameter of the `BITMAPFILEHEADER` structure. The bits for each pixel are packed together.

The bitmap begins with the bottom row of pixels and at the left side. Each row must be a multiple of 4 bytes in length. The first pixel in a row of a monochrome bitmap is encoded in the most-significant bit of the first byte in the row. The first pixel in a row of a 16-color bitmap is encoded in the most-significant 4 bits of the first byte in the row. The first pixel in a row of a 256-color bitmap is encoded in all 8 bits of the first byte in the row (each pixel occupies 1 byte in this case). Twenty-four bits-per-pixel bitmaps use groups of 3 bytes for each pixel. The 3 bytes contain the red, green, and blue intensity values for the pixel.

As soon as you have a file containing a bitmap, you can add a BITMAP resource statement to your application's resource script (.rc) file. You usually do this via whatever environment tool you are using. For example, in Visual C++ the act of creating a bitmap in the resource editor will include a reference to it in the resource script. If the bitmap was created by some external program, you need to generate a reference to it. The BITMAP statement associates a character-string identifier or an integer with the bitmap contained in the file. The resource compiler copies the bitmap from the bitmap file (typically, such a file uses the .bmp extension) into the compiled resource (.res) file. As the program is linked, the linker inserts the compiled resources into the executable (.exe) program file.

For example, suppose you've drawn a custom brush pattern using a bitmap editor application and saved it in a file called mybrush.bmp. If you use the built-in bitmap editor of your environment, the BITMAP statement will usually be inserted for you. If you import the file into your resource set, your environment tool will also add the BITMAP statement so that in your application's resource script file, you will find a BITMAP statement of the following form:

```
resID BITMAP filename
```

The resID field specifies either an integer value or a unique character string that identifies the resource. You use this value in your program to reference the bitmap. In the example proposed, let's use the following statement:

```
RoughTexture BITMAP mybrush.bmp
```

Be aware, however, that in looking at this statement you can't tell how to access the resource. For example, most environment tools will also create a definition

```
#define RoughTexture 17
```

so the effect is as if you had the resource:

```
17 BITMAP MYBRUSH.BMP
```

It is particularly important to understand how your environment resource tool handles this when you are creating a bitmap resource from an externally-created bitmap. If it creates a #define, you will need to use MAKEINTRESOURCE when you want to name the resource; if it doesn't create a #define, you will use the string name of the resource.

When you want to create a brush based on this pattern, you use the LoadBitmap or LoadImage function to load the bitmap from the executable file. You pass the function the instance handle of the module containing the desired bitmap and a parameter identifying the desired bitmap within that module. The function returns a handle to the created device-specific memory bitmap. In this example, you can load the bitmap one of two ways, depending on how you identified the bitmap on the BITMAP statement in the resource script file. You can load it either by name:

```
hbitmap = LoadBitmap (hInstance, _T("RoughTexture")) ;
```

or by integer identifier:

```
hbitmap = LoadBitmap (hInstance, MAKEINTRESOURCE (RoughTexture)) ;
```

It is critical that you use the correct form; the two are *not* interchangeable. Note that since you can't tell by looking at your .rc file which is the correct form, you have to either rely on your environment tool or read the appropriate .h file to determine which form to use. For example, in Visual C++, if you get a list of bitmaps or are displaying the bitmap in question, it will display the name as "RoughTexture" (quotes included) if you must use the string form and as RoughTexture (no quotes) if you must use the MAKEINTRESOURCE form. We point this out because it is a frequent source of problems, particularly for people either learning Windows for the first time or those moving to an integrated development environment such as those supported by Borland or Microsoft. The Visual C++ environment, if you are creating the bitmap with its built-in bitmap editor, will actually assign a name and create the #define. (It usually suggests a name starting with IDB_, a convention you may wish to maintain.) So you will find the following declarations in your files:

```
#define IDB_RoughTexture 17   // this is in RESOURCE.H

IDB_RoughTexture BITMAP filename // this is in your resource file
```

The LoadBitmap function will not load bitmaps using 256-color palettes. This is because Windows treats bitmaps loaded via LoadBitmap as 16-color bitmaps. To load bitmaps with higher resolution, you need to use the more general LoadResource call and extract the color information.

Once you have successfully done a LoadBitMap, you can then use the handle to the bitmap to create a logical brush that has that pattern by calling the CreatePatternBrush function:

```
hbrush = CreatePatternBrush (hbitmap) ;
```

Then you use this brush the way you use the others we've discussed. You select it into a device context, draw the filled object(s), select the default brush (or a stock brush) back into device context, and, finally, delete the brush and the bitmap:

```
hbrush = CreatePatternBrush (hbitmap) ;
DeleteBitmap (hbitmap) ;
SelectBrush (hdc, hbrush) ;
Rectangle (hdc, xUL, yUL, xLR, yLR) ;
SelectBrush (hdc, GetStockBrush (WHITE_BRUSH)) ;
DeleteBrush (brush) ;
```

As shown in this example, the bitmap can be deleted any time after you've used it to create the brush. You don't have to wait until the brush is deleted to delete the bitmap on which it's based.

Bitmaps are used for more than just brush patterns. An entire bitmap can be copied to a device surface as a complex picture or a large pattern, although somewhat indirectly. You create a compatible memory device context for the destination device, select the bitmap into the memory device context, and then copy the bitmap from the memory device context to the destination device context:

```
BITMAP bm ;

GetObject (hbitmap, sizeof (bm), (LPSTR) &bm) ;
```

```
hMemoryDC = CreateCompatibleDC (hdc, bm.bmWidth, bm.bmHeight) ;
SelectBitmap (hMemoryDC, hbitmap) ;
BitBlt (hdc, 0, 0, bm.bmWidth, bm.bmHeight,
        hMemoryDC, 0, 0, SRCCOPY) ;
```

Creating and Drawing into a Blank Bitmap

Complex images may take quite a bit of work to create by hand. You may find it easier to create an uninitialized bitmap and use the drawing functions of the GDI to draw the bitmap you want. First, create the uninitialized bitmap by calling either the `CreateBitmap`, `CreateBitmapIndirect`, `CreateCompatibleBitmap`, or `CreateDIBitmap` functions. The functions look like the following:

```
HBITMAP CreateBitmap (int Width, int Height,
                      UINT Planes, UINT BitCount,
                      CONST VOID * lpBits) ;
HBITMAP CreateBitmapIndirect (CONST BITMAP * Bitmap) ;
HBITMAP CreateCompatibleBitmap (HDC hdc, int Width, int Height) ;
HBITMAP CreateDIBitmap (HDC hdc, CONST BITMAPINFOHEADER * lpInfoHeader,
                        DWORD Usage,
                        CONST VOID * lpInitBits,
                        CONST BITMAPINFO * lpInitInfo,
                        UINT Usage) ;
```

Those who know the Win16 API may notice that `CreateDiscardableBitmap` is missing from this set. This is because the concept of "discardable" storage was part of the Win16 memory management. Although the API call is retained in Win32, it is obsolete there and turns into a `CreateCompatibleBitmap` call.

Because all these functions return a device-specific bitmap, they must be provided with the format used by the device to represent colors and pixels. You specify this information explicitly when calling the `CreateBitmap` function. For a monochrome bitmap, this task is easy: Set both the `Planes` and `BitCount` parameters to 1. Setting the `lpBits` parameter to `NULL` specifies that the bitmap should not be initialized. A monochrome 8 × 8 uninitialized bitmap used for a brush pattern can be created by the following:

```
hbitmap = CreateBitmap (8, 8, 1, 1, NULL) ;
```

The same approach can be used when calling the `CreateBitmapIndirect` function, but the information is passed via the fields of the `BITMAP` structure that is passed as the function parameter.

It's a bit more difficult to create a color bitmap using these two functions and still ensure that the bitmap is compatible with the desired device. You must get the device capabilities using the `GetDeviceCaps` function and create the bitmap accordingly. However, you can let Windows do the work by using either the `CreateCompatibleBitmap` or `CreateDIBitmap` functions.

You provide the handle of a device context to all three functions. Windows uses the handle to create a bitmap that has the same number of color planes and bits per pixel as the specified device.

The `CreateCompatibleBitmap` function is the function used most often to create an uninitialized color bitmap. It doesn't accept a parameter that specifies initialization data for the bitmap, and it creates the bitmap compatible with the specified device so that you don't have to worry about color planes and bits per pixel.

The `CreateDIBitmap` function also can be used to create an uninitialized bitmap, although it's much more useful when creating an initialized color bitmap, as you'll see later in the chapter. The following statements use the `CreateDIBitmap` function to create an uninitialized bitmap:

```
BITMAPINFOHEADER bmih ;

/* Initialize the BITMAPINFOHEADER here. */
hbitmap = CreateDIBitmap (hdc, &bmih, 0, NULL, NULL, 0) ;
```

After you have the handle to a device-specific bitmap, you can select it into a compatible memory device context using the `SelectBitmap` macro API function. Similar to the others you've seen, Windows defines it in windowsx.h this way:

```
#define SelectBitmap(hdc, hbm) \
    ((HBITMAP)SelectObject((hdc), (HGDIOBJ)(HBITMAP)(hbm)))
```

You can use the `SelectBitmap` macro in place of the `SelectObject` function to make your code more understandable:

```
SelectBitmap (hMemoryDC, hbitmap) ;
```

You can retrieve the current bitmap by using the `GetCurrentObject` function:

```
HBITMAP bm = (HBITMAP)GetCurrentObject(hdc, OBJ_BITMAP);
```

All drawing functions issued on the memory device context now draw on the newly created bitmap. It's important to note that uninitialized bitmaps are just that–completely uninitialized. In particular, the pixels in the bitmap aren't cleared to any value: 0, 1, white, or black. You'll probably want to start by clearing the entire bitmap to a known color. This is easiest done by using the `PatBlt` function. "PatBlt" stands for "*Pat*tern *Block t*ransfer". The function call looks like this:

```
PatBlt (hdc, X, Y, Width, Height, Rop) ;
```

The `PatBlt` function creates a pattern on the specified device that is based on the selected brush and the pixels already on the device. When the specified device context refers to a memory device context, the pattern is applied to the selected bitmap. This function does not use a bounding rectangle to specify the area. Instead, the X and Y parameters specify one corner (in logical coordinates) of the rectangle that is to receive the pattern. The `Width` and `Height` parameters specify the width and height of the rectangle in logical units. Therefore the corner of the rectangle opposite the point (X, Y) is the point (X + `Width`, Y + `Height`).

The coordinates of any corner of the desired rectangle can be given as the X and Y parameters. The `Width` and `Height` parameters can be positive or negative. These all are logical values, and the mapping mode specifies the orientation of the axes. Therefore the upper-left corner of the rectangle can be at the point (X, Y) or (X + `Width`, Y) or (X, Y + `Height`) or (X + `Width`, Y + `Height`).

GDI determines the upper-left corner of the rectangle and copies the pattern to it. Like the area functions previously described, the top and left sides of the rectangle are included in the modified area. The right and bottom sides of the rectangle are outside the modified area.

GDI combines the colors of the pixels in the selected brush with the colors already present on the device according to a raster operation code that is similar, but not identical, to the raster operation code used when drawing lines. In general, raster operation codes describe the operation that should be applied to a source operand, a brush, and a destination operand. However, the Rop parameter to the PatBlt function cannot be an operation code that refers to a source operand. The valid operation codes for the PatBlt function that have common names are listed in Table 6.10. Any raster operation code that doesn't refer to a source operand, but only to a pattern and destination operand, can be used as the raster operation code for the PatBlt function. You must specify the ones that are not listed in Table 6.10 numerically.[4] The hexadecimal values for all 16 PatBlt raster operation codes are give in Table 6.11.

Table 6.10: Raster operation codes for the PatBlt function

ROP Code	Result
PATCOPY	Copies the brush to the destination bitmap.
PATINVERT	Combines the brush and the destination bitmap using the Boolean Exclusive OR (XOR) operation.
DSTINVERT	Ignores the brush and inverts the destination bitmap using the Boolean bitwise NOT operation.
BLACKNESS	Ignores the brush and sets the destination bitmap to all bits 0. This sets the bitmap to all-black. (Technically, a pixel value of 0 doesn't necessarily mean black.)
WHITENESS	Ignores the brush and sets the destination bitmap to all bits 1. This sets the bitmap to all-white. (Technically, a pixel value with all bits set to 1 doesn't necessarily mean white.)

Table 6.11: The Boolean operations performed by the raster operation codes usable by the PatBlt function

| | Pattern(P) | 1 | 1 | 0 | 0 | | | |
| | Dest(D) | 1 | 0 | 1 | 0 | | | |
Name						Decimal Result	Boolean Operation	ROP Code
BLACKNESS		0	0	0	0	0	D = 0	0x000042
—		0	0	0	1	1	D = ~(P | D)	0x0500A9
—		0	0	1	0	2	D = ~P & D	0x0A0329
—		0	0	1	1	3	D = ~P	0x0F0001
—		0	1	0	0	4	D = P & ~D	0x500325

[4] You can also use the header file we provide, extrops.h, which defines the extended ROP codes. It uses the notation of Appendix A; for example, the code for "PDna" is 0x00500325 and is declared as the symbol "extrop_PDna". We use this file in the GDI Explorer.

Table 6.11: The Boolean operations performed by the raster operation codes usable by the `PatBlt` function

Name	Pattern(P) 1	1	0	0	Decimal Result	Boolean Operation	ROP Code
	Dest(D) 1	0	1	0			
DSTINVERT	0	1	0	1	5	D = ~D	0x550009
PATINVERT	0	1	1	0	6	D = P ∧ D	0x5A0049
—	0	1	1	1	7	D = ~(P & D)	0x5F00E9
—	1	0	0	0	8	D = P & D	0xA000C9
—	1	0	0	1	9	D = ~(P ∧ D)	0xA50065
—	1	0	1	0	10	D = D	0xAA0029
—	1	0	1	1	11	D = ~P | D	0xAF0229
PATCOPY	1	1	0	0	12	D = P	0xF00021
—	1	1	0	1	13	D = P | ~D	0xF50225
—	1	1	1	0	14	D = P | D	0xFA0089
WHITENESS	1	1	1	1	15	D = 1	0xFF0062

Finally, to stress the point again, bitmaps are GDI objects. You should delete them as soon as they are no longer needed, ideally before your application terminates.

Next we look at an example. We create an uninitialized 16×32-pixel bitmap compatible with the display device, clear it to all-black, and draw a green X from corner to corner. The following code assumes that a common display context is retrieved by the GetDC function–particularly, that the MM_TEXT mapping mode is in effect:

```
HDC             hdc ;
HDC             hMemoryDC ;
HBITMAP         hbitmap ;
HBITMAP         hbitmapOrig ;
HPEN            hpen ;
HPEN            hpenOrig ;

hdc = GetDC (hwnd) ;
hMemoryDC = CreateCompatibleDC (hdc) ;
hbitmap = CreateCompatibleBitmap (hdc, 16, 32) ;
ReleaseDC (hwnd, hdc) ;

hbitmapOrig = SelectBitmap (hMemoryDC, hbitmap) ;
```

```
PatBlt (hMemoryDC, 0, 0, 16, 32, BLACKNESS) ;
hpen = CreatePen (PS_SOLID, 0, RGB (0, 255, 0)) ;
hpenOrig = SelectPen (hMemoryDC, hpen) ;
LineTo (hMemoryDC, 16, 32) ;
MoveToEx (hMemoryDC, 16, 0, NULL) ;
LineTo (hMemoryDC, 0, 32) ;
SelectBitmap (hMemoryDC, hbitmapOrig) ;
SelectPen (hMemoryDC, hpenOrig) ;
DeletePen (hpen) ;
DeleteDC (hMemoryDC) ;

/* Now you have the desired bitmap. */
/* When you no longer need the bitmap, delete it. */

DeleteBitmap (hbitmap) ;
```

Creating an Initialized Bitmap

Three functions can create an initialized bitmap: `CreateBitmap`, `CreateBitmapIndirect`, and `CreateDIBitmap`. The `CreateBitmap` and `CreateBitmapIndirect` functions are best for creating monochrome bitmaps. As described in the previous section, when creating a color bitmap using these functions, you must provide explicit information about the number of color planes and bits per pixel for the bitmap. This task is tedious and very device-dependent.

The `CreateDIBitmap` function enables you to specify the initial values of a color bitmap in a device-independent manner. A DIB specification is used to convert the DIB to a device-specific bitmap.

First we'll discuss creating initialized device-dependent bitmaps, and then we'll look at creating color bitmaps using DIB specifications. Let's create an initialized monochrome bitmap similar to the X described above. Because we lack green, we'll make it a white X on a black 32 × 32-pixel background. The `CreateBitmap` function call will look like the following:

```
BYTE Bits [] =  {  0x80, 0x00, 0x00, 0x01,   0x40, 0x00, 0x00, 0x02,
                   0x20, 0x00, 0x00, 0x04,   0x10, 0x00, 0x00, 0x08,
                   0x08, 0x00, 0x00, 0x10,   0x04, 0x00, 0x00, 0x20,
                   0x02, 0x00, 0x00, 0x40,   0x01, 0x00, 0x00, 0x80,
                   0x00, 0x80, 0x01, 0x00,   0x00, 0x40, 0x02, 0x00,
                   0x00, 0x20, 0x04, 0x00,   0x00, 0x10, 0x08, 0x00,
                   0x00, 0x08, 0x10, 0x00,   0x00, 0x04, 0x20, 0x00,
                   0x00, 0x02, 0x40, 0x00,   0x00, 0x01, 0x80, 0x00,
                   0x00, 0x01, 0x80, 0x00,   0x00, 0x02, 0x40, 0x00,
                   0x00, 0x04, 0x20, 0x00,   0x00, 0x08, 0x10, 0x00,
                   0x00, 0x10, 0x08, 0x00,   0x00, 0x20, 0x04, 0x00,
                   0x00, 0x40, 0x02, 0x00,   0x00, 0x80, 0x01, 0x00,
                   0x01, 0x00, 0x00, 0x80,   0x02, 0x00, 0x00, 0x40,
                   0x04, 0x00, 0x00, 0x20,   0x08, 0x00, 0x00, 0x10,
                   0x10, 0x00, 0x00, 0x08,   0x20, 0x00, 0x00, 0x04,
                   0x40, 0x00, 0x00, 0x02,   0x80, 0x00, 0x00, 0x01 } ;

hbitmap = CreateBitmap (32, 32, 1, 1, Bits) ;
```

A couple of points aren't apparent from this example. Each scan line in the bitmap must be an even number of bytes long. Notice that this is different from a DIB. Each scan line in a DIB must be a multiple of 4 bytes in length. GDI assumes that a bitmap passed to the `CreateBitmap` function is composed of an array of short integer values. Scan lines are organized in a device-specific bitmap with the top line (line 0) at the beginning of the array, line 1 immediately following it, proceeding sequentially up to line `Height-1`. This, too, differs from a DIB. In a DIB, the bottom scan line comes first in the array, followed by the next line up, and so on. One bit represent white and 0 bits represent black. The left-most bit of a scan line is in the most significant bit of the first byte of data for the row.

You can set the bits of an already-created bitmap with the `SetBitmapBits` function. In this example, `hbitmap` is the handle of the bitmap whose bits you want to set and `Count` is a DWORD containing the number of bytes in the array pointed to by the `lpBits` parameter:

```
SetBitmapBits (hbitmap, Count, lpBits) ;
```

To set the X in a bitmap, we could do

```
SetBitmapBits (hbitmap, sizeof (Bits), Bits) ;
```

We mentioned that each scan line of a device-specific bitmap must be an even number of bytes in length. Redefining the `Bits` array as an array of WORDs to ensure this necessity produces its own problems. For example, this bitmap isn't the same as the preceding one:

```
WORD Bits [] =  {  0x8000, 0x0001,
                   0x4000, 0x0002,
                   0x2000, 0x0004,
                   0x1000, 0x0008,
  .
  .
  .
```

The reason is that WORDs are stored in byte-swapped order on Intel processors. That is, the WORD 0x8000 is stored in memory as 0x00 followed by 0x80 in the next-higher memory location. We could, of course, swap the bytes in the definition of the constants (0x8000 to 0x0080), but then the pattern of the bitmap would become less obvious to those maintaining the source code.

You can use the `CreateBitmapIndirect` function to create the same bitmap with the following code. Notice the distinction between a BITMAP structure and an HBITMAP handle:

```
BITMAP   bm ;
HBITMAP hbitmap ;

bm.bmType = 0 ;
bm.bmWidth = 32 ;
bm.bmHeight = 32 ;
bm.bmWidthBytes = 4 ;
bm.bmPlanes = 1 ;
bm.bmBitsPixel = 1 ;
bm.bmBits = (LPVOID) Bits ;
hbitmap = CreateBitmapIndirect (&bm) ;
```

A BITMAP is essentially a memory-based structure that contains some state information and a reference to the bits of the bitmap. However, Windows itself does not actually process this structure. Instead, it requires a copy of the bitmap description and the contents, which is under its own control, and this copy is referenced by a bitmap handle, whose type is HBITMAP. Until you have converted a bitmap to a GDI object, Windows cannot do anything with it. Much of this is due to the original design of Windows for the 8088, in which memory management of the "virtual" memory was so critical. So, while Win32, in principle, *should* be able to reference a bitmap directly through the BITMAP structure, it in fact retains the same API and requires a bit-map handle.

Creating an Initialized Bitmap from a DIB

You can also use the CreateDIBitmap function to create the same monochrome bitmap. The CreateDIBitmap function creates a device-specific bitmap and initializes it with the image contained in a DIB. You must fill out a DIB specification to describe the size of the bitmap, the format of the image in the DIB, and the colors to use for pixel values. You can create the monochrome bitmap with the following code:

```
struct tagMonoDIBSpec {
    BITMAPINFOHEADER ih;
    RGBQUAD              Colors [2];
} mdib ;

mdib.ih.biSize = sizeof (mdib.ih) ;
mdib.ih.biWidth = 32 ;
mdib.ih.biHeight = 32 ;
mdib.ih.biPlanes = 1 ;
mdib.ih.biBitCount = 1 ;
mdib.ih.biCompression = 0 ;
mdib.ih.biSizeImage = 0 ;
mdib.ih.biXPelsPerMeter = 0 ;
mdib.ih.biYPelsPerMeter = 0 ;
mdib.ih.biClrUsed = 0;
mdib.ih.biClrImportant = 0 ;
mdib.Colors [0].rgbRed = 0 ;        // Black (0, 0, 0)
mdib.Colors [0].rgbGreen = 0 ;
mdib.Colors [0].rgbBlue = 0 ;
mdib.Colors [1].rgbRed = 0xFF ;     // White (255, 255, 255)
mdib.Colors [1].rgbGreen = 0xFF ;
mdib.Colors [1].rgbBlue = 0xFF ;

hdc = GetDC (hwnd) ;
hbitmap = CreateDIBitmap (hdc,
                          (LPBITMAPINFOHEADER) &mdib.ih,
                          CBM_INIT,
                          (LPVOID) Bits,
                          (LPBITMAPINFO) &mdib,
                          DIB_RGB_COLORS) ;
ReleaseDC (hwnd, hdc) ;
```

This last example requires some explanation. The BITMAPINFO structure mdib.ih specifies how the array of bits Bits is interpreted. It defines the array as a 32 × 32-pixel array with each pixel being represented by 1 bit. One-bit pixels require two colors, so there are only two RGBQUAD entries. Each RGBQUAD entry contains the red, green, and blue intensities for a given pixel value. One advantage of this method is that you can change the bitmap to a green cross on a black background (like the one we created by drawing it) by simply changing the element in mdib.Colors[1] to green.

The process works as follows. Windows retrieves a number of bits from the `Bits` array based on the described bit planes and bits-per-pixel. It uses this pixel value to index into the RGBQUAD array, retrieving the color of the pixel in term of red, green, and blue intensities. This RGB color value is then converted to the device-specific pixel value that produces the equivalent color on the specified device. This process is a lot of work for a monochrome bitmap, but it is invaluable when dealing with color bitmaps.

We also cheated a little in the preceding example. The origin of a device-specific bitmap is the upper-left corner of the bitmap. The origin of a device-independent bitmap is the lower-left corner. This means you need to define the array of bytes starting with the bottom row of pixels rather than the top row when creating a device-independent bitmap. We used a symmetrical figure so that we didn't have to account for that difference. You also can define the bitmap data for a device-independent bitmap in a run-length-encoded (RLE) form to save space.

You also can use the `SetDIBits` function to copy a device-independent bitmap into a bitmap of your choice. It looks like this:

```
int SetDIBits (HDC hdc, HBITMAP hbitmap, UINT StartScan, UINT NumScans,
               CONST VOID * lpBits,
               CONST BITMAPINFO * lpBitsInfo,
               UINT ColorUsage) ;
```

The parameter `StartScan` specifies the scan line number of the first row of pixels in the device-independent bitmap pointed to by `lpBits`. The `NumScans` parameter specifies how many scan lines are in the `lpBits` buffer. All `NumScans` scan lines are copied from the device-independent bitmap, converted to device-specific pixel values as described before, and stored into the bitmap identified by `hbitmap`. The `lpBitsInfo` parameter points to a `BITMAPINFO` structure that defines the format of the bits in the device-independent bitmap. The `ColorUsage` parameter specifies whether the colors in the RGBQUAD array entries are literal RGB values (as we used before) or 16-bit indices into the current realized logical palette.

Similarly, you can retrieve the pixels from a device-specific bitmap, convert them to a specified device-independent representation, and store the device-independent bitmap into a specified buffer. This is the purpose of the `GetDIBits` function:

```
int GetDIBits (HDC hdc, HBITMAP hbitmap,
               UINT StartScan, UINT NumScans,
               LPVOID * lpBits,
               LPBITMAPINFO lpBitsInfo,
               UINT ColorUsage) ;
```

There is another use of `GetDIBits`, which is obtaining the parameters of a bitmap given its handle. This is particularly useful for obtaining the dimensions of a bitmap loaded with the `LoadBitmap` function. This is discussed on page 336.

You can skip a step and write a DIB directly to the surface of a device using the `SetDIBitsToDevice` function. There is no function to copy a device-specific bitmap directly to a device surface. A device-specific bitmap must be selected into a compatible memory device context, and then the `BitBlt` function can copy all or part of the memory device context surface to the device surface. The `SetDIBitsToDevice` function looks like this:

```
int SetDIBitsToDevice (HDC hdc, int xDest, int yDest,
                       DWORD Width, DWORD Height,
                       int xSrc,  int ySrc,
                       UINT StartScan, UINT NumScans,
                       CONST VOID * lpBits,
                       CONST BITMAPINFO lpBitsInfo,
                       UINT ColorUsage) ;
```

The `hdc` parameter identifies the destination device. The `xSrc`, `ySrc`, `Width`, and `Height` parameters describe a rectangular area in the source DIB. The `xSrc` and `ySrc` parameters are in device coordinates; `Width` and `Height` are in device units. Windows translates the device-independent pixel values to the appropriate device-dependent pixel values and copies the source rectangle to the destination-device surface. The rectangle is placed on the device surface at the logical coordinates (`xDest`, `yDest`).

DIBs can be very large. You can reduce the amount of memory they require by keeping only a portion of the bitmap in memory at any given time. The `StartScan` and `NumScans` parameters identify the portion of the DIB that is currently in memory. The `StartScan` parameter identifies the number of the scan line located at the beginning of the bitmap in memory, that is, the scan line number of the first row of pixels pointed to by the `lpBits` parameter. The `NumScans` parameter specifies how many scan lines are in memory. To write a large bitmap to a device surface a small section at a time, you can repeatedly load a portion of a DIB into memory and call the `SetDIBitsToDevice` function with the `StartScan` and `NumScans` parameters set appropriately.

In Win16, it was sometimes necessary to use these techniques because it was not always possible to fit in memory at once all of a DIB or several DIBs requiring simultaneous access. In Win32, this is a far less important issue because the underlying paging system can handle the swapping. However, for *very* large images you might find yourself straining even Win32's available paging space. Or you may have a program so large that it is "thrashing" its own memory, that is, causing page faults and a page swap operation so often that the paging time dominates the execution time. Also, the time required to initially read in a very large DIB might be significant, particularly if only a small portion can be viewed at any one time. For example, you might be able to read in a "window's worth" of an image in a few seconds, but reading in the entire image might take minutes. When such performance bottlenecks arise, you might find it advantageous to consider using partial-DIB management. You also can take advantage of *multithreading* to bring in pieces of a bitmap "in the background". In this way, the user can begin to work on or see the pieces already present. We discuss multithreading in Chapter 18.

The `lpBitsInfo` parameter points to a `BITMAPINFO` structure that defines the format of the DIB. The `Usage` parameter is either `DIB_RGB_COLORS` or `DIB_PAL_COLORS`. The first indicates that colors are specified by RGB color values. The second indicates that colors are specified by indices into the currently realized color palette.

Finally, there is the `CreateDIBSection` function. This creates a DIB that an application can write to directly. We document this function here because the documentation in the Win32 API reference (at least in the editions we have) is incomplete and, in fact, incorrect.

```
HBITMAP CreateDIBSection( HDC hdc, CONST BITMAPINFO * pbitmap,
                          UINT usage, VOID ** ppbits,
                          HANDLE hSection, DWORD offset);
```

The hdc is a handle to a device context. If the usage parameter is DIB_PAL_COLORS, the logical palette of this device context is used to initialize the DIB's colors. The pbitmap reference is a pointer to a BITMAPINFO structure that specifies the DIB, including its dimensions and colors. The ppbits parameter (which does not appear in some versions of the Win32 documentation) is a pointer to a variable that receives a pointer to the bitmap's bits. The hSection value is optional and can be NULL. If it is not NULL, it must be a handle to a "mapping object" obtained from the CreateFileMapping function. The bitmap's bits will be located at offset bytes into the mapping object. You will be able to retrieve this handle by calling GetObject on the bitmap handle:

```
DIBSECTION ds;
HANDLE section;

GetObject(hbitmap, sizeof DIBSECTION, &ds);

section = ds.dshSection;
```

If the hSection parameter is NULL, the system will allocate memory for the DIB and the offset parameter will be ignored. You will not be able to retrieve this handle using the above code; the ds.dshSection member will be NULL. The DIBSECTION structure, which is not otherwise documented in the Win32 reference, is

```
typedef struct tagDIBSECTION {
     BITMAP dsBM;
     BITMAPINFOHEADER dsBmih;
     DWORD dsBitFields[3];
     HANDLE dshSection;
     DWORD dsOffset;
} DIBSECTION;
```

If you specify the hSection value when you create the DIB section, the offset parameter must be a multiple of sizeof(DWORD), since the bits will be aligned on double-word boundaries. This offset value will appear as the dsOffset field in the DIBSECTION. If the hSection value is NULL on creation, the dshSection value of the DIBSECTION will be NULL and the dsOffset value will have no meaning. If this function succeeds, it returns a handle to the newly-created bitmap; if it fails, it returns NULL.

If hSection is NULL, the system will free up the allocated storage when you call DeleteObject on the bitmap. If hSection is not NULL, you must close the hSection memory handle after calling DeleteObject.

For Windows NT, you have to guarantee that the GDI subsystem has completed drawing to the bitmap. You must call GdiFlush before accessing the bits of the bitmap via the pointer that was returned via the ppbits parameter.

One of the major useful purposes of the DIBSECTION is that it allows you to perform bitmap operations very quickly, primarily to expedite animation effects.

The BitBlt, StretchBlt, and StretchDIBits Functions

The BitBlt function (pronounced "bit blit") copies a rectangular block of bits from a source device context to a destination device context. The name is an abbreviation of "*BIT BLock Transfer*".[5] The source and destination blocks must be the same width and height. The StretchBlt function also copies a rectangular block of bits from a source device context to a destination device context. However, the StretchBlt function can stretch or compress the source rectangle to fit into a larger or smaller destination rectangle.

Like the PatBlt function you saw earlier, these functions can do much more than simply copy bits from here to there. Technically, the BitBlt function provides a superset of the functionality of the PatBlt function. The StretchBlt function provides a superset of the functionality of the BitBlt function. The StretchDIBits function provides the same functionality as the StretchBlt function, but it does it on DIBs. In the next section, we discuss even more sophisticated Blt-class instructions: PlgBlt and MaskBlt.

The basic form of the BitBlt function call is

```
BOOL BitBlt (HDC hDestDC, int X, int Y, int Width, int Height,
             HDC hSrcDC, int xSrc, int ySrc, DWORD Rop) ;
```

As you can see, this looks much like the PatBlt function discussed earlier in the chapter. The hDestDC parameter specifies the destination device context for the transfer. The X, Y, Width, and Height parameters are logical coordinates of one corner of a rectangle and the extent of the rectangle, horizontally and vertically. As with the PatBlt function, this information specifies two opposite corners of a rectangle. GDI uses this information and the mapping mode to determine the upper-left corner of the rectangle. It includes the top and left sides in the modified area. The bottom and right sides are not included in the default (GM_COMPATIBLE) mode but are included in the extended (GM_ADVANCED) mode.

The PatBlt function used two operands in the transfer: a brush (or pattern) and a rectangular area of pixels on the surface of a destination device context. The BitBlt function uses the same two parameters and adds a third: a rectangular area of pixels on the surface of a source device context. The hSrcDC parameter specifies the source device context. The source rectangle is at the (source device context) logical coordinate (xSrc, ySrc). The Width and Height parameters specify the logical width and height of the source rectangle, which has the same size as the destination rectangle.

The final parameter, Rop, specifies the raster operation code for the transfer. A raster operation code for the BitBlt and StretchBlt functions indicates the Boolean operation to use when combining a source bitmap, a pattern bitmap, and a destination bitmap. There are 256 raster operation codes.

A raster operation code (ROP) is a 32-bit value. The high-order 16 bits of the code identify the Boolean operation and is a 0-extended, 8-bit value that ranges from 0 to 255. The low-order word is a bit-encoded operation code used by the device driver in executing the requested function. Only 15 of the 256 possible ternary raster operation codes have symbolic names defined in windows.h. We give their symbolic names in Table 6.12, along with the Boolean operation they represent and the hexadecimal ROP code value. You can specify the other ROP values numerically. Or you can use the extrops.h header file–supplied with the GDI Explorer–which assigns names to all 256 ROP codes. You can also use the BLT Explorer component of the GDI Explorer to experiment with the entire set of ROP codes (although some are rather boring; for example, ROP

---

[5] For history buffs: The Digital PDP-6 computer (of the mid-1960s) had an instruction, "Block transfer", mnemonic "BLT", that copied a block of 36-bit words from one memory location to another. When an operation that transferred bits in graphics devices required a name, the name "BitBlt" was invented to designate a bit-block-transfer instead of a word-block-transfer. The name stuck.

code 0x00AA0029, which copies the destination pixel to the destination, ignoring both the source and the brush pattern).

Table 6.12: The 15 ternary ROP codes with their symbolic names

	Pixel Values								**Boolean Operation**	**ROP Code**
Pattern (P)	1	1	1	1	0	0	0	0		
Source (S)	1	1	0	0	1	1	0	0		
Dest(D)	1	0	1	0	1	0	1	0		
Name										
BLACKNESS	0	0	0	0	0	0	0	0	0	0x000042
NOTSRCERASE	0	0	0	1	0	0	0	1	~(S | D)	0x1100A6
NOTSRCCOPY	0	0	1	1	0	0	1	1	~S	0x330008
SRCERASE	0	1	0	0	0	1	0	0	S & ~D	0x440328
DSTINVERT	0	1	0	1	0	1	0	1	~D	0x550009
PATINVERT	0	1	0	1	1	0	1	0	P ^ D	0x5A0049
SRCINVERT	0	1	1	0	0	1	1	0	S ^ D	0x660046
SRCAND	1	0	0	0	1	0	0	0	S & D	0x8800C6
MERGEPAINT	1	0	1	1	1	0	1	1	~S | D	0xBB0226
MERGECOPY	1	1	0	0	0	0	0	0	P & S	0xC000CA
SRCCOPY	1	1	0	0	1	1	0	0	S	0xCC0020
SRCPAINT	1	1	1	0	1	1	1	0	S | D	0xEE0086
PATCOPY	1	1	1	1	0	0	0	0	P	0xF00021
PATPAINT	1	1	1	1	1	0	1	1	P | ~S | D	0xFB0A09
WHITENESS	1	1	1	1	1	1	1	1	1	0xFF0062

Table 6.12 demonstrates how you can determine the proper ROP code for any possible Boolean operation. Notice how the pattern, source, and destination pixel values are organized. The (0, 0, 0) combination is on the right, forming a column. The result of the chosen Boolean operation on the (0, 0, 0) bits is placed in the least-significant bit of the result. The (1, 1, 1) combination forms a column on the left, with the result placed in the most-significant bit of the result.

After you've written the result for each of the eight possible combinations of a pattern, source, and destination, you have the binary value for the high-order word of the ROP code. For example, the binary result of the WHITENESS operation is all 1s or, in hexadecimal, 0xFF. The ROP code for WHITENESS is 0xFF0062. The result of the SRCAND operation is the binary value "1 0 0 0 1 0 0 0" or, in hexadecimal, 0x88. The ROP code for SRCAND is 0x8800C6.

Now you can find the ROP code for any possible Boolean operation. Compute the result of your Boolean operation as described. The 8-bit resulting value is the Boolean operation index into the table of ROP codes listed in Appendix A. The high word of the 32-bit ROP code always equals the 0-extended, 8-bit value computed in the above manner.

One frequently used ROP code is SRCCOPY. The SRCCOPY ROP performs a straight copy of the source rectangle to the destination. A brush pattern isn't used, and the original contents of the destination do not matter.

Sixteen of the ROP codes ignore the source operand. These ROP codes were listed in Table 6.11. If you select one of those codes, then the hSrcDC, xSrc, and ySrc parameters to the BitBlt function are ignored. The BitBlt function is equivalent to the PatBlt function when it uses these ROP codes. In fact, in this case it would be better to call the PatBlt function instead. Calling PatBlt makes it clear that no source operand is involved. This is a software maintenance issue, not a functionality issue. Both functions produce the same result in this situation.

The StretchBlt Function

The StretchBlt function uses the same ROP codes as the BitBlt function, but adds a twist. Rather than your assuming that the source and destination rectangles are the same size (as with the BitBlt function), you specify two additional parameters, SrcWidth and SrcHeight, that describe the width and height of the source bitmap:

```
BOOL StretchBlt (HDC hDestDC, int xDst, int yDst,
                        int DstWidth, int DstHeight,
              HDC hSrcDC,  int xSrc, int ySrc,
                        int SrcWidth, int SrcHeight,
              DWORD Rop) ;
```

The StretchBlt function stretches or compresses the source bitmap in memory to match the size of the destination rectangle. It then combines the (possibly) stretched or compressed bitmap with the brush and the original pixel values from the destination device context according to the specified ROP code. The destination coordinates and extents are logical coordinates that are translated to device coordinates according to the mapping mode specified in the destination device context. Likewise, the source coordinates and extents are logical coordinates that are translated to device coordinates according to the mapping mode in the source device context.

The StretchBlt function duplicates rows and columns as necessary when stretching a bitmap. This preserves all the information present in the original bitmap, although it might introduce some distortion. It's more complicated to compress a bitmap without destroying the image. The stretching mode attribute of the destination device context determines the manner in which a bitmap is compressed. We discussed this function in detail in Chapter 5, "Examining a Device Context in Depth". However, there are basically four choices when using this function. The original names for these choices were rather strange and have been replaced in Win32 by more meaningful names. We mention them here because they are still available and may be used either in porting old Win16 code or by Win16 programmers who are familiar with them. Here are the mode names:

- STRETCH_ANDSCANS (BLACKONWHITE)

- STRETCH_ORSCANS (WHITEONBLACK)

- STRETCH_DELETESCANS (COLORONCOLOR)

- STRETCH_HALFTONE (HALFTONE)

Each mode specifies a different process for determining how to combine two or more rows or columns of pixels into one. These modes apply only when you are reducing the size of a bitmap. You can experiment with them in the BLT Explorer of the GDI Explorer.

STRETCH_ANDSCANS combines two rows by using a logical AND operator to combine the dropped pixels with the retained pixels. The original name, BLACKONWHITE, is based on the fact that this technique, when used on a monochrome bitmap, gives preference to black pixels over white pixels.

STRETCH_ORSCANS combines two rows by using a logical OR operator to combine the dropped pixels with the retained pixels. The original name, WHITEONBLACK, indicates that in a monochrome bitmap the retention of white pixels is favored.

STRETCH_DELETESCANS simply drops the scanlines entirely, making no attempt to preserve their color. Its original name, COLORONCOLOR, indicates that it was probably intended to be the preferred method for color bitmaps.

STRETCH_HALFTONE maps pixels from the source into blocks of pixels in the destination. The average color of the block in the destination approximates the original source pixel color.

Microsoft has confirmed a bug in Windows 95: The StretchBlt mode is ignored, and the StretchBlt is always performed with the STRETCH_DELETESCANS mode, no matter what mode you set. This may be fixed by a Service Pack by the time you read this. Check out Knowledge Base article #Q138105.

The StretchBlt function is functionally a superset of the BitBlt function in another way, too. You can invert the bitmap during the transfer–horizontally, vertically, or along both axes. When the DstWidth and SrcWidth parameters have opposite signs (after they are translated to device units), the bitmap is flipped about the vertical axis. The right side of the source bitmap appears on the left side of the destination and vice versa. When the SrcHeight and DstHeight parameters have opposite signs (after they are translated to device units), the bitmap is flipped about the horizontal axis. The top of the source bitmap appears on the bottom of the destination and vice versa. When both pairs of extents have opposite signs, the source bitmap is flipped about both axes during the transfer to the destination.

The StretchDIBits Function

The StretchDIBits function performs the same operations as the StretchBlt function, but the source bitmap is a DIB. The function has the following syntax:

```
BOOL StretchDIBits (HDC hdc, int xDst, int yDst,
                    int DstWidth, int DstHeight,
                    int xSrc, int ySrc,
                    int SrcWidth, int SrcHeight,
                    CONST VOID * lpBits,
                    CONST LPBITMAPINFO BitsInfo,
                    UINT ColorUsage,
                    DWORD Rop) ;
```

This function transfers the DIB specified by the lpBits, lpBitsInfo, and ColorUsage parameters to the logical coordinates (xDst, yDst) in the destination device context. As it does, it stretches or compresses the bitmap if necessary and combines it with the brush selected in the destination device context and the original destination bitmap according to the ROP code Rop. The xSrc, ySrc, SrcWidth, and SrcHeight parameters define the size and position of the source rectangle relative to the origin of the DIB, which is the lower-left corner. The xDst, yDst, DstWidth, and DstHeight parameters define the size and position of the destination rectangle relative to the origin of the device context.

There is no specific function for a DIB that is equivalent to the PatBlt and BitBlt functions for device-specific bitmaps. You don't need one, as you can use the StretchDIBits function to perform those operations.

The MaskBlt and PlgBlt Functions

There are two powerful operations that allow you to combine the contents of bitmaps: MaskBlt and PlgBlt. MaskBlt allows you to take the contents of one bitmap and selectively combine it with the contents of another bitmap on a per-pixel basis using any two raster operations. PlgBlt ("*PoLyGon BLock Transfer*") allows you to copy the contents of one bitmap to another based on a mask (which is a little deceptive naming). It also lets you apply a shearing or rotation operation at the same time by specifying the destination as a parallelogram.

MaskBlt and PlgBlt are not available in Windows 95.

The PlgBlt function

The PlgBlt function is the somewhat simpler of the two, so we cover it first. The PlgBlt function takes 10 parameters:

```
BOOL PlgBlt(HDC dstDC, LPPOINT pt,
            HDC srcDC, int xSrc, int ySrc,
            int Width, int Height,
            HBITMAP bm, int xMask, int yMask);
```

The dstDC parameter is the DC to which the bits are copied. The point parameter is a pointer to an array of three points, expressed in logical units, which define three of the points of the destination parallelogram. The first point, pt[0], is the upper-left corner of the parallelogram. The second point, pt[1], is the upper-right corner of the parallelogram. The third point, pt[2], is the lower-left corner of the parallelogram. The fourth point on the parallelogram, which we call pt3, is computed based on the width of the parallelogram as pt3.x = pt[2].x + pt[1].x – pt[0].x, and pt3.y = pt[2].y. The source rectangle is copied from the DC specified by the srcDC parameter, starting at the logical coordinates xSrc and

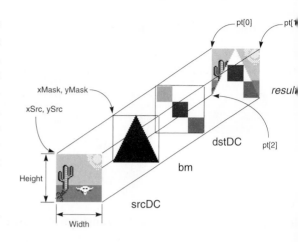

Figure 6.19: A simple masked PlgBlt operation

ySrc. The point from (xSrc, ySrc) is copied to (pt[0].x, pt[0].y). The point from (xSrc + Width - 1, ySrc) is copied to (pt[1].x, pt[1].y). The point from (xSrc, ySrc + Height - 1) is copied to the point specified by (pt[2].x, pt[2].y). This is illustrated in Figure 6.19. The bm parameter is optional; a non-NULL value specifies a monochrome bitmap that is used to mask the colors of the source rectangle. In this case, the xMask and yMask parameters specify the starting coordinate of the top-left corner of the mask within the bitmap. If the mask rectangle is smaller than the source or destination rectangles, the function replicates the mask pattern. A 1 bit in the mask causes the color to be copied from the source to the destination. A 0 bit in the mask leaves the corresponding destination pixel unchanged; this is shown more clearly in Figure 6.20. The source DC may have scaling, translation, or reflection transformations (we cover transformations starting on page 370), but not rotation or shearing. If the source and destination rectangles are not the same size, the stretching mode established by SetStretchBltMode in the destination DC will control how pixels are stretched or compressed. The destination coordinates are transformed according to the destination DC; the source coordinates are transformed according to the source DC.

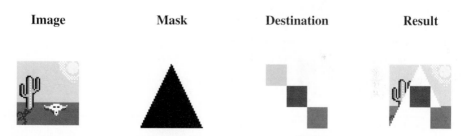

Figure 6.20: PlgBlt with a masking bitmap and no transformation

The result of the PlgBlt function is TRUE if the function succeeds and FALSE if the function fails. The function will fail if either the source or the destination DC has a rotation or shearing transformation or if the source DC is an enhanced metafile DC. It also will fail if the destination device does not support the PlgBlt

Image	Result
| 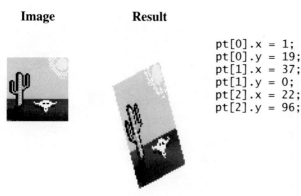 | ```
pt[0].x = 1;
pt[0].y = 19;
pt[1].x = 37;
pt[1].y = 0;
pt[2].x = 22;
pt[2].y = 96;
``` |

Figure 6.21: PlgBlt with simple transform and no masking

function. You should confirm that PlgBlt is supported by checking the RC_BITBLT capability using the GetDeviceCaps function. Finally, the PlgBlt function will fail if the DCs represent incompatible devices. PlgBlt is not implemented on Windows 95.

For example, using the GDI Explorer application you can derive the information shown in Table 6.13. This set of multipliers was used to produce the images shown (multiply the width of the bitmap by the indicated factors to obtain the points shown). There was no masking bitmap involved. Note that by using PlgBlt, we can get shearing and rotation effects on bitmaps.

Table 6.13: Multipliers for PlgBlt simple rotations

		Polygon Points					
		pt[0]		pt[1]		pt[2]	
Rotation	Image	x	y	x	y	x	y
Original	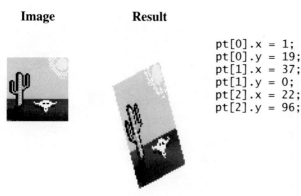	0	0	1	0	0	1
90° clockwise		1	0	1	1	0	0
180° clockwise		1	1	0	1	1	0
270° clockwise		0	1	0	0	1	1
```

Table 6.13: Multipliers for PlgBlt simple rotations

Rotation	Image	Polygon Points					
		pt[0]		pt[1]		pt[2]	
		x	y	x	y	x	y
Horizontal shear 30° counterclockwise		0	0	1	0	$\sin\theta$	1
Vertical shear 30° clockwise		0	0	1	$\sin\theta$	0	1
Rotation 30° clockwise		$\sin\theta$	0	1 + $\sin\theta$	$\sin\theta$	0	$\cos\theta$
Mirrored Transformations							
0° clockwise		1	0	0	0	1	1
90° clockwise		1	1	1	0	0	1
180° clockwise		0	1	1	1	0	0
270° clockwise		0	0	0	1	1	0
270° clockwise Vertical shear 30° clockwise		0	0	0	1	1	$\sin\theta$

The MaskBlt Function

The MaskBlt operation is complex to discuss, but simple once you see what it is doing. The basic idea of the MaskBlt is to copy pixels from one bitmap to another using a third monochrome bitmap as the mask. However, unlike PlgBlt, where a 1 bit in the mask means "copy to destination" and a 0 means "leave the destination unchanged", in MaskBlt the 1 bit means "copy with the foreground raster op" and a 0 means "copy with the background raster op". If we set the foreground raster op to copy the source and set the background raster op to copy the destination, we have exactly PlgBlt with the restriction that the copied bitmaps must be rectangular and the same size.

MaskBlt takes 12 parameters. This places it in the top 10 list of API functions with the most parameters. However, they are actually quite simple:

- A destination DC and a specification of a rectangle in it (five parameters)

- A source DC and the specification of where the transfer starts (three parameters)

- A monochrome bitmap and the specification of where the mask is found (three parameters)

- A pair of ROP codes, packed into one parameter

These are shown next:

```
BOOL MaskBlt(HDC dest, int dstX, int dstY, int width, int height,
             HDC src,  int srcX, int srcY,
             HBITMAP mask, int maskX, int maskY,
             DWORD ROP4);
```

The dest parameter is the handle of a destination DC. The bitmap selected into this DC will be modified by the MaskBlt operation. The parameters dstX, dstY, width, and height define the rectangle in the destination bitmap that will be modified. The src parameter is the handle of the source DC, and the rectangle to be copied to the destination is defined by the parameters srcX, srcY, width, and height. Note that unlike with PlgBlt, we can copy only rectangles, exactly like BitBlt. All these parameters are in logical units.

The remaining parameters give MaskBlt its power. The mask is the handle of a monochrome bitmap. The maskX and maskY parameters are offsets into the bitmap of where the mask starts. The width and height of the mask are given by the parameters width and height and are in pixels.

The final parameter is the pair of raster operations. These are ternary raster operations from Table 6.12. But those values are given as 24-bit hex numbers! How do we pack 48 bits into a single DWORD? The answer is that the *real* ternary opcode is only an 8-bit number; the low-order 16 bits are used as a specification to the device driver. In fact, the ROP4 parameter encodes the background raster op in the high byte of the high word and the foreground raster op in the low byte of the high word, and the remaining 16 bits of ROP4 are not used at all. To create a quaternary raster op, use the MAKEROP4 macro, giving it two values from Table 6.12. Note that although the documentation recommends that the low-order 16 bits be set to 0, the MAKEROP4 macro violates this specification, apparently without harm.

```
DWORD rop4 = MAKEROP4(foreground, background);
```

We said in the description of Table 6.12 that it listed only 15 of the 256 possible names. In fact, we want the pattern that is equivalent to leaving the destination unchanged, and that value is not defined in Table 6.12 Remember that example we gave on page 349 of a really boring ROP code, "copy destination to destination"? While fairly uninteresting for a BitBlt, it is far more interesting for a MaskBlt. In this case, we have to invent our own name and assign it a value. So, for example, you could write

```
#define DSTCOPY 0xAA
DWORD likePlgBlt = MAKEROP4( SRCCOPY, DSTCOPY);
```

Consider that we have effectively added the line to Table 6.12 as shown next.

		Pixel Values								Boolean Operation	ROP Code
Pattern (P)		1	1	1	1	0	0	0	0		
Source (S)		1	1	0	0	1		0	0		
Dest(D)		1	0	1	0	1	0	1	0		
Name											
DSTCOPY		1	0	1	0	1	0	1	0	D	0xAA0029

It is worth studying this example because you might, in writing a MaskBlt, have to invent another of the 256 opcodes to do what you want to do. The low-order 4 digits of the ROP code, which we don't need for MaskBlt, are as shown in Appendix A. You can also use the file extrops.h, which we supply as part of the source for the GDI Explorer. To quickly find the operator you want, you can use the ROP Finder, which is part of the BLT Explorer component of the GDI Explorer.

The MaskBlt operation has one constraint: It must cover the destination. Hence, if the mask and the size of the destination are of different sizes, the operation will fail.

In the API level 3 implementation, the GDI commands are queued for later processing. So it is not always apparent, when a function fails, exactly why it failed; this can be particularly aggravating when you are debugging. When debugging, you might want to use the GdiSetBatchLimit function with an argument of 1 to disable the GDI queuing. Then the Boolean return value from the various drawing functions will accurately reflect their success or failure.

Miscellaneous Bitmap and Drawing Functions

A few functions don't fit into the previous discussions very well. We discuss them here.

Bitmap Functions

The GetBitmapDimensionEx returns the width and height of a bitmap by updating the specified SIZE structure. You use the GetBitmapDimensionEx function like this:

```
int             Width ;
int             Height ;
SIZE            size ;

GetBitmapDimensionEx (hbitmap, &size) ;
Width = size.cx ;
Height = size.cy ;
```

This function is rather strange because it doesn't really return the bitmap's width and height. It actually returns the information that was set by the SetBitmapDimensionEx function. If no width and height were set by a prior call to the SetBitmapDimensionEx function, the GetBitmapDimensionEx function returns 0 for the width and height. If you need the real dimensions, use the GetDIBits function.

The following SetBitmapDimensionEx function call sets the bitmap dimension and returns the previous dimensions by updating the specified SIZE structure:

```
int             Width ;
int             Height ;
SIZE            size ;

SetBitmapDimensionEx (hbitmap, Width, Height, &size) ;
```

You can use these functions to associate two integers with a bitmap. Windows does not use this information.

When you actually want the dimensions of the bitmap, use the GetDIBits function or call the GetObject function, passing it the handle to a bitmap. It will fill a buffer with a BITMAP structure containing the actual dimensions of the bitmap:

```
BITMAP bm ;

GetObject (hbitmap, sizeof bm, &bm) ;

Width = bm.bmWidth ;

Height = bm.bmHeight ;
```

The FloodFill and ExtFloodFill functions don't fit in anywhere else either. The FloodFill function fills an area of a device context surface with the current brush. You specify the logical coordinates of a point on the device surface and a color that bounds the area to be filled. The FloodFill function starts at the specified point and uses the current brush to paint in all directions on the device surface until the specified color boundary is reached. Here is the function syntax for the FloodFill function:

```
BOOL FloodFill (HDC hdc, int X, int Y, COLORREF Color) ;
```

Microsoft recommends that new code use the ExtFloodFill function. The ExtFloodFill function does everything the FloodFill function does and a bit more. The syntax is somewhat different:

```
ExtFloodFill (HDC hdc, int X, int Y, COLORREF Color, UINT FillType) ;
```

When the FillType parameter is FLOODFILLBORDER, the ExtFloodFill function starts at the logical point (X, Y) and paints with the current brush until it reaches the boundary color Color. This action is identical to the FloodFill function's.

When the FillType parameter is FLOODFILLSURFACE, only the adjacent areas that are the color Color are filled with the current brush. The ExtFloodFill function starts at the point (X, Y) and paints outwardly in all directions until a color *other* than Color is encountered.

Note that the flood fill operations depend on the actual boundary colors. Thus it is very difficult to use these in a general way to draw, for example, partially overlapping circles in two different interior colors but with the same border color, where you want the second circle drawn to be visually hiding the first one. To fill an arbitrary shape, you will more likely want to use the FillPath or StrokeAndFillPath operations. Note also that flood filling with a dithered color is likely to produce unexpected results because the halftoning effects will interfere with the "edge detection" of the logical boundary. So these functions are typically far less useful than you might expect.

ScrollDC

The ScrollDC function is invaluable when you want to scroll all or part of a window containing child windows and controls. Typically, in such a case you don't want the child windows and controls to move; you want just the surface of the window underneath them to move.

The ScrollDC function takes this into account. Because it is a GDI function, it performs clipping on the scroll region. The function call looks like the following:

```
BOOL ScrollDC (HDC hdc, int dx, int dy,
               CONST RECT * ScrollRect,
               CONST RECT * ClipRect,
               HRGN UpdateRgn, LPRECT Update) ;
```

This function scrolls the device surface specified by the hdc parameter dx scroll units horizontally and dy scroll units vertically. The ScrollRect parameter is a pointer to a RECT structure that specifies the area to scroll. You can restrict the scrolling to a smaller area within the previously specified rectangle by passing a smaller rectangle as the ClipRect parameter. It contains the coordinates of a clipping rectangle. All scrolling is done within the clipping rectangle.

The ScrollDC function returns information via the last two parameters. When you pass a handle to a region as the UpdateRgn parameter, GDI sets the region to the area uncovered by the scrolling process. When you pass a pointer to a RECT structure as the Update parameter, GDI sets the rectangle to the client coordinates (independent of any mapping modes actually in effect in the DC) of the update rectangle. This is the smallest rectangle that bounds the area needing repainting. It can be later passed to InvalidateRect to force repainting.

The DrawEdge Function

The "3-D look" is pervasive in user interfaces today. Drawing those nice "3-D" edges, however, is a bit tricky, if you're doing it entirely with LineTo, that is. Of course, you could also use a bitmap, but doing this introduces the problem of mapping pixels in the bit map to the colors selected by the user in the Control Panel. This practice is recommended if you are following the GUI design guidelines. (You can accomplish this in some cases by using the LR_LOADMAP3DCOLORS option flag for the LoadImage function. But for many cases, having to create a bitmap and use LoadImage is technological overkill for what should be a simple task.) There is a composite operation, DrawEdge, that takes a rectangle and draws some portion of it using 3-D line effects. The results of three such drawings appear in Figure 6.22.

EDGE_SUNKEN   EDGE_RAISED   EDGE_ETCHED

Figure 6.22: DrawEdge effects

The DrawEdge function takes a DC, a rectangle specification, and flags to describe how the effects are to be produced:

```
BOOL DrawEdge(HDC hdc, LPRECT rect, UINT edge, UINT flags);
```

The rect parameter describes the rectangle in which the drawing takes place. The edge parameter can be any of the values given in Table 6.14. These are the values that were used to draw the illustrations of Figure 6.22.

Table 6.14: DrawEdge edge specifications

Code	Meaning
Inner border flag, one of:	
BDR_RAISEDINNER	Raised inner edge.
BDR_SUNKENINNER	Sunken inner edge.
Outer border flag, one of:	
BDR_RAISEDOUTER	Raised outer edge.
BDR_SUNKENOUTER	Sunken outer edge.
Or, use one of the following values:	
EDGE_BUMP	BDR_RAISEDOUTER | BDR_SUNKENINNER
EDGE_ETCHED	BDR_SUNKENOUTER | BDR_RAISEDINNER
EDGE_RAISED	BDR_RAISEDOUTER | BDR_RAISEDINNER
EDGE_SUNKEN	BDR_SUNKENOUTER | BDR_SUNKENINNER

The flags parameter describes which parts of the rectangle are to be drawn and chooses specific other effects. The flags values are given in Table 6.15.

Table 6.15: DrawEdge flags

Flag Value	Meaning
Base edge flags, one or more of the following:	
BF_TOP	Draws the top of the rectangle.
BF_BOTTOM	Draws the bottom of the rectangle.
BF_LEFT	Draws the left of the rectangle.
BF_RIGHT	Draws the right of the rectangle.
BF_DIAGONAL	Draws a diagonal line (always at 45° no matter what the aspect ratio of the rectangle). Interpretation depends on other flag values.
Alternatively, you can use one of the following names:	
BF_BOTTOMLEFT	BF_BOTTOM | BF_LEFT
BF_BOTTOMRIGHT	BF_BOTTOM | BF_RIGHT
BF_DIAGONAL_ENDBOTTOMLEFT	BF_DIAGONAL | BF_BOTTOM | BF_LEFT
BF_DIAGONAL_ENDBOTTOMRIGHT	BF_DIAGONAL | BF_BOTTOM | BF_RIGHT
BF_DIAGONAL_ENDTOPLEFT	BF_DIAGONAL | BF_TOP | BF_LEFT
BF_DIAGONAL_ENDTOPRIGHT	BF_DIAGONAL | BF_TOP | BF_RIGHT
BF_TOPLEFT	BF_TOP | BF_LEFT
BF_TOPRIGHT	BF_TOP | BF_RIGHT
BF_RECTBF_RECT	BF_TOP | BF_LEFT | BF_BOTTOM | BF_RIGHT
One or more of the following flags for additional effects:	
BF_ADJUST	Adjust the rectangle to leave space for client area.
BF_FLAT	Flat border.
BF_MIDDLE	Fills in the area within the borders.
BF_MONO	One-dimensional border.
BF_SOFT	Soft buttons instead of tiles.

The illustrations in Figure 6.22 were done using the DrawEdge Explorer component of the GDI Explorer. This program allows you to directly see all the visual effects of all of the various flags and options.

One strange feature of the **DrawEdge** function is its use of the "diagonal" flag, which draws a diagonal line. This diagonal line is *always* a 45° line, no matter the size of the rectangle. It is always based on the left edge of the rectangle, that is, lines will run from top left to bottom right or from bottom left to top right. The nature of the diagonal line is also modified by the presence of BF_LEFT or BF_RIGHT flags in combination with BF_TOP and BF_BOTTOM. While you may think at first that a line that ends in the top left is the same as a line that ends in the bottom right, this is not true when 3-D effects depend on the virtual "light source". For example, when the style EDGE_RAISED is chosen, a BF_DIAGONAL_ENDTOPRIGHT draws a *white* line from the lower-left corner to the top-right corner, but a BF_DIAGONAL_ENDBOTTOMLEFT draws a *black* line from the top-right corner to the bottom-left corner.

The BF_SOFT, BF_FLAT and BF_MONO flags affect specific "3-D" aspects of how the lines are actually drawn. Figure 6.23 illustrates these effects. BF_FLAT uses no 3-D effects at all.

no modifiers   BF_SOFT   BF_FLAT   BF_MONO

Basic style is EDGE_ETCHED with the BF_RECT flags set.

Figure 6.23: DrawEdge modifier effects

The BF_MIDDLE flag causes the area within the borders to be painted. The BF_ADJUST flag allows additional space for the client area of the rectangle. Since you will often want to use these borders on owner-draw objects such as buttons, you may want to reserve the client area. Using the BF_ADJUST presumably is to allow the size to be adjusted so that it lies outside the client area of the window whose client area is represented by the rectangle. We could not see a noticeable visual effect using the DrawEdge Explorer.

The GDI Batch Queue (in detail)

The final set of miscellaneous functions deals with the asynchronous nature of the GDI under Windows NT 3.*x*. Each thread has a buffer (called its "batch") in which GDI commands are accumulated. This means that if you are running a multithreaded application, not all GDI commands from one thread may have completed when control is transferred to another thread. Normally, this doesn't matter much. But if one thread is writing to a bitmap and another thread is reading from the bitmap, there is no guarantee that all of the operations have completed. The batch is flushed when any of the following occurs:

- The GdiFlush function is called.

- The batch limit, as set by GdiSetBatchLimit, has been reached.

- The batch buffers have filled up.

- A GDI function that does not return a Boolean value is called.

The batch limit is established by GdiSetBatchLimit, and can be read by GdiGetBatchLimit. To disable batching, the GdiSetBatchLimit must be called with a batch limit of 1. Since each thread has its own batch limit, you have to call `GdiSetBatchLimit` in each thread for which you want to change the batch size. Calling `GdiSetBatchLimit(0)` sets the limit to the system default.

The `GdiFlush` function forces any pending batch commands to be flushed to the device. The `GdiFlush` function returns TRUE if the batch queue was empty or all batch commands succeeded; it returns FALSE if any command in the batch failed. If a GDI function that returns a Boolean value is entered in the batch, it will return TRUE; its actual success or failure will not be determined until it is flushed from the queue. In particular, if you are debugging and your graphic commands appear to be failing, you can set the batch limit to 1, thereby disabling all batching, and get an "honest" response to the GDI Boolean functions:

```
#ifdef _DEBUG
    {
    int oldbatch = GdiSetBatchLimit(1);
    BOOL result =
#endif⁶
    your GDI request here
#ifdef _DEBUG
    if(!result)
        { /* error */
        reportError(_T("your message here"), GetLastError());
        } /* error */
    GdiSetBatchLimit(oldbatch);
    }
#endif
```

While `GetLastError` tends to return the catch-all error code "Bad parameter" (ERROR_INVALID_PARAMETER, value 87, as defined in winerror.h), it is often sufficient to identify *which* GDI function is failing.

Region Functions

A *region* is a description of an area of a device surface. It is described by a combination of one or more ellipses and polygons. You use regions mainly for two purposes: to paint the area described by a region and to clip all output to the area described by a region. You can also use a region to test for the presence of the mouse in an irregularly-shaped area.

A region is not a simple data structure like a RECT structure. It is a GDI object like a bitmap and hence must be created. When you create a region, you receive a handle to the region of type HRGN. Once you have a handle to a region, you can use the handle to manipulate the region in a number of interesting ways. You can use it directly to draw the area described by the region. You can combine one region with another region and update a third region to refer to the newly described area. You also can select a region into a device context so that all output to the device context is clipped to the area described by the selected region. You can invalidate the screen area defined by the region, thereby forcing it to redraw, or revalidate, a previously invalidated

---

[6] The rather "clever" syntactic hack here of constructing the left-hand side of the assignment statement depends on your writing a BOOL-returning GDI function immediately after the `#endif`. A bit ugly, but clever. We leave it as an exercise for the reader to turn this into a nice pair of macros to handle the encapsulation of the GDI operation.

region. You can retrieve the line, curve, or other segments of the region. You can fill or outline a region (in this sense, a region can act like a path for the restricted case of a closed polygon). You can ask if a specific coordinate is located within the region. Finally, when you're done with a region, you should delete it just as you should all GDI objects. Just don't delete one while it is selected in a device context.

The region operations are given in Table 6.16.

Table 6.16: Region operations

Operation	Explanation
CombineRgn	Combines two regions using one of the specified operations from Table 6.17.
CreateEllipticRgn	Creates a region with an elliptical shape, given the four parameters defining the bounding rectangle.
CreateEllipticRgnIndirect	Creates a region with an elliptical shape, given a reference to a RECT structure that defines the bounding rectangle.
CreatePolygonRgn	Creates a region with a polygonal shape, given an array of points that define the polygon. Specifies a mode that determines which pixels are in the region.
CreatePolyPolygonRgn	Creates one or more regions with polygonal shapes, given an array of points that define the polygons. Specifies a mode that determines which pixels are in the region.
CreateRectRgn	Creates a rectangular region, given the four coordinates of the bounding rectangle.
CreateRectRgnIndirect	Creates a rectangular region, given a reference to a RECT structure that defines the bounding rectangle.
CreateRoundRectRgn	Creates a rectangular region with rounded corners, given the four coordinates defining the bounding rectangle and the dimensions of the rounding ellipse.
DeleteRgn	Deletes a region.
EqualRgn	Tests two regions for equality.
ExtCreateRgn	Creates a region based on a transformation of an existing region. Windows 95 places some restrictions on the nature of the transformation matrix.
ExtSelectClipRgn	Combines a region with the current clipping region.
FillRgn	Fills a region with a given brush.
FrameRgn	Frames a region by drawing a border using a specified brush.
GetClipRgn	Returns a region handle to the current clipping region.

Table 6.16: Region operations

Operation	Explanation
GetPolyFillMode	Gets the polygon fill mode used by FillRgn.
GetRgnBox	Gets the bounding box of a region.
GetRegionData	Obtains the internal structure information about a region.
GetWindowRgn	Obtains the window region established by SetWindowRgn.
InvalidateRgn	Invalidates the region, eventually forcing a WM_PAINT message to be generated.
InvertRgn	Inverts the colors in the region.
OffsetRgn	Offsets the region.
PaintRgn	Paints the region using the current brush from the DC.
PathToRegion	Converts the current path in the DC to a region.
PtInRegion	Tests to see if a given coordinate is contained in the region.
RectInRegion	Tests to see if a given rectangle overlaps any part of the region.
SelectClipRgn	Selects a given region as the current clipping region.
SetPolyFillMode	Sets the polygon fill mode for FillRgn.
SetWindowRgn	Sets the window region. This will be honored by the GDI; nothing outside the window region will be written. This allows you to construct nonrectangular windows.
ValidateRgn	Validates the client area. This removes the area specified by the region from the current update region.

Several functions can be used to create a region:

- Two create an elliptical region.

- Two create a polygonal region.

- Two create a rectangular region.

- One creates a rounded rectangular area.

- One geometrically transforms a region.

- One converts a path description to a region.

You always use device coordinates when creating a region.

```
int              xUL, yUL ;
int              xLR, yLR ;
int              Count ;
int              PolyFillMode ;
int              Height ;
int              PolyCounts ;
int              Width ;
POINT            pt [10] ;
RECT             rect ;

LPXFORM xform ={1.0f, 0.0f,
                0.0f, 1.0f,
                0.0f  0.0f};
LPRGNDATA rgndata ;

hrgn = CreateEllipticRgn (xUL, yUL, xLR, yLR) ;
hrgn = CreateEllipticRgnIndirect (&rect) ;
hrgn = CreatePolygonRgn (pt, Count, PolyFillMode) ;
hrgn = CreatePolyPolygonRgn (pt, &PolyCounts,
                             Count, PolyFillMode) ;
hrgn = CreateRectRgn (xUL, yUL, xLR, yLR) ;
hrgn = CreateRectRgnIndirect (&rect) ;
hrgn = CreateRoundRectRgn (xUL, yUL, xLR, yLR, Width, Height) ;

hrgn = ExtCreateRegion (xform, Count, rgndata) ;
hrgn = PathToRegion (hdc);
```

Sometimes it's more efficient to reuse an existing region rather than create (allocate) a new one. You can reuse an existing region by calling the SetRectRgn function. It reuses the region identified by the parameter hrgn. The additional parameters specify the size of the new rectangular region. The function has the following definition:

```
BOOL SetRectRgn (HRGN hrgn, int xUL, int yUL, int xLR, int yLR) ;
```

The call SetRectRgn(hrgn, 0, 0, 0, 0) will redefine the region hrgn to be an empty rectangular region, discarding any previous region definition the handle had.

The powerhouse function for manipulating regions is the CombineRgn function:

```
int CombineRegion (HRGN hrgnDest, HRGN hrgnSrc1, HRGN hrgnSrc2,
                   int CombineMode) ;
```

This function changes the region hrgnDest to refer to the area described by a combination of the two regions hrgnSrc1 and hrgnSrc2. You specify how the two source regions are combined by the CombineMode parameter. It can be one of the five values listed in Table 6.17. The return value specifies the type of the resulting region. It can be one of the values listed in Table 6.18.

Table 6.17: Combine mode values used by the CombineRgn and ExtSelectClipRgn functions

CombineMode Value	Resulting Region (hrgnDest)
RGN_AND	Describes the overlapping areas of both the source regions (hrgnSrc1 and hrgnSrc2). This produces the intersection of the two regions.

Table 6.17: Combine mode values used by the `CombineRgn` and `ExtSelectClipRgn` functions

CombineMode Value	Resulting Region (`hrgnDest`)
RGN_COPY	Describes the same area as the region `hrgnSrc1`.
RGN_DIFF	Describes the areas of the region `hrgnSrc1` that are not in the region `hrgnSrc2`.
RGN_OR	Describes the area that is the combination of both source regions (`hrgnSrc1` and `hrgnSrc2`). This produces the union of the two regions.
RGN_XOR	Describes the area that is the combination of both source regions (`hrgnSrc1` and `hrgnSrc2`) with all overlapping area excluded. This produces an exclusive OR of the two regions.

The header file windowsx.h defines a number of macro APIs that make using the `CombineRgn` function much simpler. They look like this:

```
#define CopyRgn(hrgnDst, hrgnSrc)  \
        CombineRgn(hrgnDst, hrgnSrc, 0, RGN_COPY)
#define IntersectRgn(hrgnResult, hrgnA, hrgnB) \
        CombineRgn(hrgnResult, hrgnA, hrgnB, RGN_AND)
#define SubtractRgn(hrgnResult, hrgnA, hrgnB)   \
        CombineRgn(hrgnResult, hrgnA, hrgnB, RGN_DIFF)
#define UnionRgn(hrgnResult, hrgnA, hrgnB)       \
        CombineRgn(hrgnResult, hrgnA, hrgnB, RGN_OR)
#define XorRgn(hrgnResult, hrgnA, hrgnB) \
        CombineRgn(hrgnResult, hrgnA, hrgnB, RGN_XOR)
```

Table 6.18: Region result types

Return Value	Meaning
COMPLEXREGION	The new region has overlapping borders.
ERRORERROR	An error occurred. No new region was created.
NULLREGION	The new region is empty.
SIMPLEREGION	The new region has no overlapping borders. It is either a rectangle, ellipse, or other simple polygon.

We have used these operations in the Region Explorer component of the GDI Explorer application to produce the effects shown in Figure 6.24. In this figure, two elliptical (circular) regions that overlap are combined under the operations shown. Note that RGN_DIFF is not commutative; the left-hand circle is the first operand, and the right-hand circle is the second operand.

After you have defined a region, you can move it around by calling the `OffsetRgn` function. This moves the region X units horizontally and Y units vertically:

```
int OffsetRgn (HRGN hrgn, int X, int Y) ;
```

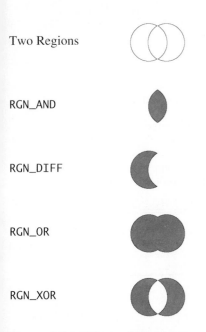

Two Regions

RGN_AND

RGN_DIFF

RGN_OR

RGN_XOR

**Figure 6.24: Effects of CombineRgn
on two overlapping regions**

You also can apply certain other transformations to a region (which we discuss when we get to ExtCreateRegion, see page 382). In full Windows NT, you can rotate, scale, offset, or shear a region. In Windows 95, you can scale and/or offset a region (but not rotate or shear it) using ExtCreateRegion. However, before we can talk about ExtCreateRegion in any detail, we need to discuss several other aspects of the GDI.

Five functions provide information about regions. You can determine whether two regions are equal to one another (EqualRgn), get the coordinate of the bounding rectangle for a region (GetRgnBox), determine whether a point is within a region (PtInRegion), and determine whether any part of a rectangle overlaps part of a region (RectInRegion). All these functions except GetRgnBox return a Boolean value. The GetRgnBox function returns one of the values COMPLEXREGION, NULLREGION, or SIMPLEREGION, as described in Table 6.18. The definitions for these functions follow:

```
BOOL EqualRgn (HRGN hrgnSrc1, HRGN hrgnSrc2) ;
int GetRgnBox (HRGN hrgn, LPRECT rect) ;
BOOL PtInRegion (HRGN hrgn, int X, int Y) ;
BOOL RectInRegion (hrgn, &rect) ;
```

One problem with regions in Win16 was that they were a "private" structure of the GDI, and you couldn't find out anything about the region except what we have already discussed. In particular, you could not find out anything about the internal structure of the region.[7] In Win32, you can find out about the actual region, including all of its components, by using the GetRegionData call. Normally you have to call this function twice: once to find out how much storage will be required to hold the region data and once to read the region data into the available storage.

```
DWORD size;
LPRGNDATA data;

size = GetRegionData(hrgn, 0, NULL);
data = (LPRGNDATA) malloc(size);
// ... deal with possibility that malloc fails...
GetRegionData(hrgn, size, data);
```

You then could modify the RGNDATA information returned and use ExtCreateRegion to create a new region that was some modification of the information. Before we can talk about ExtCreateRegion, we need to discuss something called a *transformation matrix*. That is coming.

---

[7] We looked at the internals of the region structure for Windows 3.1. See the article by Newcomer & Horn cited in "Further Reading".

You can draw in and around the area described by a region with a number of functions. The `FillRgn` function fills the surface of the device context hdc described by the region `hrgn` with the brush `hbrush`. The `PaintRgn` function also fills the area, but it uses the currently selected brush:

```
BOOL FillRgn (HDC hdc, HRGN hrgn, HBRUSH hbrush) ;
BOOL PaintRgn (HDC hdc, HRGN hrgn) ;
```

The `FrameRgn` function draws a border around the area described by a region using a specified brush. Unlike the other coordinates used by region functions, the `Width` and `Height` parameters to the `FrameRgn` function are specified in logical units. They specify the width and height of the frame to be drawn around the region. The function is defined as

```
BOOL FrameRgn (HDC hdc, HRGN hrgn, HBRUSH hbrush, int Width, int Height) ;
```

You may also want to use more advanced graphics operations to accomplish these effects by creating a path instead of a region and using `StrokePath`, `FillPath`, or `StrokeAndFillPath`.

The `InvertRgn` function inverts the colors of the area described by the region. Inverting the area a second time restores it to its original color:

```
BOOL InvertRgn (HDC hdc, HRGN hrgn) ;
```

You also can use a region to specify the clipping area of a device context. When you select a region into a device context, GDI clips all output drawn on the device context to the area specified by the clipping region. You can use the tried-and-true `SelectObject` function or the `SelectClipRgn` function to select the region into a device context. You may also use the `ExtSelectClipRgn`, which lets you perform a `CombineRgn` implicitly with the existing clipping region by specifying one of the combination modes from Table 6.17:

```
HANDLE SelectObject(HDC hdc, HRGN hrgn) ;
int SelectClipRgn (HDC hdc, HRGN hrgn) ;
int ExtSelectClipRgn(HDC hdc, HRGN hrgn, int CombineMode);
```

Unlike the other uses of the `SelectObject` function we've discussed, this `SelectObject` call does not return the previously selected region when selecting a new region into a device context. The `SelectObject`, `SelectClipRgn`, and `ExtSelectClipRgn` functions return one of the values listed in Table 6.18, which specify the type of the selected region. This means that you must explicitly cast the result of `SelectObject` to an `int` from the default, which is a `HANDLE`, if you wish to use it. A copy of the region is used for the clipping region. Therefore, you can select one region into multiple device contexts simultaneously and delete the region after selecting it into a device context.

You can specify that an area of a window has become invalid in terms of a region as well as a rectangle. The `InvalidateRgn` function marks the portion of the client area described by a region as invalid and in need of repainting. Windows adds this invalid region to the accumulating update region. When the next `WM_PAINT` message is processed, the area to be repainted will include the specified region.

You also can remove a region from the accumulating update region by calling the `ValidateRgn` function. This is useful when you have painted a region of the client area at a time other than during the processing of a `WM_PAINT` message. By marking the area as valid, Windows will not send a `WM_PAINT` message if there are no other areas in need of repainting. These functions are called as shown below. The Erase parameter specifies whether the background of the entire update region, not just the newly invalidated part of the update region, should be erased before redrawing it:

```
BOOL InvalidateRgn (HWND hwnd, HRGN hrgn, BOOL Erase) ;
BOOL ValidateRgn (HWND hwnd, HRGN hrgn) ;
```

When you are finished using a region, you should delete it. A region is a GDI object like a bitmap, a brush, a font, a palette, or a pen, and it consumes system resources. You can delete a region by calling the DeleteObject function and specifying the region handle. We prefer to use the Windows DeleteRgn macro API defined in windowsx.h. Here is its definition and an example of its use:

```
#define DeleteRgn(hrgn)  DeleteObject((HGDIOBJ)(HRGN)(hrgn))

DeleteRgn (hrgn) ;
```

Advanced Windows Graphics: Paths and Transformations

Win32 has graphical capabilities not available in 16-bit Windows: *paths* and *transformations*. Using paths you can build a complex clipping region from Bézier curves, ellipses, and rounded rectangles. But you can also create a clipping path from the path defining the outline of a text string; for example, you could clip a graphical layout by using the outline of the letters of your name. Transformations allow a Windows NT program to rotate, scale, reflect and shear–all in a single operation. They further allow the composition of these transformations to realize a single transformation that embodies all of its composite components. While shearing effects can be obtained using the PlgBlt operation, these effects apply only to bitmaps. Transformations apply to *all* graphics operators, which are handled as efficiently as possible. (Manipulating bitmaps can be very slow, and the effects when scaling comes into play can be quite ugly.)

Paths interact with the coordinate system by using coordinate transformations. Since coordinate transformations are a self-contained discussion (they don't require paths) but paths require an understanding of transformations, we first cover transformations. Note that in Windows 95, there are no transformations, except for a restricted form of the ExtCreateRegion function, so anything dealing with paths that also requires transformations means you can deal only with the "identity transformation".

Transformation Matrices

We have shown you how you can use SetViewportExtEx, SetViewportOrgEx, SetWindowExtEx, and SetWindowOrgEx to get scaling. Actually, this is the *hard* way to get scaling, but it was necessitated by the early days of the 8088. In those days, there was only the 8-bit data path to memory, the 16-bit processor architecture, no math coprocessor, and an unbelievable 4.77MHz clock.[8] Using floating-point operations to manipulate the display would have been out of the question, even *with* a math coprocessor. Today, modern processors come with on-chip floating-point units, and high-end processors have superscalar architecture (multiple instructions executed concurrently), parallel arithmetic units, and floating-point units so fast that a floating-point multiply can be done in a single machine clock cycle! So floating-point computation cost is almost an irrelevant consideration today. In Win32, we use these transformations to move from page space to device space; we talk about these spaces on below. But in Windows NT, we can use transformation matrices to manipulate our basic space.

To help you understand what a transformation matrix does, we look at some possible transformations. There is the operation of *scaling*, which changes the mapping mode to get a different correspondence between logical units and physical units. If you scale by the same amount in *x* and *y*, you have an *isotropic* mapping (almost like MM_ISOTROPIC), and if you scale differently, you have an *anisotropic* mapping (almost like MM_ANISOTROPIC). We say "almost" because you may have to scale using MM_ANISOTROPIC if you have nonsquare pixels just to get isotropic scaling in *x* and *y*, but that is a fine point. There is the operation of *translation*, which shifts the coordinates in the *x* and *y* positions. There is the operation of *rotation*, which rotates the coordinate system around its origin. Finally, there is the operation of *shearing*, which applies a linear transformation to each logical unit whose magnitude varies based on its distance from a reference point. These are all shown in Figure 6.25.

In the world of graphics, all of these transformations are captured in a simple model: the *coordinate transformation matrix.*[9] By doing matrix

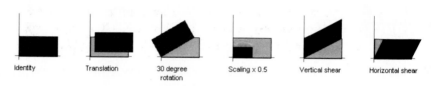

Identity   Translation   30 degree rotation   Scaling x 0.5   Vertical shear   Horizontal shear

Figure 6.25: Scaling, translation, rotation, and shearing

multiplication, you can easily combine two transformations, and when you have a composite matrix, you can quickly and easily apply it to any pair of points (x, y) to get a new pair of points (x', y'). This composition gives you the ability to compute in one step the result of applying several individual transformations, without having to apply each sequentially.

Windows deals with four coordinate spaces:

1. *World coordinate space.* In Windows NT, world coordinate space is 2^{32} units high and wide. World coordinate space is used to rotate, shear, or reflect graphical output. Note that the limitation to 2^{16} units in Window 95 is coupled to this; that is, in Windows 95, you cannot rotate or shear (or reflect) graphical output.

2. *Page coordinate space.* This was called *logical coordinate space* in earlier versions of Windows. In Windows NT, it is 2^{32} units high and wide and in Windows 95, 2^{16} units high and wide.

---

[8] Unbelievable in several ways. Those of us who worked on the timeshared mainframes and 1200-baud dial-up modems of the day found the responsiveness of the original IBM PC a pleasant surprise compared to what we normally suffered through. Many hobbyists who had come up through the slow 8-bit hobby computer chips found the speed a delight; it was unbelievably fast. It is now unbelievable that we could accomplish as much as we did on a personal computer that was so *slow*. The machine I'm writing this on is approximately 200 times faster than that original IBM PC, and over 100 times faster than the $1,000,000 DECSystem-20 I used to use (it had a whopping 4MW of memory, roughly 16MB by modern standards, and supported 60 simultaneous users). – *jmn*

[9] Transformation matrices are the core of many large graphics systems. They are well-documented in the literature, for example, Newman and Sproull's early work on graphics, Adobe Systems's PostScript Language or Foley and van Dam's book, all cited fully in "Further Reading".

3. *Device coordinate space.* In both Windows NT and Windows 95, this is 2^{16} units high and wide.

4. *Physical device coordinate space.* This is limited to the range supported by a given window, screen, printer, or plotter.

When Windows transforms graphical output from its creation through its device rendering, it progressively maps the output across each of these coordinate spaces. If you call the `SetWorldTransform` function, mapping starts in the world coordinate space; otherwise, it starts in the page space. The coordinates are then mapped to the device space under the mapping modes established by `SetMapMode` and finally to the physical device space. But if we do our scaling in world coordinates, we could use a simple mapping such as `MM_ISOTROPIC` or `MM_TEXT` to perform the next level of mapping.

The `SetWorldTransform` and all transform-related operations require that you place the DC in `GM_ADVANCED` mode using the `SetGraphicsMode` function. These are not available under Windows 95.

World-to-page space transformations are under the control of a *transformation matrix*. A transformation matrix is a 3×3 array of numbers. We won't belabor the details of matrix multiplication quite yet (see page 374), but we will observe here that in 2D space, the third column of the transformation matrix is a set of constants $(0, 0, 1)$, and these ultimately have no effect on the actual results computed. So we discard this last column, and we need only a 2×3 array to specify the transformations:

$$\begin{bmatrix} e_{11} & e_{12} & 0 \\ e_{21} & e_{22} & 0 \\ dx & dy & 1 \end{bmatrix} \text{ becomes } \begin{bmatrix} e_{11} & e_{12} \\ e_{21} & e_{22} \\ dx & dy \end{bmatrix}$$

and we can show that under a transformation any point (x, y) is converted to a new point (x', y') quite simply as

$$x' = e_{11} \times x + e_{21} \times y + dx$$

$$y' = e_{12} \times x + e_{22} \times y + dy$$

Whenever two transformation matrices are *composed* by using matrix multiplication (which requires a consistent shape between the two matrices' dimensions), the third row is provided implicitly as part of the operation.

A transformation is realized in the structure `XFORM`:

```
typedef struct   tagXFORM
    {
    FLOAT    eM11;
    FLOAT    eM12;
    FLOAT    eM21;
    FLOAT    eM22;
    FLOAT    eDx;
    FLOAT    eDy;
    } XFORM, *LPXFORM;
```

Some simple transformation matrices are shown in Table 6.19.

Table 6.19: Special cases of transformation matrices

Matrix	Operation
$\begin{bmatrix} 1 & 0 \\ 0 & 1 \\ t_x & t_y \end{bmatrix}$	Translation by an amount t_x, t_y.
$\begin{bmatrix} s_x & 0 \\ 0 & s_y \\ 0 & 0 \end{bmatrix}$	Scaling by an amount s_x, s_y.
$\begin{bmatrix} \cos\theta & \sin\theta \\ -\sin\theta & \cos\theta \\ 0 & 0 \end{bmatrix}$	Rotation counterclockwise by an amount θ.
$\begin{bmatrix} 1 & k \\ 0 & 1 \\ 0 & 0 \end{bmatrix}$	Horizontal shear by an amount k.

Remember that when you are taking the sine or cosine of an angle using the standard C math library, the angle is specified in *radians* for input to functions like `sin` and `cos` and for results from functions like `asin` and `acos`. There are 2π radians in a circle, so you can convert degrees to radians with the following *space*macros:

```
#define PI 3.141592f

#define deg_to_rad(n) \
        ((float)(((float)(n)) / (360.0f/(2.0f * PI)))

#define rad_to_deg(n) \
        ((float)((n) * (360.0f/(2.0f * PI)))
```

We can apply any combination of values here to get, in a single matrix, any amount of scaling, translation, rotation, and shearing. Furthermore, two matrices can be combined. A scaling matrix `mscale` and a translation matrix `mtrans` can be combined by using matrix multiplication to a single matrix that does the combination of scaling and translation. This is normally done with the `CombineTransform` function. Since we have used `SetWorldTransform` to establish a given transformation matrix, or we have inherited the default identity transformation, we can use `ModifyWorldTransform` to combine a transformation matrix with the current world transformation matrix in the DC, getting the effect of having performed `GetWorldTransform`, `CombineTransform`, and `SetWorldTransform`, all in one operation. So we have

```
XFORM m1 = { 1.0f,   0.0f,
             0.0f,   1.0f,
             12.0f, 24.0f};  // translation by 12 units in x and 24 units in y
XFORM m2 = {0.5f, 0.0f,
            0.0f, 0.5f,
```

```
            0.0f, 0.0f}; // scaling by 0.5 in x and y
XFORM m3;

CombineTransform(&m3, &m1, &m2);
SetWorldTransform(hdc, &m3);
```

which is the same as

```
SetWorldTransform(hdc, &m1);
ModifyWorldTransform(hdc, &m2, MWT_RIGHTMULTIPLY);
```

and this is the same as

```
SetWorldTransform(hdc, &m2) ;
ModifyWorldTransform(hdc, &m1, MWT_LEFTMULTIPLY);
```

Matrix multiplication is *not* commutative; therefore a left multiply and a right multiply of two matrices will produce two different answers.

Formally, matrix multiplication between two 3×3 matrices is defined as[10]

$$
\begin{bmatrix} a_{11} & a_{12} & a_{13} \\ a_{21} & a_{22} & a_{23} \\ a_{31} & a_{32} & a_{33} \end{bmatrix} \times \begin{bmatrix} b_{11} & b_{12} & b_{13} \\ b_{21} & b_{22} & b_{23} \\ b_{31} & b_{32} & b_{33} \end{bmatrix} \Rightarrow
$$

$$
\begin{bmatrix} (a_{11}b_{11} + a_{12}b_{21} + a_{13}b_{31}) & (a_{11}b_{12} + a_{12}b_{22} + a_{13}b_{32}) & (a_{11}b_{13} + a_{12}b_{23} + a_{13}b_{33}) \\ (a_{21}b_{11} + a_{22}b_{21} + a_{23}b_{31}) & (a_{21}b_{12} + a_{22}b_{22} + a_{23}b_{32}) & (a_{21}b_{13} + a_{22}b_{23} + a_{23}b_{33}) \\ (a_{31}b_{11} + a_{32}b_{21} + a_{33}b_{31}) & (a_{31}b_{12} + a_{32}b_{22} + a_{33}b_{32}) & (a_{31}b_{13} + a_{32}b_{23} + a_{33}b_{33}) \end{bmatrix}
$$

Using our canonical representation of a matrix, with the last column having constant values, we get

$$
\begin{bmatrix} a_{11} & a_{12} & 0 \\ a_{21} & a_{22} & 0 \\ a_{31} & a_{32} & 1 \end{bmatrix} \times \begin{bmatrix} b_{11} & b_{12} & 0 \\ b_{21} & b_{22} & 0 \\ b_{31} & b_{32} & 1 \end{bmatrix} \Rightarrow
$$

$$
\begin{bmatrix} (a_{11}b_{11} + a_{12}b_{21} + 0 \cdot b_{31}) & (a_{11}b_{12} + a_{12}b_{22} + 0 \cdot b_{32}) & (a_{11} \cdot 0 + a_{12} \cdot 0 + 0 \cdot 1) \\ (a_{21}b_{11} + a_{22}b_{21} + 0 \cdot b_{31}) & (a_{21}b_{12} + a_{22}b_{22} + 0 \cdot b_{32}) & (a_{21} \cdot 0 + a_{22} \cdot 0 + 0 \cdot 1) \\ (a_{31}b_{11} + a_{32}b_{21} + 1 \cdot b_{31}) & (a_{31}b_{12} + a_{32}b_{22} + 1 \cdot b_{32}) & (a_{31} \cdot 0 + a_{32} \cdot 0 + 1 \cdot 1) \end{bmatrix} \Rightarrow
$$

$$
\begin{bmatrix} a_{11}b_{11} + a_{12}b_{21} & a_{11}b_{12} + a_{12}b_{22} & 0 \\ a_{21}b_{11} + a_{22}b_{21} & a_{21}b_{12} + a_{22}b_{22} & 0 \\ a_{31}b_{11} + a_{32}b_{21} + b_{31} & a_{31}b_{12} + a_{32}b_{22} + b_{32} & 1 \end{bmatrix}
$$

---

[10] OK. I admit it. I'm a PostScript developer, and I've been using transformation matrices for a decade, but to be absolutely sure about what I was writing here, that I had it right for this book, I had to go back to my old college math book, *Theory and Problems of Matrices* (see "Further Reading"). A book I probably last used three decades ago. Frightening, isn't it, how time flies?–*jmn*

This can be used to show how any two transformations compose under matrix multiplication.

To compute the transformed location of any point *x, y* given a transformation matrix, we add a third column of 1 to the point and make it a 1-×-3 matrix and then apply matrix multiplication:

$$\begin{bmatrix} x & y & 1 \end{bmatrix} \times \begin{bmatrix} m_{11} & m_{12} & 0 \\ m_{21} & m_{22} & 0 \\ t_x & t_y & 1 \end{bmatrix} \Rightarrow \begin{bmatrix} (m_{11} \cdot x + m_{21} \cdot y + t_x) & (m_{12} \cdot x + m_{22} \cdot y + t_y) & 1 \end{bmatrix}$$

We can then discard the third element of the result matrix to be left with the equations

$$x' = m_{11} \cdot x + m_{21} \cdot y + t_x$$
$$y' = m_{12} \cdot x + m_{22} \cdot y + t_y$$

which are, not surprisingly, the same as the equations we gave on page 372.

The transformation matrix operations are shown in Table 6.20.

Table 6.20: Transformation matrix operations

Operation	Explanation
CombineTransform	Combine two transformation matrices M1 and M2 to produce a third one in the result parameter: M1 × M2 → result
GetWorldTransform	Copy the current transformation matrix from the DC to the matrix referenced by the parameter: CTM → result
ModifyWorldTransform	Combine the parameter xform with the current transformation matrix according to the following options:
	MWT_IDENTITY $\begin{bmatrix} 1 & 0 \\ 0 & 1 \\ 0 & 0 \end{bmatrix}$ → CTM (xform ignored)
	MWT_LEFTMULTIPLY xform × CTM → CTM
	MWT_RIGHTMULTIPLY CTM × xform → CTM
SetGraphicsMode	Sets the graphics mode for the DC.
	GM_COMPATIBLE Sets the graphics mode to be compatible with Windows 3.1 behavior.
	GM_ADVANCED Enables SetWorldTransform and ModifyWorldTransform operations and makes other changes in graphics interpretation.

Table 6.20: Transformation matrix operations

Operation	Explanation
SetWorldTransform	Sets the parameter as the world transformation in the DC: xform → CTM

Before you can use the SetWorldTransform or ModifyWorldTransform calls, you must call SetGraphicsMode(hdc, GM_ADVANCED). This enables the advanced graphics features of Win32. The default mode for a DC is GM_COMPATIBLE, which disables the world coordinate transforms as well as having the effects summarized in Table 6.21. The GM_ADVANCED mode is not supported in Windows 95. Once you have set GM_ADVANCED mode, you cannot reset the DC to GM_COMPATIBLE mode unless the transformation matrix in the DC is the identity matrix.

Table 6.21: Comparison of GM_COMPATIBLE and GM_ADVANCED

GM_COMPATIBLE	GM_ADVANCED
Font Differences	
TrueType or vector font text is always written left to right and right-side up, independent of any graphics transformations that may be in effect to invert the axes.	TrueType or vector font text fully conforms to the world-to-device transformation established in the DC.
Only the height of TrueType fonts is scaled.	Height and width are both scaled.
Nonhorizontal text can be drawn only by creating a font with a nonzero escapement and orientation.	Rotated text is drawn based on the world-to-device transformation and may be rotated, sheared, or reflected.
Raster fonts cannot be scaled.	Raster fonts scale by integer multiples but are not particularly attractive.
Rectangle Differences	
A rendering of a rectangle excludes the right and bottom edges.	A rendering of a rectangle includes the right and bottom edges.
Arc Drawing Differences	
An arc is drawn using the current arc direction set by SetArcDirection in the device space.	Arcs are always drawn counterclockwise in logical space.
Arcs do not respect page-space-to-device-space transformations that would require a flip on either axis.	Arcs fully respect the world-to-device transform that is set in the DC.

The WM_PAINT handler for a simple program that illustrates several transformations is shown in Listing 6.8. Its output is shown in Figure 6.25. When it is run under Windows 95, the rotation and shearing are not available. Take note of how we detected this. If you want a program that runs reliably under both Windows 95 and Windows NT, you must deal with exactly these issues.

Listing 6.8: Translation, scaling, rotation, and shearing

```
typedef struct {
                int    caption;
                XFORM x;
                } xforms;

xforms xf[] = {
{ IDS_IDENTITY,    { 1.0f, 0.0f,
                     0.0f, 1.0f,
                     0.0f, 0.0f}},

{ IDS_TRANSLATION, { 1.0f,  0.0f,
                     0.0f,  1.0f,
                    10.0f, 10.0f}},

#define COS30 0.86602540f
#define SIN30 0.50000000f
{ IDS_ROTATION30,
                    { COS30,  SIN30,
                     -SIN30,  COS30,
                      0.0f,   0.0f}},

{ IDS_SCALING_HALF, { 0.5f, 0.0f,
                      0.0f, 0.5f,
                      0.0f, 0.0f}},

{ IDS_SHEARV, {1.0f, sin30,
               0.0f, 1.0f,
               0.0f, 0.0f}},

{ IDS_SHEARH, { 1.0f,   0.0f,
                sin30,  1.0f,
                0.0f,   0.0f}},

{ NULL /* END OF TABLE */ }
          };


#define XFORM_SIZE 80
#define XFORM_OVERSHOOT (XFORM_SIZE / 10)

static void
drawTransform(HDC hdc, HWND errwnd, xforms * xf)
    {
    int orgdc;
    HPEN axispen = CreatePen(PS_SOLID, 1, RGB(128,128,128));
    RECT r;
    int height;
    TEXTMETRIC tm;
    HFONT f;
    TCHAR buffer[50];   // captions tend to be short

    orgdc = SaveDC(hdc);
```

```
    SetMapMode(hdc, MM_LOENGLISH);

    SelectPen(hdc, axispen);

    MoveToEx(hdc, 0, -XFORM_OVERSHOOT, NULL);
    LineTo(hdc, 0, XFORM_SIZE + XFORM_OVERSHOOT);
    MoveToEx(hdc, -XFORM_OVERSHOOT, 0, NULL);
    LineTo(hdc, XFORM_SIZE + XFORM_OVERSHOOT, 0);

    SelectPen(hdc, GetStockPen(BLACK_PEN));
    SelectBrush(hdc, GetStockBrush(LTGRAY_BRUSH));
    Rectangle(hdc, XFORM_SIZE, 0, 0, XFORM_SIZE/2);

    f = createCaptionFont(-14, "Arial");
    SelectFont(hdc, f);

    GetTextMetrics(hdc, &tm);
    height = tm.tmHeight + tm.tmInternalLeading;

    SetRect(&r, -XFORM_OVERSHOOT, -2*XFORM_OVERSHOOT,
                 XFORM_SIZE + XFORM_OVERSHOOT,
                 2*height);
    LoadString(GetWindowInstance(errwnd), xf->caption,
               buffer, DIM(buffer));
    DrawText(hdc, buffer, -1, &r, DT_CENTER | DT_CALCRECT);
    DrawText(hdc, buffer, -1, &r, DT_CENTER );
    FrameRect(hdc, &r, GetStockBrush(BLACK_BRUSH));

    if(!ModifyWorldTransform(hdc, &xf->x, MWT_LEFTMULTIPLY))
       { /* failed */
         PostMessage(errwnd, UWM_ERROR, IDS_XFORM_FAILED,
                                        xf->caption);
       } /* failed */
    else
       { /* success */
         SelectBrush(hdc, GetStockBrush(DKGRAY_BRUSH));
         Rectangle(hdc, XFORM_SIZE, 0, 0, XFORM_SIZE/2);
       } /* success */

    RestoreDC(hdc, orgdc);

    DeletePen(axispen);
    DeleteFont(f);
    }

static void
xform_OnPaint(HWND hwnd)
    {
#define XFORM_OFFSET (1.5f * XFORM_SIZE)
    HDC hdc;
    PAINTSTRUCT ps;
    int i;
    XFORM initialize = {1.2f,                  0.0f,
                        0.0f,                  1.2f,
                       (float)(XFORM_OFFSET/2.0f),
                                    (float) -XFORM_OFFSET};
```

```
XFORM translate = { 1.0f,                0.0f,
                    0.0f,                1.0f,
                    (float)(XFORM_OFFSET * 1.5f),0.0f};

int restore;

hdc = BeginPaint(hwnd, &ps);
restore = SaveDC(hdc);

if(!SetGraphicsMode(hdc, GM_ADVANCED))
   { /* no advanced mode */
    PostMessage(hwnd, UWM_ERROR, IDS_NO_GM_ADVANCED,
                                 IDS_NOT_SUPPORTED);
    return;
   } /* no advanced mode */

if(!ModifyWorldTransform(hdc, &initialize,
                            MWT_LEFTMULTIPLY))
   { /* failed transform */
    PostMessage(hwnd, UWM_ERROR, IDS_XFORM_FAILED,
                                 IDS_NOT_SUPPORTED);
    return;
   } /* failed transform */

for(i = 0; xf[i].caption != NULL; i++)
   { /* show each */
    drawTransform(hdc, hwnd, &xf[i]);
    ModifyWorldTransform(hdc, &translate,
                         MWT_RIGHTMULTIPLY);
   } /* show each */

RestoreDC(hdc, restore);
EndPaint(hwnd, &ps);
}
```

It is worth pointing out some techniques we used in doing this, as they allow you to structure graphics operations in a more reasonable manner than do strictly *ad hoc* methods. For example, note that we never SetWorldTransform. Instead, we ModifyWorldTransform, even though we have called the SetGraphicsMode function to set the GM_ADVANCED mode. This is done deliberately. In particular, it allowed us to reuse the key part of the drawing handler as a separate function to draw the illustrations on a graphics metafile, where a different coordinate transformation was in effect. Since we established the coordinate transform for the metafile outside the drawTransform handler, if the handler had done a SetWorldTransform it would have undone the metafile coordinate transformation. But by doing a ModifyWorldTransform, we will honor any existing transformation.

Another technique used heavily here is the SaveDC call. Rather than generate a large number of variables, such as "oldPen", "oldBrush", "oldFont", and the like and having to remember to deselect the user-created objects from the DC before deleting them, we simply do a RestoreDC. This restores all the objects previously selected and implicitly deselects all of the new objects. You can SaveDC to any nesting and unwind a large number of them all at once with a single RestoreDC.

An important feature to note is that we seem always to create a font and select it into the DC. This is because the default font in a DC is the "System" font, which is *not* a TrueType font. The font obtained by GetStockFont(SYSTEM_FONT) is a *raster* font. Raster fonts can be scaled only by integer multiples and will not honor most of the operations that are done with a transformation matrix. Often, when a raster font is rendered to a printer, the effects of attempting to scale it are quite ugly and completely unsuitable. So be aware that all of the fonts we create are TrueType fonts.

Finally, note that we issue an error notification by using a PostMessage call. Why go through such an elaborate indirection when it is clear that a simple MessageBox call should suffice? The reason becomes obvious if you actually issue a MessageBox call, either at the PostMessage site or when the UWM_ERROR message is processed. The message box pops up, quite probably overlaying the image that was drawn. When you dismiss the message box, the invalidated area must be redrawn. Doing this will quite possibly cause another message box to pop up, whereupon the error is encountered again. By having the parent process the message, it can implement strategies such as writing the message to another window, writing it to a debug stream via the OutputDebugString function, or ignoring it. Generally, you want to watch out for this sort of potential infinite loop when writing paint handlers.

A TrueType font can have any of the standard transformations applied to it. For example, you can apply a scaling or shearing transformation and draw text in a DC. This will produce the effect shown in Figure 6.26. The WM_PAINT handler that drew this is shown in Listing 6.9.

Figure 6.26: Text drawn with a transformation

Listing 6.9: Drawing text with a transformation

```
static void
textxform_OnPaint(HWND hwnd)
    {
     HDC hdc;
     PAINTSTRUCT ps;
     int restore;
     int localrestore;
     XFORM shear = { 1.0f,  0.0f,
                    -1.6f,  1.3f,
                     0.0f,  0.0f};

#define SHEAR_X 50.0f
```

```
#define SHEAR_Y 100.0f
    XFORM initialize = { 1.0f, 0.0f,
                         0.0f, 1.0f,
                   SHEAR_X, SHEAR_Y};

    HFONT font;
    TCHAR Message[128];

    LoadString(GetWindowInstance(hwnd), IDS_TEXTSHEAR,
                              Message, DIM(Message));
    hdc = BeginPaint(hwnd, &ps);

    restore = SaveDC(hdc);
    SetGraphicsMode(hdc, GM_ADVANCED);
    if(!ModifyWorldTransform(hdc, &initialize,
                                  MWT_LEFTMULTIPLY))
        { /* not implemented */
         PostMessage(hwnd, UWM_ERROR, IDS_TRANSFORM_FAILED,
                                  IDS_NOT_SUPPORTED);

         EndPaint(hwnd, &ps);
         return;
        } /* not implemented */

    SetBkMode(hdc, TRANSPARENT);
    SetTextAlign(hdc, TA_BASELINE);

    font = createCaptionFont(-50,"Times New Roman");
    SelectFont(hdc, font);

    //---------------------
    localrestore = SaveDC(hdc);


    SetTextColor(hdc, RGB(192,192,192));
    if(ModifyWorldTransform(hdc, &shear, MWT_LEFTMULTIPLY))
        { /* success */
         TextOut(hdc, 0, 0, Message, lstrlen(Message));
        } /* success */
    else
        { /* failure */
         PostMessage(hwnd, UWM_ERROR, IDS_SHEAR_FAILED,
                                  IDS_NOT_SUPPORTED);

         EndPaint(hwnd, &ps);
         return;
        } /* failure */

    RestoreDC(hdc, localrestore);

    //---------------------
    localrestore = SaveDC(hdc);

    TextOut(hdc, 0, 0, Message, lstrlen(Message));

    RestoreDC(hdc, localrestore);
    //---------------------

    RestoreDC(hdc, restore);
```

```
    EndPaint(hwnd, &ps);

    DeleteFont(font);
    }
```

Regions Revisited: ExtCreateRegion

Now that we've discussed transformation matrices, we can now look at the ExtCreateRegion function. This function works in principle by applying a transformation matrix to an existing region. However, it does not apply it directly to a region. Instead, you must obtain the region's representation via GetRegionData to first obtain a description of the region and then create a new region by using the region description to create a new region. Again, note that Windows 95 cannot do shearing or rotation, but in general the most interesting operations to do to a region are scaling and translation. Translation we already have by using OffsetRgn, so the major contribution of ExtCreateRegion is to allow us to scale a region. A combination of scaling and offset can be useful. For example, consider a contrived example: a program that wants to compute the "shadow" of a region, given an apparent light source. The light source is very far away and quite diffuse, but we want to simulate the shadowing by noting that the further one moves the object from the background where the shadow is cast, the smaller the shadow is relative to the size of the object casting the shadow. This can be accomplished by the following code, which for now assumes there is a constant distance between the object and the background. In a real program, in which objects can appear at different distances from the background, the scaling factor would be based on their apparent distance.

```
static void
shadow_rgn(HDC hdc, HRGN currentrgn)
{
  HRGN newrgn ;
  LPRGNDATA data ;
  DWORD size ;

  XFORM m ;

m.eM11 = MY_HSCALE_FACTOR; // factor for a fixed distance
m.eM12 = 0;
m.eM21 = MY_VSCALE_FACTOR;
m.eM22 = 0;
m.eDx = MY_HOFFSET;
m.eDy = MY_VOFFSET;

size = GetRegionData(hrgn, 0, NULL);
data = (LPRGNDATA)malloc(size);
// .. deal with malloc failure
GetRegionData(hrgn, size, data);
newrgn = ExtCreateRegion(&m, size, data);
// We may not have the region in the clipping region
ExtSelectClipRgn(hdc, newrgn, RGN_OR);
FillRgn(hdc, newrgn, ShadowBrush);
free(data);
```

Paths: Completely General Shapes for Drawing, Clipping, and Filling

A *path* is essentially a set of graphical objects represented by their outlines. A rectangle, an ellipse, a rounded rectangle, and a line can certainly be components of a path. The graphic output function Polygon takes a sequence of points and draws a line segment between pairs. The notion of path separates the act of *defining* an outline from the act of *drawing* the outline. For example, we can construct a path from, say, 0, 0 to 0, 20, then to 20, 20, then to 20, 0, and finally back to 0, 0. This path delimits a square (assuming our mapping mode is isotropic and our device has square pixels). We could *stroke* it, which would draw the outline of a square, or we could *fill* it, which would give us a square of some specific color, or we could both *stroke* and *fill* it. The Rectangle function in effect constructs a path, then strokes it with the currently selected pen, and then fills it with the currently selected brush. So why do we need a more complex method to get a square painted?

The answer is that a path is really quite general. For example, we could start at 0, 0 and draw a line to 20, 20 and then specify three pairs of control points and do a PolyBezierTo function, followed by another line, an ArcTo, a sequence of line segments drawn by Polygon, and finally another PolyBezierTo whose terminal point was 0, 0. Once we have constructed such a path, we can fill it or stroke it or both. If we are stroking a path, it does not need to form a contiguous line; it can have any number of MoveToEx calls embedded as well. Or, just to make life *really* interesting, we could convert the area defined by this path to a region, invalidate the region, and use the region in the resulting WM_PAINT handler to clip whatever we draw! The set of path-related operations is given in Table 6.22.

Table 6.22: Path operations

Function	Description
AbortPath	Closes and discards any paths in the DC. If there is an open path bracket in the DC, it is first closed and then the path is discarded.
BeginPath	Opens a path bracket in the current DC. All path-defining operations from Table 6.23 will add to this path.
CloseFigure	"Closes" the figure by drawing a line from the current position to the first point of the path being drawn. The line that is drawn is connected to the line that starts the figure by using the current line join style.
EndPath	Closes the path bracket and selects the path into the DC.
FillPath	Closes any open figure in the current path (using CloseFigure). Fills in the path's interior using the current brush from the DC and the prevailing polygon fill mode. The path is then discarded.
FlattenPath	Converts any curves in the path currently in the DC to a sequence of line segments.
GetMiterLimit	Returns the miter limit.
GetPolyFillMode	Returns the current polygon fill mode.

Table 6.22: Path operations

Function	Description
GetPath	Returns either the number of points in the path or the path and vertex data describing the currently selected path.
PathToRegion	Closes any open path and then converts the path to a region. Whether or not a point is in the region depends on the prevailing polygon fill mode. The path itself is discarded.
PolyDraw	Draws lines based on the results of GetPath.
SelectClipPath	Selects the current path as a clipping region, combining the new region with any existing region using one of the region operations defined in Table 6.17. The path itself is discarded.
SetMiterLimit	Sets the miter limit. When a path is stroked, the lines are joined with the current join mode of the pen selected into the DC. If this is PS_JOIN_MITER, the miter limit will be used to determine if a mitered or beveled corner will be produced.
SetPolyFillMode	Sets the current polygon fill mode. The polygon fill mode is used to determine how FillPath determines what areas to fill in and how PathToRegion determines which points are in the region.
StrokePath	Renders the existing closed path using the current pen in the DC. The path is then discarded.
StrokeAndFillPath	Closes any open path and then strokes the outline of the path using the current pen and fills the figure using the current brush selected in the DC. The path is then discarded.
WidenPath	Redefines the current path as being the area that would be painted if the path were drawn with StrokePath, using the currently selected pen in the DC. Flattens any curves using FlattenPath.

Table 6.23: Path-defining drawing functions

AngleArc	LineTo	Polyline
Arc	MoveToEx	PolylineTo
ArcTo	Pie	PolyPolygon
Chord	PolyBezier	PolyPolyline
CloseFigure	PolyBezierTo	Rectangle
Ellipse	PolyDraw	RoundRect
ExtTextOut	Polygon	TextOut

A path is initiated with the BeginPath function. This discards any existing path in the DC and prepares the DC to record path information. The path-defining operations shown in Table 6.23, when executed with an open path pending, will not actually draw into the DC. Instead, their effect will be realized by the addition of components to the path. A path is normally terminated by a CloseFigure call followed by an EndPath call. The CloseFigure call is not required if you do not plan to use the path for filling or clipping. However, in many cases this is exactly what you want it for. So, you most often will find the CloseFigure call preceding the EndPath call. Once you have closed a figure, you don't have to call EndPath; you can start another figure. You might do this if you were trying to draw a doughnut-like shape. You would draw the outer figure, ending up with a CloseFigure call, and then draw the inner figure, ending with another CloseFigure call. If this was all you needed, you could then call EndPath.

There is a significant difference between calling CloseFigure to close off a figure and simply drawing the geometric shape. Consider drawing a simple form like an equilateral triangle. You might decide that it would look best if you created a pen with a mitered line join. But if you draw it in this way:

```
BeginPath(hdc) ;
MoveToEx(hdc, x0, y0) ;
LineTo(hdc, x1, y1) ;  // draw line 1
LineTo(hdc, x2, y2) ; // draw line 2
LineTo(hdc, x0, y0) ; // draw line 3
EndPath(hdc) ;

StrokePath(hdc);
```

you will not see the desired effect. Lines 1 and 2 are joined with a mitered corner; lines 2 and 3 are joined with a mitered corner. But lines 3 and 1 are apparently not joined! This is because the line starts with the end caps option selected for the pen, such as flat end caps. Line 3 ends with flat end caps. But if you draw line 3 by doing a CloseFigure instead of a LineTo, then the output will be correct. Windows will join the endpoint of line 2 to the endpoint of line 1 using a straight line and will make the join using the join of the pen.

```
BeginPath(hdc)
MoveToEx(hdc, x0, y0) ;
LineTo(hdc, x1, y1) ;  // draw line 1
LineTo(hdc, x2, y2) ; // draw line 2
CloseFigure(hdc) ; // draw line 3
EndPath(hdc) ;

StrokePath(hdc);
```

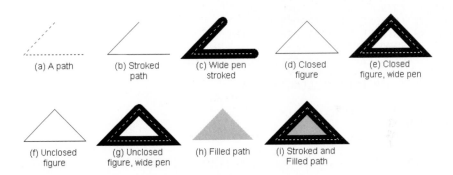

(a) A path   (b) Stroked path   (c) Wide pen stroked   (d) Closed figure   (e) Closed figure, wide pen

(f) Unclosed figure   (g) Unclosed figure, wide pen   (h) Filled path   (i) Stroked and Filled path

Figure 6.27: Paths–filled and stroked

Examples of this can be seen in Figure 6.27. Here, we will show the path when appropriate with a dashed line. Figure 6.27(a) shows a path constructed by two LineTo operations. (To get it to show, we actually stroked it with a dotted pen.) Figure 6.27(b) shows the result of stroking the path with an ordinary stock black pen. Figure 6.27(c) shows a more complex result. We create a geometric pen using ExtCreatePen, specifying a fairly thick pen, round end caps, and mitered join. When we stroke the path with this pen, we get the solid drawing shown (to show the underlying path, we stroked the path a second time with a dotted white pen). If we call CloseFigure before stroking the path with an ordinary stock black pen, we get the result shown in Figure 6.27(d). If we stroke the path with the same cosmetic pen we used previously, we get the illustration of Figure 6.27(e). Note that in this case, all the joins are mitered. As indicated, we could simply draw that third line in, which when stroked with a stock black pen would give us the result in Figure 6.27(f). Looking at this, you will not see anything substantially different from Figure 6.27(d): for a 1-pixel stock pen, the results are indistinguishable. But if we use our thick geometric pen, we get Figure 6.27(g). There is a substantial difference between the drawing of Figure 6.27(e) and Figure 6.27(g). You can see this difference by looking at the apex of the triangle. Figure 6.27(g) has a rounded top, whereas Figure 6.27(e) has a mitered top. This is because Figure 6.27(g) does not have two joined lines at its top. The CloseFigure, however, joined the lines of Figure 6.27(e), so a miter was used to render the join. It is important to understand this difference.

You can use FillPath on the same path to get the result shown in Figure 6.27(h). The interior of the figure is filled with the current brush, which we have selected as a stock gray brush. You can also use StrokeAndFillPath to both stroke and fill the path, as shown in Figure 6.27(i). Note that stroked paths place the pen symmetrically around the line defining the path, as shown by the dotted white line. In the stroking of a path, there is no equivalent of the PS_INSIDEFRAME that would draw the pen "inside" the path. The PS_INSIDEFRAME style applies only to geometric figures drawn with a bounding box, such as Rectangle, Ellipse, and Arc. The code which draws this illustration is shown in Listing 6.10.

Listing 6.10: Code to draw the filled and stroked figures of Figure 6.27

```
#define STROKE_LENGTH 50
#define STROKE_X1 (2 * STROKE_LENGTH)
#define STROKE_Y1 (STROKE_LENGTH / 2)
#define STROKE_X2 (STROKE_X1 - STROKE_LENGTH)
#define STROKE_Y2 (STROKE_Y1 + STROKE_LENGTH)
#define STROKE_X3 (STROKE_X1 + STROKE_LENGTH)
#define STROKE_Y3 STROKE_Y2
#define STROKE_SPACING (2.7f * (float)STROKE_LENGTH)

#define STROKE_VERT_GAP (STROKE_LENGTH / 5)

#define OPEN_PATH   0
#define CLOSE_PATH  1
#define DRAW_PATH   2

#define STROKE_PEN_WIDTH 15

//================================================================
HFONT createWeightedFont(int size, LPCSTR facecode, int weight)
    {
      return CreateFont(size, 0,0,0, weight, FALSE, FALSE, FALSE,
                    ANSI_CHARSET,
                    OUT_DEFAULT_PRECIS,
                    CLIP_DEFAULT_PRECIS,
                    PROOF_QUALITY,
```

```
                            VARIABLE_PITCH,
                            facecode);
    }
//================================================================
HFONT createCaptionFont(int size, LPCSTR facecode)
    {
    return createWeightedFont(size, facecode, FW_NORMAL);
    }


/****************************************************************
*                          drawPath
* Inputs:
*       HDC hDC: Display context
*       int closed: Closing option, see Effect
*       HINSTANCE hinst: Instance handle for string resource.
*                        Can be NULL if caption == 0
*       int caption: Caption to display, or 0 for no caption
* Result: void
*
* Effect:
*       Draws a path given the stroke parameters.  There are
*       three points used, which form an isosceles triangle.  They
*       are points p1, p2 and p3
*               OPEN_PATH:  p1->p2->p3
*               CLOSE_PATH: p1->p2->p3->p1  via CloseFigure
*               DRAW_PATH:  p1->p2->p3->p1  by explicit line drawing
****************************************************************/

static void drawPath(HDC hdc, int closed, HINSTANCE hinst,
                                              int caption)
    {
    RECT r;

    BeginPath(hdc);
    MoveToEx(hdc, STROKE_X1, STROKE_Y1, NULL);
    LineTo(hdc, STROKE_X2, STROKE_Y2);
    LineTo(hdc, STROKE_X3, STROKE_Y3);

    // Based on the closed parameter, select the action
    // following the second path segment
    switch(closed)
        { /* what close option? */
         case OPEN_PATH:
             // do nothing.  Path is open
             break;
         case CLOSE_PATH:
             // Close the figure; let the GDI compute the path
             // segment from p3 to p1
             CloseFigure(hdc);
             break;
         case DRAW_PATH:
             // Draw an explicit line from p3 to p1
             LineTo(hdc, STROKE_X1, STROKE_Y1);
             break;
        } /* what close option? */

    EndPath(hdc);
```

```
      // If a caption is present, draw it.
      if(caption != 0)
         { /* has caption */
          TEXTMETRIC tm;
          HFONT font = createCaptionFont(-14, _T("Arial"));
          int saved = SaveDC(hdc);
          TCHAR text[256];

          SelectObject(hdc, font);
          GetTextMetrics(hdc, &tm);
          SetRect(&r, STROKE_X2, STROKE_Y2 + STROKE_VERT_GAP,
                     STROKE_X3, STROKE_Y2 + STROKE_VERT_GAP +
                            2 *(tm.tmHeight + tm.tmExternalLeading));

          LoadString(hinst, caption, text, DIM(text));
          DrawText(hdc, text, -1, &r, DT_CENTER | DT_WORDBREAK);
          RestoreDC(hdc, saved);
          DeleteObject(font);
         } /* has caption */
      }
/****************************************************************
*                            saf_APath
****************************************************************/

static void saf_APath(HWND hwnd, HDC hdc)
     {
      int horzsave = SaveDC(hdc);
      HPEN pen;

      drawPath(hdc, OPEN_PATH, GetWindowInstance(hwnd),
                                              IDS_A_PATH);

      pen = CreatePen(PS_DOT, 0, RGB(0,0,0));
      SelectObject(hdc, pen);
      StrokePath(hdc);

      RestoreDC(hdc, horzsave);

      DeleteObject(pen);
      }
/****************************************************************
*                          saf_StrokedPath
****************************************************************/

static void saf_StrokedPath(HWND hwnd, HDC hdc)
     {
      int horzsave = SaveDC(hdc);
      HPEN pen;

      drawPath(hdc, OPEN_PATH, GetWindowInstance(hwnd),
                                              IDS_STROKED_PATH);

      pen = CreatePen(PS_SOLID, 0, RGB(0,0,0));
      SelectObject(hdc, pen);
      StrokePath(hdc);
```

```
    RestoreDC(hdc, horzsave);
    DeleteObject(pen);
    }
/*****************************************************************
*                    saf_StrokedPathWide
*****************************************************************/

static void saf_StrokedPathWide(HWND hwnd, HDC hdc)
    {
    int horzsave = SaveDC(hdc);
    int pathsave;
    LOGBRUSH blackbrush = {BS_SOLID, RGB(0,0,0), 0 };
    HPEN pen;
    HPEN whpen;

    drawPath(hdc, OPEN_PATH, GetWindowInstance(hwnd),
                                        IDS_STROKED_WIDE);

    pen = ExtCreatePen(PS_GEOMETRIC | PS_ENDCAP_ROUND |
                                        PS_JOIN_MITER,
                    STROKE_PEN_WIDTH, &blackbrush, 0, NULL);

    SelectObject(hdc, pen);

    pathsave = SaveDC(hdc);
    StrokePath(hdc);
    RestoreDC(hdc, pathsave);

    whpen = CreatePen(PS_DOT, 1, RGB(255,255,255));
    SelectObject(hdc, whpen);
    SetBkMode(hdc, TRANSPARENT);

    StrokePath(hdc);
    RestoreDC(hdc, horzsave);

    DeleteObject(pen);
    DeleteObject(whpen);
    }
/*****************************************************************
*                    saf_ClosedFigure
*****************************************************************/

static void saf_ClosedFigure(HWND hwnd, HDC hdc)
    {
    int horzsave = SaveDC(hdc);
    HPEN pen;

    drawPath(hdc, CLOSE_PATH, GetWindowInstance(hwnd),
                                        IDS_CLOSED);

    pen = CreatePen(PS_SOLID, 0, RGB(0,0,0));

    SelectObject(hdc, pen);
    StrokePath(hdc);

    RestoreDC(hdc, horzsave);
```

```
    DeleteObject(pen);
    }
/*****************************************************************
*                    saf_ClosedFigureWide
*****************************************************************/

static void saf_ClosedFigureWide(HWND hwnd, HDC hdc)
    {
    int horzsave = SaveDC(hdc);
    int pathsave;
    LOGBRUSH blackbrush = {BS_SOLID, RGB(0,0,0), 0 };
    HPEN pen;
    HPEN whpen;

    drawPath(hdc, CLOSE_PATH, GetWindowInstance(hwnd),
                                          IDS_CLOSED_WIDE);
    pen = ExtCreatePen(PS_GEOMETRIC | PS_ENDCAP_ROUND |
                                      PS_JOIN_MITER,
                       STROKE_PEN_WIDTH, &blackbrush, 0, NULL);

    SelectObject(hdc, pen);

    pathsave = SaveDC(hdc);
    StrokePath(hdc);
    RestoreDC(hdc, pathsave);

    whpen = CreatePen(PS_DOT, 1, RGB(255,255,255));
    SelectObject(hdc, whpen);
    SetBkMode(hdc, TRANSPARENT);

    StrokePath(hdc);
    RestoreDC(hdc, horzsave);
    DeleteObject(pen);
    DeleteObject(whpen);

    }
/*****************************************************************
*                    saf_UnclosedFigure
*****************************************************************/

static void saf_UnclosedFigure(HWND hwnd, HDC hdc)
    {
    int horzsave = SaveDC(hdc);
    HPEN pen;

    drawPath(hdc, DRAW_PATH, GetWindowInstance(hwnd),
                                          IDS_UNCLOSED);

    pen = CreatePen(PS_SOLID, 0, RGB(0,0,0));

    SelectObject(hdc, pen);
    StrokePath(hdc);

    RestoreDC(hdc, horzsave);

    DeleteObject(pen);

    }
```

```
/*****************************************************************
*                        saf_UnclosedWide
*****************************************************************/

static void saf_UnclosedWide(HWND hwnd, HDC hdc)
    {
     int horzsave = SaveDC(hdc);
     int pathsave;
     LOGBRUSH blackbrush = {BS_SOLID, RGB(0,0,0), 0 };
     HPEN pen;
     HPEN whpen;

     drawPath(hdc, DRAW_PATH, GetWindowInstance(hwnd),
                                            IDS_UNCLOSED_WIDE);

     pen = ExtCreatePen(PS_GEOMETRIC | PS_ENDCAP_ROUND |
                                          PS_JOIN_MITER,
                     STROKE_PEN_WIDTH, &blackbrush, 0, NULL);

     SelectObject(hdc, pen);

     pathsave = SaveDC(hdc);
     StrokePath(hdc);
     RestoreDC(hdc, pathsave);

     whpen = CreatePen(PS_DOT, 1, RGB(255,255,255));
     SelectObject(hdc, whpen);
     SetBkMode(hdc, TRANSPARENT);

     StrokePath(hdc);

     RestoreDC(hdc, horzsave);
     DeleteObject(pen);
     DeleteObject(whpen);

    }
/*****************************************************************
*                        saf_FilledPath
*****************************************************************/

static void saf_FilledPath(HWND hwnd, HDC hdc)
    {
     int horzsave = SaveDC(hdc);

     drawPath(hdc, CLOSE_PATH, GetWindowInstance(hwnd),
                                            IDS_FILLED);
     SelectObject(hdc, GetStockObject(LTGRAY_BRUSH));
     FillPath(hdc);
     RestoreDC(hdc, horzsave);
    }
/*****************************************************************
*                        saf_StrokedAndFilled
*****************************************************************/

static void saf_StrokedAndFilled(HWND hwnd, HDC hdc)
    {
     int horzsave = SaveDC(hdc);
     int pathsave;
```

```
        LOGBRUSH blackbrush = {BS_SOLID, RGB(0,0,0), 0 };
        HPEN pen;
        HPEN whpen;

        drawPath(hdc, CLOSE_PATH, GetWindowInstance(hwnd),
                                        IDS_STROKED_AND_FILLED);
        SelectObject(hdc, GetStockObject(LTGRAY_BRUSH));
        pen = ExtCreatePen(PS_GEOMETRIC | PS_ENDCAP_ROUND |
                                PS_JOIN_MITER,
                        STROKE_PEN_WIDTH, &blackbrush, 0, NULL);
        SelectObject(hdc, pen);

        pathsave = SaveDC(hdc);
        StrokeAndFillPath(hdc);
        RestoreDC(hdc, pathsave);

        whpen = CreatePen(PS_DOT, 1, RGB(255,255,255));
        SelectObject(hdc, whpen);
        SetBkMode(hdc, TRANSPARENT);

        StrokePath(hdc);

        RestoreDC(hdc, horzsave);
        DeleteObject(pen);
        DeleteObject(whpen);

    }

static void strokeandfill_OnPaint(HWND hwnd)
    {
    XFORM ShiftRight = { 1.0f,              0.0f,
                         0.0f,              1.0f,
                         STROKE_SPACING,    0.0f};
    XFORM ShiftDown  = { 1.0f,              0.0f,
                         0.0f,              1.0f,
                         0.0f,              STROKE_SPACING};
    int vertsave;
    PAINTSTRUCT ps;
    HDC hdc = BeginPaint(hwnd, &ps);

    SetGraphicsMode(hdc, GM_ADVANCED);

    vertsave = SaveDC(hdc);

    //===============================================================-
    // ROW 1
    //===============================================================-

    saf_APath(hwnd, hdc);

    ModifyWorldTransform(hdc, &ShiftRight, MWT_RIGHTMULTIPLY);

    saf_StrokedPath(hwnd, hdc);

    ModifyWorldTransform(hdc, &ShiftRight, MWT_RIGHTMULTIPLY);

    saf_StrokedPathWide(hwnd, hdc);
```

```
ModifyWorldTransform(hdc, &ShiftRight, MWT_RIGHTMULTIPLY);

saf_ClosedFigure(hwnd, hdc);

ModifyWorldTransform(hdc, &ShiftRight, MWT_RIGHTMULTIPLY);

saf_ClosedFigureWide(hwnd, hdc);

//===============================================================
// Move down to the next row
//===============================================================
RestoreDC(hdc, vertsave);

ModifyWorldTransform(hdc, &ShiftDown, MWT_RIGHTMULTIPLY);
vertsave = SaveDC(hdc);

//===============================================================
// ROW 2
//===============================================================

saf_UnclosedFigure(hwnd, hdc);

ModifyWorldTransform(hdc, &ShiftRight, MWT_RIGHTMULTIPLY);

saf_UnclosedWide(hwnd, hdc);

ModifyWorldTransform(hdc, &ShiftRight, MWT_RIGHTMULTIPLY);

saf_FilledPath(hwnd, hdc);

ModifyWorldTransform(hdc, &ShiftRight, MWT_RIGHTMULTIPLY);

saf_StrokedAndFilled(hwnd, hdc);

ModifyWorldTransform(hdc, &ShiftRight, MWT_RIGHTMULTIPLY);

//===============================================================
RestoreDC(hdc, vertsave);
EndPaint(hwnd, &ps);
}
```

A useful technique is illustrated by the contents of one of the functions that draws a thick pen figure with a white dotted line. Let's look at it in some detail.

First we save the DC so that we can restore it when all the operations are finished. We also create a separate variable to hold another SaveDC result we will need later. Further, we create a black brush for creating a geometric pen and some variables to hold pens.

```
int horzsave = SaveDC(hdc);
int pathsave;
LOGBRUSH blackbrush = {BS_SOLID, RGB(0,0,0), 0 };
HPEN pen;
HPEN whpen;
```

We then call the generic drawPath function we wrote that draws a path; the OPEN_PATH flag we defined tells the function to not close the path:

```
drawPath(hdc, OPEN_PATH, GetWindowInstance(hwnd), IDS_WIDE_STROKED);
```

We now create our wide geometric pen and select it into the DC:

```
pen = ExtCreatePen(PS_GEOMETRIC | PS_ENDCAP_ROUND | PS_JOIN_MITER,
                   STROKE_PEN_WIDTH, &blackbrush, 0, NULL);

SelectObject(hdc, pen);
```

Here's a useful technique: We want to stroke the path twice, but stroking the path will remove the path from the DC. If we first save the DC, we can stroke the path. When we restore the DC, the saved path will be restored, and we can stroke it again. So we first stroke the path with our wide pen:

```
pathsave = SaveDC(hdc);
StrokePath(hdc);
RestoreDC(hdc, pathsave);
```

Next we create a dotted white pen for drawing the path itself, select it into the DC, and stroke the path a second time. Note that we set the background mode to be transparent so that the gaps in the pen are not filled, thereby leaving the background color (black) showing through:

```
whpen = CreatePen(PS_DOT, 1, RGB(255,255,255));
SelectObject(hdc, whpen);
SetBkMode(hdc, TRANSPARENT);

StrokePath(hdc);
```

Finally, we restore the DC to its original state and delete the objects we created:

```
RestoreDC(hdc, horzsave);

DeleteObject(pen);
DeleteObject(whpen);
```

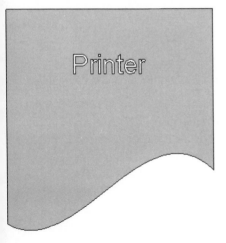

Figure 6.28: A path including text

Another example of a complex and interesting path is shown in Figure 6.28. This illustrates a symbol that is usually used in workflow diagrams to indicate a printer or a printed report. In this case, the word "Printer" appears in an outline form. This whole figure is drawn as a single path, text included. Then the path is stroked and filled. Here are some observations about this technique:

The left edge, bottom, and right edge are explicitly drawn, but the top is obtained by using the CloseFigure function.

The font is a TrueType font, not a raster font such as the System font.

After the initial MoveToEx, we do a LineTo, PolyBezierTo, LineTo, and CloseFigure call to get the box and then we do a TextOut to draw the text path. The path consists of a number of disjoint closed figures; letters such as P, i, and e have two closed figures for each letter.

The internal control points for the PolyBezierTo are $^1/_3$ and $^2/_3$ of the width of the object, with the first control point below the object and the second within it.

So that the text path is drawn properly, the background mode is set to TRANSPARENT and the polygon fill mode is set to ALTERNATE.

The figure scales itself to the size of the window by using a transformation matrix. This is all shown in Listing 6.11.

Listing 6.11: Code to draw the "Printer" box

```
static void
scale(HDC hdc, float xscale, float yscale)
    {
      XFORM scalefactor = { 1.0f, 0.0f,
                            0.0f, 1.0f,
                            0.0f, 0.0f };  // identity

      scalefactor.eM11 = xscale;
      scalefactor.eM22 = yscale;

      ModifyWorldTransform(hdc, &scalefactor, MWT_LEFTMULTIPLY);
    }

static void
translate(HDC hdc, float xdelta, float ydelta)
    {
      XFORM xlate = { 1.0f, 0.0f,
                      0.0f, 1.0f,
                      0.0f, 0.0f };  // identity

      xlate.eDx = xdelta;
      xlate.eDy = ydelta;

      ModifyWorldTransform(hdc, &xlate, MWT_LEFTMULTIPLY);
    }


#define COMPLEX_BASE 5 // base units for all dimensions

#define COMPLEX_X0 0
#define COMPLEX_Y0 0
#define COMPLEX_WIDTH (16 * COMPLEX_BASE)
#define COMPLEX_LEFT_HEIGHT (16 * COMPLEX_BASE)
#define COMPLEX_RIGHT_HEIGHT (12 * COMPLEX_BASE)
#define COMPLEX_X1 COMPLEX_X0
#define COMPLEX_Y1 (COMPLEX_Y0 + COMPLEX_LEFT_HEIGHT)
#define COMPLEX_X2 (COMPLEX_X0 + COMPLEX_WIDTH)
#define COMPLEX_Y2 (COMPLEX_Y0 + COMPLEX_RIGHT_HEIGHT)
#define COMPLEX_X3 (COMPLEX_X2)
#define COMPLEX_Y3 (COMPLEX_Y0)
#define COMPLEX_CAPTION_Y (COMPLEX_X0 + 3 * COMPLEX_BASE)
#define COMPLEX_OFFSET_Y1 (7 * COMPLEX_BASE)
#define COMPLEX_OFFSET_Y2 (5 * COMPLEX_BASE)
#define COMPLEX_FONTSIZE (-2 * COMPLEX_BASE)

#define COMPLEX_TOTAL_HEIGHT (1.5f * COMPLEX_Y1)
```

```
#define COMPLEX_DX 10.0f
#define COMPLEX_DY 10.0f

static void
complex_OnPaint(HWND hwnd)
    {
    PAINTSTRUCT ps;
    HDC hdc = BeginPaint(hwnd, &ps);
    int save = SaveDC(hdc);
    POINT pt = {COMPLEX_X0, COMPLEX_CAPTION_Y };
    SIZE size;
    RECT client;
    TCHAR caption[128];
    HFONT font = createCaptionFont(COMPLEX_FONTSIZE, _T("Arial"));
    POINT bottom[] = {
            {COMPLEX_X1 + (COMPLEX_X2 - COMPLEX_X1) / 3,
             COMPLEX_Y2 + COMPLEX_OFFSET_Y1},
            {COMPLEX_X1 + 2 * (COMPLEX_X2 - COMPLEX_X1) / 3,
             COMPLEX_Y2 - COMPLEX_OFFSET_Y2},
            {COMPLEX_X2, COMPLEX_Y2}};


    SetGraphicsMode(hdc, GM_ADVANCED);

    // Compute the scaling so it is sized to the window

    GetClientRect(hwnd, &client);
    scale(hdc, (float)client.bottom / COMPLEX_TOTAL_HEIGHT,
               (float)client.bottom / COMPLEX_TOTAL_HEIGHT);

    translate(hdc, COMPLEX_DX, COMPLEX_DY);

    LoadString(GetWindowInstance(hwnd), IDS_COMPLEX_CAPTION,
                      caption, DIM(caption));


    BeginPath(hdc);
    MoveToEx(hdc, COMPLEX_X0, COMPLEX_Y0, NULL);
    LineTo(hdc, COMPLEX_X1, COMPLEX_Y1);

    PolyBezierTo(hdc, bottom, 3);

    LineTo(hdc, COMPLEX_X3, COMPLEX_Y3);

    CloseFigure(hdc);

    // Compute a point that centers the caption
    SelectFont(hdc, font);
    GetTextExtentPoint32(hdc, caption, lstrlen(caption), &size);

    // Now center the rectangle horizontally
    pt.x += ((COMPLEX_X2 - COMPLEX_X0) - size.cx) / 2;

    SetBkMode(hdc, TRANSPARENT);
    SetPolyFillMode(hdc, ALTERNATE);
    TextOut(hdc, pt.x, pt.y, caption, lstrlen(caption));

    EndPath(hdc);
```

```
   SelectBrush(hdc, GetStockObject(LTGRAY_BRUSH));
   StrokeAndFillPath(hdc);

   RestoreDC(hdc, save);
   DeleteObject(font);
   EndPaint(hwnd, &ps);
   }
```

We can convert any path to a clipping region. For example, we can draw a path by selecting a font of an appropriate size, calling BeginPath, drawing the text into the DC using TextOut (not DrawText), and calling EndPath. For this to work as expected, we must also draw the text in TRANSPARENT mode. We can then call StrokePath to get this text rendered as an outline if we wish, producing the effect shown in Figure 6.29. In this same DC, using a different font and without creating a path, we can draw some background text; this is illustrated in Figure 6.30.

Figure 6.29: Stroked text path

If, however, instead of stroking the path, we use SelectClipPath to establish the path as a clipping region, we get the result shown in Figure 6.31. The code to accomplish all this is shown in Listing 6.12.

Listing 6.12: Code to illustrate text clipping

```
/*****************************************************************
 *                        textclip_MakePath
 *****************************************************************/
static void textclip_MakePath(HWND hwnd, HDC hdc)
    {
    RECT r;                 // client rectangle
    HFONT clipfont;         // font used to define clipping region
    HFONT oldfont;
    TCHAR text[128];

    LoadString(GetWindowInstance(hwnd), IDS_CLIPPER, text,
                                        DIM(text)) ;

    GetClientRect(hwnd, &r);

    // Scale the string so that it will fill the client area

    clipfont = createWeightedFont(r.bottom, TimesFont, FW_BOLD);

    oldfont = SelectFont(hdc, clipfont);

    // If we want the text itself to be the clipping region,
    // we must set transparent mode.

    BeginPath(hdc);
    SetBkMode(hdc, TRANSPARENT);
    TextOut(hdc, 0, 0, text, lstrlen(text));
```

```
    EndPath(hdc);

    SelectFont(hdc, oldfont);
    DeleteObject(clipfont);
    }
/******************************************************************
*                     textclip_DrawBackground
******************************************************************/
static void textclip_DrawBackground(HWND hwnd, HDC hdc)
    {
    RECT r;  // client rectangle
    HFONT bkgndfont;// font used to draw background words
    HFONT oldfont;// previous font
    POINT pt;// current output position
    TEXTMETRIC tm;// for determining font height
    int offset;// used to produce nicer appearing background
    int line;// ...
    TCHAR text[128];
    int textlen;

    GetClientRect(hwnd, &r);

    // Create a background font so that the client area will
    // contain BKGND_ROWS lines of text

#define BKGND_ROWS 30
    bkgndfont = createCaptionFont(r.bottom / BKGND_ROWS,
                                     _T("Times New Roman"));

    // We want text output to update the current position
    SetTextAlign(hdc, TA_UPDATECP);

    // Set up for the background text drawing loops
    oldfont = SelectFont(hdc, bkgndfont);
    GetTextMetrics(hdc, &tm);
    offset = 0;
    line = 0;

    MoveToEx(hdc, 0, 0, NULL);
    GetCurrentPositionEx(hdc, &pt);

    textlen = LoadString(GetWindowInstance(hwnd), IDS_BG,
                                    text, DIM(text)) ;

    while(pt.y < r.bottom)
        { /* output one row */
        // Avoid boring columnar output: offset each line by one
        // character of the string

        offset = line;

        // Now draw the row
        while(pt.x < r.right)
            { /* output background word */
            TextOut(hdc, 0, 0, &text[offset],
                        textlen - 1 - offset);
            GetCurrentPositionEx(hdc, &pt);
```

```
                offset = 0;   // make sure full word draws next time
              } /* output background word */

           // Prepare for the next row

           line = (line + 1) % (textlen - 1);
           MoveToEx(hdc, 0, pt.y + tm.tmHeight, NULL);
           GetCurrentPositionEx(hdc, &pt);
         } /* output one row */

     SelectFont(hdc, oldfont);
     DeleteObject(oldfont);
     }
/*******************************************************************
*                         textclip1_OnPaint
*******************************************************************/
static void
textclip1_OnPaint(HWND hwnd)
     {
     PAINTSTRUCT ps;
     HDC hdc = BeginPaint(hwnd, &ps);
     int restore = SaveDC(hdc);

     textclip_MakePath(hwnd, hdc);

     StrokePath(hdc);

     // Clean up the DC and delete the resources created
     RestoreDC(hdc, restore);
     EndPaint(hwnd, &ps);
     }

/*******************************************************************
*                         textclip2_OnPaint
*******************************************************************/
static void
textclip2_OnPaint(HWND hwnd, HDC hdc)
     {
     PAINTSTRUCT ps;
     HDC hdc = BeginPaint(hwnd, &ps);
     int restore = SaveDC(hdc);
     textclip_MakePath(hwnd, hdc);

     // Now set the path defined by the text to be the
     // clipping path

     StrokePath(hdc);

     textclip_DrawBackground(hwnd, hdc);


     // Clean up the DC and delete the resources created
     RestoreDC(hdc, restore);
     EndPaint(hwnd, &ps);
     }
```

```
/*****************************************************************
*                        textclip3_OnPaint
*****************************************************************/
static void
textclip3_OnPaint(HWND hwnd, HDC hdc)
    {
    PAINTSTRUCT ps;
    HDC hdc = BeginPaint(hwnd, &ps);
    int restore = SaveDC(hdc);
    textclip_MakePath(hwnd, hdc);

    // Now set the path defined by the text to be the
    // clipping path

    SelectClipPath(hdc, RGN_COPY);

    textclip_DrawBackground(hwnd, hdc);

    // Clean up the DC and delete the resources created
    RestoreDC(hdc, restore);
    EndPaint(hwnd, &ps);
    }
```

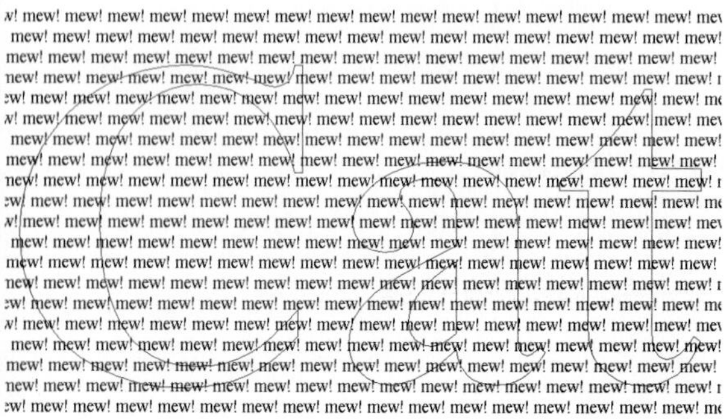

Figure 6.30: Stroked text path with background text

The code of Listing 6.12 contains three paint functions that share common functions. The function textclip_MakePath loads a string IDS_CLIPPER and uses it to create a path from a TextOut call. The function textclip_DrawBackground draws a set of lines all the way across the client area; the exact number of lines is fixed by a constant, but the height will be adjusted based on the client window size. The lines are a repeated sequence of IDS_BG strings (slightly offset on each successive line for a nice appearance). The function textclip1_OnPaint simply creates a path and strokes it (see Figure 6.29). The function textclip2_OnPaint creates the path and strokes it and then draws the background text (see Figure 6.30). Finally, textclip3_OnPaint creates the path and sets it as the clipping region so that when the background text is drawn, it is clipped to the region, thus producing the result shown in Figure 6.31.

You can find out all the details of a path by using the GetPath function. Normally, you call this twice: once to determine how much space is required and again to obtain the path information. The GetPath function returns a set of points and a parallel array indicating what each point represents. So you have to allocate two arrays to hold the information that comes back.

```
int size;
LPPOINT points;
LPBYTE types;

size = GetPath(hdc, NULL, NULL, 0);  // get number of points
```

```
points = (LPPOINT)malloc(size * sizeof(POINT));
types = (LPBYTE) malloc(size * sizeof(BYTE));
// ... write code here to deal with malloc failure...
GetPath(hdc, points, types, size);
PolyDraw(hdc, points, types, size);
```

This is exactly the same as the operation

```
StrokePath(hdc);
```

The meaning of each point is described by the value of its positionally corresponding type; so the meaning of `points[3]` is described by `types[3]`. The vertex types are given in Table 6.24.

The `PT_CLOSEFIGURE` bit is important to recognize. If you are trying to analyze the path in a program, you must mask out this value to compare the vertex type with one of the other values. For example,

Figure 6.31: Clipped background

```
if(types[i] == PT_LINETO)
```

will not necessarily give the correct test if you are not concerned with the `PT_CLOSEFIGURE` bit. The correct test to see if you have a `LineTo` operation is to do

```
if( (types[i] & ~ PT_CLOSEFIGURE) == PT_LINETO)
```

Note the careful use of parentheses! Without these parentheses, the test will always be false! (Do you understand why?)

Table 6.24: Vertex types for `GetPath` and `PolyDraw`

Vertex Type	Meaning
PT_MOVETO	The point starts a new figure.
PT_LINETO	The previous point and this point are joined by a `LineTo` operation.
PT_BEZIERTO	These points always appear in groups of three. The first of the three is the first control point of a `PolyBezierTo` function and the second of the three is the second control point of a `PolyBezierTo` function. The last point of the three is the ending point. Note that you may get several of these groups of three in a row.
PT_CLOSEFIGURE	This is a flag that is combined with any of the above using a bitwise OR operation. When present, it indicates that the corresponding point is the last point in the figure. The figure should be closed with a `CloseFigure`.

The `PolyDraw` function does not exist in Windows 95, but it can be simulated. Sample code that simulates `PolyDraw` appears in the Microsoft Knowledge Base article Q135059.

f you have used the `FlattenPath` operation, there will be no curves in the path.

The function `PathToRegion` converts the area defined by the path to a region. The current value established by `SetPolyFillMode` determines if a point is inside or outside the region. Once you have a region, you can use it for clipping. (Or you could use it for filling, but you could have used `FillPath` and avoided the extra step!)

The GDI Explorer

The GDI Explorer application that is included on the CD-ROM was used to create all the illustrations in this chapter. In addition to the examples shown, the GDI explorer contains the BLT Explorer, a way that you can test out all of the BLT operations (except those not implemented on Windows 95) under a variety of conditions. The extended BLT operations are also made available for you to study. These are the operations normally designated only by specifying the hex number, since there are no symbols defined for them. They are even assigned symbolic names in the extrops.h file, which you are free to use in your own code. If you select the BLT Explorer, the ROP Finder tab on the dialog will let you find and identify each of the 256 raster operators.

What's Next?

We devote the last few chapters to discussing output from a Windows program. So it's about time we looked into input to a Windows program. In the next chapter, we start with the basics: input from the keyboard, input from the mouse, and periodic timer message input.

Further Reading

Adobe Systems, *PostScript Language Reference Manual, Second Edition,* Addison-Wesley, 1990.

Ayres, Frank, Jr., *Theory and Problems of Matrices,* Schaum Publishing, 1962, part of the Schaum's Outline Series.

Foley, J. D. and van Dam, A., *Fundamentals of Interactive Computer Graphics,* Addison-Wesley, 1982. ISBN 0-201-144-68-9.

> The standard textbook on interactive computer graphics. Serious graphics programmers should all own it.

Glassner, Andrew S. (ed.), *Graphics Gems,* Academic Press, 1990. ISBN 0-12-286166-3.

Newcomer, Joseph M. and Horn, Bruce, "Undocumented Windows: The Windows 'Region' Structure", in *Dr. Dobb's Journal (18,3),* (March 1993).

Newman, William N. and Sproull, Robert F., *Principles of Interactive Computer Graphics, Second Edition,* McGraw-Hill, 1979.

One of the early works on computer graphics, this book was one of the first to give detailed treatment of bitmap graphical interfaces. It is still a good reference for many of the basic techniques of graphical interaction.

Chapter

7 Keyboard, Mouse, and Timer Input

Until now, we've concentrated on output under Windows. We discussed only one form of user input: input from a window scroll bar and text output, which were discussed in Chapter 4, "Displaying Text in a Window." In this chapter, we examine input from Windows devices: the keyboard, the mouse, and the timer. Like scroll bar input, keyboard, mouse, and timer input comes in the form of messages to a window procedure.

First, we explain how keyboard input works under Windows. When the user presses a key on the keyboard, Windows generates the first in a series of keyboard input messages. Because multiple applications can run concurrently, Windows needs to know which application should receive the keyboard input messages. An application may display multiple windows, so Windows also needs to know which window within an application should receive the keyboard input messages. Windows uses the concept of *input focus*, whereby it gives a keyboard message to the window that has the input focus at the time the message is retrieved from the system queue.

Keyboard messages originate as hardware-specific events. For example, a keyboard message can indicate that it was produced when the user pressed (rather than released) the third key from the left on the second row down on the keyboard. This isn't terribly useful information to most applications. Without additional information, Windows can't know the character corresponding to that key. This is provided by the *keyboard driver*, which translates the information about the physical key to a keyboard-layout-independent message. It is the job of the keyboard driver to translate the message to a hardware-independent message by producing *virtual-key-code* messages.

Virtual-key-code messages are more abstract than the original key-press messages. Virtual-key codes identify a key by its "name" function, not its location on the keyboard. For example, a virtual-key-code message could indicate that the user pressed the **F5** function key. Your application doesn't need to know the keyboard type used to enter the key press. Some keyboards have the function keys in a double column on the left. Others have the function keys in a row across the top of the keyboard; still others have two complete sets, one on the side and one across the top. Or consider the issue of internationalization. The key which is the leftmost in the lower row represents the character "w" on Belgian and French keyboards, "y" on German, Hungarian, Polish, Romanian, Slovak, Serbian, and Croatian keyboards, "ò" on Latvian keyboards, "j" on Turkish keyboards, and "z" on most of the remaining Latin-alphabet keyboards. [1] Your program doesn't need to know

---

[1] Nadine Kano's excellent book on internationalizing Windows applications (see "Further Reading") gives complete keyboard layouts for every international keyboard supported by Windows at the time the book was published.

he layout of the keyboard; the virtual-key-code message for "j" or "z" or whatever character is going to be he same, no matter which keyboard layout is used, so your program can be written without being concerned bout which keyboard layout may be used when it is run.

This coverage of hardware-independence will lead to a discussion about the differences between the ANSI character set used by Windows 95, the ANSI and Unicode character sets used by Windows NT, and the OEM character set used by the computer hardware and, therefore, by most DOS applications. The comparison of ANSI and OEM fonts starts on page 427 and the discussion of Unicode starts on page 433.

Finally, wrapping up keyboard input, we discuss the *caret*, the graphic symbol that indicates where the next typed character appears. This is often a blinking vertical bar displayed between characters. If you want to build an application that can run without a mouse, but you still want to permit the caret to be moved or you want to use the keyboard to position the caret in addition to using the mouse, you must explicitly control the caret's position using keyboard input. The built-in edit controls in Windows already do this.

The first example program in this chapter is the Key Explorer program, which displays all fields of the keyboard messages produced when you press or release a key. You can run this program and see exactly which messages are generated and in what order as you press and release different keys on the keyboard.

Next, we discuss the mouse input messages. Windows is constantly performing *hit testing* as the user moves the mouse. As the user moves the mouse, Windows sends hit test messages to the window under the new location of the cursor. The response to the hit test inquiry determines how Windows processes subsequently generated mouse messages.

We also look in depth at all the mouse messages and discuss the commonly used mouse messages (mouse movement and mouse button press and release messages). We discuss the *cursor*, which is the small bitmap that indicates where on the screen the mouse points. Windows provides several standard cursor shapes. You can also create and use your own cursors.

We wrap up the section on mouse input with a small game, the Towers of Hanoi. This application is a simple game in which you can use the mouse to move disks from one tower to another. This program uses nearly every concept we've covered so far in this book.

In the last section in this chapter, we explain how to create and use timer messages. A timer message is a message that Windows can periodically send to your application to notify the application that at least a certain interval of time has elapsed. We use timer messages in the Tower of Hanoi game to pace the automatic movement of a disk on one tower to a different tower.

Keyboard Input

Keyboard input originates when the user presses or releases a key on the keyboard. The keyboard device driver, via Windows, converts the event into a message that it places into the *system queue*. When an application with the input focus attempts to retrieve a message from its application queue and that queue is empty, Windows looks for a message for that application in the system queue. It then transfers keyboard messages from the system queue to the application's thread queue. Keyboard messages aren't placed directly into a thread queue because an earlier message in the queue might cause the input focus to move to a different thread (often a completely different application). Subsequent keyboard messages go to the application with the input focus when it asks for a new message and finds none in its thread queue.

Because Windows queues keyboard messages in the system message queue, your application is not interrupted and given the key press. It receives a message representing the key press in response to a normal call to the GetMessage function. This means that you cannot "force" your application to see a keyboard message; it sees it only when it asks for one.

Many times you won't need to process the keyboard messages in order to react to keyboard input. Windows translates some keyboard input to other types of messages. For example, the user can use the keyboard to select an item from a menu in your application. Windows then processes the keyboard messages and generates a message indicating that a menu selection was made. This process enables you to respond to the menu selection message regardless of whether the selection was made via the keyboard or the mouse.

In the next chapter, we talk about how to use edit controls for keyboard input. Edit controls are child windows that accept keyboard input and return a string representing the edited version of the characters entered. The window function for the edit control window processes the keyboard input messages and supports editing of the text. The keyboard messages are summarized in Table 7.1.

In Chapter 11, you'll read about *dialog boxes*. Dialog boxes are windows that typically contain many child window controls. Dialog boxes provide a keyboard interface to move the *input focus* from one child window control to another.

Table 7.1: Keyboard input management messages and functions

Function or Message	Usage
CharLower	Converts a NUL-terminated character string to lowercase letters.
CharLowerBuff	Converts a counted character string to lowercase letters.
CharNext	Moves forward one character (possibly several bytes) along a character string.
CharPrev	Moves backward one character (possibly several bytes) along a character string.
CharToOem	Translates a NUL-terminated ANSI or Unicode character string to an OEM character string.
CharToOemBuff	Translates a counted ANSI or Unicode character string to an OEM character string.
CharUpper	Converts a NUL-terminated character string to uppercase letters.
CharUpperBuff	Converts a counted character string to uppercase letters.
CreateCaret	Creates a keyboard input caret.
DestroyCaret	Destroys the keyboard input caret.

Table 7.1: Keyboard input management messages and functions

Function or Message	Usage
FORWARD_WM_CHAR	Message uncracker.
FORWARD_WM_DEADCHAR	Message uncracker.
FORWARD_WM_KEYDOWN	Message uncracker.
FORWARD_WM_KEYUP	Message uncracker.
FORWARD_WM_KILLFOCUS	Message uncracker.
FORWARD_WM_SETFOCUS	Message uncracker.
FORWARD_WM_SYSDEADCHAR	Message uncracker.
FORWARD_WM_SYSKEYDOWN	Message uncracker.
FORWARD_WM_SYSKEYUP	Message uncracker.
GetAsyncKeyState	Gets the key state of the key as it is at the time the call is issued.
GetCaretBlinkTime	Returns the caret blink time, in millisecond units.
GetCaretPos	Gets the current keyboard input caret position.
GetKeyboardState	Gets the keyboard state for each of 256 virtual key codes.
GetKeyboardType	Returns a type code for the keyboard.
GetKeyNameText	Returns a text name for a virtual key.
GetKeyState	Gets the key state of the key as of the last message sent.
HANDLE_WM_CHAR	Message cracker. See the OnChar handler.
HANDLE_WM_DEADCHAR	Message cracker. See the OnDeadChar handler.
HANDLE_WM_KEYDOWN	Message cracker. See the OnKey handler.
HANDLE_WM_KEYUP	Message cracker. See the OnKey handler.
HANDLE_WM_KILLFOCUS	Message cracker. See the OnKillFocus handler.
HANDLE_WM_SETFOCUS	Message cracker. See the OnSetFocus handler.
HANDLE_WM_SYSDEADCHAR	Message cracker. See the OnSysDeadChar handler.
HANDLE_WM_SYSKEYDOWN	Message cracker. See the OnSysKey handler.
HANDLE_WM_SYSKEYUP	Message cracker. See the OnSysKey handler.
HideCaret	Hides the keyboard input caret.

Table 7.1: Keyboard input management messages and functions

Function or Message	Usage
OemKeyScan	Translates an OEM character to an OEM scan code and shift state.
OemToChar	Translates a NUL-terminated OEM character string to an ANSI or Unicode character string.
OemToCharBuff	Translates a counted OEM character string to an ANSI or Unicode character string.
cls_OnChar	Message cracker handler for a WM_CHAR message. See page 427.
cls_OnDeadChar	Message cracker handler for WM_DEADCHAR message. See page 427.
cls_OnKey	Message cracker handler for WM_KEYDOWN and WM_KEYUP messages. See page 422.
cls_OnKillFocus	Message cracker handler for WM_KILLFOCUS message. See page 411.
cls_OnSetFocus	Message cracker handler for WM_SETFOCUS message. See page 411.
cls_OnSysDeadChar	Message cracker handler for WM_SYSDEADCHAR message. See page 427.
cls_OnSysKey	Message cracker handler for WM_SYSKEYDOWN, WM_SYSKEYUP messages. See page 422.
SetCaretBlinkTime	Sets the caret blink time in millisecond units.
SetCaretPos	Sets the keyboard input caret position.
SetFocus	Changes the focus so keyboard input goes to the window specified.
SetKeyboardState	Sets the keyboard state for each of 256 virtual key codes.
ShowCaret	Shows the input caret indicating where keyboard input will go.
ToUnicode	Converts a virtual key code and flag to one or more Unicode characters.
TranslateMessage	Translates a WM_KEYDOWN message to a WM_CHAR message when possible.
VkKeyScan	Translates an ANSI or Unicode character to a virtual key code and shift state.
WM_CHAR	Message reporting a character input.
WM_DEADCHAR	Message reporting a "dead" (nonspacing, usually accent) character.
WM_KEYDOWN	Message reporting a key down transition.
WM_KEYUP	Message reporting a key up transition.
WM_KILLFOCUS	Message reporting the loss of focus.

Table 7.1: Keyboard input management messages and functions

Function or Message	Usage
WM_SETFOCUS	Message reporting the acquisition of focus.
WM_SYSDEADCHAR	Message reporting a "dead" (nonspacing, usually accent) system character.
WM_SYSKEYDOWN	Message reporting a system key down transition.
WM_SYSKEYUP	Message reporting a system key up transition.

The Input Focus

We mentioned earlier in the chapter that Windows transfers a keyboard message to the application queue for the window that has the *input focus*. The keyboard is a shared resource used by all applications running under Windows. A single application often shares the keyboard among several windows. A common interface uses multiple edit controls to accept input data. (Edit controls are the small child windows into which a user enters filenames, numbers, and other textual input.) The tab key moves the input focus from one edit control to the next, so the user can type "into" the next edit control.

The active window itself or a child window of the active window always has the input focus. The title bar of the active window is highlighted (when the window has a title bar). Windows highlights the dialog frame for windows using a dialog frame (such as a dialog box). When the active window is minimized under Windows NT 3.*x*, the title bar under the icon is highlighted to indicate that the window has the input focus.

Occasionally you'll want to keep track of which window has the input focus. Windows sends the WM_KILLFOCUS and WM_SETFOCUS messages when the input focus changes. It sends the WM_KILLFOCUS message to the window function for the window losing the input focus. The wParam parameter of the message specifies the handle of the window receiving the input focus. It can be NULL. Windows sends the WM_SETFOCUS message to the window function for the window gaining the input focus. The wParam parameter to the window function specifies the handle of the window losing the input focus. It also can be NULL.

The WM_KILLFOCUS and WM_SETFOCUS messages are often misunderstood. They are *notifications* that the input focus *is* moving from one window to another. They are not queries to determine if the input focus *should* be moved. The input focus *will* be moved. You cannot intercept these messages and prevent the input focus from changing windows. Windows is in an "unstable" state when these messages are sent to your window function. For example, you cannot create dialogs or messages boxes in response to either of them.

Many times, you may want to validate the contents of a control (typically an edit control) when it loses the focus. When the contents are invalid, you would like to notify the user and force the input focus to stay on the control. You can't. In response to the WM_KILLFOCUS message, you can validate the contents of the control. If the contents are invalid, you must then post a user-defined message to the window and exit the WM_KILLFOCUS message processing. When you receive the user-defined message, you can create a message box notifying the user that the control's contents are invalid and you can set the input focus back to the control.

You can use the GetFocus and SetFocus functions to determine and change the window that owns the input focus. The GetFocus function returns the handle of the window that currently has the input focus. The SetFocus function assigns the input focus to the specified window and returns the handle of the window losing the input focus, if any. Windows directs all subsequent keyboard input to the specified window. Calling the SetFocus function generates the WM_KILLFOCUS and WM_SETFOCUS messages. Do *not* send these messages explicitly yourself. Again, they are not requests to change the focus; they are notifications that SetFocus has actually changed the focus.

You will typically write your handlers as OnSetFocus and OnKillFocus, called from the message crackers HANDLE_WM_SETFOCUS and HANDLE_WM_KILLFOCUS.

WM_SETFOCUS Message Cracker Handler

void cls_OnSetFocus(HWND hwnd, HWND oldwnd);					
	wParam		lParam		
Parameter	**lo**	**hi**	**lo**	**hi**	**Meaning**
hwnd					Window handle of the window receiving the message.
oldwnd	■	■			Handle of the window losing focus.

WM_KILLFOCUS Message Cracker Handler

void cls_OnKillFocus(HWND hwnd, HWND newwnd);					
	wParam		lParam		
Parameter	**lo**	**hi**	**lo**	**hi**	**Meaning**
hwnd					Window handle of the window receiving the message.
newwnd	■	■			Handle of the window gaining focus.

The Key Press and Release Messages

Now that you've seen how Windows determines where to send keyboard messages, we'll talk about the messages themselves. Windows generates one of two messages when a key is pressed: WM_KEYDOWN or WM_SYSKEYDOWN. It generates a complementary message when the key is released: either WM_KEYUP or WM_SYSKEYUP. When you hold down a key until the Typematic action begins, multiple key-down messages are generated, eventually followed by a single key-up message when the key is released. (Typematic keyboard action is the effect that occurs when holding a key down results in automatic repetitions of the key after an initial delay.) Each keyboard message is time-stamped when it's created. You can retrieve the time a message was created directly from the MSG structure or by calling the GetMessageTime function.

Certain key presses generate the system keyboard messages WM_SYSKEYDOWN and WM_SYSKEYUP. Typing a key along with the **Alt** key is the most frequent source of these messages. System keyboard messages generally are passed along to the DefWindowProc function. They often invoke items from the application's menu (often **Alt** plus a letter key) and the application's system menu (**Alt** plus a function key) and change the active window and therefore the location of the input focus (**Alt+Esc** and **Alt+Tab**).

Keys pressed and released without the **Alt** key usually generate nonsystem keyboard messages (WM_KEYDOWN and WM_KEYUP). If you want your application to react when the user presses or releases a key, you must process one of these messages. Windows itself doesn't care about these messages, so you can ignore them without problem. You need to process only them if you want to handle the keyboard.

It's often convenient to think about the distinction between the system keyboard messages and nonsystem keyboard messages in the following way. System keyboard messages are intended for Windows. Windows eventually will process such messages and generate other, more specific messages indicating the result of such processing. For example, Windows processes the **Alt+F4** keystroke and eventually sends a WM_CLOSE message to the window.

Nonsystem keyboard messages are intended for your application to do with as it pleases. Occasionally a key that normally generates a nonsystem keyboard message sends a system keyboard message instead. An excellent example of this is a minimized window. When a minimized (iconic) window is the active window (the title under the icon is highlighted), typically no window has the input focus. Any key pressed and released during this time generates a WM_SYSKEYDOWN and WM_SYSKEYUP message. Windows does this for the following reason. Generally, your application, when iconic, isn't expecting to receive keyboard input from a user. You usually don't want keyboard input triggering actions from your application when it is iconic. So Windows converts keystrokes that normally would be nonsystem messages into system messages. You still can intercept the messages if you want to, but typing won't unexpectedly activate your application.

You might wonder how you determine the difference between a system message that results from a key press in conjunction with the **Alt** key and a system message for a normal key, when no window has the input focus. Normally, you will never need to deal with this problem, particularly when using MDI; Windows handles it for you by routing the messages to the frame window if no child has the input focus. But if you are doing something unusual, you can examine additional information about the context of the keystroke found in the lParam parameter of each message.

The lParam *Parameter of a Keystroke Message*

The WM_KEYDOWN, WM_SYSKEYDOWN, WM_KEYUP, and WM_SYSKEYUP messages have the same format for their lParam parameter. The 32-bit lParam parameter contains the following additional information about the keystroke: the repeat count, scan-code, key-transition code, previous key state, and context code. The information is encoded in the bits of the parameter as shown in Table 7.2. The high-order 16 bits of the lParam are passed in as the flags parameter to the message cracker handler.

Table 7.2: Bit flags of the `lParam` parameter of a keystroke message and as delivered in the `flags` parameter of a handler

Bit Position		Meaning
`lParam`	`flags`	
31	15	Transition state. It is 0 when the key is being pressed. It is 1 when the key is being released.
		0 `WM_KEYDOWN` and `WM_SYSKEYDOWN` messages.
		1 `WM_KEYUP` and `WM_SYSKEYUP` messages.
30	14	Previous-key state.
		0 The message is the first `WM_KEYDOWN` message.
		1 The key was already down before this message, that is, this `WM_KEYDOWN` messages was sent as a result of Typematic action.
29	13	Context code. Generally this bit is 1 when the **Alt** key is depressed and 0 otherwise. This bit can be set in all four keyboard messages as follows:

Message	Context Code=0	Context Code=1
`WM_KEYDOWN` `WM_KEYUP`	Nonsystem key.	Some characters from non-English keyboards.
`WM_SYSKEYDOWN` `WM_SYSKEYUP`	Nonsystem key and no input focus.	System key.

Bit Position		Meaning
28-27	12-11	Reserved and used internally by Windows.
26-25	10-9	Not used.
24	8	Extended key. This bit is 1 when the key is an extended key. The extended keys on the IBM Enhanced 101- and 102-key keyboards are the keys that are duplicated on the keyboard. This bit identifies the **Alt** and **Ctrl** keys to the right of the space bar; the **Insert**, **Delete**, **Home**, **End**, **Page Up**, **Page Down**, and arrow keys to the left of the numeric keypad; and the divide (/) and **Enter** keys in the numeric keypad.
23-16	7-0	OEM Scan-code. This is the code for the key that is generated by the keyboard hardware. It is an OEM-dependent value.
0–15		Repeat count. This is the number of key presses of this key represented by the message. Windows combines multiple unprocessed successive `WM_KEYDOWN` and `WM_SYSKEYDOWN` messages for the same key into a single message and sets this field to the number of messages that were combined.

Table 7.2: Bit flags of the lParam parameter of a keystroke message and as delivered in the flags parameter of a handler

Bit Position		
lParam	flags	**Meaning**
The high-order 16 bits of lParam are passed in as the flags parameter, which is why there are 2-bit positions.		

The Virtual-key Code

Windows provides a *virtual-key-code* value in the wParam of the WM_KEYDOWN, WM_KEYUP, WM_SYSKEYDOWN, and WM_SYSKEYUP messages. A virtual-key code is a device-independent value for a specific key. Windows uses this code rather than a hardware-dependent scan code to identify a keystroke. The use of such codes isolates a Windows application from hardware dependencies caused by differences in keyboards for different languages. A given character generates the same virtual-key code no matter where that character is located on a particular keyboard or what language is in use. Table 7.3 lists the symbolic names, hexadecimal values, and keys represented by the virtual-key codes defined by Windows. Some of the codes are not defined in windows.h. We've indicated at the beginning of each subsection in the table whether the subsequent virtual-key codes are defined in windows.h. The table is presented in the order of ascending virtual-key codes.

Table 7.3: Virtual-key codes

Symbolic Name	Virtual-Key Code	Key Represented	IBM Keyboard Key
The symbolic names for the following virtual-key codes are defined in **windows.h**.			
	0x00	Undefined	
VK_LBUTTON	0x01	Left mouse button	
VK_RBUTTON	0x02	Right mouse button	
VK_CANCEL	0x03	**Control+break**	**Control+break**
VK_MBUTTON	0x04	Middle mouse button	
	0x05–0x07	Undefined	
VK_BACK	0x08	**Backspace** key	**Backspace**
VK_TAB	0x09	**Tab** key	**Tab**
	0x0A–0x0B	Undefined	
VK_CLEAR	0x0C	**Clear** key	Numeric keyboard 5 with **Num Lock** off
VK_RETURN	0x0D	**Enter** key	**Enter**
	0x0E–0x0F	Undefined	

Table 7.3: Virtual-key codes

Symbolic Name	Virtual-Key Code	Key Represented	IBM Keyboard Key
VK_SHIFT	0x10	**Shift** key	**Shift**
VK_CONTROL	0x11	**Ctrl** key	**Ctrl**
VK_MENU	0x12	**Menu** key	**Alt**
VK_PAUSE	0x13	**PAUSE** key	Pause
VK_CAPITAL	0x14	**Caps Lock** key	**Caps Lock**
	0x15-0x19	Reserved for Kanji systems	
	0x1A	Undefined	
VK_ESCAPE	0x1B	**Escape** key	**Esc**
	0x1C-0x1F	Undefined	
VK_SPACE	0x20	Space bar	Space bar
VK_PRIOR	0x21	**Page Up** key	**Page Up**
VK_NEXT	0x22	**Page Down** key	**Page Down**
VK_END	0x23	**End** key	**End**
VK_HOME	0x24	**Home** key	**Home**
VK_LEFT	0x25	← key	Left arrow ←
VK_UP	0x26	↑ key	Up arrow ↑
VK_RIGHT	0x27	→ key	Right arrow →
VK_DOWN	0x28	↓ key	Down arrow ↓
VK_SELECT	0x29	**SELECT** key	
VK_PRINT	0x2A	OEM-specific key	
VK_EXECUTE	0x2B	**EXECUTE** key	
VK_SNAPSHOT	0x2C	**Print Screen** key	**Print Screen**
VK_INSERT	0x2D	**Insert** key	**Insert**
VK_DELETE	0x2E	**Delete** key	**Delete**
VK_HELP	0x2F	**Help** key	

The symbolic names for the following virtual-key codes are the standard symbolic names, but they are not defined in `windows.h`. The virtual-key code for these keys is equal to the ASCII code for the symbol.

Table 7.3: Virtual-key codes

Symbolic Name	Virtual-Key Code	Key Represented	IBM Keyboard Key
VK_0	0x30	0 key	0 on main keyboard
VK_1	0x31	1 key	1 on main keyboard
VK_2	0x32	2 key	2 on main keyboard
VK_3	0x33	3 key	3 on main keyboard
VK_4	0x34	4 key	4 on main keyboard
VK_5	0x35	5 key	5 on main keyboard
VK_6	0x36	6 key	6 on main keyboard
VK_7	0x37	7 key	7 on main keyboard
VK_8	0x38	8 key	8 on main keyboard
VK_9	0x39	9 key	9 on main keyboard
	0x3A–0x40	Undefined	
VK_A	0x41	**A** key	A
VK_B	0x42	**B** key	B
VK_C	0x43	**C** key	C
VK_D	0x44	**D** key	D
VK_E	0x45	**E** key	E
VK_F	0x46	**F** key	F
VK_G	0x47	**G** key	G
VK_H	0x48	**H** key	H
VK_I	0x49	**I** key	I
VK_J	0x4A	**J** key	J
VK_K	0x4B	**K** key	K
VK_L	0x4C	**L** key	L
VK_M	0x4D	**M** key	M
VK_N	0x4E	**N** key	N
VK_O	0x4F	**O** key	O
VK_P	0x50	**P** key	P
VK_Q	0x51	**Q** key	Q

Table 7.3: Virtual-key codes

Symbolic Name	Virtual-Key Code	Key Represented	IBM Keyboard Key
VK_R	0x52	**R** key	R
VK_S	0x53	**S** key	S
VK_T	0x54	**T** key	T
VK_U	0x55	**U** key	U
VK_V	0x56	**V** key	V
VK_W	0x57	**W** key	W
VK_X	0x58	**X** key	X
VK_Y	0x59	**Y** key	Y
VK_Z	0x5A	**Z** key	Z

The following symbolic names are defined in `windows.h`.

	0x5B-0x5F	Undefined	
VK_NUMPAD0	0x60	Numeric keypad 0 key	Same with **Num Lock** on
VK_NUMPAD1	0x61	Numeric keypad 1 key	Same with **Num Lock** on
VK_NUMPAD2	0x62	Numeric keypad 2 key	Same with **Num Lock** on
VK_NUMPAD3	0x63	Numeric keypad 3 key	Same with **Num Lock** on
VK_NUMPAD4	0x64	Numeric keypad 4 key	Same with **Num Lock** on
VK_NUMPAD5	0x65	Numeric keypad 5 key	Same with **Num Lock** on
VK_NUMPAD6	0x66	Numeric keypad 6 key	Same with **Num Lock** on
VK_NUMPAD7	0x67	Numeric keypad 7 key	Same with **Num Lock** on
VK_NUMPAD8	0x68	Numeric keypad 8 key	Same with **Num Lock** on
VK_NUMPAD9	0x69	Numeric keypad 9 key	Same with **Num Lock** on
VK_MULTIPLY	0x6A	Multiply key	Numeric keypad *****
VK_ADD	0x6B	Add key	Numeric keypad **+**
VK_SEPARATOR	0x6C	Separator key	
VK_SUBTRACT	0x6D	Subtract key	Numeric keypad **-**
VK_DECIMAL	0x6E	Decimal key	Numeric keypad **.**
VK_DIVIDE	0x6F	Divide key	Numeric keypad **/**
VK_F1	0x70	**F1** key	**F1**

Table 7.3: Virtual-key codes

Symbolic Name	Virtual-Key Code	Key Represented	IBM Keyboard Key
VK_F2	0x71	**F2** key	**F2**
VK_F3	0x72	**F3** key	**F3**
VK_F4	0x73	**F4** key	**F4**
VK_F5	0x74	**F5** key	**F5**
VK_F6	0x75	**F6** key	**F6**
VK_F7	0x76	**F7** key	**F7**
VK_F8	0x77	**F8** key	**F8**
VK_F9	0x78	**F9** key	**F9**
VK_F10	0x79	**F10** key	**F10**
VK_F11	0x7A	**F11** key	**F11**
VK_F12	0x7B	**F12** key	**F12**
VK_F13	0x7C	**F13** key	
VK_F14	0x7D	**F14** key	
VK_F15	0x7E	**F15** key	
VK_F16	0x7F	**F16** key	
	0x80-0x87	OEM specific	
	0x88-0x8F	Unassigned	
VK_NUMLOCK	0x90	**NUM LOCK** key.	**Num Lock**

The following symbolic names are not defined in `windows.h`.

Symbolic Name	Virtual-Key Code	Key Represented	IBM Keyboard Key
VK_OEM_SCROLL	0x91	**SCROLL LOCK** key	**Scroll Lock**
	0x92-0xB9	Unassigned	
VK_OEM_1	0xBA	Keyboard specific punctuation key	;
VK_OEM_PLUS	0xBB	Plus (+) key	= +
VK_OEM_COMMA	0xBC	Comma (,) key	, <
VK_OEM_MINUS	0xBD	Minus (-) key	- _
VK_OEM_PERIOD	0xBE	Period (.) key	. >
VK_OEM_2	0xBF	Keyboard specific punctuation key	/ ?

Table 7.3: Virtual-key codes

Symbolic Name	Virtual-Key Code	Key Represented	IBM Keyboard Key
VK_OEM_3	0xC0	Keyboard specific punctuation key	` ~
	0xC1-0xDA	Unassigned	
VK_OEM_4	0xDB	Keyboard specific punctuation key	[{
VK_OEM_5	0xDC	Keyboard specific punctuation key	\	
VK_OEM_6	0xDD	Keyboard specific punctuation key	] {
VK_OEM_7	0xDE	Keyboard specific punctuation key	' "
VK_OEM_8	0xDF	Keyboard specific punctuation key	
	0xE0-0xE1	OEM specific	
VK_OEM_102	0xE2	Not-equal key	
	0xE3-0xE4	OEM specific	
	0xE5	Unassigned	
	0xE6	OEM specific	
	0xE7-0xE8	Unassigned	
	0xE9-0xF5	OEM specific	
	0xF6-0xFE	Unassigned	

Keyboard Information Functions

You may have noticed from the table that there are no virtual-key codes for the lowercase letters. Virtual-key codes represent symbols on the keyboard. The states of the **Shift** key and **Caps Lock** key determine whether the virtual-key code for a letter should be interpreted as an uppercase or lowercase letter. The WM_KEYDOWN, WM_KEYUP, WM_SYSKEYDOWN, and WM_SYSKEYUP messages don't include any information about the state of the shift keys. However, if you want to do things the hard way you can call the GetKeyState function to retrieve the current state of any virtual key. For ordinary characters, you will usually just call TranslateMessage (which we discuss shortly) and handle the WM_CHAR message it generates. Generally, the only time you need to use it for key-down messages for noncharacter codes (such as left arrow, delete, and so forth) to inquire about the state of the **Shift**, **Ctrl**, **Caps Lock**, and **Num Lock** keys, such as distinguishing a **Delete** from a **Ctrl+Delete** or **Shift+Delete**. The GetKeyState function call has the following syntax:

```
int KeyState ;

KeyState = GetKeyState (VK_SHIFT) ;
```

The high-order bit of KeyState is 1 when the key is down; otherwise, the key is up. The low-order bit represents the toggle state of the virtual key. Toggle keys, such as the **Caps Lock** and **Num Lock** keys, toggle from unset to set and back to unset with each press of the key. When the low-order bit is 1, the key is toggled; it has been pressed an odd number of times since the system started. When it is 0, the key is unset.

 The specification that "the high-order bit is set" tempts programmers to do the obvious: to test the value by saying something like if(KeyState & 0x8000).... But this is incorrect. It works fine in Win16, where integer values are 16 bits. The correct test, however, is if(KeyState < 0).... because in Win32, the correct test would have to be if(KeyState & 0x80000000).... Therefore you should not write, or make sure to correct, any code that has result-size-dependent testing of the key state. This can affect any code you are porting from Win16.

The GetKeyState function returns the state of the virtual key as it was at the time the last message was retrieved from the queue by the GetMessage function. This might not be the state of the key presently. For example, the preceding query can return a status that indicates that the **Shift** key is not down. However, there can be a message waiting in the queue indicating that the **Shift** key was subsequently pressed and is currently down. Because the message has not yet been retrieved from the queue, the new state isn't reflected in the information returned by the GetKeyState function.

This generally is exactly how you want the function to work. It usually is of more interest to know the state of a key when the current message was placed in the queue rather than how it is "right now". When you want to know whether a key is down or up at a given instant rather than know its position when the message was generated, call the GetAsyncKeyState function. The most significant bit of the returned value is 1, meaning the result is negative, when the virtual key specified by the parameter is currently down. The least significant bit is set if the specified virtual key was pressed since the last call to the GetAsyncKeyState function:

```
KeyState = GetAsyncKeyState (VK_SHIFT) ;
```

When you want to check the state of many different keys at once, you can call the GetKeyboardState function. It works similarly to the GetKeyState function but copies the state of the 256 virtual-keyboard keys to a 256-byte buffer. Windows sets the high-order bit of each byte to indicate that the key is down. The key is up when the bit is 0. For toggle keys such as **Caps Lock** the low-order bit of each byte is 1 when the key is set and 0 when unset. The only parameter is a pointer to a 256-byte buffer:

```
BYTE KeyStates [256] ;

GetKeyboardState (KeyStates) ;
```

After you've retrieved the state of all the virtual keys using the GetKeyboardState function, you can change the state of the keys. The SetKeyboardState function replaces the keyboard-state table by the one specified. The following code will clear the LEDs and BIOS flags for the **Num Lock** and **Caps Lock** keys and set the two keys to the unset state:

```
BYTE KeyStates [256] ;

GetKeyboardState (KeyStates) ;
```

```
KeyStates [VK_NUMLOCK] &= ~1 ;
KeyStates [VK_CAPITAL] &= ~1 ;

SetKeyboardState (KeyStates) ;
```

You might find it interesting to use this function to set and clear the **Num Lock** state. For example, when your user moves into a field for which only numbers are valid inputs, you could set the **Num Lock** state on to allow direct input from the numeric keypad, and when you entered a control for which numeric input was not appropriate, you could turn it off, provided you were the one that turned it on. If you do this, you should make it an option. Not all users will find this desirable (for example, most laptop computers do not have a separate numeric pad and the effect may be surprising), but many will.

You can retrieve a character string containing the name of a virtual key by calling the GetKeyNameText function. The keyboard device driver contains a list of names for all those keys with names that are longer than one character. The GetKeyNameText function returns the appropriate name for the currently installed keyboard according to the principal language supported by the keyboard driver.

You pass the function the 32-bit 1Param parameter from a keyboard message (WM_KEYDOWN, WM_KEYUP, WM_SYSKEYDOWN, and WM_SYSKEYUP), a pointer to a buffer, and the length of the buffer minus 1. You can set bit 25 of the 1Param value (the "don't care" bit) to indicate that you don't care to distinguish between left and right **Ctrl** and **Shift** keys. The function copies the 0-terminated string representing the name of the key to the specified buffer:

```
TCHAR KeyName [256] ;
int   Length;

Length = GetKeyNameText (1Param, KeyName, DIM(KeyName) - 1) ;
```

You also can inquire about the type of keyboard installed on the system. The GetKeyboardType function can return the keyboard type, the keyboard subtype, or the number of function keys on the keyboard. For example, if you want to display a graphic image of the keyboard, this function is useful if you

Table 7.4: Parameter to GetKeyboardType call

Value	Meaning
0	Return the keyboard type.
1	Return the keyboard subtype.
2	Return the number of function keys on the keyboard.

need to tell whether a system uses an IBM PC/AT-compatible (84-key) keyboard or an IBM Enhanced-compatible (101- or 102-key) keyboard. Its only parameter speci es whether the keyboard type, subtype, or number of function keys should be returned:

```
KeyboardType = GetKeyboardType (QueryType) ;
```

The QueryType parameter can be one of the values shown in Table 7.4.

Key Transition Message Crackers

Normally, you will want to use the message cracker macros HANDLE_WM_KEYUP, HANDLE_WM_KEYDOWN, HANDLE_WM_SYSKEYUP, and HANDLE_WM_SYSKEYDOWN to deal with these messages. The OnKey handlers can be used to work with both HANDLE_WM_KEYDOWN and HANDLE_WM_KEYUP being routed to the same handler, since the down parameter will indicate whether it is a WM_KEYDOWN or WM_KEYUP message. You could then choose how you process the message based on the down parameter. The handling of WM_SYSKEYDOWN and WM_SYKEYUP is similar.

```
static void
cls_OnKey(HWND hwnd, UINT vk, BOOL down, int repeat, UINT flags)
    {
      if(down)
        { /* down */
          // key down processing here
        } /* down */
      else
        { /* up */
          // key up processing here
        } /* up */
    }

LRESULT CALLBACK
myWndProc(HWND hwnd, UINT msg, WPARAM wParam, LPARAM lParam)
    {
      switch(msg)
        { /* msg */
          HANDLE_MSG(hwnd, WM_KEYDOWN, cls_OnKey);
          HANDLE_MSG(hwnd, WM_KEYUP, cls_OnKey);
        } /* msg */
      return DefWindowProc(hwnd, msg, wParam, lParam);
    }.
```

<h3 style="text-align:center">WM_[SYS]KEY[UP/DOWN] Message Cracker Handlers</h3>

void cls_OnKey(HWND hwnd, UINT vk, BOOL down, int repeat, UINT flags);					
void cls_OnSysKey(HWND hwnd, UINT vk, BOOL down, int repeat, UINT flags);					
	wParam		**lParam**		
Parameter	**lo**	**hi**	**lo**	**hi**	**Meaning**
hwnd					Window handle of the window.
vk	■	■			Virtual-key code of the key.
down					TRUE for WM_KEYDOWN, WM_SYSKEYDOWN FALSE for WM_KEYUP, WM_SYSKEYUP
repeat			■		Repeat count.
flags				■	Flags indicating key state.

Alternatively, you could use two separate procedures, one for the key down transition and another for the key up transition, and separate the code as shown next, ignoring the down parameter when you write the handler function:

```
static void
cls_OnKeyDown(HWND hwnd, UINT vk, BOOL down, int repeat,
            UINT flags)
    {
    // key down processing here
    }

static void
cls_OnKeyUp(HWND hwnd, UINT vk, BOOL down, int repeat,
            UINT flags)
    {
    // key up processing here
    }

LONG CALLBACK
myWndProc(HWND hwnd, UINT msg, WPARAM wParam, LPARAM lParam)
    {
    switch(msg)
        { /* msg */
          HANDLE_MSG(hwnd, WM_KEYDOWN, cls_OnKeyDown);
          HANDLE_MSG(hwnd, WM_KEYUP, cls_onKeyUp);
        } /* msg */
      return DefWindowProc(hwnd, msg, wParam, lParam);
    }
```

Note that in the second case, the down parameter will always be TRUE in the OnKeyDown handler and always FALSE in the OnKeyUp handler.

You should always call DefWindowProc (or your superclass procedure) via a FORWARD_ uncracker if you are intercepting system messages; otherwise, you will interfere with Windows's ability to interact properly with your application:

```
static void
cls_OnSysKeyDown(HWND hwnd, UINT vk, BOOL down, int repeat,
                UINT flags)
    {
    // Put your system key down processing here

    // If you have not completely handled the message
    // for your purposes, or have not handled it at all,
    // you must do
    FORWARD_WM_SYSKEYDOWN(hwnd, vk, repeat, flags, DefWindowProc);
    }

LONG CALLBACK
myWndProc(HWND hwnd, UINT msg, WPARAM wParam, LPARAM lParam)
    {
    switch(msg)
        { /* msg */
          HANDLE_MSG(hwnd, WM_SYSKEYDOWN, cls_OnSysKeyDown);
        } /* msg */
      return DefWindowProc(hwnd, msg, wParam, lParam);
    }
```

Note that, unlike nearly every other FORWARD_ uncracker, the parameter list for these uncrackers for keyboard messages does not follow the parameter list of its handler function exactly; in particular, it does not in-

-lude the down parameter. If you have the same handler shared for both key-up and key-down transitions, you must use the down parameter to determine which of FORWARD_WM_KEYUP, FORWARD_WM_SYSKEYUP, FORWARD_WM_KEYDOWN, or FORWARD_WM_SYSKEYDOWN you will use.

Character Messages

Most of the time you'll want to process keystroke messages only for noncharacter keys such as the "cursor movement" virtual keys VK_HOME, VK_END, VK_DOWN, VK_UP, VK_PRIOR, VK_NEXT, VK_LEFT, and VK_RIGHT. Keystroke messages aren't very convenient when you want to process character keys such as letters. As we pointed out earlier in the chapter, a VK_A virtual-key code doesn't tell you whether the character is an upper-case A, a lowercase a, or a **Ctrl+A**. You can look at the state information about the **Shift** and **Ctrl** keys, but you also need to know country-dependent information about the keyboard to properly decide what character corresponds to a particular keystroke message, because of how extended character sets are used. Fortunately, there's an easier method.

Windows provides the TranslateMessage function, which does exactly what we want. We've used it in all the example programs even though it hasn't been needed until now. The message loop looks like this:

```
while (GetMessage (&msg, 0, 0, 0))
    {
    TranslateMessage (&msg) ;
    DispatchMessage (&msg) ;
    }
```

After you've retrieved a message from the message queue by calling either the GetMessage function or the PeekMessage function, but before you call the DispatchMessage function to send the message to the ap-propriate window function, you call the TranslateMessage function and let it have a look at the message. The TranslateMessage function produces a character message for each virtual-key message that corre-sponds to a character from the ANSI (or Unicode) character set.

When you pass the TranslateMessage function a WM_KEYDOWN message and the accompanying virtual-key code specifies a key that the keyboard driver maps to an ANSI or Unicode character, the TranslateMessage function posts either a WM_CHAR or WM_DEADCHAR message to the message queue. When you pass it a WM_SYSKEYDOWN message under the same conditions, it posts either a WM_SYSCHAR or WM_SYSDEADCHAR message to the message queue. The message identifies the ANSI or Unicode character corresponding to the keystroke.

The character message is placed at the *head* of the queue. This message will be either WM_CHAR, WM_DEADCHAR, WM_SYSCHAR, or WM_SYSDEADCHAR. It will be the next message retrieved by a GetMessage or PeekMessage call. The original virtual-key message isn't changed in any way. The TranslateMessage function simply uses the information from the virtual-key message to produce a corresponding character message for keys that map to ANSI or Unicode characters.

The lParam parameter of the generated character message has the same value as the lParam parameter of the virtual-key message. Therefore, a virtual-key message containing a repeat count greater than 1 generates a character message containing the same repeat count; it does not generate multiple character messages. The wParam parameter of a character message contains the ANSI or Unicode character code for the character. So, you don't need to try to determine what ANSI or Unicode character corresponds to a particular WM_KEYDOWN message when given a particular language and the states of the **Ctrl**, **Shift**, and **Alt** keys. Instead, you can wait for the WM_CHAR message to be sent to a window function and use its wParam parameter.

The WM_DEADCHAR and WM_SYSDEADCHAR messages are a little more involved. Some keyboards have additional keys that allow diacritical marks to be entered. Diacritical marks are added to a character to distinguish that character from another, similar character. The acute accent (á), cedilla (ç), circumflex (â), grave accent (à), and umlaut (ä) are examples of diacritical marks. The user presses and releases the key representing the diacritical mark and then presses and releases the key for the character that the diacritical mark modifies. On a French keyboard, the character â (lowercase "a" with a circumflex) is typed by pressing the circumflex key, followed by the lowercase "a" key. The circumflex key is a *dead key*. That is, it doesn't represent the circumflex character itself. The key modifies the interpretation of the next key that is pressed. (The name "dead key" comes from the era of mechanical typewriters: Dead keys typed the accent mark, but did not forward-space the typewriter carriage; they did "dead spacing".) Other, more frequently used characters are typed directly. The é (lowercase "e" with an acute accent) character is a single key on a French keyboard. Figure 7.1 and Figure 7.2 show the messages generated by typing the letters é and â from the French word "théâtre" and their associated lParam.

First, for the letter é a WM_KEYDOWN message with a virtual-key code of VK_2 arrives. The VK_2 virtual-key code represents the key containing the é character. On a French keyboard, the é character is the letter produced by pressing the key corresponding to the unshifted 2 key on the main section of a U. S. keyboard. The TranslateMessage function, in conjunction with information from the installed keyboard driver (French), places a WM_CHAR message next in the queue representing the é character. The 0xE9 value is the character code for the é character from the ANSI character set. See Figure 7.1. We look at the use of the ANSI character set in more detail later. The WM_KEYUP virtual-key message occurs when the user releases the key.

Message	Virtual-Key Code or ASCII Character	lParam Parameter
WM_KEYDOWN	VK_2	0x00030001
WM_CHAR	0x00E9 (é)	0x00030001
WM_KEYUP	VK_2	0xC0030001

Figure 7.1: Keyboard messages produced when entering an é character

Next, we look at the messages generated when the user types the â character. Pressing the circumflex key (which is in the same location as the [character on a U. S. keyboard) produces a WM_KEYDOWN message with a virtual-key code of VK_OEM_6. The TranslateMessage function maps this to the diacritical mark circumflex. Because this is a diacritical mark and will modify the next character typed, a WM_DEADCHAR message is placed into the message queue. A WM_CHAR message isn't queued because there isn't a character yet–just one in progress. The user releases the circumflex key, producing the WM_KEYUP message with a virtual-key code of VK_OEM_6.

Next the "A" key is pressed, producing a WM_KEYDOWN message with a virtual-key code of VK_A. The TranslateMessage function, in conjunction with information from the installed keyboard driver (French), maps this unshifted virtual key, preceded by a dead character, to the â ANSI character. It places a WM_CHAR

Message	Virtual-Key Code or ASCII Character	lParam Parameter
WM_KEYDOWN	VK_OEM_6	0x001A0001
WM_DEADCHAR	0x005E (^)	0x001A0001
WM_KEYUP	VK_OEM_6	0xC01A0001
WM_KEYDOWN	VK_A	0x00100001
WM_CHAR	0x00E2 (â)	0x00100001
WM_KEYUP	VK_A	0xC0100001
WM_KEYUP	VK_A	0xC0100001

Figure 7.2: Keyboard messages produced when entering an â character

message containing the ANSI code for the character next in the queue. Finally, the "A" key is released and the WM_KEYUP message arrives. Figure 7.2 lists the messages that are produced by the two key presses required to enter the â character. You may also notice that bits 23-16 (the low-order byte of the high-order word) contain code 0x10 for the scan code. If you use the Keyboard Explorer on a conventional English keyboard, you will see that the "A" key produces code 0x1E, while the "Q" key produces code 0x10. This is because, on a French keyboard, the "A" is the leftmost key on the third row up, where the "Q" key is found on English keyboards.

There is one more possibility to cover. When a user presses a key containing a diacritical mark, the next key to be pressed is not known. Windows doesn't wait to see whether the next key can be validly combined with the diacritical mark corresponding to the currently pressed key. That possibility is handled when the next key is pressed. Figure 7.3 shows the messages resulting from pressing the circumflex key followed by pressing the unshifted Q key on a French keyboard. Since there is no circumflex-Q character in French, the characters must be delivered as individual character messages. The first four messages arrive as

Message	Virtual-Key Code or ASCII Character	lParam Parameter
WM_KEYDOWN	VK_OEM_6	0x001A0001
WM_DEADCHAR	0x005E (^)	0x001A0001
WM_KEYUP	VK_OEM_6	0xC01A0001
WM_KEYDOWN	VK_Q	0x001E0001
WM_CHAR	0x005E (^)	0x001E0001
WM_CHAR	0x0071 (q)	0x001e0001
WM_KEYUP	VK_Q	0xC01E0001

Figure 7.3: Messages produced when an unknown diacritical mark combination is pressed

expected. The user presses the circumflex key; this produces a WM_KEYDOWN message followed by a WM_DEADCHAR message. The user releases the key; this produces the WM_KEYUP message. Next the user presses the unshifted Q (lowercase "q") key. The TranslateMessage function, using information from the keyboard device driver, recognizes that the circumflex diacritical mark cannot be combined with a lowercase q, so two WM_CHAR messages are generated: one for the circumflex as a character, not as a diacritical mark, and one for the lowercase "q" character. Finally, the user releases the Q key, producing the WM_KEYUP message for that key.

In general, you need to process only WM_CHAR messages, not dead character messages. The final WM_CHAR message will contain the ANSI code for the letter with the diacritical mark. When the diacritical mark can't be combined with a letter, you receive two WM_CHAR messages: one for the diacritical mark as an independent character and one for the actual letter. However, a word processing application might want to display the diacritical mark (without changing the cursor position) while waiting for the user to press a letter key. After the letter key is pressed, the next WM_CHAR message arrives and you can display the letter in place of the diacritical mark.

WM_[SYS][DEAD]CHAR Message Cracker Handlers

```
void cls_OnChar(HWND hwnd, TCHAR ch, int repeat);

void cls_OnDeadChar(HWND hwnd, TCHAR ch, int repeat);

void cls_OnSysDeadChar(HWND hwnd, TCHAR ch, int repeat);
```

Parameter	wParam		lParam		Meaning
	lo	hi	lo	hi	
	l h				
hwnd					Window handle of the window.
ch (Unicode)	■				Character code of the character.
ch (ANSI)	■				
repeat			■		Repeat count.

You can use the HANDLE_WM_DEADCHAR and HANDLE_WM_SYSDEADCHAR message crackers to handle a dead-character message. The second parameter of the handler has type TCHAR, which is a type we discuss when we get to the Unicode section. For now, think of a TCHAR as being equivalent to a char. As we explain when we discuss Unicode (page 433), TCHAR is a universal name that is a Unicode character in a Unicode application and an ordinary char in an ANSI application.

The Character Sets

For the most part, Windows uses the ANSI character set. (Windows NT uses Unicode, a topic we discuss in more detail starting on page 433. But for many applications running on Windows NT, only the ANSI character set is used.) The wParam parameter of WM_CHAR messages contains the character code of the character in the ANSI character set. The ANSI character set is similar, but not identical, to the ASCII character set. To confuse the issue further, a third 8-bit character set occasionally is used–the *OEM character set*. ("OEM" stands for *Original Equipment Manufacturer*.) The OEM character set is the character set built into the underlying machine. For example, in a typical Intel-compatible Win32 platform this is the character set defined by the BIOS.

A character may be included in one character set but not in any or all of the others. For example, the ASCII character set does not include the â and é characters. However, these characters are present in the ANSI and OEM character sets. Even when a character is present in two character sets, the character may be represented by two different character codes.

The ASCII character set is likely the most familiar to microcomputer programmers. It uses a 7-bit representation for characters. This provides 128 different character codes. The codes from 0 to 31 (0x1F) and the code 127 (0x7F) are *control characters* and are not displayable. The codes from 32 to 126 (0x20 to 0x7E) represent displayable characters. Displayable characters from the ASCII character set have the same character code value in the ANSI character set. Because all English-language characters have the same character code value in both character sets, many programmers fail to properly distinguish between the ASCII and ANSI character sets.

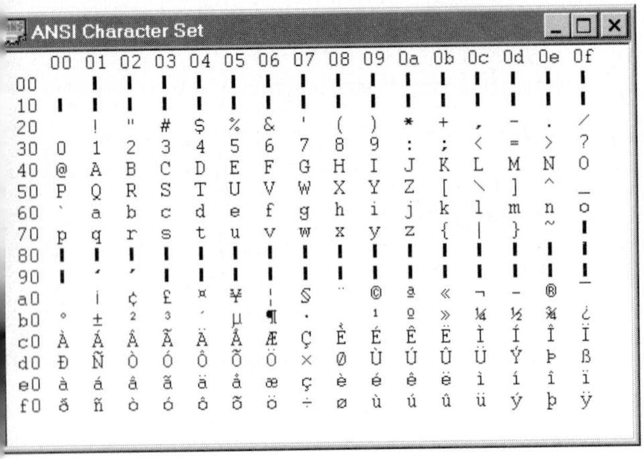

Figure 7.4: The ANSI character set

The ASCII character set does not assign code values to characters with diacritical marks and characters not used by the English language. For example, you won't find an ASCII code for the ß character, the German equivalent of ss. In fact, there are no unassigned values left in the 7-bit ASCII character code set that can be used to represent such characters. However, Windows runs on systems that use 8-bit bytes. Using 8 bits to store a character provides 128 more character codes that can be used to represent characters not found in the ASCII code set. The resulting 8-bit character set, with specific character glyphs assigned to most of the codes in the range 128..255, is the *ANSI character set*. The ANSI character set as displayed by the TextOut function on a VGA display is shown in Figure 7.4. The ANSI character codes 0 to 32 (0x1F), 0x80 to 0x90, and 0x93 to 0x9F are undefined and display on a VGA as short vertical bars. The characters with codes 0x20 to 0x7E are the same in both the ASCII and ANSI character sets. The character set known as *ISO Latin 1* is a subset of the ANSI character set. In particular, the character codes 0x80 to 0x9F are not defined in ISO Latin 1, but they are defined in ANSI. ISO Latin 1 is one of a series of international character sets specified by the International Standards Organization, and is the standard designated ISO-8859-1.[2]

One more character set of importance that you occasionally will deal with in Windows programs is the IBM extended character set. When the PC was first designed, IBM recognized that additional characters could be represented in the additional code values provided by 8-bit characters. This character set was intended for

---

[2] ISO-8859-1 is intended to support Danish, Dutch, Faroese, Finnish, French, German, Icelandic, Irish, Italian, Norwegian, Portuguese, Spanish and Swedish, and can be used also for Hawaiian and Indonesian/Malay. Other languages are supported under the standards ISO-8859-2 (Latin2), ISO-8859-3 (Latin3), ISO-8869-4 (Latin4) and ISO-8859-9 (Latin5), and ISO-6937. See *The Unicode Standard* under "Further Reading".

use with DOS programs. Most personal computers at the time lacked the ability to draw graphics. To allow a DOS program a limited ability to draw "graphics" while in text display mode, special symbols were added to the previously unassigned character codes. Symbols for playing cards, characters from non-English alphabets, and line-drawing characters are some examples of these additional characters. Figure 7.5 shows the IBM extended character set.

Windows must be able to display such characters when running DOS programs in a window. Other than for this purpose, the IBM extended ASCII character set isn't used much by Windows, with one exception. Windows calls the character set native to the system on which it's running the OEM character set. You use the OEM character set most frequently when creating and opening files. Windows 3.x and Windows 95 use the DOS operating system for their file system access[3], and files are named in DOS by certain characters from the OEM character set.

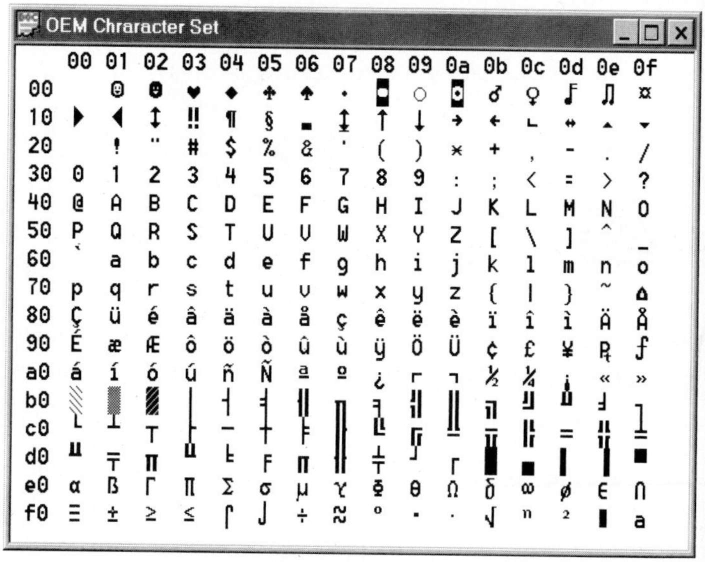

Certain characters have identical symbols but different code values in the ANSI and OEM character sets. For

Figure 7.5: The IBM extended character set

example, the French character é has the value 0xE9 in the ANSI character set, but the value 0x82 in the OEM character set for an IBM personal computer (the IBM extended ASCII character set). Creating a file under DOS with this letter as part of the filename places the 0x82 value into the directory entry. Windows 95 programs trying to match filenames will use the 0xE9 value for the é character and thus the characters will never match. Displaying the filename on the screen using the default ANSI character set font displays the short vertical bar used for unassigned character values.

The contents of files written by a Windows program and read by a DOS program, and vice versa, have the same possible problems. Characters written to files by Windows applications might be in the ANSI character set. When a file is used only by Windows applications, this isn't a problem. If you're sending the file to a Windows system that uses a different OEM code set, this actually is an advantage. The other Windows system uses the same ANSI character set, regardless of its native OEM character set. However, when the file is used by Windows applications and non-Windows applications such as DOS, the same character translation problems arise.

---

[3] You may have heard that Windows 95 is "a complete operating system that does not use DOS at all". Check out *Unauthorized Windows 95* cited under "Further Reading".

We said the characters in a file written by a Windows program might be in the Windows ANSI character set. We need to qualify this statement because Windows provides functions that translate a character string from the ANSI or Unicode character set to the OEM character set and vice versa. The CharToOem function translates the NUL-terminated string pointed to by the Src parameter from the ANSI or Unicode character set to the OEM character set. The Dst parameter specifies the location where the OEM version of the string is placed. It can be the same as the Src parameter to translate the string in place. (Note that if the source string is in Unicode, the result occupies half as many bytes when we are finished.)

```
BOOL CharToOem (LPCTSTR Src, LPSTR Dst) ;
```

Note that unlike every other string function in the C library, these translation functions specify the source parameter as the *first* parameter and the destination parameter as the *second* parameter.

The CharToOemBuff function does the same thing without requiring a NUL-terminated string. Instead, you pass a character count, giving the number of characters to be translated as the Length parameter:

```
BOOL CharToOemBuff (LPCTSTR Src, LPSTR Dst, DWORD Length) ;
```

The OemToChar and OemToCharBuff function work exactly the same as just shown, except in reverse, of course:

```
OemToChar (LPCSTR Src, LPTSTR Dst) ;
OemToCharBuff (LPCSTR Src, LPTSTR Dst, DWORD Length) ;
```

Another time you need to be concerned about character sets is when your program needs to simulate keyboard input to another application. The VkKeyScan function translates an ANSI or Unicode character to the appropriate virtual-key code and shift state values based on the currently installed keyboard. The shift state values specify the state (pressed or released) of the shift keys (**Shift**, **Ctrl**, and **Alt**) that, when used in conjunction with the specified virtual key, produce the specified ANSI character. You then can use these translated values in WM_KEYDOWN and WM_KEYUP messages that are sent to the application. The function returns an int containing the virtual-key code (VK_*) in the low-order byte and the shift state in the high-order byte:

```
SHORT VkCode = VkKeyScan (TCHAR ch) ;
```

The OemKeyScan function is similar. It translates a character from the OEM character set into OEM scan codes and states. It returns a DWORD value containing the scan code in the low-order word and shift state flags in the high-order word:

```
DWORD  dw ;
int    ScanCode;
int    ShiftState ;

dw = OemKeyScan (OemChar) ;
ScanCode = LOWORD (dw) ;
ShiftState = HIWORD (dw) ;
```

Writing an application that works properly when given characters in the ANSI character set requires a few other considerations as well. A valid ANSI character can have a value greater than 128. Watch out for sign-extension problems when assigning a char variable to an int variable. ANSI characters should use BYTE variables rather than char variables. BYTE is a typedef for unsigned char, the proper type for an ANSI character. Normal char variables are signed by default. Note that in some C code, you will find assignments of the form

```
char c;

int ch = (int)c & 0xFF;
```

These work fine if you are in an 8-bit ANSI character set, but they are a source of disaster if you are working in Unicode. You may change the char declaration to a TCHAR declaration. However, the later line of code that masks off the high-order byte may well produce an incorrect Unicode character because the possibly critical high-order 8 bits are lost. We will talk more about Unicode later in the chapter.

You can't correctly change a character from uppercase to lowercase by ORing in the value 0x20 or adding a fixed offset, or convert lowercase to uppercase via the inverse operation, when using ANSI characters. That works only for characters in the English language with values below 128. For example, consider the characters in Table 7.5. Note that although it may superficially appear that the "0x20" rule for case conversion holds for the characters of the ANSI font, it is certainly

Table 7.5: Some examples of case folding

Character	Unshifted Code ANSI	Unshifted Code OEM	Character	Shifted Code ANSI	Shifted Code OEM
a	0x61	0x61	A	0x41	0x41
à	0xE0	0x85	À	0xC0	–
æ	0xE6	0x91	Æ	0xC6	0x92
ç	0xE7	0x87	Ç	0xC7	0x80
ñ	0xF1	0xA4	Ñ	0xD1	0xA5
ˇ	0xFF	0x98	Ÿ	0x9F	–
œ	0x9C	–	Œ	0x8C	–

not true in general for ANSI characters. We have included the OEM codes to show that it is almost always *not* true in the OEM font for other than the ordinary A-Z/a-z range. We would also like to point out that several ANSI characters have no equivalent in the IBM OEM character set.

The C library functions for changing characters from uppercase to lowercase and vice versa also don't work properly on ANSI characters greater than 128. Neither function works well with Unicode characters. The multibyte and wide-string comparison routines of the standard C runtime library do not work well with non-ANSI text, although they work better than the straight 8-bit string routines. Generally, for maximum flexibility and reliability under Windows, particularly if you plan to support Unicode, you should use the Windows

API functions to do case folding, case-independent comparisons, and the like. The header file tchar.h defines some Unicode/ANSI compatible string functions (actually macro names) starting with the prefix tcs or _tcs. These are summarized in Appendix C.

To change an ANSI or Unicode character from uppercase to lowercase, use the CharLower function. The Src parameter points to a NUL-terminated string or specifies a single character. The string is translated in-place. The return value of the function is the same value passed in as Src, to simplify its use. When you want to translate a single ANSI character, place the character in the low-order byte of the low-order word (for Unicode, place the character in the low-order word) and set the high-order word to 0:

```
TCHAR Buffer [80] ;
TCHAR byt ;

CharLower (Buffer) ;
byt = LOBYTE (LOWORD(CharLower ((LPSTR) MAKELONG (byt, 0)))) ;
```

The CharUpper function performs the same action in reverse. Its parameter also can be a pointer to a NUL-terminated string or a single character:

```
TCHAR Buffer [80] ;
TCHAR byt ;

CharUpper (Buffer) ;
byt = LOBYTE (LOWORD(CharUpper ((LPSTR) MAKELONG (byt, 0)))) ;
```

The CharLowerBuff and CharUpperBuff functions convert the given string to lowercase and uppercase, respectively. The string doesn't have to be NUL-terminated because you provide the number of characters to convert as the second parameter:

```
DWORD CharLowerBuff (LPTSTR Str, DWORD Length) ;
DWORD CharUpperBuff (LPTSTR Str, DWORD Length) ;
```

The return value of these functions is the number of characters processed.

Finally, two functions accept a pointer to a string of ANSI or Unicode characters and return the next or previous character in the string. Unicode and some OEM character sets require 2 bytes to represent each character. A string containing characters from a Japanese character set is a common example. If you increment a pointer 1 byte (to skip one character) while running on a system using this type of character set, you can end up pointing in the middle of a 2-byte character sequence. The CharNext and CharPrev functions correctly skip to the next and previous characters, respectively, in a character string, even when the character set uses multibyte characters. Note that CharPrev requires that you give the starting byte of the string. This is because multibyte characters in general can take a varying number of bytes. For some multibyte sets, it may be necessary to scan the string from the beginning to determine of the previous character is 1, 2, or perhaps even more bytes before the current character. (Note that Unicode is not considered a "multibyte" character set, but rather a single-byte character set with wide bytes. This is a subtle but important distinction.)

```
LPTSTR lpCurrChar, lpNextChar, lpPrevChar, lpStartChar ;

lpNextChar = CharNext (lpCurrChar) ;
lpPrevChar = CharPrev (lpStartChar, lpCurrChar) ;
```

Windows normally displays ANSI characters on the screen. The default font for a device context is the stock object SYSTEM_FONT–a proportionally spaced font that contains ANSI characters. (There is also a fixed-pitch stock font called SYSTEM_FIXED_FONT that contains ANSI characters.)

When you want to display characters from the OEM character set, you must get the handle to the stock font OEM_FIXED_FONT and select it into the device context. Windows guarantees that this font is available to support the OEM character set. It normally doesn't provide any other fonts for the OEM character set. You can change to the OEM_FIXED_FONT with the following statement:

```
SelectFont (hdc, GetStockFont (OEM_FIXED_FONT)) ;
```

The Unicode Character Set

The problem with the 8-bit character set is that it is not large enough to represent the union of all the characters of all the various languages in the world. For some languages, the 8-bit character set is not even large enough to represent all the characters in the language. So an international committee was formed some years ago to produce a new international standard that would (attempt) to unify all the character sets. The result was Unicode[4]. Unicode is a 16-bit character set. Windows NT is implemented internally entirely in Unicode. For compatibility, it will run applications in a default 8-bit character set, but the goal is to be able to run full Unicode applications. A sampling of some of the character sets supported in Unicode is shown in Table 7.8. This is a severe abridgment of the full Unicode standard. Volume 1 alone, which does not include East Asian ideographs (that's Volume 2) is 681 pages of excruciating detail.

The presence of Unicode has introduced some new compatibility data types into the Windows programming environment. The familiar declarations of LPSTR, LPCSTR, and char have been replaced by LPTSTR, LPCTSTR, and TCHAR. These are summarized in Table 7.6. If you compile an application with the normal 8-bit mode, you will find that LPTSTR is a pointer to an 8-bit character string, LPCTSTR is a const pointer to an 8-bit char-

Table 7.6: A comparison of ANSI, Unicode, and compatible code set features

Data Type	8-bit ANSI	16-bit Unicode	Compatible
Pointer to string	LPSTR	LPWSTR	LPTSTR
const pointer to string	LPCSTR	LPCWSTR	LPCTSTR
Character	CHAR	WCHAR	TCHAR
Literal string	"abc"	L"abc"	TEXT("abc") _T("abc")
Literal character	'a'	L'a'	TEXT('a') _T('a')

acter string, and TCHAR is a char. But if you compile an application for Unicode, you will find that LPTSTR is a pointer to a 16-bit character string, LPCTSTR is a const pointer to a 16-bit character string, and TCHAR is a 16-bit (signed) character value. So you must be very careful if you want to produce an application that can

---

[4] *The Unicode Standard: Worldwide Character Encoding. Version 1.0, Volume 1.* See "Further Reading".

run in either mode with common source. You can no longer assume the 1-to-1 correspondence between address units and characters in the string. You cannot use _stricmp, _strlwr, _strupr, isupper, and other such functions from the C library, but you can use _tcsicmp, _tcslwr, _tcsupr, istupper, and similar functions listed in Appendix C. You cannot assume that adding a single 8-bit '\0' at the end of a string is going to make it a NUL-terminated string! For example, even a simple call like this is no longer valid:

```
LoadString(hInst, IDS_WHATEVER, buffer, sizeof(buffer));
```

This is because sizeof is defined as returning the number of addressable units (bytes), whereas LoadString wants a count of the number of characters that can be held in the buffer. When compiled in Unicode mode, this code would indicate the buffer is twice as long as it actually is. Instead, you must write something like

```
#define DIM(x) ( sizeof(x) / sizeof((x)[0]))

LoadString(hInst, IDS_WHATEVER, buffer, DIM(buffer));
```

Programming for Unicode requires some care, but it is certainly doable. While a full discussion of how to program for Unicode is well outside the scope of what we want to accomplish in this book, we do summarize some of the major points you need to be aware of.

There are three forms of most declarations:

1. An 8-bit character set version

2. A Unicode (16-bit) character set version

3. A compatible version that compiles differently depending on which mode you want your program to be in

Thus you can create code that can compile and run on Windows 95, using only the 8-bit set it supports, and then that can be recompiled, and it will run on Windows NT in the Unicode character set. But you can also work with 8-bit character strings on Windows NT in a Unicode application and work with 16-bit character strings in Windows 95 (albeit without direct support from the operating system). So if you were willing to go through a lot of work, you could write a Unicode application that ran on Windows 95, but you would have to implement much of the support yourself. In particular, the API calls in Windows 95 would require that you convert Unicode strings to ANSI strings "by hand" and deal explicitly in your code. This would require a lot of programming effort.

There is one Unicode API supported in Windows 95, as reported by Matt Pietrek in *Windows 95 System Programming Secrets* (see "Further Reading"). The Windows 95 MessageBox API is implemented for Unicode (MessageBoxW). This allows your Unicode-based application to check to see if you are running on Windows 95 and issue a MessageBox call stating that your program cannot run on Windows 95. This is not as useful as you might think. It works only if its input arguments are Unicode strings, which means they must be constant strings. This means that the error message can be issued only in one language, which makes internationalization difficult. We have chosen, instead, to implement the code shown in our initInstance handler.

Listing 7.1: Detecting lack of Unicode support
```
BOOL initInstance (HINSTANCE hinst, UINT resPoolID, int nCmdShow)
```

```
{
    HWND    hwnd;
    TCHAR   ClassName [MAX_RESOURCESTRING + 1] ;
    int n;
    n = LoadString (hinst, resPoolID, ClassName, DIM(ClassName)) ;
#if defined(UNICODE)
    if(0 == n)
        { /* no Unicode */
          char msg[MAX_RESOURCESTRING + 1];
          char hdr[MAX_RESOURCESTRING + 1];
          LoadStringA(hinst, IDS_NO_UNICODE, msg, DIM(msg));
          LoadStringA(hinst, IDS_APP_TITLE, hdr, DIM(hdr));
          MessageBoxA(NULL, msg, hdr, MB_OK | MB_ICONERROR) ;
          return FALSE;
        } /* no Unicode */
#endif
    VERIFY(n != 0);
```

Notice also as you read our examples that all of our code is Unicode-ready code. You will see that several applications we include have compiled Unicode versions (these are in the Unicode subdirectory under the appropriate project directory for each of the samples we have explicitly supported and checked). The TEXT macro, or its alternative form, the _T macro (see Table 7.6), prepends an L to the string or character argument that is passed in if the UNICODE symbol is defined and does nothing if the UNICODE symbol is not defined. A normal quoted string will always produce 8-bit characters, and a string preceded by L will always produce 16-bit characters.

In Windows NT, Unicode is handled by having two different API entry points: one for ANSI 8-bit codes and one for Unicode 16-bit codes. For example, the SetWindowText operation does not actually exist in Windows NT. Instead, it is a macro that compiles into either SetWindowTextA if the UNICODE symbol is undefined or into SetWindowTextW if the UNICODE symbol is defined. APIs for which Unicode entry points are defined are designated in the manuals; the actual entry points will always have an A or W suffix. So, if you happen to have on hand an 8-bit ANSI string in your Unicode application and do not wish to convert it to Unicode yourself, you could call SetWindowTextA directly. There are no functional Unicode entry points (with the exception of MessageBoxW in Windows 95) in Windows 95 or Win32s. Although the entry points are defined, they are stubs that return an error code indicating that the operation failed. In Windows 95 or Win32s, you would have to convert your Unicode strings to 8-bit strings before sending them to an API call. Of course, this means that you will end up losing some information in those cases in which there is no correspondence between a Unicode character and the ANSI subset.

Several articles have appeared in the *Microsoft System Journal* regarding how to use Unicode. These are cited in the "Further Reading" section.

Table 7.7 gives some functions you'll need to know if you are using Unicode. We do not discuss them here.

Table 7.7: Unicode translation functions

Function	Meaning
FoldString	Converts one wide-character string into another, performing one or more specified mappings.

Table 7.7: Unicode translation functions

Function	Meaning
LCMapStringW	Converts one wide-character string to another, performing locale-specific transformations.
ToUnicode	Translates a specified virtual-key code and keyboard state to a Unicode character or characters.
MultiByteToWideChar	Maps a character string from one character set to a wide character set. The source string may be an ANSI string.
WideCharToMultiByte	Maps a wide-character string to another character string. The destination string may be an ANSI string.

Table 7.8: Some of the Unicode symbol sets

Character Range		Character Set
From	To	
0x0000	0x007F	ISO 646/ANSI X3.4 characters.
0x0080	0x00FF	ISO 8859-1 "ISO Latin 1" characters.
0x0100	0x017F	ISO 8859-2, -3, -4, -9 European Latin; "ISO Latin 2, 3, 4, 5".
0x0180	0x01C3	Extended Latin.
0x01C4	0x01CC	Croatian digraphs matching Serbian Cyrillic letters.
0x01CD	0x01DC	PRC GB2312/JIS X0212 Pinyin (Latin transcription of Mandarin Chinese) diacritic-vowel combinations.
0x0250	0x02AF	IPA (International Phonetic Alphabet).
0x0300	0x036F	Generic diacritical marks.
0x0370	0x03FF	ISO 8859-7 Greek and ISO 5428 "variant and archaic" characters.
0x0400	0x04FF	ISO 8859-5 Cyrillic.
0x0530	0x058F	Armenian.
0x0590	0x05FF	ISO 8859-8 Hebrew.
0x0600	0x06FF	ISO 8859-6/ASMO 449 Arabic.
0x0900	0x097F	ISCII Devanagari (Indian).
0x0980	0x09FF	Bengali (Indian).
0x0A00	0x0A7F	Gurmukhi (Indian).

Table 7.8: Some of the Unicode symbol sets

Character Range		Character Set
From	To	
0x0A80	0x0Aff	Gujarati (Indian).
0x0B00	0x0B7F	Oriya (Indian).
0x0B80	0x0BFF	Tamil (Indian/Sri Lankan).
0x0C00	0x0C7F	Telugu (Indian).
0x0C80	0x0CFF	Kannada (Indian).
0x0D00	0x0D7F	Malayalam (Indian).
0x0E00	0x0E7F	Thai.
0x0E80	0x0EFF	Lao.
0x1000	0x105F	Tibetian.
0x10A0	0x10FF	Georgian.
0x2000	0x206F	Punctuation, em dash, en dash, direction marks.
0x2070	0x209F	Superscripts and subscripts.
0x20A0	0x20CF	Currency symbols.
0x20D0	0x20FF	Diacritical marks.
0x2190	0x21FF	Arrows.
0x2200	0x22FF	Mathematical operators.
0x2300	0x23FF	APL, miscellaneous technical symbols.
0x2440	0x245F	OCR-A, MICR (Magnetic Ink Character Recognition).
0x2600	0x26FF	Miscellaneous dingbats: weather, I-Ching, moon phases, zodiac, chess pieces, card suits, musical symbols.
0x3000	0x303F	Punctuation marks and symbols for use with Han ideographs.
0x3040	0x309F	Hiragana (Japanese).
0x30A0	0x30FF	Katakana (Japanese).
0x3100	0x312F	Bopomofo (Chinese phonetic).
0x3130	0x318F	KS C 5601 Hangul (Korean).
0x4000	0x8BFF	Chinese/Japanese/Korean ideographs.

The Caret

A *caret* is a graphic symbol, usually the approximate height of the font, that indicates where the next character you type will appear on the screen. Windows programs often use a thin vertical bar placed between two characters on the screen for this purpose, although underlines and boxes can be used. DOS programs usually refer to the caret as the "cursor" and use an underline or an inverse video box to indicate the caret position.

Windows uses the term *cursor* for a different object. The cursor is the small bitmapped image that indicates the position of the mouse. Commonly seen cursors are a small arrow and an hourglass. We look at cursors later in this chapter starting on page 472.

Like the keyboard, the caret is a system resource in Windows. Only one window can use the caret at a time. Although this obviously is more efficient in resource consumption than allowing multiple windows to use multiple carets, there are a few benefits to the user as well.

Because only one caret can be on the screen at once, there is no ambiguity as to where input will go when it is typed. It would be extremely confusing to a user to see multiple windows, all with a flashing caret, each in effect saying, "Your keystrokes will go here!" and there, and over there, and down there as well. The caret should be used only by the window that has the input focus. After all, if it doesn't have the input focus, it doesn't receive any keyboard input and, therefore, doesn't need to show the user where the input will be placed.

Windows notifies your window function when one of its windows receives the input focus by sending it a WM_SETFOCUS message. When you receive the WM_SETFOCUS message, you create the caret you want to use by calling the CreateCaret function as follows:

```
BOOL CreateCaret (HWND hwnd, HBITMAP hbitmap, int Width, int Height) ;
```

The CreateCaret function destroys the current caret (no matter which window owns it–even a window in some other application!), creates a new shape for the system caret, and assigns ownership of it to the window specified by the hwnd parameter. The hbitmap parameter determines whether the caret will be a line, a block, or a bitmap. When the parameter is (HBITMAP)0, the caret is solid, and when it is (HBITMAP)1, the caret is gray. In these two cases, the Width and Height parameters specify the width and height of the caret in logical units. When the hbitmap parameter is a handle to a bitmap, the bitmap itself defines the width and height of the caret and the Width and Height parameters are ignored.

When you want to display a thin line as a caret, you should set the Width or Height parameters to 0, not to 1. When using the MM_TEXT mapping mode on a high-resolution display, a 1-pixel-wide or 1-pixel-high line is very difficult to see. When Width or Height is 0, Windows sets the caret width or height to the system's window-border width or height. This is the value returned by the GetSystemMetrics call with the SM_CXBORDER and SM_CYBORDER indices. This will be wide (or high) enough to be visible on all displays.

The caret initially is hidden when you create it. To make it visible, you call the ShowCaret function. However, before making it visible, you probably will want to put it at the right place on the window. The SetCaretPos function moves the caret to the specified coordinates. If the window was created with the CS_OWNDC style, the coordinates are interpreted according to the current mapping mode of the DC attached to the window. If the window was not created with CS_OWNDC, the coordinates are interpreted as client (device) coordinates. The caret is moved whether or not it is visible, as long as it's owned by some window in the current task. Normally, you'll follow the caret creation with the following:

```
SetCaretPos (X, Y) ;
ShowCaret (hwnd) ;
```

You can inquire about the current position of the caret with the `GetCaretPos` function. It updates the `POINT` structure referenced by the parameter with the client-area coordinates of the position of the caret in the window containing the cursor. Client-area coordinates are device coordinates, not logical coordinates. The `CS_OWNDC` style has no effect on the value returned.

```
POINT pt ;

GetCaretPos (&pt) ;
```

As soon as the caret is visible, it begins blinking automatically. If you want to know how fast the caret is blinking, call the `GetCaretBlinkTime` function. It returns the number of milliseconds between blinks. You can change the rate at which the caret blinks by calling the `SetCaretBlinkTime` function and specifying the time in milliseconds between caret blinks. You can also change the blink rate from the Control Panel. Most users will have set a blink rate they find pleasing, so you should be prepared for some user feedback if they don't like how you change it.

The caret stays visible for the specified time and then is hidden for the same period. Because the caret is a shared system resource, you must ensure that you restore the blink rate to its original value when the window loses the input focus or becomes inactive. You can use the `GetCaretBlinkTime` to get the current value and `SetCaretBlinkTime` to change it. These functions look like the following:

```
UINT Milliseconds ;

Milliseconds = GetCaretBlinkTime () ;
SetCaretBlinkTime (Milliseconds) ;
```

Because the caret is here one (milli)second and gone the next, you must hide it before drawing on the screen or little pieces of the caret get left on the screen. This is done for you automatically when you call the `BeginPaint` function, but it must be done explicitly when drawing at any other time. You hide the caret by calling the `HideCaret` function:

```
HideCaret (hwnd) ;
```

The hwnd parameter can be either the handle of the window that owns the caret or NULL. When it is NULL, Windows hides the caret only if it is owned by a window in the current task. Calls to the `HideCaret` function accumulate. If you call it twice, you must also call the `ShowCaret` function twice before the caret becomes visible again.

Finally, when you receive a `WM_KILLFOCUS` message, you are losing the input focus and must destroy the caret. You should also restore the blink rate if you changed it. The `DestroyCaret` function destroys the current caret if it is owned by a window in the current task. It marks the caret as unowned and removes it from the screen if it is visible. It is quite simple to call, as follows:

```
DestroyCaret () ;
```

The Keyboard Explorer Program

The Key Explorer program intercepts the virtual-key-code messages and the ANSI character messages. These are the WM_CHAR, WM_DEADCHAR, WM_KEYDOWN, WM_KEYUP, WM_SYSCHAR, WM_SYSDEADCHAR, WM_SYSKEYDOWN, and WM_SYSKEYUP messages. The program displays one line on a scrolling screen for each message it intercepts. The messages are decoded and printed in a symbolic form.

Figure 7.6 shows a variety of keystrokes displayed by the Key Explorer program. The columns, from left to right, are as follows:

- Message name

- Virtual-key code or ANSI/Unicode character

- Repeat count

- Keyboard scan code

- Extended-key flag

- **Alt**-key flag

- Key Up/Down flag

- The key transition flag

It's a rather simple program. Most of the work deals with the proportionally spaced font that is used by default. We could "cheat" and use a fixed-pitch font, but for much ordinary text it is harder to read. A fixed-pitch font display also looks a bit out of place among the displays of other applications using the system default variable-pitch font. Although it's a little more effort to use a proportional font, we recommend that you get into the habit of designing a program to use one. When you plan for it from the beginning, it isn't that much additional work.

The code for the Key Explorer program follows in Listings 7.2 through 7.7. Since this code is based on our generic template, we do not show the common code that is not directly relevant to this example.

You may note that in spite of our advocacy of the message cracker macros, Listing 7.2 shows what may be appear to be an odd mixture of message cracker macros and ordinary "case decode" style. This is not accidental. The message crackers may be useful for most ordinary programming, but unusual programs such as Key Explorer that are written "close to the bare metal" of the Windows API really do, quite deliberately, want to circumvent the message cracker macros. For example, the HANDLE_WM_CHAR macro discards the lParam flag values entirely. Hence, if we used it we could not display the key's scan code, which we need to do in this program. So there may be occasions when you need to deal with raw messages, as we do here. But for those cases in which the message crackers gave us what we needed, and did not interfere with what we were trying to analyze, we used them.

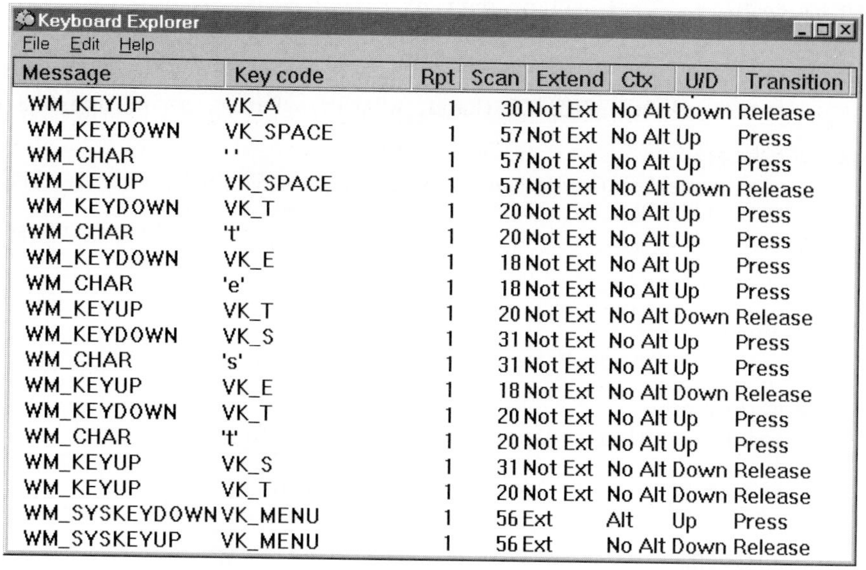

Message	Key code	Rpt	Scan	Extend	Ctx	U/D	Transition
WM_KEYUP	VK_A	1	30	Not Ext	No Alt	Down	Release
WM_KEYDOWN	VK_SPACE	1	57	Not Ext	No Alt	Up	Press
WM_CHAR	' '	1	57	Not Ext	No Alt	Up	Press
WM_KEYUP	VK_SPACE	1	57	Not Ext	No Alt	Down	Release
WM_KEYDOWN	VK_T	1	20	Not Ext	No Alt	Up	Press
WM_CHAR	't'	1	20	Not Ext	No Alt	Up	Press
WM_KEYDOWN	VK_E	1	18	Not Ext	No Alt	Up	Press
WM_CHAR	'e'	1	18	Not Ext	No Alt	Up	Press
WM_KEYUP	VK_T	1	20	Not Ext	No Alt	Down	Release
WM_KEYDOWN	VK_S	1	31	Not Ext	No Alt	Up	Press
WM_CHAR	's'	1	31	Not Ext	No Alt	Up	Press
WM_KEYUP	VK_E	1	18	Not Ext	No Alt	Down	Release
WM_KEYDOWN	VK_T	1	20	Not Ext	No Alt	Up	Press
WM_CHAR	't'	1	20	Not Ext	No Alt	Up	Press
WM_KEYUP	VK_S	1	31	Not Ext	No Alt	Down	Release
WM_KEYUP	VK_T	1	20	Not Ext	No Alt	Down	Release
WM_SYSKEYDOWN	VK_MENU	1	56	Ext	Alt	Up	Press
WM_SYSKEYUP	VK_MENU	1	56	Ext	No Alt	Down	Release

Figure 7.6: The Key Explorer program at work

Listing 7.2: Key Explorer message dispatch and handlers

```
LRESULT CALLBACK
mainFrameWndProc (HWND hwnd, UINT message, WPARAM wParam, LPARAM lParam)
{
    switch (message)
        {
        case WM_CHAR:  // Notification of an ANSI/UNICODE keypress
                mainFrame_DisplayMessage (hwnd, IDS_WM_CHAR, wParam, lParam) ;
                return HANDLE_WM_CHAR (hwnd, wParam, lParam, mainFrame_OnChar) ;

        case WM_COMMAND:  // Notification from menu or control
                return HANDLE_WM_COMMAND (hwnd, wParam, lParam, mainFrame_OnCommand) ;

        case WM_CREATE:  // Notification that a window is being created
                return HANDLE_WM_CREATE (hwnd, wParam, lParam, mainFrame_OnCreate) ;

        case WM_DEADCHAR:
                mainFrame_DisplayMessage (hwnd, IDS_WM_DEADCHAR, wParam, lParam) ;
                return HANDLE_WM_DEADCHAR (hwnd, wParam, lParam,
                                                    mainFrame_OnDeadChar) ;

        case WM_KEYDOWN:
                mainFrame_DisplayMessage (hwnd, IDS_WM_KEYDOWN, wParam, lParam) ;
                return HANDLE_WM_KEYDOWN (hwnd, wParam, lParam, mainFrame_OnKey) ;

        case WM_KEYUP:
                mainFrame_DisplayMessage (hwnd, IDS_WM_KEYUP, wParam, lParam) ;
                return HANDLE_WM_KEYUP (hwnd, wParam, lParam, mainFrame_OnKey) ;
```

```
        case WM_PAINT: // Draw all or part of client area
                return HANDLE_WM_PAINT (hwnd, wParam, lParam, mainFrame_OnPaint) ;

        case WM_SIZE:  // Window size has changed
                return HANDLE_WM_SIZE (hwnd, wParam, lParam, mainFrame_OnSize) ;

        case WM_SYSCHAR:
                mainFrame_DisplayMessage (hwnd, IDS_WM_SYSCHAR, wParam, lParam) ;
                return HANDLE_WM_SYSCHAR (hwnd, wParam, lParam,
                                                        mainFrame_OnSysChar) ;

        case WM_SYSDEADCHAR:
                mainFrame_DisplayMessage (hwnd, IDS_WM_SYSDEADCHAR,
                                                        wParam, lParam) ;
                return DefWindowProc (hwnd, message, wParam, lParam) ;

        case WM_SYSKEYDOWN:
                mainFrame_DisplayMessage (hwnd, IDS_WM_SYSKEYDOWN,
                                                        wParam, lParam) ;
                return HANDLE_WM_SYSKEYDOWN (hwnd, wParam, lParam,
                                                        mainFrame_OnSysKey) ;

        case WM_SYSKEYUP:
                mainFrame_DisplayMessage (hwnd, IDS_WM_SYSKEYUP,
                                                        wParam, lParam) ;
                return HANDLE_WM_SYSKEYUP (hwnd, wParam, lParam,
                                                        mainFrame_OnSysKey) ;

        // Note: other cases as per Skeleton application code eliminated
        // for conciseness.  See the Key Explorer code for details
        default:
                return DefWindowProc (hwnd, message, wParam, lParam) ;
    }
}

// The following are typical of all the key handlers

static void mainFrame_OnChar(HWND hwnd, TCHAR ch, int cRepeat)
{
    FORWARD_WM_CHAR (hwnd, ch, cRepeat, DefWindowProc) ;
}

void mainFrame_OnDeadChar(HWND hwnd, TCHAR ch, int cRepeat)
{
    FORWARD_WM_DEADCHAR (hwnd, ch, cRepeat, DefWindowProc) ;
}

int             mainFrame_cyPixels ;        /* Height (device units)  */
int             mainFrame_cyChar ;          /* Height (logical units) */

static BOOL
mainFrame_OnCreate (HWND hwnd, LPCREATESTRUCT lpCreateStruct)
{
    HDC         hdc ;
    HWND        hwndHeader ;
    SIZE        sz ;
    TEXTMETRIC  tm ;
```

```
    // Initialize the width table for the header

    mainFrame_ComputeMessageWidths(hwnd);

    // Create the header control
    hwndHeader = header_CreateHeader (hwnd) ;
    if (NULL == hwndHeader)
        return FALSE ;

    if (!header_AddItems (hwndHeader))
        return FALSE ;

    // Get a device context for the window
    hdc = GetDC (hwnd) ;

    // Get the metrics for the currently selected font in MM_TEXT mode
    VERIFY (GetTextMetrics (hdc, &tm)) ;
    mainFrame_cyPixels = tm.tmHeight + tm.tmExternalLeading ;

    VERIFY (SetMapMode (hdc, MM_HIENGLISH)) ;

    // Get the metrics for the currently selected font in MM_HIENGLISH mode
    VERIFY (GetTextMetrics (hdc, &tm)) ;
    mainFrame_cyChar = tm.tmHeight + tm.tmExternalLeading ;

    ReleaseDC (hwnd, hdc) ;
    return TRUE ;
}
```

We use a control called a *header control* to give us column headings. Note that we have to dynamically compute the column widths based on the strings that will be displayed; this is shown in Listing 7.6. This is due to several factors. While internationalization might be one of them, it is not the most important one (while *applications* tend to require internationalization, the internal programming is often done in the "native language" of the Windows API). The columns cannot be allocated as fixed-width (compile-time) values because this does not work between the three Win32 platforms. The "correct" widths for Windows NT 3.*x* will not work for Windows 95 or Windows NT 4.*x*. In addition, there is an undocumented value that is the size of the margin allowance. We have found that using three times the width of the space seems to work, but this is empirically determined and we cannot locate any mention of this value in any Microsoft documentation.

The algorithm for computing the width is trivial. Given an array of string ID values terminated by a 0 value, we load each string in turn, use the GetTextExtentPoint32 function to compute the width, and store the maximum width. We then compute the width of the caption, adding into the maximum width a fudge factor for the undocumented margin width and figure this value. To simplify the processing, we built this into a table of column information. Each table entry contains a pointer to the array of string IDs of possible values, the string ID of the caption, and a starting position and width for each column. The data structure and computations are shown in Listing 7.3.

Listing 7.3: Key Explorer column width computation: `columns.h`
```
// All dimensions are 1/1000ths of an inch

#define COLUMN_MESSAGE_INDENT 125
```

```
#define COLUMN_MESSAGE      0
#define COLUMN_KEYCODE      1
#define COLUMN_REPEATCOUNT  2
#define COLUMN_SCANCODE     3
#define COLUMN_EXTENDED     4
#define COLUMN_CONTEXT      5
#define COLUMN_UPDOWN       6
#define COLUMN_TRANSITION   7

typedef struct{
                int * table; // pointer to array of string IDs, 0-terminated
                int caption; // string ID of caption
                int start;   // computed by initialization
                int width;   // computed by initialization
              } widthtable;

extern widthtable column_widths[8];
```

Listing 7.4: Key Explorer column width computation: excerpts from `displayMessage.c`

```
int compute_width(HWND hwnd, widthtable * cwt)
{
 int i;
 int width = 0;
 SIZE space;
 HDC hdc = GetDC(hwnd);
 SIZE sz;
 TCHAR text[64];

 SetMapMode(hdc, MM_HIENGLISH);  // computations are stored in 1/1000ths of inch

 // allow one space as margin in our output

 GetTextExtentPoint32(hdc, _T(" "), 1, &space);

 // loop over the array of string IDs, computing the width of each string

 for(i = 0; cwt->table[i] != 0; i++)
     { /* compute each width */
       LoadString(GetWindowInstance(hwnd), cwt->table[i], text, DIM(text));
       GetTextExtentPoint32(hdc, text, _tcslen(text), &sz);
       width = max(width, sz.cx + space.cx);
     } /* compute each width */

   // Compute the width of the caption

   LoadString(GetWindowInstance(hwnd), cwt->caption, text, DIM(text));
   GetTextExtentPoint32(hdc, text, _tcslen(text), &sz);
   width = max(width, sz.cx + 3 * space.cx);   // 3 * space is fudge factor for
                                               // undocumented caption margin

   ReleaseDC(hwnd, hdc);
   return width;
}

void MainFrame_ComputeMessageWidths(HWND hwnd)
{
```

```
int i;

for(i = 0; i < DIM(column_widths); i++)
   { /* initialize each row */
    column_widths[i].width = compute_width(hwnd, &column_widths[i]);
   } /* initialize each row */

// now compute the starting position

column_widths[0].start = 0;
for(i = 1; i < DIM(column_widths); i++)
   { /* compute start */
    column_widths[i].start = column_widths[i-1].start +
                                         column_widths[i-1].width;

   } /* compute start */

// and adjust the start position of the first column

column_widths[0].start = COLUMN_MESSAGE_INDENT;
}
```

The table `column_widths`, shown in Listing 7.5, is used to set the headings in the header control, which must be set by giving the column width of each column as it is placed. It is also used to display the output which requires the column position. This is why we compute both a width and starting point. We compute the coordinates in $1/1000$ ths of an inch just to illustrate the use of the mapping modes. But the heading functions require sizes in device units, so we have to use the LPtoDP function to convert the units from the logical coordinates to pixel coordinates.

The content tables used by the `column_widths` table, which drive the length computations, are shown in Listing 7.5. The VkMap table is used to decode the virtual-key codes to a printable string. This table has 257 entries. The first 256 are for virtual key codes 0..255, and the last is a 0 entry that we use in computing the maximum column width using the `compute_widths` function shown in Listing 7.4. Only about 100 entries are actual virtual-key-code names; the remaining codes are assigned the string ID IDS_VK_UNDEFINED, which retrieves the string "Undefined". The remaining int arrays are used solely for the width computation. The `column_widths` table is used to set the headings in the header control and compute the positions of the text in the display window.

Listing 7.5: Key Explorer: setting the headings: tables from `displayMessage.c`

```
static int VkMap [] = {
   IDS_VK_UNDEFINED,   IDS_VK_LBUTTON,    IDS_VK_RBUTTON,    IDS_VK_CANCEL,
   IDS_VK_MBUTTON,     IDS_VK_UNDEFINED,  IDS_VK_UNDEFINED,  IDS_VK_UNDEFINED,
   IDS_VK_BACK,        IDS_VK_TAB,        IDS_VK_UNDEFINED,  IDS_VK_UNDEFINED,
   IDS_VK_CLEAR,       IDS_VK_RETURN,     IDS_VK_UNDEFINED,  IDS_VK_UNDEFINED,
   IDS_VK_SHIFT,       IDS_VK_CONTROL,    IDS_VK_MENU,       IDS_VK_PAUSE,
   ... // lots of detail dropped for conciseness
   IDS_VK_UNDEFINED,   IDS_VK_A,          IDS_VK_B,          IDS_VK_C,
   IDS_VK_D,           IDS_VK_E,          IDS_VK_F,          IDS_VK_G,
   IDS_VK_H,           IDS_VK_I,          IDS_VK_J,          IDS_VK_K,
   ... // lots of detail dropped for conciseness
   IDS_VK_EXSEL,       IDS_VK_EREOF,      IDS_VK_PLAY,       IDS_VK_ZOOM,
   IDS_VK_NONAME,      IDS_VK_PA1,        IDS_VK_OEM_CLEAR,  IDS_VK_UNDEFINED,
   0 // end of table for message width scan
} ;
```

```
static int msgMap[] = {IDS_WM_CHAR, IDS_WM_DEADCHAR, IDS_WM_KEYDOWN,
                       IDS_WM_KEYUP, IDS_WM_SYSCHAR, IDS_WM_SYSDEADCHAR,
                       IDS_WM_SYSKEYDOWN, IDS_WM_SYSKEYUP, 0};
static int digits[] =  {IDS_DIGITS, 0};
static int ext[] =     {IDS_EXT, IDS_NOTEXT, 0};
static int context[] = {IDS_ALT, IDS_NOALT, 0};
static int updown[] =  {IDS_UP, IDS_DOWN, 0};
static int trans[] =   {IDS_RELEASE, IDS_PRESS, 0};

widthtable column_widths[8] = {
        {msgMap,   IDS_MESSAGETITLE,     0, 0},  // WM_CHAR, etc.
        {VkMap,    IDS_KEYCODETITLE,     0, 0},  // VK_WHATEVER, etc.
        {digits,   IDS_REPEATCOUNTTITLE, 0, 0},  // repeat count: 1
        {digits,   IDS_SCANCODETITLE,    0, 0},  // scan code: 99
        {ext,      IDS_EXTFLAGTITLE,     0, 0},  // Extended/Not extended
        {context,  IDS_CONTEXTTITLE,     0, 0},  // context code: ALT, Not ALT
        {updown,   IDS_UPDOWNTITLE,      0, 0},  // up/down code
        {trans,    IDS_TRANSITIONTITLE,  0, 0},  // transition code
                              };
```

Listing 7.6: Key Explorer: setting the headings: excerpts from `mainframeHeader.c`

```
HWND
header_CreateHeader (HWND hwndParent)
{
    HINSTANCE           hinst ;
    HWND                hwndHeader ;

    // Get the application's instance handle
    hinst = GetWindowInstance (hwndParent) ;

    // Create the header control
    hwndHeader =
        CreateWindowEx (0,                       // extended window style
                        WC_HEADER,               // header control class name
                        NULL,                    // window name
                        WS_CHILD |               // window style
                        WS_BORDER |
                        HDS_HORZ,
                        0, 0, 0, 0,              // horiz, vert, width, height
                        hwndParent,              // parent window
                        (HMENU)IDC_HEADER,       // child window identifier
                        hinst,                   // application instance
                        NULL) ;                  // creation parameters

    return hwndHeader ;
}

BOOL header_Initialize (HWND hwndHeader)
{
    HWND                hwndParent ;
    RECT                rectParent ;
    HD_LAYOUT           hdl ;
    WINDOWPOS           wp ;

    // Determine the parent window
    hwndParent = GetParent (hwndHeader) ;
```

```
      // Get the client rectangle of the parent window
      GetClientRect (hwndParent, &rectParent) ;

      // Constrain the header control to its parent window's bounding rectangle
      hdl.prc   = &rectParent ;
      hdl.pwpos = &wp ;

      // Retrieves the size and position
      // of the header control within its parent's client area.
      if (!header_Layout (hwndHeader, &hdl))
          return FALSE ;

      // Set the size, position, and visibility of the header control.

      SetWindowPos (hwndHeader,
                    wp.hwndInsertAfter,
                    wp.x,
                    wp.y,
                    wp.cx,
                    wp.cy,
                    wp.flags | SWP_SHOWWINDOW) ;

      return TRUE ;
}

BOOL header_AddItems (HWND hwndHeader)
{
      HINSTANCE           hInst ;
      int                 nResult ;
      TCHAR               achBuffer [64] ;
      int i;

      hInst = GetWindowInstance (hwndHeader) ;

      for(i = 0; i < DIM(column_widths); i++)
         { /* load columns */
          VERIFY(nResult = LoadString(hInst, column_widths[i].caption,
                                          achBuffer, DIM(achBuffer)));
           header_AddItem(hwndHeader, achBuffer, column_widths[i].width);
         } /* load columns */


      return TRUE ;
}

BOOL header_AddItems (HWND hwndHeader)
{
      HINSTANCE           hInst ;
      int                 nResult ;
      TCHAR               achBuffer [64] ;
      int i;

      hInst = GetWindowInstance (hwndHeader) ;

      for(i = 0; i < DIM(column_widths); i++)
         { /* load columns */
          VERIFY(nResult = LoadString(hInst, column_widths[i].caption,
```

```
                                          achBuffer, DIM(achBuffer)));
        header_AddItem(hwndHeader, achBuffer, column_widths[i].width);
        } /* load columns */


    return TRUE ;
}

static BOOL header_AddItem (HWND hwndHeader, LPCTSTR pszText, int nWidth)
{
    int         nItem ;
    HD_ITEM     hdi;
    HDC         dc = GetDC(hwndHeader);
    POINT       pt;

    SetMapMode(dc, MM_HIENGLISH);

    hdi.mask = HDI_TEXT |       // pszText and cchTextMax member are valid
               HDI_FORMAT |     // fmt member is valid
               HDI_WIDTH ;      // cxy member is valid

    // Specify text of header item
    hdi.pszText    = (LPTSTR) pszText ;
    hdi.cchTextMax = _tcslen (pszText) ;

    // Specify the item is a left-justified string
    hdi.fmt = HDF_LEFT | HDF_STRING ;

    // Specify the width of the item, which must be in pixels

    pt.x = nWidth;
    pt.y = 0;
    LPtoDP(dc, &pt, 1);
    hdi.cxy = pt.x;

    ReleaseDC(hwndHeader, dc);

    // Insert after last item in header
    nItem = Header_GetItemCount (hwndHeader) ;
    if (-1 == Header_InsertItem (hwndHeader, nItem, &hdi))
        return FALSE ;

    return TRUE;
}
```

The drawing of the output is straightforward, as shown in Listing 7.7. When a key message comes in, we display its parameters on the screen. We do this by scrolling the window to create space, using the ScrollWindowEx function. In the space that has been created, we immediately draw the values we wish to see. For the right-justified numeric fields, we leave a half-space to the right of the digits so that they don't crowd the right margin. The one unusual feature of the drawing routine is the ValidateRect call, which appears at the end of the function in Listing 7.7. We included this call because we have actually drawn the contents of the window and don't need to redo it in the paint handler. (In fact, we don't have enough information to redo it in the paint handler. We discuss this in more detail later.) By calling ValidateRect, we keep the uncovered area from being erased for the paint handler and requiring complex data structures for the redraw.

Listing 7.7: Key Explorer display: excerpts from `displayMessage.c`

```
VOID
mainFrame_DisplayMessage (HWND hwnd, UINT Id, WPARAM wParam, LPARAM lParam)
{
    TCHAR        Buffer [64] ;
    HINSTANCE    hInst ;
    HDC          hdc ;
    HWND         hwndHeader ;
    int          Result, xPos, LabelId, length ;
    RECT         rect, rectHeader, rectScrolled ;
    SIZE         space;

    // Calculate area to be scrolled - omit header control
    GetClientRect (hwnd, &rectScrolled) ;

    // Exclude size of header
    hwndHeader = GetDlgItem (hwnd, IDC_HEADER) ;
    if (NULL != hwndHeader) {
        GetClientRect (hwndHeader, &rectHeader) ;
        rectScrolled.top += rectHeader.bottom ;     // Omit header
    }


    // Make room for the new line.
    ScrollWindowEx (hwnd, 0, -MainFrame_cyPixels,
                    &rectScrolled, &rectScrolled,
                    NULL, NULL, SW_ERASE | SW_INVALIDATE) ;

    // Erase the bottom line.
    UpdateWindow (hwnd) ;

    // Get the symbolic name of the message.
    hInst = GetWindowInstance (hwnd) ;
    VERIFY (Result = LoadString (hInst, Id, Buffer, DIM (Buffer))) ;

    // Switch to 0.001 inch units.
    hdc = GetDC (hwnd) ;
    SetMapMode (hdc, MM_HIENGLISH) ;

    GetClientRect (hwnd, &rect) ;
    SetViewportOrgEx (hdc, rect.left, rect.bottom, NULL) ;

    // Display name of message.
    TextOut (hdc, column_widths[COLUMN_MESSAGE].start,
                        MainFrame_cyChar, Buffer, Result) ;

    length = 3 ;
    switch (Id)
        { /* wId */
        case IDS_WM_CHAR:
        case IDS_WM_DEADCHAR:
        case IDS_WM_SYSCHAR:
        case IDS_WM_SYSDEADCHAR:

            // Display the ANSI/UNICODE character.
            Buffer [0] = TEXT('\'') ;
            Buffer [1] = (TCHAR) wParam ;
```

```
        Buffer [2] = TEXT('\'') ;

        switch (Buffer [1]) {
        case TEXT('\a'):
            Buffer [1] = TEXT('\\') ;
            Buffer [2] = TEXT('a') ;
            Buffer [3] = TEXT('\'') ;
            length = 4 ;
            break ;

        // dropped to save space here: identical cases for the following
        // escapes: \b, \f, \n, \r, \t, \v, \', \", \\
        // . . .
        }

        // Display ANSI/UNICODE character
        TextOut (hdc, column_widths[COLUMN_KEYCODE].start,
                            mainFrame_cyChar, Buffer, length) ;

        break ;
    case IDS_WM_KEYDOWN:
    case IDS_WM_KEYUP:
    case IDS_WM_SYSKEYDOWN:
    case IDS_WM_SYSKEYUP:

        // Display the virtual-key code.
        VERIFY (LoadString (hInst, VkMap [wParam],
                            Buffer, DIM (Buffer))) ;

        // Display virtual-key code name
        TextOut (hdc, column_widths[COLUMN_KEYCODE].start,
                            MainFrame_cyChar, Buffer, _tcslen (Buffer)) ;
        break ;
}

GetTextExtentPoint32(hdc, _T(" "), 1, &space);

// for the decoding of the parameters, refer to Table 7.2 on page 413.

// Display repeat count
// Right justify the numerals.
_itot ((int)(short)LOWORD (lParam), Buffer, 10) ;

GetTextExtentPoint32(hdc, Buffer, _tcslen(Buffer), &sz);

xPos = column_widths[COLUMN_REPEATCOUNT].start +
        column_widths[COLUMN_REPEATCOUNT].width - (sz.cx + space.cx/2);

TextOut (hdc, xPos, MainFrame_cyChar, Buffer, _tcslen (Buffer)) ;

// Display scan code.
// Right justify the numerals.
_itot (LOBYTE (HIWORD (lParam)), Buffer, 10) ;

GetTextExtentPoint32(hdc, Buffer, _tcslen(Buffer), &sz);

xPos = column_widths[COLUMN_SCANCODE].start +
            column_widths[COLUMN_SCANCODE].width - (sz.cx + space.cx/2);
```

```
TextOut (hdc, xPos, MainFrame_cyChar, Buffer, _tcslen (Buffer)) ;

    // Display extended key flag
    LabelId = (lParam & 0x01000000) ? IDS_EXT : IDS_NOTEXT ;
    VERIFY (Result = LoadString (hInst, LabelId, Buffer, DIM (Buffer))) ;
    TextOut (hdc, column_widths[COLUMN_EXTENDED].start,
                            mainFrame_cyChar, Buffer, Result) ;

    // Display context code.
    LabelId = (lParam & 0x20000000) ? IDS_ALT : IDS_NOALT ;
    VERIFY (Result = LoadString (hInst, nLabelId, Buffer, DIM (Buffer))) ;
    TextOut (hdc, column_widths[COLUMN_CONTEXT].start,
                            mainFrame_cyChar, Buffer, Result) ;

    // Display up-down code.
    LabelId = (lParam & 0x40000000) ? IDS_DOWN : IDS_UP ;
    VERIFY (Result = LoadString (hInst, LabelId, Buffer, DIM (Buffer))) ;
    TextOut (hdc, column_widths[COLUMN_UPDOWN].start,
                            mainFrame_cyChar, Buffer, Result) ;

    // Display transition state.
    LabelId = (lParam & 0x80000000) ? IDS_RELEASE : IDS_PRESS ;
    VERIFY (Result = LoadString (hInst, LabelId, Buffer, DIM (Buffer))) ;
    TextOut (hdc, column_widths[COLUMN_TRANSITION].start,
                            mainFrame_cyChar, Buffer, Result) ;

    ValidateRect (hwnd, NULL) ;
    ReleaseDC (hwnd, hdc) ;
}
```

Mouse Input

The mouse is an *optional* pointing device for Windows. In addition to mice, there are many alternative optional pointing devices, such as touch screens, touch pads, pens, light pens, drawing tablets, and the pressure-activated joystick-like device found in many laptops. Windows considers all of these to be "mouse input" devices.

The small bitmap image that represents the pointer position is called a *cursor*. As the user moves the "mouse input" device, the cursor moves correspondingly. A user can perform many different functions with the mouse, such as selecting items from a menu, clicking a push button, and indicating areas of interest in a window. But there is nothing that in any way couples cursor behavior to the keyboard that is "built into" Windows. If you want the keyboard to move the cursor, your application has to program that explicitly.

Windows supports a mouse with one, two, or three buttons. Windows refers to the buttons as the *left button* (the only button on a one-button mouse), the *middle button* (present only on a three-button mouse), and the *right button* (present on a two- or three-button mouse). Those who prefer to use the mouse with their left hands can tell Windows via the Control Panel to "swap" the mouse buttons. Then the left mouse button (the "pointer finger" button for right-handed usage) sends right-mouse-button messages and the right mouse button (the "pointer finger" button for left-handed usage) sends left-mouse-button messages. This is because the buttons are described in terms of their physical placement on the mouse, rather than their logical usage. In *The Windows Interface Guidelines for Software Design*, Microsoft has officially taken the position that the buttons are called "Button 1", "Button 2", and "Button 3", where "Button 1" is the "pointer finger" button (left button for a right-handed person), "Button 2" is the opposite button (right button for a right-handed person) and "Button 3", if present at all, is the middle button. We will continue to explain the buttons in terms of their conventional Windows nomenclature, "left", "middle," and "right", but you should simply keep in mind the idea that the buttons may be swapped and you, as the programmer, generally will not care that they have been swapped by the user.

Because a mouse is an optional device, you might want to check to see whether a mouse is present. The following GetSystemMetrics function call returns a nonzero value when a mouse is installed:

int MousePresent = GetSystemMetrics (SM_MOUSEPRESENT) ;

The number of mouse buttons can be obtained by the call

int NumberOfButtons = GetSystemMetrics(SM_CMOUSEBUTTONS) ;

The SM_CMOUSEBUTTONS code is not supported in Win16 and consequently is not available in Win32s. There is no documented way in Win16 to discover the number of buttons on a mouse.

You can tell if the mouse buttons have been swapped by using GetSystemMetrics to query the state using the SM_SWAPBUTTON code:

BOOL swapped = GetSystemMetrics(SM_SWAPBUTTON) ;

Having emphasized that the mouse (or a mouse-like pointing device) is optional, it is still one of the most important interfaces to the system, and a great deal of technology and technique must be understood for its effective use. We explore that technology and the associated techniques in the following sections.

Mouse Messages

Like keyboard input, mouse input arrives in the form of messages. These are called *mouse messages*. There are 22 different mouse messages, but only three are commonly used: WM_LBUTTONDOWN, WM_LBUTTONUP, and WM_MOUSEMOVE. Table 7.9 lists the mouse messages, divided into three groups. The 10 messages in the first group inform you of events occurring within the client area of a window. The 10 messages in the second group duplicate the first 10, except they signal actions taken in the nonclient areas of a window. The two remaining messages are the WM_NCHITTEST and WM_MOUSEACTIVATE messages. The processing for the WM_NCHITTEST message eventually generates all the other mouse messages.

Before we describe the messages in detail, let's look at how and when the messages are produced. Each time the user moves the mouse or presses and releases a mouse button, Windows sends a series of messages to the window function for the window under the cursor. The window does not need to have the input focus (that pertains to keyboard input only) and does not need to be active. Pressing any mouse button while the cursor is over an inactive window activates the window. (This is true for all areas of a window except the caption.

Table 7.9: The mouse messages

Message	Description
Client-area mouse messages	
WM_LBUTTONDBLCLK	Left button has been double-clicked in the client area.
WM_LBUTTONDOWN	Left button has been pressed in the client area.
WM_LBUTTONUP	Left button has been released in the client area.
WM_MBUTTONDBLCLK	Middle button has been double-clicked in the client area.
WM_MBUTTONDOWN	Middle button has been pressed in the client area.
WM_MBUTTONUP	Middle button has been released in the client area.
WM_MOUSEMOVE	Mouse has been moved in the client area.
WM_RBUTTONDBLCLK	Right button has been double-clicked in the client area.
WM_RBUTTONDOWN	Right button has been pressed in the client area.
WM_RBUTTONUP	Right button has been released in the client area.
Nonclient-area mouse messages	
WM_NCLBUTTONDBLCLK	Left button has been double-clicked in the nonclient area.
WM_NCLBUTTONDOWN	Left button has been pressed in the nonclient area.
WM_NCLBUTTONUP	Left button has been released in the nonclient area.
WM_NCMBUTTONDBLCLK	Middle button has been double-clicked in the nonclient area.
WM_NCMBUTTONDOWN	Middle button has been pressed in the nonclient area.
WM_NCMBUTTONUP	Middle button has been released in the nonclient area.
WM_NCMOUSEMOVE	Mouse has been moved in the nonclient area.
WM_NCRBUTTONDBLCLK	Right button has been double-clicked in the nonclient area.
WM_NCRBUTTONDOWN	Right button has been pressed in the nonclient area.
WM_NCRBUTTONUP	Right button has been released in the nonclient area.
Other mouse messages	
WM_NCHITTEST	Mouse has been moved; location as yet unknown.
WM_MOUSEACTIVATE	Mouse button has been pressed over an inactive window.

Only a left button press activates a window when the cursor is over the caption.) Simply moving the cursor over the window does not activate the window.

Unlike key presses, mouse messages can be "lost". That is, as the user moves the mouse across the client area of a window, Windows probably will not send a WM_MOUSEMOVE message reporting every pixel over which the cursor passes. The number and frequency of messages depends on the mouse hardware, the rate at which your window function can process a message, and the rate at which the mouse is moving.

Likewise, a window function can receive a button down message without a matching button up message and vice versa. Windows normally sends the button down message to the window function for the window the cursor was over when the button was pressed. The cursor might be over a different window when the button is released. If so, the button up message is sent to a different window.

Hit Testing: The WM_NCHITTEST Message

As we mentioned, moving the mouse and pressing or releasing a mouse button generates a series of messages. The first message that arrives is a WM_NCHITTEST message. The "NC" part of the message stands for "nonclient" area. This isn't because the message pertains to the nonclient area; that isn't known yet. It's because this message, like all nonclient-area messages, is nearly always processed by the DefWindowProc function and not by your window function. Windows sends the WM_NCHITTEST message to find out what part of the window is under the cursor.

The wParam parameter to a window function isn't used for a WM_NCHITTEST message. The lParam parameter contains the horizontal and vertical screen coordinates of the hot spot of the cursor. These are passed in as separate x and y parameters to the handler function when you use the message cracker. However, note that they are 16-bit values; this limits us to screens of fewer than 65,535 pixels' resolution. The hot spot of a cursor is the position within the cursor bitmap to which the cursor points. For example, the hot spot of an arrow cursor is the tip of the arrow. The hot spot of a crosshair cursor is its center. The horizontal coordinate is in the low-order word, and the vertical coordinate is in the high-order word. The DefWindowProc function processes this message and returns a value indicating the position of the cursor within a window. These values are listed in Table 7.10.

WM_NCHITTEST Message Cracker Handler

UINT cls_OnNcHitTest(HWND hwnd, int xScreen, int yScreen);					
Result			UINT, one of the HT codes from Table 7.10.		
	wParam		**lParam**		
Parameter	**lo**	**hi**	**lo**	**hi**	**Meaning**
hwnd					Window handle of the window.
xScreen			■		Horizontal coordinate, in screen coordinates.
yScreen				■	Vertical coordinate, in screen coordinates.

Table 7.10: Hit-test values returned from `DefWindowProc` as a result of a `WM_NCHITTEST` message

Value	Location of Cursor
HTBORDER	In the border of a window without a sizing border.
HTBOTTOM	In the lower horizontal border.
HTBOTTOMLEFT	In the lower-left corner of the border.
HTBOTTOMRIGHT	In the lower-right corner of the border.
HTCAPTION	In the caption (title bar).
HTCLIENT	In the client area.
HTERROR	Same as HTNOWHERE but with a beep produced.
HTGROWBOX	In the size box.
HTHSCROLL	In the horizontal scroll bar.
HTLEFT	In the left border.
HTMENU	In the menu area.
HTMINBUTTON	In the Minimize button (considered obsolete in Win32; use HTREDUCE).
HTMAXBUTTON	In the Maximize button (considered obsolete in Win32; use HTZOOM).
HTNOWHERE	Over the screen background or on a dividing line between windows.
HTREDUCE	In a minimize box.
HTRIGHT	In the right border.
HTSIZE	Synonym for HTGROWBOX.
HTSIZEFIRST	Minimum sizing border hit value.
HTSIZELAST	Maximum sizing border hit value. Note that all sizing hit values are in the range of HTSIZEFIRST through HTSIZELAST (inclusive).
HTSYSMENU	In the system menu box (close box of child windows).
HTTOP	In the upper horizontal border.
HTTOPLEFT	In the upper-left corner of the border.
HTTOPRIGHT	In the upper-right corner of the border.
HTTRANSPARENT	In a window covered by another window.

Table 7.10: Hit-test values returned from `DefWindowProc` as a result of a `WM_NCHITTEST` message

Value	Location of Cursor
HTVSCROLL	In the vertical scroll bar.
HTZOOM	In a maximize box.

When the `DefWindowProc` function returns HTNOWHERE, the cursor is considered to be over the screen background, and processing is complete. When it returns HTERROR, Windows produces a beep and considers the cursor to be over the screen background. A value of HTTRANSPARENT means the cursor is over a window covered by another window. The remaining return values can be divided into two groups: HTCLIENT and all the others. We discuss the latter group first.

Nonclient-area Mouse Messages

When the `DefWindowProc` function returns a result other than HTCLIENT, HTERROR, HTNOWHERE, or HTTRANSPARENT, the cursor is over the nonclient area of the window. The result value indicates the specific area. Windows then sends one of the nonclient-area mouse messages listed in Table 7.9, depending on why the hit-test message was sent. The wParam parameter to the subsequent nonclient-area mouse message contains the hit-test result code returned from processing the `WM_NCHITTEST` message. The lParam parameter contains the screen coordinates of the cursor with the horizontal coordinate in the low-order word and the vertical coordinate in the high-order word. If you use the HANDLE_WM_NCHITTEST message cracker, these coordinates will be passed in as separate x and y parameters.

For example, assume that the user presses the left button while the cursor is over the caption of a window. Windows first sends a `WM_NCHITTEST` message to the window function for the window under the cursor. The window function for the window typically passes the message to the `DefWindowProc` function. The `DefWindowProc` function uses the coordinates contained in the message, determines that the cursor is in the caption area, and returns HTCAPTION, indicating that the cursor is over the caption.

Because the value HTCAPTION indicates that the left button was pressed while over a nonclient area of the window, Windows next sends a `WM_NCLBUTTONDOWN` message to the window function. The `WM_NCLBUTTONDOWN` message informs the window function that the left button was pressed in a nonclient area. The wParam parameter of the message equals the hit-test result: HTCAPTION. The lParam parameter contains the screen coordinates of the cursor when the button was pressed. The LOWORD of the lParam is the *x* position and the HIWORD of the lParam is the *y* position. The `WM_NCLBUTTONDOWN` message also is typically passed to the `DefWindowProc` function, which initiates dragging of the window.

This might seem like an indirect and inefficient way to get something done. Windows sends a message to the window function just so the window function will give the message back to Windows so that Windows can perform a function it needs to do anyway. You might wonder, "Why go to all this trouble?" The reason is the great flexibility that such an approach permits. Because you can intercept any message, you can substitute your own interpretation for each message. Normally, you don't want to intercept "system" messages. After all, it's a lot of work to provide functionality already implemented in Windows. But it's a great way to extend

WM_NC*BUTTON*/WM_NCMOUSEMOVE **Message Cracker Handlers**

```
void cls_OnNCLButtonDown(HWND hwnd, BOOL dblclk,
                int xScreen, int yScreen, UINT hitCode);
```

```
void cls_OnNCMButtonDown(HWND hwnd, BOOL dblclk,
                int xScreen, int yScreen, UINT hitCode);
```

```
void cls_OnNCRButtonDown(HWND hwnd, BOOL dblclk,
                int xScreen, int yScreen, UINT hitCode);
```

```
void cls_OnNCLButtonDblClk(HWND hwnd, BOOL dblclk,
                int xScreen, int yScreen, UINT hitCode);
```

```
void cls_OnNCMButtonDblClk(HWND hwnd, BOOL dblclk,
                int xScreen, int yScreen, UINT hitCode);
```

```
void cls_OnNCRButtonDblClk(HWND hwnd, BOOL dblclk,
                int xScreen, int yScreen, UINT hitCode);
```

```
void cls_OnNCLButtonUp(HWND hwnd, int xScreen, int yScreen,
                UINT hitCode);
```

```
void cls_OnNCMButtonUp(HWND hwnd, int xScreen, int yScreen,
                UINT hitCode);
```

```
void cls_OnNCRButtonUp(HWND hwnd, int xScreen, int yScreen,
                UINT hitCode);
```

```
void cls_OnNCMouseMove(HWND hwnd, int xScreen, int yScreen,
                UINT hitCode);
```

	wParam		lParam		
Parameter	**lo**	**hi**	**lo**	**hi**	**Meaning**
hwnd					Window handle of the window.
dblclk					TRUE when called from HANDLE_WM_NC*BUTTONDBLCLK; FALSE when called from HANDLE_WM_NC*BUTTONDOWN.
xScreen			■		Horizontal position of the mouse, in screen coordinates.
yScreen				■	Vertical position of the mouse, in screen coordinates.
hitCode	■	■			Hit-test code from Table 7.10.

the functionality of your own applications. For example, assume you want to create a child window representing an object. You want to give the user the ability to move the cursor over the window, press and hold the left mouse button, and drag an outline of the child window to a new location. When the button is released, you want the child window to move to the specified location. Put the following code in the window function for the child window, and you will have just that:

```
case WM_NCHITTEST:
    return HTCAPTION;
```

When Windows asks this window function, "Where is this place in your window?", the window function responds with, "In the caption". That the window actually doesn't have a caption isn't important. Windows detects a left button press over a caption of a window and initiates the built-in window-dragging function used for dragging windows by their captions. It usually takes more than the two lines of code shown to implement such a feature.

Most of the time, you'll have no need to process the nonclient-area mouse messages. You should, however, be careful to ensure that you pass them to the DefWindowProc function. Your window won't respond to a user's actions with the cursor on the title bar, size boxes, and other areas unless Windows processes these messages. As with the OnKey handlers, you can route both the HANDLE_WM_NC*BUTTONDOWN and HANDLE_WM_NC*BUTTONDBLCLK messages to the same handler, distinguishing which one was used to invoke the handler by the Boolean dblclk parameter. There are, however, no FORWARD_WM_NC*BUTTONDBLCLK uncrackers. Instead, there are generic FORWARD_WM_NC*BUTTONDOWN uncrackers that use the dblclk parameter to determine if the message they will forward will be a WM_NC*BUTTONDOWN or a WM_NC*BUTTONDBLCLK message. This is not to say that you cannot use separate handlers for each, as shown in the following examples:

```
static void
cls_OnNCLDD(HWND hwnd,  BOOL dblclk, int x, int y, UINT hitCode)
    {
      if(dblclk)
          { /* double click */
          // double click processing here
          } /* double */
      else
          { /* single */
          // processing here
          } /* single */
      FORWARD_WM_NCLBUTTONDOWN(hwnd, dblclk, x, y, hitCode, DefWindowProc);
    }

LRESULT CALLBACK
myWndProc(HWND hwnd, UINT msg, WPARAM wParam, LPARAM lParam)
    {
      switch(msg)
          { /* msg */
          HANDLE_MSG(hwnd, WM_NCLBUTTONDOWN, cls_OnNCLDD);
          HANDLE_MSG(hwnd, WM_NCLBUTTONDBLCLK, cls_OnNCLDD);
          } /* msg */
      return DefWindowProc(hwnd, msg, wParam, lParam);
    }
```

Alternatively, you could use two separate procedures, one for the single click and another for the double click, and separate the code as shown next. Note that both handlers use the FORWARD_WM_NCLBUTTONDOWN uncracker to pass on the message.

```
static void
cls_OnNCLDown(HWND hwnd,  BOOL dblclk, int x, int y, UINT hitCode)
    {
      // processing here
      FORWARD_WM_NCLBUTTONDOWN(hwnd, dblclk, x, y, hitCode, DefWindowProc);
    }

static void
cls_OnNCLDbl(HWND hwnd, BOOL dblclk, int x, int y, UINT hitCode)
```

```
{
  // double click processing here
  FORWARD_WM_NCLBUTTONDOWN(hwnd, dblclk, x, y, hitCode, DefWindowProc);
}

LONG CALLBACK
myWndProc(HWND hwnd, UINT msg, WPARAM wParam, LPARAM lParam)
  {
    switch(msg)
        { /* msg */
          HANDLE_MSG(hwnd, WM_NCLBUTTONDOWN, cls_OnNCLDown);
          HANDLE_MSG(hwnd, WM_NCLBUTTONDBLCLK, cls_onNCLDbl);
        } /* msg */
    return DefWindowProc(hwnd, msg, wParam, lParam);
  }
```

Client-area Mouse Messages

The mouse messages of greatest interest to a Windows application are the client-area mouse messages. Windows generates these messages when the hit-test response is HTCLIENT. The wParam and lParam parameters to the window function differ from those for nonclient-area mouse messages. The lParam parameter for all client-area mouse messages contains the horizontal and vertical client area (not screen) coordinates of the cursor. The horizontal coordinate value is in the low-order word, and the vertical coordinate value is in the high-order word.

If you don't use the message cracker macros, you will have to deal with extracting these coordinates yourself. You can do this using the HIWORD and LOWORD values, as you've seen done before. But there is another way. The POINTS structure ("POINT Short") has the same format as the lParam parameter values. The lParam parameter can be viewed as a single POINTS structure or two short values packed into a long. The Windows documentation uses it both ways. The lParam parameter is defined as a point for the nonclient-area messages and as two short values for the client-area messages. It's just two different ways of describing the same data. These first two assignment statements do exactly the same thing as the third assignment does in one statement:

```
POINTS pt ;

pt.x = LOWORD (lParam) ;
pt.y = HIWORD (lParam) ;
// or
pt = MAKEPOINTS(lParam) ;
```

You may have already seen this trick in Windows 3.1 code, but using a POINT structure. The problem with a POINT structure is that it is defined as two *integer* arguments. Although this works fine in Win16, where integers are 16 bits and lParam is two 16-bit integers packed into a 32-bit value, MAKEPOINT (or any other means by which you might try to cast an lParam to a POINT) will not work at all in Win32 because it will attempt to interpret the value as two 32-bit values. The POINTS structure is defined as two short values, and the new MAKEPOINTS macro will work correctly.

Of course, if you use the message cracker functions, the value will have already been nicely split into x and y parameters to the On*Button* handlers.

WM_*BUTTON*/WM_MOUSEMOVE Message Cracker Handlers

```
void cls_OnLButtonDblClk(HWND hwnd, BOOL dblclk,
                int, int yClient, UINT keyflags);
```

```
void cls_OnMButtonDblClk(HWND hwnd, BOOL dblclk,
                int xClient, int yClient, UINT keyflags);
```

```
void cls_OnRButtonDblClk(HWND hwnd, BOOL dblclk,
                int xClient, int yClient, UINT keyflags);
```

```
void cls_OnLButtonDown(HWND hwnd, BOOL dblclk,
                int xClient, int yClient, UINT keyflags);
```

```
void cls_OnMButtonDown(HWND hwnd, BOOL dblclk,
                int xClient, int yClient, UINT keyflags);
```

```
void cls_OnRButtonDown(HWND hwnd, BOOL dblclk,
                int xClient, int yClient, UINT keyflags);
```

```
void cls_OnLButtonUp(HWND hwnd, int xClient, int yClient,
                UINT keyflags);
```

```
void cls_OnMButtonUp(HWND hwnd, int xClient, int yClient,
                UINT keyflags);
```

```
void cls_OnRButtonUp(HWND hwnd, int xClient, int yClient,
                UINT keyflags);
```

```
void cls_OnMouseMove(HWND hwnd, int xClient, int yClient,
                UINT keyflags);
```

	wParam		lParam		
Parameter	**lo**	**hi**	**lo**	**hi**	**Meaning**
hwnd					Window handle of the window receiving the message.
dblclk					TRUE if called from HANDLE_WM_*BUTTONDBLCLK; FALSE if called from HANDLE_WM_*BUTTONDOWN.
xClient			■		Horizontal position, in client area units.
yClient				■	Vertical position, in client area units.
keyFlags	■				MK_* flags from Table 7.11.

The wParam parameter for client-area mouse messages contains a value that specifies which virtual keys were held down at the time of the mouse event. This is passed into your message cracker handler as its keyflags parameter. Any combination of the MK_* (mouse key) values listed in Table 7.11 can be set.

These are bit masks, so you must be careful when determining whether two or more values are set. For example, if you want to detect that both the **Shift** *and* **Ctrl** keys are down, don't do this:

```
if (keyflags & (MK_CONTROL | MK_SHIFT)) {
    /* Gets here if either Ctrl *OR* Shift is down! */
    /* Not what is desired. */
}
```

Instead, do this:

```
if ((keyflags & MK_CONTROL) && (keyflags & MK_SHIFT))
    {
    // Gets here when both Ctrl AND Shift are down!
    }
```

Or, use nested `if` statements:

```
if (keyflags & MK_CONTROL)
    if (keyflags & MK_SHIFT)
        {
        // Ctrl+Shift keys        /* Gets here when both Ctrl AND Shift are down! */
        }
    else
        {
        // Ctrl key only
        }
```

Or, compare the explicit value:

```
if( (keyflags & (MK_CONTROL | MK_SHIFT)) ==  (MK_CONTROL | MK_SHIFT))
    {
    // Ctrl+Shift processing
    }
```

The button down and up messages are straightforward and shouldn't be confusing. You get a WM_LBUTTONDOWN when the left button is pressed while the cursor is in the client area of your window. Similarly, the WM_MBUTTONDOWN and WM_RBUTTONDOWN messages arrive when the middle and right buttons, respectively, are pressed. The WM_LBUTTONUP, WM_MBUTTONUP, and WM_RBUTTONUP messages arrive when the left, middle, and right buttons are released. This leaves the double-click messages and the WM_MOUSEMOVE messages.

Table 7.11: Mouse key values

Mouse Key Value	Meaning
MK_CONTROL	**Ctrl** key is down.
MK_LBUTTON	**Left** button is down.
MK_MBUTTON	**Middle** button is down.
MK_RBUTTON	**Right** button is down.
MK_SHIFT	**Shift** key is down.

The WM_LBUTTONDBLCLK, WM_MBUTTONDBLCLK, and WM_RBUTTONDBLCLK messages are a little different from the ones just described. Windows sends double-click messages (and their nonclient-area counterparts) only to windows that specifically request them. You request Windows to send double-click messages to a window function by specifying the CS_DBLCLKS class style when registering the window class.

A double-click is a second mouse button press that occurs within a short interval called the *double-click speed*. There is a double-click time interval that you can set from the Control Panel and that is stored in the Registration Database (reg.dat). When Windows receives a second button press that follows the first in less than this time, the second button press is considered a double-click. One question you might ask is, How does it tell a "double" click from what were intended to be two distant single clicks that occurred close together in time? In addition to the time factor, there are two system parameters you can examine via GetSystemMetrics: SM_CXDOUBLECLK and SM_CXDOUBLECLK. These are set by the display driver and are based on the resolution of the display. If the mouse moved more than these amounts in the specified *x*- or *y*-direction, then even if the mouse clicks came close together in time, they would not count as a double-click because they were "widely" separated in space.

Event	Window Has CS_DBLCLKS Style	Window Does Not Have CS_DBLCLKS Style
Right button down	WM_RBUTTONDOWN	WM_RBUTTONDOWN
Right button up	WM_RBUTTONUP	WM_RBUTTONUP
Right button down within double-click time	WM_RBUTTONDBLCLK	WM_RBUTTONDOWN
Right button up	WM_RBUTTONUP	WM_RBUTTONUP

Figure 7.7: Messages produced by a right-button double-click

Mouse messages arrive as isolated events. You can't rely on a button up message arriving immediately after the button down message. In fact, you can't rely on the button up message arriving at all unless you do mouse capture (see page 465). You can get a button up message without any previous button down message. In addition, other messages can arrive between the button press and release messages. Similarly, a double-click message arrives some unknown time after the first button press message. The message sequence for a right-button double-click is listed in Figure 7.7. Keep in mind that other messages might arrive between the messages listed.

In particular, this means that you should make any action your program makes during the processing of a double-click message be a continuation of the button down processing. For example, Windows often uses a selection technique in which a single button click selects an item for possible use, such as a filename from a list box. When you double-click on the filename, the button down message selects the file just as it does normally. Then, when the double-click message arrives, you can simply accept the selected filename. We will see how to handle this when we discuss such topics as list box notification messages in Chapter 9, page 620.

Don't try to do two totally different things based on whether the user clicks or double-clicks the mouse on a location. When you receive the button down message, you don't yet know whether it's a single button down event (in which case no double-click message will arrive) or the first button down message of a double-click sequence. To resolve this question, you would have to delay performing the single-click processing until the double-click time had expired without a double-click message arriving. This can be done, but the logic gets much more complicated and the GUI begins to appear "sluggish" because there is not an immediate feedback for the first button click.

What about triple-clicking? You've probably used some programs that do this, such as Microsoft Word. One click moves the caret, two clicks select a word, and three clicks select a paragraph. Well, in this case you would have to do most of the work yourself. When you saw the first WM_LBUTTONDBLCLK message, you would set a flag saying you were in a double-click. If you received any other WM_*BUTTONDOWN (or WM_NC*BUTTONDOWN) message, you would clear this flag. If you saw another WM_LBUTTONDBLCLK, you would first check the flag. If it was set, you would have a "triple" click. But notice that you would have to expend a lot of effort to intercept various mouse messages you might otherwise not care about and to make sure to pass them on after determining if you want to clear the flag you are maintaining. But it can be done.

The WM_MOUSEMOVE message has the same wParam and lParam parameters as the other client-area mouse messages. Windows generates WM_MOUSEMOVE messages when the user moves the mouse. Windows places these messages either in the application queue for the window under the cursor or, if a window has captured mouse input, into the application queue for the window that has captured mouse input. (Capturing mouse input is described starting on page 465.) The OnMouseMove handler looks just like the On*ButtonUp handlers and delivers the mouse position as separate x and y parameters.).

WM_MOUSEACTIVATE **Message Cracker Handler**

```
int cls_OnMouseActivate(HWND hwnd, HWND topWnd, UINT hitCode, UINT msg);
```

Result	One of the MA_* codes from Table 7.12.				
	wParam		**lParam**		
Parameter	**lo**	**hi**	**lo**	**hi**	**Meaning**
hwnd					Window handle of the window receiving the message.
topWnd	■				The handle of the top-level parent window (the window whose parent is NULL) of the window being activated.
hitCode			■		Hit-test code from the WM_NCHITTEST that generated this message.
msg				■	The message code of the message that will be sent if the return value is not an MA_*ANDEAT code.

The final mouse message is the WM_MOUSEACTIVATE message. Windows sends this message to a window function when the cursor is over an inactive window and the user presses a mouse button. The wParam parameter contains the window handle of the top-level parent window to the window being activated. The low-order word of the lParam parameter contains one of the hit-test codes previously described. The high-order word contains the mouse message identifier (WM_LBUTTONDOWN, WM_RBUTTONDOWN, etc.) that indicates what the activating event was. The OnMouseActivate handler called from the HANDLE_WM_MOUSEACTIVATE presents these as separate parameters.

Note that Windows never considers a child window to be an active window. The return value specifies whether the window should be activated and whether the mouse event should be discarded. It must be one of the values from Table 7.12. The WM_MOUSEACTIVATE message is relatively obscure, not clearly documented (in terms of its GUI implications), and often neglected. It is worth spending some time to understand exactly what it does and why it is useful.

You click the mouse while the cursor is over a window that is not active. The WM_NCHITTEST message is sent, and one of the HT codes specified in it is returned. The HT result and the resulting mouse message that would be generated are packaged up and put into a WM_MOUSEACTIVATE message. You return one of the MA_ codes shown in Table 7.12. If you do not return one of the ANDEAT variants, the message will be passed on to the window that has just been activated. Why would you not want to pass on the message? This is one of the subtleties of Windows programming that can change the entire "feel" of your application.

Table 7.12: Values returned for WM_MOUSEACTIVATE messages

Value	Meaning
MA_ACTIVATE	Activate the window.
MA_NOACTIVATE	Do not activate the window.
MA_ACTIVATEANDEAT	Activate the window and discard the mouse event.
MA_NOACTIVATEANDEAT	Do not activate the window; discard the mouse event.

Consider an application in which clicking the mouse over the client area has some effect, such as moving the caret in a text editor, drawing a pixel in a paint program, or activating some other event. This might be done, for example, when you may be displaying a picture of a chemical process with valves and controls. If you return MA_ACTIVATE, the window will be activated and brought to the top of the stack of windows. Then the WM_*BUTTONDOWN mouse message will be sent to the window. Since you might not have been able to see all of the window because it was partially obscured, you might not actually know on what you are clicking. So your editor may reposition the caret, your paint program draw a pixel, or your process control program open a valve. If you believe that, for your application, the user should be seeing all of the window before actually doing something to it, then you should return MA_ACTIVATEANDEAT. This will activate only the window and nothing else. In particular, the WM_LBUTTONDOWN message that might have been sent will not be sent. The mouse message is "eaten" by the activation process. For a large number of applications, it generally makes more sense to return MA_ACTIVATEANDEAT rather than MA_ACTIVATE. The default of DefWindowProc is to return MA_ACTIVATE.

You should think carefully about what would happen if the user wanted to "pull the window up" by clicking on it somewhere when it is buried under other windows and inactive. If there could be unwanted side effects caused by clicking on an obscured (but obviously not hidden) area, you should respond to the WM_MOUSEACTIVATE message with MA_ACTIVATEANDEAT.

You will get the WM_MOUSEACTIVATE message even if you activate the window by clicking in its nonclient area. This means that if you click on the caption bar to drag the (partially obscured) window around (perhaps to a clear space on your screen so you can see it all), and you always return MA_ACTIVATEANDEAT, you will need *two* mouse clicks to drag the window: One to activate it and bring it to the top of the stack, and another to actually "grab" it. This is not "natural". Therefore, your handler often looks like this:

```
static int mywindow_OnMouseActivate(HWND hwnd, HWND topWnd, UINT hitCode, UINT msg)
{
 if(hitCode == HTCLIENT)
    return MA_ACTIVATEANDEAT;
 else
    return MA_ACTIVATE;
}
```

This generalizes nicely; for example, you can inhibit scrolling of a window that is being activated by a click in the scroll bar by testing for HTHSCROLL or HTVSCROLL. Once the window is activated, scrolling would work as expected.

Capturing the Mouse

You typically need to *capture* the cursor when performing a "mouse drag" operation; the functions and messages relating to this are summarized in Table 7.13. Normally a mouse drag involves recording the position at which the user pressed a mouse button, tracking all mouse movements while the user holds the button down, recording the position at which the user released the button, and reacting as necessary.

However, Windows normally sends mouse messages to the window under the cursor. A window monitoring a dragging operation does not receive mouse messages once the cursor leaves that window. The user can release the mouse button outside the window and the "dragging" window never gets notified.

To solve this problem, you *capture* all mouse input using the `SetCapture` function and wait for the user to release the mouse button before releasing the captured input. Before doing something with a mouse event when you think you might have captured the mouse, you should use `GetCapture` to verify that you indeed have the mouse captured and are not getting the event from an uncaptured mouse. When you have finished using the mouse, you must call `ReleaseCapture` to release it and, incidentally, to re-enable multitasking operation of the mouse.

Table 7.13: Mouse capture operations

Operation	Explanation
`HWND SetCapture(HWND hwnd)`	Captures the mouse for the window hwnd. The window must be owned by the current thread.
`HWND GetCapture( )`	Returns the handle of the window that has the mouse capture or NULL if no window has the mouse capture.
`BOOL ReleaseCapture( )`	Releases mouse capture.
WM_CANCELMODE	Sent to a window to cancel any pending modes. `DefWindowProc` will cancel internal processing of standard scroll bar input, cancel internal processing of menus, and release the mouse capture.
WM_CAPTURECHANGED	Notifies a window that it is losing mouse capture. A window receives this even if its own thread called `ReleaseCapture`.

In addition to capturing the mouse, you may also wish to restrict the mouse so that it moves only within the client area of the screen (or some other rectangular area of the screen). You should think carefully before you do this, as it tends to violate users' expectations of what the mouse should do. However, there are times when it is exactly the correct solution. For example, you may notice in an MDI application that when you click the caption bar of a child window, you can't drag the mouse, and hence the window, outside the boundaries of the client frame. You can restrict the mouse to a rectangular area by using the `ClipCursor` function. This function takes a single parameter, a pointer to a rectangle, that expresses the constraint in screen coordinates. For example, to limit the cursor to the client area of the current window, you might use code like the following:

```
static void
draw_OnLButtonDown(HWND hwnd, BOOL dblclk, int x, int y,
                                 UINT keyflags)
```

```
  {
  RECT rect ;

  Dragging = TRUE ;
  ptOrigPos.x = x ;
  ptOrigPos.y = y ;

  SetCapture (hwnd) ;

  GetClientRect (hwnd, &rect) ;
  ClientToScreen (hwnd, (LPPOINT) &rect.left) ;
  ClientToScreen (hwnd, (LPPOINT) &rect.right) ;
  ClipCursor (&rect) ;

  }
```

When you finally release the mouse capture, you must also remove the motion restriction by calling ClipCursor with a NULL pointer:

```
static void
draw_OnLButtonUp(HWND hwnd, int x, int y, UINT keyflags)
    {
    RECT  rect ;
    POINT ptCursor;
    UINT  Nearest ;
    HWND  hwndParent ;

    if(GetCapture() != hwnd)
        return;  // we did not have the mouse
    Dragging = FALSE ;
    ReleaseCapture () ;
    ClipCursor (NULL) ;

    // ... do whatever action is required here

    }
```

Simple Drag-and-Drop

You also can use mouse capture when you want to do a drag-and-drop operation. When you click something that you can drag, the window that "owns" the draggable thing can set capture and then follow the object that is being dragged around. We usually change the cursor shape to indicate that we are doing a drag.

Drag-and-drop is a case in which you *must* capture the mouse, even though it does limit multitasking. The reason multitasking is shut down during mouse capture is to deal with exactly this situation: You need to track the mouse no matter where it goes so that you can determine the correct action to take on a "drop".

An example of a drag-and-drop application is shown in Figure 7.8, and a more elaborate one is shown in our presentation of the Tree View control in Chapter 9, page 652. The code shown that implements the simple drag-and-drop uses some features of cursor manipulation from the following section. The basic idea is that if you click the bucket icon, you can get a dipperful of water. You can then carry the dipperful to a glass and release it. Note that doing this does not require that the child windows actually be in the current application; you could drag values from one window to another. You can demonstrate this easily by running two copies of the program and discovering that you can carry the water across the applications! That is why we use registered window messages instead of simple WM_USER-based messages.

You might wonder how you "drop" something from one window onto another when it is (typically) the source window that is receiving the mouse notifications. How do you know if the recipient will accept it? You do this by receiving the mouse move messages and determining, from the screen coordinates, which window you are actually over. When there is no mouse capture, the coordinates you receive on a mouse message will never exceed the limits of the client rectangle. But with mouse capture, you can get "client coordinates" outside the client area. You can use the ClientToScreen function to convert these client coordinates to screen coordinates, and you can use the

Figure 7.8: A simple drag-and-drop application

WindowFromPoint function to retrieve the handle of the window under the point. In our case, we want to send the message to the child window, so we have to also try to get the handle of the child window in the window we have located. We do this by converting the screen point back to client coordinates in the target window and then calling ChildWindowFromPoint.

Once you have located a window, you can send this window a message telling it what to do. By using a registered window message, you know that only cooperating tasks will understand it. Any other window you send it to will pass it on to DefWindowProc, which will return 0. By careful choice of interpretation of return values, you can arrange it so that the 0 value triggers the correct behavior in your program. In our example, we have arranged that the query message returns a nonzero value if the target can accept the drop and 0 if it cannot. The choice we made in our application is to return a status code that indicates if the target can accept the drop or would accept the drop if it weren't already full. If we have the mouse over any other window, it will return 0, meaning a drop will not be accepted. Based on this, you could change the cursor shape or do as we have done: post a status message. When it is time to do the drop, we send a similar registered message to the target asking it to accept the drop. If the target accepts the drop, it returns a nonzero value; if it rejects the drop or the drop is to a window that doesn't understand the message, then DefWindowProc will return a 0. The return result can be used to determine what you do to the source, such as removing the object from a list or taking some other action (we don't do anything in our sample except post a message saying whether the drop was accepted).

For this simple example, we chose to use icons as our source and destination windows. This complicates the example somewhat because we have to override some of the built-in behavior of the STATIC class. An icon, for example, always responds to the WM_NCHITTEST message with the response HTTRANSPARENT. This means that the window will not actually receive mouse messages; the messages will be sent to the parent window instead. We had to subclass the window and override the OnNcHitTest handler to return HTCLIENT. To maintain the cursor shape of the water dipper, we had to override the WM_SETCURSOR handler to select either the empty dipper or the full dipper cursor. We overrode the WM_LBUTTONDOWN, WM_LBUTTONUP, and WM_MOUSEMOVE handlers to get the drag functionality.

Notice that the registered window messages work by simply starting up two copies of the drag-and-drop example and observing that you can dip water out of the bucket in one window and drop it into a glass in a different window. We show how to register the window messages in Listing 7.8. The key parts of the drag processing are shown in Listing 7.9, and the drop processing is shown in Listing 7.10.

Listing 7.8: Drag-and-drop: registered window messages

```
int UWM_DoDrop = 0;
int UWM_Status = 0;
int UWM_QueryDrop = 0;

// in the initInstance handler:

    UWM_DoDrop = RegisterWindowMessage(_T("Dipper.DoDrop"));
    UWM_QueryDrop = RegisterWindowMessage(_T("Dipper.QueryDrop"));
    UWM_Status = RegisterWindowMessage(_T("Dipper.Status"));
```

Listing 7.9: Drag-and-drop: drag source handler

```
HCURSOR fulldipper;
HCURSOR emptydipper;

int initializeBucket(HWND hwnd)
    {
     fulldipper = LoadCursor(GetWindowInstance(hwnd), IDC_FULL_DIPPER);
     emptydipper = LoadCusor(GetWindowInstance(hwnd), IDC_EMPTY_DIPPER);
    }

static void OnLButtonDown(HWND hwnd, BOOL dblclk, int x, int y, UINT keyflags)
    {
     HCURSOR oldCursor;
     // Set capture so we can track the mouse if the button is clicked
     // in the bucket icon
     SetCapture(hwnd);
     // choose a new icon to indicate we are carrying water
     oldCursor = SetCursor(fulldipper);
     SetWindowLong(hwnd, GWL_USERDATA, (LPARAM)oldCursor);
    }

static HWND findTarget(HWND hwnd, int x, int y)
    {
     POINT point = {x, y};

     // The mouse position is in hwnd-relative client coordinates
     // convert to screen coordinates.
     ClientToScreen(hwnd, &point);
     HWND target = WindowFromPoint(point);
     if(target == NULL)
        return NULL;

     // we may have a reference to the main window.  We want a reference
     // to one of the child windows.  Find it

     // The most general case is to transform coordinates in the target
```

```
        // window
        ScreenToClient(target, &point);
        HWND child = ChildWindowFromPoint(target, point);
        if(child == NULL)
            return target;

        return child;
    }

static void OnLButtonUp(HWND hwnd, int x, int y, UINT keyflags)
    {
        // If we have mouse capture, see if we're over a target
        if(GetCapture() == hwnd)
            { /* we have capture */
            HWND target = findTarget(x, y);

            ReleaseCapture(hwnd);
            SetCursor((HCURSOR)GetWindowLong(hwnd, GWL_USERDATA));

            // if we're over a window, send it a drop message.  If it
            // responds with an acceptance, revert to the ready message.
            // If it can't accept the drop, respond with an error message.
            if(target != NULL)
                if(!SendMessage(target, UWM_DoDrop, 0, 0))
                    SendMessage(GetParent(hwnd), UWM_Status, IDS_WASTE, 0);
                else
                    SendMessage(GetParent(hwnd), UWM_Status, IDS_READY, 0);
            } /* we have capture */
    }

static void OnMouseMove(HWND hwnd, int x, int y, UINT keyflags)
    {
        // if we have capture, see if we are over a target.  If we are,
        // indicate that we can accept a drop by posting a status message.
        // If we aren't, indicate that we are still carrying water.  If
        // the drop would be accepted but isn't feasible, indicate that as
        // well.
        if(GetCapture() == hwnd)
            { /* dragging */
            HWND target = findTarget(x, y);
            if(target != NULL)
                { /* query status */
                switch(SendMessage(target, UWM_QueryDrop, 0, 0))
                    { /* query */
                    case 0: // unknown target: DefWindowProc gave 0
                            SendMessage(GetParent(hwnd, UWM_Status,
                                                       IDS_CARRYING, 0);
                            break;
                    case QUERY_DROP_OK:
                            SendMessage(GetParent(hwnd, UWM_Status,
                                                       IDS_DROPPABLE, 0);
                            break;
                    case QUERY_DROP_FULL:
                            SendMessage(GetParent(hwnd, UWM_Status,
                                                       IDS_FULL, 0);
                            break;
                    } /* query */
                } /* query status */
            } /* dragging */
```

```
        else
            { /* no dragging */
             SendMessage(GetParent(hwnd, UWM_Status, IDS_READY, 0));
            } /* no dragging */

    }

static UINT OnNcHitTest(HWND hwnd, int x, int y)
        {
         // An icon normally returns HTTRANSPARENT so the various mouse
         // messages go to its parent; override this and make it look like
         // a normal window.
         return HTCLIENT;
        }

static BOOL OnSetCursor(HWND hwnd, HWND hwndCursor, UINT hittest, UINT msg)
        {
         // If we are in a drag, set the cursor to indicate a full dipper; if not,
         // just set the normal empty cursor
         if(GetCapture() == hwnd)
            SetCursor(fulldipper);
         else
            SetCursor(emptydipper);
         return 0;
        }

// We include a handler for the UWM_DoDrop in case we are sending it to
// the bucket, so the water drops successfully back into the bucket and
// we don't get an error message

static LRESULT dropIt(HWND hwnd, WPARAM wParam, LPARAM lParam)
        {
         return TRUE;
        }
```

Listing 7.10: Drag-and-drop: drag target handler

```
static int levels[] =
                { IDI_EMPTY_GLASS, IDI_1_GLASS, IDI_2_GLASS, IDI_3_GLASS};

#define NUM_LEVELS DIM(levels)


static LRESULT dropIt(HWND hwnd, WPARAM wParam, LPARAM lParam)
        {
         // We keep the amount of liquid in the GWL_USERDATA field.
         // Each level has a unique icon associated with it.
         int filled = GetWindowLong(hwnd, GWL_USERDATA);

         if(filled < NUM_LEVELS - 1)
            { /* not full */
             filled++;
             SetWindowLong(hwnd, GWL_USERDATA, filled);
             Static_SetIcon(hwnd, LoadIcon(GetWindowInstance(hwnd),
                                           levels[filled]));
            } /* not full */
         return TRUE;
        }
```

```
static LRESULT queryDrop(HWND hwnd, WPARAM wParam, LPARAM lParam)
    {
     int filled = GetWindowLong(hwnd, GWL_USERDATA);

     return filled < NUM_LEVELS - 1 ? QUERY_DROP_OK : QUERY_DROP_FULL;
    }

static UINT OnNcHitTest(HWND hwnd, int x, int y)
    {
     return HTCLIENT;
    }

static BOOL OnSetCursor(HWND hwnd, HWND hwndCursor, UINT hittest, UINT msg)
    {
     return 0;   // don't change the current cursor
    }
```

There are two mouse-capture-related messages your application might receive: WM_CANCELMODE and WM_CAPTURECHANGED. The WM_CANCELMODE is sent to a window to request that it cancel any internal mode it may have. If this message is passed to DefWindowProc, a ReleaseCapture will be executed. Since normally never look for this message, if it does come in, your mouse capture will be cancelled. Whene mouse capture is released, the window that had the capture will receive a WM_CAPTURECHANGED messa This notifies the window that the capture has been lost. The lParam value is the handle of the window ceiving capture, or NULL if there is no new capture being set. You can use this notification to handle the of capture and reset whatever internal state is necessary.

WM_CANCELMODE **Message Cracker Handler**

int cls_OnCancelMode(HWND hwnd);					
Result	0 if the message is processed, nonzero if it should be ignored.				
	wParam		**lParam**		
Parameter	**lo**	**hi**	**lo**	**hi**	**Meaning**
hwnd					Window handle of the window receiving the message.

WM_CAPTURECHANGED **Message Cracker Handler**

int cls_OnCaptureChanged(HWND hwnd, HWND newWnd);					
Result	0 if the message is processed, nonzero if it is being ignored.				
	wParam		**lParam**		
Parameter	**lo**	**hi**	**lo**	**hi**	**Meaning**
hwnd					Window handle of the window receiving the message.
newWnd					The handle of the window that is receiving the capture, o NULL if no window is receiving capture.

ιe Cursor

cursor is the small bitmap image that indicates where the pointing device, typically a mouse, is point-
Windows provides a number of built-in cursor shapes, and you also can create and use your own. You've
bably seen quite a few of the built-in cursors. They include the slanted arrow, hourglass, I-beam, window
ng double-arrows, and crosshair.

ιerally you should use the built-in cursors for the same purposes as Windows uses them. For example, the
ιted arrow is used to point at objects and the I-beam is used when editing text. You should change to an
ιrglass cursor when performing a lengthy operation. Nothing prevents you from coming up with "origi-
' uses for these built-in cursors except the possibility of confusing others who use your application.

of the cursor functions are summarized in Table 7.14. We do not explain all of them in this book because
ιy are little-used.

ιle 7.14: Summary of cursor support functions

ιnction	Description
ιipCursor	Limits the cursor to a particular rectangle on the screen or releas-es the restriction.
ɔpyCursor	Makes a copy of a cursor from a cursor handle.
⁻eateIconFromResourceEx	Creates a cursor from resource data.
⁻eateIconIndirect	Creates a cursor from a memory description.
ɘstroyCursor	Deletes a cursor whose handle represents a cursor that was cre-ated or loaded.
⁻awIconEx	Draws a cursor as an image.
ɘtClassLong(…, GCL_HCURSOR)	Gets the class cursor for all windows of the class.
ɘtClipCursor	Gets the current clipping rectangle set by ClipCursor.
ɘtCursor	Retrieves the handle of the current cursor. May return NULL.
ɘtCursorPos	Retrieves the current cursor position.
ɘtIconInfo	Obtains the image information about a cursor.
ɔadCursor	Loads a cursor from the resources of a module or loads a system cursor.
ɔadCursorFromFile	Loads a cursor from a file or from the file specified in the registry for a system cursor.
ɔadImage	Loads a cursor from the resources of a module; provides for size and color map variations.

Table 7.14: Summary of cursor support functions

Function	Description
LookupIconFromDirectoryEx	Locates a cursor suitable for the current display.
SetClassLong(..., GCL_HCURSOR, ...)	Replaces the class cursor for all windows of the class.
SetCursor	Sets a cursor to be the currently displayed cursor.
SetCursorPos	Positions the cursor to a particular point on the screen.
SetSystemCursor	Redefines a system cursor.
ShowCursor	Increments or decrements the show count; if ≥ 0, the cursor becomes visible, and if < 0, the cursor is hidden.
WM_SETCURSOR	Respond to this message to override the class cursor.

Custom Cursors

You can design a custom cursor for your application using one of the many cursor/icon editor applications available. There are the cursor/icon editors provided by the Microsoft, Borland, Symantec and other environments, third-party cursor/icon editors from companies such as Norton/Symantec, and innumerable freeware or shareware tools. If you are using Visual C++ or one of the other integrated development environments, you can activate the resource editor and request it to create a new cursor, and you will be put into the cursor editor. The technique for editing a cursor is very similar to designing a custom bitmap or brush pattern. After you create the cursor, you save it into a file, usually with the .cur extension.

Once you have a cursor file, there are many ways you can get it into your application. The simplest is to make it part of your resource file. To do this, a CURSOR statement must be added to your application's resource script (.rc) file. The integrated environments will do this for you as a side effect of creating the cursor, so normally you won't need to bother with it. But in some cases, you may have to hand-edit the file or at least be able to read it. The CURSOR statement associates a character string identifier or an integer with the cursor contained in the file it names. The resource compiler copies the cursor from the cursor file into the compiled resource (.res) file. After the program is linked, the linker inserts the cursor, along with the other compiled resources, into the executable (.exe) program file.

For example, suppose you've drawn a custom cursor that looks like a magnifying glass and saved it in a file called magglass.cur. In your application's resource script file, you put a CURSOR statement similar to this:

```
resID CURSOR filename
```

The resID field specifies either an integer value (either the integer itself or a symbol that is defined to be an integer) or a unique character string that identifies the resource. You use this value in your program to reference the cursor. In this example, use the statement

```
IDC_MAGGLASS CURSOR magglass.cur
```

The following statement also can be used:

```
42 CURSOR magglass.cur
```

The value 42 isn't significant and usually would be replaced by a symbolic value equated by a `#define` statement to the value 4:

```
#define IDC_MAGGLASS 42
```

To use this cursor, you call the LoadCursor function to load the cursor from the resources of the executable file. You pass it the instance handle of the module that contains the resources and a parameter identifying the desired cursor within those resources. LoadCursor returns a handle of type HCURSOR to the cursor. The function syntax, assuming you have used one of the integrated environments, is as follows:

```
LoadCursor (hInstance, MAKEINTRESOURCE(CursorName)) ;
```

You can load the cursor one of two ways, depending on how you identified it on the CURSOR statement in the resource script file. Load it either by name:

```
HCURSOR           hGlass ;
hGlass = LoadCursor (hInstance, _T("IDC_MAGGLASS")) ;
```

or by integer identifier:

```
hGlass = LoadCursor (hInstance, MAKEINTRESOURCE (42)) ;
```

which, if you have used a #define for the value IDC_MAGGLASS, could be written as

```
hGlass = LoadCursor (hInstance, MAKEINTRESOURCE (IDC_MAGGLASS)) ;
```

Predefined Cursors

It's even easier to get a handle to one of the predefined cursors. You call the LoadCursor function with the hInstance parameter set to 0 (NULL) and the CursorName set to one of the IDC_ values listed in Table 7.15. However, there is no guarantee that you will get the image shown. This is because when you call LoadCursor with an instance handle of NULL, it first passes the cursor ID to the LoadCursorFromFile function and attempts to honor the user's alternative selection of a cursor. If this succeeds, the actual cursor that is displayed is the one chosen by the user. If this fails, because the user has not set up a custom cursor, you will get a handle to a cursor whose image is shown in Table 7.15. We discuss LoadCursorFromFile on page 482. Note that the images have changed slightly between the Windows NT 3.*x* release and the Windows 95 or Windows NT 4.*x* releases. We also illustrate the bounding boxes for the 32×32 cursor to show that the sizes and relative positions of the cursors have also changed.

Displaying the Cursor

After you have the handle to a cursor, you're ready to use it. You can display a cursor in one of two ways. You can specify the cursor as a class cursor when you register the class. When you do this, Windows changes the cursor to the specified one any time the user moves the cursor into your window. Or, you can explicitly display a particular cursor whenever the cursor moves into your window or a particular part of the window.

Table 7.15: Built-in cursors

Symbolic Name	Image		Description
	API3	**API4**	
IDC_APPSTARTING OCR_APPSTARTING			Standard arrow with small hourglass.
IDC_ARROW OCR_NORMAL			Standard arrow cursor.
IDC_CROSS OCR_CROSS			Crosshair cursor.
IDC_HELP			Help cursor.
IDC_IBEAM OCR_IBEAM			Text I-beam cursor.
IDC_NO OCR_NO			Slashed circle.
IDC_SIZEALL OCR_SIZEALL			Four-way pointing arrow.
IDC_SIZENESW OCR_SIZENESW			Double arrow pointing northeast and southwest.
IDC_SIZENS OCR_SIZENS			Double arrow pointing north and south.

Table 7.15: Built-in cursors

Symbolic Name	Image		Description
	API3	API4	
IDC_SIZENWSE OCR_SIZENWSE			Double arrow pointing northwest and south-east.
IDC_SIZEWE OCR_SIZEWE			Double arrow pointing west and east.
IDC_UPARROW OCR_UP			Vertical arrow cursor.
IDC_WAIT OCR_WAIT			Hourglass cursor.

The IDC_ symbols are used with the LoadCursor function and the OCR_ symbols are used with the LoadImage function.

There appears to be no OCR_HELP symbol defined. However, the codes appear to have identical numeric values and therefore seem to represent a change in notation.

We've been using the first method in the example program. To specify a class cursor, you get a handle to the cursor (LoadCursor) and assign it to the hCursor field of the WNDCLASS structure before registering the class. The Skeleton program uses the following statement to specify the standard arrow cursor as the class cursor for its application window:

wc.hCursor = LoadCursor (NULL, IDC_ARROW) ;

The following statement, assuming there is no #define for the name IDC_MAGGLASS, would use the custom magnifying glass cursor for the class cursor:

wc.hCursor = LoadCursor (hInstance, _T("IDC_MAGGLASS")) ;

We mentioned earlier in the chapter that mouse movements and button presses and releases generate a series of messages to the window. The first message is the WM_NCHITTEST message. The second message is the WM_SETCURSOR message. Windows follows the WM_NCHITTEST message with a WM_SETCURSOR message when mouse input is not captured (see page 465) and the user either moves the mouse, presses a button, or releases a button. Windows sends a WM_SETCURSOR message to a window when the cursor moves over the window, thereby giving the window a chance to change the shape (bitmap) of the cursor.

WM_SETCURSOR Message Cracker Handler

BOOL cls_OnSetCursor(HWND hwnd, HWND hwndCursor, UINT hitCode, UINT msg);					
Result	TRUE to halt further routing of the message. FALSE to allow the message to be routed to the next parent window in the hierarch⬛				

	wParam		lParam		
Parameter	**lo**	**hi**	**lo**	**hi**	**Meaning**
hwnd					Window handle of the window receiving the message.
hwndCursor	⬛				Handle of the window that contains the cursor. This m⬛ not be the window that owns the cursor.
hitCode			⬛		One of the HT codes from Table 7.10.
msg				⬛	The mouse message that triggered this WM_SETCURSOR.

A window might change the cursor to a crosshair cursor when over one area of the window and use an ar⬛ cursor when in a different part of the window. The wParam parameter, passed to the message cracker as ⬛ hwndCursor parameter, specifies the handle of the window containing the cursor. This isn't necessarily ⬛ same window that receives the message. The lParam parameter contains the hit-test area code returned ⬛ result of processing the WM_NCHITTEST message in the low-order word. This value is passed to the mess⬛ cracker as the hitCode parameter. The high-order word contains the mouse message number that identi⬛ the mouse action that triggered the series of messages. This code is passed to the message cracker as the ⬛ parameter. You would normally get these as parameters to the OnSetCursor handler if you use ⬛ HANDLE_WM_SETCURSOR message cracker. Typically you pass the WM_SETCURSOR message to ⬛ DefWindowProc function. When the DefWindowProc function receives a WM_SETCURSOR message, it im⬛ diately passes it to the parent window, if any, for the window that just received the message. This enabl⬛ parent window to control the shape of the cursor for all its child windows that don't explicitly control t⬛ own cursors. When the window function returns TRUE, the DefWindowProc function considers ⬛ WM_SETCURSOR message processing completed.

When there is no parent window or the parent window function returns FALSE, the DefWindowProc funct⬛ sets the cursor for the window. When the hit-test area code indicates that the cursor is in a nonclient are⬛ the window, the function sets the cursor to the standard arrow cursor. When the cursor is in the client a⬛ the function sets the cursor to the class cursor, if any. As an extra bonus, this function calls the MessageB⬛ function when the hit-test area code is HTERROR and the mouse message number specifies a button do⬛ message. You also can explicitly set the cursor shape whenever you need to change it. Because the cu⬛ represents the location of the mouse pointer, you need to set its shape only for when it moves. If the mo⬛ hasn't moved, the current cursor shape generally is appropriate. You have two ways to set the cursor sh⬛ Either intercept and process the WM_SETCURSOR message described previously, or set the cursor during ⬛ processing of a WM_MOUSEMOVE message.

en you intercept the WM_SETCURSOR message, you must ensure that the cursor is set appropriately for the client and the nonclient areas of the window, even when all you really want is control over the cursor shape when the cursor is over the client area. You can examine the hitCode parameter in your etCursor handler and respond only if it is HTCLIENT, using FORWARD_WM_SETCURSOR to pass the mes- on to DefWindowProc in all other cases (see the code sample on page 480).

also can assume that control when you receive the client-area mouse movement message, MOUSEMOVE. To do this, you first must set the hCursor field of the WNDCLASS structure to NULL when reg- ring the class. This specifies that no class cursor should be used and prevents Windows from automati- y setting the cursor's shape as described previously:

```
hCursor = NULL ;
```

s has one drawback: You must now always handle the cursor yourself. This is an all-or-nothing situation. can't disable the cursor only some of the time or for only some instances of the class. Either all windows he class always have automatic handling of the cursor or none of them do.

WM_MOUSEMOVE message is the third in the series of messages resulting from a mouse movement. (Simi- y, a button press message is the third in the series of messages resulting from a button press. The first two ssages are always WM_NCHITTEST and WM_SETCURSOR. Only the third varies.) Suppose you want to set the sor's shape to the magnifying glass cursor any time it moves into the client area of a window when the dow has no class cursor. Do this by calling the SetCursor function when processing the WM_MOUSEMOVE ssage:

```
DLE_MSG(hwnd, WM_MOUSEMOVE, cls_OnMouseMove);

tic void
_OnMouseMove(HWND hwnd, int x, int y, UINT keyflags)
    {
    SetCursor (hGlass) ;
    return 0 ;
    }
```

n't worry about the overhead of repeatedly setting the cursor's shape. The cursor is changed only when specified cursor differs from the current cursor. The SetCursor function is very fast when the cursor sn't need to be changed. You can remove the cursor from the screen by calling the SetCursor function specifying NULL as the cursor handle parameter. The SetCursor function returns the HCURSOR of the viously set cursor (which may be NULL). If you will need to restore the cursor, you must save this handle.

wever, when you want the cursor temporarily removed from the screen and want it to have the same shape en you make it visible again, it's best to use the ShowCursor function. Unlike the caret hide and show ctions, this function both hides and shows the cursor. There is no HideCursor function. (Don't you just e consistency?) The function call looks like the following:

```
t ShowCursor (BOOL Show) ;
```

e ShowCursor function keeps track of the number of calls to show and hide the cursor by using a display nter. Showing the cursor (calling ShowCursor with a TRUE parameter) increments the display counter. ling the cursor (calling ShowCursor with a FALSE parameter) decrements the display counter. Windows displays the cursor only when its display counter is greater than or equal to 0. The return value of the function is the new display counter value.

The display counter initially is 0 when a mouse is installed, so the cursor initially is visible. The display counter initially is -1 when no mouse is installed, so the cursor starts out hidden when there is no mouse. You will use the ShowCursor most frequently when providing the user with a method to duplicate mouse actions with the keyboard. When the user requests to duplicate mouse actions with the keyboard, you show the cursor (because it is hidden initially on systems without a mouse), move the cursor in response to keyboard input, and hide the cursor when done. For example, you might show the cursor in response to a key-down event and hide it on the key-up event. Or you might show it on a key-down event and use a timer to hide it after one or two seconds.

Occasionally you should change the cursor at times other than upon receipt of a mouse message. In particular, you should change it just before beginning a procedure that will produce a noticeable delay to the user. During these times, you should change the cursor from its current shape to the hourglass cursor. The hourglass on the screen notifies the user that the application is busy and that he or she must wait for the operation to complete. After the lengthy operation completes, you should change the cursor back to its original shape. Don't assume that the original shape was the standard arrow cursor. You could do all this with the following code:

```
HCURSOR hOrigCursor ;
HCURSOR hwndCursor ;

// Prior to starting operation with a delay...
hwndCursor = LoadCursor(NULL, IDC_WAIT);
hOrigCursor = SetCursor (hwndCursor) ;

// Lengthy operation performed here.
// ...
// When completed, restore the cursor to its original shape.
SetCursor (horigCursor) ;
```

You might be tempted to "optimize" your code by storing the hourglass cursor or some other cursor shape in a static variable and simply reusing that handle as needed. This is not always a good idea; it requires, for example, that you respond to changes in the configuration. Consider that the user *can* use the control panel to change the cursor selection. When control returns to your program, you will still be using the old cursor shape because you have not noticed that the cursor needs to be reloaded. The cost of LoadCursor(NULL,…) is very low, and the function knows how to respond to changes in the configuration. Although we have said that it "calls LoadCursorFromFile", this call is in fact optimized internally by code that always knows if the system cursor has changed. So you don't have to worry about it. Avoid gratuitous "optimizations" that increase the complexity of your code and lower its robustness. This is particularly true when you are building reusable components, since you must then depend on your client code to notify you. This increases the complexity not only of that code but also of your interface.

This code has a problem, however. Suppose the mouse is moved out of the window during the lengthy operation and then moved back in (even if it is moved into another window in your application). The default action will be to set the cursor to the class cursor for that window. This will give the impression that the lengthy operation has finished, when in fact it has not.

To prevent this, you must write some code that handles the WM_SETCURSOR message:

```
HCURSOR currentCursor;

static BOOL
cls_OnSetCursor(HWND hwnd, HWND hwndCursor, int hitCode, UINT msg)
    {
    if(currentCursor == NULL || hitcode != HTCLIENT)
        return FORWARD_WM_SETCURSOR(hwnd, hwndCursor, hitcode,
                                    msg, DefWindowProc);
    SetCursor(currentCursor);
    return TRUE;
    }
```

Typically this handler is in the top-level window of your application. We haven't looked at dialog boxes yet, but you will also need the same code in any modal dialog box that wants to be able to set the wait cursor. The idea is to set a variable at the highest scope that could process the WM_SETCURSOR message and place in that variable the handle for the cursor you wish to have displayed. If the value in this variable is NULL, there is no cursor to set.

You may have seen in the past a trick that eliminated the need to handle WM_SETCURSOR or WM_MOUSEMOVE messages. This trick consisted of capturing the mouse before changing the cursor to the hourglass and releasing the capture after the operation completed. Don't do this. In Win16, it worked just fine because there was precisely one execution thread for the whole system. But in Windows 95 and Windows NT, the preemptive multitasking at the GUI level is shut down while the mouse is captured. This means that your lengthy operation done with a captured mouse also prevents you from, for example, reading your email and checking the status of your print job. It even limits your ability to play Solitaire during long and boring computations! It also means that if your application is running multithreaded, you may find your ability to take advantage of multithreading within your own application is curtailed. See the Synchronization Explorer (Chapter 18) for examples of these effects.

Loading Cursors from Other Sources

You can load a cursor using the LoadImage function. (The LoadImage function also will load icons and bitmaps, but in this section we concentrate on the cursors it can load.) The LoadImage function is specified as

```
HANDLE LoadImage(HINSTANCE hinst, LPCTSTR name,
                UINT type,
                int cxDesired, int cyDesired,
                UINT flags);
```

The hinst parameter specifies the module from which the cursor is to be loaded. For OEM cursors, this should be NULL.

The interpretation of the name parameter depends on the settings of the other parameters. Its interpretation is summarized in Table 7.16.

The type parameter for this discussion is always the symbol IMAGE_CURSOR. The cxDesired and cyDesired parameters indicate the desired size of the cursor. For a cursor, these values should either be 0 or set to the values desired. If 0 is specified, the values delivered by GetSystemMetrics(SM_CXCURSOR) and GetSystemMetrics(SM_CYCURSOR) will be used.

Table 7.16: Interpreting the name field of LoadImage

hinst	LR_LOADFROMFILE	Interpretation of name
not NULL	No.	A pointer to a NUL-terminated string that is the name of the resource to load.
NULL	No.	MAKEINTRESOURCE(OCR_*name*). (See Table 7.15.)
NULL	Yes.	The name of the file that contains the cursor. Applies to Win32 4.*x* only.

The flags specifies one or more of the flags shown in Table 7.17.

Table 7.17: Flag values for LoadImage of a cursor

Flag	Meaning
LR_DEFAULTCOLOR	The default flag. It basically means "not LR_MONOCHROME".
LR_CREATEDIBSECTION	Not used with cursors.
LR_DEFAULTSIZE[4]	Forces the interpretation of a 0 cxDesired and cyDesired to be the SM_CXCURSOR and SM_CYCURSOR values. Otherwise, the size is the size of the resource. If the resource contains multiple images, the cursor size will be set to the size of the first image.
LR_LOADFROMFILE[4]	The name field names a .cur file used to create the cursor.
LR_LOADMAP3DCOLORS[4]	Loads the image and replaces shades of gray with the following system color:

Gray Color	RGB	Replacement
Dark gray	128, 128, 128	COLOR_3DSHADOW
Gray	192, 192, 192	COLOR_3DFACE
Light gray	223, 223, 223	COLOR_3DLIGHT

LR_LOADTRANSPARENT[4]	Replaces all instances of the color of the first pixel in the image by one of the following two values based on the presence of the LR_LOADMAP3DCOLORS flag:

LR_LOADMAP3DCOLORS Flag	Replacement
Not present.	COLOR_WINDOW
Present.	COLOR_3DFACE

Table 7.17: **Flag values for** LoadImage **of a cursor**

Flag	Meaning
LR_MONOCHROME[4]	Loads a monochrome version of the cursor.
LR_SHARED[4]	Shares the image handle if the image is loaded more than once. Do not use for images of nonstandard sizes, images whose sizes may change after loading, or images loaded from a file.

[4] Win32 4.*x* only.

Loading System Cursors

A simpler form of loading a cursor from a file is also used to load standard system cursors. The LoadCursorFromFile function takes either a filename of a .cur file, .ani file, or a cursor ID code (via MAKEINTRESOURCE) and loads a cursor. The function is defined as

HCURSOR LoadCursorFromFile (LPCTSTR name)

The name parameter can be a pointer to a NUL-terminated file name of a cursor file for either a standard (.cur) or animated (.ani) style. However, it also can be the MAKEINTRESOURCE of one of the OCR_ names shown in Table 7.15. When this is the case, the cursor identifier is converted to a key to look up in the registry. If that key is found, the name of the file associated with it is used as the name of the file to load. This allows you to load a cursor of the type requested by the user, rather than the built-in system type. For example, if you use

        LoadCursor(NULL, IDC_WAIT) ;

you will always load the built-in hourglass cursor. But the user may have selected a special animated wait cursor, either from the standard set delivered with Windows, from a third-party vendor, or one that the user created. If you call LoadCursor with an instance handle of NULL, it will first pass the cursor ID value to LoadCursorFromFile. If that returns NULL, the built-in cursor handle will be returned.

        LoadCursorFromFile(MAKEINTRESOURCE(OCR_WAIT)) ;

For example, on one machine we use, the following entry was found for the wait cursor:

\HKEY_CURRENT_USER\Control Panel\Cursors
            Wait: REG_SZ: HOURGLAS.ANI

The mapping from OCR_ symbols to registry keys is shown in Table 7.18.

The column in the table showing the built-in cursor shows the default cursor shape. However, if Load-CursorFromFile is presented with an OCR_ value and there is no equivalent value found in the registry, the result is NULL. In that case, you should load the standard cursor.

Table 7.18: Mapping of OCR_ symbols to registry keys

The key will be found in the registry under the path: \HKEY_CURRENT_USER\Control Panel\Cursors		
Symbol	**Built-in[3]**	**Key**
OCR_APPSTARTING		AppStarting
OCR_CROSS		Crosshair
OCR_IBEAM		IBeam
OCR_NO		No
OCR_NORMAL		Arrow
OCR_SIZEALL		SizeAll
OCR_SIZENESW		SizeNESW
OCR_SIZENS		SizeNS

Table 7.18: Mapping of OCR_ symbols to registry keys

The key will be found in the registry under the path: \HKEY_CURRENT_USER\Control Panel\Cursors		
Symbol	**Built-in[3]**	**Key**
OCR_SIZENWSE		SizeNWSE
OCR_SIZEWE		SizeWE
OCR_UP		UpArrow
OCR_WAIT		Wait

[3] The symbols shown here are for API level 3. The symbols for API level 4 are slightly different and are shown in Table 7.15.

Setting System Cursors

You can change the system cursor for any of the OCR_ symbols by using the SetSystemCursor function. This function takes a handle to a cursor and an OCR_ ID and sets the system cursor to be the cursor indicated. The cursor handle that is passed in is destroyed by having the DestroyCursor function called. So when SetSystemCursor returns successfully, the cursor handle passed in is no longer valid and must not be used. The SetSystemCursor function is defined as

```
BOOL SetSystemCursor(HCURSOR cur, DWORD id);
```

The id parameter is one of the symbols from Table 7.18.

Moving the Cursor with the Keyboard

The mouse is an optional device for Windows. So a user should be able to run your application on a system lacking a mouse or other pointing device. Although some applications can't run reasonably without a mouse (drawing applications in particular), you should provide a method to duplicate mouse actions by using the keyboard. Three steps are required to do this:

1. Control the visibility of the cursor.

2. Move the cursor based on keyboard input.

3. Select items pointed to by the cursor.

We discuss only the first two. The method you use to select an item pointed to by the cursor is dependent the function of your application.

You need to control the visibility of the cursor on systems without a mouse. On such systems, the mouse c sor initially isn't visible on the screen. You need to show and hide the cursor as Windows activates and in tivates your window. You make the cursor visible by showing it when the window is activated and nonico and hide the cursor when the window is inactivated while noniconic (using the ShowCursor function). Wl Windows activates or inactivates a window, it sends a WM_ACTIVATE message to the window. The wPar parameter is nonzero when Windows is activating the window and 0 when Windows is inactivating it. 1 same message tells whether the window is iconic. The high-order word of the lParam parameter is nonze when the window is iconic; otherwise, it is 0. If you use the HANDLE_WM_ACTIVATE message cracker, you all this information as discrete parameters.

WM_ACTIVATE Message Cracker Handler

void cls_OnActivate(HWND hwnd, UINT state, HWND hActive, BOOL minimized);					
	wParam		**lParam**		
Parameter	**lo**	**hi**	**lo**	**hi**	**Meaning**
hwnd					Window handle of the window receiving the message.
state	■				Specifies if the window is being activated or deactivated:
					Value of state — **Meaning** WA_ACTIVE — Activated by other than a mouse click WA_CLICKACTIVE — Activated by a mouse click. WA_INACTIVE — Deactivated.
hActive			■		Depends on the value of state and may be NULL: **Value of state** — **Meaning of hActive** WA_ACTIVE / WA_CLICKACTIVE — Handle of the window being deactivated. WA_INACTIVE — Handle of the window being activated.
minimized		■			FALSE if the window hActive is not minimized. Nonzero (TRUE) if the window hActive is minimized.

t you must allow the user to move the cursor by using the keyboard. You do this by processing the
KEYDOWN message and looking for the virtual-key codes representing the direction (arrow) keys on the
board. These are the VK_DOWN, VK_LEFT, VK_RIGHT, and VK_UP virtual-key codes. Each time one of these
s is pressed, you move the cursor in the appropriate direction.

'll want to provide some method for accelerating the cursor motion when the user wants to move it a long
ance. It takes more than a minute to move the cursor, at one pixel per key press, all the way across the
en. This would be unacceptable performance. There are two easy ways to provide for cursor acceleration.

first approach is to use the repeat count field of the WM_KEYDOWN message as the number of units to
ve. It includes key codes repeated due to Typematic action when your application can't process the key-
rd messages as quickly as they arrive. This method moves the cursor a little more quickly than one pixel
keyboard message and is convenient when crossing a small area. The problem is that it is sensitive to
siderations such as processor speed, overall system load, and incidental aspects of what your program ac-
lly does. For example, on a modern high-speed processor, if your program is the only one running, if
re is not much overall background processing, and all you are doing is moving the cursor, your program
y be able to keep up with the Typematic key rate. But on a somewhat older processor, if your program is
of many running, if there is a lot of overall background processing, and each move of the cursor requires
rching some complex list of objects to determine a selection, the responses may be erratic; sometimes
ır program keeps up with the Typematic rate, so the repeat count stays at 1, but sometimes it falls far be-
d, and the repeat count may go up to, say, 10. This method, although easy to implement, has its hazards.

second approach is to count subsequent WM_KEYDOWN messages without an intervening WM_KEYUP message
l use the number as a (possible) increasing distance to move on the next key press. This tends to make
ır application less sensitive to factors such as processor speed and system load. The following example
ntrols the visibility of the cursor on systems without a mouse and uses both approaches for accelerating
board-controlled cursor motion:

```
atic int    RepeatRate = 1 ;
atic POINT CursorPos ;

atic void
mple_OnActivate(HWND hwnd, UINT state, HWND hActive, BOOL minimized)
    {
    if (!minimized)
       { /* not icon */
        if (GetSystemMetrics (SM_MOUSEPRESENT))
           { /* has mouse */
            if (state != WA_INACTIVE)
               { /* activating */
                ClientToScreen (hwnd, &CursorPos) ;
                SetCursorPos (CursorPos.x, CursorPos.y) ;
                SetCursor (hGlass) ;
               } /* activating */
           } /* has mouse */
       } /* not icon */
    }

atic void
mple_OnKeyDown(HWND hwnd, UINT vk, BOOL down, int repeat, UINT flags)
```

```
{
  RECT rect;

  GetCursorPos (&CursorPos) ;
  ScreenToClient (hwnd, &CursorPos) ;
  switch (vk)
    { /* vk */
      case VK_DOWN:
          CursorPos.y += RepeatRate ;
          break ;
      case VK_LEFT:
          CursorPos.x -= RepeatRate ;
          break ;
      case VK_RIGHT:
          CursorPos.x += RepeatRate ;
          break ;
      case WM_UP:
          CursorPos.y -= RepeatRate ;
          break ;
      default:
          return ;
    } /* vk */
  RepeatRate += repeat ;
  GetClientRect (hwnd, &rect) ;

  CursorPos.x = max (min (CursorPos.x, rect.right), rect.left);
  CursorPos.y = max (min (CursorPos.y, rect.bottom), rect.top);
  ClientToScreen (hwnd, &CursorPos) ;
  SetCursorPos (&CursorPos) ;
  }

static void
sample_OnKeyUp(HWND hwnd, UINT vk,  BOOL down, int repeat, UINT flags)
    {
      RepeatRate = 1 ;
    }

static LRESULT CALLBACK
sample_WNDPROC(HWND hwnd, UINT msg, WPARAM wParam, LPARAM lParam)
{
    switch(msg)
      { /* msg */
        HANDLE_MSG(WM_ACTIVATE, sample_OnActivate) ;
        HANDLE_MSG(WM_KEYDOWN,  sample_OnKeyDown) ;
        HANDLE_MSG(WM_KEYUP, sample_OnKeyUp) ;
        // ...
      } /* msg */
    return 0 ;
```

Towers of Hanoi Example Program

It's clearly time to take a break and put everything we've talked about into use. The Hanoi program is a simple, five-disk version of the Towers of Hanoi game. In this game, five disks of differing sizes form a tower on one of three pegs. The object of the game is to move the tower of disks from the left peg to the right peg,

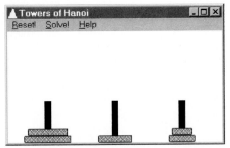

Figure 7.9: Towers of Hanoi window

using the middle peg as a temporary holding area. You can move only one disk at a time (the top one on a peg), and a larger disk cannot be placed on top of a smaller disk.

There are three menu selections. The **Reset!** command stacks all the disks in the proper order on the left-most peg. This is useful when you decide you've messed up enough and would like to start over. The **Solve!** command resets all the disks to the left-most peg and then solves the game by moving each disk to the appropriate peg until the entire tower has been moved to the right-most peg. The game moves one disk approximately every 1.25 seconds to give you time to understand the move. The **Help** command pops up a small menu that lets you select between game instructions and the **About...** box.

The pegs are simply drawn on the main application window. The WM_PAINT logic for that window redraws the pegs when needed. Each disk actually is an individual child window. The child window function draws each disk as a rounded rectangle, filling the entire client area of the child window. It's the parent window's job to keep the disk windows appropriately sized as the parent itself is resized by the user.

The child window function detects mouse button down actions and provides the logic to drag the disk from one peg to another. In this way, we implement the disk-dragging logic only once and it works appropriately no matter how many disks are used. We let Windows decide which disk (window) should receive the mouse input. Each disk window moves itself as it detects WM_MOUSEMOVE messages while the left button is held down. Figure 7.9 shows the initial display of Hanoi application. This program is based on our standard template, so only the interesting details are shown in Listing 7.11 through Listing 7.13.

Listing 7.11: Towers of Hanoi: Excerpts from `Initialization.c`

```
BOOL
initApplication (HINSTANCE hinst, UINT resPoolID)
{
    HWND        hwnd;
    TCHAR       ClassName [MAX_RESOURCESTRING + 1] ;
    WNDCLASSEX wcex ;

    VERIFY (LoadString (hinst, resPoolID, ClassName, DIM(ClassName))) ;

    // Constrain this application to run single instance
    hwnd = FindWindow (ClassName, NULL) ;
    if (hwnd) {

        // A previous instance of this application is running.

        // Activate the previous instance, tell it what the user
        // requested this instance to do, then abort initialization
        // of this instance.

        if (IsIconic (hwnd))
            ShowWindow (hwnd, SW_RESTORE) ;

        SetForegroundWindow (hwnd) ;
```

```
         // Abort this instance's initialization
         return FALSE ;
}

/****************************************************************/
/* Register one class for the main application window and a second   */
/* for the disk windows.                                             */
/****************************************************************/

wcex.cbSize         = sizeof (WNDCLASSEX) ;
wcex.style          = CS_HREDRAW | CS_VREDRAW | CS_OWNDC ;
wcex.lpfnWndProc    = mainFrameWndProc ;
wcex.cbClsExtra     = 0 ;
wcex.cbWndExtra     = 0 ;
wcex.hInstance      = hinst ;
wcex.hIcon          = LoadIcon (hinst, MAKEINTRESOURCE (resPoolID)) ;
wcex.hCursor        = LoadCursor (NULL, IDC_ARROW) ;
wcex.hbrBackground  = (HBRUSH) (COLOR_WINDOW+1) ;

wcex.lpszMenuName   = MAKEINTRESOURCE (resPoolID) ;
wcex.lpszClassName  = ClassName ;
wcex.hIconSm        = LoadImage (hinst,
                          MAKEINTRESOURCE (resPoolID),
                          IMAGE_ICON,
                          GetSystemMetrics (SM_CXSMICON),
                          GetSystemMetrics (SM_CYSMICON),
                          LR_SHARED) ;

// Register the window class and abort the initialization upon failure.
if (!internalRegisterClass (&wcex))
     return FALSE ;

/******************************/
/* Now define the disk class. */
/******************************/

/*********************************************/
/* Fetch the name of the disk window class. */
/*********************************************/

wcex.cbSize         = sizeof (WNDCLASSEX) ;
wcex.style          = CS_HREDRAW | CS_VREDRAW | CS_SAVEBITS ;
wcex.lpfnWndProc    = diskWndProc ;
wcex.cbClsExtra     = 0 ;
wcex.cbWndExtra     = UGW_DWMAXUSED ;
wcex.hInstance      = hinst ;
wcex.hIcon          = LoadIcon (hinst, MAKEINTRESOURCE (resPoolID)) ;
wcex.hCursor        = LoadCursor (NULL, IDC_ARROW) ;
wcex.hbrBackground  = GetStockObject (NULL_BRUSH) ;

wcex.lpszMenuName   = NULL ;
wcex.lpszClassName  = DiskClass ;
wcex.hIconSm        = NULL ;

// Register the window class and return success/failure status
return internalRegisterClass (&wcex) ;
}
```

```
BOOL initInstance (HINSTANCE hinst, int nCmdShow)
{
    // Initialize the Common Controls DLL
    // You must call this function before using any Common Control
    InitCommonControls () ;

    // Create the application's main frame window
    if (!createMainFrameWindow (hinst, nCmdShow))
        return FALSE ;

        return TRUE ;
}

static HWND
createMainFrameWindow (HINSTANCE hinst, int nCmdShow)
{
    HWND    hwnd ;
    TCHAR ClassName [MAX_RESOURCESTRING + 1] ;
    TCHAR Title [MAX_RESOURCESTRING + 1] ;

    // Create the main frame window
    VERIFY (LoadString (hinst, IDR_MAINFRAME, ClassName, DIM (ClassName))) ;
    VERIFY (LoadString (hinst, IDS_APP_TITLE, Title, DIM (Title))) ;

    hwnd =
        CreateWindowEx (0,                        // Extended window styles
                        ClassName,                // Address of registered class name
                        Title,                    // Address of window name
                        WS_OVERLAPPEDWINDOW|      // Window style
                        WS_CLIPCHILDREN,
                        CW_USEDEFAULT,            // Horizontal position of window
                        0,                        // Vertical position of window
                        CW_USEDEFAULT,            // Window width
                        0,                        // Window height
                        NULL,                     // Handle of parent or owner window
                        NULL,                     // Handle of menu or child-window id
                        hinst,                    // Handle of application instance
                        NULL) ;                   // Address of window-creation data

    ASSERT (NULL != hwnd) ;
    if (hwnd == NULL)
            return NULL ;

    ShowWindow (hwnd, nCmdShow) ;
    UpdateWindow (hwnd) ;

    return hwnd ;
}


/******************************************************************/
/* Create all the child windows representing the disks. */
/******************************************************************/

BOOL
mainFrame_CreateDiskWindows (HWND hwndParent)
```

```c
{
    HINSTANCE hInstance ;
    HWND      hwndChild ;
    int       i ;

    hInstance = GetWindowInstance (hwndParent) ;

    /***************************/
    /* Create the disk windows. */
    /***************************/

    for (i = NUMDISKS; i > 0; i--) {

        hwndChild = CreateWindow (
            DiskClass,              // Class of the window to create
            NULL,                   // Window caption text
            WS_CHILD | WS_VISIBLE,  // Window styles
            0, 0, 0, 0,             // No initial size
            hwndParent,             // Parent window handle
            (HMENU) i,              // Child window ID
            hInstance,              // Instance of module owning window
            NULL) ;                 // Ptr to user-defined parameters

        /*********************************************************/
        /* Insure that the window was successfully created. */
        /*********************************************************/

        if (hwndChild == NULL)
            return FALSE ;
    }
    return TRUE ;
}
```

Listing 7.12: Towers of Hanoi: Excerpts from `MainFrame.c`
mainframe.c

```c
LRESULT CALLBACK
mainFrameWndProc (HWND hwnd, UINT message, WPARAM wParam, LPARAM lParam)
{
    switch (message) {
        case WM_COMMAND: // Notification from menu or control
            return HANDLE_WM_COMMAND (hwnd, wParam, lParam, mainFrame_OnCommand) ;

        case WM_CREATE: // Notification that a window is being created
            return HANDLE_WM_CREATE (hwnd, wParam, lParam, mainFrame_OnCreate) ;

        case WM_PAINT:  // Draw all or part of client area
            return HANDLE_WM_PAINT (hwnd, wParam, lParam, mainFrame_OnPaint) ;

        case WM_SIZE:   // Window size has changed
            return HANDLE_WM_SIZE (hwnd, wParam, lParam, mainFrame_OnSize) ;

        // other cases as per skeleton...
```

```
            default:
                return DefWindowProc (hwnd, message, wParam, lParam) ;
    }
}

static void
mainFrame_OnCommand (HWND hwnd, int id, HWND hwndCtl, UINT codeNotify)
{
    switch (id) {
        case ID_APP_ABOUT:
                doAbout(hwnd);
                return ;

        case ID_APP_EXIT:
                DestroyWindow (hwnd) ;
                return ;

        case IDM_HELP_HOWTO:
                doHow(hwnd);
                return ;

        case IDM_RESET_DISKS:
            mainFrame_ResetDisks (hwnd) ;
            return ;

        case IDM_SOLVE_PROBLEM:
            {
            HMENU hmenu = GetMenu (hwnd) ;
            EnableMenuItem (hmenu, IDM_RESET_DISKS,   MF_DISABLED | MF_GRAYED) ;
            EnableMenuItem (hmenu, IDM_SOLVE_PROBLEM, MF_DISABLED | MF_GRAYED) ;
            DrawMenuBar (hwnd) ;
            mainFrame_SolveProblem (hwnd) ;
            EnableMenuItem (hmenu, IDM_RESET_DISKS,   MF_ENABLED) ;
            EnableMenuItem (hmenu, IDM_SOLVE_PROBLEM, MF_ENABLED) ;
            DrawMenuBar (hwnd) ;
            }
            return ;

        default:
            FORWARD_WM_COMMAND (hwnd, id, hwndCtl, codeNotify, DefWindowProc) ;
        }
}

static void
mainFrame_OnPaint (HWND hwnd)
{
    HBRUSH       hbrush ;
    HDC          hdc ;
    PAINTSTRUCT  ps ;
    RECT         rect ;

    /***************************************************************/
    /* The window needs to be redrawn.  Draw the three posts. */
    /***************************************************************/

    hdc = BeginPaint (hwnd, &ps) ;
```

```
hbrush = GetStockObject (BLACK_BRUSH) ;

SetRect (&rect,
    CENTERPOSTPOS - POSTWIDTH / 2, POSTHEIGHT,
    CENTERPOSTPOS + POSTWIDTH / 2, 0) ;

if (mainFrame_IntersectRect (&rect, &ps.rcPaint))
    FillRect (hdc, &rect, hbrush) ;

SetRect (&rect,
    LEFTPOSTPOS - POSTWIDTH / 2, POSTHEIGHT,
    LEFTPOSTPOS + POSTWIDTH / 2, 0) ;

if (mainFrame_IntersectRect (&rect, &ps.rcPaint))
    FillRect (hdc, &rect, hbrush) ;

SetRect (&rect,
    RIGHTPOSTPOS - POSTWIDTH / 2, POSTHEIGHT,
    RIGHTPOSTPOS + POSTWIDTH / 2, 0) ;

if (mainFrame_IntersectRect (&rect, &ps.rcPaint))
    FillRect (hdc, &rect, hbrush) ;

EndPaint (hwnd, &ps) ;


static void mainFrame_OnSize (HWND hwnd, UINT state, int cx, int cy)

HWN hwndDisk ;

/*******************************************/
/* The size of the window has changed. */
/* Map the logical coordinate system   */
/* to the new extent of the window and */
/* move the disks to their appropriate */
/* position relative to the new size.  */
/*******************************************/

/*****************************/
/* Set new scaling factors. */
/*****************************/

mainFrame_SetHanoiMappingMode (hwnd, cx, cy) ;

/*********************************/
/* (Re)position each disk window. */
/*********************************/

hwndDisk = GetFirstChild (hwnd) ;
while (hwndDisk) {
    disk_PositionDiskWindow (hwndDisk) ;
    hwndDisk = GetNextSibling (hwndDisk) ;
}
```

```
/**********************************************************/
/*                                                      */
/*                 SetHanoiMappingMode                  */
/*                                                      */
/*     Map a logical coordinate system of the form:     */
/*                                                      */
/*                    +2048 y                           */
/*           +------------------------------|           */
/*           |              ^               |           */
/*           |              |               |           */
/*           |      W i n   |   d o w       |           */
/*           |              |               |           */
/*           |              |               |           */
/*           |              |               |           */
/*           |<-------------+-------------->|           */
/*        -1024 x         (0,0)        +1023 x          */
/*                                                      */
/*     to the current physical size of the client area. */
/*                                                      */
/**********************************************************/

static void
mainFrame_SetHanoiMappingMode (HWND hwnd, int cxClient, int cyClient)
{
    HDC hdc ;

    /*****************************************************/
    /* (Re)initialize the device context mapping mode. */
    /*****************************************************/

    hdc = GetDC (hwnd) ;

    // Use the anisotropic mapping mode.
    // Arbitrarily scaled x- and y-axes.

    SetMapMode (hdc, MM_ANISOTROPIC) ;

    // The origin of the window is (still) at point (0,0).

    SetWindowOrgEx (hdc, 0, 0, NULL) ;

    /***********************************************************/
    /* Map the window origin to the point that is on the bottom */
    /* of the window vertically and in the middle of the window */
    /* horizontally.  Once the y-axis is inverted, the window   */
    /* displays quadrant one and two of a cartesian coordinate  */
    /* system.                                                  */
    /***********************************************************/

    SetViewportOrgEx (hdc, cxClient / 2, cyClient, NULL) ;

    /********************************************************/
    /* Set the logical extent of the window to 2,048 units, */
    /* both vertically and horizontally.                    */
    /********************************************************/

    SetWindowExtEx (hdc, 2048, 2048, NULL) ;
```

```
/***********************************************************************/
/* Map the 2,048 logical units to the current size of the window. */
/* The negative y-extent parameter inverts the y-axis.            */
/***********************************************************************/

    SetViewportExtEx (hdc, cxClient, -cyClient, NULL) ;
    ReleaseDC (hwnd, hdc) ;
}


/***********************************************************************/
/*                      mainFrame_IntersectRect                      */
/* This performs the same function as the Windows IntersectRect()    */
/* except that this function expects the vertical axis to increase   */
/* upwardly.  Windows' function expects it to increase downwardly    */
/* and doesn't correctly calculate the intersection.                 */
/***********************************************************************/
static BOOL
mainFrame_IntersectRect (LPRECT rect1, LPRECT rect2)
{
    int HighestLeft,    LowestRight ;
    int HighestBottom, LowestTop ;

    HighestLeft = max (rect1->left, rect2->left) ;
    LowestRight = min (rect1->right, rect2->right) ;

    if (HighestLeft >= LowestRight)
        return FALSE ;

    HighestBottom = max (rect1->bottom, rect1->bottom) ;
    LowestTop     = min (rect1->top, rect2->top) ;

    return (HighestBottom >= LowestTop ? FALSE : TRUE) ;
}


/*********************************************/
/*         mainFrame_ResetDisks             */
/* Place all disks back on the left peg.    */
/*********************************************/
static void
mainFrame_ResetDisks (HWND hwnd)
{
    HWND  hwndDisk ;
    int   i, PostPos ;

    HowMany [FIRST]  = NUMDISKS ;
    HowMany [SECOND] = 0 ;
    HowMany [THIRD]  = 0 ;

    // Move all disks to the left peg.

    hwndDisk = GetFirstChild (hwnd) ;
    while (hwndDisk) {
        disk_SetPostNum (hwndDisk, FIRST) ;
        PostPos = NUMDISKS - disk_GetDiskSize (hwndDisk) ;
```

```
    WhosOn [FIRST][PostPos] = hwndDisk ;
    hwndDisk = GetNextSibling (hwndDisk) ;
}
for (i = 0; i < NUMDISKS; i++)
    disk_PositionDiskWindow (WhosOn [FIRST][i]) ;


/***********************************************/
/*       mainFrame_SolveProblem             */
/* Move the disks in the correct order.     */
/***********************************************/

atic void
inFrame_SolveProblem (HWND hwnd)

    /***********************************************************************/
    /* Protect the current execution environment.  We raise an           */
    /* exception when the user closes the window while in the            */
    /* second level message loop.  We then terminate the program.        */
    /***********************************************************************/

    __try {
        mainFrame_ResetDisks (hwnd) ;
        disk_MoveTower (NUMDISKS, FIRST, SECOND, THIRD) ;
    }
    __except (GetExceptionCode() == STATUS_TERMINATION_REQUEST) {
        PostQuitMessage (0) ;
    }
```

sting 7.13: Towers of Hanoi: Excerpts from DiskHandling.c

```
skHandling.c

.ESULT CALLBACK
skWndProc (HWND hwnd, UINT message, WPARAM wParam, LPARAM lParam)

    switch (message)
        {
        case WM_CREATE: // Notification that a window is being created
                return HANDLE_WM_CREATE (hwnd, wParam, lParam, disk_OnCreate) ;

        case WM_LBUTTONDOWN: // Left click in windows client area...
            return HANDLE_WM_LBUTTONDOWN (hwnd, wParam, lParam, disk_OnLButtonDown) ;

        case WM_LBUTTONUP: // Left button up in windows client area...
                return HANDLE_WM_LBUTTONUP (hwnd, wParam, lParam, disk_OnLButtonUp) ;

        case WM_MOUSEMOVE: // Mouse move
                return HANDLE_WM_MOUSEMOVE (hwnd, wParam, lParam, disk_OnMouseMove) ;

        case WM_PAINT: // Draw all or part of client area
                return HANDLE_WM_PAINT (hwnd, wParam, lParam, disk_OnPaint) ;

        default:
                return DefWindowProc (hwnd, message, wParam, lParam) ;
```

```
        }
}

static BOOL
disk_OnCreate (HWND hwnd, LPCREATESTRUCT lpCreateStruct)
{
    /**********************************************************/
    /* A disk is being created.  Place it on left post. */
    /**********************************************************/

    disk_AddDiskToPost (hwnd, FIRST) ;

    return TRUE ;
}

static void
disk_OnLButtonDown (HWND hwnd, BOOL fDoubleClick, int x, int y, UINT keyFlags)
{
    HWND hwndParent ;
    RECT rect ;

    /*****************************************************************/
    /* The left mouse button is pressed while over a disk. */
    /* Prepare to drag the disk as long as it's depressed. */
    /*****************************************************************/

    /***************************************************/
    /* Only allow the topmost disk(s) to be dragged. */
    /***************************************************/

    if (!disk_IsTopDisk (hwnd))
        return ;

    /********************************************************************/
    /* Start tracking the cursor...                                  */
    /* This entails remembering from where it all started...         */
    /********************************************************************/

    ptOrigPos.x = x ;
    ptOrigPos.y = y ;
    ClientToScreen (hwnd, &ptOrigPos) ;
    GetWindowRect (hwnd, &rectOrigPos) ;

    /*******************************************/
    /* Capturing the mouse so all future      */
    /* movements are sent to this window... */
    /*******************************************/

    SetCapture (hwnd) ;

    /*********************************************************/
    /* And restricting its movement to                     */
    /* within the client area of our parent window. */
    /*********************************************************/

    hwndParent = GetParent (hwnd) ;
    GetClientRect (hwndParent, &rect) ;
```

```
        ClientToScreen (hwndParent, (LPPOINT) &rect.left) ;
        ClientToScreen (hwndParent, (LPPOINT) &rect.right) ;
        ClipCursor (&rect) ;
}

static void
disk_OnLButtonUp (HWND hwnd, int x, int y, UINT keyFlags)
{
    HDC    hdc ;
    HWND   hwndParent ;
    POINT  ptCursor ;
    RECT   rect ;
    UINT   Nearest ;

    /***********************************************************/
    /* The left mouse button was released.  Stop dragging */
    /* the disk and place it on the nearest post.  When    */
    /* the nearest post is an illegal move, place the disk*/
    /* back in its original position.                      */
    /***********************************************************/

    ReleaseCapture () ;
    ClipCursor (NULL) ;

    /***********************************************************/
    /* Determine the coordinates of the center of the disk. */
    /***********************************************************/

    GetWindowRect (hwnd, &rect) ;
    ptCursor.x = (rect.left + rect.right) / 2 ;
    ptCursor.y = (rect.top + rect.bottom) / 2 ;

    /* Convert screen coordinates to client coordinates. */

    hwndParent = GetParent (hwnd) ;
    ScreenToClient (hwndParent, &ptCursor) ;

    /* Convert client coordinates to logical coordinates. */

    hdc = GetDC (hwndParent) ;
    DPtoLP (hdc, &ptCursor, 1) ;
    ReleaseDC (hwndParent, hdc) ;

    /****************************/
    /* Find the nearest post. */
    /****************************/

    if (ptCursor.x < LEFTPOSTPOS / 2)
        Nearest = FIRST ;
    else if (ptCursor.x > RIGHTPOSTPOS / 2)
        Nearest = THIRD ;
    else
        Nearest = SECOND ;

    /***********************************************************/
    /* Remove the disk from its current post, if possible.   */
    /* If successful, place it on the nearest post.          */
    /* If the add fails, then put the disk back on the orig. post. */
    /***********************************************************/
```

```
    if (disk_RemoveDiskFromPost (hwnd) &&
        !disk_AddDiskToPost (hwnd, Nearest))
        disk_AddDiskToPost (hwnd, disk_GetPostNum (hwnd)) ;

    disk_PositionDiskWindow (hwnd) ;
}


static void
disk_OnMouseMove (HWND hwnd, int x, int y, UINT keyFlags)
{
    HWND            hwndParent ;
    POINT           ptCursor ;
    RECT            rect ;

    /************************************************************/
    /* We may be dragging the disk.  If so, calculate the    */
    /* displacement from the starting position of the drag   */
    /* to the current position of the cursor and move the    */
    /* disk so that the position that was under the cursor    */
    /* when the drag started is under the cursor now.         */
    /************************************************************/

    if (hwnd == GetCapture ()) {

        /**********************************************/
        /* Get the current position of the cursor. */
        /**********************************************/

        ptCursor.x = x ;
        ptCursor.y = y ;
        ClientToScreen (hwnd, &ptCursor) ;

        /**********************************************/
        /* Calculate the new position of the disk. */
        /**********************************************/

        rect = rectOrigPos ;
        OffsetRect (&rect, ptCursor.x - ptOrigPos.x,
                        ptCursor.y - ptOrigPos.y) ;
        hwndParent = GetParent (hwnd) ;
        ScreenToClient (hwndParent, (LPPOINT) &rect.left) ;
        ScreenToClient (hwndParent, (LPPOINT) &rect.right) ;

        /*************************************/
        /* Move the disk to its new position. */
        /*************************************/

        MoveWindow (hwnd,
                    rect.left,
                    rect.top,
                    rect.right - rect.left,
                    rect.bottom - rect.top, TRUE) ;

        /**********************************************************/
        /* Force the parent window's client area to be redrawn.  */
        /* This is necessary when the disk moves off of a peg    */
        /* so that ugly white gaps in the peg aren't left for    */
        /* indeterminate periods of time.  They eventually get   */
```

```
        /* redrawn anyway but this makes it look nicer.           */
        /*****************************************************************/

        UpdateWindow (hwndParent) ;
    }
}

static void
disk_OnPaint (HWND hwnd)
{
    HDC          hdc ;
    PAINTSTRUCT  ps ;
    RECT         rect ;
    HBRUSH       hbrush, hbrushOld ;

    hdc = BeginPaint (hwnd, &ps) ;

    hbrush = CreateSolidBrush (RGB (238, 120, 0)) ;
    hbrushOld = SelectBrush (hdc, hbrush) ;

    GetClientRect (hwnd, &rect) ;
    RoundRect (hdc, rect.left, rect.top, rect.right, rect.bottom,
        (rect.right - rect.left) / 5,
        (rect.top - rect.bottom) / 5) ;

    hbrush = SelectBrush (hdc, hbrushOld) ;
    DeleteBrush (hbrush) ;

    EndPaint (hwnd, &ps) ;
}

/*****************************************************************/
/*                                                             */
/*                   AddDiskToPost                             */
/*                                                             */
/*      Add a disk to the indicated post. A disk can only be   */
/*      added to the top of the stack of disks on a post (if   */
/*      any).  Additionally a larger disk may not be placed    */
/*      on top of a smaller disk. Return TRUE when the disk    */
/*      is added to the post and FALSE otherwise.              */
/*****************************************************************/

static BOOL
disk_AddDiskToPost (HWND hwnd, UINT PostNum)
{
    int TopDiskSize ;

    /*****************************************************************/
    /* If there are already disks on the post,                     */
    /* insure that the top disk is larger than this disk.          */
    /*****************************************************************/

    if (HowMany [PostNum]) {
        TopDiskSize =
            disk_GetDiskSize (WhosOn [PostNum][HowMany [PostNum] - 1]) ;

        if (TopDiskSize < disk_GetDiskSize (hwnd))
```

```
              return FALSE ;
       }

       /***********************************************/
       /* Add the disk to the stack on this post. */
       /***********************************************/

       WhosOn [PostNum][HowMany [PostNum]++] = hwnd ;
       disk_SetPostNum (hwnd, PostNum) ;

       return TRUE ;
}

/******************************************************************/
/*                                                              */
/*                   RemoveDiskFromPost                         */
/*                                                              */
/*     Removes this disk from its current post.  A disk can    */
/*     only be removed from a post when it is the top disk     */
/*     on the post.  Return TRUE when the disk is removed       */
/*     from the post and FALSE otherwise.                      */
/******************************************************************/

static BOOL
disk_RemoveDiskFromPost (HWND hwndDisk)
{
       /*****************************************/
       /* Determine which post the disk is on. */
       /*****************************************/

       UINT PostNum = disk_GetPostNum (hwndDisk) ;

       /*********************************************/
       /* Can only remove the disk if it's the top one. */
       /*********************************************/

       if (!disk_IsTopDisk (hwndDisk))
           return FALSE ;

       /***********************************/
       /* Remove the disk from the stack. */
       /***********************************/

       WhosOn [PostNum][--HowMany [PostNum]] = 0 ;
       return TRUE ;
}

/***************************************************/
/*                                               */
/*                   IsTopDisk                    */
/*                                               */
/* Return TRUE if the disk is the topmost on its peg. */
/* Return FALSE otherwise.                       */
/***************************************************/

static BOOL
disk_IsTopDisk (HWND hwndDisk)
```

```
{
    UINT PostNum ;

    PostNum = disk_GetPostNum (hwndDisk) ;

    return
        (WhosOn [PostNum][HowMany [PostNum] - 1] == hwndDisk) ? TRUE : FALSE ;
}
/**************************************************************/
/*                                                          */
/*                  PositionDiskWindow                      */
/*                                                          */
/* Move the window representing a disk to the proper        */
/* position in the main application window's client         */
/* area.                                                    */
/**************************************************************/

void
disk_PositionDiskWindow (HWND hwndDisk)
{
    HDC   hdc ;
    int   HorzPos, VertPos ;
    RECT  rect ;
    UINT  i, DiskSize, PostNum ;

    /**********************************************/
    /* Get the important info about this disk. */
    /**********************************************/

    DiskSize = disk_GetDiskSize (hwndDisk) ;
    PostNum  = disk_GetPostNum (hwndDisk) ;

    /**************************************/
    /* Determine its stacking position. */
    /**************************************/

    for (i = 0; i < HowMany [PostNum]; i++)
        if (WhosOn [PostNum][i] == hwndDisk)
            break ;

    /****************************************/
    /* Calculate the position of the disk. */
    /****************************************/

    SetRectEmpty (&rect) ;

    HorzPos = PostNum == FIRST ? LEFTPOSTPOS :
                    PostNum == SECOND ? CENTERPOSTPOS : RIGHTPOSTPOS ;
    VertPos = (2 * i + 1) * DISKHEIGHT ;

    OffsetRect (&rect, HorzPos, VertPos) ;
    InflateRect (&rect, DISKWIDTHUNIT * (DiskSize + 2), DISKHEIGHT) ;

    /**************************************************************/
    /* MoveWindow requires device coordinates.                  */
    /* Translate logical coordinates to device coordinates.     */
    /**************************************************************/
```

```
    hdc = GetDC (GetParent (hwndDisk)) ;
    LPtoDP (hdc, (LPPOINT) &rect, 2) ;
    ReleaseDC (GetParent (hwndDisk), hdc) ;

    MoveWindow (hwndDisk, rect.left, rect.bottom,
                rect.right - rect.left, rect.top - rect.bottom, TRUE) ;
}

/****************************************************************/
/*                                                            */
/*                      MoveTower                             */
/*                                                            */
/* Move an arbitrarily high tower of disks from one          */
/* peg to another using a third as an intermediate.          */
/****************************************************************/

void
disk_MoveTower (UINT Disks, UINT FromPeg, UINT AuxPeg, UINT ToPeg)
{
    if (Disks == 1)
        disk_MoveOneDisk (FromPeg, ToPeg) ;

    else {
        disk_MoveTower (Disks - 1, FromPeg, ToPeg, AuxPeg) ;
        disk_MoveOneDisk (FromPeg, ToPeg) ;
        disk_MoveTower (Disks - 1, AuxPeg, FromPeg, ToPeg) ;
    }
}

/****************************************************************/
/*                                                            */
/*                     MoveOneDisk                           */
/*                                                            */
/* Move the top disk from one peg to another peg. */
/****************************************************************/

static void
disk_MoveOneDisk (UINT FromPeg, UINT ToPeg)
{
    HWND hwndDisk ;

    /* Locate the top disk on the source peg. */

    hwndDisk = WhosOn [FromPeg][HowMany [FromPeg] - 1] ;

    /* Wait for a while... */

    disk_TwiddleThumbs (GetParent (hwndDisk), 1250) ;

    /* Take it off the source peg. */

    disk_RemoveDiskFromPost (hwndDisk) ;

    /* Put it on the destination peg. */

    disk_AddDiskToPost (hwndDisk, ToPeg) ;
```

```
    /* Update the display. */

    disk_PositionDiskWindow (hwndDisk) ;
}

/***************************************************/
/*                                               */
/*                  TwiddleThumbs                 */
/*                                               */
/* Twiddle our thumbs (figuratively of course)   */
/* for the specified length of time. Allow the   */
/* user to close the program while we're so      */
/* occupied.                                      */
/***************************************************/

static void
disk_TwiddleThumbs (HWND hwnd, UINT Delay)
{
    MSG msg ;

    SetTimer (hwnd, ID_TIMER, Delay, NULL) ;

    while (GetMessage (&msg, 0, 0, 0)) {
        if (msg.message == WM_TIMER) {
            KillTimer (hwnd, ID_TIMER) ;
            return ;
        }
        else if (msg.message == WM_LBUTTONDOWN ||
                 msg.message == WM_LBUTTONUP)
            continue ;

        TranslateMessage (&msg) ;
        DispatchMessage (&msg) ;
    }
    RaiseException (STATUS_TERMINATION_REQUEST,    // exception code
                    EXCEPTION_NONCONTINUABLE,      // continuable exception flag
                    0,                             // number of arguments in array
                    NULL) ;                        // address of array of arguments
}
```

Timer Input

The last remaining input device is the timer. You can ask Windows to periodically notify your application when a specified amount of time has elapsed. This notification comes in the form of a WM_TIMER message.

Your application requests the use of the timer by calling the SetTimer function and specifying how often Windows should send WM_TIMER messages (in milliseconds). When you call the SetTimer function, you actually request Windows to create a system timer event. You are not actually using the hardware timer. Windows itself uses the hardware timer to simulate multiple logical timers, each timing one system timer event.

The SetTimer function is defined as

```
UINT SetTimer (HWND hwnd, UINT idTimer, UINT IntervalTimeout,
                                        TIMERPROC TimerFunc) ;
```

Windows 3.0 was limited to eight timers. Windows 3.1 allowed up to 16. For Windows 95 and Windows NT, there is no documented limit, but it is known to be at least in the hundreds. However, if you plan to run your application on Win32s, you will be subject to the Windows 3.1 limit of 16 timers.

The only parameter with a straightforward use is the `IntervalTimeout` parameter, which specifies the (minimum) elapsed time in milliseconds between WM_TIMER messages. This is a UINT value, but under Win32s it is limited to the range 1 to 65,535.

Win16 timer intervals were limited to a 16-bit unsigned (WORD) value. If you plan to run your application on Win32s, you should limit your time interval to 65,535 milliseconds, that is, just over one minute.

However, the idea that the specification is in milliseconds can be misleading. Windows uses the hardware timer of the computer as its source of timing signals. This timer counts at a rate of one tick every 54.925 milliseconds. Windows doesn't change the rate of the hardware timer. Therefore, the actual minimum timing period is established by the hardware timer. This, plus the fact that Windows is a nonpreemptive system, has two important ramifications. First, you may get messages a little more frequently than you might expect. For example, requesting a timer message every second (1000 milliseconds) actually results in a timer message every 18 hardware clock ticks (1000/54.925 = 18.21). Eighteen clock ticks is actually 988.65 milliseconds. When the Timeout parameter is less than 55, you receive a message every clock tick (55 msec). You can't receive a timer message more frequently than one every 55 milliseconds or 18.2 messages per second.[5]

The second of these two ramifications has a number of additional implications. When another application, possibly of higher priority than your application, occupies the CPU for a period longer than your timer interval, your application won't receive a WM_TIMER message when it's due. Only when the other application finally releases control of the CPU (for example, by calling the GetMessage function) will your application get a chance to retrieve its WM_TIMER message. And even then, Windows might not give it control. Another application will relinquish control when it does a GetMessage or PeekMessage call, blocks on a synchronization object (such as a semaphore), is preempted by a higher-priority application, or has its time slice expire. But your application (or, to be precise, your thread) will execute only if it is the next thread that would be scheduled. If there are other threads in the scheduling queue ahead of yours, your thread still won't run. Note that this applies even if the other threads belong to your application. You can have high-priority threads and low-priority threads. A high-priority thread (such as handling input from the communications port) might preempt a lower priority thread (the thread that keeps the time-of-day clock in your application's window properly updated).

---

[5] You can get finer timings than this, but to do so you have to use either the multimedia timers or the DirectX support. Discussion of these topics is beyond the scope of what we can cover in this book.

Windows handles a WM_TIMER message much as it does a WM_PAINT message. Both are considered low-priority messages and are not delivered when other applications have higher-priority messages (meaning any message other than WM_PAINT and WM_TIMER) in their queues. Instead, the other applications are given control and allowed to process their messages. This can result in your application's not receiving its WM_TIMER message when due.

In fact, multiple timer periods might expire before your application gets to retrieve its WM_TIMER message from its queue. However, you'll receive only one WM_TIMER message, and it will represent all expired periods. Windows doesn't place a second WM_TIMER message in the queue, just as it doesn't place multiple WM_PAINT messages in the queue. You can, however, retrieve a WM_TIMER message from the queue just before another time period expires (which allows Windows to place a new WM_TIMER message in the empty timer queue) and, subsequently, retrieve a second WM_TIMER message almost immediately after the first.

Like the WM_PAINT message, the WM_TIMER message is not actually ever in the message queue; it is actually a flag in the thread's queue header. Therefore, there is only one flag to represent the timer. This flag is set every time the timer expires. If it is set, and there is nothing else in the queue, the GetMessage or Peek-Message function will return a WM_TIMER message.

The bottom line is that you must not rely on counting WM_TIMER messages to determine elapsed time. A WM_TIMER message might arrive as early as 54 milliseconds before the expected time or an indeterminate amount of time later. Depending on the behavior of your application and other applications that are running, the WM_TIMER message could arrive milliseconds, seconds, or minutes after it was "supposed" to arrive. When you need to know the precise amount of time that has elapsed, such as when updating a clock, use the arrival of the WM_TIMER message as a trigger to fetch the actual time and use it accordingly.

If you need really precise timings, you should use the "multimedia timers" that are now available. Although these are subject to many of the same anomalies as the regular timer, their intervals are much shorter–hence their accuracy is much higher–and they are enqueued differently. The DirectX support provides for the finer real-time intervals required for game playing and other fast-response applications. But a discussion of these timers is well beyond what the typical GUI requires. We don't go into them because we would have to discuss the multimedia services in more depth than we can devote space to in this book.

Once you have WM_TIMER messages coming into your application (at times trickling in, at other times pouring in), you might want to stop them. The KillTimer function stops the flow of timer messages. You are guaranteed not to receive a WM_TIMER message after you've called the KillTimer function. The KillTimer function not only stops the generation of new WM_TIMER messages; it also removes any that might be waiting in your message queue. You can successfully implement a one-time-only timer notification by calling Set-Timer with the appropriate delay and KillTimer when the WM_TIMER message arrives.

Now it's time to look at the other parameters to the SetTimer function. They can be used in various combinations that produce three methods in which you can use the timer.

- WM_TIMER messages are sent to a specified window function.

- WM_TIMER messages are sent to a specified callback function. You assign the ID for the system event timer.

- WM_TIMER messages are sent to a specified callback function. Windows assigns the ID for the system event timer.

We discuss these methods in more detail in the following sections.

Sending WM_TIMER Messages to a Window Function

This method is the easiest and probably the most widely used. As with the other input messages you've seen (such as WM_MOUSEMOVE and WM_KEYDOWN), Windows sends the WM_TIMER message to the window function for the window specified by the hwnd parameter in the SetTimer function call. This version of the SetTimer function call looks like this:

```
TimerId = SetTimer (hwnd, idTimer, Interval, NULL) ;
```

The idTimer parameter specifies a nonzero arbitrary number that is the timer ID. The SetTimer function returns this value when the timer is successfully created; otherwise, it returns 0. The Interval parameter specifies the (minimum) duration in milliseconds between WM_TIMER messages. The last parameter specifies the procedure-instance address of the callback function to which the WM_TIMER message should be sent. Set this parameter to NULL to get WM_TIMER messages sent to the window function.

When the WM_TIMER message arrives at the window function, the wParam parameter to the window function contains the timer ID. In the previous example, this would be idTimer. This enables you to create multiple timer events–typically for different periods–give them different ID values, and send them to the same window function. The lParam parameter contains 0 when Windows sends the WM_TIMER message to a window function. If you use a message cracker, you will get the timer ID as a parameter.

WM_TIMER Message Cracker Handler

void cls_OnTimer(HWND hwnd, UINT id);					
	wParam		lParam		
Parameter	lo	hi	lo	hi	Meaning
hwnd					Window handle of the window.
id	██	██			Timer ID number.

You use the timer ID value to indicate the particular timer to stop when calling the KillTimer function. There is no function to change the time interval for an existing timer. You must kill the existing timer and create a new one specifying the new interval. However, you can reuse the killed timer's ID:

```
KillTimer (hwnd, idTimer) ;
TimerId = SetTimer(hwnd, idTimer, NewIntervalTimeout, NULL) ;
```

Sending WM_TIMER Messages to a Callback Function

Sometimes it's more convenient to have Windows send WM_TIMER messages directly to a specific function within your application. Often, having Windows send WM_TIMER messages directly to a callback function simplifies a window function because it doesn't have to pass the message along to a WM_TIMER message function. You do this by specifying the procedure address of the function that Windows should call when the timer event occurs.

Many of the functions called directly by Windows are known as *callback functions*. You can start using the timer with the following statement:

```
TimerId = SetTimer (hwnd, idTimer, Interval, TimerFunc) ;
```

This does exactly the same as the first example does, except that now the timer messages are sent to the TimerFunc function rather than the window function for the hwnd window. If the hwnd is NULL, the idTimer parameter is ignored and a new timer ID is created and returned to you.

Because Windows calls the callback function directly, you must define the function as a callback function, as follows:

```
void CALLBACK
TimerFunc (HWND hwnd, UINT msg, UINT idTimer, DWORD Time)
    {
    /* Do WM_TIMER message processing here. */
    return ;
    }
```

The name of the function isn't significant. You can substitute any name in place of TimerFunc. Windows passes the value specified in the hwnd parameter to the SetTimer function call as the hwnd parameter to the callback function. The msg parameter is always equal to WM_TIMER because only timer messages are sent to the TimerProc function. The idTimer parameter specifies the ID of the timer. You can use it to distinguish the messages of multiple timers all directed to the same callback function. The Time parameter contains the current system time.

You also can send WM_TIMER messages to a callback function in a slightly different form. When you set the hwnd parameter to the SetTimer call to 0, the timer ID parameter is ignored. Instead, Windows assigns the timer ID value and returns it as the function return value. The timer period and procedure address parameters are used as was just described. This is the third form of the SetTimer function call:

```
TimerId = SetTimer (0, 0, Interval, TimerFunc) ;
```

When the callback function is called, the hwnd parameter to the callback function will be set to 0. The idTimer parameter will be the timer ID value assigned by Windows.

Using the Timer

Now we look at how the Hanoi program uses the timer to automatically solve the Towers of Hanoi problem. It's easy to move each disk to solve it. It's a bit more difficult to delay between disk moves in a manner suitable for the program's nonpreemptive design. Normally you would request a WM_TIMER message to be sent at the appropriate time and then return from the window function to the main application message loop. The call to GetMessage in the message loop suspends the program until the timer message arrives or the user does something to the window.

However, this approach doesn't work very well in the Hanoi program. The Hanoi program solves the Towers of Hanoi problem by recursively calling the disk_moveTower function to move smaller and smaller towers until the top disk is moved. Then, as it unwinds the recursion, the appropriate disks get moved to the appropriate pegs. We want to delay before moving each disk, but doing so by returning to the main application GetMessage loop would destroy the history kept on the stack in the form of the recursive calls. The solution is a secondary message loop. The disk_TwiddleThumbs function in the Hanoi program does just this:

```
static void
disk_TwiddleThumbs (HWND hwnd, UINT uDelay)
{
    MSG  msg ;

    SetTimer (hwnd, ID_TIMER, uDelay, NULL) ;

    while (GetMessage (&msg, 0, 0, 0))
        { /* secondary loop */
        if (msg.message == WM_TIMER) {
            KillTimer (hwnd, ID_TIMER) ;
            return ;
        }
        else if (msg.message == WM_LBUTTONDOWN ||
                 msg.message == WM_LBUTTONUP)
            continue ;

        TranslateMessage (&msg) ;
        DispatchMessage (&msg) ;
        } /* secondary loop */
    RaiseException(STATUS_TERMINATION_REQUEST,
                   EXCEPTION_NONCONTINUABLE,
                   0, NULL) ;


}
```

The SetTimer function call starts a timer. Windows sends a WM_TIMER message to the window function for the window specified by the hwnd parameter via the application message queue. While we wait for the timer message, the Hanoi program drops into a secondary message loop. The GetMessage function call suspends the program, with the current recursion depth preserved, until a message arrives. We check each message for the WM_TIMER message. When it's found, the delay is complete, so we kill the timer to prevent future WM_TIMER messages from arriving, and then return from the disk_TwiddleThumbs function.

If the message is not the WM_TIMER message, we check for left button presses and releases. When these are found, they are ignored and not dispatched to the window function for processing. This keeps the user from interfering with the automatic play by actually dragging disks around. Dispatching the mouse button messages to the window function would let the user grab and move the disks while the program is animating them. The delay loop is used when the Hanoi program is animating the display by moving the disks.

All other messages except the WM_QUIT message are handled normally. That is, they are translated and dispatched to the appropriate window function for processing. The WM_QUIT message is handled uniquely.

Structured Exception Handling

Table 7.19: Exception code format requirements

Bit Positions in Exception Code					Meaning
31	30	29	28	27-0	
1	1				Error exception.
1	0				Warning exception.
0	1				Informational exception.
0	0				Success exception.
		0			Reserved for Microsoft.
		1			User-defined exception.
			0		Reserved; must be 0.
				0000000.. FFFFFFF	Exception code.

The user can close the main application window while the game is moving the disks from peg to peg. Eventually, the close request causes the window to be destroyed, thereby placing a WM_QUIT message in the queue. The WM_QUIT message causes this secondary message loop to exit because the GetMessage function returns FALSE when it retrieves a WM_QUIT message. But if the disk_TwiddleThumbs function simply returns, the program attempts to continue solving the problem and very quickly fails because its application window has been destroyed.

To do this, we use something called *structured exception handling*, a language feature supported in the Microsoft version of C and in several other C compilers that have licensed the technology from Microsoft. Note that this is conceptually similar to, but somewhat different from, the C++ exception handling that is also supported, particularly by the MFC library.[6]

To raise an exception, we simply invoke the operation RaiseException:

```
RaiseException(EXCEPTION_INTERNAL_QUIT,
               EXCEPTION_NONCONTINUABLE,
               0, NULL) ;
```

The value of EXCEPTION_INTERNAL_QUIT must be defined in accordance with the standards Microsoft suggests. The standards are shown in Table 7.19.

Following the specification shown in Table 7.19, our chosen exception is an "informational exception" whose exception code is 0 (it is our only exception). We therefore must set the high-order 4 bits to be 0110 or 0x6:

---

[6] For a discussion of C++ and MFC exception handling, see Alan Feuer's book, cited in "Further Reading".

```
#define EXCEPTION_INTERNAL_QUIT 0x60000000
```

We certainly do not want to continue from raising this exception, so we choose to pass as the continuation flag the value EXCEPTION_NONCONTINUABLE. We have no additional information to pass to our exception handler, so when we call RaiseException we set the remaining parameters to 0 (count of additional arguments) and NULL (pointer to additional arguments).

The implementation of the **Solve!** menu item is handled by the following function:

```
static void
mainFrame_SolveProblem (HWND hwnd)
{
    /****************************************************************/
    /* Protect the current execution environment.  We raise an     */
    /* exception when the user closes the window while in the      */
    /* second level message loop.  We then terminate the program.  */
    /****************************************************************/
    __try {
        mainFrame_ResetDisks (hwnd) ;
        disk_MoveTower (NUMDISKS, FIRST, SECOND, THIRD) ;
    }
    __except (GetExceptionCode() == EXCEPTION_INTERNAL_QUIT) {
        PostQuitMessage (0) ;
    }
}
```

The effect of the __try/__except program structure is to execute the body in the __try code block. If no exception occurs, then the code in the __except block is completely ignored. Execution proceeds starting with the statement beyond the __try/__except construct and simply returns to the caller.

However, if we are in the disk_TwiddleThumbs message loop when the WM_QUIT message is received, we call RaiseException. This unwinds through any dynamically nested exception handlers (in our case, there are none up to our top-level handler) until it reaches one that invokes its exception block by having its exception filter evaluate to 1. In our case, the test

```
GetExceptionCode() == EXCEPTION_INTERNAL_QUIT
```

reads the exception code that was posted via the RaiseException function, determines that it matches, and causes the code in the __except block that follows to be executed. This causes us to post a quit message that will terminate the program execution. We don't post a WM_CLOSE or other message because the only way this exception could be received is as a consequence of a WM_QUIT message's having been received by the nested message loop.

The first parameter to the RaiseException function (which must be nonzero) is used as the exception code and returned by the GetExceptionCode function. If the exception was any other exception (including, for example, a hardware exception such as a protection fault, divide by zero, etc.), the GetExceptionCode function will not return our defined STATUS_TERMINATION_REQUEST value. This means the filter expression will be false, thereby causing the exception to be passed out to the enclosing handler. Ultimately, we may fall back to the outermost handler, the default handler. The default handler, which is established before WinMain is called, issues a MessageBox that says there was an uncaught exception and then terminates execution. If the filter expression evaluates to 1, the __except block code executes and may choose to re-raise the exception. But since we have nowhere to pass it back, we do nothing other than set msg.wParam, our return value, to 0. After the __except block is processed, execution resumes in the statement following the __except block, which in our case returns from the WinMain function.

Exceptions are an exceedingly powerful mechanism for returning control to an unknown point from within your program. Structured exceptions replace the rather primitive setjmp/longjmp mechanism that has existed in C for years. The setjmp/longjmp and the more structured CATCH/THROW of Windows 3.1 are now deemed obsolete and are not supported in Win32. Because the __try/__except mechanism is syntactically part of the language, it can deal with many issues (such as common subexpression optimization, code motion out of loops, and register value caching) that otherwise would often result in obscure bugs, particularly as more and more code optimization options were selected. You must never use setjmp/longjmp in C++ code, because this will violate the basic semantics of C++. Executing a longjmp will bypass all the block termination code essential for proper C++ object management.

You can use the exception handling mechanism with an additional feature called a *termination handler* to guarantee that allocated resources are freed properly even in the presence of errors. For example, you could protect a WM_PAINT handler:

```
__try { /* protected paint */
        hdc = BeginPaint(hwnd, &ps);
        // ... complex painting operations
        } /* protected paint */
__finally
        { /* termination handler */
        EndPaint(hwnd, &ps);
        } /* termination handler */
```

A termination handler is *always* executed when control leaves the __try block, whether it leaves the block via a goto, return, break, or an exception passing through. In this case, the EndPaint will always be executed, thereby guaranteeing that the DC is properly released. Another typical case is when you have to close files, say, after discovering that the third file in the sequence did not exist. You could do this by writing the following code:

```
HFILE file1 = 0;
HFILE file2 = 0;
HFILE file3 = 0;
__try { /* protected file block */
        file1 = OpenFile(...);
        if(file1 == 0)
            return FALSE;
        file2 = OpenFile(...);
        if(file2 == 0)
            return FALSE;
        file3 = OpenFile(...);
        if(file3 == 0)
            return FALSE;

        // some sort of file loop here:
        while(TRUE)
            { /* process files */
            // ... file operations which may
            // ... generate exceptions
```

```
            // lines must not begin with $
            if(databuffer[0] == '$')
                return FALSE;

            // ... more processing here
        } /* process files */
    } /* protected file block */
__finally
        { /* close all files */
        if(file1 != 0)
            _lclose(file1);
        if(file2 != 0)
            _lclose(file2);
        if(file3 != 0)
            _lclose(file3);
        } /* close all files */
```

This is a particularly interesting example in that it demonstrates that the various paths that return FALSE as a side effect will force the termination handler to close all the files. You've almost certainly written code that needed to do this. Remember how ugly it was? Possibly even requiring a goto? That's all history in Win32. If you are programming in C, you can use structured exception handling, and if you are programming in C++, you can use the C++ exception handling.

One serious caution about using exception handlers or termination handlers: It is much easier to design this into your program at the start than to retrofit it months into the development. Once you assume the presence of exceptions, you tend to adopt a programming style that caters to their potential occurrences. Retrofitting exceptions often introduces as many problems as it solves—code that assumed control would return to it might now be bypassed. For example,

```
        // ... open file

        processfile(file);

        // ... close file
```

may never actually execute the close-file code because an exception raised in processfile caused control to pass to a higher-level function in the call chain. To actually verify that you cannot get an exception, you must follow processfile and the functions it calls to make certain that no exceptions are raised. This includes any runtime library functions you may call. But if you assume that exceptions are a way of life, you will immediately code this as

```
        __try {
            // ... open file
            processfile(file);
        }
        __finally
        {
            // ... close file
        }
```

thus reducing the chance of an exception generating a difficult-to-diagnose bug. In many ways, writing well-structured exception-based code is as great a paradigm shift as moving from a DOS-based command-line model to a Windows event model.

Have some fun playing with the Towers of Hanoi game for a while. Most of the techniques it uses have been discussed in this and previous chapters. In the next chapter, you'll read about *controls*–the multitudes of specialized windows and window functions provided by Windows for your use, and subsequent chapters will treat various controls in depth.

Further Reading

"Internationalizing Your Win32-based Applications for Windows NT and Windows 95", *Microsoft Systems Journal*, December 1994.

The Unicode Standard: Worldwide Character Encoding. Version 1.0, Volume 1. The Unicode Consortium. Addison-Wesley, 1991. ISBN 0-201-56788-1.

Feuer, Alan, *MFC Programming*, Addison-Wesley, 1996. ISBN 0-201-63358-2.

Freytag, Asmus, "Building a Multilingual User Interface for Your Application with Win32", *Microsoft Systems Journal*, April 1995.

Kano, Nadine, and Freytag, Asmus, "The International Character Set Conundrum: ANSI, Unicode and Microsoft Windows", *Microsoft Systems Journal*, November 1994.

Kano, Nadine, *Developing International Software for Windows 95 and Windows NT*, Microsoft Press, 1995. ISBN 1-55615-840-8.

> This is a must-have book for anyone planning an international Windows application. See the extended review on page 942.

Microsoft Corporation, *The Windows Interface Guidelines for Software Design*, Microsoft Press, 1995. ISBN 1-55615-679-0.

> This book is essential reading for anyone designing a GUI. It is *not* optional. See the detailed review on page 151.

Pietrek, Matt, *Windows 95 System Programming Secrets*, IDG Books Worldwide, 1995. ISBN 1-56884-318-6.

> See the detailed review on page 273.

Schulman, Andrew, *Unauthorized Windows 95*, IDG Books Worldwide, 1994. ISBN 1-56884-305-4.

> Reveals all! Even inconvenient facts Microsoft would rather have not seen made public! See the extended review on page 274.

8 Using Controls: Overview; Static, Button, and Edit Classes

Chapter 7, "Keyboard, Mouse, and Timer Input", covers keyboard, mouse, and timer input at a low level. If you always had to handle input at that level, however, your work would quickly become tedious and error prone. Many Windows programs have common requirements. Here are just a few:

- Accept a character string from the user.

- Allow the user to edit the character string in a standard fashion.

- Allow the user to make a selection from a variety of choices.

- Allow the user to scroll items horizontally and vertically.

- Place labels on the screen.

Each Windows application could reinvent the wheel, but there's no need to do that. Many times, you can use a *control* to provide these functions. This chapter examines the following types of controls:

- Button controls such as push buttons and check boxes

- Static controls such as text labels and rectangular frames

- Edit controls, which are small windows into which the user can type and edit text

- List box controls, which provide a way for the user to select one or more items from a list of selections

- Combo box controls, which are a convenient combination of an edit control (or static control) and a list box control

- Scroll bar controls, which provide a way for the user to indicate scrolling requests

These are all Windows *base controls* that have been in Windows since Win16. There is an additional set of controls, the *common controls*, which exist in Win32 4.*x* and Windows NT. We discuss some of these controls in Chapter 9 and Chapter 10. In addition to the base controls and common controls, you can obtain from a variety of sources any number of *custom controls*, which operate very much like the base controls or common controls. These have been traditionally implemented as DLLs, but you can build custom controls right into your application. There are the *OCX controls*, which are implemented using OLE automation (**OLE** Control e**X**tension). There are *ActiveX* controls, which are "lean and mean" OCX-like controls primarily designed to be embedded in Web pages, although they are not limited to this context. One type control you will *not* find in Win32, however, is the **V**isual **B**asic e**X**tension control (VBX). These controls are strongly tied to the peculiarities of Win16 addressing and will never exist in Win32. They are replaced by OCX controls.[1]

By the end of the chapter, we'll have shown you how to create each of the base controls and how the control's parent window and the control communicate. We discuss the messages understood by each type of control as well as the messages each type of control sends to its parent window.

From the most fundamental view, a *control* is simply a child window that is based on a particular window class. Windows sends messages for a window to the window function specified when registering the class. The window functions for the predefined classes reside within Windows. The Windows *base controls* are child windows that are created from classes which Windows has defined for you. The *common controls* are child windows that are created from classes defined by the `comctl32.dll` library, which is delivered as part of Windows.

So when you create a control, you are creating a child window the same as any other child window in your application. The only difference is that Windows, a Windows-supplied DLL, a third-party vendor DLL, or you yourself provide the window function. This function determines how the control paints itself on the screen, to what input the control responds, and how it notifies its parent window when events of possible interest occur.

The window function determines what a window looks like and how it responds to input. You use the predefined window classes when you need a window that behaves in a standard way. For example, the BUTTON window class can draw its window in a number of button styles and report when the user clicks a mouse button while over the window. You receive two major benefits when you use controls. First, you don't need to write, debug, and maintain the code for the control. Second, by using standard controls where applicable, you make it much easier for a user to learn how to run and use your application. The controls in your application look and behave the same as similar controls in other Windows applications.

You should, whenever possible, use standard controls. Not only do you get a consistent set of behaviors, but your development costs drop. We also look at *owner draw*, or as they are now known, *self-draw* controls. In many cases, you can avoid the need for a custom control by taking advantage of owner draw controls.

---

[1] In principle, in Windows 95 you can run a hybrid of Win16 and Win32 DLLs, and it is certainly possible to call a 16-bit VBX control using a technique called "thunking". This technique is so complex to use for a VBX and will become obsolete so quickly that there is little point to spending any time on it.

A control handles the messy details of managing program input and notifies its parent window (by sending a message, of course) when anything of interest occurs. For example, when you click a push button, the push button control redraws the button in the down state when the WM_LBUTTONDOWN message arrives. When the WM_LBUTTONUP message arrives, the control redraws the button in the up state and sends a message to its parent window signaling that the button was pressed. We use owner-draw controls extensively in the various Explorers that accompany this text.

There are two ways to create a control:

1. You create a child window and specify a predefined class name as the window class. You can display the child window (control) within the client area of any other window: an overlapped window, a pop-up window, or another child window.

2. You create the control as part of a dialog box. Chapter 12, "Menus, Accelerators, Icons, String Resources, and MessageTable Resources", discusses creating controls within a dialog box.

Creating a Control in a Window

You will probably create most, if not all, of the controls in your application within dialogs. You will create a *dialog template* specifying all of your controls and invoke it. Those nice tabbed controls so prevalent in modern applications are done by dialogs (see Chapter 11). If you use the Microsoft Foundation Class (MFC) library in C++, you will be able to very easily create an application with what is called a "top-level dialog" or to use the CFormView class, the CRecordView class, or the CPropertyPage class. These classes are wrappers around dialogs full of controls. Other vendors' environments and class libraries have similar features. But these are only convenient ways to package the controls. What we look at here is ultimately what all of those facilities do automatically for you: create control windows. But you can create a control in the client area of any window. There is nothing special about dialogs or any of their fancy packaging that you can't do yourself with CreateWindow and the other API functions we are about to discuss.

You create a control in the client area of its parent window by calling the CreateWindow function and specifying the predefined class name as the window class. Here are the parameters to the CreateWindow function to use when creating a default push button control:

```
hDefPushbutton = CreateWindow (
    _T("button"),           /* Predefined button class */
    _T("OK"),               /* Label on the button */
    WS_CHILD |              /* Controls are always child windows */
      WS_VISIBLE |          /* Make it initially visible */
      BS_DEFPUSHBUTTON,     /* Use the default push button style */
    100,                    /* Horizontal coordinate */
    200,                    /* Vertical coordinate */
    30,                     /* Width of the push button */
    15,                     /* Height of the push button */
    hwnd,                   /* Parent window's handle */
    (HMENU) IDOK,           /* Control ID */
    hInstance,              /* Instance handle */
    NULL) ;                 /* No additional data */
```

This statement creates a child window that is 30 device units wide and 15 device units high. Windows places the window at the point (100, 200) in the client area of the hwnd window. The window belongs to the BUTTON class, one of the predefined window classes. The window class name parameter is case-insensitive. You can use the names button, Button, and BUTTON interchangeably. The button window class interprets the window name parameter of the CreateWindow function call as the label for the button.

The third parameter to the CreateWindow function call (the 32-bit window-styles parameter) has two parts: the *window* styles (these are the symbolic identifiers beginning with WS_) in the high-order word and the *control* styles in the low-order word. Window styles apply to all types of controls. Hence, you normally use the WS_VISIBLE window style when creating any type of control so that the control becomes visible when the parent window is visible. You *must* specify the WS_CHILD window style. Controls are always WS_CHILD windows. You combine window styles and control styles together using the bitwise OR operation.

The BS_DEFPUSHBUTTON is a control style, specifically, a *button style*, that applies only to windows based on the BUTTON class. The control styles you can select depend on the control class. You specify a control class to choose the general type of the control (e.g., a button, a scroll bar, or an edit control) and then specify the control styles to indicate the exact type of control. The button class specifies that we want a push button. The BS_DEFPUSHBUTTON control style specifies that we want a *default push button*. A default push button operates slightly differently and is visually distinct from a normal push button.

Child windows don't have a menu. The hMenu parameter of a CreateWindow function call that creates a child window is actually a child window *identifier,* not a menu handle. In the previous example, the value IDOK (which is defined by windows.h and is the standard identifier value for an **OK** push button) is associated with the created push button control. You must cast the child window identifier to the HMENU data type when compiling with strict type checking enabled.

A control interacts with its parent window by sending a *notification message*. You will see that there are several kinds of notification messages, and we cover them in detail. A control includes the child window identifier when it sends a message to its parent window. A parent window containing multiple controls can distinguish between the controls by their control IDs. Windows doesn't require you to use unique values for control IDs, but it's much easier to tell them apart if you do. Many development environments will not permit you to assign the same integer value to two controls.

Rather than jump right into creating controls of the various types that Windows provides, we delay a bit more and look at how you use a control. Like everything else in Windows, you send a message to a control to ask for its status or to tell it to do something. Conversely, the control sends messages to its parent window informing the parent of changes in the control. When you send a message to a control, you use the SendMessage function rather than the PostMessage function. The SendMessage function is defined as

```
LRESULT SendMessage (HWND hwnd, UINT msg,
                     WPARAM wParam, LPARAM lParam) ;
```

This function sends a message directly to the window function associated with the hwnd window. Sending a message to a window is quite different from posting a message to a window. Sending a message does not place the message in the message queue for later retrieval, as the PostMessage function does.

The `SendMessage` function call effectively calls the window function specified by the `hwnd` parameter. You call the function, which determines the appropriate window function and calls it. The called window function returns a value to the `SendMessage` function, which, in turn, passes the value back to you as its own return value. So the `lresult` variable in the previous example is set to the value returned by the `hwnd` window function when processing the `msg` message. Because of this behavior, which does not require returning to the message loop, the `SendMessage` call is often referred to as being a "synchronous" messaging mechanism. In contrast, `PostMessage`, which is essentially unpredictable as to when the message will actually be processed, is often referred to as being an "asynchronous" messaging mechanism.

The `windowsx.h` header file, first introduced in Windows 3.1, provides a set of control API macros that simplifies the sending of messages to a control. The macros pack the various parameters to a message into the proper arguments and cast the return value properly for the message being sent. These macros provide a higher-level interface for many of the API calls and messages. The message macros apply to all of the base controls and window messages. For the 32-bit "common controls", you can find a similar set of macros in `commctrl.h`. Microsoft did *not* supply a complete set of macro wrappers for all the messages, and in particular, not for many of the messages that were introduced with Win32. We have corrected this omission by adding our own file, `extensions.h`, which attempts to complete the set of functions.

 You should use these macro APIs for all Win16 development as they are much more portable to 32-bit Windows than is packing the parameters and sending the message explicitly. When you use the macros, a different macro for 32-bit Windows results in your code's packing the arguments to a message properly for the new environment. If you pack the arguments explicitly, you will have to alter your code that sends certain messages before it will work in a 32-bit Windows application. It is often best to convert an existing Win16 program to use these macros and verify that it compiles and runs under Win16, then port it to Win32. Because Win32 packs the parameters differently than Win16 does, converting the packing manually is more error-prone.

You should use the new macro APIs for all future development as they are much more portable to 32-bit Windows than is packing the parameters and sending the message explicitly. See the text inset, above.

In our discussions of controls, we provide the explicit `SendMessage` function call form for sending messages to controls (the form in which you'll see existing code communicate with controls). Also, we list the equivalent control API macro function call. However, in all examples and in all later chapters we use the wrapper calls whenever they are defined.

In addition to the `windowsx.h` wrapper calls, Windows itself defines many API calls that are higher-level wrappers for `SendMessage`. For example,

```
SetWindowText(hwnd, text)
```

is the same as

```
SendMessage(hwnd, WM_SETTEXT, 0, (LPARAM)(LPCTSTR)text);
```

and

```
SendDlgItemMessage(hdlg, id, msg, wParam, lParam);
```

is the same as

```
SendMessage(GetDlgItem(hdlg, id), msg, wParam, lParam);
```

and finally

```
SetDlgItemText(hdlg, id, text)
```

is the same as

```
SendMessage(GetDlgItem(hdlg, id), WM_SETTEXT, 0, (LPARAM)(LPCTSTR)text);
```

In addition to the generic operations, there are `windowsx.h` macros that have specific control-related names. For example,

```
Button_SetText(hButton, text);
```

is really just a wrapper around a `SetWindowText` API function.

Control Notifications

A control *notifies* its parent window when something occurs of possible interest to the parent. Most of the base controls (all but scroll bar controls) do this by sending a `WM_COMMAND` message to their parent. The low-order word of the `wParam` parameter of the message contains the ID of the control sending the message and the type of event that generated the notification. The control ID value allows you to determine which control sent the `WM_COMMAND` message. The high-order word of the `wParam` parameter of the `WM_COMMAND` message contains the *notification code*. The notification code contains additional information from the control explaining what the message means. Notification code values have different meanings depending on the type of control. The parent window's `OnCommand` handler receives the handle to the control, the control ID, and the notification code.

`WM_COMMAND` Message Cracker Handler

`void cls_OnCommand(HWND hwnd, int id, HWND hctl, UINT codeNotify);`					
	wParam		**lParam**		
Parameter	**lo**	**hi**	**lo**	**hi**	**Meaning**
`hwnd`					Window handle of the parent window receiving the message.
`id`	■				Control ID of child control; menu ID of menu item.
`hctl`			■	■	Window handle of the child control, or 0 if from a menu or accelerator.
`codeNotify`		■			Notification code from the child control, 0 if from menu, or 1 if from accelerator.

If you are familiar with how Win16 reported `WM_COMMAND` messages, you will see that the way in which the parameters are packed in Win32 is quite different. So it is very tedious and highly error-prone to take a traditional nested-`switch` Win16 application and port it directly to Win32. We urge you to use the message cracker macros and reorganize the code.

The `lParam` parameter contains the window handle of the control sending the message.

Controls aren't the only source of `WM_COMMAND` messages. Controls, menus, and accelerators all send `WM_COMMAND` messages. When possible, you should use unique IDs for controls, menu items, and accelerators. Unique IDs make it much easier to identify the source of the message. (Chapter 12, "Menus, Accelerators, Icons, String Resources, and MessageTable Resources", discusses accelerators and menus and their use of the `WM_COMMAND` message.)

Because of this "overloading" of the `WM_COMMAND` message, the Win32 *common controls* now use a `WM_NOTIFY` message. Its use, however, is very much like the `WM_COMMAND` message. The major difference is that the key information is not passed in directly via the `wParam` and `lParam` parameters. Instead, the `lParam` points to a data structure that contains notification-specific information. Each control description tells you what notification messages can occur and what data structure `lParam` references. However, all notifications have the same basic structure, an `NMHDR` structure. We'll show you each kind of notification extension for the messages we describe. To simplify processing, the `wParam` value of the `WM_NOTIFY` message contains the control ID of the control sending the message (this value is repeated in the `NMHDR` structure).

`WM_NOTIFY` Message Cracker Handler

`void cls_OnNOTIFY(HWND hwnd, int id, NMHDR * nmhdr);`

	wParam		lParam		
Parameter	**lo**	**hi**	**lo**	**hi**	**Meaning**
hwnd					Window handle of the parent window.
id	■				Control ID of the child control; menu ID of the menu item.
nmhdr			■		Reference to an NMHDR structure.

The `NMHDR` structure is defined as

```
typedef struct tagNMHDR
{
    HWND   hwndFrom;
    UINT   idFrom;
    UINT   code;           // NM_ code
}   NMHDR;
typedef NMHDR FAR * LPNMHDR;
```

The hwndFrom handle is the handle of the window that generated the notification. The idFrom duplicates the value in wParam and is the control ID of the window that generated the notification. The final field, the code, contains the notification code describing the type of the notification. For some notifications, the basic NMHDR information is all that is necessary. For other notifications, there is additional information provided. The way this is provided is by defining a structure that contains an NMHDR structure at its front. A typical example can be illustrated by an example from the Tree View control. This control defines a data structure TV_ITEM, whose details don't matter very much here (we talk about them when we look at the Tree View control; see page 652):

```
typedef struct _TV_ITEM {
    UINT        mask;
    HTREEITEM   hItem;
    UINT        state;
    UINT        stateMask;
    LPTSTR      pszText;
    int         cchTextMax;
    int         iImage;
    int         iSelectedImage;
    int         cChildren;
    LPARAM      lParam;
} TV_ITEM, FAR *LPTV_ITEM;
```

The notification for a TVN_GETDISPINFO or TVN_SETDISPINFO notification is defined by the structure

```
typedef struct _TV_DISPINFO {
    NMHDR hdr;
    TV_ITEM item;
} TV_DISPINFO;
```

This is handled by doing a type cast to the desired type:

```
LRESULT OnNotify(HWND hwnd, int id, NMHDR * nmhdr)
    {
      switch(id)
          { /* id */
          case ID_MYTREEVIEW:
              return OnMyTreeView(hwnd, nmhdr);
          // ...
          } /* id */
    }

LRESULT OnMyTreeView(HWND hwnd, NMHDR * nmhdr)
    {
      switch(nmhdr->code)
          { /* code */
          case TVN_GETDISPINFO:
              return OnMyTreeViewGetDispInfo(hwnd, (TV_DISPINFO *)nmhdr);
          // ...
          } /* code */
    }

LRESULT OnMyTreeViewGetDispInfo(hwnd, TV_DISPINFO * info)
    {
      // ...
      SetWindowText(someOtherControl, info->item->pszText);
    }
```

The OnNotify handler splits the program control flow out for each of the controls and calls an appropriate handler for the individual control. The individual control handler, such as OnMyTreeView, then has to determine what notification has occurred. In this case, we use the code value to determine which notification handler to call. When we call the notification handler, such as OnMyTreeViewGetDispInfo, we use a type cast to convert the pointer. Within the OnMyTreeViewGetDispInfo handler, we can access any of the fields of the TV_ITEM that may be required.

Using Controls

Using a control in a window requires the following steps:

1. Select a control class and a control style based on the appearance and function of the desired control.

2. Create the control at the appropriate location in the client area of a window.

3. Send the control any messages needed to set its initial value.

4. Make the control visible when it doesn't have the WS_VISIBLE window style.

5. Process WM_COMMAND messages in the parent window's window function to react to the control's changes of state.

Finally, remember that a control is simply a particular type of child window. Everything that applies to a child window applies to a control. You can't create a control as a top-level window; a control must have a parent window and a top-level window doesn't have a parent. Actions affecting the parent window also affect the control. When Windows moves the parent window, the control moves along with its parent. When you want to move the control within the client area of its parent, you call the MoveWindow function:

```
MoveWindow (hDefPushbutton, 50, 100, 30, 15, TRUE) ;
```

Generally, the MoveWindow function expects *screen* coordinates; however, when moving a child window (control), you must use *client* area coordinates. The MoveWindow function both moves and resizes a control. If you want only one of these effects, you must compute the other pair of values so that the position or size is retained. The TRUE parameter specifies that Windows should redraw the control once it has been moved to the new location. You can also use the SetWindowPos function to manipulate a control. This has an advantage in that you can *selectively* move, resize, or change the Z-order (tab order) of the control, in any combination. For those options you do not wish to change, you need not compute values.

When the parent window is resized, the control might be clipped. Windows will clip a control (as it does all WS_CHILD windows) to the parent window's boundaries. If you want controls that resize based on the parent window size, you have to resize them yourself by handling the WM_SIZE message for the parent window.

Disabling and enabling the parent window disables and enables all its child windows, controls included. You use the EnableWindow function both to enable and disable a window. You can disable a control without disabling its parent window by specifying the handle of a window and a FALSE value:

```
EnableWindow (hDefPushbutton, FALSE) ;
```

Specific controls, such as buttons, have `windows.h` wrappers. For example, `EnableWindow` has the synonym `Button_Enable`.

When you disable a control, Windows stops sending input to the control. Windows sends the input normally directed to the control to the control's parent window. For the built-in controls, Windows gives the control a grayed (lighter-colored or dim) appearance to indicate that the control is not active (for your own custom controls, you have to do this yourself). You can return the control to the active, or enabled, state by passing TRUE in the `EnableWindow` call:

```
EnableWindow (hDefPushbutton, TRUE) ;
```

Occasionally, you may wish to remove the control from the display temporarily. Instead of destroying the control and recreating it when needed, you can hide the control by calling the `ShowWindow` function with the `SW_HIDE` parameter:

```
ShowWindow (hDefPushbutton, SW_HIDE) ;
```

Make the control visible again by calling the `ShowWindow` function and specifying the `SW_SHOWNORMAL` parameter:

```
ShowWindow (hDefPushbutton, SW_SHOWNORMAL) ;
```

A control must be both enabled and visible before Windows will send it keyboard and mouse input. Note that a control that is clipped by its parent, but which has the `WS_VISIBLE` style, is considered "visible", even though you can't see it on the screen!

It is a common technique in dialog boxes and similar interfaces to either disable or hide controls that would have no effect. A general technique is to disable controls whose effect is temporarily invalid or ineffective (that is, an effect that might be later enabled is often disabled). Controls that cannot become enabled in the dialog session are often hidden entirely.

When you're done using a control, you can remove it from its parent window's client area and free all the resources it holds. Do this by destroying the control. You don't normally have to destroy the controls that you create, as Windows automatically destroys child windows when their parent window is destroyed. You destroy a control by calling the `DestroyWindow` function and specifying the handle of the control:

```
DestroyWindow (hDefPushbutton) ;
```

Fonts in Controls

All controls that paint text use a font to paint the text. Normally, the default font assigned to a control is NULL, and the control uses the default system font. However, buttons, static controls, edit controls, list boxes, and combo boxes all use the information associated with the font whenever they have to draw characters on the screen. You can explore these effects in more detail in the CtlColor Explorer.

To set a font in a control, obtain a handle to the font you wish to set. We explain all about font handles in Chapter 15. Then send the control a `WM_SETFONT` message or use the `SetWindowFont` macro from `windowsx.h`. The `lParam` to the message (the `fRedraw` argument to the macro) is TRUE to force the control to immediately redraw itself, and FALSE to defer drawing until a later time (after some other parameters have also been set).

```
HFONT font = getMyFontForThisControl();
// use one of the following:
SendMessage(hControl, WM_SETFONT, font, TRUE);
SetWindowFont(hControl, font, TRUE);
```

You can query the font that is in use in a control by using the WM_GETFONT message or the GetWindowFont macro from windowsx.h. This message returns either the font handle of the last font set by WM_SETFONT or NULL if no font has been specified for the control:

```
HFONT font = (HFONT)SendMessage(hControl, WM_GETFONT, 0, 0);
HFONT font = GetWindowFont(hControl);
```

Windows defines the following window classes:

- BUTTON
- STATIC
- EDIT
- LISTBOX
- COMBOBOX
- SCROLLBAR
- MDICLIENT

We devote all of Chapter 17, "The Multiple Document Interface", to the MDICLIENT control class. We cover the other classes in this chapter and the next two.

The STATIC Class

STATIC class controls are the simplest type of controls. They normally do not process keyboard or mouse input, and they normally do not send notification messages to their parent window. You usually use static controls to place labels near other controls, to draw a box around other controls, and to separate controls by drawing lines between them. Table 8.1 lists the static control styles.

Table 8.1: Static control styles

Style	Description
SS_BITMAP[4]	The control will hold a bitmap image. The bitmap is set using the STM_SETIMAGE message. The control will be sized to hold the bitmap unless the SS_REALSIZEIMAGE style is specified.

[1] Although the official documentation states that the text cannot be altered, we have found that a WM_SETTEXT message works perfectly well. You can check this out yourself using the Control Explorer application on the CD-ROM.
[4] These styles are available only at API level 4 and higher.

Table 8.1: Static control styles

Style	Description
SS_BLACKFRAME	Draws a "black" frame around the control using COLOR_WINDOWFRAME. See Table 8.3.
SS_BLACKRECT	Draws a filled "black" rectangle as the control using COLOR_WINDOWFRAME. See Table 8.3.
SS_CENTER	Centers the given text in the rectangle. Words that would extend past the end of a line are automatically wrapped to the beginning of the next centered line.
SS_CENTERIMAGE	If the static control contains a bitmap or icon, and the image is smaller than the client area of the static control, the rest of the client area is filled with the color of the pixel in the top left corner of the bitmap or icon. If the static control contains a single line of text, the text is centered vertically in the client area of the control.
SS_ENHMETAFILE[4]	The control will hold an image defined by an enhanced metafile. The enhanced metafile is set using the STM_SETIMAGE message. The control will be sized to hold the image unless the SS_REALSIZEIMAGE style is specified.
SS_ETCHEDFRAME[4]	Draws all four sides of the frame of the static control using the EDGE_ETCHED edge style using the DrawEdge function. See Figure 8.2, upper right-most object.
SS_ETCHEDHORZ[4]	Draws the top and bottom edges of the static control using the EDGE_ETCHED edge style using the DrawEdge function. Although this is the formal specification of the operation, we have found this is not so; see the note that follows this table.
SS_ETCHEDVERT[4]	Draws the left and right edges of the static control using the EDGE_ETCHED edge style using the DrawEdge function. Although this is the formal specification of the operation, we have found this is not so; see the note that follows this table.
SS_GRAYFRAMES	Draws a "gray" frame around the control using the COLOR_BACKGROUND color. See Table 8.3.
SS_GRAYRECT	Draws a filled "gray" rectangle as the control. See Table 8.3.
SS_ICONS	The control holds an icon. The icon can be set using the STM_SETICON message. The control will be sized to hold the icon unless the SS_REALSIZEIMAGE style is specified.
SS_LEFT	Left justifies the given text in the rectangle. Words that would extend past the end of a line are automatically wrapped to the beginning of the next left-justified line.

[1] Although the official documentation states that the text cannot be altered, we have found that a WM_SETTEXT message works perfectly well. You can check this out yourself using the Control Explorer application on the CD-ROM.
[4] These styles are available only at API level 4 and higher.

Table 8.1: Static control styles

Style	Description
SS_LEFTNOWORDWRAP	Specifies a simple static text control. Text will be displayed left-justified. Tabs are expanded. Text that extends beyond the right edge of the control will be clipped.
SS_NOPREFIX	Disables the conversion of & to an underlined character.
SS_NOTIFY[4]	Sends STN_ notifications to the parent via WM_COMMAND.
SS_OWNERDRAW[4]	Specifies that the owner of the static control will be sent a WM_DRAWITEM whenever the control needs to be redrawn.
SS_REALSIZEIMAGE[4]	Prevents a control that has the SS_ICON or SS_BITMAP style from being resized as it is loaded or drawn. If the icon or bitmap is larger than the destination area, the image will be clipped.
SS_RIGHT	Right justifies the given text in the rectangle. Words that would extend past the end of a line are automatically wrapped to the beginning of the next right-justified line.
SS_RIGHTJUST[4]	Specifies that a static control with the SS_BITMAP or SS_ICON style will have its lower-right corner held fixed when the control is resized. Only the top and left sides are adjusted to accommodate a new bitmap or icon.
SS_SIMPLE	Specifies a very restrictive control. The text is displayed left-justified and text that would exceed the rectangle size is clipped. The text cannot be modified.[1] The parent must *not* process the WM_CTLCOLORSTATIC message. The text color will not change when the control is disabled.
SS_SUNKEN[4]	Draws a "half-sunken" border around the static control.
SS_TYPEMASK	This is not actually a style you specify. It is a mask that you can use to isolate several of the styles if you are implementing a generic "owner-draw" or other custom static control. When AND'ed with the window style, it excludes the styles SS_NOPREFIX, SS_NOTIFY, SS_RIGHTJUST, SS_REALSIZEIMAGE, and SS_SUNKEN.
SS_WHITEFRAME	Draws a "white" frame around the control using the COLOR_WINDOW color. See Table 8.3.
SS_WHITERECT	Draws a filled "white" rectangle as the control using the COLOR_WINDOW color. See Table 8.3.

[1] Although the official documentation states that the text cannot be altered, we have found that a WM_SETTEXT message works perfectly well. You can check this out yourself using the Control Explorer application on the CD-ROM.
[4] These styles are available only at API level 4 and higher.

We have discovered using the Control Explorer that the SS_ETCHEDHORZ and SS_ETCHEDVERT do not perform as specified. Instead, they draw either a horizontal line between the top-left and top-right corners of the creation rectangle or a vertical line between the top-left and bottom-left corners of the creation rectangle.

Table 8.2: Static styles that can be changed via
 SetWindowLong

Style Flag	Effect
SS_NOTIFY	Enables/disables mouse clicks and enables notifications.
SS_CENTERIMAGE	Centers the bitmap or icon.
SS_NOPREFIX	Enables/disables processing of & in text.

There are 13 static class styles: three for rectangular frames, three for filled rectangles, six for controlling how text is displayed in a static control, and one for static controls in a dialog box. Some styles can be changed "on the fly", that is, by setting the GWL_STYLE field of the window using SetWindowLong. These are shown in Table 8.2. All other styles have an effect only on creation. If you want to change one of the other styles, you have to destroy the window and re-create it.

Following is a typical function that changes a style flag. This function changes the notification style of a static control. It takes a Boolean argument for the notification state and returns a Boolean indicating the previous notification state. While any nonzero value is "true", we tend to favor value-returning BOOL functions that return the actual literals TRUE and FALSE.

```
BOOL EnableNotify(HWND hwnd, BOOL mode)
    {
    DWORD style = GetWindowLong(hwnd, GWL_STYLE);
    BOOL result = (style & SS_NOTIFY) ? TRUE : FALSE;
    if(mode)
        style |= SS_NOTIFY;
    else
        style &= ~SS_NOTIFY;
    SetWindowLong(hwnd, GWL_STYLE, style);
    return result;
    }
```

We also discovered that turning off the SS_CENTERIMAGE flag when an icon is loaded in an SS_ICON control will cause the icon to be stretched to fill the entire image area. You can discover more of these effects using the Control Explorer.

The three static class styles for rectangular frames are SS_BLACKFRAME, SS_GRAYFRAME, and SS_WHITEFRAME. Each of these styles creates a rectangular box. The rectangle is not filled, and the frame of the rectangle is drawn with a Windows system color, which may not necessarily be black, gray, or white, respectively. In the 3D style, under Windows NT 3.*x*, the frame is an inset or outset outline. A set of frames is shown in Figure 8.1, in the top row.

The three static class styles for filled rectangles are SS_BLACKRECT, SS_GRAYRECT, and SS_WHITERECT. Each of these creates a rectangle filled with a Windows system color. The color used may not necessarily be black, gray, or white. In the 3D style, under Windows NT 3.*x*, the rectangle gives the appearance of being either above or below the background. A set of rectangles is shown in Figure 8.1, in the bottom row.

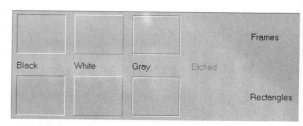

If you don't use the 3D effects in Windows NT 3.*x*, the SS_BLACKFRAME and SS_BLACKRECT styles will draw the frame and fill the rectangle, respectively, with the COLOR_WINDOWFRAME sys-

Figure 8.1: Static controls with 3-D styles

tem color. This is black in the default Windows color scheme. The SS_GRAYFRAME and SS_GRAYRECT styles draw the frame and fill the rectangle with the COLOR_BACKGROUND system color. This is the color used for the screen background (desktop). The SS_WHITEFRAME and SS_WHITERECT styles draw the frame and fill the rectangle with the COLOR_WINDOW system color. This is white in the default Windows color scheme.

The effects of these styles are shown in Figure 8.2, which was drawn under Windows 95 (the same effect is seen under Windows NT 4.*x*). The styles displayed change appearance when 3D controls are used under Windows NT 3.*x*. The 3D control library ctl3dv32.dll is used in Windows NT 3.*x* to achieve effects similar to those of Win32 4.*x*, but it implements static controls differently from the way Win32 4.*x* does. Figure 8.1 and Figure 8.2 show the differences, and Table 8.3 summarizes them.

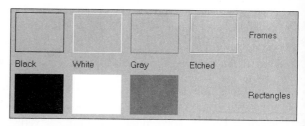

Figure 8.2: Static styles without 3.*x* 3-D interface or using 4.*x* interface

Table 8.3: 3D styles for static controls

Style	Normal Appearance	3D Appearance[1]
SS_BLACKFRAME	Rectangular box in the system "black" color, COLOR_WINDOWFRAME .	An inset box that gives the appearance of being below the background.
SS_WHITEFRAME	Rectangular box in the system "white" color, COLOR_WINDOW .	An outset box that gives the appearance of being above the background.
SS_GRAYFRAME	Rectangular box in the system "gray" color, COLOR_BACKGROUND .	An inset rectangular outline.
SS_BLACKRECT	Solid rectangle in the system "black" color, COLOR_WINDOWFRAME .	An inset box that gives the appearance of being below the background.
SS_WHITERECT	Solid rectangle in the system "white" color, COLOR_WINDOW .	An outset box that gives the appearance of being above the background.

Table 8.3: 3D styles for static controls

Style	Normal Appearance	3D Appearance[1]
SS_GRAYRECT	Solid rectangle in the system "gray" color, COLOR_BACKGROUND .	An inset rectangular outline.

[1]See the MSKB article Q125684 for more details.

The FRAME and RECT static class styles don't use the window text parameter of the CreateWindow function call. Nor do they respond to the WM_SETTEXT or WM_GETTEXT messages. The *x*- and *y*-coordinates to the CreateWindow call specify the location of the upper-left corner of the rectangle. The nWidth and nHeight parameters specify the size of the rectangle. The coordinates are relative to the upper-left corner of the parent window's client area and the width and height are in client coordinates.

Another set of styles specifies the placement of text within the static control window. You combine styles for any control by using the bitwise OR operation. The SS_LEFT, SS_CENTER, and SS_RIGHT static class styles create windows containing text that is left-justified, centered, and right-justified, respectively. The window text parameter of the CreateWindow call specifies the text to be displayed. You can use either the SetWindowText function, the Static_SetText function, or the WM_SETTEXT message to change the text.

You can change the position and size of a static control by calling the MoveWindow function or the SetWindowPos function. A static control isn't really static in the sense that it can't be changed or moved. It's termed *static* because you can put it in place and forget about it. Normally the control repaints itself when necessary and ignores all input directed at it. You can change either of these properties by using the SS_OWNERDRAW or SS_NOTIFY styles when you create the window.

Windows draws text displayed in a static control with the SS_LEFT, SS_CENTER, and SS_RIGHT styles by calling the DrawText function with the DT_WORDBREAK and DT_EXPANDTABS parameters. Thus the displayed text has embedded tabs expanded, while words that would extend past the end of a line are automatically wrapped to the next line. Text that doesn't fit within the boundaries of the control is clipped.

A control with the SS_LEFTNOWORDWRAP static class style displays its text left-justified in the rectangle. Tabs are expanded, but words are not wrapped to the next line. Instead, Windows will clip any text that extends past the end of the line.

The SS_NOPREFIX static class style disables special handling of ampersand (&) characters in the window text. Normally, Windows will remove the & characters from the text and underline the character that follows it.

The SS_SIMPLE static class style creates a simple rectangle and displays a single line of text. The text is left-justified in the rectangle. Although the official documentation states that the text cannot be altered, using the Control Explorer we were able to change the text. However, the text does not change color if the window is disabled. The parent window must not process the WM_CTLCOLORSTATIC message for this window.

You will most often use the SS_ICON static class style to put icons in dialog boxes by placing an "icon" style box in the dialog with a dialog editor. You also can use the Static_SetIcon function to set the icon dynamically, either in a dialog or in a static control you have created. A window having the style SS_ICON will normally be resized to fit the icon. Several styles modify the behavior of this style. One is the SS_CENTERIMAGE style. It causes the icon to be centered and fill the remaining client area of the static control with the same color as the pixel in the top-left corner of the icon. Another is the SS_REALSIZEIMAGE style. It prevents the window from being resized; if the icon is larger than the window, it will be clipped. And third is the SS_RIGHTJUST style. Normally, when you resize a window, the top-left corner is considered the "anchor point" and the window will resize by changing the position of the right and bottom edges. When the SS_RIGHTJUST style is used, the lower-right corner is considered the "anchor point" and the window will resize by changing the position of the top and left edges.

Static controls in Win32 can support image types that the Win16 controls could not, so Win16 programmers should take note of the added functionality. The more general STM_SETIMAGE message allows you to set one of several types of images in a static control. The form of this message is

```
(HANDLE)SendMessage(hStatic, STM_SETIMAGE, imagetype,
                    (LPARAM)(HANDLE)imagehandle);
```

There is no API wrapper defined in windowsx.h, but we have defined one in extensions.h:

```
HANDLE Static_SetImage(HWND hStatic, int imagetype, HANDLE imagehandle);
```

where imagetype indicates what type of handle is being passed. Table 8.4 shows the handles and image types. The return value of the message is either the handle to the previous image or NULL if there was no previous image.

Table 8.4: STM_SET/GETIMAGE codes

Symbol	Handle	Description
IMAGE_BITMAP	HBITMAP	Handle of a bitmap.
IMAGE_CURSOR	HCURSOR	Handle to a cursor object. The cursor is rendered as if it were an icon.
IMAGE_ENHMETAFILE	HENHMETAFILE	Handle of an enhanced metafile.
IMAGE_ICON	HICON	Handle to an icon. The icon is displayed as DrawIcon would draw it.

You can obtain the handle to the current image using the STM_GETIMAGE message. This message can take any of the following forms:

```
HBITMAP bm = (HBITMAP)SendMessage(hStatic, STM_GETIMAGE, IMAGE_BITMAP, 0);
HCURSOR cur = (HCURSOR)SendMessage(hStatic, STM_GETIMAGE, IMAGE_CURSOR, 0);
HENHMETAFILE mf = (HENHMETAFILE)SendMessage(hStatic, STM_GETIMAGE,
                                            IMAGE_ENHMETAFILE, 0);
HICON icon = (HICON)SendMessage(hStatic, STM_GETIMAGE, IMAGE_ICON, 0);
```

or you can use the API wrappers we define in extensions.h:

```
HBITMAP bm = (HBITMAP)Static_GetImage(hStatic, IMAGE_BITMAP);
HCURSOR cur = (HCURSOR)Static_GetImage(hStatic, IMAGE_CURSOR);
HENHMETAFILE mf = (HENHMETAFILE)Static_GetImage(hStatic, IMAGE_ENHMETAFILE);
HICON icon = (HICON)Static_GetImage(hStatic, IMAGE_ICON);
```

"Dynamic" Static Controls

Table 8.5: Static control notification codes

Notification Code	Meaning
STN_CLICKED	The mouse has been clicked in the static control.
STN_DBLCLK	The mouse has been double-clicked in the static control.
STN_DISABLE	The control has been disabled.
STN_ENABLE	The control has been enabled.

By tradition, a "static" control does not respond to mouse or keyboard input or notify its parent of such events. This nonresponsiveness was the reason for the original choice of the class name, "STATIC". This name choice did not stand the test of time. In fact, static controls are a handy way to mark off a space in a dialog, and by subclassing them you can intercept the mouse and keyboard messages and send notifications to the parent. One common use of static controls was to implement some sort of custom owner-draw control that needed to respond to mouse clicks in a fashion more sophisticated than an owner-draw button could. So static controls were enhanced at API level 4 to actually provide responses to certain mouse messages. While this violates the name of the control, the name should now be considered a quaint historical artifact retained for compatibility. Static controls can respond to mouse clicks and send notifications to their parents. To enable this feature, you must create the static control with the SS_NOTIFY style. Windows created with this style will respond to mouse input by returning one of the notifications by the WM_COMMAND message. These notifications are shown in Table 8.5 . Static controls respond to a limited number of messages. Table 8.6 shows the methods that apply to static controls. Not all messages will work with all control styles.

Table 8.6: Messages understood by a static control

Message	Function Description
STM_GETICON	HICON Static_GetIcon(HWND hwnd, HICON icon)[1]
	Returns the handle to the icon displayed in the static control.
STM_GETIMAGE	HANDLE Static_GetImage(HWND hwnd, int imagetype)[e]
	Returns the handle to the bitmap, icon, cursor, or enhanced metafile displayed in the static control.
STM_SETICON	HICON Static_SetIcon(HWND hwnd, HICON icon)
	Sets the icon that will be displayed in the static control. It must have an SS_ICON style.

[1]Note the strange feature that the Static_GetIcon function actually requires an icon parameter. This is in spite of the fact that the underlying message does not require such a parameter and, in fact, the parameter is not used. This bug has been present in all releases of windowsx.h and is apparently retained for backward bug compatibility. Just use NULL for the parameter value.

[e]Defined in extensions.h.

Table 8.6: Messages understood by a static control

Message	Function Description
STM_SETIMAGE	`Static_SetImage(HWND hwnd, int imagetype, HANDLE himage)`[e]
	Sets the bitmap, icon, cursor, or enhanced metafile to be displayed in the static control. The control must have the SS_BITMAP, SS_ICON, or SS_ENHMETAFILE style.
WM_ENABLE	`BOOL Static_Enable(HWND hwnd, BOOL enable)`
	Enables or disables the static control.
WM_GETFONT	`HFONT GetWindowFont(HWND hwnd)`
	Obtains the handle of the font used to draw the text.
WM_GETTEXT	`int Static_GetText(HWND hwnd, LPTSTR buff, UINT chMax) ;`
	Copies the text from a static control. The control must have a style that supports text. Returns the length of the string returned.
WM_GETTEXTLENGTH	`int Static_GetTextLength(HWND hwnd)`
	Returns the length of the text.
WM_SETFONT	`void SetWindowFont(HWND hwnd, HFONT font)`
	Sets the handle of the font used to draw the text.
WM_SETTEXT	`BOOL Static_SetText(HWND hwnd, LPCTSTR buff) ;`
	Sets the text for a static control. It must have a text style.
WM_SHOWWINDOW	`BOOL ShowWindow(HWND hwnd, UINT show)`
	Shows or hides the window.

[1] Note the strange feature that the `Static_GetIcon` function actually requires an `icon` parameter. This is in spite of the fact that the underlying message does not require such a parameter and, in fact, the parameter is not used. This bug has been present in all releases of `windowsx.h` and is apparently retained for backward bug compatibility. Just use NULL for the parameter value.
[e] Defined in `extensions.h`.

Owner-draw Static Controls

A common reason for subclassing a static control in Windows 3.*x* was to use it as some sort of custom control, usually a custom display control. Subclassing was the only way you could intercept the WM_PAINT message and handle it. This is no longer necessary at API level 4 and higher. Now you can use the SS_OWNERDRAW style. When you create a static control with this style, the control will send a WM_DRAWITEM message to the parent whenever the control needs to be redrawn. You handle the WM_DRAWITEM with an On-DrawItem handler (described more thoroughly on page 553). The CtlType field of the DRAWITEMSTRUCT has the code ODT_STATIC.

WM_DRAWITEM Message Cracker Handler (See page 552.)

```
void cls_OnDrawItem(HWND hwnd, const DRAWITEMSTRUCT * dis);
```

We can use the same reflection technique described on page 553 to avoid introducing the need for the parent to understand the child control.

In the case of static controls, there is an additional consideration. The STATIC class, like most of the control classes, is registered with the CS_PARENTDC class style (see Chapter 3, page 111). This means that the clipping region of the control is set to the clipping region of its parent, and therefore nothing prevents you from "coloring outside the lines"–that is, changing pixels outside the client area of the static control. However, the actions which *erase* the contents of the static control, such as calling InvalidateRect with a TRUE parameter, erase only the client area. This means that you either must be very careful to never draw outside the client area, or you must explicitly set a clipping region to a size no greater than the client area. We actually had to do this in the Font Explorer, because we could not control how font scaling handled the nonlinear scaling to very large sizes. The result was that some character pixels were drawn outside our custom static control.

Simple Frame Example

The following example creates a "black" frame static control. The control ID is set to the arbitrary value –1. Static controls without the SS_NOTIFY style don't send WM_COMMAND messages to their parent window, so a unique control ID usually isn't needed.

```
HWND hFrame ;
hFrame = CreateWindow (
    _T("static"), NULL,
    100, 200, 70, 40, hwnd, -1, hInstance, NULL) ;
```

The BUTTON Class

You typically create controls from the BUTTON class when you want to get a notification that the user has requested a specific action (a "push button"), or you want to accept two-valued input such as active/inactive, enabled/disabled, on/off, and yes/no. A BUTTON class window is a window that can optionally have a label. The user can click a mouse button over this window to set and unset the button. Some buttons change appearance as the user presses and releases a mouse button. Other buttons change appearance to reflect their set/unset state.

BUTTON Class Styles

Once you've chosen the BUTTON class for a control, you must select the particular style of button best suited for the task. There are 11 styles of buttons. To create a specific button style, you create a window of class BUTTON and specify the WS_CHILD window style plus the appropriate button style from Table 8.7. You should bitwise OR the WS_CHILD flag with one of these styles.

Table 8.7: BUTTON class control styles

Style	API	Description
BS_AUTOCHECKBOX	3,4	A check box-style button ☐ ☒ that automatically toggles its state when clicked.
BS_AUTORADIOBUTTON	3,4	A radio button-style button ○ ● that automatically sets the state of the button that is clicked and removes the check marks from all other radio buttons in its group.
BS_AUTO3STATE	3,4	A three-state-style button that automatically toggles through each of the three states ☐ ☒ ■ when clicked.
BS_BITMAP	4	The button displays as a bitmap.
BS_BOTTOM	4	The text displays at the bottom of the button rectangle.
BS_CENTER	4	The text is centered horizontally in the button rectangle.
BS_CHECKBOX	3,4	A small square button ☐. The rectangle is empty when not checked, and the button label is drawn to the right of the button. When checked, an X is drawn in the box ☒. Unlike a BS_AUTOCHECKBOX, the box does not change state automatically when activated.
BS_DEFPUSHBUTTON	3,4	A push button-style button drawn with a thick border that indicates the default choice.
BS_FLAT	4	Button is drawn in a "flat", rather than 3D, style.
BS_GROUPBOX	3,4	A rectangular frame surrounds (boxes in) a group of other controls. (It is not clear why this is a variety of "button"; it is actually a static control.)
BS_ICON	4	The button displays an icon.
BS_LEFT	4	The button text is left-justified in the rectangle. If the button is a radio button or check box without the BS_RIGHTBUTTON style, the text is left-justified to the right of the button.
BS_LEFTTEXT	3,4	An additional qualification of the BS_CHECKBOX, BS_RADIOBUTTON, and BS_3STATE styles. This style specifies that the text of a radio button or check box should appear on the left side of the button rather than on the default right side.
BS_MULTILINE	4	Indicates that the button will wrap long text into multiple lines if necessary in order to display the text.
BS_NOTIFY	4	Allows the button to send BN_DBLCLK, BN_SETFOCUS, and BN_KILLFOCUS notifications. A button will always send a BN_CLICKED notification independent of this style.

Table 8.7: BUTTON class control styles

Style	API	Description
BS_OWNERDRAW	3,4	A button drawn by its parent window rather than by the button window function. The button notifies its parent window when the button is clicked and when it must be drawn, inverted, and disabled.
BS_PUSHBUTTON	3,4	A small rectangular push button. The rectangle surrounds the label text.
BS_PUSHLIKE	4	Causes the button to behave like a push button. The button looks raised when it isn't pushed or checked and depressed when it is pushed or checked.
BS_RADIOBUTTON	3,4	A small circular button. ◯ The circle is filled ⦿ when the button is checked. You should group two or more radio buttons to represent mutually exclusive options. Unlike a BS_AUTORADIOBUTTON, activating this button does not affect either the button state or the state of any buttons in the group.
BS_RIGHT	4	The button text is right-justified in the rectangle. If the button is a radio button or check box without the BS_RIGHTBUTTON style, the text is right-justified to the right of the button.
BS_RIGHTBUTTON	4	An additional qualification of the BS_CHECKBOX, BS_RADIOBUTTON, and BS_3STATE styles. This style specifies that the text of a radio button or check box should appear on the left side of the button rather than on the default right side. Same as BS_LEFTTEXT.
BS_TEXT	3,4	The button displays as text. This is the default style if you don't otherwise specify a style.
BS_3STATE	3,4	This button looks like a check box with an additional state: unchecked (empty rectangle) ☐, checked (X in rectangle) ☒, and gray (solid gray rectangle) ▨. Unlike a BS_AUTO3STATE, this button does not automatically toggle through its states.
BS_TOP	4	Specifies that the text displays at the top of the button rectangle.
BS_VCENTER	4	The text is centered vertically in the button rectangle.

Modern Windows interfaces favor a "3D" style that is an attractive variant of the conventional "flat" style. However, the various versions of the CTL3D library used before API level 4 do not support the BS_LEFTTEXT style. You should try to avoid this style in your applications if you expect them to run on API level 3.

CTL3D

Table 8.8: Styles that can be changed dynamically

Style Flag	Changes
BS_BITMAP	Change with SetWindowLong(...GWL_STYLE,...).
BS_BOTTOM	Change with SetWindowLong(...GWL_STYLE,...). See note 1.
BS_CENTER	Change with SetWindowLong(...GWL_STYLE,...). See note 1.
BS_ICON	Change with SetWindowLong(...GWL_STYLE,...).
BS_LEFT	Change with SetWindowLong(...GWL_STYLE,...). See note 1.
BS_TEXT	Change with SetWindowLong(...GWL_STYLE,...).
BS_NOTIFY	Change with SetWindowLong(...GWL_STYLE,...).
BS_MULTILINE	Change with SetWindowLong(...GWL_STYLE,...).
BS_RIGHT	Change with SetWindowLong(...GWL_STYLE,...). See note 1.
BS_TOP	Change with SetWindowLong(...GWL_STYLE,...). See note 1.
BS_VCENTER	Change with SetWindowLong(...GWL_STYLE,...). See note 1.
WS_DISABLED	Change with EnableWindow.
WS_VISIBLE	Change with ShowWindow using SW_SHOW or SW_HIDE.

[1]After changing the text alignment style, you need to call InvalidateRect on the control to cause the control to redraw. In addition, for some controls (notably the group box), you must invalidate the parent window's rectangle. Use GetWindowRect to determine the screen coordinates of the control and then use ScreenToClient with the parent specified as the client in order to obtain the coordinates of the control in the parent. Then invalidate this rectangle in the control's parent window.

A button is modified by sending it messages. The complete set of button messages is shown in Table 8.9. Not all messages apply to all button styles; the applicability of a message to a particular button style is summarized in Table 8.11. A button notifies its parent of events by sending its parent a WM_COMMAND message with a notification code indicating the type of event. The notification codes are summarized in Table 8.10.

Table 8.9: Messages understood by a button control

Message	Function Description
BM_CLICK[4]	HANDLE Button_Click(HWND hwnd)[e]
	Simulates the user's clicking the button. The button receives a WM_LBUTTONDOWN message followed by a WM_LBUTTONUP message, which causes the parent to receive a BN_CLICKED notification.

[4]Available only at API level 4 and higher.
[e]These macros are defined our extensions.h file.

Table 8.9: Messages understood by a button control

Message	Function Description
BM_GETCHECK	`int Button_GetCheck(HWND hwnd)`
	Returns the checked state of the button for those buttons that have a checked state. This will be either BST_CHECKED or BST_UNCHECKED. For those buttons supporting a three-state condition, it also can be BST_INDETERMINATE.
BM_GETIMAGE[4]	`HANDLE Button_GetImage(HWND hwnd, int imagetype)`[e]
	Returns the handle to the bitmap, icon, cursor, or enhanced metafile displayed in the button control.
BM_GETSTATE	`int Button_GetState(HWND hwnd)`
	Returns a value that represents the button state. This value includes the information returned by BM_GETCHECK.
BM_SETCHECK	`void Button_SetCheck(HWND hwnd, int state)`
	Sets the checked state of the button for those buttons that have a checked state. This will be either BST_CHECKED or BST_UNCHECKED. For those buttons supporting a three-state condition, it will be BST_INDETERMINATE.
BM_SETIMAGE[4]	`BM_SETIMAGE`[4] `HANDLE Button_SetImage (HWND hwnd, int imagetype, HANDLE himage)`[e]
	Sets the specified image (bitmap, icon, cursor, or enhanced metafile) in the button control.
BM_SETSTATE	`UINT Button_SetState(HWND hwnd, UINT state)`
	Sets the button highlight state. Note that although the name suggests that this should allow you to set the same state values that are returned by BM_GETSTATE, BM_GETSTATE and BM_SETSTATE are not symmetric operations. The BM_SETSTATE message applies only to buttons that support a highlight state.
BM_SETSTYLE	`void Button_SetStyle(HWND hwnd, USHORT style, BOOL redraw)`
	Changes the style of a button. If the redraw parameter is TRUE, the button is immediately redrawn; otherwise, there is no immediate redraw.
WM_ENABLE	`BOOL Button_Enable(HWND hwnd, BOOL enabled)`
	Enables or disables the button. Returns the previous value of the enabled state.
WM_GETTEXT	`int Button_GetText(HWND hwnd, LPTSTR buffer, int count)`
	Retrieves the text of the button. Returns the actual number of characters copied.

[4]Available only at API level 4 and higher.
[e]These macros are defined our extensions.h file.

Table 8.9: Messages understood by a button control

Message	Function Description
WM_SETTEXT	BOOL Button_SetText(HWND hwnd, LPCTSTR buffer)
	Sets the text of the button.

[4]Available only at API level 4 and higher.
[e]These macros are defined our extensions.h file.

Any active button can send a BN_CLICKED notification to its parent window using the WM_COMMAND message. Table 8.10 lists the button notification codes. To get any of the other button notifications, you must create the button with the BS_NOTIFY style.

A *push button* is a small rectangular window. The frame of the window surrounds the button's label, which the button normally displays centered within its border. A push button uses the window name parameter specified in the CreateWindow function call as the label for the button. You can change the label of a button control by calling the SetWindowText function:

Table 8.10: Button notification messages

Notification Code	BS_NOTIFY style?	Meaning
BN_CLICKED	*Not required*	Button has been clicked.
BN_DBLCLK[1]	*Required*	Button has been double-clicked.
BN_SETFOCUS	*Required*	Button has received focus.
BN_KILLFOCUS	*Required*	Button has lost focus.

[1]BN_DBLCLK is the "new" name that replaces the "obsolete" name BN_DOUBLECLICKED.

BOOL SetWindowText (HWND hwnd, LPCTSTR NewLabel) ;

Any button can have one of the label position styles associated with it, although push buttons are the most common use. In Win32 4.*x*, you can cause the text to be left-, right-, bottom-, or top-justified, or you can just use the default center-horizontally and center-vertically alignment. In addition, a button control in Win32 4.*x* can be multiline. Table 8.14 summarizes the alignment options of Table 8.7.

Traditionally, the only message of any interest generated by a push button was BN_CLICKED. Thus most programmers and most books took the receipt of *any* WM_COMMAND message for a button as being equivalent to the receipt of a BN_CLICKED notification. This is a dangerous practice. Some of the new control styles cause various kinds of button notifications to be sent to the parent. For example, one new style that embeds push buttons in list controls sends a notification for the button that is *not* BN_CLICKED. Do not shortcut the precise specification of the notification. *Always* check for BN_CLICKED.

The button state can be set with either of two messages. The BM_SETCHECK message (Button_SetCheck function) lets you set the checked status of any button that has a checked state, that is, a check box or radio button. The BM_SETSTATE message (Button_SetState function) lets you set only the highlight state. You can determine the checked state of a button using the BM_GETCHECK message (Button_GetCheck function), which returns one of the values shown in Table 8.16 (page 547). The button state, which includes more than just the highlight state, can be read with the BM_GETSTATE message (Button_GetState function).

Table 8.11: Applicability of button messages for various button styles

Button Style	Message							
	BM_CLICK	BM_GETCHECK	BM_GETIMAGE	BM_GETSTATE	BM_SETCHECK	BM_SETIMAGE	BM_SETSTATE	BM_SETSTYLE
BS_AUTOCHECKBOX	✓	✓	✓	✓	✓	✓	✓	✓
BS_AUTORADIOBUTTON	✓	✓	✓	✓	✓	✓	✓	✓
BS_AUTO3STATE	✓	✓	✓	✓	✓	✓	✓	✓
BS_CHECKBOX	✓	✓	✓	✓	✓	✓	✓	✓
BS_DEFPUSHBUTTON	✓		✓	✓		✓	✓	✓
BS_FLAT	✓		✓	✓		✓	✓	✓
BS_GROUPBOX	✓[1]		✓	✓		✓		✓
BS_OWNERDRAW[2]	✓		✓	✓		✓		✓
BS_PUSHBUTTON	✓		✓	✓		✓	✓	✓
BS_RADIOBUTTON	✓	✓	✓	✓	✓	✓	✓	✓
BS_3STATE	✓	✓	✓	✓	✓	✓	✓	✓

[1]You can actually send a BM_CLICK message to a group box, and it will send its parent a BN_CLICKED notification!

[2]For messages that are not handled by the default button handler for owner-draw buttons, you can subclass the button control and handle these messages in your subclass message handler.

Using the result of the BM_GETSTATE message can be a bit tricky for values that require more than one bit to represent the value. Typically, you will use one of the BST_ symbols shown in Table 8.12 and AND it with the result of the BM_GETSTATE query. The result of this combination can then be compared to a known value, such as 0. Note carefully how parentheses were used!

You may notice that Microsoft does not provide a symbolic constant for the mask value needed for extracting the bits so you can test for the checked, unchecked, or indeterminate states. This is an unfortunate omission. Microsoft officially documents the mask value as 0x0003.

Table 8.12: Masks and values for examining the BM_GETSTATE result

Mask Value	Resulting Values	Meaning
0x0003	BST_CHECKED	Button is in the checked state.
	BST_UNCHECKED	Button is in the unchecked state.
	BST_INDETERMINATE	Button is in the indeterminate state.
BST_FOCUS	0	Button does not have the input focus.
	BST_FOCUS	Button has the input focus.
BST_PUSHED	0	Button is not pushed.
	BST_PUSHED	Button is pushed.

```
int flags = Button_GetState(hbutton);
if( (flags & 0x0003) == BST_CHECKED)
    // do something here if checked
if( (flags & 0x0003) == BST_INDETERMINATE)
    // do something here if indeterminate
if( (flags & BST_FOCUS != 0)
    // do something here if button has focus
```

Button Control Notification Messages

A button control sends a WM_COMMAND message with a notification code to its parent window. The ctlid parameter to the OnCommand handler contains the button control ID. The hctl parameter contains the window handle of the button control. The notifycode parameter contains the notification code. Table 8.13 lists the possible button notification codes. Note that nearly all are obsolete. You might encounter these codes only in an older Windows 3.*x* application that you are porting to Win32.

Problems with Buttons and the Input Focus

We mentioned earlier in the chapter that Windows sends keyboard input to the window with the input focus. This will be the top-level active window or a child window of the active window. A push button, check box, radio button, or owner-draw button receives the input focus when the user clicks the button. This is accomplished by the window function for the BUTTON class responding to the WM_LBUTTONDOWN event by performing a SetFocus operation to itself. There is no magic here; Windows doesn't know the mouse clicked on a button. Only the button itself causes the focus shift. Once a button control has the input focus, Windows sends all keyboard input directly to the control. The BUTTON controls process only one key press: the press and release of the space bar. Doing this key press is equivalent to clicking the button. The button sends a WM_COMMAND message to its parent with a notification code of BN_CLICKED. However, an interesting problem arises here.

Table 8.13: Button control notification messages

Notification Code	Meaning
BN_CLICKED	The user has clicked a button.
BN_DBLCLK	The user has double-clicked a button. To see this notification requires the BS_NOTIFY style flag.
BN_DISABLE	Obsolete. Use the BS_OWNERDRAW button style and process the WM_DRAWITEM message to draw the button in the proper state.
BN_DOUBLECLICKED	Obsolete; use BN_DBLCLK.
BN_HILITE	Obsolete; see BN_DISABLE.
BN_PAINT	Obsolete; see BN_DISABLE.
BN_UNHILITE	Obsolete; see BN_DISABLE.
BN_SETFOCUS	Button has received the focus. To see this notification requires the BS_NOTIFY style flag.
BN_KILLFOCUS	Button has lost the focus. To see this notification requires the BS_NOTIFY style flag.

Because all keyboard input flows to the control, once it has the input focus and the button control processes only the space bar key press (and then only to simulate clicking the button), you are left with the question of how you can use the keyboard to switch the input focus away from one button to another. The control would need to process at least one more key press, say the **Tab** key, in order to detect a request to give away the input focus. The answer is that you can't–at least, not directly.

One way out of this dilemma is through subclassing. You subclass the control in order to process the WM_CHAR message for the **Tab** key. When you receive the **Tab** key press message, you can set the focus to a different control by calling the SetFocus function. One advantage to using dialog boxes as opposed to creating controls yourself is that the dialog box function supports tabbing from control to control. Once again, Windows does the messy work for you. But you can get your hands dirty, if you wish.

Handling Input Focus Changes in Child Windows

The way you handle the input focus change in a control's subclass handler using the **Tab** key is to use the GetNextDlgTabItem function. This will give you the next control (or previous control) that has the WS_TABSTOP style:

HWND GetNextDlgTabItem(HWND hdlg, HWND hctl, BOOL previous)

This function gives the next control (if previous is FALSE) or previous control (if previous is TRUE) within the parent window. Although the name and documentation suggest that the parent window is a dialog, this function can apply to *any* window with child controls. So all you have to do in your subclass handler is call this function and you will get the appropriate window. The control that is returned must be enabled and visible as well. If there is no such control, the `hctl` value is returned, a condition you must check for. If `hctl` is `NULL`, the search starts at the first child window of the parent. The window list is treated as if it were circular. That is, if `hctl` is the last window in the Z-order, a forward search will proceed to the first window in the Z-order list. This is different than searching for the next child, such as by using `GetWindow` with the `GW_HWNDNEXT` option. In this case, if you asked for the next sibling of the last window, using `GetWindow` with the `GW_HWNDNEXT` option would return `NULL`. The predecessor of the first child window is the last child window.

Once you have the handle of the desired control, you can use the `SetFocus` function to change the focus to that control.

`GetNextDlgGroupItem` is a similar function to `GetNextDlgTabItem`, except that it looks for a control with the `WS_GROUP` attribute:

`HWND GetNextDlgGroupItem(HWND hdlg, HWND hctl, BOOL previous)`

Like `GetNextDlgTabItem`, this function returns the first control in the group that is visible and enabled. It works like this. First, it searches in the specified direction for a control with the `WS_GROUP` style. Then, it reverses its direction and searches within that group for the first control that is visible and enabled. If it encounters another `WS_GROUP` control before finding a visible, enabled control, it returns to the `WS_GROUP` control that started the reverse search and proceeds in the original direction, repeating this process for every `WS_GROUP` control it encounters. If it does not find a suitable control, it returns the `hctl` parameter, which you must check for. If you specify `NULL` for `hctl`, it will start with the first control in the parent window. Although the documentation explicitly talks about "dialog window", there is nothing that constrains you from applying this function to any window that has child controls. In a forward search, a control that follows `hctl` and has the `WS_GROUP` style indicates the start of the *next* group, while in a reverse search, a control with the `WS_GROUP` style is considered part of the *current* group.

You should now appreciate that there is nothing *really* special about a dialog; all the primitives you need to implement one are already present. A dialog is just a nice package that does a lot of the tedious work for you. But don't be misled by function names that suggest they work only on dialogs; they work for *any* window with child controls.

Push Buttons

You typically use push buttons to trigger an immediate action. Each time the user clicks the button, a push button sends a `WM_COMMAND` message with a notification code of `BN_CLICKED` to its parent window. A push button does not have multiple states as do other kinds of buttons. A push button can only be pushed; it cannot be checked, unchecked, or grayed. (It can, however, be *disabled*, which causes its text to display in a user-defined color selected by the Control Panel. This color is usually gray.) In Win32 4.*x*, if you specify the `BS_NOTIFY` style, you can get any of the additional notifications specified in Table 8.10 (page 539).

A *default push button* works the same as a regular push button when used in the client area of a window. (It works slightly differently when used in a dialog box.) The button window function draws a default push button with a heavier border than it uses when drawing a regular push button. You can see this in Figure 8.3.

Table 8.14: Button alignment styles

Styles	Meaning
Vertical Styles: Choose One	
BS_BOTTOM	The text is bottom-aligned in the control rectangle.
BS_TOP	The text is top-aligned in the control rectangle.
BS_VCENTER	The text is vertically centered in the control rectangle.
Horizontal Styles: Choose One	
BS_CENTER	The text is horizontally centered in the control rectangle.
BS_LEFT	The text is left-justified in the control rectangle.
BS_RIGHT	The text is right-justified in the control rectangle.
Additional Styles	
BS_MULTILINE	Text will be wrapped onto multiple lines if it is too wide.

You have probably seen both push buttons and default push buttons when an application needs an immediate answer to a question. Figure 8.3 shows three buttons: one default push button (the button labeled "Yes") and two ordinary push buttons. We show in Chapter 11 how to use the dialog message DM_SETDEFID to change the default push button dynamically.

The following code creates a default push button control and an ordinary push button control:

```
HWND hDefPushbutton ;
HWND hPushbutton ;

hDefPushbutton = CreateWindow (
    _T("button"), _T("OK"),
    WS_CHILD | WS_VISIBLE | BS_DEFPUSHBUTTON
    100, 200, 70, 40, hwnd, IDOK, hInstance, NULL) ;

hPushbutton = CreateWindow (
    _T("button"), _T("Cancel"),
    WS_CHILD | WS_VISIBLE | BS_PUSHBUTTON,
    100, 200, 70, 40, hwnd, IDCANCEL, hInstance, NULL) ;
```

The symbolic names IDOK and IDCANCEL are two of the symbolic names defined by windows.h. You typically use these codes for push buttons in a dialog box. Table 8.15 lists the complete set of codes. We use the predefined names as the button control IDs instead of making up an arbitrary value and symbolic name.

Both types of push buttons respond to the BM_SETSTATE message. You can simulate the appearance of a mouse button press on a push button by sending the BM_SETSTATE message to the button. When the wParam parameter of the message is nonzero, the button is highlighted. When the parameter is 0, the highlighting is removed. The following simulates the appearance of a click on the **Cancel** push button created earlier:

```
SendMessage (hPushbutton, BM_SETSTATE, TRUE, OL) ;
SendMessage (hPushbutton, BM_SETSTATE, FALSE, OL)
```

You can do this more clearly and simply using the Button_SetState control macro API. The following two statements produce exactly the same result as the preceding two statements, except the following more clearly describe their function and are simpler to write:

```
Button_SetState (hPushbutton, TRUE) ;
Button_SetState (hPushbutton, FALSE) ;
```

Table 8.15: Standard button codes

IDABORT
IDCANCEL
IDIGNORE
IDNO
IDOK
IDRETRY
IDYES

There is an apparent complementary message (BM_GETSTATE) and control macro API (Button_GetState) that queries the current state of a push button. However, while BM_SETSTATE can only set the highlighting state, the highlighting state of the button is only one of the many values returned by BM_GETSTATE (see Table 8.12 on page 541). The highlighting state of a push button is not too useful because a push button returns BST_PUSHED flag as nonzero only when the user is pressing the button at the time of the message.

Figure 8.3: A default push button and two push buttons

The BM_SETSTATE message controls only the appearance of the exterior of a button. It has no effect on the check state of a radio button or check box. Because this message controls only the *appearance* of the button being clicked, it does not actually cause the button to *behave* as if it had been clicked. To simulate the actual clicking of the push button, you use the BM_CLICK message or its corresponding Button_Click function. (This function is not defined in windowsx.h, but we define it for you in our extensions.h file.) When you send this message to a button, the button in turn sends itself a WM_LBUTTONDOWN message, followed by a WM_LBUTTONUP message. This results in the parent's receiving a BN_CLICKED notification. If you have subclassed the button and are handling your own responses to WM_LBUTTONDOWN and WM_LBUTTONUP, this will allow your code to respond as if the user had actually clicked the button.

Check Boxes

A *check box* is a special case of the BUTTON class. You can use a check box to allow a user to select options from your application. A check box displays as a square box with a label to one side. The default is to show the label to the right of the box. When you include the BS_LEFTTEXT button style along with the check box button style, the button displays its label to the left of the square box. (BS_LEFTTEXT is also known as the BS_RIGHTBUTTON. The name is a synonym for the same value.) You should use check boxes for options that are not mutually exclusive. You will typically use *radio buttons* for mutually exclusive options; see page 549.

However, you will often find cases in which check boxes are just the most intuitively obvious interface, except that there is some conflict. For example, selecting centered text precludes right-justified text or left-justified text, but you don't want to present the user with an odd mixture of check boxes and radio buttons (for example, you may want to present all the options in alphabetical order). In this case, you have to implement the exclusivity tests yourself. Similarly, you may find situations in which checking one option totally precludes the ability to check another option, although the "natural" presentation to the user is a set of check boxes. In this case, you have to deal with disabling the forbidden options when an overriding option is selected. Finally, there is the case in which you want to present the user with an apparent "flat" list of options, but choosing a particular option actually is the same as choosing three or five or some other combination of options. In this case, you must respond to the clicking of the "master" option value by checking or unchecking all the other options it controls and, if you want to be really clever, detecting when a sufficient set of suboptions have been selected so that you can check or uncheck the master option. You will encounter all of these specialized techniques in our various Explorer programs. We suggest reading the source code of the Explorers to discover a rich collection of GUI techniques and our favorite styles for keeping the complexity manageable.

Figure 8.4 shows three check box controls with labels describing their appearance. The check box styles are BS_CHECKBOX, BS_AUTOCHECKBOX, BS_3STATE, and BS_AUTO3STATE. The BS_CHECKBOX style creates a check box that supports two states, unchecked and checked. The BS_AUTOCHECKBOX style creates a check box that automatically toggles between these two states. The BS_3STATE style creates a check box that supports three states: unchecked, checked, and indeterminate, and the BS_AUTO3STATE style creates a check box that automatically toggles among these three states.

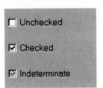

Figure 8.4: Three check box controls

A check box control sends its parent window a WM_COMMAND message with a notification code of BN_CLICKED when the user clicks the control or presses the space bar (when the control has the input focus). The BS_CHECKBOX and BS_3STATE style check boxes do not change appearance as the user clicks the check box. Only the AUTO styles automatically change appearance.

If you specify the BS_NOTIFY style, you can get any of the additional notifications specified in Table 8.10.

When you want the appearance of the BS_CHECKBOX and BS_3STATE style controls to reflect their current state, you must send a BM_SETCHECK message to the control. The BM_SETCHECK message tells the control to display the check box as unchecked, checked, or indeterminate. Table 8.16 lists the possible settings. You can also use the Button_SetCheck API wrapper from windowsx.h.

```
int prev = (int)SendMessage(hbutton, WM_SETCHECK, checkstate, 0)
// or
int prev = Button_SetCheck(hbutton, checkstate);
```

When the wParam parameter of the BM_SETCHECK message or the checkstate parameter of Button_SetCheck is BST_CHECKED, an X or check mark is placed in the check box. Any X or check mark is removed when the parameter is BST_UNCHECKED. For three-state check boxes, the parameter value

BST_CHECKED places an X or check mark in the check box. A parameter value BST_INDETERMINATE grays the check box. A value of BST_UNCHECKED returns the control to its normal (unchecked and ungrayed) state.

Table 8.16: Check box settings

BM_SETCHECK wParam **Value**	**Button Style**			
	BS_CHECKBOX BS_AUTOCHECKBOX		BS_3STATE BS_AUTO3STATE	
BST_UNCHECKED	Unchecked	☐☐	Unchecked	☐☐
BST_CHECKED	Checked	☒☑	Checked	☒☑
BST_INDETERMINATE	Checked	☒☑	Grayed	☐☐

There is a compatibility problem between API level 3 and API level 4. In API level 3, *any* nonzero value for a non–three-state check box would turn on the check mark. This was not consistent with the specification, but it worked. At API level 4, the requirement is much more precise. You must adhere to the specification. To set the check box as checked, value *must* be BST_CHECKED. This means that the following lines of code work in API level 3 and fail in API level 4:

```
#define FUNNYBIT 0x4000
Button_SetCheck(hButton, flags & FUNNYBIT);
```

For API level 4, you must recode it as

```
Button_SetCheck(hButton, (flags & FUNNYBIT) ? BST_CHECKED : BST_UNCHECKED);
```

If check boxes refuse to set properly when you run an application on Windows 95 or Windows NT 4.*x*, this is the most likely cause.

The following code creates and marks as indeterminate a three-state check box button:

```
HWND hCheckBox3 ;

hCheckBox3 = CreateWindow
    _T("button"), _T("Direction"),
    WS_CHILD | WS_VISIBLE | BS_3STATE,
    100, 200, 70, 40, hwnd, IDS_DIRECTION, hInstance, NULL) ;

SendMessage (hCheckBox3, BM_SETCHECK, BST_INDETERMINATE, OL) ;
```

You should use the Button_SetCheck control macro API rather than SendMessage to check a button. This statement is equivalent to the preceding one:

```
Button_SetCheck ( hCheckBox3, BST_INDETERMINATE) ;
```

For a button with the BS_CHECKBOX style, you have to change the state yourself. The following function can be used to toggle among the states of a BS_CHECKBOX or BS_3STATE button:

```
void toggleCheck(HWND hctl)
{
  switch(Button_GetState(hctl) & 0x0003)
    {
      case BST_CHECKED:
          if(GetStyle(hctl) & 0xF) == BS_3STATE)
              Button_SetCheck(hctl, BST_INDETERMINATE);
```

```
        else
            Button_SetCheck(hctl, BST_UNCHECKED);
        return;
    case BST_UNCHECKED:
        Button_SetCheck(hctl, BST_CHECKED);
        return;
    case BST_INDETERMINATE:
        Button_SetCheck(hctl, BST_UNCHECKED);
        return;
    }
}
```

Many times, you don't need this extra control over the appearance of a check box. It's also a bit more work to track the state of a check box and send it the proper messages so that its appearance matches its state. That's the time to use the BS_AUTOCHECKBOX and BS_AUTO3STATE styles. These check boxes work exactly as described here except that the button checks, unchecks, or sets itself indeterminate as the user clicks it.

You may still want to initially place a check mark in an automatically checked check box. You do it exactly the same as before: Send a BM_SETCHECK message to the control, preferably by using the control macro API:

```
SendMessage (hCheckBox, BM_SETSTATECHECK, BST_CHECKED, 0) ;

Button_SetCheck (hCheckBox, BST_CHECKED) ;
```

You will often use a three-state button to reflect the state of some multiple subcontrols. An example might be a control in a virus-checking program that says "Check drives". We will call this the "main control". This main control has two subselections, "Check floppy drives" and "Check hard drives". If you click the main control off, you would like to turn off the check marks in the two sub-controls as well. If you click on the main control, you also want to turn on check marks in the two subcontrols. But if you click one of the subcontrols on or off such that both are not checked, you want to set the main control to indicate a "partial" selection by using its third, "indeterminate", state. In such a case, the subcontrols will usually have the BS_AUTOCHECKBOX style and the main selection will have the BS_AUTO3STATE style. We give a specification of the desired behavior of these three buttons in Table 8.17. Note that we don't show all eight possible states. This is because we don't allow any state that has the "Virus check" button unchecked but one of the drive type buttons checked. Note that we have carefully chosen our behavior so that the act of clicking the main button, which we have made BS_AUTO3STATE, is to toggle it to its initial (unchecked) state.

Table 8.17: A specification of a three-state control example

Initial Button State			Action	New Button State		
Virus Check	Floppy	Hard	Click Which Button?	Virus Check	Floppy	Hard
☐	☐	☐	Virus Check	☒	☒	☒
☐	☐	☐	Floppy	▣	☒	☐
☐	☐	☐	Hard	▣	☐	☒
▣	☐	☒	Virus Check	☐	☐	☐

Table 8.17: A specification of a three-state control example

Initial Button State			Action	New Button State		
Virus Check	Floppy	Hard	Click Which Button?	Virus Check	Floppy	Hard
▣	☐	☒	Floppy	☒	☒	☒
▣	☐	☒	Hard	☐	☐	☐
▣	☒	☐	Virus Check	☐	☐	☐
▣	☒	☐	Floppy	☐	☐	☐
▣	☒	☐	Hard	☒	☒	☒
▣	☒	☒	Virus Check	☐	☐	☐
▣	☒	☒	Floppy	▣	☐	☒
▣	☒	☒	Hard	▣	☒	☐

Radio Buttons

Radio buttons are another special case of the BUTTON class. Radio button controls are quite similar to check box controls except that a radio button is circular ○, whereas a check box is square ☐. A radio button indicates that it is checked by displaying a solid dot in the center of the circle ◉. You typically create a *group* of radio buttons to allow the user to select one item from a collection of mutually exclusive choices. Radio buttons are named after the mechanical push buttons originally used in car radios. Pushing down one of the station selection buttons releases any other button previously pressed. In modern car radios, the buttons are done electronically, but years ago they were implemented by elaborate physical interlocks.

Figure 8.5 shows four radio buttons with one checked. A typical use of a radio button would be to indicate the direction to search (forward or backward) in a word processing application. By now, you should expect to create such a radio button with the following statement:

```
#define IDC_BACKWARD    10
#define IDC_FORWARD     11

HWND hBackwardButton ;
HWND hForwardButton ;

hBackwardButton = CreateWindow(_T("Button"),     // class name
                    _T("Backward"),   // caption
                    WS_CHILD | WS_VISIBLE | WS_TABSTOP | WS_GROUP,
                    100, 200, 70, 15,
                    hwnd,
                    (HMENU)IDC_BACKWARD,
                    hInstance,
                    NULL);
hForwardButton = CreateWindow(_T("Button"),     // class name
```

```
                              _T("Forward"),  // caption
                              WS_CHILD | WS_VISIBLE | WS_TABSTOP | WS_GROUP
                              100, 220, 70, 15,
                              hwnd,
                              (HMENU)IDC_FORWARD,
                              hInstance,
                              NULL);
```

Like a check box, a radio button sends its parent window a
WM_COMMAND message with a notification code of BN_CLICKED
when the user clicks the button. For a BS_RADIOBUTTON style,
you must send a BM_SETCHECK message to the radio button to
request it to display the "check mark" (which is actually a black
dot):

Figure 8.5: Three radio buttons

```
SendMessage (hBackwardButton, BM_SETCHECK,
                    BST_CHECKED, 0L) ;
```

Because each radio button in a group represents a mutually ex-
clusive option, you should also send BM_SETCHECK messages to all other radio buttons in the group to ensure
that their check marks are off. For this example, you uncheck the excluded option by using

```
SendMessage (hForwardButton, BM_SETCHECK, BST_UNCHECKED, 0L) ;   /* or */
```

```
Button_SetCheck (hForwardButton, BST_UNCHECKED) ;
```

This becomes inconvenient to code, so there is a special function, CheckRadioButton, that takes a range of
values representing the control IDs of the buttons in the group, and the ID of the button to be checked. All
buttons whose IDs are in the range, except the one to be checked, have their states set to BST_UNCHECKED;
then the selected button has its state set to BST_CHECKED. To use this, you give the window handle of the parent window that contains the radio buttons; for example, the state of Figure 8.5 was set by:

```
BOOL result = CheckRadioButton(hparent, ID_TOO_HOT, ID_TOO_COLD, ID_TOO_HOT);
```

The first parameter is the handle of the parent window. The second parameter is the control ID of the lowest-
numbered radio button in the group. The third parameter is the control ID of the highest-numbered radio
button in the group. The fourth parameter is the control ID of the radio button that is to be checked.

You typically use the BS_AUTORADIOBUTTON style for radio buttons in a dialog box. When all the radio buttons in a group within a dialog box have the BS_AUTORADIOBUTTON style, Windows automatically unchecks
the previously checked radio button when the user clicks an unchecked button. Windows determines what a
"group" is by searching backward through the controls, looking for a radio button with the WS_GROUP flag
set. It remembers this control as the start of the group. Windows next searches forward, looking for a control
with a WS_GROUP flag set. This marks the start of the next group, so the last control before this is considered
to be the end of the current group. Windows will turn off all radio buttons in the group except the one that
was clicked, which it turns on. By convention, a group box often follows the set of radio buttons and is of a
size to enclose the radio buttons. A group box is a button. It typically has the WS_GROUP flag set (although
this is not required, as you will see). However, you don't need a group box to do a grouping of controls. Actually, a group box is merely a decorative effect.

We've talked about how Windows searches the group in both directions. But we need to define precisely the notion of "backward" and "forward". For a dialog, this order is the order based on that in which the controls appear in the DIALOG resource (see Chapter 11). Independent of the actual *numbering* of the radio buttons, their placement in the dialog determines which one is "first" and which one is "last" in the group. The first button must have the WS_GROUP and WS_TABSTOP styles. You can change this order either by modifying the resource file in which you define the dialog or by using one of the many development environment "resource editors". Most resource editors have an option to set the *tab order*. If you are not using a dialog resource to create the controls, the tab order is the order in which the CreateWindow calls are performed. You can change this order dynamically by using the SetWindowPos function and specifying which window is to precede the window being moved. However, it is extremely unusual to do this. If you do, you are responsible for "moving" the WS_GROUP and WS_TABSTOP styles to the correct "first" control in the group.

The CheckRadioButton function we introduced earlier in this section allows you to check a radio button while simultaneously unchecking some or all other buttons in a dialog box. For example, a group of controls can represent the four cardinal directions–north, east, south, west–with control IDs assigned in that order. The following statement checks the radio button for south and unchecks the previously checked button:

```
CheckRadioButton (hDlg, IDC_NORTH, IDC_WEST, IDC_SOUTH) ;
```

The CheckRadioButton function assumes that the set of radio button IDs in a group is a *dense* set of integers, that is, in the range of integers between the lowest-numbered radio button of a group and the highest-numbered radio button of a group, every integer has an associated radio button in the group. You can have radio buttons numbered 101, 102, 103, and 104. But you will almost certainly get into trouble if you have radio buttons numbered 101, 106, 107 and 109. The actual positioning on the screen doesn't matter; the first radio button could be the highest-numbered one. For example, for Figure 8.5, *any* of the following assignments would be valid for the arrangement of buttons shown:

```
#define IDC_TOO_HOT     101
#define IDC_JUST_RIGHT  102
#define IDC_TOO_COLD    103

// ...or
#define IDC_TOO_HOT     103
#define IDC_JUST_RIGHT  102
#define IDC_TOO_COLD    101
// ...or
#define IDC_TOO_HOT     102
#define IDC_JUST_RIGHT  101
#define IDC_TOO_COLD    103
```

(there are three other permutations of ID assignments you can work out for yourself).

What matters is that the *first* control on the screen, the one whose ID is IDC_TOO_HOT, has the WS_GROUP and WS_TABSTOP styles, and the other two controls do *not* have these styles. Ideally, the control which follows the control whose ID is IDC_TOO_COLD will have the WS_GROUP style as well. This might well be a group box control, but doesn't have to be; we don't have one around the controls shown in Figure 8.5.

A button that has the BS_NOTIFY style also can send its parent a message when the user double-clicks the button. The button reports this double-click by sending its parent window a WM_COMMAND message with a notification code of BN_DBLCLICK.

Owner-draw Buttons

Maybe you've decided that no standard button looks exactly the way you'd like it to look. Technically, you'd be wrong. There *is* a standard button control that can have any appearance you wish. The catch is that you must assume the responsibility of maintaining *every* aspect of the button's appearance, including signaling when the button has the input focus and drawing the pressed and released appearance of the button as well as drawing the correct representation of a disabled button. Creating the button is as simple as before:

```
#define IDC_SPECIALBUTTON      ·39

HWND hOwnerDraw ;

hOwnerDraw = CreateWindow (
    _T("button"), NULL,
    WS_CHILD | WS_VISIBLE | BS_OWNERDRAW,
    100, 200, 70, 40,
    hwnd,
    (HMENU)IDC_SPECIALBUTTON,
    hInstance, NULL) ;
```

This button is an owner-draw button, and it operates just like all the other buttons. An owner-draw button sends a WM_COMMAND message to its parent with a notification code of BN_CLICKED when the user clicks the button. When the button needs to be redrawn, for whatever reason, it sends a WM_DRAWITEM message to its parent window.

WM_DRAWITEM Message Cracker Handler

	wParam		lParam		
Parameter	**lo**	**hi**	**lo**	**hi**	**Meaning**
hwnd					Window handle of the window.
dis			███████		Reference to a DRAWITEMSTRUCT.

`void cls_OnDrawItem(HWND hwnd, const DRAWITEMSTRUCT * dis);`

The wParam parameter of the message isn't used. The dis parameter of the handler is a pointer to a DRAWITEMSTRUCT structure, which looks like this:

```
typedef struct tagDRAWITEMSTRUCT
{
    UINT    CtlType;
    UINT    CtlID;
    UINT    itemID;
    UINT    itemAction;
    UINT    itemState;
    HWND    hwndItem;
    HDC     hDC;
    RECT    rcItem;
    DWORD   itemData;
} DRAWITEMSTRUCT;
```

It is a fairly serious violation of modularity that the parent should have to know how to draw the contents of a child window, yet this seems to be what Windows requires. This puts knowledge of the control into the parent, where it doesn't belong. In fact, if you have a control defined in a DLL, the parent class can't possibly know how to draw the child control. A fairly standard technique is to "reflect" the message back to the child by writing a handler in the parent that looks like this:

```
void cls_OnDrawItem(HWND hwnd, const DRAWITEMSTRUCT * dis)
{
   if(dis->CtlType != ODT_MENU)
       FORWARD_WM_DRAWITEM(dis->hwndItem, dis, SendMessage) ;
   else
       { /* menu in local window */
       // handle menu drawing here
       } /* menu in local window */
}
```

We must make a special test for the ODT_MENU case because owner-draw menus must be handled by the parent window (see Chapter 12, page 860), which *is* the owner of the menu.

The child control, providing it does not contain nested controls itself, will never get a WM_DRAWITEM message by any path other than this one. The OnDrawItem handler of the child control can now draw whatever it needs to draw. You should write your custom controls in this fashion. You can also get this effect for owner-draw standard controls such as buttons, combo boxes and list boxes by subclassing the control and writing your own subclass handler. You can then use the above "reflection" technique for all your owner-draw controls. This is a cleaner interface (and easier to reuse in other applications) than having the parent contain child-drawing code. The effect is that the code of the module that implements the button now has responsibility for the drawing, and we have what is technically called a "self-drawn" control.

If you are using C++ and the Microsoft Foundation Class (MFC) library, this reflection mechanism is built in. You can write the drawing code as a member function of the class handler for your class that you derive from CButton. This makes writing owner-draw (or now called "self-draw") controls quite easy. Also, you don't have to violate any abstraction boundaries to accomplish this, since it is a natural extension of the C++ class structure.

For an owner-draw button, the CtlType field will have the value ODT_BUTTON. (You also can have owner-draw combo boxes, list boxes, static controls, and menus). The CtlID field contains the control ID for the owner-draw button. For our example, this is the value IDC_SPECIALBUTTON. Owner-draw buttons don't use the itemID field.

When you design the OnDrawItem handler, you must follow a fairly stylized structure for coding it. First, you must determine why the control needs to be redrawn. The itemAction field contains the drawing action. It can be one or more of the values shown in Table 8.18 OR'ed together. To test for a value, use the bitwise AND operator:

```
        if (dis->itemAction & ODA_DRAWENTIRE)
```

The itemAction field tells you how much redrawing of the control is necessary. For example, if the option is ODA_FOCUS, you may need only to DrawFocusRect to change the focus rectangle state. The itemState field specifies the current state of the control, that is, how it should be drawn. Table 8.19 shows the bit settings.

Table 8.18: Drawing actions for the `itemAction` field of the DRAWITEMSTRUCT structure

Symbolic Name	Meaning
ODA_DRAWENTIRE	The entire control needs to be redrawn.
ODA_FOCUS	The control is either gaining or losing the input focus. Use the `itemState` field to determine whether the control should be drawn with or without the input focus.
ODA_SELECT	The control's selection status (unchecked, checked, or indeterminate) has changed. Use the `itemState` field to determine the new selection state.

You use the `itemAction` and `itemState` fields to determine how to redraw the control. For example, when the `itemAction` field has the ODA_SELECT bit set, the selection status of the control has changed. When the ODS_SELECTED bit is also set in the `itemState` field, the control has changed from unselected to selected and should be drawn as selected. As an example, check boxes and radio buttons draw a bolder border around the button when selected. It is your responsibility, as the implementer of the control, to draw the information in a way that conveys the concept of "selected". Typically, you will use the GetSysColor API to obtain the desired color. For example, you will usually draw a selected item with the COLOR_HIGHLIGHT color for its background. If you draw any text, you should do so using the COLOR_HIGHLIGHTTEXT color.

Table 8.19: Bit settings for the `itemState` field of the DRAWITEMSTRUCT structure

Symbolic Name	Meaning
ODS_CHECKED	Draws the control as "checked".
ODS_DISABLED	Draw the control as "disabled".
ODS_FOCUS	Draws the control and indicates that it has the input focus.
ODS_GRAYED	Draws the control as "grayed", indicating it is disabled (this may be the same as ODS_DISABLED–you get to specify what happens).
ODS_SELECTED	Draws the control as "selected".

The hwndItem field contains the window handle of the owner-draw button. The hDC field contains a handle to the device context that you must use when drawing the control. The rcItem field contains a clipping rectangle. You don't need to use this field when drawing an owner-draw button. Owner-draw buttons don't use the itemData field.

Once you have determined what you need to redraw, draw your custom button. You do this by selecting the required drawing objects into the specified device context and drawing the button. Be sure to restore the device context attributes to their default values and delete any GDI objects you created

before returning from processing the WM_DRAWITEM message. Normally you will draw or fill the background, then draw the text, and finally draw the focus rectangle. If you don't see the effect you expect, make sure that you haven't drawn the pieces so that one writes over (and hence erases) an earlier effect.

The font that is selected into the hDC of the DRAWITEMSTRUCT is the font established via the most recent WM_SETFONT message. If no font has been explicitly set in the control, the default font, the same one obtained by GetStockObject(SYSTEM_FONT), will be used.

Owner-draw controls represent an often-underrated Windows technique. Owner-draw buttons are a quick and easy way to get a custom button-like control. With owner-draw list boxes and owner-draw combo boxes, you can get fancy effects such as multiple colors and tabbing (although list boxes have a tabbed style, it is not terribly flexible). They have been underrated because in Windows 3.1, doing a decent owner-draw button was tedious and very difficult. However, the DrawEdge function, described in detail in Chapter 6, page 359, makes it easy to do nice-looking owner-draw buttons. In many cases the features of owner-draw list boxes can be achieved by using a restricted form of the Tree View control (see Chapter 9, page 652).

Figure 8.6 shows a sample of an owner-draw push button that uses an icon. Listing 8.1 shows the corresponding code. We will look at this code in detail. Note that in Figure 8.6, two of the buttons are inactive, while one has the focus, and the left button of the mouse has been pressed down over it. This button is shown in its "depressed" state. The icon on the depressed button is different. Since you have complete control, you can do anything you want, including changing background colors and text styles. You could, for example, paint the button background as red when it is depressed. You could use an italic font for depressed buttons or bold for default buttons or some other convention, although you risk presenting the user with an idiosyncratic GUI that may not be "obvious".

Figure 8.6: A push button with an icon

The figure shows a simple example from the Control Explorer. (In fact, the function body shown in Listing 8.1 is approximately what is found in the Control Explorer, except we dropped out some details, such as the code that logs the events, so that you can study them.) It's important to realize here that *every* detail of these buttons, including the drawing of the focus rectangle, is entirely *your* responsibility. Nothing at all is done for you. If you don't handle the WM_DRAWITEM message, you will get a blank rectangle on the screen that responds to mouse clicks. This is not entirely pointless. You can put a "nondrawing" owner-draw button on the screen, for example, along with a bitmap image, and it will respond to mouse clicks. Just nothing will display. This would allow you to make certain areas–actually, rectangular sections–"mouse aware" without having to write more code than necessary.

Listing 8.1: Code for owner-draw (self-draw) icon push button

```
static void onDrawItem(HWND hwnd, LPDRAWITEMSTRUCT dis)
{
  RECT r = dis->rcItem;   // make copy to modify
  COLORREF txcolor;       // desired text color
  HICON icon;             // icon to paint
  SIZE sz;
  TCHAR s[256];           // button caption
  POINT pos = {0,0};      // position of caption
  POINT ipos = {0, 0};    // position of icon
```

```
SIZE rsize;                    // dimensions of r (width, height)
int saved = SaveDC(dis->hDC);

int space;                     // space between icon and text
DWORD style;
RECT focus;                    // size of focus rectangle
SIZE offset = {0, 0};

// Make the rectangle a little smaller so we don't get clipped
// by our own borders

InflateRect(&r, -GetSystemMetrics(SM_CXBORDER),
               -GetSystemMetrics(SM_CYBORDER));

if(dis->itemState & ODS_SELECTED)
   { /* selected */
    txcolor = GetSysColor(COLOR_WINDOWTEXT);
    icon = (HICON) LoadImage(GetWindowInstance(hwnd),
                   MAKEINTRESOURCE(IDI_OWNERDRAW1_DOWN),
                   IMAGE_ICON,
                   GetSystemMetrics(SM_CXSMICON),
                   GetSystemMetrics(SM_CYSMICON),
                   LR_DEFAULTCOLOR);
   } /* selected */
else
   { /* unselected */
    // Determine what color to paint the text

    if(dis->itemState & ODS_DISABLED)
       txcolor = GetSysColor(COLOR_GRAYTEXT);
    else
       txcolor = GetSysColor(COLOR_WINDOWTEXT);

    // load the icon to paint
    icon = (HICON)LoadImage(GetWindowInstance(hwnd),
                   MAKEINTRESOURCE((dis->itemState & ODS_DISABLED)
                                     ? IDI_OWNERDRAW1_DISABLED
                                     : IDI_OWNERDRAW1_UP),
                   IMAGE_ICON,
                   GetSystemMetrics(SM_CXSMICON),
                   GetSystemMetrics(SM_CYSMICON),
                   LR_DEFAULTCOLOR);
   } /* unselected */

// Having chosen a text color, get ready to use it by
// setting the DC's text color to the color we have chosen

SetTextColor(dis->hDC, txcolor);

// Get the caption text and compute how large it is in
// screen units

GetWindowText(dis->hwndItem, s, DIM(s));

GetTextExtentPoint32(dis->hDC, s, lstrlen(s), &sz);

// The following code is not strictly necessary, but we
```

```
// wanted to honor the style bits that the user may have set

// Compute the width and height for later convenience
rsize.cx = (r.right - r.left);
rsize.cy = (r.bottom - r.top);

// compute a default position of icon, right justified in the
// window.

ipos.x = rsize.cx - GetSystemMetrics(SM_CXSMICON);

// The following code shows how you can honor the style flags.
// This is not strictly necessary; you can do most owner-draw
// buttons without using these techniques, but they are
// convenient to use and illustrate how to take advantage of
// flags.

// Determine the alignment based on the style flags.
// Note that since we are an owner-draw control we can use the
// API4-level flags even on Windows NT 3.x

style = GetWindowStyle(dis->hwndItem);
style &= (BS_LEFT | BS_RIGHT | BS_CENTER);

switch(style)
    { /* hstyle */
     case BS_LEFT:
            pos.x = 0;
            ipos.x = pos.x + sz.cx + space;
            break;
     case BS_RIGHT:
            pos.x = rsize.cx - sz.cx;
            ipos.x = pos.x - space
                            - GetSystemMetrics(SM_CXSMICON);
            break;
     case BS_CENTER:
            pos.x = (rsize.cx - sz.cx) / 2;
            ipos.x = pos.x + sz.cx + space;
            break;
    } /* hstyle */

style = GetWindowStyle(dis->hwndItem);
style &= ( BS_TOP | BS_BOTTOM | BS_VCENTER);

switch(style)
    { /* vstyle */
     case BS_TOP:
            pos.y = 0;
            ipos.y = 0;
            break;
     case BS_BOTTOM:
            pos.y = rsize.cy - sz.cy;
            ipos.y = rsize.cy - GetSystemMetrics(SM_CYSMICON);
            break;
     case BS_VCENTER:
            pos.y = (rsize.cy - sz.cy) / 2;
```

```
          ipos.y =
              (rsize.cy - GetSystemMetrics(SM_CYSMICON)) / 2;
          break;
   } /* vstyle */

// Note: we do not support multiline style for this control

// compute the rectangle for drawing the focus

focus.left = pos.x;
focus.top  = pos.y;
focus.right = pos.x + sz.cx;
focus.bottom = pos.y + sz.cy;
InflateRect(&r, 1, 1); // allow a little more space
                       // around the text

// For visual effect, if the button is down, shift the text over
// and down to make it look like it is being "pushed"

if(dis->itemState & ODS_SELECTED)
    { /* button down */
     offset.cx = GetSystemMetrics(SM_CXBORDER);
     offset.cy = GetSystemMetrics(SM_CYBORDER);
    } /* button down */

if(dis->itemState & ODS_SELECTED)
    { /* button down */
    DrawEdge(dis->hDC, &r, EDGE_SUNKEN,
                        BF_RECT | BF_MIDDLE | BF_SOFT);
    } /* button down */
else
    { /* button up */
     DrawEdge(dis->hDC, &r, EDGE_RAISED,
                        BF_RECT | BF_MIDDLE | BF_SOFT);
    } /* button up */

TextOut(dis->hDC, pos.x + offset.cx, pos.y + offset.cy,
                        s, lstrlen(s));

DrawIconEx(dis->hDC, ipos.x + offset.cx, ipos.y + offset.cy,
                     icon,
                     GetSystemMetrics(SM_CXSMICON),
                     GetSystemMetrics(SM_CYSMICON),
                     0, NULL,
                     DI_NORMAL);

focus.left += offset.cx; // compute new position
focus.right += offset.cx;
focus.top += offset.cy;
focus.bottom += offset.cy;

if(dis->itemState & ODS_FOCUS)
    DrawFocusRect(dis->hDC, &focus);

RestoreDC(dis->hDC, saved);
}
```

This code requires some careful study because, as far as we have been able to discover, the entire MSDN CD-ROM contains no working example of a push button other than a simple bitmap push button.

For example, we use the `DrawEdge` function to draw our raised and depressed push buttons. When we do this, we discover that the right and bottom edges of the push button simply disappear when we press the button. This effect is caused by the window we are drawing doing its usual clipping. To avoid this, we inset the rectangle we are drawing by some small amount and empirically determine that the values we use here for the `InflateRect` function are sufficient.

The `ODS_SELECTED` flag tells us if the object is "selected", which in the case of a push button means "is the button being pressed?". If the flag is set, the button should be drawn it its "pressed" state. Here we set the text color to be `COLOR_WINDOWTEXT`, thus honoring the user's color choices, and we select the icon `IDI_OWNERDRAW1_DOWN`, which is a 16 × 16 "small" icon. We use the `LoadImage` function to load it from the resource file, specifying its size by using the `GetSystemMetrics` function (rather than using the hardwired constant 16).

If the button is *not* selected, however, we have another choice to make: Do we draw it enabled or disabled? If you use the Control Explorer to disable the owner-draw button, the text goes gray, as you would "expect" from standard Windows GUI behavior. But for an owner-draw button, you must implement that yourself. The test shown here selects between two possible colors for the text, the `COLOR_WINDOWTEXT` for an enabled button and the `COLOR_GRAYTEXT` for a disabled button. Note that we once again honor the user's color choices. Otherwise, our button might look substantially different from all other buttons and controls on the screen. We also use two different icons. The "normal" icon is a solid color, but the "disabled" icon is drawn with a gray border and halftoned by adding a pattern of alternating gray pixels to the drawing, thus making the icon looked "dimmed out". The icons we use are shown in Figure 8.7.

In preparation for drawing the text, we set the text color in the DC and retrieve the actual text string. We want to draw a "focus rectangle" on the button to indicate that it has the focus. We also want this focus rectangle to look like the focus rectangle on other controls. So we have to compute its size based on the actual button text. We call `GetTextExtentPoint32` to get this information.

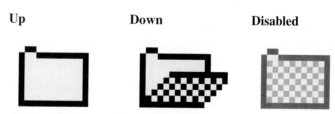

Up   **Down**   **Disabled**

Figure 8.7: Icons for owner-draw buttons

The code that follows next, as we indicate in the comments, is not strictly necessary. If you wanted to draw only one kind of button and not use any style flags at all, this code would not be necessary. However, we wanted to create a more generic example to show how you would write code to honor the style bits. The examples in Figure 8.6 were drawn with the `BS_CENTER` and `BS_VCENTER` styles selected, so when you read the code you can ignore the other cases. For `BS_CENTER`, we must compute the position based on the actual text width. We could have chosen to use the `DrawText` function as well, but computing the position of the focus rectangle is harder, so we chose this method instead. We also adjust the position of the small icon display, based on the text position, so if the text is flush right we put the icon to the left. The default, which we compute first, is to place the small icon all the way flush right in the button rectangle, but our style bit processing will change this.

We compute the focus rectangle position as shown. However, we found in practice that it looks better if we uniformly inflate the rectangle by one unit (note that some of this "fine tuning" is in no way apparent from any of the documentation provided).

Next comes one of the subtler features of doing an owner-draw push button (as opposed to many other owner-draw controls, which are more straightforward). Try this experiment with Windows: Press a push button and watch how nice it looks; it is clearly a button that moves up and down. There is something going on that you may not have noticed: The actual text of the button shifts right and down when the button is depressed. This is so "natural" in appearance that it may be that only after you've built your first owner-draw push button and found it flat, stale, and uninteresting that you realize that Windows's push buttons actually have second-order behavior. The code shows how to get that behavior. Our offset value starts out as 0, 0. However, if the push button is "selected", we change those offsets to SM_CXBORDER and SM_CYBORDER. We don't use a hardwired value here, such as "1", because on high-resolution displays a 1-pixel shift may not be noticeable.

Having done all this preparation, we are now ready to actually draw. If the button is "pressed", as indicated by the ODS_SELECTED flag, we call DrawEdge with the EDGE_SUNKEN style, which draws a "depressed" area on the screen. The BF_RECT style causes all four edges to be drawn; the BF_MIDDLE style causes the interior of the rectangle to be drawn; and the BF_SOFT style produces a more button-like appearance. If the button is not pressed, we call DrawEdge with the EDGE_RAISED style, with all other flags being the same as for the pressed case.

We next draw the text itself using the TextOut function. Here we add our offset values, which may have been modified to give the visual shift to the text. Then we draw the appropriate icon. Because we are drawing a "small" icon, we must use DrawIconEx. If we call DrawIcon, the small image will be stretched to fit a large icon space, and the results will not be at all what was intended. (Yes, we tried it, and this was what we saw!)

Finally, we may need to draw a focus rectangle. We want this rectangle to surround the text, which may have been moved by the offset value, so we add the offset value to the computed focus position. Note that we must add it to all four coordinates because a rectangle is specified by its corner coordinates, not by its top-left coordinates and a width and height. We then call DrawFocusRect to actually draw the dotted focus rectangle. Although DrawFocusRect actually does an XOR, we don't need to worry about this because we redraw the contents of the control completely. Otherwise, we would have to record the position of the previous focus rectangle (if any) and erase it. This is more complication than the problem actually requires, so we avoid it simply by overwriting the previous focus rectangle completely.

When all is done, we reset the DC to whatever values it had when we came into this function. We do this by using the RestoreDC function to restore the state, which we had saved on entry with the SaveDC function.

There's your owner-draw push button. This is a good "skeleton" from which you can derive other, more elaborate, push buttons. For example, we've "hardwired" the icons. You could instead use SetProp to attach two or three icon handles to the push button. (Remember, though, that you must use RemoveProp to remove them during the WM_DESTROY message handling.) Or you could preempt some of the built-in button style flags for your own purposes (since only the BS_OWNERDRAW value is important).

Because you have complete control, you can even have your button do things that normal buttons cannot. For example, by using SetTimer you can create an "auto-repeat" button. Here's how. Set one timer value to determine how long it takes before an auto-repeat begins. Then, if the timer fires, kill it and start a timer with another (usually shorter) interval. On every WM_TIMER message from this second timer, you simply do a SendMessage call to pass the WM_COMMAND message to the parent. This is most easily done with FORWARD_WM_COMMAND:

```
static void OnTimer(HWND hwnd, int timerid)
{
 FORWARD_WM_COMMAND(GetParent(hwnd), GetDlgCtrlID(hwnd),
                         hwnd, BN_CLICKED, SendMessage);
}
```

When you transition from "selected" back to "unselected" (and you have to keep track of this; for example, by using the GWL_USERDATA field or SetProp), you kill the pending timer. Don't worry about losing mouse clicks–the button handler has already captured the mouse.

Group Boxes

A *group box* is a rectangle used to enclose (or group together) associated buttons or controls. It typically has a label in the upper-left corner of the rectangle. It doesn't respond to mouse or keyboard input, and you'll usually never receive a WM_COMMAND message from one (except for the times when you specify BS_NOTIFY). Group boxes are, surprisingly, yet another special case of the BUTTON class–a "button" that doesn't respond to user input (this seems to be an historical artifact of the very earliest Windows implementations). Figure

Figure 8.8: A group box control surrounding two radio buttons

8.8 shows a group box created by the following example code. We set the control ID to the arbitrary value 17. Since a group box button control doesn't send WM_COMMAND messages to its parent window, you usually won't need a unique control ID, unless you want to disable or hide the group box. You would typically want to disable a group box when all the controls within it are disabled. This provides a strong visual clue to the user that no controls within it apply. Although this is most often a set of radio buttons, you should feel free to use a group box to group any set of controls.

```
HWND hGroupBox ;
#define IDC_MyControl 17

hGroupBox = CreateWindow (
    _T("button"), _T("Location"),
    WS_CHILD | WS_VISIBLE | BS_GROUPBOX,
    100, 200, 70, 40, hwnd, IDC_MyControl, hInstance, NULL) ;
```

You can change, in one of two ways, the label (text) of a button, group box, or any window. You can call the SetWindowText function, or you can send the WM_SETTEXT message to the window. Similarly, you can get the current label (text) of a window by calling the GetWindowText function or sending the WM_GETTEXT message to the window.

Any of the following statements change the window text for the hwnd window to the string pointed to by the NewLabel parameter:

```
Button_SetText(hwnd, NewLabel) ;
SetWindowText (hwnd, NewLabel) ;
SendMessage (hwnd, WM_SETTEXT, 0, (LPARAM)(LPCTSTR) NewLabel) ;
```

You can retrieve the current text for a window by calling the GetWindowText function and passing the window handle, a pointer to a buffer to hold the text, and the maximum number of characters to copy into the buffer. You can also send the window a WM_GETTEXT message to do the same thing. Both of the following statements retrieve the string currently used as the window text:

```
TCHAR Buff [128] ;
int   CharsCopied ;

CharsCopied = Button_GetText(hwnd, Buff, DIM(Buff)) ;
/* or */
CharsCopied = GetWindowText (hwnd, Buff, DIM(Buff)) ;
/* or */
CharsCopied = (int)  SendMessage  (hwnd, WM_GETTEXT,
                                   DIM(Buff),
                                   (LPARAM)(LPTSTR) Buff) ;
```

You can also determine the length of a window's text in nearly the same fashion. This is handy when you want to dynamically allocate the storage to hold the window's text. Call the GetWindowTextLength function or send a WM_GETTEXTLENGTH message to the window:

```
int Length ;

Length = Button_GetTextLength(hwnd) ;
/* or */
Length = GetWindowTextLength (hwnd) ;
/* or */
Length = (int) SendMessage (hwnd, WM_GETTEXTLENGTH, 0, 0L) ;
```

At API level 4 and higher, you can use a bitmap or icon as the group box label just by using the BS_ICON or BS_BITMAP styles and using the BM_SETIMAGE message (Button_SetImage function) to set the appropriate image. Try this with the Control Explorer to see how it looks.

As we said, one reason you may wish to assign a control ID to a group box is to allow you to enable or disable it to reflect the state of the controls inside it. For example, if you disable all the controls inside the group box you can visually make a statement to this effect by disabling the group box itself. The group box border and its text will show in a color selected by the control panel, usually a gray color.

Note that a group box does *not* force a radio button grouping on the buttons it contains. When you use the BS_AUTORADIOBUTTON style, clicking one radio button deselects all the other radio buttons in the group. The question arises, what is the group? Drawing a group box around a group *doesn't* define a group. What defines a group is a style flag called the WS_GROUP style. We discuss this again when we discuss dialog boxes in Chapter 11, but it is worth looking at here as well. By placing the group box *after* the controls it surrounds, you end up with a control containing the WS_GROUP style that delimits the end of the group. But what defines this is its position in the list of windows, *not* its geometrical relationship to the controls inside it. Suppose you were to lay down a set of three radio buttons, put in a group box larger than needed, and then add a fourth and fifth radio button to the set inside the group box. With most of the dialog editing tools you have available, you will get *two* groups of radio buttons, unless you explicitly "move" the group box to follow the radio buttons in the actual internal window order (called the "tab order").

The EDIT Class

It's a big step up from static controls to edit controls. An *edit control* is a child window that accepts keyboard input. The user can enter and edit one or more lines of text. You can allow the text to word wrap automatically to the next line or use an edit control that automatically scrolls the text–horizontally and vertically. You select the desired features of an edit control by combining edit class styles with the bitwise OR operator. There are two kinds of edit controls in Win32: the ordinary edit control and the Rich Text edit control. Here we describe the ordinary edit control in detail, but include messages and styles that apply to the Rich Text edit control as well.

The Edit Class Styles

You can create the simplest edit control with the following statement:

```
HWND hEditCntl ;
hEditCntl = CreateWindow (_T("edit"), NULL,
                          WS_CHILD | WS_VISIBLE,
                          100, 200, 70, 40,
                          hwnd, -1, hInstance, NULL) ;
```

This creates a single-line edit control. The ES_LEFT edit class style is defined as 0 so that text is left-justified in a edit control, unless you specify the ES_CENTER or ES_RIGHT styles. But these styles do not apply to a single-line edit control; if you supply them, they will be ignored. Only a multiline edit control can have centered or right-justified text.

You might have some difficulty finding the edit control we just created on the screen. By default, an edit control doesn't have a border, so all you'll see is the flashing caret at the text insertion point–and you'll see that only if the control has the focus. Finding it in order to click it would be a challenge. Most of the time, you'll want a border around the edit control window. You request one by including the WS_BORDER window style. Table 8.20 lists the edit class styles.

Table 8.20: Edit class styles

Style	Meaning
ES_AUTOHSCROLL	Automatically scrolls the text in the edit field to the right when the user enters a character at the end of the line.
ES_AUTOVSCROLL	Automatically scrolls the text in the edit field up one page when the user presses the **Enter** key on the last line.

Table 8.20: Edit class styles

Style	Meaning
ES_CENTER	Centers the text horizontally on each line of a multiline edit control. It does not center a line of text vertically.
ES_LEFT	Aligns text flush left. The only style you can use for a single-line edit control.
ES_LOWERCASE	Converts entered characters to lowercase.
ES_MULTILINE	Creates a multiline edit control.
ES_NOHIDESEL	Leaves selected text highlighted when the edit control loses the input focus.
ES_NUMBER[4]	Permits only digits to be typed in the edit control.
ES_OEMCONVERT	Converts the characters entered into the selection field from the ANSI character set to the OEM character set.
ES_PASSWORD	Displays entered characters as an asterisk (*) or the character specified by the last EM_SETPASSWORDCHAR message sent to the control.
ES_READONLY	Prevents the user from editing or entering text in the control. However, text already in the control can be selected, and selected text can be copied. Note that this is different from disabling the control: A disabled control does not permit selection or copying of its contents.
ES_RIGHT	Aligns text flush-right in a multiline edit control.
ES_UPPERCASE	Converts entered characters to uppercase.
ES_WANTRETURN	Used in combination with the ES_MULTILINE style to specify that a carriage return be inserted when the user presses the **Enter** key while entering text into a multiline edit control in a dialog box. When the user does this in a dialog box that omits this style, the dialog box's default push button is "pressed". This style has no effect on a single-line edit control.

[4]Available only at API level 4 and higher.

A user can enter text into an edit control until the edit control's rectangle is filled. You can include the ES_AUTOHSCROLL edit style to allow the user to enter more characters than can be displayed in the edit control's client area. The edit control automatically scrolls text to the right, by 10 characters, when the user types a character at the end of the line. Generally, it is not recommended that you use this technique for putting very long strings in very narrow spaces because much of the string is obscured, thus making such an interface hard to work with. You should generally size your edit control so that it can display all of the desired string in nearly all cases, using the automatic horizontal scrolling to allow the few cases of overflow that may occur.

If you plan to limit the text, one way to get a good idea of the size of the edit control is to make it large enough to hold as many W characters as needed to fill the string length. This works well for estimating sizes for Roman-based alphabets because W is the widest character.

You can step up to multiline edit controls by including the ES_MULTILINE edit class style. Multiline edit controls behave somewhat differently in dialog boxes and as child windows of "ordinary" windows. This is because edit controls in ordinary windows get all the characters typed when they have the focus, but edit controls in dialog boxes have their input filtered through the dialog procedure. The dialog procedure normally processes specific keys, such as **Tab**, **Shift+Tab**, and **Enter**, and takes specific actions. In a dialog, **Tab** shifts the focus to the next control and **Shift+Tab** shifts it to the previous control. **Enter** activates the default push button for the dialog (if one is defined).

A multiline edit control in a dialog has to deal with the conflicting requirements of the **Enter** key to terminate lines within the edit control and the **Enter** key as activator of the default push button. This is resolved in several ways:

- Use the **Ctrl+Enter** key combination to enter a newline character in the edit control, or

- Use the ES_WANTRETURN style on the edit control so that the **Enter** key enters a newline character in the edit control, or

- Subclass the control and handle the WM_GETDLGCODE message.

The special key combination **Ctrl+Enter** will always successfully enter a newline in a multiline edit control. You can also set the ES_WANTRETURN style flag, either at creation or dynamically. This flag tells the dialog box that is handling the keyboard input that the **Enter** key (the "Return" key) should be sent to the edit control, not used to activate the default push button. We defer the discussion of the WM_GETDLGCODE until Chapter 11 because it is useful for many more features in handling dialog controls; for edit controls, this message gives us the ability to intercept all the keyboard input. To simplify our discussion, we use the phrase "enter a newline character" to mean that the user has been able to enter the character. If the edit control is outside a dialog box, hitting the **Enter** key when the edit control has the focus will do the job. Inside a dialog (or a property page, or CFormView, or CRecordView, or other dialog-based context), then either **Ctrl+Enter**, **Enter** with ES_WANTRETURN, or an implementation of a WM_GETDLGCODE handler, as appropriate and available, would be used.

A multiline edit control can be quite versatile. You can specify the action taken by the control when the user enters text at the end of a line. There are two possibilities: the end of a line other than the last line in the control and the end of the last line in the control.

When the user enters text at the end of a line other than the last displayable line and the ES_AUTOHSCROLL style isn't also specified, the edit control automatically word wraps the text to the beginning of the next line. You can resize this kind of edit control, and it will appropriately word wrap the text to fit the new window size and redisplay the text. The user can enter a newline character at any time to start a new line.

When the user enters text at the end of a line other than the last displayable line, and the ES_AUTOHSCROLL style is also included, the edit control horizontally scrolls the text 10 characters to the right. The user must enter a newline character to start a new line.

The following occurs when the user enters a character at the end of the last displayable line in the control. When you use the ES_AUTOHSCROLL style, the line scrolls to the right. When you don't use the ES_AUTOHSCROLL style, the control attempts to word wrap to the next line. If you don't use the ES_AUTOVSCROLL style, the control can't scroll to a new line; it beeps and refuses the character. When you use the ES_AUTOVSCROLL style, the control scrolls its contents vertically and word wraps to the new line.

The same thing occurs when the user inserts a newline character on the last line. If the ES_AUTOVSCROLL style is set, the control scrolls vertically and the caret is positioned on the new line. When the style is not set, the control beeps and refuses to accept the newline character.

You can include the window styles WS_HSCROLL and WS_VSCROLL when you create an edit control. They add a horizontal and vertical scroll bar, respectively, to the edit control window. You can read the position of the thumb box of the vertical scroll bar by using the EM_GETTHUMB message (the Edit_GetThumb function is defined in extensions.h).

You use the ES_PASSWORD style for an edit control when you don't want the control to display the characters the user is typing. You would typically use this to enter passwords. An edit control with the ES_PASSWORD style displays an asterisk (*) for each character that the user types into the control. If you would rather the control used a different character, you can send it an EM_SETPASSWORDCHAR message with the desired character in the wParam parameter. Or you can use the Edit_SetPasswordChar function, passing the desired character. You can turn off the password processing by sending the control an EM_SETPASSWORDCHAR message with the wParam parameter set to 0 or by calling the Edit_SetPasswordChar function with a 0 character. The control then displays the actual characters typed by the user. A control with the ES_PASSWORD style does not honor the WM_COPY or WM_CUT messages.

```
SendDlgItemMessage(hdlg, IDC_EDIT, EM_SETPASSWORDCHAR, _T('*'), 0);
Edit_SetPasswordChar(GetDlgItem(hdlg, IDC_EDIT), _T('*'));
```

An edit control highlights selected text. Normally, an edit control removes the highlighting on the selected text when the control loses the input focus. (The text is still visible, but there is no indication of what text is selected). When input focus returns, the control once again highlights the selected text. The ES_NOHIDESEL edit class style causes the control to leave the selected text highlighted when it loses the input focus.

You can have the control automatically convert all characters to uppercase or lowercase as they are typed into the control by including the ES_UPPERCASE or ES_LOWERCASE styles. Remember that the case folding will be done by the CharUpper and CharLower functions, so the actual codes used for the characters will be locale-specific (see Chapter 7). These style flags may be set or cleared dynamically.

You should use the ES_OEMCONVERT style for edit controls used to enter filenames used for Windows 95. An edit control with this style converts each typed character from the ANSI character set to the OEM character set and back again to the ANSI character set. The resulting character isn't always the same as the original character; however, subsequent conversions from ANSI to OEM to ANSI do result in the same character (the first conversion may not be able to map an ANSI character to the OEM set, and may make a substitution.

Subsequent conversions of the substituted character generate an OEM character which *will* translate back to its original ANSI character). You should add this style to edit controls containing text that you want in the OEM character set. When you do an `Edit_SetText` call, Windows will translate the input string using the `OemToChar` function so that although the text you have in your buffer is in the OEM character set, the text displayed will be in the ANSI character set. When you do an `Edit_GetText` call, the contents of the edit control will first be translated by the `CharToOem` function. The string returned will be in the OEM character set. The file common dialogs already do this. A more detailed discussion of the OEM character set and the functions involved is in Chapter 7.

An edit control with the `ES_READONLY` edit style prevents the user from editing or typing into the edit control. However, selection of existing text will still work; hence, the `Copy` operation (although not `Cut` or `Paste`) will work. Table 8.21 compares edit and static control styles. The `ES_READONLY` style, once set, cannot be changed dynamically by set-

Table 8.21: `Edit` and `Static` control behavior

Control Type	Styles	User Actions Supported		
		Edit	**Select**	**Copy**
STATIC	–	No	No	No
EDIT	ES_READONLY	No	Yes	Yes
	WS_DISABLED	No	No	No

ting or clearing the style bits of the window. However, the mode can be changed on the fly either by sending an `EM_SETREADONLY` message with the `wParam` set to `TRUE` or `FALSE` to set the read-only mode or by calling the `Edit_SetReadOnly` function:

```
SendDlgItemMessage(hdlg, IDC_EDIT, EM_SETREADONLY, roflag, 0);
Edit_SetReadOnly(GetDlgItem(hdlg, IDC_EDIT), roflag);
```

The appearance of these controls with their different styles has changed several times. For example, Windows 3.*x*, with and without CTL3D, Windows NT 3.*x*, with and without CTL3DV32, and Win32 4.*x* all show slightly different appearances for disabled edit controls. If you are porting a Win16 application, the programmer may have taken advantage of the visual appearance in Win16 to get a specific effect. You may be surprised at the actual effect you see under one of the Win32 platforms.

Changing Styles

It is implementation-specific as to which style flags are examined dynamically by a window handler and which are ignored after creation. Sometimes changing flags by setting the `GWL_STYLE` field of a window using `SetWindowLong` will have an immediate effect. Sometimes it will have no effect. Sometimes you must call `InvalidateRect` after setting a flag in order to see the effect. And sometimes you must call an API function or send a message to a window to change its state, which is then reflected in its style flags. Thus some effects of changing flags are trivially achieved, while others require destroying the window and re-creating it (and ideally making sure you don't lose any of its contents or state in the process). Using the Control Explorer, you can experiment with some of these features for edit controls. Certain flags require re-creating the window, and the Control Explorer retains content and state. In practice, this happens so fast that you can hardly see it. As a result, we have introduced a completely gratuitous graphic effect to emphasize that the window is being re-created, but be aware that the time required to do this is controlled by a timer event. You can disable this feature to see how fast the re-creation actually is occurring. Table 8.22 summarizes the behavior of the various styles.

Table 8.22: Changing edit class styles

Style	Change
ES_AUTOHSCROLL	Creation time only.
ES_AUTOVSCROLL	Creation time only.
ES_CENTER	Creation time only.
ES_LEFT	Creation time only.
ES_LOWERCASE	Any time using SetWindowLong(hwnd, GWL_STYLE, ...).
ES_MULTILINE	Creation time only.
ES_NOHIDESEL	Creation time only.
ES_NUMBER[4]	Any time using SetWindowLong(hwnd, GWL_STYLE, ...).
ES_OEMCONVERT	Any time using SetWindowLong(hwnd, GWL_STYLE, ...). However, this affects only the next operation that puts text in the control. It does not change the representation of the current text in the control. Nor does it affect how GetWindowText retrieves any preexisting text.
ES_PASSWORD	Creation time only.
ES_READONLY	Any time using EM_SETREADONLY.
ES_RIGHT	Creation time only.
ES_UPPERCASE	Any time using SetWindowLong(hwnd, GWL_STYLE, ...).
ES_WANTRETURN	Any time using SetWindowLong(hwnd, GWL_STYLE, ...).
WS_DISABLED	Any time using EnableWindow(hwnd, ...).
WS_VISIBLE	Any time using ShowWindow(hwnd, ...).

[4]Available only at API level 4 and higher.

For example, to change the state of an edit control to support uppercase only input, lowercase only input, or no forced case, you could write the following:

```
#define EDIT_UPPER 0
#define EDIT_LOWER 1
#define EDIT_NONE  2

void setEditMode(HWND hwnd, int mode)
    {
```

```
DWORD style = GetWindowLong(hwnd, GWL_STYLE);
switch(mode)
    { /* mode */
     case EDIT_UPPER:
          style &= ~ ES_LOWERCASE;
          style |= ES_UPPERCASE;
          break;
      case EDIT_LOWER:
          style &= ~ ES_UPPERCASE;
          style |= ES_LOWERCASE;
          break;
      case EDIT_NONE:
          style &= ~(ES_UPPERCASE | ES_LOWERCASE);
          break;
    } /* mode */
  SetWindowLong(hwnd, GWL_STYLE, style);
}
```

Messages to an Edit Control

Of the many messages you can send to an edit control, some messages apply only to multiline edit controls. Table 8.23 lists the edit control messages.

Table 8.23: Messages understood by an edit control

Message	Description
EM_CANPASTE	Applies only to Rich Text edit controls.
EM_CANUNDO	BOOL Edit_CanUndo(HWND hwnd)
	Queries an edit control for EM_UNDO support. Returns TRUE if undo is possible and FALSE if undo cannot be executed.
EM_CHARFROMPOS[4]	int Edit_CharFromPos(HWND hwnd, int x, int y)[e]
	Given two coordinates in the client area of an edit control, returns a character position of the character nearest to those coordinates.
EM_DISPLAYBAND	Applies only to Rich Text edit controls.
EM_EMPTYUNDOBUFFER	void Edit_EmptyUndoBuffer(HWND hwnd)
	Clears the edit control's undo buffer.
EM_EXGETSEL	Applies only to Rich Text edit controls.
EM_EXLIMITTEXT	Applies only to Rich Text edit controls.
EM_EXLINEFROMCHAR	Applies only to Rich Text edit controls.

[4]Available only at API level 4 and higher.
[e]Defined in extensions.h.

Table 8.23: Messages understood by an edit control

Message	Description
EM_EXSETSEL	Applies only to Rich Text edit controls.
EM_FINDTEXT[4]	Finds the next selection in an edit control.
EM_FINDTEXTEX[4]	Finds the next selection in an edit control.
EM_FINDWORDBREAK[4]	Returns the character position of the next word break, the character class, or the delimiter determination.
EM_FMTLINES	`BOOL Edit_FmtLines(HWND hwnd, BOOL AddEOL)`
	Directs the control to add/remove soft line breaks to word-wrapped lines.
EM_FORMATRANGE	Applies only to Rich Text edit controls.
EM_GETCHARFORMAT	Applies only to Rich Text edit controls.
EM_GETEVENTMASK[4]	Applies only to Rich Text edit controls.
EM_GETFIRSTVISIBLELINE	`int Edit_GetFirstVisibleLine(HWND hwnd)`
	Returns the zero-based index of the top-most visible line in an edit control.
EM_GETHANDLE	`HLOCAL Edit_GetHandle(HWND hwnd)`
	Returns the local handle of the buffer containing the contents of the edit control. *Obsolete in Win32.*
EM_GETIMECOLOR	Gets the current Input Method Editor (IME) color. Applies only to Asian-language versions of Windows.
EM_GETIMEOPTIONS	Gets the current Input Method Editor (IME) options. Applies only to Asian-language versions of Windows.
EM_GETLIMITTEXT[4]	Returns the maximum number of characters that the user may enter into an edit control message.
EM_GETLINE	`int Edit_GetLine(HWND hwnd, int line, LPTSTR buff, int chMax)`
	Copies a line from the control to a buffer.
EM_GETLINECOUNT	`int Edit_GetLineCount(HWND hwnd)`
	Returns the number of lines in the control.

[4]Available only at API level 4 and higher.
[e]Defined in `extensions.h`.

Table 8.23: Messages understood by an edit control

Message	Description
EM_GETMARGINS[4]	Returns the left and right margin widths.
EM_GETMODIFY	BOOL Edit_GetModify(HWND hwnd)
	Returns the modification flag for the control.
EM_GETOLEINTERFACE	Applies only to Rich Text edit controls.
EM_GETOPTIONS	Applies only to Rich Text edit controls.
EM_GETPARAFORMAT	Applies only to Rich Text edit controls.
EM_GETPASSWORDCHAR	TCHAR Edit_GetPasswordChar(HWND hwnd)
	Returns the password character displayed in an edit control when the user enters text.
EM_GETPUNCTUATION	Returns the set of punctuation characters. This is available only in Asian-language versions of Windows.
EM_GETRECT	void Edit_GetRect(HWND hwnd, LPRECT rect)
	Returns the formatting rectangle of the control.
EM_GETSEL	DWORD Edit_GetSel(HWND hwnd)
	Returns the starting and ending character positions of the current selection.
EM_GETSELTEXT[4]	Applies only to Rich Text edit controls.
EM_GETTEXTRANGE	Applies only to Rich Text edit controls.
EM_GETTHUMB[4]	Returns the position of the scroll box in a multiline edit control.
EM_GETWORDBREAKPROC	EDITWORDBREAKPROC Edit_GetWordBreakProc(HWND hwnd)
	Returns the address of the current application-defined word wrap function.
EM_GETWORDBREAKPROCEX	EDITWORDBREAKPROCEX Edit_GetWordBreakProcEx(HWND hwnd)[e]
	Returns the procedure-instance address of the current application-defined extended word-wrap function.
EM_GETWORDWRAPMODE	Gets the current word-wrap mode. This is available only in Asian-language versions of Windows.

[4]Available only at API level 4 and higher.
[e]Defined in `extensions.h`.

Table 8.23: Messages understood by an edit control

Message	Description
EM_HIDESELECTION	Applies only to Rich Text edit controls.
EM_LIMITTEXT	See EM_SETLIMITTEXT.
EM_LINEFROMCHAR	`int Edit_LineFromChar(HWND hwnd, int ch)`
	Returns the line number of the line containing the character in the specified position.
EM_LINEINDEX	`int Edit_LineIndex(HWND hwnd, int line)`
	Returns the number of character positions preceding the first character on the specified line.
EM_LINELENGTH	`int Edit_LineLength(HWND hwnd, int line)`
	Returns the length of a line.
EM_LINESCROLL	`BOOL Edit_LineScroll(HWND hwnd, int hscroll,` `int vscroll)`[e]
	Scrolls the specified number of lines vertically or the specified number of characters horizontally. Applies only to multiline edit controls. Returns TRUE if sent to a multiline edit control and FALSE if sent to a single-line edit control.
EM_PASTESPECIAL	Applies only to Rich Text edit controls.
EM_POSFROMCHAR[4]	`void Edit_PosFromChar(LPPOINT pt, int charpos)`[e]
	Given a character position, which is passed in lParam, returns the client coordinates of the top-left corner of the character cell that defines that character in the pt structure whose reference is passed in wParam.
EM_REPLACESEL	`void Edit_ReplaceSel(HWND hwnd, LPCTSTR buff)`
	Replaces selected text with the specified text. The macro does not support the "undo" parameter available at API level 4.
EM_REQUESTRESIZE	Applies only to Rich Text edit controls.

[4]Available only at API level 4 and higher.
[e]Defined in `extensions.h`.

Table 8.23: Messages understood by an edit control

Message	Description
EM_SCROLL	`void Edit_Scroll(HWND hwnd, UINT quantity, UINT units)`
	Scrolls the text in a multiline edit control. The `quantity` parameter, passed in `lParam`, indicates the number of scroll units to move, as specified by `units`. The `units` parameter, passed in `wParam`, indicates the type of scroll to be done and is one of the following:
	`SB_LINEDOWN` Scroll down one line.
	`SB_LINEUP` Scroll up one line.
	`SB_PAGEDOWN` Scroll down one page.
	`SB_PAGEUP` Scroll up one page.
EM_SCROLLCARET	`BOOL Edit_ScrollCaret(HWND hwnd)`
	Scrolls the caret into view.
EM_SELECTIONTYPE	Applies only to Rich Text edit controls.
EM_SETBKGNDCOLOR	Applies only to Rich Text edit controls.
EM_SETCHARFORMAT	Applies only to Rich Text edit controls.
EM_SETEVENTMASK	Applies only to Rich Text edit controls.
EM_SETHANDLE	`void Edit_SetHandle(HWND hwnd, HLOCAL h)`
	Specifies the buffer used to hold the text. *Obsolete in Win32.*
EM_SETIMECOLOR	Sets the Input Method Editor (IME) color. Applies only to Asian-language versions of Windows.
EM_SETIMEOPTIONS	Sets the Input Method Editor (IME) options. Applies only to Asian-language versions of Windows.
EM_SETLIMITTEXT	`int Edit_LimitText(HWND hwnd, int Limit)`
	Specifies the maximum number of characters that the user may enter into an edit control. (In Windows 3.x this was the EM_LIMITTEXT message.)

[4]Available only at API level 4 and higher.

[e]Defined in `extensions.h`.

Table 8.23: Messages understood by an edit control

Message	Description
EM_SETMARGINS[4]	`void Edit_SetMargins(HWND hwnd, int which, int left, int right)`[e]
	Sets the left and right margin widths. The which parameter, passed as wParam, indicates what type of margin is being set. The lParam specifies the left and right margin widths, with the low-order word specifying the left margin and the high-order word specifying the right margin. The interpretation of wParam is one or more of the following flags:
	EC_LEFTMARGIN Set the left margin only.
	EC_RIGHTMARGIN Set the right margin only.
	EC_USEFONTINFO Use the font widths to set the margins; ignore left and right (lParam).
EM_SETMODIFY	`void Edit_SetModify(HWND hwnd, BOOL Modified)`
	Sets the modification flag for the control.
EM_SETOLEINTERFACE	Applies only to Rich Text edit controls.
EM_SETOPTIONS	Applies only to Rich Text edit controls.
EM_SETPARAFORMAT	Applies only to Rich Text edit controls.
EM_SETPASSWORDCHAR	`void Edit_SetPasswordChar(HWND hwnd, TCHAR ch)`
	Sets the character displayed by ES_PASSWORD controls.
EM_SETPUNCTUATION	Defines the set of punctuation characters. This is available only in Asian-language versions of Windows.
EM_SETREADONLY	`BOOL Edit_SetReadOnly(HWND hwnd, BOOL flag)`
	Sets or resets the read-only state of an edit control.
EM_SETRECT	`void Edit_SetRect(HWND hwnd, const RECT * rc)`
	Changes the formatting rectangle for a control, reformats the text, and repaints the control.
EM_SETRECTNP	`void Edit_SetRectNoPaint(HWND hwnd, const RECT * rc)`
	Changes the formatting rectangle for a control and reformats the text. Does not repaint the control.

[4]Available only at API level 4 and higher.

[e]Defined in `extensions.h`.

Table 8.23: Messages understood by an edit control

Message	Description
EM_SETSEL	`void Edit_SetSel(HWND hwnd, int start, int end)`
	Selects the specified characters in the control.
EM_SETTABSTOPS	`void Edit_SetTabStops(HWND hwnd, int TabCount, const int * Tabs)`
	Sets the tab-stop positions.
EM_SETTARGETDEVICE	Applies only to Rich Text edit controls.
EM_SETWORDBREAKPROC	`void Edit_SetWordBreakProc(HWND hwnd, EDITWORDBREAKPROC proc)`
	Establishes a new word-break function.
EM_SETWORDBREAKPROCEX	`void Edit_SetWordBreakProcEx(HWND hwnd, EDITWORDBREAKPROCEX proc)`[e]
	Establishes a new extended word-break function.
EM_SETWORDWRAPMODE	Sets the word-wrap mode. This is available only in Asian-language versions of Windows.
EM_STREAMIN	Applies only to Rich Text edit controls.
EM_STREAMOUT	Applies only to Rich Text edit controls.
EM_UNDO	`BOOL Edit_Undo(HWND hwnd)`
	Undoes the last edit made to the control. Returns TRUE if this was possible and FALSE if the edit could not be undone.
WM_CLEAR	Deletes the current selection. The selection is not saved in the Clipboard.
WM_COPY	Copies the selected text to the Clipboard in CF_TEXT format.
WM_CUT	Copies the selected text to the Clipboard in CF_TEXT format and then deletes the selection from the edit control.
WM_ENABLE	`BOOL Edit_Enable(HWND hwnd, BOOL Enable)`
	Enables or disables the control.
WM_GETFONT	`HFONT GetWindowFont(HWND hwnd)`
	Obtains the handle of the font used to draw the text in the control.

---

[4]Available only at API level 4 and higher.

[e]Defined in `extensions.h`.

Table 8.23: Messages understood by an edit control

Message	Description
WM_GETTEXT	`int Edit_GetText(HWND hwnd, LPTSTR buff, int chMax)`
	Replaces the contents of the buffer referenced by `buff`, passed in `lParam` with the contents of the edit control. The number of characters to be copied is specified by `chMax`, which is passed in `wParam`. Returns the actual number of characters copied.
WM_GETTEXTLENGTH	`int Edit_GetTextLength(HWND hwnd)`
	Returns the length of the text.
WM_PASTE	Replaces the current selection with the contents of the Clipboard. This has no effect if there is no CF_TEXT format data in the Clipboard.
WM_SETFONT	`void SetWindowFont(HWND hwnd, HFONT hfont)`
	Sets the font used to draw the text.
WM_SETTEXT	`BOOL Edit_SetText(HWND hwnd, LPCTSTR buff)`
	Replaces the contents of the edit control by the text referenced by `buff`, which is passed `lParam`.
WM_SHOWWINDOW	`BOOL ShowWindow(HWND hwnd, UINT show)`
	Shows or hides the window. The `show` parameter is one of the following:
	`SW_HIDE` Hides the window.
	`SW_SHOW` Shows the window.
WM_UNDO	`BOOL Edit_Undo(HWND hwnd)`
	Undoes the last edit made to the control.

[4]Available only at API level 4 and higher.
[e]Defined in `extensions.h`.

The EM_SETSEL message in Win16 specified two 16-bit positions (start and end) in the 32-bit `lParam` and used a Boolean value in `wParam` to indicate if the caret should be scrolled. The EM_SETSEL message in Win32 specifies two 32-bit positions (start and end) and does not allow a specification to scroll the caret. This is handled by a separate message, EM_SCROLLCARET. Beware of this when converting a Win16 application that uses EM_SETSEL.

Working with Selections

The text in an edit control may be *selected*. Selection is indicated by a highlighting color over the selected characters. The edit control handles the details of responding to the mouse button down, the dragging, and the mouse release, as well as the painting of the selection highlight. In addition, it supports the standard Windows keyboard shortcuts for selection, as shown in Table 8.24.

Table 8.24: Selection/caret shortcut keys

Shortcut Key	Effect
Ctrl + C	Copies the selection to the Clipboard in CF_TEXT format.
Ctrl + V	Pastes the Clipboard contents, replacing the selection. If there is no CF_TEXT data in the Clipboard, this key has no effect.
Ctrl + X	Cuts the selection to the Clipboard in CF_TEXT format.
←	Moves the caret left.
→	Moves the caret right.
↑	Multiline control: Moves up one line. Single-line control: No effect.
↓	Multiline control: Moves down one line. Single-line control: Moves caret right; same as →.
Ctrl + ←	Moves the caret left one word. The caret is left at the start of the word passed over.
Ctrl + →	Moves the caret right one word. The caret is left at the beginning of the next word, past any whitespace.
Shift + ←	Moves the selection end at the caret to the left by one position. If at the left end of the selection, extends it left; if at the right end of the selection, contracts it to the left.
Shift + →	Moves the selection end at the caret to the right by one position. If at the left end of the selection, contracts it to the right; if at the right end of the selection, extends it to the right.
Shift + ↑	Moves the caret up one line, carrying the selection end with it.
Shift + ↓	Moves the caret down one line, carrying the selection end with it.
Ctrl + Shift + ←	Moves the selection end at the caret to the left by one word. If at the left end of the selection, extends it left; if at the right end of the selection, contracts it to the left. The caret (and the end of the selection) is left at the start of the word skipped over.

Table 8.24: Selection/caret shortcut keys

Shortcut Key	Effect
Ctrl + Shift + →	Moves the selection end at the caret to the right by one word. If at the left end of the selection, contracts it to the right; if at the right end of the selection, extends it to the right.
Delete	If there is a selection, removes the contents of the selection. Otherwise, deletes the character to the right of the caret.
Ctrl + Delete	If there is a selection, removes the contents of the selection. Otherwise, deletes text from the caret position to the end of the line.
Backspace	If there is a selection, removes the contents of the selection. Otherwise, deletes the character to the left of the caret.

The edit control also handles caret management. You do not need to create, show, hide, or destroy the caret when you are using an edit control, as the control does this for you. The control creates the caret when it receives the focus and destroys the caret when it loses focus.

Normally, the user performs selection or caret motion by using the mouse. However, you may choose to do explicit management of the selection yourself; this includes the positioning of the caret. You position the caret or make a selection using the EM_SETSEL message or the Edit_SetSel macro. The value you give for the selection start positions the selection start just to the left of the character at that 0-based position (thus 0 positions the selection start to the left of the first character in the buffer). The selection end value positions the selection just to the left of that character position. If the start and end have the same value, the message simply positions the caret; otherwise, it makes a selection. If you want to specify the end of the text, you can give the value -1 for the upper bound. For example, the following selects all of the text in the control:

```
Edit_SetSel(hEdit, 0, -1);
```

and the following selects the characters in positions 11 through 17:

```
SendMessage(hEdit, EM_SETSEL, 11, 17);
```

You can retrieve the selection limits by using the EM_GETSEL message or the Edit_GetSel macro. The result of these operations is a 32-bit value whose low-order 16 bits are the selection start and whose high-order 16 bits are the selection end:

```
DWORD selection = Edit_GetSel(hEdit);
int start = LOWORD(selection);
int end = HIWORD(selection);
```

The macros don't support getting the bounds of a selection from large text buffers. In Win16, the current selection value was returned as a DWORD value, with the start position in the low-order 16 bits and the end position (the position of the character following the selection) in the high-order 16 bits. Of course, this won't work if you have an edit control larger than 65,535 characters. Edit_GetSel sends an EM_GETSEL message with both the wParam and the lParam set to NULL. It returns the same DWORD in both Win16 and Win32, but in Win32 the value is meaningless if the selection requires more than 16 bits to express the endpoints. To get the full 32-bit selection position for a large buffer, you must send the EM_GETSEL message directly (there is no API wrapper in `windowsx.h`). In that message, the wParam should contain a reference to a DWORD, which receives the start position, and the lParam should contain a reference to a DWORD, which receives the end position. In this case, the return value contains the low-order 16 bits of each of the actual values. You should not trust this return value unless you can be absolutely certain that the edit control will not have more than 65,535 characters. An example of the correct way to get the selection values for a large buffer is this:

```
DWORD start;
DWORD end;
SendMessage(hEditCtl, EM_GETSEL, (WPARAM)&start, (LPARAM)&end);
```

There is no direct way to get a copy of the selected text from an edit control. To obtain such a copy, you have to use the WM_GETTEXT message or the GetWindowText function, which copies the entire contents of the control to a buffer. You then have to copy the selection yourself.

```
LPTSTR getSelection(HWND hEdit)
{
 LPTSTR Buffer;
 int len;
 DWORD start;
 DWORD end;
 SendMessage(hEdit, EM_GETSEL, &start, &end);
 len = GetWindowTextLength(hEdit);
 Buffer = malloc((len + 1) * sizeof(TCHAR));
 if(Buffer == NULL)
     return NULL;
 GetWindowText(hEdit, Buffer, len + 1);
 // if we have the entire selection, we need to adjust the
 // sizes to compute the length
 len = end - start;
 if(start != 0)
     memmove(Buffer, &Buffer[start], len * sizeof(TCHAR));
 Buffer[len] = _T('\0');
 return realloc(Buffer, (len + 1) * sizeof(TCHAR));
}
```

Unix

If you are transitioning from a traditional Unix environment, you should be aware that the use of memmove instead of memcpy is a very important distinction. According to the ANSI standard, memcpy (and strcpy) are not guaranteed to work correctly if the source and destination areas overlap. Only memmove is guaranteed to work correctly in this situation. This change was made to allow the most frequent use of memcpy and strcpy to be optimized, perhaps generated inline using string move instructions, on any architecture. The case of left-to-right or right-to-left move does not matter if the source and destination do not overlap. However, the old Unix versions of strcpy and memcpy did work correctly for overlapping areas (with a significant performance penalty for this flexibility). In order to not break existing Unix code, the Unix compilers often implement these functions with the older specification. Hence, the change has often gone unnoticed by Unix programmers. Microsoft and the other compiler vendors do not have this commitment, and in particular, there is no guarantee that memcpy with overlapping source and destination will work correctly on all possible Windows NT platforms. For example, it may work correctly on the Intel architecture but introduce difficult-to-find bugs when ported to another architecture. This behavior may even vary from compiler to compiler. Do not use memcpy or strcpy on overlapping areas. You Have Been Warned.

You can replace the text highlighted by the selection rectangle (whether or not it is showing) by using the EM_REPLACESEL message. This message removes the text that lies between the low and high selection bounds (if there is no selection, nothing is removed). It then inserts at the caret position its string argument:

```
SendMessage(hEdit, EM_REPLACESEL, 0, (LPARAM)Buffer);
```

or

```
Edit_ReplaceSel(hEdit, Buffer);
```

The wParam parameter is unused at API level 3 and must be 0. At API level 4, it is the "undoable" flag. That is, if it is 0 the replacement does not become part of the undo state maintained by the edit control. If it is non-zero, the replacement is undoable. The undoable flag is not supported in the Edit_ReplaceSel macro. You must send the message directly:

```
SendMessage(hEdit, EM_REPLACESEL, TRUE, (LPARAM)Buffer);
```

There is no way to detect, in an ordinary edit control, if the user has changed the selection. Sometimes this matters. For example, you may want to enable or disable the Copy and Cut icons on a toolbar if there is no selection. Since you can't tell if there is a selection change, you don't know when to enable or disable the icons. There are two ways to handle this. One is to take advantage of what is called "idle time" and update the controls in response to a WM_ENTERIDLE message. This is, in effect, polling each edit control to see if it has the focus and has a selection or asking the control which has the focus if it has a selection. The other technique is to subclass the edit control, intercept any messages that could result in a selection change, and take your action based on the current selection. We did this in our MDI example in Chapter 17, and the code appears there in detail. See Listing 17.8 on page 1190 and the discussion on page 1210.

Setting Contents, Copy, Cut, and Paste

The remaining messages that alter the text in an edit control are the *Window Messages* (WM_*): WM_SETTEXT, WM_COPY, WM_CUT, WM_CLEAR, and WM_PASTE.

You normally set the text of an edit control by sending it a WM_SETTEXT message. This is usually wrapped in a more convenient API wrapper, such as SetWindowText, Edit_SetText, SetDlgItemText, or SetDlgItemInt. This message, or its equivalent API wrapper functions, completely replaces the contents of the edit control text with the NUL-terminated string, which is passed as the argument. A copy of this string is made and stored in the edit control, so once the SendMessage or API function returns, you can reuse or deallocate the space or exit the scope level in which the space was defined. The SetDlgItemInt formats its integer argument as a string and then calls SetDlgItemText referencing that string.

You can copy the currently selected text from an edit control to the Clipboard by sending the WM_COPY or WM_CUT messages to the control. The WM_COPY message copies the selected text to the Clipboard in CF_TEXT format. The WM_CUT message does the same and then deletes the selected text in the control.

```
SendMessage (hEditCntl, WM_COPY, 0, 0) ;
SendMessage (hEditCntl, WM_CUT, 0, 0) ;
```

Neither the WM_COPY nor the WM_CUT messages will have any effect if the edit control has the ES_PASSWORD style. For controls with the ES_PASSWORD style set, these messages return a 0 result.

You might also want to use the WM_CLEAR message. It deletes the selected text from the control without copying it to the Clipboard:

```
SendMessage (hEditCntl, WM_CLEAR, 0, 0) ;
```

Of course, it's nice to be able to retrieve text from the Clipboard and paste it into the control. The WM_PASTE message does just that. It places the text at the current caret position or replaces the current selection:

```
SendMessage (hEditCntl, WM_PASTE, 0, 0) ;
```

The WM_PASTE message requires that there be an entry in the Clipboard in CF_TEXT format. If there is no CF_TEXT object in the Clipboard, the WM_PASTE message is ignored. Normally, you will enable only the paste menu item, toolbar icon, or other mechanism in your GUI that allows a paste if a paste is actually possible. This is often not a serious consideration; most edit controls appear in a dialog, where there is no menu. Thus, there is usually no object that needs to be enabled. Edit controls implement the standard Windows accelerator keys, which are shown in Table 8.24.

The WM_COPY, WM_CUT, WM_CLEAR, and WM_PASTE messages do not have edit control message API equivalents. However, the windowsx.h header file does define message cracker macros for these messages. You can use the message forwarding macros as a portable way to send these messages to an edit control. Here are the message forwarding macro statements equivalent to the preceding four lines of code:

```
FORWARD_WM_COPY   (hEditCntl, SendMessage) ;
FORWARD_WM_CUT    (hEditCntl, SendMessage) ;
FORWARD_WM_CLEAR  (hEditCntl, SendMessage) ;
FORWARD_WM_PASTE  (hEditCntl, SendMessage) ;
```

Working with Multiline Edit Controls

The edit control messages listed in Table 8.23 refer to the contents of the edit control in two ways: the offset from the beginning of the edit control's text and the line number (in a multiline edit control). Line numbers begin at 0. You can retrieve the number of lines in a multiline edit control using either of these statements:

```
Lines = SendMessage (hEditCntl, EM_GETLINECOUNT, 0, 0) ;
```

```
Lines = Edit_GetLineCount (hEditCntl) ;
```

You can retrieve each line, one at a time, by using code like this:

```
LPTSTR Buffer [128] ;
int  i ;
int  LineLength ;

for (i = 0; i < Lines; i++)
    {
    LineLength = Edit_GetLine (hEditCntl, i, Buffer, DIM(Buffer)) ;
    // text which is copied is not NUL-terminated.
    Buffer [LineLength] = _T('\0') ;
    // Do something with the line because
    // it's going away shortly.
    }
```

The EM_GETLINE message is somewhat unusual. It requires three parameters: the line number to retrieve, the buffer pointer, and the maximum length. However, you can send only the first two via the message (in Win32, you can retrieve a line whose number is greater than 32,767). The third value required, the maximum length of the buffer, is stored in the first 16 bits of the buffer itself. This value is overwritten by the text that is retrieved. You cannot have lines in your edit control that are longer than 65,535 characters. The Edit_GetLine macro wrapper nicely handles this. You give it a pointer to the buffer and the maximum length, and it will handle the ugly type casting and store the length value in the first 16 bits of the buffer.

Note also that our code uses an LPTSTR, meaning that it could be used for both Unicode and ANSI, depending on whether the UNICODE symbol is defined at compilation time. Thus we cannot simply use the sizeof operator to determine the buffer size, which could be 128 bytes or 256 bytes. The message requires a character count. So we must divide the sizeof the buffer by the sizeof a TCHAR, using the DIM macro for convenience, to obtain the character count that will fit in the buffer. A minor point, but one that is important: If you were to switch to Unicode, your program will quite possibly crash if you overrun your buffer.

Another odd–and undocumented–feature is that the length you give must be one character longer than the maximum line length you can retrieve. Although the EM_GETLINE message does not put a terminating NUL byte at the end of the string, it assumes that you probably will want to do this. Hence, it will not copy more than the character count minus one character to the buffer. This means that you can be guaranteed that after the line length is returned, you can still safely store the NUL byte within the buffer. The effects of EM_GETLINE are shown in Figure 8.9.

Buffer before call (8-bit ANSI coding):

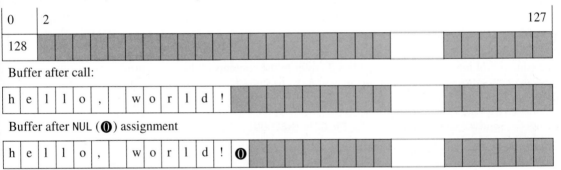

Buffer after call:

Buffer after NUL (●) assignment

Figure 8.9: Buffer behavior for EM_GETLINE

If you are allocating your buffer dynamically, and particularly if you use the EM_LINELENGTH message to get the length of any specific line, remember that your buffer must have max(sizeof(short), (length + 1) * sizeof(TCHAR)) bytes. Note that if you have an ANSI application and the line has length 0, this turns into max(2, (0 + 1)*1) bytes. Otherwise, you will allocate only 1 byte and storing the count word will clobber the second byte. Some allocators, such as the MFC debug-mode allocator, will detect this as a buffer overrun and report an error. Yes, it hit us when writing the Control Explorer.

If you want to allocate a buffer "just big enough" to hold a line, there is a message, EM_LINELENGTH, that will give you the length of the line. However, it also is unusual in that it does not want a line index. Instead, it wants the offset of a character position in the line. It will return the line length of the line that contains that character position. However, you more likely have a line index. How do you use EM_LINELENGTH? You convert the line index to a character position by sending an EM_LINEINDEX message to the control:

```
int pos = Edit_LineIndex(hEdit, index);
int pos = (int)SendMessage(hEdit, EM_LINEINDEX, line, 0);
```

The resulting value is the character position of the first character in the line. So you now have a character in the line and can ask the line length:

```
int len = Edit_LineLength(hEdit, pos)
```

You can then allocate your buffer of size max(sizeof(short), (len + 1) * sizeof(TCHAR)) bytes (see the inset above) and proceed as shown in the EM_GETLINE example.

Line Scrolling and Formatting

How text appears in an edit control depends on several properties of the edit control. The font that is used to display the text is by default the system font; however, you can use SetWindowFont to establish the handle for a font that is used to display the text. In an edit control, all of the text is displayed in the same font. (If you need multiple font display, you must use a Rich Text edit control.) For an edit control without ES_AUTOHSCROLL, the text will be clipped by the control and you will not be able to see any of the text that extends beyond the right edge of the window. For multiline controls, the text will be either word-wrapped or allowed to extend beyond the visible area of the window. When a multiline control is created with the ES_AUTOHSCROLL style, a horizontal scroll bar will appear at the bottom of the control whenever text extends beyond the horizontal dimensions of the area. Otherwise, the text will be line-wrapped, preferentially at word breaks. (If there are no word breaks, it will be wrapped wherever necessary to fit the lines in the space available.)

Normally, the area in which the text is formatted, called the *formatting rectangle*, is the same size as the client area of the edit control. However, you can change the formatting rectangle to be smaller than or larger than the client area by using either the EM_SETRECT message (Edit_SetRect function) or EM_SETRECTNP message (Edit_SetRectNoPaint function) to specify a different rectangle. The EM_SETRECTNP (Edit_SetRectNoPaint) does not trigger a repainting of the contents of the edit control; it is up to you to trigger that by some other means, such as explicitly invalidating the client area. This is available for those cases in which you may want to defer the repainting until you have done some other computations. When the formatting rectangle is set, the lines may be formatted to be wider than the client area. In this case, the horizontal scroll bar will appear if the ES_AUTOHSCROLL style was set. Word breaks and line wrapping are determined by the formatting rectangle, not by the size of the client area. You can always reset the formatting rectangle by using GetClientRect to get the bounds of the client area and then using that rectangle to establish the new formatting rectangle.

You can set the tab stops of a multiline edit control by using the EM_SETTABSTOPS message or calling the Edit_SetTabStops function. (The default for a tab stop is 32 dialog box units, that is, eight average character widths of the system font.) When you put text into the edit control, any tab characters in the text will generate whitespace to force the character following the tab to start at the position of the next tab stop. The EM_SETTABSTOPS message does not cause Windows to redraw the text. But you can call the InvalidateRect function to invalidate the client area of the control and thus force the control to be redrawn using the new tab positions. As in all other contexts of tabs in Windows, you can tab only forward, not backward. If the text exceeds the column width established, the tab will move to the next available tab position following the current position.

Table 8.25 summarizes the parameters to the EM_SETTABSTOPS message and to its API wrapper, Edit_SetTabStops.

Table 8.25: EM_SETTABSTOPS/Edit_SetTabStops behavior

EM_SETTABSTOPS	wParam	lParam	
Edit_SetTabStops	TabCount	Tabs	**Effect**
	0	Ignored	Tab stops are set every 32 dialog box units (every 8 characters).
	1	LPINT	Tab stops are set evenly spaced every Tabs[0] dialog box units.
	> 1	LPINT	Tab stop i is set to Tabs[i] dialog box units.

You can play with the tab stop settings using the Control Explorer. Select the **Edit** control tab and then click the **Send Messages** button. To send an EM_SETTABSTOPS message, select the **Tabs** control tab. Note, however, that you can't actually put a tab into the edit control because the **Tab** key is interpreted by the dialog as a request to move to the next control in the dialog. To get around this, use the **Set DlgCodes** button and add the DLGC_WANTTAB style to the edit control. The edit control is actually subclassed to a handler that will return the correct dialog code. You can then use the **Tab** key to insert a tab and see the effects.

The formatting rectangle defines a space in which formatting is done. But some fonts (particularly those for script-style characters) contain "overhang" graphics, graphics that are outside the character's actual spacing. For example, in some decorative fonts, the letter "Q" has a tail that effectively "underlines" the "u" that follows. If, for whatever reason, this "Q" appeared as the last character on a line, the formatting rectangle would clip the overhang. To allow for these fonts, Windows enables you to set the margins of the edit control. By default, the margins are set to be wide enough to accommodate the largest horizontal overhang in the font currently used in the edit control, so the case we just described should not arise. You could, of course, end up with the opposite problem: margins that are far too wide, having been set to accommodate some unusual character in the font (for example, finding a "Q" at the end of a word in English is unusual).

To give you flexibility, Windows at API level 4 and higher allows you to change the margins by sending an EM_SETMARGINS message to the edit control. You can set either the left margin, the right margin, or both margins, or you can tell the control to revert to its default behavior, using the current font. This is done by explicitly sending the message. There is no API wrapper for this message in windowsx.h. The value in lParam is usually created by using MAKELONG to combine the 16-bit left margin value and 16-bit right margin value into a single 32-bit value. The value in wParam can be one of the values shown in Table 8.26. It determines how the lParam value is used. This message does not return a meaningful value. The Edit_SetMargins API wrapper is defined in extensions.h.

```
SendMessage(hEdit, EM_SETMARGINS, EC_LEFTMARGIN | EC_RIGHTMARGIN,
            MAKELONG(left, right));
Edit_SetMargins(hedit, EC_LEFTMARGIN | EC_RIGHTMARGIN, left, right) ;
```

Table 8.26: EM_SETMARGINS codes

wParam	LOWORD(lParam)	HIWORD(lParam)	Effect
EC_LEFTMARGIN	Left margin.	Ignored.	Sets the left margin.
EC_RIGHTMARGIN	Ignored.	Right margin.	Sets the right margin.
EC_LEFTMARGIN | EC_RIGHTMARGIN	Left margin.	Right margin.	Sets both margins.
EC_USEFONTINFO	Ignored.	Ignored.	Uses the font information to set the margins.

Word breaks are handled by one of two functions, which you must write (there is a default word-break function that is locale-specific). A word-break function is intended to extend the rather simplistic notion of what constitutes a word break to some more powerful and application-specific definition. For example, you may have a control in which the user is supposed to type in a designator such as a "part number" or a "telephone number". You don't want a part number such as "302 AB 7" to break; you want it treated as a complete "word". Similarly, you might not want a telephone number, such as (412) 555-1212, to break at the space following the area code; you want the entire telephone number to be treated as a complete "word". To change the definition of a "word" for this purpose, you use the word-break function.

To establish a word-break function, you first must write one. It looks like this:

```
int CALLBACK MyEditWordBreakProc(
    LPTSTR  text,    // pointer to edit text
    int  CurPos,     // index of starting point
    int  len,        // length in characters of edit text
    int  action      // action to take
  )
  {
   int pos;
   BOOL isdel;

   switch(action)
      { /* action */
       case WB_ISDELIMITER:
           // look for beginning of word to the
           // right of the current position
           isdel = . . .
           // return TRUE if Windows should treat
           // the character at text[CurPos] as a
           // delimiter and FALSE if it should not
           return (int)isdel;
           break;
       case WB_LEFT:
           // look for beginning of word to the
           // left of the current position
           pos = . . .
           return pos;
       case WB_RIGHT:
           // look for beginning of word to the
           // right of the current position
```

```
        pos = . . .
        return pos;
    } /* action */
}
```

We have "simplified" this example by omitting all of the complex code. You would write the code that did a complex scan to determine if the character at CurPos is part of a "part number" or "telephone number" and, if so, either return the character position of the beginning or ending of the "word" or indicate by TRUE or FALSE that the character that otherwise would be treated as a punctuation mark is not a punctuation mark.

Having written this function, you would then associate it with one or more edit controls by using the EM_SETWORDBREAKPROC message or Edit_SetWordBreakProc function:

```
SendMessage(hEdit, EM_SETWORDBREAKPROC, 0, (LPARAM) MyEditWordBreakProc) ;
SetWordBreakProc(hEdit, MyEditWordBreakProc) ;
```

If your special tests decide that the text is not one of the special names you need to process, you can call the default word-break procedure. To do this, you have to have saved the original word-break procedure address. You can get this with EM_GETWORDBREAKPROC or the Edit_GetWordBreakProc function before setting your word-break procedure. You can use any of the techniques we have discussed for how to store window-specific data, such as using the GWL_USERDATA word to hold the old function pointer, or use GWL_USERDATA to hold a pointer to a structure in which you store the old function pointer, or use SetProp to attach the old function pointer as a property.

Having set the formatting rectangle and optionally established the word break procedure, you can take advantage of the formatting that has been done; for example, to lay out the text for printing. You can send the EM_FMTLINES message (or call the Edit_FmtLines function) to an edit control to cause it to insert or remove soft line breaks. A soft line break is the sequence defined as two carriage returns followed by a line feed (in C, the string "\r\r\n"). A soft line break is set any place the formatting has forced a word wrap. When you issue an WM_GETTEXT message or use the Edit_GetText function after you request that soft line breaks be set, the buffer you get back will contain these soft line breaks. You can remove them from the edit control by using the EM_FMTLINES message and requesting that they be removed. If you write your own word-break procedure, you must treat both the hard line break (a single carriage return followed by a line feed; in C, the string "\r\n") and the soft line break both as "word" delimiters.

In the message, the wParam value is TRUE to insert soft line breaks and FALSE to remove them. For the function, the AddEOL parameter carries the same information:

```
SendMessage(hEdit, EM_FMTLINES, TRUE, 0) ;

Edit_FmtLines(hEdit, TRUE) ;
```

Coordinate Mapping

Coordinates in an edit control can be in several different coordinate systems. One is the simple, one-dimensional coordinate system, "position in buffer". A second is the two-dimensional coordinate system, "line in control, character position in line". And a third is the physical coordinate system of "pixel in client area". This latter is mostly interesting if you are subclassing an edit control to get some special effect not otherwise achievable. You can map between any of these coordinate systems. Table 8.27 shows the possible mappings.

Table 8.27: Edit control coordinate mappings

From	To	
	Use Message	
`int BufferPosition`	`POINTS pt`	
	`pt = (POINTS)SendMessage( hEdit, EM_POSFROMCHAR,` `                    BufferPosition, 0 );`	
	`int LineIndex`	
	`LineIndex = SendMessage( hEdit, EM_LINEFROMCHAR,` `                    BufferPosition, 0) ;`	
	`int ColumnIndex`	

	`ColumnIndex = BufferPosition -`
	`                    SendMessage(hEdit, EM_LINEINDEX,`
	`                        LineIndex, 0 ) ;`	

–	`int LineIndex`	
	`LineIndex = SendMessage( hEdit,` `                    EM_GETFIRSTVISIBLELINE, 0, 0 ) ;`	

`int LineIndex`	`int LineStart`
	`(buffer position of first`
	`character of line)`	

	`LineStart = SendMessage(hEdit, EM_LINEINDEX,` `                    LineIndex, 0 ) ;`	
`int LineIndex` `int ColumnIndex`	`int BufferPosition`	
	`BufferPosition = LineIndex + ColumnIndex ;`	
`POINTS pt`	`int LineIndex` `int ColumnIndex`	

	`LONG pos = SendMessage(hEdit, EM_CHARFROMPOS,`
	`                    MAKELONG(pt.x, pt.y));`
	`int LineIndex = HIWORD ( pos ) ;`
	`int ColumnIndex = LOWORD ( pos ) ;`	

`selection`	`int BufferPosition`	

	`int BufferPosition;`
	`LONG end;`
	`SendMessage(hEdit, EM_GETSEL,`
	`                    (WPARAM)&BufferPosition,`
	`                    (LPARAM)&end);`	

The EM_POSFROMCHAR message (Edit_PosFromChar function) returns a DWORD that contains the signed *x*-coordinate in the low-order word and the signed *y*-coordinate in the high-order word. You can cast this to a POINTS (short-point) structure:

```
typedef struct tagPOINTS
{
    SHORT   x;
    SHORT   y;
} POINTS, * PPOINTS, * LPPOINTS;
```

Note that the point may be outside the client area of the edit control:

```
POINTS pt = (POINTS)SendMessage (hEdit, EM_POSFROMCHAR, pos, 0) ;
// The coordinates are found in pt.x and pt.y
```

If the position is beyond the end of the buffer, the position that is returned is the coordinate of where the next character would be "drawn".

The EM_CHARFROMPOS computes a character position from a mouse position. The EM_CHARFROMPOS message (or Edit_CharFromPos, defined in our extensions.h file) takes the *x, y* position in its lParam and returns a value that encodes the line index and column position of the character. The return value is -1 if the point specified is outside the client area of the control.

```
LONG val = SendMessage (hEdit, EM_CHARFROMPOS, 0, MAKELONG(x, y));
if (val != -1)
    { /* valid point */
      int line = HIWORD(val) ;
      int col = LOWORD(val) ;
      // compute the buffer position of the character
      // under the mouse
      int pos = Edit_LineIndex ( hEdit, line)  + col ;
      // . . . do something with coordinates
    } /* valid point */
```

Edit Control Notification Messages

An edit control sends a WM_COMMAND message with a notification code to its parent window. The id parameter to the OnCommand message handler is the edit control ID. The hctl parameter is the window handle of the edit control. The codeNotify parameter is the notification code. Rich Text edit controls use both the WM_COMMAND and WM_NOTIFY messages to send messages to the parent window. Table 8.28 lists the edit control notification codes that appear with WM_COMMAND, and Table 8.29 lists the Rich Text edit control notification codes that appear with WM_NOTIFY. The parameters for an OnNotify handler are the same as the parameters for an OnCommand handler.

Table 8.28: Edit control WM_COMMAND notification codes

Notification code	Meaning
EN_CHANGE	Control contents have changed.
EN_ERRSPACE	Error allocating additional memory.
EN_HSCROLL	Control scrolls horizontally.
EN_IMECHANGE	Control has a change of status of the Input Method Editor (IME). This is available only in Asian-language versions of Windows.

Table 8.28: Edit control `WM_COMMAND` notification codes

Notification code	Meaning
EN_KILLFOCUS	Control loses the input focus.
EN_MAXTEXT	Attempt to exceed character limit (set by `EM_SETLIMITTEXT` or by hitting the control limit if `ES_AUTOHSCROLL` was not set).
EN_SETFOCUS	Control obtains the input focus.
EN_UPDATE	Control contents will change.
EN_VSCROLL	Control scrolls vertically.

`WM_COMMAND` Message Cracker Handler (See page 520)

```
void cls_OnCommand(HWND hwnd, int id, HWND hctl, UINT codeNotify);
```

`WM_NOTIFY` Message Cracker Handler (See page 521)

```
void cls_OnNotify(HWND hwnd, int id, NMHDR * nmhdr);
```

Table 8.29: Rich Text edit control `WM_NOTIFY` notification codes

EN_CORRECTTEXT	EN_OLEOPFAILED	EN_SAVECLIPBOARD
EN_DROPFILES	EN_PROTECTED	EN_SELCHANGE
EN_MSGFILTER	EN_REQUESTRESIZE	EN_STOPNOUNDO

The EN_UPDATE notification code indicates that the user has changed the contents of an edit control, but Windows has not yet displayed the change on the screen. The EN_CHANGE notification code follows. It indicates that the user has changed the text of an edit control and Windows has displayed the change. Normally, you use the EN_UPDATE message to respond to a change where you must interact with the user before the change appears, and you use EN_CHANGE when you can interact with the user after the change has been displayed. You generally don't need to respond to both.

One approach you might take to input validation is to save a copy of the contents of the edit control. When the user makes a change, you respond to the EN_UPDATE message by verifying that the input is correct, for example, by checking its syntax or comparing it to some known valid set of values. If the input is correct, you make a copy of it and replace the "backup copy" with this new contents of the edit control. If the change the user made is not valid, you replace the contents with the backup copy and beep. But be careful! The act of replacing the contents triggers another EN_UPDATE message!

Classic input validation in most systems simply validates after every keystroke. For example, if you expect a telephone number, you might demand that the first character be a "(", the next three characters be digits, the fifth character be a ")", the next three characters be digits, the next character be a hyphen, and the next four characters be digits. If the user types an invalid key, you simply beep and ignore it. You might think that such methods could be simulated in Windows by intercepting the WM_CHAR messages by subclassing the edit control. But in Windows, this doesn't work because the user can use the cursor keys or the mouse to reposition the input caret and effectively type characters out of sequence. So you can't assume that keystrokes come in representing the sequential entry of characters. Hence, you also must not implement any form of validation that would prohibit the user from creating the input text in any order.

To handle this in Windows, you must use the EN_UPDATE notification. When you receive the EN_UPDATE notification, you read the current text in the control, parse it according to whatever rules you have established, and either accept it or reject it. If you accept it, you don't need to do anything special. If you reject it, you must restore the previous text (which you must store somewhere). Again, you must be careful because this will trigger another EN_UPDATE notification. This could lead to an infinite recursion unless you can guarantee that setting the old text value cannot possibly generate an error.

The EN_HSCROLL and EN_VSCROLL notification codes signal that the user has clicked the edit control's horizontal and vertical scroll bars, respectively, although the change has not yet been displayed on the screen.

An edit control informs its parent window when it gains and loses the input focus by sending it WM_COMMAND messages with the EN_SETFOCUS notification codes.

The edit control notifies its parent of error conditions. It sends the EN_MAXTEXT notification code when the user attempts to enter more than the specified number of characters into an edit control. It uses this code also when the user attempts to type past the end of an edit control that doesn't have the ES_AUTOHSCROLL style. The EN_ERRSPACE notification code indicates that the control could not allocate additional memory.

There is a difference between the EM_SETLIMITTEXT and the absence of the ES_AUTOHSCROLL style. The EM_SETLIMITTEXT limits the total number of characters that can be typed into the control by counting the number of characters. Without the ES_AUTOHSCROLL, the number of characters is limited by the size of the edit control itself. Thus, if you think that you are limiting the number of characters by limiting the edit control size, remember that with variable-pitch fonts, you might be limiting yourself to the equivalent of, say, only 9 capital "I" characters or 3 capital "W" characters. The actual limit in any edit control is the lesser of the limit set by EM_SETLIMITTEXT and the maximum width of text if you don't use ES_AUTOHSCROLL.

You should not rely on ES_AUTOHSCROLL as a solution for minimizing the size of an edit control. Very few interfaces can be more frustrating to deal with than an edit control whose size is consistently shorter than the typical input string that will be typed (unless it is an edit control without ES_AUTOHSCROLL that is consistently shorter than the typical input string!). ES_AUTOHSCROLL should be thought of as a way of being safe in the very rare cases in which a string might exceed the available screen space. This is one of those esthetic areas where you must be very aware of the impact of your decision on the end user.

Summary

There are many kinds of controls available in Windows. We have chosen a somewhat arbitrary breakdown of the categories to create separate chapters. This chapter has covered what we have classed as "scalar" controls–those which return or accept a single value (we think of the string values of the static and edit controls as being single values for this purpose). In the next chapters we will cover two other classes of controls, which we have split into "array" controls–those controls which can hold more than a single value–and "slider" controls–those controls which provide some sort of linear numeric input or output.

9 Using Controls: ListBox, ComboBox, ImageList, and TreeView Classes

The previous chapter covered "simple value" controls, such as check boxes and edit controls. Next, we examine controls that let us view and scroll many kinds of objects. The simplest of these is the LISTBOX class, which allows us to have a simple scrollable list. A more general control, based on the list box, is the COMBOBOX class. This gives us an edit control or a static control combined with a scrollable list of values. The most popular form of the COMBOBOX is the "drop-down" style because it uses as little screen space as possible when it is not actually needed. As dialogs and interactions become more complex, the ability to save screen space becomes important.

The list box is rather simplistic, and in many cases, you would like to show columnar data. The List View control (whose formal class name is SysListView) is a combination of a list box-like facility combined with the Header control (whose formal class name is SysHeader) that gives you a simple columnar list. But since it was intended to support facilities like the Windows 95 or Windows NT 4.*x* Explorer, it gives you several alternative representations, such as icon displays. We discuss the Header control in Chapter 7, page 443.

The Tree View control (whose formal class name is SysTreeView32) gives the nested, expandable tree views familiar from the Explorer directory view. The Tree View control can utilize a facility called the "Image List" to simplify the display of iconic information, so we also cover image lists (although they are not actually a control).

The LISTBOX Class

The LISTBOX class creates a control that contains and displays a list of items. A list box can display its contents in a single column or in multiple columns.

When a single-column list box contains more items than can be displayed in the control's client area, you can add a vertical scroll bar to scroll the other items into view. A multiple column list box doesn't need a vertical scroll bar because the items in the list snake from the bottom of one column to the top of the column immediately to the right. You can, however, request a horizontal scroll bar to scroll to additional columns of items.

A list box normally allows the user to select only one item at a time. However, you can create a list box that allows the user to select multiple items. There are two variants. The one actually called "multiple selection" allows the user to click an item and turn it on and off. The other multiple-selection list box is officially an "extended selection" list box. In this case, the user can either click one item and drag it along the list box, highlighting the items as the mouse is dragged over them, or use the **Ctrl** key with a mouse click to toggle the list box item selection so that it works just like a multiple-selection list box. There is even a list box, often used for display purposes when you don't want selection as an option, that does not support selection (this is only in API level 4 and higher). You can examine all of these by using the Control Explorer.

Finally, you can create an owner-draw list box in the same way that you can create an owner-draw button. You don't draw the list box; you draw just the items in the list box. An owner-draw list box can have all items be the same height or each item vary in height. Owner-draw list boxes are very powerful and flexible. For example, for many years, prior to the introduction of the TreeView control class, the hierarchical file display shown in a traditional **File/Open** dialog was done using an owner-draw list box. The hierarchical-style display is so common that it is now implemented as a standard common control, the Tree View (see page 652).

The LISTBOX Class Styles

You can create a standard list box with the following statement:

```
#define IDC_LISTBOX   42  // arbitrary control ID

HWND hListBox ;

hListBox = CreateWindow (
    _T("listbox"), NULL,
    WS_CHILD | WS_VISIBLE | LBS_STANDARD,
    100, 200, 300, 60, hwnd, IDC_LISTBOX, hInstance, NULL) ;
```

This creates a single-column list box with a border around it. The control sends notification messages to its parent window when the user selects an item in the list box. The list box keeps its contents sorted alphabetically. The list box also has a vertical scroll bar. You get all these features by specifying the LBS_STANDARD list box class style.

Table 9.1 shows the LISTBOX class styles.

Table 9.1: LISTBOX **class styles**

Style	Meaning
LBS_DISABLENOSCROLL	Shows a disabled vertical scroll bar for the list box when the box does not contain enough items to scroll. When you do not specify this style, the scroll bar is hidden when the list box does not contain enough items to require scrolling.
LBS_EXTENDEDSEL	Allows the user to easily select contiguous items as well as separate items in a list box.
LBS_HASSTRINGS	Creates a list box that contains strings. All list boxes except owner-draw list boxes have this style by default. An owner-draw list box can either have or omit this style. If this style is selected, the list box maintains the storage for the strings.
LBS_MULTICOLUMN	Creates a multicolumn, horizontally scrollable list box. The LB_SETCOLUMNWIDTH message sets the width of the columns.
LBS_MULTIPLESEL	Allows the user to select multiple items.
LBS_NOINTEGRALHEIGHT	Allows a list box to display a partial item. Normally, a list box resizes itself to display only complete items.
LBS_NOREDRAW	Doesn't redisplay the contents of the list box when items are added or deleted. You can add or remove this style at any time by sending the WM_SETREDRAW message.
LBS_NOSEL[4]	Indicates that the list box is for purposes of displaying information. Selection is not permitted.
LBS_NOTIFY	Notifies the parent window whenever the user clicks or double-clicks an item.
LBS_OWNERDRAWFIXED	Creates an owner-draw list box containing items with a constant height.
LBS_OWNERDRAWVARIABLE	Creates an owner-draw list box containing items that can vary in height.
LBS_SORT	Alphabetically sorts the strings in a list box. For an owner-draw list box, you can implement any sort criteria you want.
LBS_STANDARD	LBS_NOTIFY I LBS_SORT I WS_BORDER I WS_VSCROLL
LBS_USETABSTOPS	Expands tab characters when drawing an item.
LBS_WANTKEYBOARDINPUT	Sends a WM_VKEYTOITEM or WM_CHARTOITEM message to the parent window whenever the user presses a key while the list box has the input focus.
WS_BORDER	Draws the list box with a border.

[4]Available only at Win32 API level 4 and higher.

Table 9.1: LISTBOX class styles

Style	Meaning
WS_HSCROLL	The list box could have a horizontal scroll bar.
WS_VSCROLL	The list box could have a vertical scroll bar.

[4]Available only at Win32 API level 4 and higher.

A basic list box is rather plain. There is no border around the displayed items, and the box displays the items in the order they were added. The list box doesn't notify its parent window when the user selects items. And, finally, the list box does not scroll, so it must be large enough to display all items. You receive this basic list box when you create a window of the LISTBOX class and specify only the WS_CHILD window style.

Generally, this box is a little too plain. You'll want to add a few optional styles. Adding the WS_BORDER style produces a list box with a border around the list of items. (Actually, it requests a border around a window, but a list box is a child window.) Note that in some cases, such as using the ctl3dv32.dll library under Windows NT 3.*x*, a border is required for proper 3D appearance.

It's convenient to let the list box notify its parent window when the user selects items in it. When you add the LBS_NOTIFY style, a list box sends a WM_COMMAND message each time the user selects an item. Without this style, you would have to explicitly query the list box (by sending it messages) to determine which items were selected.

You can add a vertical scroll bar to a list box by including the WS_VSCROLL style. The scroll bar allows the user to scroll through the list of items so that the list box doesn't have to be large enough to display every item at once. Adding a horizontal scroll bar is a bit tricky. We talk about how to do one on page 619.

Frequently, it's convenient to display the items in a list box in sequence. A list box with the LBS_SORT style sorts all items added to the list box. Sort order is determined by the "code page" for localized national language support; thus, collating sequence follows the expected national standard.[1]

Because the notification, sort, scroll, and border styles are frequently used together, windows.h defines LBS_STANDARD as the combination of these four styles:

```
#define LBS_STANDARD \
    (LBS_NOTIFY | LBS_SORT | WS_VSCROLL | WS_BORDER)
```

Creating a list box of the proper size is a bit more complicated than it is for most controls. First, you have to decide how many items you want the box to display. The vertical height of the box is then the number of items times the height of a character in the font the box uses. (This is the tmHeight field from the TEXTMETRIC structure.) The width of the list box should be one of two values. One possible value is that it should be at least as wide as the longest string in the box. When you include the WS_VSCROLL style, you

---

[1] For more information on international sorting orders, see O'Donnell, S. M., *Programming for the World: A Guide to Internationalization*, and Kano, N, *Developing International Software for Windows 95 and Windows NT*, both cited in "Further Reading".

should increase the width by the width of the vertical scroll bar. (This is the value returned by the GetSystemMetrics function when you specify the SM_CXVSCROLL parameter.) Or, in those few cases in which you cannot reasonably make the list box sufficiently wide or cannot predict how wide it needs to be, you should add a horizontal scroll bar. We discuss this on page 619.

A list box normally lets the user select only one item. The selected item is always the last item chosen. Selecting a new item deselects the previously selected item. You can allow the user to select more than one item from a list box by including either the LBS_MULTIPLESEL style or the LBS_EXTENDEDSEL style. The LBS_MULTIPLESEL style allows the user to select more than one item. Clicking an item toggles its selection state. The user can select any number of items, but each item must be individually selected. The LBS_EXTENDSEL style also allows the user to select more than one item from the list box. However, additional support is added to allow the user to easily select multiple contiguous items in the list box, as well as multiple noncontiguous items. Basically, you use the LBS_MULTIPLESEL style when the user must select each item individually. You use the LBS_EXTENDSEL style when the user can press the **Shift** key and select multiple contiguous items with a single mouse action, or use the **Ctrl** key and select multiple discontiguous items.

The LBS_NOSEL style allows you to specify a list box that allows the user to view information but not to select anything.

The selection styles are mutually exclusive; you may select only one of them or none of them. The behavior of the list box at the user interface is summarized in Table 9.2.

Table 9.2: Selection style behavior

Style	Selection Ability	
None	Single selection; new selection removes previous selection.	
LBS_NOSEL	No selection available.	
LBS_EXTENDEDSEL	Multiple selection; the click effect is determined by the shift state, as follows:	
	None	Click removes all existing selection highlights and highlights the new selection.
	Shift	Click extends the existing selection from its anchor point to the item being selected.
	Ctrl	Click toggles item selection state.
	Drag	Extends the selection from its anchor point, where the mouse was clicked, down to the item that is under the mouse. When the mouse is released, the highlighted items become the new selection.
LBS_MULTIPLESEL	Multiple selection; clicking an item toggles its selection state.	

You would generally use the LBS_MULTICOLUMN style when creating a list box that contains a large number of narrow items but has a large amount of horizontal screen space available. You may have already seen a multicolumn list box. The list view in a Windows 95 or Windows NT 4.*x* Explorer window, for example, displays the directory entries in a multicolumn list box. A multicolumn list box displays items starting in the left-most column. When it is filled (top to bottom), it displays the remaining items in a second column immediately to the right of the first. You don't need to vertically scroll a multicolumn list box, but you may need to horizontally scroll it. When all items can't be displayed in the client area of the box, you should include the WS_HSCROLL window style. This adds a horizontal scroll bar to the list box. If the list box is not a multicolumn list box, you will have to do some additional work to cause the horizontal scroll bar to appear.

Of course, a multicolumn list box needs to know the width of a column. All columns will be the same width. You set this width by sending a LB_SETCOLUMNWIDTH message to the box.

You can create an owner-draw list box just as you can create owner-draw buttons; however, you're responsible for drawing only the individual items in an owner-draw list box, not the entire control. Owner-draw list boxes fall into two main categories: those containing items that all have the same height (indicated by the LBS_OWNERDRAWFIXEDL style) and those containing items that can vary in height (indicated by the LBS_OWNERDRAWVARIABLE style).

Normally, an owner-draw list box doesn't assume that items added to the list box are strings. When you add an item, an owner-draw list box normally just stores the 32-bit value. The LBS_HASSTRINGS list box style indicates that the items added to the box are pointers to strings and that the box should maintain the storage for the string. When the box has both the LBS_HASSTRINGS and the LBS_SORT styles, the box sorts the strings. When the box has the LBS_SORT style without the LBS_HASSTRINGS style, the box sends multiple WM_COMPAREITEM messages to its parent window to determine the relative positions of items in the box.

A list box with the LBS_WANTKEYBOARDINPUT style notifies its parent window when it receives WM_KEYDOWN and WM_CHAR messages. It receives these messages only when it has the input focus. The owner of a list box with the LBS_HASSTRINGS style receives WM_VKEYTOITEM messages but not WM_CHARTOITEM messages from the box. The owner of a list box without the LBS_HASSTRINGS style receives WM_CHARTOITEM messages but not WM_VKEYTOITEM messages from the box.

When the list box receives a WM_KEYDOWN message, it sends a WM_VKEYTOITEM message to its parent window. The low-order word of the wParam parameter of the WM_VKEYTOITEM message contains the virtual-key code from the WM_KEYDOWN message. The high-order word of the wParam parameter contains the current caret position. The lParam contains the handle of the list box.

When the list box receives a WM_CHAR message, it sends a WM_CHARTOITEM message to its parent window. The low-order word of the wParam parameter of the WM_CHARTOITEM message contains the character. The high-order word of the wParam parameter contains the current caret position. The lParam contains the handle of the list box, as does the WM_VKEYTOITEM message.

The parent window can use the WM_VKEYTOITEM and WM_CHARTOITEM messages in any way it wants.[2] When the parent window function uses these messages, it should return one of the values shown in Table 9.3. You could use these messages to create a list box that supports the selection of multiple items by keyboard input of wildcard characters.

Table 9.3: Return values from processing WM_VKEYTOITEM and WM_CHARTOITEM

Return Value	Effect
-2	The parent has selected the proper item in the list box; no further processing is required.
-1	The list box should execute the default action for the key (for a character key, select the next item in the list box that starts with that key).
>=0	The list box should execute the default action for the key on the item whose index is returned.

WM_VKEYTOITEM Message Cracker Handler
WM_CHARTOITEM Message Cracker Handler

```
void cls_OnVKeyToItem(HWND hwnd, UINT vk, HWND hList, int CaretPos);
void cls_OnCharToItem(HWND hwnd, UINT ch, HWND hList, int CaretPos);
```

| Parameter | wParam | | lParam | | Meaning |
	lo	hi	lo	hi	
hwnd					Window handle of the window.
vk	■				OnVKeyToItem: 8-bit virtual-key code (high-order 8 bits are 0).
ch	■				ANSI: OnCharToItem: character code (high-order 8 bits are 0).
					Unicode: OnCharToItem: character code.
hList			■		Handle to the list box.
CaretPos		■			The current position of the list box caret.

---

[2] For more details on proper use of these messages, also check out the Microsoft Knowledge Base article Q108941 found on the MSDN CD-ROM or online on various Microsoft-supported services.

A list box with the LBS_USETABSTOPS style expands tab characters when it draws its strings. A default tab stop is set for every 32 horizontal dialog units. The size of a dialog unit varies based on the system font and can be different horizontally and vertically. To calculate the number of pixels in a dialog unit, you first must call the GetDialogBaseUnits function to obtain the number of pixels, horizontally and vertically, in a dialog base unit, not a dialog unit. A dialog base unit is a unit of measurement that derives from the height and average width of characters in the system font.

```
DWORD   dw ;
int     HorzBaseUnit ;
int     VertBaseUnit ;

dw = GetDialogBaseUnits () ;
VertBaseUnit = HIWORD (dw) ;
HorzBaseUnit = LOWORD (dw) ;
```

A horizontal dialog unit is equal to one fourth the horizontal dialog base unit value. A vertical dialog unit is equal to one eighth the vertical dialog base unit value. The inverse may not be true, however. That is, 4 horizontal dialog units may not equal 1 horizontal dialog base unit because of truncation during the integer division. So you should always multiply the number of dialog units by the dialog base unit value before dividing the product by 4 or 8 (depending on the axis). For example, the following code calculates the distance in pixels between the default tab stops:

```
PixelDist = (32 * HorzBaseUnit) / 4 ;
```

The following doesn't calculate the proper value when the horizontal dialog base unit value isn't evenly divisible by 4:

```
PixelDist = 32 * (HorzBaseUnit / 4) ;    /* Wrong! */
```

You can change the tab-stop positions of a list box control with the LBS_USETABSTOPS style. You send the control an LB_SETTABSTOPS message with the wParam parameter set to the number of tab stops in the list. The lParam parameter points to an array of integers containing the tab-stop positions in dialog units, not dialog base units. You can tab forward only–not backward–so the tab stops in the array must be listed in increasing order. Tab stops in list boxes are awkward to use in general. Usually, you will find that using a variety of alternatives will be easier and produces a better result. Owner-draw list boxes give you better control of alignment. Header windows and list views are most often what are being simulated with tab stops. Ultimately, you may wish to use a third-party "grid control" for more elaborate displays.

Table 9.4: LB_SETTABSTOPS parameters

wParam	lParam	Meaning
> 1	LPINT	lParam points to array of wParam tab stops.
1	LONG	lParam in distance of equally-spaced tabs.
0	NULL	Tabs every 2 dialog units.

The lParam parameter of the LB_SETTABSTOPS message is interpreted differently when the wParam parameter is less than 2 (because no array of tab stops is required). When the wParam parameter equals 1, the lParam parameter contains the distance between equally spaced tab stops. You can also set a default tab stop of 2 dialog units by setting both wParam and lParam to 0. This is summarized in Table 9.4.

Finally, the LBS_NOREDRAW list box class style creates a list box with its redraw flag turned off. This type of box doesn't update its display when an item is added or deleted. Obviously, this list box isn't very useful unless you can make the list box update its display sooner or later. You can turn the redraw flag of the list box control back on again by sending the control a WM_SETREDRAW message with the wParam parameter set to a nonzero value:

```
SendMessage (hListBox, WM_SETREDRAW, TRUE, OL) ;
```

```
/* or */
```

```
SetWindowRedraw (hListBox, TRUE) ;
```

Normally, a list box redraws its contents every time a new item is added. This can cause much unnecessary redrawing and flickering when you're initially filling or refilling a list box. To avoid this, create the list box with the LBS_NOREDRAW style and add all but the last item to the list box. Next, call SetWindowRedraw with a redraw parameter of TRUE. Finally, add the last item to the list box. You should note that it's the addition of the final item that causes the list box to be drawn. The WM_SETREDRAW message only sets or clears the redraw flag; it does not redraw the list box. Later, you can clear the redraw flag before refilling the list box with new or additional elements.

```
SetWindowRedraw (hListBox, FALSE) ;
```

Occasionally, you may not know which item is the last item to be added to a list box until after you've added the item. In this case, add all the items with the redraw flag set to FALSE. Then set the redraw flag to TRUE and force the list box to redraw itself by calling the InvalidateRect function as follows:

```
InvalidateRect (hListBox, NULL, TRUE) ;
```

The LBS_DISABLENOSCROLL list box style controls the disappearance of the scroll bar. Without this style, the box hides its vertical scroll bar when it does not contain enough items to require scrolling. With this style, the box disables, but does not hide, its vertical scroll bar when it does not contain enough items to require scrolling. This is particularly useful if your list box is changing its contents in response to some other control setting; the user does not see the scroll bar snap in and out of existence. It also means that if you are computing the horizontal scroll bar width, you do not need to determine whether the scroll bar would be present. (This is a bit tricky. You have to do geometric computations based on the font height and list box size.) Instead, you can always assume its presence.

Messages to a List Box Control

By now you should be expecting that you interact with a list box by sending it messages. List boxes, along with combo boxes, are among the richest of the built-in controls. There are 36 messages unique to list box controls, as listed in Table 9.5.

Most list box messages return the value LB_ERRSPACE or LB_ERR to indicate an error in the request. The list box returns LB_ERRSPACE when it can't allocate enough memory for the box items. It returns LB_ERR when the action requested by the message can't be successfully completed and LB_OKAY[3] when it is successfully completed.

---

[3] Note the inconsistent spelling. Everywhere else, the spelling is "OK"!

Table 9.5: List box messages

Message	Function Action
LB_ADDFILE	`int Listbox_AddFile(HWND hwnd, LPCTSTR filename)`[e]
	Adds a filename to a list box that may already contain filenames.
LB_ADDSTRING	`int ListBox_AddString(HWND hwnd, LPCTSTR str)`
	`int ListBox_AddItemData`[1]`(HWND hwnd, LPARAM data)`
	Adds a string to the list box. The `ListBox_AddItemData` is used for owner-draw list boxes without the LBS_HASSTRINGS style and is a wrapper for LB_ADDSTRING.
LB_DELETESTRING	`int ListBox_DeleteString(HWND hwnd, int index)`
	Deletes a string from the list box.
LB_DIR	`int ListBox_Dir(HWND hwnd, UINT attrs, LPCTSTR FileSpec)`
	Adds a list of files to the list box. The files are selected by the `attrs` flags.
LB_FINDSTRING	`int ListBox_FindString(HWND hwnd, int indexStart, LPCTSTR Find)`
	`int ListBox_FindItemData(HWND hwnd, int indexStart, LPARAM data)`[1]
	Returns the index of the item in the list box that matches the specified prefix. The search starts at the specified index and wraps around to index 0, continuing around if necessary.
LB_FINDSTRINGEXACT	`int ListBox_FindStringExact(HWND hwnd, int indexStart, LPCTSTR Find)`
	Returns the index of the item in the list box that exactly matches the specified string.
LB_GETANCHORINDEX[4]	`int ListBox_GetAnchorIndex(HWND hwnd)`[e]
	Returns the index of the first selection of a multiple selection in a multiple-selection list box. The selection spans the anchor index to the caret index (either of these may be the larger value).

[1]When a list box is created with one of the LBS_OWNERDRAW styles but without the LBS_HASSTRINGS style, there is no provision for a string. Instead, the LB_ADDSTRING, LBS_FINDSTRING, and LB_INSERTSTRING operations take the 32-bit value and store it as item data. The value can be retrieved either by using the ListBox_GetText or the ListBox_SetItemData and ListBox_GetItemData calls.

[4]Available only at Win32 API level 4 and higher.

[e]Defined in `extensions.h`.

Table 9.5: List box messages

Message	Function Action
LB_GETCARETINDEX	`int ListBox_GetCaretIndex(HWND hwnd)`
	Returns the index of the item in the list box that has the focus rectangle.
LB_GETCOUNT	`int ListBox_GetCount(HWND hwnd)`
	Returns the number of items in the list box.
LB_GETCURSEL	`int ListBox_GetCurSel(HWND hwnd)`
	Returns the index of the selected item.
LB_GETHORIZONTALEXTENT	`int ListBox_GetHorizontalExtent (HWND hwnd)`
	Returns the scrollable width of the list box.
LB_GETITEMDATA	`LRESULT ListBox_GetItemData(HWND hwnd, int index)`
	Returns the 32-bit value associated with the item.
LB_GETITEMHEIGHT	`int ListBox_GetItemHeight(HWND hwnd, int index)`
	Returns the height in pixels of the specified item in a variable-height owner-draw list box. Returns the height in pixels of all items in all other list boxes.
LB_GETITEMRECT	`int ListBox_GetItemRect(HWND hwnd, int index, LPRECT rect)`
	Returns the bounding rectangle in list box client-area coordinates for the specified item.
LB_GETLOCALE	`LCID ListBox_GetLocale(HWND hwnd)`[e]
	Returns the locale identifier for the list box.
LB_GETSEL	`int ListBox_GetSel(HWND hwnd, int index)`
	Returns the selection state of an item.
LB_GETSELCOUNT	`int ListBox_GetSelCount(HWND hwnd)`
	Returns the number of selected items.

[1]When a list box is created with one of the LBS_OWNERDRAW styles but without the LBS_HASSTRINGS style, there is no provision for a string. Instead, the LB_ADDSTRING, LBS_FINDSTRING, and LB_INSERTSTRING operations take the 32-bit value and store it as item data. The value can be retrieved either by using the ListBox_GetText or the ListBox_SetItemData and ListBox_GetItemData calls.

[4]Available only at Win32 API level 4 and higher.

[e]Defined in `extensions.h`.

Table 9.5: List box messages

Message	Function Action
LB_GETSELITEMS	`int ListBox_GetSelItems(HWND hwnd, int Items, LPINT Indices)`
	Fills an array with the indices of the selected items in a multiselection list box.
LB_GETTEXT	`int ListBox_GetText(HWND hwnd, int index, LPTSTR Buffer)`
	Copies the string for the specified item into the specified buffer.
LB_GETTEXTLEN	`int ListBox_GetTextLen(HWND hwnd, int index)`
	Returns the length of a string in the list box.
LB_GETTOPINDEX	`int ListBox_GetTopIndex(HWND hwnd)`
	Returns the index of the first visible item.
LB_INITSTORAGE[4]	`int ListBox_InitStorage(HWND hwnd, int itemcount, int stringBytes)`[e]
	Initializes a storage space for holding the list box data.
LB_INSERTSTRING	`int ListBox_InsertString(HWND hwnd, int index, LPCTSTR str)`
	`int ListBox_InsertItemData(HWND hwnd, int index, LPARAM data)`[1]
	Inserts an item at the specified position.
LB_ITEMFROMPOINT[4]	`int ListBox_ItemFromPoint(HWND hwnd, int x, int y)`[e]
	Returns the index of the nearest item, given client coordinates of a point.
LB_RESETCONTENT	`BOOL ListBox_ResetContent(HWND hwnd)`
	Removes all items from a list box.
LB_SELECTSTRING	`int ListBox_SelectString(HWND hwnd, int indexStart, LPCTSTR Find)`
	`int ListBox_SelectItemData(HWND hwnd, int indexStart, LPARAM data)`[1]
	Selects the first item that matches a prefix.

[1]When a list box is created with one of the LBS_OWNERDRAW styles but without the LBS_HASSTRINGS style, there is no provision for a string. Instead, the LB_ADDSTRING, LBS_FINDSTRING, and LB_INSERTSTRING operations take the 32-bit value and store it as item data. The value can be retrieved either by using the ListBox_GetText or the ListBox_SetItemData and ListBox_GetItemData calls.

[4]Available only at Win32 API level 4 and higher.

[e]Defined in `extensions.h`.

Table 9.5: List box messages

Message	Function Action
LB_SELITEMRANGE	`int ListBox_SelItemRange(HWND hwnd, BOOL Select,` `int first, int last)`
	Selects consecutive items in a multiple-selection list box. Limited to list boxes containing 65,536 items or fewer. Available in all versions of Windows.
LB_SELITEMRANGEEX	`int ListBox_SelItemRangeEx(HWND hwnd, int first,` `int last)`
	Selects consecutive items in a multiple-selection list box. In Windows 95, limited to list boxes containing 65,536 items or fewer. In Windows NT, limited to $2^{31} - 1$ entries. Not available in Win32s.
LB_SETANCHORINDEX[4]	`int ListBox_SetAnchorIndex(HWND hwnd, int index)`[e]
	Sets the index of the first selection of a multiple selection. Returns 0 if successful and LB_ERR if there is an error.
LB_SETCARETINDEX	`int ListBox_SetCaretIndex(HWND hwnd, int index)`
	Sets the focus rectangle to the specified item and scrolls the item into view.
LB_SETCOLUMNWIDTH	`void ListBox_SetColumnWidth(HWND hwnd, int ColumnWidth)`
	Sets the width of all columns in a multicolumn list box.
LB_SETCURSEL	`int ListBox_SetCurSel(HWND hwnd, int index)`
	Selects an item and scrolls it into view.
LB_SETHORIZONTALEXTENT	`void ListBox_SetHorizontalExtent(HWND hwnd,` `int cxExtent)`
	Sets the width, in pixels, of the contents of a list box with the WS_HSCROLL style.
LB_SETITEMDATA	`int ListBox_SetItemData(HWND hwnd, int index,` `LPARAM data)`
	Associates a 32-bit value with the specified item.

[1]When a list box is created with one of the LBS_OWNERDRAW styles but without the LBS_HASSTRINGS style, there is no provision for a string. Instead, the LB_ADDSTRING, LBS_FINDSTRING, and LB_INSERTSTRING operations take the 32-bit value and store it as item data. The value can be retrieved either by using the ListBox_GetText or the ListBox_SetItemData and ListBox_GetItemData calls.

[4]Available only at Win32 API level 4 and higher.

[e]Defined in extensions.h.

Table 9.5: List box messages

Message	Function Action
LB_SETITEMHEIGHT	`int ListBox_SetItemHeight(HWND hwnd, int index, short cy)`
	Sets the height in pixels of the specified item in a variable-height owner-draw list box. Sets the height in pixels of all items in all other list boxes.
LB_SETLOCALE	`LCID ListBox_SetLocale(HWND hwnd, LCID locale)`[e]
	Determines the sorting order for list boxes that have the LBS_SORT attribute.
LB_SETSEL	`int ListBox_SetSel(HWND hwnd, BOOL Select, int index)`
	Sets the selection state for an item in a multiple-selection list box.
LB_SETTABSTOPS	`BOOL ListBox_SetTabStops(HWND hwnd, int cTabs, LPINT Tabs)`
	Sets the tab-stop positions.
LB_SETTOPINDEX	`int ListBox_SetTopIndex(HWND hwnd, int indexTop)`
	Scrolls the list box until the specified item is at the top of the list box.

[1]When a list box is created with one of the LBS_OWNERDRAW styles but without the LBS_HASSTRINGS style, there is no provision for a string. Instead, the LB_ADDSTRING, LB_FINDSTRING, and LB_INSERTSTRING operations take the 32-bit value and store it as item data. The value can be retrieved either by using the ListBox_GetText or the ListBox_SetItemData and ListBox_GetItemData calls.
[4]Available only at Win32 API level 4 and higher.
[e]Defined in extensions.h.

Many messages require an item index. Items in a list box are numbered from 0.

Even though you usually think of a list box as containing strings, items in a list box are actually composed of two parts: an optional string and an associated 32-bit item data value. A typical list box (that is, a list box other than an owner-draw list box without the LBS_HASSTRINGS style) almost always uses the string component and frequently ignores the associated 32-bit item data value. An owner-draw list box without the LBS_HASSTRINGS style has only the 32-bit item data value, no associated string.

Typically, you use the 32-bit value to store some useful encoded representation associated with the string. For example, you might store a set of strings such as "1200", "2400", "4800", "9600", "14.4K", or "28.8K" to represent serial line speeds. You would then associate, in the item data, a value such as BAUD_1200, BAUD_2400, etc. (values defined for the COMMPROP structure), which represent those strings. It is almost always a bad idea to make any fixed mapping between the list box index and some other value. If you do so, your code will tend to break in unexpected ways when a new feature is added to the list box. Another common association is to put a 32-bit pointer to a data structure as the item data for a string. When you ask for the current selection, you can retrieve the pointer to the information structure by retrieving the item data and casting it to a pointer of the correct type.

Regardless of the type of list box, you can always get and set the associated 32-bit value for a list box item. You get the 32-bit associated value for an item by sending the LB_GETITEMDATA message to the list box with the wParam parameter set to the index of the item:

```
DWORD ItemValue ;

ItemValue = SendMessage (hListBox, LB_GETITEMDATA, Index, 0L) ;
ItemValue = ListBox_GetItemData (hListBox, Index) ;
```

You can change the associated 32-bit value by sending the LB_SETITEMDATA message to the list box. The wParam parameter contains the index of the item to change, and the lParam parameter contains the new value to be associated with the specified item:

```
SendMessage (hListBox, LB_SETITEMDATA, Index, ItemValue) ;
ListBox_SetItemData (hListBox, Index, ItemValue) ;
```

 List boxes in Win32 4.*x* are limited to 32,767 entries. You cannot use a value for any list box operation, including ListBox_GetItemData and ListBox_SetItemData, that exceeds this limit, in spite of the fact that these parameters are 32-bit values.

Adding, Inserting, and Deleting Items from a List Box

You add a new string to a list box by sending it an LB_ADDSTRING message. The wParam parameter isn't used. The lParam parameter points to the string to be added. When a new string is added to an owner-draw list box without the LBS_HASSTRINGS style, the lParam parameter is treated as an uninterpreted 32-bit item value rather than as a pointer to a string:

```
SendMessage (hListBox, LB_ADDSTRING, 0, (LPARAM)(LPCTSTR)String) ;
SendMessage (hOwnerDraw, LB_ADDSTRING, 0, ItemValue) ;
ListBox_AddString (hListBox, String) ;
ListBox_AddItemData(hOwnerDraw, ItemValue) ;
```

Note that the ListBox_AddItemData could have been written as

```
ListBox_AddString (hOwnerDraw, ItemValue) ;
```

A list box adds a new item to the end of the list. When the box has the LBS_SORT style, the item is placed at the appropriate position in the list. The sorting order is normally determined by the "locale" information established when Windows is installed; this means the sort order will follow the prevailing international standard for character order. However, when you must run with one language and sort using another (for example, an application that runs using Canadian English but which must display lists of Canadian names using the Canadian French collating sequence), you will have to override the sort order using the LB_SETLOCALE message. This is discussed in more detail on page 637.

Note that an owner-draw list box without the LBS_HASSTRINGS style doesn't have an associated string, but it can have the LBS_SORT style. Such a list box sends a WM_COMPAREITEM message to its parent window one or more times. Windows sets the wParam parameter of the WM_COMPAREITEM message to the control ID of the list box sending the message. The lParam parameter points to a COMPAREITEMSTRUCT structure that looks like this:

```
typedef struct tagCOMPAREITEMSTRUCT {
    UINT    CtlType ;
    UINT    CtlID ;
    HWND    hwndItem ;
    UINT    itemID1 ;
    DWORD   itemData1 ;
    UINT    itemID2 ;
    DWORD   itemData2 ;
} COMPAREITEMSTRUCT ;
```

Like we did for WM_DRAWITEM (see page 553), we can "reflect" the WM_COMPAREITEM message to the subclass window handler. We don't need to test for the ODT_MENU case because the WM_COMPAREITEM message only applies to list boxes and combo boxes. If we have subclassed a standard list box control with a subclass handler such as mySpecialListBoxProc, we can write an OnCompareItem handler in the subclass to do the comparison and thus get maximum reuse from the implementation:

```
switch(msg)
    {
     HANDLE_MSG(hwnd, WM_COMPAREITEM, wnd_OnCompareItem);
     // ...and other cases here
    }

int wnd_OnCompareItem(HWND hwnd,
                const COMPAREITEMSTRUCT * cis)
    {
     return FORWARD_WM_COMPAREITEM(cis->hwndItem, cis, SendMessage);
    }
```

In the module that implements the special list box, we can call the original window procedure of the list box via the baseProc pointer we have saved when we subclassed it:

```
LRESULT CALLBACK
mySpecialListBoxProc(HWND hwnd, UINT msg, WPARAM wParam, LPARAM lParam)
    {
     switch(msg)
        { /* msg */
         HANDLE_MSG(hwnd, WM_COMPAREITEM, mySpecial_OnCompareItem);
         // ... other cases
        } /* msg */
     return CallWindowProc(baseProc, hwnd, msg, wParam, lParam);
    }
```

If every list box we can have that is owner-draw without strings is properly subclassed, the above code completely handles all comparison requests.

The CtlType field contains the value ODT_LISTBOX, which specifies an owner-draw list box. The CtlID field contains the control ID for the list box. The hwndItem field contains the window handle of the list box. The itemID1 and itemID2 fields contain the indices of the list box items to be compared. The itemData1 and itemData2 contain the associated 32-bit values for each item. The parent window of the list box must process the WM_COMPAREITEM message. It must return –1 when item 1 sorts before item 2; 0 when item 1 and item 2 sort equally; and 1 when item 1 sorts after item 2.

WM_COMPAREITEM Message Cracker Handler

```
int cls_OnCompareItem(HWND hwnd, const COMPAREITEMSTRUCT * cis);
```

Result	0 if both items are equal -1 if item1 < item2 1 if item1 > item2				
Parameter	**wParam**		**lParam**		**Meaning**
	lo	**hi**	**lo**	**hi**	
hwnd					Window handle of the window containing the control.
cis			▮		COMPAREITEMSTRUCT reference.

You can use this flexibility for several purposes. For example, if your item data is a reference to a structure containing either a mixture of text and binary data or multiple text fields, you can use it to get sorting based on information that could not be contained in a purely textual representation of the data. Also, with it you can sort according to a different set of rules than the one the LBS_SORT option with LBS_HASSTRINGS would use. The default rule is to use locale-specific sorting based on the "locale" specification established for Windows. You can extend this to use a nonlocal locale, such as sorting a list according to one set of language rules while running under a different locale using the LB_SETLOCALE message. But in some cases, there is no locale in the formal Windows sense that can be used. An example might be sorting bibliographic data in accordance with the American Library Association (ALA) rules for filing, which has special treatment of diacritical marks. In this latter case, you have no choice but to use an owner-draw list box without LBS_HASSTRINGS, since there is no "built-in" locale for "ALA". A more common sorting problem might be sorting a set of hex or decimal numbers that do not have leading spaces or tabs and that must be displayed flush-right. Or in another example, sorting a set of dates and displaying them in chronological order but using the current prevailing date format, which might be "03.01.96" or "1/3/96" or "3-Jan-96". The text string representation of a date often bears no resemblance to the key necessary for correct sorting. In the case of locale-specific strings, you can't depend on the strings having a textual representation guaranteed to sort properly (prime examples are names of months, names of weekdays, and general date layout).

You can insert an item into a specified position in the list box by sending an LB_INSERTSTRING message to the box. The box will place the new item in the position specified by the wParam parameter of the message; the item formerly at that position, and all items whose index is higher, are "shifted down" by one item position to make room for the new item. When the wParam parameter is -1, the item is added to the end of the list. As when adding items, the lParam parameter contains either a far pointer to the string to be inserted or the 32-bit value to associate with the item. Items inserted into a sorted list box are inserted at the specified location regardless of the position to which they would sort. The following statements insert an item into a list box at the ItemIndex position. The first inserts a string into an ordinary list box. The second inserts a 32-bit value into an owner-draw list box. We also show the windowsx.h API equivalents.

```
SendMessage (hListBox, LB_INSERTSTRING, ItemIndex, (LPARAM)(LPCTSTR)String) ;
SendMessage (hOwnerDraw, LB_INSERTSTRING, ItemIndex, ItemValue) ;
// or...
```

```
ListBox_InsertString (hListBox, ItemIndex, String) ;
ListBox_InsertString (hOwnerDraw, ItemIndex, ItemValue) ;
```

When you add or insert an item into an owner-draw list box, the box needs to determine the display size of the item. When a user clicks the mouse button while in the list box, an owner-draw list box uses the size of each item to calculate the item that should be selected. Because the parent window of an owner-draw list box draws the items, the list box sends it a WM_MEASUREITEM message requesting the size of the item.

WM_MEASUREITEM Message Cracker Handler					
void cls_OnMeasureItem(HWND hwnd, MEASUREITEMSTRUCT * mis);					

Parameter	wParam		lParam		Meaning
	lo	hi	lo	hi	
hwnd					Window handle of the window containing the control.
mis			■		Pointer to a MEASUREITEMSTRUCT to be updated.

An owner-draw list box with the LBS_OWNERDRAWFIXED sends the WM_MEASUREITEM message to its parent only once because all items are the same size. It does this when it is created rather than waiting until the first item is added or inserted into the list box. When the list box is in a dialog box, the WM_MEASUREITEM message will arrive before the WM_INITDIALOG message. Because most dialog functions initialize when the WM_INITDIALOG message arrives, you must take care that the WM_MEASUREITEM message processing logic doesn't rely on variables that are not initialized until later. An owner-draw list box with the LBS_OWNERDRAWVARIABLE style sends a WM_MEASUREITEM message to its parent window for each item when that item is added to or inserted in the list box.

MFC

There is a problem when using the Microsoft Foundation Classes and LBS_OWNERDRAWFIXED windows in dialogs. Well, this really isn't a bug as much as a design mismatch. What you'd like to do is have your subclassed owner-draw window class respond to the reflected WM_MEASUREITEM. The problem is that this message is sent *when the window is created by the dialog handler*; however, the MFC interception and processing is not activated until after the WM_INITDIALOG handler performs the necessary subclassing during the data exchange. So the message is effectively lost. If you are doing your own subclassed list box control in MFC (and this is the natural way to implement your control) and you need LBS_OWNERDRAW with other than the default height, you *must* use the LBS_OWNERDRAWVARIABLE style so that you get the messages *after* the subclassing. This design mismatch is both subtle and incredibly difficult to discover unless you have been warned.

The wParam parameter of a WM_MEASUREITEM message contains the control ID of the list box sending the message. The lParam parameter contains a far pointer to a MEASUREITEMSTRUCT structure, which looks like this:

```
typedef struct tagMEASUREITEMSTRUCT {
    UINT    CtlType ;
    UINT    CtlID ;
    UINT    itemID ;
    UINT    itemWidth ;
    UINT    itemHeight ;
    DWORD   itemData ;
} MEASUREITEMSTRUCT ;
```

As we did for WM_DRAWITEM (see page 553) and WM_COMPAREITEM, we can "reflect" the WM_MEASUREITEM message to the subclass window handler. And like WM_DRAWITEM, a WM_MEASUREITEM may also apply to a menu, and we must make the special check for menus. The handler function should process the WM_MEASUREITEM message by setting the appropriate fields in the structure and returning. The WM_MEASUREITEM message and the MEASUREITEMSTRUCT structure are common to all owner-draw controls (buttons, list boxes, combo boxes, and menus). The following discusses the structure only in reference to list boxes.

The CtlType field contains the value ODT_LISTBOX. The CtlID field contains the control ID for the list box. The itemID field contains the index of the item being measured for variable-height list boxes; it isn't used for fixed-height list boxes. The itemWidth field isn't used by list boxes. You specify the height of a list box item by setting the itemHeight field. This is the height of all items in a fixed-height list box and the height of the itemID item in a variable-height list box, expressed in device units (pixels). The itemData field contains the value that was passed to the list box in the lParam parameter of the LB_ADDSTRING or LB_INSERTSTRING message. This is a pointer to a string if the list box has the LBS_HASSTRINGS style; otherwise, it is the application-supplied 32-bit value.

It's handy to be able to delete an item from a list box once you've added or inserted it. You do this by sending a LB_DELETESTRING message to the box, with the wParam parameter containing the index of the item to delete:

```
SendMessage (hListBox, LB_DELETESTRING, ItemIndex, 0L) ;
ListBox_DeleteString (hListBox, ItemIndex) ;
```

Deleting an item from an owner-draw list box that doesn't have the LBS_HASSTRINGS style causes the box to send a WM_DELETEITEM message to its parent window. The only datum associated with items in such a list box is the 32-bit application-supplied value. An application may have allocated storage for each item in the list box and could use the handle to the storage as the 32-bit item value. The WM_DELETEITEM message gives the parent window a chance to release any storage allocated for the deleted item. This message is also sent for each item in the list box control when the list box is destroyed.

WM_DELETEITEM Message Cracker Handler

void cls_OnDeleteItem(HWND hwnd, const DELETEITEMSTRUCT * dis);					
	wParam		lParam		
Parameter	**lo**	**hi**	**lo**	**hi**	**Meaning**
hwnd					Window handle of the window containing the control.
dis			███		Reference to a DELETEITEMSTRUCT.

The list box sends a WM_DELETEITEM message to its parent window to inform the parent window that the item has been removed from the box. Usually, this is handled by the same reflection mechanism we described on page 553. We do not need to make a special test for ODT_MENU because a WM_DELETEITEM is never sent for an owner-draw menu (see Chapter 12, page 860). The wParam contains the control ID of the control sending the message. The lParam parameter contains a far pointer to a DELETEITEMSTRUCT structure that looks like this:

```
typedef struct tagDELETEITEMSTRUCT {
    UINT        CtlType ;
    UINT        CtlID ;
    UINT        itemID ;
    HWND        hwndItem ;
    DWORD       itemData ;
} DELETEITEMSTRUCT ;
```

The CtlType field contains the value ODT_LISTBOX, which specifies an owner-draw list box. The CtlID field contains the control ID for the list box. The itemID field contains the index of the deleted list box item. The itemData field contains the item's associated 32-bit value. The parent window of the box should use this information to free any allocated storage for the deleted item (or, by using the reflection method, inform the subclass handler for the box that it should free the storage).

You can delete all items from a list box by sending it a LB_RESETCONTENT message:

```
SendMessage (hListBox, LB_RESETCONTENT, 0, 0L) ;

ListBox_ResetContent (hListBox) ;
```

An owner-draw list box without the LBS_HASSTRINGS style sends a WM_DELETEITEM message (as described above) to its parent window for each item in the list box.

Selecting an Item in a Single-selection List Box

Generally, you don't need to select items in a list box. The user selects one or more items, the list box sends notification messages alerting you to the user's actions, and you use these notifications to retrieve the selected item or items from the list box.

Occasionally, you may want to establish a default selection, for example, the same item or items that the user selected the last time the list box was used. To do so is simple. However, you select an item differently in a single-selection list box than you do in a multiple-selection list box. We look first at selecting an item in a single-selection list box.

Selecting an item in a single-selection list box is the simplest case. You use the ListBox_SetCurSel macro to send the LB_SETCURSEL message to the box. The wParam parameter contains the index of the item to select. This message deselects any previously selected item, selects the specified item, and scrolls it into view:

```
SendMessage (hListBox, LB_SETCURSEL, ItemIndex, 0L) ;
ListBox_SetCurSel (hListBox, ItemIndex) ;
```

You can deselect all items in a list box by using an index parameter of –1.

You can also select the first item in a list box that begins with a specified prefix string. You send an LB_SELECTSTRING message to the list box with the wParam parameter containing the index of an item. The search starts with the item immediately after the item specified in the wParam parameter. The search is circular. That is, when it reaches the end of the list box, it continues with the first item in the list box and searches up to the item specified in the wParam parameter. When you specify -1 for the wParam parameter, the search starts with the first item in the list box.

The lParam parameter normally contains a pointer to a NUL-terminated prefix string. The lParam parameter is interpreted differently for owner-draw list boxes that don't have the LBS_HASSTRINGS style. When the box also omits the LBS_SORT style, the lParam value is compared with the 32-bit item data value provided when the items were added or inserted into the list box. When the list box includes the LBS_SORT style, the box sends WM_COMPAREITEM messages to its owner to determine which item matches the specified prefix string. In either case, the box returns the index of the selected item or the value LB_ERR when no such item is found. Here is an example of both usages:

```
SelectedItem = SendMessage (hListBox,
                            LB_SELECTSTRING,
                            StartIndex,
                            (LPARAM)(LPCSTR)Prefix) ;
SelectedItem = SendMessage (hOwnerDraw,
                            LB_SELECTSTRING,
                            StartIndex,
                            ItemValue) ;
SelectedItem = ListBox_SelectString (hListBox,
                            StartIndex,
                            Prefix) ;
SelectedItem = ListBox_SelectString (hOwnerDraw,
                            StartIndex,
                            ItemValue) ;
```

The first statement selects the first item in the list box that begins with the same characters as are in the Prefix string. The second statement selects the first item in the list box that has the same 32-bit value as specified by the ItemValue parameter. Both searches begin with the item after the StartIndex item.

Determining the Selection in a Single-selection List Box

Eventually, you'll want to retrieve the item that the user has selected. The item may or may not be the one you initially selected. Retrieving the item is easy for a single-selection list box. Send the LB_GETCURSEL message to the control to determine which item, if any, is selected. Neither the wParam nor the lParam parameter is used:

```
SelectedItem = SendMessage (hListBox, LB_GETCURSEL, 0, 0) ;

SelectedItem = ListBox_GetCurSel (hListBox) ;
```

The SelectedItem variable contains the index of the currently selected item or the value LB_ERR if no item is selected.

Selecting Items in a Multiple-selection or Extended-selection List Box

You select or deselect one item or all items in a multiple-selection list box by sending the list box a LB_SETSEL message. When the wParam parameter is nonzero, the specified item is selected and highlighted. When the wParam parameter is 0, the specified item is deselected and highlighting is removed. When the lParam parameter is -1, all items in the list box are selected or deselected, depending on the wParam parameter. To select or deselect a single item, you place the index of the item in the low-order word of the lParam

Table 9.6: LB_SETSEL/ListBox_SetSel parameters

```
ListBox_SetSel(hListBox, select, index)
SendMessage(hListBox, LB_SETSEL, wParam, lParam)
```

select (wParam)	index (lParam)	Effect
FALSE	-1	Deselects all elements of the list box.
TRUE	-1	Selects all elements of the list box.
FALSE	>= 0	Deselects the item specified by index.
TRUE	>= 0	Selects the item specified by index.

parameter. Selecting and deselecting a single item in a multiple-selection list box doesn't affect any other items that may be selected. This is summarized in Table 9.6.

The first pair of the following statements deselects all items in the list box. Both statements in the second pair select the index item:

```
SendMessage (hListBox, LB_SETSEL, FALSE, MAKELPARAM(-1, 0)) ;
ListBox_SetSel (hListBox, FALSE, -1) ;

SendMessage (hListBox, LB_SETSEL, TRUE, MAKELPARAM(Index, 0)) ;
ListBox_SetSel (hListBox, TRUE, Index) ;
```

You may want to select or deselect a group of consecutive items in a multiple-selection list box. You could select or deselect them one at a time using the LB_SETSEL message, but it's easier to send one message: LB_SELITEMRANGE. The wParam parameter is identical to the LB_SETSEL message: nonzero to select items in the specified range and 0 to deselect them. The low-order word of the lParam parameter contains the index of the first items in the range. The high-order word contains the index of the last item in the range. This limits the message's usefulness to list boxes containing fewer than 65,536 items. For those containing more than 65,536 items, you must use the LB_SELITEMRANGEEX message. For this message, the wParam is the index of the first item in the range and the lParam is the index of the last item in the range. If the first item is greater than the second item, the selection is removed from the specified range of items. The following statement selects the first 10 items in a multiple-selection list box:

```
SendMessage (hListBox, LB_SELITEMRANGE, TRUE, MAKELPARAM(0, 9));
SendMessage (hListBox, LB_SELITEMRANGEEX, 0, 9) ;

ListBox_SelItemRange (hListBox, TRUE, 0, 9) ;
```

Note that LB_SELITEMRANGEEX has no equivalent API call in windowsx.h.

The following statements are all equivalent ways to deselect the first 10 items in a multiple-selection list box:

```
SendMessage (hListBox, LB_SELITEMRANGE, FALSE, MAKELPARAM(0, 9));
SendMessage (hListBox, LB_SELITEMRANGEEX, 9, 0) ;
ListBox_SelItemRange (hListBox, TRUE, 0, 9) ;
```

Determining the Selection in a Multiple-select List Box

Determining the selection in a multiple-selection list box is a bit trickier than in a single-selection list box. In a single-selection list box, there is either no selection or precisely one selection. The focus always determines the selection, so the focus is always unique. The LB_GETCURSEL message (ListBox_GetCurSel macro) will return either the actual selection or LB_ERR if there is no selection.

When a list box can have multiple selections, however, the "current selection" may not actually be an active selection. You can see this using the Control Explorer, as shown in Figure 9.1. The selection rectangle is over item 3, as reported by LB_GETCURSEL, but the actual selections are 0 and 1. The messages displayed at the bottom show the most recent messages received by the parent and report on the current status. In this figure, you can see that the items 0 and 1 had been selected. We then clicked item 3, thereby selecting it, and clicked once again to deselect it. Notice that LB_GETCURSEL shows the "current selection" as being 3, even though it is not selected. You have to use a different technique to determine the active selections.

You can determine whether a particular item in a multiple-selection list box is selected by sending the LB_GETSEL message to the list box. The wParam parameter contains the item index. The lParam parameter isn't used:

```
int Result ;

Result = (int)SendMessage (hListBox, LB_GETSEL, Index, 0) ;
Result = ListBox_GetSel (hListBox, Index) ;
```

Be careful with the returned value; it isn't a Boolean value. The returned value is positive when the specified item is selected and 0 when the specified item is not selected. The returned value is negative when a error occurs. (The value is actually LB_ERR, which is defined to be -1.)

You can retrieve the selection state of each item in a multiple-selection list box by sending a LB_GETSEL message for each item. It's more efficient, however, to ask once and get the selection state of all items in the list box. You first send the LB_GETSELCOUNT message to the list box to retrieve the number of selected items in a multiple-selection box.

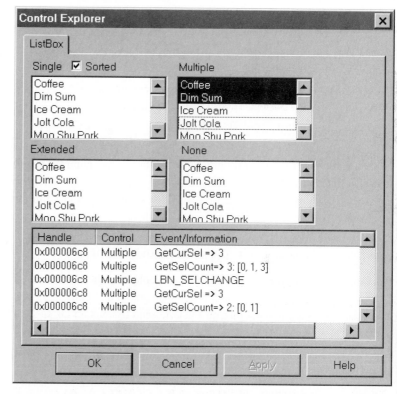

Figure 9.1: Selection in a multiple-selection list box

```
int     ItemCount ;
LRESULT Items, ItemsReturned ;
Items = SendMessage (hListBox, LB_GETSELCOUNT, 0, 0) ;

ItemCount = ListBox_GetSelCount (hListBox) ;
```

You use the returned value to allocate dynamic storage sufficient to hold the returned number of integers (Items * sizeof (int)). You then send a LB_GETSELITEMS message to the multiple-selection list box and retrieve the selection state of every item in the box. The lParam parameter of the message contains a pointer to the dynamically allocated buffer. The wParam parameter specifies the maximum number of integers that the buffer can hold (which is Items in this example). The box fills the buffer with an array of integers, each of which specifies the index of a selected item. The box returns the actual number of integers placed in the buffer:

```
int * Buffer;
Buffer = (int *)malloc(Items * sizeof(int));

ItemsReturned = SendMessage (hListBox, LB_GETSELITEMS,
                                Items, (LPARAM) Buffer) ;
ItemsReturned = ListBox_GetSelItems (hListBox, Items, Buffer) ;
```

Once you know which items are selected, you can retrieve them. First, it's useful to find out how long each string is, especially when you want to dynamically allocate the storage to hold the string. Send the LB_GETTEXTLEN message with the wParam parameter set to the item index. The lParam parameter isn't used. The box returns the length of the string, in bytes, excluding the terminating NUL character or the value LB_ERR when an error occurs:

```
Length = SendMessage (hListBox, LB_GETTEXTLEN, Index, 0) ;
Length = ListBox_GetTextLen (hListBox, Index) ;
```

After you've allocated a buffer to hold the string, send an LB_GETTEXT message to have the list box copy the string for the item into the buffer. The wParam parameter of the message contains the item index. The lParam parameter contains a far pointer to the buffer receiving the string. The box returns the length of the string, in bytes, excluding the terminating NUL character or LB_ERR when an invalid item is specified. The following code copies the string for the Index item of a list box into the buffer pointed to by the Buffer parameter:

```
Length = SendMessage (hListBox, LB_GETTEXT, Index, (LPARAM) Buffer) ;
Length = ListBox_GetText (hListBox, Index, Buffer) ;
```

We like to write programs based on the philosophy that the less information duplicated, the better. Thus, we don't bother keeping track of the number of items in a list box at any given time. When you need to know how many items are in a list box, just ask it. Send the box an LB_GETCOUNT message, and it will return the number of items in it:

```
DWORD cItems ;
int   nItems ;

cItems = SendMessage (hListBox, LB_GETCOUNT, 0, 0) ;
nItems = ListBox_GetCount (hListBox) ;
```

File Names in List Boxes

One message is very useful for filling a list box with strings, if the strings are a list of files from the current directory: LB_DIR. The lParam parameter contains a pointer to a file-specification string. This string is a pattern; it can contain wildcard characters. The wildcard characters are a question mark (?), which means "match any single character", and an asterisk (*), which means "match any number of characters". You can use the file-specification *.* to match all files.

The LB_DIR and CB_DIR messages in Windows 95 do *not* support long filenames! If you need to support long filenames, you will have to use the GetShortPathName function to convert the long filename to the 8.3-compatible format. However, the list box will display only short filenames in Windows 95. See the MSKB article Q131286.

The wParam parameter contains a file attribute value. Only a file with an attribute specified by this parameter and that matches the file specification are added to the list box. Table 9.7 lists the file attributes.

Table 9.7: File attributes

wParam Value	File Type
DDL_ARCHIVE	Include files with the archive bit set.
DDL_DIRECTORY	Include subdirectories.
DDL_DRIVES	Include disk drives.
DDL_EXCLUSIVE	Exclude normal files from the list.
DDL_HIDDEN	Include hidden files.
DDL_READONLY	Include read-only files.
DDL_READWRITE	Include read/write files with no additional attributes.
DDL_SYSTEM	Include system files.

Normally, all read/write files with no additional attributes are always included in the list. You can request that the names of additional files also be included by using the bitwise OR operation to combine the appropriate values. For example, the value DDL_READWRITE | DDL_READONLY | DDL_DIRECTORY | DDL_ARCHIVE includes all files normally listed by the command prompt dir command: read/write files, read-only files, files with the archive bit, and subdirectories. When you want only a specific type of file, you must add the value DDL_EXCLUSIVE. For example, to get a list containing only subdirectories, you use the

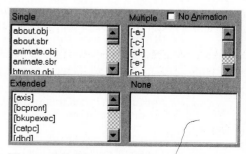

Figure 9.2: List boxes filled by using the LB_DIR message.

value DDL_DIRECTORY | DDL_EXCLUSIVE. This includes subdirectories but excludes read/write files. Figure 9.2 shows the list box display from the Control Explorer application. This is the List Box Explorer component. The top-left list box was filled using with the options DDL_READWRITE | DDL_READONLY | DDL_ARCHIVE. The bottom-left list box was filled using the options DDL_DIRECTORY | DDL_EXCLUSIVE. The top-right list box was filled using the options DDL_DRIVES | DDL_EXCLUSIVE.

You should include the LBS_SORT list box class style for a list box filled by a LB_DIR message when you mix files, subdirectories, and drives. This style sorts all the matching filenames (alphabetically), followed by the list of disk drives, followed by subdirectories. The left list box in Figure 9.2 is sorted, but the right one is not. Because it's easier to find a file alphabetically, the file list box was sorted. Sorting the directory list box would place the drives before the subdirectories. Users will select a subdirectory more often than they will select a drive letter. The list box is sorted to place the subdirectories ahead of the drive letter, thus making the subdirectories entries more accessible.

The LB_ITEMFROMPOINT message is convenient if you are implementing a drop-aware list box. Given two values, the x- and y-coordinates of a point, where 0, 0 is the upper-left corner of the client area of the list box, this message will return a DWORD whose low-order value is the index of the nearest item to that point. The high-order word is 0 if the specified point is in the client area of the list box and is 1 if the point is outside the client area. Note that this limits this message to working only on list boxes containing fewer than 65,536 items. Essentially you can query on each WM_MOUSEMOVE what list box item you are over. On a WM_LBUTTONUP, you can use the ListBox_InsertString or ListBox_InsertItemData functions to insert the data you are dropping into the list box. If the data came from the same list box, you will have to remember that if it was originally at an index higher than the one you drop it into, then the item you will delete (assuming the drag-and-drop is a move) will be one position higher than it started. To convert a mouse move to an item position, you might use code of this form:

```
static void mylist_OnMouseMove(HWND hWnd, int x, int y, UINT keyflags)
    {
     int index;
     DWORD value;
     value = SendMessage(hWnd, LB_ITEMFROMPOINT, 0, MAKELPARAM(x, y));
     if(HIWORD(value) == 0)
        { /* over something */
         int index = LOWORD(value);
         // if we can drop our object onto the list box
         // item we are over, use the application-
         // defined IDC_DROP cursor to show dropability
         // Otherwise use the stock circle-slash cursor
         // to indicate no dropping allowed.
         if(CanDropOn(hWnd, index))
            SetCursor(LoadCursor(GetWindowInstance(hWnd), IDC_DROP));
         else
            SetCursor(LoadCursor(NULL, IDC_NO));
        } /* over something */
     else
        { /* not over anything */
         SetCursor(LoadCursor(NULL, IDC_NO));
        } /* not over anything */
    }
```

A list box that is going to have a large number of items can be loaded more efficiently if you preallocate storage using the LB_INITSTORAGE message. This is discussed in more detail on page 637.

Establishing a Horizontal Scroll Bar

A horizontal scroll bar is occasionally useful on a list box (or on the list box of a combo box). A horizontal scroll bar requires that you use the WS_HSCROLL style. But the scroll bar will *not* appear automatically if a line of the list box is wider than the list box itself (it *does* appear automatically for edit controls!). You must actually measure each line in the list box and set the scroll bar yourself.

For an owner-draw list box, you can compute the maximum width as you do the drawing, but this means the horizontal scroll bar will not appear until you scroll into view a line whose display space is wider than the list box. The alternative is somewhat simpler, but has a bit more overhead. Each time an item is added to or deleted from a list box, you scan all the elements of the list box and compute the maximum width required. This can be done by using a function like that shown in Listing 9.1. There are several points to observe about this code. The code is not designed to work with owner-draw list boxes. It is intended to be "generic", that is, to work with any list box (that is not owner-draw), so it does not assume the default font or a known upper bound on string length. If you know the font (or know that you are always using the system font), you don't need to deal with the font issues. If you know a compile-time maximum string length, you can omit the first pass that computes a buffer size.

Listing 9.1: Computing list box width

```
int computeHorizontalExtent(HWND hListBox)
    {
     int i ;
     int count = ListBox_GetCount(hListBox) ;
     HFONT font ;
     HDC dc ;
     int width = 0 ;
     LPTSTR Buffer;
     int saved ;

     // first, we must make sure we have a buffer
     // large enough to hold the longest string
     for(i = 0; i < count; i++)
        { /* compute buffer size */
          int len = ListBox_GetTextLen(hListBox, i) ;
          width = max (width, len) ;
        } /* compute buffer size */

     // If the list box is empty, just return 0
     if (width == 0)
        return 0;

     // Allocate a buffer to hold the string
     // including the terminating NUL character
     Buffer = malloc ((width + 1) * sizeof(TCHAR)) ;
     if (Buffer == NULL)
        return 0 ;

     // We will need a DC for string length computation
```

```
    dc = GetDC(hListBox) ;

    // Save the DC so we can restore it later
    saved = SaveDC(dc) ;

    font = GetWindowFont (hListBox) ;

    // If our font is other than the system font,
    // select it into the DC
    if (font != NULL)
        SelectFont (dc, font);

    // We now compute the longest actual string length
    width = 0 ;
    for(i = 0; i < count; i++)
        { /* compute buffer size */
          SIZE sz ;
          ListBox_GetText(hListBox, Buffer) ;
          // Compute string length.  Use lstrlen instead
          // of strlen for Unicode compatibility
          GetTextExtentPoint32 (dc, Buffer,
                                 lstrlen(Buffer), &sz);
          width = max (width, sz.cx ) ;
        } /* compute buffer size */

    // we no longer need the buffer or DC; free them
    free (Buffer) ;
    RestoreDC(dc, saved) ;
    ReleaseDC(hListBox, dc) ;

    // Deal with the (possible) presence of a
    // scroll bar
    width += GetSystemMetrics(SM_CXVSCROLL) ;
    return width;
    }

int MyList_AddString(HWND hListBox, LPCSTR str)
    {
    int index = ListBox_AddString(hListBox, str) ;
    int extent = computeHorizontalExtent(hListBox) ;
    ListBox_SetHorizontalExtent(hListBox, extent) ;
    return index ;
    }
```

List Box Notification Messages

A list box control, like button and edit controls, sends notifications to its parent window via WM_COMMAND messages. The notification has the same form that you've already seen.

Table 9.8 shows the list box notification codes.A list box sends a WM_COMMAND message with the LBN_DBLCLK, LBN_SELCANCEL, or LBN_SELCHANGE notification codes to its parent window only when the list box is created with the LBS_NOTIFY list box class style.

A list box sends an LBN_SELCHANGE notification each time the user selects or deselects an item in the list box. It sends an LBN_DBLCLK notification when the user double-clicks an item in the box. An

LBN_SELCHANGE notification occurs each time the user presses an arrow key in a multiple-selection list box, even if the selection doesn't change. A list box does not send this notification when you explicitly change the selection by sending an LB_SETCURSEL message.

You can use the LBN_SELCHANGE notification to monitor each selection change and keep track of

Table 9.8: List box notification codes

Code	Meaning
LBN_DBLCLK	User has double-clicked an item.
LBN_ERRSPACE	List box cannot allocate enough memory.
LBN_KILLFOCUS	List box is losing the input focus.
LBN_SELCANCEL	User has canceled the selection in a list box.
LBN_SELCHANGE	The selection in a list box has changed.
LBN_SETFOCUS	List box is gaining the input focus.

which items are selected at any given time. Alternatively, you can wait for the double-click notification or other external signal (such as a notification from a push button) and retrieve the selected items from the list box at that time.

You can use the Control Explorer to watch the notification messages flow as the result of mouse clicks and keyboard actions. See Figure 9.1.

One serious caution here, which we've mentioned before in the context of the WM_LBUTTONDOWN and WM_LBUTTONDBLCLK messages. These messages work so that you first get a WM_LBUTTONDOWN. If there is a second click within the time/space limits that determine it is a double click and the CS_DBLCLKS style is set for the window, the second click will be reported as a WM_LBUTTONDBLCLK. For a list box, the WM_LBUTTONDOWN message to the list box generates an LBN_SELCHANGE notification to the parent window. The WM_LBUTTONDBLCLK message will send an LBN_DBLCLK message to the parent. So you can't have LBN_DBLCLK do something totally different from what an LBN_SELCHANGE would do because the LBN_SELCHANGE will have already occurred. Typically, you have your LBN_DBLCLK call the same handler as for your OK button. In the case of a multiple-selection box, the second mouse click, the one reported via the LBN_DBLCLK, does not toggle the selection again. However, for a list box with LBS_MULTIPLESEL, if the item on which you click was already selected, the first click (reported as LBN_SELCHANGE) deselects the item, and the second click (reported as LBN_DBLCLK) leaves it deselected. This may surprise you if you aren't expecting it.

The list box sends an LBN_ERRSPACE notification when it can't allocate enough memory during a request such as adding or inserting an item into the list box. Often the parent window does not know how to respond, so you end up writing a subclass handler and subclassing the list box. You then reflect this notification to your subclass handler, as we have already described for the WM_DRAWITEM message (see page 553).

The list box sends an LBN_SETFOCUS notification code to its parent as it gains focus and an LBN_KILLFOCUS notification as it loses focus. A list box control, like other controls, can receive the input focus after a Set-Focus function call. Once you give it the input focus, there isn't a keystroke to take the input focus away again. (After all, the control doesn't have the faintest idea where the input focus should go, even if it did know that now was the time to give away the input focus.) You'll have to provide some method of transferring the input focus via the keyboard when you create multiple controls in a window. You have the same problem with edit controls, and the same approach solves the problem. Use subclassing to watch for a key-stroke, preferably the **Tab** and **Shift+Tab** keys, and when the keystroke(s) is detected, circularly pass the input focus from one control to the next in a window. Fortunately, the most common usage of these controls is in dialog boxes and their derivatives such as property pages, so the dialog class handles all this for you. But if you are creating these controls in an ordinary window and writing a window handler for it, you will have to do the subclassing yourself.

The COMBOBOX Class

The COMBOBOX class creates a single control consisting of a list box plus a selection field similar to a static or edit control. The selection field is always visible. The list box can be displayed at all times or can remain hidden until the user selects a "drop-down" icon next to the selection field. You use a combo box much as you would an edit control and a list box. Many of the combo box styles have parallel list box control and edit control styles. Nearly all the messages you send to a combo box have equivalent list box and edit control messages. A combo box sends all the notification codes described for a list box plus a few additional ones. You can create one type of combo box with the following statement:

```
#define IDC_COMBOBOX    49

HWND hComboBox ;

hComboBox = CreateWindow (
    _T("combobox"), NULL,
    WS_CHILD | WS_VISIBLE | CBS_DROPDOWN,
    100, 200, 300, 60, hwnd, IDC_COMBOBOX, hInstance, NULL) ;
```

The COMBOBOX Class Styles

Some styles affect the operation of the selection field whereas others affect the list box. Most are equivalent to the previously described edit control styles and list box styles. Table 9.9 lists the combo box styles.

Table 9.9: COMBOBOX class styles

Style	Meaning
CBS_AUTOHSCROLL	Automatically scrolls the text in the selection field to the right when the user enters a character at the end of the line.
CBS_DISABLENOSCROLL	Displays a disabled vertical scroll bar, rather than hiding the scroll bar, when the associated list box does not contain enough items to require scrolling.
CBS_DROPDOWN	Creates a combo box similar to CBS_SIMPLE, except the list box remains hidden until the user selects the drop-down icon to the right of the selection field.
CBS_DROPDOWNLIST	Creates a combo box similar to CBS_DROPDOWN, except the selection field does not accept input. It displays the current list box selection.

Table 9.9: COMBOBOX class styles

Style	Meaning
CBS_HASSTRINGS	Creates an owner-draw combo box that contains strings. The combo box maintains the storage for the strings.
CBS_LOWERCASE[4]	Converts characters typed into the edit control to lowercase.
CBS_NOINTEGRALHEIGHT	Allows a combo box to display a partial item. Normally, a combo box resizes itself to display an integral number of items.
CBS_OEMCONVERT	Converts the characters entered into the selection field from the ANSI character set to the OEM character set and then back to ANSI. Applies only to CBS_SIMPLE- or CBS_DROPDOWN-style combo boxes.
CBS_OWNERDRAWFIXED	Creates an owner-draw combo box containing items of identical height.
CBS_OWNERDRAWVARIABLE	Creates an owner-draw list box containing items that can vary in height.
CBS_SIMPLE	Creates a simple combo box. The list box is always displayed below the selection field, which contains the currently selected item in the list box. That is, the "drop-down" is always "dropped". The user can type into the selection field when the combo box has the input focus.
CBS_SORT	Sorts the strings in a combo box alphabetically.
CBS_UPPERCASE[4]	Converts characters typed into the edit control to uppercase.

[4]Available only in Win32 4.x and higher levels.

There are three types of combo boxes. You pick one of the CBS_SIMPLE, CBS_DROPDOWN, or CBS_DROPDOWNLIST styles to select the type you want. The CBS_SIMPLE style creates a combo box composed of an edit control as the selection field and a list box that is always displayed below the edit control. The user can type into the selection field control when the combo box has the input focus. When an item in the list box matches what the user has typed into the selection field, the box scrolls to display the matching item at the top of the list box. The user can select an item from the box by using the mouse or the down arrow and up arrow keys (when the combo box has the input focus). When the user selects an item from the list box, the combo box displays the selected item's string in the selection field.

The CBS_DROPDOWN style creates a combo box similar to the CBS_SIMPLE style, except the list box is normally hidden; only the selection field is displayed. The user can display the list box below the selection field by clicking the icon to the right of the selection field. This causes the list box to drop down below the selection field, thereby temporarily overlaying the screen contents. Clicking the icon a second time hides the list box. When the combo box has the input focus, the **Alt+,** key combination displays the list box and the **Alt+–** key combination hides it.

When the list box has dropped down, the combo box operates like a CBS_SIMPLE combo box. In addition, the user can still select items from the list box even when it is hidden and when the combo box has the input focus. Pressing the down arrow or up arrow keys when the combo box has the input focus places the string for the next or previous item in the hidden list box into the selection field.

The CBS_DROPDOWNLIST looks like a CBS_DROPDOWN combo box, but operates a little differently. The user can drop down the list box and select items as before. However, the selection field is a static text control rather than an edit control. Items selected from the list box are displayed in the static text control but cannot be edited. When the combo box has the input focus, the user can select an item in the list box by typing the first letter of the item.

You would typically use a CBS_DROPDOWN combo box to allow the user to select one of a number of possible items from a list box while simultaneously allowing the user to specify an item not in the list box. Using a CBS_DROPDOWNLIST combo box forces the user to choose only from the list of items in the list box. Rarely, if ever, would you want to create a CBS_SIMPLE style list box.

All the other combo box styles have a matching edit control style or list box style, so we won't cover the same ground again. The styles have the same meaning for the edit field or list box field part of the combo box as they do for an independent edit control or list box control.

Note, however, that the list box of a combo box is not the same as an ordinary list box. Several features of list boxes are missing. For example, you cannot double-click an item in a drop-down list or set tab stops or even (in API level 3) set a horizontal scroll bar. And although the combo box appears to be implemented as an edit control and a list box, the "list box" is actually owned by the desktop! This strange feature will certainly surprise you if you try to do anything fancy with the list box (like subclassing it!). It allows the drop-down to fall over the boundary of the window that contains the combo box control; otherwise, it would be clipped by its parent window, an undesirable effect. If you have to do anything *really* sophisticated to the list box component of a combo box, you may have to implement your own list box instead. And, finally, there are no "owner-draw" combo boxes *except* those with the style CBS_DROPDOWNLIST. This is because there are no "owner-draw" edit controls, so when the edit control tries to draw the owner-draw item you end up with strange-looking output. However, the system and much of the tooling are willing to let you actually create windows with either CBS_DROPDOWN or CBS_SIMPLE style and with one of the owner-draw styles as well. It just displays the edit control contents incorrectly.

Messages to a Combo Box Control

Most of the messages to a combo box control are very similar to those you saw for edit controls and list box controls. Table 9.10 lists the combo box messages.

You can send the CB_SETEDITSEL message to a combo box to select a range of characters in the edit control of a combo box. The wParam parameter isn't used. The low-order word of the lParam parameter contains the start character position, and the high-order word contains the end character position. If the start position is set to -1, the selection is removed. If the end position is set to -1, the selection includes the last character in the edit control. The following line selects the entire string in the edit control of a combo box:

```
SendMessage (hComboBox, CB_SETEDITSEL, 0,
                    MAKELPARAM (0, -1)) ;
ComboBox_SetEditSel(hComboBox, MAKELPARAM(0, -1));
```

Table 9.10: Combo box messages

Message	Function Action
CB_ADDSTRING	`int ComboBox_AddString(HWND hwnd, LPCTSTR str)`
	`int ComboBox_AddItemData`[1]`(HWND hwnd, LPARAM data)`
	Adds an entry to the list box.
CB_DELETESTRING	`int ComboBox_DeleteString(HWND hwnd, int index)`
	Deletes a string from the list box.
CB_DIR	`int ComboBox_Dir (HWND hwnd, UINT attrs, LPCTSTR FileSpec)`
	Adds a list of files to the combo box.
CB_FINDSTRING	`int ComboBox_FindString(HWND hwnd, int indexStart, LPCTSTR Find)`
	`int ComboBox_FindItemData`[1]`(HWND hwnd, int indexStart, LPARAM data)`
	Returns the index of the first matching item starting at indexStart, whose initial substring matches the Find string.
CB_FINDSTRINGEXACT	`int ComboBox_FindStringExact(HWND hwnd, int indexStart, LPCTSTR Find)`
	Returns the index of the first matching item starting at indexStart, whose entire string matches the Find string.
CB_GETCOUNT	`int ComboBox_GetCount(HWND hwnd)`
	Returns the number of items in the list box.
CB_GETCURSEL	`int ComboBox_GetCurSel(HWND hwnd)`
	Returns the index of the selected item.
CB_GETDROPPEDCONTROLRECT	`void ComboBox_GetDroppedControlRect(HWND hwnd, LPRECT rect)`
	Returns the screen coordinates of the visible (dropped-down) list box associated with the combo box.

[1]When a combo box is created with one of the CBS_OWNERDRAW styles but without the CBS_HASSTRINGS style, there is no provision for a string. Instead, operations such as CB_ADDSTRING and CB_INSERTSTRING take the 32-bit value and store it as item data. It can be retrieved either by using the ComboBox_GetText or the ComboBox_GetItemData calls.

[4]Available only in Win32 API level 4 and higher.

[e]These functions are defined in extensions.h.

Table 9.10: Combo box messages

Message	Function Action
CB_GETDROPPEDSTATE	`BOOL ComboBox_GetDroppedState(HWND hwnd)`
	Returns a nonzero value if the list box associated with a combo box is visible or a 0 otherwise.
CB_GETDROPPEDWIDTH[4]	`int ComboBox_GetDroppedWidth(HWND hwnd)`
	Returns the width of the combo box drop-down, in pixels.
CB_GETEDITSEL	`DWORD ComboBox_GetEditSel(HWND hwnd, int index)`
	Returns the start and end positions of the selected text in the edit control of a combo box.
CB_GETEXTENDEDUI	`UINT ComboBox_GetExtendedUI(HWND hwnd)`
	Returns a nonzero value if the combo box has the extended user interface.
CB_GETHORIZONTALEXTENT[4]	`int ComboBox_GetHorizontalExtent`[e]`(HWND hwnd)`
	Returns the scrollable width of the list box.
CB_GETITEMDATA	`LRESULT ComboBox_GetItemData(HWND hwnd, int index)`
	Returns the 32-bit value associated with the item.
CB_GETITEMHEIGHT	`int ComboBox_GetItemHeight(HWND hwnd, int index)`
	Returns the height of items in the list box associated with the combo box.
CB_GETLBTEXT	`int ComboBox_GetLBText(HWND hwnd, int index, LPTSTR Buffer)`
	Copies the string for an item in the list box of a combo box to a specified buffer.
CB_GETLBTEXTLEN	`int ComboBox_GetLBTextLen(HWND hwnd, int index)`
	Returns the length of a string for an item in the list box associated with a combo box.

[1]When a combo box is created with one of the `CBS_OWNERDRAW` styles but without the `CBS_HASSTRINGS` style, there is no provision for a string. Instead, operations such as `CB_ADDSTRING` and `CB_INSERTSTRING` take the 32-bit value and store it as item data. It can be retrieved either by using the `ComboBox_GetText` or the `ComboBox_GetItemData` calls.

[4]Available only in Win32 API level 4 and higher.

[e]These functions are defined in `extensions.h`.

Table 9.10: Combo box messages

Message	Function Action
CB_GETLOCALE	`LCID ComboBox_GetLocale`[e]`(HWND hwnd)`
	Returns the locale identifier for the combo box.
CB_GETTOPINDEX[4]	`int ComboBox_GetTopIndex`[e]`(HWND hwnd)`
	Returns the index of the first visible item in the list box.
CB_INITSTORAGE[4]	`int ComboBox_InitStorage`[e]`(HWND hwnd, int count, int stringBytes)`
	Initializes a storage space for holding the list box data. `count` is the number of items to add and `stringBytes` is the number of bytes to allocate for strings.
CB_INSERTSTRING	`int ComboBox_InsertString(HWND hwnd, int index, LPCTSTR str)`
	`int ComboBox_InsertItemData`[1]`(HWND hwnd, int index, LPARAM data)`
	Inserts an item at the specified position.
CB_LIMITTEXT	`int ComboBox_LimitText(HWND hwnd, int Limit)`
	Sets the maximum number of characters that the user can enter into the edit control of a combo box.
CB_RESETCONTENT	`BOOL ComboBox_ResetContent(HWND hwnd)`
	Removes all items from the list box and clears the edit control contents.
CB_SELECTSTRING	`int ComboBox_SelectString(HWND hwnd, int indexStart, LPCTSTR Find)`
	`int ComboBox_SelectItemData`[1]`(HWND hwnd, int indexStart, LPARAM data)`
	Selects the first item that matches the specified prefix. The text in the edit control of the combo box is updated to contain the newly selected item's string.

[1]When a combo box is created with one of the CBS_OWNERDRAW styles but without the CBS_HASSTRINGS style, there is no provision for a string. Instead, operations such as CB_ADDSTRING and CB_INSERTSTRING take the 32-bit value and store it as item data. It can be retrieved either by using the `ComboBox_GetText` or the `ComboBox_GetItemData` calls.

[4]Available only in Win32 API level 4 and higher.

[e]These functions are defined in `extensions.h`.

Table 9.10: Combo box messages

Message	Function Action
CB_SETCURSEL	`int ComboBox_SetCurSel(HWND hwnd, int index)`
	Selects an item and scrolls it into view. The text in the combo box edit control or static control is changed to the selected item.
CB_SETDROPPEDWIDTH[4]	`int ComboBox_SetDroppedWidth`[e]`(HWND hwnd, int width)`
	Sets the minimum width of the combo box drop-down list, in pixels.
CB_SETEDITSEL	`void ComboBox_SetEditSel(HWND hwnd, int start, int end)`
	Selects all the characters in the edit control of a combo box that are within the specified start and end character positions.
CB_SETEXTENDEDUI	`void ComboBox_SetExtendedUI(HWND hwnd, BOOL extend)`
	Selects either the default user interface or the extended user interface for a combo box with the CBS_DROPDOWN or CBS_DROPDOWNLIST style.
CB_SETHORIZONTALEXTENT[4]	`void ComboBox_SetHorizontalExtent`[e]`(HWND hwnd, int width)`
	Sets the width, in pixels, of the contents of the list box if the combo box was created with the WS_HSCROLL style.
CB_SETITEMDATA	`int ComboBox_SetItemData(HWND hwnd, int index, LPARAM data)`
	Associates a 32-bit value with the specified item.
CB_SETITEMHEIGHT	`int ComboBox_SetItemHeight(HWND hwnd, int index, short cy)`
	Sets the height of items in the list box associated with a combo box or the height of the edit control or static text control associated with a combo box.
CB_SETLOCALE	`LCID ComboBox_SetLocale`[e]`(HWND hwnd, LCID locale)`
	Determines sorting order for combo boxes that have the CBS_SORT attribute.

[1]When a combo box is created with one of the CBS_OWNERDRAW styles but without the CBS_HASSTRINGS style, there is no provision for a string. Instead, operations such as CB_ADDSTRING and CB_INSERTSTRING take the 32-bit value and store it as item data. It can be retrieved either by using the ComboBox_GetText or the ComboBox_GetItemData calls.

[4]Available only in Win32 API level 4 and higher.

[e]These functions are defined in `extensions.h`.

Table 9.10: Combo box messages

Message	Function Action
CB_SHOWDROPDOWN	BOOL ComboBox_ShowDropdown(HWND hwnd, BOOL show)
	Shows or hides the drop-down list box on a CBS_DROPDOWN- or CBS_DROPDOWNLIST-style combo box.
WM_ENABLE	int ComboBox_Enable(HWND hwnd)
	Enables or disables the combo box.
WM_GETTEXT	int ComboBox_GetText(HWND hwnd, LPTSTR Buffer, int chmax)
	Sets the contents of Buffer to the text in the edit or static control of the combo box. Returns the length of the text.
WM_GETTEXTLENGTH	int ComboBox_GetTextLen(HWND hwnd)
	Returns the length of the text in the edit or static control.
WM_SETTEXT	BOOL ComboBox_SetText(HWND hwnd, LPCTSTR text)
	Sets the text in the edit control or static control.
WM_SHOWWINDOW	BOOL ShowWindow(HWND hwnd, int mode)
	Shows or hides the combo box.

[1]When a combo box is created with one of the CBS_OWNERDRAW styles but without the CBS_HASSTRINGS style, there is no provision for a string. Instead, operations such as CB_ADDSTRING and CB_INSERTSTRING take the 32-bit value and store it as item data. It can be retrieved either by using the ComboBox_GetText or the ComboBox_GetItemData calls.

[4]Available only in Win32 API level 4 and higher.

[e]These functions are defined in extensions.h.

You can retrieve the start and end character positions of the selected text in the edit control of a combo box by sending the box the CB_GETEDITSEL message. The wParam and lParam parameters aren't used. The combo box returns the starting character position in the low-order word of the returned long value. The end character position is in the high-order word. As with an edit control, if there is no selection, the start and end positions will be the same and indicate the character index before which the caret appears:

```
DWORD dw ;
int   xStart, xEnd ;

dw = (DWORD) SendMessage (hComboBox, CB_GETEDITSEL, 0, 0) ;
xStart = LOWORD (dw) ;
xEnd = HIWORD (dw) ;
```

or you can use the API macro wrapper:

```
dw = ComboBox_GetEditSel (hComboBox) ;
xStart = LOWORD (dw) ;
```

```
xEnd = HIWORD (dw) ;
```

One problem with edit controls, whether alone or in a combo box, is that you receive no notification of when the user has changed the selection. This can become important, for example, if you need to enable or disable toolbar icons for operations such as Cut and Copy based on whether a nonempty selection has been made. This can be solved by subclassing the control and intercepting certain mouse and keyboard operations and checking for the presence or absence of a selection. We show this in some detail in our MDI example in Chapter 17 (page 1210), so we won't discuss it here.

You can limit the number of characters that a user can type into the edit control of a combo box by sending the combo box a CB_LIMITTEXT message specifying the maximum number of characters to accept. The wParam parameter contains the maximum number of characters the user can enter. The 1Param parameter isn't used. These statements prevent the user from entering a string longer than what the buffer can hold (allowing for a NUL character at the end of the string):

```
TCHAR Buff [40] ;

SendMessage (hComboBox, CB_LIMITTEXT, DIM(Buff) - 1, 0) ;
```

You also can use the API macro wrapper:

```
ComboBox_LimitText(hComboBox, DIM(Buff) - 1);
```

You send the CB_GETLBTEXTLEN and CB_GETLBTEXT messages to a combo box to retrieve the length of a string in the list box of a combo box and the string itself, respectively. The wParam parameter of both messages contains the index of the desired item. The 1Param parameter isn't used when retrieving the length of the string. During a CB_GETLBTEXT message, it contains a pointer to the buffer to which the combo box copies the string:

```
Length = SendMessage (hComboBox, CB_GETLBTEXTLEN, index, 0) ;
SendMessage (hComboBox, CB_GETLBTEXT, index, (LPARAM)(LPTSTR)Buff) ;
```

or, alternatively, you can use the recommended API macros:

```
Length = ComboBox_GetLBTextLen(hComboBox, index);
ComboBox_GetLBText(hComboBox, index, Buff);
```

 In Windows NT, the length returned by the CB_GETLBTEXTLEN will be *at least* the size of the buffer required. Depending on certain interactions (largely unspecified in the Microsoft documentation) between Unicode and non-Unicode components of a system, the length returned may be larger than the actual length required. One condition under which it does occur is when there is a mixture of an ANSI application and the common dialogs (which use Unicode). The true length will be returned by the CB_GETLBTEXT message.

Generally, you want to let the user drop-down the hidden list box of a combo box that was created with the CBS_DROPDOWN or CBS_DROPDOWNLIST styles. If you need to, however, you can explicitly show and hide the list box. You send the CB_SHOWDROPDOWN message to the combo box with the wParam parameter set to TRUE to display the list box if it's not already visible. Setting the wParam parameter to FALSE hides the list box if it is displayed. This statement displays a hidden list box of a drop-down style combo box:

```
SendMessage (hComboBox, CB_SHOWDROPDOWN, TRUE, 0) ;
```

Or you can use the recommended API macro:

```
ComboBox_ShowDropdown (hComboBox, TRUE) ;
```

You can determine whether the list box associated with a combo box is visible (dropped-down) using the CB_GETDROPPEDSTATE message. The wParam and lParam are not used and must be 0. This message returns a nonzero value if the list box is visible; otherwise it is 0.

```
BOOL Visible ;
Visible = (BOOL) SendMessage (hComboBox, CB_GETDROPPEDSTATE, 0, 0) ;
Visible = ComboBox_GetDroppedState (hComboBox) ;
```

When the list box associated with a combo box is visible, you can retrieve the screen coordinates of the list box by sending the CB_GETDROPPEDCONTROLRECT message to the combo box. The combo box will update the specified RECT structure with the coordinates:

```
RECT rect ;
SendMessage (hComboBox,
             CB_GETDROPPEDCONTROLRECT, 0, (LPARAM)(LPRECT)&rect) ;
```

or

```
ComboBox_GetDroppedControlRect(hComboBox, &rect) ;
```

Smart Drop-down Lists

You can set the height and width of the list box that drops down. Typically, you will set the height when the "default size" of the combo box is longer than the size needed to hold the number of items in the list. Rather than have a large blank white space following the last item, you could shorten the box height so that it is just large enough to hold the set of items currently in it.[4] You should "remember" the actual height originally set so that you don't set a value larger than this height, since you could possibly exceed the screen height for a long combo box list. You can set the width to be a "minimum allowable" width. The actual width of the drop-down list of a combo box is the larger of the edit control (or static control) or the minimum width specified.

Specifying the minimum width is simple. Use the CB_SETDROPPEDWIDTH message, specifying the minimum width of the drop-down, in pixels, in the wParam (this has no API equivalent):

```
SendMessage(hComboBox, CB_SETDROPPEDWIDTH, (WPARAM)width, 0);
```

---

[4] You will discover that some of this functionality, but by no means all of it, is built into API level 4. The only problem we find is that when the list box is empty, the full-height list box, instead of just a one-entry list box, always drops down. We find this visually disturbing. You will also find a much more sophisticated version of this adjustment code in the GDI Explorer. Here we set the maximum height so that the box displays showing the maximum number of possible elements: choosing the larger of the space above the combo box or the space below the combo box. This means that the actual size can change depending on the vertical position of the combo box when it is dropped down! Check out the idcombo.cpp source file.

You can find the current setting of the width by using the CB_GETDROPPEDWIDTH message. This message, which has no API macro equivalent, returns the minimum allowable drop-down width in pixels. The operation of reading or setting the dropped width is supported only at API level 4 and higher.

Figure 9.3: Normal drop-down with fewer items than height (API level 3)

Setting the height is a bit more difficult. As we said, you probably want to retain the original setting (such as that established by the dialog template) as a maximum allowable height. There are many ways to do this. The simplest is if you are programming in a language such as C++. You subclass the combo box control (in MFC, you make a derived class of CComboBox) and store the original height in a member variable of that new class.

When programming at the straight API level, however, you need a separate variable to hold the information. Rather than clutter up your code with an assortment of static variables that retain this information, there are several common ways to associate a value with a control. The simplest is to use the GWL_USERDATA datum that every window class has. You can use the SetWindowLong function to store any 32-bit value in this word and the GetWindowLong function to retrieve it. Since this is a 32-bit value, you can store anything you want. In the example that follows, we store an integer value that is the original height. In more elaborate cases, you can store a pointer to a structure of window-related information. Every window class, including the built-in classes, has a GWL_USERDATA datum.

Another way to associate a value with a control is to use the SetProp function to store a property associated with the window. This property can hold any 32-bit value; however, the SetProp function expects a HANDLE value, so you must cast your value to be a HANDLE type. You can use the GetProp function to retrieve the value. Like SetProp, it assumes the value is a HANDLE and you must cast it to some other type if that is not what is being returned. However, you must also remember to remove the property from the window as the window is being destroyed. Otherwise, the property will simply be disconnected and remain in existence, consuming memory unnecessarily. Thus, if you use this technique, you must have an OnDestroy handler that does a RemoveProp for every property you have attached. If you attach properties conditionally, it doesn't matter if you remove nonexistent properties. So you can remove all the properties without actually first testing for their existence. You must use this technique if someone else is already using (or you suspect someone *might* be using) the GWL_USERDATA field for some other purpose.

Figure 9.4: Smart drop-downs with 0, 2, and 10 entries

Figure 9.4 shows a sample of the effect and Listing 9.2 shows the code. Note that we store the original combo box width and height and have added an option to double the drop-down list box height. We set this up so that if the list box is empty, we will show a list box that has one (empty) element. Visually, it is better to drop down a small empty list than to drop down a list of 0 height. This gives some feedback that the system is indeed responding to the drop-down request but has nothing to show. Our "smart drop-down" code limits this empty list to one line.

Listing 9.2: Sample code for smart drop-down

```
void cls_OnDropdown(HWND hDlg, HWND combo)
{
    int items;
    int lineheight;
    HDC dc;
    TEXTMETRIC tm;
    RECT r;
    int required_height;
    int permitted_height;
    HFONT font;

    // Compute the size of the combo box
    // This assumes that the combo box is NOT
    // owner-draw!
    items = ComboBox_GetCount(combo);
    dc = GetDC(combo);
    font = GetWindowFont(combo);
    if(font != NULL)
        SelectObject(dc, font);
    GetTextMetrics(dc, &tm);
    ReleaseDC(combo, dc);
    lineheight = tm.tmHeight + tm.tmExternalLeading;
    required_height = (2 + max(items, 1)) * lineheight;
    permitted_height = (int)
                    LOWORD(GetWindowLong(combo, GWL_USERDATA));

    ComboBox_SetDroppedWidth(combo,
                (int)HIWORD(GetWindowLong(combo, GWL_USERDATA)));

    // If the required height is less than or equal to the saved
    // height, use the required height.  If it is greater, use
    // the saved height
    ComboBox_GetDroppedControlRect(combo, &r);
    ScreenToClient(hDlg, (LPPOINT)&r.left);
    ScreenToClient(hDlg, (LPPOINT)&r.right);

    if(required_height <= permitted_height)
        { /* smaller than default setting */
         r.bottom = r.top + required_height;
        } /* smaller than default setting */
    else
        { /* larger than default setting */
         r.bottom = r.top + permitted_height;
        } /* larger than default setting */

    MoveWindow(combo, r.left, r.top,
                    r.right - r.left, r.bottom - r.top, TRUE);
}

// The GWL_USERDATA values were set in the OnInitDialog handler:

BOOL cls_OnInitDialog(HWND hDlg, HWND focus, LPARAM lParam)
    {
    RECT r;

    // ...
```

```
    GetWindowRect(GetDlgItem(hDlg, IDC_COMBO), &r);
    ScreenToClient(hDlg, (LPPOINT)&r.left);
    ScreenToClient(hDlg, (LPPOINT)&r.right);
    SetWindowLong(GetDlgItem(hDlg, IDC_COMBO), GWL_USERDATA,
                MAKELONG(r.bottom - r.top, r.right - r.left));
}
```

You can enable and disable the combo box *extended user interface* by sending the CB_SETEXTENDEDUI message to a combo box. Set the wParam parameter to TRUE to select the extended user interface and FALSE to select the standard user interface. The lParam parameter is not used and must be 0. The following example selects the extended user interface for the specified combo box:

```
SendMessage (hComboBox, CB_SETEXTENDEDUI, (WPARAM) TRUE, 0L) ;
ComboBox_SetExtendedUI (hComboBox, TRUE) ;
```

The extended user interface for combo boxes differs from the standard user interface in the following ways:

- Clicking the static control of a CBS_DROPDOWNLIST style combo box displays the associated list box.

- Pressing the down arrow key displays the list box. The **F4** key is disabled.

- Scrolling in the static control is disabled when the list box is not visible (the arrow keys are disabled).

Adding, Inserting, and Deleting Items from a Combo Box

You add, insert, and delete items from the list box of a combo box exactly the same way as you do for an ordinary list box control except that names of the messages have changed. You use the CB_ADDSTRING, CB_INSERTSTRING, and CB_DELETESTRING messages rather than the LB_* counterparts. You also use the CB_DIR message to fill the list box of a combo box with filenames.

The CB_DIR and LB_DIR messages in Windows 95 do *not* support long filenames! If you need to support long filenames, you must use the GetShortPathName function to convert the long filename to the 8.3-compatible format. However, the list box will display only short filenames in Windows 95. See the MSKB article Q131286.

The list box of an owner-draw combo box sends the same WM_MEASUREITEMW messages to the parent window of the combo box, as does a normal list box. It also sends WM_COMPAREITEM messages to the parent window of the combo box when the combo box has the CBS_SORT style and doesn't have the CBS_HASSTRINGS style. It sends WM_DELETEITEM messages when the combo box doesn't have the CBS_HASSTRINGS style. You should handle these messages exactly as you would for a list box. See page 607 (WM_COMPAREITEM), page 610 (WM_MEASUREITEM), and page 611 (WM_DELETEITEM).

Selecting an Item in a Combo Box

You select and deselect an item in the list box of a combo box as you do a single-selection list box, except that the message names change to CB_SETCURSEL, CB_SELECTSTRING, and CB_GETCURSEL. The combo box messages have the same parameters as do their corresponding regular list box messages. Combo boxes, however, do not have multiple-selection modes. So any messages dealing with multiple selection in list boxes have no corresponding messages in combo boxes.

Combo Box Notification Messages

A combo box control (buttons, edit controls, and list boxes) sends notifications to its parent window via WM_COMMAND messages. The HIWORD(wParam) contains the notification code, which is passed to the OnCommand handler as its codeNotify parameter. Table 9.11 shows the combo box notification codes.

Table 9.11: Combo box notification messages

Code	Meaning
CBN_CLOSEUP	The list box of a combo box has been hidden.
CBN_DBLCLK	User has double-clicked an item in the list box of a CBS_SIMPLE combo box. You cannot receive this message from a combo box with a drop-down list box.
CBN_DROPDOWN	The list box of a combo box is about to become visible.
CBN_EDITCHANGE	User has changed the text in the edit control of a combo box. The display has already been updated.
CBN_EDITUPDATE	User has changed the text in the edit control of a combo box. The display has not yet been updated.
CBN_ERRSPACE	The list box of a combo box cannot allocate enough memory.
CBN_KILLFOCUS	The combo box is losing the input focus.
CBN_SELCHANGE	The selection in the list box of a combo box has changed.
CBN_SELENDCANCEL	The combo box selection has been canceled.
CBN_SELENDOK	The combo box selection has been accepted.
CBN_SETFOCUS	The combo box is gaining the input focus.

Many of these notification codes are similar to others already discussed. CBN_DROPDOWN alerts the combo box's parent window that the list box of a drop-down combo box is about to become visible. A combo box notifies its parent window just before displaying a change in the edit control of a combo box by sending a WM_COMMAND message with a CBN_EDITUPDATE. It sends a CBN_EDITCHANGE immediately after displaying the change.

A combo box notifies its parent window when it gains and loses the input focus with CBN_SETFOCUS and CBN_KILLFOCUS, respectively. A combo box with the CBS_DROPDOWN or CBS_DROPDOWNLIST styles removes the drop-down list box from the display when it loses the input focus. One use of CBN_GETFOCUS is to issue a CB_SHOWDROPDOWN, so that when the control gets the focus it drops down.

A combo box sends a CBN_SELENDCANCEL when the user selects an item in the list box and then clicks outside the combo box to hide the dropped-down list box. You should ignore the user's selection.

A combo box sends a CBN_SELENDOK when the user selects an item in the list box and then presses the **Enter** key or clicks the down arrow key to hide the dropped-down list box. You should accept the user's selection.

Finally, a combo box sends a CBN_CLOSEUP when the list box of a combo box is hidden. A CBN_CLOSEUP follows a CBN_SELENDCANCEL or CBN_SELENDOK.

Combo Boxes and List Boxes Are Not Interchangeable

There are times when you may decide that a list box is not the right control and you want to use a combo box instead, or vice versa. You must be very careful when making such a change; neither the style flags nor the messages are interchangeable. Table 9.12 shows this. You must change the names of set styles or called message functions.

Table 9.12: Comparison of list box and combo box styles

Numeric Code	List Box	Combo Box
0x0001	LBS_NOTIFY	CBS_SIMPLE
0x0002	LBS_SORT	CBS_DROPDOWN
0x0003	–	CBS_DROPDOWNLIST
0x0004	LBS_NOREDRAW	–
0x0008	LBS_MULTIPLESEL	–
0x0010	LBS_OWNERDRAWFIXED	CBS_OWNERDRAWFIXED
0x0020	LBS_OWNERDRAWVARIABLE	CBS_OWNERDRAWVARIABLE
0x0040	LBS_HASSTRINGS	CBS_AUTOHSCROLL
0x0080	LBS_USETABSTOPS	CBS_OEMCONVERT
0x0100	LBS_NOINTEGRALHEIGHT	CBS_SORT
0x0200	LBS_MULTICOLUMN	CBS_HASSTRINGS
0x0400	LBS_WANTKEYBOARDINPUT	CBS_NOINTEGRALHEIGHT
0x0800	LBS_EXTENDEDSEL	CBS_DISABLENOSCROLL
0x1000	LBS_DISABLENOSCROLL	–
0x2000	LBS_NODATA	CBS_UPPERCASE
0x4000	LBS_NOSEL	CBS_LOWERCASE
0x180..0x1A9	LB_ messages	–
0x140..0x161	–	CB_ messages

Improving Performance for List Boxes and Combo Boxes

A list box, whether a LISTBOX class or the list box of a COMBOBOX class, will dynamically allocate storage for the strings or items it is storing. However, each time it expands its storage, it must allocate new storage, copy the existing list box information to the new storage space, and then free the old storage space. This results in severe time penalties when you are loading up a list box with a large number of entries. To improve performance, the LB_INITSTORAGE or CB_INITSTORAGE message tells the control to preallocate an amount of storage. Doing this lets you avoid the unnecessary allocate-copy-free cycle when items are added. To preallocate storage for a number of items, you can send a message

```
SendMessage(hListBox, LB_INITSTORAGE, 1000, 15000);
```

```
SendMessage(hCombo, CB_INITSTORAGE, 1000, 15000);
```

which preallocates enough space in the control for 1,000 list box items and allows for 15,000 bytes for character strings (that is, each item would take around 15 bytes). The return value is the maximum number of items that you can add before the list box needs to do its next allocation or LB_ERRSPACE if there is not enough memory to satisfy this request. Microsoft recommends that you do this any time you expect to have more than 100 items in a list box. If your list box is owner-draw without the LBS_HASSTRINGS or CBS_HASSTRINGS style, the lParam value can be 0. If, in the course of filling the list box, your estimates turn out to be low, the normal allocation mechanism will come into play. If they are high, the extra space will not be reclaimed until some other operation (another LB_INITSTORAGE or CB_INITSTORAGE, perhaps) frees the space. In Windows 95, the maximum number of items that can be preallocated in a list box is 32,767.

Setting Locales for List Boxes and Combo Boxes

When a list box or a combo box has the LBS_SORT or CBS_SORT style, the control arranges the strings "in sorted order". But what is "sorted order"? Different languages have different rules for how characters are arranged. For example, in Spanish, *ll* sorts between *l* and *m*. In German, the single character ß sorts as if it were the two characters *ss*. In Czech, the pair *ch* sorts as a single character between *h* and *i*. In Danish and Norwegian, *ä* sorts after *z* and before *ö*, while in French *ä* sorts after *a* and before *b*. All of these assorted rules are handled by what is called a *locale*; when you install Windows, you get to choose the "native language" it will use. Doing this causes the correct fonts to be loaded and sets up the operations for character comparison and translation (what constitutes uppercase and lowercase, for example, and what character codes are letters). All of these character relationships are defined by the locale. We discussed comparison and translation in Chapter 7 starting on page 427. List boxes and combo boxes use the language-dependent comparison routines to support the LBS_SORT and CBS_SORT styles.

The default sort order for a list box or a combo box is based on the default locale. But there are times when you may have to support more than one locale. In a bilingual country such as Canada, the sort order for names might want to follow the local conventions, which may follow the French collating sequence, yet the "native" language for Windows might be either French or English. In this case, you will need to override the default locale information for a list box or combo box using the LB_SETLOCALE or CB_SETLOCALE messages.

These allow the list box or combo box to use a different language than the one installed on Windows. Even if you are doing your own comparisons using an owner-draw list box without LBS_HASSTRINGS, you might want to use the CompareStringW API call, which wants a locale ID. In this case, you can write your code to be locale-independent by using the LB_GETLOCALE or CB_GETLOCALE messages to obtain the locale ID set for the list box or combo box.

You create a locale ID by using the MAKELCID macro. This takes two parameters—a language ID and a sort ID—and makes a 32-bit locale ID. The language ID consists of a primary language ID and a sublanguage ID composed using the MAKELANGID macro. The primary language ID can be one of the identifiers shown in Table 9.13. The sublanguage is SUBLANG_DEFAULT unless a specific sublanguage is required, and the sort ID is typically SORT_DEFAULT, although some languages that have more than one sort ID will have other options. The sort order can be any of the values from Table 9.14. We show the encoding of a locale ID in Figure 9.5. Of course, with every release of Windows the number of languages supported may differ, so Table 9.13 is a snapshot of only one instant in time of what is an ever-expanding list of supported languages.

31		20	19	16	15		10	9		0
reserved			sort ID		sublanguage ID			language ID		

```
MAKELCID(MAKELANGID(languageID, sublanguageID), sortID)
```

Figure 9.5: Layout of locale ID

Table 9.13: Languages supported by Win32

95	NT	Language id	Sublanguage ID
	✓	LANG_AFRIKAANS	
	✓	LANG_ALBANIAN	
	✓	LANG_ARABIC	SUBLANG_ARABIC_ALGERIA
			SUBLANG_ARABIC_BAHRAIN
			SUBLANG_ARABIC_EGYPT
			SUBLANG_ARABIC_IRAQ
			SUBLANG_ARABIC_JORDAN
			SUBLANG_ARABIC_KUWAIT
			SUBLANG_ARABIC_LEBANON
			SUBLANG_ARABIC_LIBYA
			SUBLANG_ARABIC_MOROCCO
			SUBLANG_ARABIC_OMAN
			SUBLANG_ARABIC_QATAR
			SUBLANG_ARABIC_SYRIA
			SUBLANG_ARABIC_TUNISIA
			SUBLANG_ARABIC_UAE
			SUBLANG_ARABIC_YEMEN

Table 9.13: Languages supported by Win32

95	NT	Language id	Sublanguage ID
	✓	LANG_BASQUE	
✓	✓	LANG_BULGARIAN	
	✓	LANG_BYELORUSSIAN	
	✓	LANG_CATALAN	
✓	✓	LANG_CHINESE	SUBLANG_CHINESE_HONGKONG
			SUBLANG_CHINESE_SIMPLIFIED
			SUBLANG_CHINESE_SINGAPORE
			SUBLANG_CHINESE_TRADITIONAL
✓	✓	LANG_CROATIAN	
✓	✓	LANG_CZECH	
✓	✓	LANG_DANISH	
✓	✓	LANG_DUTCH	SUBLANG_DUTCH
			SUBLANG_DUTCH_BELGIAN
✓	✓	LANG_ENGLISH	SUBLANG_ENGLISH
			SUBLANG_ENGLISH_AUS
			SUBLANG_ENGLISH_CAN
			SUBLANG_ENGLISH_CARRIBEAN
			SUBLANG_ENGLISH_EIRE
			SUBLANG_ENGLISH_JAMAICA
			SUBLANG_ENGLISH_NZ
			SUBLANG_ENGLISH_SAFRICA
			SUBLANG_ENGLISH_UK
			SUBLANG_ENGLISH_US
	✓	LANG_ESTONIAN	
✓	✓	LANG_FINNISH	
✓	✓	LANG_FRENCH	SUBLANG_FRENCH
			SUBLANG_FRENCH_BELGIAN
			SUBLANG_FRENCH_CANADIAN
			SUBLANG_FRENCH_LUXEMBOURG
			SUBLANG_FRENCH_SWISS

Table 9.13: Languages supported by Win32

95	NT	Language id	Sublanguage ID
✓	✓	LANG_GERMAN	SUBLANG_GERMAN
			SUBLANG_GERMAN_AUSTRIAN
			SUBLANG_GERMAN_LIECHTENSTEIN
			SUBLANG_GERMAN_LUXEMBOURG
			SUBLANG_GERMAN_SWISS
✓	✓	LANG_GREEK	
	✓	LANG_HEBREW	
✓	✓	LANG_HUNGARIAN	
✓	✓	LANG_ICELANDIC	
	✓	LANG_INDONESIAN	
✓	✓	LANG_ITALIAN	SUBLANG_ITALIAN
			SUBLANG_ITALIAN_SWISS
✓	✓	LANG_JAPANESE	
✓	✓	LANG_KOREAN	SUBLANG_KOREAN
			SUBLANG_KOREAN_JOHAB
	✓	LANG_LATVIAN	
	✓	LANG_LITHUANIAN	
✓	✓	LANG_NEUTRAL	SUBLANG_DEFAULT
			SUBLANG_NEUTRAL
			SUBLANG_SYS_DEFAULT
✓	✓	LANG_NORWEGIAN	SUBLANG_NORWEGIAN_BOKMAL
			SUBLANG_NORWEGIAN_NYNORSK
✓	✓	LANG_POLISH	
✓	✓	LANG_PORTUGUESE	SUBLANG_PORTUGUESE
			SUBLANG_PORTUGUESE_BRAZILIAN
✓	✓	LANG_ROMANIAN	
✓	✓	LANG_RUSSIAN	
✓	✓	LANG_SLOVAK	
✓	✓	LANG_SLOVENIAN	
	✓	LANG_SORBIAN	

Table 9.13: Languages supported by Win32

95	NT	Language id	Sublanguage ID
✓	✓	LANG_SPANISH	SUBLANG_SPANISH
			SUBLANG_SPANISH_ARGENTINA
			SUBLANG_SPANISH_BOLIVIA
			SUBLANG_SPANISH_CHILE
			SUBLANG_SPANISH_COLOMBIA
			SUBLANG_SPANISH_COSTARICA
			SUBLANG_SPANISH_DOMINICAN
			SUBLANG_SPANISH_ECUADOR
			SUBLANG_SPANISH_GUATEMALA
			SUBLANG_SPANISH_MEXICAN
			SUBLANG_SPANISH_MODERN
			SUBLANG_SPANISH_PANAMA
			SUBLANG_SPANISH_PARAGUAY
			SUBLANG_SPANISH_PERU
			SUBLANG_SPANISH_URUGUAY
			SUBLANG_SPANISH_VENEZUELA
✓	✓	LANG_SWEDISH	
	✓	LANG_THAI	
✓	✓	LANG_TURKISH	
	✓	LANG_UKRANIAN	

Table 9.14: Sort order IDs

Sort Order Key	Meaning
SORT_CHINESE_BIGS	Chinese BIGS order.
SORT_CHINESE_UNICODE	Chinese Unicode order.
SORT_DEFAULT	Default sort code for country.
SORT_JAPANESE_UNICODE	Japanese Unicode order.
SORT_JAPANESE_XJIS	Japanese XJIS order.
SORT_KOREAN_KSC	Korean KSC order.
SORT_KOREAN_UNICODE	Korean Unicode order.

To continue an example we mentioned earlier, assume you have done a Windows installation for Canadian English, but you want a list box in sorted order according to French Canadian sorting rules. You could accomplish this by sending the following message to the list box:

```
SendMessage(hListBox, LB_SETLOCALE,
            MAKELCID(MAKELANGID(LANG_FRENCH,
                        SUBLANG_FRENCH_CANADIAN),
                SORT_DEFAULT)), 0);
```

Note that there is no ListBox_ or ComboBox_ API equivalent for these messages.

Image Lists

Image lists are not a control class. Structurally, image lists look like an extension to the GDI facilities, so perhaps should have been discussed in that chapter. However, we decided that because image lists are so central to many of the Win32 controls, such as list view and tree view, that we would include the discussion in this chapter, where we can readily give the context for understanding them. Also, image lists are actually supported by commctl32.dll, the library that supports many of the Win32 controls. This makes it easy to couple the discussion to that of the other controls supported by that library.

An image list is simply a collection of same-sized images that packages the images and their support operations into a single package. With image lists, you don't need to maintain handles on icons, bitmaps, or memory DCs or understand the mysteries of BitBlt. In many cases, the sort of imaging that was done by owner-draw list boxes can now be handled by the built-in functionality of list view and tree view controls using the image lists to get nice icons.

Some facilities you might want to use, such as drag-and-drop list views or tree views, cannot easily be done without image lists (of course, you can program *anything*, no matter how tedious, but why bother?). When we look at the tree view class, for example, we show how to implement a drag-and-drop facility in surprisingly few lines of code.

You can create an image list by starting with an empty image list and adding icons and bitmaps. An image list stores the images as a single large image internally, so there is a functional limitation. That is, neither the sum of all the widths nor the maximum height of an image can exceed 32K pixels. All images must be the same size, and you must know the dimensions when you create the image list. An image list is referenced by its *handle*, a datum of type HIMAGELIST.

Image lists come in two flavors: *nonmasked* and *masked*. An image from a nonmasked image list is copied directly to its destination using the equivalent of a BitBlt(...SRCCOPY) operation. Every pixel of the image transfers to the destination. An image from a masked image list is accompanied by a second bitmap, a monochrome bitmap called the *mask*. This bitmap is used to determine which pixels of the destination to replace. If a bit in the mask is 1, the destination pixel remains unchanged. If a bit in the mask is 0, the image pixel is copied to the destination.

The operations to manage image lists are shown in Table 9.15.

Table 9.15: Operations for managing image lists

Function	Function Prototype Description
ImageList_Add	`int ImageList_Add(HIMAGELIST hlist, HBITMAP image, HBITMAP mask)`
	Adds one or more images to the image list. The number of images contained in the bitmap is computed from the values used to create the image list and the size of the bitmap. The return value is the index of the image (or the first image, if there were multiple images in the bitmap) or -1 if there was an error. If the image list is a masked image list, the `mask` parameter specifies the bitmap that is the mask; otherwise, it is ignored.
ImageList_AddIcon	`int ImageList_AddIcon(HIMAGELIST hlist, HICON icon)`
	An abbreviation for `ImageList_ReplaceIcon(hlist, -1, icon)`.
ImageList_AddMasked	`int ImageList_AddMasked(HIMAGELIST hlist, HBITMAP image, COLORREF color)`
	Adds images to an image list and generates the mask bitmap based on a selected background color in the image. Returns the index of the first image added or -1 if there was an error.
ImageList_BeginDrag	`BOOL ImageList_BeginDrag(HIMAGELIST hlist, int index, int hotspotX, int hotspotY)`
	Creates a temporary drag image and puts it in a separate image list within the image list `hlist`. This temporary image will be manipulated with `ImageList_DragMove`. The return value is nonzero if successful or FALSE if there is an error.
ImageList_Create	`HIMAGELIST ImageList_Create(int width, int height, UINT flags, int initsize, int growsize)`
	Creates an image list to hold images of the specified width and height. The `initsize` parameter tells what the initial allocation should be (the number of images to allocate) and the `growsize` parameter tells the number of new slots that should be created when the current allocation is exceeded. The `flags` parameter specifies the type of the image list, and is one of the following:

Value	Meaning
ILC_COLOR	Uses the default behavior if none of the other ILC_COLOR* flags are specified. The usual default is ILC_COLOR4, but for some old display drivers, the default is ILC_COLORDDB.

Table 9.15: Operations for managing image lists

Function	Function Prototype Description	
Only one of these color values can be specified	ILC_COLOR4	Uses a 4-bit DIB section (16 colors) to hold the image list bitmaps.
	ILC_COLOR8	Uses an 8-bit DIB section (256 colors) to hold the image bitmaps.
	ILC_COLOR16	Uses a 16-bit DIB section (32K or 64K colors) to hold the image bitmaps (some display cards use only 15 of the 16 bits for color values).
	ILC_COLOR24	Uses a 24-bit DIB section (16M colors) to hold the image bitmaps.
	ILC_COLOR32	Uses a 32-bit DIB section (depending on the encoding, this usually means 30 bits of color information, or 1G colors).
	ILC_COLORDDB	Uses a device-dependent bitmap. The number of colors depends on the device characteristics.
	ILC_MASK	Uses a mask. The image list contains two bitmaps: a color bitmap for the image and a monochrome bitmap for the mask. If this flag is not included, the image list will contain only one bitmap, the image bitmap.
ImageList_Destroy	BOOL ImageList_Destroy(HIMAGELIST hlist)	
	Destroys the image list. Returns a nonzero value if successful or FALSE if there is an error.	
ImageList_DragEnter	BOOL ImageList_DragEnter(HWND owner, int x, int y)	
	Initiates a dragging operation. The specified window is locked against updates. The drag image is displayed at the specified coordinates. The coordinates are relative to the upper-left corner of the window (*not* the client area) and expressed in device units. Returns a nonzero value if successful or FALSE if an error occurs.	
ImageList_DragLeave	BOOL ImageList_DragLeave(HWND owner)	
	Unlocks the specified window and hides the drag image. The window can now be updated.	

Table 9.15: Operations for managing image lists

Function	Function Prototype Description
`ImageList_DragMove`	`BOOL ImageList_DragMove(int x, int y)`
	Moves the drag image to the new coordinates specified by x and y. This function is usually used in the `WM_MOUSEMOVE` (`OnMouseMove`) handler.
`ImageList_DragShowNolock`	`BOOL ImageList_DragShowNolock(BOOL show)`
	The `show` parameter specifies whether to show (TRUE) or hide (FALSE) the drag image. Returns a nonzero value if successful or FALSE if there is an error.
`ImageList_Draw`	`BOOL ImageList_Draw(HIMAGELIST hlist, int index, HDC dc, int x, int y, UINT style)`
	Allows you to draw a selected image in a DC. The `index` value specifies which image from the list will be drawn. It is drawn at the logical coordinates specified by x and y. The `style` is one of the following values (note that some values have more than one name):

Value	Meaning
`ILD_BLEND25` `ILD_FOCUS`	Draws the image, blending in 25% of the system highlight color. Has no effect if the image list does not have a mask.
`ILD_BLEND` `ILD_BLEND50` `ILD_SELECTED`	Draws the image, blending in 50% of the system highlight color. Has no effect if the image list does not have a mask.
`ILD_MASK`	Draws the mask only.
`ILD_NORMAL`	Draws the image using the selected background color (see `ImageList_SetBkColor`). If the background color is the value `CLR_NONE`, the image is drawn "transparently" using the mask.
`ILD_TRANSPARENT`	Draws the image "transparently" using the mask. The image list background color (see `ImageList_SetBkColor`) is ignored. Has no effect if the image list does not have a mask.

Table 9.15: Operations for managing image lists

Function	Function Prototype Description
ImageList_DrawEx	BOOL ImageList_DrawEx(HIMAGELIST hlist, int index, HDC dc, int x, int y, int dx, int dy, COLORREF bkg, COLORREF fg, UINT style)
	Draws the image in the specified DC. The image is drawn with the specified style (the same styles as ImageList_Draw). The image is blended with the specified foreground and background colors. The background color is used only if the image list has a mask (created with the ILC_MASK flag). The background color can be one of the following:

	RGB(r, g, b)	Any application-defined color.
	CLR_NONE	No background color. The image is drawn transparently.
	CLR_DEFAULT	Default background color (see ImageList_SetBkColor).

The foreground color is used only if the style includes ILD_BLEND25 or IDL_BLEND50 (or one of their synonyms).

	RGB(r, g, b)	Any application-defined color.
	CLR_NONE	No blend color. The image is blended with the color of the destination DC.
	CLR_DEFAULT	Default foreground color. Uses Get-SysColor(COLOR_HIGHLIGHT)

Function	Function Prototype Description
ImageList_EndDrag	BOOL ImageList_EndDrag()
	Ends a drag operation. Returns a nonzero value if successful or FALSE if there is an error.
ImageList_ExtractIcon	HICON ImageList_ExtractIcon(HINSTANCE hinst, HIMAGELIST hlist, int index)
	Creates an icon or cursor based on the image and mask in the image list. The hinst parameter is currently unused and must be set to 0 (or NULL). An abbreviation for ImageList_GetIcon(hlist, index, 0).
ImageList_GetBkColor	COLORREF ImageList_GetBkColor(HIMAGELIST hlist)
	Retrieves the current background color established by the ImageList_SetBkColor call.

Table 9.15: Operations for managing image lists

Function	Function Prototype Description
`ImageList_GetDragImage`	`HIMAGELIST ImageList_GetDragImage(LPPOINT pt, LPPOINT hotspot)`
	Retrieves the temporary image list created by the `ImageList_BeginDrag` operation. It also retrieves the current drag position, which is stored in `pt`, and the offset of the drag image relative to the drag position (the `hotspot`). Either `pt` or `hotspot` can be NULL if the value is not needed.
`ImageList_GetIcon`	`HICON ImageList_GetIcon(HIMAGELIST hlist, int index, UINT flags)`
	Creates an icon or cursor based on the image and mask selected by `index`. The `flags` value is one of the ILD_* values used by `ImageList_Draw`.

	`ILD_BLEND25, ILD_FOCUS`
	`ILD_BLEND50, ILD_SELECTED, ILD_BLEND`
	`ILD_MASK`
	`ILD_NORMAL`
	`ILD_TRANSPARENT`

`ImageList_GetImageCount`	`int ImageList_GetImageCount(HIMAGELIST hlist)`
	Returns the number of images in the image list.
`ImageList_GetImageInfo`	`BOOL ImageList_GetImageInfo(HIMAGELIST hlist, int index, IMAGEINFO FAR * info)`
	Retrieves information about an image.
`ImageList_LoadBitmap`	`HIMAGELIST ImageList_LoadBitmap(HINSTANCE hinst, LPCTSTR resource, int width, int growsize, COLORREF mask)`
	Loads a bitmap from the executable or DLL specified by `hinst`. The height of the images is determined by the height of the bitmap. The number of images is determined based on the width of the bitmap and the `width` parameter. The `growsize` determines how many slots will be created each time the image list needs to be expanded. If the `mask` parameter is `CLR_NONE`, no mask bitmap will be generated. If a color is specified, each pixel in that color will be changed to black and its corresponding position in the mask bitmap will be set to 1.

Table 9.15: Operations for managing image lists

Function	Function Prototype Description
ImageList_LoadImage	HIMAGELIST ImageList_LoadImage(HINSTANCE hinst, LPCTSTR resource, int width, int growsize, COLORREF mask, UINT type, UINT flags)

Creates an image list from a bitmap, cursor, or icon resource. If the hinst parameter is NULL (0), the resource parameter must be a MAKEINTRESOURCE of one of the OCR_ symbols defined in Table 7.15 on page 475, OBM_ symbols defined in Table 12.14 on page 883, or OIC_ symbols defined in Table 12.19 on page 913. If the flags parameter specifies LR_LOADFROMFILE, the resource parameter is the filename of the file containing the image; otherwise, it is the string name or MAKEINTRESOURCE of the resource ID for the resource in the specified hinst. The width parameter specifies the width of each image. The height and number of images can be inferred from the file. The growsize parameter determines how many slots will be created each time the image list needs to be expanded. The mask parameter determines the color to be used to generate the mask for a masked image list. If it is the special value CLR_NONE, no mask is generated. The type field can be one of the following values:

Type	Image Loaded
IMAGE_BITMAP	A bitmap.
IMAGE_CURSOR	A cursor.
IMAGE_ICON	An icon.

The flags value controls how the image is loaded. It can be a combination of any of the following bits:

Flag	Meaning
LR_DEFAULTCOLOR	Uses the color format of the display.
LR_LOADDEFAULTSIZE	Uses the widths specified by the system metrics (codes SM_CXICON, SM_CXSMICON, SM_CXCURSOR) if the width parameter is 0. If this flag is not set and the width is 0, the size is set to the size of the image in the resource or, in the case of multiple images, to the first image.
LR_LOADFROMFILE	The resource parameter is the filename of a .bmp, .ico, or .cur file.

Table 9.15: Operations for managing image lists

Function	Function Prototype Description	
	`LR_LOADMAP3DCOLORS`	Searches the color table of the image and replaces particular shades of gray with the corresponding "3D-look" color. See Table 12.22 on page 916.
	`LR_LOADTRANSPARENT`	Replaces all pixels in the image that have the same color as the pixel in the top-left corner with the current `COLOR_WINDOW` value.
	`LR_MONOCHROME`	Loads a black-and-white version of the image.
	`LR_SHARED`	Shares the image handle if the image is loaded multiple times.
`ImageList_Merge`	`HIMAGELIST ImageList_Merge(HIMAGELIST hlist1, int index1, HIMAGELIST hinst2, int index2, int dx, int dy)`	
	Creates a new image by combining the image designated by `index1` in image list `hlist1` with the image designated by `index2` in image list `hinst2`. During the combination, the second image will be offset by an amount dx, dy before combining and the second image will be drawn transparently over the first. The mask for the new image is the result of a bitwise OR of the two masks. A new image is created and placed in a new image list. That new image list handle is returned.	
`ImageList_Read`	`HIMAGELIST ImageList_Read(LPSTREAM stream)`	
	Reads an image list from a stream.	
`ImageList_Remove`	`BOOL ImageList_Remove(HIMAGELIST hlist, int index)`	
	Removes the image at index position `index` from the image list. If `index` is –1, all images are removed.	
`ImageList_RemoveAll`	`BOOL ImageList_RemoveAll(HIMAGELIST hlist)`	
	Synonym for `ImageList_Remove(hlist, -1)`.	
`ImageList_Replace`	`BOOL ImageList_Replace(HIMAGELIST hlist, int index, HBITMAP image, HBITMAP mask)`.	
	Replaces the image at position index with the new `image` value. If the image list is not masked, the `mask` parameter is ignored.	

Table 9.15: Operations for managing image lists

Function	Function Prototype Description
ImageList_ReplaceIcon	`int ImageList_ReplaceIcon(HIMAGELIST hlist, int index, HICON icon)`
	Replaces the image at position `index` with the new icon or cursor image. If the image list is masked, the icon or cursor mask will be used to generate the mask. Returns the index for the replacement or `-1` if there is an error. After the replacement, the icon or cursor can be destroyed because the bits have already been copied to the image list.
ImageList_SetBkColor	`COLORREF ImageList_SetBkColor(HIMAGELIST hlist, COLORREF color)`
	Sets the background color to use for drawing images. If the color parameter is `CLR_NONE`, the images are drawn transparently using the mask.
ImageList_SetDragCursorImage	`BOOL ImageList_SetDragCursorImage( HIMAGELIST hlist, int index, int hotspotX, int hotspotY)`
	Creates a new drag image by combining the specified image (which is often a mouse cursor image) with the current drag image. The `hotspot` parameters define the hotspot within the new image.
ImageList_SetIconSize	`BOOL ImageList_SetIconSize(HIMAGELIST hlist, int width, int height)`
	Sets a new size for the images in an image list. This removes all existing images from the list.
ImageList_SetOverlayImage	`BOOL ImageList_SetOverlayImage(HIMAGELIST hlist, int index, int overlay)`
	Adds the index of an image to the list of images that can be used as overlay masks. Up to four images can be in this list. An overlay mask is drawn using `ImageList_Draw` or `ImageList_DrawEx` and specifying the index of the overlay mask using the `INDEXTOOVERLAYMASK` macro.
ImageList_Write	`BOOL ImageList_Write(HIMAGELIST hlist, LPSTREAM stream)`
	Writes the image list to a stream.

You create an image list using the `ImageList_Create` function. Here is when you make some fundamental decisions about how your image list will work. You specify the width and height of the images (*all* images will be this size). You also decide whether your image list contains masked images. Following is a call that creates a masked image list capable of holding small icons:

```
HIMAGELIST icons = ImageList_Create(GetSystemMetrics(SM_CXSMICON),
                                    GetSystemMetrics(SM_CYSMICON),
                                    ILC_COLOR | ILC_MASK,
                                    20,  // initial allocation
                                    4);  // grow size
```

This creates an image list that can hold up to 20 images. When the twenty-first image is added, four slots will be added, so you will have an image list that can hold up to 24 images. When the twenty-fifth image is added, another four slots will be added. Because there is a fairly high cost in reallocating the number of images, you ideally should allocate an initial size that is as close as possible to the actual number of images you will put into the image list. For lists that will fluctuate in size or be added to at various times by user actions over which you have no control (you might be supporting a user-definable toolbar, for example), the number of slots to grow is based on how efficient you want subsequent additions to be. A larger number wastes a bit of space to get higher performance.

The image size is essentially fixed at creation time. You can use the ImageList_SetIconSize to change the image size, but all existing images will be discarded.

Having now created an image list, you can add images to it. The images can be from bitmap resources, with potentially multiple images for each bitmap resource. Or they can be from icon resources, cursor resources, system cursors, system icons, system bitmaps, bitmap (.bmp) files, cursor (.cur) files, or icon (.ico) files. They also can be from bitmaps, icons, or cursors created on the fly in your program. If you have a handle to a bitmap, you can use ImageList_Add or ImageListAdd Masked, while for icons or cursors, you can use ImageList_AddIcon. The major difference here arises when you are using a masked image list. A bitmap requires that you supply a matching monochrome mask bitmap, whereas for cursors and icons, the masking bitmap is intrinsic to the representation. In the simple case of a bitmap, the ImageList_AddMasked function takes a bitmap and a specification of what color should be used to compute the mask. When an image is added with ImageList_AddMasked, a mask bitmap of the same size as the image is created. All pixels in the original bitmap that match the specified color are changed to black (RGB(0, 0, 0)) and the corresponding bit in the mask bitmap is set to 1. A copy of the bitmap, cursor, or icon is made by the ImageList_Add* functions, so you can delete the objects after calling them.

A common source of these bitmap representations is a resource segment, so the ImageList_LoadImage function is provided to handle the details of loading the resource, calling the appropriate ImageList_Add* function, and deleting the loaded resource. ImageList_LoadBitmap is a convenient wrapper around the ImageList_LoadImage function.

You may even want to load bitmaps, cursors, or icons directly from the files generated by tools, such as icon editors or paint programs, without these being first converted to resources. This is particularly important if you want to allow your end user to add new images. End users typically have no way to get these graphical representations into your resource segment. ImageList_LoadImage allows you to specify the LR_LOADFROMFILE flag, which uses the "resource name" as a filename to load the image.

When you are finished with an image list, you use ImageList_Destroy to delete it and reclaim all the resources it has used, including bitmap space, memory DCs, and other internal allocations.

Once you have created an image list, you can use it for various purposes. You can treat it much like a GDI resource and use it for your own drawing, using ImageList_Draw or ImageList_DrawEx in your OnPaint handler. However, the real reason for image lists is to support controls such as the tree view and list view controls and operations such as drag-and-drop. For that, we defer discussion of the drag-and-drop related features to those sections. The use of image lists for tree view drag-and-drop starts on page 672.

The `TreeView` Class

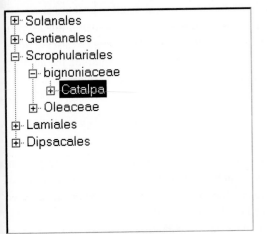

Figure 9.6: A tree view control

The tree view class (official class name "SysTreeView") provides the support necessary to support tree-structured displays with the ability to "open" a level of the hierarchy. We will look at the tree view styles in depth in this section, and explore some of the issues of using a tree view control. A nearly "fully loaded" tree view control is illustrated in Figure 9.6 .[5]

You create a tree view control using the special name WC_TREEVIEW in the CreateWindow(Ex) call. (We generally refer to a tree view control by its common name, "tree control", partly in deference to the MFC library for which the CTreeView class is something a bit different from the CTreeCtrl class.) The WC_TREEVIEW name is defined in the commctrl.h file. You can use any of the styles from Table 9.16. These can be changed at any time by using the SetWindowLong function. The control in Figure 9.6 is created by the code

```
HWND htree = CreateWindow(WC_TREEVIEW,        // class name
                   NULL,                       // caption
                   WS_BORDER | WS_VISIBLE | WS_CHILD |
                   TVS_HASBUTTONS | TVS_HASLINES | TVS_LINESATROOT,
                   left,                       // left
                   top,                        // top
                   width,                      // width
                   height,                     // height
                   hwnd,                       // parent window
                   (HMENU)IDC_TREE,            // control ID
                   hInstance,                  // instance handle
                   NULL);                      // parameters
```

We show the effects of other style combinations in Figure 9.7.

Elements in a tree view control are designated by *handles*. These are conceptually the same as handles to other Windows-maintained objects. You use these handles to designate items within a tree control. A list box uses integers as "handles"; you manipulate items in a list box by their position. In a tree control, because two items that appear to be adjacent on the screen may not at all be adjacent because they contain hidden

---

[5] The pervasive example used in this section is based on a botanical classification scheme. This was a natural choice as a consequence of living with a person who has spent most of her professional life as a librarian in botanical libraries.

Table 9.16: Tree view class styles

Style	Meaning
TVS_DISABLEDRAGDROP	Tree view controls with this style will not send TVN_BEGINDRAG notifications to their parents.
TVS_EDITLABELS	Tree view controls with this style allow the user to edit the contents of the "label" of an entry.
TVS_HASBUTTONS	The tree view control has "buttons" to the left of each entry that can be used to open and close the tree level.
TVS_HASLINES	The tree view control has vertical lines that connect levels.
TVS_LINESATROOT	The topmost hierarchy has lines. If TVS_HASLINES is not specified, but TVS_HASBUTTONS *is* specified, the top-most hierarchy has buttons but not lines.
TVS_SHOWSELALWAYS	The selection remains highlighted even when the tree view control does not have the focus.

subitems, a simple linear index is no longer sufficient. Operations that create items in a tree control return a handle, which is of type HTREEITEM, and most operations that work on tree controls take an HTREEITEM parameter to designate to which item they apply. There is a special value, of type HTREEITEM, called TVI_ROOT. This value can be used in some contexts where you would use an HTREEITEM. It represents the root of the tree.

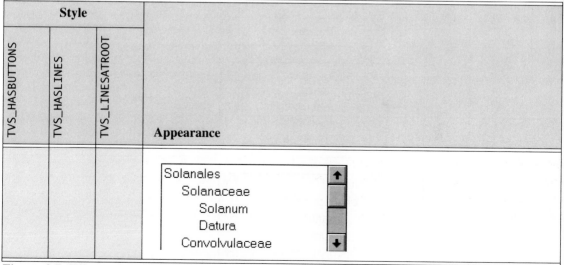

Figure 9.7: Effects of style bits on tree view controls

Style			
TVS_HASBUTTONS	TVS_HASLINES	TVS_LINESATROOT	**Appearance**
✓			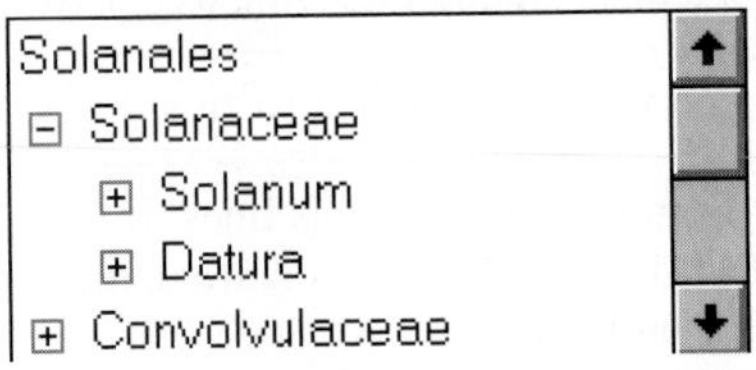 Solanales / ⊟ Solanaceae / ⊞ Solanum / ⊞ Datura / ⊞ Convolvulaceae
	✓		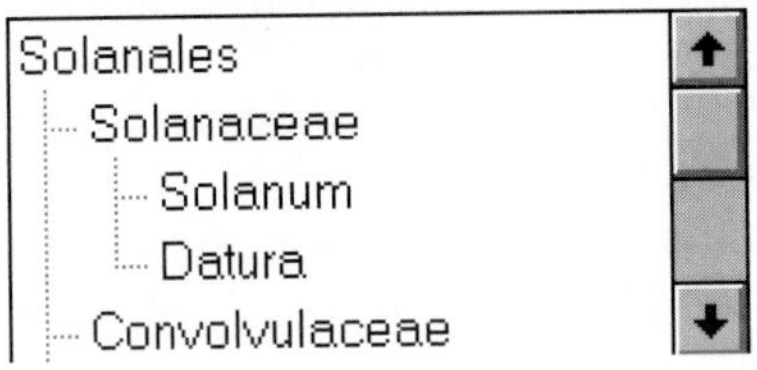 Solanales / ─ Solanaceae / ─ Solanum / ─ Datura / ─ Convolvulaceae
✓	✓		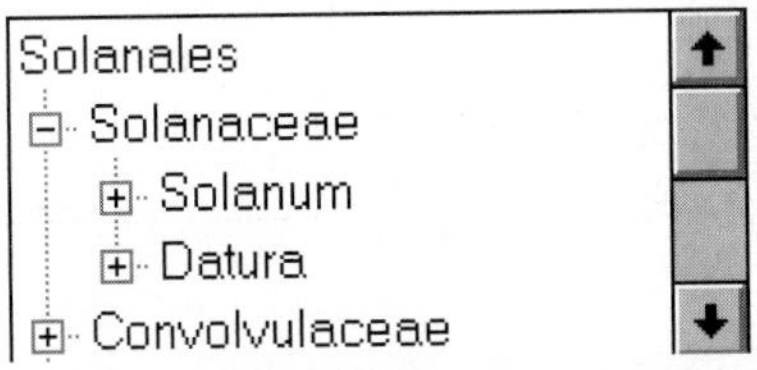 Solanales / ⊟─ Solanaceae / ⊞─ Solanum / ⊞─ Datura / ⊞─ Convolvulaceae
✓		✓	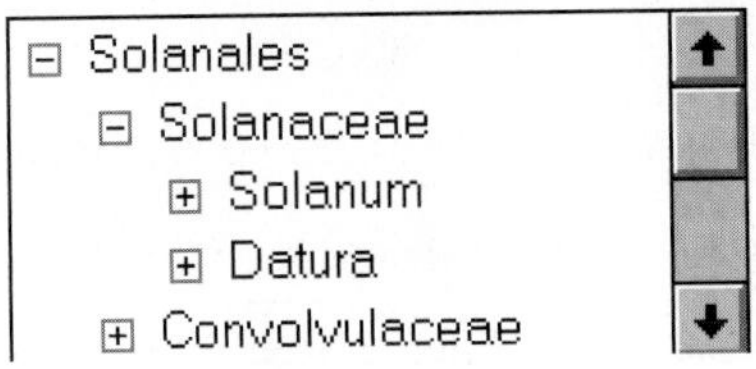 ⊟ Solanales / ⊟ Solanaceae / ⊞ Solanum / ⊞ Datura / ⊞ Convolvulaceae
	✓	✓	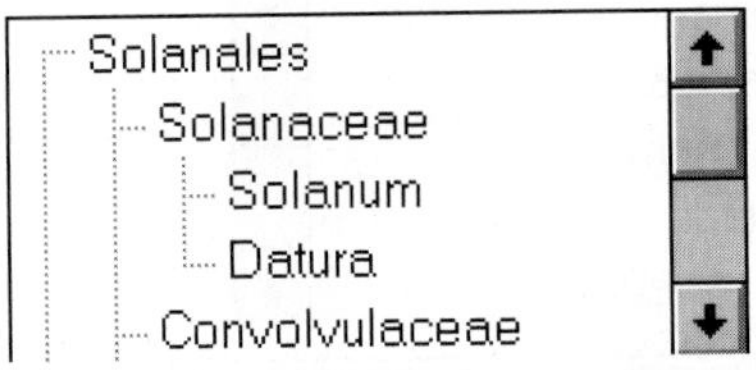 ─ Solanales / ─ Solanaceae / ─ Solanum / ─ Datura / ─ Convolvulaceae

Figure 9.7: Effects of style bits on tree view controls (Continued)

Style			
TVS_HASBUTTONS	TVS_HASLINES	TVS_LINESATROOT	**Appearance**
✓	✓	✓	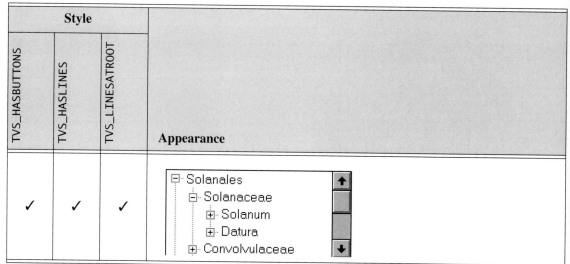

Figure 9.7: Effects of style bits on tree view controls (Continued)

Messages to Tree View Controls

You manipulate tree controls by sending any of the messages described in Table 9.17. The macro functions that wrap these messages are defined in `commctrl.h`.

Table 9.17: Tree view messages

Message	Function Action
TVM_CREATEDRAGIMAGE	`HIMAGELIST TreeView_CreateDragImage(HWND hwnd, HTREEITEM item)`
	Creates a "dragging bitmap" for the specified item, creates an image list to hold the bitmap, and puts the bitmap in the image list. The resulting image list can be used with image list operations.
TVM_DELETEITEM	`BOOL TreeView_DeleteItem(HWND hwnd, HTREEITEM item)`
	`BOOL TreeView_DeleteAllItems(HWND hwnd)`
	Deletes the selected item and all its subitems. If the item handle is TVI_ROOT, all items in the control are deleted. The `TreeView_Delete-AllItems` macro provides TVI_ROOT as the handle.
TVM_EDITLABEL	`HWND TreeView_EditLabel(HWND hwnd, HTREEITEM item)`
	Begins in-place editing of the text of the specified item. If the item is not already selected, it will be. Returns a handle to the edit control. The control must have the focus before this message is sent. This will generate a TVN_BEGINLABELEDIT notification to the parent window.

Table 9.17: Tree view messages

Message	Function Action
TVM_ENDEDITLABELNOW	BOOL TreeView_EndEditLabelNow(HWND hwnd, BOOL cancel)
	Ends in-place editing of the text of the item being edited. The cancel parameter, if TRUE, discards the current changes; if FALSE, it saves them. Generates a TVN_ENDLABELEDIT notification to the parent window.
TVM_ENSUREVISIBLE	BOOL TreeView_EnsureVisible(HWND hwnd, HTREEITEM item)
	Forces the selected item to be visible. This will expand any parent nodes in the tree if necessary and scroll the selected line into view on the control. If an item needs to be expanded, the parent window will receive TVN_ITEMEXPANDING and TVN_ITEMEXPANDED notifications.
TVM_EXPAND	BOOL TreeView_Expand(HWND hwnd, HTREEITEM item, UINT action)
	Expands or collapses the display of the selected item. Does *not* trigger TVN_ITEMEXPANDING or TVN_ITEMEXPANDED notifications to the parent window. The action is one of the following:

Flag	Meaning
TVE_COLLAPSE	Collapses the list.
TVE_COLLAPSERESET	Collapses the list and removes the child items. Requires that TVE_COLLAPSE also be specified.
TVE_EXPAND	Expands the list.
TVE_TOGGLE	Collapses or expands the list as appropriate.

Message	Function Action
TVM_GETCOUNT	int TreeView_GetCount(HWND hwnd)
	Returns the count of the items in the tree control.
TVM_GETEDITCONTROL	HWND TreeView_GetEditControl(HWND hwnd)
	Returns a handle to the edit control being used to edit the text of an item or NULL if there is an error.

Table 9.17: Tree view messages

Message	Function Action
TVM_GETIMAGELIST	`HIMAGELIST TreeView_GetImageList(HWND hwnd, UINT type)`
	Retrieves the image list. The `type` parameter determines which list is retrieved, as follows:

Type	Meaning
TVSIL_NORMAL	Retrieves the handle to the normal image list, which contains the images for the selected and nonselected modes for an item.
TVSIL_STATE	Retrieves the handle for the state image list for user-defined states.

Message	Function Action
TVM_GETINDENT	`int TreeView_GetIndent(HWND hwnd)`
	Returns the indentation amount used for nested items. The distance is expressed in pixels.
TVM_GETISEARCHSTRING	`int TreeView_GetISearchString(HWND hwnd, LPCSTR str)`
	Retrieves the incremental search string.
TVM_GETITEM	`BOOL TreeView_GetItem(HWND hwnd, TV_ITEM FAR * item)`
	Retrieves the information about an item and its attributes.
TVM_GETITEMRECT	`BOOL TreeView_GetItemRect(HWND hwnd, HTREEITEM item, LPRECT rect, BOOL textonly)`
	If the item is visible, the `rect` structure is modified to hold the bounding rectangle dimensions and the return value is TRUE. If the item is not visible, the return value is FALSE and the `rect` is unchanged. If the `textonly` parameter is TRUE, the bounding rectangle is the rectangle for the text; otherwise, it is the bounding rectangle for the entire line.
TVM_GETNEXTITEM	`HTREEITEM TreeView_GetNextItem(HWND hwnd, HTREEITEM item, UINT flag)`
	Retrieves an item based on a specified relationship to the item passed as a parameter. The next previous macro is one of a family of macros that are based on the flag type, as follows:

Flag	Macro Meaning
TVGN_CARET	TreeView_GetSelection The handle to the currently selected item or NULL if none is selected.

Table 9.17: Tree view messages

Message	Function Action
	TreeView_GetChild The first child in the control. When flag is specified with the message or the TreeView_GetNextItem macro instead of using the TreeView_GetChild macro, the item parameter must be NULL.
TVGN_CHILD	
TVGN_DROPHILITE	TreeView_GetDropHilite The handle of the item that is the target of a drag-and-drop operation or NULL if there is no target.
TVGN_FIRSTVISIBLE	TreeView_GetFirstVisible The handle of the first visible item in the list.
TVGN_NEXT	TreeView_GetNextSibling The handle of the next sibling window (at the same level of the tree) or NULL if there is no next sibling.
TVGN_NEXTVISIBLE	TreeView_GetNextVisible The next visible item that follows the specified item. The specified item must be visible.
TVGN_PARENT	TreeView_GetParent The handle of the parent item or NULL if the item specified is the root.
TVGN_PREVIOUS	TreeView_GetPrevSibling The handle of the previous sibling or NULL if there is no previous sibling.
TVGN_PREVIOUSVISIBLE	TreeView_GetPrevVisible The handle of the first visible item that precedes the specified item or NULL if there is no such item. The specified item must be visible.
TVGN_ROOT	TreeView_GetRoot The top-most entry of the control or NULL if the control is empty.
TVM_GETVISIBLECOUNT	int TreeView_GetVisibleCount(HWND hwnd) Returns a count of the number of items fully visible in the client area of a tree control.

Table 9.17: Tree view messages

Message	Function Action
TVM_HITTEST	HTREEITEM TreeView_HitTest(HWND hwnd, LPTV_HITTESTINFO hti)
	Returns the handle of the item that contains the point specified by the pt member of the TV_HITTESTINFO structure.
TVM_INSERTITEM	HTREEITEM TreeView_InsertItem(HWND hwnd, LPTV_INSERTITEMSTRUCT tis)
	Inserts a new item in the tree control. The TV_INSERTITEMSTRUCT specifies the attributes of the new item. Returns the handle of the new item or NULL if the insertion failed.
TVM_SELECTITEM	BOOL TreeView_Select(HWND hwnd, HTREEITEM item, UINT flag)
	Selects the specified item and either scrolls it into view or redraws it in the style specified. The flag parameter indicates the type of highlighting to be performed. There are also special macros that implicitly supply the flags shown, as follows:

Flag	Highlight
TVGN_CARET	TreeView_SelectItem Selects the specified item. If the item is in a collapsed part of the tree, enough of the tree will be expanded to make the selected item visible. The item also will be scrolled into visibility. Sending this message will generate TVN_SELCHANGING and TVN_SELCHANGED notifications.
TVGN_DROPHILITE	TreeView_SelectDropTarget Redraws the item in the style that indicates it is the target of a drag-and-drop operation.
TVGN_FIRSTVISIBLE	TreeView_SelectSetFirstVisible Scrolls the display so that the specified item is the first one visible in the client area. *As far as we have been able to determine using the Control Explorer, this statement is not true. The specified item will become visible, but it is not necessarily the first line in the client area.*

Table 9.17: Tree view messages

Message	Function Action
TVM_SETIMAGELIST	`HIMAGELIST TreeView_SetImageList(HWND hwnd, HIMAGELIST imagelist, UINT type)`

Sets the normal or state image list. If the `imagelist` parameter is NULL, the images are removed from the control. Following are the values that can be specified:

Type	Meaning
TVSIL_NORMAL	Sets the handle to the normal image list, which contains the images for the selected and nonselected modes for an item.
TVSIL_STATE	Sets the handle for the state image list for user-defined states.

Message	Function Action
TVM_SETINDENT	`void TreeView_SetIndent(HWND hwnd, int indent)`

Sets the indentation level used for nested tree items. The indentation level is specified in units of pixels.

Message	Function Action
TVM_SETITEM	`int TreeView_SetItem(HWND hwnd, const LPTV_ITEM item)`

Sets some or all of the attributes of the specified tree item. The TV_ITEM structure contains the values, and the `mask` member of that structure indicates which values are to be set.

Message	Function Action
TVM_SORTCHILDREN	`BOOL TreeView_SortChildren(HWND hwnd, HTREEITEM item, int recurse)`

Sorts the child items of the specified item. The `recurse` parameter is reserved and must be 0.

Message	Function Action
TVM_SORTCHILDRENCB	`BOOL TreeView_SortChildrenCB(HWND hwnd, LPTV_SORTCB sort, int recurse)`

Sorts the child items of the specified item using a user-specified callback function that is specified as part of the TV_SORTCB structure. The `recurse` parameter is reserved and must be 0.

Inserting Items in a Tree View

Many tree controls will never be edited. Instead, they will be solely for display purposes. These are the easiest controls to work with. You simply load the data into the control and you're done. Examples of these simple controls are in our Font Explorer, where we show you all the details of a font using a tree control. Rather than overwhelm you with data, we present only top-level concepts and let you expand them to any level of detail you need.

To put items in a tree control, you may want first to make sure the tree control is empty (just in case some other program state has changed that is going to cause the tree control to be reloaded with new data). This is done something like the way you initialize a list box using `ListBox_ResetContent` or a combo box using `ComboBox_ResetContent`. For a tree control, you accomplish this by deleting the root item and all the items below it. You send the `TVM_DELETEITEM` message or use one of the macro wrappers. For the designated item to delete, you can use either the actual handle to the root element of the tree, if you have it, or the special designator `TVI_ROOT`. All three of the following methods are identical; the two macros just generate the `SendMessage`:

```
SendMessage(htree, TVM_DELETEITEM, 0, TVI_ROOT) ;
TreeView_DeleteItem(htree, TVI_ROOT) ;
TreeView_DeleteAllItems(htree) ;
```

Having thus ensured that the data we are loading into the control will be the only data in the control, we can now start to add the data. To add information to a tree control, we need to specify several of its attributes. Unlike with a list box or combo box, an item in a tree control has a very rich set of attributes. We specify these using a `TV_INSERTSTRUCT` structure to hold the information.

```
typedef struct _TV_INSERTSTRUCT {
    HTREEITEM hParent;
    HTREEITEM hInsertAfter;
    TV_ITEM item;
} TV_INSERTSTRUCT, FAR *LPTV_INSERTSTRUCT;
```

To insert an item, we must initialize the fields of a `TV_INSERTSTRUCT` object. Two key fields are `hParent` and `hInsertAfter`. If the `hParent` field is set to either the value `TVI_ROOT` or `NULL`, the insertion will be at the root of the tree control. The first item thus inserted will be the root item of the tree. Subsequent insertions using `TVI_ROOT` or `NULL` may be done before or after this item; in the former case, the first item of the tree will possibly change. All items inserted this way will be siblings. If no item contains subitems, you have something very much like a "rich list box".

To determine where an item inserts, you set the `hInsertAfter` field to be the handle of the item after which the new item should appear. You may also use the special item designators shown in Table 9.18. The `TVI_LAST` "item handle" causes the new item to be the last item under the specified parent (the equivalent of `ListBox_AddString` to a list box without the `LBS_SORT` style). Unlike list boxes or combo boxes, tree controls are not implicitly sorted. You can either use the "item handle" `TVI_SORT` to cause the new item to be

Table 9.18: TV_INSERTSTRUCT insertion order codes

Item Code	Meaning
TVI_FIRST	Inserts the new item as the first item under the parent.
TVI_LAST	Inserts the new item as the last item under the parent.
TVI_SORT	Inserts the new item in sorted order in the list under the parent.

inserted in the list in sorted order, or you can later send the tree control a message to sort its elements.

Thus far we have told how and where to insert the item, but we haven't yet said anything about the contents of the item. This is handled by the `TV_ITEM` structure, which is inside the `TV_INSERTSTRUCT`. A `TV_ITEM` is defined as follows, and the details are provided in Table 9.19:

```
typedef struct _TV_ITEM {
    UINT        mask;
    HTREEITEM   hItem;
    UINT        state;
    UINT        stateMask;
    LPTSTR      pszText;
    int         cchTextMax;
    int         iImage;
    int         iSelectedImage;
    int         cChildren;
    LPARAM      lParam;
} TV_ITEM, FAR *LPTV_ITEM;
```

Table 9.19: The TV_ITEM structure

Field	Meaning
mask	Indicates which fields are valid on operations that set values or which fields are desired on operations that retrieve values.

Flag	Fields
TVIF_CHILDREN	The cChildren field will be set or retrieved.
TVIF_HANDLE	The hItem member is valid. This is used to specify the item on both set and retrieve operations.
TVIF_IMAGE	The iImage member is valid on a set or is requested on a retrieve.
TVIF_PARAM	The lParam member is valid on a set or is requested on a retrieve.
TVIF_SELECTEDIMAGE	The iSelectedImage member is valid on a set or is requested on a retrieve.
TVIF_STATE	The state field, subject to the stateMask, will be set; otherwise, the entire state field will be retrieved.
TVIF_TEXT	The pszText field is a valid pointer. For a retrieve, the cchTextMax must also be a valid value.

Field	Meaning
hItem	For operations that require the specification of an item, this is the HTREEITEM.
state	Indicates the state of the item. To set a bit, the corresponding bit in stateMask must be a 1. The state bit value, 0 or 1, will be set only for those bits that are selected by stateMask. On retrieval, the entire state value is retrieved and stateMask is ignored.

Bit	Meaning
TVIS_BOLD	Item is displayed in boldface type.

Table 9.19: The TV_ITEM structure

Field	Meaning	
	TVIS_CUT	Item is selected as part of a cut (and paste) operation.
	TVIS_DROPHILITED	The item is highlighted to indicate it is a possible drop target in a drag-and-drop operation.
	TVIS_EXPANDED	The item is expanded. This applies only to items that have child items.
	TVIS_EXPANDEDONCE	The list of child items has been expanded at least once. If this bit is set, the sending of TVN_ITEM-EXPANDING and TVN_ITEMEXPANDED notifications is suppressed.
	TVIS_FOCUSED	The item has the focus and is surrounded by a standard focus rectangle. Only one item at a time can have the focus.
	TVIS_SELECTED	The item is selected.
	INDEXTOOVERLAYMASK	This macro can be used to specify a value that is the index of an overlay image. You must set the TVIS_OVERLAYMASK value in the stateMask field.
	INDEXTOSTATEIMAGEMASK	This macro can be used to specify a value that is the index of a user-defined state image. You must set the TVIS_STATEIMAGEMASK value in the stateMask field.
stateMask	Specifies which members of the state field are valid and should be changed on a set operation. Ignored for retrieve operations. For many operations that implicitly retrieve item information, in particular WM_NOTIFY messages that contain TV_ITEM values, the value of this field is undefined and should not be depended on. Uses the same TVIS_ values as state, plus the following:	

Bit	Meaning
TVIS_OVERLAYMASK	The overlay image is used as part of the drawing operation. The index of the overlay mask is specified as part of the state member; see "The Overlay Image List" on page 675. If this value is specified, Microsoft suggests that no other TVIS_ value should be specified. Our experience with the Control Explorer suggests that this is not a restriction. The index of the overlay must be specified using the INDEXTOOVERLAYMASK macro to form the value for the state field.

able 9.19: The TV_ITEM structure

Field	Meaning	
	TVIS_STATEIMAGEMASK	The state image is used when the item is drawn. The index of the state image is specified as part of the state member; see "The State Image List" on page 672. If this value is specified, Microsoft suggests that no other TVIS_ value should be specified. Our experience with the Control Explorer suggests that this is not a restriction. The index of the state image mask must be specified using the INDEXTOSTATEIMAGEMASK macro to form the value for the state field.
pszText	If the TVIF_TEXT flag is set in mask, this must point to a valid NUL-terminated string or it must be the special value LPTSTR_TEXTCALLBACK. When the callback value is specified, the parent window will receive a TVN_GETDISPINFO notification message and must supply the appropriate text. The parent window will also receive a TVN_SETDISPINFO notification if the item changes.	
cchTextMax	When text is being retrieved, the pszText field must point to a buffer to receive the text string. This field specifies the length of the buffer, in characters. The value is ignored when setting text.	
iImage	The index of the icon image in the tree control's image list to display for a nonselected item. The special value I_IMAGECALLBACK can be used to indicate that the parent window should receive a TVN_GETDISPINFO notification to supply the index value on the fly.	
iSelectedImage	The index of the icon image in the tree control's image list to display for a selected item. The special value I_IMAGECALLBACK can be used, as in the iImage field.	
cChildren	A flag that indicates that the item has child items. One of the following values apply:	

	Value	Meaning
	0	The item has no child items.
	1	The item has one or more child items.
	I_CHILDRENCALLBACK	The parent window has responsibility for keeping track of the number of child items. The tree control will query the parent by sending a TVN_GETDISPINFO notification.

Field	Meaning	
lParam	A 32-bit value associated with the item. You get to determine what this means.	

Typically, you will set the mask to have the TVIF_TEXT flag and the pszText member to point to the string to be stored. The hItem, state, stateMask, cchTextMax, and cChildren members are completely ignored. You can set the lParam value at the time you insert a new item, as well as choose the images via the iImage and iSelectedImage members (see "Image Lists", page 672) by selecting the appropriate TVIF_ flag value for mask.

The result of calling TreeView_InsertItem is a handle to the item just inserted (or NULL if there was an error). You may then employ this handle to insert new items under the item represented by the handle. An example of this is shown in Listing 9.3.

Listing 9.3: Inserting multiple levels in a tree view
```
void buildDictionary(HWND htree)
{
 HTREEITEM letter;

 letter = addEntry(htree, TVI_ROOT, _T("A"));
 addEntry(htree, letter, _T("Aardvark"));
 addEntry(htree, letter, _T("Abalone"));

 letter = addEntry(htree, TVI_ROOT, _T("B"));
 addEntry(htree, letter, _T("Baobab") );
 addEntry(htree, letter, _T("Banana"));
 if(GetStyle(htree) & TVS_HASBUTTONS)
     InvalidateRect(htree, NULL); // force buttons to draw
}

HTREEITEM addEntry(HWND htree, HTREEITEM parent, LPCTSTR text)
{
 TV_INSERTSTRUCT str;
 str.hParent = parent;
 str.item.mask = TVIF_TEXT;
 str.hInsertAfter = TVI_SORT;
 str.item.pszText = (LPTSTR)text;
 return TreeView_InsertItem(htree, &str);
}
```

If you have the TVS_HASBUTTONS style set and you add an element under an element that is not already displaying a button, the button that you would expect to appear does not appear. You must invalidate the entry to force it to redraw. You can do this by using the TVM_GETITEMRECT (TreeView_GetItemRect) operation and invalidating only that rectangle. Or you can do as we did in Listing 9.3 and simply invalidate the entire client area. Otherwise, the buttons will not appear until the user does something to force their appearance, such as collapse and expand the enclosing entry or click the item.

Selecting an Item

You can select an item in a tree control by giving the item handle. Do this with the TVM_SELECTITEM message or the TreeView_Select or TreeView_SelectItem macros.

```
SendMessage(hTree, TVM_SELECTITEM, TVGN_CARET, hitem);
TreeView_Select(hTree, hitem, TVGN_CARET);
TreeView_SelectItem(hTree, hitem);
```

Consistency in naming conventions is not a strong point of the API. Note that the general wrapper for the TVM_SELECTITEM message is called TreeView_Select, while the very specific one that sets the selection caret is called by the same name as the message, TreeView_SelectItem.

If you specify a NULL parameter for hitem, the selection highlight is removed. If the handle supplied is for an item that is nested in the tree, the tree will be expanded if necessary so that item would be visible. However, making a selection does not necessarily force the selection to be visible in the control. Our experiments with the Control Explorer suggest that if the tree has to be expanded to make the item visible, the item will be scrolled into view. However, if the subtree that contains the item is already expanded but simply scrolled off the visible control area, the selection will occur but the item will not be forced to scroll to visibility.

If you want to ensure that the item selected becomes visible, use the TVGN_FIRSTVISIBLE flag to the TVM_SELECTITEM message. Any of the following three equivalent statements will accomplish this:

```
SendMessage(hTree, TVM_SELECTITEM, TVGN_FIRSTVISIBLE, hitem);
TreeView_Select(hTree, hitem, TVGN_FIRSTVISIBLE);
TreeView_SelectSetFirstVisible(hTree, hitem);
```

There is a significant difference in behavior between what is specified in the documentation and what we have observed using the Control Explorer. The documentation claims that the TVGN_FIRSTVISIBLE option "scrolls the tree view vertically so that the given item is the first visible item". As far as we can tell, what *really* happens is that the tree view is scrolled vertically so that the given item becomes visible. In our demo data example in the Control Explorer, random samplings gave us positions of the specified item from four to seven lines from the top of the control.

There is one last selection type: drag-and-drop highlighting. This is established by one of the following statements:

```
SendMessage(hTree, TVM_SELECTITEM, TVGN_DROPHILITE, hitem);
TreeView_Select(hTree, hitem, TVGN_DROPHILITE);
TreeView_SelectDropTarget(hTree, hitem);
```

The most common form of selection is that the user will use the mouse to select an item in the tree control. If, for some reason, you want to prohibit the user from changing the selection, you must handle the TVN_SELCHANGING notification of the WM_NOTIFY message. If you return TRUE, the selection will not change. In this manner, you can inhibit selection on a case-by-case basis. Since you will be given both the old and new items, you can determine, based on your requirements, if you should inhibit changes *from* the old item or changes *to* the new item. If you return FALSE for the message, the selection will proceed as it normally should and the new item will be selected. At that point, you will receive a TVN_SELCHANGED notification.

Getting Information about an Item

To get information about an item for which you have the handle, you initialize a TV_ITEM structure to have its hItem member refer to that item and set the mask member to indicate which values you want retrieved. If the mask includes TVIF_STATE, the entire state will be retrieved, independent of any settings in the stateMask. An example of how to retrieve the information is shown in Listing 9.4.

Listing 9.4: Retrieving tree item information

```
// The following code retrieves the text and state flags for an item
//
TV_ITEM item;
TCHAR text[256];
```

```
memset(item, 0, sizeof(item));

item.hItem = item_we_want_to_know_about;
item.mask = TVIF_TEXT | TVIF_STATE;

item.pszText = text;
item.cchTextMax = DIM(text);

TreeView_GetItem(htree, &item);
```

The item handle used in the hItem member of the TV_ITEM structure must be a real handle. You can't use the special handle TVI_ROOT. If you do, you will get a memory access violation. If you want the information on the first item in the tree control, you must do
    item_we_want_to_know_about = TreeView_GetRoot(htree);
If the resulting handle is NULL, the tree control is empty.

Microsoft has been inconsistent in its interpretation of the stateMask field. For example, for the TVM_GETITEM message, the stateMask is ignored and all the state bits are returned in the state field. But for the list view control, the stateMask determines which bits are returned! If you don't initialize the stateMask field (for example, to 0xFFFFFFFF) on an LVM_GETITEM message, you will not get all the bits of the state that you might expect. Microsoft *does* document this behavior, but the inconsistency of the behavior between the tree view and the list view may cause you problems, especially if you assume a certain consistency between the two.

Tree View Notifications

A tree control communicates with its parent using the WM_NOTIFY message. The lParam value is a pointer to a structure that contains an NMHDR structure and extensions based on the type of message. You check the code field of the NMHDR structure to determine which notification you have received. Based on that information, you cast the pointer to one of the types shown in Table 9.20 to determine specific information about the event you are being notified about.

Table 9.20: Tree View notifications

Notification Code	NMHDR Structure	Description
TVN_BEGINDRAG	NM_TREEVIEW	A drag-and-drop operation initiated by the left mouse button has started.
TVN_BEGINLABELEDIT	TV_DISPINFO	A label edit is about to start. Return TRUE to cancel the label edit.
TVN_DELETEITEM	NM_TREEVIEW	An item is being deleted.
TVN_ENDLABELEDIT	TV_DISPINFO	Label editing is ending.
TVN_GETDISPINFO	TV_DISPINFO	The parent window must provide information needed to display or sort an item.
TVN_ITEMEXPANDED	NM_TREEVIEW	An item has expanded or collapsed.

Table 9.20: Tree View notifications

Notification Code	NMHDR Structure	Description
TVN_ITEMEXPANDING	NM_TREEVIEW	A request has been made to expand or collapse an item. Return TRUE to inhibit the expansion or collapse.
TVN_KEYDOWN	TV_KEYDOWN	The user has pressed a key when the tree control has the focus.
TVN_SELCHANGED	NM_TREEVIEW	The selection has changed.
TVN_SELCHANGING	NM_TREEVIEW	The selection is about to change. Return TRUE to inhibit the change of selection.
TVN_SETDISPINFO	TV_DISPINFO	The parent must update information. Sent when label editing has finished for an item whose string pointer was LPSTR_TEXTCALLBACK.

Notifications Using the **NM_TREEVIEW** *Structure*

A reference to an NM_TREEVIEW structure is sent for the TVN_BEGINDRAG, TVN_BEGINRDRAG, TVN_DELETEITEM, TVN_ITEMEXPANDING, TVN_ITEMEXPANDED, TVN_SELCHANGING, and TVN_SELCHANGED notifications. This structure is defined as follows:

```
typedef struct _NM_TREEVIEW {
    NMHDR       hdr;
    UINT        action;
    TV_ITEM     itemOld;
    TV_ITEM     itemNew;
    POINT       ptDrag;
} NM_TREEVIEW, FAR *LPNM_TREEVIEW;
```

The validity of various fields in the NM_TREEVIEW structure depends on the type of notification, as does the validity of members of the embedded TV_ITEM structures. This validity is summarized in Table 9.21. For any member not mentioned, its value is undefined. Note in particular that the stateMask member of the TV_ITEM members is undefined and cannot be depended on for any useful information. The action field is defined only for those notifications indicated.

TVN_BEGINDRAG and TVN_BEGINRDRAG are sent for any control that does not have the TVS_DISABLEDRAGDROP style whenever the left or right mouse buttons are used to initiate a drag operation. The left button initiates what is referred to as a "default drag" operation (usually a move operation, but the choice is application-specific). The right button usually pops up a menu of options to associate with the dragging operation (see *The Windows Interface Guidelines for Software Design*, pp. 78–81).

TVN_DELETEITEM is sent in response to a TVM_DELETEITEM (TreeView_DeleteItem) operation. Only the itemOld.hItem and itemOld.lParam values are valid. If you had allocated any storage to represent this item (and typically you store the pointer to this storage as the lParam value of the item), this is your last chance to free up that storage. When you return from this notification, the item will be deleted from the tree control; you may have lost your only reference to the allocated storage.

Table 9.21: `NM_TREEVIEW` field validity

Notification	itemNew				itemOld				action
	hItem	mask	state	lParam	hItem	mask	state	lParam	
TVN_BEGINDRAG TVN_BEGINRDRAG	✓		✓	✓					
TVN_DELETEITEM					✓			✓	
TVN_ITEMEXPANDED TVN_ITEMEXPANDING	✓		✓	✓					TVE_COLLAPSE TVE_COLLAPSERESET TVE_EXPAND TVE_TOGGLE
TVN_SELCHANGED TVN_SELCHANGING	✓	✓	✓	✓	✓	✓	✓	✓	TVC_BYKEYBOARD TVC_BYMOUSE TVC_UNKNOWN

TVN_ITEMEXPANDED and TVN_ITEMEXPANDING are sent whenever an item is being expanded or collapsed. For TVN_ITEMEXPANDING, you can return TRUE to keep the item from expanding or collapsing or FALSE to permit the item to expand or collapse. You can determine what state it is in by examining the `itemNew.state` field and the nature of the request from the `action` field. TVN_ITEMEXPANDED is sent if the expansion or collapse is permitted to complete. Note that if you do not respond to TVN_ITEMEXPANDING yourself, the WM_NOTIFY will be sent to DefWindowProc, which will return 0 (FALSE), thus allowing the operation to proceed.

TVN_SELCHANGED and TVN_SELCHANGING are sent when an item is being selected. These might result from the user's clicking the mouse over the item or from sending a TVM_SELECTITEM message or calling the TreeView_Select macro with the TVGN_CARET option (the TreeView_SelectItem macro is the same as TreeView_Select(htree, TVGN_CARET)). You can determine the states of the new and old items by examining the values of `itemNew` and `itemOld`. The TVN_SELCHANGING notification is sent before the selection is changed. If you return TRUE, the change in selection will be suppressed and you will not get the TVN_SELCHANGED notification.

Notifications Using the `TV_DISPINFO` *Structure*

The TVN_BEGINLABELEDIT, TVN_ENDLABELEDIT, TVN_GETDISPINFO, and TVN_SETDISPINFO notifications all pass a TV_DISPINFO structure, as follows:

```
typedef struct _TV_DISPINFO {
    NMHDR hdr;
    TV_ITEM item;
} TV_DISPINFO;
```

You can defer certain decisions until display time. When the tree control needs to display certain information, it does not have that information readily at hand and thus is forced to call the parent window to obtain it. There are many reasons you might want to do this. For example, you might have a very large database. Preloading the tree from the database may take an inordinate amount of time. Having spent all that time, you find you have consumed a vast amount of memory to hold all the information. By marking certain information as "callback" information, you simply indicate that the tree control should call the parent when the information is needed. This "on demand" approach can minimize both load time and storage required, at the expense of more complex programming.

Table 9.22: Tree view callback values

Field	Callback Value
pszText	LPSTR_CALLBACK
iImage	I_IMAGECALLBACK
iSelectedImage	I_IMAGECALLBACK
cChildren	I_CHILDRENCALLBACK

The values that can be used for callback and their designations are shown in Table 9.22. To force a callback using TVN_GETDISPINFO, use the specified callback value in place of any other value you might use. Note that the name LPSTR_CALLBACK should in principle be LPTSTR_CALLBACK because it would work equally well in a Unicode environment. However, in a Unicode application you would have to return a Unicode string.

You can test these callbacks by using the Control Explorer; select under the "Tests" category the option for "Callbacks". Then when a TVN_GETDISPINFO notification occurs, you are presented with a dialog that lets you supply the needed value. You next supply the value. The Control Explorer will remember the value you supplied. The next TVN_GETDISPINFO that is issued for this same information will use this stored value. If you find yourself in an apparent infinite loop, use the **Cancel** response to disable the "Callbacks" option.

You also will be presented, on a TVN_SETDISPINFO notification, with a description of the information supplied.

The sketch of some simple code to respond to the request to provide the text for an entry is shown in Listing 9.5. What is important to note here is that we actually check to make sure the mask field is requesting text. We might also add additional tests for the other callback values. You should be aware that a notification could request more than one value type.

Listing 9.5: Responding to a TVN_GETDISPINFO notification

```
// After responding to the WM_NOTIFY and determining which control
// you respond to the TVN_GETDISPINFO with this function

void OnGetDispInfoMyTree(HWND hwnd, TV_DISPINFO * info)
{
  if(info->item.mask & TVIF_TEXT)
     { /* return text */
      // based on the following parameters:
      //      info->item.hItem
      //      info->item.state
      //      info->item.lParam
      // compute a string and set it into
      //      info->item.pszText
      // but do not exceed
      //      info->item.cchTextMax
```

```
        } /* return text */

    if(info->item.mask & TVIF_IMAGE)
        { /* return image */
        // compute new image value and store it...
        // info->item.iImage = whatever ;
        } /* return image */
}
```

The design of the Control Explorer's TVN_GETDISPINFO handler was an interesting experience. For one thing, popping up the dialog violates some basic assumptions that Microsoft makes, that is, that there will be no user interactions during the processing of the notification. Here are some of the failure modes I encountered while I was developing the TVN_GETDISPINFO handler:

- The first time I tried it, I typed in the string desired and clicked **OK**. The result was that I got an immediate TVN_GETDISPINFO notification again. Why? Because the dialog partially overlapped the tree control. Thus when it closed, it forced a new WM_PAINT, which required the display string again!
- I tried moving the dialog out of the way before closing it. No luck. Moving the dialog uncovered the tree control, which generated a WM_PAINT, which generated a TVN_GETDISPINFO, *recursively*, so I now had two dialogs on the screen!
- I tried to deal with this by resizing the tree control so that it was smaller and not overlapped by the window. It didn't matter. The act of resetting the focus apparently causes a repaint. I couldn't get out of the loop.
- I decided to store the value so that it was requested only once. Then I could handle the later notifications simply by returning the saved value. So I added a cache of values and stored the new item values when the dialog completed. This didn't work because between the time the query-the-user dialog terminates and the time the control returns to the TVN_GETDISPINFO handler, *another* TVN_GETDISPINFO notification is generated!
- The current implementation requires that I do an explicit SendMessage *before* the dialog closes, thereby forcing the new information into the cache so that it is available for subsequent notifications.
- When I added the message logging, I started getting another case in which the dialog was popping up. It turns out that doing a TVM_GETITEM to get the text so that it can be displayed in the logging window forces yet another request for the text. The logging code had to be modified to account for the case of being in a TVN_GETDISPINFO handler.

These are some of the issues you may also have to be aware of if you are doing unusual things in response to such notifications. Much of this behavior has to be inferred from observation; it is simply not documented anywhere. Also, I wanted to point out that the overly complex model for the callbacks that is used in the Control Explorer is *not* a good model to follow. This is because the complexity is forced by the need to have a general-purpose demonstration program that violates certain basic assumptions, rather than the clean implementation that is actually necessary in practice. – *jmn*

Notifications Using the TV_KEYDOWN Structure

The TVN_KEYDOWN notification passes a TV_KEYDOWN structure, as follows:

```
typedef struct _TV_KEYDOWN {
    NMHDR hdr;
    WORD wVKey;
    UINT flags;
} TV_KEYDOWN;
```

If you wish to implement a more sophisticated response to a key down event, you can handle this notification. If you do not handle this, the default is to select the next visible item whose text starts with the key that was pressed. If you are doing very sophisticated tree controls or want a different kind of behavior, you can process this notification.

Image Lists

There are three image lists you can use in a tree control (see "Image Lists" on page 642): *normal, state,* and *overlay.* These allow you to associate an image with the content of an item (the *normal* image list) or with the state of the tree (the *state* image list) and also to overlay (*overlay* image list) a normal image with another image (from the same normal image list), thus creating a "combined" image. With these three image lists, you can produce highly informative iconic representations of information in the tree.

The Normal Image List

The *normal* image list is used to determine the icon that is displayed with an entry. An entry can display one of two icons from this list. One is displayed when the item is normal; it is set by the iImage field of the TV_ITEM structure. The other is displayed when the item is selected; it is set by the iSelectedImage field of the TV_ITEM structure. You may specify these values at any time, either when the item is created or by using the TreeView_SetItem function or TVM_SETITEM message.

The value you use to identify an image is its index in the image list. You must establish the image list using the TreeView_SetImageList function or the TVM_SETIMAGELIST message, specifying the TVSIL_NORMAL option. Once you set an image list for a tree control, the display of the images is not optional; every item will have an image displayed beside it. If you have not established the iImage or iSelectedImage values, you will see image number 0 displayed. So you might find it convenient to always place a blank image in position 0 so that "nothing" displays (but there will be extra space, even though you don't see anything!).

But what about the case in which you want to display an icon that indicates, for example, with an open file folder that the subdirectory has been expanded or with a closed folder that the subdirectory is unexpanded? Or what if you want to put a "+" in the folder to indicate there are contents to examine? In any case, you have to do some additional programming. You must respond to notifications such as TVN_EXPANDED and actually change the iImage or iSelectedImage (or both) in the item. But there is another way to do this that deals with the structure of the tree, not its contents.

The State Image List

The second image list you can use is the *state* image list. You set the state image list by using the TreeView_SetImageList function or the TVM_SETIMAGELIST message but specifying the TVSIL_STATE option. The state image list is limited to 16 entries, the first one of which cannot be used. You can now have, in any one tree control, up to 16 unique states of each item (including state 0, which means "no state"). For the "no state" case (unlike the case for a normal image list), nothing is displayed. For states 1 through 15, the image in the state image list indexed by that value is displayed to the left of the item (which still has its selected and unselected images).

We show an example in Figure 9.8. In this figure, we have no normal image list, only a state image list. This illustration was done using the Control Explorer. There is a "Demo" button that preloads the botany example. There also is a special-option check box, "Use State Image List", that invokes some special code in the Control Explorer that reacts to the TVN_ITEMEXPANDED notification. So unlike with many of the Explorer operations, we have taken some control away from the user and built it into the Explorer to get the desired

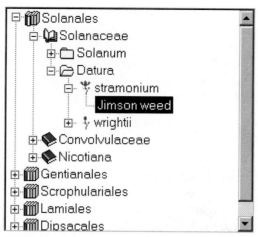

Figure 9.8: A tree view using a state image list

effect. (Otherwise, we'd have to let you respond to the TVN_ITEMEXPANDED message "by hand" and do the operations that change the images. You can still do this, of course, and experiment with the low-level actions, but the demo looks more attractive and is more fun when run automatically.)

The state image list is a separate image list. We create our "botany" state image list by using the ImageList_LoadImage function:

```
HIMAGELIST stlist;
stlist = ImageList_LoadImage(hinst,
                MAKEINTRESOURCE(IDB_BOTLIST),
                16,               // Bitmap width of each image
                1,                // grow size
                RGB(0,0,128),     // DKBLUE is masking color
                IMAGE_BITMAP,     // type of resource
                0);               // flags
```

This is a masked image list. We generate the mask automatically by designating what color should be used for the masking color; in this case, dark blue, RGB(0, 0, 128). The bitmap we use is almost the one shown in Figure 9.9. To enhance legibility, we have set the background color in the figure to a

Figure 9.9: The state image list bitmap
IDB_BOTLIST

light gray (the dark blue of the original did not reproduce well for publication). The image at position 0 was made visible (a big red X) so that you can see that setting the state value to 0 produces no image, not just a blank image because the first entry was blank. You can easily see that selecting a state value of 0 really does mean "blank state" and the image at position 0 in the bitmap is not used.

To establish this image list as a state image list, you must call TreeView_SetImageList and specify the TVSIL_STATE value:

```
TreeView_SetImageList(htree, stlist, TVSIL_STATE);
```

When you load your tree control, you use the 1Param field of the item to hold information that is specific to that item. This information can be a simple integer or a pointer to a more complex structure. For our simple example here, we store a code indicating in which level of the tree the item appears (order, family, genus, or species). Using this code, we can tell which state icon we will display for that level. We chose to have two icons for each level of the tree: one to indicate the unexpanded state of the tree and one to indicate its expanded state. We handle this by the handler shown in Listing 9.6.

Listing 9.6: A tree view control using a state image list

```
LRESULT OnNotify(HWND hwnd, int id, NMHDR * hdr)
{
 if(id == IDC_TREE)
      return OnNotifyTree(hwnd, hdr);
 // ...
}

LRESULT OnNotifyTree(HWND hwnd, NMDHR * hdr)
{
 switch(hdr->code)
     { /* code */
      case TVN_ITEMEXPANDED:
          OnExpandedTree((NM_TREEVIEW *)hdr);
          return 0;
      // ...
     } /* code */
}

void OnExpandedTree(NM_TREEVIEW * tvh)
{
 int state = 0;
 TV_ITEM tv;

 switch(tvh->itemNew.lParam)
     { /* decode action */
      case DEMO_ORDER:
              state = IMAGE_BOOKS_UNSELECTED;
              break;
      case DEMO_FAMILY:
              state = IMAGE_BOOK_UNSELECTED;
              break;
      case DEMO_GENUS:
              state = IMAGE_FOLDER_UNSELECTED;
              break;
      case DEMO_SPECIES:
              state = IMAGE_FLOWER_UNSELECTED;
              break;
     } /* decode action */
 // state is now our "base state".  If it is 0 we are done, but if it is
 // nonzero, we need to determine if we should show the expanded or
 // unexpanded version.
 if(state != 0)
     { /* show expand state */
      if(hdr->itemNew.state & TVIS_EXPANDED)
          state++;  // select next image, the expanded image
     } /* show expand state */
```

```
// We now have a state value.  We need to set the item
tv.mask = TVIF_STATE | TVIF_HANDLE;
tv.hItem = hdr->itemNew.hItem;
tv.state = INDEXTOSTATEIMAGEMASK(state);
tv.stateMask = TVIS_STATEIMAGEMASK;
TreeView_SetItem(tvh->hdr.hwndFrom, &tv);
}
```

The Overlay Image List

The third image list that you can use is the *overlay* image list. This is not actually a full-fledged image list. Instead, it is a specification of which entries in an image list can be overlays for that image list. This "image list" is limited to no more than four entries numbered 1 through 4; as with the state image list, selecting entry 0 means there is no overlay. And as with the state image mask selection, the overlay image selection is done by encoding the value in the `state` field of the TV_ITEM. Selecting overlay image 0, as we said, means there is no overlay. Selecting overlay image 1 through 4 causes the tree view's drawing algorithm to go to a data structure associated with the image list. From this list,

Figure 9.10: Using an overlay mask (1)

the tree view's drawing algorithm chooses the image to be overlaid based on the value stored in that data structure. Usually you use an overlay mask when you have some set of standard notations that you want to use with your images. For example, you might have a big red X indicating that the elements below the item are bogus or that the item cannot be expanded. You might have a dozen different images, so to X them out would require doubling your images, a bit inconvenient. Instead, you have your dozen "base images" and one big red X. To X-out an item, you select the X as an overlay image (for example, index number 1) and then set the state to indicate that the current item is to be X-ed out. The code fragments necessary to do this are shown in Listing 9.7.

Figure 9.11: Using an overlay mask (2)

For example, suppose you choose image number 25 to be overlay image 1. For the current item, you select image number 14 to be your `iImage` (unselected image) and image number 7 to be your `iSelectedImage`. Setting the overlay image of the current item to be 1 will cause the image that is displayed to be drawn as either image 14 or image 7 (depending on the selection state). Then image 25 will be *overlaid* on top of the first image. This is shown in Figure 9.10. The unselected image is a sheet-of-paper icon; the selected image is a user-is-looking-at-this icon, and the overlay mask, which we have set on the first item, is the red X. You can set up this experiment with the Control Explorer. You will discover that selecting the first item will display the selected image, but the red X will be kept on top of it, as shown in Figure 9.11.

Listing 9.7: Handling an overlay image

```
// During image list setup
#define BIG_RED_X 25    // 25th entry in the bitmap
#define RED_X_OVERLAY 1 // desired entry in the overlay mask

HIMAGELIST images;
// ...
// During initialization code:
    images = ImageList_LoadImage(...) ;
    ImageList_SetOverlayImage(BIG_RED_X, RED_X_OVERLAY);

    TreeView_SetImageList(htree, images, TVSIL_NORMAL);

// a subroutine to select the X-ing

void setBigRedX(HWND htree, HTREEITEM item, BOOL set)
{
  TV_ITEM tvi;
  tvi.hItem = item;
  tvi.mask = TVIF_STATE;
  tvi.stateMask = TVIS_OVERLAYMASK;
  tvi.state = (set ? INDEXTOOVERLAYMASK(RED_X_OVERLAY) : 0);
  TreeView_SetItem(htree, &tvi);
}
```

Implementing Drag-and-Drop Features

Revolutionize modern systematic botany! Cause furor at international botanical conventions! Take our botanical hierarchy example and use drag-and-drop to change it all around! Be the first on your block to be declared the modern Linnaeus!

Well, not quite. But there *are* situations in which rearranging a list or tree (remember, you can create a tree with no children and have just a list!) is an appropriate and desirable facility to present to your users. You can implement simple drag-and-drop with surprisingly little effort in a tree control, and a fancy drag-and-drop without much more effort.

The abstract description is quite simple. If you have a selected item, clicking the mouse over it and dragging the mouse out will notify the parent window that an apparent drag operation has been initiated. The parent, of course, is free to ignore this notification. But if you want to implement a drag-and-drop capability, you can follow some simple steps to make it all work:

1. Respond to the WM_NOTIFY TVN_BEGINDRAG notification by setting up some data structures to manage the drag operation, creating an image to represent the drag, capturing the mouse, and hiding the mouse cursor.

2. In the WM_MOUSEMOVE handler, if you are in a drag, move the "cursor"–actually, the special image you have created–to represent the drop position.

3. In the WM_LBUTTONUP handler, if you are in a drag, locate the position where the drop is to take place and implement the drop operation.

We have provided an implementation of drag-and-drop in the Control Explorer. While actions are taking place, you can see what is executing in the logging window, which records the key events in the operation.

To play with this, go to the "Tests" option and select "Implement drag and drop". This option will not work until you have an image list associated with the control. To do this, you must click the **Image List** button. This gives you a "canned" image list so that you can play with drag-and-drop.

We have discovered that the extant examples of implementing drag-and-drop have problems. For example, one article on the subject is simply obsolete (see the bug inset that follows), while another oversimplifies the problem. Our example attempts to show a much more general solution that handles many of the more interesting cases.

There is an article on the MSDN-CD ROM entitled "Cleverly Coding with Chicago's Gadgets, Part I: Image Lists and Tree Views". This represents a very early release of some of the software. In fact, the product release does not support the operations used in the example shown in that article. Note particularly how dragging of the image is initiated. The article proposes using a now-nonexistent function called `ImageList_StartDrag`. Study our example for the correct code.

For example, we support a copy operation as well as a move operation using the recommended Microsoft practice of **Ctrl+**drag to indicate a copy. We handle automatic scrolling if you are trying to drag from one location in the tree to another that is not currently visible. And we deal with the unusual condition of how to copy or move to the very first or very last item of the control, which Microsoft does not address. (It turns out that you can get direct support for one or the other, but not for both!)

There is a generalization of this that would allow you to copy or move an item from one tree control to another (or even from one tree control to some other control!). The tree-to-tree generalization follows naturally from the algorithm presented. The difference between the simple drag-and-drop and the tree-to-tree drag-and-drop is that when handling the mouse move, you have to do your target tests in the destination tree view and you must handle the drop operation in terms of the destination tree view.

Starting the Drag Operation

To start the drag operation, you must respond to the `TVN_BEGINDRAG` notification message, which comes in the `WM_NOTIFY` message. We decode these messages through a series of function calls, ultimately getting routed to our specific handler. The dispatch code is sketched in Listing 9.8.

Listing 9.8: Decoding the TVN_ notification messages

```
static LRESULT CALLBACK
myWndProc(HWND hwnd, UINT msg, WPARAM wParam, LPARAM lParam)
{
  switch(msg)
      { /* msg */
        HANDLE_MSG(WM_NOTIFY, OnNotify);
        // ... other message types
      } /* msg */
}

LRESULT OnNotify(HWND hwnd, UINT id, NMHDR * hdr)
{
    switch(id)
```

```
      { /* id */
       case ID_TREE: // the ID of our tree control (not very imaginative...)
            return OnNotifyTree(hwnd, hdr);

       // ... other control notification tests
      } /* id */
}

LRESULT OnNotifyTree(HWND hwnd, NMHDR * hdr)
{
    switch(tvh->hdr.code)
        { /* code */
         case TVN_BEGINDRAG:
             return doStartDrag(hwnd, (NM_TREEVIEW *)hdr);
         case NM_DBLCLK:  // See page 697
             return doStartEdit(hwnd, hdr);
         // ... other notification handlers go here
        } /* code */
}

void doStartDrag(NM_TREEVIEW * tvh)
{
  // See Listing 9.9
}
```

Having arrived at our handler, we must initiate the dragging operation. This consists of the following steps:

1. Detect if we are doing a move or copy operation by recording the state of the **Ctrl** key (GetKeyState).

2. Create a drag image to represent the object we are going to drag (TreeView_CreateDragImage).

3. Turn off the selection highlight of the currently selected item (TreeView_SelectItem).

4. Initialize the image list drag parameters (ImageList_BeginDrag).

5. Start the drag operation (ImageList_DragEnter).

6. Turn off the normal mouse cursor (ShowCursor).

7. Capture the mouse (SetCapture).

For the code, you can go directly to Listing 9.9 on page 680. Here, we examine each of these steps in detail. We assume that because we have captured the mouse, we can treat this operation as a single-threaded task and use some static state to hold the information about the dragging operation. A more complex solution would be to attach the state to the window using any of the techniques we discuss elsewhere in this book. (In the Control Explorer, we have written the code in C++, and we attach this state to the C++ class instance, which makes it local to the window.) To simplify this, we keep all the state in a structure designated treedragger.

We use the GetKeyState function to obtain the state of the keyboard at the time of the last message (the mouse click). We query a particular key, such as the **Ctrl** key, by giving its virtual-key code name. If the key is depressed, the return value is negative. The key we want is designated VK_CONTROL.

We then create the little image that is dragged around to indicate where the object being dragged is going to land. If you have an image list, this is easy. You call `TreeView_CreateDragImage`. It returns a handle to an image list that contains a specially constructed drag image. There are many convenient functions for manipulating this image. If you *don't* have an image list, this won't work, and you will have to implement your own means of tracking what is going on. This can be very painful to do. This is why Microsoft encourages the use of image lists. (Also, this is why the Control Explorer won't let you run drag-and-drop until you have assigned an image list to the control. The example would have become unwieldy if we had to implement all the support that image lists already provide.) Since the example won't really run properly if there isn't an image list, we protect ourselves by placing an `ASSERT` statement after the drag image list creation.

You might decide that creating a tiny image list, say, one pixel wide, would do the job. We tried it. It doesn't work if you use the `TVS_HASBUTTONS` style because the amount of horizontal space that is allowed for the button is controlled by the image list, if one is present. The consequence of this is that you cannot have an image list smaller than about 12 pixels; this produces a fairly ugly effect. You can use the Control Explorer to select an alternative image list–we provide a "single blank entry" image list–and see the result. If you then add a state list, the effect is somewhat improved although of questionable acceptability.

We turn off the selection highlight next. This reduces some screen clutter and eliminates some other problems. While there appears to be no built-in GUI interface that allows multiple-selection in a tree control, you can set the `TVIS_SELECTED` flag on any number of items in the list and they will highlight. We found that it took a lot of work to track the proper setting of this bit, particularly for a copy, so we eliminated the problem by turning selection off.

When we do the drag, our drag image, like any cursor, must have a "hot spot" (although this is a simulated cursor, we want the same sort of behavior). The hot spot is the coordinate that represents where the cursor "really is". We set our hot spot in the top-left corner of the image, but we have to establish this. Depending on the nature of your tree contents and the images you have chosen to use, you may set your hot spot somewhere else, perhaps in some place indicated by the particular image you are using. In this case, you would write a more elaborate computation for the hot spot.

To compute the hot spot, we first need to know the bounding rectangle of the item we have just picked up. Then we adjust the "logical" hot spot so that it is always in the same place no matter where the mouse was when we clicked it. Consider the case in which we click the mouse near the top-left edge of the item. We want our hot spot to be the top-left corner of the image. This corner is some small number of pixels to the left of the mouse cursor and a few pixels above it. So we adjust the hot spot to be relative to the current mouse position by offsetting a small distance. If we click the mouse near the bottom-right edge of an item, we still want the hot spot in the same place, that is, the top-left corner of the image. But now that corner is a much larger number of pixels to the left of the mouse cursor and a larger number of pixels above it, compared to the first case. That's what the computation of the hot spot is dealing with.

Next, we get the "item rectangle" of the item we wish to drag. We call `TreeView_GetItemRect` and pass in the handle of the control, the handle of the item, and a pointer to a rectangle to receive the parameters. We also pass in a `Boolean` value that limits that rectangle to a bounding rectangle of the text only. (Otherwise, we would have a rectangle for the entire line. This would be fine, but `TreeView_CreateDragImage` has already computed an image based on the text alone.) With the values of the bounding rectangle, we are able to use the `ImageList_BeginDrag` function to establish the image to use and the hot spot. According to the Microsoft documentation, this creates yet another temporary image list (apparently a component of the drag image), which is used to support the drag operation.

Now that we have the image properly constructed, we need to display it. This is accomplished with the `ImageList_DragEnter` function, which locks the window whose handle we pass in against updates (particularly important in a multithreaded environment!) and displays the drag image. Because our drag image is now our "cursor", we should turn off the actual mouse cursor, which we do using `ShowCursor`. We also capture the mouse with `SetCapture` so that we continue to get mouse messages, even if the mouse is dragged outside the window (see Chapter 7, particularly the section starting on page 465). All of this is shown in Listing 9.9.

Listing 9.9: The doStartDrag function

```
typedef struct {
                BOOL dragging;
                BOOL copying;
                HIMAGELIST DragImage;
                HWND htree;
                } drag_state;

drag_state treedragger;

void doStartDrag(HWND hwnd, NM_TREEVIEW * tvh)
{
        treedragger.htree = tvh->itemNew.hItem;
        treedragger.copying = GetKeyState(VK_CONTROL) < 0;

        treedragger.DragImage = TreeView_CreateDragImage(tvh->itemNew.hItem);
        ASSERT(treedragger.DragImage != NULL);  // just in case...

        TreeView_SelectItem(NULL);  // remove active selection

        TreeView_GetItemRect(tvh->hdr.hwndFrom,
                        tvh->itemNew.hItem,
                        &rc,
                        TRUE);  // text only

        ImageList_BeginDrag(treedragger.DragImage,
                        0,                         // use first image
                        tvh->ptDrag.x - rc.left,   // coords of image hot spot
                        tvh->ptDrag.y - rc.top);   // ...

        ImageList_DragEnter(nmtv->hdr.hwndFrom,
                        tvh->ptDrag.x,
                        tvh->ptDrag.y);

        ShowCursor(FALSE);
        SetCapture(hwnd);
        treedragger.dragging = TRUE;
}
```

Dragging the Item

We are now dragging an item around. When we move the mouse, we see a display very much like that of Figure 9.12. The small image of "Solanales" that is hanging off to the right is the drag image. The position that is highlighted is the position into which it will be dropped when the mouse button is released.

That brings us to the next point of drag-and-drop: computing the "drop target". This can be as easy, or as hard, as you want to make it. In the Control Explorer, we support two kinds of drag-and-drop: a relatively naive version that simply drops one item into the position occupied by another and a "smart" version that doesn't let us violate the tree hierarchy. We explore the simpler version first and then show how you can write something more complex.

We determine the drop target during the mouse move operation. The code for this is shown in Listing 9.10. Because this code is processed in the parent window and the parent window may have captured the mouse for various reasons, we react to the mouse move only if we are in an active drag-and-drop dragging operation. We determine if we are by checking the `treedragger.dragging` status, rather than simply querying if `GetCapture() == hwnd`. The latter test is not sufficient if we are supporting dragging in more than one window or even cross-window dragging. In these cases, we would probably need to determine which window was the source and which was the destination and therefore we would need to store additional information in the `treedragger` structure. Depending on the sophistication of our drag-and-drop operation, we might need a quite different handler code for each of the windows in which we support dragging. The code shown in Listing 9.10 works only if we are dragging within a single window and there is only one window represented by `treedragger`.

The first thing we do in the move handler is move the drag image. This is done with the `ImageList_DragMove` function, where we specify the new coordinates of the hot spot of the image. One implication of this call is that, because it does not take an image list as a parameter, it must be storing the current image list (the one established by `ImageList_DragEnter`, in fact) in a static storage location or a thread-local storage location somewhere deep in the image list code. Since we cannot tell if the allocation is static or thread local, we should be careful not to have some other thread manipulate the image list module while we are doing the drag.

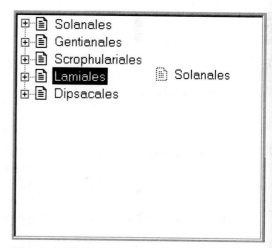

Figure 9.12: A drag operation in action

Next, we determine if the image hot spot is over some target item in the tree view. We do this by setting the x and y parameter values into a `TV_HITTESTINFO` structure and sending a `TVM_HITTEST` (`TreeView_HitTest`) query. The return value is either an `HTREEITEM` handle for the tree item we are "near", or `NULL`, meaning we are not near any tree item.

When we first tested this code in the Control Explorer, with a tree that was expanded, we copied an item that was in the expanded list into one of its child nodes. (As you will see later in this example, this involves copying all the child nodes.) But since the child node was constantly expanding, the copy operation kept finding more and more to copy. And because the copy operation is recursive, we eventually ran out of stack space. So we avoid this by simply not allowing a tree to be copied into any part of its own subtree–at least not if we're going to allow a recursive copy! The isParent test, shown in Listing 9.11, allows us to avoid this situation by forcing the target to be NULL if we violate this restriction. Because of how isParent is coded, however, a node is implicitly a parent of itself. We did want to allow the original node to be selectable as a target. One reason for doing this is that we want to provide a consistent GUI behavior. Another is that in the case of a copy-drag (as opposed to a move-drag), allowing an item to be "dropped" onto its source makes perfect sense. We deal with this by making an explicit test. That is, if the target is the source, we don't call isParent and therefore the target remains a valid selection. If we are doing a drag-move, we will eventually reject this selection in the OnLButtonUp handler.

Once we have determined what the drop target is–even if it is NULL–we need to highlight the tree to indicate this. Here's where we need to be aware of the fact that our cursor is only a *simulated* cursor, not a real one. To draw the highlight, the tree control will request a DC from Windows. Ordinarily, requesting a DC will blank out the mouse cursor so that the cursor does not disturb whatever is being drawn and whatever is being drawn does not disturb the cursor. But with a *simulated* cursor, this automatic action doesn't happen. GDI doesn't know about that drag image on the screen, and in particular, it doesn't know that it should hide it. You have to do that yourself. This is done with the ImageList_DragShowNolock, which hides or shows the drag image depending on its Boolean parameter.

Having hidden the drag image, we can now call TreeView_SelectDropTarget, passing in the handle of the desired item. If there is already a drop target highlighted, its highlight will be removed and the selected target will receive the highlight. If the selected target is NULL, nothing will be highlighted (but the existing highlight will be removed, which is what we want to have happen here). We can then use ImageList_DragShowNolock to redisplay the drag image.

That's all there is to simple dragging. But what about more complex dragging? For example, not letting the user violate the tree hierarchy by permitting only the exchange of child nodes at the same level. Or the fact that certain kinds of nodes might be permitted only under certain parent nodes? Or allowing a child node to be dropped on an empty parent, thus indicating the parent is a permissible drop target? And what if the drop target is not visible and we want the tree control to scroll automatically for us? All of these and more are possible variations you can do. We shortly show you how to implement a smart drag-and-drop and an autoscroll operation. But for now, we will leave our simple example alone and proceed to showing how to implement the drop operation.

Listing 9.10: Handling mouse move during a drag-and-drop
```
void OnMouseMove(HWND hwnd, int x, int y, UINT flags)
{
    if(treedragger.dragging)
        { /* handle drag */
          TV_HITTESTINFO hti;
          HTREEITEM target;
```

```
          ImageList_DragMove(x, y);

          hti.pt.x = x;
          hti.pt.y = y;
          target =  TreeView_HitTest(treedragger.htree, &hti);

          if(target != treedragger.DragItem &&
              isParent(treedragger.htree, target, treedragger.DragItem))
                  target = NULL;

          ImageList_DragShowNolock(FALSE); // hide the image
          TreeView_SelectDropTarget(treedragger.htree, target);
          ImageList_DragShowNolock(TRUE); // make it visible again

          } /* handle drag */
}
```

Listing 9.11: The isParent function
```
BOOL isParent(HWND htree, HTREEITEM target, HTREEITEM dragee)
    {
     if(dragee == NULL)
        return FALSE;     // no dragee, shouldn't even be here
     if(target == NULL)
        return FALSE;     // hit root of tree without finding dragee
     if(dragee == target)
        return TRUE;       // we would be copying into a subtree! No!
     return isParent(TreeView_GetParent(htree, target), dragee);
    }
```

Dropping the Item

The drop operation was surprisingly difficult to get right. The sample code we started with always dropped the dragee just after the target. This meant that you could never, ever drag an item to the first position in the list because no matter how hard you tried, the item would end up dropping below the target and thus be at best the second item. Of course, this could be "fixed" by then dragging the first item to the second position, but that seemed clumsy. Inverting the sense of the insertion resulted in something equally unsatisfactory; although you could now drag an item to the front of the list, it was impossible to drag an item to the *end* of the list! Slightly more sophisticated fiddling revealed that we actually had to determine if the item being dragged was being dragged *upward* in the list or *downward* in the list! But doing this gave some very "intuitively obvious" behavior–if you drag an item to position 3 of the list it actually becomes the new third item in the list.

To do the drop right in all cases requires several additional considerations that we've already outlined for the mouse move handler. The most crucial is, is it legitimate to drop this kind of node in this position? But the case that is omitted from all the sample code we've seen is that in which the node in question has child nodes. In the simple examples, only a simple drop was done and therefore only one node was copied. For our example, we wanted to copy the entire subtree. Otherwise, the subtree would be lost when the source node was deleted.

The resulting drag-drop code is shown in Listing 9.12.

The first things we do are just the bookkeeping overhead: resetting everything we set up initially to enable dragging. Thus we call `ImageList_EndDrag` and `ImageList_DragLeave` to terminate use of the temporary image lists (and delete them). We reenable the mouse cursor using `ShowCursor`, and we release the mouse with `ReleaseCapture`. Finally, we destroy explicitly the temporary image list created by `TreeView_GetDragImage` by calling `ImageList_Destroy`.

Now we can actually do the drop. We retrieve the (unique) item that has the drop highlight that we set during mouse motion by calling `TreeView_GetDropHilight`. This will return either the handle of an item or `NULL`. If it returns the handle of an item, we proceed with the drop logic; otherwise, we didn't have a drop target and no drop is done.

Well, almost. We could be smart in the mouse move logic and not allow a node to be selected as a drop target if it is the node we're actually dragging. On the other hand, to be consistent with the user expectations of the GUI, we should permit this, if for no other reason than it gives the user a "no drop" option that is symmetric with much of the rest of the Windows GUI. So that's what we do here. In addition to testing the target for `NULL`, we make sure that our drop target is not the object being dragged. (If you try this in the Control Explorer, you will discover that it feels "natural" to see the drop target selected even if it is the node you're dragging.)

To "drop" an item, we insert it into the tree using `TreeView_InsertItem`. This requires that we give a parent node (which might be `TVI_ROOT` if we are inserting into the top-most level of the tree) and an `hInsertAfter` handle that tells where the inserted node should go in the child list of the parent. It is the computation of these two values that becomes tricky. For the moment, the computation of the parent node for the `TreeView_InsertItem` is simple: It is the parent of the node that is the drop target. We will see in our hierarchy-preserving drag-and-drop that the parent might *be* the drop target because we are dropping a child node onto it. (Note that in the simple code we're presenting here, there is no way to drop a node onto another node and make it a child of that node. You would have to provide a special interface, such as via the right-button-drag option or the **Shift** key, to indicate a child drop, which we haven't implemented here.)

After performing some experiments that attempted to show us what seemed to be an "intuitively obvious" interface, we ended up with the interface you can play with. It has the property that the dropped item appears in the position in the tree view in which it is dropped. If you drag an item to the third position, it will appear in the third position after the drop.

Remember this as a GUI designer. These interfaces are *not* "intuitively obvious". If you've ever had to train a nontechnical person in the use of Windows, you already understand this. What we *really* have is a set of conventions that more-or-less work. This set of conventions requires that the users be *trained* to understand them. To the degree you can minimize this training by following conventions, you succeed. To the degree that you can minimize this training by *violating* the GUI conventions, you succeed. But if your violation or conformance results in a system in which users make certain kinds of errors frequently, it means the GUI design is wrong. It's important to get it as right as possible the first time. One reason for this is that the existing base of users will be unhappy with your new, improved, and less-error-prone release simply because it is *different* than the previous release. You don't have the luxury of "throwing one away".

One of the guiding principles of software design is the maxim popularized by Fred Brooks, "plan to throw one away. You will anyway". Unfortunately, everybody remembers this bit of folklore, but nobody seems to have ever read the actual book. The result of this misinterpretation is a degree of incredible sloppiness in design and programming, based on the premise that there will always be a chance to redo it. This means that a number of really poorly designed GUIs exist, which are badly implemented, and virtually unmaintainable. Fred's actual admonition was that you will *have* to throw one away, no matter how good a job you do, because systems, needs, and expectations evolve. He goes on to say, in the book, "Delivering that throwaway to customers buys time, but it does so only at the cost of agony for the user, distraction for the builders while they do the redesign, and a bad reputation for the product that the best redesign will find hard to live down" (page 116 of the 1975 edition). Anyone who can quote the "throwaway" maxim without being able to quote this significant supplement is a hazard to a project. Fred *never* intended this maxim to be justification for poor design or implementation, and in fact says quite the opposite. See "Further Reading" for the full citation. – *jmn*

This behavior comes at the expense of some complexity. For example, if you drag-move an item *downward* in the list, it will be removed from the source position. This means that for it to end up in the third position, it has to be inserted *after* the second item in the list. But if you are going to remove it, the second item in the resulting list is the *third* item in the current list, so the drop target itself (the third item) is the predecessor. If you are moving an item *upward* in the list, then for it to become the third item in the list it should be inserted after the second item, that is, be the *predecessor* of the drop target. But in a drag-copy of an item downward, the source is *not* removed, so the node after which you insert it is the predecessor of the drop target, as in an upward move.

We first make a couple of simple tests. We must have a non-NULL target. Also, unless we are doing a drag-copy, the target must not be our source, `DragItem`. If these two criteria are met, we can successfully drop the `DragItem` on the target.

We do a drop by inserting a *copy* of the node into the tree at the selected target position. After we have done this, if we are in a drag-move, we delete the source node (`DragItem`); otherwise, we leave it in place. So we first obtain a copy of the item. We do this first because we will show in a more complex example that we need the information about the source to determine what the target should be (when we are forcing the tree hierarchy to be maintained). For this simpler example, it wouldn't make much difference which order we did the computations in: getting a copy of the node or determining the final target.

We first compute an assumed parent/predecessor pair:

```
tvins.hParent = TreeView_GetParent(target);
tvins.hInsertAfter = TreeView_GetPrevSibling(target);
if(tvins.hInsertAfter == NULL)
    tvins.hInsertAfter = TVI_FIRST;
```

We have to make a special case where the `hInsertAfter` ends up being NULL. If this is the case, we want to insert *before* the node, but the insert doesn't have a previous sibling. This can happen only for the first node in the list. (Remember, this applies at any level of the tree. At the top-most level, this would be the first entry in the tree, but for a child list, it would be the first entry in the child list.) If `hInsertAfter` is NULL, the node is inserted at the *end* of the list, so we use the special designator `TVI_FIRST` to force it to be inserted after the "front" of the list, that is, to become the first node in the list. If we do nothing to upset this computation, the `hInsertAfter` now represents the predecessor of the node we are going to insert.

We now have to account for the downward motion of a node under a drag-move. This is done by this code:

```
if(isDownSibling(treedragger.DragItem, target))
 { /* Drag down */
  if(!treedragger.copying)
    tvins.hInsertAfter = target;
 } /* Drag down */
```

The isDownSibling function is shown in Listing 9.13. Finally, we insert a new item representing the DragItem in its new position:

```
tvins.item = tvi;                    // copy entire item across
newitem = TreeView_InsertItem(treedragger.htree, &tvins);
```

 The above code carries a serious implication: A tree item loses its original "identity" when it is dragged around. Thus, if you have cleverly stored away the HTREEITEM handles for critical data items you plan to manipulate, query, or otherwise use and you permit drag-and-drop, you are now in deep trouble. Those original handles, for a drag-move, are now rendered invalid. Using them might generate an access error. It is a good idea to never store the handles to any tree items beyond what is needed for immediate processing (for example, it is OK to store them while loading up the tree view). They should not be retained over possible user interactions. Instead of storing handles, you should have a well-defined search criterion that can uniquely identify a node not by its handle but by its contents (such as a unique lParam field or a unique value in a structure referenced by the lParam field).

You could think that we're done, except for deleting the source on a drag-move. Unfortunately, this is not true. What we just did was copy exactly one node of the tree across. If that node has child nodes, we have to copy them, recursively, as necessary. The code to do this is almost straightforward and is shown in Listing 9.14. What we do is walk along the child list of the source node, picking up each immediate child node in turn, creating a copy of it, and inserting it at the end (TVI_LAST) of the new node. For each node we add to the child list, we call copyChildren recursively to copy *its* children. We did find it necessary to clear the TVIS_SELECTED bit because we would otherwise end up with potentially several nodes marked as being "selected".

Now, if we are in a drag-move operation, we can delete the original source node. This is simple:

```
TreeView_DeleteItem(treedragger.htree, treedragger.DragItem);
```

This almost works. Actually, in terms of deleting the source node (and all of its child nodes), it works perfectly. We did discover one "bug" in the tree code, however. If the node we are deleting is the last child node in a subtree, the parent is still displayed with a little button indicating that it can be collapsed. The parent node does not get any notification that its last child has been deleted. So the user is left with this incorrect button still being displayed. This is entirely too ugly. So we fix it by getting the parent node and then, after the deletion, seeing if there are any child nodes. If there are none, we clear the TVIS_EXPANDED bit from the state, thereby causing the "collapsed" box to be displayed.

 This bug inset refers to the preceding paragraph that describes the failure of the tree view to remove the "collapse" button from a parent whose last child has been deleted. We debated whether this is a "bug" or a "pitfall" and decided that it is closer to being a "bug", since the tree view control should have handled this itself. You should be aware of this bug/pitfall whenever you delete a node from a tree view and be prepared to handle it. There is a complementary bug that fails to make a button appear when a previously childless node has a child node attached. This can be solved by invalidating the rectangle in which that line appears (using TVM_GETITEMRECT or TreeView_GetItemRect) or simply invalidating the entire control. When the area is redrawn, the proper button will appear.

The code that clears the TVIS_EXPANDED bit is very simple because of the stateMask field. We simply set the TVIF_STATE flag in the TV_ITEM to indicate that we are changing (only) the state value. We set the entire state field to 0 (which includes the TVIS_EXPANDED value) and set the stateMask to have only the TVIS_EXPANDED bit set. When we call TreeView_SetItem, only those bits masked by stateMask will be changed, that is, only the TVIS_EXPANDED bit will be affected. That bit will be set to the value in state and therefore will be cleared.

We finish up by clearing any drop-highlight state in the tree and resetting the treedragger.dragging flag to indicate the drag is now over.

Listing 9.12: Well-behaved drop code

```
void OnLButtonUp(HWND hwnd, int x, int y, UINT keyflags)
{
    if(treedragger.dragging)
       { /* handle drop */
        HTREEITEM target;
        HTREEITEM newitem;
        TV_ITEM tvi;
        TCHAR buffer [256];
        TV_INSERTSTRUCT tvins;

        ImageList_EndDrag();

        ImageList_DragLeave(treedragger.htree);

        ShowCursor(TRUE);   // restore mouse cursor

        ReleaseCapture();

        ImageList_Destroy(treedragger.DragImage);
        treedragger.DragImage = NULL;

        // Proceed with the drop...
        target = TreeView_GetDropHilight(treedragger.hTree);
        if(target != NULL &&
            (treedragger.copying || target != treedragger.DragItem))
           { /* do drop */
            tvi.mask = TVIF_TEXT | TVIF_IMAGE | TVIF_SELECTEDIMAGE |
                                 TVIF_PARAM | TVIF_STATE | TVIF_CHILDREN;
            tvi.hItem = DragItem;
            tvi.pszText = buffer;
            tvi.cchTextMax = DIM(buffer);
            TreeView_GetItem(treedragger.hTree, &tvi);   // get the current item

            tvins.hParent = TreeView_GetParent(treedragger.htree, target);
            tvins.hInsertAfter = TreeView_GetPrevSibling(treedragger.htree,
                                                              target);
            if(tvins.hInsertAfter == NULL)
                tvins.hInsertAfter = TVI_FIRST;

            if(isDownSibling(treedragger.htree, treedragger.DragItem, target))
               { /* Drag down */
                if(!treedragger.copying)
                    tvins.hInsertAfter = target;
               } /* Drag down */
```

```
            tvins.item = tvi;   // copy entire item across
            tvins.stateMask = 0xFFFFFFFF;    // deliver all state bits
            newitem = TreeView_InsertItem(treedragger.htree, &tvins);

            copyChildren(treedragger.htree, newItem, treedragger.DragItem);

            if(!treedragger.copying)
                { /* delete source */
                  HTREEITEM parent = TreeView_GetParent(treedragger.htree,
                                                 treedragger.DragItem);

                  TreeView_DeleteItem(treedragger.htree, treedragger.DragItem);

                  if(parent != NULL)
                      { /* check child state */
                        // See if, after delete, there are any children
                        if(TreeView_GetChild(treedragger.htree, parent) == NULL)
                            { /* no children left */
                              TV_ITEM tvp;
                              tvp.mask = TVIF_STATE;
                              tvp.hItem = parent;
                              tvp.state = 0;
                              tvp.stateMask = TVIS_EXPANDED;
                              TreeView_SetItem(treedragger.htree, &tvp);
                            } /* no children left */
                      } /* check child state */
                } /* delete source */
            TreeView_SelectDropHilight(treedragger.hTree, NULL);
            treedragger.dragging = FALSE;
          } /* do drop */
      } /* handle drop */
}
```

Listing 9.13: The isDownSibling function for a tree view

```
BOOL isDownSibling(HTREE htree, HTREEITEM source, HTREEITEM target)
    {
    while(source != NULL)
        { /* scan up */
          source = TreeView_GetNextSibling(htree, source);
          if(source == target)
              return TRUE;
        } /* scan up */
    return FALSE;
    }
```

Listing 9.14: The copyChildren function for a tree view

```
void copyChildren(HWND htree, HTREEITEM to, HTREEITEM from)
    {
    HTREEITEM child = TreeView_GetChild(htree, from);
    HTREEITEM newchild;
    while(child != NULL)
        { /* copy children */
          TV_ITEM newitem;
          TCHAR buffer[256];
          TV_INSERTSTRUCT tvins;
          newitem.mask = TVIF_TEXT | TVIF_IMAGE | TVIF_PARAM |
                      TVIF_STATE | TVIF_SELECTEDIMAGE | TVIF_CHILDREN;
```

```
        newitem.hItem = child;
        newitem.pszText = buffer;
        newitem.cchTextMax = DIM(buffer);
        TreeView_GetItem(htree, &newitem);

        tvins.hParent = to;
        tvins.hInsertAfter = TVI_LAST;
        tvins.item = newitem;
        tvins.stateMask = 0xFFFFFFFF;
        tvins.item.state &= ~TVIS_SELECTED;   // make sure to lose selection bit
        newchild = TreeView_InsertItem(htree, &tvins);

        copyChildren(htree, newchild, child);
        child = TreeView_GetNextSiblingItem(htree, child);
    } /* copy children */
}
```

"Smart" Drag-and-Drop

Doing a drag-and-drop is a bit more complex than the conventional Windows literature suggests. The drag-and-drop we describe in the previous section isn't a very "smart" drag-and-drop. It will not enforce the tree hierarchy. Our example is a botanical example, where in effect each level of the tree has a "type" (in the programming language sense) and there is no cross-type assignment permitted. Our previous example allowed the user to "cast" any level of the tree into any other level of the tree, thereby violating the fundamental structure of systematic botany. You can imagine many other applications where the type structure of the tree must be preserved. How hard is that to do?

The answer is, not very hard at all, compared to writing the rest of the code. We encode in each tree item an integer that represents its level in the tree; the highest level nodes have the highest numbers and the deepest nodes have the lowest numbers. We encoded this in the lParam field of the TV_ITEM structure, but in a more general system you might have the lParam field referencing a data structure in which the information is encoded. You might even choose more sophisticated "type" systems. For example, the resource editor of the Microsoft Visual C++ environment has levels for various resources such as bitmaps, dialogs, icons, and menus. You cannot drop a menu into the bitmap folder. Exactly how you choose to implement your system is application-specific, but we hope the style we used in the Control Explorer will give you some suggestions.

To enable the "smart" drag-and-drop in the Control Explorer, click the **Smart D&D** check box. New code will now come into play. This new code not only enforces the tree hierarchy; it also gives us the ability to drop a child node on an empty parent and have the child inserted into the parent's previously empty child list. Our simpler drag-and-drop implementation offered no such capability. The smart drag-and-drop code does assume that the tree starts out with the correct hierarchy, so if you've been playing with the structure without smart drag-and-drop, you should probably click the **Demo** button to get a valid tree rebuilt.

Only a few lines of code need to be added to the mouse move handler. Rather than leave their insertion as an "exercise for the reader", we show them in bold in Listing 9.15. Note that we have also added a BOOL smart field to the treedragger structure.

Listing 9.15: Handling mouse move during "smart" drag-and-drop

```
void OnMouseMove(HWND hwnd, int x, int y, UINT flags)
```

```
{
    if(treedragger.dragging)
        { /* handle drag */
        TV_HITTESTINFO hti;
        HTREEITEM target;

        ImageList_DragMove(x, y);

        hti.pt.x = x;
        hti.pt.y = y;
        target = TreeView_HitTest(treedragger.htree, &hti);

        if(target != treedragger.DragItem &&
            isParent(treedragger.htree, target, treedragger.DragItem))
                target = NULL;

        if(treedragger.smart && target != NULL)
            { /* be smart */
            // This is almost too easy.  We've encoded the level in the
            // lParam field, so we can only select the target if the
            // lParam fields are identical
            if(treeLevel(treedragger.htree, target) !=
                    treeLevel(treedragger.htree, DragItem))
                { /* not same level */
                // Are we trying to drop a child on an empty parent?
                if(treeLevel(treedragger.htree, target) !=
                        treeLevel(treedragger.htree, DragItem) + 1)
                    { /* not compatible */
                    target = NULL;   // can't do it
                    } /* not compatible */
                } /* not same level */
            } /* be smart */

        ImageList_DragShowNolock(FALSE); // hide the image
        TreeView_SelectDropTarget(treedragger.htree, target);
        ImageList_DragShowNolock(TRUE); // make it visible again

        } /* handle drag */
}
```

Listing 9.16: The treeLevel function

```
int treeLevel(HWND htree, HTREEITEM item)
    {
    TV_ITEM tvi;
    tvi.hItem = item;
    tvi.mask = TVIF_PARAM;
    TreeView_GetItem(htree, &tvi);
    return (int)tvi.lParam;
    }
```

The drop operation likewise requires some enhancement. We check to see if we are dropping on a "compatible" target node. A "compatible" target node is a node either at the same level in the tree hierarchy (treeLevel values are the same) as the DragItem or whose level in the tree would make it an immediate parent node of the DragItem. If the node would become a parent node of our DragItem, we reset the parent node for the insertion. We implement the treeLevel function, shown in Listing 9.16, to compute the actual level of a tree node.

Listing 9.17: Well-behaved drop code, enhanced for "smart" drop

```
void OnLButtonUp(HWND hwnd, int x, int y, UINT keyflags)
{
    if(treedragger.dragging)
        { /* handle drop */
        HTREEITEM target;
        HTREEITEM newitem;
        TV_ITEM tvi;
        TCHAR buffer [256];
        TV_INSERTSTRUCT tvins;

        ImageList_EndDrag();

        ImageList_DragLeave(treedragger.htree);

        ShowCursor(TRUE);   // restore mouse cursor

        ReleaseCapture();

        ImageList_Destroy(treedragger.DragImage);
        treedragger.DragImage = NULL;
        target = TreeView_GetDropHilight(treedragger.hTree);

        if(target != NULL &&
            (treedragger.copying || target != treedragger.DragItem) &&
            (!treedragger.smart ||
                ( treeLevel(target) == treeLevel(DragItem) ||
                  treeLevel(target) == treeLevel(DragItem) + 1)))
        { /* do drop */
          tvi.mask = TVIF_TEXT | TVIF_IMAGE | TVIF_SELECTEDIMAGE |
                              TVIF_PARAM | TVIF_STATE | TVIF_CHILDREN;
          tvi.hItem = DragItem;
          tvi.pszText = buffer;
          tvi.cchTextMax = DIM(buffer);
          TreeView_GetItem(treedragger.hTree, &tvi);  // get the current item

          tvins.hParent = TreeView_GetParent(treedragger.htree, target);
          tvins.hInsertAfter = TreeView_GetPrevSibling(treedragger.htree,
                                                            target);
          if(tvins.hInsertAfter == NULL)
             tvins.hInsertAfter = TVI_FIRST;

          if(treedragger.smart)
             { /* smart */
             // Determine where and how to insert it.  If we inserting at
             // the same level, we use the parent of the target.  If we
             // are inserting a child level the parent *is* the target
             if(treeLevel(treedragger.htree, target) ==
                      treeLevel(treedragger.htree, treedragger.DragItem) + 1)
                { /* child insert */
                tvins.hParent = target;
                } /* child insert */
             } /* smart */

          if(isDownSibling(treedragger.htree, treedragger.DragItem, target))
             { /* Drag down */
```

```
            if(!treedragger.copying)
                tvins.hInsertAfter = target;
            } /* Drag down */

        tvins.item = tvi;  // copy entire item across
        tvins.stateMask = 0xFFFFFFFF;    // deliver all state bits
        newitem = TreeView_InsertItem(treedragger.htree, &tvins);

        copyChildren(treedragger.htree, newItem, treedragger.DragItem);

        if(!treedragger.copying)
            { /* delete source */
              HTREEITEM parent = TreeView_GetParent(treedragger.htree,
                                                treedragger.DragItem);

              TreeView_DeleteItem(treedragger.htree, treedragger.DragItem);

              if(parent != NULL)
                  { /* check child state */
                    // See if, after delete, there are any children
                    if(TreeView_GetChild(treedragger.htree, parent) == NULL)
                        { /* no children left */
                        TV_ITEM tvp;
                        tvp.mask = TVIF_STATE;
                        tvp.hItem = parent;
                        tvp.state = 0;
                        tvp.stateMask = TVIS_EXPANDED;
                        TreeView_SetItem(treedragger.htree, &tvp);
                        } /* no children left */
                  } /* check child state */
            } /* delete source */
        TreeView_SelectDropHilight(treedragger.hTree, NULL);
        treedragger.dragging = FALSE;
        } /* do drop */
    } /* handle drop */
}
```

Automatic Scrolling in Drag-Drop

The "direct manipulation" interface has become a buzzword of GUI design. Why have some "indirect" way of accomplishing a task when a way of directly manipulating the object(s) in question is easier to learn, to understand, and to use? The problem with this thinking is that it does not take reality into account. Reality points out nasty little issues. What if we have drag-drop, but you can't see the drop point when you pick the object up and you somehow have to make it visible before you can do the drop? With only one input means, the mouse, you now have a problem. The only means to make the target visible is to use the mouse, but the mouse has its paws full dragging your object. You can't have it do both simultaneously, at least not with the conventional interfaces. We shudder to think of the "two mouse" interface, with left-hand and right-hand mice, requiring coordination that would be nearly superhuman (the pat-your-head-and-rub-your-stomach class of problems). Yet would we *really* want to go back to a mode whereby we typed in commands that said "copy this thing to that place", where we had to designate "this thing" and "that place" by typing their *names*? Probably not. But the implication is that as a GUI designer, you *must* be prepared to make sure that direct manipulation interfaces are effective.

Another example is the resizing of a window. You simply grab an edge and drag it along until the desired size is reached. But in the case of the Control Explorer, we wanted to be able to resize the tree window so that we could capture screen dumps and have them all be the same size. This required adding a size box "on demand" to the tree view control and using it to resize the window (see Chapter 10, page 712 for the details of how this actually works). But a problem arose. How do we get screen snapshots taken on different days to be size-compatible? The solution was to provide direct *feedback* on the window size. (This turned out not to work on Windows 95 because Windows 95 handles window resize differently from Windows NT. So our screen snapshots for the tree control were done on Windows NT.) Thus, in addition to ensuring that we can accomplish the task using direct manipulation, it is essential that we provide continuous, often *quantitative*, feedback to the user as to what is happening–for example, the drop-target highlighting.

We have now shown that the tree view has a natural paradigm, easily taught and easily used, for moving items around: drag-and-drop. But a tree view can be arbitrarily long, much longer than the window. We need to provide a way to have the window scroll while we are dragging so that the target can be found. We do this in a way that is compatible with a style found in most document processing programs. That is, if you drag near the top of the window, the contents will scroll downward, thus making the previously hidden contents visible. If you drag near the bottom of the window, the contents will scroll upward. Now you *can* accomplish two functions with a single mouse interface: both dragging and scrolling.

To do this, we use a timer. When the hot spot is within a specified distance of the top or bottom of the window, we initiate a timer, which begins to send periodic messages to our window (see Chapter 7, page 504 for more about timers). On each timer message, we scroll the window. We actually use two different time intervals: If we are near an edge, but still within the window, we scroll "slowly"; if we are outside the window, we scroll more quickly. Microsoft suggests another strategy in *The Windows Interface Guidelines for Software Design* (page 82), that of using the velocity of the mouse motion to determine the velocity of the scroll. We decided to use a simpler interface here because we have sometimes found that these velocity-based computations are difficult for users to get used to. We could have implemented a multistep velocity based on the distance the user moves the mouse outside the window, that is, the further the mouse is from the window, the faster the scroll rate. We *do* leave this as an Exercise For The Reader.

We set the timer using a callback function because we need fairly evenly-spaced timer intervals. Jeffrey Richter points out in one of his "Windows Q&A" columns (see "Further Reading") that there are some features of how the timer works that influence minimum intermessage time. In particular, he includes a program that tests the timer and he reports that the smallest quantization of a timer on Windows 95 is 55ms, and on Windows NT it is 10ms. He further reports that actions such as dragging a window around on the screen can profoundly affect the *actual* intermessage time. If you're really concerned about timers, you should check out the article. Because the timer message is the second-lowest priority message in the system, a thread will receive a WM_TIMER message only if there is nothing else in its queue. But in a drag, you are generating mouse-move messages. Combine this with the timer quantization, and you can see that the scrolling could become quite irregular, based on how much mouse traffic is coming in. This can be processor-dependent, platform-dependent, and/or operating-system-dependent.

To avoid the queue behavior of the WM_TIMER message, we instead use the callback function to enqueue our own notification message using PostMessage. Because the callback is not affected by the queued messages, we will see a more regular scrolling since our own messages will arrive with far more regularity than the timer messages.

 Measurement is an art. Richter's article is a very important reference, since he shows just how to determine the resolution, accuracy, and precision of a timer. If you have a solid grounding in undergraduate physics, much of this will be obvious: what are we measuring, how accurately are we measuring it, how precise are our measurements, and how reproducible are our measurements? And, finally, *is what we are measuring the correct thing to be measuring to predict behavior*? Unfortunately, most operating systems do not provide accurate or reproducible measurement tools with sufficient resolution for many measurements we would find interesting. This topic is covered in more depth in my Dr. Dobb's article, "Profiling for Performance", cited in "Further Reading"– *jmn*

We store the direction of our autoscroll in the `treedragger` structure, and we add a new field, `ScrollDirection`. We then add a call to the `checkAutoScroll` function shown in Listing 9.18 to the very end of the `OnMouseMove` handler.

In `checkAutoScroll`, we first see if the window has a scroll bar and, if so, if the scroll bar has a nonempty range:

```
SCROLLINFO si;
BOOL hasscroll = GetScrollInfo(treedragger.htree, SB_VERT,
                                          &si, SIF_RANGE);

if(hasscroll && si.nMin != si.nMax)
    { /* has scroll bar */
```

If we actually have a displayable, nonempty scroll bar, we form a POINT structure using the x and y parameters of the OnMouseMove handler. Next, we get the client rectangle of the tree view control and use the PtIn-Rect function to ask if we are within the window. (Because we have mouse capture, we will get mouse messages even when the mouse coordinates are outside the window.) If we are within the window, we will initiate a "slow" scroll to reveal the hidden information; if we are outside the window, we will initiate a "faster" scroll. We could be even more sophisticated and use the distance the mouse is outside the window to determine velocity, but this code should give you the basic idea of how to handle it.

To initiate the autoscroll when we are inside the window, we define two regions called the "scroll zones", one at the top of the window and one at the bottom. We choose to use the height of a horizontal scroll bar as the defining region simply because this is a number that scales nicely for various display sizes. (We wouldn't choose a fixed number of pixels because in high-resolution displays, the scroll zone would be very thin, and in low-resolution displays, it would be very large.) The *Windows Interface Guidelines for Software Design* suggests using twice the scroll bar height. We tried this, but it seemed to offer too much space, so we chose to use only the height itself. If the hot spot is within the window, but not within the scroll zones, we terminate any scrolling action we may have already set by calling the `autoScroll` function with the `SCROLL_OFF` parameter. The `autoScroll` function and its definitions appear in Listing 9.19 on page 696.

If the code we pass to `autoScroll` is SCROLL_OFF, we cancel any pending timer. Otherwise, we use the code to choose an interval to represent "slow" or "fast" scrolling and set a timer with a specified callback function. We store the timer ID in the `treedragger` structure, in a new field, `timer`. We store the desired direction of the scroll in the `treedragger` structure, in a new field, `ScrollDirection`.

The only reason we have to use a timer callback is to avoid the one-second quantization that Windows imposes on us for WM_TIMER messages. So we use it only to post a message about scrolling back to our main window. When the posted message is processed, we call the onScrollRequest handler. The callback and onScrollRequest functions are shown in Listing 9.20.

The onScrollRequest is called from our basic message dispatcher function:

```
case UWM_SCROLL:
            onScrollRequest(hwnd);
            return 0;
```

All this function really does is send a WM_VSCROLL message to the tree view, whose direction is based on the value we had stored in treedragger.ScrollDirection. The only trick here is the same one we had to address in dealing with highlighting: The "cursor" we're dragging isn't a *real* cursor; it's a *simulated* cursor drawn on the screen with ordinary GDI calls. This means that when we actually scroll the window, the ScrollWindow function that does the real work scrolls the entire contents of the window, *including the image of the simulated cursor.* But on the next mouse move, we use the ImageList_DragMove function to move the image. This function knows it has to erase the image from its previous location. That location is now probably blank, thus causing the XOR operation that was supposed to erase the image to actually draw it again. Then ImageList_DragMove will redraw it at the new position. The result is that a simple autoscroll can leave *three* images of the drag cursor on the screen:

1. The one that was scrolled out from under the hot spot

2. The one that was drawn based on the assumption that an XOR would erase the one that was already there

3. The one that was drawn by the request to draw in the new position

This Does Not Look Good.

The solution is the same one we had to apply for highlighting. That is, we must use the ImageList_DragShowNolock function to hide the drag cursor, *then* do our scrolling, and finally use ImageListDragShowNolock to redisplay the image.

We also have to add the following lines to the start of the OnLButtonUp handler:

```
if(treedragger.timer != 0)
    { /* kill timer */
     KillTimer(treedragger.timer);
     treedragger.timer = 0;
    } /* kill timer */
```

Drag-and-Drop Summary

This completes our "thorough" example of how to implement a realistic set of drag-and-drop functionality for a tree control. At this point, you have a good framework for doing drag-and-drop. However, the requirements of your application will strongly dictate how complex the operations such as mouse move and drop ultimately have to become to support what you need. By showing you at least the places where you need to plug in your own code, we hope we have helped you identify the key places you may need to modify.

The Control Explorer is written in C++. The code you see here is a C transcription of the C++ code from the Control Explorer, less the logging and debugging features that Control Explorer needs but which serve no purpose in a real tree control implementation.

Listing 9.18: The checkAutoScroll function: Initiating autoscrolling in a tree view

```
void checkAutoScroll(HWND hwnd, int x, int y)
        {
        SCROLLINFO si;
        BOOL hasscroll = GetScrollInfo(treedragger.htree, SB_VERT,
                                           &si, SIF_RANGE);

        if(hasscroll && si.nMin != si.nMax)
           { /* has scroll bar */
           // If we have a scroll bar, see if the mouse is in the window
           POINT pt;
           RECT rc;

           pt.x = x;
           pt.y = y;
           GetClientRect(treedragger.htree, &rc);
           if(PtInRect(&rc, pt))
              { /* in window */
              // See if we're in the "scroll zone". WIGSD suggests
              // 2xscroll height, but we choose 1xscroll height
              if(pt.y < rc.top + GetSystemMetrics(SM_CYHSCROLL))
                 { /* scroll up */
                  autoScroll(hwnd, SB_LINEUP, SCROLL_SLOWLY);
                 } /* scroll up */
              else
              if(pt.y > rc.bottom - GetSystemMetrics(SM_CYHSCROLL))
                 { /* scroll down */
                  autoScroll(hwnd, SB_LINEDOWN, SCROLL_SLOWLY);
                 } /* scroll down */
              else
                 autoScroll(0, SCROLL_OFF);
              } /* in window */
           else
              { /* outside window */
              if(pt.y < rc.top)
                 { /* fast up */
                  autoScroll(hwnd, SB_LINEUP, SCROLL_FASTER);
                 } /* fast up */
              else
              if(pt.y > rc.bottom)
                 { /* fast down */
                  autoScroll(hwnd, SB_LINEDOWN, SCROLL_FASTER);
                 } /* fast down */
              } /* outside window */
           } /* has scroll bar */
        }
```

Listing 9.19: The autoScroll function: setting the autoscroll timer

```
#define SCROLL_OFF      0
#define SCROLL_SLOWLY   1
#define SCROLL_FASTER   2

#define SCROLL_TIMER    1  // Timer ID of scroll timer
```

```
void autoScroll(HWND hwnd, int SBcode, int timecode)
    {
    int time;
    if(timecode == SCROLL_OFF)
        { /* stop scroll */
        if(treedragger.timer != 0)
            { /* kill active timer */
            KillTimer(hwnd, treedragger.timer);
            timer = 0;
            } /* kill active timer */
        return;
        } /* stop scroll */

    treedragger.ScrollDirection = SBcode;

    if(timecode == SCROLL_SLOWLY)
        time = 250;
    else
        time = 100;

    treedragger.timer = SetTimer(hwnd, SCROLL_TIMER, time, timerProc);
    }
```

Listing 9.20: The timer callback and the onScrollRequest handler

```
#define UWM_SCROLL (WM_USER + 101)

void CALLBACK timerProc(HWND hwnd, UINT msg, UINT id, DWORD ticks)
    {
    PostMessage(hwnd, UWM_SCROLL, 0, 0);
    }

void onScrollRequest(HWND hwnd)
    {
    POINT pt;

    ImageList_DragShowNolock(FALSE); // hide image
    SendMessage(treedragger.htree, WM_VSCROLL,
                    MAKELONG(treedragger.ScrollDirection, 0),
                    (LPARAM)NULL);
    ImageList_DragShowNolock(TRUE); // show image

    GetCursorPos(&pt);
    checkAutoScroll(hwnd, pt.x, pt.y);
    }
```

Label Editing

A tree control provides a capability for "label editing". This lets the user edit the contents of the text "in place". Under older interaction styles, the user might double-click an entry and have a dialog box pop up. The new contents of the label would be typed into the dialog box and either the **OK** or the **Cancel** button would be clicked. If **OK** was clicked, the contents of the label would be updated; if **Cancel** was clicked, no change would be made.

Such interfaces are clumsy to use. A better method would be to enable direct manipulation to achieve the same effect. A tree control gives us such a method.

To enable label editing, the tree control must be created with, or later set to have, the TVS_EDITLABELS style. Like the other TVS_ styles, this can be changed at any time using the GetStyle and SetWindowLong API functions. The following function lets you change the edit-label style at any time:

```
BOOL enableEditLabels(HWND htree, BOOL enable)
{
DWORD style = GetStyle(htree);
BOOL old = (style & TVS_EDITLABELS) != 0;
if(enable)
    style |= TVS_EDITLABELS;
else
    style &= ~TVS_EDITLABELS;

SetWindowLong(htree, GWL_STYLE, style);
return old;
}
```

Of the many ways of choosing to actually initiate the editing of a label, the use of the left-mouse-double-click is the one most consistent with the GUI standards. To deal with this, you must respond to the WM_NOTIFY message with the NM_DBLCLK notification code. We already installed the code to handle this in Listing 9.8, so we concentrate here only on the code for the double-click handler.

Normally, double-clicking a tree item expands the tree. However, we want a double-click to initiate the editing of the label. This means we will need to provide some other means of doing the expansion. Hence, we must use the TVS_HASBUTTONS style if we have a true tree display (as opposed to having a simple one-level tree that lets us take advantage of all these other features). To open a top-level item, we must also specify TVS_LINESATROOT.

You may wish to limit the editing selectively. Perhaps some levels are uneditable, or some particular entries are uneditable. For your application, you get to decide the policies for editing. If you return 0 from the double-click handler, the double-click is assumed to have been unhandled by your code and the default tree control action (expand or collapse the tree) will ensue. If you return a nonzero value, you are telling the tree control that you have done something special and it should *not* take its default action. The choice is very simple. If the control is the TVS_EDITLABELS style, initiate label editing; otherwise, return 0 because nothing special has happened. Our doStartEdit handler is shown in Listing 9.21.

Listing 9.21: The tree view NM_DBLCLK handler
```
LRESULT doStartEdit(HWND hwnd, NMHDR * pNMHDR)
{
    HWND htree = pNMHDR->hwndFrom;

    if(GetStyle(htree) & TVS_EDITLABELS)
        { /* edit labels */
          HTREEITEM target = TreeView_GetSelectedItem(htree);
          if(target != NULL)   // and maybe other tests for editability...
              { /* edit its label */
                HWND editctrl = TreeView_EditLabel(htree, target);
                if(editctrl != NULL)
                    { /* subclass it */
                      WNDPROC oldptr = SubclassWindow(editctrl, editWndProc);
                      SetWindowLong(editctrl, GWL_USERDATA, (DWORD)oldptr);
```

```
            } /* subclass it */
          return editctrl != NULL;
        } /* edit its label */
      } /* edit labels */
    return 0;
}
```

You get back the handle of an edit control. This edit control can be subclassed. We show you how to do this. However, it is not necessary unless you want to do something like filter keystrokes or perform other sophisticated operations. The handlers for the subclassed edit control are very simple and are shown in Listing 9.22.

Listing 9.22: Handlers for subclassed edit control
```
static void
edit_OnDestroy(HWND hwnd)
    {
    DWORD oldproc = ::GetWindowLong(hwnd, GWL_USERDATA);
    if(oldproc != 0)
        SetWindowLong(hwnd, GWL_WNDPROC, oldproc);
    }

static LRESULT CALLBACK
editWndProc(HWND hwnd, UINT msg, WPARAM wParam, LPARAM lParam)
    {
    switch(msg)
        { /* msg */
        HANDLE_MSG(WM_DESTROY, edit_OnDestroy);
        // ... your handlers go here
        } /* msg */
    return CallWindowProc((WNDPROC)::GetWindowLong(hwnd, GWL_USERDATA),
                                      hwnd, msg, wParam, lParam);
    }.
```

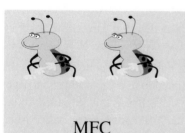

MFC

Here's a bug so bad it deserves *two* bug icons. Not only is there a bug, but the bug fix has a bug (actually, it has about five or six, depending on how you want to count, but that wouldn't leave us any space to write about it). The Control Explorer, like most of our Explorers, is written in C++ using MFC. We could not get label editing to work properly. Pressing the **Esc** key dismissed the dialog, and pressing the **Enter** key activated the default push button! This bug took a long time to track down, but ultimately, while trying to understand what was going wrong, we discovered *Knowledge Base* article Q125645. This article explains what goes wrong when you use an edit control as part of a "property page" in MFC. It also gives the code necessary for the workaround. Unfortunately, this code contains more bugs than it pretends to fix, and it doesn't even fix the problem! Perhaps by the time you read this, Microsoft will have figured out a fix, but it has persisted through two major compiler releases, and we can't be sure it even *can* be fixed because of the implications for other controls. So what we give in Listing 9.23 is our successful workaround. It lets us use edit controls—and in particular, the in-place edit controls for editing labels in tree views—in an MFC property page. You Will Not Find This Solution Anywhere Else...

Listing 9.23: Using edit controls and tree view label edit in an MFC property page
```
// This code is a substantial rewrite of the (very incorrect) code found
// in Knowledge Base Article Q125645, 17-Jan-96, titled
// FIX: Edit Control in Property Page Does Not Get Return Keys
//
BOOL CTree::PreTranslateMessage(MSG * pMsg)
{
```

```
if(pMsg->message == WM_KEYDOWN &&
    (pMsg->wParam == VK_RETURN ||
     pMsg->wParam == VK_ESCAPE))               // jmn: added ESC test
        { /* special key */
        static const TCHAR editclassname[] = _T("edit");
        // jmn: we add +1 not for the NUL, which is already accounted for
        // by the DIM size, but to guarantee that a class name like "editor"
        // is not truncated to "edit" and appear to be equal.
        TCHAR focusname[DIM(editclassname) + 1];  // jmn: DIM, not sizeof!
        HWND hFocus = ::GetFocus();
        ::GetClassName(hFocus, focusname,
                           DIM(focusname));    // jmn: DIM, not sizeof!

        if(lstrcmpi(focusname, editclassname) == 0)
            { /* edit control */
            if(::GetWindowLong(hFocus, GWL_STYLE) & ES_WANTRETURN)
                { /* ES_WANTRETURN */
                ::TranslateMessage(pMsg);           // jmn: must do this
                ::DispatchMessage(pMsg);            // here and return
                return TRUE;                        // TRUE, not FALSE
                } /* ES_WANTRETURN */
            } /* edit control */
        // It may not be an edit control, but honor the WM_GETDLGCODE status
        // that it may be issuing
        if(::SendMessage(hFocus, WM_GETDLGCODE, 0, 0) &
            (DLGC_WANTALLKEYS | DLGC_WANTCHARS | DLGC_WANTMESSAGE)) // jmn:
                                                    // added
                                                    // WANTCHARS

            { /* deal with it here */
            ::TranslateMessage(pMsg);           // jmn: must do this
            ::DispatchMessage(pMsg);            // here and return
            return TRUE;                        // TRUE, not FALSE
            } /* deal with it here */
        } /* special key */
return CPropertyPage::PreTranslateMessage(pMsg);
}
```

An important feature of the code in Listing 9.23 is that the MFC class that implements the tree control in the Control Explorer is called CTree. The PreTranslateMessage virtual function intercepts a message right after ::GetMessage has read it and before ::TranslateMessage and ::DispatchMessage are called. In the case of property pages, the class CPropertyPage, it too has overridden the PreTranslateMessage virtual method and does special processing, one feature of which is to call the PreTranslateMethod of the CPropertySheet (the container in which all those property pages appear). The CPropertySheet's PreTranslateMethod interferes with the proper handling of **Enter** and **Esc** relative to edit controls. There is no way to defeat this without defeating *all* special message processing, so we have to call ::Translate-Message and ::DispatchMessage directly here and tell the caller that we have indeed done everything required. We have not tested this solution out in all possible contexts, but it works correctly for edit controls, and the Control Explorer seems to otherwise work correctly.

Stop the Presses

We can't stop the presses. Books have rock-solid publication deadlines. But mere weeks before we went to press, Microsoft released, in beta, a new version of comct132.dll as part of the Internet Explorer 4.0

beta release. There was simply not enough time to research all the new features within the time we had left
We recommend the two excellent *Microsoft Systems Journal* articles by Strohm Armstrong, cited in "Furthe
Reading". Tree view controls now support an owner-draw ability and a partial-expansion ability, among
other new features. Keep an eye on our Web site for updated Explorers.

Tree Control Summary

Tree controls are very powerful and flexible controls. That power and flexibility comes at a certain cost in the
complexity of programming them. We have shown you a number of advanced techniques for using tree controls that you should find useful in the future.

Further Reading

Armstrong, Strohm, "Previewing the Common Controls DLL for Microsoft Internet Explorer 4.0, Part I",
Microsoft Systems Journal 11, 10 (October 1996).

Armstrong, Strohm, "Previewing the Common Controls DLL for Microsoft Internet Explorer 4.0, Part II",
Microsoft Systems Journal 11, 11 (November 1996).

> These two excellent articles cover the late-breaking release that came out in beta far too late to
> research for this book. At the time we went to press, this material was still not official product
> release, but it almost certainly will be by the time you hold this book in your hands. Keep an eye on
> our Web site for updated Explorers.

Brooks, Fred, *The Mythical Man-Month: Essays on Software Engineering*, Addison-Wesley, 1975. ISBN 0-
201-00650-2.

Brooks, Fred, *The Mythical Man-Month: Essays on Software Engineering* (anniversary edition), Addison-
Wesley, 1995. ISBN 0-201-83595-9.

> This eminently readable book should be on the must-read list of *every* software builder. Fred Brooks
> managed the IBM OS/360 effort, and if anyone has an understanding of how hard it is to build large
> software, Fred is preeminent in that area. My edition is the 1975 edition, but it was recently re-
> issued in an updated "anniversary" edition. The famous quote about "Plan to throw one away; you
> will anyway" is one of the most-quoted and least-understood lines of the legacy of this book. When
> you read the chapter that contains this quote, you will see that he is saying something quite different
> than the popular interpretation, and far more important. See the "flame" inset on page 685. This
> book outlines almost all the critical basic principles of software design and management. *–jmn*

Microsoft Corporation, *The Windows Interface Guidelines for Software Design*, Microsoft Press, 1995.
ISBN 1-55615-679-0.

> A must-have, must-read book. See the review on page 151.

Newcomer, Joseph M., "Profiling for Performance", *Dr. Dobb's Journal* 18, 1 (January 1993), pp. 80-87, 106.

> This article covers some of the more subtle points of performance measurement. I also recommend
> any good undergraduate physics lab technique manual. I started doing performance measurement in
> 1969, and brought my then-recent expertise of physics lab technique to bear on the subject. *–jmn*

O'Donnell, Sandra Martin, *Programming for the World: A Guide to Internationalization*, Prentice-Hall, 1994.

A critical book if you're planning an international application. See the review on page 942.

Richter, Jeffrey, *Windows Q&A*, in *Microsoft Systems Journal,* February 1995. Also published on the MSDN CD-ROM.

This article points out some undocumented facets of how timers work, particularly the quantization of WM_TIMER messages.

C h a p t e r

10 Using Controls: Scroll Bar, Trackbar, Up/Down, and Progress Classes

There are several controls that provide a "continuous" input or output mechanism to the user. These controls are used to provide a way of translating "sliding" values between the user interface and the program. The SCROLLBAR class implements a window that has the same appearance as the standard scroll bars that appear on the edges of a window when the WS_HSCROLL or WS_VSCROLL styles are specified.

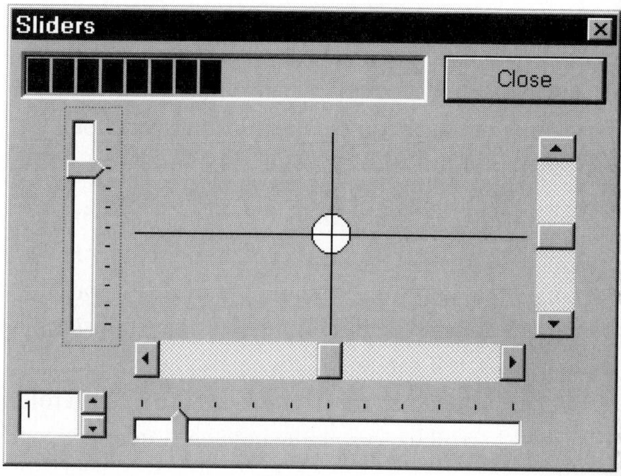

A special case of the SCROLLBAR class we describe, the "sizing box", behaves totally unlike any other control you will see. It is sufficiently odd that we thought we should take time to explain it.

The trackbar controls, also known as "slider

Figure 10.1: Sliding controls

controls", work very much like scroll bars, but have a more "modern" look, more like a high-tech volume control on an audio mixer console. They support actual calibration marks and an overall nicer appearance. A slider control also is "self-maintaining", a feature that makes them easier to use than scroll bars.

The up/down control, sometimes called a "spin" control, allows you to adjust a value by small amounts quickly. A spin control is most often associated with an edit control, so you can either enter a value directly or "nudge" it with the up/down control.

The progress bar control is included here because it is a "sliding" control; it is an output-only control. This type of control is used to show a percentage-of-completion for some task. This is an important user feedback mechanism.

A sample of all of these controls is in Figure 10.1, one of the demonstrations found within the Control Explorer application.

The SCROLLBAR Class

Scroll bar *controls* are different from the *standard scroll bars* discussed in Chapter 4, page 177. Scroll bar controls and standard scroll bars work very similarly, but sometimes it's necessary to distinguish between them.

You create standard scroll bars by including the WS_HSCROLL or WS_VSCROLL window styles when you create a window. A standard scroll bar is not within the client area of the window and lies on the right or bottom edge of the window. A standard scroll bar is not an actual control but rather is a piece of the nonclient area that Windows paints to look exactly like a scroll bar control. Although it appears to behave just like a scroll bar control, it is in fact a simulation of one. This is not a situation the ordinary user can detect.

A scroll bar *control* is a child window just like the other controls we have discussed. Unlike a standard scroll bar, which must appear on either the right edge or bottom edge of a window, you can place a scroll bar control anywhere in the client area of its parent window. You create a scroll bar control by creating a child window based on the predefined window class SCROLLBAR and including one of the two scroll bar class styles, SBS_VERT (for a vertical scroll bar) or SBS_HORZ (for a horizontal scroll bar).

You can create a scroll bar control with any desired size, unlike a window scroll bar. Often, though, you'll want to create a scroll bar control in the standard Windows size. You can retrieve the appropriate scroll bar system metric and size the scroll bar control appropriately. For example, the following code creates a scroll bar control that looks like a horizontal standard scroll bar. It has the standard scroll bar height for a horizontal window scroll bar, and it lies across the bottom of the client area of its parent. Despite the similarities to a standard scroll bar, it is a scroll bar control. The scroll bar control is actually in the client area of the parent. A standard scroll bar lies in the nonclient area of a window.

```
int Height ;
RECT rect ;

GetClientRect (hwnd, &rect) ;
Height = GetSystemMetrics (SM_CYHSCROLL) ;
hScrollBar = CreateWindow (
    _T("scrollbar"), NULL,
    WS_CHILD | WS_VISIBLE | SBS_HORZ,
    0, rect.bottom - Height, rect.right, Height,
    hwnd, IDC_SCROLLBAR, hInstance, NULL) ;
```

If you want to create a "window" that appears to look like a window with standard scroll bars, but which actually uses scroll bar controls, perhaps the easiest way is to create *four* windows. One window represents what you want the user to think of as "the window." It will probably have a caption; the usual system menu;

minimize, maximize, and close buttons; and the like. In its client area, you create three other windows that have the first window as a parent: two scroll bar controls and another window that is the "logical client" area. Responding to a WM_SIZE message becomes a bit more complex. You have to resize all three of the child windows to keep up the illusion of a single logical window, but this is merely tedious, not subtle.

Because standard scroll bars are standard sizes, you have to use the technique just described if you are trying to create a window for a touch-screen or other so-called "kiosk" application, where you want to have scroll bars that are large enough to touch with a low-resolution device (a finger on a touch screen). Standard scroll bars cannot be resized for such purposes.

The SCROLLBAR Class Styles

One set of styles determines the type of scroll bar control to create: a horizontal scroll bar (SBS_HORZ), a vertical scroll bar (SBS_VERT), a size box (SBS_SIZEBOX), or a size grip (SBS_SIZEGRIP). You use the other styles to control the size and placement of the scroll bar or size box. Table 10.1 lists the SCROLLBAR class styles.

Table 10.1: SCROLLBAR class styles

Style	Meaning
SBS_BOTTOMALIGN	Creates a horizontal scroll bar control with the system scroll bar height. Aligns the bottom edge of the scroll bar with the bottom edge of the rectangle specified in the CreateWindow call. Must be used with the SBS_HORZ style.
SBS_HORZ	Creates a horizontal scroll bar control.
SBS_LEFTALIGN	Creates a vertical scroll bar control with the system scroll bar width. Aligns the left edge of the scroll bar with the left edge of the rectangle specified in the CreateWindow call. Must be used with the SBS_VERT style.
SBS_RIGHTALIGN	Creates a vertical scroll bar control with the system scroll bar width. Aligns the right edge of the scroll bar with the right edge of the rectangle specified in the CreateWindow call. Must be used with the SBS_VERT style.
SBS_SIZEBOX	Creates a size box of the size specified in the CreateWindow call.
SBS_SIZEBOXBOTTOMRIGHTALIGN	Creates a size box with the system size box width and height. Aligns the lower-right corner of the size box with the lower-right corner of the rectangle specified in the CreateWindow call. Must be used with the SBS_SIZEBOX or SBS_SIZEGRIP styles.
SBS_SIZEBOXTOPLEFTALIGN	Creates a size box with the system size box width and height. Aligns the upper-left corner of the size box with the upper-left corner of the rectangle specified in the CreateWindow call. Must be used with the SBS_SIZEBOX style.

Table 10.1: SCROLLBAR class styles

Style	Meaning
SBS_SIZEGRIP	The same as SBS_SIZEBOX, but with a raised edge. *The previous sentence is the "official" documentation. However, it appears to be incorrect; see our bug note on page 713.*
SBS_TOPALIGN	Creates a horizontal scroll bar control with the system scroll bar height. Aligns the top edge of the scroll bar with the top edge of the rectangle specified in the CreateWindow call. Must be used with the SBS_HORZ style.
SBS_VERT	Creates a vertical scroll bar of the size specified in the CreateWindow call.

You can use the various alignment flags to quickly and easily create standard-sized scroll bars aligned to any edge of the scroll bar control's parent window. For example, the following code creates the same scroll bar as the previous example, but with a little less effort:

```
RECT rect ;

GetClientRect (hwnd, &rect) ;
hScrollBar = CreateWindow (
    _T("scrollbar"), NULL,
    WS_CHILD | WS_VISIBLE | SBS_HORZ | SBS_BOTTOMALIGN,
    0, 0, rect.right, rect.bottom,
    hwnd, IDC_SCROLLBAR, hInstance, NULL) ;
```

The SBS_SIZEBOX and SBS_SIZEGRIP scroll bar class styles create a small gray size box. The SBS_SIZEGRIP style creates it with a raised-edge appearance. Pressing and holding the left mouse button over such a control begins a resize operation on the control's parent window. For example, creating an SBS_SIZEBOX or SBS_SIZEGRIP style control with the SBS_SIZEBOXBOTTOMRIGHTALIGN style creates a sizing control that works identically to grabbing and dragging the lower-right corner of a sizing frame around the parent window. This is discussed in more detail on page 712.

According to at least one article, in some implementations of Win32 the SBS_SIZEBOXBOTTOMRIGHTALIGN style has a bug: According to the article on the MSDN CD-ROM entitled "Scroll Bar Controls in Win32", the positioning of the size box is off by 3 pixels in both directions. The workaround for this problem is to add 3 pixels to the xWidth and yHeight parameters specified in the CreateWindow call. Exactly how one copes with this if Microsoft should fix the bug (assuming it is not declared as a "feature" and made permanent) is left unstated.

Messages to a Scroll Bar Control

You can modify the internal values of a scroll bar by sending it messages or by calling API functions. Table 10.2 lists the scroll bar messages and their API functions. Historically, some of these functions are actual API functions, implemented as part of Windows (earlier versions of Windows did not support the full set of SBM_ messages shown here). The ScrollBar_ functions are windowsx.h macros that "wrap" the Send-Message function.

Table 10.2: Messages understood by a scroll bar control

Message	Function Description
SBM_ENABLE_ARROWS	BOOL ScrollBar_Enable(HWND hwnd, UINT flags)[x]
	Enables the scroll bar arrows. Uses one of the ESB_ codes from Table 10.4.
SBM_GETPOS	int ScrollBar_GetPos(HWND hwnd)[x]
	Returns the current scroll box position.
–	int GetScrollPos(HWND hwnd, int sbar) *(This function is considered obsolete in Win32; use* SetScrollInfo.*)*
SBM_GETRANGE	BOOL ScrollBar_GetRange[x](HWND hwnd, LPINT minpos, LPINT maxpos)
	Gets the current range set for the scroll bar control.
–	BOOL GetScrollRange(HWND hwnd, int sbar, LPINT min, LPINT max) *(This function is considered obsolete in Win32; use* SetScrollInfo.*)*
SBM_GETSCROLLINFO	BOOL GetScrollInfo(HWND hwnd, int sbar,[1] LPSCROLLINFO scrollinfo)
	Obtains the scroll position, scroll range, tracking position, or page distance.
SBM_SETPOS	int ScrollBar_SetPos(HWND hwnd, int pos, BOOL redraw)[x]
	Sets the current scroll box position.
–	int SetScrollPos(HWND hwnd, int sbar, int pos, BOOL redraw) *(This function is considered obsolete in Win32; use* SetScrollInfo.*)*
SBM_SETRANGE	BOOL ScrollBar_SetRange(HWND hwnd, int minpos, int maxpos, BOOL redraw)[x] // with redraw parameter FALSE
	Sets the range of the scroll bar control but does not redraw it.
–	BOOL SetScrollRange(HWND hwnd, int sbar, int min, int max, BOOL redraw) *(This function is considered obsolete in Win32; use* SetScrollInfo.*)*
SBM_SETRANGEREDRAW	BOOL ScrollBar_SetRange(HWND hwnd, int minpos, int maxpos, BOOL redraw)[x] // with redraw parameter TRUE
	Sets the range of the scroll bar control and redraws it.

[x]These are defined in `windowsx.h`.

[1]For this value, use SB_CTL for a scroll bar control.

Table 10.2: Messages understood by a scroll bar control

Message	Function Description
SBM_SETSCROLLINFO	`int SetScrollInfo(HWND hwnd, int sbar,`[1] `LPSCROLLINFO scrollinfo, BOOL redraw)`
	Takes a SCROLLINFO structure that is used to set information.
WM_ENABLE	`BOOL EnableWindow(HWND hwnd, BOOL enable)`
	Enables or disables the scroll bar.
WM_SHOWWINDOW	`BOOL ScrollBar_Show(HWND hwnd, UINT mode)`[x]
	Shows or hides the scroll bar. The mode parameter is one of following:
	SW_HIDE Hides the window.
	SW_SHOW Shows the window.

[x]These are defined in `windowsx.h`.
[1]For this value, use SB_CTL for a scroll bar control.

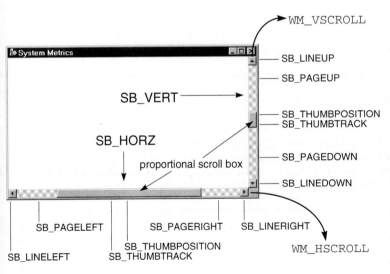

Figure 10.2: Scroll bar notifications and how they are generated

A scroll bar represents a range of values. These values can represent anything that is convenient to your application. When the user drags the *scroll box* (formerly called "the thumb box"), the scroll bar sends messages to its parent window. These messages continually keep the parent window informed of the position of the scroll box within the control's range of values. When the user clicks the mouse above or below the scroll box or in the arrows at the end of the scroll bar, the scroll bar sends messages to its parent window. These are illustrated in Figure 10.2 and discussed in detail starting on page 711. In addition to responding to mouse events, a scroll bar control will respond to keyboard events when it has the focus. We summarize these actions in Table 10.5 on page 711.

Setting Scroll Bar Parameters

Your application must set the scrolling range of a scroll bar control. You also must adjust the scroll box position of a scroll bar each time the user drags and releases it. Basically, a scroll bar control operates the same as do the standard scroll bars we explain in Chapter 4, page 177.

You use slightly different parameters to the scroll bar functions when you use them on a scroll bar control. For the standard scroll bars, you specify the handle of the window and one of SB_VERT or SB_HORZ to indicate which of the scroll bars you are going to affect. When you are dealing with a scroll bar control, you specify the handle of the control itself and give the value SB_CTL to indicate that you are working directly on a scroll bar control.

You call the SetScrollInfo function to set the range of values for a scroll bar almost like you do for a standard scroll bar. This sends an SBM_SETSCROLLINFO message to the scroll bar, whose lParam value is a pointer to a SCROLLINFO structure.

```
typedef struct tagSCROLLINFO {
    UINT cbSize ;        // size of this structure, in bytes
    UINT fMask ;         // flags of what to set or get
    int  nMin ;          // minimum scrolling position
    int  nMax ;          // maximum scrolling position
    UINT nPage ;         // page size (scroll box size control)
    int  nPos ;          // current position of scroll box
    int  nTrackPos ;     // immediate position during drag
} SCROLLINFO;
```

The fMask parameter represents one or more of the flags from Table 10.3. To set a value, you must set its corresponding flag and set the value in the structure. To get a value, you must set its corresponding flag. After the call, only those fields whose flag was set are modified. Note that SIF_DISABLENOSCROLL applies only to SetScrollInfo and SIF_TRACKPOS applies only to GetScrollInfo.

Table 10.3: SCROLLINFO flag values

Bit Mask Name	Meaning
SIF_ALL	SIF_PAGE | SIF_POS | SIF_RANGE | SIF_TRACKPOS
SIF_DISABLENOSCROLL	Only for SetScrollInfo. If the parameter values make the scroll bar unnecessary, disable the scroll bar instead of removing it.
SIF_PAGE	The nPage member gets or sets the page size for the proportional scroll box.
SIF_POS	The nPos member contains the scroll box position.
SIF_RANGE	The nMin and nMax members contain the parameters defining the scroll range.
SIF_TRACKPOS	The nTrackpos member contains the current 32-bit tracking position (ignored for SetScrollInfo).

For example, to set the range of a scroll bar control to the values 1 through 100, you can use

```
SCROLLINFO si;
si.cbSize = sizeof(si) ;
si.nMin = 1 ;
si.nMax = 100 ;
si.fMask = SIF_RANGE ;
SetScrollInfo (hScrollBar, SB_CTL, &si, TRUE) ;
```

The first parameter specifies the window handle of the scroll bar control. The SB_CTL value as the second parameter identifies the window handle as the handle of a scroll bar control rather than the handle of a standard scroll bar. The third parameter is a pointer to the SCROLLINFO structure. The final parameter indicates whether Windows should redraw the scroll bar.

Retrieving Scroll Bar Parameters

The GetScrollInfo function will retrieve scroll bar parameters. You must initialize the cbSize member and set the fMask to indicate which values you wish to retrieve. The members of the SCROLLINFO structure that are selected by the fMask will be modified; the rest will remain unchanged.

The GetScrollInfo function returns FALSE if the sbar parameter is SB_HORZ or SB_VERT and the corresponding scroll bar is not being displayed. In this case, none of the values specified by the fMask member is modified. You must check the return value.

To avoid the previous pitfall, you must handle the case in which the standard window scroll bars might not be displayed. Here is a sample of code that guarantees that the position value will be valid (and perhaps even correct) after a GetScrollInfo call:

```
SCROLLINFO si;
si.cbSize = sizeof(SCROLLINFO) ;
si.fMask = SIF_POS;
if(!GetScrollInfo(hwnd, SB_VERT, &si))
    si.nPos = 0;   // since scroll bar hidden, assume not needed and
                   // we are showing the entire contents, so logically
                   // we are at the start of the scroll range
// ... si.nPos is now valid even if the scroll bar was hidden
```

Enabling Scroll Bar Arrows

The SBM_ENABLE_ARROWS message will selectively enable the arrows at each end of the scroll bar. For example, you might indicate that the scroll bar is at the beginning of its range or that you do not permit reverse scrolling. You do this by disabling the top or left arrow, respectively, using the following:

```
SendMessage(hScrollBar, SBM_ENABLE_ARROWS, flags, 0);
```

or alternatively

```
ScrollBar_Enable (hScrollBar, flags) ;
```

where flags is one of the values from Table 10.4.

Table 10.4: ScrollBar_Enable values

Name	Meaning
ESB_ENABLE_BOTH	Enables both arrows of a scroll bar.
ESB_DISABLE_LTUP	Disables the left arrow of a horizontal scroll bar or the up arrow of a vertical scroll bar.
ESB_DISABLE_RTDN	Disables the right arrow of a horizontal scroll bar or the down arrow of a vertical scroll bar.
ESB_DISABLE_BOTH	Disables both arrows of a scroll bar.

Scroll Bar Notifications

Unlike most other controls, a scroll bar control does not send a WM_COMMAND message with a notification code. Instead, it sends a WM_HSCROLL or WM_VSCROLL message just like a standard scroll bar. You can tell the difference between a WM_HSCROLL or WM_VSCROLL message from a standard scroll bar and one from a scroll bar control by the lParam parameter of the message, the value that comes in as the hctl parameter to the message handler. This value is the window handle of the scroll bar control when the message is from a scroll bar control. It is NULL when the message is from a standard scroll bar. This means the parent window will receive a WM_HSCROLL or WM_VSCROLL message with one of the notification codes shown in Figure 10.2 or, for keyboard messages, one of the notification codes shown in Table 10.5. In addition, whenever the scrolling action stops, the parent window will receive a message with the notification SB_ENDSCROLL. If the user drags the scroll box, a sequence of SB_THUMBTRACK notifications will be sent. When the scroll box is released by the release of the mouse button, an SB_THUMBPOSITION notification will be sent.

Table 10.5: Notifications from a scroll bar control as a result of keystrokes

Key	OnHScroll or OnVscroll sbcode Value
PageUp	SB_PAGEUP
PageDown	SB_PAGEDOWN
← or ↑	SB_LINELEFT/SB_LINEUP
→ or ↓	SB_LINERIGHT/SB_LINEDOWN
Home	SB_TOP
End	SB_BOTTOM

The special variants of the scroll bar class, the SBS_SIZEBOX and SBS_SIZEGRIP style controls, do not send a WM_COMMAND, WM_HSCROLL, or WM_VSCROLL message. Instead, these controls directly resize the parent window, thereby causing the parent window to receive WM_SIZE messages, a topic we discuss further on page 712.

WM_HSCROLL, WM_VSCROLL **Message Cracker Handlers–Scroll Bars**

```
void cls_OnHScroll(HWND hwnd, HWND hctl, UINT code, int pos);
```

```
void cls_OnVScroll(HWND hwnd, HWND hctl, UINT code, int pos);
```

	wParam		lParam		
Parameter	**lo**	**hi**	**lo**	**hi**	**Meaning**
hwnd					Window handle of the parent window.
hctl			■	■	Window handle of the scroll bar control (0 for standard scroll bars).
code	■				SB_ code.
pos		■			Position for SB_THUMBTRACK and SB_THUMBPOSITION.

Keyboard Notifications

A scroll bar control can process keystrokes when it has the input focus. Table 10.5 lists the associated LOWORD(wParam) values in a WM_HSCROLL or WM_VSCROLL message generated by keyboard input.

The messages have the same meaning for a scroll bar control as they do for a standard scroll bar. The SB_TOP, SB_LEFT, SB_BOTTOM, and SB_TOP scroll bar notifications are produced by scroll bar controls only, not by standard scroll bars. They scroll to the top or bottom of a vertical scroll bar or to the left or right of a horizontal control bar. (There are actually only two values, which might more properly have been called "upper limit" and "lower limit". However, they were named for the scroll bar orientation, so it is easier to remember SB_LEFT than the fact that the left of a horizontal scroll bar is designated the "top".) A scroll bar control must have the WS_TABSTOP window style set in order to receive the input focus when it's clicked with the mouse. If the user holds a key down and it begins to auto-repeat, it will send a sequence of notifications. When a key is released, you will receive an SB_ENDSCROLL notification.

Using the Size Box

Figure 10.3: A size grip control

There are two special variations of a scroll bar. These are selected by the SBS_SIZEBOX and SBS_SIZEGRIP style flags. The SBS_SIZEGRIP control for Windows 95 is illustrated in Figure 10.3 (we don't bother to show an SBS_SIZEBOX control because it is simply a boring gray rectangle).

The size box and size grip controls are a bit unusual in how they operate and are generally not well-documented. The size controls do not operate like other scroll bars. They work by actually resizing the parent window, thus resulting in Windows's sending WM_SIZE messages to the parent window. Hence, clicking a size control and dragging the mouse generates a series of window size operations, much like clicking and dragging on a sizing frame does. What makes these controls even stranger is that they do not work at all like you would expect if you create one in the top-left corner of a window. You might expect in this case that the control would act by dragging along the top-left corner, making the window shrink or grow at the top or left and leaving the bottom and right anchored in position. It does not. It acts the same way whether you create it in the top-left corner or the bottom-right corner: It drags around the bottom-right corner. You can even create it without either of the SBS_SIZEBOXTOPLEFTALIGN or SBS_SIZEBOXBOTTOMRIGHTALIGN styles, in which case it will be created with a size based on the rectangle specified. So you are likely to find this control "intuitively obvious" for your users only when it is anchored at the bottom-right of its parent window. You can experiment with all of these effects using the Control Explorer application. Note that in the Explorer we also use the WM_GETMINMAXINFO message to limit the window size, particularly in the case in which the control has neither alignment specified. An important observation is that the OnSize handler has responsibility for seeing that the control moves in sync with the window. You have to compute a position from the bottom-right corner of the window and move the size box there yourself, as shown in Listing 10.1. Note also that you must force the area that is about to be uncovered to repaint or you will get little bits of the size box left behind on the screen.

All available documentation claims that a size grip, SBS_SIZEGRIP, is "just like" a size box, SBS_SIZEBOX. Using the Control Explorer, we have determined that this is simply not true. We have done a number of experiments and could not get the SBS_SIZEGRIP style to work as documented. In particular, all of our experience has shown that WM_SIZE messages are sent to the SBS_SIZEGRIP control, not to its parent. You can try the same experiments and see the same effects by using Spy++.

Listing 10.1: Managing the size box

```
static void OnSize(HWND hwnd, UINT nType, int cx, int cy)
{
    RECT r;     // size box window rectangle
    RECT inv;   // invalid rectangle
    HWND sb = GetDlgItem(hwnd, IDC_SCROLLBAR);
    int fudge = 3;   // compensate for 3-pixel bug

    // This code depends upon the fact that our scroll bar
    // has a known ID.  We don't actually know if it has
    // generated the WM_SIZE message, but no matter how we
    // get resized we have to keep it visible

    // This code only handles bottom right alignment.
    // If you care, see the Control Explorer source for
    // the fully general case

    GetWindowRect(sb, &r);
    if(is95())
        fudge = 0;   // apparently only Win95 doesn't have the 3-pixel bug

    // invalidate the parent window area that is being uncovered.
    inv = r;
    ScreenToClient(hwnd, (LPPOINT)&inv.left);
    ScreenToClient(hwnd, (LPPOINT)&inv.right);
    InflateRect(&inv, fudge, fudge);
    InvalidateRect(hwnd, &inv);
```

```
MoveWindow(sb, cx - r.right - r.left + fudge,
               cy - r.bottom - r.top + fudge,
               r.right - r.left,
               r.bottom - r.top, TRUE);
}
```

The Trackbar Control

The trackbar control (official class name, `msctls_trackbar`) works in a fashion very much like a scroll bar, except that it is "self-maintaining", that is, you don't have to do the elaborate computations to set its value and maintain it. Hence, unlike the example on page 215, you don't have to do an explicit setting of the trackbar position in response to every WM_HSCROLL or WM_VSCROLL message.

You create a trackbar control using the special name TRACKBAR_CLASS in the CreateWindow(Ex) call. You can use the styles from Table 10.6, but obviously some are in conflict with others. For example, it is worth noting that the value TBS_BOTH is a completely separate value from the result of combining TBS_TOP | TBS_BOTTOM or TBS_LEFT | TBS_RIGHT. When a trackbar control is created, it has a set of default values that are shown in Table 10.10 on page 723.

```
HWND hTrackbar = CreateWindow(TRACKBAR_CLASS,        // class name
                      NULL,                           // window caption
                      WS_CHILD | WS_VISIBLE |
                      TBS_HORZ | TBS_AUTOTICKS,        // styles
                      0,                              // left
                      rect.bottom - Height,           // top
                      rect.right,                     // width
                      Height,                         // height
                      hwnd,                           // parent
                      (HMENU)IDC_TRACKBAR,            // child ID
                      hInstance,                      // instance handle
                      NULL) ;                         // parameters
```

A sampler of trackbar controls created with various styles is shown in Table 10.7.

Table 10.6: Trackbar class styles

Style	Meaning
TBS_AUTOTICKS	Creates a control that provides for a tick mark for each position of the control or some integer multiple of the positions (see UDM_SETTICKFREQ).
TBS_BOTH	Causes the tick marks to be displayed on both sides of the control (regardless of orientation, vertical or horizontal).
TBS_BOTTOM	Causes the tick marks to be displayed on the bottom of the control. The same value as TBS_RIGHT, but used for horizontal trackbars.
TBS_ENABLESELRANGE	When specified at creation time, allows a range of values to be specified. The endpoints of the range are indicated by small triangles in the tick mark position.

Table 10.6: Trackbar class styles

Style	Meaning
TBS_FIXEDLENGTH	When TBS_ENABLESELRANGE is specified, causes the thumb box to change size based on the selection range. If the TBS_FIXEDLENGTH style is specified, the thumb box size does not change with the selection range. *As far as we can determine, there is no variable-width thumb box and this style does nothing.*
TBS_HORZ	Causes the track bar to be oriented with the thumb box moving in a horizontal direction.
TBS_LEFT	Causes the tick marks to be displayed on the left of the control. The same value as TBS_TOP, but used for vertical trackbars.
TBS_NOTHUMB	Causes the trackbar control to not have a thumb box.
TBS_NOTICKS	Creates a trackbar that has no tick marks.
TBS_RIGHT	Causes the tick marks to be displayed on the right of the control. The same value as TBS_BOTTOM, but used for vertical trackbars.
TBS_TOP	Causes the tick marks to be displayed on the top of the control. The same value as TBS_LEFT, but used for horizontal trackbars.
TBS_VERT	The track bar will be oriented with the thumb box moving in a vertical direction.

Table 10.7: Some selected trackbar control styles

Tick Marks									
TBS_AUTOTICKS	TBS_NOTICKS	TBS_BOTH	TBS_TOP	TBS_BOTTOM	TBS_ENABLESELRANGE	TBS_NOTHUMB	WS_BORDER	TBS_HORZ	
✓			✓					✓	
✓				✓				✓	

Table 10.7: Some selected trackbar control styles

| TBS_AUTOTICKS | Tick Marks | | | | TBS_ENABLESELRANGE | TBS_NOTHUMB | WS_BORDER | TBS_HORZ | |
	TBS_NOTICKS	TBS_BOTH	TBS_TOP	TBS_BOTTOM					
✓		✓						✓	
✓		✓			✓			✓	
	✓		✓					✓	
		✓						✓	
		✓				✓		✓	
✓				✓			✓	✓	

Using Trackbars

Trackbars work very much like scroll bars. The user can "grab" the slider with the mouse and drag it around. The user also can click in the area to the left or right of the slider and cause it to move by a "page" distance. One difference between scroll bars and trackbars is that a trackbar does not have a mouse "line" advance.

Like a scroll bar, a trackbar sends WM_HSCROLL and WM_VSCROLL messages to its parent. These encode information about the state of the trackbar. The message handlers look almost identical to the message handlers for scroll bars.

WM_HSCROLL, WM_VSCROLL Message Cracker Handlers–Trackbars

```
void cls_OnHScroll(HWND hwnd, HWND hctl, UINT code, int pos);
```

```
void cls_OnVScroll(HWND hwnd, HWND hctl, UINT code, int pos);
```

Parameter	wParam lo	wParam hi	lParam lo	lParam hi	Meaning
hwnd					Window handle of the parent window.
hctl			■	■	Window handle of the trackbar control.
code	■				TB_ code.
pos		■			Position for TB_THUMBTRACK and TB_THUMBPOSITION.

As with a scroll bar, only the low-order 16 bits of the trackbar value are provided in the pos parameter during a tracking operation. If you are using a trackbar with a range larger than 16 bits, you will have to send an explicit TBM_GETPOS message (Trackbar_GetPos function) to the control to retrieve the 32-bit value. The notification codes that can be sent by a trackbar are shown in Table 10.8 and illustrated in Figure 10.4.

Table 10.8: Trackbar notification codes in an WM_HSCROLL or WM_VSCROLL message

User Action	Notification Code in WM_HSCROLL or WM_VSCROLL
Clicks the mouse to the left of the slider of the horizontal trackbar.	TB_PAGEUP (TB_PAGELEFT[1])
Clicks the mouse above the slider of the vertical trackbar.	TB_PAGEUP
Clicks the mouse to the right of the slider of the horizontal trackbar.	TB_PAGEDOWN (TB_PAGERIGHT[1])
Clicks the mouse below the slider of a vertical trackbar.	TB_PAGEDOWN
Clicks the mouse on the slider and drags it.	TB_THUMBTRACK
Releases the mouse button.	TB_THUMBPOSITION, followed by TB_ENDTRACK
Presses the **Home** key.	TB_TOP (TB_LEFT[1])
Presses the **End** key.	TB_BOTTOM (TB_RIGHT[1])

[1]The name is not part of the base commctrl.h definitions but has been defined for your convenience in the extensions.h file included on the CD-ROM.

Table 10.8: Trackbar notification codes in an WM_HSCROLL or WM_VSCROLL message

User Action	Notification Code in WM_HSCROLL or WM_VSCROLL
Presses the → key.	TB_LINEDOWN (TB_LINERIGHT[1])
Presses the ↑ key.	TB_LINEUP (TB_LINELEFT[1])
Presses the ↓ key.	TB_LINEDOWN (TB_LINERIGHT[1])
Presses the ← key.	TB_LINEUP (TB_LINELEFT[1])
Presses the **PageDown** key.	TB_PAGEDOWN (TB_PAGERIGHT[1])
Presses the **PageUp** key.	TB_PAGEUP (TB_PAGELEFT[1])
Releases key.	TB_ENDTRACK

[1]The name is not part of the base commctrl.h definitions but has been defined for your convenience in the extensions.h file included on the CD-ROM.

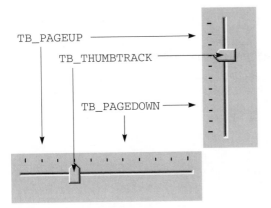

TB_PAGEUP

TB_THUMBTRACK

TB_PAGEDOWN

Figure 10.4: Trackbar messages and their sources

What you need to be aware of here is the nature of these messages and their order. If the user holds the mouse down in the "page" area to the left or right of the slider, a sequence of messages with the notification appropriate for that area will be sent. When the user releases the mouse button, the TB_ENDTRACK notification will be sent. The same sequence happens when the user clicks the slider and drags it. The TB_ENDTRACK notification indicates that the slider has been released.

The trackbar controls have a built-in keyboard interface that works very much like the one for scroll bar controls (see page 712). When a key is held down and goes into its auto-repeat mode, a sequence of notifications is sent. When the key is released, a TB_ENDTRACK message is sent.

Trackbar Messages

Once you have created a trackbar control, you can set its range and position using the messages or the API equivalent functions we have defined in extensions.h (on the CD-ROM that accompanies this book). These messages and functions are described in Table 10.9.

Table 10.9: Messages that can be sent to a trackbar control

Message	Function[1] Meaning
TBM_CLEARSEL	`void Trackbar_ClearSel (HWND hwnd, BOOL redraw)`
	Clears the current selection in the trackbar.
TBM_CLEARTICS[2]	`void Trackbar_ClearTicks (HWND hwnd, BOOL redraw)`
	Clears the tick mark array.
TBM_GETCHANNELRECT	`void Trackbar_GetChannelRect (HWND hwnd, LPRECT rc)`
	Retrieves the bounding rectangle for the trackbar's *channel*, the area over which the slider moves. This also contains the highlight when there is a selection.
TBM_GETLINESIZE	`int Trackbar_GetLineSize (HWND hwnd)`
	A 32-bit value that specifies the amount to move the slider on a `TB_LINEUP` (or `TB_LINELEFT`[3]) or `TB_LINEDOWN` (or `TB_LINERIGHT`[3]) notification message.
TBM_GETNUMTICS[2]	`int Trackbar_GetNumTicks (HWND hwnd)`
	Returns a count of the number of tick marks in the control.
TBM_GETPAGESIZE	`int Trackbar_GetPageSize (HWND hwnd)`
	A 32-bit value that specifies the amount to move the slider on a `TB_PAGEUP` (`TB_PAGELEFT`[3]) or `TB_PAGEDOWN` (`TB_PAGERIGHT`[3]) notification.
TBM_GETPOS	`int Trackbar_GetPos (HWND hwnd)`
	Returns the current 32-bit position value of the slider.
TBM_GETPTICS[2]	`LPINT Trackbar_GetPTicks (HWND hwnd)`
	Returns a pointer to the tick mark array.
TBM_GETRANGEMAX	`int Trackbar_GetRangeMax (HWND hwnd)`
	Returns the 32-bit upper bound of the slider range.
TBM_GETRANGEMIN	`int Trackbar_GetRangeMin (HWND hwnd)`
	Returns the 32-bit lower bound of the slider range.

[1]The macro forms are defined in the file `extensions.h`, which is on the CD-ROM that accompanies this book.

[2]Microsoft is inconsistent in the naming. Compare the style flags that are spelled "TICKS" with the messages that are spelled "TICS". We have decided, in our naming of the macros, to use the correct spelling of the word.

[3]Symbols not defined by Microsoft but defined in `extensions.h`.

Table 10.9: Messages that can be sent to a trackbar control

Message	Function[1] Meaning
TBM_GETSELEND	`int Trackbar_GetSelEnd (HWND hwnd)`
	Returns the upper limit of the selection. If the trackbar doesn't have the TBS_ENABLESELRANGE style, this message returns a 0.
TBM_GETSELSTART	`int Trackbar_GetSelStart (HWND hwnd)`
	Returns the lower limit of the selection. If the trackbar doesn't have the TBS_ENABLESELRANGE style, this message returns 0.
TBM_GETTHUMBLENGTH	`int Trackbar_GetThumbLength (HWND hwnd)`
	Returns the length of the slider, measured along the track direction (that is, the height of the thumb on a vertical control or the width of the thumb on a horizontal control).
TBM_GETTHUMBRECT	`void Trackbar_GetThumbRect (HWND hwnd, LPRECT rc)`
	Causes the `rc` structure to be filled in with the bounding rectangle of the thumb.
TBM_GETTIC[2]	`int Trackbar_GetTick (HWND hwnd, WORD index)`
	Given the index of a tick mark, returns its position (measured in units along the scale from the minimum to the maximum of the range) or -1 if the `index` value does not specify a valid tick index.
TBM_GETTICPOS[2]	`int Trackbar_GetTickPos (HWND hwnd, WORD index)`
	Returns the tick position of the tick or –1 if the `index` parameter is not a valid tick mark index. The distance in client coordinates of the trackbar control in the direction of the slider movement.
TBM_SETLINESIZE	`int Trackbar_SetLineSize (HWND hwnd, int size)`
	Sets the line size used when processing a TB_LINEUP (or TB_LINELEFT[3]) or TB_LINEDOWN (or TB_LINERIGHT[3]) notification message. The return value is the previous line size setting.
TBM_SETPAGESIZE	`int Trackbar_SetPageSize (HWND hwnd, int size)`
	Sets the page size used when processing a TB_PAGEUP (or TB_PAGELEFT[3]) or TB_PAGEDOWN (or TB_PAGERIGHT[3]) notification message. The return value is the previous page size setting.

[1]The macro forms are defined in the file extensions.h, which is on the CD-ROM that accompanies this book.

[2]Microsoft is inconsistent in the naming. Compare the style flags that are spelled "TICKS" with the messages that are spelled "TICS". We have decided, in our naming of the macros, to use the correct spelling of the word.

[3]Symbols not defined by Microsoft but defined in extensions.h.

Table 10.9: Messages that can be sent to a trackbar control

Message	Function[1] Meaning
TBM_SETPOS	`void Trackbar_SetPos (HWND hwnd, BOOL move, int pos)`
	Sets the position to the indicated value. The move parameter appears to have no effect. See the bug note on page 722.
TBM_SETRANGE	`DWORD Trackbar_SetRange (HWND hwnd, BOOL redraw, WORD lo, WORD hi)`
	Sets the lower and upper bounds of the trackbar range. This message can be used only if the values are in the range 0..65,535. Otherwise, you must use TBM_SETRANGEMIN and TBM_SETRANGEMAX to set the 32-bit values.
TBM_SETRANGEMAX	`void Trackbar_SetRangeMax (HWND hwnd, BOOL redraw, int hi)`
	Sets the 32-bit upper bound of the trackbar range.
TBM_SETRANGEMIN	`void Trackbar_SetRangeMin (HWND hwnd, BOOL redraw, int lo)`
	Sets the 32-bit lower bound of the trackbar range.
TBM_SETSEL	`void Trackbar_SetSel (HWND hwnd, BOOL redraw, WORD lo, WORD hi)`
	Sets the start and end values of the selection. The trackbar must have the TBS_ENABLESELRANGE style for this to have any effect. This can be used only if the values are in the range 0..65,535.
TBM_SETSELEND	`void Trackbar_SetSelEnd (HWND hwnd, BOOL redraw, int hi)`
	Sets the end value of the selection. The start value is left unchanged. The trackbar must have the TBS_ENABLESELRANGE style for this to have any effect.
TBM_SETSELSTART	`void Trackbar_SetSelStart (HWND hwnd, BOOL redraw, int lo)`
	Sets the start value of the selection. The end value is left unchanged. The trackbar must have the TBS_ENABLESELRANGE style for this to have any effect.
TBM_SETTHUMBLENGTH	`void Trackbar_SetThumbLength (HWND hwnd, UINT size)`
	Sets the size of the thumb, in device units (pixels). *Appears to have no effect.*
TBM_SETTIC[2]	`BOOL Trackbar_SetTick (HWND hwnd, LONG pos)`
	Sets the position of the tick mark. Returns TRUE if successful; FALSE otherwise.

[1]The macro forms are defined in the file `extensions.h`, which is on the CD-ROM that accompanies this book.

[2]Microsoft is inconsistent in the naming. Compare the style flags that are spelled "TICKS" with the messages that are spelled "TICS". We have decided, in our naming of the macros, to use the correct spelling of the word.

[3]Symbols not defined by Microsoft but defined in `extensions.h`.

Table 10.9: Messages that can be sent to a trackbar control

Message	Function[1] Meaning
TBM_SETTICFREQ[2]	void Trackbar_SetTickFreq (HWND hwnd, WORD freq, int offset)
	Sets the tick mark frequency for a control that uses the TBS_AUTOTICKS[2] style. The default frequency, 1, puts a tick at each value position. A higher value places the tick marks at the frequency specified. The meaning of the offset parameter is unknown; see page 732.

[1]The macro forms are defined in the file extensions.h, which is on the CD-ROM that accompanies this book.
[2]Microsoft is inconsistent in the naming. Compare the style flags that are spelled "TICKS" with the messages that are spelled "TICS". We have decided, in our naming of the macros, to use the correct spelling of the word.
[3]Symbols not defined by Microsoft but defined in extensions.h.

Simple Trackbars

When a trackbar control is created, it has a number of default attributes, shown in Table 10.10. You can change these by sending messages to the control. For a simple trackbar, the two parameters you are most likely to want to change are the position and the maximum range (the minimum range is usually left at 0).

You can change the range and position of a trackbar just like you can for a scroll bar. Although there are no direct API functions for changing these values, the macros defined in extensions.h package the messages nicely.

The position value is set by sending the TBM_SETPOS message or using the Trackbar_SetPos function. This message has an odd definition, and in fact the documentation may be out of date. The documentation states that this takes a 32-bit signed value for the position and a Boolean argument that tells it to either set the position (TRUE) or simply verify that the slider is within the range specified (FALSE). If the Boolean value is FALSE, the documentation claims that the slider is not actually moved to the position indicated by the position value. But if it is not within the range of the control, it will be forced to be just within the range (a too-large value is set to the upper limit and a too-small value is set to the lower limit). As far as we have been able to determine, it is impossible to create a situation in which the position goes outside the bounds. We also have determined that the Boolean value appears to have no effect on the behavior of the message (see the bug inset below).

Using the Control Explorer, we were unable to create any situation in which the position ever went outside the bounds of the trackbar. If you change either the upper limit or the lower limit, a TBM_GETPOS message will show you that the position is immediately forced into conformance. Furthermore, the setting of the Boolean value appeared to have no effect on the TBM_SETPOS message. Whether the value was TRUE or FALSE did not influence its behavior, which was to set the position to the value specified in the message. If the position value was out of range of the limits, the actual value set would be forced to within the limits. This was true on Windows/NT 3.51, Windows/NT 4.0, and Windows 95.

You set the range by using either the TBM_SETRANGE message or Trackbar_SetRange function (if both endpoints of the range are in the range 0..65535) or by using the individual messages TBM_SETRANGEMIN and TBM_SETRANGEMAX or functions Trackbar_SetRangeMin and Trackbar_SetRangeMax (for endpoints requir-

Table 10.10: Trackbar initial values

Value	Default
Range minimum	0
Range maximum	0
Position	0
Selection start	0
Selection end	0
Tick frequency	1
Line size	1
Page size	10

ing more than 16 bits to represent them). You also must use the TBM_SETRANGEMIN and TBM_SETRANGEMAX messages if you need negative values, since the TBM_SETRANGE treats the two values as unsigned 16-bit integers.

The messages and API functions all take a `Boolean` argument that indicates whether the control should be immediately redrawn to reflect the change. If you pass a FALSE value, the control will not be redrawn. You will eventually either have to send a message with a TRUE redraw value or invalidate the rectangle of the control and call `UpdateWindow` to force the control to redraw.

If the position value is outside the range being set, it will be forced to be within the range.

You can query the range using the TBM_GETRANGEMIN or TBM_GETRANGEMAX messages or their function equivalents, `Trackbar_GetRangeMin` and `Trackbar_GetRangeMax`.

Setting the Line and Page Sizes

A trackbar automatically handles the notification messages for movement and handles the keyboard shortcuts that invoke them. In particular, the current position is implicitly changed. The question is, by how much? While a scroll bar can be used to advance, for example, a document by 20 lines, it may internally be advancing a buffer pointer by 782 bytes to accomplish this. A trackbar control tends to want to do uniform advancement in response to a "page" request; this is seen as a fast way to move by some increment. You can use the TBM_SETPAGESIZE message (`Trackbar_SetPageSize` function) to establish the page size that is used. The TBM_GETPAGESIZE message (`Trackbar_GetPageSize` function) retrieves the value. The default page size for a trackbar control is 10.

Although there is no "line" interface from the mouse, a trackbar control that has the focus will respond to keyboard input, in particular, to the arrow keys (see Table 10.8). These will generate "line" notifications. You can set the line size using the TBM_SETLINESIZE message (`Trackbar_SetLineSize` function) to set the line size and the TBM_GETLINESIZE message (`Trackbar_GetLineSize` function) to retrieve the line size.

When the slider is advanced by the line size or page size, it is done by simply adding or subtracting the line size or page size to the current position. Thus, if the page size is 10 and the current position is 44, the result of a page advance is position 54 (44 + 10), not 50 (moving up to the nearest multiple of a page size).

Trackbars with Selection

To provide visual feedback to your user, you can use a trackbar with *selection*. This allows you to highlight a particular region of the trackbar that represents some range of interesting values. An example is shown in Figure 10.5. This particular control was created with the styles TBS_BOTTOM | TBS_ENABLESELRANGE |

Figure 10.5: A trackbar with a selection

TBS_HORZ. The range is indicated not only by the highlighting shown but also by the small triangular tick marks indicating the endpoints of the range.

The selection values can be set together or independently. The messages and API functions all take a Boolean argument that indicates whether the control should be immediately redrawn to reflect the change. If you pass a FALSE value, the control will not be redrawn. You will eventually either have to send a message with a TRUE redraw value or invalidate the rectangle of the control and call UpdateWindow to force the control to redraw.

The TBM_SETSEL message or Trackbar_SetSel function sets both the lower and upper selection values, provided both are in the range 0..65535. You can change any one value independently using TBM_SETSELSTART or TBM_SETSELEND messages or the Trackbar_SetSelStart or Trackbar_SetSelEnd functions. You must use these functions if your trackbar uses a range outside the limits 0..65535. You can retrieve the limits of the selection using the TBM_GETSELSTART and TBM_GETSELEND messages or the Trackbar_GetSelStart and Trackbar_GetSelEnd function wrappers.

The selection may be cleared either by explicitly setting the lower and upper values to 0 or by sending the control the TBM_CLEARSEL message or using the Trackbar_ClearSel function wrapper.

Tick Marks

Microsoft has been inconsistent in their spelling of the term "tick". For example, all the messages spell it "TIC", while the styles spell it "TICK". According to *Webster's Seventh New Collegiate Dictionary*, G & C Merriam Company 1963, a **tic** is defined as a "local and habitual spasmodic motion of particular muscles, *esp.* of the face", whereas a **tick** is defined as "a small spot or mark, *esp.* one used to direct attention to something, to check an item on a list, or represent a point on a scale". We have chosen to use the proper spelling in our macros and use the incorrect spellings only when we must refer to the symbols defined by Microsoft.

The topic of tick marks is rather poorly covered in the available documentation. The documentation we have available as we write this is not only sketchy; it also is incomplete, ambiguous, misleading, and in some cases simply incorrect. The usual caveats in dealing with reverse-engineering apply here: We can tell you what the current release *does*, but we can't tell you why it does it. We don't know if the anomalies we see are the result of deliberate design decisions that were incorrectly documented or errors in the implementation. We *can* tell you that for the releases of commctl32.dll we are using,[1] the behavior is consistent and not at all what might be expected. Worse still, we cannot tell you what the future holds. Will the documentation be corrected to reflect the behavior? Will the behavior be corrected to reflect the documentation? Will the anomalous cases we have analyzed be declared bugs and fixed or be declared "correct" behavior (the standard Microsoft phrase: "This behavior is by design")? All we can do here is warn you of several pitfalls and "raise your consciousness" that this is an area to deeply suspect. We have chosen to summarize each of the bugs with a "bug insert" to draw your attention to each problem. But we explain these in more detail in the accompanying prose. We cover a simple example and then discuss the bugs and anomalies starting on page 728.

---

[1] Windows/NT 3.51: Library version 3.51. Windows 95: Library version 4.00.950. Windows/NT 4.0: Library version 4.00.

Simple Tick Marks

Figure 10.6: Tick frequency of 1, range 0..100

If you simply need the tick marks spaced in a linear fashion, you can create the trackbar with the TBS_AUTOTICKS style. You will get one tick mark for each position in the range. If the range is a reasonable size, the

Figure 10.7: Tick frequency of 5, range 0..100

tick marks are often so close together that they form what appears to be a solid line, as shown in Figure 10.6. In such cases, you need to place the tick marks further apart, such as every 5 units, as shown in Figure 10.7, or every 20 units, or whatever value you think makes a good-looking control. To set the tick mark spacing, you send the control the TBM_SETTICFREQ message or use the Trackbar_SetTickFreq function. A control created with the TBS_AUTOTICKS style will also adjust the tick marks if the lower or upper bounds are changed to maintain the spacing. If you change the range, you will have to force the control to redraw with the new tick marks (see page 728).

Custom Tick Marks

Perhaps the most interesting case of tick marks is the desire to create tick marks in specific places. These may represent calibration points, nonlinear scales, or scales with "coarse-and-fine" gradations. You might even want to have a control whose tick marks are changed by some external setting. We show an example of a nonlinear scale in Figure 10.8, which shows how to create a logarithmic scale. Of course, the trackbar itself has no idea of what those tick marks mean, so it continues to report its position in a linear fashion. It is your responsibility to provide any external nonlinear response to a physical trackbar position. The code shown in Listing 10.2 illustrates how we did this for Figure 10.8.

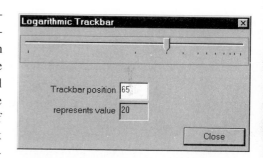

Figure 10.8: A trackbar control with a logarithmic scale

This simple case is handled by using the TBM_CLEARTICS message (Trackbar_ClearTicks function) to remove all existing tick marks except the two at the far ends of the control (which are always present whenever you have tick marks enabled). You can then use the TBM_SETTIC message (Trackbar_SetTick function) to set each of the values at which you wish to have a tick mark displayed.

Listing 10.2: Code to implement a logarithmic trackbar

```
static BOOL log_OnInitDialog(HWND hDlg, HWND hwndFocus, LPARAM lParam)
{
    HWND trackbar = GetDlgItem(hDlg, IDC_TRACKBAR);
    int hi;
    int page;
    double logupper;
```

```
    // assorted initialization here...
    Trackbar_SetRangeMin(trackbar, 0);
    Trackbar_SetRangeMax(trackbar,100);
    Trackbar_SetPageSize(trackbar, 10);

    // Having set the values we can now use them...
    hi = Trackbar_GetRangeMax(trackbar);
    page = Trackbar_GetPageSize(trackbar);

    // Assume low is 0!
    double logupper = log10((double)hi);
    for(int i = page; i < hi; i += page)
        { /* set ticks */
         int tick = (int)((double)hi * log10((double)i) / logupper + 0.5);
         Trackbar_SetTick(trackbar, tick);
        } /* set ticks */
      return TRUE;   // return TRUE unless you set the focus to a control
}
static BOOL recursion = FALSE;

static void setValue(HWND hDlg)
{
    HWND trackbar = GetDlgItem(hDlg, IDC_TRACKBAR);
    int pos = Trackbar_GetPos(trackbar);
    int val;

    // Set the edit control to reflect the new setting.
    // Avoid the infinite recursion caused by the resulting EN_CHANGE
    // notification
    recursion = TRUE;
    SetDlgItemInt(hDlg, IDC_POS, pos, FALSE);
    recursion = FALSE;

    // Compute the logical value represented by the physical position
    val = (int)
                (pow(10, (log10((double)Trackbar_GetRangeMax(trackbar)) * (double)pos)
                       /
                  (double)(Trackbar_GetRangeMax(trackbar))) + 0.5);
      SetDlgItemInt(hDlg, IDC_VAL, val, FALSE);
    }

static void OnHScroll(HWND hwnd, UINT SBCode, UINT Pos, HWND Ctl)
{
    if(Ctl != NULL)
       { /* control */
        switch(GetDlgCtrlID(Ctl))
           {/* ctlid */
            case IDC_TRACKBAR:
               setValue();
               return;
            // ...other WM_HSCROLL sources processed here...
           } /* ctlid */
       } /* control */
    else
       { /* standard scroll bar */
        // ... handle standard scroll bar here (horizontal scrolling)
       } /* standard scroll bar */
```

```
}

static void OnCommand(HWND hDlg, UINT id, HWND ctl, UINT codeNotify)
{
    switch(id)
        { /* id */
        case IDC_POS:   // respond to user type-in
            OnPos(hDlg, ctl, codeNotify);
            return;
        // ... other cases here
        } /* id */
}

static void OnPos(HWND hDlg, HWND ctl, UINT codeNotify)
{
    switch(codeNotify)
        { /* notification */
        case EN_CHANGE:
            if(!recursion)   // avoid infinite recursion
                setValue(hDlg);
            return;
        // ... possibly other events noted here
        } /* notification */
}
```

This code has several useful and/or interesting features to point out. The most important, of course, is the way in which the logarithmic tick marks are constructed and interpreted. We use the "page size" for convenience here; the first page, 10% of the value, uses 50% of the distance. Note in Figure 10.8 that the tick marks form a fairly obvious logarithmic scale, except for the gap between 90 and 100 on the right, which seems larger than the gap between 80 and 90. Part of this is due to pixel quantization, and part of it appears to be due to how the control sets its endpoints. The computation of a physical position p of the trackbar from a logical value v in the range $0..h$ is computed by

$$p = \frac{\log v}{\log h} \times h$$

which is computed for each value at a page-sized interval in the range in the `OnInitDialog` handler. This gives us the tick marks. When we get a notification from the trackbar, we have to convert the linear position p into a value v. Solving the above equation for v, knowing p, we get

$$v = 10^{\left(\frac{p \times \log h}{h}\right)}$$

which is the computation we perform in the `setValue` function.

A tricky bit of Windows programming is required when we need to copy the value of the trackbar position to an edit control but want the user to be able to use the edit control to set some other value and reflect this value back to the trackbar. In our case, we have enabled the edit control; if the user types in a value, we set the trackbar to that position. We react to a change in the edit control by processing the EN_CHANGE notification sent to the parent via a WM_COMMAND message. We then set the trackbar value and call the `setValue` function to place a copy of the current trackbar position (interpreted as both a linear and logarithmic value) in the appropriate display windows. *But this triggers an* EN_CHANGE *notification on the edit control when we set the edit control value.* This calls the handler, which calls `setValue`, which sets the value, which causes n EN_CHANGE event, which then repeats the whole process and rapidly eats up the entire stack. This is a common problem in programming Windows using edit controls in this way. We protect ourselves by having piece of state information to indicate that we are in a recursive call. In a single-threaded environment and a modal dialog box (thus guaranteeing that only one instance of the edit control can exist), we can (as we have hown here) get away with using a single static variable, recursion, to block the recursive call. It is important that you set this recursion indicator before sending the WM_SETTEXT message that would trigger the reursive call and clear it afterwards so that user-initiated changes will get processed. (Edit_SetText, SetWindowText, SetDlgItemText, and SetDlgItemInt are all just convenient wrappers around the WM_SETTEXT message.)

To be fully general, we have to deal with the fact that all scroll bar events, which could include standard scroll bars, up/down control events, and trackbar events, filter through a single WM_HSCROLL handler. We herefore have to split out which control caused the event, just like in WM_COMMAND. However, unlike WM_COMMAND, we do not get the control ID passed in. Instead, we have to use the GetDlgCtrlID function to obtain the control ID from the control handle, which *is* passed in. To be completely general, we need to deal with messages from the standard scroll bars, as we showed in Listing 10.2.

Problems with Tick Marks in Trackbar Controls

There are numerous problems with the tick marks in trackbar controls. We list here most of the ones we have discovered. Since Microsoft often "fixes" bugs by declaring the behavior as being "by design", these may persist well into the future; on the other hand, some may actually be fixed. Only time will tell. A significant issue here is that if you are writing code, you should use the Control Explorer to see exactly what the behavior is. If it is not as we describe here, you may have to distribute the latest version of commct132.dll with your application. Otherwise, you must be cognizant of at least these problems we have discovered, particularly if you have to support legacy Win32 systems that may still have these problems.

The TBS_AUTOTICKS style suggests that the tick marks will be automatically updated whenever the range changes. This is almost true. The tick marks are recomputed, but are not displayed until an event occurs that forces the control to be redrawn.

When the TBS_AUTOTICKS style is selected, the documentation states that as the range changes, the tick marks will be automatically updated. This is almost true. The tick marks are not automatically redisplayed until some event occurs that will cause the control to be redrawn. For any control with TBS_AUTOTICKS style, the recommended practice is that you call InvalidateRect(NULL) after changing either the lower or upper bound of the range so that the change is immediately visible. However, using the TBM_SETTICFREQ message (Trackbar_SetTickFreq function) causes the new tick marks to be immediately redisplayed.

The TBM_SETTIC message states an explicit requirement that the tick value be a positive integer. This statement appears to be an error in the documentation.

The `TBM_SETTIC` message (`Trackbar_SetTick` function) states that the tick value must be a positive integer. This would make it impossible to set tick marks for trackbar controls whose ranges included negative values. Using the Control Explorer, we were able to construct a trackbar whose range was -100..100 and that had tick marks at negative positions. This restriction appears to be a documentation error.

The TBM_GETNUMTICS message (`Trackbar_GetNumTicks` function) will return a value 2 larger than the number of actual tick marks that you can access using TBM_GETPTICS (`Trackbar_GetPTicks`), TBM_GETTIC (`Trackbar_GetTic`), or TBM_GETTICPOS (`Trackbar_GetTickPos`).

With any style except `TBS_NOTICKS`, you get two "free" tick marks at the lower and upper limit positions. Any tick marks you set are in addition to these tick marks. The `TBM_GETNUMTICS` message (`Trackbar_GetNumTicks` function) returns the *actual* number of tick marks displayed. But you cannot ask for information about the two "built-in" tick marks. You cannot ask about the value used by the lowest tick mark using `TBM_GETTIC` (`Trackbar_GetTic`) or about its position using `TBM_GETTICPOS` (`Trackbar_GetTickPos`). Nor can you ask about the value or position of the highest tick mark. You can ask only about the values of tick marks you have created, either by explicitly setting them with `TBM_SETTIC` (`Trackbar_SetTick`) or by using the `TBS_AUTOTICKS` style (but there are more bugs with this style; just keep reading). So the 0th tick mark is the lowest-numbered tick mark you have created.

The TBM_GETPTICS message (`Trackbar_GetPTicks` function) will return NULL when the number of tick marks is 2. This fact is not documented. The number of valid elements in the array pointed to is two smaller than the number of tick marks claimed by TBM_GETNUMTICS (`Trackbar_GetNumTicks`).

Given the above observation, that the value returned by `TBM_GETNUMTICS` message (`Trackbar_GetNumTicks` function) represents the actual number of tick marks displayed, we find a problem with the `TBM_GETPTICS` message (`Trackbar_GetPTicks` function). This operation returns a pointer to an array "containing the positions of tick marks for a trackbar". There is a boundary condition: When the number of ticks returned by `TBM_GETNUMTICS` (`Trackbar_GetNumTicks`) is 2, the pointer returned by `TBM_GETPTICS` (`Trackbar_GetPTicks`) is NULL. When the pointer is non-NULL, the values returned represent only the number of tick marks you have set, not including the two "free" endpoint tick marks. Thus the valid array subscripts are 0..*numticks* – 3. If you attempt to access values in the range 0..*numticks* – 1, you'll discover that the values at the end of the array may be garbage, may appear to be valid, or may not exist at all. In the latter case, an attempt to access them will result in an Access Violation (it happened to us during the testing)!

The values returned in the TBM_GETPTICS message (Trackbar_GetPTicks function) are anomalous. For the TBS_AUTOTICKS style, they do not correctly reflect the frequency value established by TBM_SETTICFREQ (Trackbar_SetTickFreq).

The next anomaly arises when we examine the contents of the array returned by TBM_GETPTICS. When the TBS_AUTOTICKS style is set, the tick marks are placed at intervals established by the TBM_SETTICFREQ message (Trackbar_SetTickFreq function). The array, unfortunately, does not reflect this. No matter what frequency is actually established (and you can tell that it is established by looking at the tick marks actually displayed), the values returned by the array reflect a frequency of 1.

The documentation does not state the type of the pointer or when the pointer returned by TBM_GETPTICS (Trackbar_GetPTicks) is no longer valid. Assume that any operation that modifies the ticks structure will invalidate this pointer.

The pointer returned by TBM_GETPTICS (Trackbar_GetPTicks) is an LPINT pointer, a fact unspecified in the current documentation.

The pointer returned is valid only briefly. If you do any operation such as TBM_CLEARTICS (Trackbar_ClearTicks) or TBM_SETTIC (Trackbar_SetTick), the array might be reallocated internally. Therefore you should not store this pointer but only use it locally. If you are doing anything that could change the number of ticks and hence reallocate the pointer, you must first copy *numticks – 2* integer values to an array of your own so that you can continue to use them while you change the tick marks. For example, if you want to "double" the number of tick marks, you might want to loop over the existing set of tick marks and add tick marks representing half the interval between two existing tick marks. This would mean either computing an array of tick marks to be set and then setting them after the loop completes or setting the ticks within the loop. If you choose to set the tick marks in the body of the loop, and the loop was using the array reference returned by TBM_GETPTICS, the array is changed out from under the loop. Not only will you get loop anomalies, but a reallocation could invalidate the pointer and cause an Access Violation or other failures.

The values returned by TBM_GETTICPOS (Trackbar_GetTickPos) and TBM_GETTIC (Trackbar_GetTick) are supposed to be -1 if the tick mark index is not a valid index. This is not true. You cannot depend upon this value being -1 to indicate an invalid index.

When the TBS_AUTOTICKS style is used, operations such as TBM_GETTICPOS (Trackbar_GetTickPos) and TBM_GETTIC (Trackbar_GetTick) are supposed to return -1 if the tick mark index is "not valid". This is simply not true. These operations will return a value different from -1 for any tick mark index up to the maximum valid tick mark index at frequency 1. For example, if you set the lower bound of the range of the trackbar to 0 and the upper bound to 100 and set the frequency (with TBM_SETTICFREQ or Trackbar_SetTickFreq) to 3, you would expect to have 33 divisions in the scale. TBM_GETNUMTICS (Trackbar_GetNumTicks) returns 35, counting the two endpoints. You can ask for the tick value for any tick mark up to index number 98 (the 99th tick mark, that is, 101 – 2) and still get a valid value. You can ask for the position of any tick mark in the range 0..98 and receive the same value at any frequency. As far as we can tell, the frequency information is being totally ignored in the current releases.

You might also expect that "a valid index" represents any value in the range of 0..*numticks* – *1*. Actually, a "valid index" is any value in the range of 0..*numticks* – 3. This means that when TBM_GETNUMTICS (Trackbar_GetNumTicks) returns 2, there are no valid indices.

The value returned by TBM_GETTICPOS (Trackbar_GetTickPos) is not clearly documented.

The value returned by TBM_GETTICPOS (Trackbar_GetTickPos) is not adequately documented. The documentation states that this operation "returns the physical position, in client coordinates, or the specified tick mark, or –1 if [the parameter] does not specify a valid index". It does not state what form is used for this value. For example, an experienced Windows programmer might expect that the value returned would be a physical position, that is, an *x, y* coordinate, packed, as is traditional in Windows, with the *x*-value in the LOWORD component of the result and the *y*-value in the HIWORD of the result. This is not what you get. The result is actually the *offset* of the tick mark position, in client coordinates, along the axis of the slider. Thus, for a horizontal trackbar, the value returned is an *x* offset, and for a vertical trackbar, the value returned is a *y* offset. Both values are expressed as 32-bit integers. Also, note our earlier observation that TBM_GETTICPOS does not work correctly for TBS_AUTOTICKS trackbars.

The value returned by TBM_GETTIC (Trackbar_GetTick) is supposed to be -1 if the tick mark index is not a valid index. If you have a trackbar that has a negative range, then -1 could be a perfectly valid value.

Trackbars can have negative lower limits. If you query the value of a tick mark at a particular position (tick mark index) and –1 is a valid tick mark value, you will not be able to distinguish this valid value from the value returned for an invalid tick mark index. Beware of this if you are writing any code that wants to support a "generic" trackbar control where you may not have control of the range.

The TBM_SETTICFREQ message (Trackbar_SetTickFreq function) is specified as taking two parameters, a frequency value and an offset value. As far as we have been able to determine, the offset value has no effect.

The TBM_SETTICFREQ message (Trackbar_SetTickFreq function) is specified as taking two parameters, a frequency value and an offset value. We have been unable to determine if the offset value has any effect. Although Microsoft documents the existence of this parameter, the documentation does not explain it. It may well be obsolete or possibly not yet implemented. We recommend setting this value to 0 in case there is a change in the future. We have included the parameter in our Trackbar_SetTickFreq macro, since we have no information on its validity.

The TBM_SETTHUMBLENGTH message appears to have no effect. The TBS_FIXEDLENGTH style appears to have no effect.

The TBM_SETTHUMBLENGTH message (Trackbar_SetThumbLength function) appears to have no effect. It neither changes the thumb length nor does it have a visual effect. There appears to be no variable-width slider. This also means that the TBS_FIXEDLENGTH style flag is meaningless. We have been unable to produce any effect that hints that a variable-width slider is possible.

You can set multiple tick marks in the same position using TBM_SETTIC (Trackbar_SetTick). The tick marks returned are in the order they were set, not in sorted order.

The tick marks do not form a "set" in the mathematical sense. If you use the TBM_SETTIC message (Trackbar_SetTick function) to set a value that is already in the tick mark array, you will get duplicate entries in the tick mark array. You can see this using the Control Explorer. Thus the TBM_GETNUMTICS (Trackbar_GetNumTicks) value will reflect not the number of discrete tick marks displayed, but the number of tick marks in the array (plus the two "free" endpoint tick marks). The tick marks in the array are in the order they were set; they are not maintained in any sorted order.

You can set multiple tick marks in a control that was created with the UDS_NOTICKS style. If you do, UDM_GETNUMTICS will return 0, but UDM_GETPTICS will return a non-NULL pointer.. The UDM_GETTIC and UDM_GETTICPOS messages will return the same values they returned if the UDS_NOTICKS style were not present, but no tick marks will be displayed.

If you create a trackbar with the UDS_NOTICKS style, you would think that operations such as UDM_SETTIC (Trackbar_SetTick) and UDM_GETPTICS (Trackbar_GetPTicks) would fail. They do not. In fact, everything works pretty much as it would if the UDS_NOTICKS style were not specified, including the fact that UDM_GETPTICS (Trackbar_GetPTicks) returns a valid pointer. But you can't find out how many elements are in the array returned because UDM_GETNUMTICS (Trackbar_GetNumTicks) returns 0.

Stop the Presses

We can't stop the presses. Books have production deadlines. But mere weeks before we went to press, Microsoft released a new version of `comctl32.dll`, as part of the Internet Explorer 4.0 beta release. A track bar control can now support up to two "buddy" controls (in a fashion similar to Up/Down buddy controls see page 739). You can add Tool Tips to trackbars. We recommend the two excellent articles by Strohm Armstrong cited in "Further Reading".

Up/Down Controls

The up/down control (official class name `msctls_updown`), also known as a "spin" control, is another type of "slider" input control. You can think of the simplest form (shown in Figure 10.9) as a scroll bar without the thumb and page capabilities, just the endpoint arrows. Usually, an up/down control is paired with another control, such as a static control, an edit control, or a list control, to give visual feedback. An example of a pair of these controls is shown in Figure 10.10. You can couple the behavior by using your own code or automatically couple them by using a feature called the "buddy" control feature.

Figure 10.9: An up/down control

There are at least three ways to create an up/down control. The most common is that it is in a dialog template and is automatically created when the dialog is created. There is also the old standby, `CreateWindow(Ex)`. To specify the class name, you should use the name `UPDOWN_CLASS` defined for you in `commctrl.h`. A typical creation of an up/down control by this method is shown a little further along. You can specify any of the standard window styles (although `WS_CHILD` is essential) and any of the up/down control styles from Table 10.11. Finally, you can use the `CreateUpDownControl` API call which is implemented in `comctl32.dll`, which we will also discuss shortly.

Figure 10.10: An up/down control paired with an edit control

Before you can create an up/down control, you must be certain the common control DLL is loaded. Do this by calling `InitCommonControls()` during your application initialization. This is already done for you by our standard template files.

We show some selected effects of using these styles in Table 10.11. These demonstrate the effects on the buddy control, in this case a coupled edit control. In the figures, the up/down controls that appear to the right of the edit control when neither `UDS_ALIGNLEFT` nor `UDS_ALIGNRIGHT` are specified appear there because they have been placed there explicitly. For those controls for which an explicit alignment has been specified, it doesn't matter where the control is when it is created. When the buddy attachment is made, the control is repositioned so that the specified alignment is maintained. There is no requirement other than visual convention (and ease of use!) that an up/down control be physically near the values it is manipulating.

To create a window in the usual fashion, you can use `CreateWindow(Ex)`:

```
HWND updown = CreateWindow(UPDOWN_CLASS,           // class name
                           NULL,                   // window caption
                           WS_CHILD | WS_VISIBLE |
                           UDS_HORZ | UDS_SETBUDDYINT,// styles
                           0,                      // left
                           rect.bottom - Height,   // top
                           rect.right,             // width
                           Height,                 // height
                           hwnd,                   // parent
                           (HMENU)IDC_UPDOWN,      // child ID
                           hInstance,              // instance handle
                           NULL) ;                 // parameters
```

However, once you've created a window in this way, you will need to send it messages to initialize its state, such as its lower and upper bounds, its current position, and the handle of its buddy control. This is often more easily handled by using the `CreateUpDownControl` function, which is implemented in the `comctl32.dll` file:

```
WINCOMMCTRLAPI HWND WINAPI CreateUpDownControl(
                           DWORD Style,        // Style flags
                           int x,              // leftmost position
                           int y,              // top position
                           int cx,             // width
                           int cy,             // height
                           HWND hParent,       // parent window handle
                           int ID,             // control ID
                           HINSTANCE hInst,    // instance handle
                           HWND hBuddy,        // buddy handle or NULL
                           int Upper,          // upper limit
                           int Lower,          // lower limit
                           int Pos);           // initial position
```

The `Style` flags must include the `WS_CHILD` style; otherwise, the creation will fail. This function creates an up/down control and initializes all of the values passed as parameters.

 If you specify the `UDS_AUTOBUDDY` style and also specify the hBuddy parameter to `CreateUpDownControl`, you will find very odd behavior. If the window handle passed as hBuddy is not the immediate predecessor and one of the alignment styles `UDS_ALIGNLEFT` or `UDS_ALIGNRIGHT` is specified, the window that *is* the immediate predecessor will be resized to make space for the up/down control. However, the explicit UDM_SETBUDDY operation done after creation will resize the actual buddy control and move the up/down control to the specified alignment. This results in an anomalous resizing of some control other than the intended one. If the handle specified by the parameter hBuddy *is* the immediate predecessor and one of the alignment options is specified, the auto-buddy operation will resize the immediate predecessor window to make room for the up/down control. Then the UDM_SETBUDDY operation will resize the *already resized* window, thus resulting in the window's being too small. The Control Explorer goes out of its way to keep this from happening because it allows for multiple re-creations of the windows and tries to fiddle everything back to a "clean" initial state before each creation. But until we put the special code checks in, this is what we saw happening.

Table 10.11: Up/down class styles

Style	Meaning
UDS_ALIGNLEFT	Positions the up/down control next to the left edge of its buddy window. The buddy window is moved to the right and its width is decreased so that there is room for the up/down control.

Table 10.11: Up/down class styles

Style	Meaning
UDS_ALIGNRIGHT	Positions the up/down control next to the right edge of its buddy window. The buddy window width is decreased so that there is room for the up/down control.
UDS_ARROWKEYS	When the control has the focus, using the arrow keys will change the position.
UDS_AUTOBUDDY	At the time the control is created, it selects the immediate Z-order predecessor as its buddy window.
UDS_HORZ	Creates a horizontal up/down control.
UDS_NOTHOUSANDS	If present, suppresses the formatting of the value with a thousands separator. This style has meaning only when the UDS_SETBUDDYINT style is also present. Applies only when the base for conversion is not 16.
UDS_SETBUDDYINT	Whenever the value changes, a printable version of the current position is formatted and sent to the buddy window using the WM_SETTEXT message. If UDS_NOTHOUSANDS is not specified, the text will have thousands separators; if the conversion base is 16, the value will be in hexadecimal. There is a special case for a list box buddy; see page 741.
UDS_WRAP	Normally, the up/down control stops when it reaches the end of its range. When this style is specified, the value will "wrap" from the highest value to the lowest or from the lowest to the highest, depending on the direction in which it is currently stepping.

Messages to Up/Down Controls

You modify various values of an up/down control by sending messages. The complete list of messages is given in Table 10.12. We supply, in the file extensions.h, a collection of API wrappers (similar to those found in windowsx.h for the base messages) that package these up into more mnemonic and convenient packages, where you don't have to worry about parameter packing issues.

Table 10.12: Messages that can be sent to an up/down control

Message	Function[1] Meaning
UDM_GETACCEL	int UpDown_GetAccel (HWND hwnd, int count, LPUDACCEL accels)
	Copies accelerator information to the accels array. Returns the number of accelerators retrieved. To query the number of accelerators, use a count of 0 and an accels pointer of NULL.

[1]The macro forms are defined in the file extensions.h, which is on the CD-ROM that accompanies this book.

Table 10.12: Messages that can be sent to an up/down control

Message	Function[1] Meaning
UDM_GETBASE	`int UpDown_GetBase (HWND hwnd)`
	Returns the radix (10 or 16) used when formatting the text for a buddy control.
UDM_GETBUDDY	`HWND UpDown_GetBuddy (HWND hwnd)`
	Retrieves the handle of the currently associated buddy control. The result is NULL if there is no associated control.
UDM_GETPOS	`int UpDown_GetPos (HWND hwnd)`
	The current value of the control representing its current position is in the low-order 16 bits. If there is an error (no buddy control, text of buddy control is not a number), the high-order 16 bits are nonzero.
UDM_GETRANGE	`DWORD UpDown_GetRange (HWND hwnd)`
	Returns the current range settings. The low-order 16 bits are the maximum position for the control, and the high-order 16 bits are the minimum position for the control.
UDM_SETACCEL	`BOOL UpDown_SetAccel (HWND hwnd, int count, LPUDACCEL accels)`
	Sets new accelerator values. Result is TRUE if successful; FALSE if there is an error.
UDM_SETBASE	`int UpDown_SetBase (HWND hwnd, int base)`
	Sets the radix (10 or 16) to be used when formatting text for a buddy control. The result is the previous setting of the radix. If the base parameter is not 10 or 16, the return value is 0.
UDM_SETPOS	`int UpDown_SetPos (HWND hwnd, int pos)`
	Sets a new position value. If there is a buddy control, the value is also set to the buddy control. The return value is the previous position.
UDM_SETRANGE	`void UpDown_SetRange (HWND hwnd, short high, short low)`
	Sets the maximum and minimum positions for the control. The positions must be less than or equal to UD_MAXVAL and greater than or equal to UD_MINVAL.

[1]The macro forms are defined in the file `extensions.h`, which is on the CD-ROM that accompanies this book.

Using Up/Down Controls

The behavior of an up/down control differs in some ways from the behavior of a trackbar control or a scroll bar control. In a scroll bar control, the top arrow (for a vertical scroll bar) or the left arrow (for a horizontal scroll bar) moves the position towards the lower bound; this is always done by decreasing the value. The opposing arrows increase the value to the upper bound.

An up/down control does not require that its upper bound be higher than its lower bound. In fact, it often is the case that you need to have a "lower bound" that is greater than its "upper bound". For up/down controls the relation of the values determines which direction the arrow moves the value. For a default up/down control, the lower bound is 100 and the upper bound is 0. Thus the up arrow on a vertical control moves the value "up" to the upper bound by decrementing it until the upper bound (0) is reached and the down arrow moves the value "down" to the lower bound by incrementing it until the lower bound (100) is reached.

This default seems unnatural, but it is based on a desire to have the arrows on the default up/down control exhibit the same behavior as the arrows on a scroll bar of the same orientation. But unlike with a scroll bar you can use the UDM_SETRANGE message (UpDown_SetRange function) to change the bounds so that the arrows have the opposite effect. If you've been playing with the Control Explorer and other Explorers on the CD-ROM that comes with this book, you will see that the coupled edit control-up/down control is a favorite of ours. Nearly every one of the up/down controls required explicit initialization via UDM_SETRANGE to complement its range so that the up arrow would increase the value and the down arrow would decrease it.

A very unfortunate feature of up/down controls is that they are limited to 16-bit values and a maximum range of 32,767. This seems an odd restriction to impose in a 32-bit world, especially because these controls are natural interfaces for a number of applications (such as moving around in databases) where the 16-bit limit makes their use somewhere between difficult and impossible.

You interact with up/down controls by sending them messages. You can also use any of the UpDown_ functions shown in Table 10.12. The UDM_GETRANGE message (UpDown_GetRange function) retrieves the two 16-bit range endpoint values, where the *low*-order word of the result is the *high* end of the range and the *high*-order word of the result is the *low* end of the range. It is worth pointing this out because it is different from other ranges returned as 16-bit values in Windows.

The position of the control is set by the UDM_SETPOS message (UpDown_SetPos function). The value that is passed in is constrained to be within the limits set. If it exceeds the limits, the actual value set is just within the appropriate boundary. You can retrieve the position using the UDM_GETPOS message (UpDown_GetPos function). Only the low-order 16 bits of the result returned by UDM_GETPOS are valid. The high-order 16 bits are 0 if the operation succeeded and nonzero if there was an error. An "error" includes not having a buddy control or discovering that the text of the buddy control does not form a valid number. Setting and retrieving the position has other implications when a buddy control is used; see the buddy control discussion starting on page 739.

Notifications from Up/Down Controls

An up/down control can be treated much like a scroll bar or trackbar control. You receive WM_HSCROLL and WM_VSCROLL messages from it, just like you do from a scroll bar or a trackbar. However, the only notifications you receive in the messages are SB_THUMBPOSITION and SB_ENDSCROLL. There appear to be no line or page messages sent by an up/down control. This means the position information delivered in the pos parameter to the handler reflects the current value (at least the low-order 16 bits of it, which is currently all there are) of the up/down control.

Since all scrolling messages from scroll bars (including the standard scroll bars), trackbars, and up/down controls go to the same OnHScroll or OnVScroll handler, you have to split out the handling based on which control generated the event, much like you have to do in a WM_COMMAND handler.

Listing 10.3: Sample code to handle an up/down control

```
static void OnVScroll(HWND hwnd, UINT SBCode, UINT Pos, HWND Ctl)
{
  if(Ctl != NULL)
     { /* control */
       switch(GetDlgCtrlID(ScrollBar))
           {/* ctlid */
            case IDC_SPINVALUE:
                // ... handle the control which spins the value
                OnMySpinValue(hwnd, SBCode, Pos, Ctl);
                return;
              // ...other WM_VSCROLL sources processed here...
           } /* ctlid */
     } /* control */
  else
     { /* standard scroll */
       // ... handle window scrolling here
     } /* standard scroll */
}

static void OnMySpinValue(HWND hwnd, UINT SBCode, UINT Pos, HWND ctl)
{
  switch(SBCode)
     { /* SBCode */
       case SB_THUMBPOSITION:
                // do something with the value, such as...
                SetDlgItemInt(hwnd, IDC_VALUE, Pos, TRUE);
                break;
       case SB_ENDSCROLL:
                // ... do something when the action stops
                // (whatever is appropriate)
                break;
     } /* SBCode */
}
```

For example, in the code in Listing 10.3, you can respond to each SB_THUMBPOSITION message and update a control (IDC_VALUE) to reflect the current position. But if updating related material would be time consuming (for example, if the up/down control was representing page numbers in a document), you would not want to redraw the related material until the user had stopped holding the control down. In this case, you respond to the SB_ENDSCROLL event by actually locating the page in the document and drawing it on the screen.

An up/down control provides another notification. Before sending the WM_HSCROLL or WM_VSCROLL message, the control sends a WM_NOTIFY message. The NMHDR parameter of the handler references an NM_UPDOWN structure, as follows:

```
typedef struct _NM_UPDOWN
{
    NMHDR hdr;
    int iPos;
    int iDelta;
} NM_UPDOWN, FAR *LPNM_UPDOWN;
```

Instead of responding to the WM_HSCROLL or WM_VSCROLL messages, you can decode the WM_NOTIFY message and dispatch directly to your handler. There is currently only one notification code defined,

UDN_DELTAPOS. But you should always check to be sure you are processing this code. Your handler for a no-tification event for an up/down control will look something like the code shown in Listing 10.4.

Listing 10.4: Handling the WM_NOTIFY:UDN_DELTAPOS message

```
static void OnHandleMySpinControl(HWND hwnd, int id, LPNM_UPDOWN udh)
{
  if(udn->hdr.code == UDN_DELTAPOS)
     { /* delta */
     // Set the value to the static control
     DWORD range = UpDown_GetRange(hwnd);
     // Get the limits.  Note that we don't care which is which...
     int high = max((short)LOWORD(range), (short)HIWORD(range));
     int low  = min((short)LOWORD(range), (short)HIWORD(range));
     BOOL wrap = (BOOL)(GetStyle(hwnd) & UDS_WRAP);
     int newvalue = udh->iPos + udh->iDelta;

     if(newvalue < low)
        newvalue = wrap ? high : low;
     else
     if(newvalue > high)
        newvalue = wrap ? low : high;

     SetDlgItemInt(hwnd, IDC_VALUE, newvalue, TRUE);
     // ... possibly do other interesting things
     } /* delta */
}
```

The iPos member of the NM_UPDOWN structure is the *current* position of the control at the time the mouse was clicked (or a repeat event occurred) and *before being modified and sent via* WM_HSCROLL *or* WM_VSCROLL. The iDelta member of the NM_UPDOWN structure represents the amount by which the value will be modified; currently, it is limited to either 1 or -1. We discovered using the Control Explorer that a control that has the UDS_WRAP style processes the wrap *after* the WM_NOTIFY, so as you see in Listing 10.4, we added code to handle the wrap, since we will not process the WM_VSCROLL message.

Typically, if you process the WM_NOTIFY message you will not process the WM_HSCROLL or WM_VSCROLL messages, and vice versa. Tooling such as that available in the Microsoft development environments makes it somewhat easier to respond to the WM_NOTIFY messages, at least when programming in C++. In pure C code, there does not seem to be any particular advantage of one method over the other.

Buddy Controls

An up/down control can be used as a stand-alone control. But, as we have shown in the code in Listing 10.3, you might want to update a control to reflect the value. In fact, this is so common that there is a built-in capability to handle this: the "buddy control" feature. The "buddy control" is a control that is coupled to the up/down control. Changes in the up/down control can be reflected to the buddy, and changes in the buddy can influence the behavior of the up/down control.

We first show you a set of simple examples. Then we explore some of the problems and issues of proper buddy control usage.

Establishing a Buddy

If you have an up/down control, you can couple it to its "buddy control" by sending the handle of the buddy control to the up/down control using the UDM_SETBUDDY message (UpDown_SetBuddy function). The result returned is the previous buddy control handle. To remove a buddy control association, you send the up/down control a NULL handle.

Once a buddy has been established, the up/down control's behavior depends on the buddy-related style bits. If the UDS_ALIGNLEFT style or the UDS_ALIGNRIGHT style is set in the up/down control, the control is moved to be aligned with its buddy. The width of the control is retained, and its height is adjusted to be the height of the control with which it is aligned. These styles are illustrated in Figure 10.11 and Figure 10.12. If you don't specify one of the alignment styles and you want the up/down control near the buddy control, you have to align the up/down control with its buddy yourself. Notice that if you use the Up/Down Control Explorer, which is part of the Control Explorer application on the CD-ROM, we position the up/down control in a place disjoint from any of its potential buddy controls. This does not prevent it from having one of the selected controls as a buddy. It just means that there is no physical proximity of an up/down control and its buddy, a point we wished to emphasize.

Setting the Buddy Value

Whenever an up/down control changes, it can automatically update the contents of its buddy control. If the UDS_SETBUDDYINT style was used when the control was created, the text representing the numeric value is formatted and sent to the buddy control with a WM_SETTEXT message. For decimal numbers, the text is formatted with thousands separators (for example, in the United States, commas) whenever there are more than three digits. You can suppress this feature by using the UDS_NOTHOUSANDS style. If you create the control with this style, thousands separators will not be used. This style cannot be changed on the fly; in fact, none of the up/down control styles can be changed once the control is created. The text is formatted as a decimal number (with possible thousands separators) if the radix is 10 and as a hexadecimal number (the UDS_NOTHOUSANDS style is ignored) with a leading 0x if the radix is 16. You select the radix using the UDM_SETBASE message (UpDown_SetBase function), and you can query the current base using the UDM_GETBASE message (UpDown_GetBase function). There are only two valid radix values: 10 and 16. If you attempt to set any other value, the request is ignored and the value returned is 0, not the previous setting of the radix.

You can't use the UDS_SETBUDDYINT style in any case in which what you are displaying is not expressible as simple integer; for example, if you are using the up/down control to modify a date or time. We show an example of this in Chapter 13, Listing 13.7 (page 990), where we modify a date. In this case, we don't use a buddy control.

Retrieving the Position

The presence of a buddy control does more than provide some feedback. The buddy control contents can be modified, either directly by the user (such as via an edit control) or by the program. Whenever the up/down control is queried for its position by UDM_GETPOS (UpDown_GetPos), it retrieves the contents of the buddy control via a `WM_GETTEXT` message (or for a list box, `LB_GETCURSEL`) and converts the value to an integer, which is the value it returns. You can verify this behavior using the Control Explorer. If the buddy control contains an invalid number, it appears that the value of the buddy control is ignored and the most recent internal value is used. The parser used is able to understand thousands separators. However, if there is an error, the high-order 16 bits of the value returned by `UDM_GETPOS` (`UpDown_GetPos`) are nonzero.

List Box Buddies

There is one documented special case, which you can also play with in the Control Explorer. That is, if the buddy is a list box, then the messages used are `LB_SETCURSEL/LB_GET-CURSEL` instead of `WM_SET-TEXT/WM_GETTEXT`. An example of a buddy control with `UDS_ALIGNLEFT` style is shown in Figure 10.12. Notice that the height of the up/down control, at the left, has been adjusted to match the height of the list box. If you change the limits of the up/down control that is attached to the left of the list box, you can get the arrows of the up/down control to move the selection in the opposite direction of the scroll bar arrows. While a strange thing to do, this demonstrates that you can get such behavior.

UDS_ALIGNLEFT	UDS_ALIGNRIGHT	UDS_NOTHOUSANDS	UDS_SETBUDDYINT	UDS_HORZ	Base	Effect
			✓		10	1,000
✓			✓		10	1,000
✓			✓	✓	10	1,000
	✓		✓		10	1,000
		✓	✓		10	1000
			✓		16	0x03E8

Figure 10.11: Selected styles and their effect on up/down controls

We did discover one anomaly that seems to apply only to a list box buddy. If the up/down control is coupled to a list control and the limit of the up/down control is greater than the number of elements in the list, the `UDS_WRAP` feature is inoperative. This is because the buddy limits the range to the valid indices for the list box, say, 0..7, while the up/down control limit might be 0..100. If you increment the value to 7, it will increment no further. So although it has hit its logical end, it has not hit the upper limit, and will not wrap back to

Figure 10.12: List box buddy

0. If you want your list box control to cycle from the last element back to the first element, you must set the upper limit of the control to have the range 0..*n*, where *n* is the highest valid index into the list box.

Auto-buddy

Because most controls are used in dialog boxes, a special feature, particularly nice for dialogs, is the UDS_AUTOBUDDY style. If a control has this style set, it automatically locates, during its creation, its immediate predecessor sibling and declares that sibling to be its buddy control. This buddy is established at the time of creation of the control. If you need to change the buddy, you must use an explicit UDM_SETBUDDY (UpDown_SetBuddy) operation. This means you can, in a dialog, easily set the buddy control just by using the "tab order" of the controls. The control that logically precedes the up/down control in tab order will be its buddy. (Note that this has absolutely nothing to do with the physical placement of the controls within the dialog layout!)

Using the UDS_AUTOBUDDY style has some hazards if you are not using it in a dialog. We already pointed out one pitfall on page 734. If you are doing a CreateUpDownControl call, the buddy control will be the last one in the Z-order, since a new window is created at the end of the Z-order (that's why it works for dialogs). So you either have to create the buddy immediately preceding the creation of the up/down control or use SetWindowPos to force the desired buddy window to the end of the Z-order. Since the Z-order also dictates the behavior of the **Tab** key, this could have undesired side effects. Your best choice under such conditions is simply to use an explicit UDM_SETBUDDY (UpDown_SetBuddy) operation.

Buddy Control Pitfalls

Buddy controls have another often nasty feature. That a buddy control can have its value changed by the up/down control it is paired with, via WM_SETTEXT, can induce other effects. Edit controls, the most popular buddy control, are prone to these problems. In particular, during dialog creation you may find WM_COMMAND messages coming in with the EN_CHANGE and EN_UPDATE notifications, caused by the buddy control text being changed. These come in before all the controls have been created and before your WM_INITDIALOG handler has been called to initialize the rest of your controls and data structures. You usually discover this feature when you get an access violation as your dialog starts up. If you haven't seen this problem before, it takes a bit of thinking to figure out just what is going on. There is only one solution we've discovered for this: an "initialization complete" flag that tells when dialog initialization has completed and it is safe to start processing EN_CHANGE and EN_UPDATE notifications. For the case of single-threaded modal dialogs, you can use a simple Boolean variable. For more elaborate cases, such as the C++/MFC CFormView class, we add the Boolean variable as a member variable in the class, set it to FALSE in the constructor, and set it to TRUE just before returning from the OnInitDialog method. In pure C, you can accomplish this by using the GWL_USERDATA word (which starts out as 0) and setting it to 1 upon completion. (If you're using it to point to a data structure, just put the Boolean value in your data structure.) We also set the value to FALSE in the OnDestroy handler, particularly important for modeless dialogs whose structure may be allocated only once with new or malloc. Or you can use SetProp and GetProp (don't forget to do RemoveProp in the

OnDestroy handler). But it seems almost always necessary to handle this "start-up transient". Careful examination of the code for our various Explorers will show that much of it has this protective code in place. We show a simple example for a single-threaded modal dialog handler in Listing 10.5.

Listing 10.5: Single-threaded modal dialog EN_CHANGE protection

```
BOOL initialized = FALSE;

static void OnEditControl(HWND hwnd, UINT ctlid, HWND hctl, UINT codeNotify)
{
 switch(codeNotify)
    { /* code */
      case EN_CHANGE:
           if(!initialized)
              return;

           // ...
           break;
      case EN_UPDATE:
           if(!initialized)
              return;

           // ...
           break;
    } /* code */
}

static BOOL OnInitDialog(HWND hDlg, HWND hfocus, LPARAM lParam)
{
    // ... your normal initialization
    initialized = TRUE;
    return TRUE;   // if no change in focus
}

static void OnDestroy(HWND hwnd)
{
 // ... whatever you normally would destroy here...
 initialized = FALSE;
}
```

Up/Down Accelerators

The rate at which the up/down control advances does not have to be constant. In the default control, we have discovered three threshold values that are used. The values that control this behavior are called accelerators. They have absolutely nothing to do with the keyboard accelerators used for menu shortcuts. You can change these values by using the UDM_SETACCEL message (UpDown_SetAccel function) and examine them by using the UDM_GETACCEL message (UpDown_GetAccel function). These accelerators operate by specifying a time interval in seconds and an increment rate. If you hold the mouse down on an up/down control for the specified number of seconds, the rate at which the control increments changes from 1 (the initial value) to the value specified by the accelerator. A sample set of accelerator values, those provided by a default up/down control, are shown in Figure 10.13. Initially, the increment is 1; after 2 sec, the increment rate becomes 5 units, and after 5 sec the increment rate becomes 20 units, where it remains for the duration of the cycle.

nSec	nInc
0	1
2	5
5	20

Figure 10.13: Accelerator values in an up/down control

To retrieve the current set of accelerators, you send a UDM_GETACCEL message, giving the count of the number of accelerators you have allocated space for and a pointer to the allocated space, which will be an array of UDACCEL structures. The return result tells you the actual number of accelerators copied into that space. There is a slight problem here, however. You need to know how much space to allocate to get all the accelerators. Here is a method for getting this information. Although it is undocumented, we tried it and it worked (and it is consistent with many other interfaces in Win32). Namely, if you send a message with a count of 0 and a NULL pointer, the message will return the actual number of accelerators currently present. You then can allocate storage and retrieve the accelerators. The code to retrieve accelerators is shown in Listing 10.6.

The UDACCEL structure is quite simple:

```
typedef struct _UDACCEL {
    UINT nSec;
    UINT nInc;
} UDACCEL, FAR *LPUDACCEL;
```

The nSec member tells how many seconds to wait, and the accompanying nInc member tells how fast to increment the control. It is possible that making the first entry be other than (0, 1) will result in strange behavior.

Listing 10.6: Retrieving up/down control accelerators

```
static void modifyAccelerators(HWND hupdown)
{
    int n = UpDown_GetAccel(hupdown, 0, NULL);
    LPUDACCEL accels = (LPUDACCEL)malloc(n * sizeof(UDACCEL));

    if(accels == NULL)
        return;  // or raise exception, or issue error msg...

    UpDown_GetAccel(hupdown, n, accels);
    // modify the accelerators here...
    UpDown_SetAccel(hupdown, n, accels);
    free(accels);
}
```

The Progress Bar Control

Figure 10.14: A progress bar control

The progress bar control (official class name msctls_progress32), shown in Figure 10.14, allows you to keep the user informed of how well something is progressing. It is one of the simplest controls. This is because unlike every other control we've seen, *it has no styles*. Well, it has all the standard *window* styles, but there are no *progress bar* styles. So you can create such a control with or without a border, visible or hidden, enabled or disabled, or with any other window style, but there are no other control-specific styles you can give. We even thought of including an empty "progress bar styles" table just so that the table of contents would be symmetrical, but we decided that this was probably gratuitous. A progress bar also has no notification messages. A progress bar is as completely passive and simple a control as exists anywhere in Windows (except for the WS_EX_ styles that allow mouse events to be reflected to the parent). You create a progress bar via CreateWindow(Ex), using the name PROGRESS_CLASS.

Table 10.13 shows the messages that can be sent to a progress bar control.

Table 10.13: Messages that can be sent to a progress bar control

Message	Function[1]	Meaning
PBM_DELTAPOS	`int Progess_DeltaPos (HWND hwnd, int delta)`	
	Advances the progress bar by the `delta` amount. Returns the previous value.	
PBM_SETPOS	`int Progress_SetPos (HWND hwnd, int pos)`	
	Sets the current position of the progress bar to be `pos`. Returns the previous value.	
PBM_SETRANGE	`DWORD Progress_SetRange (HWND hwnd, int low, int high)`	
	Sets the range of the progress bar to be the two parameters specified. The low-order 16 bits of the result are the previous low value, and the high-order 16 bits are the previous high value.	
PBM_SETSTEP	`int Progress_SetStep (HWND hwnd, int step)`	
	Sets the size used by the PBM_STEPIT message.	
PBM_STEPIT	`int Progress_StepIt (HWND hwnd)`	
	Advances the progress bar by the current step amount. If the maximum range of the progress bar is reached, the current position is set to 0. Returns the previous position.	

[1]The macro forms are defined in the file extensions.h, which is on the CD-ROM that accompanies this book.

The simplest usage is to set a range value that represents endpoints of your range, usually a lower limit of 0 and an upper limit as large as 65,535.[2] The lower bound must be less than the upper bound. The return value from sending the PBM_SETRANGE value is the previous range or 0 (MAKELONG(0, 0)) if an illegal pair of range values is given. If a nonzero value is returned, the LOWORD is the previous lower bound and the HIWORD is the previous upper bound. Having set the range, you can now send a succession of PBM_SETPOS messages

---

[2] Yes, in the era of 32-bit operating systems and 32-bit values, we still have a foolish 16-bit limitation here, a serious inconvenience, particularly if you want to use the progress bar for files. However, Microsoft has realized how absurd this is and has released a new version, in beta as we go to press with this book, that supports 32-bit ranges. See "Stop the Presses" on page 746.

indicating where the current position along the progress line should be. The control figures out how much space should be filled in and draws the appropriate amount of filled-in space, as shown in Figure 10.14.

However, the additional messages allow us an even simpler interface. Having set the range (and possibly the initial position), you can use the PBM_DELTAPOS message (Progress_DeltaPos function) to add its parameter value to the current position. This value can be signed, so it can move the progress bar in either direction. You also can use the PBM_SETSTEP message (Progress_SetStep function) to set an implicit step value. The parameterless PBM_STEPIT message (Progress_StepIt function) will then add this value successively until the maximum limit is reached. When the maximum limit is reached or exceeded, the current position is reset to be one "step" unit higher than the lower limit value.

Stop the Presses

We can't; publication deadlines are inflexible. But Microsoft just released, within weeks of our going to press, a beta version of comct132.dll, which has support for 32-bit ranges in progress bar controls. See the article by Strohm Armstrong in the *Microsoft Systems Journal* that we cite in "Further Reading". The 32-bit progress bar control appears in Part II of the series.

The Control Explorer

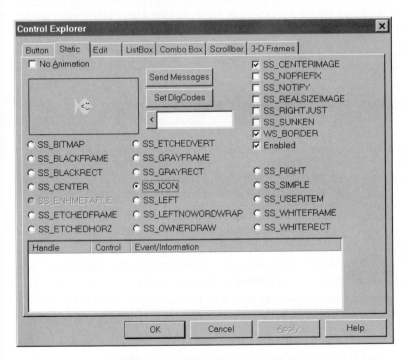

With the Control Explorer application, you can play with the various controls. You can create controls of various styles and send them an assortment of messages, seeing what values are returned. You can also interact with the controls, seeing what events are sent to the parent as a consequence of your actions. For each control class, you can watch the events generated and send your own messages. Samples of the Control Explorer are also shown in Figure 10.15. All of the illustrations in these chapters on controls were produced using the Control Explorer.

Figure 10.15: The Control Explorer screen (static control)

Further Reading

Armstrong, Strohm, "Previewing the Common Controls DLL for Microsoft Internet Explorer 4.0, Part I", *Microsoft Systems Journal* 11, 10 (October 1996).

Armstrong, Strohm, "Previewing the Common Controls DLL for Microsoft Internet Explorer 4.0, Part II", *Microsoft Systems Journal* 11, 11 (November 1996).

These two excellent articles cover the late-breaking release that came out in beta far too late to research for this book. At the time we went to press, this material was still not official product release, but it almost certainly will be by the time you hold this book in your hands. Keep an eye on our Web site for updated Explorers.

Further Reading

Chapter

11 Dialog Boxes

Let's take another step in the trek for Windows enlightenment. You may have noticed we're slowly emerging from the Windows swamp of bitblts, pens, brushes, and other low-level, although extremely powerful, graphical operations, and heading toward easier-to-use prepackaged functions.

The first step in our emergence was controls. Controls are prepackaged objects that provide a window with a certain appearance and behavior. In Chapters 8 through 10, you saw how to create controls by calling the CreateWindow function for each control. Using a control to obtain information from a user lifts part of the burden from you; no longer do you need to monitor mouse movements, button clicks, and simple editing tasks. You can use the appropriate control and let it do the dirty work. However, even with controls, you are left with much work to do.

For example, you need a parent window to nurture the controls. Controls are only children, after all. You must place each control at its proper position in a window. You must coordinate the interaction between controls. Recall that one particular problem was the issue of passing the input focus from one control to another. Managing the interaction and display of multiple controls in a window is a common task performed by nearly all Windows applications. Windows provides a prepackaged solution to many of the problems of control management: the *dialog box*.

In this chapter, we explore the many variations of a dialog box. First, we define a dialog box and explain the various components to a dialog box (for example, the dialog-class window function, the dialog function, and the dialog template). Next, we explain the two different types of dialog boxes–modal and modeless–and when you should use each. Then we explain the different functions you can use to create a dialog box.

Windows provides standard, prewritten dialog box templates and dialog functions for commonly used features of a window, including these for the following user interactions:

- Displaying available colors from which the user can select one color

- Displaying a list of available fonts; the available styles, such as bold or italic; the font's point size; and other font features from which the user can select a font

- Displaying a list of filenames that match specified extensions, directories, and drives, allowing the user to select a file for input or output

- Displaying a list of currently available printers and allowing the user to select a printer

- Displaying information about the default printer and its configuration and enabling the user to specify how to print output and start a print operation

- Displaying information about page layout, such as margins, paper size, and paper orientation, allowing the user to select an output page layout

- Displaying information about the configuration of the serial ports and allowing the user to set the bit rate, parity, number of data bits, and number of start bits for each available port

- Requesting that an application search (typically) for a specified string in the specified manner and direction using such factors as case sensitivity, word match, and the direction of search

- Requesting that an application search for an old string and replace it with a specified new string

This chapter demonstrates how you can write your own dialog functions. Chapter 13 shows how to use the printer setup, how to print, and how to work with page setup dialogs.

What Is a Dialog Box?

A *dialog box* is a pop-up window that contains controls. You use a dialog box whenever you need to display information or request information from the user. We've included one dialog box (the **About...** dialog box) in every example program so far. It displays a few lines of text and contains a push button you click when you're done reading the dialog box text.

You display a dialog box by calling one of the dialog box creation functions and passing a *dialog box template* and the address of a dialog function. A dialog box template describes the appearance of the dialog box: the size of the pop-up window, the window styles used to create the pop-up window, a list of the controls to create in the pop-up window, their sizes and locations, the font to use for text in the controls, and similar parameters. The dialog box creation functions use the specified dialog box template to create a window based on the description in the template. The specified dialog function processes some of the messages for the pop-up window and the controls in the pop-up window.

When Windows creates the pop-up window for a dialog box, it creates the window based on the *dialog window class*. The dialog window class is predefined by Windows, as are the button, list box, and other predefined control classes. The dialog window class specifies a function inside Windows itself as the window function for the windows of that class, that is, of the class "dialog box window". This window function provides a keyboard interface to the controls; for example, you can tab between controls and use the arrow keys to select a particular control in a group of controls. The controls in a dialog box send the messages described in Chapters 8 through 10 to this window function, not to the dialog function you specify when you create the dialog box. This window function passes some of the messages to your specified dialog function for processing.

There are three ways to create a dialog box template:

1. You can use one of a number of dialog editors that are on the market. The Resource Editor application provided with the Microsoft Visual C++ and similar tools in other development environments allow you to graphically lay out the appearance of a dialog box. When

you're satisfied with the appearance of a dialog box, these tools allow you to save a description of the dialog box in a text file. This file is usually, but does not have to be, an .rc file (*Resource Compiler input file*).

2. Because the dialog box template is actually a text file, you can also use a text editor to create the file. Occasionally you might create (or edit) the text file "by hand" to make a change not easily performed by a dialog editor.

3. You can build a data structure in memory and pass the address of the data structure to a dialog box creation function. The data structure describes the dialog box and each of the controls to create in the dialog box. Typically, you would use this method only when you don't know the form of the dialog until runtime. To demonstrate this method, we create an **About...** dialog box in the example program later in this chapter using a dialog box template data structure.

The first two methods produce a text file that forms the application's resource definition file. You compile the application's resource definition file using the Resource Compiler that produces an output (.res) file containing a binary version of the resource definitions. (In case you're curious, the Resource Compiler compiles the text dialog box templates into this very same data structure that you can construct using the third method.)

As you link your Windows application, the Linker inserts the compiled resource definitions (.res file) in the executable program (.exe) file.[1] You create a dialog box either by calling one of the dialog box creation functions and indicating which one of the dialog box templates from the application's resource definitions to use or by calling one of the dialog box "indirect" creation functions and pointing to the data structure to use.

If you are coming from a Win16 environment, the Resource Compiler worked somewhat differently there. Depending on a command-line switch, the rc program either acted as a resource *compiler*, taking an .rc file and creating an .res file, or as a resource *binder*, taking an .res file and an .exe file and either adding the resources to the executable file or replacing the existing resources of the executable with the new .res file. In Win32, this is all done by the Linker.

Dialog Functions and Callback Functions

A dialog function is a callback function somewhat like a window function but also very much like a timer callback function.

Failing to declare a function to be a callback function often causes your program to operate improperly. Any time we have strange, unpredictable problems with a Windows application, we immediately check to see whether all window and callback functions have the proper linkage type, and as a result we often end up fixing the problem quickly. A notable symptom is the generation of a General Protection Fault (GPF) (exception code 0xC0000005), whereupon you find yourself in the middle of some piece of assembly code that makes no sense. Be sure you add the CALLBACK attribute to your callback function declarations.

---

[1] Actually, it first converts the .res file into a linkable COFF file (Common Object File Format) and then links *that* into the executable. But this is a fine point.

Modal and Modeless Dialog Boxes

A dialog box can be one of two forms: modal or modeless. Displaying a *modal dialog box* stops the application and forces the user to respond to the dialog box. A modal dialog box disables its owner window when the dialog box is displayed. Because a disabled window cannot receive keyboard or mouse input, the user cannot continue interacting with the owner window, but must respond to the dialog box. When the dialog box terminates, it enables its owner window, thereby once again allowing it to process input.

Displaying a *modeless dialog box* does not stop the application and does not force the user to respond to the dialog box. A modeless dialog box does not disable its owner window, so the user can interact both with the owner window and the modeless dialog box. For example, a paint program might display its painting tools in a modeless dialog box. The user could draw in the application window and also select new painting tools from the modeless dialog box.

You may have heard that if you use the Microsoft Foundation Class (MFC) library version 4 (or later), "there are no modal dialog boxes". This is true only at the low-level implementation level. If you invoke a modal dialog box, the library actually creates a modeless dialog box and "fakes modality". This is necessary in order to support OCX controls. The point is that although modal dialog boxes are not created by API functions, neither you the programmer nor the user can tell that the library is faking the modality.

Modal Dialog Boxes

Most dialog boxes are *modal* dialog boxes. The **About...** dialog box in all the example programs you've seen so far is a modal dialog box. The **File Open...** and **Save As...** dialog boxes contained in many Windows applications are modal dialog boxes. In each case, Windows suspends execution of the application until the user responds to the display or request for information. As you saw in the Towers of Hanoi program, you can't simply stop and wait for an event. Even though Win32 is preemptive, an application waiting in a tight loop ties up processor resources, keeps memory resources locked in place because the process is active, and, on laptops, interferes with power-save and low-power handling.

Using a modal dialog box gives the appearance that an application stops and waits for input. You display a modal dialog box by calling one of the `DialogBox`, `DialogBoxParam`, `DialogBoxIndirect`, or `DialogBoxIndirectParam` functions. These functions create and display a modal dialog box and do not immediately return control but seemingly suspend. Because the newly created dialog box disables input to its owner window, all mouse and keyboard input for the application flows to the window function for the dialog box window, which then passes most of the input to the dialog function.

The dialog function processes messages from the controls in the dialog box. Eventually, it should decide to terminate. For example, a dialog box often terminates when the user clicks a provided **OK** or **Cancel** push button. The dialog function terminates the dialog box by calling the `EndDialog` function and specifying a return value. That return value is used as the return value from the suspended function call that originally created the dialog box.

It's important to realize that the `EndDialog` function doesn't actually terminate the dialog box. It sets a flag requesting that the dialog box be terminated. The `EndDialog` function then returns to its caller, the dialog function. Windows terminates the dialog box when the dialog function returns from processing the current message. Control then returns from the original call to the `DialogBox` (or equivalent) function. The value of the `DialogBox` (or equivalent) function is–just to repeat the point–the argument provided to the `EndDialog` function.

The `DialogBox` function (and its companion functions) avoids returning immediately to its caller by starting a secondary message loop similar to the one in the Towers of Hanoi program. This secondary message loop keeps messages flowing through Windows and avoids halting other applications. However, messages may arrive and be dispatched from this secondary message loop to the owner window of the dialog box; only keyboard and mouse input has been disabled, not messages in general.

It is this secondary message loop that makes it impossible for a modal dialog to handle the event notifications from OCX controls. If you want to use OCX controls and you are coding without using MFC, you will find that life becomes very complex very quickly. If you plan to use OCX controls, we strongly urge you to write your application using MFC.

For example, `WM_TIMER` messages could still be sent to the window function that is "suspended" on the call to the `DialogBox` function. Messages sent from another application or even the dialog function itself are also delivered to the owner window function. This can lead to problems if your code expects global and static variables to have the same value before and after the call to the `DialogBox` function. Other messages that arrive during the indeterminate delay produced by creating a modal dialog box could possibly change such variables.

You specify the window styles for a dialog box in the dialog box template. You can also select from a few dialog styles unique to a dialog box window. A dialog box must be a pop-up window. It cannot have the `WS_CHILD` window style. Windows disables all child windows when their parent windows are disabled. A `WS_CHILD`-style modal dialog box would disable its parent, which would disable itself as well. Then, because neither the parent nor the child window could receive input, the dialog box could never terminate. If you are using the MFC class library, you should note that the dialog templates that you use for an MFC `CFormView` or `CPropertyPage` actually *require* the `WS_CHILD` style. That is because these "dialog boxes" are handled specially by the MFC code as modeless dialogs.

The recommended styles for a modal dialog box are `DS_MODALFRAME`, `WS_CAPTION`, and `WS_SYSMENU`. Creating a window with these styles produces an overlapped window with a border that represents a modal dialog box. The window has a title bar, a system menu, and a close button. Including the system menu allows the user to terminate the dialog box via the **Close** command on the system menu (or its equivalent: double-clicking on the system menu icon) as well as by using a control to signal completion (like an **OK** or **Cancel** push button).

You can also create dialog boxes with `WS_THICKFRAME` borders for more sophisticated applications that want a resizable dialog. You further can create dialog boxes with menus. We will deal with these topics later. Table 11.1 shows other dialog styles.

Table 11.1: Dialog box styles

Style	Meaning
DS_3DLOOK [4]	Uses a nonbold font and draws 3D borders around controls. Not required for any application marked for Windows 4.0 or higher.
DS_ABSALIGNDS_ABSALIGN	Indicates the coordinates are screen coordinates. If this style is not present, Windows assumes the coordinates specifying the dialog box position are client coordinates relative to the parent of the dialog.
DS_CENTER [4]	Centers the dialog in the screen *working area* (the working area is that part not obscured by the tray).
DS_CENTERMOUSE [4]	Forces the mouse to the center of the dialog box.
DS_CONTEXTHELP	Includes the question mark "button" in the caption of the dialog. Enables context-sensitive help via the WM_HELP message.
DS_CONTROL	Creates a dialog box that works as a child window of another dialog box.
DS_FIXEDSYS [4]	Uses the SYSTEM_FIXED_FONT instead of the SYSTEM_FONT.
DS_LOCALEDIT	Obsolete; applies only to Win16 applications. Ignored in Win32.
DS_MODALFRAME	Creates a dialog modal frame around the window.
DS_NOFAILCREATE [4]	Creates the dialog even if errors exist, such as errors in creating a child control.
DS_NOIDLEMSG	Suppresses WM_ENTERIDLE messages sent to the owner.
DS_SETFONT	Used only for the "indirect" forms; indicates that the DLGTEMPLATE contains the font name and size information.
DS_SETFOREGROUND	Forces the dialog to the foreground (using the SetForegroundWindow function internally).
DS_SYSMODAL	Creates a system-modal dialog box with the WS_EX_TOPMOST style. However, this style alone has no effect on other windows in the system (you must specify MB_SYSMODAL in the creation call).

[4] Win32 4.*x* API only.

Modeless Dialog Boxes

A *modeless* dialog box does *not* disable its owner window when it is created. A modeless dialog appears as a separate and peer window to its owner window. The user can interact with the dialog box controls (an interaction that results in messages arriving at the dialog function) and concurrently, use the owner window (which sends messages to its window function). You will most often use modeless dialogs for tool configuration windows and for debugging output windows. You will use them implicitly in property pages. In MFC-based libraries, you will find them in the CFormView, CRecordView, or CPropertyPage classes.

You create a modeless dialog box by calling the CreateDialog, CreateDialogIndirect, CreateDialogParam, or CreateDialogIndirectParam function. These functions create and display a modeless dialog box, but unlike the functions for a modal dialog box, they return immediately from the call. They do not wait for the dialog box to process input and terminate.

Because these functions return immediately, they obviously don't create a secondary message loop like a modal dialog box. Instead, a modeless dialog box receives messages dispatched by the original message loop (usually in the WinMain function). However, this leads to the first real change to a message loop that's been a steadfast and stable companion until now.

The IsDialogMessage *Function*

One of the main reasons for using a dialog box is to let Windows handle the details of moving the input focus from control to control and selecting controls via keyboard input. Windows does this only for a modeless dialog box when you call the IsDialogMessage function as part of the message loop. This function determines whether a given message is for a specified modeless dialog box, and if so, it processes the message. The IsDialogMessage function converts keyboard messages into commands to dialog box controls. For example, when the function detects a **Tab** key press, it moves the input focus to the next control (or group of controls) in the dialog box. A down arrow or up arrow key press selects the next or previous control in a group, such as the next radio button in a group of radio buttons.

You use this function by altering your message loop as follows:

```
while (GetMessage (&msg, 0, 0, 0)
    if (hdlg == NULL || !IsDialogMessage (hdlg, &msg)) {
        TranslateMessage (&msg) ;
        DispatchMessage (&msg) ;
    }
```

The hdlg variable is the handle of the currently active modeless dialog. We will show in the next section how this variable is set and maintained.

The use of IsDialogMessage is not limited to the message loop for supporting modeless dialogs. You can also use the IsDialogMessage function to provide a dialog-box-like keyboard interface to those controls that you create in any window. To provide a keyboard interface to an ordinary window containing controls, pass the window handle rather than the dialog box handle to the IsDialogMessage function.

Once you retrieve a message, you must check to see whether it's for a modeless dialog box. You typically create a modeless dialog box only when it's needed; consequently, the foregoing example assumes that the global variable hdlg contains the dialog box handle when the modeless dialog box exists. Only when the modeless dialog box exists do you pass the message to the IsDialogMessage function. The IsDialogMessage function processes only those messages intended for the specified dialog box. It returns a nonzero value when it processes a message and 0 otherwise. You must not pass a message processed by the IsDialogMessage function to the `TranslateMessage` or `DispatchMessage` functions. Of course, when the message isn't processed by the `IsDialogMessage` function, it needs to be translated and dispatched as normal.

Eventually, you'll want to terminate the modeless dialog box. You terminate a modeless dialog box just as you do all windows: by calling the `DestroyWindow` function. Do *not* call `EndDialog` for a modeless dialog box.

Using Multiple, Concurrent Modeless Dialog Boxes

When you have more than one modeless dialog displayed concurrently, you need to call the `IsDialogMessage` function for the currently active one in order to provide all with a keyboard interface. You can maintain a global variable with each modeless dialog box's handle in it. Then, for each message, you can check each variable for a nonzero value and, if the value is nonzero, call the `IsDialogMessage` function. But there is an easier way.

It's easier to keep a single global dialog box handle such as `hdlg`, as shown in the previous code fragment. The `IsDialogMessage` function processes keyboard input messages. Such messages are sent only to the active window. Only one window can be active at any given time. So when Windows activates a modeless dialog box, you can place the dialog box handle in the single global variable. When Windows deactivates a modeless dialog box, you set the global variable to 0. You then need test only one variable when calling the `IsDialogMessage` function in your message loop. You can implement this approach as follows:

1. Modify your message loop to call `IsDialogMessage` if the `hdlg` variable is non-NULL (as we have shown).

2. Add a user-defined message handler to set the global variable.

3. Add a handler in your modeless dialogs to send a user-defined message to their parent stating their activation status.

While this may seem a bit more complex than manipulating a single global variable directly from the dialog itself, it is far more flexible. For example, it allows you to create reusable dialogs (building up your personal collection of "common dialogs") for which you don't have to know the actual variable name of the dialog box handle used in the main message loop. It allows you to create modeless dialogs that execute in separate threads, since each thread can maintain its own modeless dialog variable and you don't need to know how it does that in your dialog. And you can put your favorite dialogs in DLLs, and they don't need to know anything about how they are handled by their parents.

Modify your main message loop:

```
HWND hdlgActive ;     /* Global variable */
    .
    .
    .
    while (GetMessage (&msg, 0, 0, 0)
        if (hdlgActive == NULL ||
            !IsDialogMessage (hdlgActive, &msg))
            { /* normal processing */
             TranslateMessage (&msg) ;
             DispatchMessage (&msg) ;
            } /* normal processing */
    .
```

Define a user-defined message, such as the following, where we chose WM_USER + 17 as the value:

```
#define UWM_MODELESS_HANDLE (WM_USER + 17)
```

Add an activation handler to your modeless dialog:

```
void dlg_OnActivate(HWND hdlg, UINT state,
                    HWND ActDeact, BOOL minimized)
    {
     if(state)
        { /* activating */
         SendMessage(GetParent(hdlg), UWM_MODELESS_HANDLE, 0, (LPARAM)hdlg);
        } /* activating */
     else
        { /* deactivating */
         SendMessage(GetParent(hdlg), UWM_MODELESS_HANDLE, 0, 0);
        } /* deactivating */
    }
    .
    .
    // In the modeless dialog function...
    switch (msg)
        { /* msg */
        case WM_ACTIVATE:
            HANDLE_WM_ACTIVATE(hDlg, wParam, lParam, dlg_OnActivate) ;
            return FALSE ;
```

Write a handler for the message in the parent window:

```
void mywindow_OnModelessHandle(HWND hwnd, WPARAM wParam, LPARAM lParam)
    {
     hdlgActive = (HWND)lParam;
    }
```

Handle the message in the parent window:

```
        switch(msg)
            { /* msg */
            HANDLE_MSG(hwnd, WM_whatever, ...);
            // ... etc.
            case UWM_MODELESS_HANDLE:
                mywindow_OnModelessHandle (hwnd, wParam, lParam);
                return 0;
            } /* msg */
```

This example uses another of the message cracker handlers, HANDLE_WM_ACTIVATE, whose parameters are shown in the following box.

To be fully general, you should use RegisterWindowMessage and register a specific window message; then your dialogs are truly reusable, since not even the message number is hardwired. We discuss this further on page 759.

Making the dialog visible on the screen

When a modeless dialog receives the focus, it may be partially or almost totally obscured by having been dragged off the screen. So you might want to cause it to become visible. The Win32 4.*x* API provides a

WM_ACTIVATE Message Cracker Handlers

```
void cls_OnActivate(HWND hwnd, UINT state, HWND ActDeact,
                    BOOL minimized);
```

Parameter	wParam lo	wParam hi	lParam lo	lParam hi	Meaning
hwnd					Window handle of the window receiving message.
state	■				Activate state of hwnd:
					WA_ACTIVE — Activated by some method other than a mouse click (for example, by a call to the SetActiveWindow function or by use of the keyboard interface to select the window).
					WA_CLICKACTIVE — Activated by a mouse click.
					WA_INACTIVE — Deactivated.
ActDeact			■		Depends on the value of the state parameter:
					WA_INACTIVE — The handle of the window being activated.
					WA_ACTIVE / WA_CLICKACTIVE — The handle of the window being deactivated.
minimized		■			The minimized state of the window being activated or deactivated. A nonzero value indicates the window is minimized.

message to do this: DM_REPOSITION. You send this message to a dialog after you resize it or if you have changed the focus to it. It repositions the dialog so that it is entirely within the area of the desktop. An example of this might be triggering a modeless dialog from a menu item or toolbar command:

```
void mainframe_OnShowToolbox(HWND hwnd)
    {
    if(!IsWindow(htoolbox))
        htoolbox = CreateDialog(...);
    else
        { /* refocus it */
        BringWindowToTop(htoolbox);
        SetFocus(htoolbox);
        SendMessage(htoolbox, DM_REPOSITION, 0, 0);
        } /* refocus it */
    }
```

This will force the toolbox to full visibility if it has been dragged out of the way.

Using Registered Window Messages

You may have seen a flaw in the above example: We set our user-defined message to a constant value. This means that every application we write has to reserve this value in case it uses one of our modeless dialogs. Eventually, we might end up with a list of dozens of message numbers that are "reserved" for some purpose by some code or DLL that we might possibly consider using in the future. Keeping track of all of this becomes difficult or impossible. Eventually, you will end up with two completely different dialogs that send the same user-defined message value to their parents for totally different purposes. When that happens, you can't use the dialogs in the same application. Of course, it is easy to change one of the dialogs, but if the dialog was in a DLL, now it will send a different message to its parent in every application that uses it. As a result, every application that is already compiled for that DLL will stop working!

There is a cleaner solution to this problem than having to maintain a long list of pre-assigned message numbers for user-defined messages: the *Registered Window Message*.

Windows reserves the message numbers less than `WM_USER` and between 0x8000 and 0xBFFF for its own purposes. You may use any message number in the range `WM_USER` through 0x7FFF for your own purposes. Windows also reserves messages in the range 0xC000 through 0xFFFF to be *registered* message codes. You can register a window message by giving a character string name to it and calling the `RegisterWindowMessage` function. The value you get back is a value that is "globally unique" for your current Windows session. You can't predict what this value will be, but you can be assured that no other registered window message will have it. Depending on the order in which you run applications, you might get different values after you reboot. But within each Windows session, you can be certain that for a given string name the values are unique. Hence, you can even have two separate applications registering the same string, which will give them the same message number. These two applications can now send messages to each other.

One disadvantage of the registered window message is that you cannot use its value in a `switch` statement because a `switch` statement requires that all the cases be compile-time constants. You have to add an explicit test of the message number, comparing it to the variable that holds the registered message value (and do this for each registered message you wish to process).

A typical place to register a window message is in the `initInstance` function for your application. Here's an example. First, we define a string name and put it in some header file, such as `modeless.h`:

```
#define RWM_MODELESS_HANDLE "Modeless.Handle"
```

The string you choose should contain enough characters to be unique. Here we elected to use two words separated by a period, but any characters can appear in the string, including spaces.

Next, we declare a variable to hold the registered message ID:

```
int ModelessMessageID = 0;
```

Add a line to our `initInstance` handler to register the message:

```
300L initInstance(UINT nCmdShow)
    {
    // .. other initialization (see Chapter 2)
    ModelessMessageID = RegisterWindowMessage (RWM_MODELESS_HANDLE);
    // eventually return a value TRUE or FALSE...
    }
```

In the message decoding, we add a line to handle the registered message. Note that we put it into the default case of the switch, but we could have as easily chosen to place it as a test before the switch statement:

```
switch(msg)
    { /* msg */
    HANDLE_MSG(hwnd, WM_whatever, ...);
    HANDLE_MSG(hwnd, WM_somethingelse, ...);
    default:
        if(msg == ModelessMessageID)
            mywindow_OnModelessID (hwnd, wParam, lParam);
        else
        if(msg == ...) // more registered messages
            mywindow_On... // call handler
        break;
    } /* msg */
```

We defined the mywindow_OnModelessID handler as shown in the following. We don't encourage writing code inline in the switch statement. Such programs, as we have observed earlier, are harder to read and maintain. The efficiency considerations of code size or speed are almost totally irrelevant.

```
void mywindow_OnModelessID(HWND hwnd, WPARAM wParam, LPARAM lParam)
    {
    hdlg = (HWND)lParam;
    }
```

We need to put this efficiency argument in perspective. Nearly all messages are generated as a consequence of user input. Thus the performance is constrained primarily by user perception. Let's take a look at this quantitatively. A mouse is approximately two feet from the ear. The speed of sound in air is approximately 1100 ft/sec. The mouse-click-down signal is virtually instantaneous, insofar as the computer hardware is concerned, but the user won't detect the mouse click aurally for approximately 2 ms. The neural path between the fingertip and the brain is approximately 3 ft. The speed of neural propagation is approximately 300 ft/sec. The tactile feedback of the mouse click takes 10 ms to arrive at the brain. This does not even take into consideration the time for the perceptual processing in the brain. Take these numbers and figure out what percentage of the total time is represented by the additional function call to process the message. Essentially, the overhead of the function call is, in the worst case, on a very slow processor, perhaps 300 ns. On a modern high-performance processor, it could be five times faster. There is no need to "optimize" the performance by writing hard-to-maintain code, since the perceptual time swamps any possible code improvement by four to six orders of magnitude.

Creating a Dialog Box

Table 11.2 lists the functions that create a dialog box. You must select the proper function based on the type of dialog box (modal or modeless) you wish to create, the source of the dialog box template (a dialog resource or DLGTEMPLATE structure), and the need to pass an application-defined parameter to the dialog function.

Table 11.2: Dialog box creation functions

Function	Type	Parameter	Source of Dialog
DialogBox	Modal	No	Resource file.
DialogBoxParam	Modal	Yes	Resource file.
DialogBoxIndirect	Modal	No	LPDLGTEMPLATE.
DialogBoxIndirectParam	Modal	Yes	LPDLGTEMPLATE.
CreateDialog	Modeless	No	Resource file.
CreateDialogParam	Modeless	Yes	Resource file.
CreateDialogIndirect	Modeless	No	LPDLGTEMPLATE.
CreateDialogIndirectParam	Modeless	Yes	LPDLGTEMPLATE.

These functions have similar parameters and every function returns an int value. We'll look at these functions as a group. The parameters are explained in Table 11.3. Here are the functions:

```
DialogBox               (HINSTANCE hInstance,
                         LPCTSTR TemplateName,
                         HWND hwndOwner,
                         DLGPROC DialogFunc) ;

DialogBoxParam          (HINSTANCE hInstance,
                         LPCTSTR TemplateName,
                         HWND hwndOwner,
                         DLGPROC DialogFunc,
                         LPARAM InitParam) ;

DialogBoxIndirect       (HINSTANCE hInstance,
                         LPCDLGTEMPLATE dlgTemplate,
                         HWND hwndOwner,
                         DLGPROC DialogFunc) ;

DialogBoxIndirectParam  (HINSTANCE hInstance
                         LPCDLGTEMPLATE dlgTemplate
                         HWND hwndOwner
                         DLGPROC DialogFunc
                         LPARAM InitParam)

CreateDialog            (HINSTANCE hInstance
                         LPCTSTR TemplateName
                         HWND hwndOwner,
                         DLGPROC DialogFunc)

CreateDialogParam       (HINSTANCE hInstance
                         LPCTSTR TemplateName
                         HWND hwndOwner
                         DLGPROC DialogFunc
                         LPARAM InitParam)
```

```
CreateDialogIndirect        (HINSTANCE hInstance
                             LPCDLGTEMPLATE dlgTemplate
                             HWND hwndOwner,
                             DLGPROC DialogFunc) ;

CreateDialogIndirectParam (HINSTANCE hInstance
                             LPCDLGTEMPLATE dlgTemplate
                             HWND hwndOwner
                             DLGPROC DialogFunc
                             LPARAM InitParam)
```

Table 11.3: Dialog box creation parameters

Parameter	Description
hInstance	Specifies the handle of the module instance that contains a dialog resource template. Normally, this is the hInstance parameter that Windows passed to your WinMain function. However, you could create a DLL that contains dialog templates used by an application. You would then specify the handle of the DLL (which you get from the LoadLibrary function) because it would contain the desired dialog template.
You will use one of the two following parameters, depending on whether you are doing a "nonindirect" or an "indirect" creation:	
TemplateName	The "name" of the dialog template. This can be either the string name or an integer that is made into a name using the MAKEINTRESOURCE macro.
DlgTemplate	A pointer to a block of memory that contains a dialog template. You will either call a "nonindirect" dialog function and specify the resource in the resource file or an "indirect" dialog and specify a pointer to a memory resource in the same format.
hwndOwner	Specifies the handle of the window that owns the dialog box.
DialogFunc	Specifies the address of the dialog function. You must declare the dialog function as a CALLBACK function that returns a BOOL value. The example uses the identifier DialogFunc for the name of the dialog function, but the name isn't significant.
The following is used only for the "–Param" versions of the calls:	
InitParam	A 32-bit value that you must cast to an LPARAM. This value will be sent as the lParam value in the WM_INITDIALOG message.

message

(defined within Windows)

Windows dialog box procedure
`LRESULT DialogProc(...)`

Your dialog box function
`BOOL MyDlgProc(...)`

TRUE

FALSE

Default dialog box procedure
`LRESULT DefDialogProc(...)`

Default window procedure
`LRESULT DefWindowProc(...)`

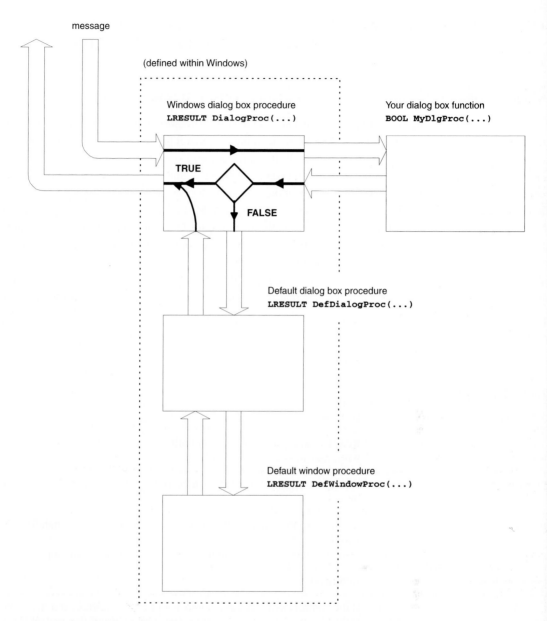

Figure 11.1: Dialog-handling functions and their relationships

Here, for example, is a typical dialog function declaration. We call it `MyDlgProc`. You should choose an appropriate name for each of your dialogs. Note the *very important* presence of the `CALLBACK` linkage type declaration!

```
BOOL CALLBACK
MyDlgProc (HWND hdlg, UINT msg, WPARAM wParam, LPARAM lParam) ;
```

Unlike a window function, a dialog function must *not* call the `DefWindowProc` function to process unwanted messages. A dialog function must return a `FALSE` value to indicate that it has not processed the message or at least wants the normal processing to occur as well. It returns a nonzero value when it processes a message and doesn't want the normal processing for that message. The built-in dialog-class window function actually receives the message first. It calls your dialog function, passing it the message and allowing the dialog function to process the message. When the dialog function returns `FALSE`, the dialog-class window function provides the default processing for the message. This is shown in Figure 11.1. The most important exception to the rule that you return `TRUE` to indicate no further processing is required and `FALSE` to indicate that further processing is required is the `WM_INITDIALOG` message, although there are a few other messages that have special return value requirements (see Table 11.9 on page 793). You may also wish to handle user-defined messages (particularly in modeless dialogs) that return specific values; we show how to do this on page 793.

Table 11.4 shows the default handling for dialog messages. This is the action that will be taken if you return `FALSE` from your dialog function. For all other messages not listed in Table 11.4, the message is passed directly to `DefWindowProc` (see Table 3.1 on page 105).

Table 11.4: DefDlgProc actions

Message	Processing
DM_GETDEFID	Returns the control ID of the default push button, if one exists; otherwise, returns 0.
DM_SETDEFID	Sets the control whose ID is in wParam to be the new default push button.
WM_ACTIVATE	*Activating:* Restores input focus to the control whose handle was saved. *Deactivating:* Saves the handle of the control that has the input focus.
WM_CHARTOITEM	Returns 0.
WM_CLOSE	If the control currently has a control with code IDCANCEL *and* that control is disabled, this beeps and returns. Otherwise, if the control is enabled, it posts a WM_COMMAND message with the control ID IDCANCEL.
WM_COMPAREITEM	Returns 0.
WM_ERASEBKGND	Fills the dialog box client area using the brush returned by the WM_CTLCOLORDLG message (see Chapter 17, page 1211) or the default window color.

Table 11.4: DefDlgProc actions

Message	Processing
WM_GETFONT	Returns the handle of the application-defined dialog box font (see DS_SETFONT).
WM_INITDIALOG	Returns FALSE.
WM_LBUTTONDOWN	If a combo box has the input focus, this sends it a CB_SHOWDROPDOWN message requesting that it hide its drop-down list box. The message is then passed to DefWindowProc.
WM_NCDESTROY	Releases any application-defined font for any dialog that has the DS_SETFONT style. The message is then passed on to DefWindowProc.
WM_NCLBUTTONDOWN	If a combo box has the input focus, this sends it a CB_SHOWDROPDOWN message requesting that it hide its drop-down list box. The message is then passed to DefWindowProc.
WM_NEXTDLGCTL	Sets the input focus to a control. The message is ignored if the focus is not on a control.

wParam	lParam lo	lParam hi	Effect
HWND	1		Handle of the control that gets focus.
0	0		Next feasible WS_TABSTOP control.
!= 0	0		Previous feasible WS_TABSTOP control.

Message	Processing
WM_SETFOCUS	Sets the focus to the control whose window handle has been saved. If no handle has been saved (see the WM_ACTIVATE action, above in this table, and WM_SHOWWINDOW and WM_SYSCOMMAND, below in this table), the focus is set to the first enabled, visible control in the dialog.
WM_SHOWWINDOW	If the dialog is being hidden, saves the handle of the control that has the focus. The message is then passed to DefWindowProc.
WM_SYSCOMMAND	If the dialog is being minimized, saves the handle of the control that has the focus. The message is then passed to DefWindowProc.
WM_VKEYTOITEM	Returns 0.

A dialog box function is a callback function, like a window function or a timer callback function. It processes messages for the dialog box much as a window function processes messages for a window. However, it typically processes only the WM_INITDIALOG, WM_COMMAND, WM_HSCROLL, WM_VSCROLL, and WM_NOTIFY messages. It may also handle the WM_DESTROY message if it has to free up resources it has allocated. But a dialog function is, after all, just another message handler. It can handle all of the usual window messages, including notifications that the color scheme has changed and that the system is shutting down, as well as your own user-defined messages.

The WM_INITDIALOG message arrives at the dialog function before the dialog box is displayed. You use this message to set the input focus to a specific control and perform any required initialization. The controls in the dialog box send WM_COMMAND messages, WM_NOTIFY messages, WM_VSCROLL messages, or WM_HSCROLL messages to the dialog function when the user alters them. The WM_COMMAND and WM_NOTIFY messages contain the notification codes described in Chapters 8 through 10.

 You might see a WM_COMMAND message arriving *before* a WM_INITDIALOG message. You have to be prepared to accommodate this situation. In particular, you can use some of the common controls (such as the "auto-buddy" feature on spin controls), which will generate WM_COMMAND messages when they are created long before the WM_INITDIALOG message comes through.

You don't always need to specify a dialog function when you create a dialog box. Normally, a dialog box uses the dialog-class window function somewhere inside Windows. This window function passes messages to your dialog function, that is, the function specified by the DialogFunc parameter. This is the default behavior if you don't explicitly declare a class in the dialog box template.

You can specify a *private dialog class* when you define a dialog box. You do this with the CLASS statement in a dialog box template. When you specify a private window class for a dialog box, the window function specified when the class was registered processes messages for the dialog box rather than the dialog-class window function inside Windows. All messages that are not explicitly processed by the private-class window function for a dialog box must be passed to the DefDlgProc function. Calling the DefWindowProc function is not a suitable substitute. The call to the DefDlgProc function looks nearly identical:

```
return DefDlgProc (hdlg, msg, wParam, lParam) ;
```

Using CreateWindow versus CreateDialog

There are two ways to create a window that contains numerous controls. The first is the brute force method. You can call the CreateWindow function to create the window. You then repeatedly call the CreateWindow function to create each control. This approach requires either that the CreateWindow calls are explicitly written in your code or that you build an application-specific data structure that you interpret to build the window and the controls.

The second, and better, approach uses dialog templates and CreateDialog (or one of the other dialog creation functions). Rather than build an application-specific data structure, you build a Windows-defined dialog template. In this template you can specify an application-defined window class. You call one of the dialog creation functions and specify the dialog template. Windows interprets the dialog template and creates the window and all the child controls for you. Because you specified an application-defined class, Windows sends all messages for the created window to the window function defined when you registered the class. Several development platforms support this technique directly, such as Microsoft Visual C++. In Visual C++, when you invoke the AppWizard to create a new application, you check the item that says to create an application as a "top-level dialog". In this way, all of the necessary code to accomplish this will be generated (in fact, the InitInstance handler will create the modal dialog and run it).

These two approaches differ in several ways. The template approach is less work and easier to modify as requirements change than is the explicit window/control creation approach. When you use the template approach, however, you must register the application-defined window class and request at least DLGWINDOWEXTRA bytes of window extra area. The first DLGWINDOWEXTRA bytes of window extra area are used by the DefDlgProc function. The brute force approach requires no window extra area because you are really just creating a window with some controls in it. You don't call the DefDlgProc function for such windows; therefore you do not need to reserve the window extra area.

Passing Parameters When Creating a Dialog Box

A philosophy we have found very useful in constructing dialogs is that *no dialog should access any static variable (except for static, read-only tables) and should never access any variables by name in any module other than its own.* Following this philosophy would in general make it hard for a dialog to actually *do* anything, so there has to be a way to pass parameters in to a dialog. This philosophy often is critical to the success of Win32 applications. Early Windows 3.*x* examples were not always "thread safe", and using multiple threads in Win32 while following the Windows 3.*x* style could result in the corruption of critical information. Although we are not going to discuss multithreading issues here (see Chapter 18), the philosophy we use for dialogs makes it easier to add full thread safety later. Perhaps the simplest test to decide what a dialog should and should not access from within its code is to think about what would happen if you wanted to put it into a DLL. You should think of DLL code as having *no* access to your program symbols. It can communicate only by what is passed in, what it can pass back, and messages it can send and receive.

One of the important ways of passing information into a dialog is via the *dialog parameter*. The InitParam parameter specified in the CreateDialogIndirectParam, CreateDialogParam, and DialogBoxParam function calls is passed as the lParam parameter of the message. Windows sends the WM_INITDIALOG message to the dialog function before displaying the dialog box.

Quite often, you'll use this additional parameter when creating a private-class dialog box, as already described. We frequently use a dialog box template as a convenient method for describing a series of similar windows we wish to create. We pass a unique parameter each time we create a window based on a specific template. The private-class window function uses the parameter to tailor each generic window created, based on the template, to the task at hand.

For example, you might create a number of identical windows, each of which displays the current and desired temperature for different areas of one or more ovens on an assembly line. Every window might also contain a control that allows the user to set the temperature. Even though each control might have a different range, each window operates in the same fashion. The range of a control contained in such a window could be specified by the extra parameter. The template specifies the appearance of a window, and the extra parameter can contain or, more often, point to, additional window-specific information used by the window function. We talk much more about this throughout this chapter.

We've described three different ways to specify the dialog box template. Most of the time, you'll probably use a dialog editor to design a rough approximation of the final dialog box. You may also edit the dialog box template, which is produced by the dialog editor, with a text editor in order to position controls exactly. Alternatively and much less frequently, you can create a *dialog template* (DLGTEMPLATE) structure in memory and provide a pointer to the structure. There are several articles describing how to build these dialog templates. However, based on the number of problems we see reported in the forums by people who are trying this, it is *not* a trivial exercise! We will show how to construct a simple dialog template in memory starting on page 770.

The WM_INITDIALOG Message

Windows sends a WM_INITDIALOG message to a dialog function immediately before displaying the dialog box. The wParam parameter contains the window handle of the first control in the dialog box that can be given the input focus. This parameter contains the application-specific data passed in as the InitParam when you call the CreateDialogIndirectParam, CreateDialogParam, DialogBoxIndirectParam, or DialogBoxParam function. If you did not call one of the -Param versions of these functions, the lParam value is NULL.

WM_INITDIALOG Message Cracker Handler

BOOL cls_OnInitDialog(HWND hwnd, HWND hFocus, LPARAM lParam);				
Result	TRUE to allow hFocus to actually get the focus. FALSE if you have set the focus yourself.			

	wParam		**lParam**		
Parameter	**lo**	**hi**	**lo**	**hi**	**Meaning**
hwnd					Window handle of the dialog.
hFocus	███				Handle of the first window to receive focus.
lParam			███		Value passed in to –Param version of functions; 0 if "non-Param" functions are called.

When the OnInitDialog handler returns a nonzero value, Windows sets the input focus to the control identified by the wParam parameter (or the hFocus parameter of the message handler function). When your OnInitDialog handler explicitly sets the input focus to a control (using the SetFocus function), you must return a FALSE value to prevent Windows from setting the focus. You must also ensure that your dialog function returns this value to its caller:

```
BOOL MyDialogFunc(HWND hwnd, UINT msg, WPARAM wParam, LPARAM lParam)
    {
    switch(msg)
        { /* msg */
        case WM_INITDIALOG:
            return (BOOL)HANDLE_WM_INITDIALOG(hwnd, wParam, lParam,
                                              mydialog_OnInitDialog);
        } /* msg */
    }
```

When you define a private dialog class, you often don't need to use a dialog function. The dialog window function (which you specified when you registered the private dialog class) typically handles all the messages. In this case, you usually pass NULL as the dialog function parameter in a call to CreateDialog/DialogBox.

Windows sends a WM_INITDIALOG message first to the window function for the dialog box. This can be either the standard system dialog class window function or a private dialog class window function you've defined. Your private class dialog function can process the message or pass the message to the DefDlgProc function. When you process the message (by returning TRUE or FALSE), Windows considers the message process complete and doesn't forward the message further.

When your private dialog class window function passes the message to the DefDlgProc function (as you should do for all unprocessed messages and as the standard system dialog class window function does), Windows checks to see if you specified a dialog function on the CreateDialog or DialogBox call. If you did, Windows sends the WM_INITDIALOG message to the dialog function, allowing it a chance to process the message. If you did not, *no* WM_INITDIALOG message is sent.

A private dialog class window function gets a chance to process the message before Windows sends it to the dialog function.

What to Do in the WM_INITDIALOG Handler

Your WM_INITDIALOG handler will do one or more of the following actions:

- Store initial values in the controls. These are typically check boxes, radio buttons, edit controls, and text controls, but of course any control, including your own custom controls, can have initial values set here. You also may want to change the captions on buttons.

- Change the caption of the dialog.

- Enable, disable, hide, or make visible various controls based on the input data.

- Create a structure on the heap that holds additional information for the dialog while it is executing and attach a pointer to this structure to the dialog.

- Attach a pointer to the creation parameter to the dialog.

- Set the focus to a particular control.

Because all of this happens before the dialog box displays, you can change the status, caption, color, position, or any other property of a control without the user's being subjected to annoying "flicker". The dialog box will not become visible until you have returned from the OnInitDialog handler.

We'll examine several of these cases and see what the code looks like. We pick a relatively simple example: ordering a pizza. The goal is to create a dialog that allows the selection of one of three sizes (small, medium, or large) and a selection of toppings, such as extra cheese, salami, or pineapple. In addition, we have a database of people's favorite pizzas, so if we know the name of a person or a style of pizza we can get a "standard pizza" immediately. The design includes a feature that lets us change the standard pizza for a given pizza style designator.

The program is based on our standard Skeleton program (Chapter 2), with the addition of two dialogs: one to select the name of a person (or "Other") and the other to order the actual pizza. This version won't support adding new pizza-eaters to the database. Nor does it store the database across invocations. We haven't yet seen all the API functions we need to implement these features. For now, we will explore the basics of creating a dialog box, specifically, an interesting set of techniques for dealing with such boxes.

Creating a Dialog Box Template in Your Resource Definition File

You can create the dialog box template by hand using a text editor or by using the dialog editor component of your development environment. All of the major development environments provide resource editors, and a dialog is one kind of resource that you can create and edit. However, we want to show you what those tools are doing. Occasionally, you may need to go in and modify a resource manually or will have to read a resource script. So we devote some space here to explaining the details of these automatically generated files.

Here is the definition for the **About...** dialog box used by the `Skeleton` application:

```
IDD_ABOUTBOX DIALOG DISCARDABLE  22, 17, 204, 83
STYLE DS_MODALFRAME | DS_CONTEXTHELP | WS_POPUP |
            WS_VISIBLE | WS_CAPTION | WS_SYSMENU
CAPTION "About "
FONT 8, "System"FONT
BEGIN
    DEFPUSHBUTTON       "OK", IDOK, 166, 63, 32, 14,
                        WS_GROUP
    ICON                IDR_MAINFRAME, IDC_STATIC, Resource:
                        3, 2, 18, 20
    LTEXT               "FileDescription",
                        IDC_ABOUT_FILEDESCRIPTION,
                        30,2,118,8
    RTEXT               "ProductVersion",
                        IDC_ABOUT_VERSION, 180, 2, 17, 8
    LTEXT               "LegalCopyright",
                        IDC_ABOUT_LEGALCOPYRIGHT,
                        30,10,168,8
    LTEXT               "Comments",
                        IDC_ABOUT_COMMENTS, 30, 18, 168, 8
    CONTROL             "", IDC_STATIC, "Static",
                        SS_BLACKRECT, 2, 31, 200, 1
    LTEXT               "OSVERSION", IDC_ABOUT_OSVERSION,
                        4, 34, 196, 8
    LTEXT               "ProcessorVersion",
                        IDC_ABOUT_PROCESSORVERSION,
                        4, 42, 196, 8
    CONTROL             "", IDC_STATIC ,"Static",
                        SS_BLACKRECT, 2, 52, 200, 1
    LTEXT               "LegalTrademarks",
                        IDC_ABOUT_LEGALTRADEMARKS,
                        3,57,156,18
    LTEXT               "Version ", IDC_STATIC,
                        152, 2, 28, 8
END
```

The DIALOG statement begins the definition of a dialog box template in a resource script file. This dialog box template has the identifier IDD_ABOUTBOX. You can't actually tell at this point if the dialog is identified by an integer or by a string. This is a somewhat unfortunate property of the resource syntax. It leads to much confusion, particularly if you have followed the advice of many early Windows programming books, which were based on earlier tooling. The earlier tooling created only dialog resources that had string names. The problem is to determine which of the two following methods is correct to use to create this dialog:

```
DialogBox(hInstance, _T("IDD_ABOUTBOX"), hWnd, aboutFunc);
DialogBox(hInstance, MAKEINTRESOURCE(IDD_ABOUTBOX), hWnd, aboutFunc) ;
```

If you use the wrong one, your dialog will not come up! This is one of the most common problems we see in the online forums. The answer is almost always, "You used the wrong form of the call to create the dialog". It turns out that, in principle, the only way to actually tell is to look at the set of .h files included in the resource (.rc) file. If you were to find a line like this one:

```
#define IDD_ABOUTBOX 17
```

then you can be sure that the MAKEINTRESOURCE form is the one you want. This is because there is a preprocessor (a rather simplistic one that superficially resembles the standard C preprocessor) that has transformed the DIALOG declaration into

```
17 DIALOG ...
```

so that the "name" is really an integer! This is not always apparent. However, the Microsoft development environment makes this fairly evident. If you ask for the "properties" display while editing a dialog and select the entire dialog box, the name will be displayed either with or without quotation marks. If there are no quotation marks around the dialog name, the "name" is an integer and you must use MAKEINTRESOURCE. If there are quotation marks, the "name" is a string and you must use the string form. Table 11.5 summarizes the notation and calling styles.

Table 11.5: Options for creating a dialog

Displayed As	Invoke By
"IDD_ABOUTBOX"	DialogBox(…, _T("IDD_ABOUTBOX"), …)
IDD_ABOUTBOX	DialogBox(…, MAKEINTRESOURCE(IDD_ABOUTBOX), …)

The DIALOG statement primarily defines the position and size of the dialog box. The position is expressed in client coordinates (pixels) relative to the parent of the dialog. The size is expressed in *dialog units*. A dialog unit is $1/4$ (horizontally) or $1/8$ (vertically) of the system *dialog base unit*. A dialog base unit is derived from the size of a character in the system font. Windows uses dialog units, rather than pixels, to display a dialog box in the same relative size independent of the type of display used (this is because the system font automatically "scales" to keep approximately the same visual appearance independent of the resolution). Also included are the load options and memory options used to indicate when to load the resource and whether the resource must be fixed in memory or can be discarded. Normally, you will make your dialog resources DISCARDABLE. However, you will want to make them PRELOAD and FIXED if you are writing a program that executes from floppy disks, such as an installation program.

The CAPTION statement specifies the text that should appear on the title bar for the dialog box window. In most dialog editors, you simply check off the style box to indicate that the dialog will have a caption, and then type the caption into the appropriate field. This generates the CAPTION statement in the dialog resource.

The STYLE statement lists the window and dialog box styles for the dialog box window. Omitting this statement implies the use of the WS_BORDER, WS_POPUP, and WS_SYSMENU styles. In most resource editors, you simply click the appropriate set of check boxes to generate the components of a STYLE statement.

You could include a MENU statement to define a menu for the dialog box, but doing so is unusual. A dialog box almost never has or needs a menu. Normally you specify this only if you have a top-level dialog (where the dialog box is your entire application) or some very unusual modeless dialog that you want to look like a full-fledged window. In the former case, your development environment tooling (such as Microsoft's App-Wizard) will generate this for you.

The optional (and in this example, omitted) CLASS statement specifies a private dialog box window class. Omitting this statement causes the dialog box to use the Windows standard dialog class. To specify that an application window class should be used for a dialog box, include a CLASS statement that specifies an integer or string, enclosed in double quotation marks, that identifies the class of the dialog box like this:

```
CLASS   "MySpecialClass"
```

You must register this class prior to creating the dialog box. When you register a class used by a dialog box, the cbWndExtra field of the WNDCLASS structure used to register the class must be set to DLGWINDOWEXTRA. It can be a larger value. The DefDlgProc function uses the first DLGWINDOWEXTRA bytes of the extra window area.

Optionally, you can include a FONT statement. This statement specifies the font used by Windows to draw text in the dialog box. The font must have already been loaded before the dialog is created, either during system startup or explicitly by calling the LoadFont function. You specify the size of the font in points and the name of the typeface like this:

```
FONT   12, "MS Sans Serif"
```

You can add an optional EXSTYLE statement. This allows you to set extended styles for the dialog. You can specify any of the WS_EX_ styles. One of these, shown in Table 3.6 on page 124, is the WS_EX_TOPMOST style, which forces the dialog to be the topmost window. For a modal dialog, this style is not particularly useful because it forces the window to be topmost even when the application is not the active one. But for a modeless tool dialog, it guarantees that the tool dialog will "float" above all other windows, including sibling modeless dialogs that aren't "topmost" windows.

You can add a LANGUAGE statement; this changes the default language for the dialog. The LANGUAGE statement requires both a language and a sublanguage specification, using the language codes shown in Table 9.13 on page 638:

```
LANGUAGE language, sublanguage
```

Following all of these specifications, the BEGIN and END statements delimit the beginning and ending of the list of controls that are contained in the dialog box. A dialog box can have up to 255 controls. Although the control IDs themselves are 16-bit values, the control limit is 255. This is generally practical.

There are many different dialog control statements. Most define a specific type of control. One, however, the CONTROL statement, can be used to define any control, whether or not it is a built-in control, a user-defined window, or even (starting with Microsoft's VC++ 4.0) the unique 128-bit ID of an OCX control.

Table 11.6: Dialog control statements

Statement Type	Window Class	Implied Window Style
AUTOCHECKBOX	Button	BS_AUTOCHECKBOX | WS_TABSTOP
AUTO3STATE	Button	BS_AUTO3STATE | WS_TABSTOP
AUTORADIOBUTTON	Button	BS_AUTORADIOBUTTON | WS_TABSTOP
CHECKBOX	Button	BS_CHECKBOX | WS_TABSTOP
COMBOBOX	Combobox	CBS_SIMPLE | WS_TABSTOP
CONTROL	User-specified	WS_CHILD | WS_VISIBLE
CTEXT	Static	SS_CENTER | WS_GROUP
DEFPUSHBUTTON	Button	BS_DEFPUSHBUTTON | WS_TABSTOP
EDITTEXT	Edit	ES_LEFT | WS_BORDER | WS_TABSTOP
GROUPBOX	Button	BS_GROUPBOX | WS_TABSTOP
ICON	Static	SS_ICON
LISTBOX	Listbox	LBS_NOTIFY | WS_BORDER | WS_VSCROLL
LTEXT	Static	SS_LEFT | WS_GROUP
PUSHBOX	Button	BS_PUSHBOX | WS_TABSTOP
PUSHBUTTON	Button	BS_PUSHBUTTON | WS_TABSTOP
RADIOBUTTON	Button	BS_RADIOBUTTON | WS_TABSTOP
RTEXT	Static	SS_RIGHT | WS_GROUP
SCROLLBAR	ScrollBar	SBS_HORZ
STATE3	Button	BS_3STATE | WS_TABSTOP

All control statements, except COMBOBOX, CONTROL, EDITTEXT, LISTBOX, and SCROLLBAR, have the following form:

```
Control-type    "text", id, xUL, yUL, width, height, style, extended-style
```

The **About...** box uses the following statement to define a default push button control:

```
DEFPUSHBUTTON "OK", IDOK, 166, 63, 32, 14, WS_GROUP
```

The COMBOBOX, EDITTEXT, LISTBOX, and SCROLLBAR statements omit the text parameter and have this form:

```
Control-type id, xUL, yUL, width, height, style, extended-style
```

When you want to specify every possible parameter for a control, you use the CONTROL statement. It allows you to specify the text and the window class for the control in addition to all the normal parameters:

```
CONTROL text, id, class, style, xUL, yUL, width, height, extended-style
```

The text parameter specifies the text to be displayed for controls that use it. For example, for a button the text is the label on the button. For a static text control, the text is the text that is displayed. The id parameter specifies the control ID. A control sends this value as part of a WM_COMMAND or WM_NOTIFY notification message to its parent window.

The xUL, yUL, width and height parameters are given in dialog units. The coordinates (xUL, yUL) specify the upper-left corner of the control.

The style parameter is optional on all statements other than the CONTROL statement. It can be any style valid for the specified type of control. These are the same styles you use when creating a control by calling the CreateWindow function.

The class parameter of the CONTROL statement must be a predefined name, character string, or integer value that indicates the window class used by the control. A CONTROL statement implies the use of the WS_CHILD and WS_VISIBLE styles. You don't need to mention them explicitly.

As new control styles were added to Windows over its evolution, new resource statements were not added to define them. Therefore most of the controls added since Windows 3.0 had to be declared in the resource script using the CONTROL statement. For example, to declare an automatic (auto) radio button or an auto check box, you actually had to do something of the following form. Fortunately, much of this detail work was handled by the resource editor, which knew how to generate all the right forms for declaring the controls.

```
CONTROL    "Radio1", IDC_RADIO1, "Button",
                BS_AUTORADIOBUTTON | WS_GROUP |
                WS_TABSTOP, 9, 31, 94, 11
CONTROL    "Check1", IDC_CHECK1, "Button",
                BS_AUTOCHECKBOX | WS_GROUP |
                WS_TABSTOP, 10, 54, 99, 9
```

The most recent releases of the Microsoft tooling added new statements for all the controls, as shown in Table 11.6, so the use of the CONTROL statement will not be as prevalent as it once was. However, if you are getting resources built by earlier versions of the tooling, either from Win16 or the early releases of Win32, you will find these statements in your resource script.

We have not yet discussed the WS_GROUP and WS_TABSTOP styles. The dialog-class window function provides a keyboard interface to move the input focus from one control to another in a dialog box, but you have to tell it which controls should receive the input focus and which never need the input focus. Because you already know that you move from control to control by using the **Tab** key, you should be able to guess that the WS_TABSTOP style identifies those controls that should have the input focus.

When the user presses the **Tab** key, the dialog box window function moves the input focus from the control that currently has it to the next control in the dialog box that has the WS_TABSTOP style. Controls that should never have the input focus, such as static text controls, should not use the WS_TABSTOP style. The input focus moves from tab stop to tab stop in the order in which the controls are defined in the dialog template. (Actually, the focus moves in what is called the "Z-order" of the child windows of the dialog, and when the last child window is encountered, the search begins again at the front of the list. This order is exactly the order in which the lines appear in the dialog resource.) Using your dialog editor, you can change this order by using a feature called "set tab order". This feature allows you to arrange the controls so that the progression (using the **Tab** key) is the one you desire. All dialog editing tools we know of have this feature.

You get the chance to initially set the input focus to a specific control when your dialog function receives the WM_INITDIALOG message. During the processing for this message, you can set the input focus to a particular control and return FALSE. When you return TRUE, Windows sets the input focus to the first control in the dialog box that has the WS_TABSTOP style.

The dialog-class window function provides a second-level keyboard interface to controls as well. After you move the input focus to a group of controls, such as radio buttons, by pressing the **Tab** key, you can then use the arrow keys to move the input focus from one radio button to the next within the group. You mark the beginning of such a group of groups by setting the WS_GROUP style on the first control in the group. Repeatedly pressing the down arrow key moves the input focus from the first control that has the WS_GROUP style up to, but not including, the next control that has the WS_GROUP style and back again to the first control in the group.

Another keyboard interface is based on the text labels for controls in a dialog box. An ampersand (&) character in a control's text is removed and signals that the following letter should be underlined. You can move the input focus directly to a control by pressing the key corresponding to an underlined letter. You can disable this feature by including the SS_NOPREFIX style on the control containing an ampersand in its text. This permits an ampersand character to be displayed as part of a control's text without having to double it. For controls that don't have identifying text, such as list boxes or combo boxes, you place a static text control physically near the list box or combo box and put a caption in the static control that has an ampersand. You then arrange the tab order so that the static control immediately precedes the control in question in the tab order, as well as being physically near it. Now when you press the key corresponding to the underlined letter (or use the **Alt**-shifted key, if you were in a control that cared about key strokes), you will move to the control following the static control. All of this behavior is built into the internal dialog box procedure.

Normally, you don't need to concern yourself with the mechanics of passing the input focus from control to control; you just need to set the WS_GROUP and WS_TABSTOP styles appropriately and let Windows do the work. When you specify a private dialog class, however, you may want to take over even at this level. Windows provides two functions that determine the next (or previous) control in a group or tab stop.

The GetNextDlgGroupItem function searches for the next (or previous) control within a group of controls in the dialog box, based on the WS_GROUP style:

GetNextDlgGroupItem (hdlg, hCtl, Direction) ;

The GetNextDlgTabItem function searches for the next (or previous) control that has the WS_TABSTOP style:

GetNextDlgTabItem (hdlg, hCtl, Direction) ;

The hCtl parameter specifies the control used as the starting point for the search. The Direction parameter is TRUE to search for the next control and FALSE to search for the previous control.

You can set the ID of a control to any value that makes sense for your application. Occasionally, you'll want to use certain predefined values rather than arbitrary ones. As an example, we examine the **OK** and **Cancel** push buttons often used to terminate a dialog box.

Normally, the user clicks one of the push buttons to close the dialog box. Doing so sends a WM_COMMAND message that contains the control ID for the button clicked. However, a dialog box provides a keyboard interface as well as a mouse interface. Pressing the space bar when a button has the input focus is equivalent to clicking the button. The button sends a WM_COMMAND message containing its control ID to its owner window with the BN_CLICKED notification code. Nothing needs to be done to explicitly support the space bar keyboard interface. However, things work differently when the user presses the **Enter** key.

Table 11.7: WM_COMMAND messages generated by dialog handler

Action	Focus On	Default Push Button?	Effect		
			OnCommand Parameters		
			ID	**hwndCtl**	**codeNotify**
Enter	Button	–	Current button sends WM_COMMAND to dialog.		
			Button ID	Current button	BN_CLICKED
Enter	Non-Button	No	Dialog receives WM_COMMAND.		
			IDOK	NULL	0
Enter	Non-Button	Yes	Dialog receives WM_COMMAND.		
			Default button ID.	NULL	BN_CLICKED
Escape	–	–	Dialog receives WM_COMMAND.		
			IDCANCEL	NULL	0
System menu: **Close**	N/A	N/A	Dialog receives WM_COMMAND.		
			IDCANCEL	NULL	0

The following behavior is summarized in Table 11.7:

- When the user presses the **Enter** key while a push button has the input focus, a dialog box sends a WM_COMMAND message with the ID field set to the control ID for the push button with the input focus, thereby sending the notification code BN_CLICKED.

- When the user presses the **Enter** key, no push button has the input focus, and a default push button exists in the dialog box, a dialog box sends a WM_COMMAND message with the ID field set to the control ID for the default push button and the notification code set to BN_CLICKED.

- When the user presses the **Enter** key, no push button has the input focus, and there is no default push button in the dialog box, a dialog box sends a WM_COMMAND message with the ID field set to the control ID value IDOK and the notification code set to 0, as if the notification came from a menu.

- When the user presses the **Esc** or **Ctrl-Break** keys or closes the dialog box using the system menu (on a dialog box with the WS_SYSMENU and WS_CAPTION styles), a dialog box sends a WM_COMMAND message with the ID field set to the control ID value IDCANCEL and the notification code set to 0, as if the notification came from a menu.

You can simplify your program logic by using these predefined control IDs on the appropriate controls. By using the control ID value IDOK for an **OK** push button and the control ID value IDCANCEL for a **Cancel** push button, you don't need additional logic to support the dialog box keyboard interface. Generally, you want to use these control IDs any time you are using one of the object-based libraries, such as MFC, because they have built-in support for these messages already. The full set of standard button ID codes is given in Table 8.15 on page 545.

You can find out which push button is the default by sending the dialog a DM_GETDEFID message. The value returned is the ID of the button that is the default or 0 if no button has the default:

```
int defbutton = SendMessage(hdlg, DM_GETDEFID, 0, 0);
```

You can change the default push button by sending a DM_SETDEFID message. The wParam of the message specifies the control ID of the push button that is to be the new default push button. The default push button property is removed from any previous button that may have had it. For example, to set the text of the **Cancel** button to **Close** and make that the new default button, you would use code like that shown in Listing 11.1. Note that you send the DM_SETDEFID message to the *dialog*, not to the *control*. You can find out the control ID of the current default push button by sending the DM_GETDEFID message to the dialog.

Listing 11.1: Changing the default push button and caption
```
static void CancelToClose(HWND hwnd, BOOL makedefault)
    {
    TCHAR CloseText[128];
    if(LoadString(GetWindowInstance(hwnd),
                IDS_CLOSE_CAPTION,
                CloseText, charactersof(CloseText)) != 0)
      { /* change caption */
       SetDlgItemText(hwnd, IDCANCEL, CloseText);
      } /* change caption */
    if(makedefault)
       SendMessage(hwnd, DM_SETDEFID, IDCANCEL, 0) ;
    }
```

Each of the control styles shown in Table 11.6 has an implied set of style flags. But suppose you don't want one of those flags? Perhaps, for some reason, you don't want the WS_TABSTOP style that some controls imply. Or, in a more credible example, you may want a CONTROL-specified control without the WS_VISIBLE style. How do you turn off a style?

Turning off a style involves one of the more obscure and certainly inconsistent pieces of syntax in any Windows tool. To turn *off* an implied style, you simply include it in the "OR" list with the prefix NOT. As a C programmer, you would never discover this. But it emphasizes that although the statements in a resource file might superficially resemble pieces of the C language, they are actually a resource definition language that has its own syntax and semantics. Take, for example, the following statement, which creates a custom control of class "funny" that is a visible child control:

```
CONTROL "", IDC_FUNNY_CTL, "funny", , 10, 20, 30, 40
```

and the following, which creates a control that is a child control but not visible:

```
CONTROL    "", IDC_FUNNY_CTL, "funny", NOT WS_VISIBLE, 10, 20, 30, 40
```

or, to emphasize the strange syntax, one that creates a control with a border and a tab stop, but which is not visible:

```
CONTROL    "", IDC_FUNNY_CTL, "funny",
           WS_BORDER | WS_TABSTOP | NOT WS_VISIBLE
           10, 20, 30, 40
```

The Pizza-ordering Program

Having now explained how to construct dialogs, we can construct a pizza-ordering program. To do this, we use two different dialog boxes and use them to illustrate a number of useful dialog box techniques.

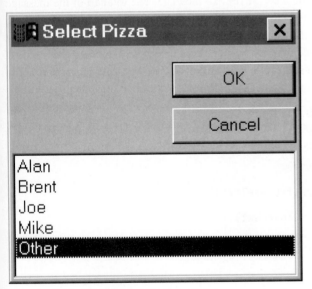

Figure 11.2: The pizza selection dialog

We construct a dialog that selects one of a set of predefined pizza types by a pizza name. In this case, we use the name of the person who wants the pizza. However, we also could use names like "Fully loaded" or "Veggie" as generic names for classes of pizzas. We add a simple top-level menu item (pardon the pun) to our basic `Skeleton` code: "**Pizza!**". When we select this menu item, it brings up the choice dialog. We then click one of the pizza-selection names and click **OK**, or click **Cancel** to terminate the whole process. If we choose a name, we will next see a dialog that gives us a set of "configuration options" for ordering the pizza. (No, you can't order a pizza with 32MB of RAM and 4GB of disk.) Figure 11.2 shows the selection menu.

One thing that might not be apparent at first glance is that this dialog has a *sizing* border! (This may not be obvious at first because the difference is subtle and does not show up particularly well in black-and-white reproduction.) We can resize this dialog! This facility allows us to illustrate a variety of useful techniques. The resizing is more evident when we look at the actual resource declaration, shown in Listing 11.2. Note the WS_THICKFRAME style that is used instead of the WS_DLGFRAME style.

Before we cover the resizing, however, we'll look at the more ordinary aspects of implementing this dialog. We first need to look at the declaration of a pizza structure, as shown in Listing 11.3.

The structure is fairly straightforward. A Boolean value indicates if the structure represents a "standard" pizza (one defined from the database) or an "other" pizza for which we do not yet have an entry (we don't provide for creating a new entry in this program). An integer encodes the size–large, medium, or small–using one of the SIZE_ constants we define later in the file.[2] A name is assigned to any standard pizza, and we allow for future Unicode support by declaring it an LPTSTR. A Boolean flag indicates whether we want to limit selections to strictly vegetarian. Finally, a DWORD of flags allows us up to 32 toppings, of which we specify only 12 for this example. In addition to the user-visible part of the specification, we have an internal field that is set to TRUE if the user decides to redefine the standard. Otherwise, any other modifications are made only for this order and not recorded permanently.

Listing 11.2: The pizza selection dialog template
```
IDD_SELECTPIZZA DIALOG DISCARDABLE  0, 0, 87, 90
STYLE DS_3DLOOK | DS_CENTER | WS_POPUP | WS_VISIBLE |
                 WS_CAPTION | WS_SYSMENU | WS_THICKFRAME
CAPTION "Select Pizza"
FONT 8, "MS Sans Serif"
BEGIN
     LISTBOX           IDC_SELECTIONS,0,41,87,49,LBS_SORT |
                       LBS_NOINTEGRALHEIGHT | WS_VSCROLL |
                       WS_TABSTOP
     DEFPUSHBUTTON     "OK",IDOK,37,6,50,14
     PUSHBUTTON        "Cancel",IDCANCEL,37,24,50,14
END
```

Listing 11.3: The PIZZA structure and its constants
```
typedef struct {
          BOOL standard;      // true if standard pizza
          short size;         // size of pizza
          LPTSTR name;        // name of standard
          BOOL veggie;        // TRUE for veggie-only
          DWORD toppings;     // topping flags

          // Output parameters only:
          BOOL update_standard;   // TRUE if user asks
                                  // to change
          } PIZZA, *LPPIZZA;

#define SIZE_ERR    (-1)    // used internally

#define SIZE_SMALL  0
#define SIZE_MEDIUM 1
#define SIZE_LARGE  2
```

---

[2] You may wonder why we are not using enum values for this. It turns out that an enum field has some particularly nasty properties when you try to move cross-platform between Win32 and Win16. As we would like to avoid problems in the future, we have to be concerned with similar problems between 64-bit and 32-bit platforms in a few years. So we explicitly use a platform-independent type such as short, thereby reducing our potential problems.

```
#define TOPPING_XCHEESE      0x00000001
#define TOPPING_PEPPERONI    0x00000002
#define TOPPING_SAUSAGE      0x00000004
#define TOPPING_ONIONS       0x00000008
#define TOPPING_MUSHROOMS    0x00000010
#define TOPPING_ANCHOVIES    0x00000020
#define TOPPING_PINEAPPLE    0x00000040
#define TOPPING_HOTPEPPERS   0x00000080
#define TOPPING_BLACKOLIVES  0x00000100
#define TOPPING_GREENOLIVES  0x00000200
#define TOPPING_BACON        0x00000400
#define TOPPING_SALAMI       0x00000800

#define TOPPING_MEATS \
            (TOPPING_PEPPERONI | TOPPING_SAUSAGE | \
             TOPPING_BACON | TOPPING_SALAMI)

#define TOPPING_ALL 0x00000FFF
```

Having now established our basic data structure, we can deal with establishing a database of pizzas from which we can read descriptions to load up our selection box. To keep this example simple, we build the database as a data structure in memory. Listing 11.4 shows the sample data. We arranged this table so that all but the last entry have a "standard" flag of TRUE; the last entry defines the default pizza used for "other". The end-of-table mark is a NULL name pointer.

Listing 11.4: The sample pizza database

```
PIZZA PizzaTable[] = {
  {TRUE, SIZE_MEDIUM, _T("Joe"),   FALSE,
                                   TOPPING_PEPPERONI |
                                   TOPPING_ANCHOVIES |
                                   TOPPING_HOTPEPPERS |
                                   TOPPING_BLACKOLIVES},
  {TRUE, SIZE_MEDIUM, _T("Brent"),FALSE,
                                   TOPPING_PEPPERONI,
                                   TOPPING_SAUSAGE |
                                   TOPPING_ONIONS |
                                   TOPPING_XCHEESE |
                                   TOPPING_MUSHROOMS},
  {TRUE, SIZE_MEDIUM, _T("Alan"),  FALSE,
                                   TOPPING_SAUSAGE |
                                   TOPPING_XCHEESE},
  {TRUE, SIZE_MEDIUM, _T("Mike"),  FALSE,
                                   TOPPING_GREENOLIVES |
                                   TOPPING_MUSHROOMS |
                                   TOPPING_SAUSAGE |
                                   TOPPING_XCHEESE |
                                   TOPPING_ONIONS},
// END OF TABLE:
  {FALSE, SIZE_MEDIUM, NULL,       FALSE,
                                   TOPPING_PEPPERONI}
                  };
```

We load up our list box in the OnInitDialog handler, shown in Listing 11.5. Note that this code does not need to know the name of the table of pizzas; it obtains the name from the lParam value. This means that we've created the dialog with the DialogBoxParam call, as indeed we will show in Listing 11.7. To use the lParam value, you have to cast it to whatever type it is; in this case, we cast it to an LPPIZZA value.

We center the window, using our `centerWindow` function. We load up our list box in a relatively straightforward fashion. It is a sorted list box, so we have no guarantee that what we put in it will appear in any particular correspondence with the order of the original input table (in fact, we have deliberately constructed our table so that there is no correlation!). Hence, we need some way to associate a list box entry with its `PIZZA` structure. We do this by using the `ListBox_SetItemData` call. Given the index of the string we've just inserted, we can associate that string with its original `PIZZA` structure as shown in Listing 11.3. No other part of the system will need to know how the original structures are created except the caller of the selection code. The fact that this implementation uses an array in memory is completely invisible to all other processing. Therefore we can replace the fixed table with something more flexible–such as code that reads and writes files, an ODBC-compliant database, or the Registry–and construct an array in memory. Only this `OnInitDialog` handler and its caller need to be concerned about how the set of `PIZZA` objects is represented.

When the loop terminates, the index i is pointing to the last entry in the table, our "default" entry. So we add it to the table, using the string `IDS_OTHER` to indicate our "other" selection. We use `ListBox_SetItemData` to associate the entry with this last entry in the array. Finally, lacking any other criteria for selection, we set the current selection to always be the default "other" entry.

We use `GetDlgItem` extensively. Given the ID of a control, we can get its handle by calling `GetDlgItem` on its parent window, passing in the ID. If a control of that ID exists in the window (strictly speaking, if a child window of the hwnd parameter has that ID), we get its HWND; if there is no such window, we get NULL. If more than one window exists with the same ID, we will get the handle to the first one it finds. (But we don't know what the search algorithm is, so it is the first window it finds according to a *unspecified search algorithm*.) Although the name implies it is a function that works on dialog windows, it in fact works on any window that has child windows, whether the child windows are controls or otherwise.

There is an inverse operation, `GetDlgCtrlID`, that, when given a window handle, returns to you the control ID. For all non-negative control IDs, assuming that all child window IDs are unique within the parent, the following two relationships hold:

```
GetDlgCtrlID(GetDlgItem(parent, id)) == id
```

and

```
GetDlgItem(parent, GetDlgCtrlID(hwnd)) == hwnd
```

Listing 11.5: Pizza selection `OnInitDialog` handler

```
static BOOL select_OnInitDialog(HWND hwnd,
                     HWND hwndFocus, LPARAM lParam)
  {
    int i;
    int index;
    LPPIZZA pizza = (LPPIZZA)lParam;
    TCHAR otherstr[256];
      HWND selections = GetDlgItem(hwnd, IDC_SELECTIONS);

    // Center the dialog window
    centerWindow (hwnd, NULL) ;


    for(i = 0; pizza[i].name != NULL; i++)
```

```
    { /* load standard pizzas */
     index = ListBox_AddString(selections,
                 pizza[i].name);
     ListBox_SetItemData(selections, index,
                 &pizza[i]);
    } /* load standard pizzas */

// Now that we've loaded up all the standard
// names, load up the "Other" case.
// Use the specs of the last entry to set
// the default

LoadString(GetWindowInstance(hwnd), IDS_OTHER,
           otherstr, DIM(otherstr));
index = ListBox_AddString( selections, otherstr);
ListBox_SetItemData( selections,index, &pizza[i]);
ListBox_SetCurSel( selections, index );

return TRUE;
}
```

We have now loaded up the list box; the user will make a selection and click **OK**. Our OnOK handler is shown in Listing 11.6. We use ListBox_GetCurSel to find the index of the current selection. Although it is not possible to have "no selection", we want to make this code robust in case a programmer we've never met makes a modification (such as adding a multiple select list box). So we actually check for LB_ERR and proceed only if we have a valid index. If we have a valid index, we request the item data for that entry and cast it to an LPPIZZA. This gives us a pointer to the actual PIZZA data structure associated with that list box selection. Finally, we call EndDialog. We cast our pointer to be an int; this will be the value returned by the DialogBoxParam call! If we do not have a valid index, the call will return NULL. For the IDCANCEL button, we also return a NULL to our caller. We see the DialogBoxParam call in Listing 11.7.

Listing 11.6: Pizza selection OnOK handler
```
static void select_OnOK(HWND hwnd)
    {
    LPPIZZA pizza = NULL;
    int index;
    HWND selections = GetDlgItem(hwnd, IDC_SELECTIONS);

    index = ListBox_GetCurSel( selections );
    if(index != LB_ERR)
        { /* has selection */
         pizza = (LPPIZZA)ListBox_GetItemData(
                 selections,
                 index);
        } /* has selection */
    EndDialog(hwnd, (int)pizza);
    }
```

Listing 11.7: Calling the pizza selection dialog
```
LPPIZZA getPizzaSelection(HWND hwnd)
    {
    return (LPPIZZA)DialogBoxParam (
                    GetWindowInstance(hwnd),
                    MAKEINTRESOURCE(IDD_SELECTPIZZA),
```

```
            hwnd,
            selectProc,
            (LPARAM)PizzaTable);
}
```

This is all we really needed to do a selection. But we have added some complexity to the dialog to illustrate how we can build a dynamically resizable dialog. If you don't need to see how to resize a dialog, you can skip the next section and resume on page 789. The techniques shown here can be applied to any window that contains controls, but most often it is a dialog. If you will be using class libraries that support dialog variants, such as the MFC CFormView, you may find the ability to resize a dialog useful.

Resizable Dialogs

We can create an ordinary window with a resizing border using the WS_THICKFRAME style. We also can create a dialog with a resizing border by replacing the WS_DLGFRAME style with WS_THICKFRAME. In most development environments, this is an option you can select in the dialog editor.

WM_SIZE Message Cracker Handler

```
void cls_OnSize(HWND hwnd, UINT state, int cx, int cy);
```

Parameter	wParam		lParam		Meaning	
	lo	hi	lo	hi		
hwnd					Window handle of the window	
state					The indicator of the new window state:	
					SIZE_MAXHIDE	Sent to all pop-up windows when any other window is maximized.
					SIZE_MAXIMIZED	The window has been maximized.
					SIZE_MAXSHOW	Sent to all pop-up windows when any other window has been restored to its previous size.
					SIZE_MINIMIZED	The window has been minimized.
					SIZE_RESTORED	The window has been resized, but it is neither maximized nor minimized.
cx					The new width of the client area.	
cy					The new height of the client area.	

The problem with any resizable window, dialogs included, is that unless you take special action, the resizing of the parent window leaves the child windows untouched. If you make the window very large, you simply end up with the same controls, in their original positions, in the upper left of the window's new client area. And if you make it smaller, perhaps extremely tiny, the controls will be clipped by the parent window. This means that some or all controls will simply disappear under the edge of the parent. Neither feature seems to make the ability to resize a dialog (or any other window containing child windows) particularly valuable.

But child windows are just windows. They can, themselves, be resized or moved. That's what we're going to do now: We're going to expand that list box both vertically and horizontally so that it fills the available client area and the **OK** and **Cancel** buttons will "float" with the right edge of the window.

To do this, we must handle the WM_SIZE message. A WM_SIZE message comes in any time the window size has changed, informing us of the new size of the window. Note that the size is limited to only 16 bits, even in Win32. This is because the size is always expressed in default client units–pixels–so we are limited to windows of 65,535 pixels in each dimension. This is not a serious limitation, however, since it depends on the actual screen size (which is currently around 1600 pixels maximum dimension).

The only case of a resize notification of no interest to us is the SIZE_MINIMIZED. Should we receive this code, we ignore it. In some cases, however, you will want to take special actions when a window is minimized.

When we are doing sophisticated resizable dialogs, what ends up inside the OnSize handler is usually a long, tedious set of graphical transformations that compute new rectangles for various controls, then move the controls to the new locations. You may, for example, have two list boxes side by side instead of the one we have here. You may want them to remain equal-sized and yet still fill the entire lower part of the dialog. In addition, you may have controls that affect each list box positioned above each list box, and you may want the controls for the right-hand list box to float so that they are always aligned above that list box, no matter how its resizing has changed its position. You could have controls that float (as our buttons will), controls that resize themselves, or controls that do both under some complex algorithm of your own devising. All things are possible; it is only a question of your patience.

We have some specialized knowledge of our dialog that we are going to apply. We know there are only two buttons, situated on the right, and a single list box at the bottom. We want to resize the list box to fill the new area and float the buttons horizontally. The code to do this is shown in Listing 11.8.

We first check to see if our window has been iconized. If it has been, we simply return without bothering to do anything. Next, we call the select_MoveButton routine to move the **OK** and **Cancel** buttons so that they are always positioned at the right edge of the window. If we wanted to allow for a margin, we could do so by adding in that computation.

Let's look at select_MoveButton in more detail. We get the client rectangle for our window (this means that the origin will be the .top and .left fields in the rectangle and will always be 0, 0). We also get the *window* rectangle of the control we are about to move. The window rectangle includes all of the area of the window and is expressed in *screen* coordinates. For controls with borders (and in the case of edit controls, margins), there can be a serious discrepancy between the control's *client* area and its *window* area. Since we want to move the control itself, not just its client space, we need to know the size of the entire control.

But GetWindowRect returns *screen* coordinates; the MoveWindow call will want *client* coordinates when moving a child window. We can convert from screen coordinates to client coordinates by using the Screen-ToClient function. This function takes two arguments. The first is a handle of the window that is the window whose client area is to be used for the basis of the conversion. The second is a pointer to a POINT structure that contains the *x, y* coordinates to be converted. We can convert in one of two ways. Either this way:

```
POINT pt;
    pt.x = rect.left;
    pt.y = rect.top;
    ScreenToClient(hwnd, &pt);
    rect.left = pt.x;
    rect.top = pt.y;

    pt.x = rect.right;
    pt.y = rect.bottom;
    ScreenToClient(hwnd, &pt);
    rect.right = pt.x;
    rect.bottom = pt.y;
```

or we can recognize that the layout of a RECT is conveniently the layout of two POINT structures and write

```
ScreenToClient(hwnd, (LPPOINT)&rect.left);
ScreenToClient(hwnd, (LPPOINT)&rect.right);
```

We have now converted the button coordinates from screen coordinates to client coordinates in the parent window. We compute in the SIZE variable the actual size of the button, in client coordinates. Finally, we call MoveWindow, moving the button in question to a position client.right – sz.cx but retaining the original top position and size so that the button will always be positioned with its right edge against the right edge of the parent.

Returning to the main body of select_OnSize, we get the window rectangle of the selections list box and convert that to client coordinates just as we did with the button. We compute a new width for the list box–the entire width of the client window. Then we compute a new height for the list box–the distance from the current list box top to the new client area bottom. If the latter value is negative (for example, we dragged the bottom of the parent to a position higher than the top of the list box), we don't do anything. Otherwise, we resize the list box using MoveWindow, thereby causing it to stretch out to fill the area.

With any resizable list box, it is usually important to specify the LBS_NOINTEGRALHEIGHT style. Doing this allows us to stretch the list box vertically and still fill the entire area. If we omit this style, the list box almost always ends a bit short of the bottom of the client area, except when the client area being used is *exactly* large enough to hold a list box that is an integer multiple of its line height. This is usually an ugly effect, which is why we chose to include the LBS_NOINTEGRALHEIGHT style.

Listing 11.8: OnSize handler for pizza selection

```
static void select_OnSize(HWND hwnd, UINT state, int cx, int cy)
    {
    RECT client;
    RECT r;
    SIZE sz;
```

```
    if(state == SIZE_MINIMIZED)
        return; // ignore iconic change

    // Move the OK and Cancel buttons so they are
    // again flush against the right edge of the
    // window

    select_MoveButton(hwnd, IDOK);
    select_MoveButton(hwnd, IDCANCEL);

    // Next, resize the list box to fit the
    // remaining area:

    GetClientRect(hwnd, &client);
    GetWindowRect (
              GetDlgItem (hwnd, IDC_SELECTIONS), &r);

    ScreenToClient(hwnd, (LPPOINT)&r.left);
    ScreenToClient(hwnd, (LPPOINT)&r.right);

    sz.cx = client.right - client.left;
    sz.cy = client.bottom - r.top;

    // If the size should be negative, the list
    // box is invisible so don't
    // even try to resize it.

    if(sz.cy > 0)
        { /* resize list box */
          MoveWindow(GetDlgItem(hwnd, IDC_SELECTIONS),
                        r.left, r.top,
                        sz.cx, sz.cy, TRUE);
        } /* resize list box */
    }
static void select_MoveButton(HWND hwnd, UINT id)
    {
    RECT client;
    RECT r;
    SIZE sz;

    GetClientRect(hwnd, &client);
    GetWindowRect(GetDlgItem(hwnd, id), &r);

    // We how have the window coordinates of
    // the button.  Convert them
    // to client coordinates

    ScreenToClient(hwnd, (LPPOINT)&r.left);
    ScreenToClient(hwnd, (LPPOINT)&r.right);

    sz.cx = r.right - r.left;
    sz.cy = r.bottom - r.top;

    MoveWindow(GetDlgItem(hwnd, id),
                    client.right - sz.cx,
                    r.top,
                    sz.cx, sz.cy, TRUE);
    }
```

Limiting the Resizing

We still have a problem with the selection box given in the previous example. We can resize it horizontally so that the buttons are clipped (because of our algorithm, the left edge of the button is clipped by the left border of the parent), and we can resize it vertically so that the list box completely disappears and eventually the buttons become invisible as well. This is probably not desirable.

We can limit the size a window can take on as a consequence of a resizing operation by handing the WM_GETMINMAXINFO message. The WM_GETMINMAXINFO message is sent to a window any time Windows wants to verify the limits for a resizing operation. One is sent during window creation, well before the WM_CREATE message, and you will receive a flurry of them any time you are dragging the window for resizing. You set values in the fields of the MINMAXINFO structure that constrain the width and/or height. For example, you could constrain the width only, but not the height, or the height only, but not the width. Or you could set a minimum width and a maximum height (but leave the maximum width unconstrained and the minimum height unconstrained). You could even set the minimum width and height to be in a specific ratio.

WM_GETMINMAXINFO Message Cracker Handler

```
void cls_OnGetMinMaxInfo(HWND hwnd, LPMINMAXINFO mmi);
```

Parameter	wParam		lParam		Meaning
	lo	hi	lo	hi	
hwnd					Window handle of the window.
mmi					Pointer to a MINMAXINFO structure.

Following is the MINMAXINFO structure:

```
typedef struct tagMINMAXINFO {   // mmi
    POINT ptReserved;
    POINT ptMaxSize;
    POINT ptMaxPosition;
    POINT ptMinTrackSize;
    POINT ptMaxTrackSize;
} MINMAXINFO;
```

The fields in the structure are explained in Table 11.8. The field of interest to us is the ptMinTrackSize. We need to set this value so that the user cannot resize the window to clip the listbox entirely (in fact, we will want to retain one line of text visible in the list box) and cannot clip the buttons. Because we have only two buttons, of the same size and vertically aligned, our code can be simpler than the general case might be. The code for our OnGetMinMaxInfo handler is shown in Listing 11.9.

Table 11.8: Fields of the MINMAXINFO structure

Field	Usage
ptReserved	Reserved; do not use.

Table 11.8: Fields of the MINMAXINFO structure

Field	Usage
PtMaxSize	Specifies the maximum width (.x) and maximum height (.y) of the maximized window.
ptMaxPosition	Specifies the left position (.x) and top position (.y) of the maximized window.
ptMinTrackSize	Specifies the smallest width (.x) and smallest height (.y) to which a window can be dragged.
ptMaxTrackSize	Specifies the largest width (.x) and largest height (.y) to which a window can be dragged.

Listing 11.9: The pizza selection OnGetMinMaxInfo handler

```
static void select_OnGetMinMaxInfo(HWND hwnd, LPMINMAXINFO mmi)
    {
    POINT limit;
    RECT r;
    int lineheight;

    // We don't want the window to get any narrower
    // than the size of the OK button, plus the width
    // of its frame

    GetWindowRect(GetDlgItem(hwnd, IDOK), &r);
    limit.x = r.right - r.left + 2 * GetSystemMetrics(SM_CYFRAME);

    // Get the position and size of the list box in
    // client coordinates

    GetWindowRect( GetDlgItem( hwnd, IDC_SELECTIONS), &r) ;
    ScreenToClient(hwnd, (LPPOINT)&r.left) ;
    ScreenToClient(hwnd, (LPPOINT)&r.right) ;

    // Find out how high one line is in the list box:

    lineheight = ListBox_GetItemHeight ( GetDlgItem(hwnd, IDC_SELECTIONS), 0);

    // Don't forget to add the thickness of the top
    // and bottom borders and the caption bar height!
    // Remember, this is the *window* height we're
    // computing!

    limit.y = r.top + lineheight +
                2 * GetSystemMetrics(SM_CYBORDER) +
                GetSystemMetrics(SM_CYCAPTION) +
                2 * GetSystemMetrics(SM_CYFRAME);

    // Set our new limit value in the MINMAXINFO
    // structure:

    mmi->ptMinTrackSize = limit;

    }
```

We first obtain the window size (not the client area size) of the push button using GetWindowRect. Because the **OK** and **Cancel** buttons are the same size and vertically aligned, we could use either one for our dimensions; we chose the **OK** button. The dialog must be large enough to show this button in its client area, and no smaller. But the MINMAXINFO structure wants a *window* size, not a *client area* size. So, because we have a resizable dialog, we know we have to add the width of the window borders. But how wide is a window border for a resizable window? We use the GetSystemMetrics function and give it the SM_CYFRAME (width of a vertical resizing border) code; the value will be the width of a sizing border, in pixels. We store this value in limit.x. Because we have chosen our button width as the constraining minimum size, our width computation is finished.

Computing the height is a bit trickier. We do not reposition the list box; instead we simply let it grow vertically. Therefore we want our minimum height to be the *y*-position of the top of the list box plus the height of one line of the list box. Because we are not doing an owner-draw-variable list box, we know that all the elements are the same height. So our minimum height in the client area is the client coordinate of the top of the list box, plus the height of the list box border, plus the height of one line of list box content. We first get the client coordinate of the top of the list box using GetWindowRect and ScreenToClient, as before. Then we use ListBox_GetItemHeight to get the height of an arbitrary element of the list box, for example, the one at position 0. We can get the height of a horizontal border by using GetSystemMetrics(SM_CYBORDER), remembering that a list box has both a top and bottom border. This gives us a maximum position (top plus line height plus two border heights), in client area coordinates. We also must add the height of the top and bottom resizing borders, as expected. Further, we must add the height of the caption (SM_CYCAPTION). We now have a minimum height in *window* coordinates, as required. Having done this computation, we can now store the result in the mmi->ptMinTrackSize field. If you run this sample, you will see that our size is now constrained so that no control is clipped.

Handling Double-click Activation

At this point, we are lacking one basic GUI feature that a user might expect: double-click activation. Clicking twice on a name in the selection list should be the same as clicking once and then clicking **OK**. Unless we take special action, however, we won't get double-click activation. We need to add a double-click handler for the list box. We do this by adding a line to the WM_COMMAND handler and creating a list box handler, as shown in Listing 11.10.

Listing 11.10: The Pizza OnCommand handler showing double-click support

```
static void select_OnCommand(HWND hwnd, int id, HWND hwndCtl, UINT notifycode)
    {
    switch(id)
        { /* id */
        case IDOK:
                select_OnOK(hwnd);
                return;
        case IDCANCEL:
                EndDialog(hwnd, (int)NULL);
                return;
        case IDC_SELECTIONS:
                select_OnSelection(hwnd, hwndCtl, notifycode);
```

```
                return;
        } /* id */
    }

static void select_OnSelection(HWND hwnd, HWND hwndCtl, UINT notifycode)
    {
    switch(notifycode)
        { /* notifycode */
         case LBN_DBLCLK:
                select_OnOK(hwnd);
                return;
        } /* notifycode */
    }
```

The listing shows the OnCommand handler. If the **OK** button is clicked, control goes to the OnOK handler, which will terminate the dialog and return a pointer to a PIZZA structure. If **Cancel** is clicked, EndDialog is called, returning a NULL pointer. To support the double-click, we add a handler for the OnSelection event. Note that we pass the notification code on to this handler. In the handler, we decode the notification code. We are not currently interested in any of the list box events except LBN_DBLCLK, which indicates the user has double-clicked an entry. Recall from our discussion in Chapter 7 (page 462) that a double-click event is always preceded by the normal single-click event, so by the time we see the LBN_DBLCLK notification, the normal mouse click selection of the list box item has already occurred. All we do for the double-click is simulate the **OK** button's having been clicked by calling the OnOK handler.

Our selection interface is now complete.

Window-related Data and How to Manage It

Windows is an "object-based" system in which windows form the primary objects. The "methods" of a window are the messages it processes. By doing subclassing, we can achieve an object-based inheritance of functionality. But what about data? Object-based languages have objects that have both methods and instance-specific data, yet C as a language has no "object-based" data mechanism. Certainly Windows does not appear to support window-specific data beyond that inherited from its WNDCLASS or dealing with the position and size of the window itself. How can we associate window-specific data with a window?

One idea that might occur to you is to build tables in memory, whether arrays or linked lists, whose purpose is to match window handles to window-specific data. This is certainly possible, but it is both inelegant and cumbersome. There are several other ways we can associate data with a window: window-extra words, properties, and GWL_USERDATA.

Whenever you create a window, a data structure is created by the USER module that represents all of the information about that window. Much of this information is available to you by using the GetWindowLong or GetWindowWord functions. This information includes

- the handle of its sibling window (GWL_HWNDNEXT),

- the handle of the first window of its child list (GWL_CHILD),

- the handle of its owner window (GWL_OWNER), and

- the instance handle of its creating application (GWL_HINSTANCE).

Other key information about the window, such as its state (minimized, maximized, or normal), its physical position on the screen, and the size of its client area, can be tested with other API functions (IsIconic, IsZoomed, GetWindowRect, GetClientRect).

But these are not the only properties a window can have. When you register a window class, a field of the WNDCLASS structure, cbWndExtra, can be set to nonzero. This value is the number of "window-extra" bytes that will be allocated in the internal window structure, *just for you*. What you do with these window-extra bytes is up to you. In the past, programmers were discouraged from allocating more than 4 bytes because of the severe space constraints of Windows 3.*x*. This concern is reduced for Win32 programming, but you still should not be overly profligate of this space. This is particularly true on Windows 95, which has large amounts of space but doesn't have the virtually unlimited space of Windows NT for storing internal window structures. It is also more convenient and marginally more efficient to access your own data structure rather than using [Get/Set]Window[Word/Long] function calls. So we assume that you are using only a small amount of window-extra bytes, enough for one or two pointers (typically).

To get window-extra bytes, you must set the cbWndExtra field before you register the class:

```
WNDCLASS wc;
// ... normal initialization of WNDCLASS
wc.cbWndExtra = sizeof(VOID *);
return RegisterClass(&wc);
```

To access this space, you call [Get/Set]WindowLong (for a LONG value) or [Get/Set]WindowWord (for a WORD value), specifying your window handle and an offset into the extra byte space. Positive offsets are offsets into your private window-extra space. Negative offsets for these functions access built-in fields (whose position in the structure may not be related to the actual offset value provided). Be careful, though. Windows does not actually check that you are giving a valid positive offset. If you give an offset that is beyond the space you have allocated, you could overwrite critical internal information or retrieve meaningless information.

To associate a structure with a window, you would typically allocate sizeof(void *) bytes of window-extra space to the window class when you register it. Then on creation, you might do something like this:

```
int mywindow_OnCreate(HWND hwnd, LPCREATESTRUCT cs)
    {
    MyWindowData * data;
    // ... whatever else you want to do
    data = malloc(sizeof(MyWindowData));
    if(data == NULL)
        return -1;  // abort creation process
    // initialize the fields of the data variable here
    SetWindowLong(hwnd, MWL_DATA, (LPARAM)data);
    // eventually, return 0 or -1
    }
```

where you have defined the structure MyWindowData as being a **struct** that holds all the window-specific data for your window. The offset MWL_DATA is defined by you (MWL stands for "My Window Long", similar to the naming convention we suggested for user-defined messages):

```
#define MWL_DATA 0
```

If you had allocated more than one pointer's worth of space, you might have other MWL_ offsets for your own window-specific information.

Whenever we want the data pointer associated with a window, we can get it by writing

```
MyWindowData * data = (MyWindowData *) GetWindowLong(hwnd, MWL_DATA);
```

This is so common to need and so clumsy to write that you are best served by writing a separate function declaration and declaring it *inline,* if your compiler supports doing this (for example, in Microsoft compilers the __inline keyword tells the compiler you would like to inline a function). An inline function is just as efficient as a macro but without the annoying properties of a macro. For example, the parameters are evaluated only once, thereby giving consistent results in the presence of side effects. An inline function is not compiled as a separate function but rather expanded directly in the place it is called. There are usually some restrictions on inline functions, as follows:

- Recursive inline functions, for example, generally ignore the inline property and are compiled out-of-line like any other function. (Microsoft compilers support inline compilation of recursive functions if the recursion depth can be computed at compile time and does not exceed a programmer-specifiable limit.)

- Functions called via function pointers are compiled out-of-line (although they may also be expanded inline where possible).

- Some compilers when compiling in "debug" mode compile the functions out-of-line to make debugging easier.

- A function whose body is "too large" may be compiled out-of-line.

We can write the inline function like this, without any loss of efficiency over writing a macro:

```
static __inline MyWindowData * GetMyData(HWND hwnd)
    {
     return (MyWindowData *) GetWindowLong(hwnd, MWL_DATA);
    }
```

and get the data pointer by placing in each function where we need it the declaration:

```
static void OnSomeHandler(HWND hwnd)
    {
     MyWindowData * data = GetMyData(hwnd);
```

In the case of dialog boxes, you have only one additional consideration. Each dialog window has a number of extra bytes already allocated, defined by the DLGWINDOWEXTRA value. So if you want extra bytes with a dialog window, you must register a private dialog class, and add however many bytes you want to the value DLGWINDOWEXTRA. Your first offset will be DLGWINDOWEXTRA. This becomes rather complicated to deal with, and can be avoided by using the GWL_USERDATA field instead.

The GWL_USERDATA Field

The technique we've described is so common that Microsoft has, in Win32, added a special field to *every* window class, the GWL_USERDATA field. If you want to add only one pointer to a window, even a window of a built-in class such as a LISTBOX, you can use the GWL_USERDATA field. We are going to store a pointer to the selected PIZZA structure with the window, and we are going to be able to retrieve it any time we need it with the getPizza function:

```
static __inline LPPIZZA getPizza( HWND hwnd )
{
    return (LPPIZZA)GetWindowLong(hwnd, GWL_USERDATA) ;
}
```

Returning Values from a Dialog

Generally, you return a value TRUE or FALSE from a dialog procedure. You return TRUE if you've handled the message and don't want the default dialog processing to continue, and FALSE if you want normal dialog processing to continue. For most messages, if you return FALSE, the DefDlgProc function will handle the message, passing it on to DefWindowProc as appropriate, as indicated in Table 11.4. However, for some messages, you return a value with a different meaning. These messages are shown in Table 11.9.

Table 11.9: Dialog handler messages that have unusual return values

Message	Return Value
WM_CHARTOITEM	Returns an int cast to a BOOL, which represents the index in the list box to be selected.
WM_COMPAREITEM	Returns an int cast to a BOOL. The value represents the result of the comparison.
WM_CTLCOLORBTN WM_CTLCOLORDLG WM_CTLCOLOREDIT WM_CTLCOLORLISTBOX WM_CLTCOLORMSGBOX WM_CTLCOLORSCROLLBAR WM_CTLCOLORSTATIC	Return an HBRUSH cast to a BOOL. This is the brush used to paint the background of the control.
WM_INITDIALOG	TRUE to indicate that you have not changed the focus to a different control and that the default action, setting the focus to the initial control, should be taken. FALSE to indicate that you have changed the focus and the default action should *not* be taken.
WM_QUERYDRAGICON	Returns an HICON cast to a BOOL.
WM_VKEYTOITEM	Returns an int cast to a BOOL, which represents the index in the list box to be selected.

But what if you want to add your own user-defined messages to a dialog? These messages might also require nonstandard return values. Consider the case in which you want to send a message that returns a pointer to a string:

```
LPTSTR result = (LPTSTR)SendMessage(hdlg, UWM_MYMESSAGE, 0, 0);
```

You can't just return the value cast to a BOOL because there is no guarantee that the value is actually preserved by the dialog handler. There is, however, a way to accomplish this: Use one of the special dialog "extra" fields, DWL_MSGRESULT. To return your own value, you simply set this field to the value you want to return and it will be returned to the SendMessage function:

```
BOOL MyDialogProc(HWND hdlg, UINT msg, WPARAM wParam,
                                  LPARAM lParam)
  {
    switch(msg)
       {
        case UWM_MYMESSAGE:
           {
             LPTSTR result = ...; // computes value
             SetWindowLong(hdlg, DWL_MSGRESULT, (LPARAM)result);
             return TRUE;
           }
```

This is nicely packaged in a macro, SetDlgMsgResult, found in `windowsx.h`. The macro is defined as

```
BOOL SetDlgMsgResult(HWND hdlg, UINT msg, LPARAM result)
```

The msg parameter is the input parameter to the dialog procedure. If the message is any of those shown in Table 11.9, then the result of this function is the result parameter cast to a BOOL. If it is any other message, the result is stored in the DWL_MSGRESULT field and the return value is TRUE. This allows you to use it safely to return any value. The example we presented could now be rewritten as

```
BOOL MyDialogProc(HWND hdlg, UINT msg, WPARAM wParam, LPARAM lParam)
  {
    switch(msg)
       {
        case UWM_MYMESSAGE:
           {
             return OnMyMessage(hdlg, wParam, lParam);
           }
        // ...
       }
  }

BOOL OnMyMessage(HWND hdlg, WPARAM wParam, LPARAM lParam)
  {
     LPTSTR result = ...; // computes value
     return SetDlgMsgResult(hdlg, UWM_MYMESSAGE, result);

  }

}
```

If you are porting an application from Win16, you may find the symbol DWL_USER, used in the Win16 source, is undefined. In Win16, the only window class that had a user-data long word defined was the Dialog class. The designator for this word was DWL_USER. This designator can now be replaced by GWL_USERDATA.

Using Properties

We've already discussed how to use window *properties* to store information with a window. We expand on this discussion here. Table 11.10 lists the property and atom functions.

Table 11.10: Property and atom functions

Function		Description
ATOM	AddAtom(LPCTSTR)	Adds an atom to the local atom table.
ATOM	DeleteAtom (ATOM)	Deletes the atom from the local atom table.
int	EnumProps(HWND, PROPENUMPROC)	Calls the enumeration function for each property associated with the window.
int	EnumPropsEx (HWND, PROPENUMPROC, LPARAM)	Calls the extended enumeration function for each property associated with the window.
ATOM	FindAtom(LPCTSTR)	Returns the handle for the atom, if it exists in the local atom table.
UINT	GetAtomName (ATOM, LPTSTR, int)	Retrieves the atom name for the atom.
HANDLE	GetProp(HWND, LPCTSTR)	Returns the window property named by the string.
ATOM	GlobalAddAtom(LPCTSTR)	Adds an atom to the global atom table.
ATOM	GlobalDeleteAtom(ATOM)	Deletes an atom from the global atom table.
ATOM	GlobalFindAtom(LPCTSTR)	Returns the handle for the global atom, if it exists.
LPCTSTR	MAKEINTATOM(int)	Converts an integer to a value usable by the functions that want an atom name.
HANDLE	RemoveProp (HWND, LPCTSTR)	Removes the specified property from the window.
BOOL	SetProp(HWND, LPCTSTR, HANDLE)	Attaches a property to the window using the specified name, or replaces the value if the property is already attached.

The property functions are somewhat misleading because they reference setting and returning HANDLE values. In fact, they can set and return any HANDLE-*sized* value, which in the case of Win32 means any 32-bit value. You can use these functions to store a Boolean, integer, single-precision floating-point, or pointer value with any window. In their simplest form, they take a pointer to a string that is the name of the atom. For example, if the GWL_USERDATA word is already in use or you want to leave it alone for the user of your control or window, you would still need a way of attaching window-specific data to the window for your own purposes. You might, for example, be doing a sophisticated owner-draw list box that you would like other programmers to be able to use without either interfering with your data or having your need for GWL_USERDATA imposed on them. So instead of using GWL_USERDATA, which is now unavailable, or creating a whole new window with cbWndExtra bytes, which might be impossible, you can attach your information using a property. This is particularly useful both for dialog boxes and the controls you are putting in them, which is why we're spending time discussing it here.

You attach a property using the SetProp function. For example, instead of using

```
SetWindowLong(hwnd, MWL_DATA, (LPARAM)data);
```

or

```
SetWindowLong(hwnd, GWL_USERDATA, (LPARAM)data);
```

you could call

```
SetProp(hwnd, _T("MyData"), (HANDLE)data);
```

and to retrieve the data, you would use the GetProp function. Instead of writing

```
return (MyWindowData *) GetWindowLong(hwnd, MWL_DATA);
```

or

```
return (MyWindowData *) GetWindowLong(hwnd, GWL_USERDATA);
```

you would write

```
return (MyWindowData *) GetProp(hwnd, _T("MyData"));
```

However, unlike the window-extra bytes or the GWL_USERDATA, there is one additional action you *must* take. In your OnDestroy handler for the window, you *must* call RemoveProp to free up the resources consumed by the property:

```
static void mywindow_OnDestroy(HWND hwnd)
    {
    MyWindowData * data = GetMyData(hwnd);
    free(data);
    RemoveProp(hwnd, _T("MyData"));
    }
```

As you may gather from the calls, each requires looking up the string name in a property table. The string comparison is case-insensitive, so the names "MyData", "mydata", and "MYDATA" are all equivalent. The first one that is added defines the actual string stored, but all the strings will compare as equal. But a string comparison is somewhat inefficient, and if we were doing this often we might begin to see this cost in overall performance. So we can use a more efficient mechanism to encode these names: the *atom*.

An *atom* is just a 16-bit unique ID for a string. You create an atom by using the AddAtom or AddGlobalAtom functions. They have roughly the same effect, except that AddAtom adds the atom to the *local atom table*, which is private to your process, and AddGlobalAtom adds the atom to the *global atom table,* which is shared. You will read more about global atoms when we discuss OLE and OLE controls, so for now we concentrate only on the local atom table operations. The global atom table behaves just like the local atom table except if two different processes register the same global atom string they will receive exactly the same integer atom value.

Having registered the string and received an atom ID in return, you can now use this atom ID in any of the property function calls. To use the ATOM value as a parameter in a call that wants an LPCTSTR, you must use the MAKEINTATOM function to cast the atom value into a form that both passes compiler type checking and tells the function that what has been passed in is not a true string pointer, but the actual atom token.

When you are done with an atom, you must call DeleteAtom. Atoms are reference-counted, so every AddAtom call must have a matching DeleteAtom call. For example, you could do an AddAtom call in the OnInitDialog handler and a DeleteAtom call in the OnDestroy handler. You would store the atom handle itself in a

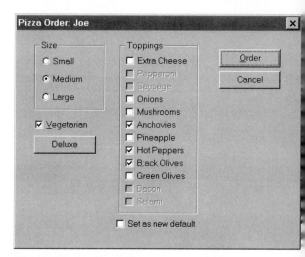

Figure 11.3: The pizza-ordering dialog

static variable. If your dialog was modeless and you could have multiple instances, the second AddAtom call would return the same atom value as the first. If both dialogs were closed, the second DeleteAtom call would decrement the reference count to 0 and the atom would be removed. When the dialog was re-created, the AddAtom might return a completely different integer, but it would be guaranteed valid until all instances of the dialog were again closed.

We list all the functions here for completeness, but we don't explain the enumeration functions, as they are very rarely used.

Initializing the Pizza Dialog

Having now examined the many ways we can attach window data to a window, we can study how the pizza ordering dialog is initialized. The dialog is shown in Figure 11.3. Its dialog resource appears in Listing 11.11. The OnInitDialog handler for the pizza ordering dialog is shown in Listing 11.12.

Listing 11.11: The pizza order dialog template
```
IDD_PIZZA DIALOG DISCARDABLE  0, 0, 229, 169
STYLE DS_MODALFRAME | WS_POPUP | WS_CAPTION | WS_SYSMENU
CAPTION "Pizza Order"
FONT 8, "MS Sans Serif"
```

```
BEGIN
    DEFPUSHBUTTON     "&Order",IDOK,163,14,50,14
    PUSHBUTTON        "Cancel",IDCANCEL,163,31,50,14
    CONTROL           "Small",IDC_SMALL,"Button",
                          BS_AUTORADIOBUTTON,20,19,33,10
    CONTROL           "Medium",IDC_MEDIUM,"Button",
                          BS_AUTORADIOBUTTON,20,33,40,10
    CONTROL           "Large",IDC_LARGE,"Button",
                          BS_AUTORADIOBUTTON,20,47,34,10
    GROUPBOX          "Size",IDC_STATIC,14,7,57,55
    CONTROL           "Extra Cheese",IDC_XCHEESE,"Button",
                          BS_AUTOCHECKBOX | WS_TABSTOP,88,19,53,9
    CONTROL           "Pepperoni",IDC_PEPPERONI,"Button",
                          BS_AUTOCHECKBOX | WS_TABSTOP,88,29,53,9
    CONTROL           "Sausage",IDC_SAUSAGE,"Button",
                          BS_AUTOCHECKBOX | WS_TABSTOP,88,39,53,9
    CONTROL           "Onions",IDC_ONIONS,"Button",
                          BS_AUTOCHECKBOX | WS_TABSTOP,88,49,53,9
    CONTROL           "Mushrooms",IDC_MUSHROOMS,"Button",
                          BS_AUTOCHECKBOX | WS_TABSTOP,88,59,53,9
    CONTROL           "Anchovies",IDC_ANCHOVIES,"Button",
                          BS_AUTOCHECKBOX | WS_TABSTOP,88,69,53,9
    CONTROL           "Pineapple",IDC_PINEAPPLE,"Button",
                          BS_AUTOCHECKBOX | WS_TABSTOP,88,79,53,9
    CONTROL           "Hot Peppers",IDC_HOTPEPPERS,"Button",
                          BS_AUTOCHECKBOX | WS_TABSTOP,88,89,53,9
    CONTROL           "Black Olives",IDC_BOLIVES,"Button",
                          BS_AUTOCHECKBOX | WS_TABSTOP,88,99,53,9
    CONTROL           "Green Olives",IDC_GOLIVES,"Button",
                          BS_AUTOCHECKBOX | WS_TABSTOP,88,109,53,9
    CONTROL           "Bacon",IDC_BACON,"Button",
                          BS_AUTOCHECKBOX | WS_TABSTOP,88,119,53,9
    CONTROL           "Salami",IDC_SALAMI,"Button",
                          BS_AUTOCHECKBOX | WS_TABSTOP,88,129,53,9
    PUSHBUTTON        "Deluxe",IDC_DELUXE,14,82,50,14
    CONTROL           "&Vegetarian",IDC_VEGGIE,"Button",
                          BS_AUTOCHECKBOX | WS_TABSTOP,15,69,60,9
    GROUPBOX          "Toppings",IDC_STATIC,83,7,63,136
    CONTROL           "Set as new default",IDC_SET_DEFAULT,
                          "Button",
                          BS_AUTOCHECKBOX | WS_TABSTOP,81,146,70,10
END
```

Listing 11.12: The pizza ordering `OnInitDialog` handler

```
static BOOL
PizzaDlg_OnInitDialog (HWND hwnd, HWND hwndFocus,
                                      LPARAM lParam)
{
    LPPIZZA pizza = (LPPIZZA)lParam;

    // Set a reference to the pizza structure in
    // the dialog

    SetWindowLong(hwnd, GWL_USERDATA, lParam);

    // Center the dialog window
    centerWindow (hwnd, NULL) ;
```

```
    setToppings(hwnd, pizza->toppings);

    setSize(hwnd);

    CheckDlgButton(hwnd, IDC_VEGGIE, pizza->veggie);

    setVeggieMode(hwnd);

    if(!pizza->standard)
        { /* not standard pizza */
         ShowWindow(
                     GetDlgItem(hwnd, IDC_SET_DEFAULT),
                     SW_HIDE);
        } /* not standard pizza */
    else
        { /* standard pizza */
         EnableWindow(GetDlgItem(hwnd, IDC_SET_DEFAULT),
                                  FALSE);
        } /* standard pizza */

#define SEP _T(": ")
    if(pizza->name != NULL)
        { /* has name */
         int captionlen = GetWindowTextLength(hwnd);
         int newlen;
         LPTSTR newname;

         newlen = captionlen + lstrlen(SEP) + lstrlen(pizza->name);

         newname = (LPTSTR)malloc( (newlen + 1) * sizeof(TCHAR));
         if(newname != NULL)
             { /* allocated buffer */
              GetWindowText(hwnd, newname, captionlen + 1);
              lstrcat(newname, SEP);
              lstrcat(newname, pizza->name);
              SetWindowText(hwnd, newname);
              free(newname);
             } /* allocated buffer */
        } /* has name */

    return TRUE ;
}
```

When we create the dialog box for ordering a pizza, we use DialogBoxParam and pass in, as the additional parameter, a pointer to the PIZZA structure we obtained from the selection dialog. This parameter is in turn passed into the OnInitDialog handler as its lParam value. We cast this to an LPPIZZA value and store it in the local variable "pizza". We then call SetWindowLong to store this pointer as part of the window structure, using the GWL_USERDATA field of the window. We then must transfer the internal state of the PIZZA structure to the controls. This allows the controls to reflect the actual values that are coming in. This is one of the most common operations you will perform in your OnInitDialog handler.

We call setToppings to select all the appropriate check boxes for the toppings we want and setSize to select the correct radio button for the size (we show these in more detail later in the chapter). Then we call

CheckDlgButton to set the state of the "Vegetarian only" check box, IDC_VEGGIE. We call a function setVeggieMode that represents an important aspect of any GUI: enabling only those controls permitted by the current selection. We also look at this in more detail soon, but we want to cover the overall structure of the OnInitDialog handler before plunging into the details.

We have two kinds of pizza orders: the "standard" ones that are in our database and the "other". If we have given a "standard" order and then make changes, we offer the user the option of changing the default order for that pizza selection. But for the "other", we don't allow the changes to be reflected back. So if the pizza is not a standard pizza, we completely hide the check box that lets the user change the default setting. Finally, if we have a standard pizza, we change the caption to reflect the name of the standard pizza. Since we have not changed the focus to any other control, and in fact want the default focus, we return TRUE.

Setting Initial Control Values

We showed you one example of how to set a control value in the dialog based on the input values by using CheckDlgButton to set the "Vegetarian only" check box. The setToppings function, given a bit mask of toppings, does all the work of setting the entire set of check boxes for toppings. For the initial setting, we just pass in the bit mask of topping selections that came in via the PIZZA structure (we show you later in the chapter why we need to pass the bit mask explicitly). The setToppings function and part of the table it uses are shown in Listing 11.13.

Listing 11.13: setToppings function for pizza dialog

```
#define ALLTOPPINGS(x) (x) = 0; \
                      ToppingMap[(x)].id != 0; (x)++

static const struct {int id;
                     DWORD mask;} ToppingMap[] = {
   { IDC_XCHEESE,    TOPPING_XCHEESE      },
   { IDC_PEPPERONI,  TOPPING_PEPPERONI    },
   // ...
   { IDC_BACON,      TOPPING_BACON        },
   { IDC_SALAMI,     TOPPING_SALAMI       },
   { 0, 0 }  // end of table
                                     };

static void setToppings(HWND hwnd, DWORD toppings)
{
    int i;

    // Set the current buttons
    for( ALLTOPPINGS(i) )
        { /* set each button */
          CheckDlgButton(hwnd, ToppingMap[i].id,
                 (toppings & ToppingMap[i].mask)
                                     ? BST_CHECKED
                                     : BST_UNCHECKED);
        } /* set each button */

}
```

Since we found that we used the same for-loop in several places to scan the toppings table, we created a macro ALLTOPPINGS that handles the iteration; it takes one argument: the name of the variable used as a counter. The ToppingMap table is simply a set of pairs of a control ID and a bit mask that encodes the topping. We set the selection of toppings by passing in a DWORD of the flags for the toppings we want to set and then iterating across the table. For every entry in the table that has a corresponding bit set in our input bit mask, we turn on the check mark; if there is no bit, we turn it off.

The size is set similarly. The setSize code is shown in Listing 11.14. Note that we use different representations for the abstract property (SIZE_SMALL, for example) and the control (IDC_SMALL). This decouples the choice of representation (the SIZE_ symbols) from the choice of GUI (a set of radio buttons). Suppose we decided that there were additional sizes such as "child", "personal", "family", "frat party", and "football team celebration" and that the radio buttons were now not suitable. We could change the GUI to use, say, a drop-down list combo box without the clients of the dialog having any idea how the GUI represented the information. It is usually a good idea to maintain such separations, although it necessitates a transformation each way. Unlike with the toppings, we have chosen here to illustrate a different method: using a switch statement. If we anticipated the addition of many different new sizes, we might have chosen to implement this using a table just as we did for the toppings.

Listing 11.14: setSize: setting the pizza size

```
static void setSize(HWND hwnd)
    {
      int ctl = 0;
      LPPIZZA pizza = getPizza(hwnd);

      if(pizza == NULL)
          return;

      switch(pizza->size)
          { /* size */
           case SIZE_SMALL:
                   ctl = IDC_SMALL;
                   break;
           case SIZE_MEDIUM:
                   ctl = IDC_MEDIUM;
                   break;
           case SIZE_LARGE:
                   ctl = IDC_LARGE;
                   break;
          } /* size */

      if(ctl != 0)
          CheckRadioButton(hwnd, IDC_SMALL, IDC_LARGE, ctl);
    }
```

The code is quite straightforward. We simply decode which SIZE_ came in and set the ctl variable to indicate which radio button should be checked. The CheckRadioButton function takes a lower and upper bound of radio button control IDs and an ID of the control to be checked and checks that control while turning off all the others in the set.

The "Set as new default" check box is handled differently, depending on whether the pizza order is a standard or "other" order. If it is an "other" order, we hide the option using the ShowWindow function. This takes a window handle and one of a series of display options shown in Table 11.11, although only the SW_SHOW and SW_HIDE are useful for controls in dialogs. For a standard pizza, we will enable the check box only if a change has been made in the pizza configuration. Since at startup no change has been yet made, we want to disable the control initially. We can do this simply by calling the EnableWindow function or one of its control-specific wrappers such as Button_Enable. Here we call EnableWindow directly. We want to emphasize this point: Because controls are windows, we can perform any window operation we want on them. The most common operations are ShowWindow and EnableWindow, often set up in the WM_INITDIALOG handler, but you can also move and resize the controls, as we've already shown.

Table 11.11: ShowWindow options

ShowWindow Option	Description
SW_HIDE	The window is made invisible.
SW_MAXIMIZE	Maximizes the window. This has the same effect as clicking the "zoom" button in the caption bar.
SW_MINIMIZE	Minimizes the window. If the window is a top-level window, it activates the next top-level window in the Z-order.
SW_RESTORE	Makes the window visible and activates it. The window is restored to its original size and position. This operation should be used when restoring a minimized window.
SW_SHOW	The window is made visible if not already visible. Its state (minimized, maximized, normal) is otherwise unchanged.
SW_SHOWDEFAULT	Shows the window according to the SW_ flag value that was passed in the STARTUPINFO structure passed to the CreateProcess call that started the application.
SW_SHOWMAXIMIZED	The window is made visible if not already visible and is maximized. The window is also activated. This has the same effect as clicking the "zoom" button in the caption bar.
SW_SHOWMINIMIZED	The window is made visible if not already visible, and it is made iconic. It is also activated. This has the same effect as clicking the "iconize" button in the caption bar.
SW_SHOWMINNOACTIVE	Shows the window as a minimized window. The window is not activated, and the current active window remains active.
SW_SHOWNA	Shows the window in its current state. The window is not activated and the current active window remains active.
SW_SHOWNOACTIVATE	Makes the window visible if it is not already visible, but does not activate it. The window is displayed in its current state.

Table 11.11: ShowWindow options

ShowWindow Option	Description
SW_SHOWNORMAL	The window is made visible if not already visible, and it is set to the "normal" size, that is, neither minimized nor maximized.

Changing the Caption Text

Although we can give a dialog box a caption when we create the dialog, we are not constrained to treat that as a design-time constant. We can choose to replace the caption of a dialog at any time simply by calling the SetWindowText function to pass in a new string. Here we illustrate how to use the existing dialog caption and how to append some additional information to it.

We have a caption associated with the dialog box. We would also like to display the name of the currently selected pizza if we are ordering a standard pizza. We could choose to put this text in a static text control in the dialog, but we've already shown you how to do that. Instead we're going to show you something new. We are going to append the name of the standard pizza to the dialog title, separated by a colon and space.

If we were always going to display a name, we could include the colon and space as part of the dialog title. But for the "other" order we don't display a name, so we've decided instead to add the separator explicitly. However, there is no "concatenate window text" operation that we can call on. Instead, we have to explicitly get the existing text, use lstrcat to append to it whatever other strings we want to append, and then use SetWindowText to replace the existing caption with our new caption.

We can do this in one of two ways: We can allocate a fixed buffer on the stack and get the window text into it, or we can dynamically allocate a buffer. Since we haven't yet shown you how to do dynamic allocation for this purpose, we'll show you the more general method so that you can see how it is done.

To dynamically allocate a buffer, we need a buffer that is long enough to hold the existing text, the name we're going to add, and the separator, not forgetting the terminal NUL character. We are able to compute the caption length of the existing caption by calling the GetWindowTextLength function. This returns the number of characters (*not* bytes!) in the current caption. We compute a new length that is the sum of the caption length, the separator length, and the length of the name of the standard pizza. We then allocate enough *bytes* to hold all the *characters* by multiplying the number of characters needed by the size of a TCHAR to get the number of bytes to allocate.

If the allocation of the memory fails, we do nothing; the caption will remain unchanged. But if the allocation succeeds, we read the existing caption into the buffer, concatenate the separator, concatenate the pizza selection name, and finally, use SetWindowText to make this string the new caption. When SetWindowText returns, it has made a copy of the string, and we can safely free up the string we allocated.

You should always be conscious of Unicode, even if you're programming in Windows 95. Some future release of a non-NT Win32 platform might support Unicode, or you may need to suddenly convert your application to support Unicode on Windows NT. To support Unicode, we made the following changes over what you would do if you were programming without Unicode considerations:

- Include the standard header file tchar.h. For Unicode, make sure the_UNICODE symbol is defined[3] before you include this file.

- Declare all constant strings (and character constants) with the _T or TEXT macro, which will declare them as either 8-bit or 16-bit characters, as appropriate.

- Do all allocations taking into consideration sizeof(TCHAR).

- Use the Windows operations lstr- operations, or the tcs- operations defined in tchar.h, instead of the C library str- operations; lstr- and tcs- operations will compile differently for ANSI and Unicode modes, whereas the str- operations are strictly ANSI (8-bit character).

Enabling and Disabling Controls

One of the guiding principles of GUI design is that options that are not available simply are not presented. You can accomplish this by one of two methods: hiding the option entirely or disabling it. We already showed how you can hide an option that can never become feasible (if we invoke the dialog for a nonstandard pizza, we can never change the default) and how the OnInitDialog will disable a control that currently has no meaning. But what about controls whose meaning changes depending on dynamic conditions that occur after OnInitDialog?

There are several approaches to this problem. We first show what appears to be a simple one. Then we explain why it is not really the best approach and make some additional changes that implement a cleaner solution.

The simplest way to enable and disable controls is to respond to the conditions that change their state and call functions that enable and disable controls when that condition ensues. We call setVeggieMode to reflect the state of the vegetarian mode to the controls, disabling all controls defined as "meat"[4]. The code for set-VeggieMode is shown in Listing 11.15. We call setVeggieMode during the OnInitDialog *after* we've set the state of the control. Whenever the "Vegetarian only" button is clicked, we call it again. (Remember, this is an *auto* check box, so each click will change its state. All we need to do is read that state.) The OnCommand handler dispatches IDC_VEGGIE events to setVeggieMode as well, as illustrated by the fragment shown in Listing 11.15.

Listing 11.15: setVeggieMode code and button handler
```
static void setVeggieMode(HWND hwnd)
{
    int i;
    BOOL veggie = IsDlgButtonChecked(hwnd, IDC_VEGGIE);
```

---

[3] Note that the symbol is preceded by an underscore, which is inconsistent with the symbol UNICODE required by windows.h. See the note on page 1325.

[4] You may notice that we do not consider "anchovies" as "meat". It is left as an exercise for the reader to implement the several forms of vegetarianism as more extensive options.

```
    for( ALLTOPPINGS(i) )
       { /* set veggie enables */
       BOOL  meat = (ToppingMap[i].mask &
                                      TOPPING_MEATS) ;
       EnableWindow(
                GetDlgItem(hwnd, ToppingMap[i].id),
                (meat && veggie ? 0 : 1)) ;
       if(meat && veggie)
          CheckDlgButton(hwnd, ToppingMap[i].id,
                                      FALSE);
       } /* set veggie enables */
}
static
void pizzaDlg_OnCommand (HWND hwnd, int id,
                         HWND hwndCtl, UINT codeNotify)
{
    switch (id) {
        case IDC_VEGGIE:
                setVeggieMode(hwnd);
                break;
        ...
```

To set the "veggie mode", we first read the state of the "Vegetarian only" check box. We don't look at all at the state of the PIZZA structure that was used to set the initial state. The state has changed, and we need to find out the current state. We then walk over the table of controls. If the control in question is a "meat" control (as defined by the TOPPING_MEATS mask), we disable the control if we are in "veggie mode" and enable it if we are not in "veggie mode". If we have a control that is a meat control and we are in "veggie mode", we also ensure the control is not checked.

To set the "Deluxe" pizza, we simply turn on all the bits in the bit mask. If in "veggie mode", we remove the bits that represent meats and then we call setToppings, passing this new bit mask as the value to set. You can examine this code in the source file.

Saving the State of the Dialog

After we finally click **OK**, we need to capture the state of the controls. Note that until now, we have not actually saved any state back to the PIZZA structure. In our OnOK handler, we call the function savePizzaState that updates the PIZZA structure that was passed in. The code for savePizzaState is shown in Listing 11.16.

Listing 11.16: savePizzaState function
```
static void savePizzaState(HWND hwnd)
{
 LPPIZZA pizza = getPizza(hwnd);

 if(pizza == NULL)
    return;

 pizza->toppings = getToppings(hwnd);
 pizza->veggie = IsDlgButtonChecked(hwnd, IDC_VEGGIE);
 pizza->size = getSize(hwnd);
 pizza->update_standard = IsDlgButtonChecked(hwnd, IDC_SET_DEFAULT);
}
```

We first call `getToppings` to get a bit map that represents the topping check boxes that are currently set. This is the inverse operation of `setToppings` and uses the same table. We update the `toppings` field with this value. The state of the `IDC_VEGGIE` control is saved as the `veggie` field. The `getSize` operation returns us a `SIZE_` value to store in the size field. If the check box for saving the configuration as a new standard is checked, the `update_standard` field will be set to TRUE. We're done. Well, almost. We just talked about how to get the value of the check box for saving the configuration, but we haven't yet done anything about actually setting that check box!

Using Idle Time to Update Controls

We have seen one way to update the controls: At a point where the state has changed, we call a function that updates the control state. This paradigm works only for fairly simple situations. A classic problem in maintaining the enable/disable/visible state of various controls or menu items is that the conditions that influence them are often complex. Distributing the decisions to enable or disable controls across all the places that *might* influence the controls eventually results in those places becoming inconsistent. The decision to enable or disable a control may come to depend on several conditions, not all of which are always apparent. This can result in code's becoming quite fragile under continued modification. As more complex conditions arise that would influence a control, it is not easy to remember all the places where calls need to be made. This is a classic "reactive" paradigm. It essentially encodes in the internals of an application the same command-driven approach that we no longer support at the user interface. What we want is a paradigm that works internally just like the user interface works externally.

`WM_ENTERIDLE` Message Cracker Handler

```
void cls_OnEnterIdle(HWND hwnd, UINT source, HWND SourceWnd);
```

| Parameter | wParam | | lParam | | Meaning |
	lo	hi	lo	hi	
hwnd					Window handle of the window that is receiving the message.
source					The source of the idle message:
					MSGF_MENU	The idle state comes from displaying a menu.
					MSGF_DIALOGBOX	The idle state comes from displaying a dialog box.
SourceWnd					The meaning of this handle depends on the source value:
					MSGF_MENU	The handle of the window that owns the menu that is being displayed.
					MSGF_DIALOGBOX	The handle of the dialog box that is being displayed.

There is such a paradigm. It requires that we make a change in the main loop of our main window. But otherwise, it works very much like a WM_PAINT handler.

To deal with controls, we treat controls like paintable entities. We keep enough state around to be able to recreate, at any instant, the exact configuration of how the controls should be enabled, disabled, or visible, plus any other state we would like to maintain. We trigger the "painting" with a WM_ENTERIDLE message. A WM_ENTERIDLE message is sent to the parent of a dialog by the dialog when nothing else is happening. We can get any number of WM_ENTERIDLE messages, possibly several in a row. What we do is "reflect" the WM_ENTERIDLE message back down to the dialog. A sample OnEnterIdle handler for the main frame is shown in Listing 11.17.

Listing 11.17: Main frame OnEnterIdle handler

```
static void
MainFrame_OnEnterIdle(HWND hwnd, UINT source,
                       HWND SourceWnd)
    {
     if(source == MSGF_DIALOGBOX)
         FORWARD_WM_ENTERIDLE(SourceWnd, source, NULL, SendMessage);
     else
         FORWARD_WM_ENTERIDLE(hwnd, source, SourceWnd, DefWindowProc);
    }
```

The main frame's OnEnterIdle handler forwards the WM_ENTERIDLE message to the dialog box that originated it; if it is from a menu, it passes it on to the DefWindowProc.

A dialog box can receive a WM_ENTERIDLE from its parent (given our main frame handler), from its own menu (if it has one), or from a child dialog box (if it has one). We can easily distinguish these cases by looking at the parameters that come in; a reflected message has a source window of NULL. We don't bother to check for this in the OnEnterIdle handler in our dialog, shown in Listing 11.18, because it has no menu and it has no child dialogs. The complete control flow of the message and its dispatching is shown in Figure 11.4.

Listing 11.18: Dialog OnEnterIdle handler

```
static void
pizzaDlg_OnEnterIdle(HWND hwnd, UINT source, HWND SourceWnd)
    {
     LPPIZZA pizza = getPizza(hwnd);
     int size;
     BOOL enable = FALSE;
     DWORD toppings;

     if(!pizza->standard)
         return; // nothing to do for 'other'

     // See if the size changed

     size = getSize(hwnd);

     enable |= (size != pizza->size);

     // See if any of the toppings changed

     toppings = getToppings(hwnd);

     enable |= (toppings != pizza->toppings);
```

```
// See if the veggie state changed

enable |= ((BOOL)
            (IsDlgButtonChecked(hwnd, IDC_VEGGIE))
          != ((BOOL)pizza->veggie));

if(enable != (BOOL)IsWindowEnabled(Enable:
            GetDlgItem(hwnd, IDC_SET_DEFAULT)))
    EnableWindow(GetDlgItem(hwnd, IDC_SET_DEFAULT),
                                        enable);
if(!enable && IsDlgButtonChecked(hwnd, IDC_SET_DEFAULT))
    CheckDlgButton(hwnd, IDC_SET_DEFAULT, FALSE);
}
```

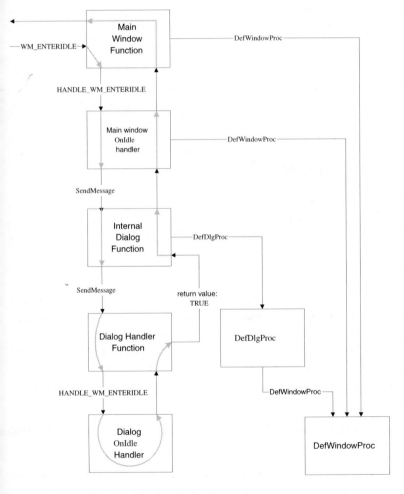

Figure 11.4: Message routing for WM_ENTERIDLE

To implement the control update, we first get a pointer to the PIZZA structure. For this handler, we update only the "Set as new default" check box status, enabling it if the configuration is changed from the original. But we could handle other controls here. For example, we could simply ignore any changes to the "Vegetarian only" check box, and update the controls by calling setVeggieMode during idle time.

We start out by assuming the "Set as new default" control will be disabled and hence set the enable value to FALSE. If we don't have a standard pizza, we simply return, as the control is already invisible. If we do have a standard pizza, we query the current control settings for the size, the toppings, and the vegetarian-only state. If any one of them has changed from the original values, we enable the "Set as new default" control, which allows the user to check it. We optimize the screen behavior by first checking to see if the state of the control is the same as the state we are going to set it to. If it is, we don't call the EnableWindow function. This reduces screen flicker, particularly because of the frequency of WM_ENTERIDLE messages. If we have disabled the check box and it was checked, we clear the check mark. If you are changing button captions, you should read the current button caption using GetWindowText and compare it to the text you are about to set. If they are the same, don't call SetWindow-Text. While making this comparison may seem unnecessary, the overall effect is far more satisfactory because control flicker is reduced.

Some Remaining Problems

If the user has checked the "Set as new default" button, then set the configuration back to its original state, and then modified the configuration again, the check mark remains unset, since we cleared it when we disabled the check box. We can use the GWL_USERDATA field of the check box to record its value and restore this value if the box is enabled. This is left as an exercise for the reader.

If the user changes the default configuration and then decides to cancel the order, it may be that the only purpose of bringing up the dialog was to change the default configuration. In this case, we would like to retain the changes even if the user cancels. This means that we would have to treat this dialog unlike most dialogs, where we copy the controls back on **OK** and leave the original values on **Cancel**.

Creating a Dialog Box Using DLGTEMPLATE Structure

The disadvantage to using a dialog box template that is defined as program resource is that it is static. You must determine its size and contents when the program is assembled. However, you can create a DLGTEMPLATE structure at runtime. A DLGTEMPLATE structure defines the contents of a dialog box. As it turns out, the resource compiler actually compiles the text description of a dialog box into a DLGTEMPLATE structure that is placed into the program's resources.

It's a bit inaccurate to claim that the DLGTEMPLATE structure defines the contents of a dialog box. The DLGTEMPLATE structure itself defines only the header for a complete dialog box definition. Even then, the definition is incomplete because the header contains three variable-length strings, a concept that can't be expressed in a C structure. An entire *dialog box template* consists of the DLGTEMPLATE structure and one or more DLGITEMTEMPLATE structures, which represent the controls contained in the dialog box. You have to construct each dialog box template "on the fly" by writing the bytes in memory, keeping track of where you are, and proceeding from there for the next set of bytes.

A sketch of the options of a dialog template is shown in Figure 11.5. We explain this figure, but you should refer to it for clarification as needed.

The DLGTEMPLATE itself has the fields you might expect: style and position values. The style field holds the style bits, which can be any of the styles we show in Table 11.1, and the dwExtendedStyle field holds the extended (WS_EX_) style bits. The x and y fields designate the initial position of the dialog in dialog box units relative to the parent, and the cx and cy fields define the width of the dialog in dialog box units. Note, however, if you specify the DS_ABSALIGN style, the x and y values are absolute screen positions in screen units.

Following the DLGTEMPLATE in memory are at least three, possibly four, descriptors. The first descriptor is for the menu. If the dialog does not have a menu, the WORD immediately following the DLGTEMPLATE is 0x0000, indicating there is no menu. If it has a menu, then one of two forms of menu description can be used. If the WORD immediately following the DLGTEMPLATE is 0xFFFF, the WORD immediately following is the integer ID of the menu in the resource of the executable whose HINSTANCE is passed to the dialog creation function. Otherwise, the DLGTEMPLATE is followed by a *Unicode string,* which is the *name* of the menu in the resource of the executable whose HINSTANCE is passed in.

	DWORD	style		Style flags.
	DWORD	dwExtendedStyle		Extended style flags.
DLGTEMPLATE:	WORD	cdit		Count of dialog items.
	WORD	x		Position of top-left corner.
	WORD	y		Position of top-left corner.
	WORD	cx		Width of dialog.
	WORD	cy		Height of dialog.
Menu:	0x0000	0xFFFF	Unicode string name of menu	Choose one of the representations to the left.
		Menu ID		
			L'\0'	
Dialog class:	0x0000	0xFFFF	Unicode string name of private dialog class	Choose one of the representations to the left.
		Class atom		
			L'\0'	
Title:			Unicode caption string	If the dialog does not have WS_CAPTION, this string is ignored.
			L'\0'	
Font:			Font size	Only if DS_SETFONT is specified.
			Unicode string name of font	
			L'\0'	
Controls:				DLGITEMTEMPLATEs

Figure 11.5: DLGTEMPLATE layout

This is very important to understand: a DLGTEMPLATE is *always* written using Unicode strings, *even if your application is not a Unicode application!* This includes an application intended *only* for Windows 95! Hence, you must use the explicit Unicode versions of the functions that work on strings. String values you use must be declared as LPWSTR or LPCWSTR, *not* as LPTSTR or LPCTSTR. String constants *must* be declared using the L-style declarations, not using _T().

The Unicode string encoding is also used in Windows 95. Since Windows 95 doesn't support the Unicode versions of the API, you will have to use the wide-character-string library functions such as wcscpy, wcscat, and wcscmp. If you use these in an application you are initially targeting to Windows NT, you will have a program that is portable across both Win32 platforms.

The second descriptor specifies the class of the dialog. If the WORD following the menu descriptor is 0x0000, the dialog is assumed to be using the built-in dialog class handler. If the WORD following the menu descriptor is 0xFFFF, the WORD that follows it is the *atom* that represents the private window class that will be used. Remember that RegisterClass, if successful, returns an atom that is the atom for the class. You can save this atom and use it to construct a dialog template. If the WORD following the menu descriptor is neither 0x0000 nor 0xFFFF, then it is the first character of a NUL-terminated Unicode string that is the name of the class to use. This class must be registered before the dialog creation function is called.

The third descriptor is the title string, which is a NUL-terminated Unicode string. This descriptor must always be present, *even if the dialog style does not include the WS_CAPTION style!* If the dialog does not include this style, the title string will be set but not displayed.

If the dialog style includes the DS_SETFONT style, a fourth descriptor is required: the font descriptor. If the style does not include DS_SETFONT, this descriptor is omitted. The first WORD of this descriptor is the font size in points. Next comes the name of the font as a NUL-terminated Unicode string.

Following the descriptors is some number of *dialog item templates*, represented by DLGITEMTEMPLATE structures. Like the DLGTEMPLATE structure, these structures contain variable-length string data. The DLGITEMTEMPLATE structure is only the header for each control. The layout for a DLGITEMTEMPLATE is shown in Figure 11.6.

The information in a DLGITEMTEMPLATE is quite similar to that of a DLGTEMPLATE. The first field is the style, which includes whatever style flags are appropriate for the control being created. Unlike a control statement in a DIALOG defined in a resource file (see Table 11.6), there are no implied styles here. If you want a button to have a WS_TABSTOP style, you must include that style explicitly. Remember that the control styles (the low-order 16 bits of the style) are interpreted differently for each control. If you change the control class, be sure to change the styles to be consistent with that class! The dwExtendedStyle field is the same as in the DLGTEMPLATE, thereby allowing you to specify any of the extended (WS_EX_) window styles. The x, y, cx, and cy fields specify the position and size of the control in dialog box units. The new field for a DLGITEMTEMPLATE is the id field, which specifies the ID to be assigned to the control. You can set this to any integer value; for example, IDOK for creating an **OK** push button or IDC_MYCONTROL for some control of your own.

Figure 11.6: DLGITEMTEMPLATE layout

DLGITEMTEMPLATE	DWORD	`style`		Style flags.
	DWORD	`dwExtendedStyle`		Extended style flags.
	WORD	`x`		Position of top-left corner (horizontal).
	WORD	`y`		Position of top-left corner (vertical).
	WORD	`cx`		Width of dialog.
	WORD	`cy`		Height of dialog.
	WORD	`id`		Control ID.
Control class:		`0xFFFF`	Unicode string name of class.	Choose one of the representations to the left.
		Class atom.		
			`L'\0'`	
Text:		`0xFFFF`	Unicode text.	Choose one of the representations to the left.
		String ID.		
			`L'\0'`	
Creation parameters:			Length.	

Table 11.12: Atoms for built-in control classes

Control Class	Class Atom Value
`Button`	0x0080
`ComboBox`	0x0085
`Edit`	0x0081
`ListBox`	0x0083
`ScrollBar`	0x0084
`Static`	0x0082

Following the `DLGITEMTEMPLATE` are two descriptors. The first names the class of the control. If the `WORD` following the `DLGITEMTEMPLATE` is `0xFFFF`, the `WORD` that follows it is the atom for the class of the control (see the discussion of `RegisterClass` for the `DLGTEMPLATE`). If the `WORD` is not `0xFFFF`, it is the first character of a NUL-terminated Unicode string that names the class, for example, `L"BUTTON"`. Note, however, that you can't actually construct a "compile-time" template; you must create it at runtime. The built-in classes have predefined atoms that identify them, which are shown in Table 11.12. So if you are creating a button, you don't need to put in the variable-length string `L"BUTTON"`. Instead, you can write a word `0xFFFF` followed by the word `0x0080`. You will get the same effect.

The second descriptor is the control text. If the `WORD` following the class atom or class name string is `0xFFFF`, the `WORD` that follows it is the ID of a resource in the `HINSTANCE` passed into the dialog creation function. The interpretation of this resource ID depends on the type of control being created; for example, for a

STATIC control with the SS_ICON style, this is the resource ID of an icon to be loaded into the control. If the word is not 0xFFFF, the WORD following the class atom or class name string is the first Unicode character of a NUL-terminated Unicode string that is the actual text. If the string is of length 0, then the NUL character is the first (and only) character of the string.

Creating a Dialog Box Template: An Example

In working up the example for this topic, we created a single module that lets you create a dialog template in memory. It handles all of the strange situations in building a dialog template. (One crucial one is undocumented; we had to discover it the hard way!) The code as is implemented is the file dlgtemplate.c and its matching header file dlgtemplate.h. You can use these in your own application to build dialog templates.

We set several goals. First, we wanted you to create a dialog template and item templates as simply and painlessly as possible. Second, we wanted them all packed up in a single module. Third, we wanted the calls to resemble as closely as possible the actual dialog item statements from the resource file. The purpose of the last goal was to allow you to take a resource statement and easily convert it to a call.

Before we show how we accomplished this, we need to talk more about the Unicode functions and the Unicode representation. In Windows NT, the operating system is implemented entirely in terms of Unicode. However, for easy support of ordinary 8-bit ANSI applications, a parallel set of API functions accepts 8-bit ANSI strings and converts them internally to Unicode strings before calling the "real" function. These functions are distinguished by having the suffix letter "A" (for "ANSI") appended to the end of the function name. The Unicode functions are defined by having the suffix letter "W" (for "Wide") appended to the end of the function name. So when you call a function like lstrcpy, you may be calling either lstrcpyW or lstrcpyA, depending on whether you defined the symbol UNICODE. However, that is just a convenience; the windows.h include set simply defines the "visible" API names in terms of either the A or W names. The A and W suffix names are the actual names exported by the Windows operating system. So you can call a specific function simply by naming it with its A or W suffix. No matter with which mode we have compiled our source file (UNICODE or not), lstrcpyA will copy 8-bit strings terminated with a single NUL byte and lstrcpyW will copy 16-bit strings terminated with a single NUL character (16-bit). You can generally tell which functions have this property because they are marked in the reference manual with the annotation Unicode. All such functions have both A and W variants. In addition, a number of the macros available have their normal, A, and W variants. We will use one of them: MAKEINTRESOURCEW.

Unfortunately, this doesn't work for Windows 95. Windows 95 has very limited Unicode support. Key among the missing functions is the lstrcpyW function. So if you write an application that you expect will run on Windows 95, you have to use the C library functions for working with Unicode strings. As long as you are not depending on collating sequence, you can use the C runtime wide-character functions to manipulate Unicode, such as wcslen, wcscpy, wcscat, and wcscmp (but only if you are checking for equality).

Let's look at a DIALOG declaration to see how we might convert this to a function call. We include in the following illustration three declarations–EXSTYLE, MENU, and CLASS–that our **About...** box doesn't use to show how we will allow for those in the future. We use our own **About...** dialog box specifications for the actual example (remember, we want it to look the same!). When we need to illustrate a feature we don't use, we show the unused feature in italics.

```
IDD_ABOUTBOX DIALOG DISCARDABLE  22, 17, 204, 83
   STYLE DS_MODALFRAME | DS_CONTEXTHELP | WS_POPUP |
              WS_VISIBLE | WS_CAPTION | WS_SYSMENU
   EXSTYLE extended-style
   MENU menuid
   CLASS classname
   CAPTION "About "
   FONT 8, "System"
```

We convert this to a procedure call that looks like the following. We indicate unused features by passing NULL or 0 values.

```
LPDLGTEMPLATE templ;
LPDLGITEMTEMPLATE item;
#define DLGTEMPLATE_SIZE 2048

templ = DIALOG(&item, DLGTEMPLATE_SIZE,
               22, 17, 204, 83,  // x, y, cx, cy
               DS_MODALFRAME | DS_CONTEXTHELP |
               WS_POPUP | WS_VISIBLE | WS_CAPTION |
               WS_SYSMENU,      // style
               0,               // extended style
               NULL,            // menu
               NULL,            // class
               L"About ",       // caption
               L"System",       // font
               8);              // font height
```

The specification of the DIALOG function is given in Table 11.13.

Table 11.13: The DIALOG function

```
LPDLGTEMPLATE * DIALOG(LPDLGITEMTEMPLATE * item, UINT size,
                       int x, int y, int cx, int cy,
                       DWORD style, DWORD exstyle,
                       LPCWSTR menu, LPCWSTR class,
                       LPCWSTR caption,
                       LPCWSTR font, int height);
```

Parameter	Description
LPDLGITEMTEMPLATE * item	If successful, places in this variable a pointer to the location where the first dialog item will be added; this will be used by the individual control-creation functions. If unsuccessful, the effect on this location is undefined.
UINT size	The dialog template is built into memory, which is allocated by the DIALOG function. You must tell it how large the template will be. If you pass in 0, a default value (4096) will be used. Otherwise, the amount of space passed in via this parameter defines the size. *There is no checking for overflow! You must be sure this value is large enough!*

Table 11.13: The DIALOG function

`int x`	Position of the top-left corner of the dialog (horizontal).
`int y`	Position of the top-left corner of the dialog (vertical).
`int cx`	Width of the dialog in dialog units.
`int cy`	Height of the dialog in dialog units.
`DWORD style`	The style bits.
`DWORD exstyle`	The extended style bits.
`LPCWSTR menu`	The menu to be used with the dialog. It can be one of three types of values:
	`NULL` — No menu is used.
	`LPCWSTR` — Name of menu resource.
	`MAKEINTRESOURCEW(id)` — Integer resource ID of menu to be used.
`LPCWSTR class`	The class of the dialog. It can be one of three types of values:
	`NULL` — Use the default dialog box class.
	`LPCWSTR` — Name of the registered class.
	`MAKEINTRESOURCEW(atom)` — Class atom of the registered class.
`LPCWSTR caption`	The caption. If no caption is used, you can pass in `NULL`.
`LPCWSTR font`	The font to use. If you do not wish to specify a font, you can pass in `NULL`. If you pass in `NULL`, the `DS_SETFONT` style will be removed if it is present.
`int height`	Font height in points. If font is `NULL`, this value is ignored.

The implementation of this function is shown in Listing 11.19, along with the "helper" functions it uses.

Listing 11.19: The DIALOG function implementation

```
#define DLGTEMPLATE_WORKING_SIZE 4096

/************************************************
appendString
************************************************/

__inline LPWORD appendString(LPWORD ptr, LPCWSTR text)
```

```
      {
       LPWSTR str = (LPWSTR)ptr;
       wcscpy(str, text);
       ptr = (LPWORD)(str + wcslen(str) + 1);
       return ptr;
      }
/******************************************************
setClassAtom
******************************************************/

__inline LPWORD setClassAtom(LPDLGITEMTEMPLATE item,
                             WORD classatom)
      {
       LPWORD ptr = (LPWORD)&item[1];
       *ptr++ = 0xFFFF;
       *ptr++ = classatom;
       return ptr;
      }


/******************************************************
setClassName
******************************************************/

__inline LPWORD setClassName(LPDLGITEMTEMPLATE item,
                             LPCWSTR classname)
      {
       LPWORD ptr = (LPWORD)&item[1];
       ptr = appendString(ptr, classname);
       return ptr;
      }
/******************************************************
setResourceID
******************************************************/

__inline LPWORD setResourceID(LPWORD ptr, short id)
      {
       *ptr++ = 0xFFFF;
       *ptr++ = (WORD)id;
       return ptr;
      }

/******************************************************
DIALOG
******************************************************/

LPDLGTEMPLATE DIALOG(LPDLGITEMTEMPLATE * item,
                UINT size, int x, int y, int cx, int cy,
                DWORD style, DWORD exstyle,
                LPCWSTR menu, LPCWSTR class,
                LPCWSTR caption, LPCWSTR font,
                int height)
      {
       LPDLGTEMPLATE dlg;
       LPWORD ptr;
```

```
   if(size == 0)
      size = DLGTEMPLATE_WORKING_SIZE;
   dlg = (LPDLGTEMPLATE) malloc(size);
   if(dlg == NULL)
      return NULL;

   dlg->x = x;
   dlg->y = y;
   dlg->cx = cx;
   dlg->cy = cy;

   dlg->cdit = 0;   // no dialog items yet

   dlg->style = style;
   if(font == NULL)
      dlg->style &= ~ DS_SETFONT;
   else
      dlg->style |= DS_SETFONT;

   dlg->dwExtendedStyle = exstyle;
   dlg->cdit = 0;

   ptr = (LPWORD) &dlg[1];

   if(menu == NULL)
      *ptr++ = 0; // no menu
   else
   if(HIWORD(menu) == 0)
      ptr = setResourceID(ptr, LOWORD(menu));
   else
      ptr = appendString(ptr, menu);

   if(class == NULL)
      *ptr++ = 0;
   else
   if(HIWORD(class) == 0)
      ptr = setResourceID(ptr, LOWORD(class));
   else
      ptr = appendString(ptr, class);

   ptr = appendString(ptr, (caption == NULL ? L"" : caption));

   if(font != NULL)
      { /* has font */
      *ptr++ = height;
      ptr = appendString(ptr, font);
      } /* has font */

   if(item != NULL)
      *item = (LPDLGITEMTEMPLATE) ptr;Template:

   return (LPDLGTEMPLATE)dlg;
}
```

The first thing we do is check the size to see if the caller passed in a 0, indicating that we can choose the size. If we are told to choose the size, we set the size to a default value. We then call `malloc` to get some space; if this fails, we return NULL. If it succeeds, we copy the parameter values into the newly allocated space. We initialize the cdit field of the dialog template to 0, thereby indicating that this dialog has no controls. It will be the responsibility of the caller to increment this field as controls are added.

Next, we check to see if the user has passed in a font name. If the font name is NULL, we turn off the DS_SETFONT bit in the styles; this bit is valid only if a font has been specified. If a font has been specified, we force the DS_SETFONT bit on because this is required in order to use the font. The caller should be very careful not to alter the DS_SETFONT style bit once the dialog has been created.

We next append the variable-length portions of the text to the dialog template. To do this, we need a WORD pointer to the first position past the end of the dialog template. We get this by computing the address of dlg[1] and then casting that address to an LPWORD pointer.

Our first field is the menu identifier. If no menu was passed in, we simply store a 0 word and increment the pointer. We have carefully read the specification of the MAKEINTRESOURCE family of macros. They store the 16-bit resource ID in the lower word and 0 in the upper word of the fictitious string pointer they create. The string pointer is fictitious because it doesn't *actually* point to a string; it simply allows the macro to lie to the compiler about what the type is so that the parameter passes type checking. The MAKEINTRESOURCEW macro creates an LPCWSTR-type result whose high-order word is 0. We next check that condition here. If we have one of these values, we call a function setResourceID. This function, when given a pointer and a 16-bit value, lays down the sequence 0xFFFF, value, at the position indicated by the pointer. The function returns an updated pointer. We use this technique throughout this code. If the value is anything else, it is assumed that it is a valid string pointer, and the appendString function is called to append the Unicode string. It will return an updated pointer.

We repeat this process for the class parameter. For the caption parameter, we allow the caller to pass in NULL, but the DLGTEMPLATE requires an actual string. So if the caller passes in a NULL, we pass on a pointer to a 0-length string. If the font is not NULL, we append the height and the font string.

We expect that the caller will pass in an LPDLGITEMTEMPLATE * pointer, but in case it is NULL, we avoid an access fault by checking for this condition. However, since it is fairly complex to determine the actual end of the dialog template, the caller will find life easier if a reference is passed in. We store the location where the first dialog item should be placed in this location. We then return a pointer to the dialog template itself.

We're going to use these helper functions again for the controls, so let's take a look at them. We've chosen to declare them as inline functions because they are so simple.

The setClassAtom function is very simple. It takes as a reference an LPDLGITEMTEMPLATE (because the class atom is the first value that follows the template) and returns an LPWORD for the location where the next descriptor can be written. It simply stores 0xFFFF and the input class atom value immediately following the DLGITEMTEMPLATE. The setClassName function is similar, except it calls appendString to write the string value. The setResourceID function works just like setClassAtom, except it takes a current position pointer instead of a dialog item template address.

The appendString function contains some interesting code. First, it casts the current pointer from being a word pointer to a Unicode string pointer. It then copies its text input argument to the location defined by that pointer. Note that it doesn't matter whether this is compiled as a Unicode or ANSI application; it calls wcscpy, which always does a Unicode string copy. Finally, it computes a new pointer value. It takes the string pointer and adds to it the string length, using the wcslen function. This string length is in *characters*, not bytes. But under the rules of arithmetic of C, if you have a pointer p to an n-byte structure and add a value k to p, the actual address computed is the address of p + n × k bytes. So this properly adds the number of bytes required for the number of Unicode characters (plus one for the NUL character) to the address str and then casts the result to an LPWORD.

We can now create our base dialog by issuing the call shown in Listing 11.24.

Creating Controls in the Dialog

Our base dialog is now done, but it isn't very interesting. It has no controls. It will, in fact, come up, and you can use the system menu to close it, but by most standards it is really boring. Let's add some controls.

To add controls, we must increment the cdit field of the DLGTEMPLATE to indicate that a control has been added. We have a choice to make here: Do we automatically update the field, thus requiring the caller to pass in a DLGTEMPLATE reference, or do we require the caller to do this explicitly? Since we can use these control functions to create DLGITEMTEMPLATEs that are *not* part of a DLGTEMPLATE, and which we might want to re-assemble later, we chose not to get the DLGTEMPLATE involved. Now you can call these functions to create controls anywhere in memory and assemble your own full dialog template out of the precomputed pieces. All you have to remember is to set the cdit count in the DLGTEMPLATE correctly.

All of the specialized control constructors call one basic constructor, CONTROL, so we look at that one first. The code for CONTROL is shown in Listing 11.20, and its specification is given in Table 11.14.

Table 11.14: Parameters to the CONTROL function

```
LPDLGITEMTEMPLATE CONTROL(LPDLGITEMTEMPLATE item,
                          LPCWSTR text, short id,
                          LPCWSTR classname,
                          DWORD style,
                          int x, int y, int cx, int cy,
                          DWORD exstyle)
```

Result: LPDLGITEMTEMPLATE	The location following this template at which a new template can be constructed.
Parameter	**Description**
LPDLGTEMPLATE item	Address of where the item is to be created in memory.
LPCWSTR text	Text to be associated with the item. The text can be one of the forms:

NULL	No text. Internally substitutes L"".
LPCWSTR	Name of the class.
MAKEINTRESOURCEW(atom)	Class atom of the class.

short id	Control ID.	
LPCWSTR classname	Class name of control to be created. It may be one of the following:	
	LPCWSTR	Name of the class.
	MAKEINTRESOURCEW(atom)	Class atom of the class.
DWORD style	Style bits for the control. The WS_CHILD style will be added automatically.	
int x	Horizontal position of top-left corner of the control, in dialog units.	
int y	Vertical position of top-left corner of the control, in dialog units.	
int cx	Width of the control, in dialog units.	
int cy	Height of the control, in dialog units.	
DWORD exstyle	Extended style bits.	

Listing 11.20: The CONTROL function

```
LPDLGITEMTEMPLATE CONTROL(LPDLGITEMTEMPLATE item,
                          LPCWSTR text, short id,
                          LPCWSTR classname,
                          DWORD style,
                          int x, int y, int cx, int cy,
                          DWORD exstyle)
  {
  LPWORD ptr = (LPWORD) &item[1];

  item->style = WS_CHILD | style;
  item->dwExtendedStyle = exstyle;
  setItemPos(item, x, y, cx, cy);
  item->id = (WORD)id;

  if(HIWORD(classname) != 0)
      ptr = setClassName(item, classname);
  else
      ptr = setResourceID(ptr, LOWORD(classname));

  if(HIWORD(text) != 0)
      ptr = appendString(ptr, text);
  else
      ptr = setResourceID(ptr, LOWORD(text));

  ptr = noParms(item, ptr);

  return (LPDLGITEMTEMPLATE)ptr;
  }
```

Let's compare a CONTROL statement from the resource file with the way we would add a control to a template with the CONTROL function. Here's a line from the resource file of the sample programs:

```
CONTROL "",IDC_STATIC, "Static", SS_BLACKRECT, 2, 31, 200, 1
```

Compare this with how we call it in our sample program:

```
templ->cdit++;
item = CONTROL(item, L"",
                IDC_STATIC,
                L"Static",
                SS_BLACKRECT | WS_VISIBLE,
                2, 31, 200, 1,
                0);
```

The only significant changes are that we must increment the control count field `templ->cdit`, pass the current item pointer into the `CONTROL` function, and (because there are no implicit or default styles) add the `WS_VISIBLE` style explicitly. We also cannot default any parameters, so the extended style value must be explicitly provided as 0.

Now we look at what the code actually does. First, it computes the address just past the area that represents a `DLGITEMTEMPLATE` and stores it in `ptr`. Then it stores the style, extended style, and position values. We can pass in a class name as either a `MAKEINTRESOURCEW(atom)` or as a quoted string such as `L"Static"`. We detect which of these values has been passed in and all either `setClassName` or `setResoureceID`. The text can be passed in either as a string or as a resource ID, so we perform the same test and store the appropriate format. Finally, we must lay down the count of the number of window creation parameters, which is, in this implementation, always 0. To do this, we call a function `noParms`. Finally, we return a pointer that is the pointer to the place we can lay down the next `DLGITEMTEMPLATE`.

The `noParms` function is very important. All of the documentation available simply refers to the fact that "creation parameters follow" without stating anything about what those parameters look like. But the examples in the Microsoft references all write a 0 and have the comment "no creation parameters". It is still not clear what value goes in here: a word count, a byte count, or what. But we discovered one thing (after spending hours trying to track down why some controls worked and others took memory reference exceptions): In a compiled `.res` file, *every* `DLGITEMTEMPLATE` *is an even number of words in length!* This fact appears to be undocumented in any available Microsoft documentation (although we hope this error will be corrected). Once we wrote the `noParms` procedure to compute the actual length of the item template and added an occasional padding word to make the length work out correctly, our example worked immediately. The code is quite simple and is shown in Listing 11.21.

Listing 11.21: The noParms function

```
__inline LPWORD noParms(LPDLGITEMTEMPLATE item,
                          LPWORD ptr)
  {
   *ptr++ = 0;     // no parameters
   if( (((LPWORD)item) - ptr) & 1)
      *ptr++ = 0;

   return ptr;
  }
```

The `noParms` function takes a pointer to the `DLGITEMTEMPLATE` and a current pointer position, from which it computes whether the `DLGITEMTEMPLATE` plus its variable-length descriptors uses an even number of words. If the difference is odd (the low-order bit is 1), we append one more 0 word. The updated pointer is returned.

This pointer will be the position at which the next DLGITEMTEMPLATE would start if we were creating a sequence of them.

For full generality, we would need to add a function that lets us specify additional arguments. We don't have that here. But one of the consequences of the noParms function is that a DLGITEMTEMPLATE will end with either one or two 0 words, and we can't tell without doing a length computation whether the terminal 0 word is the parameter count or the padding word. Don't assume that you can add parameters by "backing up" one word and then writing them, unless you correctly determine that backing up one word is sufficient.

Adding Other Control Functions

The parameter order for the CONTROL function was done so that the parameters corresponded to the parameter list of the CONTROL statement in the resource file. We want to support other resource statements with functions, so we have added a function for each of the resource statements listed in Table 11.6. We show some examples in Listing 11.22. All of these are written in terms of the basic CONTROL function. To specify the classes for these built-in classes, we use the class atom values we show in Table 11.12 and the MAKEINTRESOURCEW macro to encode them.

Listing 11.22: Control functions

```
LPDLGITEMTEMPLATE DEFPUSHBUTTON(LPDLGITEMTEMPLATE item,
                        LPCWSTR text, short id,
                        int x, int y, int cx, int cy,
                        DWORD style, DWORD exstyle)
    {
     return CONTROL(item, text, id,
                MAKEINTRESOURCEW(0x0080),
                style | BS_DEFPUSHBUTTON,
                x, y, cx, cy,
                exstyle);
    }

LPDLGITEMTEMPLATE LTEXT(LPDLGITEMTEMPLATE item,
                LPCWSTR text, short id,
                int x, int y, int cx, int cy,
                DWORD style,
                DWORD exstyle)
    {

     return CONTROL(item, text, id,
                MAKEINTRESOURCEW(0x0082),
                SS_LEFT | style,
                x, y, cx, cy,
                exstyle);
    }

LPDLGITEMTEMPLATE LISTBOX(LPDLGITEMTEMPLATE item,
                        short id,
                        int x, int y, int cx, int cy,
                        DWORD style,
                        DWORD exstyle)
    {
```

```
     return CONTROL(item, L"", id,
                    MAKEINTRESOURCEW(0x0083),
                    style,
                    x, y, cx, cy,
                    exstyle);
}
```

Some of the functions explicitly add style flags; for example, the LTEXT function explicitly adds the SS_LEFT style. Other functions supply the arguments that are required by the CONTROL function that are not passed in because they have no meaning and no equivalent in the resource statements. For example, the LISTBOX function does not take a text argument, but passes in an empty string (L"") to the CONTROL statement.

Using these functions, we can create the **About...** dialog box "on the fly". A portion of the code from the aboutbox.c file is shown in Listing 11.23.

Listing 11.23: Creating the **About...** box

```
LPDLGTEMPLATE makeAboutBoxTemplate()
    {
    LPDLGTEMPLATE templ;
    LPDLGITEMTEMPLATE item;
    //  See the code on page 76 for the creation of
    //  the DLGTEMPLATE 'templ'
//=====================================================
// DEFPUSHBUTTON "OK", IDOK, 166,63,32,14, WS_GROUP
//=====================================================

    templ->cdit++;
    item = DEFPUSHBUTTON(item, L"OK", IDOK,
                    166, 63, 32, 14,
                    WS_GROUP |
                    WS_TABSTOP | WS_VISIBLE, 0);

//=====================================================
//    ICON IDR_MAINFRAME, IDC_STATIC, 3,2,18,20
//=====================================================

    templ->cdit++;
    item = ICON(item, MAKEINTRESOURCEW(IDR_MAINFRAME),
                IDC_STATIC, 3, 2, 18, 20,
                WS_VISIBLE, 0);

//=====================================================
// LTEXT "FileDescription", IDC_ABOUT_FILEDESCRIPTION,
//        30,2,118,8
//=====================================================

    templ->cdit++;
    item = LTEXT(item, L"FileDescription",
                IDC_ABOUT_FILEDESCRIPTION,
                30, 2, 118, 8, WS_VISIBLE, 0);

// ... some LTEXT examples omitted...
```

```
/=========================================================
/ CONTROL "", IDC_STATIC, "Static", SS_BLACKRECT,
/                     2,31,200,1
/=========================================================

    templ->cdit++;
    item = CONTROL(item, L"", IDC_STATIC, L"Static",
                   SS_BLACKRECT | WS_VISIBLE,
                   2, 31, 200, 1, 0);

/ (for the remainder of the code, see the source file)

    return templ;
    }
```

The way we construct and call the dialog is shown in Listing 11.24. Note that it is the responsibility of the caller to free the dialog template created by makeAboutBoxTemplate.

Listing 11.24: Calling the indirect dialog

```
static void MainFrame_OnAppAbout(HWND hwnd)
    {
    HINSTANCE hinst = GetWindowInstance (hwnd) ;
    LPDLGTEMPLATE temp = makeAboutBoxTemplate();
    if(temp != NULL)
        { /* call it */
        int error;
        DialogBoxIndirect (hinst, temp, hwnd, (DLGPROC) AboutDlgProc) ;
        error = GetLastError();
        free(temp);  // release it
        } /* call it */
    }
```

The Message Box

Many times, you won't need to create a dialog box to prompt the user for simple replies. Windows supplies a *message box* for those times when you need to display a line or two of text to the user and get a simple response, such as **Yes**, **No**, or **Retry**.

A message box (displayed by the MessageBox function) is a window that contains a caption and a message that you supply along with a number of predefined icons and push buttons. The user responds to the message box by clicking one of the push buttons. The MessageBox function returns a value indicating which button was pressed. The function call looks like this:

```
ButtonID = MessageBox (hwndOwner, Message, Caption, Flags) ;
```

The hwndOwner parameter identifies the window that owns the message box window. Generally, you set this to the handle of the window that makes the MessageBox function call. When you call MessageBox from a dialog function, you should use the dialog box handle. Windows gives the input focus to the hwndOwner window when the message box is destroyed.

Suppose you don't want this window to receive the input focus when the message box is destroyed or when you don't have a window handle (such as during program initialization in the WinMain function prior to creating a window and entering the message loop). Just pass a NULL value for the hwndOwner parameter. *Don't* use the handle returned by the GetDesktopWindow function as the hwndOwner parameter to the MessageBox function. If you do, the message box displays, but the user will not able to respond to it, and the system will hang. Once your application has a main window, you must *not* call MessageBox with a NULL handle unless you explicitly specify the MB_TASKMODAL flag (see page 828). If you do not specify MB_TASKMODAL with a NULL owner handle, your main window *will not be disabled*. And, if you have forced some window to be "always on top", it will be on top of all windows, including message boxes. The result: Not only is your parent window not disabled, but you don't see the message box![5]

The Message parameter is a pointer to a NUL-terminated string containing the message to appear in the client area of the message box. The Caption parameter is a pointer to a NUL-terminated string used for the caption of the message box window.

The flags parameter contains bit flags that indicate the contents and style of the message box. You choose which push buttons should be displayed in a message box by selecting from the values shown in Table 11.15, and you can determine which of these buttons is the default by using one of the styles shown in Table 11.16. You can add in the MB_HELP style to any other selection using the OR operator. Making the **Help** button the default button does not cause the message box to return, but instead causes the help system to be invoked. You can cause a predefined icon to appear in the message box by choosing one of the icon flags shown in Table 11.17. (Observe that there has been a change in appearance between API level 3 and API level 4 and there is no guarantee that these images will remain the same in future releases.) You can choose the modality by including one of the values from Table 11.18. For special purposes, you can include one or more of the flags specified in Table 11.19. The set of flag choices is summarized in Table 11.20.

Table 11.15: Message box button selection codes

Flags	Button Captions				Return Values
	1	**2**	**3**	**4**	**Return Values**
MB_ABORTRETRYIGNORE	**Abort**	**Retry**	**Ignore**	**Help**[1]	IDABORT, IDRETRY, IDIGNORE
MB_OK	**OK**	**Help**[1]			IDOK
MB_OKCANCEL	**OK**	**Cancel**	**Help**[1]		IDOK, IDCANCEL
MB_RETRYCANCEL	**Retry**	**Cancel**	**Help**[1]		IDRETRY, IDCANCEL
MB_YESNO	**Yes**	**No**	**Help**[1]		IDYES, IDNO

---

[5] This is a realistic scenario. It happened to me when I was trying to use a commercial subroutine library that issued MessageBox calls with a NULL handle but no MB_TASKMODAL flag! *–jmn*

Table 11.15: Message box button selection codes

	Button Captions				
Flags	**1**	**2**	**3**	**4**	**Return Values**
MB_YESNOCANCEL	**Yes**	**No**	**Cancel**	**Help**[1]	IDYES, IDNO, IDCANCEL
MB_HELP[4]					Does not return. Invokes the help system.

[1] The **Help** button is present if the MB_HELP style is also specified.
[4] Win32 4.x and higher only.

Table 11.16: Default button selection codes

Button Indicator	**Button Selection**	**Default Result**
MB_DEFBUTTON1	MB_ABORTRETRYCANCEL	IDABORT
	MB_OK	IDOK
	MB_OKCANCEL	IDOK
	MB_RETRYCANCEL	IDRETRY
	MB_YESNO	IDYES
	MB_YESNOCANCEL	IDYES
MB_DEFBUTTON2	MB_ABORTRETRYCANCEL	IDRETRY
	MB_OK	MB_HELP	–
	MB_OKCANCEL	IDCANCEL
	MB_RETRYCANCEL	IDCANCEL
	MB_YESNO	IDNO
	MB_YESNOCANCEL	IDNO
MB_DEFBUTTON3	MB_ABORTRETRYCANCEL	IDCANCEL
	MB_OKCANCEL	MB_HELP	–
	MB_RETRYCANCEL	MB_HELP	–
	MB_YESNO	MB_HELP	–
	MB_YESNOCANCEL	IDCANCEL

Table 11.16: Default button selection codes

Button Indicator	Button Selection	Default Result
MB_DEFBUTTON4[4]	MB_ABORTRETRYCANCEL | MB_HELP	–
	MB_YESNOCANCEL | MB_HELP	–

[4] Win32 4.*x* and above only.

Table 11.17: Message box icon codes

Icon Code	Usage	Icon API3	Icon API4
MB_ICONASTERISK	Obsolete; use MB_ICONINFORMATION.		
MB_ICONERROR	An icon indicating an error.		
MB_ICONEXCLAMATION	Obsolete; use MB_ICONWARNING.		
MB_ICONHAND	Obsolete: use MB_ICONERROR.		
MB_ICONINFORMATION	An information icon.		
MB_ICONQUESTION	A question-mark icon.		
MB_ICONSTOP	Obsolete; use MB_ICONERROR.		
MB_ICONWARNING	An icon indicating a warning.		

The MessageBox call produces up to four push buttons in the message box, depending on the selection. You can specify which push button is the default for the message box by including one of the MB_DEFBUTTON values from Table 11.16. If no explicit value is specified, the default is as if MB_DEFBUTTON1 was specified.

You can also control the urgency of a message box by including one of the modality flags from Table 11.18. The default MB_APPLMODAL message box type creates a message box that disables its owner window. The user must respond to the message box before the owner window can be used. The user can switch to and use other windows of the current application as well as the windows of other applications. This is the default unless you specify one of the other modal types.

Table 11.18: MessageBox modality flags

Modality Flag	Effect
MB_APPLMODAL	Disables its owner window. Other windows in the application can still be used.
MB_TASKMODAL	Disables all top-level windows in the current task if the hwndOwner is NULL.
MB_SYSTEMMODAL	All applications are suspended until the message box is dismissed.

The MB_TASKMODAL message box type creates a message box similar to the MB_APPLMODAL type. However, when the hwndOwner parameter to the MessageBox function is NULL, an MB_TASKMODAL message box disables all the top-level windows of the current application. The user can switch to other applications but must respond to the message box before continuing with the current application.

The MB_SYSTEMMODAL message box type creates a message box that suspends *all* applications until the user responds to the message box. This type should be used only to report the most significant of system-wide errors, those that can result in a serious compromise of system integrity. Do not use it for anything less.

You can display an icon in a message box along with your message. Choose from the icon codes shown in Table 11.17; these values are ORed into the flags. Since the release of the original Windows system, the names and appearances of the icons have changed. Consequently, the header files contain a number of synonyms for the icons, many of which are now considered obsolete. We show the obsolete synonyms in the table because you are likely to encounter them if you are porting Win16 code.

The MB_ICONINFORMATION type displays an icon resembling the international symbol for information. It is generally used when you wish to alert the user to some situation. The MB_ICONWARNING type displays an exclamation-point icon. It is generally used when you wish to alert the user that a condition has arisen that is nonfatal, but that means the operation being performed may not complete as expected. The MB_ICONERROR type displays a stop sign icon. It is generally used when a condition has arisen that makes it impossible for the current operation to proceed. The MB_ICONQUESTION type displays a question mark icon. It is generally used when you need a confirmation from the user.

If you set the MB_ICONERROR flag along with the MB_SYSTEMMODAL flag, you will not get any icons in the message box. This combination of flags tells Windows that something critical has happened in your application and that the application needs to notify the user. Windows does the least amount of processing it can in order to ensure it can display the message box. Typically these flags are used only when displaying a message box that must be displayed even under very low memory conditions or when a system failure may be imminent.

Finally, you can add one or more of the flags shown in Table 11.19. We don't cover these in detail becaus their use is generally uncommon (unless, of course, you are working in Hebrew or Arabic or are writing N system services).

Table 11.19: Miscellaneous MessageBox flags

Flag	Function
MB_RIGHT[4.x]	Text in the message box is right-justified.
MB_RTLREADING[4.x]	Text will be displayed with right-to-left reading order on Hebrew and Arabic systems.
MB_SERVICE_NOTIFICATION [NT]	Windows NT Service Notification. The message is displayed on the default desktop, even if no user is logged into the system.
MB_DEFAULT_DESKTOP_ONLY [NT]	The desktop must be a default desktop (a desktop that belongs to a user once the user has logged in).
MB_SETFOREGROUND	The message box becomes the foreground window (via SetForegroundWindow).

[4.x] Win32 4.x only.
[NT] Windows NT only.

Table 11.20: Summary of MessageBox flags

Button Configuration (Choose One)	Button Default (Choose One)	Icon (Choose One)	Modality (Choose One)	Miscellaneous (Add in One or More)
MB_ABORTRETRYIGNORE	MB_DEFBUTTON1[*]	MB_ICONERROR	MB_APPLMODAL[*]	MB_HELP
MB_OK[*]	MB_DEFBUTTON2	MB_ICONINFORMATION	MB_TASKMODAL	MB_RIGHT[4]
MB_OKCANCEL	MB_DEFBUTTON3	MB_ICONQUESTION	MB_SYSTEMMODAL	MB_RTLREADING[4]
MB_RETRYCANCEL	MB_DEFBUTTON4[4]	MB_ICONWARNING		MB_SETFOREGROUND
MB_YESNO		no icon[*]		MB_SERVICE_NOTIFICATION[NT]
MB_YESNOCANCEL				MB_DEFAULT_DESKTOP_ONLY[NT]

[*] Default if no explicit value given.
[4] API level 4 only.
[NT] Windows NT only.

he MessageBox function returns either 0 when the message box cannot be created or one of the values in
`able 11.21 to indicate the button that the user selected.

Table 11.21: Values returned from the MessageBox function

Button Pressed	Value
Abort	IDABORT
Cancel	IDCANCEL
Ignore	IDIGNOREID
No	IDNO
OK	IDOK
Retry	IDRETRY
Yes	IDYES

The MessageBox Explorer

The MessageBox Explorer application, shown in Figure 11.7, allows you to experiment with all the features
of the MessageBox call. You can set all of the parameters of the MessageBox call, including the body text.
The escape characters \r, \t, and \n are all handled when they appear in the body text. You also can try set-
ing the parent window to NULL and see the effects if MB_TASKMODAL is not set.

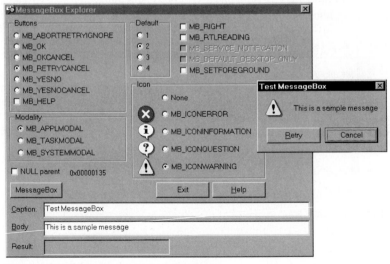

Figure 11.7: The MessageBox Explorer

12 Menus, Accelerators, Icons, String Resources, and MessageTable Resources

Menus, accelerators, icons, and strings can all be specified in the resource-definition file for a Windows application. This chapter examines each of these resources. However, this is not the first time we've used a menu or string resources. You can think of message resources as a special kind of string resource.

Each of the example programs you've seen so far has contained a menu. You've been able to select the "**About** *ApplicationName...*" menu item from the **Help** pop-up menu of all example programs to request the About box to be displayed. We've placed nearly all of the string literals we've used in the example programs into the resource-definition files.

The first section in this chapter explains how to define, create, use, and destroy menus used by a Windows application. First, we discuss the various methods for defining a menu. Once you have a menu definition, you can create a menu based on that definition. When you create a menu, you can associate the menu with a window. When you no longer need a menu, you disassociate the menu from a window and destroy the menu.

You can shortcut this process. When you create a window, you can specify a menu definition and let Windows create the menu and associate the menu with the new window. Windows will also destroy the menu associated with a window when it destroys the window.

You can alter a menu after you create it. Windows provides functions to add, insert, and delete items in a menu. You can also temporarily disable a menu item. The user can't select a disabled menu item. You typically gray a disabled menu item to indicate visually that the menu item isn't currently applicable. You aren't restricted to text labels in a menu. You can also use a bitmap as a menu item, or even draw a custom image of your menu item.

Windows applications typically have a system menu that contains a number of predefined selections such as restore and maximize. You can also change the system menu for your application both by deleting predefined menu items and adding your own custom menu items.

There are two example programs for this chapter: the Menu Demo program and the Menu Explorer program. The Menu Demo program, written in C, shows basic menu handling techniques. The Menu Explorer program, which is in C++, lets you play with nearly all of the menu API functions. We define most of the menus in these example programs in the resource-definition files. We also define, in the Menu Demo program, one menu using a data structure compiled into the program.

In the second section, we discuss *keyboard accelerators*. A keyboard accelerator is a keystroke that the user can use to quickly make a menu selection. In addition to demonstrating the use of menus, the Menu Explorer example program uses keyboard accelerators.

We then discuss *icon resources* and *string resources*. You can load icons and character strings from your application resources at runtime.

Finally, we discuss *message tables*, a special kind of resource that allows you to more easily write internationalized applications.

Menus, icons, strings, and messages that you define in your application's resource definition file can be changed without changing the source code for the application. They can even be changed by the end user if that end user has an appropriate tool. There are many third-party tools that let the user localize the application to a particular language.

Menus

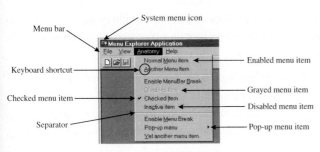

Figure 12.1: Anatomy of a menu

You've used menus before, but now we're going to see how all those effects are produced. The anatomy of a menu is shown in Figure 12.1. A menu consists of a set of *items*. A menu item has style and state descriptions; for example, the top-level menu bar in most applications consists of a set of pop-up menu items. Any menu, whether the top-level menu bar or a pop-up menu, has one or more items in it. These may be ordinary enabled menu items, grayed menu items, separator items, and further pop-up items. In a pop-up menu, a menu item may have an additional state that is displayed, called its *checked* state. Within a pop-up menu, there may be *separator* items.

A user may select a menu item in various ways. For example, clicking the top-level menu item causes its associated pop-up menu to drop down; we show this in Figure 12.1. Holding the mouse button down and dragging down to a particular item and releasing the mouse button selects that item. An item also can be selected by clicking the top-level menu item and then clicking the item in the displayed menu. Using the **Alt** key in combination with a letter selects the menu item with the corresponding underlined letter. Once a menu item drops down, just typing a letter will select the menu item with the corresponding shortcut letter designated (the **Alt** key is not required). If there is no designated letter, the first letter of the menu text is used for the selection. As the programmer, you won't know and won't be able to (without a lot of extra work) find out which of these methods is used, as they produce essentially identical effects. No matter which of these methods is used, you will see them identically. However, there is a keyboard shortcut method that goes, in effect, directly to the menu item: the *accelerator key*. This is a virtually separate mechanism from the menu system, and we discuss it separately (see page 905).

When the user selects an item from a menu, Windows sends a WM_COMMAND message to the window function associated with the window that owns the menu. The message specifies the *menu ID*, which is similar to a control ID, for the menu item that the user selected. Your application responds to the message by performing the requested function.

You can also define certain keystrokes as shortcuts to select a menu item. These are called *accelerator keys.* You associate a keystroke with a menu ID value. When the user presses an accelerator key, Windows sends (almost) the same message to the window function as it does when the user selects the menu item with the same menu ID.

There are several types of menus. A *top-level* menu is the horizontal list of items displayed just below the caption of a window. Entries in a menu are displayed either as text or as bitmaps. An entry in a top-level menu can be either a *command menu item* or a *pop-up menu item.*

Windows uses the terms *menu, command menu item,* and *pop-up menu item* in a special sense. A *menu* is a top-level menu and is the menu Windows displays in a bar immediately under a window's caption. The Windows documentation occasionally refers to a top-level menu as the *menu bar.*

The items on a top-level menu must be *pop-up menu items* or *command menu items.* Selecting a label corresponding to a pop-up menu item produces a vertically displayed menu that "pops up" below the selected label. For example, the **File** label present on the menus of many Windows applications represents a pop-up menu. When the user selects **File**, its pop-up menu appears, offering file-related, additional choices such as **New**, **Open...**, **Close**, **Save...**, and so on.

Command menu items can be present on a top-level menu, although they are most often found on pop-up menus. Command menu items represent a final selection. When the user selects a command menu item, Windows sends a WM_COMMAND message to the window function identifying the menu item that the user selected.

Typically, Windows applications use the following conventions in the labels for pop-up menu items and command menu items used in a top-level menu:

- A menu item in the top-level menu that produces an immediate response ends with an exclamation point. For example, an **Exit!** menu item indicates that selecting it will cause the application to terminate without further menus popping up.

- A menu item that causes a dialog box to appear requesting additional information should end with an ellipsis (three periods). For example, an **Open...** menu item indicates that selecting it will causes a dialog box to appear, no doubt requesting the name of the file to open.

- A pop-up menu item has no special suffix code on its caption text.

Windows does not supply a suffix automatically; it is your responsibility to adhere to the GUI standards and supply it.

If you have an *accelerator* associated with a menu (we talk about those starting on page 905), you should include the description of the accelerator on the right edge of the menu. For example, the **Exit** item under the **File** menu should say that **Alt+F4** is the accelerator. Also, you will typically find that the **New** item under the **File** menu has **Ctrl+N** as the accelerator. It is your responsibility to put this information in the menu item text.

An entry in a pop-up menu that has a u symbol, the cascaded menu symbol, at its right edge is not a command menu item, but another pop-up menu. You don't insert the symbol; that is done for you by Windows, unless you are doing an owner-draw menu item. When you're drawing an owner-draw item and want to use the cascaded menu symbol, you can use the built-in bitmap OBM_MNARROW, described on page 884.

A label on a pop-up menu item should have no suffix. When the user selects a pop-up menu item, Windows displays the list of items in the pop-up menu and waits for the user to make a selection. A pop-up menu can, itself, contain command menu items and other pop-up menu items. When the entry selected from the pop-up menu is a command menu item, Windows sends a WM_COMMAND message to the application notifying it of the user's choice.

When the user selects an entry in a pop-up menu and that entry is another pop-up menu, Windows displays the specified second-level pop-up menu to the right of the original pop-up window. The user can then select an entry from this second-level pop-up window. You can create menus with more than one level of pop-up menus. Multiple levels of pop-up windows are called *cascading menus*.

A pop-up menu and a cascading pop-up menu are normally owned by another menu. The user selects a pop-up menu item from the owner menu and Windows displays the pop-up menu. You can also explicitly request Windows to display a pop-up menu at an arbitrary location on the screen whenever you wish. Generally, you'll display this pop-up menu at a fixed location, at the current cursor position, or a position relative to a location in the application's client area, usually in response to a right-mouse-button notification. This particular type of pop-up menu is not associated with another menu. Such a pop-up menu is called a *floating pop-up menu*. These are the menus that are normally invoked with a right-mouse-button click and are application- and context-specific.

Operations on a menu can be performed in one of two modes: *by position* or *by command*. In most menu functions, you specify the mode by adding the MF_BYPOSITION or MF_BYCOMMAND flags into a "flags" value. In many of the Win32 4.*x* functions there is a separate Boolean parameter, byPosition, that you set to TRUE to operate on a menu by position and FALSE to operate on a menu by command ID.

Generally you want to operate on a menu by command ID. This is not only more reliable but also has the added feature that when a command ID is specified, the entire menu tree is searched for a menu item that has the designated menu ID. Hence, even if the menu item you want to modify is in a pop-up menu, or even a pop-up menu *within* a pop-up menu, then to perform the operation successfully you need only the top-level menu handle (usually for the main window's menu, which you can get with `GetMenu`).

For some operations, however, you need a menu position. For example, in the Win32 3.*x* API the only way you can manipulate a pop-up menu item within a menu is by specifying its position, since this API does not support IDs for pop-up menus. (The 4.*x* API does, however, so you should seldom need a by-position approach if you can program exclusively in the level 4 API.) This often leads to dangerously fragile code and requires some additional programming effort to build robust and reliable applications that continue to work in the presence of maintenance. We show an example of how to do this in Listing 12.3 on page 877.

Defining and Creating a Menu

Now let's look at the three ways you can define a menu:

- Define a menu in a resource file.

- Create a menu dynamically.

- Create a menu from a memory template.

The most common method is defining an application's menus in the application's resource-definition file. This allows you to change a menu–for example, into a different language–by changing only the resource-definition file. You don't need to make any changes to your source code or to relink the application.

Here's a good design rule you can use in designing menus: *You, the programmer, do not own the shape of the menu.* The "shape" of the menu, that is, the specification of the top-level items, what items appear under which top-level item, and so on, is often controlled by "outside forces"–management, marketing, competition, the desires and (usually highly vocal) opinions of the end users, evolving in-house standards, and even evolving Microsoft GUI standards. The menu might be rearranged significantly between two major releases of the software. Here are some particularly nasty and unfounded assumptions:

- The **File** menu is the first menu (easily violated if you are using the Multiple Document Interface; see Chapter 17).

- The **Edit** menu is the second menu item (for much the same reason as the **File** menu). However, you can't even assume that it is the one just to the right of **File** because some views may not support the concept of cut/copy/paste, and the menu item is dropped entirely.

- The **Window** menu is the next-to-right-most menu item. (We discuss this further in Chapter 17.)

- The **Help** menu is the last menu item. (This may not be true if you add debugging menu items during development. These are often most conveniently placed beyond the standard "product" menu.)

We've seen all these as problems. So, your code should have as little dependency as possible on the actual menu shape. Always using the "by command" option is a significant step in this direction. Our basic design rule is *if you have any constant that defines a menu position, or assume a menu is in any relative position to either end of the menu bar, your program is unmaintainable.* Many years of programming Windows, particularly maintaining (or attempting to maintain) existing code, have only confirmed this rule.

 Never encode any test in your program that requires a specific text string be found in the menus, and *never* put a string constant in your program that you will use to change a menu. A user with a resource editor can actually change the resources even in your delivered executable and even for a language that Microsoft does not currently support, such as Esperanto. If you expect that the strings you encode in the resource will be the strings found at execution, you are living dangerously. We show you how to deal with this when we get to the discussion of string resources later in the chapter.

We should start using appropriate terminology from the beginning, so we point out that you actually define a *menu template* in a program's resource-definition file. When you create a *menu*, you can specify a *menu template* and Windows builds a menu based on the description in the template. But the template and the menu are *not* the same. You can use one template to create six identically-shaped, but individual, menus.

You don't *need* to use a menu template to create a menu. You can create a menu dynamically. You can create an empty menu and add, insert, and change items within that menu. Typically, you would create a menu dynamically when you want a user-defined menu. That is, you don't know what the menu should look like until the user runs the application.

Finally, you can define a menu template by creating an in-memory data structure. Actually, the resource compiler compiles the text menu template in a resource-definition file into this same data structure. You can then create a menu based on the template described by this data structure.

Defining a Menu Template in Your Resource Definition File

Menus (of all types) are often defined in an application's resource definition (.rc) file by one or more MENU statements. Each MENU statement must be followed by the BEGIN keyword and one or more MENUITEM and/or POPUP statements and terminated by the END keyword. Like dialogs, a menu resource is named either by a string or by an integer. Also, the same issues we discussed on page 336 with respect to resource naming apply. The following example defines a menu identified by the symbolic integer value EXAMPLEMENU.

In your header file, for example, resource.h:

```
#define EXAMPLEMENU          42

#define IDM_NEW             101
#define IDM_OPEN            102
#define IDM_CLOSE           103
#define IDM_SAVE            104
#define IDM_SAVEAS          105
#define IDM_EXIT            106
#define IDM_HELP            111
```

In your resource file, for example, yourapp.rc:

```
EXAMPLEMENU MENU DISCARDABLE
BEGIN
```

```
    POPUP       "&File"
    BEGIN
        MENUITEM "&New...",      IDM_NEW
        MENUITEM "&Open...",     IDM_OPEN
        MENUITEM "&Close",       IDM_CLOSE
        MENUITEM "&Save",        IDM_SAVE
        MENUITEM "Save &As...",  IDM_SAVEAS
        MENUITEM SEPARATOR
        MENUITEM "E&xit",        IDM_EXIT
    END
    MENUITEM "&Help",  IDM_HELP, HELP
END
```

The MENU or MENUEX statement begins the menu resource definition. A MENU or MENUEX statement has the following syntax:

```
menuID MENU [load-option] [memory-options]
optional-statements
BEGIN
    item-definitions
END

menuID MENUEX
BEGIN
    item-definitions
END
```

The menuID parameter specifies a name or integer that you use to identify the menu resource. The *load-option* parameter has no meaning in Win32 but will be recognized so that you can maintain a dual Win16/Win32 code base or more easily port a Win16 application to Win32. The *memory-options* parameter, if present, is DISCARDABLE. Windows creates a menu from the menu resource template. The DISCARDABLE option applies to the menu resource *template*, not to the actual menu created from the resource. Changes to a menu aren't lost when the menu template is discarded.

You may encounter additional declarations when porting Win16 applications to Win32; in particular, the keywords PRELOAD and LOADONCALL as load options, and MOVEABLE and FIXED as memory options. These have no meaning in Win32 applications. They are recognized for compatibility, but they are ignored.

The *optional-statements* can be any of LANGUAGE, CHARACTERISTICS, or VERSION and apply only to the MENU declaration, not the MENUEX declaration. Except for the LANGUAGE statement, these optional statements exist primarily for tools that work on resources, such as the Microsoft Resource Editor that is part of the Visual C++ environment. The LANGUAGE statement contains an ID of a language and an optional sublanguage from the selection we gave in Table 9.13, page 638.

Each POPUP statement defines a pop-up menu. A POPUP statement contains a text string that specifies the name of the pop-up menu and, optionally, one or more keywords that control the appearance of the pop-up menu name. A POPUP statement must be followed by a BEGIN keyword and one or more MENUITEM and/or POPUP statements and terminated by the END keyword just like a MENU statement. The syntax of a MENUITEM or POPUP depends on whether it is declared within a MENU or MENUEX statement. Older tools constructed only MENU resources.

We look at the more limited form first because the MENUEX form of the statements is essentially an extension (hence the -EX suffix) of functionality (but with a slightly different set of keywords). A POPUP statement in a MENU declaration has the following syntax:

```
POPUP       "text" [, option-list]
BEGIN
    item-definitions
END
```

A MENUITEM statement in a MENU declaration has the following syntax:

```
MENUITEM "text", ItemID [, option-list]
```

The text parameter specifies the character string that is displayed for the pop-up menu. The following discussion applies to the text parameter in both statements.

The string can contain the escape character \t. The \t character inserts a tab character into the string. It is used to align text in columns. Tabs should be used for this purpose; adding space characters generally won't work when you are using a variable-pitch font. Windows uses a variable-pitch font for menu text. The width of a text string depends on the characters in the string rather than the number of characters. Tab characters should be used only in text parameters for items in a pop-up menu, not in the menu bar. Normally you use \t to separate the accelerator name from the menu name. We explain this more when we discuss keyboard accelerators; in particular, see page 909. You can insert a double quotation mark (") into the string by including two double quotation marks ("").

You may encounter a \a escape sequence if you are porting older Win16 code to Win32. This escape sequence is no longer supported in Win32. It caused the menu item to be flushed to the right end of the menu bar, an action now accomplished via the MFT_RIGHTJUSTIFY flag on the menu item. Hence, you must use the MENUEX declaration (currently Win32 4.x only).

An ampersand (&) in the string causes the character that follows it to be underlined. A single ampersand is not displayed. You display an ampersand as part of the text by inserting two ampersands (&&). Windows considers an underlined character in text for a menu to be a *mnemonic* for the item. The same applies to the first letter in the text when no character is underlined. The user can select a top-level menu item by pressing a letter key while also pressing the **Alt** key. Upon receiving such a keystroke, Windows searches the top-level menu for a menu item with a mnemonic that matches the key press. When it finds one, Windows sends a message to the window identifying the selected menu item. If the menu item is a command menu item, it is "executed" by sending the appropriate WM_COMMAND message to the top-level window. If the item is a pop-up menu, the menu is displayed and, within this menu, items will be displayed. You can use the **Alt** key or ordinary unshifted keys to select one of these menu items. Each MENUITEM statement defines the text of a menu item and the menu ID, an integer value that is sent to the window that owns the menu when the user selects the menu item. It also optionally defines one or more keywords that control the appearance of the menu item.

The items are displayed as listed in the menu definition. The "File" text string will be displayed as the left-most item in the menu. The "Help" text string will be the right-most item and will have a vertical separator to its left (because the HELP optional keyword was used).

The ItemID parameter of a MENUITEM statement specifies the menu item's ID, an integer that is similar to the control ID parameter of a control. This integer value is sent to the window that owns the menu when the user selects the item's name. When the user selects an enabled MENUITEM item (other than a SEPARATOR) from a menu, Windows sends a WM_COMMAND message to the window function for the window that owns the menu. The wParam parameter of the message contains the ItemID value. When the user operates a control, the control sends a WM_COMMAND message with the wParam parameter set to the control ID value. For this reason, it's convenient, although not necessary, to avoid using identical values for control and menu IDs.

The options listed in Table 12.1 control the appearance of the menu text and can be specified as the option-list parameters of the MENUITEM and POPUP statements that can appear under a MENU declaration, although not all options are valid in all cases. You can include one or more options separated by spaces or commas.

Table 12.1: MENUITEM and POPUP options in a MENU declaration

Option	Description
CHECKED	The item is initially displayed with a check mark (✓) to the left of the text.
GRAYED	The item is initially inactive, cannot be selected, and appears on the menu in a gray or lightened color (as set by the Control Panel). This option cannot be combined with INACTIVE.
HELP	The item has a vertical separator to the left of the text. This option is valid only on MENUITEM statements.
INACTIVE	The item is initially inactive and cannot be selected, but appears on the menu in the normal menu-text color. The option cannot be combined with GRAYED.
MENUBARBREAK	This option is identical to MENUBREAK, except that a vertical bar separates a new column from the old when used on an entry in a pop-up menu.
MENUBREAK	The item begins on a new line when used on top-level menu items. When used on an entry in a pop-up menu, this item begins a new column in the pop-up menu. No dividing line separates the new column of items from the old.
SEPARATOR	The item is an inactive item, represented by a horizontal line drawn across the width of the menu. This attribute cannot be combined with any other attribute and has no text or menuID.

There is a special form of the MENUITEM statement that looks like the following:

MENUITEM SEPARATOR

This statement creates a horizontal bar in the menu. The bar is inactive and cannot be selected. You use this statement to separate two menu items in a pop-up menu. The example menu definition used this statement to separate the **Exit** menu item from the file manipulation menu items.

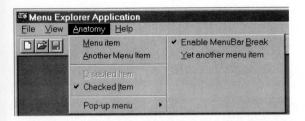

Figure 12.2: The effect of the MENUBARBREAK style

You can force a vertical break by using the MENUBREAK or MENUBARBREAK keywords. The effect is shown in Figure 12.2, which is the result of selecting the **Enable MenuBar Break** item from the menu of Figure 12.1. This sets a menu bar break on the menu item shown. The MENUBREAK style forces the break, and the MENUBARBREAK forces the break and includes the vertical separator bar.

Win32 4.x Menus

The MENUEX statement is supported only for Windows 95 and Windows NT 4.x applications. Since you may still have to support "legacy" Windows NT 3.5x systems, there will be a transition period during which the MENUEX statement and its associated capabilities are not supported under Windows NT. So you will have to decide if the limitation to Windows 95 and Windows NT 4.x and the exclusion of Windows NT 3.x is acceptable. If so, you can use the MENUEX statements. You should then explicitly check during your initInstance function that you are indeed running on a Windows 4.x platform.

You might think that using the linker option/SUBSYSTEM:Windows,4.0 would be sufficient to keep your application from running under Windows NT 3.5x. It is not. Check out the Knowledge Base article Q125705, "Application Version Marking in Windows 95", which explains that using this switch also allows applications to execute on Windows NT 3.5x and higher.

When you declare a menu with the MENUEX statement, the syntax of a MENUITEM and POPUP differs somewhat from that of the MENU statement. A MENUITEM statement is of this form:

```
menuID MENUEX // show we are in a MENUEX
    MENUITEM "text", id, type, state
```

The text and id values are identical to those used by a MENUITEM in a MENU declaration. However, the type and state fields are different. The type field specifies the type of the menu item and is a bit field, not a keyword. You can use bit field operators to build the type field you wish to use. The bits are defined in the file winuser.h, and you must include this file explicitly in your resource file. (For example, the Microsoft environment lets you specify which files to include. Other environments have similar capabilities.) The bits can be any of those shown in Table 12.2. The state flags are also encoded as a set of bits and can be any of the bits shown in Table 12.3.

The bits are combined using any of the operators shown in Table 12.4. Note that *unlike* the limitations imposed on style bits for a dialog or controls, a much more complete set of arithmetic and Boolean operators is provided, and parentheses can be used to combine terms. For example, the two MENUITEMs in the following example have the same bits:

```
#define StdBits (MFS_DISABLED | MFS_CHECKED)
MyMenu MENUEX
```

```
BEGIN
  MENUITEM "This", IDM_THIS, MFT_STRING, MFS_DISABLED
  MENUITEM "That", IDM_THAT, MFT_STRING, StdBits & ~ MFS_CHECKED
END
```

Table 12.2: Menu types for MENUITEMs in MENUEX declarations

Flag	Description
MFT_BITMAP	The menu item will be a bitmap.
MFT_MENUBARBREAK	Places the menu item on a new line if it is in a menu bar or in a new column if it is a pop-up menu. When a pop-up menu is broken into multiple columns, a vertical bar will separate the columns.
MFT_MENUBREAK	Places the menu item on a new line if it is in a menu bar or in a new column if it is a pop-up menu. When a pop-up menu is broken into multiple columns, there is no vertical bar separator between the columns.
MFT_OWNERDRAW	The menu item will be drawn by the window that owns the menu.
MFT_RADIOCHECK	Displays a checked menu item using the radio button mark ●, provided the checked bitmap has not been overridden by an explicit bitmap. See SetMenuItemInfo.
MFT_RIGHTJUSTIFY	Right-justifies the menu item and all items to its right. This is valid only for top-level menus.
MFT_SEPARATOR	The menu item is a horizontal line drawn across the width of the menu. This option is valid only for pop-up menus, not top-level menus. It cannot be combined with MFT_BITMAP or MFT_STRING. The text string is ignored.
MFT_STRING	The menu is displayed using a string.

The *type* flags determine the representational properties of the menu. The property MFT_STRING indicates that the menu is an ordinary menu item; the text string will be displayed. The MFT_BITMAP indicates that the menu will have a bitmap; you will have to set the bitmap handle using the SetMenuItemInfo before it can properly display. The MFT_OWNERDRAW flag indicates that the menu is owner-draw; like owner-draw controls, you have complete responsibility for drawing the pixels of the menu item. The owner of the menu will get WM_MEASUREITEM and WM_DRAWITEM messages when the menu item needs to be drawn. We show a detailed example of this on page 860. Finally, the MFT_SEPARATOR flag indicates that the menu item is a disabled, nonselectable separator line.

Table 12.3: Menu states for MENUITEMs in MENUEX declarations

Flag	Description
MFS_CHECKED	The menu item is checked.
MFS_DEFAULT	The menu item will be the default. There is only one default menu item in any pop-up menu.

Table 12.3: Menu states for MENUITEMs in MENUEX declarations

Flag	Description
MFS_DISABLED	The menu item is disabled (it cannot be selected), but it is not grayed out.
MFS_ENABLED	The menu item is enabled.
MFS_GRAYED	The menu item is disabled (it cannot be selected), and it is grayed out.
MFS_HILITE	The menu item is highlighted.
MFS_UNCHECKED	Removes any check mark.
MFS_UNHILITE	Removes any highlighting from the menu item. This is the default state.

Table 12.4: Valid operators for bit fields within MENUEX declarations

Op	Description
+	Addition.
–	Subtraction.
–	Unary minus (signed negation).
~	Unary bitwise complement (NOT).
&	Bitwise AND.
|	Bitwise OR.
( )	Parentheses for grouping.

A POPUP statement in the context of a MENUEX declaration is also quite different from a POPUP statement in a MENU declaration:

```
menuID MENUEX // show we are in a MENUEX
       POPUP "text" [, id [, type
                        [, state [, helpID ]]]]
```

A POPUP statement in the context of a MENU declaration supports only text and a set of simple options. A POPUP statement in the context of a MENUEX declaration supports an extensive set of options, including the ability to attach an ID to the pop-up *and* attach a help ID. This is a significant change from the traditional pop-up menus of Windows 3.*x* and Windows NT 3.*x*. In the original design of Windows, a pop-up menu did not have an ID, since it could not send a message to its owner. This led to a serious problem with identifying the menu so that you could modify its properties, such as enabling or disabling it, making other state changes to it, or changing its text. The Windows 4.*x* interface allows you to attach a menu ID to a pop-up menu, thereby making it more readily (and reliably) accessible for manipulation by the menu API functions. (See our warning about the "menu shape" on page 835.)

A comparison of the features of the POPUP and MENUITEM declarations for MENU and MENUEX is shown in Table 12.5.

Table 12.5: Comparison of MENU and MENUEX features

		Availability and Format	
Declaration	**Parameter**	**MENU**	**MENUEX**
POPUP	"text"	✓	✓
	id		✓
	type		MFT_BITMAP
		MENUBARBREAK	MFT_MENUBARBREAK
		MENUBREAK	MFT_MENUBREAK
			MFT_OWNERDRAW
			MFT_RADIOCHECK
			MFT_RIGHTJUSTIFY
		Implied	MFT_STRING
	state	CHECKED	MFS_CHECKED
			MFS_DEFAULT
		GRAYED	MFS_GRAYED
		INACTIVE	MFS_DISABLED
			MFS_ENABLED
			MFS_HILITE
			MFS_UNCHECKED
			MFS_UNHILITE
	helpid		✓
MENUITEM	text	✓	✓
	ItemID	✓	✓
	type	BITMAP	MFT_BITMAP
		HELP	
		MENUBARBREAK	MFT_MENUBARBREAK
		MENUBREAK	MFT_MENUBREAK

Table 12.5: Comparison of MENU and MENUEX features

Declaration	Parameter	Availability and Format	
		MENU	MENUEX
			MFT_OWNERDRAW
			MFT_RADIOCHECK
			MFT_RIGHTJUSTIFY
		SEPARATOR	MFT_SEPARATOR
		implied	MFT_STRING
	state	CHECKED	MFS_CHECKED
			MFS_DEFAULT
		GRAYED	MFS_GRAYED
		INACTIVE	MFS_DISABLED
			MFS_ENABLED
			MFS_HILITE
			MFS_UNCHECKED
			MFS_UNHILITE

Creating a Menu Dynamically in Win32 3.x

The API functions used to create and modify menus are somewhat different in Win32 3.x and Win32 4.x. We discuss them separately because you may need to support applications under the older Windows NT 3.x interface. This section discusses the Win32 version 3.x interface (Windows NT 3.1, 3.5, and 3.51). The Win32 version 4.x interface (Windows 95 and Windows NT 4.x) discussion starts on page 849.

Several of these functions are identical in Win32 3.x and Win32 4.x. The remaining functions are still supported under Windows 95 and Windows NT 4.x. Microsoft simply states that these functions are no longer the "preferred" way of doing menu manipulation but they are retained for compatibility. This gives them the option of removing these functions in some future release of Win32, so you should use the recommended functions for all new code. The differences between the two interfaces are summarized in Table 12.10.

To create a menu dynamically, you call the CreateMenu function to create an empty menu. The function call returns a handle to the new menu:

```
HMENU CreateMenu () ;
```

If you want a popup menu, you call CreatePopupMenu instead:

```
HMENU CreatePopupMenu () ;
```

Either of these returns a handle to an empty menu that can be used by any menu-manipulating function. A menu created by CreateMenu becomes a pop-up menu if it is added as a pop-up menu item to another menu.

Appending, Inserting, and Modifying Menu Items in Win32 3.*x*

When you have a handle to an empty menu, you can add command menu items and pop-up menu items to the menu with the AppendMenu function and the InsertMenu function. The AppendMenu function appends a new item to the end of a menu. Here is the syntax of the function call:

```
BOOL AppendMenu (HMENU hmenu, INT Flags, UINT NewItemID, LPCTSTR NewItem) ;
```

The NewItemID is the identifier of the new command item. However, if Flags includes the MF_POPUP flag, the NewItemID is the handle of the pop-up menu that is associated with the position that is being replaced, which must be cast to a UINT. The function returns TRUE if it succeeds and FALSE if it fails. The GetLastError function will return an error code explaining the failure. The interpretation of NewItem depends on the Flags value. Since the most common usage is a pointer to a string, the parameter is declared as an LPCTSTR. For other types, you will have to do an explicit cast to the LPCTSTR type to avoid compile-time warnings or errors.

An example of the effect is shown in Figure 12.3. Here we show one line of how we might construct the familiar **File** menu if we were doing it dynamically. Of course, we would not actually wire the string constant into our call; we would load a string from the string table.

```
AppendMenu(hFileMenu, MF_STRING, IDM_SAVEAS, _T("Save &As..."))
```

Before	**After**
Open... Close	Open... Close Save As...

Figure 12.3: AppendMenu **in action**

The InsertMenu function inserts a new item at a specified position in a menu, moves the item at the specified position, and moves all following items down the menu. The function call looks much the same as the AppendMenu call, with the addition of the ItemID parameter:

```
BOOL InsertMenu (HMENU hmenu, UINT ItemID, UINT Flags,
                 UINT NewItemID, LPCTSTR NewItem) ;
```

As with AppendMenu, the NewItemID can be either the integer identifier of a command menu item or the menu handle of a pop-up menu item (if MF_POPUP is specified in Flags) cast to a UINT. The NewItem parameter is interpreted in the same way as for AppendMenu. This is summarized in Table 12.6.

An example of the effect is shown in Figure 12.4. Here we show one line of how we might insert an element into the familiar **File** menu if we were doing it dynamically. We show how we would do it using both MF_BYPOSITION and MF_BYCOMMAND. The two statements are equivalent. As with the AppendMenu call, we would not actually use the string constants shown, but would load the strings from a string table resource.

```
InsertMenu(hFileMenu, IDM_SAVEAS, MF_BYCOMMAND | MF_STRING,
                      IDM_SAVE, _T("&Save..."))

InsertMenu(hFileMenu,  2, MF_BYPOSITION | MF_STRING,
                      IDM_SAVE, _T("&Save..."))
```

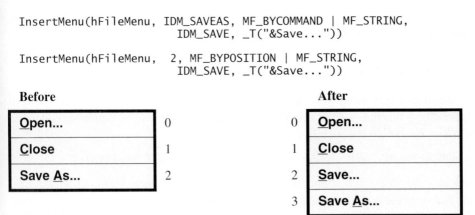

Figure 12.4: InsertMenu in action

The ModifyMenu function uses the same parameters as the InsertMenu function. The ModifyMenu function changes an existing menu item by replacing the existing menu item with a completely new menu item. When the existing menu item is a pop-up menu item, the function destroys the previously defined pop-up menu and releases the memory containing the menu. (This means you cannot share, without risk, a pop-up menu that is in another pop-up menu. You should create two copies of the menu so that if one is destroyed by ModifyMenu, the other remains safe.) A ModifyMenu function call is defined as

```
BOOL ModifyMenu (HMENU hmenu, UINT ItemID, UINT Flags,
                 UINT NewItemID, LPCTSTR NewItem) ;
```

If the Flags parameter does not include the MF_POPUP flag, the NewItemID is the identifier of the new command menu item. If Flags does includes the MF_POPUP flag, the NewItemID is the handle of the pop-up menu that will be associated with the menu item that is being replaced; it must be cast to a UINT. The NewItem type depends on the Flags field. This is all summarized in Table 12.6.

An example of the effect is shown in Figure 12.5. Here we show one line of how we might change the menu item if the "**Show Ruler**" item were selected. We show how we would do it using both MF_BYPOSITION and MF_BYCOMMAND. The two statements are equivalent for this example. As with the previous examples, we would not actually use the string constants shown but would load the strings from a string table resource.

 It is almost always a serious mistake to use MF_BYPOSITION with a hard-wired constant, even one that is defined by using a #define. Under long-term maintenance of the code, a change in the menu arrangement requires a change in the constant, a situation not readily apparent, even to the original author. The consequence of using MF_BYPOSITION is the introduction of obscure bugs. You should never use MF_BYPOSITION unless you have just computed the exact position. See our warning about the menu shape on page 835.

```
ModifyMenu(hViewMenu, IDM_SHOWRULER, MF_BYCOMMAND | MF_STRING,
                      IDM_HIDERULER, _T("Hide &Ruler"))

ModifyMenu(hViewMenu,  2, MF_BYPOSITION | MF_STRING,
                      IDM_HIDERULER, _T("Hide &Ruler"))
```

Before

Toolbar	0
Status Bar	1
Show Ruler	2

After

0	Toolbar
1	Status Bar
2	Hide Ruler

Figure 12.5: ModifyMenu **in action**

The AppendMenu, InsertMenu, and ModifyMenu functions have the parameters shown in Table 12.6.

Table 12.6: Menu function parameters

Parameter	Description	
hMenu	Specifies the handle of a menu to which you're appending, inserting, or modifying a menu item.	
ItemID	Specifies an existing item in the menu. You can specify an item by its current position in the menu or by its menu ID. The interpretation depends on the flags that are included in the Flags parameter:	
	MF_BYPOSITION	ItemID is a position of the menu item.
	MF_BYCOMMAND	ItemID is the ID of the menu item.
Flags	One or more of the following flags (not all combinations are permitted; see Table 12.7):	
	MF_BITMAP	The item is a bitmap. The NewItem parameter is interpreted as a bitmap handle.
	MF_BYPOSITION	Interprets ItemID as a menu position. For InsertMenu, a position of -1 appends to the end of the menu.
	MF_BYCOMMAND	Interprets ItemID as a command ID.
	MF_CHECKED	The bitmap is displayed with a check mark. If the SetMenuItemBitmaps function has been used to set the bitmaps, the "checked" bitmap is displayed.
	MF_DISABLED	The menu item is disabled. It cannot be selected, but it is not grayed.
	MF_ENABLED	The menu is enabled. The MF_DISABLED and MF_GRAYED states are removed.
	MF_GRAYED	The menu item is disabled. It cannot be selected, and it is displayed in the "grayed" color.

Table 12.6: Menu function parameters

Parameter	Description	
	MF_MENUBARBREAK	The menu item is placed on a new line (for a menu bar) or starts a new column (for a pop-up menu). The columns are separated by a visible separator line. See Figure 12.2.
	MF_MENUBREAK	The menu item is placed on a new line (for a menu bar) or starts a new column (for a pop-up menu). The columns are not separated by a visible separator line.
	MF_OWNERDRAW	The item is an owner-draw menu item. The NewItem parameter is an arbitrary 32-bit value that is passed to your WM_MEASUREITEM and WM_DRAWITEM handlers.
	MF_POPUP	The item is a pop-up menu. The NewItem parameter is the handle of a pop-up menu.
	MF_SEPARATOR	The item is a separator, a horizontal line drawn the width of the menu. A separator is disabled and cannot be selected.
	MF_STRING	Interprets NewItem as a pointer to a string.
	MF_UNCHECKED	The item is displayed as an unchecked menu item. If SetMenuItemBitmaps has been used to define the bitmaps, the "unchecked" bitmap is displayed.
NewItemID	Specifies the item ID of the new item. The interpretation is based on the bits in the Flags parameter:	
	Flags Bit	**Interpretation of NewItemID**
	MF_POPUP	The handle to a pop-up menu item, cast as a UINT.
	Not MF_POPUP	The menu item ID of the command menu item.
NewItem	The interpretation depends on which flags are set:	
	Flags bit	**Interpretation of NewItem**
	MF_BITMAP	A bitmap handle, cast to an LPCTSTR.
	MF_OWNERDRAW	An arbitrary 32-bit value you interpret in your WM_MEASUREITEM and WM_DRAWITEM handlers, cast to an LPCTSTR.
	MF_STRING	A pointer to a NUL-terminated text string.

Table 12.7: Permitted combinations of menu flags

Select only one of the choices from each of the following sets:	
state:	MF_DISABLED, MF_ENABLED[*], MF_GRAYED
image:	MF_BITMAP, MF_STRING[*], MF_OWNERDRAW, MF_SEPARATOR
break:	MF_MENUBREAK, MF_MENUBARBREAK
check mark:	MF_CHECKED, MF_UNCHECKED[*]
selection:	MF_BYPOSITION, MF_BYCOMMAND[*]
pop-up:	MF_POPUP, *no flag*[*]

[*]The default if not specified.
Note that the MF_POPUP alternative is to specify no flag at all. There is no "not-a-pop-up" flag for the nonpop-up case.

The Flags parameter contains additional flags that specify the type of the new item that will be added, inserted, or replaced in the menu. It also can contain flags describing the initial appearance of the new item. You can specify more than one flag parameter by combining multiple flags using the C bitwise OR operator, subject to the limitations shown in Table 12.7.

The NewItem parameter identifies the actual item to be displayed as the menu selection. It is either a pointer to a NUL-terminated character string, a handle to a bitmap, or an arbitrary 32-bit value.

The MF_BYCOMMAND flag is actually not needed in the examples because it is the default value.

Creating a Menu Dynamically: Win32 4.*x*

To create a menu dynamically in Win32 4.*x,* you call the CreateMenu function to create an empty menu. The function call returns a handle to the new menu:

```
HMENU CreateMenu () ;
```

If you want a pop-up menu, you call CreatePopupMenu instead:

```
HMENU CreatePopupMenu () ;
```

Either of these returns a handle to an empty menu that can be used by any menu-manipulating function. A menu created by CreateMenu becomes a pop-up menu if it is added as a pop-up menu item to another menu.

The MENUITEMINFO Structure

The key to most of the important menu operations in Win32 4.*x* is the MENUITEMINFO structure. This structure is used to both set and retrieve settings of a menu. Although many of the older Win32 3.*x* operations (such as EnableMenuItem) are still available, the new SetMenuItemInfo and GetMenuItemInfo functions allow you much more flexibility than the Win32 3.*x* set does.

The definition of the MENUITEMINFO is shown as follows. See Table 12.8 for the details of each field.

```
typedef struct tagMENUITEMINFO {
    UINT    cbSize;
    UINT    fMask;
    UINT    fType;
    UINT    fState;
    UINT    wID;
    HMENU   hSubMenu;
    HBITMAP hbmpChecked;
    HBITMAP hbmpUnchecked;
    DWORD   dwItemData;
    LPTSTR  dwTypeData;
    UINT    cch;
} MENUITEMINFO, * LPMENUITEMINFO;
```

Table 12.8: MENUITEMINFO fields

Field	Description		
UINT cbSize	The size of the structure, in bytes. Must be initialized before any call that uses this structure.		
UINT fMask	A bit mask that determines which fields will be set or retrieved in the menu item. It can be any of the following:		
	MIIM_CHECKMARKS	Retrieves or sets the hbmpChecked and hbmpUnchecked members.	
	MIIM_DATA	Retrieves or sets the dwItemData member.	
	MIIM_ID	Retrieves or sets the wID member.	
	MIIM_STATE	Retrieves or sets the fState member.	
	MIIM_SUBMENU	Retrieves or sets the hSubMenu member.	
	MIIM_TYPE	Retrieves or sets the fType and dwTypeData members.	
UINT fType	The menu item type. It can be one or more of the flags described in Table 12.2, which have been renamed to be MFT_ flags:		
	MFT_BITMAP	The menu is a bitmap menu.	
	MFT_MENUBARBREAK	There will be a break before the menu item. Columns are separated by a vertical bar.	
	MFT_MENUBREAK	There will be a break before the menu item. No separator will be displayed.	

Table 12.8: `MENUITEMINFO` **fields**

Field	Description	
UINT fType (continued)	MFT_OWNERDRAW	The item is an owner-draw item.
	MFT_RADIOCHECK	The default "checked" bitmap is a bullet.
	MFT_RIGHTJUSTIFY	The menu will be right-justified in the top-level menu.
	MFT_RIGHTORDER	*This bit is currently undocumented by Microsoft, but it appears in the header file. It may apply to right-to-left languages such as Hebrew or Arabic.*
	MFT_SEPARATOR	The menu item is a separator bar.
	MFT_STRING	The menu item is a string.
UINT fState	The menu item state. It can be one or more of the values described in detail in Table 12.3, which are renamed to be MFS_ flags:	
	MFS_CHECKED	If set, the item is "checked".
	MFS_DEFAULT	If set, the item is the default menu item.
	MFS_DISABLED	If set, the documentation claims that the item is disabled, but not grayed. Microsoft currently defines this constant as being MFS_GRAYED, thus eliminating the concept of disabled-but-not-grayed menu items.
	MFS_ENABLED	This is a 0 constant that can be used to indicate the menu item is enabled. You must not use MF_DISABLED or MF_GRAYED if you specify this value.
	MFS_GRAYED	If set, the item is disabled and grayed.
	MFS_HILITE	If set, the item is highlighted.
	MFS_UNCHECKED	This is a 0 constant used to explicitly indicate that the item is "unchecked".
	MFS_UNHILITE	This is a 0 constant used to explicitly indicate that the item is not highlighted.
UINT wID	The 16-bit value that identifies the menu item. The high-order 16 bits are unused and must be 0.	
HMENU hSubMenu	Handle to the pop-up menu for this menu item. If the menu item is not a pop-up, this will be NULL.	

Table 12.8: MENUITEMINFO fields

Field	Description
HBITMAP hbmpChecked	A handle to the bitmap to display if the item is "checked". This defaults, if NULL, to a check mark (✓), unless the MFT_RADIOCHECK flag is set, in which case it is a bullet (●).
HBITMAP hbmpUnchecked	A handle to the bitmap to display if the item is "unchecked". This defaults, if NULL, to no bitmap.
DWORD dwItemData	An application-defined 32-bit value associated with the menu item.
LPTSTR dwTypeData	The contents of the menu item. The meaning depends on the menu item type: <table><tr><th>Menu Item Type</th><th>Interpretation of dwTypeData</th></tr><tr><td>MFT_BITMAP</td><td>Handle of a bitmap to display.</td></tr><tr><td>MFT_OWNERDRAW</td><td>Arbitrary 32-bit value.</td></tr><tr><td>MFT_SEPARATOR</td><td>Not used; can be NULL.</td></tr><tr><td>MFT_STRING</td><td>A pointer to the buffer that contains the text to be set or that will receive the text when retrieved.</td></tr></table>
UINT cch	The length of the item text, when retrieving information about an MFT_STRING menu item. Set to 0 for other menu types. Ignored for SetMenuItemInfo.

Whenever you use a MENUITEMINFO structure, you must initialize its cbSize field to be the size of the structure:

```
{
 MENUITEMINFO mif;
 mif.cbSize = sizeof(MENUITEMINFO);
```

This is required. The menu functions will fail if this field is not properly initialized.

The fields that will be set via a SetMenuItemInfo or retrieved via a GetMenuItemInfo must be indicated by setting the fMask field. This can be any of the flags shown in Table 12.8, combined using the bitwise OR operator. If you are using the InsertMenuItem or SetMenuItemInfo functions, you must then initialize the fields selected by the fMask field to the values you want to set. If you are using the GetMenuItemInfo function, then after you call the function, the fields you selected with the fMask will contain the values retrieved from the menu item. Unselected fields will be unchanged. If you did not explicitly initialize them, their contents are unpredictable, especially if (as we illustrated earlier in the chapter) the structure is a local variable.

It is also worth pointing out yet another instance where the Hungarian notation is completely inconsistent with the declaration type, showing once again that Hungarian notation is a seriously flawed idea. The dwTypeData field would be assumed to be a DWORD, but it is an LPTSTR, and the wID field would be assumed to be a WORD (16 bits), but it is a UINT (32 bits). This shows that the idea is so bad that even Microsoft, who tries to promote it, can't get it right.

Appending, Inserting, and Modifying Menu Items in Win32 4.*x*

When you have a handle to an empty menu, you can add command menu items and pop-up menu items to the menu with the InsertMenuItem function:

```
BOOL InsertMenuItem (HMENU hmenu, UINT ItemID,
          BOOL byPosition, LPMENUITEMINFO lpmenuinfo) ;
```

The hmenu parameter is a handle to the menu into which the item is being inserted. The ItemID parameter is either a position or a menu ID; its interpretation depends on the byPosition Boolean parameter. If byPosition is FALSE, the ItemID is the ID of the menu item before which to insert the new menu item. If byPosition is TRUE, the ItemID is the position at which to insert the new menu item; the menu item at that position and all the ones that follow are moved down to make room for the insertion. The return value is TRUE if the operation succeeds and FALSE if it fails. In case of failure, GetLastError will give you more information about the failure.

For example, to insert a menu item for a **Save...** menu, given we have partially constructed a menu, we can use InsertMenuItem, shown as follows. The effect is shown in Figure 12.6. The following code is intended to be illustrative rather than an example of a full menu-building operation. For example, we use a literal string for the text instead of loading a string from a resource file. (Doing this will lead us into serious trouble as soon as the product goes international.)

```
void addSave(HMENU hmenu)
    {
    MENUITEMINFO saveitem = {
               sizeof(MENUITEMINFO),  // cbSize
               MIIM_ID | MIIM_STATE |
               MIIM_TYPE,             // fMask
               MFT_STRING,            // ftype
               MFS_DISABLED,          // fState
               IDM_SAVE,              // wID
               NULL,                  // hSubMenu
               NULL,                  // hbmpChecked
               NULL,                  // hbmpUnchecked
               0,                     // dwItemData
               _T("&Save..."),        // dwTypeData
               0} ;                   // cch
    InsertMenuItem(...//see discussion for parameters)
    }
```

```
InsertMenuItem(hFileMenu, IDM_SAVEAS, FALSE, &saveitem);

InsertMenu(hFileMenu,  2, TRUE, &saveitem);
```

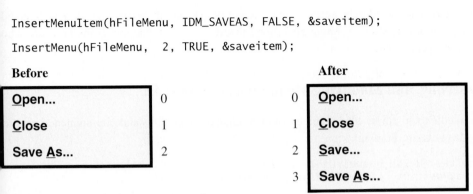

Figure 12.6: InsertMenuItem in action

Modifying a menu item is fairly straightforward but for simple modifications is amazingly verbose. Instead of an assortment of API functions, we can use SetMenuItemInfo to modify any menu item, including all of the properties that cannot be modified in any other way, such as the ID of a pop-up menu item. If we make the reasonable assumption that all menu IDs are unique, then all we need to do is fill in a MENUITEMINFO structure with the fields we wish to change, set the fMask field, and call SetMenuItemInfo. Note, however, that for some properties we may need to call GetMenuItemInfo to retrieve the existing status, such as the fState field values. For example, to gray out a menu item, we can use the code shown in Listing 12.1.

Listing 12.1: Using SetMenuItemInfo

```
void grayMenuItem(HMENU hmenu, UINT id, BOOL state)
    {
    MENUITEMINFO mif;
    mif.cbSize = sizeof(MENUITEMINFO);
    mif.fMask = MIIM_STATE;
    GetMenuItemInfo(hmenu, id, FALSE, &mif);
    if(state)
        { /* enable */
        mif.fState &= ~ (MFS_GRAYED | MFS_DISABLED);
        mif.fState |= MFS_ENABLED;
        } /* enable */
    else
        { /* disable */
        mif.fState &= ~ (MFS_ENABLED | MFS_DISABLED);
        mif.fState |= MFS_GRAYED;
        } /* disable */
    SetMenuItemInfo(hmenu, id, FALSE, &mif);
    }
```

Generally, for such simple modifications you will want to use one of the specialized API functions, such as

```
EnableMenuItem(hmenu, id, MF_BYCOMMAND | MF_GRAYED)
```

or

```
EnableMenuItem(hmenu, id, MF_BYCOMMAND | MF_ENABLED)
```

The overhead of doing the full `SetMenuItemInfo` call is necessary, however, if you are modifying one of the many attributes that have no equivalent in the Win32 3.*x* API, such as the ID of a pop-up menu, or setting a type that has no equivalent in the earlier API.

We could change the ID and text of a menu item using `SetMenuItemInfo`. For example, to change a menu item that says "**Show Ruler**" to one that says "**Hide Ruler**", we could use the following code:

```
static void setHideRuler(HWND hwnd)
    {
    TCHAR HideText[MAX_MENU_SIZE] ;
    MENUITEMINFO hideruler = {
                sizeof(MENUITEMINFO),    // cbSize
                MIIM_TYPE | MIIM_ID,     // fMask
                MFT_STRING,              // fType
                MFS_ENABLED,             // fState
                IDM_HIDE_RULER,          // wID
                NULL,                    // hSubMenu
                NULL, NULL,              // bitmaps
                0,                       // dwItemData
                HideText,                // dwTypeData
                0};                      // cch
    HMENU hmenu = GetMenu(hwnd);
    LoadString(GetWindowInstance(hwnd), IDS_HIDE, HideText, DIM(HideText));
    SetMenuItemInfo(hmenu, IDM_SHOW_RULER, FALSE, &hideruler);
    }
```

As an example, we use the Menu Explorer application to insert a bitmap menu item, use `SetMenuItemInfo` to change its "checked" bitmap to a 👍 symbol, and change its status to "checked". The result is shown in Figure 12.7.

Figure 12.7: A custom check mark bitmap menu item

Radio Button Menu Items

Radio button menu items are a variant on the check mark style for a menu item intended to show a set of disjoint choices. The ordinary check marked menu item shows a ✓ symbol beside the menu item. You can set any other bitmap you want, but a common bitmap is a bullet, •, which is usually used to indicate an exclusive choice of a set of menu items. For example, you may have a menu **Character** that allows you to set certain characteristics of the fonts being displayed. When the menu drops down, you might get a menu like that shown in Figure 12.8. The use of the separators to mark off the mutually exclusive selections and the use of the radio button check mark give a strong visual clue that these choices are mutually exclusive.

You could use the `GetMenuItemInfo` and `SetMenuItemInfo` functions to individually deal with each of the plain, bold, italic, and bold italic menu options, turning off the `MFS_CHECKED` state for all but the one selected and setting it for the one selected. You could set your own custom bitmap to represent the bullet. But the bullet is so common that the special MFT_RADIOCHECK style is used to get a bullet check mark. And as with radio buttons, there is an easier way to turn on one of a set of choices while turning off all the others: Check-MenuRadioItem.

```
BOOL CheckMenuRadioItem(HMENU hmenu,
                UINT first,
                UINT last,
                UINT selected,
                UINT flags)
```

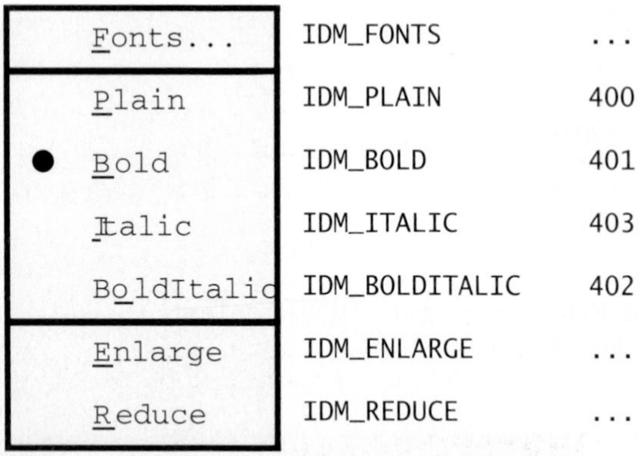

To use CheckMenuRadioItem, if you want to use ID codes, you have to arrange your ID codes so that the set of mutually exclusive menu items forms a continuous set within a range. For example, we could set the values illustrated in Figure 12.8. We show only the IDs for the radio menu items. Note that they do *not* have to be in order. In fact, they don't even have to represent menu items that are physically adjacent if you are using MF_BYCOMMAND, although it makes a lot of sense visually to arrange your menu this way. To select the **Bold** menu item, you could call CheckMenuRadioItem with the following parameters:

Fonts...	IDM_FONTS	...
Plain	IDM_PLAIN	400
● Bold	IDM_BOLD	401
Italic	IDM_ITALIC	403
BoldItalic	IDM_BOLDITALIC	402
Enlarge	IDM_ENLARGE	...
Reduce	IDM_REDUCE	...

Figure 12.8: A Character menu and its IDs

```
CheckMenuRadioItem(GetMenu(hwnd),   // menu.
                IDM_PLAIN,       // first ID of group
                IDM_ITALIC,      // last ID of group
                IDM_BOLD,        // ID to check
                MF_BYCOMMAND);   // values are IDs
```

This will set the MFS_CHECKED and MFT_RADIOCHECK flags in the selected menu item and clear them from the other menu items in the range.

Default Menu Items

You can set a menu item to be a *default* menu item. If the user double-clicks a menu and that menu contains a default menu item, the effect will be as if the user had dropped down the menu and selected that menu item. There can be only one default menu item for a given menu. A default menu item is displayed in boldface when the menu is visible.

If you are creating your menu from a resource file and you are using the MENUEX resource, then the MENUITEM resource can take a set of flags, one of which is the MFS_DEFAULT flag. See Table 12.3 and the discussion on page 840. If you are not using this technique or you wish to change the default menu item, you can do so with the SetMenuItemInfo function, using code very much like that in Listing 12.1. There is a simpler interface, however: the SetMenuDefaultItem function. It has the form

```
BOOL SetMenuDefaultItem(HMENU hmenu, UINT item, BOOL byPosition);
```

The interpretation of the `item` parameter is based on the `byPosition` parameter. If `byPosition` is FALSE, `item` is the ID of the menu item that will become the new default menu item in hmenu. If `byPosition` is TRUE, `item` is the position of the menu item that will become the new default menu item in hmenu. If `item` is (UINT)-1, there will be no default menu item.

You can discover which menu item is the current default menu item by using the `GetMenuDefaultItem` function:

```
UINT GetMenuDefaultItem(HMENU hmenu, BOOL byPosition, UINT flags)
```

If there is no default menu item, the value returned is (UINT)-1. If the `byPosition` flag is TRUE, the value returned will be the position of the default item in the menu. If the `byPosition` flag is FALSE, the value returned will be the ID of the menu item that is the default menu. The `flags` can be either one or more of the values shown in Table 12.9 or 0. Note that the case in which the default menu item is a pop-up is handled specially; you should note carefully the `GMDI_GOINTOPOPUP` flag if you ever set a default menu item to be a pop-up.

A lot of Windows API functions were specified before Microsoft understood the difference between signed and unsigned integers. Unfortunately, this confusion is pervasive and infests even the new Win32 API functions. The formal specification of `GetMenuDefaultItem` is that it returns a UINT value, yet the documentation claims that if it fails, the return value is -1, an impossible value for a UINT. You would expect that you might be able to write
```
            if(GetDefaultMenuItem(hmenu, FALSE, 0) == -1)
```
but if you do, the compiler will (quite correctly) complain that you are comparing a UINT to a signed value. This is why we always try to use explicit casts when we specify such values; you *can* validly write
```
            if(GetDefaultMenuItem(himenu, FALSE, 0) == (UINT)-1)
```

Table 12.9: `GetDefaultMenuItem` flags

Flag	Description
GMDI_GOINTOPOPUP	If present and the default menu item is a pop-up, recurses into the pop-up menu searching for a default menu item within it. If the default menu item is a pop-up and that pop-up does *not* contain a menu item, the return value identifies the pop-up. If not present, the first default menu item in the hmenu parameter is returned. If there is no default menu item in the menu, (UINT)-1 is returned.
GMDI_USEDISABLED	If present, will consider menu items that are disabled or grayed. If not present, disabled and grayed menu items are ignored. If the only default menu items are disabled or grayed, the return value is (UINT)-1.

Summary: A Comparison of Win32 3.*x* and Win32 4.*x* Menu Capabilities

The Win32 4.*x* menu system gives you much more capability than the Win32 3.*x* system. However, you may have to support the Win32 3.*x* system for your existing application platform base, at least for some time. Alternatively, if you choose to support only the Win32 4.*x* interface, you will have a "more modern" GUI interface that is easier to program.

Here is a summary of the major features of the Win32 4.*x* menu system:

- You can attach an ID to a pop-up menu, thereby making it easy to locate and modify its state.

- You will automatically get WM_HELP messages when the user hits the **F1** key while a menu item is selected.

- You have a new check-mark style built in, MFT_RADIOCHECK, along with its API function, CheckMenuRadioItem.

- Right-justified menus in the top-level menu bar are done differently than the 3.*x* API, using the MFT_RIGHTJUSTIFY flag.

- All of the menu features can be specified either in the resource file using the MENUEX resource type or in a menu template using the MENUEX_TEMPLATE_HEADER and MENUEX_TEMPLATE_ITEM structures.

- You can get a "default" menu item that is selected by double-clicking the top-level menu item.

The differences in the functions used in the two interfaces are summarized in Table 12.10.

Table 12.10: A comparison of Win32 3.*x* and Win32 4.*x* menu functions

Win32 3.*x* Function	Win32 4.*x* Function
AppendMenu	InsertMenuItem
ChangeMenu (obsolete)	SetMenuItemInfo
CheckMenuItem	SetMenuItemInfo
CreateMenu[*]	CreateMenu
CreatePopupMenu[*]	CreatePopupMenu
DeleteMenu[*]	DeleteMenu
DestroyMenu[*]	DestroyMenu
DrawMenuBar[*]	DrawMenuBar
EnableMenuItem[*]	EnableMenuItem
	SetMenuItemInfo
GetMenu[*]	GetMenu
GetMenuCheckMarkDimensions	GetMenuCheckMarkDimensions[1]
	GetSystemMetrics(SM_CXMENUCHECK)

Table 12.10: A comparison of Win32 3.*x* and Win32 4.*x* menu functions

Win32 3.*x* Function	Win32 4.*x* Function
GetMenuItemCount*	GetMenuItemCount
GetMenuItemID*	GetMenuItemID
GetMenuState	GetMenuItemInfo
GetMenuString	GetMenuItemInfo
GetSubMenu*	GetSubMenu
GetSystemMenu*	GetSystemMenu
HiliteMenuItem*	HiliteMenuItem
	SetMenuItemInfo
InsertMenu	InsertMenuItem
LoadMenuIndirect*	LoadMenuIndirect: MENUITEMTEMPLATE
	LoadMenuIndirect: MENUEX_TEMPLATE_ITEM
ModifyMenu	SetMenuItemInfo
RemoveMenu*	RemoveMenu
SetMenu*	SetMenu
SetMenuItemBitmaps	SetMenuItemInfo
TrackPopupMenu*	TrackPopupMenu
	TrackPopupMenuEx
	CheckMenuRadioItem
	GetMenuContextHelpId
	GetMenuDefaultItem
	GetMenuItemRect
	MenuItemFromPoint
	SetMenuDefaultItem

*No change between API level 3 and API level 4.

[1]Although GetMenuCheckMarkDimensions currently exists at API level 4, it is not recommended by Microsoft for future work. You're now supposed to use the GetSystemMetrics calls.

Bitmap Menu Items

You can use four different types of symbols to represent an item in a menu: a bitmap, an owner-draw item, a separator, and a character string, the most common.

In the 3.*x* API, you specify the type of the item being appended, inserted, or modified by specifying *one* of the following flags as the Flags parameter to the AppendMenu, InsertMenu, and ModifyMenu functions: MF_BITMAP, MF_OWNERDRAW, MF_SEPARATOR, or MF_STRING, as suggested in Table 12.7. The MF_STRING flag is assumed if you don't specify one of these flags.

The MF_BITMAP flag specifies that the item is a bitmap. The NewItem parameter contains a handle to the bitmap. Windows displays the bitmap image as the item in the menu.

In the 4.*x* API, you use the InsertMenuItem, SetMenuItemInfo, and GetMenuItemInfo, the fType field of the MENUITEMINFO structure will have the MFT_BITMAP flag set. The dwTypeData field will contain the bitmap handle to be set or the existing bitmap handle after a GetMenuItemInfo.

Owner-Draw Menu Items

For AppendMenu, InsertMenu, and ModifyMenu, the MF_OWNERDRAW flag specifies that the item is an owner-draw item. An owner-draw item can look like anything you desire.

For InsertMenuItem, SetMenuItemInfo, and GetMenuItemInfo, the fType field of the MENUITEMINFO structure will have the MFT_OWNERDRAW flag set.

Windows will ask you once how big the item is–when the menu item is first displayed–and will notify you each time the menu item needs to be drawn. You can then draw anything you like to represent the item. Note that whatever you draw, it must be the same each time; you can't change the size. However, you *can* call ModifyMenu or SetMenuItemInfo to "replace" the menu item with one that is identical in all respects except for the size. The WM_MEASUREITEM message will be sent again for the "new" menu item.

Windows sends a WM_MEASUREITEM message to the window that owns a menu containing an owner-draw menu item when the menu item is displayed for the first time. The lParam of this message contains a pointer to a MEASUREITEMSTRUCT structure that looks like the following:

```
typedef struct tagMEASUREITEMSTRUCT
   {
   UINT         CtlType;
   UINT         CtlID;
   UINT         ItemID;
   UINT         itemWidth;
   UINT         itemHeight;
   DWORD        itemData;
   } MEASUREITEMSTRUCT;
```

Unlike the trick we described on page 553 for "reflecting" owner-draw messages such as WM_MEASUREITEM messages to the owner-draw control, or to a subclass of a built-in control that is done as owner-draw, we have no "class" to which we can reflect a WM_MEASUREITEM for a menu. We have to handle it in the window that contains the menu. Menus are not "objects" in the Windows sense; they cannot receive messages.

When using the Microsoft Foundation Classes (MFC), you will find that the CMenu class is a class that is a set of *virtual methods* that reflect the various owner-draw messages into the class. This elaborate mechanism does not exist when you are programming in C. Other C++ systems provide similar mechanisms. This greatly simplifies how owner-draw menus are handled because it is the derived menu class that knows how to draw itself, rather than placing the responsibility on an unrelated piece of code, the "owner".

MFC

WM_MEASUREITEM **Message Cracker Handler**

`void cls_OnMeasureItem(HWND hwnd, MEASUREITEMSTRUCT * mis);`

Parameter	wParam		lParam		Meaning
	lo	hi	lo	hi	
hwnd					Window handle of the window.
mis					Pointer to a MEASUREITEMSTRUCT to be updated.

The CtlType field of the structure contains the value ODT_MENU. The CtlID field is not used for a menu item. The ItemID field contains the menu ID for the menu item. The itemData field contains the 32-bit value specified as the NewItem parameter of an AppendMenu, InsertMenu, or ModifyMenu function call or of the dwItemData field of the MENUITEMINFO for a SetMenuItemInfo or InsertMenuItem function.

You must update the itemHeight *and* itemWidth fields of the MEASUREITEMSTRUCT before returning from processing the WM_MEASUREITEM message. The itemWidth and itemHeight fields must contain the width and height of the menu item. Of all the owner-draw items you will encounter, only a menu item requires that you specify the itemWidth.

Windows sends a WM_DRAWITEM message to the window that owns a menu when an owner-draw item needs to be drawn. The lParam parameter of the message contains a pointer to a DRAWITEMSTRUCT structure. This structure is defined as follows:

```
typedef struct tagDRAWITEMSTRUCT
  {
    UINT        CtlType;
    UINT        CtlID;
    UINT        ItemID;
    UINT        itemAction;
    UINT        itemState;
    HWND        hwndItem;
    HDC         hDC;
    RECT        rcItem;
    DWORD       itemData;
  } DRAWITEMSTRUCT;
```

The CtlType field of the structure contains the value ODT_MENU. The CtlID field is not used for a menu item. The ItemID field contains the menu ID for the menu item. The itemAction field contains bit settings hat describe the drawing action that is required. The `itemState` field contains flags that describe the appearance of the menu item after it has been drawn. For example, the `ODS_CHECKED` flag is set when the menu tem should be drawn with a check mark. The `ODS_GRAYED` flag is set when the menu item should be drawn grayed.

The `hwndItem` field contains the handle of the menu containing the item. The `hDC` field contains a handle of a device context that you must use when drawing the item. You must ensure that the device context is restored to its initial state before returning from processing the `WM_DRAWITEM` message. That is, any changes made to the device context (by selecting different pens or brushes) must be reversed (by selecting the original pen or brush or using `RestoreDC`) before you return.

The `rcItem` field is a rectangle in the `hDC` device context that describes the boundaries of the item to be drawn. Windows does *not* clip the drawing of a menu item to this rectangle. When you draw the menu item, you must not draw outside of this rectangle. The `itemData` field contains the 32-bit value specified as the `NewItem` parameter of an `AppendMenu`, `InsertMenu`, or `ModifyMenu` function call or of the `dwItemData` field value that was set on an `InsertMenuItem` or `SetMenuItemInfo` function.

`WM_DRAWITEM` Message Cracker Handler

```
void cls_OnDrawItem(HWND hwnd, const DRAWITEMSTRUCT * dis);
```

| Parameter | wParam | | lParam | | Meaning |
	lo	hi	lo	hi	
hwnd					Window handle of the window.
dis			███████		Reference to a `DRAWITEMSTRUCT`.

We show an owner-draw menu handler in Listing 12.2. This is a quite elaborate example, adapted from the code of the Menu Explorer application that accompanies this chapter. It takes a data structure that specifies each of the colors to be used (text, highlighted text, menu background, highlighted menu background), the width and height of the menu item, and the text to be displayed. In addition, the handle of a bitmap to be used for checked menu items is provided. This example is chosen because it shows how you might start a simple owner-draw menu scheme that looks much like a text menu.

Listing 12.2: An owner-draw menu handler

```
typedef struct {
        int width;                   // menu width
        int height;                  // menu height
        COLORREF text;               // unselected menu text color
        COLORREF background;         // unselected menu bkg color
        COLORREF hilitetext;         // selected menu text color
        COLORREF hilitebackground;// selected menu bkg color
        COLORREF gray;               // grayed menu text color
        HBITMAP  bmcheck;            // checked bitmap
        LPCTSTR  s;                  // caption
        } odinfo;
```

```
void menu_OnMeasureItem(HWND hWnd, LPMEASUREITEMSTRUCT mis)
    {
     int checkwidth = LOWORD(GetMenuCheckMarkDimensions());
     odinfo * mi = (odinfo *)mis->itemData;
     SIZE size;

     if(mi->height == 0 || mi->width == 0)
        { /* get text height */
         HDC dc = GetDC(hWnd);
         GetTextExtentPoint32(dc, mi->s, lstrlen(mi->s), &size);
        } /* get text height */

     if(mi->height > 0)
        mis->itemHeight = mi->height;
     else
        mis->itemHeight = size.cy;

     if(mi->width > 0)
        mis->itemWidth  = mi->width;
     else
        mis->itemWidth  = size.cx;
    }

void menu_OnDrawItem(HWND hwnd, LPDRAWITEMSTRUCT dis)
    {
     odinfo * mi = (odinfo *)dis->itemData;
     COLORREF text;  // text color
     COLORREF bkg;   // background color
     int rop;

     int saved = SaveDC(dis->hDC);

     if(dis->itemState & ODS_SELECTED)
        { /* item is selected */
         text = mi->hilitetext;
         bkg = mi->hilitebackground;
         rop = MERGEPAINT;
        } /* item is selected */
     else
        { /* unselected */
         text = mi->text;
         bkg = mi->background;
         rop = SRCAND;
        } /* unselected */

     // In either case, if the item is grayed, show it in
     // the "gray" color
     if(dis->itemState & ODS_GRAYED);
        text = mi->gray;

     RECT r = dis->rcItem;
     CSize checksize;
     checksize.cx = LOWORD(GetMenuCheckMarkDimensions());
     checksize.cy = HIWORD(GetMenuCheckMarkDimensions());
```

```
    HBRUSH br = CreateSolidBrush(bkg);
    FillRect(dis->hDC, &dis->rcItem, br);

    SetBkMode(dc, TRANSPARENT);
    SetTextColor(dc, text);

    TextOut(dc, r.left, r.top, mi->s, lstrlen(mi->s));

    // Now draw the checkmark if the item is checked
    if(dis->itemState & ODS_CHECKED)
        { /* draw checkmark */
          HDC memDC;
          memDC = CreateCompatibleDC(dc);
          HBITMAP oldbm = SelectObject(memDC, mi->bmcheck);
          BitBlt(dc, dis->rcItem.left, dis->rcItem.top,
                               checksize.cx, checksize.cy,
                               memDC, 0, 0, rop);
        } /* draw checkmark */
    RestoreDC(dc, saved);
}
```

Separator Menu Items

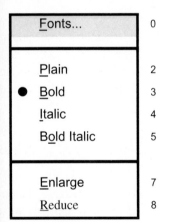

Figure 12.9:
Separators in
menus

The MF_SEPARATOR flag specifies that the item is a horizontal dividing line. For menu items created by InsertMenuItem or modified by SetMenuItemInfo, this is indicated by the fType field having the MFT_SEPARATOR flag set.

This is equivalent to an item created by a MENUITEM SEPARATOR statement in a resource definition file. You cannot gray, disable, or highlight this type of menu item. The idNewItem and NewItem parameters are ignored when you specify this flag.

A separator menu item occupies a position in the menu, although not as much physical space as a regular menu item. This position is counted in the GetMenuItemCount result and affects anything that uses MF_BYPOSITION. The menu in Figure 12.9 contains 9 items numbered 0 through 8. Menu items 1 and 6 are separator items.

String Menu Items

The MF_STRING flag specifies that the item is a character string. This is the most frequently used type. The NewItem parameter contains a pointer to the character string. Windows displays the string using the system font. When you don't specify either MF_BITMAP, MF_OWNERDRAW, MF_SEPARATOR, or MF_STRING, the MF_STRING flag is assumed.

For menus created with InsertMenuItem or modified by SetMenuItemInfo, a string menu item is designated by having the MFT_STRING flag set in the fType field. If this flag is set, the dwTypeData field of the MENUITEMINFO structure is a reference to the text string.

Controlling the Appearance of an Item on a Menu in Win32 3.*x*

Several flags control the appearance of a menu item: MF_CHECKED, MF_DISABLED, MF_ENABLED, MF_GRAYED, MF_MENUBARBREAK, MF_MENUBREAK, and MF_UNCHECKED. The MF_CHECKED, MF_DISABLED, MF_GRAYED, MF_MENUBARBREAK, and MF_MENUBREAK flags have the same effect as the corresponding option in a menu template in a resource definition file.

The MF_ENABLED flag enables an item so that the user can select it. It also restores a grayed item to its normal appearance. The MF_UNCHECKED flag specifies that an item should not have a check mark displayed next to it. This flag is the default value. You also can supply custom check mark bitmaps for an item using the Set-MenuItemBitmaps function. If you do so, the MF_UNCHECKED flag requests that Windows display the "check mark off" bitmap next to the menu item. In this case, you must also have the MF_USECHECKBITMAPS flag set for the menu item; otherwise, the built-in check mark bit map is used.

To set the check mark state, you call the CheckMenuItem function, passing it the value MF_CHECKED or MF_UNCHECKED, along with the usual flags such as MF_BYPOSITION or MF_BYCOMMAND, a menu handle, and a position or menu ID.

Controlling the Appearance of an Item on a Menu in Win32 4.*x*

For menu items created by the MENUEX resource, you specify the state flags directly as the bit names and use the Boolean operators to compose them. These same flags are used in InsertMenuItem and SetMenuItemInfo and returned by GetMenuItemInfo to indicate the state of the menu item. The flags are MFS_CHECKED, MFS_DEFAULT, MFS_DISABLED, MFS_GRAYED, MFS_HILITE, MFS_UNCHECKED, and MFS_UNHILITE and are discussed in detail in Table 12.3.

You can set the default menu item status by calling the SetMenuDefaultItem function, as discussed in detail on page 856, by setting explicitly the MFS_DEFAULT flag in the resource file, or by using the SetMenuItemInfo function.

You can change the bitmaps used for check boxes by using the bitmap fields in the MENUITEMINFO structure and calling SetMenuItemInfo or by using the SetMenuItemBitmaps function (although this latter form is officially considered obsolete). You also can designate a menu item using the MFT_RADIOCHECK flag or the CheckMenuRadioItem function.

Creating a Menu Based on a Template

There is a third and seldom-used method to create a menu. You can create a data structure and provide a pointer to the data structure as the only parameter to the LoadMenuIndirect function. The data structure consists of a header (a MENUITEMTEMPLATEHEADER or MENUEX_TEMPLATE_HEADER structure) followed by one or more MENUITEMTEMPLATE or MENUEX_TEMPLATE_ITEM structures.

We first describe the Win32 3.*x* structures. The Win32 4.*x* API supports both the MENUITEMTEMPLATEHEADER and MENUEX_TEMPLATE_HEADER structures. You cannot "mix and match" these. If you use a MENUITEM-

TEMPLATEHEADER, you must follow it with only MENUITEMTEMPLATE entries. If you use a MENUEX_TEMPLATE_HEADER, you must follow it with only MENUEX_TEMPLATE_ITEM entries.

The Win32 3.x Menu Templates

The MENUITEMTEMPLATEHEADER header structure is defined as follows:

```
typedef struct
  {
    UINT versionNumber;
    UINT offset;
  } MENUITEMTEMPLATEHEADER;
```

The versionNumber field specifies the version number of the menu template and must be set to 0 for a MENUITEMTEMPLATEHEADER. The offset field specifies the offset in bytes from the end of the header to the first MENUITEMTEMPLATE structure. This field should be set to 0 when the first MENUITEMTEMPLATE structure immediately follows the header. A MENUITEMTEMPLATE structure is defined as follows:

```
typedef struct
  {
    WORD   mtOption;
    WORD   mtID;
    WCHAR  mtString[1];
  } MENUITEMTEMPLATE;
```

However, the structure definition can't actually be used as it is defined. It allocates only one character for the menu item string. Each mtString field in a MENUITEMTEMPLATE structure must be an array of characters exactly large enough to contain the string, including the terminating NUL character. A subsequent MENUITEMTEMPLATE structure immediately follows the NUL character. And note also that in Win32–even Windows 95–the characters are Unicode 16-bit characters, independent of the mode in which your application has been compiled.

The mtOption field contains one or more menu flag settings. You've seen most of them already. They are MF_CHECKED, MF_END, MF_GRAYED, MF_HELP, MF_MENUBARBREAK, MF_MENUBREAK, MF_OWNERDRAW, and MF_POPUP.

The MF_END menu flag specifies that a menu item is the last menu item at a particular nesting level. The MF_END flag must be specified in the mtOption field of the last MENUITEMTEMPLATE structure in the template to indicate the end of the menu template. Also, the MF_END flag must also be specified for the last menu item in each pop-up menu defined in the template to indicate the end of the pop-up menu.

Normally, you'll allocate dynamic storage and create the header and menu item templates in that storage. The Menus example program in this chapter defines a menu template in static data just to provide an example of its use. You wouldn't normally define such a template in static data.

The Win32 4.x Menu Templates

A MENUEX_TEMPLATE_HEADER is defined as shown as follows. We illustrate this definition as a set of comment lines because, in fact, this structure is not defined anywhere in Windows. It is expected that you will lay down the bytes in memory in the order this "structure" defines:

```
// typedef struct {
//      WORD wVersion;
//      WORD wOffset;
//      DWORD dwHelpID;
// } MENUEX_TEMPLATE_HEADER;
```

The first 16 bits of the structure must contain the value (WORD)1, which indicates that this is an extended menu template. The next 16 bits are an unsigned offset to the first MENUEX_TEMPLATE_ITEM structure, *measured relative to the end of this field!* If you have been programming using a MENUITEMTEMPLATEHEADER, note that this is different from the interpretation of the wOffset field in that header. This means that if your first template immediately follows the dwHelpID value, then the value of wOffset should be 4. The last 32 bits of a MENUEX_TEMPLATE_HEADER is the help ID for the menu bar or the pop-up menu.

Usually, the header is immediately followed by a sequence of MENUEX_TEMPLATE_ITEM structures. These structures are defined approximately by the following comment, but it is expected that you will be laying down the data consecutively. In any case, the text field is variable length. So this structure cannot be accurately described by a C structure.

```
// typedef struct {
//      DWORD dwType;
//      DWORD dwState;
//      UINT uId;
//      WORD bResInfo;
//      WCHAR szText[1];   // variable-length text string
//      // DWORD dwHelpID;
//      } MENUEX_TEMPLATE_ITEM;
```

This structure, like the MENUEX_TEMPLATE_HEADER, has no real definition in any of the header files.

The first 32 bits of the item template are the dwType field and can be any of the MFT_ flags (in legal combinations) from Table 12.2. The next 32 bits of the item template are the dwState field and can be any of the MFS_ flags (in legal combinations) from Table 12.3. The next 32 bits represent the menu item ID, which is limited to 16 bits, so the high-order 16 bits of this UINT are unused and must be

Table 12.11: bResInfo field values

Code	Interpretation
0x0000	Menu item is not a pop-up, and is not the last item.
0x0080	Menu item is the last menu item in the menu bar or pop-up.
0x0001	Menu item is a pop-up menu.
0x0081	Menu item is a pop-up menu and the last menu item.

0. The next 16 bits are an indication of whether the menu item is the last item in a pop-up or the menu bar and whether the menu item itself is a pop-up menu. It can be one of the values shown in Table 12.11.

Following the bResInfo field is the text of the menu item. It is a NUL-terminated *Unicode* field; it *must* be a Unicode field, even if the application is an ANSI application. This field is as long as necessary. If the bResInfo field is 0x0001, indicating that the menu item is a pop-up menu, it will have an additional 32 bits following the text string, which is the help ID of the menu itself. If the menu item is not a pop-up menu item, this field is omitted.

The MENUEX_TEMPLATE_ITEM structures must be a multiple of 8 bytes in length. If an odd number of words is in a MENUEX_TEMPLATE_ITEM, an additional 2 bytes of zeroes must be added to ensure correct size. Note that failure to do this could cause a Windows 95 system to lock up.

You must be very careful when constructing these headers. According to the Knowledge Base article Q131281, if LoadMenuIndirect is called in Windows 95 with invalid data, the system hangs. Under Windows NT the response is to return NULL, and GetLastError will return ERROR_INVALID_DATA. What is dismaying is that the behavior that hangs Windows 95 is reported as being "by design", that is, this call is designed to crash Windows 95 in the presence of bad data. You Have Been Warned!

Creating the Menu from a Template

After you've created the data structure, you can create a menu based on the structure by calling the LoadMenuIndirect function and passing it a pointer to the menu template, like this:

```
HMENU hmenu ;

hmenu = LoadMenuIndirect (lpMenuItemTemplateHeader) ;
```

Note that because the first word of the template contains the value 0 (MENUITEMTEMPLATEHEADER) or 1 (MENUEX_TEMPLATE_HEADER), the call can distinguish which type of structure is being passed in.

Class and Window Menus

You can associate a menu with an overlapped or pop-up window in a number of different ways. Most commonly, you specify a class menu and a menu when you create the window. A child window cannot have a menu.

You specify a class menu when you register a window class. The lpszMenuName field of the WNDCLASS structure contains a pointer to a NULL-terminated character string. The string specifies the resource name of a menu that is defined in the application resource definition file. For example, to define a menu called TestMenu as the class menu, do the following. First, in the resource definition file define the following menu template:

```
TestMenu MENU
BEGIN
/* Menu items go here. */
END
```

Then, in your class registration code add the following assignment statement:

```
wc.lpszMenuName = _T("TestMenu") ;
```

You also can use an integer value to identify a menu template in your resource definition file, like this:

```
#define IDM_TESTMENU    42

IDM_TESTMENU MENU
BEGIN
/* Menu items go here. */
END
```

And in your class registration code, add the following assignment statement:

```
wc.lpszMenuName = MAKEINTRESOURCE (IDM_TESTMENU) ;
```

When you create an overlapped or pop-up window and the hmenu parameter of the CreateWindow function call is NULL, the class menu is used as the menu for the window. If there is no class menu (the lpszMenuName member of the WNDCLASS structure used to register the window class was set to NULL), the window will have no menu.

You can create a window and give it a specific menu regardless of whether a class menu is specified for the window class. You do this by passing the handle to the menu to be used by the window as the hmenu parameter of the CreateWindow function call. Because this requires a handle to a menu rather than the name or integer ID of the menu template definition in the resource definition file, you have a little more flexibility when it comes to the source of the menu.

All the previously described methods can be used to define the menu template. When you define the menu template in the resource definition file, you must explicitly load the menu template to obtain a handle to the menu itself. Notice the distinction between the menu template and the menu.

You can load a menu template from the resource definition file, create a menu based on the template, and obtain the handle to the created menu by calling the LoadMenu function. You must pass the instance handle of the module containing the menu template resource (this is normally the application's instance handle) and the name or integer ID of the menu template. Assuming that the hInstance variable contains the application's instance handle, the following statement retrieves a menu handle to the TestMenu menu already defined:

```
HMENU hmenu ;

hmenu = LoadMenu (hInstance, MAKEINTRESOURCE (IDM_TESTMENU)) ;
```

You also can use the CreateMenu function to obtain a handle to a menu that you explicitly build. The Load-MenuIndirect function also returns a *menu handle*. You can use any of these menu handles when creating a window to give it a menu:

```
hwnd = CreateWindow (lpClassName, lpWindowName,
                     WS_OVERLAPPEDWINDOW,
                     CW_USEDEFAULT, 0,
                     CW_USEDEFAULT, 0,
                     0,
                     hmenu,
                     hInstance, NULL) ;
```

Initializing a Menu before It Is Displayed

You may want to initialize the items in a menu just before Windows displays the menu. For example, suppose you have a menu containing the items "**Cut**" and "**Paste**" to move text to and from the Clipboard. A user shouldn't be able to cut text from your window to the Clipboard unless some text is selected (highlighted). Conversely, when the Clipboard is empty or does not contain data of a type that can be pasted, the **Paste** option shouldn't be valid. An application should prevent the user from selecting menu items that aren't valid.

Since the **Paste** option should be grayed when the Clipboard is empty or of unknown format, we need to actually set the state of the menu item to indicate to the user that the menu selection isn't currently valid and to prevent the user from selecting the menu item. You don't want to keep checking the Clipboard and changing the state of the menu item to match. Most of the time, the menu won't be displayed, so why bother trying to keep current the state of items on the menu? Instead, you should update the state of all menu items just before Windows displays the menu to the user. Windows sends the window that owns the menu a WM_INITMENU message just before displaying the menu.

Windows sends the WM_INITMENU message when the user clicks the menu bar with the mouse or presses a menu key. The wParam parameter of the message contains the handle of the pop-up menu that is about to be displayed and is passed into the OnInitMenu handler. The lParam parameter isn't used.

WM_INITMENU Message Cracker Handler

```
void cls_OnInitMenu(HWND hwnd, HMENU hmenu);
```

| | wParam | | lParam | | |
Parameter	lo	hi	lo	hi	Meaning
hwnd					Window handle of the window.
hmenu	███	███			Handle of the menu that is about to be displayed.

You process this message by enabling, disabling, graying, checking, or unchecking the menu items in the menu, as appropriate. For example, assuming the paste menu item has the menu ID IDM_PASTE, the following code checks the Clipboard and enables the menu item when it contains text and grays the menu item when it does not:

```
void class_OnInitMenu(HWND hwnd, HMENU hmenu )
{
  if (GetMenu (hwnd) != hmenu)
    return ; // not the main menu

  EnableMenuItem (hmenu, IDM_PASTE,
              IsClipboardFormatAvailable (CF_TEXT)
                            ? MF_ENABLED : MF_GRAYED) ;
}
```

When you receive a WM_INITMENU message, you should check to ensure the message pertains to the menu you want to initialize. It's possible for a window function to receive a WM_INITMENU message for a menu other than the menu owned by the window. For example, the Menus example program in this chapter creates a floating pop-up menu when the user presses the right mouse button while in the client area of the window. Just before Windows displays the floating pop-up menu, it sends a WM_INITMENU message to the application's main window function. In this case, however, the wParam parameter specifies the handle to the floating pop-up menu, not the menu displayed on the menu bar. Of course, you may need to initialize the pop-up menu items as well, so instead of returning (as we do in our example), you would determine which pop-up menu was activated and modify its state.

Altering a Menu

As you've just (briefly) seen, you can change the appearance of a menu dynamically. We show the Win32 functions for menu manipulation in Table 12.12, indicating which API supports them (the Win32 4.*x* API supports the older forms, but has declared some of them "obsolete"). The two sets of functions are contrasted in Table 12.10.

Table 12.12: Functions used to manipulate menus

API		Function	Description
3	**4**	**Function**	**Description**
✓	✗	AppendMenu	Appends an item to the end of a menu.
✓	✗	CheckMenuItem	Adds or removes a check mark by a menu item.
	✓	CheckMenuRadioItem	Sets a "radio button"-style mark to one of a set of menu items; the check mark is removed from all other menu items in the set.
✓	✓	CreateMenu	Creates an empty menu.
✓	✓	CreatePopupMenu	Creates an empty pop-up menu.
✓	✓	DeleteMenu	Deletes an item from a menu. If the item is a pop-up, the pop-up menu handle is invalidated and the memory containing the menu is released.
✓	✓	DestroyMenu	Destroys a menu, thereby freeing any memory that the menu occupied.
✓	✓	DrawMenuBar	Redraws the menu bar of a window.
✓	✓ ✦	EnableMenuItem	Enables, disables, or grays a menu item.
✓	✓	GetMenu	Returns the menu handle associated with the specified window.
✓	✗	GetMenuCheckMarkDimensions	Retrieves the dimensions of a default check mark bitmap.
	✓	GetMenuDefaultItem	Returns the ID or position of the default menu item.
✓	✓	GetMenuItemCount	Retrieves the number of items in a menu.

Legend:

✓	Available and supported.
✗	Available but considered obsolete and should not be used. Use InsertMenuItem, SetMenuItemInfo, and/or GetMenuItemInfo.
✦	Function also available via SetMenuItemInfo or GetMenuItemInfo.
▨	Not available.

Table 12.12: Functions used to manipulate menus

API			
3	**4**	**Function**	**Description**
✓	✓	`GetMenuItemID`	Returns the handle of a menu item.
	✓	`GetMenuItemInfo`	Retrieves detailed information about a menu item (command or pop-up).
	✓	`GetMenuItemRect`	Obtains the coordinates of the rectangle for the menu item.
✓	✗	`GetMenuState`	Retrieves status flags for a menu item.
✓	✓ ✚	`GetMenuString`	Copies a menu item label into a buffer.
✓	✓	`GetSubMenu`	Returns a pop-up menu handle.
✓	✓	`GetSystemMenu`	Provides access to the system menu.
	✓	`GetSystemMetrics` `(SM_CXMENUCHECK)`	The width of the menu check mark.
	✓	`GetSystemMetrics` `(SM_CYMENUCHECK)`	The height of the menu check mark.
✓	✓ ✚	`HiliteMenuItem`	Changes highlighting of a top-level menu item.
✓	✗	`InsertMenu`	Inserts an item at a specified position in a menu.
	✓	`InsertMenuItem`	Inserts a menu item into a menu.
✓	✓	`IsMenu`	Tests a handle to see if it is a valid menu handle.
✓	✓	`LoadMenu`	Loads a menu from the resource segment of an instance.
✓	✓	`LoadMenuIndirect`	Returns a menu handle for a menu template.
	✓	`MenuItemFromPoint`	Given a `POINT` structure, returns the index of the menu at that point.
✓	✗	`ModifyMenu`	Modifies an item in a menu.

Legend:

✓	Available and supported.
✗	Available but considered obsolete and should not be used. Use `InsertMenuItem`, `SetMenuItemInfo`, and/or `GetMenuItemInfo`.
✚	Function also available via `SetMenuItemInfo` or `GetMenuItemInfo`.
	Not available.

Table 12.12: Functions used to manipulate menus

API		Function	Description
3	**4**		
✓	✓	RemoveMenu	Removes a pop-up menu item from a menu but does not invalidate the pop-up menu handle or release the memory containing the menu.
✓	✓	SetMenu	Sets the menu for a window.
	✓	SetMenuDefaultItem	Sets the default item for the menu.
✓	✗	SetMenuItemBitmaps	Associates bitmaps with a menu item.
	✓	SetMenuItemInfo	Sets detailed information about a menu item (command or pop-up).
✓	✓	TrackPopupMenu	Displays and tracks a pop-up menu.
	✓	TrackPopupMenuEx	Displays and tracks a pop-up menu.

Legend:

✓	Available and supported.
✗	Available but considered obsolete and should not be used. Use InsertMenuItem, SetMenuItemInfo, and/or GetMenuItemInfo.
✚	Function also available via SetMenuItemInfo or GetMenuItemInfo.
	Not available.

We discussed the AppendMenu, InsertMenu, and ModifyMenu functions earlier in the chapter.

The DeleteMenu function deletes an item from the menu identified by the hmenu parameter. The ItemID parameter specifies the item to delete. You can specify the item by its position or menu ID just as in the InsertMenu and ModifyMenu functions. The Flags parameter must be set to either MF_BYPOSITION or MF_BYCOMMAND (the default value). Deleting a pop-up menu calls DestroyMenu on the menu handle for the associated pop-up menu and releases all storage used by the pop-up menu. The following statement deletes the **Show Ruler** menu item from an earlier example:

```
DeleteMenu (hViewMenu, IDM_SHOWRULER, MF_BYCOMMAND) ;
```

The RemoveMenu function has the same parameter as the DeleteMenu function. The RemoveMenu function deletes the specified item from the menu but doesn't otherwise affect the removed item. If the item is a pop-up menu, the menu handle for the associated pop-up menu remains valid and the pop-up menu can still be used. To continue to use the pop-up menu, you'll have to save the menu handle for the pop-up menu prior to removing it from the menu.

You can retrieve the pop-up menu handle for a pop-up menu by calling the GetSubMenu function. You specify the menu handle for the menu containing the pop-up menu, such as the hmenu parameter, and the position

Table 12.13: Bits returned by `GetMenuState`

Bit	Meaning
MF_BITMAP	Menu item is a bitmap.
MF_CHECKED	Menu item has a check mark.
MF_DISABLED	Menu item is disabled.
MF_GRAYED	Menu item is grayed.
MF_HILITE	Menu item is highlighted.
MF_MENUBARBREAK	Menu item is a menu-bar-break item.
MF_MENUBREAK	Menu item is a menu-break item.
MF_POPUP	Menu item is a pop-up item. Bits 7..15 (the high-order byte of the low-order word) contain the item count of the menu.

For command menus, the `MF_POPUP` flag is not set and the low-order 16 bits may include the following flags:

MF_OWNERDRAW	Menu item is an owner-draw item.
MF_SEPARATOR	Menu item is a separator.

of the pop-up menu item within the menu, such as the nPos parameter. The `GetSubMenu` function retrieves a handle by position only. The first item is at position 0. You cannot retrieve the menu handle for a pop-up menu by command because a pop-up menu in the Win32 3.*x* implementation does not have a menu ID. The function is defined as

```
HMENU GetSubMenu
(HMENU hmenu, int Pos) ;
```

The hmenu parameter is a menu handle and the Pos parameter is the index of the menu item to be retrieved (0-based). If the menu item at the indicated position is a pop-up menu item, the handle of that menu will be returned. If the menu item is a command menu item or the value Pos is out of range for the menu, the return value will be NULL.

Enabling, Disabling, and Graying an Item on a Menu

When you need only to enable, disable, or gray an item on a menu, it's more convenient to use the `EnableMenuItem` function rather than to modify the menu item with the `ModifyMenu` function. Modifying an item actually replaces the item with a new item. The `EnableMenuItem` function changes only the state of an existing menu item:

```
BOOL EnableMenuItem (HMENU hmenu, UINT ItemID, UINT Enable) ;
```

The hmenu parameter specifies the menu handle of the menu containing the item to enable, disable, or gray. The `ItemID` parameter specifies the item. You can specify the item by position or by menu ID. The `Enable` parameter specifies the action to take as well as the form of the `ItemID` parameter. You should choose one flag from each of the following groups:

- MF_BYCOMMAND (default) or MF_BYPOSITION

- MF_ENABLED (default), MF_DISABLED, or MF_GRAYED

When the Enable parameter is 0, the item with the menu ID specified by the ItemID parameter is enabled. The following statement grays the C++ menu item in a menu of language types:

```
EnableMenuItem (hmenu, IDM_CPLUSPLUS, MF_BYCOMMAND | MF_GRAYED) ;
```

When you change an item in the menu bar, the changes are not immediately displayed. You must call the DrawMenuBar function to force the menu bar to be displayed with the changes. Notice that this function requires the *window* handle for the window containing the menu bar, not the menu handle for the menu:

```
BOOL DrawMenuBar (HWND hwnd) ;
```

Think of the DrawMenuBar function as serving the same purpose that InvalidateRect does in the client area. Like InvalidateRect, DrawMenuBar *forces* the menu bar to be redrawn, so you should issue it only if you *know* the menu bar has changed; otherwise, you will get an annoying flicker of the menu bar.

Checking and Unchecking a Menu Item

You can also change the appearance on an existing menu item by placing or removing a check mark next to the item. Typically, you'll group together a number of mutually exclusive items and place a check mark next to the item the user last selected. When the user selects a different item in the group, you should uncheck the previously checked item and check the latest selection.

You initially check a menu item by specifying the CHECKED option flag on the MENUITEM for the menu template in the resource definition file. You can include the MF_CHECKED menu flag when dynamically creating a menu. You use the CheckMenuItem function to check and uncheck an existing menu item.

```
CheckMenuItem (hmenu, ItemID, Check) ;
```

The hmenu parameter specifies the menu handle of the menu containing the item to check or uncheck. The ItemID parameter specifies the item. You can specify the item by position or by menu ID. The Check parameter specifies the action to take as well as the form of the ItemID parameter. You should choose one flag from each of the following groups:

- MF_BYCOMMAND (default) or MF_BYPOSITION

- MF_UNCHECKED (default) or MF_CHECKED

When the Check parameter is 0, the item with the menu ID specified by the ItemID parameter is unchecked. The CheckMenuItem function returns the previous state of the menu item. The return value is MF_CHECKED, or MF_UNCHECKED, representing the previous state, or –1 if the menu item does not exist. The following statement checks the C language menu item of a language-selection menu:

```
CheckMenuItem (hmenu, IDM_C, MF_BYCOMMAND | MF_CHECKED) ;
```

There are two small restrictions when using this function:

- You cannot check an item on a top-level menu. You can check and uncheck either a menu item or a pop-up menu as long as it is contained in a pop-up menu.

- Because a pop-up menu in Win32 3.*x* doesn't have a menu ID, you must specify the pop-up menu by position in order to check it. This restriction goes away in the Win32 4.*x* API, but to do so creates a program that will not run under Win32 3.*x*.

Figure 12.10: A pop-up menu with a menu item leading to a cascading pop-up menu

The Menu Demo example program has a **Direction** pop-up menu defined as part of the menu used as the default class menu. When the user selects this item, Windows displays a pop-up menu containing four directions plus a cascading pop-up menu item that offers four diagonal directions on its pop-up window. Figure 12.10 shows the second-level menu, and Figure 12.11 shows the cascading pop-up menu with an item in it checked.

We use the code in Listing 12.3 to check and uncheck the items in the **Direction** menu as the user selects a new direction. When a direction from either the pop-up menu or the cascading pop-up menu is selected, we uncheck all items on the **Direction** menu rather than keep track of which direction was previously selected. We then check the selected item (wParam contains its menu ID). The code we show is a bit complicated, and there are good reasons for that. We need to examine the task a bit more carefully before we can explain the actual code.

When the newly selected item is one of the directions on the cascading pop-up menu, we also check the pop-up menu (**Diagonals**) that leads to the cascading pop-up menu. Otherwise, we ensure the **Diagonals** pop-up menu is unchecked as well. You must refer to a pop-up menu item by position when checking and unchecking it. You will see that with the Win32 4.*x* interface, you can refer to a pop-up directly by its ID. But when programming in the Win32 3.*x* API, you must use the actual position. This can result in some very fragile code.

For example, we could take advantage of the fact that we "know" that the **Directions** menu is the third (index 2) position in the top-level menu bar and that the **Diagonals** menu is in the sixth (index 5) position in the **Directions** menu. We could have coded the checkDiagonalMenu function in the following Listing 12.3 much more simply as

```
CheckMenuItem(GetSubMenu(GetMenu(hwnd),2), 5, MF_BYPOSITION | check);
```

which would work perfectly well, *as long as the arrangement of the menus is never changed, including the presence or absence of separators!* This is hardly ever true in real applications. Our goal is to show you not only how to write Windows programs that *work*, but also how to write Windows programs whose long-term maintenance costs are reasonable. This means that we write code that may take a bit longer to write but which has a long-term payback in reduced maintenance.

You could argue that the use of the constants 2 and 5 is clearly a bad idea, and a #define should be used to give these names. It turns out that this offers very little improvement. The person who changes the menu layout must *know* that you have used MF_BYPOSITION to modify the menu, that there are symbolic constants, and which header file defines them so that they can be changed. In practice, this information is never discoverable until the menus stop working as expected.

We do make some assumptions here: that there *is* a **Diagonals** menu and it *is* in the **Directions** menu. With a bit more work, we could even eliminate these assumptions.

The key function is the getSubmenuPosition function. Given a menu, this searches the menu items in the menu looking for a pop-up menu item that contains, somewhere in it (at any level), a particular ID. It does this by using the GetSubMenu and GetMenuState functions. If GetSubMenu is applied to a menu item that is not a pop-up, it returns NULL. If the menu item is a pop-up, GetSubMenu returns the handle to the pop-up menu. Given that we have a handle to the menu, we use GetMenuState to ask for the "state" of any particular menu item. This state can be in one of two forms. If the MF_POPUP flag is set, indicating that the item is a pop-up menu, the low-order byte of the low-order word contains a subset of the flags shown in Table 12.13. If the MF_POPUP flag is not set, the menu item is a command menu item, and the additional flags of MF_OWNERDRAW and MF_SEPARATOR may be present. If the menu

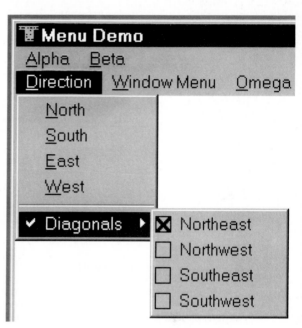

Figure 12.11: A cascading pop-up menu

item does not exist–for example, we use MF_BYCOMMAND and the submenu does not have any item (at any depth) with that ID–then GetMenuState is defined as returning the UINT value 0xFFFFFFFF. Our algorithm uses the knowledge of this return value to locate the desired submenu. If we find the desired ID in the submenu, we now have in hand the position of the submenu in the parent menu and we can return that position as our result. Otherwise, we return –1, thereby indicating that we could not find the desired menu item. Given that we have computed the actual position, we can now safely use MF_BYPOSITION to modify the menu item.

The getSubmenuPosition function is one of those functions that you find that you write once and then include in your favorite library or cut-and-paste into every application thereafter. With proper usage, you can effectively write code that doesn't break under menu rearrangement.

Listing 12.3: Menu manipulation by position

```
#define ALLDIRECTIONS(i)  i = IDM_NORTH; \
                          i <= IDM_SOUTHWEST; \
                          i++

void menu_OnCommand(HWND hwnd, UINT ctlid, HWND hctl, int codeNotify)
{
 // The menu item:
```

```
//      Menu item                       ID*
//      Directions                      ---
//      0    North                      741
//      1    South                      742
//      2    East                       743
//      3    West                       744
//      4    ------------------         ---
//      5    Diagonals >                ---
//                          0  Northeast 745
//                          1  Northwest 746
//                          2  Southeast 747
//                          3  Southwest 748
//      * Actual IDs might change but the order
//        shown here must be maintained; in
//        particular, the first and last values
//        of the range must be the names used in
//        the ALLDIRECTIONS macro.
int i;
int sm;
HMENU hSubMenu;
HMENU hMenu = GetMenu(hwnd);

switch (ctlid)
   { /* ctlid */
    case IDM_NORTH:
    case IDM_SOUTH:
    case IDM_EAST:
    case IDM_WEST:
        uncheckAllDirections(hwnd);
        // Check the selected direction
        CheckMenuItem (hmenu, ctlid, MF_BYCOMMAND | MF_CHECKED) ;
        checkDiagonalMenu(hwnd, MF_UNCHECKED);
        return;

    case IDM_NORTHEAST:
    case IDM_NORTHWEST:
    case IDM_SOUTHEAST:
    case IDM_SOUTHWEST:
        hmenu = GetMenu (hwnd) ;
        uncheckAllDirections(hwnd);

        // check the current diagonal direction
        CheckMenuItem (hmenu, ctlid, MF_BYCOMMAND | MF_CHECKED) ;
        // check the "Diagonals" menu
        checkDiagonalMenu(hwnd, MF_CHECKED);
        return;
   } /* ctlid */
}

/////////////////////////////////////////////////////////////
void uncheckAllDirections(HWND hwnd)
{
 HMENU hmenu;
 int i;
 hmenu = GetMenu (hwnd) ;
        for (ALLDIRECTIONS(i))
            { /* uncheck all */
```

```
              CheckMenuItem (hmenu, i, MF_BYCOMMAND | MF_UNCHECKED) ;
           } /* uncheck all */
}

//////////////////////////////////////////////////////////////
// checkDiagonalMenu
//      HWND hwnd: Top-level window handle
//      UINT check: MF_CHECKED or MF_UNCHECKED
// EFFECT:
//      Sets the checkmark on the "Diagonals"
//      menu on or off
void checkDiagonalMenu(HWND hwnd, UINT check)
{
  int sm;
  HMENU hmenu = GetMenu(hwnd) ;
  HMENU hSubMenu;

  // First, locate the position of the
  // "Directions" menu in the main menu
  sm = findSubmenuPosition(hmenu, IDM_NORTH) ;
  if(sm == -1)
      return ; // error, should not occur

  // Now locate the position of the "Diagonals"
  // submenu in the "Directions" menu
  hSubMenu = GetSubMenu(hmenu, sm);
  sm = findSubmenuPosition(hSubMenu, IDM_NORTHWEST) ;
  if(sm == -1)
      return ; // error, should not occur
  CheckMenuItem (hSubMenu, sm, MF_BYPOSITION, check) ;
}

//////////////////////////////////////////////////////////////
//      findSubmenuPosition
//      HMENU hmenu: Menu in which we are
//                    searching for submenu
//      UINT id: ID for item in submenu
// RETURNS: int
//      The position in the hmenu where the
//      submenu containing 'id' is found.  Value
//      is -1 if no submenu containing the id
//      can be found

int findSubmenuPosition(HMENU hmenu, UINT id)
{
  int i;
  HMENU hSubMenu;

  for (i = 0;
       i < GetMenuItemCount(hmenu);
       i++)
      { /* find submenu */
       hSubMenu = GetSubMenu(hmenu, i);
       if(hSubMenu == NULL)
          continue ; // not a pop-up
       if(GetMenuState(hSubMenu, id, MF_BYCOMMAND) == 0xFFFFFFFF)
          continue;  // not in this menu
```

```
        return i;
    } /* find submenu */
return -1;
}
```

Using a Bitmap as a Menu Item

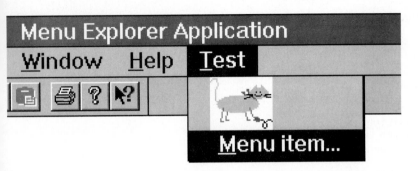

Figure 12.12: A bitmap menu

Menu templates specified in an application's resource definition file cannot specify a bitmap for a menu item. But you can specify a bitmap as a menu item when you append, insert, or modify a menu item using the AppendMenu, InsertMenu, ModifyMenu InsertMenuItem, or SetMenuItemInfo func-

tions. You could, for example, include the menu item in the resource file as an ordinary string menu item and then, during your initInstance function, use ModifyMenu or SetMenuItemInfo to change it to a bitmap menu item. You've seen all the parameters of these functions before. The only missing ingredient is the bitmap.

You can create the bitmap in any of the ways we've previously described. You can load it from the application's resources. You can also create a memory device context, select a bitmap into the device context, and draw anything you like. When you have a bitmap handle for the bitmap containing the image for the menu item, you append, insert, or modify the menu item while specifying the MF_BITMAP menu flag. The NewItem parameter to the AppendMenu, InsertMenu, or ModifyMenu function call contains the bitmap handle.

The following example loads a bitmap with the integer ID IDB_GRAYCAT from the application's resources and appends it to the menu specified by the hmenu parameter. Just to be different, we use the InsertMenu function to append the new menu item. Your code would be clearer if you used the AppendMenu function instead. The effect of this is shown in Figure 12.12.

```
HMENU           hmenu ;
HBITMAP         hbitmap ;

hBitmap = LoadBitmap (hInstance,
                MAKEINTRESOURCE (IDB_GRAYCAT)) ;
InsertMenu (hmenu, -1, MF_BYPOSITION | MF_BITMAP,
                IDM_GRAYCAT, (LPCSTR) hbitmap) ;
```

Using a Bitmap as a Custom Menu Item Check Mark

When you check an item on a menu, Windows displays its standard check mark (✓) to the left of the item's text. When you uncheck an item, Windows removes the standard check mark and doesn't display a symbol next to the text.

Rather than use a standard check mark, you can provide your own bitmap, and Windows will display it next to an item when that item is checked. You can also provide a second bitmap that Windows displays when the item is not checked.

Figure 12.10 shows checked and unchecked menu items that use the standard Windows check mark. Figure 12.11 shows a menu that uses two custom check marks. We create the checked and unchecked bitmaps during the WM_CREATE message processing. The internal application function createCheckmarkBitmaps creates the two bitmaps. We call the GetMenuCheckMarkDimensions function to determine the proper size of the check mark bitmaps. It returns a DWORD value that contains the height and width (in pixels) of the default check mark bitmap. The width is in the low-order word, and the height is in the high-order word.

Figure 12.13: An example of custom menu item check marks

```
DWORD dw ;

dw = GetMenuCheckMarkDimensions ()
Width = LOWORD (dw) ;
Height = HIWORD (dw) ;
```

The default check mark bitmap can be obtained by using LoadBitmap and specifying the OBM_CHECK. A listing and image of all the standard bitmaps available are given in Table 12.14.

We create two bitmaps that are exactly the size of the default check mark bitmap and that are compatible with the current display device. We select these bitmaps (one at a time, of course) into a memory device context and draw the checked and unchecked images into the bitmaps. We then instruct Windows to use these newly created bitmaps as the checked and unchecked check mark bitmaps for the menu items on the cascading pop-up menu.

Listing 12.4: Creating custom check mark bitmaps
```
void
createCheckmarkBitmaps (HWND hwnd)
{
    DWORD   dw ;
    HBITMAP hbitmapOrig ;
    HBRUSH  hbrush, hbrushOrig ;
    HDC     hdc, hMemoryDC ;
    HPEN    hpenCross, hpenFrame, hpenOrig ;
    WORD    Width, Height ;

    hdc = GetDC (hwnd) ;
    // Create a compatible memory device context.
    hMemoryDC = CreateCompatibleDC (hdc) ;
    // Get the proper size of a checkmark.
    dw = GetMenuCheckMarkDimensions () ;
    Width = LOWORD (dw) ;
    Height = HIWORD (dw) ;

    // Create two uninitialized bitmaps.
    // One for the checked bitmap and one for the unchecked bitmap.
```

```
    hbitmapChecked = CreateCompatibleBitmap (hdc, Width, Height) ;
    hbitmapUnchecked = CreateCompatibleBitmap (hdc, Width, Height) ;
    ReleaseDC (hwnd, hdc) ;
    /*************************************************************/
    /* Draw a rectangle in the system menu text color.          */
    /* The inside of the rectangle is filled with the           */
    /* system menu text color.                                  */
    /* The checked bitmap has an X drawn in this rectangle.     */
    /*************************************************************/

    hbrush = CreateSolidBrush (GetSysColor (COLOR_MENU)) ;
    hpenFrame = CreatePen (PS_INSIDEFRAME, 0, GetSysColor (COLOR_MENUTEXT)) ;
    hpenCross = CreatePen (PS_SOLID, 2, GetSysColor (COLOR_MENUTEXT)) ;
    hbitmapOrig = SelectBitmap (hMemoryDC, hbitmapUnchecked) ;
    hbrushOrig  = SelectBrush (hMemoryDC, hbrush) ;
    hpenOrig    = SelectPen (hMemoryDC, hpenFrame) ;

    // Initialize the unchecked bitmap.
    PatBlt (hMemoryDC, 0, 0, Width, Height, PATCOPY) ;
    // Create the unchecked image.
    Rectangle (hMemoryDC, 1, 1, wWidth - 1,Height - 1) ;

    // Initialize the unchecked bitmap.
    SelectBitmap (hMemoryDC, hbitmapChecked) ;
    PatBlt (hMemoryDC, 0, 0, Width, Height, PATCOPY) ;
    // Create the checked image.

    Rectangle (hMemoryDC, 1, 1, wWidth - 1, wHeight - 1) ;
    SelectPen (hMemoryDC, hpenCross) ;
    MoveToEx (hMemoryDC, 2, 2, NULL) ;
    LineTo (hMemoryDC, Width - 2, Height - 2) ;
    MoveToEx (hMemoryDC, Width - 2, 2, NULL) ;
    LineTo (hMemoryDC, 2, Height - 2) ;

    // Free the resources.
    SelectBitmap (hMemoryDC, hbitmapOrig) ;
    SelectBrush (hMemoryDC, hbrushOrig) ;
    SelectPen (hMemoryDC, hpenOrig) ;
    DeleteDC (hMemoryDC) ;
    DeleteBrush (hbrush) ;
    DeletePen (hpenFrame) ;
    DeletePen (hpenCross) ;
}
```

For Win32 3.*x*, the SetMenuItemBitmaps function associates two bitmaps with a menu item. You have to specify the menu handle, the item within that menu, one of the two familiar (by now) flags–MF_BYCOMMAND or MF_BYPOSITION–the handle to a bitmap containing the unchecked image, and the handle to a bitmap containing the checked image:

```
for (ALLDIRECTIONS(i))
    SetMenuItemBitmaps (hmenuClass, i, MF_BYCOMMAND,
                        hbitmapUnchecked, hbitmapChecked );
```

Bitmaps are GDI objects, so you should delete them when you're finished using them. In this case, we need them until the application window is destroyed. When we receive the WM_DESTROY message, we delete the two bitmaps:

```
DeleteBitmap (hbitmapChecked) ;
DeleteBitmap (hbitmapUnchecked) ;
```

You can also use LoadBitmap to load several *predefined* bitmaps. These bitmaps are called "OEM bitmaps" and start with the symbol OBM_. Table 12.14 shows the symbols, *none of which are defined unless you define the symbol* OEMRESOURCE *before you include* windows.h. You can use these bitmaps to render controls, pieces of your own custom controls, owner-draw controls, or anything else you need. To load one of them, you call LoadBitmap, but instead of specifying an instance handle, you specify NULL as the first parameter and the MAKEINTRESOURCE of one of the names in Table 12.14 as the second parameter. You will see from the table that the API level 4 images are consistently smaller than the API level 3 images.

```
HBITMAP check = LoadBitmap(NULL,MAKEINTRESOURCE(OBM_CHECK));.
```

If you are using precompiled headers, you cannot simply do a #define OEMRESOURCE in the file in which you wish to use these symbols. The symbols are actually defined by the precompiled header. Instead, you must do a #define OEMRESOURCE in the "main" file that causes the precompiled header to compile. For our example files, this is the StdSDK.h file, and in MFC it is the stdafx.h file. If you get a compiler error that you have an undefined symbol, and you are using precompiled headers, make sure you have made the modification in the correct files. You may have to force a complete rebuild to get the precompiled header to be correct.

Table 12.14: The OEM bitmaps

Symbol	Bitmap		Explanation
	API 3	**API 4**	
OBM_BTNCORNERS	▢ ◻ ▪	●	Bitmaps for "corner" markers. The arrangement for API 3 appears to be a 12w × 12h bitmap, a 14w × 12h bitmap, and a 10w × 10h bitmap.
OBM_BTSIZE	▢	▨	Sizing button; API 3 is 18 × 18; API 4 is 16 × 16.
OBM_CHECK	✓	✔	Default check mark; API 3 is 18 × 18; API 4 is 15 × 15.
OBM_CHECKBOXES	☐☒▣☒⊙⊚⊙⊚▨▨	☐☑▣⊙⊙⊙⊙▨▨	A collection of check box symbols. Each API 3 symbol is 16 × 16 pixels; each API 4 symbol is 13 × 13 pixels.
OBM_CLOSE	▭ ▭	▦ ▦	Two "close" buttons.
OBM_COMBO	↓	▼	The drop-down arrow for a combo box.

Table 12.14: The OEM bitmaps

Symbol	Bitmap		Explanation
	API 3	API 4	
OBM_DNARROW			A down arrow button in its normal state.
OBM_DNARROWD			A down arrow button in its depressed state.
OBM_DNARROWI			A down arrow button in its disabled state.
OBM_LFARROW			A left arrow button in its normal state.
OBM_LFARROWD			A left arrow button in its depressed state.
OBM_LFARROWI			A left arrow button in its disabled state.
OBM_MNARROW			The arrow used to indicate cascaded items in a menu.
OBM_OLD_CLOSE			A pair of close buttons with an "antique look" (Windows 2.0!).
OBM_OLD_DNARROW			A down arrow.
OBM_OLD_LFARROW			A left arrow.
OBM_OLD_REDUCE			A minimize button with an "antique look".
OBM_OLD_RESTORE			A restore button with an "antique look".
OBM_OLD_RGARROW			A right arrow.
OBM_OLD_UPARROW			An up arrow.

Table 12.14: The OEM bitmaps

Symbol	Bitmap		Explanation
	API 3	**API 4**	
OBM_OLD_ZOOM			A zoom button with an "antique look".
OBM_REDUCE			A "reduce" button.
OBM_REDUCED			A "reduce" button in its depressed state.
OBM_RESTORE			A "restore" button.
OBM_RGARROW			A right arrow button in its normal state.
OBM_RGARROWD			A right arrow button in its depressed state.
OBM_RGARROWI			A right arrow button in its disabled state.
OBM_SIZE			A sizing box corner.
OBM_UPARROW			An up arrow button in its normal state.
OBM_UPARROWD			An up arrow button in its depressed state.
OBM_UPARROWI			An up arrow button in its disabled state.
OBM_ZOOM			A zoom button.

In Win32 4.*x*, you can set the bitmaps using the SetMenuItemInfo call, specifying the MIIM_CHECKMARKS in the fMask field of the MENUITEMINFO structure and placing the bitmap handles in the hbmpChecked and hbmpUnchecked fields of the MENUITEMINFO structure. Refer to Table 12.8 for more details on the MENUITEMINFO structure.

Menu Messages

The messages shown in Table 12.15 all apply to working with menus. Many of them, such as WM_ENTERMENULOOP and WM_EXITMENULOOP, are very specialized and will hardly ever be of interest except in specialized circumstances. Others, such as WM_DRAWITEM and WM_MEASUREITEM, are uncommon *until* you do them the first time (owner-draw menus can become addicting). Others, such as WM_INITMENUPOPUP and WM_MENUSELECT, are very common.

Table 12.15: Menu messages and their handlers

Message and Handler	Description
WM_COMMAND	Sent whenever an item is selected from the menu.
	void cls_OnCommand(HWND hwnd, int id, HWND hctl, UINT codeNotify)
WM_DRAWITEM	Sent whenever an owner-draw menu item must be drawn. It is also sent for other owner-draw items such as list boxes, combo boxes, buttons, and static controls.
	void cls_OnDrawItem(HWND hwnd, const LPDRAWITEMSTRUCT * dis)
WM_ENTERIDLE	Sent to the owner window of a menu that is entering an idle state. A menu enters an idle state when no messages are waiting in its queue after it has processed one or more previous messages. This message is also sent from modal dialog boxes.
	void cls_OnEnterIdle(HWND hwnd, UINT src, HWND hsrc)
WM_ENTERMENULOOP	Sent just before the modal message loop for the menu is entered. The isPopupMenu argument tells if this is for a menu from the menu bar (FALSE) or a floating pop-up menu (TRUE).
	void cls_OnEnterMenuLoop(HWND hwnd, BOOL isPopupMenu)[e]
WM_INITMENU	Sent only when a menu is first accessed; only one message is generated for each access. For example, moving the mouse across several menu items while holding down the button does not generate new messages.
	void cls_OnInitMenu(HWND hwnd, HMENU hmenu)
WM_INITMENUPOPUP	Sent any time a pop-up is about to become active. It passes information about the pop-up to be activated.
	void cls_OnInitMenuPopup(HWND hwnd, HMENU hmenu, UINT item, BOOL sysmenu)

[e]Defined in the extensions.h file we include on the CD-ROM.

Table 12.15: Menu messages and their handlers

Message and Handler	Description
WM_EXITMENULOOP	Sent just after the modal message loop for the menu is exited. The isPopupMenu argument tells if this is for a menu from the menu bar (FALSE) or a floating pop-up menu (TRUE).
	`void cls_OnExitMenuLoop(HWND hwnd, BOOL isPopupMenu)`[e]
WM_MEASUREITEM	Sent whenever the size of an owner-draw menu item must be computed. It is also sent for other owner-draw items such as list boxes, combo boxes, buttons, and static controls.
	`void cls_OnMeasureItem(HWND hwnd, LPMEASUREITEMSTRUCT mis)`
WM_MENUCHAR	Sent when a menu is active and the user presses a key that does not correspond to any mnemonic or accelerator key.
	`DWORD cls_OnMenuChar(HWND hwnd, UINT ch, UINT flags, HMENU hmenu)`
WM_MENUSELECT	Sent each time a new item is selected from a menu. This allows you to track the menu selections, for example, by displaying an explanation in a status line.
	`void cls_OnMenuSelect(HWND hwnd, HMENU hmenu, int item, HMENU hpopup, UINT flags)`

[e]Defined in the `extensions.h` file we include on the CD-ROM.

Maintaining Menu State

Over the years, we have developed several styles of programming for dealing with the user interface. One important style is that the GUI should be separate from the actual application code. This means that the style of programming shown in Figure 12.14 is highly desirable. Note that in this model, the GUI *queries* the program state and the algorithms *manipulate* the program state. There is no direct coupling between the "working" code and the GUI. This allows you, as the GUI designer, to maintain a certain independence. If you change from using cascaded menus to using modeless dialog boxes, toolbars, or other GUI techniques, you don't have to constantly fiddle with your code to get it to communicate. If, however, you use the "forbidden" path shown, every change in the GUI involves searching all the code for all the places the GUI was queried directly for the state or that the GUI was set based on some internal computations.

A classic error is to use the menus to hold state. In this model, whenever you change state in the program, you immediately reflect it to the menu system by enabling, disabling, or checking menu items. This approach is very fragile. It means you have to know how to get the menu, what menu items are involved, and how to detect which menu is active (critical in using the Multiple Document Interface). You also have to maintain code that actually remembers to update the menu items with exactly the same algorithm in all

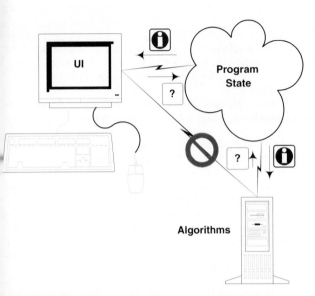

Figure 12.14: The relationship of the GUI to the program

cases. Years of maintenance of code written this way will give you a great desire to come up with alternatives that are more reliable as well as more robust under maintenance.

Although in this model there is no direct *data* path between the GUI and the algorithms, there is a *command* or *event* path; a user-initiated action can notify the algorithms to react. While traditionally this is done almost entirely by the WM_COMMAND, WM_HSCROLL, or WM_VSCROLL messages (and in API level 4, the WM_NOTIFY message as well), we usually limit the actual coupling to a set of known function names to be called as a consequence of each notification. The message handlers then have only to call the appropriate function, making each handler exactly one line of code.

The best solution to the menu state problem that we have found is to set the menu state *only* in response to a WM_INITMENUPOPUP command. At no other time is any direct manipulation done to the menus. Whenever a WM_INITMENUPOPUP message is received by the main window, it immediately queries the program state and sets the state of all the menu items that may require a state change. This is done in the OnInitMenuPopup handler.

WM_INITMENUPOPUP Message Cracker Handler

```
void cls_OnInitMenuPopup(HWND hwnd, HMENU hmenu, UINT item, BOOL sysmenu);
```

Parameter	wParam		lParam		Meaning
	lo	hi	lo	hi	
hwnd					Window handle of the window.
hmenu	■				Handle of the pop-up menu about to be displayed.
item			■		Integer offset of the item that contains the pop-up.
sysmenu				■	TRUE if the pop-up is the system (control) menu; FALSE otherwise.

There are two approaches you can take when you get this message. You can recursively walk the tree of menus starting with hmenu and, for each menu item, query whatever program state is necessary to set it properly. Or you can simply set the program state for all controls in all possible menus. Note that if you choose the first approach, you *must* write a recursive menu walk because, as we've pointed out, the shape of the menus can change. We've found that the simplest approach is often the easiest to implement: Simply set all the menu states for all the menu items you care about.

Do not be misled into false optimizations. In particular, you should attempt to avoid *ever* using the `item` parameter. It is a common mistake to know that, for example, the **Window** menu is the fourth-from-the-left or next-to-last menu item and then react only to setting the **Window** menu items if `item == 3` or if `item == GetMenuItemCount(GetMenu(hwnd)) - 1`. These computations hardly ever survive. For example, if you want to add a **Debug** menu item during development, you might well place it to the right of all menus, including **Help**, which the GUI standard suggests is (normally) the right-most menu item. This will break any code that uses the second test. And you will find that inevitably you must add a new menu item somewhere in the top-level menu; hence, the **Window** menu is now the fifth from the left. If you hardwired the constant, you are in serious trouble, but even if you used a `#define` statement to define the offset, you have to remember to find this declaration and change it. This hardly ever happens. As we pointed out in Chapter 11 in the inset on page 760, the human reaction times are such that any ordinary sets of queries to the program state are virtually instantaneous and produce no user-detectable delay in dropping down the menu. Do not be misled by false "optimizations" that save imperceptible time at the cost of increased maintenance complexity, a "fragile" GUI, and increased maintenance cost. Simple is also cheap.

The Microsoft Foundation Class library performs the recursive treewalk for you, calling what are called "CMDUI" handlers. The amount of internal message routing is incredible, and you *still* can't tell the difference in user interface performance.

Putting all the code in one place has additional advantages. Since the code is all in one place, only one place has to be maintained to keep the GUI intact. And since this `OnInitMenuPopup` code *must* be called whenever the menus are dropped down, there is no danger that someone has changed the state and forgotten to call the notification function that updates the GUI. In fact, no one has to remember to call notification code. (This is a common problem in doing dialogs, which often do not have any automated way to cause control state to be made consistent with the program state.)

A typical `OnInitMenuPopup` handler consists of a set of `EnableMenuItem`, `CheckMenuItem`, and similar calls, each of which usually looks at a small number of program variables. However, for some states, it isn't quite as easy. A typical scenario is when there are multiple windows active (such as in the Multiple Document Interface), but you want to know what menu state applies to the currently active window. In this case, we recommend doing a `SendMessage` to query the window directly. A common alternative is that whenever a window receives the focus, it sets in some global variables the appropriate state that the GUI can query. This is unreliable, since it requires that each window know what state it must manipulate, and this state will change as your program evolves and the number of window classes that might exist changes. Often a window has to know about the state that other classes might set so that it can clear the state; this is a serious violation of modularity. Typical queries we make via `SendMessage` include querying the active window for its ability to cut, copy, paste, and undo and for whether it needs to be saved. A sample `OnInitMenuPopup` handler is shown in Listing 12.5. When we discuss MDI, we show you how the `getActiveWindow` function is actually written.

Listing 12.5: A sample `OnInitMenuPopup` handler

```
void main_OnInitMenuPopup(HWND hwnd, HMENU hmenu, UINT item, BOOL sysmenu)
    {
    HWND active = getActiveWindow(hwnd);
    EnableMenuItem(GetMenu(hwnd), IDM_CUT, MF_BYCOMMAND |
          SendMessage(active, UWM_QUERY_CUT, 0, 0)
                              ? MF_ENABLED : MF_GRAYED);
    // similar to above for Copy, Paste, Undo...

    // the target window typically checks its modification flag
    // to reply to the next message
    EnableMenuItem(GetMenu(hwnd), IDM_SAVE, MF_BYCOMMAND |
          SendMessage(active, UWM_QUERY_SAVE, 0, 0)
                              ? MF_ENABLED : MF_GRAYED);

    // This queries some program state which is global
    EnableMenuItem(GetMenu(hwnd), IDM_LOAD_MYSTUFF,
          MF_BYCOMMAND |
                (mystuffLoadable() ? MF_ENABLED : MF_GRAYED);
    }
```

The lessons that led to the adoption of this style were often painful.[1] This style represents very good defensive programming.

Tracking the Menu Selection

A very common user interface is to display an explanation of the menu item in a status line at the bottom of the window. Ideally, a brief sentence is more informative than the brief one-or-two-word description given as the menu text. This is handled by the `WM_MENUSELECT` message.

`WM_MENUSELECT` Message Cracker Handler

`void cls_OnMenuSelect(HWND hwnd, HMENU hmenu, int item, HMENU hpopup, UINT flags);`

Parameter	wParam		lParam		Meaning	
	lo	hi	lo	hi		
hwnd					Window handle of the window.	
hmenu			■	■	Depends on the presence of MF_POPUP in `flags`.	
					MF_POPUP	The handle of the main menu.
					not MF_POPUP	The handle of the pop-up menu containing the menu item selected.

---

[1] I once fixed a problem in a program I was asked to modify, where some menu items were inconsistently being enabled or disabled depending on what the user had done recently. There were 23 sites in the source code that called `EnableMenuItem` for one particular menu item. There were at least six *different* computations of enabling the menu item. And there *should* have been, in this model, about 27 sites in the source code that called `EnableMenuItem`. I didn't even try to fix the code in its own style. I moved all the computations to a newly written `OnInitMenuPopup` handler, determined the *actual* correct algorithm (only three locations in the code did it correctly!). The actual code for one menu item was three lines long, and could have been written in one very complex line. I chose the simpler, clearer implementation. When I finished doing this for all the menu items, the menu maintenance problems disappeared. The entire `OnInitMenuPopup` handler was about 40 lines of code. – *jmn*.

WM_MENUSELECT Message Cracker Handler

```
void cls_OnMenuSelect(HWND hwnd, HMENU hmenu, int item, HMENU hpopup, UINT flags);
```

Parameter	wParam		lParam		Meaning
	lo	hi	lo	hi	
item					Depends on the presence of MF_POPUP in flags.
					MF_POPUP — The menu index of the pop-up menu in the main menu. See also hmenu and hpopup.
					not MF_POPUP — The identifier of the menu item.
hpopup					Depends on the presence of MF_POPUP in flags.
					MF_POPUP — GetSubMenu(hmenu, item)[1]
					not MF_POPUP — NULL
flags					One or more of the following flags:
					MF_BITMAP — Menu item is a bitmap menu item.
					MF_CHECKED — Menu item is checked.
					MF_DISABLED — Menu item is disabled.
					MF_GRAYED — Menu item is grayed.
					MF_HILITE — Menu item is highlighted.
					MF_MOUSESELECT — Item was selected using the mouse.
					MF_OWNERDRAW — Menu item is owner-drawn.
					MF_POPUP — Menu item is a pop-up menu.
					MF_SYSMENU — Menu item is the system menu.
					If flags has the value 0xFFFFFFFF and hmenu is NULL, the menu has been dismissed. Note that the value is sign-extended from 0xFFFF by the macro.

[1]The HANDLE_WM_MENUSELECT macro does this computation for you.

In your handler, you can look at the flags parameter and, if the menu is not a pop-up, you will have in the item parameter the command identifier for the menu. You can then map this to a string that you can display. The simplest way to "map the identifier to a string" is to carefully choose the menu identifiers so that you can assign the same integer value to a *resource string*, a topic we discuss in more detail starting on page 923. You can then load the string and display it. We show a sample of this code in Listing 12.6; this is a slight variant of the code used in the MDI Demo discussed in Chapter 17. The hinst variable is the instance handle to the resources and displayStatusLine is a function of your own that actually does the display of the text. The sample uses the include file shown in Listing 12.7 and the resource file shown in Listing 12.8. We deliberately chose large numbers for the menu items and strings so that it is unlikely that adding ordinary string resources will cause a problem. The large numbers also serve as an indicator that something special is being done. While we could have used small numbers such as 1, 2, or 3, this makes it hard to see the special menu prompting strings all in one place, a desirable property from the maintenance viewpoint.

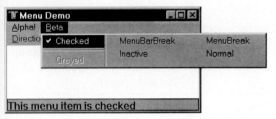

Figure 12.15: Dynamic menu tracking window

Do not be tempted to store the strings in memory or preload them into your own cache of prompt strings or even use string constants in memory. These are false optimizations. For example, if you preload the strings, then if you later add the ability to switch languages dynamically, you need to remember to invalidate your cache and reload it. The Load-String operation maintains a cache for you, and nearly every modern program uses this technique. It does not seem to introduce any perceptible performance degradation at the GUI level. If you reassign hinst to refer to a different language resource set, the code continues to work correctly. We talk more about this in the STRINGTABLE section.

Listing 12.6: Tracking the menu
```
static void main_OnMenuSelect(HWND hwnd, HMENU hmenu, int item,
                              HMENU hpopup, UINT flags)
   {
    if(flags == 0xFFFFFFFF)
       { /* menu dismissed */
         displayStatusLine(_T(""));
            return;
       } /* menu dismissed */

    if(!(flags & MF_POPUP))
       { /* command item */
         TCHAR msg[256];
         LoadString(hinst, item, msg, DIM(msg));
         displayStatusLine(msg);
       } /* command item */
   }
```

Listing 12.7: The header file for resources for menu tracking
```
#define ID_NEW        40000
#define ID_OPEN       40001
#define ID_CLOSE      40002
#define ID_SAVE       40003
#define ID_SAVEAS     40004
//... and so on
```

Listing 12.8: The resource file for menu tracking
```
    ...
    POPUP &File
       BEGIN
            MENUITEM "&New\tCtrl+N"    ID_NEW
            MENUITEM "&Open\tCtrl+O"   ID_OPEN
            MENUITEM "&Close"          ID_CLOSE
            MENUITEM "&Save\tCtrl+S"   ID_SAVE
```

```
        MENUITEM "Save &as"          ID_SAVEAS
      //... and so on

STRINGTABLE
    BEGIN
        ID_NEW "Creates an empty document"
        ID_OPEN "Opens an existing document"
        ID_CLOSE "Closes the currently active document"
        ID_SAVE  "Saves the currently active document"
        ID_SAVEAS "Saves the document under a new name"
        ...
```

The problem becomes only slightly more complex if there isn't a status line, as the code in Listing 12.6 presumes. In the Menu Demo program, we have only a normal window and need to display the status line when tracking the menu. We do this by handling the WM_ENTERMENULOOP and WM_EXITMENULOOP messages. When we enter a menu loop, we create a tracking window, and when we exit the menu loop, we destroy the window. This window is shown at the bottom of Figure 12.15.

WM_[ENTER/EXIT]MENULOOP* **Message Cracker Handler**					
`void cls_OnEnterMenuLoop(HWND hwnd, BOOL isTrackPopup);` `void cls_OnExitMenuLoop(HWND hwnd, BOOL isTrackPopup);`					
	wParam		**lParam**		
Parameter	**lo**	**hi**	**lo**	**hi**	**Meaning**
hwnd					Window handle.
isTrackPopup	■				TRUE if tracking a floating pop-up menu. FALSE if tracking an ordinary pop-up menu.

*These message crackers are not defined in windowsx.h but are in our supplied extensions.h file.

The code to create, update, and destroy the status window is shown in Listing 12.9. There are several interesting features to note about this code:

- Additional text is included in each prompt. These strings support "flyover help", which is implicitly supported by the tool bar. The flyover help prompt is the text that follows a \n (newline) character in the string. We use the _tcschr function to locate this newline character and, if that character is found, replace it with a NUL character.

- In mainframe_OnExitMenuLoop, we need to call InvalidateRect after we destroy the window. To determine the correct rectangle, we use GetWindowRect to get the area covered by the tracker window in screen coordinates and then ScreenToClient to convert these to client-relative coordinates of the parent.

- Because we create the child window for the menu tracker with a known ID, IDW_TRACKER, we can use GetDlgItem to locate the child window. GetDlgItem is not restricted to being used only for dialogs; it gets its name from that common usage, but it will locate any child window of a window. Note that this means we don't need to assign a global variable to hold the window handle; we can recover it any time we need it.

Listing 12.9: Dynamic menu tracking window

```
#define IDW_TRACKER 1 // The only child window we have

static void
mainframe_OnExitMenuLoop( HWND hwnd, BOOL isTrackPopup);
{
 HWND htracker = GetDlgItem(hwnd, IDW_TRACKER);
 if(htracker != NULL)
    { /* remove it */
      RECT r;
      GetWindowRect(htracker, &r);
      DestroyWindow(htracker);
      ScreenToClient(hwnd, (LPPOINT)&r.left);
      ScreenToClient(hwnd, (LPPOINT)&r.right);
      InvalidateRect(hwnd, &r, TRUE);
    } /* remove it */
 FORWARD_WM_EXITMENULOOP(hwnd, isTrackPopup, DefWindowProc);
}

// void mainframe_OnEnterMenuLoop (HWND hwnd, HMENU hmenu, UINT item, BOOL sysmenu)
//

static void
mainframe_OnEnterMenuLoop (HWND hwnd, BOOL isTrackPopup)

{
     RECT r;
     GetClientRect(hwnd, &r);

     r.top = r.bottom - GetSystemMetrics(SM_CYCAPTION);

     CreateWindowEx(0,                                  // Extended styles
                 _T("Static"),                          // class name
                 _T(""),                                // caption
                 WS_BORDER | WS_CHILD | WS_VISIBLE | SS_LEFT, // styles
                 r.left,                                // origin x
                 r.top,                                 // origin y
                 r.right - r.left,                      // width
                 r.bottom - r.top,                      // height
                 hwnd,                                  // parent
                 (HMENU)IDW_TRACKER,                    // ID
                 GetWindowInstance(hwnd),               // instance
                 NULL);                                 // parms

     FORWARD_WM_ENTERMENULOOP(hwnd, isTrackPopup, DefWindowProc);
}

static void
mainframe_OnMenuSelect(HWND hwnd, HMENU hmenu, int item, HMENU hmenuPopup, UINT flags)
{
 HWND htracker = GetDlgItem(hwnd, IDW_TRACKER);
 if(htracker != NULL)
    { /* show prompt */
      if((flags & MF_POPUP) == 0)
         { /* menu item */
           TCHAR prompt [256];
           LPSTR newline;
```

```
            LoadString(GetWindowInstance(hwnd), item, prompt, DIM(prompt));
            newline = _tcschr(prompt, _T('\n'));
            if(newline != NULL)
                *newline = _T('\0');   // drop flyover help prompt
            SetWindowText(htracker, prompt);
        } /* menu item */
    else
        { /* pop-up */
          SetWindowText(htracker, _T(""));
        } /* pop-up */
    } /* show prompt */
 FORWARD_WM_MENUSELECT(hwnd, hmenu, item, hmenuPopup, flags, DefWindowProc);
}
```

Using a Floating Pop-up Menu

Nearly all pop-up menus you use in a Windows application are owned by the menu on the menu bar. However, Windows also provides the TrackPopupMenu and TrackPopupMenuEx functions that allow you to display a pop-up menu anywhere on the screen. Because the pop-up isn't "attached" to a menu item on the menu bar but can float around and be displayed anywhere on the screen, it's called a *floating* pop-up menu. These are most often in response to a WM_CONTEXTMENU message being received.

To use the TrackPopupMenu or TrackPopupMenuEx functions, you first need a handle to a pop-up menu. All the menu functions you've used so far create a top-level menu. Although a top-level menu can contain pop-up menus, the top-level menu itself is not a pop-up and cannot be used with the TrackPopupMenu or TrackPopupMenuEx function.

The easiest way to get the handle to a pop-up menu is to define a menu in the resource definition file that contains the desired pop-up menu. You then can load the menu and retrieve the handle to the pop-up menu using the GetSubMenu function. For example, the following code retrieves the handle to the pop-up **File** menu contained in the EXAMPLEMENU menu described at the beginning of this chapter:

```
HMENU hmenu ;
HMENU hPopup ;

hmenu = LoadMenu (hInstance,
            MAKEINTRESOURCE (EXAMPLEMENU)) ;
hPopup = GetSubMenu (hmenu, 0) ;
```

You can also create an empty pop-up menu by calling the CreatePopupMenu function, like this:

```
hPopup = CreatePopupMenu () ;
```

You then can append and insert menu items into the pop-up menu using the AppendMenu and InsertMenu functions. This is usually how you would create a pop-up menu dynamically.

Note that if you use only CreateMenu, you will *not* get correct behavior! You *must* use CreatePopupMenu. You also must not use a MENU resource, but in fact must use a POPUP menu contained within a MENU resource. The Knowledge Base article Q75254 documents the problems you may encounter using TrackPopupMenu. If you use a menu that does not have the MF_POPUP flag set, you will get your menu displayed only as a single vertical bar.

You display a floating pop-up menu by specifying the pop-up menu handle as the hmenu parameter to the TrackPopupMenu or TrackPopupMenuEx function. The TrackPopupMenu function syntax is as follows:

```
BOOL TrackPopupMenu (HMENU hmenu, UINT Flags,
                     int x, int y,
                     int Reserved,
                     HWND hwnd,
                     LPRECT lprect) ;
```

The Flags parameter specifies the screen-position and mouse-button flags. You can select at most one of each of the groups of flags shown in Table 12.16 and combine them using the C bitwise OR operator.

Table 12.16: TrackPopupMenu flags

Flag	Description
Choose one of the following alignment flags:	
TPM_CENTERALIGN	Centers the floating pop-up menu horizontally about the coordinate specified by the x parameter.
TPM_LEFTALIGN	Aligns the left side of the floating pop-up menu with the coordinate specified by the x parameter.
TPM_RIGHTALIGN	Aligns the right side of the floating pop-up menu with the coordinate specified by the x parameter.
Choose one of the following mouse-button flags:	
TPM_LEFTBUTTON	The floating pop-up menu tracks the left mouse button.
TPM_RIGHTBUTTON	The floating pop-up menu tracks the right mouse button.
In API level 4 and higher, you can also specify one of the following vertical alignment flags:	
TPM_TOPALIGN	Aligns the top of the floating pop-up menu with the coordinate specified by the y parameter.
TPM_VCENTERALIGN	Centers the floating pop-up menu vertically about the coordinate specified by the y parameter.
TPM_BOTTOMALIGN	Aligns the bottom of the floating pop-up menu with the coordinate specified by the y parameter.
In API level 4 and higher, you can specify which alignment is to be favored if the desired alignment cannot be met. (For example, the mouse was clicked too close to an edge or, for TrackPopupMenuEx, the exclusion rectangle interferes with the placement.)	
TPM_VERTICAL	If the specified alignment cannot be managed, favors the vertical alignment over the horizontal alignment.
TPM_HORIZONTAL	If the specified alignment cannot be managed, favors the horizontal alignment over the vertical alignment.

Table 12.16: TrackPopupMenu flags

Flag	Description
In API level 4 and higher, you can suppress the sending of messages to the parent window:	
TPM_NONOTIFY	Does not send notification messages to the window. Suppresses WM_INITMENU and WM_EXITMENULOOP messages but not WM_MENUSELECT messages.
TPM_RETURNCMD	Does not send a WM_COMMAND message to the window. Instead, returns the ID of the selected menu item as the return value of the function.

The x parameter specifies the horizontal screen coordinate to which the floating pop-up menu should be aligned. The screen-position flag specifies how the menu will be aligned with this coordinate. The y parameter specified the vertical screen coordinate of the top of the floating pop-up menu. The Reserved parameter is reserved and must be set to 0. The hwnd parameter specifies the handle of the window that owns the pop-up menu. This window normally receives WM_INITMENU and WM_INITMENUPOPUP messages just before the pop-up menu is displayed and receives the WM_ENTERMENULOOP and WM_EXITMENULOOP messages bracketing the menu loop. The WM_COMMAND message that results from the user's selecting a command menu item is also sent to this window. The lprect points to a RECT structure that contains the screen coordinates of a rectangle in which the user can click a mouse button without dismissing the floating pop-up menu. You can specify NULL for this parameter to request that Windows dismiss the floating pop-up menu if the user clicks outside the pop-up.

The TrackPopupMenu function normally *posts* WM_COMMAND messages to its owner window. This means that the TrackPopupMenu function returns before the owner window receives the WM_COMMAND message. You cannot tell, in this mode, if the user has selected a command menu item or merely caused an action that has dismissed the menu. The result indicates only whether the function successfully popped up the menu, not the result of any action taken subsequently. If, at API level 4 or higher, you specify the TPM_RETURNCMD flag, no message is posted. Instead, you get as the return value either the menu ID of the selected item or 0 if the user did not make a selection (the menu was dismissed). This feature is not available in API level 3, and if you want to support the older API, you must be cautious about using this feature.

The TrackPopupMenuEx function is defined as

```
BOOL TrackPopupMenuEx (HMENU hmenu, UINT Flags,
                       int x, int y,
                       HWND hwnd,
                       LPTPMPARAMS  params) ;
```

The x, y, hmenu, and hwnd parameters are all as defined for the TrackPopupMenu function. Flags can be any of the values shown in Table 12.16.

The TPMPARAMS structure is defined as

```
typedef struct tagTPMPARAMS {
    UINT cbSize;
    RECT rcExclude;
    } TPMPARAMS, * LPTPMPARAMS;
```

The cbSize member must be initialized to sizeof(TPMPARAMS). The rcExclude member contains the screen coordinates of a rectangle that the floating pop-up menu should not overlap. You can specify NULL for the params parameter to indicate that there is no limitation.

Like the TrackPopupMenu function, the TrackPopupMenuEx function will *post* its WM_COMMAND messages to the owner window. Hence, you must return to your message loop before you can execute the command (if any) that was selected. The TPM_RETURNCMD flag can be used to bypass this messaging. If the flag is set, you will get the ID of the menu item returned as the value of TrackPopupMenuEx.

The following code is excerpted from the example program in this chapter. We compiled in a static menu template. When the user presses the right mouse button in the client area of the application window, Windows sends a WM_RBUTTONDOWN message to the window. When we receive the WM_RBUTTONDOWN message, we convert the client area coordinates of the mouse click into screen coordinates. We display the floating pop-up menu with its upper-left corner at this location.

We create a menu based on the compiled-in menu template by calling the LoadMenuIndirect function. After we create the menu, we retrieve the handle to the first item, which is a pop-up menu, by calling the Get-SubMenu function.

We display the floating pop-up menu at the point where the user clicked the button by calling the TrackPopupMenu function. The TrackPopupMenu function starts a secondary message loop and doesn't return until the user is done with the menu, having either selected an item from it or dismissed the menu without making a selection. Note that for the sake of this example, we have put the actual strings in the program; this program could not be localized for another country with code like this in it. The strings *must* be Unicode strings even if the rest of the application is ANSI-only, even in Windows 95. Note also that the MF_POPUP flag is set. If you try to use TrackPopupMenu without having the MF_POPUP flag set for the menu, the floating pop-up menu will display as a simple vertical bar. This behavior is documented in the Knowledge Base article Q75254, which documents several problems you may encounter in using TrackPopupMenu incorrectly. Within each level of menu (there are two here: the top-level pop-up and the items that are within it) the *last* item in the list must have the MF_END flag set. As a result, the MF_END flag appears twice in our definition: once to end the pop-up list and once to end the list of items within it.

```
void class_OnRButtonDown(HWND hwnd, BOOL dblclk,
                         int x, int y,
                         UINT keyflags)
{
  static struct {

    // The MENUITEMTEMPLATEHEADER structure.

    MENUITEMTEMPLATEHEADER mith ;

    // Define a pop-up menu.

    UINT        mtOption1 ;
    WCHAR       mtString1 [15] ;
```

```
        // Define the first menu item within
        // the pop-up menu.

        UINT          mtOption2 ;
        UINT          mtID2 ;
        WCHAR         mtString2 [16] ;

        // Define the second menu item within
        // the pop-up menu.

        UINT          mtOption3 ;
        UINT          mtID3 ;
        WCHAR         mtString3 [5] ;

} MenuTemplate = {
    { 0, 0 },  // version 0, offset to first item 0
    MF_POPUP | MF_END,       // mtOption1
    L"Floating popup",       // mtString1[15]
    // menu items            ------------------
    0,                       // mtOption2
    IDM_ABOUT,               // mtID2
    L"About MenuDemos",      // mtString2[16]
                             // ---------------
    MF_END,                  // mtOption3
    IDM_EXIT,                // mtID3
    L"Exit"                  // mtString3[5]
  } ;
  HMENU hmenu ;
  HMENU hSubMenu ;

  ClientToScreen (hwnd, &pt) ;

  hmenu = LoadMenuIndirect ((LPSTR) &MenuTemplate) ;
  hSubMenu = GetSubMenu (hmenu, 0) ;

  TrackPopupMenu (hSubMenu,
                  TPM_LEFTBUTTON | TPM_CENTERALIGN,
                  x, y, 0, hwnd, NULL ) ;
  DestroyMenu (hmenu) ;
  }
}
```

Figure 12.16 shows a floating pop-up menu that has been constructed in the Menu Explorer (its definition is shown in the left-hand box in the screen capture, which was done under Windows NT 3.51). It has been activated by the right mouse button and is awaiting the user's selection.

After the `TrackPopupMenu` or `TrackPopupMenuEx` functions return, we destroy the top-level menu by calling the `DestroyMenu` function. Because the destroyed menu contains the pop-up menu as a menu item, the pop-up is also destroyed. This frees all the memory occupied by the menu.

Most of the time, you won't need to explicitly destroy a menu. Windows destroys a window's menu when the window is destroyed. However, you need to destroy all menus you create that are not owned by a window, such as our example floating pop-up menu.

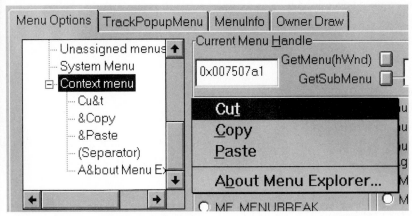

Figure 12.16: A floating pop-up menu

Using Multiple Top-level Menus

Sometimes, you may have multiple menus that can be used by a single window, although not simultaneously, of course. But when the user selects a particular application function, it may be more appropriate to change the menu bar of the window to a completely new menu that is more appropriate to the new state. You can do this by calling the SetMenu function. You specify the window handle and the menu handle for the new menu:

```
BOOL SetMenu (HWND hwnd, HMENU hmenu) ;
```

The previous menu for the window isn't destroyed, and the previously obtained handle to the old menu is still valid.

The example program allows the user to change the menu for the application window from the menu specified when the window was created to the menu specified when the class was registered and back again. The class menu is specified by the following statement:

```
wc.lpszMenuName = MAKEINTRESOURCE (IDM_CLASSMENU) ;
```

Just before creating the main application window, we load both the class menu and the window's menu. When we create the application's window, we specified hmenuWindow as the window's menu:

```
/**************************************************/
/* Load the menus for the window.                 */
/* Specify the window menu when creating the      */
/* window. This overrides the default class       */
/* menu.                                          */
/**************************************************/

hmenuWindow = LoadMenu (hInstance, MAKEINTRESOURCE (IDM_WINDOWMENU)) ;
hmenuClass  = LoadMenu (hInstance, MAKEINTRESOURCE (IDM_CLASSMENU)) ;

/*********************************************/
/* Create the application's main window. */
/*********************************************/
```

```
hwnd = CreateWindow (
          ClassName ,
          WindowTitle ,
          WS_OVERLAPPEDWINDOW,
          CW_USEDEFAULT, 0,
          CW_USEDEFAULT, 0,
          0,
          hmenuWindow,
          hInstance,
          NULL) ;
```

Each menu contains one item that results in the opposite menu's replacing the current menu as the menu for the window. This menu swapping is triggered by a WM_COMMAND message that has the wParam parameter equal to the menu ID IDM_CLASSMENUITEM or IDM_WINDOWMENUITEM:

```
void class_OnCommand(HWND hwnd, int ctlid,
                     HWND hctl, UINT codeNotify)
    {
    switch (ctlid)
        { /* ctlid */
        case IDM_CLASSMENUITEM:
            SetMenu (hwnd, hmenuClass) ;
            haccCurr = 0 ;
            return ;

        case IDM_WINDOWMENUITEM:
            SetMenu (hwnd, hmenuWindow) ;
            haccCurr = haccWindow ;
            return ;
        } /* ctlid */
    }
```

When the application terminates, we no longer need and must destroy the two menus we created. Windows will automatically destroy the menu *currently* used by the window, but it could destroy either depending on which is the current menu. Rather than keep track of which menu is in use, we wait for the WM_DESTROY message, which indicates that the window is being destroyed, and then we remove the current menu, whichever one it is, from the window. We will then destroy both menus explicitly.

You can call the SetMenu function, specifying NULL as the new menu handle, and the window no longer owns a menu. So once you set the menu handle for a window to NULL, you can explicitly destroy all the top-level menus you've created without being concerned about Windows's attempting to destroy a menu a second time.

```
void class_OnDestroy(HWND hwnd)
    {
    SetMenu (hwnd, NULL) ;
    DestroyMenu (hmenuClass) ;
    DestroyMenu (hmenuWindow) ;
    PostQuitMessage (0) ;
    }
```

A more complicated way to achieve the same goal is to determine which menu is associated with the window (by calling the GetMenu function). Windows will destroy that menu, so we destroy the other menu. This method allows Windows to destroy the menu associated with the window:

```
void class_OnDestroy(HWND hwnd)
    {
    hmenu = GetMenu (hwnd) ;
    if (hmenu == hmenuClass)
        DestroyMenu (hmenuWindow) ;
    if (hmenu == hmenuWindow)
        DestroyMenu (hmenuClass) ;
    PostQuitMessage (0) ;
    }
```

The System Menu

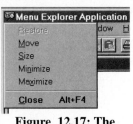

Figure 12.17: The system menu (API level 4)

A window created with the WS_SYSMENU window styles has a system menu icon to the left of the title bar. The user can click this icon, and the system menu will pop up, as shown in Figure 12.17. The system menu typically contains the **Restore**, **Move**, **Size**, **Minimize**, **Maximize**, **Close**, and (at API level 3 only) **Switch To** items. You can use the functions previously described to delete, insert, and modify items in the system menu as well as in your own menus.

When you add items to the system menu, you must make sure the menu IDs for the new items do not conflict with the IDs used by the normal system menu items. Windows reserves for its own use all menu IDs greater than or equal to 0xF000 (61440).

To change the system menu, you first need a handle to the menu. The GetSystemMenu function returns the menu handle for the system menu used by the window specified by the hwnd parameter. The call is defined as

```
HMENU GetSystemMenu (HWND hwnd, BOOL Revert) ;
```

All applications initially use the *standard system menu*. The first time you call the GetSystemMenu function with the Revert parameter set to FALSE, the function makes a copy of the standard system menu, attaches this menu to your window as the window's system menu, and returns the menu handle of the copy.

The system menu is copied only during the first call. Second and subsequent calls to the GetSystemMenu function with the Revert parameter set to FALSE return the handle of the copy of the system menu currently in use. This menu isn't necessarily identical to the standard system menu because you may have made modifications to it.

Calling the GetSystemMenu function with the Revert parameter set to TRUE destroys the (possibly modified) copy of the system menu (if a copy was ever made) and resets the menu of the original, unmodified system menu. In this case, it returns a NULL value so you cannot use this function to modify the original system menu.

Windows sends a WM_SYSCOMMAND message, rather than a WM_COMMAND message, when the user selects an item from the system menu. The wParam parameter of the WM_SYSCOMMAND message specifies the menu ID for the selected menu item. Windows defines the system menu IDs listed in Table 12.17.

WM_SYSCOMMAND Message Cracker Handler

```
void cls_OnSysCommand(HWND hwnd, UINT id, int x, int y);
```

Parameter	wParam lo	wParam hi	lParam lo	lParam hi	Meaning
hwnd					Window handle of the window.
id	■	■			ID of the system menu item (see Table 12.17).
x			■		Indicates the horizontal mouse position (in screen coordinates) of the mouse if the mouse was used to choose the menu; see the y-coordinate value.
y				■	Indicates the vertical mouse position (in screen coordinates) of the mouse if the mouse was used to choose the menu:
					0 — Menu was chosen by keyboard mnemonic. The x coordinate is meaningless.
					-1 — Menu was chosen by keyboard accelerator. The x coordinate is meaningless.
					> 0 — Menu was chosen by the mouse; this is the y-coordinate. The x-coordinate is the horizontal mouse position.

Table 12.17: System menu item IDs

Menu ID	Description
SC_CLOSE	Closes the window.
SC_CONTEXTHELP	Changes the cursor to the "help" cursor. If the user clicks a control in a dialog box, the window will receive a WM_HELP instead of a WM_COMMAND message.
SC_DEFAULT	Selects the default item, if the user double-clicks the system menu. The default item is SC_CLOSE.
SC_HOTKEY	Activates the window associated with the application-specified hot key.
SC_HSCROLL	Scrolls the window horizontally.
SC_ICON	Same as SC_MINIMIZE.
SC_KEYMENU	Retrieves a menu through a keystroke.

Table 12.17: System menu item IDs

Menu ID	Description
SC_MAXIMIZE	Maximizes the window.
SC_MINIMIZE	Minimizes the window.
SC_MONITORPOWER	Handles power-save features; sets the state of the display.
SC_MOUSEMENU	Retrieves a menu through a mouse click.
SC_MOVE	Moves the window.
SC_NEXTWINDOW	Moves to next window.
SC_PREVWINDOW	Moves to previous window.
SC_RESTORE	Restores the window to its previously saved size.
SC_SCREENSAVE	Executes the screen-saver application. The user specifies this application in the Desktop section of the Control Panel.
SC_SIZE	Resizes the window.
SC_TASKLIST	Executes or activates the Task Manager (API level 3 only).
SC_VSCROLL	Scrolls the window vertically.
SC_ZOOM	Same as SC_MAXIMIZE.

Windows uses the four low-order bits of the predefined system menu IDs internally. When you want to test the id parameter of a WM_SYSCOMMAND message to see if it's a message from one of the system menu items, you must ignore the low-order 4 bits of the id value as follows:

```
void class_OnSysCommand(HWND hwnd, UINT id, int x, int y)
    {
    if ((id & 0xFFF0) == SC_MAXIMIZE)
        // Prevents the user from
        // maximizing the window.
        return ;
    FORWARD_WM_SYSCOMMAND(hwnd, id, x, y, DefWindowProc) ;
    }
```

If you add your own menu items to the system menu and, therefore, intercept the WM_SYSCOMMAND message, you must make sure you pass all unprocessed messages to the DefWindowProc function. If you don't, the standard system menu commands will be effectively disabled. They will look active to the user, but selecting them will have no effect.

Rather than throw away messages from the SC_MAXIMIZE menu item like we do in the previous example, you should gray the menu item to indicate to the user that the application has deliberately disabled the maximize option. For other menu items, you may even want to remove them entirely. You might do this, for example, for the **Close** item of the system menu of a child window that you don't want the user to close. In this case, you may also have to remove the second separator of an adjacent pair.

The `Menus` Example Program

The `Menus` example program is shown in Figure 12.10, Figure 12.11 and Figure 12.15. It uses most of the menus and menu items we've described so far. It also uses keyboard accelerators and string resources, which we describe next.

The Menu Explorer

The Menu Explorer application allows you to experiment with the menu system. You can create menus, modify existing menus, and use the various menu functions to see what really happens on each of the various functions. You can construct an owner-draw menu (or at least twiddle the parameters), assign custom check mark icons, and try out the various API level 4 operations such as `SetMenuItemInfo` and `GetMenuItemInfo`. You can watch the menu-related messages that are sent to your main window.

Accelerators

You can define *accelerator keys* by defining an *accelerator table* in your application's resource definition file or in an accelerator table you construct dynamically. An accelerator key gives the user a quick method for selecting an item from a menu by using a single keystroke.

The first step toward using accelerator keys is to inform the user which key press corresponds to which menu item. Generally, you do this by placing the name of the accelerator key to the right of the text for a menu item. You separate the menu text from the accelerator key description with a tab character (\t). Figure 12.18 shows the **Edit** menu of the example program with five accelerators listed. The declarations for the menu items are shown on page 909. The declarations for the actual accelerators are shown on page 906.

Figure 12.18: A menu showing accelerator keys

Creating an Accelerator Table

After you create the menu that informs the user of the accelerator keys, you must create an accelerator table. An *accelerator table* maps accelerator keys to their corresponding command menu items. You can either define an accelerator table in your resource definition file using the `ACCELERATORS` statement or create one "on the fly" in your program by using the `CreateAcceleratorTable` function.

The text in a menu item that describes the corresponding accelerator key is descriptive only. Windows doesn't use it to determine which keys are accelerator keys. That information is in the accelerator table.

An accelerator table resource begins with the accelerator table name field followed by the ACCELERATORS keyword. As with the other resources you've seen, the name field can be either a unique character string or an integer value. We used the same integer value for the accelerator table as we used for the corresponding menu. Resource ID values need be unique only within a resource type such as a menu, a string, an accelerator, or a dialog.

You list the accelerator keys between BEGIN and END keywords. Each accelerator key definition has the following form:

```
key, accelID, [keytype[,]] [NOINVERT] [ALT] [SHIFT] [CONTROL]
```

The example program defines the following accelerator table:

```
IDM_WINDOWMENU ACCELERATORS
BEGIN
    "Z",        IDM_UNDO,    VIRTKEY, CONTROL
    "X",        IDM_CUT,     VIRTKEY, CONTROL
    "C",        IDM_COPY,    VIRTKEY, CONTROL
    "V",        IDM_PASTE,   VIRTKEY, CONTROL
    VK_DELETE,  IDM_DELETE,  VIRTKEY
END
```

The key field specifies the keystroke to be used as the accelerator key. You can define this key in one of three ways:

- *Literal character.* A single ASCII character enclosed in quotation marks ("A") that defines the specified character key as an accelerator key. The uppercase A character is the accelerator key in this example. You can precede the character by a caret (^) to indicate that the corresponding control character is the accelerator key. For example, "^A" defines **Ctrl+A** as the accelerator key.

- *Numeric ASCII code.* An integer value representing the ASCII character with that numeric value. The keytype field must be ASCII.

- *Numeric virtual key code.* An integer value representing the virtual key with that numeric value. Generally, you'll use the symbolic names listed in windows.h rather than an explicit number (for example, VK_DELETE). The alphanumeric keys don't have symbolic names in windows.h. You can define these keys by placing the uppercase letter or the number in double quotation marks (for example, "Z" or "5"). Alphabetic virtual keys must be uppercase letters. The keytype field must be VIRTKEY.

The accelID field contains the accelerator ID that identifies the accelerator. Windows sends this value as the wParam parameter of a WM_COMMAND or WM_SYSCOMMAND message or the ctlid parameter to an OnCommand or OnSysCommand handler, sent when the user presses an accelerator key. When an accelerator entry is a shortcut for a menu selection, you'll generally specify the same value for the menu ID and the accelerator ID.

The `keytype` field must be `ASCII` or `VIRTKEY`. It can be omitted only when defining a character within double quotation marks. The `keytype` is assumed to be `ASCII` in that case.

The `NOINVERT` option specifies that a corresponding top-level menu item, if any, is not inverted when the accelerator key is pressed. This option has an effect only when the corresponding menu item is a top-level menu item. Without this option, Windows highlights the top-level menu item when the accelerator is used.

The `ALT`, `SHIFT`, and `CONTROL` options can be used only when the `keytype` field is `VIRTKEY`. They specify that the **Alt**, **Shift**, or **Ctrl** key must be down when the character is pressed to activate the accelerator.

Generally, you should define a shifted accelerator key using the virtual key code rather than using the ASCII code. This is because of the processing of the `SHIFT` keyword. When you specify an ASCII character, either in double quotation marks (`"A"`) or as an integer value (`65`), Windows performs a case-sensitive match of the key press and the specified ASCII code. When they match, Windows then checks to see whether the **Shift** key is down. This may define a different accelerator key than you expect.

Take, for example, an uppercase A defined as an ASCII accelerator with the `SHIFT` option specified. Pressing the **A** key with the **Shift** key down and **Caps Lock** off activates the accelerator. Pressing the **A** key with the **Shift** key down and **Caps Lock** on does not activate the accelerator. In the latter case, pressing the **A** key with **Caps Lock** on normally produces an uppercase A. The **Shift** key down as well converts the uppercase A to a lowercase a, which fails the case-sensitive character test. Pressing the **A** key with **Caps Lock** on and the **Shift** key up produces an uppercase A. However, when Windows checks the state of the **Shift** key (for the `SHIFT` option test) it finds the **Shift** key up, so the accelerator isn't activated.

You can't solve this dilemma by specifying an ASCII lowercase a with the `SHIFT` option either. This defines an accelerator that is activated only when the user presses the **A** key while **Caps Lock** is on and the **Shift** key is pressed.

Defining an accelerator as a virtual key bypasses these difficulties. A *virtual key* specifies a key on the keyboard as opposed to a character code. Definitions using virtual keys aren't affected by the state of the **Caps Lock** key.

Loading an Accelerator Table

To use an accelerator table, you must have a handle to it. You can get this either from the `CreateAcceleratorTable` call or by loading a resource. You load an accelerator table resource by calling the `LoadAccelerators` function. It returns a handle to the accelerator table:

```
HACCEL  haccel ;

haccel = LoadAccelerators (hInstance, MAKEINTRESOURCE (IDM_WINDOWMENU)) ;
```

Because you must load the accelerator table before you use it, you generally load the table during your program initialization code (where you often load menus and create windows).

Sometimes you may want to load the table during the `WM_CREATE` message processing for the window. Generally you load an accelerator table during the `WM_CREATE` message processing when you also load a menu for the window. The main consideration is that the application's message loop uses the accelerator table handle. You'll have to ensure that the handle is valid when the message loop uses it.

Creating Accelerator Tables Dynamically

You can also create an accelerator table by using the `CreateAcceleratorTable` function. This takes a pointer to an array of ACCEL values and a count of how many entries are in the table.

```
HACCEL CreateAcceleratorTable(LPACCEL lpaccel, int Count)
```

An ACCEL value is a structure that encodes the necessary accelerator information:

```
typedef struct tagACCEL {
    BYTE fVirt;
    WORD key;
    WORD cmd;
        } ACCEL;
```

The fVirt member is a combination of the flags shown in Table 12.18. The key member is the character code or virtual key code, and the cmd member is the code that will be sent when the accelerator is selected by that keystroke combination.

Table 12.18: ACCEL flags

fVirt Value	Description
FALT	The **Alt** key must be held down for the accelerator.
FCONTROL	The **Ctrl** key must be held down for the accelerator.
FNOINVERT	The top-level menu item will not be highlighted when this accelerator is selected.
FSHIFT	The **Shift** key must be held down for this accelerator.
FVIRTKEY	The key member specifies a virtual key code. If this flag is not specified, the key member specifies an ASCII key code.

You can obtain the contents of an accelerator table, given the handle, by using the `CopyAcceleratorTable` function. This takes the following arguments:

```
int CopyAcceleratorTable (HACCEL haccel, LPACCEL lpaccel, int count);
```

If the lpaccel parameter is NULL, then the result of the function is the number of accelerator table entries in the table. If it is not NULL, then the result is the number of entries actually copied. Typically, you will call this function once with a NULL parameter to determine how much storage to allocate and then call it again with a reference to the newly allocated storage. An example is shown in Listing 12.10.

Listing 12.10: Using CopyAcceleratorTable
```
LPACCEL getCopy(HACCEL haccel)
    {
     int Length;
     LPACCEL tbl;
```

```
Length = CopyAcceleratorTable(haccel, NULL, 0);
tbl = malloc(Length * sizeof(ACCEL));
if(tbl != NULL)
   { /* do copy */
    CopyAcceleratorTable(haccel, tbl, Length);
   } /* do copy */
 return tbl;
}
```

If you create an accelerator table, you must eventually destroy it using `DestroyAcceleratorTable`. A table that is loaded using `LoadAccelerators` does not need to be explicitly destroyed.

Displaying Accelerators in the Menu

Accelerator tables are independent of menus. The text in the menu that indicates what accelerator is associated with it is just that–text. It does not get changed if you change accelerator tables. Its presence does not create an accelerator key or configure an acceleration table. This can be a maintenance nightmare. If you add a new menu item, you must remember which item is supposed to have an accelerator to also go to the accelerator table and then add the new accelerator key specification. It is as bad if you make a change; you must check two (or perhaps even more!) places for consistency. If you change accelerator tables or add or delete accelerators (by either loading a new table or creating a new table dynamically), you have to change the text of the command menu items yourself. You would do this either by loading a new menu that shows the new accelerators or by changing each of the entries in the menu to correspond to the new accelerator table.

Generally, the set of accelerators is determined by your resource file, so you can "hardwire" the text of the accelerator into the menu. For example, the accelerator table shown on page 906 would be represented in its menu declarations by text of the following form:

```
MENUITEM "&Undo\tCtrl+Z", IDM_UNDO
MENUITEM SEPARATOR
MENUITEM "Cu&t\tCtrl+X", IDM_CUT
MENUITEM "&Copy\tCtrl+C", IDM_COPY
MENUITEM "&Paste\tCtrl+V", IDM_PASTE
MENUITEM "Cle&ar\tDelete", IDM_DELETE
```

Using the `CopyAcceleratorTable` function, you could get the complete set of current accelerators. You could then either walk the menu tree recursively, removing any accelerator text you find (the text after the tab character, by convention), checking the accelerator table for a match, and adding the text back in. Or you could handle the `WM_INITMENUPOPUP` message and modify the current menu at that point. The latter is often useful for internationalization, where the mnemonics for accelerators could change based on the local language.

In the fully general case, you might not put *any* accelerator text on a menu item. You then could write code that went through an accelerator table and attached any accelerator text to the menu by decoding the accelerator table and using the appropriate menu functions.

Accelerators and the Message Loop

You must modify the standard message loop to use accelerators in an application. After you've retrieved a message, you call the `TranslateAccelerator` function. This function examines the message specified by the `lpMsg` parameter to see whether it contains a keyboard-input message. If it does, the function also determines if the key press corresponds to one of the accelerators defined in the accelerator table specified by the `haccel` parameter. The function call looks like this:

```
BOOL TranslateAccelerator (HWND hwnd, HACCEL haccel, LPMSG lpMsg) ;
```

When it finds an accelerator keystroke, it converts the message into a `WM_COMMAND` or `WM_SYSCOMMAND` message. The message contains the accelerator ID that is associated with the key press, and the function sends the message to the window specified by the `hwnd` parameter.

The `TranslateAccelerator` function sends a `WM_SYSCOMMAND` message when the accelerator ID corresponds to an item in the system menu. It sends a `WM_COMMAND` message for all other accelerators. The low-order word of the `wParam` parameter contains the accelerator ID from the accelerator table entry that matched the keystroke. The high-order word of the `wParam` parameter contains 1 to indicate that the message originates from an accelerator. The same word contains 0 when the message is from a menu. If the message came from a control, the value would be the notification code.

`WM_COMMAND` Message Cracker Handler

```
void cls_OnCommand(HWND hwnd, int id, HWND hctl, UINT codeNotify);
```

Parameter	wParam		lParam		Meaning
	lo	hi	lo	hi	
hwnd					Window handle of the parent window.
id	■				Control ID of the child control; menu ID of the menu item.
hctl			■		Window handle of the child control; 0 if from the menu or accelerator.
codeNotify		■			Notification code from the child control; 0 if from the menu and 1 if from the accelerator.

Commands in accelerator tables do not have to correspond to any command menu items in the menu owned by the `hwnd` window. You can define accelerator keys that correspond to actions not present on a window's menu.

The `TranslateAccelerator` function returns a nonzero value when the message is an accelerator key message. When the `TranslateAccelerator` function returns nonzero, the message has been completely processed and you must not pass it to the `TranslateMessage` and `DispatchMessage` functions. When the `TranslateAccelerator` function returns 0, you must process the message normally. A typical message loop that handles accelerators looks like this:

```
while (GetMessage (&msg, 0, 0, 0))
    if (!TranslateAccelerator (hwnd, haccel, &msg))
        {
        TranslateMessage (&msg) ;
        DispatchMessage (&msg) ;
        }
```

The message loop in the example program is a little different because we switch menus dynamically. The menu specified when the application window is created has a corresponding accelerator table for items in the **Edit** menu. Those accelerators should be active only when the corresponding menu is being used. The application uses the `haccCurr` variable to hold the current accelerator table handle. When the variable is 0, accelerator keystrokes are not translated.

```
while (GetMessage(&msg, 0, 0, 0))
    if (haccCurr == NULL ||
        !TranslateAccelerator (hwndMain, haccCurr, &msg))
        {
        TranslateMessage (&msg) ;
        DispatchMessage (&msg) ;
        }
```

Accelerators without Menu Items

Although we have talked about accelerators as if they are connected to command menu items, in fact, an accelerator doesn't need to have a command menu item associated with it. The fact that an accelerator sends a `WM_COMMAND` message is actually independent of any menu item. You could have commands associated with the keyboard that had no equivalent in menus. Although this tends to violate GUI standards, it is sometimes very useful, particularly in a debugging mode where you can "hide" diagnostic commands on shortcut keys for your own convenience. For example, add the accelerator line

```
"D", IDM_DEBUG_INFO, VIRTKEY, CONTROL
```

to your accelerator table definition. You then can use the **Ctrl+D** key code to invoke the `debugInfo` procedure in your program by including the following code:

```
void cls_OnCommand(HWND hwnd, int id, HWND hctl, UINT codeNotify)
    {
    switch(id)
        { /* id */
        case IDM_DEBUG_INFO:
            debugInfo(hwnd);
            return;
        // other cases here
        } /* id */

    }

void debugInfo(HWND hwnd)
    {
    // your debugging display code goes here
    )
```

Icon Resources

Most Windows applications display icons as part of their graphical user interface. An *icon* is a small image used to represent a component of your application. Most applications use an icon to represent the application's main window when the window is minimized. Some applications display icons in the client area of their windows. The Windows Program Manager displays icons in the program group windows to represent applications. You also can display an icon as part of a dialog box.

Defining an Icon Resource

A program typically defines the icons that it uses in the application's resource definition file. The ICON statements in this file define a name or integer ID for the icon and specify the name of a file that contains the icon. An ICON statement has the following syntax:

nameID ICON [*load-option*] [*memory-option*] *filename*

Like many other resources you've seen, the nameID field specifies either a unique name or an integer value that identifies the resource. The *load-option* field is ignored in Win32 and is recognized only for compatibility with earlier resource files (see the note on page 837). The *memory-option* field can be DISCARDABLE. These attributes have the same meaning as in all the other resources.

The *filename* field is the name of the file that contains an icon resource. The filename is not surrounded by double quotation marks. The following example defines an icon resource for a warning icon. The icon is identified by the name WarnIcon and the bitmap image(s) for the icon are contained in the file warnicon.ico:

WarnIcon   ICON   warnicon.ico

An icon file may contain a number of bitmap images. Each image in the file represents the same icon but one that is drawn at a different resolution for display on a particular display device.[2] When you use the icon in your application, you first load the icon from the application resources. Then, you ask for it by name or integer ID. Windows selects the image of the icon that best matches the current display device.

For example, you can distribute your application with icons drawn for several different styles:

- A standard icon, 32×32 pixels, in 16 colors

- A high-resolution color icon, 32×32 pixels, in 256 colors

- A large, high-resolution color icon, 48×48 pixels, in 256 colors

- A small icon, 16×16 pixels, in 16 colors

You write the application as if there were only one icon image and supply the various images. Windows examines the various images of the icon and selects the one that best matches the resolution and colors supported by the system display device and (in the case of the small icon) the user's selected icon display option.

You create an icon file using an icon editor. Most development environments have an editor that can create an icon file containing one or more icon images; for example, the Visual C++ development environment

---

[2] In case you're wondering, those "icon files" you download or get through shareware that contain hundreds of icons are in fact ordinary .exe or .dll files with huge resource files bound in. Each resource file contains hundreds of ICON statements.

from Microsoft. Icon files typically have an .ico extension. Even though this is the recommended extension, it isn't mandatory.

When you run the resource compiler to compile your resource definition file, the compiler *copies* the icon images from all icon files listed on ICON statements into the compiled resource definition (.res) file. These resources are then bound into the executable program file.

Loading an Icon Resource

Before you can display an icon, you must load it. You load an icon from the application's resources using the LoadIcon function. The following code shows two methods to load the same icon. Which one you select depends on how you identified the icon in the resource definition file.

```
#define IDI_WARNICON    42

HICON hicon ;

hicon = LoadIcon (hInstance, _T("WarnIcon")) ;
hicon = LoadIcon (hInstance, MAKEINTRESOURCE (IDI_WARNICON)) ;
```

Windows also defines several predefined icons. You access these icons also by calling the LoadIcon function. In this case, you specify 0 as the hInstance parameter. The nameID parameter must be one of the values listed in Table 12.19. The names indicated as obsolete are rooted in early Windows history and make little sense, considering the images. We include these because you may encounter them if you are porting earlier Windows applications or are working on a Win32 application written before the later tooling releases regularized the names.

Table 12.19: Predefined Windows icons

| Value | Icon | | Icon Shape |
	API3	API4	
IDI_APPLICATION OIC_SAMPLE			Default application icon.
IDI_ASTERISK			Obsolete; use IDI_INFORMATION.
IDI_ERROR OIC_ERROR			Indicates a serious warning message. The sense is, "Stop! Are you sure you want to proceed?"
IDI_EXCLAMATION			Obsolete; use IDI_WARNING.
IDI_HAND			Obsolete; use IDI_ERROR.

Table 12.19: Predefined Windows icons

Value	Icon		Icon Shape
	API3	**API4**	
IDI_INFORMATION OIC_INFORMATION			Indicates an informative message; the preferred name; replaces IDI_ASTERISK.
IDI_QUESTION OIC_QUES			Question mark. Indicates that the message is a query.
IDI_WARNING OIC_WARNING			Exclamation point. Indicates a warning message. Preferred usage; the preferred name; replaces IDI_EXCLAMATION.
IDI_WINLOGO OIC_WINLOGO			Windows logo.

The IDI symbols are used for LoadIcon. The OIC symbols, which are defined only if the OEMRESOURCE symbol is defined before windows.h is included, are used for LoadImage.

The LoadIcon function returns a handle to the specified icon when the function is successful; otherwise, it returns (HICON)NULL.

Table 12.20: Summary of icon support functions

Function	Description
CopyIcon	Creates a copy of an icon.
CreateIcon	Creates an icon.
CreateIconFromResource	Creates an icon from a resource description of the bits of the icon.
CreateIconFromResourceEx	Creates an icon from a resource description of the bits of the icon.
CreateIconIndirect	Creates an icon from a description in memory.
DestroyIcon	Destroys an icon.
DrawIcon	Draws an icon.

Table 12.20: Summary of icon support functions

Function	Description
DrawIconEx	Draws an icon.
GetIconInfo	Retrieves an icon description from an icon handle.
LoadIcon	Loads an icon from a module's resources.
LoadImage	Loads an icon from a module's resources or from a .ico file.
LookupIconIdFromDirectory	Searches RT_GROUP_ICON resources for the best icon for the current display device. (This is used by LoadIcon and LoadImage to find an icon.)
LookupIconIdFromDirectoryEx	Searches RT_GROUP_ICON resources for the best icon for the current display device, given a desired size.
Static_GetIcon	API wrapper around an STM_GETICON message.
Static_SetIcon	API wrapper around an STM_SETICON message.
STM_GETICON	Retrieves the handle of an icon from an SS_ICON static control.
STM_GETIMAGE	Retrieves the handle of an icon from an SS_ICON static control.
STM_SETICON	Sets an icon handle in an SS_ICON static control.
STM_SETIMAGE	Sets an icon handle in an SS_ICON static control.

Displaying an Icon Resource

There are a number of ways you can display an icon. You can specify a handle to an icon when registering a window class, and Windows will display the icon when a window of that class is minimized. You can also override Windows's default behavior and display whatever you like when a window is minimized. This display could be an icon or an image drawn using the GDI drawing functions. You can also display an icon in a dialog box with very little effort. We look at each method.

Class Icons

A frequently displayed icon is the icon that represents the application when it is minimized. By default, Windows displays the icon specified as the class icon for a window when the window is minimized. Most of the example programs so far have specified the default application icon as the class icon. You specify the class icon by setting the hIcon field of the WNDCLASS structure used when registering the window class to the handle of the icon. Here is the statement we've been using in most of the examples:

```
wc.hIcon = LoadIcon (0, MAKEINTRESOURCE(resPoolID)) ;
```

The `LoadImage` Function

The `LoadIcon` function is quite limited in what it can accomplish. A more powerful function is the `LoadImage` function, which can be used to load cursors, icons, and bitmaps. In this chapter, we concentrate only on the `LoadImage` features for loading icons.

The `LoadImage` function is specified as

```
HANDLE LoadImage(HINSTANCE hinst, LPCTSTR name,
                 UINT type,
                 int cxDesired, int cyDesired,
                 UINT flags);
```

The `hinst` parameter specifies the module from which the cursor is to be loaded. For OEM cursors, this should be NULL.

The interpretation of the `name` parameter depends on the settings of the other parameters and is summarized in Table 12.21.

Table 12.21: Interpreting the name field of `LoadImage`

hinst	LR_LOADFROMFILE	Interpretation of name
not NULL	no	A pointer to a NUL-terminated string that is the name of the resource to load.
NULL	no	MAKEINTRESOURCE(OCR_*name*)
NULL	yes	The name of the file that contains the cursor. Win32 4.*x* only.

The `type` parameter for this discussion is always the symbol `IMAGE_CURSOR`. The `cxDesired` and `cyDesired` parameters indicate the desired size of the cursor. For a "normal" (32 × 32) icon, these values should either be 0 or set to the values returned by `GetSystemMetrics` for the codes `SM_CXICON` and `SM_CYICON` (these are the values that will be used if you specify 0). For any other size icon, you must specify explicit sizes. To get a "small icon" (16 × 16), you should explicitly use the `GetSystemMetrics` values for `SM_CXSMICON` and `SM_CYSMICON`. If more than one icon is stored under the same resource ID, you will get the one that matches your request.

The `flags` parameter specifies one or more of the flags shown in Table 12.22.

Table 12.22: Flag values for `LoadImage` of an icon

Flag	Meaning
LR_DEFAULTCOLOR	The default flag. It basically means "not LR_MONOCHROME".
LR_CREATEDIBSECTION	Not used with icons.

[4]Available only in the Win32 API level 4 and higher.

Table 12.22: Flag values for LoadImage of an icon

Flag	Meaning
LR_DEFAULTSIZE[4]	Forces the interpretation of a 0 cxDesired and cyDesired to be the SM_CXICON and SM_CYICON values. Otherwise, the size is the size of the resource. If the resource contains multiple images, the size is set to the size of the first image.
LR_LOADFROMFILE[4]	The name field names a .ico file used to create the icon.
LR_LOADMAP3DCOLORS[4]	Loads the image and replaces shades of gray with the following system color:

Gray Color	RGB	Replacement
Dark gray	128,128,128	COLOR_3DSHADOW
Gray	192,192,192	COLOR_3DFACE
Light gray	223,223,223	COLOR_3DLIGHT

Flag	Meaning
LR_LOADTRANSPARENT[4]	Replaces all instances of the color of the first pixel in the image by one of the following two values based on the presence of the LR_LOADMAP3DCOLORS flag:

LR_LOADMAP3DCOLORS	Replacement
no	COLOR_WINDOW
yes	COLOR_3DFACE

Flag	Meaning
LR_MONOCHROME[4]	Loads a monochrome version of the icon.
LR_SHARED[4]	Shares the image handle if the image is loaded more than once. Do not use for images of nonstandard sizes, images whose sizes may change after loading, or images loaded from a file.

[4]Available only in the Win32 API level 4 and higher.

Drawing Icons Yourself

You can render an icon into a DC at any time. The DrawIcon function is defined as

```
BOOL DrawIcon (HDC hdc, int xUL, int yUL, HICON hicon) ;
```

The DrawIcon function draws the icon specified by the hicon parameter on the device specified by the hdc parameter. The function draws the icon with its upper-left corner at the logical coordinates specified by the xUL and yUL parameters. It requires that the mapping mode of the specified device context be MM_TEXT.

You can also use the DrawIconEx function. This function allows you to draw either an icon or a cursor. The parameters for DrawIconEx are more elaborate than those for DrawIcon and are shown in Table 12.23.

Table 12.23: DrawIconEx parameters

```
BOOL DrawIconEx(HDC hdc, int xLeft, int yTop, HICON hicon,
                int Width, int Height, UINT frame,
                HBRUSH hbr, UINT flags);
```

Parameter	Description
HDC dc	The device context.
int xLeft	The logical coordinate of the left edge of the icon.
int yTop	The logical coordinate of the top edge of the icon.
HICON hicon	The handle to an icon, cursor, or animated cursor. Must have been loaded by Load-Image, LoadCursor, or LoadIcon.
int Width	The logical width of the icon or cursor. Ignored when DI_DEFAULTSIZE is specified in the flags parameter.
int Height	The logical height of the icon or cursor. Ignored when DI_DEFAULTSIZE is specified in the flags parameter.
UINT frame	Index of the desired frame in an animated cursor.
HBRUSH hbr	NULL or a valid brush handle. If a valid brush handle, this is used with an internally allocated off-screen bitmap. The background color is drawn into the off-screen bitmap, the icon or cursor is drawn into the bitmap, and then the bitmap is copied to the device with BitBlt. If NULL, the icon or cursor is drawn directly into the device context.
UINT flags	**One or more of the following flags:**

DI_COMPAT	Draws the cursor or icon using the system default image rather than the user-specified image.
DI_DEFAULTSIZE	Draws the cursor or icon in its default size, ignoring the Width and Height parameters.
DI_IMAGE	Performs the raster operation defined by the image part of the icon. The mask is ignored.
DI_MASK	Performs the raster operation defined by the mask part of the icon. The image part is ignored.
DI_NORMAL	DI_IMAGE | DI_MASK

In particular, note the ability to specify a background brush. This allows "flicker-free" drawing by causing the icon or cursor to be drawn in an off-screen bitmap and then block-transferred in its entirety to the destination. The mechanism of creating, copying, and freeing the off-screen bitmap is entirely handled within the DrawIconEx function.

The following code draws the icon specified by the hicon variable, centered in the client area of a window. The icon has been previously attached to the window using the SetProp function and the atom ID MY_ICON_PROPERTY.

```
void class_OnPaint(HWND hwnd)
   {
   HDC            hdc ;
   int            xUL;
   int            yUL ;
   HICON          hicon ;
   PAINTSTRUCT ps ;
   RECT           rect ;

   hdc = BeginPaint (hwnd, &ps) ;
   // Draw the icon centered in the window.

   hicon = GetProp(hwnd, MAKEINTRESOURCE ( MY_ICON_PROPERTY )) ;

   if(hicon != NULL)
       { /* draw the icon */
       GetClientRect (hwnd, &rect) ;
       xUL = (rect.right   - GetSystemMetrics (SM_CXICON)) / 2;
       yUL = (rect.bottom - GetSystemMetrics (SM_CYICON)) / 2;
       DrawIcon (hdc, xUL, yUL, hicon);
       } /* draw the icon */
   EndPaint (hwnd, &ps) ;
   }
```

If you pass to DrawIcon an HCURSOR instead of an HICON, you will get a badly rendered cursor image. In particular, the cursor image of the stock arrow cursor (IDC_ARROW) is rendered as a solid black arrow instead of the white outlined arrow that actually appears. If for some reason you need to render into a window an image that is a cursor, you can use one of several methods:

- If you are running with the Win32 4.x API, you can place a static control where you want the cursor image drawn and then send the STM_SETIMAGE message to the static control:

   ```
   SendMessage(hwnd, STM_SETIMAGE, IMAGE_CURSOR, hcursor)
   ```

- If you are running with the Win32 3.x API, need a method that is compatible across both platforms, or don't want to use a static control, use DrawIconEx[3]:

   ```
   void paintCursor(HDC hdc, HCURSOR cur, int x, int y)
      {
      HBRUSH br = GetStockBrush(WHITE_BRUSH);

      DrawIconEx(hdc, x, y, (HICON)cur, 0, 0, 0, br,
             DI_DEFAULTSIZE | DI_NORMAL);
      }
   ```

---

[3] With minor embellishments, this is the code that was used to draw the cursors that appear in Table 7.15. After rendering the code into a bitmap, the bitmap was placed on the Clipboard, from which it was pasted into this document.

Switching to a Different Icon

You can use icon resources and dynamically change the icon displayed by a window that is minimized. There are two completely different ways to do this; which you use depends on to which interface you are programming. To make life more complicated, the Win32 3.*x* and Win32 4.*x* methods are mutually incompatible. Win32 3.*x* does not support the only way that works in Win32 4.*x*, and Win32 4.*x* does not support the only way that works in Win32 3.*x*. So you will have to check the version of Windows you are running and handle the change appropriately.

Displaying Different Icons in Win32 3.*x*

To allow your program to change the display icon, you specify that the window has no class icon when you register the class. Do this by setting the hIcon field of the WNDCLASS structure to NULL when you register the class. When a window does not have a class icon, Windows sends a WM_PAINT message to the window whenever the icon needs to be drawn. When you receive the WM_PAINT message, you must first determine if the window is iconic. If it is, you use the DrawIcon function to draw the desired icon. For example, to change the icon used by a window, you can use the same code we previously used but use it in the normal WM_PAINT handler:

```
void class_OnPaint(HWND hwnd)
   {
   HDC          hdc ;
   int          xUL ;
   int          yUL ;
   PAINTSTRUCT  ps ;
   RECT         rect ;

   hdc = BeginPaint (hwnd, &ps) ;

   if(IsIconic(hwnd))
      { /* iconic window */
       HICON hicon ;
       // Draw the icon centered in the window.

       hicon = GetProp(hwnd, MAKEINTRESOURCE ( MY_ICON_PROPERTY )) ;
       if(hicon != NULL)
          { /* draw the icon */
           GetClientRect (hwnd, &rect) ;
           xUL = (rect.right  - GetSystemMetrics (SM_CXICON)) / 2;
           yUL = (rect.bottom - GetSystemMetrics (SM_CYICON)) / 2;
           DrawIcon (hdc, xUL, yUL, hicon);
           } /* draw the icon */
      } /* iconic window */
   else
      { /* normal window */
       // your normal window drawing code here
       } /* normal window */
   EndPaint (hwnd, &ps) ;
   }
```

Actually, under the 3.*x* interface you can draw *anything* in the space of the iconized window; for example, a scaled image of what was in the image. However, since this feature is no longer supported in the 4.*x* interface, we don't describe it here.

Displaying Different Icons in Win32 4.*x*

The Win32 4.*x* interface does not support drawing in an iconized window. Therefore, you can't draw an icon–or anything else–in an iconic window. However, you *can* change the icon that is displayed. If you send an STM_SETICON or STM_SETIMAGE message to a top-level window, the icon you set overrides the class icon specified for the window, and that icon will be displayed. You can use the Static_SetIcon function as well, although the name suggests it applies only to static controls. It really is just a wrapper around the STM_SETICON message.

If you want to change the little icon that appears at the top left of the caption bar, which is also the icon used in Win32 4.*x* for the minimized window, you have to create a 16 × 16 icon in the same icon resource as the icon you used to register the window class. When you supply the icon handle as part of the WNDCLASS structure, this small icon will be used for the caption bar. The icon on the top left of the caption bar will also be changed by the STM_SETICON or STM_SETIMAGE messages.

Displaying an Icon in a Dialog Box

You can easily display an icon in a dialog box. Creating an icon control is similar to creating a push button list box, and other types of controls. You include an ICON control statement in the body of the dialog box definition. An ICON control statement looks like the following:

ICON *text*, *ID*, *x*, *y*, *width*, *height*, [*style*]

The text field specifies the name of an icon resource defined somewhere else in the resource definition file. This is the name (or integer number) of the icon *resource*, not the name of the icon *file*. Earlier in the chapter, we defined a warning icon resource named "WarnIcon". The file containing the icon was called warnicon.ico. You could display that icon in a dialog box using the following statement:

ICON "WarnIcon", IDC_ICONDISPLAY, 10, 20, 1, 1

The *ID* parameter specifies the control ID of the icon control. Many times you can set this to an arbitrary value (we often use -1, also known as IDC_STATIC in the Microsoft developer environment) because icon controls are usually static controls. An icon control will generally never send a notification message to a dialog function unless you have selected the SS_NOTIFY style (see Chapter 8, page 532). By setting the control ID to a unique value, however, you can manipulate the icon control from your dialog code; for example, to show it, hide it, or cause it to display different icons.

The *x* and *y* parameters specify the upper-left corner of the control. As with the other dialog box controls, these coordinates are specified in dialog units. The *width* and *height* parameters are ignored. A static icon control automatically sizes itself. The optional style parameter can only be SS_ICON.

The method you must use to change the icon that is displayed by a static icon control varies depending on the version of Windows. You send the STM_SETICON message to associate an icon with a static icon control. The wParam parameter contains the handle of the icon to be displayed. The lParam parameter is not used and must be 0. If you need the flexibility of the Win32 4.x interface, you can send the STM_SETIMAGE message with the type IMAGE_ICON.

We prefer when possible to use the appropriate control APIs defined in windowsx.h to change the icon that is displayed by a static icon control–the Static_SetIcon control API, which is a wrapper around the STM_SETICON message. Unfortunately, there is no API wrapper for STM_SETIMAGE message.

We use the following code in the example program to display the predefined information icon as part of an **About...** dialog box. Here is a simple dialog box definition:

```
IDD_ABOUTBOX      DIALOG LOADONCALL MOVEABLE DISCARDABLE 40, 40, 144, 65
STYLE WS_CAPTION | DS_MODALFRAME
CAPTION "About Menus"
BEGIN
    CTEXT "Microsoft Windows", IDC_STATIC,  0,  6, 144,  8
    CTEXT "Menus Example Application", IDC_STATIC,  0, 18, 144,  8
    CTEXT "Copyright \251 Brent Rector, 1995", IDC_STATIC,  0, 30, 144,  8
    DEFPUSHBUTTON "OK", IDOK,  50, 45,  32, 14, WS_GROUP
    ICON  "", IDC_ICONDISPLAY, 114, 42,   1,  1
END
```

We don't specify an icon resource name on the ICON statement in the dialog box definition. When the dialog function receives an WM_INITDIALOG message, we send an STM_SETICON message to the static control specifying the icon to display. We use the control APIs to send the messages. Here is the relevant code:

```
BOOL about_OnInitDialog(HWND hdlg, HWND hfocus, LPARAM lParam)
    {
    HICON hicon;
    HWND hwndIcon;
    // Update the static icon control with
    // the new icon.
    hicon = LoadIcon (NULL, IDI_INFORMATION) ;
    hwndIcon = GetDlgItem (hdlg, IDC_ICONDISPLAY) ;
    Static_SetIcon (hwndIcon, hicon) ;
    return TRUE ;
    }
```

You might wonder if you can retrieve the handle of the icon currently displayed by a static icon control. Yes, you can. You can send an STM_GETICON message to a static icon control. The return value is the icon handle if successful and 0 if the static icon control has no associated icon or if an error occurred. If you are using the Win32 4.x API, you also can send the STM_GETIMAGE message to a static control. Here we use the windowsx.h API wrapper to send the STM_SETICON message. This function wrapper, for unknown reasons, requires a second parameter, which is never used, so we specify it as NULL:

```
HICON hicon ;

Static_GetIcon (GetDlgItem(hdlg, IDC_ICONDISPLAY), NULL);
```

You can be even more flexible. You can write a generic **About...** box, put it in a DLL, and have it send a message to its parent querying the icon. There is even a message that does this already: WM_QUERYDRAGICON.

Normally, this message is sent only to windows that have no default icon and it must return a "dragging cursor" or an icon. You can use this in your **About...** box code instead of using LoadIcon. You send this message to the parent requesting an icon to display. In this way, the **About...** box can be independent of your application.[4] You need to intercept this message in your parent and return an appropriate icon.

String Resources

We've been using string resources in all the example programs since we described the Skeleton program in Chapter 2, even though we've not emphasized their use. You should define the character strings used by a Windows application as string resources rather than as compile literals into the code and data. You define string resources in the application's resource definition file. Separating the character strings used by an application from the code provides a number of benefits. First, we look at how you define string resources and then we review some reasons for their use.

Defining a String Resource

You can include one or more STRINGTABLE statements in the resource definition file. The resource compiler creates one string table from all the STRINGTABLE statements, so string IDs must be unique across all string resources within a given executable or DLL.

A STRINGTABLE statement looks like the following:

```
STRINGTABLE [load-option] [memory-option]
BEGIN
stringID    string
    .
    .
    .
END
```

The optional *load-option* parameter has no meaning in Win32 and is ignored; it is recognized only for compatibility with resources created with earlier tooling. The optional *memory-option* parameter is DISCARDABLE. One or more string resource definitions are specified between the BEGIN and END keywords.

The *stringID* parameter specifies an integer value that identifies the string resource. The *string* parameter contains characters enclosed by double quotation marks. You can define a character in the string using a C-style octal or hex escape sequences. For example, you can insert an end-of-line character (line-feed) by specifying \012 or \x0A. We include a copyright symbol (©) in the **About...** dialog box text by specifying \251. Here are the string resource definitions from the Menus program. This program uses these string resources when registering its window class and when creating its main application window.

```
STRINGTABLE
BEGIN
    IDS_CLASSNAME       "MenuExampleClass"
    IDS_WINDOWTITLE     "Menu Example"
END
```

---

[4] For example, see Newcomer, J. M., "A Generic About... Box", cited in the "Further Reading" section.

You should try to assign string ID values consecutively (most resource editors take care of this for you). The resource compiler allocates one *string segment* for every 16 strings. (It groups the string resources by dividing the *stringID* value by 16 and putting all the strings whose quotient is the same value into the same string segment.) The strings associated with the string ID values 0 to 15 are placed into one segment, the strings associated with the string ID values 16 to 31 are placed into another segment, and so on. Windows loads the entire segment when a string resource is loaded. Assigning the string IDs 16 and 32 to two strings causes the resource compiler to allocate two segments, one for each string. When you load both strings, Windows allocates memory to hold both segments and must read each one from the executable file. Only one segment will be used when you use consecutive ID values within the same group. This is almost an irrelevant consideration in Win32, but it did affect performance in Win16.

You load a string when it's required by calling the **LoadString** function. The function call looks like this:

```
Chars = LoadString (hInstance, stringID, Buffer, BufferMax) ;
```

The **hInstance** parameter specifies the handle of the module that contains the string resources. Normally, you specify the application's instance handle as this parameter. You can load strings, as well as other resources, from a DLL by specifying the DLL's instance handle. The **stringID** parameter is the integer identifier defined as the string ID for the string in the resource definition file. The **Buffer** parameter is a pointer to the buffer that receives the string. The **BufferMax** parameter specifies the maximum number of characters (*not* bytes–think Unicode) to be copied to the buffer. This includes the terminating NUL character, so you generally specify the buffer size (in TCHAR units). The Menus program loads the window title from the string resources when drawing the program's icon:

```
Length = LoadString (hInst, IDS_WINDOWTITLE,
                     Buffer,
                     DIM (Buffer)) ;
```

Localization and Strings

Localization is the process of tailoring an application for a different linguistic/cultural market than the one for which it was originally designed. One aspect of localization is translating character strings from one language to another. Windows can run on many different computers, including computers that have other than English language or even Roman alphabet keyboards (for example, Greek, Cyrillic, Hebrew, and Arabic). Generally speaking, users prefer applications that operate in their native language. Translating messages displayed by an application becomes much simpler when all character strings are separated from the code and collected together in the resource definition file. You can produce localized versions of a well-designed application by translating the strings and recompiling the resource definition file. The code for the application need not be touched.

Of course, designing a program for ease of localization involves more than separating the strings from the code. Compared to English, many languages require more space for a string. Buffers allocated to hold resource strings must be large enough to hold a string that varies in length based on the language used. When you design a dialog box in English, you need to leave room for text to expand when the application is translated into other languages. When you allocate buffers for user input, you should be generous; don't assume that the answer will be a short English word from the known vocabulary you are working with. This applies also to buffers created to hold the strings returned from list boxes and combo boxes. Don't assume that the vocabulary is the English vocabulary; instead, allocate a buffer either very large, or based on the actual size of the string to be copied.

Short phrases in English (ten or fewer characters) often take up to three times as much space when translated into other languages. Slightly longer phrases in English (up to 20 characters) generally take twice as much space when translated into other languages. Relatively long phrases (around 50 characters) increase in size by 50% when translated from English. You need to plan for this expansion when writing a Windows application and allocate sufficiently large buffers.

You should use the `lstrcmp` and `lstrcmpi` functions to compare strings in a Windows program rather than the C functions `strcmp` and `strcmpi`. The C functions do not take into account the current language selected by the Windows user. The `lstrcmp` and `lstrcmpi` functions compare two strings, taking into account the ordering of the alphabet for the current language, diacritical marks, and a few other special cases. The `lstrcmpi` function ignores the effect of the case of the character on the string comparison, but effects caused by diacritical marks are still significant. The `lstrcmp` family of functions also compiles conditionally under the UNICODE definition (see Chapter 7). While the `tcscmp` family of functions also compiles conditionally under _UNICODE,[5] it does not handle the language selection issue, doing a straight character code comparison instead.

The current language also affects the definition of which character values are alphabetic, numeric, lowercase, and uppercase. You should use the `IsCharAlpha`, `IsCharAlphaNumeric`, `IsCharLower`, and `IsCharUpper` functions to test the corresponding attribute of a character.

We previously discussed the character case translation functions `CharLower`, `CharLowerBuff`, `CharUpper`, and `CharUpperBuff`. You should use these functions to translate a string from uppercase to lowercase or vice versa. These functions translate characters based on the currently installed language.

The code in a application must not make certain assumptions when using string resources. For example, your code shouldn't reuse one string in multiple contexts. Even though the same word or phrase might apply in English, other languages may use completely separate words and phrases, thus requiring multiple strings. You shouldn't convert a word from the singular to the plural by modifying it. The rules for plurals vary by language, and some languages have different words for the singular and plural. Each should be separately defined as a string resource. Don't construct sentences out of stock phrases you store in the string resources; for example, "Unable to", ["Open", "Read", "Write", "Close"], "file" (filename here) "error code" (error code number here) (text of error code here). In some other language, the word order in the sentence may change. The endings of the words may change depending on the context (so you can't use the same string you used for the **Open** menu item in the **File** menu). In general, you should use complete sentences with placeholders for the parameters.[6]

---

[5] Microsoft is not consistent in its naming conventions. For `windows.h` and other Windows-based files, the correct symbol to define is UNICODE. But for `tchar.h`, the correct symbol to define is _UNICODE.

[6] In my first effort at this, in a DOS application, back in 1986, I didn't know about these rules. The result was a large "resource file" that was extremely difficult to translate, especially to German where the verb is at the end of the sentence. In retrospect, I should have created an even *larger* "resource file" that followed these rules. *–jmn*

For many cases, a simple parameterized string handles most cases of localization. *Don't* substitute individual words in the string. However, such values as the error code and the filename can be substituted:

```
STRINGTABLE
  BEGIN
     IDS_FILE_ERROR_HEADING  "File operation error"
     IDS_OPEN_FAILURE        "Unable to open file %s, error code %d"
     IDS_CLOSE_FAILURE       "Unable to close file %s, error code %d"
     IDS_READ_FAILURE        "Unable to read file %s, error code %d"
END
```

You could use this string in a function very much like that shown in Listing 12.11. This illustrates a number of useful techniques.

You must also be careful not to re-use the same word in different senses. For example, in English the word "read" can be used in any of the following sentences:

- Unable to **read** file *name*

- Successfully **read** the filename

- **Read** the file now?

- **Read** these instructions carefully...

- Filename has been **read**.

In other languages, the forms of the verb can change based not only on whether it is an infinitive and whether it is the present, past, or future tense. An entirely different word might be used to indicate that the *computer* is going to read a file and a request that the *user* read instructions (some languages differentiate between personal and impersonal forms of actions, for example). Do not "optimize" your resource file by attempting to reuse words just because they are there; evaluate them in context. Unfortunately, the inability to actually annotate a resource file in most resource editors means that this critical information of which form is being used is often lost days or weeks after the decisions are made. You often end up putting the annotations in manually, and the resource editors often discard them. The tooling is not as sophisticated as it should be.

Listing 12.11: Using LoadString
```
int reportFileError(int ErrorMsg, LPTSTR filename, int ErrorCode)
    {
    TCHAR format[256];
    TCHAR message[550];
    TCHAR heading[256];
    LoadString(hInstance, ErrorMsg, format, charactersof(format));
    wsprintf(message, format, filename, ErrorCode);
    LoadString(hInstance, IDS_FILE_ERROR_HEADING,
               heading, DIM(heading));
    return MessageBox(GetFocus(), message, heading,
                            MB_RETRYCANCEL | MB_ICONERROR);
    }
```

Knowing that filenames are limited to 255 characters, we can allocate 256 characters to a buffer to hold the longest possible filename string. While there is no actual limit to string resources in Win32, there was once a limit of 256 characters to a string, and this limit is still almost always large enough (and because you have to specify the string length explicitly, you won't get an array overrun if the string is too long; it will be truncated). Allowing for the longest possible string we could generate by formatting, we get a maximum length of the resulting string as 255 + 256 + 10, so we just round up to a conveniently larger number (550) to hold the result. We load the string (in this case, we don't check for failure to load) for the error message, which is actually a format string we can pass to `wsprintf`. We then call `wsprintf` with this format string and the arguments that are the filename and internal error code. Next, we issue a `MessageBox` with the resulting string as the body of the message. But we also need a caption for the `MessageBox`! So we load the heading string from the resource file as well. The result of this function is the result of the `MessageBox`, that is, `IDRETRY` or `IDCANCEL`.

In fact, even resource strings are sometimes not adequate for formatting messages, which is why Win32 has introduced `Message` resources. We discuss these in the following section.

Although using string resources requires a bit more foresight and effort than including the string in the code as a literal, that effort is often repaid many times over during the maintenance of the application. When you get into the habit of using string resources, you'll find them a natural and convenient mechanism.

`FormatMessage` Function and `MESSAGETABLE` Resources

String resources are often insufficient for full internationalization of an application. For example, the word order in a sentence can change. Microsoft has addressed this need by providing two facilities: the `FormatMessage` function and the `MESSAGETABLE` resource.

Because `FormatMessage` can operate without using any `MESSAGETABLE` resources, in fact, by using ordinary `STRINGTABLE` resources, we look at it in some detail first. Then, we show how you can construct international applications using `MESSAGETABLE` resources.

The `FormatMessage` function allows you to take a set of variable text (or values in general) and a formatting string and place the variable text into the formatting string in positions that are unrelated to the order of the format requests. This is different from `wsprintf` or `sprintf`, where the formatting strings encode the parameter positions. For example, you might have a formatting string from the string table that said

`"%d warning(s), %d error(s)"`

so if you load this formatting string into a variable `fmt`, you must format it as

`wsprintf(msg, fmt, Warnings, Errors);`

However, for reasons that are completely contrived to illustrate this point, if we wanted to change the message to present the information in a different order, we couldn't do that using `wsprintf`. For example, the message cannot be changed to say

`"%d error(s), %d warning(s)"`

because the substitution is that the first parameter is the number of warnings and the second parameter is the number of errors, so the message would now be incorrect.

Using `FormatMessage`, however, we would use a formatting string

`"%1!d! warning(s), %2!d! error(s)"`

where the %1 indicates the first parameter is substituted and the %2 indicates the second parameter is substituted. The `!d!` indicates that the parameters are to be formatting using %d formatting. (For more details of the syntax, see Table 12.25; we don't want to take time right here to explain it.) The actual `FormatMessage` call would be the following:

```
int args[2];
#define MSGLEN 128
TCHAR msg[MSGLEN];
args[0] = Warnings;
args[1] = Errors;
FormatMessage(FORMAT_MESSAGE_FROM_STRING |
              FORMAT_MESSAGE_ARGUMENT_ARRAY,
              fmt, 0, 0,
              msg,
              DIM(msg),
              (va_list *)args);
```

We look at this simple `FormatMessage` call's argument list, without going into the complete argument list description. Table 12.24 describes the parameters we have used so far. You'll find the complete description in Table 12.26.

Table 12.24: Simple `FormatMessage` parameters

Parameter	Description
DWORD Flags	FORMAT_MESSAGE_FROM_STRING | FORMAT_MESSAGE_ARGUMENT_ARRAY
LPVOID source	LPTSTR reference to the format string.
DWORD messageID	Ignored.
DWORD languageID	Ignored.
LPTSTR buffer	Pointer to buffer for formatted result.
DWORD size	Number of characters in buffer.
va_list * args	Pointer to array of argument values.

The `Flags` parameter sets up some indicators that give meaning to the remaining parameters. For this simple example, we need only the two flag values shown.

The `source` pointer is a reference to the formatting string. The next two parameters, `messageID` and `languageID`, are ignored in this form of the call. We explain them later when we talk about the full `FormatMessage` call.

The `buffer` is a pointer to the place to put the formatted result. When we discuss the full `FormatMessage` call, you will see that you can ask `FormatMessage` itself to allocate a buffer that is large enough to hold the message. For now, assume that you have to reference a sufficiently large buffer. The `size` parameter tells how many characters are in the buffer. We've also discovered if the buffer isn't large enough to hold your formatted string,

`FormatMessage` leaves the buffer *unmodified* and returns a 0 value. You must check the return value; if you don't, you won't know what is in that buffer unless you actually set it to some initial value. If your buffer was too small, the `GetLastError` call will return the value `ERROR_INSUFFICIENT_BUFFER` (defined in `winerror.h`).

The last parameter must be cast to a "`va_list *`" type. Normally, you would have to include the `stdarg.h` file to get this symbol defined, but Windows defines it for you. You don't get any of the other variable-argument-list support, but we'll show how to do that later. Because we specified the `FORMAT_MESSAGE_ARGUMENT_ARRAY` flag, this isn't really a `va_list` reference anyway; just a pointer to an array of 32-bit values. Each value in the array represents one of the parameter substitutions that can be made, starting with %1 meaning element [0], %2 meaning element [1], and so on.

A Formatted `MessageBox` Function

You will probably find `FormatMessage`, even in its simpler form, a bit clumsy to use, so instead you can create a variable-argument function that formats and issues a message using a `MessageBox`. We do this in Listing 12.12, which illustrates several useful techniques.

Listing 12.12: A generic `FormatMessage`/`MessageBox` function

```
#include <STDARG.H>
// ...
// formatMessageBox
// Inputs:
//     HWND parent: Parent window of message box.
//     HINSTANCE hinst: Instance handle of resource
//                      file.  Ignored, and can be NULL,
//                      if fmt and caption are passed as
//                      a string
//     UINT flags: MB_ flags for MessageBox call
//     LPCTSTR caption: Caption for message box.  Can be
//                      either an LPCTSTR reference, or
//                      a MAKEINTRESOURCE reference.  If
//                      MAKEINTRESOURCE is used, must
//                      supply a non-NULL hinst if it
//                      is different from the instance
//                      handle of hwnd.
//     LPCTSTR fmt: Formatting string for message box
//                  body.  Can be either an LPCTSTR
//                  reference or a MAKEINTRESOURCE
//                  reference.  If MAKEINTRESOURCE is
//                  used, must supply a non-NULL hinst
//                  if different from instance handle
//                  of hwnd.
//         ...      The parameters to the formatting
//                  string.  There must be at least as
//                  many as required by the fmt string
// Effect:
//     Calls FormatMessage to format the body of the
//     MessageBox call, then displays the message box.
// Return value: int
//     The result of the MessageBox call.  Will be -1
//     if a resource could not load.
```

```
// Limitations:
//      If MAKEINTRESOURCE is used for both caption and
//      fmt, the resource strings must be in the same
//      module.
//
int __cdecl formatMessageBox(HWND parent,
                    HINSTANCE hinst,
                    UINT flags, LPCTSTR caption,
                    LPCTSTR fmt, ...)
    {
    LPTSTR result;
    TCHAR localfmt[256];
    TCHAR localcaption[256];
    va_list args; );
    DWORD fmtval;
    int retval;

    va_start(args, fmt);

    fmt = getString(hwnd, hinst, fmt, localfmt, DIM(localfmt));
    if(fmt == NULL)
        return -1;

    caption = getString(hwnd, hinst, caption, localcaption, DIM(localcaption));
    if(caption == NULL)
        return -1;

    fmtval = FormatMessage(FORMAT_MESSAGE_FROM_STRING |
                        FORMAT_MESSAGE_ALLOCATE_BUFFER,
                        fmt, // source string
                        0,   // ignored
                        0,   // ignored
                        (LPTSTR)&result,
                        0,
                        &args);
    if(fmtval != 0)
        { /* OK */
         retval = MessageBox(parent, result, caption,flags);
         LocalFree(result);
        } /* OK */
    else
        { /* error */
         DWORD err = GetLastError();
         FormatMessage(FORMAT_MESSAGE_ALLOCATE_BUFFER |
                        FORMAT_MESSAGE_FROM_SYSTEM,
                        NULL,
                        err, // error code
                        0,   // default language id
                        (LPTSTR)&result,
                        0,   // buffer initial size
                        NULL); // no arguments
        MessageBox(parent, result, caption, MB_ICONSTOP | MB_OK);
         retval = -1;
         LocalFree(result);
        } /* error */
    va_end(args);
    return retval;
    }
```

```
// getString
//   Inputs:
//        HWND hwnd: Window handle.  Used to
//                   GetWindowInstance if the hinst is
//                   needed and is NULL
//        HINSTANCE hinst: Instance handle of the
//                         resource from which we get
//                         the string
//        LPCTSTR str: A string pointer or a
//                     MAKEINTRESOURCE of a string ID
//        LPTSTR buffer: If str is a MAKEINTRESOURCE
//                       this is a reference to a buffer
//                       into which the string will be
//                       loaded.
//        int size: The length of buffer, in characters.
//
// RESULT: LPCTSTR
//        if str is a string pointer, then str
//        if str is a MAKEINTRESOURCE handle, then buffer
//        if any error, then NULL
// EFFECT:
//        If necessary, a string will be loaded and
//        placed in buffer

LPCTSTR getString(HWND hwnd, HINSTANCE hinst,
            LPCTSTR str, LPTSTR buffer, int size)
    {
    if(HIWORD(str) == 0)
        { /* MAKEINTRESOURCE ( str ) */
         if(hinst == NULL)
             hinst = GetWindowInstance(hwnd);
         if(LoadString(hinst, LOWORD(str), buffer, size) == 0)
             return NULL ;
         return buffer ;
        } /* MAKEINTRESOURCE ( fmt )*/
    else
        return str ;
    }
```

Observe that this is the first place we've actually tried to emulate what MAKEINTRESOURCE-accepting API functions do. The test is simple: If the high-order 16 bits of the "address" are 0, then we interpret the low-order 16 bits as a resource ID. Since the first 65,536 memory locations are not mapped into the process space, there will never be a valid pointer less than the value 0x00010000.

We allow the programmer who is using the formatMessageBox function to specify either string argument references or MAKEINTRESOURCE references, where the integer is the STRINGTABLE ID of a string. If the user specifies two literal strings, the instance parameter is not needed and we can pass in a NULL; otherwise, the LoadString operations need to know the instance handle of the resource. We *could* get this from the window handle by doing GetWindowInstance(hwnd), but this would limit us to having our message strings in the same file as our application. We want to allow for resource-only DLLs that hold localized messages, so we require an explicit instance handle. If this handle is NULL and it is needed, *then* we use the GetWindowInstance call. You can see this in the helper function getString. This function converts a "string reference" to a pointer to a string. If the reference is already a pointer, it simply returns that pointer;

otherwise, it loads the string from the resource file referenced by its hinst parameter. If this is successful, it returns the pointer to the buffer. Any error returns NULL.

The formatMessageBox function itself is a function of a variable number of parameters. Hence, we place the explicit __cdecl linkage declaration. This overrides any default linkage type the programmer may later set for the project, thereby guaranteeing that this function will always compile correctly as a function with a variable number of parameters. Only the __cdecl linkage supports this. The other linkage types, such as __stdcall and __fastcall (a Microsoft-specific extension supported by some other vendors as well), require a fixed number of arguments.

The va_start and va_end calls are required as part of the protocol for dealing with variable-length argument lists. These are defined in the include file stdarg.h, which you must include explicitly. Note that some environments, such as MFC, already include this as part of the standard include library. If you aren't programming in MFC, you may need to include it explicitly. The name used as the second argument to va_start is the name of the right-most parameter to the function, in our case, fmt.

Having obtained our formatting and caption strings, we now format the message using the FORMAT_MESSAGE_FROM_STRING flag. Note that we no longer use the FORMAT_MESSAGE_ARGUMENT_ARRAY flag because we have a real variable-length argument list pointer, a va_list; we pass a reference to its pointer, &args. The buffer and length parameters are somewhat different also. We are taking advantage of a feature we have not yet discussed: the automatic allocation of the buffer. When we specify the FORMAT_MESSAGE_ALLOCATE_BUFFER flag, instead of passing in a pointer to the result buffer, we pass in a pointer to a pointer to the result buffer (which we must cast to make the compiler happy). For the length, we pass in an initial suggested length (in characters), which we simply set to 0. If the formatting is successful, we pop up a message box and return its value; if the formatting is unsuccessful, we pop up a far less useful (to the user) message box that reports the failure of the FormatMessage call. The point of this implementation was to show you a use of GetLastError and the FORMAT_MESSAGE_FROM_SYSTEM option. When we pass in the FORMAT_MESSAGE_FROM_SYSTEM flag, the result buffer will contain the text of the system error in the default locale for which Windows was installed. So you don't need your own private message table for system errors.

We call the LocalFree function to release the buffer that FormatMessage allocated. The only difference between GlobalFree and LocalFree in Win32 is that LocalFree wants a pointer, while GlobalFree wants a handle. Writing LocalFree(mem) is a convenient substitute for writing GlobalFree(GlobalHandle(mem)).

The FormatMessage Format String

You can provide the format string to FormatMessage along with the FORMAT_MESSAGE_FROM_STRING flag. This string could be a literal or, as you saw in Listing 12.12, you can load the string from the STRINGTABLE resource. Another source, which we discuss beginning on page 936, is a MESSAGETABLE resource. The final source is the system message table, which you can access by specifying the FORMAT_MESSAGE_FROM_SYSTEM flag. The formatting string is a sequence of characters and escape sequences. Like the well-known sprintf function, the characters that are not part of an escape sequence are just transferred directly to the output buffer. Characters that are part of an escape sequence cause some action, either the insertion of a character or the formatting of an input parameter.

Table 12.25: FormatMessage format string

Format String	Description
%0	Message text line is not terminated by a newline sequence. This has otherwise no effect, and can appear anywhere in the formatting string.
%*n*	The *n*th input parameter is interpreted as a string and replaces the %*n*. This is the same as specifying %*n*!s!. The value *n* can be in the range 1..99.
%*n*!*sprintf*!	The *n*th input parameter is interpreted according to the *sprintf* formatting string and replaces the %*n*!*sprintf*! sequence. The * designator can be used for either width or precision or both; the (*n*+1)st input parameter is used for the first * and the (*n* + 2)nd input parameter is used for the second *. Floating-point specifiers (e, E, f, and g) are not supported.
%%	A % is placed in the formatted message text.
%n	A hard line break is placed in the formatted message text.
%*space*	A space is placed in the formatted message text.
%.	A single period is placed in the formatted message text.
%!	An exclamation point is placed in the formatted message text. This can be used to insert an exclamation point after an insertion without any confusion with interpreting the exclamation point as the start of a formatting specification.

The full FormatMessage specification

The FormatMessage function is more powerful than being simply a "fancy sprintf" replacement. In particular, it gives you access to a resource called a *message table* resource. This resource can contain messages keyed not only by a message ID, but also by a severity ID, an application code, and a language. And, in a very handy feature, it can deliver to you the actual localized text of system error messages. If you ever used the strerror function in C to obtain a string message for a file error code, you know how useful this can be in delivering a meaningful error message to the user. But the problem with strerror was that the strings were compiled in; if you shipped the product to Germany, France, Italy, or Japan, the user had no choice but to see the messages in English. *All* of the error codes returned by GetLastError have strings, but the strings are determined by Win32 and are based on whatever localization is currently in effect. So the same executable image, *without even changing resource definitions*, will return, for any system error, a French message for a French-speaking Canadian and an English message for an English-speaking Canadian who may even be sharing the same Win32 machine. This is done based on their current localization as set by the Control Panel or by the application itself. (An example might be a shared terminal in a bank. The banking application might have an icon for each supported language. Whoever steps up to it clicks the icon and gets the preferred language. And error messages from the system, formatted using `FormatMessage` and `FORMAT_MESSAGE_FROM_SYSTEM`, will come out in the current language).

The `FormatMessage` function allows you to extend this flexibility to your own application, while maintaining a single "database" of messages. Rather than have three, or seven, or seventeen string resource files (plus the inevitable danger of having them get out-of-sync), you have one message table file that contains, for each message, its text in each of the languages you support. When you run the message table compiler, you will get a warning message if you forgot to add the text in one of the languages.

From this message file, you can get a header file that your program uses. The program associates your names for the messages with an integer code. You also get a set of binary message files, one for each supported language, that can be included in your resource file, as well as several resource files compiled into one resource or several resource files compiled into separate resource-only DLLs.

Table 12.26 describes all of the parameters of the `FormatMessage` function. First, we look at how `FormatMessage` can access this table and then we look at how to construct a message table.

Table 12.26: Full `FormatMessage` parameters

Parameter	Description
DWORD Flags	The high-order bits are used as flags to control the interpretation of the remaining parameters. The flags may be combined using the OR operation.
	FORMAT_MESSAGE_ALLOCATE_BUFFER
	Changes the interpretation of the `buffer` and `size` parameters. If this flag is present, `buffer` is treated as a pointer to an LPTSTR, which is set to point to the allocated storage upon successful completion. You must call `LocalFree` to free up this storage. The `size` parameter is treated as an initial estimate of the space required (it may be 0). If this flag is absent, the `buffer` parameter is treated as a pointer to the actual storage to be filled. The `size` parameter is the number of *bytes* available in the buffer (Unicode programmers take note!).
	FORMAT_MESSAGE_ARGUMENT_ARRAY
	Changes the interpretation of the `args` parameter. If this flag is present, `args` is treated as a pointer to a set of 32-bit values. If this flag is absent, `args` is treated as a `va_list` pointer.
	FORMAT_MESSAGE_IGNORE_INSERTS
	If this flag is present, the `args` parameter is ignored and the message string is copied uninterpreted to the buffer. This allows you to retrieve the formatting string without actually doing any formatting.
	FORMAT_MESSAGE_FROM_STRING
	If this flag is present, the `messageID` and `languageID` parameters are ignored, and the `source` parameter is a pointer to the NUL-terminated formatting string.

Table 12.26: Full FormatMessage parameters

Parameter	Description
	FORMAT_MESSAGE_FROM_HMODULE If this flag is present, the source parameter is a module handle for the message-table resources. If source is NULL, the current process application file's resources are used.
	FORMAT_MESSAGE_FROM_SYSTEM If this flag is present, the function will search the system message table. This flag may be specified with the FORMAT_MESSAGE_FROM_HMODULE flag. If neither the FORMAT_MESSAGE_FROM_HMODULE nor FORMAT_MESSAGE_FROM_STRING flags is specified, but this flag is specified, the function ignores the source parameter and just checks the system message table.
	The low-order 8 bits of the flags are interpreted as a maximum line length:
	0 No width restrictions. Only the line breaks encoded in the message string will be set in the output buffer.
	1 to 254 Line breaks in the message string are ignored. The line is formatted with line breaks inserted as necessary to maintain the line length, and only hard line breaks (%n) are retained.
	FORMAT_MESSAGE_MAX_WIDTH_MASK Line breaks in the message string are ignored. Hard line breaks are retained. No additional line breaks are generated.
LPVOID source	Source reference. Interpretation depends on the flags.
	FORMAT_MESSAGE_FROM_STRING LPCTSTR string pointer.
	FORMAT_MESSAGE_FROM_HMODULE Module handle for message resources.
DWORD messageID	A 32-bit message identifier. Ignored if the flags contain FORMAT_MESSAGE_FROM_STRING.
DWORD languageID	A 32-bit language ID. See Chapter 9, page 637. Ignored if the flags contain FORMAT_MESSAGE_FROM_STRING.
LPTSTR buffer	The interpretation of this depends on the presence of the FORMAT_MESSAGE_ALLOCATE_BUFFER flag. If the flag is present, this is an LPTSTR * pointer. The pointer it references will be set to point to the allocated buffer. If the flag is absent, this is an LPTSTR to the actual buffer.

Table 12.26: Full FormatMessage parameters

Parameter	Description
DWORD size	The interpretation of this depends on the presence of the FORMAT_MESSAGE_ALLOCATE_BUFFER flag. If the flag is present, this is a specification of the initial allocation to use (it can be 0). If the flag is absent, it is the number of characters available in the buffer.
va_list * args	The interpretation of this depends on the presence of the FORMAT_MESSAGE_ARGUMENT_ARRAY flag. If the flag is present, this is a pointer to an array of 32-bit argument values. If the flag is absent, this is a pointer to a va_list.

The flags of interest here are the FORMAT_MESSAGE_FROM_SYSTEM and FORMAT_MESSAGE_FROM_HMODULE. If the FORMAT_MESSAGE_FROM_HMODULE flag is set, then the source parameter is an LPVOID cast of a module handle. This handle could be either your own application's instance handle or the instance handle of a DLL (typically a resource-only DLL, but it might be a localization DLL that has locale-specific code as well). The 32-bit messageID and the 32-bit languageID select the message from the table using the correct language. For the language, you can specify a locale ID, such as LOCALE_USER_DEFAULT. The effect is to format the message according to the formatting string and the parameters.

If the FORMAT_MESSAGE_FROM_SYSTEM flag is present and the message is not found in your message resource (or you don't specify the FORMAT_MESSAGE_FROM_HMODULE flag at all), then FormatMessage will search the system message table for the messageID code and otherwise proceed as expected, honoring the other flags such as FORMAT_MESSAGE_ALLOCATE_BUFFER.

If you just want to retrieve the message text string without actually doing a substitution (for example, you may pass it on later to FormatMessage using the FORMAT_MESSAGE_FROM_STRING flag), you can include the FORMAT_MESSAGE_IGNORE_INSERTS flag. In this case, the argument pointer can be NULL because it is ignored.

Having shown you how to access the message table, we next look at how to construct one.

The MESSAGETABLE Resource

You can insert into your resource file a special resource that can be used by the FormatMessage function. This is a MESSAGETABLE resource. A MESSAGETABLE statement in the resource file names a file that is a binary MESSAGETABLE file. The binary file is created by the *Message Compiler*, a tool provided as part of the Windows development environment. The Message Compiler takes a message description file and produces the binary file. Typically, you place the MESSAGETABLE resource in a resource-only DLL.

The MESSAGETABLE source file is described in Table 12.27. There is an initial *header section* that establishes some overall parameters for the message format. For example, you could change the keywords for severity to be other strings than the default set shown. This would be convenient if your preferred language of discourse was not English. You could also add language codes for other languages. There are two sources for these codes, and they are inconsistent. One is the file winnls.h (*National Language Support*). This file defines the constant 1 to represent the United States (CTRY_UNITED_STATES) (this is suggestive of the source of the default value English assumed by the `LanguageNames` keyword shown in Table 12.27, but this is inconsistent with nearly all other usage in Windows). Windows nearly everywhere expects *localeIDs,* which are defined by the symbols in `winnt.h`, which we already listed in detail in Chapter 9 (Table 9.13, page 638). Unfortunately, the message compiler does not support a `#include` directive or a `#define` directive, so you must look up the values in `winnt.h` and put them explicitly in the declaration.

Table 12.27: Message text file format

Keyword/Value	Description
Header Section	
`MessageIdTypedef=type`	Sets the `typedef` name that is used in a cast operation for each message code.
`SeverityNames=(name=value)`	Defines a set of names used for the `Severity` keyword and associates a value with each name. The only allowable values are 0, 1, 2, and 3. The default set of names, if you don't declare any, is as follows:

Success	0x0
Informational	0x1
Warning	0x2
Error	0x3

Keyword/Value	Description
`FacilityNames=(name=value)`	Defines a set of names used for the `Facility` keyword and associates a value with each name:

System	0x0FF
Application	0xFFF

Keyword/Value	Description
`LanguageNames=(name=value:filename)`	Defines a set of names used for the `Language` keyword and associates a value and a filename. The filename is used to generate the output file for that language:

English	English=1:MSG00001

Keyword/Value	Description
`OutputBase=number`	Sets the output radix for the message constants put in the include file. Possible values are 10 and 16.
Message Section	
`MessageId=value` `MessageId=+value`	This is the first declaration in any message definition. The value is optional; if it isn't specified, the value is one higher than the preceding `MessageId` for the same facility. If the value is preceded by a + the value is the sum of the preceding `MessageId` for the same facility and the number following the +. The `MessageID` must fit in 16 bits.

Table 12.27: Message text file format

Keyword/Value	Description
`Severity=severityname`	The severity of the message, using one of the names defined in the header or the default names. This field is optional and defaults to the last explicit value specified, initially `Success`.
`Facility=facilityname`	The facility code of the message, using one of the names defined in the header or the default names. This field is optional and defaults to the last explicit value specified, initially `Application`.
`SymbolicName=name`	The symbolic name associates a named constant with the message code. This named constant is placed in the header file.
`OutputBase=number`	The output base for the constant; values permitted are 10 and 16.

Following each message definition is a sequence of language-specific lines. A message can span several lines and contain embedded whitespace, new lines, and blank lines.

`Language=languagename`	One of the language names defined in the header.
`message text`	Any number of message lines. The contents include all the formatting codes specified in Table 12.25.
`.`	A line containing exactly one character: a period. No whitespace can surround this period. If you want a line that starts with a period, use the `%.` escape sequence.

The format of a message code is shown in Figure 12.19. The message compiler generates a header file that contains the symbolic names for each error code. Each error code that has a `SymbolicName` field generates a declaration of this form:

```
#define name ((type)0xnnnnnnnn)// with MessageIdTypedef
#define name 0xnnnnnnnn         // no MessageIdTypedef
```

The `type` is what is declared in the `MessageIdTypedef` declaration in the header. If there is no declaration, no type casting is done. The message code is used in the `messageID` parameter of the `FormatMessage` call when the `FORMAT_MESSAGE_FROM_HMODULE` flag and/or the `FORMAT_MESSAGE_FROM_SYSTEM` flag is used.

Once the message file is created, it is run through the Message Compiler `MC`. The output is a header file that is used by your application to get the symbolic codes. The output also is a series of binary files that can be named with a `MESSAGETABLE` statement:

```
id MESSAGETABLE filename
```

3 3	2	2	2		1	1	
1 0	9	8	7		6	5	0
Sev	C	R	Facility			Code	

Sev	Severity code
	00 Success
	01 Informational
	10 Warning
	11 Error
C	Customer code flag: 0 for Microsoft, 1 for customer
R	Reserved, must be 0
Facility	Facility code
Code	The message id for the facility

Figure 12.19: Message code format

The `.mc` file should have a name that is unique within your project. Don't, for example, use a name that corresponds to an existing `.rc` or `.h` file in your project; if you do, the files will be overwritten when you run the MC compiler.

One output from the MC compiler is an `.rc` file that you can include in your resource script (usually by putting the `#include` statement in explicitly using the environment tools). This will include all the languages in your resource file.

Another option is to create resource-only DLLs for each of the languages. You create a `.rc` file that contains only the MESSAGETABLE declaration:

```
1 MESSAGETABLE filename.BIN
```

where `filename` is the filename specified in the `LanguageNames` section of the header. Your DLL will have a single procedure, shown in Listing 12.13. The `#pragma` shown suppresses the compiler warnings about unreferenced parameters. This `#pragma` is for the Microsoft C compilers; other compilers may have a different way of disabling this message.

Listing 12.13: Resource-only DLL source code
```
#include <windows.h>
#pragma warning(disable:4100)
BOOL WINAPI DllEntryPoint(HINSTANCE hInstance,
```

```
                            DWORD reason,
                            LPVOID reserved)
    {
    return TRUE;
    }
```

The entry point to a DLL in Win16 was called `LibMain`. Because the parameters are quite different in Win32, a different naming convention was chosen. See Chapter 11.

You build a language-specific DLL by compiling the code shown in Listing 12.13, compiling a resource file with the `MESSAGETABLE` in it (plus any other language-specific resources, if appropriate), and building an executable of the two. You can load a language-specific DLL by calling the `LoadLibrary` function, specifying the name of the DLL. The handle returned from the `LoadLibrary` function is the handle that you use as the `source` parameter in the `FormatMessage` function with the `FORMAT_MESSAGE_FROM_HMODULE` flag set. To switch languages, you call `LoadLibrary` again. You must call `FreeLibrary` on a library that you've loaded. An example of a function that handles this is shown in Listing 12.14. What you might do is create a menu dynamically whose menu item data was the 32-bit language identifier. Then if any language were chosen, you would call `loadNewLanguage` with the associated language identifier; it would return `TRUE` if it succeeded and `FALSE` if it failed. If it succeeded, it would have changed the `langlib` variable, which you would pass in to `FormatMessage` as the module handle.

Listing 12.14: Using `LoadLibrary` for resource-only DLLs

```
HINSTANCE langlib = NULL;

BOOL loadNewLanguage(LCID lcid)
    {
    TCHAR lang[4];
    TCHAR filename[256];
    HINSTANCE hmodule;

    GetLocaleInfo(lcid, LOCALE_SABBREVLANGNAME, lang, DIM(lang) );
    lang[3] = _T('\0');
    wsprintf(filename, _T("MyApp%s"), lang);
    hmodule = LoadLibrary(filename);
    if( hmodule == NULL)
        return FALSE;
    if(langlib != NULL)
        FreeLibrary(langlib);
    langlib = hmodule;
    return TRUE;
    }
```

The `GetLocaleInfo` function with the option `LOCALE_SABBREVLANGNAME` returns a three-character locale abbreviation. This abbreviation is the two-character abbreviation specified by the ISO 639 language standard plus a third letter that indicates the sublanguage. For example, for U. S. English the abbreviation string is "ENU", so this code will try to load the file named `MyAppENU`. DLL. If it fails, as indicated by a return value less than HINSTANCE_ERROR, it returns FALSE. Otherwise, it frees the currently loaded library (if any) and sets the library to be the newly loaded library and then returns TRUE.

To create individual language DLLs, you can look at the output from your MC run. For example, if the header contains the declaration

```
LanguageNames=(English=9:MSGENG
               German=7:MSGGERM
               Spanish=0x0a:MSGSPAN
               French=0x0c:MSGFRENCH)
```

then you will get in the output directory the files `msgeng.bin`, `msggerm.bin`, `msgspan.bin`, and `Nmsgfrench.bin`. You will also get a file with the same name as your input file and the extension `.rc` that contains the following lines:

```
LANGUAGE 0xa,0x0
1 11 MSGSPAN.bin
LANGUAGE 0x7,0x0
1 11 MSGGERM.bin
LANGUAGE 0xc,0x0
1 11 MSGFRENCH.bin
LANGUAGE 0x9,0x0
1 11 MSGENG.bin
```

This creates four resources of type 11 (the code for an RT_MESSAGETABLE resource) whose contents are defined by the filenames given. This is designed to incorporate all your language strings into a single resource, which may not be what you want (or you wouldn't be trying to create individual DLLs). What you would have to do is extract each pair of lines (the LANGUAGE line and the line that follows it) and place them in separate resource files, which would then be compiled and linked into each of the DLLs.

Further Reading

If you are interested in localization issues, following are some books we recommend. Reviews are by Joseph M. Newcomer, who has used all of them except *The Unicode Standard, Volume 2:*

Harbison, Samuel P. and Steele, Jr., Guy L., *C: A Reference Manual, Fourth edition*, Prentice-Hall, 1995.

> This is one of the best reference works I've found for the C language.[7] One of its charms is that it is not afraid to point out the Dark Corners of C semantics, and indicate where different compilers have sometimes made different choices about how to implement them. The latest edition includes the ISO C Amendment 1 (1994), which covers facilities for writing portable international programs. I particularly recommend the discussion of extended character sets in Chapter 12. It also covers issues of writing C code compatible with both C and C++.

---

[7] The fact that both authors are friends of mine is not a factor in this evaluation, but public disclosure is important. I now own all four editions, and it is one of the books I keep at hand near the computer.

Kano, Nadine, *Developing International Software for Windows 95 and Windows NT*, Microsoft Press, 1995. ISBN 1-55615-840-8.

> This is *the* single most important reference you will need. Although it does not go into as much background detail in some areas as O'Donnell's book, it tells you a lot (well, almost everything) about what you need to know to internationalize in Windows. Extensive appendices show keyboard layouts, formatting options for locale IDs, and other exquisite detail. There is no other single source for all this information.

Newcomer, Joseph M., "A Generic About... Box", *Dr. Dobb's Sourcebook: Windows Programming* #218, Fall 1994.

> Many of of the techniques of this article are found in our `Template` application's **About...** box.

O'Donnell, Sandra Martin, *Programming for the World: A Guide to Internationalization*, Prentice-Hall, 1994. ISBN 0-13-722190-8.

> Although this book is primarily Unix-centric and specifies some solutions in terms of Unix code, it is an excellent introduction to the issues of internationalization. It is a good companion volume to Kano's book, as it often gives more background and motivation for many issues.

The Unicode Consortium, *The Unicode Standard: Worldwide Character Encoding, Version 1.0, Vol. 1*, Addison-Wesley, 1991. ISBN 0-201-56788-1.

The Unicode Consortium, *The Unicode Standard: Worldwide Character Encoding, Version 1.0, Vol. 2*, Addison-Wesley, 1992. ISBN 0-201-60845-6.

> More detail than you could ever need on languages you've never heard of, but for those languages you need, this is the definitive and indispensable reference for Unicode. This documentation is thorough. In addition to the background and technical descriptions of how concepts like diacritical marks are handled, each glyph is shown in its character map and each language is shown in its entirety. Volume 1 includes Latin, Cyrillic, Greek, Hebrew, and Arabic as well as other alphabets used across Europe, Africa, and India. Volume 2 covers the unified character codes for Chinese, Japanese, and Korean ideographs.

Chapter

13 Printing

Sooner or later you'll want to print information from a Windows application. In many ways, printing a page on a printer is very similar to painting a window on the display. You determine the available colors and the size of the printer's display surface. You create, rather than borrow, a device context (DC) for the printer. And you print text and graphics using the same GDI functions used to draw on the display.

However, in a few ways, printing on a printer is quite different from drawing on the display. Multiple applications may wish to print concurrently, but only one can use the printer at a time. Output from different applications must be collected into separate documents. A printer prints on one page at a time. Your application must indicate when it is done drawing on one page and ready to begin drawing on the next page. This step is unnecessary when drawing on the video display.

Although we've tried to provide example programs that paint the screen efficiently, it hasn't dominated the design of an application. Printers are extremely slow devices in comparison to video displays. Because a printing operation can take a considerable amount of time, you should give the user a method to halt a lengthy printing operation.

The first topic in this chapter is an overview of the printing process for a Windows application. Programming for printing is one of the more complex tasks programmers face when writing Windows applications. Getting the actual printing done isn't so hard. However, along with printing your output, you must do the following:

- Properly perform the initialization required before you can print.

- Decide at runtime the capabilities of the installed device driver for the desired printer and tailor your printing logic to the driver's capabilities.

- Handle the assorted errors that can occur.

- Check whether the user has requested printing to be canceled.

The overview provides you with a high-level conceptual view of the Windows printing process. After we present the overview, we examine each of the steps of the printing process in detail and show you how to implement the steps in a Windows application.

In the detailed examination, we explain how to print using the default printer on a Windows system. Because some users may have more than one printer, we also explain how to print using any installed printer. Once you decide which printer to use, you can create a DC for the printer.

You draw on the surface of a printer DC just as you draw on the surface of a display context for the system display.

Throughout this chapter, we continually and deliberately use the phrase "draw a page" rather than "print a page". We do this for two reasons. First, the verb *print* still connotes alphanumeric output. It sounds rather strange to say that you are printing an ellipse that is filled with a pattern brush in a specified color. Historically, we've always printed text and drawn figures. Considering the numerous fonts that can be available on a Windows system, much text output also appears drawn rather than printed.

Second, Windows considers the printer's display surface as randomly accessible. That is, you can draw anywhere on a page at any time. You don't need to draw the top line first, followed by the second line, and so on, to the bottom of the page. If you like, you can draw the page from the bottom up, left to right, right to left, or in any other order. The surface of the printer DC is the printable area of a single page on the associated printer. It is not uncommon to draw the headers and footers first and then fill in the "body" later. It also is not uncommon when printing "electronic forms" to draw the entire form (headings, boxes, borders, decorations, and the like) as part of the page initialization and then draw the text on top of the fixed form. Each page is effectively a completely random-access space on which you draw. However, like drawing on the screen, those pieces drawn later will usually "overwrite" the earlier pieces. Sometimes this means that you draw the "body text" first and then lay down on top of this text the borders, outlines, headers, footers, and other "decorations".

Some printers (such as laser printers) can hold an entire page in memory and can accept output for the page in any order. Many printers, however, cannot accept output in any order except the traditional top to bottom order. Because Windows permits you to draw a page in any order, yet some printers require output to the printer to be in a specific order, Windows shoulders the burden of converting and reordering your drawing requests as necessary. This means that the drawing requests you make aren't necessarily what the printer receives, and the printer probably won't receive the requests in the order you make them. Thus there is a distinct difference between your drawing a page and the printer's printing the page.

We also created a DLL that you can incorporate into your own applications. It allows you to specify callbacks for formatting headings, footings, and each "line" of output. If you want to draw the entire page yourself (for example, if "lines" aren't a reasonable model), then you can treat the entire page as a single "line". The DLL provides for all the necessary setup of the printing task after you have used the common setup dialogs to choose a printer and a page setup.

Printing changed considerably beginning with Windows version 3.1. Setting up printing in the older versions of Windows required coding that resembled magic; you copied the arcane code and hoped it worked. Win32 has rendered almost all of this code obsolete. In fact, most of it won't even work. This won't impact you much in writing new code. But if you are porting an older program, you should plan on rewriting the printing setup "from scratch" and largely ignore the printer initialization code that was there. The new code is far simpler, easier to maintain, and will very probably work correctly the first time you compile it.

An Overview of the Printing Process

An application must complete a number of steps to print in the Windows environment. You must select a printer. You must obtain a DC for the printer. You must open and close the *document* and for each page you must open and close each *page*. There are some "housekeeping" functions that allow you to terminate the document and that allow you to tell Windows how to query the user for cancellation. All of these functions are summarized in Table 13.1. In the discussion that follows, you should refer to Figure 13.1 to see how each component relates to the printing process. When appropriate, you may provide a menu item for **Page Setup...** that allows the user to choose page margins, paper size, and other such features for the printer. If you do not provide this option or the user has not called it, you should assume some defaults appropriate to your application. For more on page setup, see "The Page Setup Dialog" starting on page 1015.

You must decide whether the application should print using the current printer or give the user the ability to select one of the installed printers. You use the `PrintDlg` function to obtain a DC for the printer. The sections in this chapter entitled "Using the Default Printer" (page 950) and "Using Any Installed Printer" (page 951) discuss this task in more detail.

After you create a DC for a printer, you establish an *abort function* by calling the `SetAbortProc` function. You specify the printer DC handle and the address of a function:

```
int SetAbortProc (HDC hdc,
ABORTPROC AbortFunc) ;
```

The `SetAbortProc` function does not, as you might think, set (establish) an abort procedure that Windows calls when it wants to abort a print operation. Instead, GDI periodically calls this "abort" function to *ask* your application if it wishes to abort the current print request. Technically, it's not mandatory for a Windows printing application to specify an abort function. For all practical purposes, however, you must *always* use an

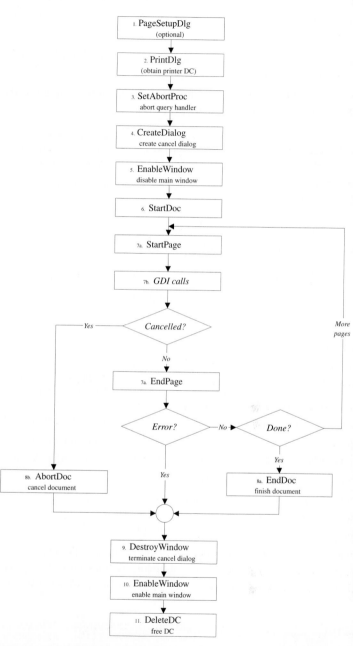

Figure 13.1: Printing logic

abort function because some printer drivers require it and will fail without it. We discuss the abort function in the sections "Allowing Other Program Interactions while Printing" (page 975) and "The Abort Function" (page 976).

At this point, you normally create a modeless dialog box used to interact with the user, such as to tell the user what page is printing and what device it is printing on and to accept a cancellation request from the user. Next, you signal the beginning of a new document by calling the StartDoc function. You specify the printer DC handle and a pointer to a DOCINFO structure.

Under Win16, there was a particular function, Escape, that was used to invoke many of the printing operations, such as setting the abort procedure, starting a new page, and ending the document. These have all been super-seded by API functions with similar names. The Escape mechanism is supported in Win32 for backward com-patibility, but it should not be used for any new code. You should try to replace it in any code you are porting. We do not discuss the Escape function in this book.

Table 13.1: Document printing and setup functions

Function	Description
AbortDoc	Terminates a print job.
EndDoc	Ends a print job.
EndPage	Ends a page.
PageSetupDlg	Allows the user to configure page setup, such as choosing margin sizes, paper orien-tation, paper size, and the like. Optional.
PrintDlg	Allows the user to set up and configure printing options. Its most important usage is to obtain a DC for printing.
SetAbortProc	Establishes a procedure that is called to check for user termination of the printing process.
StartDoc	Starts a print job.
StartPage	Notifies the printer driver to prepare to receive output for a new page.
ResetDC	Updates a DC, thereby allowing new functionality that was not supported by any es-cape function under previous versions of Windows. For example, you can use this function to change orientation or paper bins in the middle of a print job.

There are a number of other printer-related APIs you will see, such as OpenPrinter, ClosePrinter, WaitForPrinterChange, StartDocPrinter, EndDocPrinter, StartPagePrinter, and EndPagePrinter. These functions are concerned with controlling, administering, and spooling to network printers and are of pri-mary interest to those writing network printing services. They do not actually have anything to do with drawing pages.

```
DOCINFO di ;

StartDoc (hdc, &di) ;
```

The DOCINFO structure looks like this:

```
typedef struct {
    int         cbSize ;
    LPCSTR      lpszDocName ;
    LPCSTR      lpszOutput ;
} DOCINFO ;
```

The cbSize field of the DOCINFO structure must be initialized to the size of the structure. The lpszDocName field points to a NUL-terminated string that specifies the name of the document. This string must not be longer than 32 characters including the terminating NUL character. You can set the lpszOutput field to point to a NUL-terminated string that specifies the name of an output file to which Windows redirects the printer output. Normally, you set this field to NULL, thereby sending the output to the device associated with the specified DC.

The StartDoc function call initializes the printer device driver and invokes whatever other operations your system may require to initialize printing. Internally, Windows NT and Windows 95 operate somewhat differently, and the configuration of your network, including the existence of a local printer and location of printer servers, additionally complicate a detailed discussion. In fact, one of the nicer features of the Windows printer abstraction is that you don't *have* to know exactly what happens inside the operating system to deal with setting up a printing request!

The name you specify in the DOCINFO structure usually appears in the Print Manager as the title of the document. It may also appear on a "break page" if your printing environment uses these to separate output on shared printers.

Once you've signaled the beginning of a document, you must call the StartPage function at the beginning of each page. The StartPage function prepares the printer driver to accept data and disables changes to the printer's device mode (made by calling the ResetDC function). Changes to the DC's *mode* remain disabled until you call the EndPage function. Hence you cannot change device modes, such as the paper orientation, printer input tray, or paper size, in the midst of drawing a page. You can change printer device modes only at page boundaries. You can change other properties of the DC, such as the mapping mode, background color, and origin.

Now you can draw the page of the document using the appropriate GDI output functions (TextOut, Rectangle, and so on). The output produced by these GDI functions may or may not be sent to the printer at this time, but usually it is sent later. Windows may need to record an application's GDI function calls in order to print the page properly.

After you finish drawing the first page, you call the EndPage function to signal the device that you are done. This signals the end of one page and the beginning of a new page. You always call the EndPage function at the end of a page. You repeat this process of drawing a page (via GDI output operations on a printer DC) and calling the EndPage function until you've printed all pages. You then issue the EndDoc function call to signal the end of the document. When you have completed printing, you call `DestroyWindow` to delete the modeless dialog box that was presented to the user.

This is the basic outline for a Windows printing application. You specify an abort function, you signal the beginning of a document, you repeatedly indicate the beginning of a page, draw each page, indicate when the page is complete, and finally signal that you have completed the document.

However, a lot of work went on behind the scenes. Contrary to intuition, GDI may have done very little work when you called the drawing functions and nearly all the work during the `EndPage` function call that signals the end of a page. We discuss soon what GDI actually does when you call its drawing functions and what it does when you signal the end of a page.

We mentioned that GDI may record the GDI function calls that an application uses when drawing a page and that the output from these function calls may not be sent directly to the printer. GDI makes this recording, when necessary, because an application can draw anywhere on the page at any time using the GDI output functions. For example, an application can draw the heading at the top of the page as the last output operation for a page.

Many printers, especially dot-matrix printers and some ink-jet printers, can print a page only line-by-line sequentially from the top of the page to the bottom. GDI, however, doesn't know what should be printed on the first line until the application signals that the page is completely drawn. In this situation, Windows must print the output at the top of the page before printing the output at the bottom of the page. But you have *drawn* the output at the top of the page long after you have *drawn* the output at the bottom of the page. Somehow the output produced by an application's GDI function calls must be reordered (and sometimes even broken into multiple, smaller pieces) before they are sent to the printer.

When GDI needs to reorder an application's printer output, it records the application's GDI function calls in a disk-based *metafile* until the application signals that it has completed drawing the page. So GDI very quickly processes the `TextOut`, `LineTo`, `Polygon`, and similar function calls used when drawing the page. All it needs to do is write a record in the metafile. This is one time where intuition leads one astray. Little work is required when drawing a complex page in this situation because the page isn't actually drawn.

You've probably guessed the other time when intuition leads you astray. When you signal the end of a page (by calling the `EndPage` function), you are not simply generating a form feed and skipping to the next page. It is during the `EndPage` function call that GDI begins the process of converting the recorded output function calls in the disk-based metafile into actual printer output. GDI finds out from the printer device driver the size of each *band* on a page. A band might be as small as the area on a dot-matrix printer printed by one pass of the printing head or as large as the entire page on a laser printer with sufficient memory.

For each band on a page, GDI sets a clipping region to the area of the band and replays the disk-based metafile. This technique is called *banding*. Replaying the metafile executes all the recorded GDI functions for the page with the clipping region, restricting the generated output to that which is within the current band. Only the drawing requests from the GDI functions that affect the area described by the current band are sent to the printer driver. The printer device driver converts the device-independent drawing requests for the clipped area into the proper device-dependent commands and data for the particular printer. The printer device driver gives the device-dependent printer commands and data for the band back to GDI.

Normally, GDI saves each band of output (device-dependent printer commands and data) in another disk file called a *spool file*. It copies each band of output for the page into this spool file until the page is complete. Once an entire page of output is spooled, GDI notifies the print spooler that it needs to print a page of the document. The print spooler is the component that actually copies the output data from the spool file to the serial, parallel, or network port to which the printer is connected. It does this as a background operation allowing other applications to run while it is printing.

Now, GDI has reordered your drawing requests, converted the device-independent drawing requests into device-dependent information, and given the device-dependent printer output to the print spooler, which will print it. Control finally returns from the EndPage function that ended the page. You can see that an EndPage function call does much more than just eject a page!

This discussion so far has assumed the worst case in which a printer cannot accept drawing requests for a page in any order. Some printers can accept an entire page of output and create an image of the page in their own memory. When using a printer that doesn't require banding, GDI doesn't create the metafile because it isn't needed. In this case, GDI passes the application's drawing requests directly to the printer device driver as the application makes the TextOut, LineTo, Polygon, and other function calls. It doesn't hold the requests until the page is complete. The printer device driver converts the device-independent drawing requests into the device-dependent commands and data for the specified printer and gives the resulting output back to GDI, which spools the output as described previously.

One complication with printing as compared to drawing on the system display is that not all GDI output functions can be used on all printers. Windows allows you to use only a subset of the GDI output functions when writing to a metafile. Basically, these are the functions that only produce output and do not ask for information from the DC. Only the functions listed in Table 13.2 can be used when drawing on a printer via a metafile. Of particular note is that the DrawText function *cannot* be used if a metafile is necessary.

Some early Win16 documentation incorrectly stated that DrawText was a permitted operation in writing to a metafile. The result is that some code that was written for Win16 applications may use DrawText. It will work correctly on nonbanding printers.Be careful of this if you are porting a Win16 application.

This overview, of course, describes the process when nothing goes wrong. There are numerous places where something could fail. Errors must be handled. Also, the user should be given a method to abort the print job; this requires the cooperation of the application.

We next look at each step required to add printing to a Windows application. The first step is selecting the printer on which to print. The most common (and simplest) choice is the "currently selected printer", so we start with it.

Table 13.2: GDI output functions usable in a metafile

Arc	OffsetWindowOrgEx	SetBkColor
ArcTo	PatBlt	SetBkMode
BitBlt	Pie	SetDIBitsToDevice
Chord	PolyBezier	SetMapMode
CloseFigure	PolyBezierTo	SetMapperFlags
CreateBrushIndirect	PolyDraw	SetPaletteEntries
CreateDIBPatternBrush	Polygon	SetPixel
CreateFontIndirect	Polyline	SetPixelV
CreatePalette	PolylineTo	SetPolyFillMode
CreatePatternBrush	PolyPolygon	SetROP2
CreatePenIndirect	PolyPolyline	SetStretchBltMode
CreateRegion	RealizePalette	SetTextAlign
DeleteObject	Rectangle	SetTextCharacterExtra
Ellipse	ResizePalette	SetTextColor
Escape *(obsolete)*	RestoreDC	SetTextJustification
ExcludeClipRect	RoundRect	SetViewportExtEx
ExtTextOut	SaveDC	SetViewportOrgEx
FloodFill	ScaleViewportExtEx	SetWindowExtEx
IntersectClipRect	ScaleWindowExtEx	SetWindowOrgEx
LineTo	SelectClipRgn	StretchBlt
MoveToEx	SelectObject	StretchDIBits
		TextOut

Using the Default Printer

The simplest way to get a DC for the default printer is to use the PrintDlg function in a very limited mode–so limited, in fact, that it doesn't even present a dialog to the user. To get a DC for the current, or *default,* printer, the code shown in Listing 13.1 works well.

Listing 13.1: Getting the default printer

```
HDC getDefaultPrinterDC()
    {
    PRINTDLG pdsetup;

    memset (&pdsetup, 0, sizeof (PRINTDLG));
    pdsetup.lStructSize = sizeof (PRINTDLG);
    pdsetup.Flags = PD_RETURNDEFAULT | PD_RETURNDC ;

    if (PrintDlg (&pdsetup))
        return pdsetup.hDC;
    else
        return NULL;
    }
```

The unusual feature of calling the print "dialog" this way is that it doesn't actually pop up a dialog at all; it just asks the print dialog handler to do all the work to determine the default printer and return this information, along with a DC. So the user won't see anything happen at all. However, internally you will have a DC to the default printer.

The `getDefaultPrinterDC` function returns either the handle to a printer DC for the current default printe or 0. When it returns 0, you should issue a message to the user stating that the print request could not be completed. If you need to report more detail, you can call the function `CommDlgExtendedError` to get a value that is the last error experienced by the common dialogs. These error codes are explained with each of the common dialogs, and the symbols are defined in the header file `cderr.h`.

Using Any Installed Printer

To allow the user to choose any printer and change the various settings, you will normally use the `PrintDlg` function to create an actual dialog and to interact with the user. To use the `PrintDlg` function, you set up some values in the structure that configures it, the `PRINTDLG` structure. Our previous example set only two fields before the call and retrieved a value from a third after the call. But the `PRINTDLG` structure has a large number of options that we have to look at in more detail. The structure is defined in `commdlg.h` as follows:

```
typedef struct tagged {
    DWORD       lStructSize;
    HWND        hwndOwner;
    HANDLE      hDevMode;
    HDC         hDC;
    DWORD       Flags;
    WORD        nFromPage;
    WORD        nToPage;
    WORD        nMinPage;
    WORD        nMaxPage;
    WORD        nCopies;
    HINSTANCE   hInstance;
    DWORD       lCustData;
    LPPRINTHOOKPROC lpfnPrintHook;
    LPSETUPHOOKPROC lpfnSetupHook;
    LPCTSTR     lpPrintTemplateName;
    LPCTSTR     lpSetupTemplateName;
    HANDLE      hPrintTemplate;
    HANDLE      hSetupTemplate;
} PRINTDLG;
```

Think of `PrintDlg` features at three levels: the basic functionality, such as getting a DC; the intermediate functionality, such as page selection; and the advanced features, such as defining your own dialog's templates and handler. We cover these levels independently, first developing the simpler interactions and then explaining the more complex features. In the tables that follow, we've added some codes to suggest what we think the levels are: B for basic, I for intermediate, and A for advanced. This should help you sort out the intimidating complexity and know what you can safely ignore for most ordinary printing tasks.

To understand the fields and flags of the `PRINTDLG` structure, first refer to Figure 13.2 to see what a Print dialog looks like.

The `PrintDlg` function serves another closely related purpose: to allow for printer selection. This is the "print setup dialog" and is shown in Figure 13.3. The major data structures are the same, so the functionality of printer setup became part of the `PrintDlg` functionality.

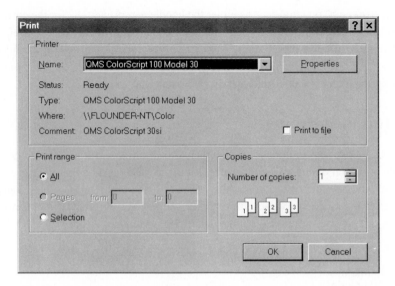

Figure 13.2: A PrintDlg print dialog

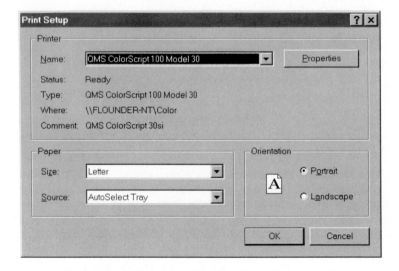

Figure 13.3: A PrintDlg setup dialog

Table 13.3: Fields of PRINTDLG structure

	Field	Description	
		Input (Set before the Call)	**Output (The Value after the Call)**
B	DWORD lStructSize	Length of the structure.	Unchanged.
B	HWND hwndOwner	The window that owns the dialog box or NULL if the dialog box has no owner.	Unchanged.
B	HANDLE hDevMode	A global handle to a memory object that is a DEVMODE structure used to set the dialog controls and that receives values from those structures, or NULL.	A possibly different DEVMODE handle, depending on user selections. Fields in the DEVMODE structure indicate the values chosen by the user. May be NULL if the printer driver does not support DEVMODE.
B	HANDLE hDevNames	A global handle to a memory object that is a DEVNAMES structure, or NULL.	A possibly different DEVNAMES handle for the selected printer; may be NULL.
B	HDC hDC	Ignored.	DC or IC returned.
B	DWORD Flags	Flags indicating what services are requested in the dialog box.	Flags indicating what options were selected by the user.
I	WORD nFromPage	Value initializing the dialog box. Must not be less than nMinPage.	Value chosen by the user.
I	WORD nToPage	Value initializing the dialog box. Must not be greater than nMaxPage.	Value chosen by the user.
I	WORD nMinPage	Value setting the lower limit for page selection.	Unchanged.
I	WORD nMaxPage	Value setting the upper limit for page selection.	Unchanged.
I	WORD nCopies	Value setting the initial number of copies.	Either 1 or the number of copies selected by the user. If 1, check the DEVMODE dmCopies field.

B	Basic functionality; of interest for most calls.
I	Intermediate functionality; selection.
A	Advanced functionality; templates and hook functions.

Table 13.3: Fields of PRINTDLG structure

		Description
		The following fields are specified on input and remain unmodified:
A	HINSTANCE hInstance	Instance handle for dialog box templates, if they are used, or NULL.
A	DWORD lCustData	Value to be passed to the hook function as the lParam value of the WM_INITDIALOG message. Ignored if there is no hook function enabled.
A	LPPRINTHOOKPROC lpfnPrintHook	Pointer to a CALLBACK function that "hooks" messages sent to the Print dialog.
A	LPSETUPHOOKPROC lpfnSetupHook	Pointer to a CALLBACK function that "hooks" messages sent to the Print Setup dialog.
A	LPCTSTR lpPrintTemplateName	Either the string name of your custom Print dialog template found in the hInstance module or a MAKEINTRESOURCE for its ID.
A	LPCTSTR lpSetupTemplateName	Either the string name of your custom Print Setup dialog template found in the hInstance module or a MAKEINTRESOURCE for its ID.
A	HANDLE hPrintTemplate	A handle to an in-memory dialog structure (see DialogBoxIndirect in Chapter 11) used for the Print dialog.
A	HANDLE hSetupTemplate	A handle to an in-memory dialog structure used for the Print Setup dialog (see DialogBoxIndirect in Chapter 11, particularly the discussion starting on page 770).
B	Basic functionality; of interest for most calls.	
I	Intermediate functionality; selection.	
A	Advanced functionality; templates and hook functions.	

Table 13.4: PRINTDLG Flags Values

	Flag	Description
B	PD_ALLPAGES	A value used to check if the **All** radio button was selected. See page 959 for the description of how to use this value (it isn't a bit value!).
B	PD_COLLATE	If set, and other criteria are met, will cause the **Collate** check box to be checked when the dialog comes up. Upon return, indicates the state of this check box as set by the user.

Table 13.4: PRINTDLG Flags Values

	Flag	Description
I	PD_DISABLEPRINTTOFILE	If set, disables the **Print to file** check box when the dialog comes up. Ignored if the PD_HIDEPRINTTOFILE flag is set.
A	PD_ENABLEPRINTHOOK	Enables the print hook. Requires that a function pointer be set in the lpfnPrintHook field.
A	PD_ENABLEPRINTTEMPLATE	The dialog box will be created from the template named by the lpPrintTemplateName field in the hInstance module.
A	PD_ENABLEPRINTTEMPLATEHANDLE	The hInstance field contains a handle to an in-memory dialog template (see Chapter 11, particularly the discussion starting on page 770). The lpPrintTemplateName field is ignored.
A	PD_ENABLESETUPHOOK	Enables the setup hook. Requires that a function pointer be set in the lpfnSetupHook field.
A	PD_ENABLESETUPTEMPLATEHANDLE	Indicates that the hInstance is a handle to an in-memory dialog template used for a setup dialog. The lpSetupTemplateName field is ignored.
I	PD_HIDEPRINTTOFILE	Hides (and disables) the **Print to file** check box.
I	PD_NOPAGENUMS	Disables the **Pages** radio button and its associated edit controls.
I	PD_NOSELECTION	Disables the **Selection** radio button.
I	PD_NOWARNING	Suppresses all warning messages, including those indicating why the dialog may not have come up. Use the CommDlgExtendedError function to get an error code.
I	PD_PAGENUMS	If set on input, causes the dialog to come up with the **Pages** radio button selected. When PrintDlg returns, this is set if the user selected the **Pages** radio button.
B	PD_PRINTSETUP	Causes the system to display a Print Setup dialog (not normally used under Win32).
I	PD_PRINTTOFILE	If set on input, causes the dialog to come up with the **Print to file** check box already checked. When PrintDlg returns, this indicates if the user selected the **Print to file** option.
B	PD_RETURNDC	If set on input, causes PrintDlg to allocate a DC for the printer in the hDC field. Unchanged on output.

Table 13.4: PRINTDLG Flags Values

	Flag	Description
B	PD_RETURNDEFAULT	Causes PrintDlg to return the DEVMODE and DEVNAMES values structures for the default printer. The hDevNames and hDevMode fields must be NULL when this flag is specified; otherwise, the function will fail. On successful completion, these fields will have handles to the structures.
A	PD_RETURNIC	If set on input, causes PrintDlg to allocate an information context (IC) for the printer in the hDC field.
I	PD_SELECTION	If set on input, causes the dialog to come up with the **Selection** radio button checked. When PrintDlg returns, this flag is set if the user chose the **Selection** radio button.
I	PD_SHOWHELP	If set, the dialog will have a **Help** button. If this is set, the hwndOwner must be set.
A	PD_USEDEVMODECOPIES	If the selected printer does not support multiple copies, disables the **Copies** edit control and the **Collate** option.
B	Basic functionality; of interest for most calls.	
I	Intermediate functionality; selection.	
A	Advanced functionality; templates and hook functions.	

Not all of the useful information comes back in the PrintDlg structure; only the basic information is returned here. If you care about what size paper the user has chosen, what orientation has been chosen, and many other setup details, you have to also refer to the *device mode* structure. This structure is returned as a HANDLE in the PrintDlg structure. By using GlobalLock, you can get a pointer to this structure and examine it to discover many other parameters of the printer. You'll need to do this, for example, to determine how many lines you can draw on the page. We touch briefly the DEVMODE structure here but save the details for later (see page 959).

One other important printer dialog is the *page setup dialog*. You use this to set up properties such as margins and paper orientation. You don't need to call it, but most applications that want to conform to the GUI standards will want it. We discuss it starting on page 1015.

Getting the Printer DC for Any Printer

Normally, you will ask the user to select a printer and other printing options. It is often unwise to assume that the user will want to write to the default printer. In the days when a user had one printer physically attached to the machine, this may have been valid, but today a user may have normal access to two or more printers. Increasingly common is the locally connected personal laser or inkjet printer, the networked color printer, and the fax modem. As the economics of printers change, the likelihood that the user will have access to even more printers is even greater. What you *don't* want to do is require that the user go back to the Control Panel each time to change the default printer! The printing decision is often based on a print-by-print run draft to the local printer and final to the color printer; draft to the local printer and final to the fax. Having to go back to the control panel each time is clearly a major inconvenience. It also leaves the default printer set up incorrectly for the next printing operation, which might be from a different application hours later.

Because you normally want the user to be able to select the printer and the options, a normal printing operation should put up a print dialog very much like that shown in Figure 13.2. After the user has selected the options desired, control returns from PrintDlg. If the return indicates success, the printing operation can start.

Listing 13.2 shows an example of code that responds to a **Print** menu request. It obtains a DC and calls your printing function, passing in the pointer to the PRINTDLG structure that was used to initialize the printer. Because the PRINTDLG structure is maintained as static storage, the settings that the user chooses–particularly the printer and its options–are available on the next print request. Once the printer has been obtained, you call the startPrintJob function to perform the initial setup of the printing task, including posting the dialog with the "**Cancel**" button and establishing the abort procedure. Then startPrintJob calls the function printLoop, which actually does the printing. Finally, we call endPrintJob to clean up and close off the printing task.

Listing 13.2: Initiating printing
```
static PRINTDLG pd;

void cls_OnPrint()
    {
     if (!getPrinterDC (&pd))
        return;
     if (!startPrintJob (&pd))
        return;
     printLoop (&pd);
     endPrintJob (&pd);
    }
```

Listing 13.3: The getPrinterDC function
```
BOOL getPrinterDC(PRINTDLG * pd)
    {
     if(pd->hDevNames == NULL && pd->hDevMode == NULL)
        { /* needs initialization */
         memset(pd, 0, sizeof(PRINTDLG));
         pd->lStructSize = sizeof(PRINTDLG);
         pd->Flags = PD_RETURNDEFAULT;
         if(!PrintDlg(pd))
            { /* failed */
             DWORD err = CommDlgExtendedError();
             reportPrinterError(err); // you write this
             return FALSE;
            } /* failed */
         pd->Flags &= ~ PD_RETURNDEFAULT;
        } /* needs initialization */
     pd->Flags |= PD_RETURNDC;
     // set up any other options you want here, such
```

```
    // as page numbers, selection, collate, etc.
    if(!PrintDlg(pd))
        {/* failed or canceled */
         DWORD err = CommDlgExtendedError();
         if( err == 0)
            { /* canceled */
             return FALSE;
            } /* canceled */
          reportPrinterError(err);
          return FALSE;
        } /* failed or canceled */
    return TRUE;
    }
```

Listing 13.3 shows the actual details of obtaining a printer DC. We first check to see that the two handles, hDevMode and hDevNames, have been initialized. If they have not been, we want to initialize the PRINTDLG structure to refer to the default printer. We do this as we previously did, by setting only the PD_RETURNDC flag and calling PrintDlg. When PrintDlg is called with this flag, it does not actually pop up a dialog but simply obtains the necessary parameters from the currently selected printer and sets the hDevMode and hDevNames fields, among others. If this is not successful, we call our own function reportError, which does whatever is appropriate to report an error. Since there is no dialog, the only reason for failure is that the operation did not complete internally.

Once we have an initial printer setting, either by obtaining the default printer or by using the printer last selected, we can set any application-specific state, such as whether page numbers or selection printing is permitted. Then we call PrintDlg with the PD_RETURNDC flag set. The Print dialog box will be displayed, configured according to our input parameters. If this is the first time we called getPrinterDC, it will come with the default printer configured. The user is free to select another printer or choose a different set of options for the current printer.

When control returns, the value of PrintDlg will be either FALSE or a nonzero (TRUE) value. A result of FALSE could occur for many reasons, including illegal input parameters, failure to create the dialog, or the result of the user's having selected the **Cancel** button. To determine the real cause, you call CommDlgExtendedError, which returns 0 if the user hit the **Cancel** button and a nonzero value if there was an error. If the user hit **Cancel**, we return quietly; otherwise, we again call our reportPrinterError function, which handles error reporting. A simple reportPrinterError function is

```
void reportPrinterError(DWORD err)
    {
    TCHAR caption[256];
    TCHAR message[256];

    LoadString (hInstance, IDS_PRINT_ERROR_CAPTION,
                caption, DIM(caption));
    LoadString (hInstance, IDS_PRINT_ERROR_BODY,
                message, DIM(message));
    MessageBox (GetFocus(), message, caption,
        MB_ICONERROR | MB_OK);
    }
```

This uses the following resources:

```
STRINGTABLE
BEGIN
    IDS_PRINT_ERROR_CAPTION    "Printing Error"
    IDS_PRINT_ERROR_BODY       "Print request failed"
END
```

Checking for Selection Options

Checking for the selection option uses the symbol PD_ALLPAGES. This is not a bit value; in fact, it is defined as the value 0. It is intended to be used as follows:

```
switch(pd.Flags & (PD_SELECTION | PD_PAGENUMS))
    { /* selection type */
    case PD_ALLPAGES
        // .. whatever you need to indicate all
        // .. pages
        break;
    case PD_SELECTION:
        // .. whatever you need to indicate the
        // .. current selection
        break;
    case PD_PAGENUMS:
        // .. whatever you need to indicate the
        // .. range is page numbers
        break;
    } /* selection type */
```

Determining Device Mode Values

The PRINTDLG contains only some simple values, such as page limits. Your printer may support many other features, such as alternative paper sizes, alternative paper trays, and landscape/portrait layout. If you plan to support internationalization, you also have to be prepared to handle paper in a variety of formats such as Letter, Legal, A4, and others, as those shown in Table 13.6.

This additional information is device-dependent. For example, not all printers support all paper sizes or support landscape printing. You have to actually check the parameters. The user can change these from the PrintDlg by clicking the **Properties** button associated with the printer selection.

This device-dependent information is found in the DEVMODE structure, whose handle is found in the PRINTDLG structure. The DEVMODE structure is shown next and explained in Table 13.5. Note that not all drivers support the DEVMODE structure. You must be prepared to accept that even after a PrintDlg call, this value may be NULL.

```
typedef struct tagDEVMODE {
    BCHAR     dmDeviceName [CCHDEVICENAME] ;
    WORD      dmSpecVersion ;
    WORD      dmDriverVersion ;
    WORD      dmSize ;
    WORD      dmDriverExtra ;
    DWORD     dmFields ;
    short     dmOrientation ;
```

```
    short       dmPaperSize ;
    short       dmPaperLength ;
    short       dmPaperWidth ;
    short       dmScale ;
    short       dmCopies ;
    short       dmDefaultSource ;
    short       dmPrintQuality ;
    short       dmColor ;
    short       dmDuplex ;
    short       dmYResolution ;
    short       dmTTOption ;
    BCHAR       dmFormName[CCHFORMNAME];
    WORD        dmLogPixels;
    DWORD       dmBitsPerPel;
    DWORD       dmPelsWidth;
    DWORD       dmPelsHeight;
    DWORD       dmDisplayFlags;
#if(WINVER >= 0x400)
    DWORD       dmICMMethod;
    DWORD       dmICMIntent;
    DWORD       dmMediaType;
    DWORD       dmDitherType;
    DWORD       dmReserved1;
    DWORD       dmReserved2;
#endif // WINVER >= 0x400
} DEVMODE ;
```

Table 13.5: The DEVMODE structure

Field	Description
dmDeviceName	The user-visible name of the printer. This name is unique for each type of printer in the system. A BCHAR value is an unsigned character value that has the same width as a TCHAR.
dmSpecVersion	The version number of the data specification that this structure is based on.
dmDriverVersion	The driver version assigned by the printer driver developer. For example, by convention, Windows NT 3.5 or 3.51 drivers have designations such as 0x350 or 0x351, and Windows 95 drivers have designations like 0x400. But it is the driver developer's choice to make a number that corresponds to the intended operating system environment.
dmSize	The size, in bytes, of the DEVMODE structure, not including the private data that follows.
dmDriverExtra	The number of bytes of driver-specific data that follows this structure. The first byte of this data is found by adding dmSize to the address of this structure.

Table 13.5: The DEVMODE structure

Field	Description
dmFields	A set of bit flags indicating which other fields of the DEVMODE structure are meaningful. Before attempting to use one of the fields so designated, you should check this field to see if its flag is set. If it isn't, the value in that field is likely gibberish and you shouldn't depend on it.

Flag	Field
DM_ORIENTATION	dmOrientation
DM_PAPERSIZE	dmPaperSize
DM_PAPERLENGTH	dmPaperLength
DM_SCALE	dmScale
DM_COPIES	dmCopies
DM_DEFAULTSOURCE	dmDefaultSource
DM_PRINTQUALITY	dmPrintQuality
DM_COLOR	dmColor
DM_DUPLEX	dmDuplex
DM_YRESOLUTION	dmYResolution
DM_TTOPTION	dmTTOption
DM_COLLATE	dmCollate
DM_FORMNAME	dmFormName
DM_LOGPIXELS	dmLogPixels
DM_BITSPERPEL	dmBitsPerPel
DM_PELSWIDTH	dmPelsWidth
DM_PELSHEIGHT	dmPelsHeight
DM_DISPLAYFLAGS	dmDisplayFlags
DM_DISPLAYFREQUENCY	dmDisplayFrequency
DM_ICMMETHOD	dmICMMethod
DM_ICMINTENT	dmICMIntent
DM_MEDIATYPE	dmMediaType
DM_DITHERTYPE	dmDitherType

Table 13.5: The DEVMODE structure

Field	Description	
dmOrientation	The orientation of the paper:	
	DMORIENT_PORTRAIT	Portrait orientation (long axis vertical).
	DMORIENT_LANDSCAPE	Landscape orientation (long axis horizontal).
dmPaperSize	The paper size, expressed as a code. See Table 13.6.	
dmPaperLength	If present, overrides the dmPaperSize value. Specifies the length in units of 0.1 mm (approximately 0.004 inch).	
dmPaperWidth	If present, overrides the dmPaperSize value. Specifies the width in units of 0.1 mm (approximately 0.004 inch).	
dmScale	Indicates the scaling as a percentage, that is, 100 is 100%.	
dmCopies	Specifies the number of copies on printers that support multiple-page copies (for example, most laser printers). If set, the nCopies member of the PRINTDLG will be 1 and the actual number of copies selected will be found here.	
dmDefaultSource	Reserved[1]; must be 0.	
dmPrintQuality	The printer resolution. Either a negative value from the following set or a positive value that is a device-dependent resolution in dots per inch (DPI).	
	DMRES_HIGH	High resolution.
	DMRES_MEDIUM	Medium resolution.
	DMRES_LOW	Low resolution.
	DMRES_DRAFT	Draft resolution.
	>0	X-resolution in DPI.
dmColor	One of the following values:	
	DMCOLOR_COLOR	Color printer.
	DMCOLOR_MONOCHROME	Monochrome printer.
dmDuplex	Selects single-sided or double-sided printing for those printers capable of it. Possible values are as follows:	
	DMDUP_SIMPLEX	No duplex printing.
	DMDUP_HORIZONTAL	*Undocumented.*
	DMDUP_VERTICAL	*Undocumented.*

Table 13.5: The DEVMODE structure

Field	Description	
dmYResolution	If this is present, as indicated by the DM_YRESOLUTION, it is the *y*-resolution, in dots per inch, of the printer. If this is present, the dmPrintQuality field will be the *x*-resolution in dots per inch.	
dmTTOption	Specifies how TrueType fonts should be printed (see Chapter 15). This member can be one of the following:	
	DMTT_BITMAP	Print TrueType fonts using graphics. This is the default for dot-matrix and many inkjet printers.
	DMTT_DOWNLOAD	Download TrueType fonts as "soft fonts". This is the default for most Hewlett-Packard printers that support the Printer Control Language (PCL).
	DMTT_SUBDEV	Substitute device fonts for TrueType fonts. This is the default for PostScript printers.
dmCollate	Specifies whether document collation should be done when printing multiple copies:	
	DM_COLLATE_TRUE	Enabled.
	DM_COLLATE_FALSE	Disabled.
dmFormName	Windows NT 3.*x*: Name of form to use. Windows 95: Not used. Windows NT 4.*x*: We don't know; it is undocumented.	
dmLogPixels	Logical pixels per inch. Not used by printers.	
dmBitsPerPel	Color resolution of the display device. Not used by printers.	
dmPelsWidth	Width of device surface in pixels. Not used by printers.	
dmPelsHeight	Height of device surface in pixels. Not used by printers.	
dmDisplayFlags	Display mode. Not used by printers.	
dmDisplayFrequency	Displays refresh frequency. Not used by printers.	

The following fields are specified for Windows 4.*x*. They are not supported under Windows NT 3.5*x*.

dmICMMethod	Specifies how ICM (color matching) is handled. For non-ICM applications, specifies only if ICM is disabled. For ICM applications, indicates how to handle ICM support. Can be one of the following values. The printer driver must support this. Most printers support only DMICMMETHOD_NONE or DMICMMETHOD_SYSTEM. PostScript drivers support all values.	
	DMICMMETHOD_NONE	ICM is disabled.

Table 13.5: The DEVMODE structure

Field	Description	
dmICMMethod (cont.)	DMICMMETHOD_SYSTEM	ICM is handled by Windows.
	DMICMMETHOD_DRIVER	ICM is handled by the device driver.
	DMICMMETHOD_DEVICE	ICM is handled by the device.
	>DMICMMETHOD_USER	Driver-defined.
dmICMIntent	Used primarily by non-ICM applications:	
	DMICM_SATURATE	Optimize for color saturation. Typical for business graphics.
	DMICM_CONTRAST	Optimize for contrast. Typical for scanned photographs.
	DMICM_COLORMETRIC	Attempt to match requested color.
	>DMICM_USER	Driver-defined.
dmMediaType	Specifies the media type. One of the following values:	
	DMMEDIA_STANDARD	Plain paper.
	DMMEDIA_GLOSSY	Glossy paper.
	DMMEDIA_TRANSPARENCY	Transparency film.
	>DMMEDIA_USER	Driver-defined.
dmDitherType	Specifies how dithering is to be done. One of the following values:	
	DMDITHER_NONE	No dithering.
	DMDITHER_COARSE	Coarse brush dithering.
	DMDITHER_FINE	Fine brush dithering.
	DMDITHER_LINEART	High contrast dithering; not suitable for continuous color images.
	DMDITHER_GRAYSCALE	Gray-scale-only device.
	>DMDITHER_USER	Driver-defined value.
dmReserved1	Reserved; must be 0.	
dmReserved2	Reserved; must be 0.	

[1] In spite of the official specification that this is "reserved" and must be 0, we have found several drivers that fill in nonzero values here. It is modified by changing the "Source" selection in the Print Setup dialog, such as Manual Feed, Envelope Feed, and Upper Tray.

Table 13.6: Paper size codes in DEVMODE dmPaperSize

Paper Code	Size[1]
DMPAPER_9X11	9×11 in (229×280 mm).
DMPAPER_10X11	10×11 in (254×280 mm).
DMPAPER_10X14	10×14 in (254×356 mm).
DMPAPER_11X17	11×17 in (280×432 mm).
DMPAPER_15X11	15×11 in (381×280 mm).
DMPAPER_A2	A2, 420×594 mm ($16^1/_2 \times 23^3/_8$ in.).
DMPAPER_A3	A3, 297×420 mm ($11.7 \times 16^3/_4$ in.).
DMPAPER_A3_EXTRA	A3 extra, 322×445 mm ($12^{11}/_{16} \times 17^1/_2$ in.).
DMPAPER_A3_EXTRA_TRANSVERSE	A3 extra transverse, 322×445 mm ($12^{11}/_{16} \times 17^1/_2$ in.).
DMPAPER_A3_TRANSVERSE	A3 transverse, 295×420 mm ($11^5/_8 \times 16^3/_4$ in.).
DMPAPER_A4	A4, 210×297 mm ($8^1/_2 \times 11.7$ in.).
DMPAPER_A4_EXTRA	Super A4, $9.27 \times 12^{11}/_{16}$ in. (236×322 mm).
DMPAPER_A4_PLUS	A4 Plus, 210×330 mm ($8^1/_2 \times 13$ in.).
DMPAPER_A4SMALL	A4 small, 210×297 mm ($8^1/_2 \times 11.7$ in.).
DMPAPER_A4_TRANSVERSE	A4 transverse, 210×297 mm ($8^1/_2 \times 11.7$ in.).
DMPAPER_A5	A5, 148×210 mm ($5.8 \times 8^1/_2$ in.).
DMPAPER_A5_EXTRA	A5 extra, 174×235 mm ($6.85 \times 9^1/_4$ in.).
DMPAPER_A5_TRANSVERSE	A5 transverse, 148×210 mm ($5.8 \times 8^1/_2$ in.).
DMPAPER_A_PLUS	Super A4 transverse, 227×356 mm ($8^{15}/_{16} \times 14$ in.).
DMPAPER_B4	B4, 250×354 mm ($9^{27}/_{32} \times 14$ in.).
DMPAPER_B5	B5, 182×257 mm ($7^{11}/_{64} \times 10^1/_8$ in.).
DMPAPER_B5_EXTRA	B5 extra, 201×276 mm ($7^{29}/_{32} \times 10^{55}/_{64}$ in.).
DMPAPER_B5_TRANSVERSE	B5 transverse, 182×257 mm ($7^{11}/_{64} \times 10^1/_8$ in.).
DMPAPER_B_PLUS	Super B, 305×487 mm ($12 \times 19^{11}/_{64}$ in.).
DMPAPER_CSHEET	C, 17×22 in. (432×559 mm).

Table 13.6: Paper size codes in DEVMODE dmPaperSize

Paper Code	Size[1]
DMPAPER_DSHEET	D, 22 × 34 in. (559 × 864 mm).
DMPAPER_ENV_9	#9 envelope, $3^7/_8 \times 8^7/_8$ in.
DMPAPER_ENV_10	#10 envelope, $4^1/_8 \times 9^1/_2$ in.
DMPAPER_ENV_11	#11 envelope, $4^1/_2 \times 10^3/_8$ in.
DMPAPER_ENV_12	#12 envelope, $4^3/_4 \times 11$ in.
DMPAPER_ENV_14	#14 envelope, $5 \times 11^1/_2$ in.
DMPAPER_ENV_B4	B4 envelope, 260 × 353 mm.
DMPAPER_ENV_B5	B5 envelope, 176 × 250 mm.
DMPAPER_ENV_B6	B6 envelope, 176 × 125 mm.
DMPAPER_ENV_C3	C3 envelope, 324 × 458 mm.
DMPAPER_ENV_C4	C4 envelope, 229 × 324 mm.
DMPAPER_ENV_C5	C5 envelope, 162 × 229 mm.
DMPAPER_ENV_C6	C6 envelope, 114 × 162 mm.
DMPAPER_ENV_DL	DL envelope, 110 × 220 mm.
DMPAPER_ENV_INVITE	Invitation envelope, 220 × 220 mm.
DMPAPER_ENV_ITALY	Italy envelope, 110 × 230 mm.
DMPAPER_ENV_MONARCH	Monarch envelope, $3^7/_8 \times 7^1/_2$ in.
DMPAPER_ENV_PERSONAL	$6^3/_4$ envelope, $3^5/_8 \times 6^1/_2$ in.
DMPAPER_ESHEET	E, 34 × 44 in. (864 × 1118 mm).
DMPAPER_EXECUTIVE	Executive, $7^1/_2 \times 10^1/_4$ in. (184 × 267 mm).
DMPAPER_FANFOLD_LGL_GERMAN	German Legal fanfold, $8^1/_2 \times 13$ in. (216 × 330 mm).
DMPAPER_FANFOLD_STD_GERMAN	German Standard fanfold, $8^1/_2 \times 12$ in. (216 × 305 mm).
DMPAPER_FANFOLD_US	U. S. Standard fanfold, $14^7/_8 \times 11$ in. (378 × 280 mm).
DMPAPER_FOLIO	Folio, $8^1/_2 \times 13$ in. (216 × 330 mm).
DMPAPER_ISO_B4	B4 ISO, 250 × 353 mm ($9^{27}/_{32} \times 13^{29}/_{32}$ in.).
DMPAPER_JAPANESE_POSTCARD	Japanese postcard, 140 × 148 mm ($5^1/_2 \times 5^{53}/_{64}$ in.).

Table 13.6: Paper size codes in DEVMODE dmPaperSize

Paper Code	Size[1]
DMPAPER_LEDGER	Ledger, 17×11 in. (432×280 mm).
DMPAPER_LEGAL	Legal, $8^1/_2 \times 14$ in. (216×356 mm).
DMPAPER_LEGAL_EXTRA	Legal extra, $9^1/_2 \times 15$ in. (241×381 mm).
DMPAPER_LETTER	Letter, $8^1/_2 \times 11$ in. (216×280 mm).
DMPAPER_LETTER_EXTRA	Letter extra, $9^1/_2 \times 12$ in. (248×305 mm).
DMPAPER_LETTER_PLUS	Letter plus, $8^1/_2 \times 11$ in. (216×280 mm).
DMPAPER_LETTERSMALL	Letter small, $8^1/_2 \times 12.69$ in. (216×322 mm).
DMPAPER_LETTER_TRANSVERSE	Letter transverse, $8^1/_2 \times 11$ in. (216×280 mm).
DMPAPER_NOTE	Note, $8^1/_2 \times 11$ in. (216×280 mm).
DMPAPER_QUARTO	Quarto, 215×275 mm ($8^1/_2 \times 10^{53}/_{64}$ in.).
DMPAPER_STATEMENT	Statement, $5^1/_2 \times 8^1/_2$ in. (140×216 mm).
DMPAPER_TABLOID	Tabloid, 11×17 in. (280×432 mm).
DMPAPER_TABLOID_EXTRA	Tabloid extra, 11.69×18 in. (297×457 mm).

[1]Converted sizes in parentheses, either English or Metric, are approximate sizes only.

The dmDeviceName field contains the name of the device that the driver supports. For example, "PCL / HP LaserJet" is the name of one driver. You can use this to indicate the printer you're printing on. The dmSize field contains the size, in bytes, of the DEVMODE structure. This value does not include the length of any device-dependent data that may follow the structure. The dmDriverExtra field contains the size, in bytes, of the device-specific data that follow the DEVMODE structure. Unless you are constructing an application that requires or expects a specific kind of printer, you will not look at any of this extended information.

The dmFields field contains a set of flags that indicate which of the remaining fields in the DEVMODE structure have been initialized. Not all printer drivers support all possible options.

Hazards with Device Mode Values

We were dismayed to find many anomalies and inconsistencies in our viewing of the DEVMODE structure. Much of this is undoubtedly due to inadequate documentation. Some may be due to historical artifacts. We summarize here some of the more glaring errors we found.

Setting the `dmTTOption`

Presumably, if you wanted to force TrueType fonts to download instead of letting device substitution work, you could set the `dmTTOption` field to `DMTT_DOWNLOAD`. We found this did not work for our printers. If you set the `dmTTOption` field in the DEVMODE structure (remembering to set the `DM_TTOPTION` flag), the value we set was ignored and in fact was *reset* to `DMTT_DOWNLOAD`. However, if we went into the printer setup and changed the option to select TrueType font downloading, this change was remembered, but it was not reflected in any way in the `dmTTOption` field. This appears to be an artifact of the printer driver, but it indicates the kind of problems you are likely to find. You can check this out on your machine using the Print Explorer.

The `dmPaperSize` field

If you examine the `DeviceCapabilities` page in the Print Explorer, you will find that it will give you, for each printer, a list of paper names and their associated integer values that are used in the `dmPaperSize` field. We found inconsistencies on one of our printers, as shown in Table 13.7.

Table 13.7: Anomalies in the `DEVMODE` `dmPaperSize` field

Integer	Driver Reports Name	"Official" Name	"Official" Integer
42	B5	DMPAPER_ISO_B4	13
43	Invoice	DMPAPER_JAPANESE_POSTCARD	6 ("Statement")
44	#10 envelope	DMPAPER_9X11	20
45	Monarch envelope	DMPAPER_10X11	37
46	DL envelope	DMPAPER_15X11	27
47	C5 envelope	DMPAPER_ENV_INVITE	28

The above information was obtained for a DataProducts LZR-960 printer running under Windows NT 3.51.

The columns on the left are what the driver reports back for the paper. The "official" name indicates the value that is defined in `wingdi.h` for the corresponding integer; that is, we find

```
#define DMPAPER_ISO_B4 42
```

The "official" integer is the one we might expect to find for the paper type reported; that is, we find the declaration

```
#define DMPAPER_B5 13
```

So you should be somewhat suspicious of some of these values, particularly with older drivers. The driver in question was running on Windows NT 3.51, and the integer values 42 and higher are defined only for Windows 4.0 and higher.

The `dmDefaultSource` Field

This field is defined in the DEVMODE structure as being "Reserved, must be 0", while the DeviceCapabilities API documentation refers the reader to the DEVMODE definition for additional information. We examined several printers with the Print Explorer and found the values shown in Table 13.8. Note that the only consistency seems to be the values 15 (use Print Manager default settings) and 4 (Manual Feed). In the absence of documentation of any form on this field, we can offer only that it seems highly device-dependent but is selectable based on values you can present to the user (or that the user selects from the print dialogs). There seem to be no predefined symbols you could use if you wished to set this up in the DEVMODE structure, and of course localization makes a string comparison to the bin names a meaningless test.

Table 13.8: Sample values of the `dmDefaultSource` field

	Bin Name Reported		
Integer Value	**LZR 960**	**QMS-PS2220**	**QMS-100 30si**
4	Manual Feed	Manual Feed	Manual Feed
15	Print Manager Settings	Print Manager Settings	Print Manager Settings
256	Upper Tray	Lower Tray	
257	Lower Tray	Upper Tray	
258	Envelope Feeder	Bypass Tray	
52685			(unknown)

Setting Device Mode Values

After you get a structure by getting the default printer, you can change values in it to indicate your own choices. If you set a field, you must set its corresponding flag in the `dmFields` field. Note again that a printer driver may not honor your specification.

In Listing 13.4, we change the orientation of the paper on a laser printer by setting the `dmOrientation` field to DMORIENT_LANDSCAPE. Note that we must also set the `dmFields` field have its DM_ORIENTATION bit set to indicate that we have initialized the `dmOrientation` field (the bit may already be set, but we must make sure it *is* set). When we look at the **Options...** of the printer, we will see that its orientation is Landscape.

Listing 13.4: Setting properties in the DEVMODE structure

```
HDC getLandscapePrinterDC()
    {
    PRINTDLG pd;
    LPDEVMODE dm;

    memset (&pd, 0, sizeof (PRINTDLG));
```

```
    pd.Flags = PD_RETURNDEFAULT;
    if (!PrintDlg (&pd))
        return NULL;
    if (pd.hDevMode == NULL)
        return NULL;
    pd.Flags &= ~PD_RETURNDEFAULT;
    dm = (LPDEVMODE) GlobalLock (pd.hDevMode);
    if (dm == NULL)
        return NULL;
    dm.dmOrientation = DMORIENT_LANDSCAPE;
    dm.dmFields |= DM_ORIENTATION;
    GlobalUnlock (pd.hDevMode);
    pd.Flags |= PD_RETURNDC;
    if (!PrintDlg (&pd))
        return NULL;
    return pd.hDC;
}
```

The remaining fields you initialize to the values appropriate for the printer you are using.

Another useful function is the DeviceCapabilities function. It returns various capabilities of the printer such as the number of bins, number of copies, available paper sizes, orientation, and level of duplex support.

If you pass the handle to an initialized DEVMODE structure in the PRINTDLG structure to the PrintDlg function and the dmDeviceName field of the DEVMODE structure does not contain the name of a device supported on the user's system, the PrintDlg function will return an error. It's best to allow the user to select the printing device from those available on the system. You can determine the name of the selected device by examining the dmDeviceName field after the PrintDlg function returns.

Be sure you don't "remember" the global handle you pass in the hDevMode field of the PRINTDLG structure, that is, make a copy of it anywhere. The PrintDlg function can allocate a different global memory block and return this new handle in the updated PRINTDLG structure. In this case, the original handle that you "remembered" has already been freed. You are required, after you are done with the DEVMODE block, to free the handle present in the hDevMode field after the PrintDlg function returns–even if the PrintDlg function returns a 0 value, which may be, but is not necessarily, an error return.

Similarly, the hDevNames field contains a global memory handle to a movable global memory block. In this case, the global memory referenced by the handle contains a DEVNAMES structure. You pass three strings in the DEVNAMES structure to initialize the dialog box controls: the driver name, the printer name, and the output port name. When the PrintDlg function call returns, the fields of the DEVNAMES structure contain the strings specifying the device selected by the user. You can use these strings to create a printer DC or an IC for the selected device. The DEVNAMES structure looks like this:

```
typedef struct tagDEVNAMES {
    UINT      wDriverOffset ;
    UINT      wDeviceOffset ;
    UINT      wOutputOffset ;
    UINT      wDefault ;
    /* The variable length strings are stored here  */
} DEVNAMES ;
```

The wDriverOffset field contains the offset from the beginning of the DEVNAMES structure to a NUL-terminated string that specifies the device driver's filename without the extension.

The wDeviceOffset field contains the offset from the beginning of the structure to a NUL-terminated string that specifies the name of the device. This string must be identical to the string used in the dmDeviceName field of the DEVMODE structure, including the 32 bytes maximum length restriction.

The wOutputOffset field contains the offset from the beginning of the structure to a NUL-terminated string that specifies the device name of the output port; for example, "LPT1".

The wDefault field contains a flag value, DN_DEFAULTPRN, that indicates whether the strings identify the default printer. When you pass a DEVNAMES structure to the PrintDlg function and you set the DN_DEFAULTPRN flag, the PrintDlg function verifies that the user has not changed the default printer since the last print operation. When the PrintDlg function returns, the wDefault field is changed when the user changed the printer selection. In this case, the DN_DEFAULTPRN flag is set if the user selected the default printer and is not set if a specific printer was selected. The **Print...** dialog box reserves the other bits in the wDefault field for its own use.

An example of how to display the contents of the DEVNAMES structure is shown in Listing 13.5. The result of the display for one of our printers (running under Windows NT 3.51) is shown in Figure 13.4, which has been spread out a bit to illustrate the fields. We also show the actual memory layout of the memory that starts at the address of the DEVNAMES structure. The structure shown is for the ANSI version of the application.

[winspool]	[QMS-PS2220]	[Ne00:]	Default
wDriverOffset	wDeviceOffset	wOutputOffset	wDefault
0x0008	0x0011	0x001C	0x0001

memory:

00	02	04	06	08	11	1c
0008	0011	001C	0001	w i n s p o o l ◉	Q M S - P S 2 2 2 0 ◉	N E 0 0 : ◉

Figure 13.4: Sample DEVNAMES display

It's worth noting the very peculiar-looking type casts that are required to properly address the information. This represents a strong prejudice we have to not "break" the type system by converting a pointer without careful casting that makes it explicit.

```
(LPCTSTR)&((LPCSTR)dn)[dn->wDriverOffset]
```

By casting the LPDEVNAMES pointer dn to be an LPCSTR (8-bit string), we are able to subscript it. The LPCSTR, when subscripted by an integer value, adds that number of 8-bit bytes to the base address to arrive at the address of the 8-bit value specified by the subscript. The address, rather than the value, is used, as specified by the & operator. But this gives us a pointer to an 8-bit ANSI string. Because of Unicode, we must cast this again as an LPCTSTR. While in principle this doesn't matter much in a formatting string given to wsprintf, it is a good habit to document precisely what you are doing when you start playing games with the C type system.

You can set the hDevNames field or the PRINTDLG structure to 0 to request that the PrintDlg function allocate the DEVNAMES string and initialize its fields to the appropriate values based on the printer name specified in the DEVMODE structure. When the hDevMode and hDevNames fields are 0, the PrintDlg function allocates a DEVMODE structure and a DEVNAMES structure. It initializes the DEVNAMES structure with values for the current default printer. If you use the PageSetupDlg function to set up page parameters, you should copy the hDevMode and hDevNames values you get back from that function in its PAGESETUPDLG function to initialize the corresponding fields of the PRINTDLG. In this case, you had best ensure you have set all the fields to 0 values first and then set the lStructSize field, provided you are using the code we use in Listing 13.4, which won't initialize the structure unless those two handles are NULL. Note also that if you have used the PageSetupDlg, you should make sure that you have consistent devices between the two structures. For example, if neither is initialized, just call the function. If one is initialized, replace the handles in the structure you are about to pass with the handles in the other one so that changes the user made in one setup call are reflected to the other. Remember that you must free up the handles before overwriting them with a different handle.

As with the hDevMode handle, the hDevNames global memory handle can be different from the handle passed to the PrintDlg function when the function call returns, even when the function call returns 0. The original handle has already been freed, but you must free the returned handle when you are done with it if it is nonzero.

You don't have to use the strings returned in the DEVNAMES structure to create a DC or IC for the specified device using CreateDC. Although this was common in Win16, and absolutely necessary before PrintDlg was introduced, it is not necessary in Win32. You can, as we have already explained, ask the PrintDlg function to create the DC or IC for you. You specify the PD_RETURNDC or PD_RETURNIC flag in the Flags field of the PRINTDLG structure. The PrintDlg function returns a DC handle or IC handle in the hDC field of the PRINTDLG structure.

Listing 13.5: Displaying the contents of the DEVNAMES structure
```
void showDevNames(HWND hdlg, int ctlid, HANDLE hDevNames)
{
    if (hDevNames != NULL)
       { /* has devnames */
        TCHAR s[256];
        LPDEVNAMES dn;
        dn = (LPDEVNAMES)GlobalLock(hDevNames);
        wsprintf (s, _T("[%s] [%s] [%s] %s"),
              (LPCTSTR)&((LPCSTR)dn)[dn->wDriverOffset],
              (LPCTSTR)&((LPCSTR)dn)[dn->wDeviceOffset],
              (LPCTSTR)&((LPCSTR)dn)[dn->wOutputOffset],
                 dn->wDefault & DN_DEFAULTPRN
                          ? _T("Default") : _T(""));
        GlobalUnlock (hDevNames);
        SetDlgItemText (hdlg, ctlid, s);
       } /* has devnames */
    else
```

```
    { /* no devnames */
     SetDlgItemText (hdlg, ctlid, _T("NULL"));S
    } /* no devnames */
}
```

Three Elements Required in a Printing Windows Application

A printing Windows application must have three elements not needed by nonprinting applications. The first is basically an initialization process. You determine which printer is installed on the system. You create a DC for the printer. You retrieve various metrics about the printing surface (the "page") and the sizes of characters in the font(s) you use when printing. In other words, you first retrieve information about the printer upon which you're going to print and then use this information to format each page properly. We retrieved practically the same information about the system display and used it to format window output.

The second element consists of functions you must add solely to allow the user to interact with your own application while your application is busy printing. Users are frequently rather fickle folks. A user instructs your application to print a file. The application finds out on which printer to print. It sets the printer to the proper mode. The application retrieves the metrics for the printer and the printer's fonts. The application merrily prints along and . . . the user decides to cancel the print request.

Whoops! All that work, and you haven't given the user a way to cancel a long-running print request! This is not the time to extol on the elegant design of your printing code or the precision with which you place each unwanted word on each unwanted page. Users find themselves in the position of the sorcerer's apprentice, having started something they can no longer control.

In addition to the *abort function*, you must add an *abort dialog function* to allow the user to interact with your application, specifically, to allow the user to cancel a long-running print request. This terminology is confusing but is the standard for these functions.

The abort *function* is not the same as the abort *dialog function*. The abort function allows the user to continue to interact with the application while it is printing. The abort dialog function allows the user to cancel an in-progress print request. To make matters worse, the abort dialog function interacts with the abort function, so we must describe the two functions together to some extent.

The third element to add to your application is the easiest conceptually. You simply add the code to print each page. This task is very similar to formatting a display in a window. The main difference is the additional error checking you must include when printing. For example, you never run out of "paper" when drawing on the system display. You have to gracefully handle such problems when printing.

Obtaining Information about a Printer

After you have a DC for a printer, you can find out information about the device. For example, we call the `GetDeviceCaps` function in the example program to get the height and width of the printable area on the device. Some selected `GetDeviceCaps` codes are summarized in Table 13.9. We also call the `GetTextMetrics` function to obtain the height of a character in the default font for the device. If we were doing a simple "line printer emulation", we could use the following code to compute the number of lines that will fit on a page:

```
cxPage = GetDeviceCaps (hdc, HORZRES) ;
cyPage = GetDeviceCaps (hdc, VERTRES) ;
GetTextMetrics (hdc, &tm) ;
cyChar = tm.tmHeight + tm.tmExternalLeading ;

// Compute 1/4" margins (LOGPIXELSY / 4) at top and
// bottom (2 * 1/4")

margins = 2 * (GetDeviceCaps (hdc, LOGPIXELSY) / 4);
LinesPerPage = (cyPage - margins) / cyChar;
```

Table 13.9: Selected GetDeviceCaps codes

Code	Description
HORZSIZE	Width, in mm, of the printable area.
VERTSIZE	Height, in mm, of the printable area.
HORZRES	Width, in pixels, of the printable area.
VERTRES	Height, in pixels, of the printable area.
LOGPIXELSX	Number of pixels per horizontal logical inch.
LOGPIXELSY	Number of pixels per vertical logical inch.
RASTERCAPS	The raster capabilities of the printer, expressed as a set of bit options. Selected options are as follows:
	RC_BANDING Printer requires banding support.
	RC_BITBLT Printer can handle bitmaps.
	RC_SCALING Printer supports scaling.

It is worth pointing out that the HORZRES and VERTRES values are the *printable* area of the page. It is up to the device driver to determine what its printer can actually do. (Very few printers can print a full $8^{1}/_{2} \times 11$ inch page on Letter paper. An exception is a printer called *full bleed*–a technical term from the printing industry meaning edge-to-edge printing. Many color printers do support full bleed printing.) An example of actual values is shown in Table 13.10. The values shown in the **Value** column are those reported by GetDeviceCaps. The sizes are computed directly (unshaded boxes) or based on the computation of 25.4 mm/inch (shaded boxes). The HORZSIZE and VERTSIZE values are computed based on the LOGPIXELSX and LOGPIXELSY values. Note minor discrepancies due to roundoff errors. Hence, the computation of the margins value in the previous example is for $^{1}/_{2}$-inch margins in the printable area. A computation of the *real* margin would require using information from the DEVMODE, based on the paper size. In our example, however, the dmPaperLength and dmPaperWidth fields of the DEVMODE are *not* set. Only the dmPaperSize is set, thereby leaving it up to us to compute the actual size from the DMPAPER_LETTER value using a lookup table.

Table 13.10: Sample `GetDeviceCaps` values

Parameter	Value	Units	Size	
HORZRES	202	mm	202 mm	7.95 in.
VERTRES	267	mm	267 mm	10.51 in.
HORZSIZE	2391	pixels	202 mm	7.97 in.
VERTSIZE	3150	pixels	267 mm	10.50 in.
LOGPIXELSX	300	pixels/in.		
LOGPIXELSY	300	pixels/in.		

All values in this table are for the version 3.10 driver for a QMS-2200PS printer configured for Letter paper (8½-×-11 in. page), DEVMODE dmPaperSize reporting DMPAPER_LETTER, running on Windows NT release 3.51. Your Mileage May Vary. Shaded values are computed dimensions. Dimensions for HORZSIZE and VERTSIZE are computed based on LOGPIXELSX and LOGPIXELSY.

Another attribute of a printer that's often very important is whether the device can print bitmaps. You call the `GetDeviceCaps` function specifying the `RASTERCAPS` parameter to return a value that describes the raster capabilities of the device. When the `RC_BITBLT` bit is set in the returned value, the device accepts bit-block transfers and can print bitmaps:

```
if (GetDeviceCaps (hdc, RASTERCAPS) & RC_BITBLT)
    {
    // The device supports bit-block transfers.
    }
```

Remember, there's really nothing special about a printer DC when compared to the display contexts we've been using all along. You can switch fonts, change mapping mode, change pens and brushes, and change colors on color printers by selecting the right objects into a printer DC just as you can for a display context.

One point to remember is that the `EndPage` function call resets the attributes of the specified DC to their default values. Brushes, pens, fonts, and other changed attributes must be reselected into the DC after *each* `EndPage` function call.

Allowing Other Program Interactions while Printing

When you print in a Windows application, your main printing logic need not do anything special to allow mouse interactions to continue. As you issue each GDI output function to draw on the page, GDI simply adds a record to the disk-based metafile and returns to the printing logic. The majority of the work begins when you signal the completion of a page by making an `EndPage` function call.

When you call the `EndPage` function, GDI replays the metafile containing the output for the page and issues the drawing requests to the device driver once for each band on the page (which, as we've pointed out, may be only one band for many page printers). The device driver converts the drawing requests into the appropriate printer control sequences and data and gives this information back to GDI. GDI then stores the actual printer output in a spool file. When the entire page has been spooled (or printed), the call to EndPage function returns.

The Abort Function

Converting the metafile to printer output and spooling it can be an extremely lengthy operation. GDI gives the application a chance to abort this lengthy operation by periodically calling a specified function while processing the EndPage function call. This function is called the *abort function*.

In Win16 applications, which were nonpreemptive, the abort function had another critical role: It informed the system that other tasks could now run. Otherwise, *nothing* else could happen while the user was printing. Win32 uses preemptive multitasking and does not require this feature of the abort function, although, as we will show, it helps the preemptive scheduler if you explicitly release the processor instead of waiting for your application to be preempted by the scheduler.

Although Windows doesn't require a printing Windows application to have an abort function, you should always include one. Without an abort function, the print request cannot be canceled. And without an abort function, the print request will always fail when an out-of-disk-space error occurs.

The primary purpose of an abort function (as indicated by its name) is to give your application the chance to abort the print request. GDI calls the abort function; this means the abort function is a CALLBACK-linkage function.

The abort function returns a nonzero value to indicate that GDI should continue processing the still-outstanding EndPage function call. That is, when the abort function returns a nonzero value, GDI continues replaying the metafile, spooling output for a page and periodically calling the abort function. Control returns to the caller of the EndPage function call only after GDI finishes spooling the page without encountering an error and without the abort function's requesting an abort.

The abort function returns FALSE to indicate that GDI should stop processing the outstanding EndPage function call and abort the print job. When the abort function returns FALSE, GDI stops replaying the metafile, aborts the print request, and, supposedly, returns to the caller of the EndPage function call the SP_APPABORT error code that indicates that the abort function aborted the print job. We say "supposedly" because although the documentation states that an error code will be returned in this situation, we've never received one. We've always found that GDI does abort the print job when the abort function requests an abort, but the EndPage return code still indicates that no error or abort was encountered.

The abort function has a second purpose. You can (and should!) include a special second-level message loop in the logic of the abort function. It allows your program to process other messages while GDI generates your application's printer output. In particular, it allows the WM_LBUTTONDOWN message that is clicked over the **Cancel** button on the dialog to be processed, thereby allowing the user to cancel the print job.

GDI periodically calls your abort function where you handle messages using the special second-level message loop. This allows your application to retrieve any pending messages. After each pending message is processed, control returns to the second-level message loop in your abort function. When there are no more pending messages, the PeekMessage returns FALSE. The loop terminates, and the abort function returns TRUE to GDI, which continues the generation of the printer output.

The abort function has a third purpose. GDI also calls the abort function when two conditions are met:

- There is insufficient space on the disk drive specified by the TEMP environment variable.

- More space will eventually become available if only your application will release control and wait for a while.

When GDI calls an abort function because of insufficient disk space, you can take this opportunity to alert the user that the disk is full. Meanwhile, the output is usually being written to the printer by the spooling system, so disk space may come free. The user may also choose to free up some space by explicitly deleting unused files or moving files to another drive.[1] If you return a TRUE value, the GDI will again attempt to write. This may return control to you again if the disk is still full. Although Win32 systems are preemptive multitasking, it would be nice to explicitly say, "I really can't do anything else until some other task runs," and then release control of the processor without having to wait for the task to be preempted. The secondary message loop is such an indicator to the operating system.

This process continues until a file is completely printed. When the system finishes using a spool file, it deletes the spool file, which frees additional disk space. This time, when the abort function returns to GDI, GDI finds additional space available, and the application can continue printing.

Note that this is a major improvement over not using an abort function in your application. When an out-of-disk-space error occurs in an application that has specified no abort function, the EndPage function call returns an SP_OUTOFDISK error regardless of whether disk space could become available.

The following steps are required to use an abort function:

1. Define the abort function.
2. Notify GDI of the existence of the abort function for a print job.

We next look at each step, beginning with the abort function, which is often called AbortFunc. You must define this function as follows (with the qualification, of course, that you can call it practically anything):

```
BOOL CALLBACK AbortFunc (HDC hdc, int nCode)
{
    /* Function body */
}
```

The hdc parameter identifies the printer DC. The nCode parameter indicates whether an error has occurred. It is 0 if no error has occurred. It is the value SP_OUTOFDISK when insufficient disk space is available and more disk space will become available if the application delays and allows other applications to run. As it

---

[1] You might want to use a MessageBox call to do this. If you read the description of the MessageBox call, it suggests that the MB_SYSTEMMODAL flag should be used "to notify the user of serious, potentially damaging, errors that require immediate attention (for example, running out of memory)". Of course, if you use a system-modal message box here, the user *won't* be able to switch to another task to free up some disk space. Worse still, if you had used it to notify the user of a lack of memory, or virtual memory, the user would be unable to shut down any other tasks in the system! *Don't* use a system-modal message box unless you are utterly certain you know that it is the only choice! It is only very rarely the correct choice.

turns out, however, there is no real need to check the value of this parameter. You generally want to do the same thing no matter why GDI calls the abort function.

An abort function has the following basic structure:

```
BOOL CALLBACK AbortFunc (HDC hdc, int nCode)
{
    MSG msg ;

    while (PeekMessage (&msg, 0, 0, 0, PM_REMOVE))
        {
        TranslateMessage (&msg) ;
        DispatchMessage (&msg) ;
        }

    return TRUE ;
}
```

GDI calls the abort function periodically. In it, you repeatedly call the PeekMessage function as long as it returns a nonzero value. The PeekMessage function returns a nonzero value when it retrieves a message from the application message queue. (The message is also removed from the queue because the PM_REMOVE parameter was specified. Without this parameter, the message would be retrieved, but not removed, from the queue.)

For each retrieved message, you translate and dispatch it just as you do in a standard message loop. So far, in fact, nothing is different from a standard message loop. However, things change a little bit when the Peek-Message function finds no message to retrieve.

When the PeekMessage function finds no message in the queue, it will return a 0 (FALSE) value. Before returning FALSE, however, it notifies the scheduler that it is desirable to release control and allow scheduling of other applications. This allows these other applications to retrieve their messages from their message queues. After all applications have had a chance to run (the preemptive nature of Win32 does not require that they run until their message queues are empty), your application again gets a chance to run. The call to the Peek-Message function will return a FALSE value if there are still no messages in your application's queue.

Both the GetMessage and PeekMessage functions return a message currently in the application's message queue and, if there are none, notify the scheduler to allow other applications to run. The difference is that the GetMessage function never returns until a message is available for the calling application; it is a "blocking call". The PeekMessage function returns FALSE if these is no message available; it is a "nonblocking call". You must be careful about using PeekMessage in other contexts, however. Because your application looks "active", laptop power management software usually refuses to go into its power-down-if-idle-too-long state; your application has defeated the ability of the laptop to conserve the battery power. Many problems that were handled in Win16 by using PeekMessage are better handled in Win32 by other mechanisms, such as multiple threads.

In the AbortFunc function, the FALSE value from PeekMessage terminates the while loop. The abort function then returns TRUE, indicating that GDI should continue printing.

The abort function can return FALSE to abort the print job; however, this doesn't work quite as you might expect. When GDI calls the abort function with the nCode parameter set to the value SP_OUTOFDISK and the abort function returns FALSE, the current in-progress EndPage function call (the one that triggered this call to the abort function) returns the error code SP_APPABORT. The print job is aborted.

When GDI calls the abort function with the nCode parameter set to 0 (the normal situation) and the abort function returns FALSE (to abort the current print request), the in-progress EndPage function call does not return an error, as the documentation states it does. Instead, GDI quits generating output for the page terminated by the aborted EndPage call, but the EndPage call itself appears successful to the printing logic in your application.

This leads to a common problem with the initial versions of many Windows printing applications. Requesting that a print job be aborted by returning FALSE from the abort procedure aborts the printer output generation for the current page and terminates the print request as requested. Because the EndPage function returns successfully in this situation (contrary to the documentation), an application's printing logic, thinking no errors were encountered, draws the next page and executes another EndPage function call. This results in GDI's eventually calling the abort function again, which immediately aborts that page as well. This process continues until the application has "printed" the entire document.

Of course, it's much more efficient to signal the printing logic to stop printing when the abort function aborts the print job. The abort function cancels the output for the current page, but you want to indicate to the printing logic that no additional pages should be printed. Unfortunately, there's no way to do this as a return value from an EndPage function call. You must use a technique that is a last resort–a global variable. You'll see how to do this in the Print DLL example program.

You set the abort function for a print job by calling the SetAbortProc function. You pass the printer DC handle and the procedure address of the abort function. Here is a typical call to set the abort function for a print job:

```
SetAbortProc (hdc, AbortFunc) ;
```

You must set the abort function for a print job before starting the job with the StartDoc function call. You don't need to set the abort function to NULL or to another function when printing is complete because GDI calls the abort function only during the EndPage function call. It never calls it when you're not printing.

The previous simple abort function doesn't provide a means to actually abort the print job. Instead, it always returns TRUE, thereby indicating that the print job should continue. Providing the capability to abort a print job complicates the abort function only a little. We soon show you an abort function that allows the user to abort a print job, but first we look at a different function: the abort dialog function.

The Abort Dialog Function

For a user to abort a print job, you must supply a method for the user to indicate that an abort is desired. You could conceivably provide a menu selection or a control on the application window that allows the user to do this. However, such an approach has many drawbacks, as you'll see in this section. The typical approach is to provide a modeless dialog box that has a **Cancel** push button. The application creates and displays the modeless dialog box when it begins printing. If the user clicks the push button, the print job is canceled. When the application finishes printing, the modeless dialog box is destroyed.

Because a dialog box has an associated dialog function, the function for the dialog box used to abort a print job is often called the *abort dialog function*. You have to be careful to distinguish between the *abort function* and the *abort dialog function*. They work together closely but are two different functions.

The abort dialog function is generally quite simple. Its only purpose is to set a flag indicating that the user has requested to abort the print job. Here is a very simple abort dialog function:

```
BOOL Aborted      = FALSE ; // The global abort flag
HWND hAbort = 0 ;

void abort_OnCommand(HWND hdlg, int id, HWND hctl, UINT codeNotify)
    {
    switch(id)
        { /* id */
        case IDOK:
        case IDCANCEL:
            Aborted = TRUE ;
            return;
        } /* id */
    }

BOOL CALLBACK
AbortDlgFunc (HWND hdlg, UINT msg, WPARAM wParam, LPARAM lParam)
{
    switch (message) {
        case WM_INITDIALOG:
            Aborted = FALSE ;
            hAbort = hdlg ;
            return TRUE ;

        case WM_COMMAND:
            HANDLE_WM_COMMAND(hdlg, wParam, lParam, abort_OnCommand);
            return TRUE;

        case WM_DESTROY:
            hAbort = 0 ;
            return TRUE ;
    }
    return FALSE ;
}
```

The Aborted global variable contains a Boolean value indicating whether the user has aborted the print job. The hAbort global variable contains the handle to the modeless abort dialog box window. It contains 0 when the dialog box doesn't exist. These two global variables are used by the abort dialog function and the abort function. The Aborted variable will also be used by the main printing logic.

The abort dialog function sets both variables during the WM_INITDIALOG message processing. The Aborted flag is set to FALSE to indicate that the print job hasn't yet been aborted. (Actually, it hasn't even begun because one of the first things you do is create and display the dialog box before starting printing.) The dialog window handle (provided by the hdlg parameter) is saved in the hAbort global variable. Because a valid window handle is always a nonzero value, testing hAbort for nonzero is equivalent to determining if the modeless dialog box exists. Of course, to maintain the validity of this test, you need to reset hAbort to 0 when the dialog box is destroyed. You do this in the WM_DESTROY message processing logic.

A `WM_COMMAND` message with a control ID equal to the value `IDOK` or `IDCANCEL` indicates that the user has either clicked the **Cancel** push button, pressed the **Enter** key, pressed the **Esc** key, or closed the dialog box via the system menu. In other words, we're giving the user many ways to cancel the print job. You may wish to restrict the user to fewer ways. Regardless of the ways you decide to allow the user to enter the cancel request, the dialog function simply sets the `Aborted` variable to `TRUE`, thus indicating that the user requested an abort.

After you create the abort dialog box, you should disable your application's window. Disabling the window prevents it from receiving keyboard and mouse input. This is very important! When GDI calls your abort function, the abort function dispatches all messages in your application's message queue before releasing control to other applications.

One of these messages could be for the application's window and could cause the application to attempt to modify the data being printed, thereby resulting in the printed output for later pages being inconsistent with earlier pages. But it also means that the user could perform another print request (maybe even multiple requests) before the application manages to complete the first one. The application or user might attempt to delete a file that it's currently printing; this attempt would fail because the print loop would still have the file open. The user might even use the system menu to close (terminate) the application!

That produces a real mess because the application's window(s) would be destroyed while it's running in a secondary message loop (the `PeekMessage` loop). Eventually, control would return from the `DispatchMessage` call in the abort function, which, in turn, would try to return to GDI. GDI then would return from the `EndPage` function call into the application's window function, which is performing the print request. Assuming the application made it this far without crashing, you would now be running in a window function where the window handle given to the window function would be invalid (because the application was terminated) and the window would no longer exist.

By your disabling the application's window, all mouse and keyboard input to your application is funneled through the abort dialog function. This prevents the endless problems that can arise as a result of messages that cause your application to be reentered while it's busy printing. After the printing is complete (or aborted), you enable the application window just prior to destroying the abort dialog box. This allows the application to once again receive mouse and keyboard input.

A (Slightly) More Complex Abort Function

No matter how complex you make the abort dialog function (the Print DLL displays the page it is printing in the abort dialog box), it maintains two pieces of information that are visible outside the function. They are the handle to the dialog box and the Boolean abort flag, both of which the abort function uses. To demonstrate this, here is the entire abort function for the Print DLL:

```
BOOL CALLBACK
AbortFunc (HDC hdc, int nCode)
{
    MSG msg ;

    while (PeekMessage (&msg, 0, 0, 0, PM_REMOVE))
```

```
        if (!hAbort || !IsDialogMessage (hAbort, &msg))
           {
            TranslateMessage (&msg) ;
            DispatchMessage (&msg) ;
           }

    return (!Aborted) ;
}
```

The PeekMessage loop has changed slightly from the basic abort function. After the PeekMessage function retrieves a message, we check to see whether the abort dialog box currently exists. If it does, the message might be a keyboard message intended for the dialog box (for example, if the user presses **Enter** or **Esc**). The IsDialogMessage function examines the message and, if it's for the specified dialog box, completely processes the message. When the dialog box doesn't currently exist or the message isn't intended for the dialog box, the message is translated and dispatched normally. Basically, we've added the normal lines of code required to provide a keyboard interface to a modeless dialog box.

After giving other applications a chance to run, the abort function returns the proper value to GDI indicating whether the user has aborted the print job. If the user hasn't (Aborted is FALSE), the abort function returns TRUE, thus indicating that GDI should continue generating the printer output for the page. When the user has aborted the print job (Aborted is TRUE), the abort function returns FALSE, thereby indicating that GDI should stop generating output for the current page. Remember that the EndPage function doesn't return any indication that the print job was aborted by the abort function except in the special circumstance of an insufficient disk space error. You'll need to test the value of the Aborted flag in the printing logic and halt printing there, too.

Printing a Document

Here is a skeletal version of the logic to print a document. We removed the error checking from this template to highlight the structure of the process. You can look at similar code in the Print DLL to see much of the necessary error handling. The code assumes that the abort function has been set already:

```
DOCINFO docinfo ;
      .
      .
      .
Aborted = FALSE ;
PrintError = FALSE ;

docinfo.cbSize       = sizeof (docinfo) ;
docinfo.lpszDocName  = lpFileName ;
docinfo.lpszOutput   = NULL ;

Status = StartDoc (hdc, &docinfo) ;

while (!Aborted && !PrintError)
    { /* print loop */
     // Break out of loop if all pages
     // have been printed.
```

```
    if (endOfFile() || whateverTestYouLike())
        break ;

    /* Otherwise draw the page. */
    .
    .
    .

    /* Signal the end of the page.                  */
    /* The abort function gets called many times     */
    /* during the execution of this next statement. */

    if (EndPage (hdc)) < 0
        PrintError = TRUE ;
    } /* print loop */
if (!PrintError)
    if (Aborted)
        AbortDoc (hdc) ;

    else
        EndDoc (hdc) ;
```

Notice that this logic stops attempting to print pages as soon as either the Aborted flag or the PrintError flag is TRUE. It isn't absolutely necessary to stop printing when only the Aborted flag is TRUE because the printing of each page would be aborted by the abort function. If you're printing a very long document, however, it could take quite a while for the print logic to draw each page to the metafile, only for the information to be discarded. It is best to avoid doing unnecessary work, so we stop drawing pages as soon as we detect that the user has aborted the request.

Finally, once you've printed all pages in the document, you signal the end of the document by calling the EndDoc function. There are three situations that must be handled here:

1. No errors were encountered and the print request was not aborted by the abort function. In this case, you must call the EndDoc function to end the document.

2. GDI encounters an error during the processing of an EndPage function call. The EndPage function will return an error code, thus causing the PrintError flag to be set to TRUE. In this case, you must not call the EndDoc function or the AbortDoc function because GDI has already ended (aborted) the document.

3. The user requests that the print request be aborted. Therefore the abort function signals GDI to abort the current page and the EndPage function call immediately returns, indicating that no error was encountered. The Aborted flag is TRUE, but the PrintError flag is still FALSE. In this case, you must call the AbortDoc function to abort the document.

Error handling is the most complex part of the print logic for a Windows application. The Print File example uses structured exception handling liberally to recover properly from errors and to release all allocated resources.

The order in which you call the various interrelated and interacting components of a Windows printing application is also important. Here is a suggested ordering for the steps required to print from a Windows application, as illustrated in Figure 13.1:

1. `PageSetupDlg`: Allow the user to do a page setup and be sure to set up values that represent the defaults if the user does not do a page setup.

2. `PrintDlg`: Create a DC for the printer.

3. `SetAbortProc`: Set the abort function for the print job.

4. `CreateDialog`: Create the modeless abort dialog box.

5. `EnableWindow`: Disable the application's window.

6. `StartDoc`: Signal the beginning of the document.

7. Repeatedly

    (a) `StartPage`: Signal the beginning of a new page,

    (b) draw each page, and

    (c) `EndPage`: Signal the completion of the page.

8. `EndDoc/AbortDoc`: Signal the end of the document.

    (a) `EndDoc`: completion if no printing errors were encountered, or

    (b) `AbortDoc` if the printing was canceled, or

    (c) Neither of the above if a printing error occurred.

9. `DestroyWindow`: Destroy the modeless abort dialog box.

10. `EnableWindow`: Enable the application's window.

11. `DeleteDC`: Delete the created printer DC.

This is all there is to printing in its basic form–other than a myriad of things that could go wrong!

Using Custom Dialog Templates and Hook Functions

Using a Custom Dialog Template

The goal of the common dialogs is to make it easy to get a consistent "look and feel" across all applications. So why would you want to do a custom dialog that would give your application a unique "look and feel"? Generally, you wouldn't want to use a custom dialog for printing, but what if the general print dialog template didn't quite make sense for your application? For example, you might be doing a calendar application where the print choices might be "All months", "Selected months", and "Months", and the edit controls would accept strings like "Jan 97", "01/97", or "97/01". While the "look and feel" actually would be consistent with other applications, the actual details of how the controls are handled would be quite different *for your custom features.* You still want the printer options, printer selection, and other features of the dialog.

Fortunately, Microsoft makes this easy for you. The templates for the common dialogs are all defined in a set of resource script files. You can copy one of these into your project. For example, under Microsoft Visual C++ the print and print setup dialog templates are found in the file `include\prnsetup.dlg` under the compiler directory (although other vendors or other releases of Microsoft compilers may put this elsewhere). In this file, the name of the print dialog template is PRINTDLGORD and the name of the print setup dialog template is PRNSETUPDLGORD.

To use one of these templates, you must copy the template into your resource file and must also force the file `dlgs.h` to be included in your resource compilation. This file defines all the control IDs. If you don't include it in your resource file, most resource editors will be unable to load your resource file.

Once you have made the copy and set up the header file, you can open your resource script and edit the print dialog resource. However, one restriction on editing is absolutely crucial: You *may not* delete any control already present in the dialog. Nor may you use its ID for any other purpose. If you wish to make a control disappear, you must mark it as "disabled" and remove its "visible" flag. For your editing convenience, you may move such disabled, invisible controls off to some unused corner of the dialog, but they *must* be present. The common dialog handler for PrintDlg will assume that all these controls exist. If they do not, PrintDlg will fail, most likely with a PDERR_INITFAILURE code (from CommDlgExtendedError()).

You can now add your own custom controls. When you are setting up for PrintDlg, you must set the following flags and values in the PRINTDLG structure to cause your custom template to be used:

```
pd.Flags |= PD_ENABLEPRINTTEMPLATE;
pd.hInstance = your_instance_handle_here;
pd.lpPrintTemplateName = MAKEINTRESOURCE(PRINTDLGORD);
```

We use MAKEINTRESOURCE because the symbol PRINTDLGORD is defined in `dlgs.h`. Of course, you can change the name if you have more than one kind of print dialog; we just have one and chose to retain its original name.

You may also wish to set

```
pd.lCustData = (LPARAM)your_custom_data_pointer_here;
```

to add your own custom data (usually a pointer) to the dialog setup, a topic we discuss in the next section. You can see this using the Print Explorer. Set the values shown in Table 13.11 and click the **PrintDlg** button.

Table 13.11: Print Explorer settings for custom print template

Tab	Field	Value	Represents	Computed As
PRINTDLG	nMinPage	23940	Jan 1995	1995 * 12 + 0
PRINTDLG	nMaxPage	24023	Dec 2001	2001 * 12 + 11
PRINTDLG	nFromPage	23952	Jan 1996	1996 * 12 + 0
PRINTDLG	nToPage	23963	Dec 1996	1996 * 12 + 11
PRINTDLG Flags	PD_ENABLEPRINTHOOK	✓		

Table 13.11: Print Explorer settings for custom print template

Tab	Field	Value	Represents	Computed As
PRINTDLG Flags	PD_ENABLEPRINTTEMPLATE	✓		
PRINTDLG Flags	PD_PAGENUMS	✓		

We set up the custom printing range so that we encode the month as the number of months from January, year 0 (00000). Hence, January 1995 is computed as shown. We discuss this in more detail in the next section. The result is shown in Figure 13.5. The customizations that we have added are shown circled.

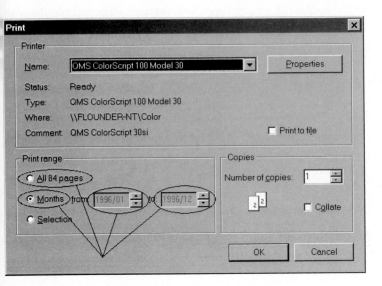

Figure 13.5: A custom print dialog

Using a Hook Function

Generally a custom dialog is not terribly useful unless you can actually deal with your custom controls. For example, you might set the PRINTDLG nMinPage and nMaxPage values of a calendar application to some span of months, for example, January of the previous year to December of two years from now. You might also set the nFromPage and nToPage values to be January and December, respectively, of the current year. But you want to display the limits according to the prevailing date format selected by the user or the site and interpret input according to the localized standard date notation. This means you will have to have your own edit controls for specifying the "from" and "to" dates, load them when the dialog is created, respond to changes in them, and store them when the dialog terminates. Even though the dialog looks otherwise identical to the ordinary print dialog, these two controls are different.

To allow you to deal with custom controls, you can specify a *hook function* in the PRINTDLG setup. You must set the lpfnPrintHook or lpfnSetupHook fields in PRINTDLG to get a custom print dialog hook or a custom print setup dialog hook. You must also set the PD_ENABLEPRINTHOOK or PD_ENABLESETUPHOOK flags so that your hook function will be called. For example, to enable our custom hook function, printHook, we do the following setup before calling PrintDlg:

```
pd.lpfnPrintHook = printHook
pd.Flags |= PD_ENABLEPRINTHOOK;
```

A hook function is a dialog function that is called whenever a message is received by the standard common print dialog handler. It looks to see if you have enabled the hook function, and if you have, it calls your hook function. If you return TRUE, the common dialog handler returns TRUE; if you return FALSE, the common dialog handler performs its normal handling. Your hook function will be called before any other processing, with one exception: The WM_INITDIALOG message will be processed first by the common dialog function and *then* by your hook function.

This does complicate things a bit because of the way the message cracker macros and handlers are specified. The HANDLE_WM_COMMAND message, for example, always evaluates to a FALSE value. Normally when we write a dialog handler, we write

```
case WM_COMMAND:
     HANDLE_WM_COMMAND(hdlg, wParam, lParam, dlg_OnCommand);
     return TRUE;
```

but in the case of a hook function, this would mean that *all* WM_COMMAND messages, including the ones for the controls we have left alone, would be treated as if they were processed in our hook function. This is not what we want; we want all the other controls to work normally.

Table 13.12: Common Dialog control ranges

Name	Hex	Decimal
ctlFirst	0x400	1024
ctlLast	0x4FF	1279

The simplest solution is to choose control IDs for our custom controls that are well outside the range of controls used by the common dialogs, a range of controls defined by the symbols ctlFirst and ctlLast in the file dlgs.h. Unfortunately, most resource editors don't let you use symbolic values, even on initial assignment, so you must look up these values and choose a control value outside the range. The control values and their hex and decimal equivalents are shown in Table 13.12. You then can do a simple discrimination:

```
static BOOL handled;

BOOL CALLBACK myHookFunc(HWND hdlg, int msg, WPARAM wParam, LPARAM lParam)
{
 switch(msg)
    { /* msg */
     case WM_COMMAND:
             HANDLE_WM_COMMAND(hdlg, wParam, lParam, dlg_OnCommand);
             return handled;
     // .. other messages here
    } /* msg */
}

void dlg_OnCommmand(HWND hdlg, int id, HWND hctl, UINT codeNotify)
{
 if(ctlFirst <= id && id <= ctlLast)
    { /* dlgs.h control */
     handled = FALSE;
     return;
    } /* dlgs.h control */
  // .. one of our controls
  switch(id)
     // .. handle controls here
  handled = TRUE;
  return;
}
```

This solution is inelegant, and potentially not thread-safe, because of the use of a shared static variable between the two functions. However, if you are printing, it is unlikely you will have two separate threads both trying to print, so thread safety is not likely to have any practical impact on your code. Of course, you must then make sure that only one thread can actually initiate printing.

For a more elegant, and thread-safe, solution you could use SetProp and GetProp to store the "handled" property with the dialog window. However, you must remember to RemoveProp when the window is destroyed.

We have taken a simple approach here: All standard controls operate normally, and our new controls are handled by our new code. In some cases, you may wish to override the behavior of some built-in controls, either replacing it entirely (probably not a good idea) or taking special actions (not uncommon). You would simply set the handled flag to indicate whether standard processing is to proceed.

The Microsoft Foundation Class library does not correctly support writing common dialog hook functions. The problem is if you intercept any message for an existing control, MFC gratuitously returns TRUE, thus indicating you have completely handled the message *even if your purpose is simply to note what control was changed and you want the common dialog to do whatever it is supposed to do*. In the Font Explorer, we discovered this after much tedious debugging. You may want to read our code to see how we intercepted the messages and translated them to MFC. Unfortunately, this appears to be an intrinsic design limitation up to and including MFC 4.*x*.

MFC

While you may be tempted to avoid the use of the message cracker macros entirely–after all, the problem of returning a value is simply an artifact of the definition of the HANDLE_WM_COMMAND macro–remember that we might see, in a few years, a Win64 API for 64-bit machines. And the conversion trauma may be just as bad as the Win16/Win32 conversion has been. A little more work now can reduce the amount of work in the future, and robustness-under-maintenance is one of our goals.

In our hook function, we can handle all the details of converting date strings in the edit controls to integers that encode the dates. This is more complicated than you might imagine because you have to deal with localization. For example, if you allow "Jan-96" you must allow all of the short-month-abbreviations for all possible countries. Windows provides support for this with such API calls as EnumCalendarInfo, but a detailed discussion of this topic is well beyond the scope of this book. We recommend *Developing International Software for Windows 95 and Windows NT*, by Nadine Kano (see the review on page 942).

Without going into all the details of the locale-specific information, we present an implementation of the modified Print dialog in Figure 13.5. To simplify our setting of dates, we do not allow the user to modify the dates directly by typing in text. Instead, we provide "spin controls", known formally in Windows as "up-down controls", that allow the user to modify the internal, but not the external, representation. To avoid having to include locale-specific date conversion here, we simply represent the date as a numeric year and month based on the Gregorian calendar, for example, "1996/01". A truly internationalized application would have to support local calendars, not just the Gregorian calendar.

Although we have "replaced" the existing page edit controls, we cannot remove them. If you bring up the dialog in your dialog editor, you will find that the original from-page and to-page controls have been moved to the lower-left corner of the dialog and set to be both "disabled" and "invisible". But we can't remove them, and in fact we must actually use them, as we show you when we discuss the IDOK handler.

If you use the Print Explorer application we include on the CD-ROM, you will find that you cannot set the PD_ENABLEPRINTTEMPLATE flag without setting the PD_ENABLEPRINTHOOK flag to the same state. Setting or clearing one will set or clear the other. This is because the Print Explorer has a built-in special test case of the custom dialog we are describing here and requires both flags be set. It would not work correctly if only one were set. If you set the flags, a button called "Dates" is enabled. This button stores some encoded date values in the page controls.

The encoding[2] we use for dates is $(year * 12) + (month - 1)$. We export from our handler three functions to handle the encoding:

1. encodeYYMM takes a year and month and delivers an encoded integer.
2. decodeYY takes an encoded date and returns the year.
3. decodeMM takes an encoded date and returns the month.

Of course this would be "simplified" if we simply used the low-order 2 digits of the year. Unfortunately, this fails utterly when the end-of-century boundary is passed; incrementing the encoded date for 99/12, 1199, gives the value 1200, thus resulting in the decoded string 100/1. We could, of course, take the resulting year mod 100, resulting in the decoded string 00/1. But if we were to actually parse the input string, as we might want to do, life becomes immediately more complex. It is generally a bad idea to truncate dates internally, and you should be very careful about how you deal with external truncation.[3]

We first modified the dialog template by adding the up-down controls and the edit controls. We made the edit controls "disabled" so that they do not respond to user input or to cut or paste operations. This saves us from having to deal with arbitrary changes in the text. We then wrote the hook handlers, which are in the file printhook.c. The hook function itself is printHook and is shown in Listing 13.6. We need to handle the WM_INITDIALOG, WM_COMMAND, and WM_VSCROLL messages.

Listing 13.6: The printHook function

```
static BOOL handled;
// The above variable is set by the WM_COMMAND and WM_VSCROLL handlers because
// they cannot return a value.  This represents a defect in the design of
// the message cracker macros
```

---

[2] It would have been easier to encode it as $(year * 100) + month$. Then you could type the values in yourself. For example, "199601" would represent January 1996. The only problem with this is that 199,601 exceeds 32,768. The up-down controls are limited to ranges of 32,768 with an absolute maximum value of 32,767 (it seems we keep getting stuck with 16-bit limits, despite being in a 32-bit environment). Since we wanted to use the up-down controls, we had to deal with this limit. Hence, the denser encoding, which is virtually unreadable in its raw form. The denser encoding also works better for dealing with wraparound; we don't have to make any special boundary checks as we would with the more-readable encoding. For example, if we had chosen the "readable" encoding, then when the control went to 199613, we would have to change it to be 199701, and when it went to 199600, we would have to change it to be 199512. This is a lot of extra complexity.

[3] It is a constant source of annoyance to me that a database tool I use to maintain bibliographic data will not let me record the original publication date of any science fiction story written before 1900. Even though it supports a full 4-digit year internally, it carefully does not permit the user to enter other than 2-digit years. I had to add a separate "century adjust" flag and set it to -100 in the records for Jules Verne and H. G. Wells, among others. Date-sorting is on the sum of the year and the century adjust flag; printout has to cope as well. I therefore strive to never create this same error in my own code. – *jmn*

```
JINT CALLBACK printHook (HWND hwnd, UINT msg, WPARAM wParam, LPARAM lParam)
    {
    switch(msg)
        { /* msg */
        case WM_INITDIALOG:
                return (BOOL)HANDLE_WM_INITDIALOG(
                                hwnd, wParam, lParam, printhook_OnInitDialog);
        case WM_COMMAND:
                HANDLE_WM_COMMAND (hwnd, wParam, lParam, printhook_OnCommand);
                return handled;
        case WM_VSCROLL:
                HANDLE_WM_VSCROLL (hwnd, wParam, lParam, printhook_OnVScroll);
                return handled;
        } /* msg */
    return 0;
    }
```

The first function we look at is the OnInitDialog handler function. For the common dialogs, the lParam of this function contains a pointer to the appropriate input structure, in this case, the PRINTDLG structure. The printhook_OnInitDialog function is shown in Listing 13.7, along with the support functions that initialize the controls. The setBuddy function associates an up-down control with some other control (in our case, an edit control). However, as we explain on page 992, we cannot use the built-in "buddy" notion because of its inherent limitations, so we implement our own using the GWL_USERDATA field.

Listing 13.7: The printhook_OnInitDialog function

```
static BOOL printhook_OnInitDialog(HWND hwnd, HWND hfocus, LPARAM lParam)
    {
    LPPRINTDLG pd = (LPPRINTDLG)lParam;

    SetWindowLong (hwnd, GWL_USERDATA, lParam);

    setBuddy (GetDlgItem (hwnd, IDC_SPINSTART),
                            GetDlgItem (hwnd, IDC_STARTMONTH));
    setBuddy (GetDlgItem (hwnd, IDC_SPINEND),
                            GetDlgItem (hwnd, IDC_ENDMONTH));

    setDateData (hwnd, IDC_STARTMONTH, pd->nFromPage);
    setDateData (hwnd, IDC_ENDMONTH,   pd->nToPage);
    setDateSpin (hwnd, IDC_SPINSTART, pd->nMinPage,
                        pd->nMaxPage, pd->nFromPage);
    setDateSpin (hwnd, IDC_SPINEND,    pd->nMinPage,
                        pd->nMaxPage, pd->nToPage);

    return TRUE;
    }

static void setDateData(HWND hwnd, int ctl, int date)
    {
    TCHAR strdate[256];
    if(date == 0)
        lstrcpy (strdate, _T(""));
    else
        wsprintf (strdate, _T("%d/%02d"),
                    decodeYY(date), decodeMM(date));
```

```
    SetDlgItemText (hwnd, ctl, strdate);
    }

static void setDateSpin(HWND hwnd, int ctl, int minval, int maxval, int val)
    {
    SendDlgItemMessage (hwnd, ctl, UDM_SETRANGE, 0, MAKELONG (maxval, minval));
    SendDlgItemMessage (hwnd, ctl, UDM_SETPOS, 0, val);
    }

static void setBuddy(HWND spin, HWND buddy)
    {
    SetWindowLong (spin, GWL_USERDATA, (LPARAM) buddy);
    }
```

The printhook_OnCommand function looks unnecessarily complicated for all that it does. This is because we will eventually want it to do more. For example, we would someday like to enable those edit controls and let the user type in an arbitrary date string, such as "Jan-97", and we will need to put handlers in for the edit control change notifications. Just because a feature is not currently in a version does not mean that it is not a good idea to structure the code so that it is easier to add it later.

The IDOK handler, shown in Listing 13.8, is a bit unusual in that it seems to be doing something rather pointless: storing the values of our controls into invisible, disabled, and unused controls. Appearances can be deceiving. This is one of the cases you must watch out for whenever you are modifying the behavior of a common dialog. Those controls are invisible and disabled because the common dialog handler still assumes that they are present and useful. It will fail if it can't find the controls it expects. When it does find them, it uses them, even if they are invisible and disabled.

Although we are handling the IDOK control notification, we still return FALSE to the common dialog, requesting that it continue its ordinary processing. Part of its ordinary processing is to grab the values stored in the controls for the first and last pages and store those values in nFromPage and nToPage, respectively. What seems obvious is that we should store the values of our up-down controls in nFromPage and nToPage, but if we do, they will be overwritten by the values from the hidden edit controls. And if we return TRUE, then PrintDlg will assume that we have copied *all* of the important control information out and won't bother to do so. So our only recourse is to let PrintDlg do what it wants to do. What *we* do is set the values of the up-down controls into the hidden, disabled edit controls so that the correct values will be returned to the caller.

How do we know which controls? We can inspect the print dialog template that we have copied into our resource file and discover that the two controls we moved aside are called edt1 and edt2. Not the most memorable of names; in fact all the controls in the common dialogs have names like this. You have to actually look at the dialogs in detail to see what the controls actually are used for. And, of course, there is the potential for such short names to conflict with names you've already declared. If you discover that after adding dlgs.h to your compilation, you are getting odd compilation errors (particularly ones dealing with integer syntax or similar messages), make sure you don't have a variable name that looks like one of the symbols in dlgs.h.

Listing 13.8: The printhook_OnCommand and printhook_OnOK functions
```
static void printhook_OnCommand(HWND hwnd, int id, HWND hctl, UINT codeNotify)
    {
```

```
     LPPRINTDLG pd = (LPPRINTDLG)GetWindowLong(hwnd, GWL_USERDATA);
     handled = FALSE;
     if(ctlFirst <= id && id <= ctlLast)
         { /* dlgs.h control */
          return;
         } /* dlgs.h control */

     switch(id)
         { /* id */
          case IDOK:
                    printhook_OnOK(hwnd);
                    break;
         } /* id */
     }

static void printhook_OnOK(HWND hwnd)
     {
     SetDlgItemInt (hwnd, edt1, getSpinValue (hwnd, IDC_SPINSTART), FALSE);
     SetDlgItemInt (hwnd, edt2, getSpinValue (hwnd, IDC_SPINEND), FALSE);
     handled = FALSE;  // we want normal handling
     }

static int getSpinValue(HWND hwnd, UINT id)
     {
     return (int)LOWORD(SendDlgItemMessage(hwnd, id, UDM_GETPOS, 0, 0));
     }
```

The last function of importance is the handler for the WM_VSCROLL messages. The OnVScroll handler is shown in Listing 13.9. We get WM_VSCROLL messages because our up-down controls are vertical. We could set a style flag that makes the control be horizontal, in which case we would get WM_HSCROLL messages.

Unlike a scroll bar control, an up-down control adjusts its own value. So we don't need to decode the code parameter to the OnVScroll handler. We merely query the position using the UDM_GETPOS message, which returns the current position in the low-order 16 bits of the return value. We then call the formatting function to store the result in the appropriate control.

To determine the appropriate control, we designate a "buddy" control using the same naming convention Windows uses. A "buddy" control is a control that is associated with an up-down control. Usually, either you create your up-down control with the UDS_AUTOBUDDY style, thereby making the control immediately preceding it in the Z-order be its buddy, or you use the UDM_SETBUDDY message to establish a buddy control. You also can set the UDS_SETBUDDYINT style, which causes the up-down control to send a WM_SETTEXT message to its buddy control to display its integer value. In our case, we can't use this flag because our formatting is more complex than a simple integer.

A buddy window also introduces additional complications. For example, the message to read the current position value does *not* read the up-down control position if there is a buddy control. Instead, it converts the text of the buddy control to an integer and returns that value. This is so the user can edit the text of the associated control and see that change reflected in the up-down control's position. Unfortunately, there is no style flag that turns this feature off if it isn't appropriate. Because we have fancier formatting than a simple integer, a buddy control would destroy our ability to read the up-down control's position. So although we need the idea, we don't want the "semantic baggage" that comes along with it. We "roll our own" buddy control concept by storing the handle of the buddy control in the GWL_USERDATA field of the up-down control.

We could have chosen to subclass our buddy control and intercept the WM_SETTEXT and WM_GETTEXT messages, changing the format from what the up/down control sets to the appropriate text. But this adds more
complication than we want to deal with. After all, to actually set the text requires sending a WM_SETTEXT
message to the control, which we *don't* want reinterpreted, so we have to detect the recursive call and handle
it properly. There is a alternative way to handle this.

The code is actually quite simple. If the scrolling message is not from one of our recognized controls, we
simply return FALSE to the caller of the hook and allow normal processing to occur. If it is one of our controls, we get the handle of its buddy and its position value and call the formatting function to put the value
into the edit control.

Listing 13.9: The printHook_OnVScroll handler

```
static void printhook_OnVScroll(HWND hwnd, HWND hctl, UINT code, int pos)
    {
    int buddy;
    int val;

    handled = FALSE;

    switch(GetDlgCtrlID(hctl))
        { /* which */
        case IDC_SPINSTART:
        case IDC_SPINEND:
                buddy = (HWND)GetWindowLong(hctl,GWL_USERDATA);
                break;
        default:
                return;
        } /* which */

    handled = TRUE;
    val = (int)LOWORD(SendMessage(hctl, UDM_GETPOS, 0, 0));

    setDateData(hwnd, GetDlgCtrlID(buddy), val);
}
```

A General Printing DLL

We have found that over the years we've written the same printing code again and again, with only slight
variations. Printing can be roughly characterized as being either "graphics" printing or "line printer emulation" printing (with plenty of exceptions, of course, but those two models seem to capture most of what
we've done). We've captured this experience in a fairly general DLL. While this DLL is not the ultimate
printing solution, it covers a large number of the cases we've encountered.

The printing solutions we've captured in this DLL include these:

- The basic printer setup after the printer DC has been obtained via PrintDlg

- The placement of headers and footers is handled, including accounting for the changes
  in the area in which you can print

- Headers and footers in a different font from the rest of the page

- Pagination, including notification of the abort dialog as to which page is being printed

- Handling termination, abort, and error conditions

- A callback to set up the DC for each page

- A callback that occurs just before the page is closed

- Lines of the page body, including

  - Lines in different fonts

  - Lines of the page body in mixed fonts

  - Lines of the page body that include graphical icons

Like most complex operations, this requires a detailed setup structure. To allow for flexibility, we incorporated several expansion features. In addition, this is a good example of the integration of a number of techniques we discussed in earlier chapters. Next, we look at how we do this.

The Goals of the Print DLL

With the print DLL, we wanted to encapsulate all the requirements for printing and then have it call your application to format each line. In the default cause, we wanted a simple "line printer" emulator, where all you had to do was a single TextOut call and increment the vertical position. In particular, handling pagination would be automatic. We wanted to make it easy to have left-justified, right-justified, and centered headings and to force a new page when needed. And it would maintain the "Printing page *n*" display in the abort dialog.

After looking a bit more at the problem, we wanted to give you the ability to use your own abort dialog and to change fonts and other parameters for formatting the headers, footers, and page body. We also wanted to leave it up to you to format the individual lines, including the use of such features as boldface, italic, icons, and the like on each line or even to format the entire body yourself (if, for example, you were printing some graphics). Finally, we wanted to make this a DLL that you could use in binary form, not some piece of code you had to keep cutting and pasting into your applications.

These were the goals. Here's what we had to do to realize them.

The Input Structure

The input structure is the PrintIt structure. The structure is shown in Table 13.13, and the PrintData member prdata is described in detail in Table 13.14.

Table 13.13: The PrintIt structure

Type and Name	Description
DWORD lStructSize	Length of the structure, in bytes.

Table 13.13: The PrintIt structure

Type and Name	Description		
`PrintData prdata`	A `PrintData` structure that holds information passed to formatting routines. See Table 13.14.		
`PAGESETUPDLG * psu`	If you have used `PageSetupDlg` and want the results used, store a pointer to the `PAGESETUPDLG` structure here. If this is non-NULL, the `psu->rtMargin` field will be used to compute margins. If it is NULL, the margins will be the physical limits of the page.		
`DWORD Flags`	A set of option flags, one or more of the following:		
	`PrintIt_ENABLETEMPLATE`	Use the template specified by the `hInst` and `Template` fields.	
	`PrintIt_ENABLEHOOK`	Use the hook function specified by the Hook field.	
`HINSTANCE hInst`	If `PrintIt_ENABLETEMPLATE` is set, this is the instance handle of the module that contains the dialog template. If the flag is not set, this field is ignored.		
`LPCTSTR Template`	If `PrintIt_ENABLETEMPLATE` is set, this is the name (or `MAKEINTRESOURCE` ID) of the template in the module.		
`BOOL (CALLBACK *Hook)(HWND hdlg, int msg, WPARAM wParam, LPARAM lParam)`			
	If `PrintIt_ENABLEHOOK` is set, this is the address of a CALLBACK function for your dialog hook.		
`BOOL Aborted`	A flag your custom hook function can set to TRUE to indicate that printing should be terminated. On input, its value indicates the current Aborted state, and on return, its value is ORed into the Aborted flag.		
`int (CALLBACK *FormatLine)(LPPrintData data)`			
	Called to format each line of output. The return value is one of the following:		
	`PI_Continue`	Continue processing.	
	`PI_Stop`	Terminate printing.	
	`PI_NewPage`	Continue processing; the next line will be on a new page.	

```
int (CALLBACK *TopLeft)(LPPrintData data, LPTSTR buffer, int length)
int (CALLBACK *TopCenter)(LPPrintData data, LPTSTR buffer, int length)
int (CALLBACK *TopRight)(LPPrintData data, LPTSTR buffer, int length)
int (CALLBACK *BottomLeft)(LPPrintData data, LPTSTR buffer, int length)
int (CALLBACK *BottomCenter)(LPPrintData data, LPTSTR buffer, int length)
int (CALLBACK *BottomRight)(LPPrintData data, LPTSTR buffer, int length)
```

Table 13.13: The PrintIt structure

Type and Name	Description
	Any of these function pointers can be NULL. If NULL, no action will be taken. If non-NULL, the corresponding function will be called to obtain a string to be formatted for the appropriate heading. The buffer parameter points to a place where you can put a string, and length is the number of characters you can put in the buffer. The return value can be one of the following values. A negative value is one of the predefined symbols. A value greater than or equal to 0 is the height, in logical units, of the heading that you have formatted. You may change any DC parameters, and they will be used for the formatting with PH_Continue. Then the DC will be restored.

PH_Continue	Heading string is in the buffer; it must be displayed.
PH_Stop	Terminate printing.
>= 0	Height, in logical units, of the header line you've formatted.

`int (CALLBACK *Query)(LPPrintData data)`

	Queries the state of the printing. This is called before each FormatLine call. This is primarily to keep from having an extra blank page at the end of the file or before an operation that would start a new page. At the point this is called, the DC is not valid for drawing, as a StartPage has not been performed. If this is NULL, no query will be made.

PQ_Continue	No action required; follow normal behavior.
PQ_NewPage	Start a new page; the next FormatLine call will be for the first line of the new page.
PQ_Stop	Terminate printing.

`void (CALLBACK *PrepareDC)(LPPrintData data)`

	If present, called after every StartPage to set up the DC.

`void (CALLBACK *FinishPage)(LPPrintData data)`

	If present, called right before every EndPage to handle any special end-of-page formatting needs. Returns one of the following values:

PF_Continue	No action required; follow normal behavior.
PF_Stop	Terminate printing.

Table 13.13: The PrintIt structure

Type and Name	Description
DWORD error	When an error return happens, this contains the result of a GetLastError call.

Table 13.14: The PrintData structure

Type and Name	Description
PRINTDLG * pd	A pointer to a PRINTDLG structure that was used to obtain a DC. The hDC field of this structure must be valid. Upon completion of the printing, this DC will be released and the hDC field will be set to NULL.
LPCTSTR DocName	The name of the document. This is the name set in the DOCINFO structure passed to StartDoc. If NULL, a generic name will be used.
LPCTSTR OutputName	The output name, normally NULL. This is the name set in the DOCINFO structure passed to StartDoc.
LPVOID UserData	A pointer to any data you want to pass on to the formatting functions.
HWND Owner	The parent window for the Abort dialog. You can send your user-defined messages to this dialog window. In most cases, this requires that you use your own dialog template.
The following fields are ignored on input. They are set to specific values when the callback functions are called.	
int pageno	The current page number.
int ypos	The current vertical page position for the next line, in device units.
int dy	The line height of the printer DC using the font that was set in it when doPrintIt was called or after PrepareDC was called. This is the base-line-to-baseline distance and is typically the result of computing tm.tmHeight + tm.tmExternalLeading of the TEXTMETRIC structure.
RECT page	The current printable area of the page, excluding headings, in device units. The printable area will be modified by the margins set by the PageSetupDlg function and stored in the psu field. When the heading functions are called, this contains the entire area of the page. Only when all heading functions have completed is this updated to exclude the heading space.

Table 13.15: `PrintIt.DLL` functions

Result	Function	Arguments and Description
DWORD	doPrintIt	(LPPrintIt pr)
		Sets up printing and calls specified functions until requested to terminate.
HDC	prDC	(LPPrintData prd)
		In-line convenience function that returns the DC for use within the formatting functions.
DWORD	getPrintItError	(DWORD errorcode, LANGID langid, LPTSTR Buffer, int length)
		If the return result from doPrintIt is nonzero, converts it to a printable error message string.

A simple example of printing uses very few of these fields. For example, to simply print the lines of a file, we can set the structure as shown in Listing 13.10.

Listing 13.10: Simple `PrintIt` DLL usage

```
void myapp_OnPrint(HWND hwnd)
{
 PRINTDLG pd;
 PrintData pr;

 memset(&pd, 0, sizeof(PRINTDLG));
 pd.lStructSize = sizeof(PRINTDLG);
 pd.Flags = PD_RETURNDC;
 if(!PrintDlg(&pd))
     { /* PrintDlg error or cancel */
       DWORD err = CommDlgExtendedError();
       if(err != 0)
          { /* error */
           // .. handle error here
          } /* error */
       return;
     } /* PrintDlg error or cancel*/

 memset(&pr, 0, sizeof(PrintData));
 pr.lStructSize = sizeof(PrintData);
 pr.prdata.pd = &pd;
 pr.prdata.DocName = filename;  // name of file
 pr.prdata.UserData = (LPVOID)filehandle;  // file handle
 pr.Owner = hwnd;
 pr.FormatLine = myPrintLine;
 pr.TopLeft = myTopLeft;
 pr.BottomRight = myBottomRight;
 result = doPrintIt(&pr);
 if(result != 0)
     { /* doPrintIt error */
       TCHAR errmsg[256];
```

```
        TCHAR caption[256];
        getPrintItError(result,
                    MAKELANGID(LANGUAGE_NEUTRAL, SUBLANG_NEUTRAL),
                    errmsg,
                    sizeof(errmsg) / sizeof(TCHAR));
        if(pr.error != 0)
           { /* add to message */
             if(lstrlen(errmsg) < DIM(errmsg) - 3)
                 lstrcat(errmsg, _T("\r\n"));
             if(lstrlen(errmsg) < DIM(errmsg) - 1)
                 FormatMessage(FORMAT_MESSAGE_FROM_SYSTEM,
                             NULL,
                             pr.error,
                             MAKELANGID(LANG_NEUTRAL, SUBLANG_NEUTRAL),
                             &errmsg[lstrlen(errmsg)],
                             DIM(errmsg) - lstrlen(errmsg));
          LoadString(hInst, IDS_PRINTING_ERROR, caption, DIM(caption));
          MessageBox(hWnd,  errmsg, caption, MB_ICONSTOP | MB_OK );
         } /* doPrintIt error */
}

//----------------------
int CALLBACK myPrintLine(LPPrintData prd)
    {
     TCHAR Buffer[256];
     if(!myReadLine((HFILE)prd->prdata.UserData, Buffer, DIM(Buffer)))
         return PI_Stop; // end of file hit
     TextOut(prDC(prd), prd->page.left, prd->ypos, Buffer, lstrlen(Buffer));
     prd->ypos += dy;
     return PI_Continue;
     }
//————————————————————

int CALLBACK myTopLeft(LPPrintData prd, LPTSTR Buffer, int length)
    {
     lstrcpyn(Buffer, prd->DocName, length);
     return PH_Continue;
  }

//————————————————————-

int CALLBACK myBottomRight(LPPrintData prd, LPTSTR Buffer, int length)
    {
     TCHAR pageno[10];
     wsprintf(pageno, _T("%d"), prd->page);
     lstrcpyn(Buffer, pageno, length);
     return PH_Continue;
  }
```

The Query Function

The code in Listing 13.10 is almost right. It has one small defect: The myPrintLine function doesn't handle embedded form-feed ("\f") characters in the file. We could change it so that if myReadLine encountered a form-feed character, it would make sure that that character was the only one placed in the buffer. We also would change myPrintLine to recognize this:

```
if(Buffer[0] == _T('\f'))
    return PI_NewPage;
```

but this isn't quite right either because in preparing to format the line, the DLL has automatically made sure that it will start on a new page if necessary. But if the "line" would cause a page eject, it should be detected *before* we actually try to print the line! It wouldn't be sufficient to say, "Well, if we're already at the top of a new page, don't do anything", because the nature of the output might be to change a heading under these conditions. So we added the Query function to the structure. This function may be called even when there is no valid page to draw on (so don't try to draw on the page in this function!). The DLL calls this function under two conditions: There is no open page and it would like to know if it should quit; or there is an open page and it would like know if it should start a new one. One precaution you should take is that it may be called twice for the same line: once to see if it should start a new page if no page is active, and once after it has started a page to see if it should start a new page or quit.

```
int myQuery(LPPrintData prd)
    {
    HFILE f = (HFILE)prd->UserData;
    TCHAR ch;
    if(_lread(f, &ch, sizeof(TCHAR)) == 0)
        return PQ_Stop;   // end of file reached

    if(ch == _T('\f'))
        return PQ_NewPage; // force new page

    _llseek(f, -sizeof(TCHAR), 1); // re-read character
                                   // next time

    return PQ_Continue;   // no special action required
    }
```

Unicode warning: This application assumes that it is either an ANSI application reading ANSI files or a Unicode application reading Unicode files. Therefore it assumes that it is reading a TCHAR. If you want an ANSI application that can read Unicode files or a Unicode application that can read ANSI files, you'll have to modify this behavior. This is left as an "exercise for the reader".

Writing the **PRINTIT.DLL** Callbacks

The FormatLine Callback

The FormatLine callback is called for each "line" to be formatted. You can turn this into a "FormatPage" function simply by always returning PI_NewPage.

When the function is called, you are passed a PrintData object. In this object, you will find the current page number in the pageno field, which may be useful, and the current line position in the ypos field, which is essential. This latter value is expressed *in device units*. If you are using any mapping mode other than MM_TEXT, you must call the DPtoLP function to convert this position to a logical coordinate in your space. If you have established a PrepareDC function, you can set the mapping mode there, and your mapping mode will be the prevailing one. However, if you called doPrintIt with the unmodified hDC you got from Print-

Dlg, then its mapping mode is MM_TEXT. You will have to change the mapping mode yourself. Note that *any* changes you make to the DC will be reset after you return, so you will need to make them again on the next FormatLine call.

You use the ypos to determine where to print the next line. How you do alignment is up to you. Remember that you can't call DrawText (a function that is not valid for metafile recording) if the GetDeviceCaps (RASTERCAPS) has the RC_BANDING bit set, so it is best to avoid the DrawText function entirely if you expect maximum portability of your application. After you have printed your line, you must advance ypos by the amount of *physical* space you've used for the line.

If you want to print several "grouped" lines and want to make sure they will all fit, the bottom field is the device coordinate position of the bottom of the printable area, *less any space used for footers.* If the amount of physical space you require is greater than page.bottom - ypos, you should return PI_NewPage and make sure that you will be in a position to reformat the data again. For example, if you had to read a file before determining the number of lines, such as you might have to do if the lines would "wrap", you should back up the file to where it was before returning.

The value page.top is the top of the printable area, less any space for headers and margins. The meaning of these

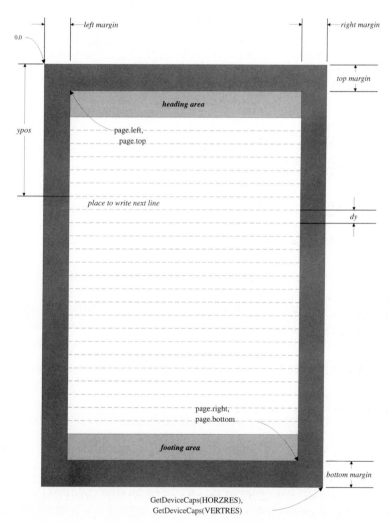

fields is shown in Figure 13.6. Note that either the heading area or footing area could have a height of 0.

Figure 13.6: FormatLine's view of the page

The PrintIt Code

Developing the `PrintIt` DLL code required a fairly careful knowledge of the topics we've explored so far, so we use it as an example of how to bring all this knowledge together. In particular, we deal with a lot of the side conditions of coordinate transformations that are essential to proper printing.

The doPrintIt Function

The `doPrintIt` function is the external interface. It is shown in its entirety in Listing 13.12. Because we are creating a DLL, we want this function to be an exported function, so we must add the `_declspec(dllexport)` declaration as shown. Note that we can now call this function from either C or C++ code. The bilingual header file, `printit.h`, allows for this, as shown in Listing 13.11.

Listing 13.11: A header file suitable for C and C++

```
#ifdef __cplusplus
extern "C" {
#endif

__declspec(dllexport)
DWORD APIENTRY doPrintIt(LPPrintIt pd);
__declspec(dllexport)
DWORD APIENTRY getPrintItError(DWORD error, LANGID langid,
                               LPTSTR Buffer, int length);

#define PRINTIT_PAGE_NOTIFICATION_MSG ("Printit.PageNotification")
#ifdef __cplusplus
           }
#endif
```

Note the inclusion of the declaration `extern "C"`, which depends on whether the preprocessor symbol `__cplusplus` is defined. This allows the code, which is written in C, to be called from a C++ program. If compiled with a C compiler, the `extern "C"` declaration will not be included and an ordinary C external function is declared. If compiled with a C++ compiler that defines the symbol `__cplusplus`, the `extern "C"` declaration will cause the compiler to generate the function with an ordinary C (nonmangled) name.

This function first checks the fields for validity, returning error codes for any of the following problems:

- The structure has the wrong size value.

- The `PRINTDLG hDC` field is NULL (it must be a valid DC handle).

- The `FormatLine` function pointer is NULL (this is the key formatting function callback and must be defined).

The `SetLastError` function is used to set the return error code to 0 to indicate that the error is not a system error but a DLL-defined error. The `doPrintIt` function will return a nonzero error code for system errors that are encountered as well. But in this case, it does not do a `SetLastError`; it leaves the error code that was set by the failed operation.

Next, a structured termination handler, the `__try...__finally` construct, is used to guarantee that no matter how control leaves, including exceptions that may be raised for other reasons, the printing operation will be cleanly terminated. A termination handler's code will *always* be executed. If the code in the __try clause contains a return, a break from a containing loop or case, a goto that transfers control out of the scope of the _try, or raises an exception, the control will *always* pass through the __finally clause before the control actually reaches its destination. The termination handler calls endPrint and then deletes the DC and sets the DC handle to NULL. If there is an abort dialog active, it is also terminated and the owner window is enabled.

Within the __try clause, we nest an exception handler. If any of the functions called throws an exception, control will pass to the _except clause, where we set the return code to be the exception code that was raised. If the cause was an EndPage failure, we must set the PrinterError flag. Note the advantage of using the exception clause and the termination clause: We don't have to check the return results for validity, thus simplifying the code and reducing the chance of an error.

We have defined a simple throw macro that wraps exception raising, defined as

```
#define throw(e) RaiseException ( (e),\
                   EXCEPTION_NONCONTINUABLE, 0, 0);
```

Listing 13.12: The doPrintIt function

```
_declspec(dllexport)
DWORD APIENTRY doPrintIt(LPPrintIt pr)
    {
    DWORD result = 0;

    if(pr->lStructSize != sizeof(PrintIt))
        { /* wrong version */
         return PRINTERR_STRUCTSIZE;
        } /* wrong version */

    pr->error = 0;   // assume no error until proven otherwise

    if(pr->prdata.pd->hDC == NULL)
        { /* no DC */
         SetLastError(0);
         return PRINTERR_NO_DC;
        } /* no DC */

    if(pr->FormatLine == NULL)
        { /* no fmt line */
         SetLastError(0);
         return PRINTERR_NO_FMTLINE;
        } /* no fmt line */

    __try
        {
        __try
            {
             startPrint(pr);
             printLoop(pr);
            }
        __except(checkFilter(GetExceptionCode()))
            {
             result = GetExceptionCode();
             pr->error = GetLastError();
```

```
                // Was it the EndPage that failed?
                if(result == PRINTERR_ENDPAGE_FAILED)
                    PrinterError = TRUE;
            }

        }
    __finally {
                endPrint(pr->prdata.pd->hDC);

                DeleteDC(pr->prdata.pd->hDC);
                pr->prdata.pd->hDC = NULL;

                if(hAbort != NULL)
                    DestroyWindow(hAbort);

                if(pr->prdata.Owner != NULL)
                    EnableWindow(pr->prdata.Owner, TRUE);
            };
    return result;
    }
```

The checkFilter Function

The checkFilter function constitutes the *exception filter*. This function checks to see if the exception should be handled by the current handler or if it is unrecognized and must be handled by some earlier exception handler that is outside our scope. The function is shown in Listing 13.13. An exception filter can return several values to indicate how the exception should be handled:

- EXCEPTION_EXECUTE_HANDLER will cause the handler to execute. We return this value if we recognize the exception as a printer DLL exception.

- EXCEPTION_CONTINUE_SEARCH will bypass the exception handler and pass the exception to the next higher exception handler. We return this value if we do not recognize the exception as a printer DLL exception.

- EXCEPTION_CONTINUE_EXECUTION causes execution to resume at the point where the RaiseException was called. We do not return this value.

Because the 2 high-order bits of the error code indicate severity and can be any value, we mask them off so that only the low-order bits participate in the comparison.

Listing 13.13: The checkFilter function

```
int checkFilter(int code)
    {
#define errmask ~0xC0000000
    if((code & errmask) > (PRINTERR_FIRST & errmask) &&
        (code & errmask) < (PRINTERR_LAST & errmask))
        return EXCEPTION_EXECUTE_HANDLER;

    return EXCEPTION_CONTINUE_SEARCH;
    }
```

The printLoop Function

The core printing effort is the printLoop function, shown in its entirety in Listing 13.14. This function performs some setup and then executes the printing loop.

We want to be able to update the display in the modeless dialog, indicating the current page being displayed, and we want to allow you to supply your own function, so we notify the dialog of a page number change by sending a message to the dialog. We can't predict what WM_USER-based symbols you might be using, so instead we use a *registered* window message, which we establish by calling RegisterWindowMessage. The integer returned is guaranteed to be a system-wide unique message ID value. So if you register the same message string (which is defined in the PrintIt.h header file), you will be able to test to see if we've sent this message to your dialog.

Next, we establish the coordinates of the actual printable area on the page. This is by default 0..GetDeviceCaps(hdc, HORZRES) horizontally and 0..GetDeviceCaps(hdc, VERTRES) vertically. However, if you have used the PageSetupDlg call to ask the user for margin information, we adjust the margins by the distance specified in the PAGESETUPDLG rtMargin structure. The values in this structure must be converted from 0.01 mm or 0.001 inch dimensions to device units, our canonical representation. We store the printable area less the selected margins in a local structure baseMargins, which we use to reset the Print-Data structure for each new page.

Having performed all the necessary setup, we now execute the printing loop. The loop continues indefinitely until either one of our callback functions returns a "stop" code or the Aborted flag is set. We don't bother to check the PrinterError as our earlier (and simpler) examples did because anything that could cause an error will throw an exception that will eventually be handled by the _except clause in the doPrintIt function.

To avoid leaving extra blank pages, especially if you have indicated in a callback that a new page should be created, we keep an "open page" flag. This helps us avoid leaving an extra blank page on boundary conditions, such as a form-feed printing on the first line of a page or an end-of-file occurring on the first line of a new page. If the current page is *not* open, we "open" it by calling the StartPage function, calling your PrepareDC function if you supplied one, and then drawing the page headings and footings by using the supplied callback functions. We *could* have left all the details of formatting the page headings and footings up to you. However, since left, centered, and right-justified text are so common, we provide the necessary detail work for you. If your needs are more elaborate, you can draw your own page heading and footing when the callback gets control.

To "open" a page, we first set the printable area to be the entire page less any explicitly defined margins. We want to be sure we aren't about to start a page that will need to be immediately closed if the next formatting call detects an end-of-file condition (leaving an extra blank page at the end of the output, a condition we're trying to avoid). So we call your Query function if it is given. You can return one of the PQ_ codes to indicate the action. If you determine that an end-of-file condition would occur, you can return PQ_Stop.

If the Query function doesn't indicate end-of-file, we call the StartPage function to inform the printing subsystem that we are starting a new page. You may want to change the mapping mode or set other DC parameters, so if you provide a PrepareDC function, we call it, passing in the PrintData pointer. You can set up the DC, and these values will be maintained for each line printed. We then increment the page number and send a message to the abort window notifying it of the new page number. The default abort dialog we provide actually displays this information, but of course you are free to ignore it in your own function.

Next, we call your callback functions to set the headings. We had a choice here of having a single function you provided and passing in one of six codes or letting you provide six different functions; we chose to have one function for each header segment. The functions return either a negative number, one of the codes indicated in Table 13.13, or a number >= 0, which is the height of the heading or footing, *in logical units*. This saves you from having to worry about details such as mapping modes in each of the header callbacks. If you return a PH_Continue code, we assume that you have filled in the buffer and we use that text to draw the heading in the appropriate place on the page. If you have changed the font or mapping mode in the DC, we take this into account. We convert the prevailing font height to physical units and return that value to the heading computation logic. Note that we take the max of the heights so that you can use multiple fonts, and the header will allow enough space to accommodate the tallest. Remember that a line of text is specified by its top-left corner, and note that we have to convert from the bottom value for the footings so that the footings appear in the right place. The doHeading function takes care of all of the necessary transformations from logical to physical units. If an exception is thrown by the heading functions, we simply return from the printing loop.

If the page is already open, we also call your Query callback to determine if a new page or end-of-file condition will occur. We then take appropriate action to terminate the page or the printing operation.

Finally, having guaranteed that the page is active and that there is something to format, we call your FormatLine function. Note that we do this in a context that saves the DC first and then restores it after the line has been formatted. This means that you can feel free to do anything you want to the DC, and the changes will be cleaned up before you are called to format the next line. The ypos value, which you must maintain, indicates where the next line will be drawn. Remember that the ypos value is in physical device units, so if you modify it you must remember to convert to physical units. Note that the DC is restored in the termination clause so that the return statement executed when the PI_Stop code is returned will reset the DC before returning from printLoop.

If the new ypos would fall below the computed bottom margin, we are at the end of a page. If you have supplied a FinishPage callback, we call it. If the FinishPage does not return PF_Stop, we call the EndPage function and mark the page state as "closed." If EndPage should fail, we throw an exception. If FinishPage returns PF_Stop, we return. Note that we don't have to do anything special to end the current page because the termination handler will close off any open page. However, we do use a local Boolean needFinish to keep us from calling the FinishPage callback a second time from the termination handler.

Listing 13.14: The printLoop function

```
static void printLoop(LPPrintIt pr)
    {
    HDC hdc = pr->prdata.pd->hDC;
    TEXTMETRIC tm;
    int savedDC;
    RECT basemargins;   // margins for each new page
```

```
int bottommargin;
BOOL needFinish = FALSE;

PageNotificationMessage =
        RegisterWindowMessage(PRINTIT_PAGE_NOTIFICATION_MSG);
basemargins.right = GetDeviceCaps(hdc, HORZRES);
basemargins.left = 0;
basemargins.top = 0;
basemargins.bottom = GetDeviceCaps(hdc, VERTRES);

if(pr->psu != NULL)
    { /* has page setup */
      RECT margin;
      int hres = GetDeviceCaps(hdc, LOGPIXELSX);
      int vres = GetDeviceCaps(hdc, LOGPIXELSY);

      margin = pr->psu->rtMargin;

      if(pr->psu->Flags & PSD_INHUNDREDTHSOFMILLIMETERS)
          { /* mm */
            margin.top = (margin.top * 1000) / 2540;
            margin.bottom = (margin.bottom * 1000) / 2540;
            margin.left = (margin.left * 1000) / 2540;
            margin.right = (margin.right * 1000) / 2540;
          } /* mm */

      // Now normalize to device resolution
      margin.top = (margin.top * vres) / 1000;
      margin.bottom = (margin.bottom * vres) / 1000;
      margin.left = (margin.left * hres) / 1000;
      margin.right = (margin.right * hres) / 1000;

      basemargins.top += margin.top;
      basemargins.left += margin.left;
      basemargins.right -= margin.right;
      basemargins.bottom -= margin.bottom;
    } /* has page setup */

pr->prdata.pageno = 0;

_try
  while(TRUE)
    { /* main loop */
    if(Aborted)
       break;

    if(!pageopen)
        { /* open page */
          int hh; // heading height, in device units
          int fh; // footing height, in device units

          pr->prdata.page = basemargins;

          if(pr->Query != NULL)
              { /* ask about new page */
                switch(pr->Query(&pr->prdata))
                    { /* query */
```

```
            case PQ_Continue:
                    break;
            case PQ_Stop:
                    return;
            case PQ_NewPage:
                    break;        // since we're already
                                  // planning a
                                  // new page, nothing
                                  // special needed
        } /* query */
    } /* ask about new page */

if(StartPage(hdc) < 0)
    throw (PRINTERR_STARTPAGE_FAILED);

// If the programmer has specified a DC setup
// function, call it here
if(pr->PrepareDC != NULL)
    { /* DC setup */
    (pr->PrepareDC)(&pr->prdata);
    } /* DC setup */

GetTextMetrics(hdc, &tm);
pt.x = 0;
pt.y = tm.tmHeight + tm.tmExternalLeading;
LPtoDP(hdc, &pt, 1);
pr->prdata.dy = pt.y;

pageopen = TRUE;
needFinish = TRUE;
pr->prdata.pageno++;

SendMessage(hAbort, PageNotificationMessage,
                0, pr->prdata.pageno);

// Set the page heading and footing
hh = 0;
fh = 0;
__try
    { /* try-headings */
      hh = doHeading(pr,
                    pr->prdata.page.top,
                    pr->TopLeft, PH_LEFT);
      hh = max(hh, doHeading(pr,
                            pr->prdata.page.top,
                            pr->TopCenter,
                            PH_CENTER));
      hh = max(hh, doHeading(pr,
                            pr->prdata.page.top,
                            pr->TopRight,
                            PH_RIGHT));
      fh = doHeading(pr, pr->prdata.page.bottom,
                    pr->BottomLeft,
                    PH_BOTTOM | PH_LEFT);
      fh = max(fh, doHeading(pr,
                            pr->prdata.page.bottom,
                            pr->BottomCenter,
                            PH_BOTTOM | PH_CENTER));
```

```
            fh = max(fh, doHeading(pr,
                            pr->prdata.page.bottom,
                            pr->BottomRight,
                            PH_BOTTOM | PH_RIGHT));
            pr->prdata.page.top += hh;
            pr->prdata.page.bottom -= fh;
            pr->prdata.ypos = pr->prdata.page.top;
            bottommargin = pr->prdata.page.bottom - pr->prdata.dy;
            if(pr->prdata.ypos > bottommargin)
                { /* impossible margins */
                  throw(PRINTERR_MARGINS);
                } /* impossible margins */
            } /* try-headings */
          __except(checkFilter(GetExceptionCode
              {
              // doHeading threw an exception
              throw(GetExceptionCode());
              }


      } /* open page */
    else
       { /* already open */
       if(pr->Query != NULL)
          { /* query need new page */
          switch(pr->Query(&pr->prdata))
              { /* query */
              case PQ_Continue:
                      break;       // yes, print it
              case PQ_Stop:
                      return;      // stop printing
              case PQ_NewPage:
                                   // force new page
                      if(pr->FinishPage != NULL)
                          switch(pr->FinishPage(&pr->prdata))
                              { /* finish */
                              case PF_Stop:
                                  needFinish = FALSE;
                                  return;
                              case PF_Continue:
                                  break;
                              } /* finish */

                      if(EndPage(hdc) < 0)
                        throw(PRINTERR_ENDPAGE_FAILED);
                      pageopen = FALSE;
                      continue;
              } /* query */
          } /* query need new page */
       } /* already open */

    // Ask the caller to format the line
    __try
       { /* format line */
       savedDC = SaveDC(hdc);
       switch(pr->FormatLine(&pr->prdata))
          { /* fmt codes */
          case PI_Continue:
                  break;
```

```
                    case PI_Stop: // stop printing, e.g., EOF
                            return;
                    case PI_NewPage: // force page break
                            pr->prdata.ypos = bottommargin + 1;
                            break;
                } /* fmt codes */
            } /* format line */
        __finally
            {
            RestoreDC(hdc, savedDC);
            }

    if(pr->prdata.ypos > bottommargin)
        { /* end of page */
        if(pr->FinishPage != NULL)
            switch(pr->FinishPage(&pr->prdata))
                { /* finish */
                case PF_Stop:
                        needFinish = FALSE;
                        return;
                case PF_Continue:
                        break;
                } /* finish */
        if(EndPage(hdc) < 0)
            throw (PRINTERR_ENDPAGE_FAILED);
        pageopen = FALSE;
        } /* end of page */
    } /* main loop */
__finally
    { /* check page close */
    if(pageopen)
        { /* force end of page */
        if(needFinish && pr->FinishPage != NULL)
            pr->FinishPage(&pr->prdata);
        if(EndPage(hdc) < 0)
            throw (PRINTERR_ENDPAGE_FAILED);
        pageopen = FALSE;
        } /* force end of page */
    } /* check page close */
}
```

The doHeading Function

The doHeading function, shown in Listing 13.15, is interesting because it shows how we have to deal with the difference between logical and physical coordinates. Like formatLine, each call to a header function saves and restores the DC. It is important that you do not save or restore the DC in your callback function because the changed DC is normally used to format the heading. But if you have formatted the heading and changed any of the DC parameters to do so, you must return the space you have used, *in logical coordinates.* Your changed DC is necessary to perform the logical-to-physical conversion. This may not be apparent if you are using the default MM_TEXT mapping mode, where logical and physical points are identical. But if you are changing mapping modes, it will be critical. The restoration of the DC is handled by a termination handler, so even if the header function throws an exception, the DC will be restored.

A heading function returns either a negative number or a number >= 0. A non-negative number returned means you have done all the necessary formatting and are returning the height that you used in logical units. We convert the logical value returned to a physical offset and return that physical offset (which the caller uses to adjust the printable area). Note that because `return` goes through the termination handler, we don't need to explicitly reset the DC. However, if the code was `PH_Continue`, we need to compute the actual text height that we will return. Then we format the text you have provided in the buffer. We first compute a logical distance for right-justified or centered text that is based on the mapping mode of the DC and its current font (both of which you are free to change). We also compute a base position in physical units for the left, center, or right of the text. We then convert this physical position based on the physical margins to a logical offset for the `TextOut` and adjust the physical `ypos` by the physical height of the line.

Listing 13.15: The doHeading function

```
static int doHeading(LPPrintIt pr, int ypos,
                     LPPrintItHeaderFunc fn, UINT which)
    {
    TCHAR line[256];
    HDC hdc = pr->prdata.pd->hDC;
    int savedDC;

    if(fn == NULL)
        return 0;

    savedDC = SaveDC(hdc);
    _try
        {
        POINT pos;
        SIZE sz;
        int adjust;

        sz.cx = 0;   // not needed, but why confuse LPtoDP
        sz.cy = fn(&pr->prdata, line, DIM(line));

        switch(sz.cy)
            { /* fn val */
              case PH_Stop:
                    throw (PRINTERR_STOP_REQUESTED);
              case PH_Continue:
                    break;
              default:
                    LPtoDP(hdc, (LPPOINT)&sz, 1);
                    return sz.cy;
            } /* fn val */

        // Get the text size in logical coordinates

        GetTextExtentPoint32 (hdc, line, lstrlen(line), &sz);

        switch(which & ~ PH_BOTTOM)
            { /* which */
              case PH_CENTER:
                    pos.x = pr->prdata.page.left +
                            (pr->prdata.page.right - pr->prdata.page.left) / 2;
                    adjust = sz.cx / 2;
                    break;
```

```
    case PH_RIGHT:
            pos.x = pr->prdata.page.right;
            adjust = sz.cx;
            break;
        default:
            pos.x = pr->prdata.page.left;
            adjust = 0;
            break;
    } /* which */

    DPtoLP(hdc, &pos, 1);
    pos.x -= adjust;
    pos.y = ypos;   // vertical physical coordinate

    LPtoDP(hdc, (LPPOINT)&sz, 1);

    // Handle the case of being on the bottom by
    // computing the top of the text box
    // (ypos will be the bottom of the text box
    // for bottom line output)
    if(which & PH_BOTTOM)
        ypos -= sz.cy;

    TextOut(hdc, pos.x, pos.y, line, lstrlen(line));
    return sz.cy;
    }
  _finally
    {
     RestoreDC(hdc, savedDC);
    }
 }
```

The startPrint Function

The startPrint function, shown in Listing 13.16, looks very much like the simple example we gave earlier, with two minor exceptions. One is that we use either a built-in resource that is part of our DLL or a resource you provide in the PrintIt structure by giving the name and instance handle of the resource. The other is that, in case of an error, we throw an exception.

To load our own resource, we need the instance handle for the DLL itself. We store this when the DLL is initialized. The DLL initialization function, which most DLLs have, is shown in Listing 13.17. This one is the simplest initialization function; it stores only the instance handle in a static variable. This function is called each time a new thread attaches to the DLL. Because each client of the DLL gets a private copy of the data, the instance handle must be initialized for each client. (This function is also called whenever a thread detaches from the DLL, but we don't need to do anything special because no thread-specific or task-specific resources are allocated.)

Listing 13.16: The startPrint function

```
static void startPrint(LPPrintIt pr)
    {
     DOCINFO di;
     HINSTANCE dlginst = hInst;
     LPCTSTR dlgname = MAKEINTRESOURCE(IDD_ABORT);
```

```
di.cbSize = sizeof(DOCINFO);
di.lpszDocName = pr->prdata.DocName;
di.lpszOutput = NULL;

if(pr->Flags & PrintIt_ENABLETEMPLATE)
    { /* use template */
      dlgname = pr->Template;
      dlginst = pr->hInst;
    } /* use template */

hAbort = CreateDialogParam(dlginst, dlgname,
                           pr->prdata.Owner,
                           (DLGPROC)abortDlgFunc,
                           (LPARAM)pr);

if(hAbort == NULL)
    throw (PRINTERR_ABORTDLG_FAILED);

if(SetAbortProc(pr->prdata.pd->hDC, abortFunc) < 0)
    throw (PRINTERR_SETABORT_FAILED);

ShowWindow(hAbort, SW_NORMAL);
UpdateWindow(hAbort);

if(pr->prdata.Owner != NULL)
    EnableWindow(pr->prdata.Owner, FALSE);

if(StartDoc(pr->prdata.pd->hDC, &di) < 0)
    throw (PRINTERR_STARTDOC_FAILED);

pageopen = FALSE;
}
```

Listing 13.17: The DllEntryPoint function
```
static HINSTANCE hInst;

BOOL WINAPI DllEntryPoint(HINSTANCE hinstDLL, DWORD fdwReason, LPVOID lpReserved)
    {
    hInst = hinstDLL; // save for future activities

    return TRUE;
    }
```

Using an External Abort Dialog Template and Hook Function

You can provide your own custom abort dialog template. If you use the same control IDs as the built-in one, then all you need to do is put the name (or MAKEINTRESOURCE of the ID) of the resource in the Template field and set the PrintIt_ENABLETEMPLATE flag in the Flags field. The built-in function will simply set the page number, device, and port information. We have carefully designed this so that (unlike with the common dialog functions) you don't have to have all the controls present, enabled or not; you can drop whatever controls you don't want. If you have other information you'd like to display, you can pass it in via the UserData field. Then when your OnInitDialog handler is called, you will be passed a pointer to the complete PrintIt structure that you can store in the GWL_USERDATA field and use as needed to update the information you display. You can also call `RegisterWindowMessage`, passing in the name of the string for the page number notification message. Each time `StartPage` is called, the `printLoop` function will also send a message to the abort dialog indicating the new page number. You can ignore this message or use it to display the page number.

A set of functions that provide for a different handler is shown in Listing 13.18.

Listing 13.18: A custom abort dialog handler

```
static void custom_OnCommand(HWND hdlg, int id, HWND hctl, UINT codeNotify)
    {
    LPPrintIt prt = (LPPrintIt)GetWindowLong(hdlg, GWL_USERDATA);
    if(id == IDCANCEL)
        { /* aborted */
        if(prt != NULL)
            prt->Aborted = TRUE;
        } /* aborted */
    }


static void custom_OnPageNotify(HWND hdlg, int page)
    {
    TCHAR fmt[256];
    TCHAR msg[256];
    if(LoadString(GetWindowInstance(hdlg), IDS_PRINTING_PAGE,
                        fmt, DIM(fmt)) == 0)
        return;
    wsprintf(msg, fmt, page);
    SetDlgItemText(hdlg, IDC_PAGENO, msg);
    }

static BOOL custom_OnInitDialog(HWND hdlg, HWND hfocus, LPARAM lParam)
    {
    LPDEVNAMES dn;
    LPPrintIt prt = (LPPrintIt)lParam;

    SetWindowLong(hdlg, GWL_USERDATA, lParam);

    prt->Aborted = FALSE;
    centerWindow(hdlg);

    dn = (LPDEVNAMES)GlobalLock(prt->prdata.pd->hDevNames);
    if(dn != NULL)
        { /* locked */
        SetDlgItemText(hdlg, IDC_PRINTER,
            (LPCTSTR)&((LPCSTR)dn)[dn->wDeviceOffset]);

        GlobalUnlock(prt->prdata.pd->hDevNames);
        } /* locked */

    return TRUE;
    }

BOOL CALLBACK CustomHook(HWND hdlg, int msg, WPARAM wParam,LPARAM lParam)
    {
    static int NotificationMessage = 0;
```

```
if(NotificationMessage == 0)
   NotificationMessage =
       RegisterWindowMessage(PRINTIT_PAGE_NOTIFICATION_MSG);
if(msg == NotificationMessage)
   { /* page notification */
    custom_OnPageNotify(hdlg, lParam);
    return TRUE;
   } /* page notification */

switch(msg)
   { /* msg */
    case WM_COMMAND:
            HANDLE_WM_COMMAND(hdlg, wParam, lParam, custom_OnCommand);
            return TRUE;
    case WM_INITDIALOG:
            return (BOOL)HANDLE_WM_INITDIALOG(hdlg, wParam, lParam,
                                               custom_OnInitDialog);
   } /* msg */
 return FALSE;
}
```

Calling doPrintIt with a Custom Dialog and Hook

When you call doPrintIt with a custom dialog and hook, you initialize the structure as already explained, except for the additions shown in Listing 13.19. In this example, the variable hInst represents the instance handle of the module that contains the template.

Listing 13.19: Adding a custom abort dialog and hook

```
PrintIt prt;

// Other setup here as shown earlier...

prt.Flags |= (PrintIt_ENABLEHOOK | PrintIt_ENABLETEMPLATE);
prt.hInst = hInst;
prt.Template = MAKEINTRESOURCE(IDD_CUSTOMPRINTING);
prt.Hook = CustomHook;
```

The Page Setup Dialog

A common attribute in setting up a print request is dealing with the more boring details of margin setup and page layout. For example, we noted that the printable area on a page might be less than the actual page size. You may also want to establish your own margins, which may or may not include space for the page headings (what you do with the information is up to you). You can change the margins and page orientation, as well as select optional paper trays for printers that have multiple paper sources. A sample page setup dialog is shown in Figure 13.7. In this dialog, we have set the orientation to landscape mode (the long edges of the paper are the top and bottom) and the left and right margins to $1/2$ in.

The Page Setup Dialog uses the following PAGESETUPDLG structure, which is explained in more detail in Table 13.16.

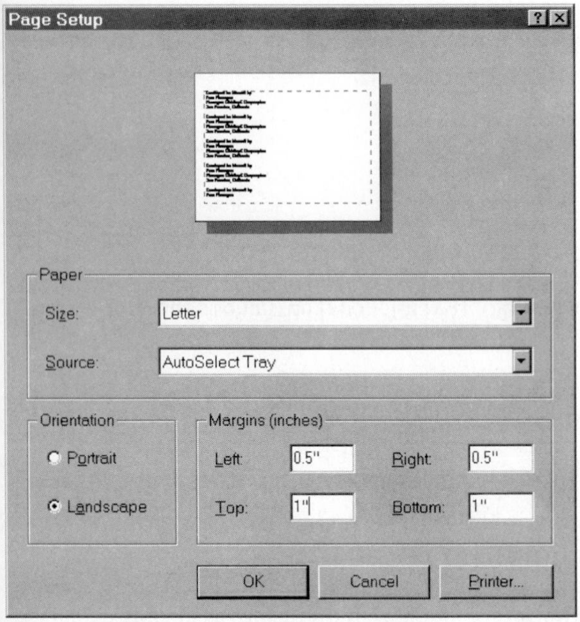

Figure 13.7: Sample page setup dialog

```
typedef struct tagPSD {
    DWORD            lStructSize;
    HWND             hwndOwner;
    HGLOBAL          hDevMode;
    HGLOBAL          hDevNames;
    DWORD            Flags;
    POINT            ptPaperSize;
    RECT             rtMinMargin;
    RECT             rtMargin;
    HINSTANCE        hInstance;
    LPARAM           lCustData;
    LPPAGESETUPHOOK  lpfnPageSetupHook;
    LPPAGEPAINTHOOK  lpfnPagePaintHook;
    LPCTSTR          lpPageSetupTemplateName;
    HGLOBAL          hPageSetupTemplate;
} PAGESETUPDLG, * LPPAGESETUPDLG;
```

After initializing the PAGESETUPDLG structure, you can call the PageSetupDlg function quite simply by passing in a reference to this structure. Upon completion, the return value from Page-SetupDlg will be FALSE if the user cancelled or closed the dialog and not FALSE if it completed successfully. If the result is not FALSE, the fields in the PAGESETUPDLG are set according to the specifications in Table 13.16 and Table 13.17.

Table 13.16: Fields of the PAGESETUPDLG structure

Field	Description
DWORD lStructSize	Size of this structure, in bytes.
HWND hwndOwner	Handle to the window that is the owner of the dialog or NULL if no owner.
HGLOBAL hDevMode	Handle to a global memory object containing a DEVMODE structure. On input, if this is non-NULL, the values are used to initialize the controls.
HGLOBAL hDevNames	Handle to a global memory object containing a DEVNAMES structure. On input, if this is non-NULL, the values are used to initialize the controls.
DWORD Flags	A set of flag options, as described in Table 13.17.
POINT ptPaperSize	The width (cx) and height (cy) of the page. The units are expressed in either hundredths of millimeters or thousandths of inches, depending on the setting of Flags as either PSD_INHUNDREDTHSOFMILLIMETERS or PSD_INTHOUSANDTHSOFINCHES.
RECT rtMinMargin	The minimum setting for the left, right, top, and bottom margins, expressed in the same units as ptPaperSize. This value is ignored if the PSD_MINMARGINS flag is not set.

Table 13.16: Fields of the PAGESETUPDLG structure

Field	Description
RECT rtMargin	The actual margins established for the left, right, top, and bottom margins. Set these and include the PSD_MARGINS flag in the Flags member before calling the dialog to get the initial values. On successful return, these values will be the values established by the user.
HINSTANCE hInstance	Instance handle for the custom dialog template. This will work the same way as described for custom print dialog templates; see page 984 for more discussion. Ignored if the PSD_ENABLEPAGESETUPTEMPLATE flag is not set.
LPARAM lCustData	A 32-bit value you can use to pass additional information to your custom dialog hook function. You can access this by using the lParam field of the OnInitDialog handler, which is a pointer to the PAGESETUPDLG structure. This works the same as for custom print dialog templates; see page 984 for more discussion.
LPPAGESETUPHOOK lpfnPageSetupHook	A pointer to a procedure for a custom hook function. This allows you to intercept all the messages of the dialog and act on them. This value is ignored unless the PSD_ENABLEPAGESETUPHOOK flag is set.
LPPAGEPAINTHOOK lpfnPagePaintHook	A pointer to a PagePaintHook function. This function will receive a sequence of WM_PSD_* messages whenever the image needs to be redrawn. This value is ignored unless the PSD_ENABLEPAGEPAINTHOOK flag is set.
LPCTSTR lpPageSetupTemplateName	A reference to the resource for a custom template. This can be either a string name or a MAKEINTRESOURCE value. The template will be found in the instance specified by the hInstance data member. This value is ignored if the PSD_ENABLEPAGESETUPTEMPLATE flag is not set.
HGLOBAL hPageSetupTemplate	The handle of a dialog box resource in memory (see Chapter 11, particularly the discussion starting on page 770). This is ignored if the PSD_ENABLEPAGESETUPTEMPLATEHANDLE flag is set.

Table 13.17: Flags of the PAGESETUPDLG structure

Flag	Meaning
PSD_DEFAULTMINMARGINS	Sets the minimum allowable margins for the page to be the printer's minimum margins. Ignored if PSD_MARGINS and PSD_MINMARGINS are also set.[1]
PSD_DISABLEMARGINS	Disables the margin controls.
PSD_DISABLEPAGEPAINTING	The sample page is drawn as a simple blank page without indications of margins or text.

Table 13.17: Flags of the PAGESETUPDLG structure

Flag	Meaning
PSD_DISABLEPAPER	Disables the paper selection; user cannot select paper size or source.
PSD_ENABLEPAGEPAINTHOOK	Enables the hook function specified in the lpfnPagePaintHook field. If this flag is set, the PSD_DISABLEPAGEPAINTING flag is ignored.
PSD_ENABLEPAGESETUPHOOK	Enables the hook function specified in the lpfnPageSetupHook field.
PSD_ENABLEPAGESETUPTEMPLATEHANDLE	Indicates that the hPageSetupTemplate contains a handle to a dialog box template. If this flag is set, the lpPageSetupTemplateName field is ignored.
PSD_INHUNDREDTHSOFMILLIMETERS	The values in the dimensions are interpreted as units of 0.01 mm. If this flag is set and the PSD_RETURNDEFAULT flag is also set, the values returned for the ptPaperSize and rtMargin will be in 0.01 mm units. If this flag is set on input, it will override the default locale-specific units. On return, this flag indicates which units the user selected.
PSD_INTHOUSANDTHSOFINCHES	The values in the dimensions are interpreted as units of 0.001 in. If this flag is set and the PSD_RETURNDEFAULT flag is also set, the values returned for the ptPaperSize and rtMargin will be in 0.001-in. units. If this flag is set on input, it will override the default locale-specific units. On return, this flag indicates which units the user selected.

If neither the PSD_INHUNDREDTHSOFMILLIMETERS or PSD_INTHOUSANDTHSOFINCHES flag is set, the default units are determined by the locale.

Flag	Meaning
PSD_INWININTLMEASURE	Not implemented.
PSD_MARGINS	If this value is set, the controls for the initial margins will be set from the values in the rtMargin field. This flag is cleared when the function returns.
PSD_MINMARGINS	If this value is set, a value set less than a corresponding value in rtMinMargin will be replaced by that value from the rtMinMargin field. No warning is given to the user.
PSD_NOWARNING	Disables warning messages. The only warning message is if there is no system default printer.
PSD_RETURNDEFAULT	Initializes the hDevMode, hDevNames, ptPaperSize, and rtMargin fields based on the system default printer. No dialog box is displayed.

Table 13.17: Flags of the PAGESETUPDLG structure

Flag	Meaning
PSD_SHOWHELP	Displays the **Help** button. When this button is pressed by the user, the owner receives a WM_HELP message. The hwndOwner field must be set.

[1] We have noticed that for some laser printers, the default minimum margins are returned as 0 in all dimensions, even though the printer itself cannot image all of the physical page. This should therefore be treated as a suspect value.

Page Setup Custom Painting Hook

You can draw in the page layout area in order to create a display suitable for your problem domain. For example, if you have a report that has two columns and optional headings, you may want to create additional controls on the page setup dialog (like we did for the print dialog) to control these options and give the user a display that shows what the page should look like. Even if you don't create a set of custom options, you may want to create a picture that represents your output more accurately.

A sample of a custom page setup layout is shown in Figure 13.8. This is a sample obtained from the Print Explorer by checking the PSD_ENABLEPAGEPAINTHOOK option. The text shown is on pale yellow paper and is shown as three columns of text. The column outlines and sample text are drawn by our own handler.

To create a special handler to do this, you write a hook function to handle the messages for painting that is defined as

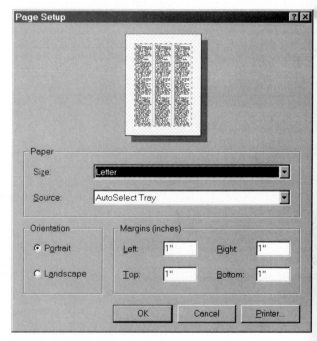

Figure 13.8: A custom page setup dialog

```
UINT APIENTRY PagePaintHook(HWND hctl, UINT msg, WPARAM wParam, LPARAM lParam)
```

The documentation from Microsoft states that the first parameter to the PagePaintHook function is the handle to the page setup dialog. We initially believed this, but our code didn't work. Some poking about using Spy++ revealed that the first parameter to the PagePaintHook is the handle to the static control that represents the rectangle in which the page image is drawn. Once we changed our code to recognize this situation, it worked correctly.

In the handler, we receive a number of messages that indicate what needs to be drawn. These messages are described in Table 13.18. They are sent any time the OnPaint handler for the window that is the sample is called. We use the WM_PSD_FULLPAGERECT message, described in Table 13.18, to paint the page background yellow and the WM_PSD_GREEKTEXTRECT message to draw the three column outlines and place the simulated text within them. The details can be read in the source code of the Print Explorer.

The messages shown in Table 13.18 are sent to the paint hook function in the order shown in the table. You can check out the effects of these options in the Print Explorer by using the **Page Setup** tab.

Table 13.18: Messages sent to the PagePaintHook function

Message	Parameters	Description
WM_PSD_PAGESETUPDLG	LOWORD(wParam)	A paper-type designator; one of the DM_PAPER_* values from Table 13.6.[3]
	HIWORD(wParam)	A paper type and orientation flag. These flags do not have symbolic values assigned, so only the hex constants are documented:

Flag Value	Meaning
0x0001	Paper in landscape mode; dot matrix printer.[1]
0x0003	Paper in landscape mode; HP-PCL printer.
0x0005	Paper in portrait mode; dot matrix printer.
0x0007	Paper in portrait mode; HP-PCL printer.
0x0009	Envelope in landscape mode; undocumented (PostScript?).[2]
0x000B	Envelope in landscape mode; HP-PCL printer.
0x000D	Envelope in portrait mode; dot matrix printer.
0x0019	Envelope in landscape mode; dot matrix printer.
0x001D	Envelope in portrait mode; undocumented (PostScript?).[2]
0x001F	Envelope in portrait mode; HP-PCL printer.

Table 13.18: Messages sent to the `PagePaintHook` function

Message	Parameters	Description
	LPARAM	LPPAGESETUPDLG reference. You can use this to get the `lCustData` value and all other parameters such as current margins.
	returns	TRUE to suppress messages until the next time the image needs to be redrawn; FALSE to continue to receive messages for this drawing sequence.
		The dialog box is about to draw the sample page. The hook procedure can use this message to prepare to draw the contents of the sample page.
WM_PSD_FULLPAGERECT	wParam	Handle of a DC to be used for painting.
	lParam	LPRECT that contains the coordinates (in pixels) of the sample page.
	returns	TRUE to suppress messages until the next time the image needs to be redrawn; FALSE to continue to receive messages for this drawing sequence.
		The dialog box is about to draw the sample page. This message specifies the bounding rectangle of the sample page.
WM_PSD_MINMARGINRECT	wParam	Handle of a DC to be used for painting.
	lParam	LPRECT that contains the coordinates (in pixels) of the minimum margin rectangle on the sample page.
	returns	TRUE to suppress messages until the next time the image needs to be redrawn; FALSE to continue to receive messages for this drawing sequence.
		The dialog box is about to draw the sample page. This message specifies the margin rectangle for the minimum margins.
WM_PSD_MARGINRECT	wParam	Handle of a DC to be used for painting.
	lParam	LPRECT that contains the coordinates (in pixels) of the margin rectangle on the sample page.
	returns	TRUE if you draw the margin rectangle; FALSE if you want the dialog handler to draw the margin rectangle for you.
		The dialog box is about to draw the margin rectangle. The message specifies the margin rectangle for the actual margins.

Table 13.18: Messages sent to the `PagePaintHook` function

Message	Parameters	Description
WM_PSD_GREEKTEXTRECT	wParam	Handle of a DC to be used for painting.
	lParam	LPRECT that contains the coordinates (in pixels) of the greek text rectangle on the sample page.
	returns	TRUE if you draw the greek text; FALSE if you want the dialog handler to draw the greek text for you.
	The dialog box is about to draw the greek text inside the margin rectangle.	
WM_PSD_ENVSTAMPRECT	wParam	Handle of a DC to be used for painting.
	lParam	LPRECT that contains the coordinates (in pixels) of the envelope stamp rectangle on the sample page.
	returns	TRUE if you draw the envelope stamp image; FALSE if you want the dialog handler to draw the image for you.
	The dialog box is about to draw in the envelope-stamp rectangle of an envelope sample page. This message is sent for envelopes only.	
WM_PSD_YAFULLPAGERECT	wParam	Handle of a DC to be used for painting.
	lParam	LPRECT that contains the coordinates (in pixels) of the envelope stamp rectangle on the sample page.
	returns	TRUE if you draw the envelope stamp image; FALSE if you want the dialog handler to draw the image for you.
	The dialog box is about to draw the return address portion of an envelope sample page. This message is sent for envelopes and other paper sizes.	

[1]We are not at all sure why printers are divided into the two categories "HPPCL" and "dot matrix" when there are so many different kinds of technologies available. What is even stranger is that all of our printers that are PostScript printers return some of these values as one of the "dot matrix" values, while other values are returned with codes that do not appear in our version of the documentation. While ordinarily this could be explained in terms of 8088 history, the PageSetupDlg was not introduced until the Win32 interface. The nomenclature is thus completely inexplicable, and its utility, particularly when it designates PostScript printers as "dot matrix", is suspect.

[2]In using the Print Explorer, we discovered that there is very little consistency in the values returned. We found at least these two values coming back, but no documentation to explain them. In addition, we discovered that some envelopes return codes indicating they are ordinary paper.

[3]In using the Print Explorer, we discovered that selecting a paper type in the drop-down list will sometimes result in this message's receiving a paper type that appears to have little, if any, correlation with the paper type selected. We are dismayed by this and offer no conjectures as to the cause. But be aware that you may not be able to trust this value at all. We got different discrepancies, in some cases, between Windows NT 3.5, Windows 95, and Windows NT 4.*x*. Some well-established printers such as the venerable Apple LaserWriter, for some very common paper types, return for this value completely undocumented and well out-of-range paper codes. We find this all very suspect.

The Print Explorer

Much of the information used to create this chapter was gleaned from intensive study of the `PRINTDLG`, `PAGESETUPDLG`, and `PrintIt` structures and their associated operations using an application we developed called the Print Explorer, which is included in the CD-ROM that accompanies this book. This application comes complete with source code (written in C++), and you can use it to test any problems you may have with printing. In addition, all of the code that appears here and complete examples of how to use custom templates and other interesting features appear in the Print Explorer. The Print Explorer was the testbed used to test all the code, including the `PrintIt` DLL.

14 Memory Management

Windows controls the allocation of system memory. Both Windows itself and Windows applications allocate and release memory blocks frequently during their lifetimes. Because many applications can run concurrently under Windows, dynamic storage requests can vary in amount instant by instant from practically none to more than the amount of memory available in the computer.

The performance of Windows and applications running under it depends to a great extent on the amount of available memory. Excessive memory usage by an application can cause Windows to discard and reload pages unnecessarily. Generally, this is an indication that you should allocate memory as needed and free it as quickly as possible–always good advice.

Often, you will find that memory allocation is not a major component of your task. You allocate some space now and again–a few tens of thousands of bytes–and free it as needed. In the course of execution, you may do a few thousand allocations. But this doesn't mean you have a really memory-intensive application. If this describes your application, the next section is all you need to read.

But what if your application is memory-intensive, for example, allocating hundreds of thousands of small objects or working with huge bitmaps? Or what if it may be expected to run for days or even weeks once it has been started? You will need to understand the system memory architecture in great detail so that you can work *with* it instead of *against* it (or to rephrase this, so that it can work with *you*, instead of against you). You will need to understand how paging works, how to avoid page faults, how to deal with allocating your own memory heaps and then allocating within the heaps, how to avoid memory fragmentation, and a number of other details. We tell you a lot of those details in this chapter. But unlike Win16, you don't *need* to know those details to get a program up and running. You don't even have to *care* about those details unless you have a memory-intensive application where performance and reliability are serious issues. [1]

Dynamic Memory Allocation–The Simple Approach

If you want to allocate storage in C, call `malloc`. To free it, call `free`. If you are programming in C++, use the new operator to allocate storage and the `delete` operator to free it. In a few cases, such as using the Clipboard, the API function states that a global memory handle is required to pass information in. Call

---

[1] This is a very realistic problem. The document production system used to create this book can expand its memory requirements–editing only one chapter–until it has consumed hundreds of megabytes of virtual memory, and it must be shut down and restarted every few hours of editing just because it has fragmented memory so badly that simple operations can sometimes cause over a minute of paging activity! It simply ignores the properties of the virtual memory system, and works very much against it.

GlobalAlloc to allocate the memory. When you are done with it, do a GlobalFree. (But you must *not* do this when you use the Clipboard.) Do not use GlobalAlloc unless you are working with an API function that *requires* a global memory handle. Generally, avoid GMEM_MOVEABLE memory unless it is required by the API function you are calling.

If you've been a Win16 programmer, this concludes the chapter on simple memory allocation. If you're not a Windows programmer and need to call GlobalAlloc, you need to read the next section to see how the basic memory allocation API functions operate. But even experienced Windows programmers should read the section on how to implement efficient memory-intensive applications under Win32.

Some Details about Simple Memory Allocation

We are going to assume that you, as a C or C++ programmer, know about malloc and free or new and delete. These work as you would expect under Windows.[2] The only detail we need to explain here is the notion of *memory handles* and how you use them.

Windows uses the notion of *handle* for managing resources administered by the system. You have already seen how the GDI uses handles to represent pens, brushes, bitmaps, and other resources, and the handle we use for many API functions, the *instance handle* for our running application. Windows also administers memory and represents a memory location with a *memory handle*. The original purpose of its doing this, in Win16, was to allow the system to shift the positions of objects in physical (real) memory. Much folklore and tradition surrounds the use of memory handles in Win16. In Win32, all physical memory is handled by the virtual memory component of the operating system, and this process is invisible to the application. The other reason for shifting objects in the address space (as opposed to physical memory) is to allow *compaction* of the blocks of memory, a topic we will discuss later in the chapter. That is not done in Win32. But the handle does represent a resource, so the idea is still used.

Within the heap, allocated memory blocks are one of three types: *fixed*, *moveable*, or *discardable*. The type of a memory block greatly affects how your application must access the information contained in the block.

First, we look at the three types of memory blocks. Then we discuss how to allocate a block of each type from the heap.

---

[2] We emphasize this because if you started programming Win16 in the early days, malloc and free did *not* work as you might expect. In fact, they basically didn't work at all. Later releases of the compiler gave only passing support to these until very late in the history of Win16. A huge mythology arose concerning the "right" and "wrong" ways to handle memory in Windows. With the release of Windows 3.1 and the compiler and runtime support that accompanied it, much of this mythology became irrelevant, but it persisted throughout the literature, including Microsoft's documentation. Many programmers fled screaming from the complexity and went back to programming non-Windows applications. So if you've heard rumors about how hard it is to allocate memory in Windows, they simply are no longer true. And if you had a bad experience with early Windows programming, be assured that you no longer have to deal with such complexity just to get a block of ordinary memory to write something into.

Fixed, Moveable, and Discardable Memory Blocks

Fixed Memory Blocks

You're probably already familiar with *fixed memory blocks* because they're the type used by most memory allocation schemes. This is what you get in a traditional allocator when you call `malloc` or `new`. When you allocate a fixed memory block with `GlobalAlloc`, Windows returns the address of the memory block. (Technically, it returns a handle to the block that, for fixed blocks only, happens to be the same as its address.) The address of the block never changes from the time you allocate it until you free it.

You get a fixed memory block by using `malloc`, `new`, or `HeapAlloc`, or by using `GlobalAlloc` with the `GMEM_FIXED` flag. Using fixed memory blocks was discouraged in versions of Windows prior to 3.1 and must be avoided in any Win32 application you expect to run under Win32s. Otherwise, they have no significance, since the storage compaction algorithms that Win16 used, which would move blocks around to compress the heap, simply don't exist in Win32. If you plan to run under Windows 95, Windows NT, or later versions of the Win32 operating system, you can ignore all the folklore that restricts the use of fixed memory blocks. In fact, it is *moveable* memory blocks in Win32 that have a limitation; we discuss this a little later in the chapter. There is no limit on how many fixed memory blocks you can have, up to the 2GB limit[3] or the limit of your paging system, whichever comes first. And in an era in which you can buy a 2GB or larger disk drive for much less than we used to pay for 40MB drives, it may be only some Win32 implementation restrictions that keep you from devoting all of it to being a paging device!

Moveable Memory Blocks

The second type of memory block is the *moveable memory block*. This is normally used only for special allocations, such as handles which must be passed to certain API functions (the Clipboard and multimedia functions being the most common). You should generally avoid the use of moveable memory blocks in Win32 unless absolutely required by the API function you are calling because the Win32 implementation limits you to no more than 65,535 moveable memory blocks. You cannot get a moveable memory block using `malloc` or `HeapAlloc`. You must either use `GlobalAlloc` with the `GMEM_MOVEABLE` flag or, if in C++, implement your own `new` operator for a class and have it call `GlobalAlloc` with the `GMEM_MOVEABLE` flag.

When you allocate a moveable memory block, Windows doesn't return the address of the block. Instead, it returns a *handle* to the block, an `HGLOBAL`. The handle uniquely identifies that particular memory block. When you want the address of the block, you must convert the handle to an address. You *lock* the memory block to do this using `GlobalLock`.

Locking a block has no effect on moveable, nondiscardable memory blocks other than returning the address of the block. Normally, a Windows application will allocate a block and immediately lock it. The application then can use the block whenever it needs to. When the application no longer needs the storage, it should unlock and free the block.

---

[3] No, this is not a typo. That's 2GB, not 4GB; see page 1042.

Freeing the block returns its space to the default heap for subsequent allocations. *Unlocking* a block doesn't *free* it. You must free the block before the storage can be used in a subsequent memory allocation. Some global memory handles, such as those used to pass Clipboard data, must remain unlocked once you have stored the Clipboard information into the memory, but you must not *free* them yourself.

Discardable Memory Blocks

The third kind of memory block is the *discardable memory block*. Windows can reallocate a discardable memory block to a 0 length (thus releasing the space it occupied for other uses) when it needs space to satisfy an allocation request. Doing this destroys all data contained in the memory block. You typically use a discardable memory block to hold information that is convenient to keep in memory but that can easily be recreated when necessary.

You cannot get a discardable memory block using `malloc` or `HeapAlloc`. You must either use `GlobalAlloc` with the GMEM_MOVEABLE and GMEM_DISCARDABLE flags or, if in C++, implement your own new operator to call `GlobalAlloc` with the GMEM_MOVEABLE and GMEM_DISCARDABLE flags.

When you allocate a discardable memory block, Windows returns a handle to the block, just like it does for a moveable block. When you lock the block prior to accessing it, Windows returns the address of the block. The handle returned when allocating a discardable memory block remains valid even after the block is discarded; this can occur at any time the block is unlocked. When you lock a discarded memory block, Windows returns a NULL pointer because the data in the block no longer exists. You then must reallocate the block from its current 0 length back to the size required and recreate the contents of the block. Windows will not discard a locked block, so you must unlock the block if you want Windows to have an opportunity to discard the storage.

The original goal of using discardable memory blocks permits Win16 to satisfy allocation requests that might otherwise fail. The Win32 goal is to allow the system to postpone for as long as possible the need to allocate more virtual memory to the application.

When insufficient memory is available to satisfy a memory allocation request, Windows attempts to coalesce free blocks in order to create a large enough block. If this can't be done, Windows begins discarding discardable memory blocks one by one until either a large enough free block can be created or no more discardable blocks exist. In the first case, the memory allocation succeeds, but one or more discardable memory blocks may have to be recreated when needed. In the second case, Windows will attempt to allocate more virtual memory to the application. If this succeeds, the memory allocation will succeed; otherwise, the memory allocation request fails. Note that a later reallocation of a discarded memory block can itself cause this process to take place, possibly discarding other discardable blocks to create enough space to create the one you want. What is not clear from any documentation we have been able to find is exactly what criteria Win32 uses to decide to discard memory.

A discardable *resource* can be replaced by reloading the resource from the resource segment of the module. This happens transparently. That is, if you call a resource loading function and the existing copy of the resource has been discarded, a new copy will be loaded. A discardable data segment will have to be recreated by its owner. Hence, if you are the owner of a discardable memory segment, the locking operation could legitimately return a NULL pointer. You could assume this meant that the storage had been discarded, or you could use the `GlobalFlags` function to see if it returned a status with the `GMEM_DISCARDED` bit set. At that point, you would have to recreate its contents.

We mentioned that in Win32 you can have only 65,535 moveable memory blocks in a process. Discardable memory blocks are also counted as moveable memory blocks, since they also have the `GMEM_MOVEABLE` flag.

Managing Memory Blocks Using the `Global-` Functions

To allocate a chunk of memory, you call `GlobalAlloc`, passing in a size request and a number of flags specifying the type of memory to be allocated. What `GlobalAlloc` returns is an `HGLOBAL` handle, which is a non-zero value if the operation succeeded and a 0 (`NULL`) value if it failed.

```
HANDLE hMem ;

hMem = GlobalAlloc (flags, size) ;
```

The `flags` parameter specifies one or more flags describing the type of the memory block, plus a few other options. The `size` parameter specifies the number of bytes to be allocated. Table 14.1 lists the flags that the `GlobalAlloc` function uses.

Most of the flags that were once passed to `GlobalAlloc` are now obsolete and are ignored. We list only the ones that exist in Win32.

Unless you allocated *fixed* memory using the `GMEM_FIXED` flag, this handle does not yet let you access the memory you have been allocated. First, you must *lock* the memory. When you lock the memory using `GlobalLock`, you get an `LPVOID` pointer. You typically cast this pointer to the pointer type you want. (If you are programming in C++, you *must* cast it, or the compiler will give you an error message. C++ is less forgiving than C about assignments from `LPVOID`.) If you lock a `GMEM_FIXED` block, you get back the same handle you gave it, since the handle already represents locked memory. When you are done reading or writing the storage, you can call `GlobalUnlock` to release it, while retaining its handle until you need it again. When you are finally done with the storage entirely, you release it by calling `GlobalFree`.

As with all other Win32 handles, memory handles are 32-bit values. This may cause you problems when you are porting an application from Win16. Clever programmers often packed two 16-bit memory handles into a single 32-bit `DWORD`. But you can't pack two 32-bit memory handles into a `DWORD` no matter how hard you try. If this technique was used in a Win16 application, you will have to pass in the `DWORD` a pointer to a `struct` *containing* two handles.

Generally, Windows programmers tend to couple the locking of storage with its allocation and the unlocking of it with its deallocation and ignore any other details of when to unlock it. Unless the API function requires that you not hold onto the storage (the classic example being the Clipboard), this has no impact on either the correctness or performance of your Win32 application. But you should try to avoid the use of moveable memory unless absolutely necessary.

Locking is determined by looking at the *lock count*. Only memory that is *discardable* maintains a lock count. Each lock operation on discardable memory increments the lock count, and each unlock operation decrements the lock count. An unlock operation on storage whose lock count is already 0 has no effect. Operations such as `GlobalFree` will fail if the lock count is nonzero. Even using discardable memory, which is unusual in Win32, it is rare to have a lock count greater than 1.

When using certain facilities, such as the Clipboard, the system returns a memory handle; `GetClipboardData` and `PrintDlg` are two functions we've encountered that do this. You must explicitly lock the handle, copy out what you need, and unlock the handle. In the case of the Clipboard, the system "owns" the memory handle; once you've put something into the Clipboard, you must not keep the handle locked and you must not free it. Each function will tell you the rules for supplying memory handles to it or how to treat memory handles you receive from it.

The handle functions are summarized in Table 14.1. We indicate with a check mark (✓) the ones you will most commonly use.

 Win16 programmers will see that this table is *much* shorter than the equivalent table for Win16 memory management. Many of the API functions of Win16 are totally obsolete and have no equivalent. All of the `Local-` functions of Win16 are *identical* to the `Global-` functions, and the names are retained only for compatibility. We do not mention them here.

 In a Win32s application, if you call `GlobalAlloc` with `GMEM_FIXED` you will severely impact the performance of the underlying Win16 system. If you ever plan to run your application under a Win32s system, you must specify `GMEM_MOVEABLE`. If you require `GMEM_FIXED`, you may want to test what version of the system you are running on and refuse to run on a Win32s system. Check out the MSKB article Q114611 for more details.

For example, to set information in the Clipboard you must allocate a global memory handle, which has the `GMEM_MOVEABLE` flag set:

```
BOOL stringToClipboard(HWND hwnd, LPCTSTR str)
    {
    HGLOBAL h;
    LPTSTR p;

    if(!OpenClipboard(hwnd))0
        return FALSE;

    __try
        { /* Clipboard opened */
        h = GlobalAlloc(GMEM_MOVEABLE | GMEM_DDESHARE,
                            (lstrlen(str) + 1) * sizeof(TCHAR));
        if( h == NULL)
            return FALSE;

        p = (LPTSTR) GlobalLock(h);
        if(p == NULL)
            { /* lock failed */
            GlobalFree(h);
```

```
            return FALSE;
         } /* lock failed */

      lstrcpy(p, str);
      GlobalUnlock(h);
      EmptyClipboard ( ) ;
      SetClipboardData (CF_TEXT, h);
      } /* Clipboard opened */
   __finally
      {
      CloseClipboard();
      }
   return TRUE;
   }
```

Table 14.1: Default heap (Global-) functions

Result	Function	Parameters and Description	
✓	HGLOBAL	GlobalAlloc	(UINT flags, DWORD size)
			Allocates storage and returns a global handle to it; NULL if the allocation fails. The flags can be any of the following:
✓			GMEM_FIXED — Allocates a fixed block of memory. The resulting HGLOBAL is actually an LPVOID to the allocated storage.
✓			GMEM_MOVEABLE — A moveable memory block; use GlobalLock to obtain the pointer.
✓			GMEM_DDESHARE — Generally meaningless in Win32 but can be used as a hint to some implementations that the memory will be shared via the Clipboard or DDE.
			GMEM_DISCARDABLE — The storage is discardable. Some Win32 implementations may ignore this flag.
✓			GMEM_ZEROINIT — Initializes the memory to 0.
✓			GHND — GMEM_MOVEABLE | GMEM_ZEROINIT
✓			GPTR — GMEM_FIXED | GMEM_ZEROINIT
✓	LPVOID	GlobalAllocPtr *	(UINT flags, DWORD size)
			Allocates and locks storage and returns a pointer to the storage; NULL if the allocation fails. The flags are the same as for GlobalAlloc.

✓ Indicates the most commonly used API functions or flags.

* These are defined in windowsx.h.

Table 14.1: Default heap (Global-) functions

Result	Function	Parameters and Description	
HGLOBAL	GlobalDiscard	(HGLOBAL handle)	
		Releases the storage but retains the handle, which can be re-allocated.	
UINT	GlobalFlags	(HGLOBAL handle)	
		Returns the flags associated with the memory handle. Can be one of the following:	
		GMEM_DDESHARE	Generally meaningless; used as a hint.
		GMEM_DISCARDABLE	The memory block could be discarded.
		GMEM_DISCARDED	The memory block has been discarded.
		In addition, the following value is defined:	
		GMEM_LOCKCOUNT	A bit mask that can be used to extract the lock count from the returned result.
✓ BOOL	GlobalFree	(HGLOBAL handle)	
		Releases the storage that had been allocated. The handle is no longer valid after this is called.	
✓ BOOL	GlobalFreePtr *	(LPVOID ptr)	
		Unlocks the handle that represents ptr and then does a GlobalFree on the handle.	
HGLOBAL	GlobalHandle	(LPVOID ptr)	
		The pointer must refer to the first byte of the memory block in the handle (the result of the GlobalLock call). Returns the handle; returns NULL if ptr does not refer to the first byte of a global allocation.	
✓ LPVOID	GlobalLock	(HGLOBAL handle)	
		Locks the memory object by incrementing its lock count and returns a pointer to its storage. The pointer remains valid until the storage is unlocked.	

✓ Indicates the most commonly used API functions or flags.

* These are defined in windowsx.h.

Table 14.1: Default heap (Global-) functions

Result	Function	Parameters and Description	
HGLOBAL	GlobalReAlloc	`( HGLOBAL handle, DWORD size, UINT flags )`	
		Reallocates the storage associated with a handle. If the new size is smaller than the current size, the information beyond the end of the new storage will be lost. Note that the handle returned may be different than the handle passed in; you should assume that the handle passed in is no longer valid after this call. The `flags` value specifies how to reallocate the object	
		GMEM_MODIFY	Ignores `size`, changes the attributes of memory according to the `flags` parameter.
		If GMEM_MODIFY is *not* specified, `flags` can be one of the following:	
		GMEM_MOVEABLE	If the size is 0, discards the storage. The handle must have a 0 lock count *and* be moveable and discardable.
		GMEM_NOCOMPACT	Prevents memory from being discarded to satisfy the allocation request.
		GMEM_ZEROINIT	If expanding storage, initializes the new storage to zero.
		If GMEM_MODIFY *is* specified, `flags` can be one of the following:	
		GMEM_DISCARDABLE	If the storage was previously allocated as moveable or if the GMEM_MOVEABLE value is also specified, the storage is reallocated as discardable memory.
		GMEM_MOVEABLE	Changes a fixed memory object to a moveable memory object.
DWORD	GlobalSize	`( HGLOBAL handle )`	
		Returns the size, in bytes, of the global memory object. This is the actual size and may be larger (by some allocation quantum) than the requested size.	

✓ Indicates the most commonly used API functions or flags.

* These are defined in windowsx.h.

Table 14.1: Default heap (Global-) functions

Result		Function	Parameters and Description
✓	BOOL	GlobalUnlock	(HGLOBAL handle)
			Decrements the lock count on the memory object. If the lock count was decremented to 0, returns FALSE, indicating the storage was actually unlocked; otherwise, returns TRUE.
✓	BOOL	GlobalUnlockPtr *	(LPVOID ptr)
			GlobalUnlock(GlobalHandle(ptr))

✓ Indicates the most commonly used API functions or flags.

* These are defined in windowsx.h.

Note the use of the __finally clause to guarantee that the Clipboard is always closed. Refer to the discussion of structured exception handling in Chapter 7, page 510.

The specification of the flags in GlobalAlloc is obtained directly from the specification of the SetClipboardData function: "It must be allocated by GlobalAlloc using the GMEM_MOVEABLE and GMEM_DDESHARE flags". Actually, the GMEM_DDESHARE flag is largely meaningless in Win32. It is used by some Windows NT implementations as a hint that the operating system can use to optimize DDE and Clipboard performance.

In Win16, setting the GMEM_DDESHARE flag meant that the storage you allocated would not be released when your application terminated; it would remain allocated. This allowed you to pass the handle to some other running application, which then had to take responsibility for explicitly freeing the storage before it terminated. This is no longer possible in Win32. Whatever storage you allocate is private to your application and *will* be freed when your application terminates, *except* for memory handles given to the Clipboard. Memory sharing in Win32 is handled by memory-mapped files.

Allocating a Fixed Memory Block

The malloc and HeapAlloc functions always return fixed memory blocks. The default implementation of the new operator is to return a fixed memory block. You can also use GlobalAlloc to allocate a fixed memory block.

A memory block allocated by GlobalAlloc will be a fixed memory block unless you specify the GMEM_MOVEABLE flag; however, your code will be easier to understand if you specify the GMEM_FIXED flag. The following statement allocates a 1K block of fixed global memory:

```
hMem = GlobalAlloc (GMEM_FIXED, 1024) ;
```

You can request that the block be initialized to 0 when it's allocated like this:

```
hMem = GlobalAlloc (GMEM_FIXED | GMEM_ZEROINIT, 1024) ;
```

The windows.h header file also defines the symbol GPTR, which can be used to allocated a fixed block that is initialized to 0:

```
hMem = GlobalAlloc (GPTR, 1024) ;
```

The symbol GPTR (for global pointer) refers to the handle returned by the GlobalAlloc function when a fixed memory block is allocated. The "handle" of a global fixed block is always the address of the allocated memory. You don't need to lock a fixed block to obtain its address.

You can call GlobalLock and lock a fixed global memory handle if you wish. The GlobalLock function returns a pointer identical to the one returned by the GlobalAlloc function. Or you can cast the result of an allocation to immediately be a pointer. In the following example, str1, str2, and str3 end up with pointers to blocks of storage of size MyLimit:

```
LPTSTR str1 = (LPTSTR)GlobalAlloc(GMEM_FIXED, MyLimit) ;
LPTSTR str2 = (LPTSTR)GlobalLock(GlobalAlloc(GMEM_FIXED, MyLimit));
LPTSTR str3 = (LPTSTR)GlobalAllocPtr(GMEM_FIXED, MyLimit);
```

Allocating a Moveable Memory Block

A memory block will be moveable when you specify the GMEM_MOVEABLE flag. Generally, in Win32 the concept of a moveable memory block has no meaning because there are no compaction algorithms involved. However, some API functions still formally specify that the block of memory referenced by the handle must be moveable. The following statement allocates a 1K block of moveable global memory:

```
hMem = GlobalAlloc (GMEM_MOVEABLE, 1024) ;
```

You can request that the block be initialized to 0 when it's allocated like this:

```
hMem = GlobalAlloc (GMEM_MOVEABLE | GMEM_ZEROINIT, 1024) ;
```

The windows.h header file also defines the symbol GHND, which can be used to allocate a moveable block that is initialized to 0:

```
hMem = GlobalAlloc (GHND, 1024) ;
```

The symbol GHND (for global handle) indicates that the handle returned by the GlobalAlloc function is a handle whose value has no relationship to the address of the allocated memory. You can't convert it to an address directly (although you may divine how to do this, your answer may apply only to one particular release of one version of one of the 32-bit operating systems). You must *lock* the block to obtain the address of the block. You lock a block by calling the GlobalLock function and passing it the handle of the block. The GlobalLock function returns a pointer to the memory block. You should cast the result of GlobalLock if you need other than an LPVOID pointer.

```
HGLOBAL    hMem ;
LPVOID     lp ;

hMem = GlobalAlloc (GHND, 1024) ;
lp = GlobalLock (hMem) ;
```

Allocating a Discardable Global Memory Block

A memory block will be discardable when you specify both the GMEM_MOVEABLE and GMEM_DISCARDABLE flags. The following statement allocates a 1K block of discardable global memory:

```
hMem = GlobalAlloc (GMEM_DISCARDABLE | GMEM_MOVEABLE, 1024) ;
```

You can request that the block be initialized to 0 when it's allocated like this:

```
hMem = GlobalAlloc (GMEM_DISCARDABLE | GMEM_MOVEABLE | GMEM_ZEROINIT, 1024) ;
```

You must lock a discardable global memory block before accessing it to prevent Windows from discarding it while you are using it. You lock a block by calling the GlobalLock function and passing it the handle of the memory block. The GlobalLock function returns a pointer to the memory block. Windows will not discard a memory block as long as it's locked:

```
HGLOBAL hMem ;
LPVOID  lp ;

hMem = GlobalAlloc (GMEM_DISCARDABLE | GHND, 1024) ;
lp = GlobalLock (hMem) ;
```

Allocating a Shareable Memory Block

You can't allocate a shareable memory block.

Windows applications have a limited means of sharing global data. In Win32, all of your data is private to your application, and passing a pointer to your private address space to another application is a meaningless operation. You may discover that in porting a Win16 application, the application felt free to allocate memory and then pass either the handle or a pointer to the memory to some other task. *This does not work under Win32.* Memory sharing in Win32 is done by *memory-mapped files*, a topic beyond the scope of this book.

In Win32, the GMEM_DDESHARE flag essentially has no meaning. However, for some implementations of Win32 the presence of this flag can be used by the operating system to optimize the performance of some API functions, such as the Clipboard. Your application could run successfully without ever specifying this flag, but it might run a bit faster if it uses it.

Locking and Unlocking Memory Blocks

You use locking and unlocking only on moveable and discardable memory blocks you get from GlobalAlloc or from other API functions such as GetClipboardData, PrintDlg, and others. You should never try to apply these functions to memory you get from malloc, HeapAlloc, or a default implementation of new.

The primary purpose of the GlobalLock function is to return the address of the block specified by the supplied handle. The GlobalLock function returns 0 when the lock request fails. A lock request can appear to fail even when the supplied handle is valid if you are locking a discardable block that Windows has already discarded. Windows does not invalidate the handle to a discarded block; it simply resizes the block to a 0 length (which discards the block's contents and releases the space). The still-valid handle refers to a 0-length block, and a 0-length block has no address.

The GlobalLock function will fail when you supply an invalid handle. A handle is invalid when the block to which it refers has already been freed or when the handle doesn't refer to any block (that is, it is a garbage value, possibly from being obtained from an uninitialized stack variable). The function increases the lock count only when locking discardable blocks. This prevents the block from being discarded. Similarly, the GlobalUnlock function decreases the lock count only for discardable blocks. This allows an unlocked block to be discarded if necessary.

When GlobalLock is applied to a fixed memory block, the result is the same as the handle. This is not true when you apply it to a moveable handle.

After you've obtained the address of a dynamic storage block with GlobalLock, it will not change as long as the block remains locked. You can lock a block once at the start of an application and keep it locked the entire time the application is running. Once you unlock the block, however, there is no guarantee that the next time you lock it you will get the same address back. So if you are doing dynamic locking and unlocking, you must not store the pointer to the locked storage anywhere that will allow it to be used after the storage is unlocked. While Win32 in principle does no storage compaction, it does manipulate memory maps, and certain unlocked storage, such as the Clipboard, is under its control, not yours. The Clipboard and other such memory has the additional feature that, between one lock event and the next one, some other process or thread (even a thread of your own program) can change the contents. As a result, even holding onto the handle of such storage is likely to result in a failure.

The windowsx.h header file provides a number of macro APIs that are quite convenient when you are writing protected-mode Windows applications. Typically, such applications allocate global memory and immediately lock it so as to obtain a pointer to the memory. The GlobalAllocPtr macro API combines these otherwise separate steps into one call. The macro definition looks like this:

```
#define GlobalAllocPtr(flags, size) \
        (GlobalLock(GlobalAlloc((flags), (size))))
```

You pass the desired memory allocation flags as the flags parameter to the GlobalAllocPtr macro and the number of bytes as the size parameter. The macro combines the allocation and lock function calls.

Similarly, you can release global memory given a pointer to the memory by using the GlobalFreePtr macro. windowsx.h defines it this way:

```
#define GlobalFreePtr(lp) \
        (GlobalUnlockPtr(lp), \
        (BOOL)GlobalFree(GlobalPtrHandle(lp)))
```

Reallocating a Memory Block

We've been discussing the attributes of a memory block as if they are specified once and then remain constant for the life of the block. Although this is normally the case, it needn't be so. For memory that you've allocated with GlobalAlloc, you can change either its size or its attributes. The GlobalReAlloc function can change not only the size of a memory block (as the C runtime function realloc can do). It also can change the type (moveable, discardable, or fixed) of the block.

The most common use for this function is to change the size of a previously allocated memory block. To do so, you specify the handle of the block, the new size, and an option indicating whether memory should be discarded to satisfy this request. You can specify either GMEM_NOCOMPACT to suppress any attempt to discard memory or 0 to indicate that memory can be discarded if necessary.

You can use this ability to increase (or decrease) the size of a memory block to minimize memory use by an application. For example, you might need to maintain a table in an application but may not know the actual size of the table (number of items) until the application runs. You can call the GlobalAlloc function to allocate a table that's large enough to hold the number of items used in a typical run of the program. If you need more room, you just call GlobalReAlloc to increase the size of the table. In fact, once you build the table and know its size, you can call GlobalReAlloc to free any unused space. For example, the following code allocates a block of storage, loads it with some data, and then reallocates it, allowing memory to be discarded:

```
#define MAX_ITEMS 100000

HGLOBAL hMem = GlobalAlloc(GHND, MAX_ITEMS * sizeof(item));
item * items = GlobalLock(hMem);
int count = 0;
    // .. load up the table
    for(count = 0; count < MAX_ITEMS; count++)
        { /* load it */
        // .. read an item
        // if end-of-file, break
        items[count].field = something;
        // ...
        } /* load it */
    GlobalUnlock(hMem);
    hMem = GlobalReAlloc (hMem, count * sizeof(item), 0) ;
}
```

Alternatively, you could have written

```
hMem = GlobalReAlloc (hMem, count * sizeof(item), GMEM_NOCOMPACT) ;
```

You can ask that a reallocated block be initialized to 0 by specifying the GMEM_ZEROINIT flag. Only the additional bytes in the block (if the block is increasing in size) are initialized to 0. When you shrink a block, it is truncated, but the remaining data remains untouched.

You can even reallocate a fixed memory block to a larger or smaller sized fixed block. In a sense, it becomes temporarily moveable during the reallocation. To reallocate a fixed block, you must specify the block's handle, the new size, and the GMEM_MOVEABLE flag. Do *not* include the GMEM_MODIFY flag. This example changes the size of a fixed block to 2,048 bytes:

```
hMemNew = GlobalReAlloc (hMem, 2048, GMEM_MOVEABLE) ;
```

When the fixed block's size is increased, insufficient room may exist at the end of the existing block. The GMEM_MOVEABLE flag allows Windows to move the fixed block to a new location. The returned value is the handle of the new fixed block and may not be the same as the block's previous handle. Because the new block is fixed, it won't be moved again unless reallocated or made moveable.

The same statement can be used on a locked, moveable block to change its size. The GMEM_MOVEABLE flag indicates in this case that the block can be moved, even though it is presently locked. Again, the returned handle may be different from the original handle.

A special case exists for discardable blocks. A call to the GlobalReAlloc function specifying a discardable block, a new size of 0, and the GMEM_MOVEABLE flag causes the block to be discarded. In fact, the GlobalDiscard function is actually a macro that does just this:

```
#define GlobalDiscard (hMem) \
     GlobalReAlloc ((hMem), 0, GMEM_MOVEABLE) ;
```

You use the GMEM_MODIFY flag to change the memory flags for a block. With this flag, you can make a fixed block moveable or discardable. You also can change a moveable block to a discardable block and vice versa; however, you cannot change a moveable or discardable block to a fixed block. The first of the following two statements makes a block moveable. The second makes a block discardable:

```
hMemNew = GlobalReAlloc(hMem, 2048, GMEM_MODIFY | GMEM_MOVEABLE);
```

```
hMemNew = GlobalReAlloc(hMem, 2048, GMEM_MODIFY | GMEM_DISCARDABLE) ;
```

Freeing a Memory Block

When you're done using a dynamically allocated memory block that you got from GlobalAlloc, you return it to Windows by calling the GlobalFree function. The GlobalFree function returns the storage occupied by the block to the free space in the default heap. A block must have a lock count of 0 before it can be freed successfully (this limitation applies only to discardable blocks, which are the only kind for which a lock count is kept). Here is a typical call to the GlobalFree function. The function returns 0 when successful. It returns the hMem parameter when the block cannot be freed.

```
hMem = GlobalFree (hMem) ;
```

If you don't have the handle, you can call the windowsx.h function GlobalFreePtr:

```
hMem = GlobalFreePtr (ptr) ;
```

Other Default Heap Functions

There are various other memory functions for memory you get from GlobalAlloc; most of these you'll use rarely, if at all. They were far more important under early versions of Windows (pre-Win32) and have at best vestigial usefulness, except in special cases.

The GlobalFlags, GlobalHandle, and GlobalSize functions return information about a memory block. The GlobalFlags function requires the handle to a memory block and returns a UINT value describing the block's memory allocation flags in the high byte of the low-order word and the lock count of the block in the low byte of the low-order word. The memory allocation flags can be one of the flags listed in Table 14.1. These flags must be tested by logically ANDing the flag against the returned value, *not* against the extracted high byte of the returned value. For example, to see if a block has been discarded, you do this:

```
if (GlobalFlags (hMem) & GMEM_DISCARDED)
    {
    /* Block has been discarded, rebuild it. */
    }
```

The lock count is in the low byte. You can extract this value by logically ANDing the returned value with the mask GMEM_LOCKCOUNT, as follows:

```
LockCount = GlobalFlags (hMem) & GMEM_LOCKCOUNT ;
```

Don't attempt to free a block based on its lock count! This does not work. Locking a block does not increment its lock count unless it's a discardable block.

You can obtain the handle for a global memory block given its address. The GlobalHandle function requires the address of a global memory block and returns an HGLOBAL. The GlobalHandle function returns 0 when no handle exists for the specified address.

The GlobalSize function returns a DWORD value that is the current size of the global memory block specified by the supplied handle or 0 if an error occurs:

```
DWORD Size ;

Size = GlobalSize (hMem) ;
```

A memory block is often allocated slightly larger than the size requested. The GlobalSize function returns the *actual* size of the allocated block. You should check to see if the block has been discarded before calling the GlobalSize function about the block. Because discarded blocks have a size of 0, you can't tell from the return value of the GlobalSize function whether the block has been discarded or an error occurred. Alternatively, you could call GetLastError to obtain additional information.

Dynamic Memory Allocation–When Performance Matters

With the advent of really fast processors (the typical "low-end" contemporary personal computer is more than 50 times faster than the big mainframes of a couple of decades back), a lot of "efficiency" considerations have given way to a desire to write clean, easily understood, and easily maintained code. In most cases, adding a thousandth of a second to the processing of a mouse click so that the code reads well is a very good trade-off. But when efficiency matters, it often matters *a lot*. You turn on every optimization your compiler supports. If you're careful, you even turn on the "dangerous" optimizations, such as those that ignore "aliasing" through multiple pointers. And you get code that, at the instruction level, is as tight and fast as a really first-class optimizing compiler can produce (and all of the serious development environments that we know of have really first-class optimizing compilers). And your application *still* runs like a dog. What's wrong?

There are usually two base causes for this: your algorithm and your memory access patterns. There are "good" algorithms and "bad" algorithms. You might have an algorithm that, when iterating over a set of elements, takes one pass over all the elements for each element it processes, thus requiring n^2 accesses of the information. For small values of n this doesn't matter, but if n gets to be very large, your time goes up as the square of the number of elements. So you should check your algorithm to make sure that you aren't executing really tight, fast code on a slow algorithm. Also, you should be wary of something that is often glossed over in discussions of complexity. We talk about "order-n^2" sort algorithms and "order-n log_2 n" sort algorithms and point out that the second is superior to the first in performance. But the formal definition of an "order-n log_2 n" algorithm is that time is *proportional* to n log_2 n. An unstated consideration is that the constant of proportionality could be large. Make sure you don't have a large constant of proportionality. See the inset below for an anecdote.

But assuming that you have good code and a good algorithm, and it still runs like a dog, you are left with only two conclusions: The problem really is hard to solve and under the best of conditions will take a really long time, or there is some other factor.

The Constant of Proportionality: A True Story

Once, many years ago, I was working on a compiler-like application that had to print out lengthy cross-references. The cross-references had to be printed out in sorted order, including within each subcomponent. This meant that for each component, all its fields had to be sorted, and then within each field, all references, both by object name and field name, had to be sorted, and so on. This was in the days before C was popular, so we didn't have qsort. In a hurry to concentrate on the other details of the problem, I wrote the six-line bubble sort, knowing that I would have to replace this n^2 algorithm with a better algorithm before I released the system. It worked fine on all my small test cases, so I threw a large input file at it. My program printed out the message "Starting cross-reference listing"; 10 minutes later, it was still computing. Of course, the problem was my horrible sort algorithm. So I hauled out my trusty $n \log n$ sort subroutine, dusted it off, and replaced the bubble sort by the "fast" sort. My new version of the program printed out the message "Starting cross-reference listing" and 7 minutes later had still produced no output. I started probing with the debugger and discovered that the program was still spending most of its time in the sort subroutine. After a bit of instrumentation was added, I found that it was spending nearly all of its time in the equivalent of strcmp! While the algorithm was now $n \log n$, the relatively slow string-compare was giving me a large constant of proportionality. I solved the problem by sorting the entire symbol table exactly once, then going through it in sorted order and adding to each symbol entry an integer which represented the position in the overall sort order. For each substructure and its cross-references, I then sorted by comparing not strings, but the integers I assigned. The entire cross-reference phase, which generated over 30 pages of output and called the sort routine hundreds of times, ran to completion in under 1 minute (on a 256K machine with about 10% of the speed of a typical modern personal computer system and 5% of the speed of the machine I'm working on right now!). The algorithm was fine. The constant of proportionality was, as I computed later, about 50 times smaller for the second representation.– *jmn*

In many cases, the "other factor" is how you use memory. Your key algorithms may have the property that in a Win32 virtual memory environment, they are causing page faults and disk traffic at a rate hundreds or thousands of times more than a slightly different algorithm.

One classic case of how memory can affect a program is the computation of SPECmarks, a standard performance measurement, on high-end workstations. One test in the SPEC suite was a FORTRAN program that did matrix inversion. One vendor wrote a special program that read the FORTRAN program, analyzed it, and wrote a new FORTRAN program that computed the same result. But the second program was rewritten to execute all the loops in a way that would maximize the number of cache hits and minimize the number of page faults. This resulting program ran 20 times faster. All you had to do was give the rewrite program some parameters that defined the cache behavior and the page size, and it would rewrite the program to be optimal on whatever machine it was running.

Performance Evaluation

Some years ago we wrote a high-performance storage allocator (see *IDL: The Language and Its Implementation*, Chapter 14, for more details; see "Further Reading"). A product group in the company measured their system and found that it was spending something like 20% of its time in the allocator, as measured by sampling the program counter. We analyzed their algorithms and our allocator and could not find any reason for this high number. Eventually we discovered that a subroutine they were calling in an inner loop–a subroutine which they hadn't written– would allocate a small, variable-length, working buffer, then before returning would deallocate it. The effect was that although the allocator was very fast, calling it several hundred thousand times in an inner loop was definitely a bad idea. No one was aware of this allocation except the original author of the subroutine, who never expected that it would be called in a deeply-nested inner loop, and therefore felt that calling the allocator was acceptable. The use of the storage allocator should have been part of the external specification of the subroutine's behavior, except that this was supposed to be an "implementation detail" invisible to the caller. In terms of performance, its impact was *not* invisible! Moral: it doesn't matter how fast the allocator is if you overuse it.–*jmn*

We're not going to look at cache hits, but we *are* going to look at using special memory management and algorithm changes to minimize page faults, which on a Win32 system can buy a *lot* of performance. First, we discuss how Windows organizes system memory. Next, we discuss alternatives of how to allocate and use dynamic memory in the Win32 environment.

System Memory Organization

All Win32 applications operate in protected mode used by Windows, which on Intel platforms is often called the "386 enhanced mode"; although this processor is largely obsolete, the mapped memory architecture it introduced has become established as the *de facto* standard for all subsequent Intel and Intel look-alike processors. Win32 on Intel platforms runs in the enhanced mode, which allows you to run applications whose individual or aggregate memory requirements exceed the physical memory available on the processor, by using *virtual memory*. Windows NT also operates on non-Intel platforms, which have their own approaches to how memory is mapped, so Win32 can actually be configured to use virtual memory on a variety of platforms. Remember that Win32 is the *specification* of an API. In principle, it should be possible to implement significant parts of it on other, even non-Microsoft, platforms.

Virtual memory permits the use of disk space as part of the logical address seen by an application. Theoretically, Win32 can address 4 *giga*bytes (2^{32}, or 4,294,967,296, bytes) of virtual memory. On a more practical note, your paging file might be 50 to 200MB for a typical 16MB or 32MB configuration, or even larger if you have a more substantial configuration. Only the *lower* 2GB of virtual memory are actually available to you; the upper 2GB are reserved for the Win32 operating system. This is not currently felt to be a major limitation.[4]

Of course, nothing comes free. You pay a penalty to gain more "memory" than the computer actually contains. A disk access is much slower than a memory access. When a program refers to a memory location that is currently not in main memory but in the swap file, Windows must find space in (or create space in) main memory to hold the page containing the referenced location.

If Windows has to make room for the page, it may first have to remove a different page from memory by writing a copy of the page to the *swap file* (called *swapping out* the page). Windows reads the page containing the referenced location into the free space in main memory (called *swapping in* the page). It fixes up the memory mapping tables used by the hardware so that the page appears in your address space in the place it is supposed to be. Finally, Windows allows the program that tried to reference the now-present location to try again, and the program continues on–until the next time it references a location not presently in memory. Of course, while it is waiting for the page to swap out or swap in, it tries to run some other application that is ready to run and whose pages are already present.

---

[4] In the mid-1960s, IBM introduced their 360 line, which had a potential for 16MB of main memory. Many outsiders thought this absurdly high, since the low-end system came with 32K and the major mainframes had 512K. In fact, "virtual memory" was thought to be pointless because there was little if any need to support programs that wouldn't fit in the massive 256K main memories that were becoming available. Does this sound familiar?

Because of the paging just described, as well as other overhead required to support mapped memory, an application running on any machine that supports mapped memory runs more slowly than it would on a "bare machine". This is one of the reasons that "instruction timings" are often meaningless. Interactions with the level 1 cache, level 2 cache, page tables, and the address translation unit (called the "Translation Lookaside Buffer", or TLB, in many architectures) all change a simple "MOVE EAX,data" instruction so that it might execute in as little as 5 ns (the clock time of a 200MHz processor, assuming the level 1 cache already holds the data) or 40 ms (take a disk with a 10 ms typical seek time, write out one 4,096K block, and read in another, and there's 20 ms already, not counting rotational latency or other considerations!).

Of particular note is that the virtual address space of any one process can be larger than the amount of physical memory. The heap could become so large that only part of it could reside in memory at any one time. Windows, using the memory management hardware of the processor, copies *pages* of the application to and from a swap file on disk. On most architectures, a *page* is a 4,096-byte chunk of memory, but this is not a fixed number. Other architectures (a concern of anyone writing a Windows NT program, for example) might support different page sizes. You can discover the page size on any Win32 system by calling the GetSystemInfo function. Pages that aren't currently being used are swapped to disk, while those in use are held in memory. Because of the hardware memory management features of the 80386 and above microprocessors for Windows 95 and Windows NT and the non-Intel workstations on which Windows NT runs, this process can be done without the cooperation of the application.

There is potential here for introducing a serious performance penalty. For example, consider the use of the ordinary malloc/free functions in C or the new/delete operators in C++. After some large number of allocations and deallocations, you may find that your key pieces of information are scattered rather widely throughout memory. The consequence of this is that accessing them in sequence, as you might do if you have a linked list of objects, could result in touching a different page for each object. Under conditions of heavy load, your quick-and-fast list traversal algorithm could be generating a paging operation for each object!

Here's a classic case of virtual memory mismanagement. In the late 1960s, a major vendor delivered a FORTRAN compiler on its first virtual memory architecture. The compiler writers had allocated a 1MB "hash table" for the symbols because "everyone knew" that larger hash tables gave better performance. The compiler was a dog. When the developers investigated why, they discovered that the hashing algorithm tended to allocate one symbol per page . . . so a symbol lookup almost always generated a page fault. Of course, this was less noticeable on the "big" 750K development machine, which had very few users. But it showed up badly on the "regular" 512K customer mainframes that had 40 simultaneous users. I know. I used one of those customer mainframes, and the FORTRAN users had a serious impact on all of us.

Unfortunately, the field gets older, but not smarter. Although this problem was well-known in 1968, in 1996 a certain document production system from a major vendor does virtual memory management so badly that after only a few hours of editing of a single chapter it has consumed several hundred megabytes of swap space, causing Windows NT to issue repeated warnings of low swap space. Before the warnings start, performance has suffered badly. A simple menu dropdown can take over half a minute, during which the disk works frantically; other operations are often worse. The end result is that after a few hours of editing the program has to be restarted just to get a fresh virtual memory image of manageable size! *–jmn*

Fortunately, there is a way around this. The technique has had various names in history, such as "local heaps", "collections", "arenas", and "pools". Win32 calls it *dynamic heaps*. We investigate the techniques for optimizing dynamic allocation of small objects as well as how to manage large objects starting on page 1050.

The Local Heap, the Global Heap, and `malloc/new` (Win16 programmers only!)

If you are a Win16 programmer, you will want to read this section to understand the differences between Win16 and Win32 allocation. If you're not a Win16 programmer, this section is somewhere between unnecessary and confusing. If you *are* a Win16 programmer, you need to read this section to see how Win32 compares to Win16 (it's simpler). If you are new to Windows programming, you can skip over this section and go right to the section "Supporting Multiple Heaps" that follows on page 1045, in which we contrast the historical Win16 allocation mechanisms with the Win32 allocation mechanisms.

In Win16, every task had a *local heap* and a *global heap*. The local heap was in a data segment that was limited to 64K and had to hold the stack, the statically allocated programmer variables, and all the constant strings, and still somehow support heap allocation. There was a separate set of API functions to manage the local heap, such as `LocalAlloc`, `LocalFree`, `LocalLock`, and `LocalUnlock`. There was a great deal of folklore surrounding the engineering decisions as to when to use the local heap.

In Win32, the concept of local heap is meaningless. There is only one heap for each application. For compatibility, the API function names are retained, but in fact they always refer to the same heap as their "global" name counterparts. The `LocalFlags` function will return flag values that can be successfully used with the old LMEM_ symbols (for example, GMEM_DISCARDABLE is defined as 0x100, but LMEM_DISCARDABLE is defined as 0xF00). If you use the old `Local-` functions with the LMEM_ symbols, your program will operate correctly. This was done so that older Win16 applications could be easily ported. About the only use for the `Local-` functions is the ability of `LocalFree` to take a pointer to storage instead of requiring a handle.

Starting with Windows 3.1, most programmers began to ignore the local heap entirely. Since many interesting large programs did not need to run multiple instances (and some, for reasons of sharing files and other resources, didn't want to allow multiple instances), most programmers abandoned the "medium model" of programming that permitted multiple instances of an application to run. They returned to the "large model", which simplified life considerably for the programmer at the cost of limiting the user to one running instance of the program at a time. Distinctions such as "near" and "far" pointers could be largely ignored if you programmed in large model. And `malloc` and `new` would allocate from the far heap, making them much more civilized. Generally, programming in the large model was the accepted way to write large applications. Those programmers who needed to support multiple-instance applications could still use the global heap. However, they had to call the "far" allocation functions, such as `_fmalloc`, and deal with all the subsequent problems that arose because many of the standard C library functions couldn't access "far" data. A number of apparently gratuitous copies of global data to stack locations were *necessary* because of the problems of "near" (16-bit) and "far" (segmented 32-bit) pointers.

A significant problem with `GlobalAlloc` was that it would consume one "selector", and there were only 8,192 selectors *system-wide*. And it was *slow* to allocate global memory; you didn't want to do this for small objects, such as a buffer to hold some useful information during a function call. The early C compilers, however, implemented `malloc` as `GlobalAlloc`, thus making it every bit as inefficient of time and selectors as direct `GlobalAlloc` usage. You may even find yourself porting a C application written using this philosophy and wondering why the programmer went to all that trouble. The reason was: It was necessary at the time.

Microsoft, Borland, and others released compilers whereby `malloc` would allocate using `GlobalAlloc` only to get new large chunks of memory and then suballocate those until they were exhausted, thus implementing what many programmers had done. However, the *books* about Windows programming hardly ever mentioned this. Someone reading about Windows programming for the first time might think that `GlobalAlloc` and `LocalAlloc` were the only way of life. The folklore that `malloc` would not work persisted for years after the newer compilers were released.

Another problem with `malloc` was that it was one of the worst-possible implementations of a storage allocator, both for intrinsic performance and for paging performance. The old C runtime `malloc` used the so-called "first fit" algorithm. That is, it scanned free storage until it found a block big enough to hold the allocation; if the block was larger, it was split and the difference returned to the free list. To make things worse, the traditional implementation did not even keep a list of free storage. Instead, it simply traversed all the storage blocks in the heap, allocated and unallocated, until it found an unallocated block large enough to satisfy the allocation request. This meant that if you had a lot of allocations, the `malloc` code touched *every memory block, both allocated and free,* until it found a free block large enough to satisfy the request. Hence, *every page in the heap up to the one satisfying the request was touched.* This is a truly awful algorithm in a paging environment. Programmers who wrote applications that had large heaps usually wrote or bought replacements for `malloc`.

What is interesting is that in Win32, we are back to the situation whereby `malloc` is defined to be equivalent to `GlobalAlloc`. However, `GlobalAlloc` is *not* the same functionality as was found in Win16. For example, it does not allocate a "selector"; the concept of a selector is meaningless in the Win32 linear address space. `GlobalAlloc` has been completely rewritten to be a far more efficient implementation than the Win16 allocator, and `malloc` no longer has to circumvent it. And, apparently, unlike the old `malloc`, the `GlobalAlloc` function does *not* need to scan the entire heap to find an available memory block.

Finally, in Win16 there was *The* Global Heap. There was exactly one global heap, system-wide. *All* running applications used the single global heap. You could even allocate storage from the global heap and pass a pointer to this storage to another application, which could then access the contents. The global heap was paged by the underlying Windows 3.1 paging mechanism.

In Win32, there is no single global heap. Every application has its own "global" heap, called the *default heap,* from which allocations are performed. The addresses in the application are private and cannot be handed to any other application. (Well, you can, but it won't do you any good; they are always *interpreted* relative to the current task. So if you pass a pointer to your location 0xE140C000 to some other application, it will read or modify the contents of *its* location 0xE140C000, which is probably not what you expect.) In general, you cannot pass a pointer or handle from one process to another.

Supporting Multiple Heaps

Win16 programmers often implemented their own memory allocation subroutines. This was not always necessary, especially after the C runtime system began to support `malloc` and `new` in the way a C programmer would expect them to.

There were at least two other sound reasons for doing your own allocator, however. One is that `malloc`, as traditionally implemented, was one of the worst-performing storage allocation algorithms around (if you have skipped the previous section, we describe its problems there). In Win32, that is no longer the case. Also, `malloc` tended to fragment storage rather badly. The result was more and more unusable blocks in memory, thereby making `malloc`'s already bad implementation perform even more poorly. Programmers often implemented their own allocators to get around these problems.

Considerations When Using the Default Heap

An application should allocate only sufficient default heap for its purposes and free it as quickly as possible. There are several competing constraints you should take into consideration when using the default heap.

First and foremost is a concept developed in the late 1960s to explain and attempt to control the scheduling of tasks in a virtual memory environment: the *working set*. The working set is that collection of pages necessary to support the program during a single time slice in a multitasking environment. If your code requires calling 10 functions to complete an operation–say, the result of a user menu selection–where each function is on a different page, then you need the page that holds the code doing the function calls as well as one page for each function called. This means your *code working set* to complete the function call is 11 pages. If your algorithm is in a loop that requires touching 10 objects, where each object is on a different page, then your *data working set* is 10 pages. Assuming that none of the data we just mentioned are in the stack, you'll need (at least) one more page for your stack. As we have described it, your working set in the previous example is a minimum of 22 pages (90,112 bytes)–11 code pages and 11 data pages. By monitoring the recent history of your program, the operating system determines what pages were most recently touched and assumes that these will be the pages you will need for the next timeslice and then generally will not schedule your process unless all of the pages of the working set are in memory. Of course, the next time your process executes, the user may select a completely different operation, thus requiring a different set of pages be in memory, but the operating system cannot be prepared for this. The working set model is generally considered a good predictor of your program's behavior. The major problem arises when your working set becomes very large. If, during the last timeslice, your program touched 150 different pages, the system will want to make sure that all 150 pages are back in memory before your process can run again. This may cause delays, as some of those pages may have to be paged back in, since they had been removed to make room for the pages of other processes that were running while your process was waiting for its next turn at the processor.

What you should do is arrange your system to minimize both working sets. The smaller your working set is, the fewer pages need to be present to run your application. This means that getting all the pages in takes less time and your code will more likely run to completion within its timeslice without causing a page fault. If your working set is large and varies greatly over time, the chances of completing your timeslice without a page fault are very low. Consequently, your application will have to relinquish control of the system until the page it wants can be brought in. In extreme cases, the only page available to be replaced is another page in your working set, so you have to wait while *that* page is paged out before the desired page is brought in. To make the situation even nastier, the *next* page you plan to access may be exactly the one that was just paged out! When you get into this situation, the condition is known as "thrashing", since the system spends most of its time thrashing about moving pages in and out and very little actually executing code. Of course, while your application is waiting, *other* applications can run. They, too, can exhibit the same behavior. Ultimately, such a system spends *all* of its time moving pages to and from disk, as the many large applications fight for the scraps of memory space that are available. This condition has the rather colorful, and accurate, designation of a "feeding frenzy".

Next we look at some ways in which you could get your application into trouble. Then we examine how you can avoid them.

Page Thrashing–Random Access

In the Win32 linear address space, suppose you do a large number of allocations, then some deallocations, and then some more allocations, and the objects you allocate have pointers to each other in some way (for example, a linked list structure). You may find that many data structures end up having a pointer to a structure on another page. When your working set becomes larger than the physical memory *available to your application*, Windows begins swapping pages of your application out to the disk. Note that because multitasking is going on, the amount of space available to *your* application may be considerably less that the amount of physical memory actually available. It is the job of Windows to try to optimize overall system response. This may mean keeping some pages of other applications in memory as well. So you could start paging long before your virtual memory size exceeds the physical memory size of the processor. In an extreme case, traversing a linked list could cause one page fault on each pointer access. In fact, there is a known algorithm that, given knowledge of the underlying paging algorithm expressed as some simple parameters, will allocate and access memory to give the *worst* possible paging performance. (This algorithm was developed in the late 1960s as a torture test for the then-new virtual memory architectures.) But many applications can come close to this algorithm simply by accident. You would like to have related data structures "near" each other as much as possible so that, for example, list traversals would be fast. You would like to reduce memory fragmentation so that you do not clutter up your heap with small, unusable segments that have to be touched on each malloc. And you would like very much to have an allocator that does not traverse every block, in linear fashion, searching for a block that satisfies a request. If your code feels sluggish, it may not be the code itself that is bad, or even, necessarily, your algorithm. It may be the interaction of your algorithm with the default heap and the operating system paging algorithms.

Page Thrashing–Sequential Access

Another source of problems is when you are dealing with really large data structures, such as image bitmaps. Consider the layout shown for a $1200 \times 1600 \times 32$ bitmap image. This image consumes 7.68MB of virtual memory, or 1,875 4K pages. The first few scan lines are shown in Figure 14.1. Each scan line requires two, or sometimes three, pages. An algorithm that did a transformation that scanned the entire image, top to bottom and left to right, would touch all 1,875 pages. With a multipass algorithm, after it finished with the lower-right corner, it would start again at the top-left corner. But that was the least recently used page, so there is an excellent chance it has been paged out. So a second pass is almost guaranteed to cause 1,875 page faults if the working set can't hold all 1,875 pages! If a paging operation were to take, say, 10 ms (an optimistic number), such an algorithm could spent 18 sec just *waiting* for pages *on each pass*. This would limit us to about 3 passes per minute. Thirty passes would take 56,250 page faults, or nearly 10 min of paging time (and that was with the *optimistic* page time assumption).

n this case, you have to redesign your multipass algorithm to make multiple passes across, say, the first 10 scan lines, then the next 10, and so on. This would encompass only a dozen pages, a working set that would almost certainly not be paged out. But working this way, we would do all 30 passes across the image, taking only 1,875 page faults at worst or, with our 10-ms assumption, 18.75 sec of paging across the whole image for all 30 passes! When working with large data objects such as images in Win32, you have to start thinking this way.[5]

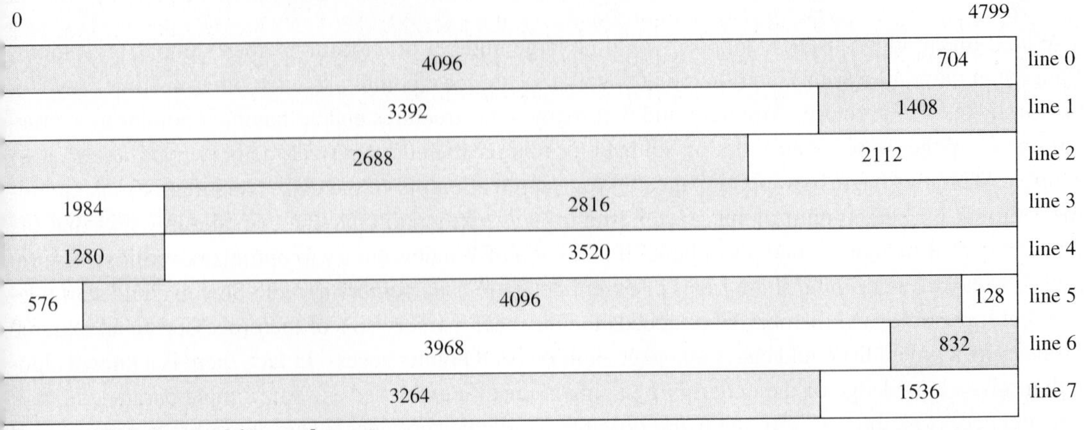

Figure 14.1: Image bitmap layout

Synchronization Bottlenecks

Finally, there is one really subtle problem that arises because of Win32's *multithreading* capability. You can have in your application several *threads of control*. These act like mini-timeslicing mechanisms *within your application*. A background thread can run for a while, block on some condition, and finally resume when the condition is met. For example, serial I/O is handled by having a thread block on the serial port; when input is received, the thread awakens and handles it. Often, it handles the input by sending a message to another thread (usually the "main thread" that is handling the GUI) informing it that serial input is ready. Another case might be in image processing. That is, you run the image processing algorithm in the background thread, while leaving the interface "lively" and still talking to the user. If the user is not doing anything, the user's thread blocks on the GetMessage call, while the background thread runs full speed (it doesn't have to keep calling PeekMessage). If the user wants to abort the background thread, the background thread itself can be terminated by the user thread (of course, you have to deal with handling the partially completed operation, but that's not a Windows problem).

Now consider what happens in a preemptive multitasking environment like Win32 when the preemption is at the thread level. At any instant, your executing thread can be preempted by any other task in the system, *in-*

---

[5] With adding complexity, you can also take into account the behavior of the level 1 and level 2 caches that sit between the physical memory and the processor. But this requires knowing the exact model of processor chip and support chip(s), since these values are often quite different, even within a single family such as the Intel processor line. Any algorithm that tries to take advantage of this information has to be reconfigurable for different platforms. Even then, the introduction of a new processor family or even support chipset can cause problems.

cluding a thread in your own application. Here's what would happen if the storage allocator didn't understand multithreading. Your first thread is deep into the storage allocator. It has found an available chunk of storage. Just as it is about to mark this chunk as allocated, control is forcefully wrested from it and another thread starts executing. This thread asks the allocator for a block of exactly the same size. Since the first thread has not yet modified the allocation blocks to reserve the block it found, the current thread finds *the same block.* It is able to successfully allocate it. Eventually, control returns to the first thread, which continues doing what it was doing, *to exactly the same block* because that is the block it was working on when it lost control. Oops. Two threads now each think they have the same block. Finding a bug like this can be a nightmare. It is often timing-sensitive and nonreproducible. Just every so often, for no apparent reason, your application either crashes or (worse still!) silently corrupts some information.

Well, the C runtime and Windows recognize this possibility, so they *serialize* access to the storage allocator data structure by using a synchronization lock. When the first thread enters the allocator, it sets the "this storage is busy" lock. When the second thread enters the allocator, it tries to set the lock and fails because the lock is already set. So it waits until the lock comes free. When the first thread completes, it releases the lock, allowing the second thread to proceed. Since the first thread has completely finished its allocation, the data structures are known to be intact and the second thread (which has now set the lock to block out anyone else from that data structure) can be guaranteed to find a different block.

This works fine until you have two memory-intensive threads competing for the use of the default heap. Then they both find that they are always waiting for the same resource. This is even more serious when you are running a multiprocessor configuration because your application could potentially have two threads that are concurrently executing in your one process. If they are forced to wait on each other's allocation access, you end up turning your multiprocessor into a single processor, except you've got the additional overhead of the locks and the scheduling that they incur because the threads are always blocking on each other, so you end up with subuniprocessor performance. This is generally not what you expect after spending extra money to get that multiprocessor computer.

Gas stations learned long ago how to deal with this: You don't have a single gas pump because you end up with long lines of customers waiting for the one resource. Instead, you have four or six or ten pumps (we'll ignore for the moment the issue of different grades of gasoline for simplicity) and you can then have four or six or ten customers pumping gas simultaneously. In fact, if on the average you have as many pumps as you have simultaneous customers, and customers don't arrive too quickly, nobody ever has to wait in line at all.[6] Multithreading is an old idea. But if you have a single heap and a lot of threads, you begin to feel a bit like you're buying gas at a one-pump station on a major turnpike on a holiday weekend. Your algorithms may be the best you can write. The compiler optimizations may be as tight as they can be. You may even have worried about issues like fragmentation and paging. But if you've got all your threads blocking on memory allocation all the time, your program will run verrrry slooooowly.

All applications allocate memory from the default heap, but each application and DLL can have one or more private heaps, called *dynamic heaps*. We look at them next.

---

[6] Yes, we know the result from queuing theory that if the expected interarrival time equals the expected service time, the queue grows to infinite size.

Dynamic Heaps

You can create additional heaps, called *dynamic heaps*, as you need them. The heaps are managed by the functions shown in Table 14.2.

Table 14.2: Dynamic heap functions

Result	Function	Parameters and Description
HANDLE	GetProcessHeap	( )
		Returns a handle to the default process heap. This handle can be used for all Heap- functions.
DWORD	GetProcessHeaps	(UINT count, LPHANDLE handles)
		Returns the handles to all the heaps for the process. The return value is the number of heaps available in the process. If the return value is greater than count, then the buffer is too small; no handles are returned. A return value of 0 indicates failure.
LPVOID	HeapAlloc	(HANDLE heap, DWORD flags, DWORD size)
		Allocates a block of size bytes from the heap whose handle is given. The flags may be 0 or one or more of the following:
		HEAP_GENERATE_EXCEPTIONS
		Raises an exception instead of returning NULL. Not needed if specified on HeapCreate.
		HEAP_NO_SERIALIZEHEAP_NO_SERIALIZE
		Threads will not serialize. Not needed if specified on HeapCreate.
		HEAP_ZERO_MEMORYHEAP_ZERO_MEMORY
		The storage returned will be set to 0.

Table 14.2: Dynamic heap functions

Result	Function	Parameters and Description
UINT	HeapCompact	(HANDLE heap, DWORD flags)
		"Compacts" the heap. This actually means that it coalesces adjacent free blocks and decommits (releases to the operating system) any large free blocks of memory in the heap. The return result is the size of the largest committed free block in the heap or 0 if the operation failed; use Get-LastError for additional information. GetLastError may return the code NO_ERROR, meaning the heap was full and there was no uncommitted storage. *Not implemented on Windows 95.* The flags may be 0 or the following:
		HEAP_NO_SERIALIZE
		Threads will not serialize. Not needed if specified on HeapCreate.
HANDLE	HeapCreate	(DWORD flags, DWORD initsize, DWORD limit)
		Creates a heap whose maximum size is limit and whose initial size is initsize. Additional pages will be committed to the heap as needed, until limit is reached. The flags will affect all operations that will be performed on the heap and can be 0 or one or more of the following:
		HEAP_GENERATE_EXCEPTIONS
		All allocations will raise an exception instead of returning NULL.
		HEAP_NO_SERIALIZE
		Threads will not serialize on subsequent operations on the heap.
BOOL	HeapDestroy	(HANDLE heap)
		Deletes the heap passed in.
BOOL	HeapFree	(HANDLE heap, DWORD flags, LPVOID addr)
		Frees the storage referenced by addr. The storage must have been allocated from the heap whose handle is passed in. The flags can be 0 or the following:
		HEAP_NO_SERIALIZE
		Threads will not serialize. Not needed if specified on HeapCreate.

Table 14.2: Dynamic heap functions

Result	Function	Parameters and Description
BOOL	HeapLock	(HANDLE heap)
		Locks the heap against other threads. If it returns TRUE, the heap is locked; if FALSE, use GetLastError to find out more information. You must use this function before a HeapWalk if serialization is required. *Not implemented on Windows 95.*
LPVOID	HeapReAlloc	(HANDLE heap, DWORD flags, LPVOID addr, DWORD size)
		Reallocates the block at location addr to become size bytes in the heap whose handle is given. The flags may include any of the following:
		HEAP_GENERATE_EXCEPTIONS
		Raises an exception instead of returning NULL. Not needed if specified on HeapCreate.
		HEAP_NO_SERIALIZE
		Threads will not serialize. Not needed if specified on HeapCreate.
		HEAP_REALLOC_IN_PLACE_ONLY
		May not move data to reallocate to a larger size.
		HEAP_ZERO_MEMORY
		If the block is being increased in size, the additional storage will be set to 0.
DWORD	HeapSize	(HANDLE heap, DWORD flags, LPVOID addr)
		Returns the actual size, in bytes, of the storage referenced by addr. The storage must be allocated from the indicated heap. The flags can be 0 or the following:
		HEAP_NO_SERIALIZE
		Threads will not serialize. Not needed if specified on HeapCreate.

Table 14.2: Dynamic heap functions

Result	Function	Parameters and Description
BOOL	HeapUnlock	(HANDLE heap)
		Unlocks the heap locked by HeapLock. Other threads may now access it. Returns TRUE if successful, and FALSE if failure. Use GetLastError to get additional information. *Not implemented on Windows 95.*
BOOL	HeapValidate	(HANDLE heap, DWORD flags, LPVOID addr)
		Attempts to check the heap for consistency. If a heap control block is damaged, returns FALSE. If addr is non-NULL, checks only that block for damage; otherwise, validates the entire heap. If the heap or block is intact, returns TRUE. *Not implemented on Windows 95.* The flags may be 0 or the following:
		HEAP_NO_SERIALIZE
		Threads will not serialize. Not needed if specified on HeapCreate.
BOOL	HeapWalk	(HANDLE heap, LPPROCESS_HEAP_ENTRY entry)
		Enumerates memory blocks in a heap. If the heap is shared with other threads, you must call HeapLock before starting the walk and HeapUnlock after you are done. *Not implemented on Windows 95.*

The HeapCreate function creates a dynamic heap. You typically specify the maximum heap size you will require. If you can't predict this, you may find that you will eventually be unable to allocate from your heap because you've used it all up. So you have to either be prepared to deal with running out of heap gracefully (by not crashing, but by reporting to the user that all the heap is used up) or allocate another heap to keep allocations going. Or, you can just set this parameter to 0, in which case, the size of the heap will be limited only by available memory. Assume for the moment that you can accurately predict an upper bound of storage. For example, you might find that 256K is going to be enough. In addition, you can specify how much memory the heap should *commit* initially, that is, how much space the operating system should allocate to the heap at creation (as opposed to allocating by page faulting as the unused pages are touched). The following call creates a 256K heap (0x40000) with a 16K (0x4000) initial allocation:

```
HANDLE itemheap = HeapCreate(0, 0x4000, 0x40000);
```

The value returned is a handle to the heap, or 0 (NULL) if the heap creation failed; you can use GetLastError to find out more information. The heap itemheap is what you are going to use to allocate certain items. You may allocate only one kind of value in this heap, or you may allocate several related kinds of values. Or you may use the heap to allocate every kind of storage you need within one thread, and you can improve the single-thread performance by setting the HEAP_NO_SERIALIZE flag. This suppresses all interlocks that would keep multiple threads from stepping on each other. By limiting the heap to a single thread, you eliminate the need to synchronize access to it (more on this later in the chapter!) How you use the heap is now up to you.

Table 14.3: Allocation responses when
HEAP_GENERATE_EXCEPTIONS is specified

| | HEAP_GENERATE_EXCEPTIONS | | |
Request	At Creation Time	At Allocation Time	Effect
Satisfied	–	–	Returns a pointer.
Unsatisfied	Yes	No	Raises an exception.
Unsatisfied	Yes	Yes	Raises an exception.
Unsatisfied	No	No	Returns NULL.
Unsatisfied	No	Yes	Raises exception.

When you are done with the heap, you can call Heap-Destroy. When this function is called, the heap is destroyed, all the pages are decommitted, and the heap handle becomes invalid. You must not have any outstanding pointers into the heap that will be used, as they will most likely generate memory access faults.

To allocate a memory object on the heap, you call HeapAlloc, passing in the handle to a heap, a set of flags (which may be 0), and a size request. What happens next depends on the flags you used when you created the heap, the flags you use on the HeapAlloc call, and whether there is enough memory to satisfy the request.

If there is enough memory to satisfy the request, you will get back a non-NULL value that is a pointer to the storage. The amount of storage you actually get may be slightly larger than the amount you requested because of internal rounding up to a nearest multiple-of-something (the exact value may depend on which implementation of Win32 you are running under). You can use this storage as you would any dynamically allocated block.

An early article by Randy Keith, "Managing Heap Memory in Win32", found on the MSDN CD-ROM, suggested that the roundup was to a multiple of 16 bytes, plus 16 bytes of additional overhead. When we used the ClassHeap explorer option of the Heap Explorer, we found that under Windows NT release 3.51, the allocation quantum was 8 bytes plus an additional 8 bytes required for storage management overhead. This undoubtedly represents a release-specific change since his article was written.

If there is not enough memory to satisfy the request, either you will get a NULL pointer returned or an exception will be raised. If, when you created the heap, you specified the HEAP_GENERATE_EXCEPTIONS flag, you will always get an exception when an allocation fails. Otherwise, you will get an exception only if you specified the HEAP_GENERATE_EXCEPTIONS flag on the HeapAlloc call. This is summarized in Table 14.3. If an exception is raised, it will be one of those shown in Table 14.4. You can get this code by calling the GetExceptionCode function as you call the exception filter or in the handler of your exception processing.

You can reallocate storage by calling HeapReAlloc. In addition to the flag values HEAP_GENERATE_EXCEPTIONS, HEAP_NO_SERIALIZE, and HEAP_ZERO_MEMORY, which act just like Heap-Alloc (except HEAP_ZERO_MEMORY affects only the new memory if the block is expanded), you can supply the HEAP_REALLOC_IN_PLACE_ONLY flag. This constrains the reallocation to not change the address of the memory block if it has to be expanded. If sufficient adjacent storage is free, the allocation will succeed; otherwise, it will return NULL or raise an exception according to the behavior specified in Table 14.3. The return value, on success, is a pointer to the reallocated storage. If the HEAP_REALLOC_IN_PLACE_ONLY flag is set, this is the same as the input address.

You can use the Get-ProcessHeap to get a handle for the default heap, so all of the heap functions can apply to the default heap as well. If you want to do debugging or performance analysis, you can get handles to all the heaps by calling the GetProcessHeaps function. As with many of the API functions that require allocation, you can use this function to deter-

Table 14.4: Heap exceptions

Exception	Description
STATUS_NO_MEMORY	The allocation failed because there was insufficient memory in the heap.
STATUS_ACCESS_VIOLATION	The allocation failed because of a memory access violation. This may indicate either heap corruption or an invalid parameter to the operation.

mine how much space you need to allocate for the handles. Note the restriction that if the count is less than the number of process heaps, the heap handles will *not* be written to the buffer.

```
HANDLE hdefault;
LPHANDLE hstorage;
int n;
n = GetProcessHeaps(1, &hdefault);
hstorage = (LPHANDLE)GlobalAllocPtr(n * sizeof(HANDLE));
GetProcessHeaps(n, hstorage);

// .. do whatever you want to the heaps

GlobalFreePtr(hstorage);
```

Of the remaining functions, the one that is often useful for analyzing your storage patterns is HeapWalk, which we use in our Heap Explorer. This function returns a description of each block of storage. It is implemented only in versions of Windows NT and not on the Windows 95 platform. The PROCESS_HEAP_ENTRY is as follows:

```
typedef struct _PROCESS_HEAP_ENTRY {
    PVOID lpData;
    DWORD cbData;
    BYTE cbOverhead;
    BYTE iRegionIndex;
    WORD wFlags;
```

```
    union {
        struct {
            HANDLE hMem;
            DWORD dwReserved[ 3 ];
        } Block;
        struct {
            DWORD dwCommittedSize;
            DWORD dwUnCommittedSize;
            LPVOID lpFirstBlock;
            LPVOID lpLastBlock;
        } Region;
    };
} PROCESS_HEAP_ENTRY, *LPPROCESS_HEAP_ENTRY,
          *PPROCESS_HEAP_ENTRY;
```

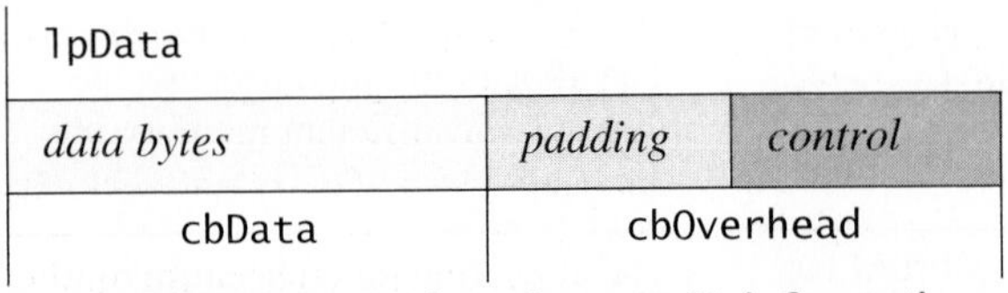

Figure 14.2: Interpretation of HeapWalk information

The interpretation of the information for most memory blocks is shown in Figure 14.2. An ordinary memory block, which has the PROCESS_HEAP_ENTRY_BUSY flag set, consists of cbData bytes allocated at the address lpData, with cbOverhead bytes of "overhead". This overhead includes the space required to reach the next allocation quantum boundary, plus space required for the heap control structures.

The interpretation of the wFlags field is given in Table 14.5.

Table 14.5: PROCESS_HEAP_ENTRY: wFlags values

Value	Description		
0	Frees storage.		
PROCESS_HEAP_REGION	The first of a region of contiguous virtual memory used by the heap. A heap has one or more regions. The other fields are interpreted as follows:		
	lpData	First address used by the region.	
	cbData	Total size of reserved address space.	
	cbOverhead	Size of heap control structure that describes the region.	
	dwCommittedSize	Current memory commitment in the region.	
	dwUnCommitted-Size	Uncommitted memory in the region.	
	lpFirstBlock	Pointer to the first valid memory block in the region.	
	lpLastBlock	Pointer to the last valid memory block in the region.	

Table 14.5: PROCESS_HEAP_ENTRY: wFlags values

Value	Description	
PROCESS_HEAP_UNCOMMITTED_RANGE	The memory block represents an uncommitted range of memory. The other fields are interpreted as follows:	
	lpData	First address in the uncommitted block.
	cbData	Total size of the uncommitted block.
	cbOverhead	Size of the heap control structure that describes the uncommitted block.
PROCESS_HEAP_ENTRY_BUSY	The heap element is an allocated block. The other fields are interpreted as follows and as given in Figure 14.2:	
	lpData	First address in the allocated block.
	cbData	Total size of the data portion of the block.
	cbOverhead	Additional information used to maintain the heap data structure.
	hMem	Valid only if the element is moveable.
PROCESS_HEAP_ENTRY_MOVEABLE	Valid only if PROCESS_HEAP_ENTRY_BUSY is set. Represents GMEM_MOVEABLE memory allocated in the default heap. The hMem value is the handle that describes the current entry.	
PROCESS_HEAP_ENTRY_DDESHARE	Valid only if PROCESS_HEAP_ENTRY_BUSY is set. Represents GMEM_DDESHARE memory allocated in the default heap.	

Heap Serialization

The default heap is implicitly serialized. The operations such as GlobalAlloc, GlobalFree, GlobalReAlloc, GlobalSize, GlobalHandle, GlobalFlags, GlobalLock, and GlobalUnlock all work correctly even when multiple threads are accessing the default heap. The default heap is protected by a synchronization object that keeps more than one thread from accessing it. As mentioned earlier in the chapter, however, this can lead to a serious performance bottleneck if you are writing multithreaded memory-intensive applications because all accesses to the heap must go through this single lock.

By creating additional heaps, you can avoid this bottleneck. The simplest approach is to create a heap for each thread and create each heap with the HEAP_NO_SERIALIZE flag set. Subsequent heap operations will not be serialized; no mutual exclusion will take place. Thus a thread has immediate access to its heap, and since no other thread is accessing that heap (this is done by design–and you have to make sure this is true), the unserialized access is safe. Hence, there is no synchronization, and you don't even have the overhead of a thread setting a lock that no other thread will block on.

It is essential under this scenario either that you do not allow any thread to access the heap other than the one you intend or, if you want to use more than one thread, that you provide an external synchronization mechanism. However, by creating one or more heaps that are private to a thread, you can eliminate the need to synchronize as well as the bottlenecks that could arise.

Locality of Reference

Performance of most virtual memory systems, from the hardware caches and pipelines through the virtual memory paging algorithms, is related to a concept called *locality of reference*. This principle states that "the future will be just like the past". That is, your next instruction or memory reference will, with very high probability, be within a small number of bytes of one of the past several memory references. The determination of "a small number of bytes" is based on the sizes of the instruction pipeline, instruction cache, processor cache, level 2 cache, and the like. The parameters dictating the behavior of these architectural features are based on careful studies of "typical" instruction and data reference patterns. Your data access performance may be very architecture-dependent; an algorithm that screams on one Win32 platform may run like a dog on another. There can even be substantial differences between two versions of the same nominal chip or even between two systems using the same chip but implemented by two different vendors. So it is generally difficult for you to write an application that can take maximum advantage of all of the architectural variations available.

Paging performance, on the other hand, is something you have a good chance of controlling. Usually the only interesting parameter is the page size, which you can determine with the GetSystemInfo function. In addition, by careful use of dynamic heaps, you can force many data structures to be "near" each other so that the references are on the same page.

For example, you might allocate a dynamic heap to serve for a symbol table. Symbol tables often exhibit the property that they grow during the processing of input but can be completely discarded at a certain point. You could even allocate heaps for individual subcomponents. This strategy means that all of the information for a particular object, such as a symbol table entry or a database record descriptor, are on the same page. In a more general system, which has just the default heap, there is a good chance that, based on previous allocations and deallocations, each string or object referenced could be on a separate page. This would increase your working set and open up the possibility of page faults.

In addition, when the database is closed, or the function compiled, or whatever event transpires to free up all the storage, you can free it up all at once by destroying the entire heap with HeapDestroy. This results in less fragmentation of the default heap because everything is in the separate heap.

Reducing Heap Fragmentation

If you have an application that allocates objects of many different sizes, one side effect of this is fragmentation of the heap. This is a particular problem with algorithms like first-fit, which have a tendency to fragment blocks.

Consider a situation in which you have allocated blocks of sizes 20, 40, 40, 60, 40, and 80. Memory looks like Figure 14.3(a). After some deallocations, your storage resembles Figure 14.3(b). Now the question is where to allocate a block of 20 units. You have several choices. You could allocate it at the tail of the storage, that is, at the start of the highest free area. Or you could allocate it at the first block that is found in an address-order scan, the first block that is found on a free list, or the block that is the nearest fit. Under the HeapAlloc strategy, the block that is allocated results in the allocation shown in Figure 14.3(c). What can't be determined from this figure is *why* it was allocated there. It was the last block freed, so perhaps the allocation occurred because the allocator tries to use the smallest block to try to preserve large blocks when possible or because this was the first block found on the free list. Further experimentation, which we did with the Heap Explorer, seems to reveal a tendency to favor splitting smaller blocks over splitting larger blocks. This is an algorithm that will tend to generate small fragments but preserve large blocks in case they are needed. We have been unable to deduce the exact algorithm used here. One feature we did discover is that on deallocation, adjacent free blocks appear to be immediately coalesced, at least on our small example. So we aren't certain why the HeapCompact function would be useful.

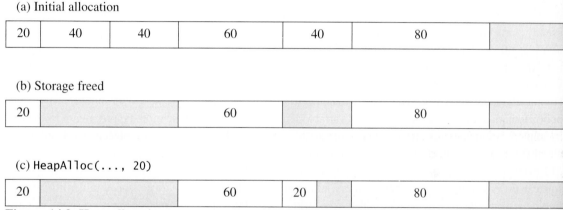

(a) Initial allocation

| 20 | 40 | 40 | 60 | 40 | 80 | |

(b) Storage freed

| 20 | | 60 | | 80 | |

(c) HeapAlloc(..., 20)

| 20 | | 60 | 20 | | 80 | |

Figure 14.3: Heap allocation

Another strategy for reducing heap fragmentation is to create "homogeneous heaps", that is, heaps in which all objects are the same size. This strategy is extremely useful if you have two or three kinds of objects that have frequent allocations and deallocations. By using multiple heaps, you can avoid having lots of little fragments left over because objects of one kind are, say, one allocation quantum longer than objects of another type. In so doing, not only do you generate locality of reference, but there is also, essentially, *no* fragmentation of any of the heaps. If you balance this with a heap that holds the odd-sized objects (such as strings), you can get a substantial improvement in performance, both in allocation performance and in paging performance. The allocation performance improvement comes about because the system never has to search for a nearest match in size or a best match. Instead, all available chunks in the homogeneous heap are either of the correct size or a multiple of the correct size. You can read more about the design of self-adaptive heaps in the cited works in the "Further Reading" section. Our best deduction in examining the behavior of HeapAlloc is that it is an algorithm quite similar to the ones described.

Reducing storage fragmentation also enhances long-term reliability. If you have a system in which you have several different sizes of objects and use a single heap, you have a fundamentally entropic situation. Eventually, you will end up with storage fragmented into blocks of the smallest size or into blocks that are residual fragments that are too small to allocate for any of your data structures. Long before your application consumes the available address space, it will grow to consume all of the available virtual memory. This not only affects its own performance; it also affects overall system performance. When all available virtual memory is consumed, an allocation request will fail. At this point, your application will stop working. It may stop "gracefully", popping up a message box saying that it has run out of memory. Or it may stop rather ungracefully by taking a memory access fault as you try to use a NULL pointer as a valid reference. Neither case is acceptable to the user. If your application is one that is up for days or weeks, this can be a major annoyance.[7]

Using separate heaps for each type of object seriously reduces the entropy of the system; storage does not fragment nearly as badly, or at all in some cases. Allocating variable-length objects, however, remains a weak point. You may even have to implement your own storage compaction model to handle this, depending on how serious the problem is.

A common application class that requires this reliability is the *NT System Service*, a type of application that usually starts up with the system or at logon and simply continues to run until the system is shut down or the user logs off. System services represent user-level components that are logically a part of the "operating system" (at least from the user's viewpoint). They should be expected to run reliably as long as the system is up, which can be weeks or months. There is one school of thought that says the only way to achieve this is with completely static allocation. The less extreme position requires that every object type should have its own pool. Both positions agree that the use of variable-length objects is a problem. Some programmers avoid it by implementing compaction for the heap of variable objects. Others force variable objects into fixed-length chunks; for example, declaring that all strings have a maximum length of 512 bytes and always allocating 512 bytes to a string even if it holds only one character. While such profligacy may offend those who try to squeeze every last byte out of their memory, in fact it pays off in *significantly* enhanced reliability because freeing a string *always* creates a complete free-string object that can hold "any" string necessary. For those who need the occasional long string, a "short string heap"/"long string heap" of fixed-size strings works well. A far more difficult alternative is the approach that "chains" together lots of short objects into a single long object. Since this requires strings to behave in a very unnatural way, it would defeat most of the built-in string handling code.

Using C++

All of these strategies apply to C programming. But what if you are using C++? How can you take advantage of these strategies?

---

[7] Note that nearly *any* application has this property; for example, a word processor program. Think of "exit" as an obsolete concept left over from the Dark Days of DOS. Think of your application as something that will be in the user's Startup group (loads when the user logs in) and will terminate when the power company has its next power flicker (or the operating system crashes, which of course Cannot Possibly Occur). This gives you a whole new perspective on what it means to write reliable software. One of the critical components in the reliability is the heap. In particular, heap fragmentation can become your limiting factor.

One feature of C++ that makes this easy is the ability to redefine the new and delete operators on a per-class basis. By creating classes that use their own new and delete operators that call HeapAlloc, you can allocate objects and components on a private heap.

There are two ways you can handle this. One calls for assigning a unique heap to each class; another calls for sharing a common heap across several classes. Both of these methods apply not only to deriving classes from existing classes (as we show here), but also to your own classes.

If you are using a unique heap, you can define the class as shown in Listing 14.1 and write a fairly straightforward implementation as shown in Listing 14.2.

Listing 14.1: Private heaps using new and delete: class definition 1

```
class CMyData {
    public:
        CMyData();
        ~CMyData();
        LPVOID operator new(size_t size);
        void operator delete(LPVOID s);
        void setString(LPCTSTR s);
        LPCTSTR getString();
    private:
        static HANDLE heap;
        LPCTSTR s;
                };
```

Listing 14.2: Private heaps using new and delete: implementation 1

```
HANDLE CMyData::heap = NULL;

CMyData::CMyData()
    {
    s = NULL;
    }

CMyData::~CMyData()
    {
    if(s != NULL)
        { /* deallocate */
        ::HeapFree(heap, 0, (LPVOID)s);
        } /* deallocate */
    s = NULL;
    }

LPVOID CMyData::operator new(size_t size)
    {
    if(heap == NULL)
        { /* allocate heap */
        heap = ::HeapCreate(0, 0, 0);
        if(heap == NULL)
            AfxThrowMemoryException();
        } /* allocate heap */

    LPVOID p = ::HeapAlloc(heap, 0, size);
    if(p == NULL)
```

```
        AfxThrowMemoryException();
      return p;
    }

void CMyData::operator delete(LPVOID p)
    {
      if(p != NULL && !::HeapFree(heap, 0, p))
        AfxThrowMemoryException();
    }
```

This is fairly straightforward. From Listing 14.1, notice that we have only one component of the class that requires dynamic allocation: a string pointer. The structure has a constructor and destructor, and we define new and delete operators. In addition, we have made the string component private, thus making it inaccessible except through the methods setString and getString. This limits the allocation to be the kind of allocation we want to use.

Since this class will have its own private heap, we need a handle for that heap. We declare this as a static class member. This means that all instances of the class will share the one static instance and hence the one heap handle.

The implementation of the constructor shown in Listing 14.2 is fairly obvious: It simply sets the one interesting member value, the string pointer, to NULL. The destructor is a bit more complex: If the reference to the string is non-NULL, we call HeapFree to release it. Except for calling HeapFree instead of delete, we have nothing new here from the C++ viewpoint.

We do add one declaration, however. The static heap handle heap is declared and initialized to NULL. This defines the one instance of the static variable.

The new operator introduces something different from a normal class. It wants to allocate from the private heap, but it must first *have* a private heap. So it checks the static variable heap. If that variable is NULL, we have not allocated a heap, so we call HeapCreate to create one. Note that we commit no initial memory, set no upper bound, and set no flags. If this function is being implemented in MFC, as we have done, we can call the library function AfxThrowMemoryException. If you are using a different class library, you can raise here an exception appropriate to your library.

We create the heap with no flags so that it will not raise exceptions on failure and will serialize all accesses. This implementation of our private heap is therefore more likely to be used for reducing heap fragmentation than for eliminating synchronization bottlenecks. If we had added the HEAP_NO_SERIALIZE flag, then no subsequent operations would be serialized by the heap itself. We do not specify HEAP_GENERATE_EXCEPTIONS because C and C++ exceptions do not interact well unless you are careful, and we wanted to avoid that discussion here.

After the heap itself has been created, we call HeapAlloc to allocate the storage for an instance of our object. The storage is allocated in our private heap. If the allocation succeeds, we return the pointer it gives us; otherwise, we raise an exception by calling AfxThrowMemoryException.

The delete operator calls HeapFree to release a non-NULL pointer. If the deallocation fails for some reason, we throw an exception. Note that the delete operator does not do anything to the string referenced by the string pointer; we will extend it shortly to handle this case.

This simple implementation works well, but it has one problem: Once we've allocated the heap, it stays. Nothing gets rid of it. When our process terminates, its resources will be reclaimed by the system. If we have a small heap that will be used throughout the program, we suffer no penalties by not releasing it. In fact, if the heap itself will often go to a 0 allocation, we actually *gain* efficiency by not having to constantly destroy and recreate the heap as we oscillate between 0 and 1 item in the heap.

A slightly better implementation from the viewpoint of memory allocation is shown in Listing 14.3. The differences in the implementation are set out in boldface type. Here we add one more static class variable, count, which counts the number of allocations we have on the heap. The count is incremented on each new operator and decremented on each delete operator. If the count ever reaches 0, the heap itself is deleted. As we said, if your heap will tend to have a small number of objects in it, and go empty often, this is *not* an efficient strategy. But if your heap tends to grow and you at some point free up all the objects and then may or may not need the heap again, the automatic deallocation is reasonable.

Listing 14.3: Implementations of new and delete with automatic heap reclamation

```
class CMyData {
    public:
        CMyData();
        ~CMyData();
        LPVOID operator new(size_t size);
        void operator delete(LPVOID s);
        void setString(LPCTSTR s);
        LPCTSTR getString();
    private:
        static HANDLE heap;
        static DWORD count;
        LPCTSTR s;
                    };

DWORD CMyData::count = 0;

LPVOID CMyData::operator new(size_t size)
    {
      if(heap == NULL)
        { /* allocate heap */
          heap = HeapCreate(0, 0, 0);
          if(heap == NULL)
            AfxThrowMemoryException()
        } /* allocate heap */

      LPVOID p = HeapAlloc(heap, 0, size);
      if(p == NULL)
        AfxThrowMemoryException();
      count++;
      return p;
    }

void CMyData::operator delete(LPVOID p)
    {
      if(!HeapFree(heap, 0, p))
        AfxThrowMemoryException();
      count--;
      if(count == 0)
```

```
        { /* deallocate */
         if(!HeapDestroy(heap))
             AfxThrowMemoryException();
    heap = NULL;
        } /* deallocate */
 }
```

You can begin to work theme-and-variation on this. For example, the Heap Explorer has a conditional flag that is checked to determine if automatic deallocation should be done; this flag is set from the GUI to allow you to see the effects of this. You can add explicit operations to your own heap allocator to set or clear such a flag, or you can add explicit methods to free the heap. You can implement heap-deallocation conditionally on the allocation count, refusing to free the heap if the count is nonzero. Or you can always force deallocation, freeing up the entire heap. In this way, you wouldn't have to free up all the individual items in the heap. You might want to support both styles: aggressive deallocation (deallocate the heap as quickly as possible) or lazy deallocation (deallocate the heap only occasionally, if at all). The right way to do this depends on the requirements of your application.

One interesting approach taken in several applications is to *never* explicitly deallocate an object and to implement the world's simplest allocator. This allocator would simply increment a pointer by the allocation size to determine the next allocatable block and return the previous value of the pointer, working in a private heap. Once the entire collection of objects was no longer required, the entire simple heap would be freed in a single operation by the pointer's being set back to the starting position. This works if you tend to almost always do allocations, with few free operations, and have a "clean" point where you can deallocate everything at once. Experiments with such systems have measured performance improvements by factors of 2 to 5 in total program performance over conventional heap management strategies! It always pays to study your overall system memory architecture, looking for such places where specialized allocators can be used.

We have one other operation we wish to do: We want to store the strings that the string pointer references in the same heap. Note that because the strings are always associated one-to-one with the objects, we don't need to keep a separate allocation count of the strings. The string is a private data member that can be accessed only by the setString and getString methods. We cannot assign to this private data member a reference to a string that is not in our own private heap. The setString and getString operators are shown in Listing 14.4. You might choose to implement getString as an inline function for efficiency.

Listing 14.4: The setString and getString methods
```
void CMyData::setString(LPCTSTR str)
    {
    LPTSTR p;

    // If we call setString(NULL), delete the string reference and replace
    // it with NULL; if we pass in a string pointer, free any existing string
    // and create a new string, copying the contents of the parameter into
    // the newly-allocated space.
    if(str != NULL)
        { /* create new string */
        p = (LPTSTR)HeapAlloc(heap, 0,
                (lstrlen(str) + 1) * sizeof(TCHAR));
        if(p == NULL)
            AfxThrowMemoryException();
```

```
          lstrcpy(p, str);
        } /* create new string */
    else
        { /* delete string */
        p = NULL;
        } /* delete string */

    // Free up whatever string we were referencing in preparation for
    // replacing it by the new string, or NULL, as appropriate
    if(s == NULL)
        HeapFree(heap, 0, (LPVOID)s);
    // The private data member s now references the new string or is NULL
    s = p;
    }

LPCTSTR CMyData::getString()
    {
    return s;
    }
```

Thread-Local Storage

A special kind of storage is *thread-local storage*. This type of storage can be used in any application but is most useful in DLLs (we discuss how to use it in DLLs in Chapter 16, page 1145). It is handled by the functions listed in Table 14.6.

Table 14.6: Thread-local storage functions

Function	Description
DWORD TlsAlloc( )	Allocates a thread-local storage index that is used for other Tls operations.
BOOL TlsFree(DWORD TlsIndex)	Releases the thread-local storage index referenced by TlsIndex.
LPVOID TlsGetValue(DWORD TlsIndex)	Retrieves the value for the calling thread's local storage.
BOOL TlsSetValue(DWORD TlsIndex, LPVOID TlsValue)	Stores a value in the calling thread's local storage for the specified TlsIndex.

Typically, thread-local storage is allocated when a process is started or when a DLL is attached to a process (see Chapter 16). It is a compromise between statically allocated storage, which is global to all threads, and stack-allocated storage, which is private to each thread.

For example, if you were using multiple threads, you couldn't write the function shown in Listing 14.5 and expect that it would work if called from multiple threads. This is important. You quite likely will find code like this in a legacy system because it is easy to write and utterly reliable in a single-threaded environment.

However, it doesn't work in a multithreaded environment such as Win32 supports. With preemptive multitasking, then between the time the first call completed and the static variable was copied, another thread might get control and *also* call the function, thus overwriting the static buffer. When the first thread got control, it would find the wrong text in its buffer and not realize it.[8]

Listing 14.5: Thread-unsafe code

```
LPCTSTR formatWhatever(int parm)
    {
    static TCHAR msg[MAX_MESSAGE_LENGTH];
    wsprintf(msg, _T("...%d..."), parm);
    return msg;
    }
```

A variant of this *looks* like it might be safe. It is often used when you want to use more than one call to a string function in a context such as a wsprintf. This variant guarantees that up to a certain limit, there will be no reuse of the static buffers. This is shown in Listing 14.6. Superficially, this looks like it might be thread-safe because each thread should increment the variable i and thus guarantee that each thread return a unique string from the array msgs. However, if you examine it carefully you will realize that the act of incrementing i is itself preemptible. Hence, it is entirely possible that when the first thread fetches the value i, it will be preempted. The second thread then fetches the *same* value, increments it, and puts it back. Then the first thread increments the value it fetched and puts it back into the variable, thus using the *same* value as the second thread already computed. So while this technique allows the code to be *serially reusable*, it does not allow the code to be *re-entrant*. This is a subtle but extremely important distinction. Unless you add some sort of external synchronization mechanism that prevents two threads from using this code at the same time, you cannot use it. And adding an external synchronization mechanism simply to support a simple string formatting operation is overkill. You'll pay a serious penalty in performance and complexity for introducing such a mechanism. And if you fail to use it, the consequences are serious: You won't get the expected result and could even generate memory access faults under the right (well, under the *wrong*) conditions.[9]

Listing 14.6: Another thread-unsafe implementation

```
LPCTSTR formatWhatever(int parm)
    {
    static int current = 0;
    static TCHAR msgs[MAX_MSG][MAX_MESSAGE_LENGTH];
    i++;
    wsprintf(msgs[current], _T("...%d..."), parm);
    return msgs[current];
    }
```

---

[8] Actually, the situation is much worse. Assume, for example, that the first thread starts formatting the text and then the second thread gets control and overwrites the buffer. The first thread then regains control and continues filling in the buffer. Now the buffer is a mix of the results of the first and second threads' execution. This is what the first thread sees. If the first thread returns a string *shorter* than had already been formatted by the second thread, then when the second thread gets control and completes, only the portion already formatted by the first thread will be returned. Confused? Think about how hard it would be to debug this, since it is so timing-dependent that it may happen only occasionally, and trying to use the debugger would immediately change the nature of the result! A failure of this type, deep in the kernel of an operating system, once caused a system crash about once a week. I found it by accident. *—jmn.*

[9] There is even a special name for these kinds of bugs: *Heisenbugs*, a pun on the Heisenberg Uncertainty Principle, which in effect states that an attempt to measure a system perturbs it so that complete knowledge of the system is not possible. See *The New Hacker's Dictionary*, cited in "Further Reading".

Using Thread-Local Storage

Thread-local storage is intended to support small, fast allocation. Each thread is guaranteed a certain minimum number of thread-local storage slots, each of which can hold a 32-bit value. This value is defined for a specific Win32 release by the symbol TLS_MINIMUM_AVAILABLE. For Windows NT release 3.*x* and Windows 95, this value is 64.

The strategy for using thread-local storage requires careful explanation and use because it isn't quite what you think it might be. Every thread gets, implicitly, an array that we will call "tls", which is in effect LPVOID tls[TLS_MINIMUM_AVAILABLE]. But the array elements are allocated by a single, global array of flags. If you ask for an allocation of a thread-local slot by calling TlsAlloc, it gives you an available slot. This slot is now reserved in *all* threads, both those already existing and those that will be created. When you free a thread-local slot by using TlsFree, it is now made available in *all* threads, those already existing and those that will be created, so if any thread is still using that slot, you are probably in deep trouble. The usual discipline is that the thread-local storage slots are allocated when your process starts up and never deallocated. This strategy doesn't work for DLLs; we look at that in more detail in Chapter 16.

Because thread-local slot allocation requires synchronization and could be a performance bottleneck if done too often, you want to do it only once, during a startup situation, whether process startup or thread initialization. Because thread-local slots are scarce resources, you don't want to allocate very many to a thread; in fact, you usually want to allocate only one. This one can then be used to point to some more complex structure on the heap. The reason you want to use thread-local allocation is that it implicitly changes with the thread; if you are preempted, you know that your thread-local value is safe. The other thread is using *its* thread-local value.

Remember that the thread-local slot allocation must be done *globally* to all threads. You don't want to do thread-local slot allocation each time as each thread starts. Listing 14.7 shows the formatting function of Listing 14.5, rewritten to be thread-safe. The use of the global variable may seem to violate a number of guidelines we've given, but in fact it is the equivalent of a const declaration; once initialized, it doesn't change.

Listing 14.7: Thread-safe formatting function

```
int myFormatSlot = TLS_OUT_OF_INDEXES;

BOOL initialize(HINSTANCE hInstance)
    {
    // ... lots of other initialization here
    myFormatSlot = TlsAlloc();
    if(myFormatSlot == TLS_OUT_OF_INDEXES)
        return FALSE; // initialization failed
    // ...
    }

LPCTSTR formatWhatever(int parm)
    {
    LPTSTR buffer;
    buffer = (LPTSTR)TlsGetValue(myFormatSlot);
    if(buffer == NULL)
        { /* not allocated or failure */
```

```
        if(GetLastError() != 0)
            return NULL; // error return
        buffer = (LPTSTR)malloc(MAX_MESSAGE_LENGTH * sizeof(TCHAR));
        if(buffer == NULL)
            return NULL; // error return
        TlsSetValue(myFormatSlot, buffer);
        } /* not allocated or failure */
    wsprintf(buffer, _T("...%d..."), parm);
    return buffer;
    }
```

The code shown in Listing 14.7 contains several notable features. First, we use a global variable to hold the index of the thread-local storage, which we've already discussed. This is initialized in the application initialization function and used in the formatWhatever function to access the thread-local storage slot. If the thread-local slot is not initialized or there was an error, the result will be a NULL value; it is necessary to check which of these occurred. Normally, a correctly executing function will not change the error code returned by GetLastError, but TlsGetValue will set the GetLastError result to 0 if it succeeded. Thus it is possible to tell whether the NULL result is the result of an error or an uninitialized variable. If the result is NULL, we call the allocator to allocate a buffer of the appropriate maximum size and use TlsSetValue to store this. Thus this operation need be done only once. Finally, we return the value of the buffer pointer. No matter which thread is executing, it will now get the correct pointer to its thread-local buffer. The malloc function *is* thread-safe and therefore cannot be corrupted by preemption.

Because thread-local storage is supposed to be as efficient as possible, the Tls functions do virtually no error checking. Passing in an incorrect value as a Tls index will most likely produce incorrect and possibly terminal (memory-access-fault) effects.

Note that in this fragment, we do not free the storage. Calling TlsFree will release the thread-local storage slot. *It will not free up any resources referenced by that slot.* This means that at the point where you must free the storage, you must also free up any resources. If we wanted to free up the myFormatSlot, we would have to do something like this:

```
void freeMyFormatSlot()
    {
    LPCTSTR buffer = TlsGetValue(myFormatSlot);
    if (buffer != NULL)
        free(buffer);
    TlsFree(myFormatSlot);
    }
```

However, it is more common to simply allocate the slots once and never free them, since they are potentially used anywhere at any time up to program termination.

The management of thread-local objects seems to violate many principles of abstraction. In particular, adding thread-local storage requires that for the initialization of the application and some other event, such as termination of the application or termination of the last of the possible threads that might use the storage, you must know the name of the variable and how it is used. Tracking thread-local assignments is a manual process and offers an excellent opportunity for error. Fortunately, there are ways to avoid this; we discuss these next.

The thread Attribute

Several compilers implement automatic thread-local storage management. For Microsoft C, this is done by adding the thread attribute to a variable declaration like so:

```
__declspec(thread) LPTSTR buffer;
```

This is often simplified by adding this macro declaration:

```
#define threadLocal __declspec(thread)
```

thus allowing you to write

```
threadLocal LPTSTR buffer;
```

The __declspec(thread) attribute can apply *only* to data declarations of static extent. This means only those variables you declare at file level or declare within a block with the static attribute can be thread-local. Stack variables, of course, are implicitly thread-local, since they are declared within the thread's private stack.

Using compiler-managed thread-local storage allows us to rewrite the code of Listing 14.7 in a more compact form, as shown in Listing 14.8. This code handles all of the necessary Tls API function calls. It also uses a number of clever techniques to avoid having a limit set by the TLS_MINIMUM_AVAILABLE value. This is by far the easiest way to manage your thread-local storage in C. It does not work in C++, but there is in C++ a CThreadLocal template class that can "wrap" a C++ class and thus provides a similar capability for any C++ object declared with static scope. This template is described in Technical Note 58 on the MSDN CD-ROM.

The use of __declspec(thread) does have a cost, however. This is a Microsoft-specific extension and may not be supported in all compilers. One reason for choosing the macro implementation, however, is that some alternative C compilers support compiler-managed thread-local storage with a slightly different keyword. You could use conditional compilation to isolate the compiler-specific dependencies into a single header file. If cross-compiler portability is not of major concern, you can use whatever thread-local storage mechanism your compiler supports. However, cross-compiler portability is often a major concern in developing Windows NT applications; in particular, you have to be concerned with compilers not yet written for architectures on which Windows NT does not yet run.

Listing 14.8: Using __declspec(thread) for thread-local storage
```
LPCTSTR formatWhatever(int parm)
    {
    static threadLocal LPTSTR buffer;
    if(buffer == NULL)
        { /* not allocated */
        buffer = (LPTSTR)malloc(MAX_MESSAGE_LENGTH * sizeof(TCHAR));
        if(buffer == NULL)
            return NULL; // error return
        } /* not allocated */
    wsprintf(buffer, _T("...%d..."), parm);
    return buffer;
    }
```

Sharing Thread-Local Storage

You can't share thread-local storage. That's the point of thread-local storage. In particular, you can't create thread-local storage that is shared by "some" threads but not "others"; it is private to each thread. You can't set the thread-local storage of any other thread explicitly. Instead, you have to somehow convince that thread that it should set its thread-local storage for you. This is often done by sending a message to the window associated with the thread. But that works only if there *is* a window associated with the thread. More often, threads are "worker threads" that have no associated window. In this case, you probably should use shared memory variables, and you must deal explicitly with the synchronization issues.

Thread-Local Storage Summary

We have thus far avoided talking about threads. However, when you write DLLs, you can't avoid them. We talk more about how to use thread-local storage in a DLL in Chapter 16, page 1145. There you will discover that unfortunately the __declspec(thread) mechanism *doesn't* work in DLLs, and your only choice will be to use the explicit Tls API functions.

The Heap Explorer

Included on the CD-ROM for this book is the complete source and executable of the Heap Explorer. It has two parts: the basic Heap Explorer, which lets you play with allocation and deallocation to see what happens to a heap; and another, the ClassHeap explorer, which implements a class-private heap in C++ and a graphical display of the heap it implements.

For exquisitely detailed heap information, you also can use the Process Walker. The Process Walker is a program written by Microsoft and is distributed as part of the Win32 SDK Tools. It also is found in source form on the MSDN CD-ROM.

Summary

We can't offer you the Universal Right Solution to storage management. If storage management *is* your bottleneck in performance, the techniques for optimizing it depend very much on the nature of your data and algorithms. We pointed out some of the issues and suggested some of the approaches you might take. Using the HeapWalk function to collect information is a very useful technique, but it is only one of several tools. One technique we have found very useful in memory-intensive applications is to replace all heap calls by a call on our own function. This function can then record information about what is being allocated, how often, by which call sites, how long the information remains allocated, and the like. Any or all of this information can be useful.

Further Reading

Here are some suggestions. They are certainly biased by one author's experience.

Keith, Randy, "Managing Heap Memory in Win32", on the MSDN CD-ROM.

A good overview of the Win32 allocation system, in far more detail than most programmers need to know. An excellent detailed study of heap overheads, internal representations, and the like, all of which could be useful if you are trying to debug an obscure memory-damage problem or if you really want to take advantage of deeper knowledge of how the allocator internals work.

Nestor, John R., Newcomer, Joseph M., Stone, Donald L., and Gianinni, Paola, *IDL: The Language and Its Implementation*, Prentice-Hall, 1990.

The Interface Description Language (IDL) is a language-independent, object-oriented, multiple-inheritance data definition language. This book describes the language and the challenges the authors faced in creating an efficient (in both time and space) implementation of a system based on this definition language. Of particular note is the implementation of the storage allocator, based on but considerably extending the work of Weinstock, cited below.

Newcomer, J. M., "Heap Storage Damage Detection", *The C User's Journal*, October 1989.

Several techniques for debugging storage, including techniques that can be applied for performance analysis, appear in this article.

Raymond, Eric S., *The New Hacker's Dictionary, Second edition*, MIT Press, 1993. ISBN 0-262-68079-3.

This delightful book is a compilation of the old MIT-AI definition list, updated to modern terminology, including Unix, MS-DOS, and other cultures. I (*jmn*) was one of the major contributors to the first edition, so this review is definitely biased . . . but you should enjoy the book anyway.

Weinstock, C. B., *Dynamic Storage Allocation Techniques*, Ph.D. Dissertation, Computer Science Department, Carnegie Mellon University, April 1976. (Available through the microform service of the National Technical Information Service, NTIS).

Weinstock, C. B., and Wulf, W. A., "An Efficient Algorithm for Heap Storage Allocation", *SIGPLAN Notices*, October 1988.

For those who would like more about storage allocation in general, a fairly exhaustive study of the performance of storage allocation was done by Weinstock, in which he presents a high-performance allocator that minimizes storage fragmentation. The later paper by Weinstock and Wulf is a distillation of the Ph.D. research. The details of an implementation of a high-performance allocator based on this work are what is described in the book by Nestor, Newcomer, Gianinni, and Stone.

Storage allocation has always been a significant issue in system architecture. Detailed studies of storage allocation in the LISP environment generated dozens of significant papers in the late 1970s and early 1980s.

Chapter

15 Fonts

Windows provides a graphical user interface. An application can take advantage of the graphical nature of this interface to display text output in more than one font. Windows always displays text using the font currently selected into the device context specified when you call the DrawText, ExtTextOut, TabbedTextOut, and TextOut functions.

Because fonts and font terminology aren't familiar to most programmers, especially those new to a graphical environment, the first part of this chapter defines the terminology used by Windows when referring to a font. This terminology is slightly different than that used by a typographer.

Early versions of Windows had two types of fonts: raster (fonts represented by bitmaps) and vector (fonts represented by a list of line segments). Windows 3.1 introduced a third type of font that is supported in all versions of the Win32 interface–TrueType. All fonts in all applications in Win32 are TrueType fonts, with a few exceptions such as the system font. You can use the Font Explorer program to discover the nature and properties of fonts in your system.

The font type greatly affects how you can use the font and how much GDI can modify the font. In some cases, GDI can synthesize the font you want from one of the fonts available to GDI. For example, GDI typically synthesizes bold, italic, underline, and strikeout variations of a raster font. The size of a character in a raster font can be increased only by integer multiples. Characters in a TrueType font can be continuously scaled.

After we define the terminology and the restrictions and capabilities of the various types of fonts, we show you how to list the fonts available on a system. A user can add fonts to a Windows system, so you don't know exactly which fonts are available until your application runs.

Next, we show you how to request a particular font. Windows uses the concept of a *logical font*. A logical font is a description of the ideal font you would like to use. In this less-than-perfect world, you request Windows to use draw text using your ideal font and Windows tries to honor your request as best it can. For example, your ideal font might scale to $28\frac{1}{4}$ pixels high on the device under whatever mapping mode you are using; Windows will most likely choose a 28-pixel rendering.

Finally, we talk about the Font Explorer, which lets you discover all of the properties of fonts in the system.

What Is a Font?

A *font* contains the glyphs for the characters in a particular character set. A *glyph* is a symbol or pictograph for an object. The objects of interest in this discussion are the symbols for the characters in a character set. The glyphs in a font have a particular typeface and size.

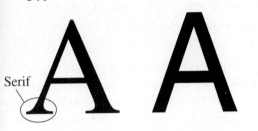

Serif font: Times New Roman   Sans serif font: Arial

Figure 15.1: Serif and sans serif fonts

A *typeface* is classified based on the appearance of the glyphs. Two characteristics distinguish the most commonly used typefaces. One is whether the glyphs have *serifs*–smaller lines that finish a letter's main stroke, as at the top and bottom of the letter M. Fonts without serifs are called *sans serif* fonts. These are shown in Figure 15.1. The other characteristic is the width of the characters. If the characters all have the same width, the font is a *fixed pitch, fixed width,* or *monospaced* font. If the characters can have different widths, the font is a *variable pitch, variable width,* or *proportionally spaced* font. Samples of some common TrueType fonts are shown in Figure 15.2. The comparisons of the width of the "W", "i", and vertical bar "I" symbols should give you an idea of relative character widths.

	Serif		Sans Serif	
Monospaced	Wide ediW | | | |	Courier New	Wide ediW | | | |	Lucida Console
Proportionally Spaced	Wide ediW ||||	Times New Roman	Wide ediW ||||	Arial

Figure 15.2: Font characteristics

Other typefaces are quite distinctive and don't require the classifications just discussed. Some typefaces resemble script handwriting, others contain decorative symbols, and still others contain elaborate glyphs for characters such as those used in Old English type.

Windows classifies typefaces in five *font families:* Decorative, Modern, Roman, Script, and Swiss. The Decorative font family includes typefaces such as Old English, Symbol, and WingDings. The Modern font family includes monospaced typefaces such as Courier, Elite, and Pica. The Roman font family includes typefaces with proportional spacing and serifs. Typical Roman typefaces include Times New Roman and New Century Schoolbook. The Script font family includes typefaces that resemble script handwriting, such as Cursive. The Swiss font family includes typefaces with variable-width strokes that are sans serif, such as Arial.

Factoids

The actual glyphs of a font are not protected under U. S. copyright law. The font *name*, however, is protected by trademark laws. The name "Helvetica", for example, is a registered trademark of Linotype AG or its subsidiaries and may not be used to describe a font product without a license from the owner of the trademark. Before you can sell a font you have created, you have to make sure the name you use to describe it is not a registered trademark of another font company. But the glyphs themselves are not protected. For example, fonts that have an appearance similar to (or even exactly the same as) Helvetica can use other nontrademark-infringing names such as "Swiss" (the word "Helvetica" is actually the Latin word for "Swiss"). Typeface companies are very protective of their font names.

The term *typeface* has had many interpretations. Sometimes it includes the notion of bold, italic, and bold italic, that is, Times New Roman, **Times New Roman Bold,** *Times New Roman Italic*, and ***Times New Roman Bold Italic*** are, by one classification scheme, four separate typefaces. Under another interpretation Times **New** *Roman* is a single "typeface", in any form. There seem to be varying interpretations of the term depending upon whether the reference is to traditional hand-set type or to electronic typography, and even within electronic typography, different vendors have used the term in different ways, not all of which are considered correct by typographers.

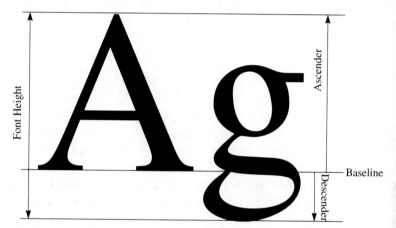

Figure 15.3: Font dimensions

A Windows program takes the latter definition, and specifies the name of a typeface and specifies separately whether the typeface should be normal, italic, or bold.

A *font* in the typographic sense is all of the characters of one size of one typeface. The size of a font is specified in *points*. A point is approximately $1/72$ inch.[1] We use the term *point* from here on as if it were exactly $1/72$ inch. The size of a font is measured from the top of the *ascenders* to the bottom of the *descenders* (see Figure 15.3). Therefore, a 24-point Times New Roman font is $24/72$ inch high. An 8-point Times New Roman font is a completely different font because it has a different size.

---

[1] All references to points always say "approximately $1/72$ of an inch". Here's the real value, as taken from *The Handbook of Chemistry and Physics, 39th Edition* (Chemical Rubber Company, 1963): A point is 0.01389 inch, or 0.035278 cm. This yields a value of 71.99424 points to the inch. Now You Know.

Just to emphasize the point, Windows has two representations: externally, to the user, it uses the term "font" in such a way that an 8-point Times New Roman Bold font and an 8-point Times New Roman Italic font are considered one "font" with slightly different attributes. A typographer considers them two different fonts (because in setting type, they come out of two different physical drawers). Internally, when you create a font, the font *handle* for each font is different, thus conforming more to what a typographer thinks.

Types of Windows Fonts

Windows supports three types of fonts: *raster*, *stroke* (or *vector*), and *TrueType*.

Raster Fonts

In a *GDI raster font*, each character is stored as a bitmap pixel image of the character with a fixed height and width. Hence, a raster font is designed to be used on a specific device that has a matching *aspect ratio*. The aspect ratio is the ratio of the width and height of a pixel on a device. You can display characters from a raster font on a device that has a different aspect ratio, but the characters look compressed or expanded.

Windows can use a GDI raster font as a template to create, or *synthesize*, a font with larger character sizes. This is one of many ways GDI can synthesize a slightly different font from a GDI-based font. GDI synthesizes a larger point size raster font from the bitmap for a smaller font by duplicating rows and columns of the bitmap an integer number of times. Officially, GDI expands the height of a GDI raster font up to eight times. It expands the width up to five times. You can use the Raster Font Explorer component of the Font Explorer application to discover this is not so. For example, some fonts stop scaling at 8 multiples, while others stop scaling at 11 multiples. We were able to scale the MS Sans Serif font by a factor of 20, the highest magnification the Font Explorer program allows. And some fonts, at higher magnifications (sometimes beyond 8, sometimes beyond 11; this appears to be font-dependent) seem to invoke a font substitution mechanism that uses what appears to be a TrueType font for the higher magnifications (it appears to be Arial). We can find no documentation anywhere of this observable behavior, and cannot explain its basis.

GDI cannot synthesize a smaller raster font from a larger font because it doesn't remove rows and columns from the bitmap. Therefore GDI raster fonts are available only in certain sizes. If you want a 4-point GDI raster font and the smallest font is 8-point, you're out of luck. Similarly, GDI can't synthesize a 9-point font from an 8-point font because only integral multiples are allowed.

Although GDI can synthesize fonts with large point sizes (within the previously described limits), they tend to look poor when they get too large. Because rows and columns are duplicated, large-point-size raster fonts that are synthesized have a blocky or coarse appearance. Figure 15.4 shows some characters from various GDI raster fonts, magnified until the original bitmap representation becomes obvious. You should also examine Figure 15.5, which shows that a font does not necessarily retain its appearance in various scalings. This set of images was created in the Font Explorer, using the FixedSys font at several multiples of its nominal font height (which is 15 pixels).

Raster fonts have a significant performance advantage: They are pre-computed bitmaps. As you will see, the other font representations require that Windows render the bitmap "on the fly", that is, create the appropriate bitmap as needed. Raster fonts already *are* bitmaps and can therefore be quickly copied to where they are needed. The performance is one reason that certain key Windows fonts such as System, MS Dialog, and MS Dialog Light are raster fonts: They are used everywhere and performance matters.

Since raster fonts are prerendered to specific sizes, in early (pre-3.0) Windows programming you had to have *screen raster fonts* and totally separate *printer raster fonts*. Not all raster fonts had equivalents in screen and printer representations. This made early Windows printing quite a challenge. Today, raster fonts for printers are almost unheard of. Only the few critical Windows system fonts and a few historic kept-for-compatibility-with-earlier-applications screen raster fonts can be found.

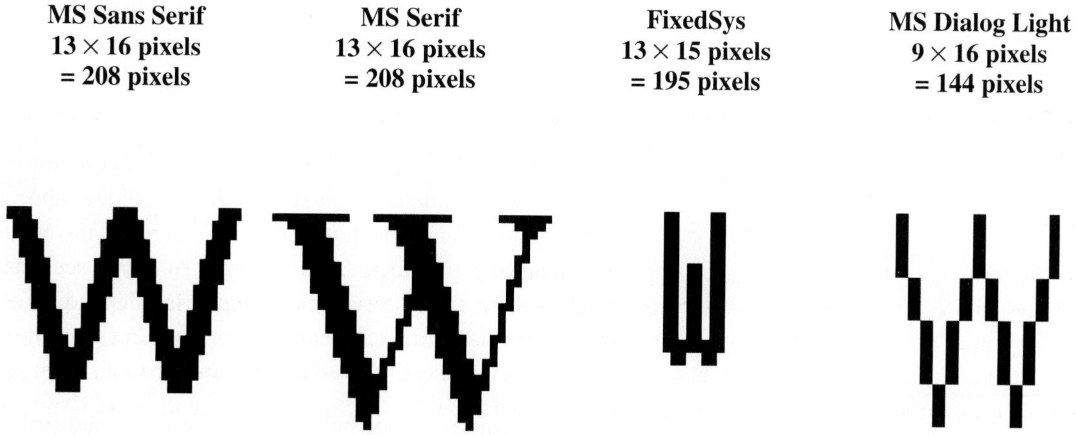

MS Sans Serif	MS Serif	FixedSys	MS Dialog Light
13 × 16 pixels	13 × 16 pixels	13 × 15 pixels	9 × 16 pixels
= 208 pixels	= 208 pixels	= 195 pixels	= 144 pixels

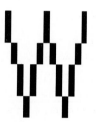

Dimensions are given as the scaling factor × original font height = new font height. MS Dialog Light would not scale above 9.

Figure 15.4: Characters from selected GDI raster fonts

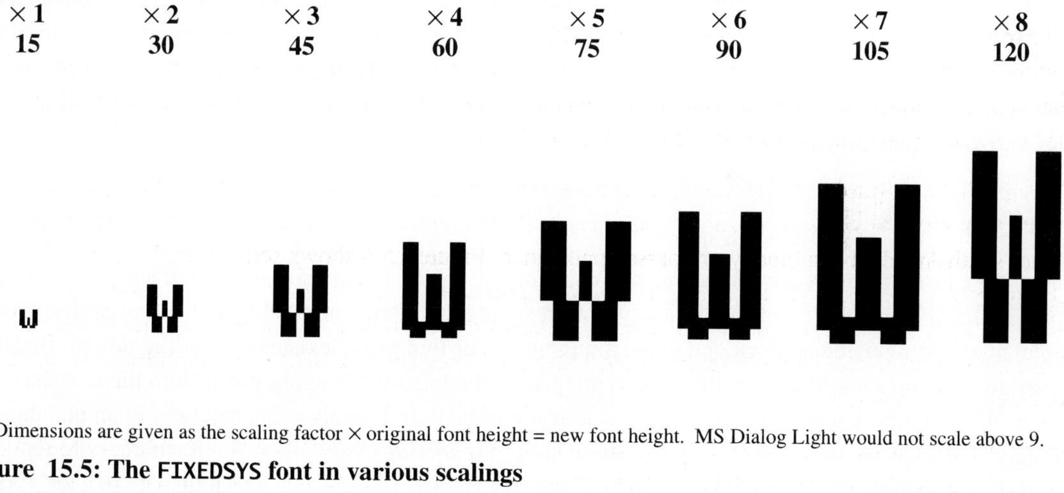

× 1	× 2	× 3	× 4	× 5	× 6	× 7	× 8
15	30	45	60	75	90	105	120

Dimensions are given as the scaling factor × original font height = new font height. MS Dialog Light would not scale above 9.

Figure 15.5: The FIXEDSYS font in various scalings

Stroke or Vector Fonts

GDI stroke fonts were an early attempt to solve the problems with raster fonts. Unlike GDI raster fonts, in which characters are represented by a pixel bitmap, GDI stroke fonts are represented by an array of vectors or line segments. (This is why they are sometimes called *vector fonts*.) A GDI stroke font can be scaled to any size, and it displays appropriately on all devices no matter what their aspect ratios. Because the characters are composed of line segments, however, they look considerably less dense than an equivalent raster font. Stroke fonts are rare in Win32. The only stroke fonts in a stock Win32 installation are those kept for compatibility with legacy code.

Raster fonts in a small point size generally look better than equivalently sized stroke fonts, while stroke fonts in a large point size look better than equivalently sized synthesized raster fonts. Figure 15.6 shows the same two characters from a GDI stroke font using the same point size. If you look closely, you can see the individual line segments that comprise the characters.

Figure 15.6: Two characters from a GDI stroke font

We have found using the Raster Explorer component that the same undocumented font substitution techniques appear to be used at higher magnifications. For example, the Modern typeface gets rendered in a variety of fonts (we see what appears to be Times New Roman and Arial, depending on the scaling). Figure 15.6 came from the Font Explorer, which uses GDI scaling to scale up a smaller font.

GDI also can synthesize bold, italic, underlined, and strikeout fonts from normal GDI raster fonts and GDI stroke fonts. GDI synthesizes a bold font by increasing the *weight* (or thickness) of the lines or strokes that comprise the character. GDI synthesizes an italic font by skewing the characters so that they appear slanted. The base of the character remains in place, while the upper portion of the character is shifted to the right, with the greatest amount of shift at the top of the character. GDI synthesizes an underlined font by drawing a solid line below the baseline of each character cell. GDI synthesizes a strikeout font by drawing a solid horizontal line through each character cell.

TrueType Fonts

Rendering a raster from a vector description is challenging. As the feature size of a detail such as a serif approaches the pixel resolution of the device, you start seeing the effects of pixel quantization. Serifs, for example, might be rendered as thick and ugly (rounding up) or thin or nonexistent (rounding down). Because of how font features might map to the underlying pixels, the left serif hanging down from the crossbar of a capital "T" might be 1 pixel wide but the right serif might be 0 or 2 pixels wide, resulting in an unbalanced and ugly character. We would not like to see these kind of renderings very often. But it isn't easy to render a font well, particularly when you have to render it quickly enough to refresh a screen display in a WM_PAINT handler or format 60 pages per minute on a printer. Adobe Systems pioneered this technology when it introduced a system called PostScript®, which has a very fast font-rendering engine. PostScript is a "page description language" used in laser printers and other similar high-quality printers. The font description they use is known as "Adobe Type 1 Fonts". This rendering engine also is available in some implementations of Windows as a screen rendering engine known as "Adobe Type Manager". The other major font rendering engine you will encounter is the TrueType rendering engine, which is built into all contemporary versions of Windows. Microsoft and Adobe have agreed on a font description standard called OpenFont that allows fonts to be shared between PostScript Type 1 font engines and Windows TrueType engines. We have already seen some of the font technology discussed in Chapter 4. We examine the TrueType/OpenFont technology in more depth next.

TrueType fonts, introduced with Windows 3.1, provided a solution to the problems of font scalability just described. Windows stores a TrueType font as a collection of points and *hints* that define the character outline. Hints are algorithms that distort the outline of a character when scaling it in order to improve the appearance of the bitmaps at specific resolutions. When an application requests a TrueType font, the TrueType rasterizer uses the outline and the hints to produce a bitmap (raster font) of the size requested by the application.

Fine detail rendering is only a part of the problem. Typical hints deal with how to scale thicknesses of vertical and horizontal lines, maintain symmetry of fine details (serifs are only one such detail) in the presence of pixel roundoff, avoiding losing thin features entirely, and other considerations about visual appearance. The problem in typography is that visually, linear scaling will produce ugly effects at even relatively small magnifications larger or smaller than the nominal design size. Much of this perceived ugliness is based on the nonlinearities of the human perceptual system. This is why the simplistic stroke fonts were never very satisfactory.

 If you would like to learn more about font design, you should consult Don Knuth's book on typeface design, *MetaFont*, in which he describes a program that takes an analytic description of a font and renders a bitmap that maintains the sort of aesthetics that a typographer would want. The major difference between Knuth's MetaFont program and rendering engines such as TrueType and PostScript is that TrueType and PostScript can render with incredibly high performance while still handling hinting. Since Knuth's methods are nonproprietary, they are carefully documented and explained. You will get considerable insight into font technology from his books and articles.

TrueType fonts offer many advantages over raster and vector fonts. You can rotate and scale TrueType fonts by nearly any amount. In contrast, raster fonts cannot be rotated, and they can be scaled only in integer multiples of their base size. TrueType fonts look nice at all sizes due to their hints. Your application can use a TrueType font on the screen and on a printer and have the characters look the same. They also will be rendered in the best possible format independent of the relative differences in resolution between the typical screen and the typical printer. Figure 15.7 shows some characters from a TrueType font. Nearly all fonts in Win32, except the specialized raster fonts and legacy stroke fonts mentioned earlier in the chapter, are TrueType fonts. The fonts shown in Figure 15.7 still show quantization (but much less than that of scaled raster fonts!) because they are actual screen captures and are done at the resolution of the screen pixels. Compare these to Figure 15.8, where the characters (whose point size is chosen to approximate the size of that in the image display of Figure 15.7) are rendered by the high-resolution printer engine used to typeset this book. TrueType can render for any device at its natural resolution, and you, as a programmer, generally don't need to be aware of the differences in devices.

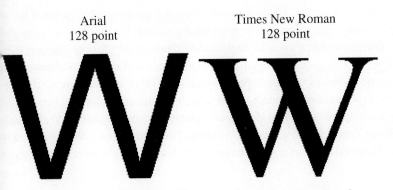

Arial
128 point

Times New Roman
128 point

Figure 15.7: Characters from a TrueType font, screen-rendered

Font Resources

Windows stores raster and vector fonts in font resource files, which have the `.fon` file extension. TrueType font resource files have a `.fot` file extension. A TrueType font also has a related font-information file with the same base file name as the `.fot` file but which uses the `.ttf` file extension. Font resource files are typically stored in the Windows system subdirectory. This is the directory returned by the `GetSystemDirectory` function. A font resource file actually is a dynamic link library that contains no code and no data, only a font directory resource and all the individual font resources for the font named by the file. You will generally never see any of these, since you will use operations such as `CreateFont` to access these resources only indirectly. You typically install fonts using a font installation utility, such as the Control Panel. Unless you plan to go into font management software design, it is unlikely you will ever need to deal with fonts at other than the level of already-available installers.

Device Fonts

A *device font* is a font that is recognized by a graphical output device. Most video display adapters don't have any device fonts. For such devices, Windows converts text output to a bitmap representing the text and sends the bitmap to the device. A laser printer, however, might store many different device fonts. Some laser printers even come equipped with hard drives or the ability to connect hard drives as font repositories. When you display text on a device using a device font, Windows needs only to send the characters to the device. Windows does not need to convert the text to a bitmap. The device converts text to the appropriate bitmap when it receives the character data. GDI cannot synthesize a different font from a device font, as it has no access to or understanding of the internal representation of the device font.

Some printers support the downloading of fonts. TrueType fonts work especially well on such printers. Windows can download a TrueType font to the printer, after scaling it to the required size. Subsequently, Windows sends only the characters that are printed, plus an indication of which font should be used when the font needs to change. Doing this requires considerably less work (and is therefore much more efficient) than converting each character to a bitmap and sending each bitmap to the printer.

The most likely device font you will encounter is an Adobe Type 1 font, the representation used for PostScript printers, or a downloadable HP printer font. The Adobe Type Manager, which exists for some versions of Windows, also renders these Type 1 fonts on the screen.

Using a Stock Font

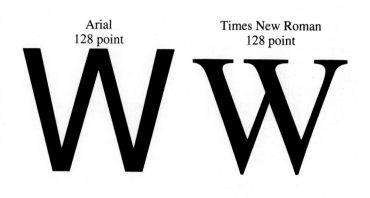

Arial
128 point

Times New Roman
128 point

Figure 15.8: Characters from a TrueType font, printer-rendered

To display text in a font, you obtain a handle to the font, select it into a device context, and write the text. The easiest way to obtain a handle to a font is to retrieve a handle to one of the *stock fonts*. Windows provides the six stock fonts listed in Table 15.1. The font samples shown are all taken at the same resolution and scaling; whatever differences you see are entirely due to the differences in the fonts. You should note in particular the effect that selecting the OEM font has on the characters with codes above 127 (a few of which are shown).

Table 15.1: The Windows stock fonts

Symbolic Name	Description
ANSI_FIXED_FONT	A fixed-pitch (width) Courier font containing the characters from the ANSI character set. ANSI_FIXED_FONT ®²¶¼Äåýø
ANSI_VAR_FONT	A variable-pitch (width) sans serif font containing characters from the ANSI character set. ANSI_VAR_FONT ®²¶¼Äåýø
DEVICE_DEFAULT_FONT	A font preferred by the device. Specifying this font for a display device that doesn't have a device font is equivalent to requesting the SYSTEM_FONT. DEVICE_DEFAULT_FONT ®²¶¼Äåýø
OEM_FIXED_FONT	A fixed-pitch Terminal font containing characters from the OEM character set. Windows uses this font when displaying DOS applications running in a window. OEM_FIXED_FONT «▨╠╝─σ²º

Table 15.1: The Windows stock fonts

Symbolic Name	Description
SYSTEM_FIXED_FONT	A fixed-pitch font containing characters from the ANSI character set. This is the font used as the system font by Win16 prior to version 3.0. (It is rarely used in Win32 for any purpose.) **SYSTEM_FIXED_FONT** ®²¶¼Äåýø
SYSTEM_FONT	A variable-pitch font containing characters from the ANSI character set. Windows uses this font to display window captions, dialog boxes, message boxes, and menu items. SYSTEM_FONT ®²¶¼Äåýø

You get a handle to a stock font the same way you get a handle to a stock pen or brush: You call the GetStockObject function and pass one of the symbolic names listed in Table 15.1. As soon as you have the handle to the font, you select the font into a device context by calling the SelectObject function.

windowsx.h defines the more convenient GetStockFont and SelectFont macro APIs, which are defined in terms of the GetStockObject and SelectObject function like this:

```
#define SelectFont(hdc, hfont)   \
   ((HFONT)SelectObject((hdc),(HGDIOBJ)(HFONT)(hfont)))
#define GetStockFont(i)    ((HFONT)GetStockObject(i))
```

We prefer the more mnemonic macro APIs, so we use them throughout the examples in this chapter. They also cast their results, which is nice when you are using STRICT type checking.

For example, the lazy way to display aligned columns of information in a window is to switch to a fixed-pitch font and align the columns by padding with spaces. You can do that like this:

```
HFONT   hfontFixed ;
HFONT   hfontPrev ;

hfontFixed = GetStockFont (SYSTEM_FIXED_FONT) ;
hfontPrev  = SelectFont (hdc, hfontFixed) ;
TextOut (hdc, 10, 10, "AAA     BBB     III", 17) ;
TextOut (hdc, 10, 20, "XXX     YYY     WWW", 17) ;
SelectObject (hdc, hfontPrev) ;
```

The system stock font is the only font guaranteed to be available. However, you still can call the GetStockFont function for any of the other stock fonts. If the requested stock font isn't available, the GetStockFont function returns a handle to the system font.

You don't need to delete a stock font, just as you don't need to delete stock pens and stock brushes. An attempt to delete a stock object is ignored, so you don't have to try to be careful about attempting to delete stock fonts.

Enumerating Fonts

Although retrieving a handle to a stock font is the easiest way to get a handle to a font, the selections available are somewhat limited. Many additional fonts might be available for a particular device, and you can call the EnumFontFamilies or EnumFontFamiliesEx functions to find out which fonts are available. A *font family* is a set of fonts sharing the same text name string.

The EnumFontFamilies or EnumFontFamiliesEx functions are used in two ways:

- To return information about one randomly selected font from each available font family available on a specified device

- To return information about each font in a specified font family that is available on a device

The EnumFonts function was used for this purpose in versions of Windows prior to 3.1. It is still provided for backwards compatibility with applications written for earlier versions of Windows. You likely will not encounter it in practice, unless you are porting an old legacy application. When writing new applications that must run under Windows NT 3.*x*, you should use the EnumFontFamilies function. It is recommended that you use EnumFontFamiliesEx for the 4.*x* level API, such as Windows 95 or Windows NT 4.*x*.

The EnumFontFamilies(Ex) function differs from the EnumFonts function in that it retrieves the style names associated with a TrueType font. You must use the EnumFontFamilies or EnumFontFamiliesEx functions to retrieve information about unusual font styles present on a system such as Monotype Sorts and WingDings.

Typically, you call the EnumFontFamilies(Ex) function once to obtain the names of each available font family for a specified device. Then you call it once for each font family returned by the first call. These subsequent calls obtain information about each font in the specified font family.

In either case, the EnumFontFamilies(Ex) function retrieves information about a font and passes it to a callback function. The EnumFontFamilies(Ex) function continues retrieving information about each font meeting the specified criteria (device and typeface name, if any) and passing that information to the callback function until either all matching fonts have been enumerated or the callback function returns 0.

The EnumFontFamilies function has the following function prototype:

```
int EnumFontFamilies (HDC hdc, LPCTSTR Family,
                FONTENUMPROC FontFunc,
                LPARAM lParam) ;
```

- The hdc parameter to EnumFontFamilies specifies the device context handle for a device. The fonts that are enumerated may depend on which fonts are available for the particular device represented by the DC.

- The Family parameter is a pointer to a NUL-terminated character string that specifies the family name for the desired fonts. When you specify NULL as this parameter, the EnumFontFamilies function randomly selects one font from each available font family and enumerates it. When you specify a family name, the EnumFontFamilies function enumerates each font with the specified font family that is available on the device.

- The FontFunc parameter is the procedure address of the callback function.

- The lParam parameter is a pointer to application-supplied data. You can specify any value you like for this parameter, and it is passed to the callback function. This provides a clean mechanism to pass data from an EnumFontFamilies function call to a callback function without resorting to global data and flags.

To enumerate one font from each typeface name available on a device, you call the EnumFontFamilies function like this:

```
EnumFontFamilies (hdc, NULL, lpfnFontFunc, lParam) ;
```

To enumerate all fonts for a specific typeface name, such as Courier New, you call the EnumFontFamilies function like this:

```
EnumFontFamilies (hdc, _T("Courier New"), FontFunc, lParam) ;
```

The callback function must be defined as a CALLBACK function. In the following example, the callback function is arbitrarily called FontFunc, but it can be called whatever you want. The EnumFontFamilies callback function has the following form:

```
int CALLBACK
FontFunc (const LPENUMLOGFONT NewLogFont,
          const LPTEXTMETRIC NewTextMetric,
          int FontType, LPARAM lParam) ;
```

The lpNewLogFont parameter to the callback function is a pointer to an ENUMLOGFONT structure, which in earlier versions of Windows was referred to as a NEWLOGFONT structure. The NEWLOGFONT structure isn't defined in any header file, but Win32 defines the ENUMLOGFONT structure. It contains a LOGFONT structure and two additional members as well as information about the logical attributes of a particular font. This structure is passed only to the callback function of EnumFontFamilies and is otherwise unavailable.

We describe the LOGFONT structure in detail later in the chapter. Of particular interest at this point is the lfFaceName field of a LOGFONT structure, which contains the font's typeface name.

An ENUMLOGFONT contains a LOGFONT structure plus the elfFullName and elfStyle fields:

```
typedef struct tagENUMLOGFONT
{
    LOGFONT        elfLogFont;
    BYTE           elfFullName[LF_FULLFACESIZE];
    BYTE           elfStyle[LF_FACESIZE];
} ENUMLOGFONT, FAR* LPENUMLOGFONT;
```

The elfFullName field contains the full name for the font. This name includes the font name and the style name. The elfStyle field contains the style name for the font. For example, when enumerating the Arial bold italic font, the lfFaceName contains the string "Arial", the lfStyle contains the string "Bold Italic", and elfFullName contains the string "Arial Bold Italic".

Typically, you save the typeface name from each LOGFONT structure passed to the callback function as a result of a call to the EnumFontFamilies function. Do this with NULL specified as the Family parameter. This is how you obtain a list of all available typefaces for a device.

The NewTextMetric parameter is a pointer to a NEWTEXTMETRIC structure when the font is a TrueType font. If the font is not a TrueType, this parameter points to a TEXTMETRIC structure. The NEWTEXTMETRIC structure is identical to the TEXTMETRIC structure except that four additional fields are present at the end of the structure. These structures contain information about the physical attributes of a particular font. The fields of the TEXTMETRIC structure contain the same values they would contain if you selected the font into the specified device context and called the GetTextMetrics function. All the size fields of the TEXTMETRIC structure, with the exception of the tmDigitizedAspectX and tmDigitizedAspectY fields, contain values given in logical units. Therefore many values in the TEXTMETRIC structure depend on the current mapping mode of the device context when the EnumFontFamilies function is called.

The FontType parameter contains a bit-encoded value that indicates the type of font. Three symbolic names are defined in the windows.h header file for this parameter: DEVICE_FONTTYPE, RASTER_FONTTYPE, and TRUETYPE_FONTTYPE.

You must use the AND (&) operator to test the FontType value, using the DEVICE_FONTTYPE RASTER_FONTTYPE, and TRUETYPE_FONTTYPE constants to determine the font type. If the RASTER_FONTTYPE bit is set, the font is a raster font. If the TRUETYPE_FONTTYPE bit is set, the font is a True-Type font. If neither bit is set, the font is a vector font.

A third bit, DEVICE_FONTTYPE, is set when a device (for example, a laser printer) supports downloading TrueType fonts or when the font is a device-resident font. It is set to 0 if the device is a display adapter, dot-matrix printer, or other raster device. An application can also use the DEVICE_FONTTYPE mask to distinguish GDI-supplied raster fonts from device-supplied fonts. GDI can simulate bold, italic, underline, and strikeout attributes for GDI-supplied raster fonts, but not for device-supplied fonts.

The lParam parameter to the callback function is the value provided as the lParam argument on the EnumFontFamilies function call.

The EnumFontFamiliesEx function should be used for all Win32 applications that will run on the version 4.x and higher APIs. However, this function is not supported on Windows NT 3.x. The EnumFontFamiliesEx function, implemented in the Win32 4.x API, is recommended for new code. It is defined as

```
int EnumFontFamiliesEx (HDC hdc, LPLOGFONT lf,
                        FONTENUMPROC FontFuncEx,
                        LPARAM lParam, DWORD flags)
```

Like EnumFontFamilies, it takes an HDC parameter that defines a DC as well as a procedure pointer, in this case to a slightly different callback. The LPARAM parameter is passed into the callback. The DWORD flags parameter is reserved and must be 0. However, instead of a string's name being passed in, a pointer to a LOGFONT structure is given. The fields of this LOGFONT are interpreted as shown in Table 15.2.

Table 15.2: The LOGFONT fields used by EnumFontFamilies(Ex)

Field	Interpretation
lfCharSet	If set to DEFAULT_CHARSET, enumerates all fonts in all character sets. If set to any other valid value, enumerates only fonts in the specified character sets.

Table 15.2: The LOGFONT fields used by EnumFontFamilies(Ex)

Field	Interpretation
lfFaceName	If set to an empty string, enumerates one font in each available typeface name. If set to a typeface name, enumerates all fonts with the same name.
lfPitchAndFamily	Must be set to 0 for all versions of the operating system except Hebrew and Arabic. For these fonts, the value MONO_FONT must be used.

The callback function for EnumFontFamiliesEx is

```
int CALLBACK
FontFuncEx (const LPENUMLOGFONTEX NewLogFont,
            const LPNEWTEXTMETRICEX NewTextMetric,
            int FontType, LPARAM lParam) ;
```

The ENUMLOGFONTEX structure contains a LOGFONT structure and three additional fields:

```
typedef struct tagENUMLOGFONTEX
{
    LOGFONT      elfLogFont;
    BCHAR        elfFullName[LF_FULLFACESIZE];
    BCHAR        elfStyle[LF_FACESIZE];
    BCHAR        elfScript[LF_FACESIZE];
} ENUMLOGFONTEX, FAR *LPENUMLOGFONTEX;
```

The NEWTEXTMETRICEX structure is defined as

```
typedef struct tagNEWTEXTMETRICEX
{
    NEWTEXTMETRIC    ntmTm;
    FONTSIGNATURE    ntmFontSig;
}NEWTEXTMETRICEX;
```

What is odd about this specification is that if you actually write the callback this way, your application will not compile. Microsoft has defined the callback function as requiring the function prototype as follows:

```
int CALLBACK
FontFuncEx (const LPLOGFONT LogFont,
            const LPTEXTMETRIC TextMetric,
            int FontType, LPARAM lParam) ;
```

Therefore you must cast these inside the function as shown here:

```
int CALLBACK
FontFuncEx (const LPLOGFONT LogFont,
            const LPTEXTMETRIC TextMetric,
            int FontType, LPARAM lParam)
    {
    const LPENUMLOGFONT newLogFont =
                    (const LPENUMLOGFONT)LogFont;
    const LPNEWTEXTMETRICEX newTextMetric =
                    (const LPNEWTEXTMETRICEX)TextMetric;
    //...
```

Defining a Logical Font

The `EnumFontFamilies` function tells you what fonts are available for a given device, but it doesn't return a handle to a font, only information about available fonts. To obtain a handle to a font, you must call the `CreateFont` or `CreateFontIndirect` function.

The `CreateFont` function is the most unwieldy function in the Windows API. It has 14 parameters, and a typical call looks like this:

```
HFONT   hfont ;

hfont = CreateFont (Height,
                    Width,
                    Escapement,
                    Orientation,
                    Weight,
                    Italic,
                    Underline,
                    StrikeOut,
                    CharSet,
                    OutputPrecision,
                    ClipPrecision,
                    Quality,
                    PitchAndFamily,
                    Facename) ;
```

A common way of calling `CreateFont` in Win16 was to specify 0 values for nearly everything; for example, `CreateFont(height, 0, 0, 0, 0, 0, 0, 0, 0, 0, 0, 0, 0, NULL)`. The problem with this was that it would apply the heuristic mapping technique and usually select the default system font in Windows 3.0. But when TrueType was introduced in Windows 3.1, instead of a standard Windows installation having six fonts, it was not uncommon to find a Windows installation with 60 fonts (one of the authors has 350 fonts on one machine). Quite often some other font would be the first font found in the heuristic match the font mapper did, and you might find that on some installations, the status line (for example) would come out in script font, while other text came out in even stranger fonts. You may even find vestiges of this technique if you are porting legacy code. Whenever possible, try to be as specific as possible, down to an explicit typeface name. Otherwise, you won't know what your end user will actually get.

A call to the `CreateFontIndirect` function is much more Spartan, is easier to do correctly, and is more efficient. You pass only one parameter–a pointer to a `LOGFONT` structure. This structure contains 14 fields, one corresponding to each parameter passed to the `CreateFont` function. A call to the `CreateFontIndirect` function typically looks like this:

```
HFONT      hfont ;
LOGFONT    logfont ;

hfont = CreateFontIndirect (&logfont) ;
```

The `CreateFont` and `CreateFontIndirect` functions create a *logical font*, which is, in many ways, your description of the ideal font you want to use. When you select a logical font into a device context by calling the `SelectFont` function (or the lower-level `SelectObject` function), Windows compares the logical font to the actual fonts available for the device and uses the one that matches the logical font most "closely". (The actual comparison is done using different weights for different attributes, and various penalties are assessed for various mismatches.) In this way, logical fonts are similar to logical brushes and pens. The actual font, brush, and pen are chosen based on the capabilities of the device when the GDI object is selected into the device context.

The fields in a LOGFONT structure (and the parameters to the CreateFont function) all have a default value of 0. You can initialize all fields in a LOGFONT structure to 0, create a font based on the structure, select the font into a device context, and receive a usable default font. More often, you'll want to set most fields to 0 and specify nonzero values for only a few fields. Doing this enables Windows to match the logical font to the available fonts for a device with the comparison, taking into account the attributes you consider important without penalizing mismatches on the attributes for which you specify a default value.

The LOGFONT Structure

A LOGFONT structure is defined as follows:

```
typedef struct tagLOGFONT
    {
    int         lfHeight ;
    int         lfWidth ;
    int         lfEscapement ;
    int         lfOrientation ;
    int         lfWeight ;
    BYTE        lfItalic ;
    BYTE        lfUnderline ;
    BYTE        lfStrikeOut ;
    BYTE        lfCharSet ;
    BYTE        lfOutPrecision ;
    BYTE        lfClipPrecision ;
    BYTE        lfQuality ;
    BYTE        lfPitchAndFamily ;
    TCHAR       lfFaceName [LF_FACESIZE] ;
    } LOGFONT;
```

The NEWLOGFONT structure is almost identical:

```
struct tagNEWLOGFONT {                      /* nlf */
    int     lfHeight;
    int     lfWidth;
    int     lfEscapement;
    int     lfOrientation;
    int     lfWeight;
    BYTE    lfItalic;
    BYTE    lfUnderline;
    BYTE    lfStrikeOut;
    BYTE    lfCharSet;
    BYTE    lfOutPrecision;
    BYTE    lfClipPrecision;
    BYTE    lfQuality;
    BYTE    lfPitchAndFamily;
    TCHAR   lfFaceName[LF_FACESIZE];
    TCHAR   lfFullName[2 * LF_FACESIZE]; /* TrueType only */
    TCHAR   lfStyle[LF_FACESIZE];        /* TrueType only */

} NEWLOGFONT;
```

The fields of the LOGFONT structure are interpreted as shown in Table 15.3.

Table 15.3: Fields of the LOGFONT structure

Field	Explanation
lfHeight	This is the desired height of the font in logical units. Hence this value depends on the mapping mode of the device context in which you select the font. When the value is set to 0, GDI arbitrarily searches for a 12-point font. When it is set to a positive number, the number specifies the height of the character cell. (The height of the character cell corresponds to the TEXTMETRIC tmHeight measurement.) When it is set to a negative number, the absolute value of the number specifies the height of a character, not the character cell. Applications that specify font height in points typically set this field to a negative number, as points are a measurement of character height, not cell height. (The height of a character corresponds to the TEXTMETRIC tmHeight minus the tmInternalLeading measurement.)
lfWidth	This is the desired average width of characters in the font in logical units. This value depends on the mapping mode of the device context in which you select the font. When the value is set to 0 (the typical value), GDI searches for the font with the smallest difference between the digitization aspect ratio for the font and the aspect ratio of the device. When you specify a nonzero value, Windows might have to use a font designed for a different aspect ratio in order to honor the request.
lfEscapement	This specifies the angle in tenths of a degree between the line on which characters are written (baseline of a character) and the horizontal axis. The default is 0. It specifies that characters are written horizontally, left-to-right. Setting this value to 900 (90 degrees) requests that characters be written upward. Values of 1800 (180 degrees) and 2700 (270 degrees) request that characters be written right-to-left and downward, respectively.
lfOrientation	This specifies the orientation of the character. • The field is ignored for TrueType fonts. • GDI stroke (vector) fonts use the lfOrientation field when the escapement is a multiple of 90 degrees. For these fonts, the field specifies the angle, in tenths of a degree, between the baseline of a character and the horizontal axis, measured counterclockwise from the horizontal axis. The value 0 specifies that the character is written with its baseline parallel to the horizontal axis, right side up. A value of 1800 specifies that a character is written with its baseline parallel to the horizontal axis, but upside down. Values of 900 and 2700 specify that the character is rotated 90 degrees (lying on its back) or 270 degrees (lying on its front). • Some devices can rotate characters, but many cannot. Some devices can rotate only in multiples of 90 degrees. You should call the GetDeviceCaps function with the TEXTCAPS index to determine a device's capabilities. If the TC_CR_90 bit is set, the device can do rotations of 90 degrees. If the TC_CR_ANY bit is set, the device can rotate the characters by an arbitrary amount.

Table 15.3: Fields of the LOGFONT structure

Field	Explanation
lfWeight	This is the font weight in *inked pixels* per 1,000. The field can be set to any integer value between 0 and 1,000. Typical values are 400 for a normal font and 700 for a bold font. The following font weight symbolic names are defined in the windows.h header file:

Symbolic name	Value
FW_DONTCARE	0
FW_THIN	100
FW_EXTRALIGHT	200
FW_ULTRALIGHT	200
FW_LIGHT	300
FW_NORMAL	400
FW_REGULAR	400
FW_MEDIUM	500
FW_SEMIBOLD	600
FW_DEMIBOLD	600
FW_BOLD	700
FW_EXTRABOLD	800
FW_ULTRABOLD	800
FW_BLACK	900
FW_HEAVY	900

Field	Explanation
lfItalic	A nonzero value specifies an italic font. GDI can synthesize an italic font from a GDI font. You must call the GetDeviceCaps function and specify the TEXTCAPS index to determine whether a device can italicize a device font. When the TC_IA_ABLE bit is set in the returned value, the device can italicize characters.
lfUnderline	A nonzero value specifies an underlined font. GDI can synthesize an underlined font from a GDI font. You must call the GetDeviceCaps function and specify the TEXTCAPS index to determine whether a device can underline a device font. When the TC_UA_ABLE bit is set in the returned value, the device can underline characters.

Table 15.3: Fields of the LOGFONT structure

Field	Explanation
lfStrikeOut	A nonzero value specifies a strikeout font. GDI can synthesize a strikeout font from a GDI font. You must call the GetDeviceCaps function and specify the TEXTCAPS index to determine whether a device can underline a device font. When the TC_SO_ABLE bit is set in the returned value, the device can create strikeout characters.
lfCharSet	This specifies the font's character set. A 0 value requests the ANSI character set. The following character set symbolic names are defined in the windows.h header file (those marked with [4] apply only to API level 4):

ANSI_CHARSET	
ARABIC_CHARSET[4]	
BALTIC_CHARSET[4]	
CHINESEBIG5_CHARSET	
DEFAULT_CHARSET	The DEFAULT_CHARSET value is not used by the font mapper. You specify this value when you want the font name and size to fully describe the logical font. You must be careful when using this value. If the specified font name does not exist, GDI can substitute a font in any character set.
EASTEUROPE_CHARSET[4]	
GB2312_CHARSET	
GREEK_CHARSET[4]	
HANGEUL_CHARSET	
HEBREW_CHARSET[4]	
JOHAB_CHARSET[4]	
MAC_CHARSET[4]	
OEM_CHARSET	
RUSSIAN_CHARSET[4]	
SHIFTJIS_CHARSET	
SYMBOL_CHARSET	
THAI_CHARSET[4]	
TURKISH_CHARSET[4]	

Table 15.3: Fields of the LOGFONT structure

Field	Explanation	
lfOutPrecision	This specifies how closely GDI must match the requested font with an available font for a device when comparing the fonts' heights, widths, escapements, orientations, and pitches. This value controls how the font mapper chooses a font when more than one font has the specified name. When you ask for a font that has a given name, there may be a device font with that name, a raster font with that name, and a TrueType font with that name. The following output precision symbolic names are defined in the windows.h header file:	
	OUT_CHARACTER_PRECIS	Obsolete.
	OUT_DEFAULT_PRECIS	Font choice does not matter.
	OUT_DEVICE_PRECIS	Choose the device font whenever possible.
	OUT_RASTER_PRECIS	Choose a raster font whenever possible.
	OUT_STRING_PRECIS	Not used by the font mapper, but can be returned during font enumerations.
	OUT_STROKE_PRECIS	Choose a stroke (vector) font whenever possible. Not used by the font mapper in Windows NT, but can be returned during font enumerations.
	OUT_TT_PRECIS	Choose a TrueType font whenever possible.
	OUT_TT_ONLY_PRECIS	Choose a TrueType font, even when the face name matches a raster or vector font.
lfClipPrecision	This specifies how to clip characters that are partly outside of the clipping region. The following clipping precision symbolic names are defined in the windows.h header file:	
	CLIP_CHARACTER_PRECIS	Obsolete.
	CLIP_DEFAULT_PRECIS	Clipping precision does not matter.
	CLIP_EMBEDDED	You must specify the CLIP_EMBEDDED value to use an embedded read-only TrueType font.

Table 15.3: Fields of the LOGFONT structure

Field	Explanation
	CLIP_LH_ANGLES — Fonts do not always rotate in the same direction when you do not combine the CLIP_LH_ANGLES value with any of the other clip precision values. Normally (that is, when the CLIP_LH_ANGLES bit is not set), device fonts always rotate counterclockwise. The rotation of other types of fonts depends on whether the orientation of the coordinate system is left-handed or right-handed. Setting the CLIP_LH_ANGLES bit causes all fonts to depend on the orientation of the coordinate system.
	CLIP_MASK — Not used.
	CLIP_STROKE_PRECIS — Not used by the font mapper, but may be returned during font enumerations.
	CLIP_TT_ALWAYS — Not used.
lfQuality	This specifies how GDI attempts to match the logical font to an available physical font. Three symbolic names are defined in Windows.h:
	DEFAULT_QUALITY — Specifies that the appearance of the font does not matter.
	DRAFT_QUALITY — Permits GDI to scale a GDI font, if necessary. For a raster font, this choice may result in a font with a coarse appearance and, therefore, a lower quality than font obtained via PROOF_QUALITY. GDI synthesizes bold, italic, strikeout, and underlined fonts, if necessary.
	PROOF_QUALITY — Prevents GDI from scaling a GDI raster font. The font nearest to but not larger than the requested size is chosen. This results in characters with the best possible appearance, but they might be smaller than what was requested. GDI synthesizes bold, italic, strikeout, and underlined fonts, if necessary.
lfPitchAndFamily	This specifies the pitch and the family for the font. The low-order two bits indicate the pitch of the font, and the high-order four bits indicate the font family. You can use one of the following symbolic names to specify the pitch:

Table 15.3: Fields of the LOGFONT structure

Field	Explanation		
	Symbolic Name	**Description (Windows Font)**	
	DEFAULT_PITCH	Don't care.	
	FIXED_PITCH	Fixed-pitch font requested.	
	VARIABLE_PITCH	Variable-pitch font requested.	

It is possible to request a variable-pitch font and receive a fixed-pitch font. Although the GDI font-mapping scheme penalizes such a choice, a fixed-pitch font might be the best selection available. However, when you request a fixed-pitch font, variable-pitch fonts are assessed a far greater penalty because the application probably doesn't handle variable-pitch fonts properly. It's less likely that GDI would choose a variable-pitch font when you request a fixed-pitch font than it is that GDI would choose a fixed-pitch font in response to a variable-pitch font request.

Field	Explanation		
lfPitchAndFamily *(continued)*	The font family describes the general appearance of the font. You specify a family when you want a certain appearance for the characters but don't care which exact typeface is used. The windows.h header file contains the following symbolic names for font families. You combine these with the pitch values described just above by using the bitwise OR (|) operator. They correspond to the five families described at the beginning of this chapter:		
	Symbolic Name	**Description**	**Sample Font**
	FF_DECORATIVE	Novelty font.	Old English, WingDings
	FF_DONTCARE	Don't care.	N/A
	FF_MODERN	Modern fonts have a constant character spacing and may or may not have serifs.	Pica, Elite, Courier New
	FF_ROMAN	Roman fonts have variable character spacing and serifs.	Times New Roman, New Century SchoolBook
	FF_SCRIPT	Script fonts resemble handwriting.	Script, Cursive
	FF_SWISS	Swiss fonts have variable character spacing and are sans serif.	MS Sans Serif, Arial

Table 15.3: Fields of the LOGFONT structure

Field	Explanation
	You should select one symbolic name for the pitch and one symbolic name for the font family, join them together by using the Boolean OR operator, and assign the result to this field.
lfFaceName	This field contains a NUL-terminated string that specifies the desired typeface. When the NULL string is specified (when the first character is 0), GDI chooses a device-dependent default typeface. This is a character array LF_FACESIZE characters in length; therefore the string cannot exceed LF_FACESIZE -1 characters.

The Font-matching Scheme

When you select a logical font into a device context, GDI matches the description of the logical font against each available font for the device. Each font is assigned a penalty that equals all the weighted penalties for each attribute of the font that does not match the requested value. GDI chooses the font with the smallest penalty. When two fonts have the same smallest penalty (because the penalty might consist of different components for each font even though the sum is equal), GDI chooses the font that has the greatest number of certain attributes in common with the logical font. Basically, GDI attempts to choose the font that has the fewest differences from the requested logical font. However, it's more important for certain attributes to match than it is for others.

Penalties are weighted. Some penalties are so severe that any font matching the corresponding attribute is chosen over all fonts that do not match the attribute. Penalties are assessed as described in the following paragraphs. We've listed the attributes in descending order of importance and weighted penalty. Normally, no penalty is assessed when a DEFAULT_* (0) value is used for an attribute.

There are two exceptions to this rule:

1. The lfCharSet field of the LOGFONT structure is the most important attribute when matching fonts. Because the ANSI_CHARSET symbolic name is defined as 0, however, setting this field to 0 (which normally requests the default for an attribute) is equivalent to explicitly requesting the ANSI character set. You should use the DEFAULT_CHARSET value only when you specify the name and size of an existing font.

2. The three stroke fonts provided with Windows 3.0 (Modern, Roman, and Script) are marked as belonging to the OEM character set, but they actually contain characters from the ANSI character set. They are deliberately mismarked so that GDI chooses a stroke font in preference to a raster font only as a last resort. These fonts appear in Win32 only for compatibility with legacy applications.

Suppose you request an ANSI font in a specific size and either you specify a raster font or the only possible matches are all raster fonts, but no such raster font is available. GDI will choose a smaller raster font that can be scaled to a size near the requested size over a stroke font that can be scaled to any size. This is because raster fonts typically use the ANSI character set, and the penalty for mismatched character sets is far greater than that assessed for mismatched character sizes. You must specify OEM_CHARSET when you want a GDI stroke font.

Typically, you will use TrueType fonts rather than stroke fonts. TrueType fonts offer better scaling and rotation capabilities that do stroke fonts. They also look better. It is rare to encounter a font other than a True-Type font in Win32, aside from the few exceptions we've already discussed.

Setting the lfPitchAndFamily field to FIXED_PITCH isn't as important as the proper character set, but it's far more important than any of the other attributes. When you ask for a fixed-pitch font, GDI probably will choose a font with the requested character set, a fixed pitch, and all other attributes mismatched in preference to a font with the requested character set, a variable-pitch font, and all other attributes exactly as requested. This is a result of the assumption that an application that requests a fixed-pitch font probably doesn't properly display text in a variable-pitch font.

The lfFaceName field is next in importance. Suppose you specify a typeface and a font in that typeface is available in the requested character set (and it has a fixed pitch that also was requested) but all other attributes don't match. GDI probably will choose that font over other fonts that match all other attributes but fail to match the requested typeface name. You should always specify a value for the lfFaceName field.

Somewhat less important than the lfFaceName attribute is the lfFamily attribute. This attribute is considered when a NULL string is specified for lfFaceName (when no explicit typeface is requested) and the lfFamily field is set to a value other than FF_DONTCARE (when an explicit typeface family is requested). A font that has a matching character set, fixed pitch (if specified), a NULL typeface string, and an explicit family requested, but no other attributes that match, is more likely to be chosen over a font that belongs to a different family that matches all other attributes.

Next, GDI compares the requested height (lfHeight—which should always be specified) of a font against the size of a font after it has been scaled. The weights are such that GDI chooses a smaller font than requested and scales it up in size rather than choosing a larger font than requested and using it as is. Generally, you receive a font larger than requested only when there is no smaller font. When you request PROOF_QUALITY, however, a font slightly larger than requested might be chosen in preference over a font much smaller than requested. This is because requesting PROOF_QUALITY prevents GDI from scaling a smaller raster font. Since TrueType fonts scale continuously, this rule applies only to raster fonts.

Matching a fixed-pitch font when a variable-pitch font is requested results in a penalty. This penalty lies between that assessed for choosing a font with a smaller height than requested and that for choosing a font with a greater height than requested. Basically, when a variable-pitch font is desired, GDI is more likely to choose a smaller-than-requested fixed-pitch font over a larger-than-requested variable-pitch font.

The width of the font is less important than its height. A small penalty is assessed, but generally it is less than the penalty for mismatched height and the penalty for a fixed-pitch font when a variable-pitch font is requested. Typically, you specify a width only to deliberately request a font designed for a device with a different aspect ratio.

GDI assesses a modest penalty when scaling of either the height or width of a font is required. However, a relatively substantial penalty is assessed when a font must be scaled both vertically and horizontally. The greater the difference between the scaling factors for the height and width, the greater the penalty.

Differing font weights are assessed a small penalty, but it generally isn't significant compared to the penalties just discussed.

Lack of italics assesses an even smaller penalty. Although GDI can synthesize an italic font from a GDI-based font, a real italic font is preferred when one is available.

Finally, strikeout and underlining mismatches are assessed small penalties, for the same reason given for the italic penalty.

When all penalties are summed, two fonts might have the same total penalty, but due to different factors. GDI selects the font of the two that does not have the following penalties (listed in order from most severe to least severe): italic synthesis required, bold synthesis required, strikeout synthesis required, underline synthesis required, vertical scaling required, and horizontal scaling required.

Generally, if you specify a TrueType face name and a height, you will almost always get an exact match. However, if the font does not exist on the machine at the time the `CreateFont` call is made, these rules are applied in an attempt to locate the best-match font.

Getting Information about a Font

From the preceding discussion, you can likely see that the font you receive when you select a logical font in a device context might differ greatly in some ways from the font you requested. You might want to call the `GetTextMetrics` function to find out the attributes of the font you actually received.

However, you don't need to worry about receiving a different-than-expected font when you create a font based on the logical-font information returned by a call to the `EnumFontFamilies` function. When you select such a font into the device context specified when enumerating the fonts, you receive exactly the font described by the `LOGFONT` structure. GDI still performs the font-matching procedure, but the logical font description exactly matches an available font, so the desired font is used. After all, the `EnumFontFamilies` function initialized the `LOGFONT` structure to describe an available font exactly.

Once you have created the font, you may want to select it into a device context later. At that time, you may need to inquire about its various parameters or get information about text that would be rendered in the selected font. Functions for these purposes are shown in Table 15.4. We discuss only some of them here; the rest are either very simple or very special-purpose. For example, the `GetAspectRatioFilterEx` function is useful only on displays with "nonsquare" pixels, such as the CGA and EGA displays. This was important at one time in the history of Windows, but both types of displays are obsolete and are not even supported under Win32. This function is retained for those unusual displays that may have nonsquare pixels, but we've not seen any in modern times. The `GetFontData` function is used to get font information when you have to embed a TrueType font in a document so that it can print at some remote site. Discussing this concept is well beyond the scope of this book, since it almost always applies to OLE-based compound documents, a topic which by itself can barely be covered in an entire book the size of this one. The `GetCharacterPlacement` function looks useful, but it has a huge number of options that apply only to non-Latin languages, a topic beyond the expertise of either author. We have a special `GetCharacterPlacement` explorer in Font Explorer just so you can experiment yourself.

Table 15.4: Font and character information functions

Result	Function	Parameters and Explanation
BOOL	GetAspectRatioFilterEx	(HDC dc, LPSIZE aspectratio)
		Returns the aspect ratio of pixels on the screen. "Square" pixels will return the same values for cx and cy.
BOOL	GetCharABCWidths	(HDC dc, UINT firstchar, UINT lastchar, LPABC abc)
		Returns in the abc object or array the A, B, and C widths of the characters in the range firstchar to lastchar.
BOOL	GetCharABCWidthsFloat[NT]	(HDC dc, UINT firstchar, UINT lastchar, LPABCFLOAT abcf)
		Returns in the abcf object or array the A, B, and C widths of the characters, in floating point, in the range firstchar to lastchar.
DWORD	GetCharacterPlacement[4,x]	(HDC dc, LPCTSTR string, int count, int maxextent, LPGCP_RESULTS * results, DWORD flags)
		Retrieves information about a character string, including character widths, caret positioning, ordering, and glyph rendering.
BOOL	GetCharWidth32	(HDC dc, UINT firstchar, UINT lastchar, LPINT buffer)
		Returns, in the array referenced by buffer, the widths of all characters in the range.
BOOL	GetCharWidth[NT]	(HDC dc, UINT firstchar, UINT lastchar, LPINT buffer)
		Obsolete; use GetCharWidth32.

[4]Available only in Win32 API 4 and higher.
[NT]Available only in Windows NT.

Table 15.4: Font and character information functions

Result	Function	Parameters and Explanation
BOOL	GetCharWidthFloat	(HDC dc, UINT firstchar, UINT lastchar, PFLOAT buffer)
		Returns the widths of the characters in the range firstchar to lastchar, as floating-point values.
DWORD	GetFontData	(HDC dc, DWORD table, DWORD offset, LPVOID buffer, DWORD count)
		Retrieves the description of a TrueType font. Usually used to save the font as part of a document.
DWORD	GetFontLanguageInfo[4]	(HDC dc)
		Returns information describing characteristics of the currently selected font. If the return value is 0, the font is a "normal" Latin font.
DWORD	GetGlyphOutline	(HDC dc, UINT char, LPGLYPHMETRICS gm, DWORD count, LPVOID buffer, CONST MAT2 * mat2)
		Returns the detailed font outline description. Usually used by applications that need to do very fancy font rendering, for example, producing 3-D display fonts from ordinary fonts.
DWORD	GetKerningPairs	(HDC dc, DWORD numpairs, LPKERNINGPAIR pairs)
		Returns the number of kerning pairs if pairs is NULL; otherwise, fills the pairs array with all the kerning pairs for the font.
UINT	GetOutlineTextMetrics	(HDC dc, UINT count, LPOUTLINETEXTMETRIC otm)
		Returns in the parameter specified by otm the outline text metrics. Since this is a variable-length structure, you must call it first with otm set to NULL to get the length of the buffer required.
BOOL	GetRasterizerCaps	(LPRASTERIZER_STATUS status, UINT count)
		Returns in status an indication of whether TrueType fonts are installed.

[4]Available only in Win32 API 4 and higher.
[NT]Available only in Windows NT.

Table 15.4: Font and character information functions

Result	Function	Parameters and Explanation
DWORD	GetTabbedTextExtent	`(HDC dc, LPCTSTR string, int count,` `int tabcount, LPINT positions)`
		Given a number of tab positions and a string that contains tabs, computes the text extent of the string when tabs are expanded according to the tabs in the `positions` array.
int	GetTextCharExtra	`(HDC dc)`
		Retrieves the intercharacter spacing, also known as "track kerning".
BOOL	GetTextExtentExPoint	`(HDC dc, LPCTSTR str, int charcount,` `int maxextent, LPINT fit, LPINT dx, LPSIZE size)`
		Returns information about the partial string extents.
BOOL	GetTextExtentPoint	`(HDC dc, LPCTSTR str, int count, LPSIZE size)`
		Obsolete; use GetTextExtentPoint32.
BOOL	GetTextExtentPoint32	`(HDC dc, LPCTSTR str, int count, LPSIZE size)`
		Computes the width and height, in logical units, of the specified string.
int	GetTextFace	`(HDC dc, int count, LPTSTR buffer)`
		Retrieves the face name of the currently selected font.
BOOL	GetTextMetrics	`(HDC dc, LPTEXTMETRIC tm)`
		Returns the text metrics for the current font selected in the DC. These include the font height and internal leading, among other parameters.
DWORD	SetMapperFlags	`(HDC dc, DWORD flags)`
		Specifies whether the font mapper should try to match a font's aspect ratio. Returns the previous value of the mapper flags.
int	SetTextCharacterExtra	`(HDC dc, int extra)`
		Sets the intercharacter spacing, "track kerning," to the specified number of logical units.

[4]Available only in Win32 API 4 and higher.
[NT]Available only in Windows NT.

We've used the `GetTextMetrics` function in earlier examples in this book to retrieve information about character sizes. The `GetTextMetrics` function returns information about characters in the current font of the specified device context. Similarly, the `GetTextExtentPoint32` function returns the height and width of a character string based on the currently selected font. You must select the desired font into a device context before calling these two functions to return information about characters in that font.

The `GetTextFace` function copies the typeface name of the selected font into a specified buffer. In this typical function call, the `hdc` parameter specifies the device context, the `Count` parameter specifies the buffer length, and the `FaceName` parameter is a pointer to a buffer:

```
int Chars ;

Chars = GetTextFace (hdc, Count, FaceName) ;
```

The `GetTextMetrics` function initializes a `TEXTMETRIC` structure with metrics about the font currently selected in a device context. Many of the structure's fields correspond to fields in the original `LOGFONT` structure. The fields in the `TEXTMETRIC` structure, however, contain the values for the chosen font. These can differ from the values you requested in the `LOGFONT` structure. The `TEXTMETRIC` structure is described in much more detail in Chapter 4.

 A bug in Windows 3.0 and carried forward for compatibility caused the `GetTextMetrics` function to return the `tmDigitizedAspectX` value in the `tmDigitizedAspectY` field and vice versa. If you are porting esoteric legacy code, you may run into this. However, the `TEXTMETRIC` structure passed to the `EnumFontFamilies` callback function has the `tmDigitizedAspectX` and `tmDigitizedAspectY` values placed in the correct fields. That is, the `GetTextMetrics` function returns these values swapped, but the `EnumFontFamilies` function returns them properly.

All size values in the `TEXTMETRIC` structure are in logical units, except for the `tmDigitizedAspectX` and `tmDigitizedAspectY` fields, which represent a dimensionless ratio. All size values in a `NEWTEXTMETRIC` are in logical units, except for the aspect fields, as in the `TEXTMETRIC`, and the new fields shown in Table 15.5, which are in "notional units". A TrueType font is defined according to an internal coordinate system that is used to describe the points and vectors for each glyph. By default, a TrueType font is defined in a 2048×2048 coordinate system. The TrueType font rendering engine maps this font coordinate system, in which the coordinates are in *notional units*, to the device coordinates, using the logical font size, the current mapping mode, the transformation matrix, and other characteristics of the DC.

The `NEWTEXTMETRIC` is the same as the `TEXTMETRIC` structure, but it is passed into the enumeration function only for TrueType fonts. The `NEWTEXTMETRIC` structure is defined as shown in Figure 15.9, where the highlighted structure members are identical to those of the `TEXTMETRIC` structure.

Kerning

Kerning is a technique by which the space between characters is adjusted. Kerning may be done to adjust the line width or, more commonly, to give a more pleasing appearance. A character has a property, its *bounding box,* which is the smallest rectangle that encloses all the pixels that make up that character. In terms of hand-set

```
typedef struct tagNEWTEXTMETRIC
    {
    LONG  tmHeight;
    LONG  tmAscent;
    LONG  tmDescent;
    LONG  tmInternalLeading;
    LONG  tmExternalLeading;
    LONG  tmAveCharWidth;
    LONG  tmMaxCharWidth;
    LONG  tmWeight;
    LONG  tmOverhang;
    LONG  tmDigitizedAspectX;
    LONG  tmDigitizedAspectY;
    WCHAR tmFirstChar;
    WCHAR tmLastChar;
    WCHAR tmDefaultChar;
    WCHAR tmBreakChar;
    BYTE  tmItalic;
    BYTE  tmUnderlined;
    BYTE  tmStruckOut;
    BYTE  tmPitchAndFamily;
    BYTE  tmCharSet;

    DWORD ntmFlags;              // NEWTEXTMETRIC
    UINT  ntmSizeEM;
    UINT  ntmCellHeight;
    UINT  ntmAvgWidth;

    } NEWTEXTMETRIC, * PNEWTEXTMETRIC,
                     * LPNEWTEXTMETRIC;
```

Figure 15.9: NEWTEXTMETRIC structure

lead type, the bounding box corresponds to the smallest size a rectangular type slug can be and still enclose the actual character glyph. Early typesetting, both hand-set lead and electronic, placed a character, moved forward by the bounding box distance (implicit in lead type), and then placed the next character. In a "hot-lead" Lino-Type machine, the slugs could then be spread apart by *wedges* to achieve flush-right line justification. Two types of wedges were used: *intraword* and *interword*. Wedges were arranged mechanically so that spaces tended to appear wider between words; but in some cases, the letters would be spread as well. In such a system, kerning could increase spacing, but never decrease it. In very special cases, type slugs for hand-set type could be cast with the character actually overhanging the body of the slug. This would allow two characters to overlap.

Table 15.5: Additional fields of the NEWTEXTMETRIC structure

Field	Description
ntmFlags	Specifies the nature of the font. It can be any combination of the following bits:
	0x00000001 Italic

Table 15.5: Additional fields of the NEWTEXTMETRIC structure

Field	Description	
	0x00000002	Underscore
	0x00000004	Negative
	0x00000008	Outline
	0x00000010	Strikeout
	0x00000020	Bold
ntmSizeEM	The size of an "em square" for the font. This is expressed in "notional units," the units for which the font was defined.	
ntmCellHeight	The height of the font in notional units.	
ntmAvgWidth	The average width of the font in notional units.	

All other fields of the NEWTEXTMETRIC structure are identical to those of the TEXTMETRIC structure.

The effect of bounding box placement can be either visually pleasing or disturbing. We read text more readily if the visual "whitespace" between characters is approximately equal. For example, the space between two vertical characters such as "MN" represents a certain area of whitespace. But if we place characters like "AV" or "A.V.", the *apparent* whitespace between the two characters is much wider. Typographers worry very much about such details. The appearance, and elegance, of a typeface often depends critically on the relationship of whitespace to black space in intraword spacing. Typography is a centuries-old skill, and the art of letter forms is thousands of years old, so this relationship has been studied intensely. Reading is often our primary means of communication. The choice of font often determines the comfort (and sometimes even the effectiveness) of communication. Fonts that are too small, too crowded, or too widely spaced, or that fail in some other way to meet these rather subtle aesthetic criteria can lead to the user experiencing fatigue, interpretation of the text being subject to error, and other degradation of the communication supposedly embodied by the text. Typography is ultimately an art form that combines pragmatism with aesthetics.

To deal with one of the many issues of overall document appearance, the concept of *kerning* was introduced. There are two kinds of kerning: *pair*, which defines the relationship between two adjacent characters and depends on the actual character glyphs, and *track*, which is a constant amount of space added between all characters, much like the hot-lead LinoType machine we just described. The goal of kerning is to maintain a balance of whitespace and black space along the line of printing. If you want to produce "visually optimal" output, you will want to be aware of what kerning can do for you.

TrueType and ABC Widths

Most TrueType fonts implicitly use a simplistic approximation to pair kerning. This approach contributes to their good appearance while allowing Windows to display them quickly. It also means that you can get very

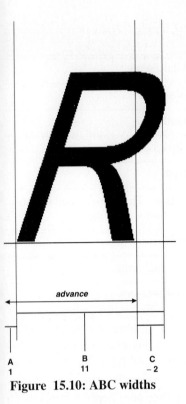

A   B   C
1   11   – 2

Figure 15.10: ABC widths

good output without having to do any kerning yourself, as the system will do the kerning for you. Generally, you will not need to look at the details of kerning unless you are doing something special with type; for example, working with headlines, large signs, and other uses that emphasize character spacing. In writing applications that require good visual appearance, such as in the aforementioned cases, you will want to do more precise kerning.

The approximate pair kerning of TrueType fonts is based on a set of values called the "ABC widths". These are illustrated in Figure 15.10. The A width is an offset from the nominal start of the character position to the start of the black space defining the character. The B width defines the vertical borders of the bounding box of the glyph. The C width is the distance between the rightmost edge of the glyph and the nominal end of the character. Note that as shown in the figure, either the A or C widths can be negative. The character shown is from the 10-point Arial Narrow font. The *advance width* is the distance the character advances the character position. It is equal to the B width plus the A and C widths. The advance width of the character shown is 10 units.

When a string is drawn with one of the output operations, such as TextOut, the character starts at the position given by the coordinates to the text output operation (either implicit or explicit). After the character is drawn, the logical coordinates are advanced by the advance width and the resulting logical coordinates are where the next character starts.

Note the implication of this: If you have a character with a negative A width and you start drawing it at position (0, 0) in a window with default coordinates, the left edge of the character will be clipped by the left edge of your window. If you have chosen your window width to be exactly the string width and the last character in the string has a negative C width, the right-most character will be clipped by the right edge of the window.

One way to avoid this is provided by built-in controls, such as the Static controls. These controls are created from a class that has the CS_PARENTDC flag set. This flag causes the clipping region of the control to be set to the clipping region of the parent window. Thus small errors in the computations of fonts, which also can happen as a consequence of pixel roundoff error for small fonts, will not clip one or two pixels from the beginning or end of the string.

However, your application may need to be more precise. In particular, if you are writing an application that is producing large letters, the clipping may ultimately be done by the printer, which cannot print any pixels outside its physical margins. Having the freedom of not being clipped by the window doesn't matter; you'll lose the left or right edges of your characters. Here you need to use the ABC width information.

The Font Explorer program has a special dialog just to let you play with kerning; it is called the Kerning Explorer. One thing we learned in writing the Font Explorer was to avoid using fonts scaled by the mapping

Much of the documentation of the CS_PARENTDC incorrectly states that it causes the window to inherit the device context of its parent. This is not true; it inherits the clipping region of its parent. This documentation error, which has been pervasive in much of the Windows literature, is pointed out by the Knowledge Base article Q111005.

modes, that is, mapping modes such as MM_ISOTROPIC, which is what we used to implement the large character displays of the Font Explorer. TrueType fonts scale well from an aesthetic viewpoint. This means that the hints provided result in nonlinear scalings, particularly at very large and very small sizes. When we scaled the fonts for display, we discovered that the nonlinear scaling often resulted in apparent misplacements and overhangs. If you work with the Kerning Explorer, remember that the various numbers we show for small fonts represent how those fonts will be rendered in MM_TEXT mode (in fact, we carefully go out of our way to make sure this is done correctly). But when they are rendered in magnified mode, you'll see how the nonlinearities affect the fonts. To eliminate these nonlinearities, you can choose larger font sizes, which get scaled less and thus will show you more accurate representations.

All of Font Explorer uses MM_TEXT mapping mode for its computations. The ABC widths, however, will change in nonlinear ways with larger point sizes. You can use Font Explorer to choose different point sizes and then look at the ABC widths.

If you want to properly place a font, use the GetCharABCWidths API function to get the ABC width values of the first character of the string. You can then advance your starting horizontal position either by the negative of the A width, or alternatively by the negative of the A width only if the A width is negative. This will guarantee that you don't lose the left edge of the first character. Code to do this is shown in Listing 15.1. This code assumes that you have not created the window hwnd with the CS_PARENTDC class style. In this example, the HDC parameter has the desired font selected into it. We can't depend on that font being a TrueType font, but the GetCharABCWidths will return FALSE if the font does not support the ABC parameters. Be careful. If the function returns FALSE, the ABC structure is not modified and will therefore contain whatever random values were found on the stack. An example of one workaround we do in Font Explorer is shown in Listing 15.2.

Listing 15.1: Computing correct starting position
```
void drawString(HWND hwnd, HDC dc, LPCTSTR str)
    {
     ABC abc;
     RECT r;
     GetClientRect(hwnd, &r);
     if(GetCharABCWidths(dc, str[0], str[0], &abc))
        { /* TrueType font */
         r.left -= abc.abcC;
        } /* TrueType font */
      TextOut(dc, r.left, r.top, str);
    }
```

Listing 15.2: Handling non-TrueType fonts
```
void wnd_OnPaint(HWND hwnd)
```

```
    {
    ABC abc;
    LPCTSTR str;
    PAINTSTRUCT ps;
    HDC dc = BeginPaint(hwnd, &ps);
    // Get the string into str
    // Select the desired font into the dc

    if(!GetCharABCWidths(dc, str[0], str[0], &abc))
        { /* not TrueType */
         SIZE sz;
         abc.abcA = abc.abcC = 0;
         GetTextExtentPoint32(dc, str, 1, &sz);
         abc.abcB = sz.cx;
        } /* not TrueType */
    // ...
    //
    // Use variable 'abc' values here (doesn't matter
    // if font was TrueType or not)
    // ...
    EndPaint(hwnd, &ps);
    }
```

Pair Kerning

Because of the choices of ABC widths, TrueType fonts that are displayed by the operations such as TextOut will use the advance width to place the characters. Doing this will cause those characters with negative A or C widths (such as italic fonts) to implicitly kern. However, this is not the same as the precise kerning that takes into consideration the relationship of the shapes of two adjacent characters. For advanced typography, the simplistic kerning done by TrueType is not adequate. However, TrueType fonts encode *pair kerning data*. This is information that you can use to do precise pair kerning. It comes in two forms: either integer or floating-point (currently floating-point is supported only under Windows NT). The floating-point representations are intended to handle even more precise kerning information by being able to represent abstract "fraction pixels". Font Explorer will show you the floating-point pairs. However, what we've seen so far indicates that the floating-point kerning is currently the same value as the integer kerning; but then we haven't looked at all fonts in all sizes.

To obtain the pair kerning information, you must use the GetKerningPairs function. This function requires that you have a buffer large enough to hold all the kerning pairs for a font; it won't return a partial set of kerning pairs. The usual way this is handled is shown in Listing 15.3. This function returns either an array of KERNINGPAIR information or NULL. A NULL value could mean the allocation failed. It also could mean that the font is not a TrueType font or it is a TrueType font with no kerning data. You must always be prepared to deal with non-TrueType fonts in your application.

A KERNINGPAIR structure is shown next:

```
typedef struct tagKERNINGPAIR {
    WORD wFirst;
    WORD wSecond;
    int  iKernAmount;
} KERNINGPAIR, *LPKERNINGPAIR;
```

The words wFirst and wSecond represent the first and second characters of a pair. Not all pairs of characters have kerning data; in this case, you assume a kerning value of 0. Once you've obtained the kerning pair list, you can see if the character pair of interest is in the list. Do this by searching the array for an entry wFirst equal to your first character and wSecond equal to your second character. If you find such an entry, the iKernAmount is the amount to add (it is usually negative) to your current character position to obtain a new character position. These values are always expressed in logical units and are relative to the currently selected font in the dc parameter of the GetKerningPairs function. Thus, if you select a new font into the DC, you must get new kerning pair data for formatting text. This is true even if the font is the same font but in a different size. If you had an 18-point font and now have a 36-point font, you can't get the correct kerning data by multiplying all the existing data by 2. This is because of the nonlinear scaling. If you have kerning data for a display, you can't use it to format for a printer.

You may even notice that your text when displayed is not quite "right", particularly in smaller font sizes. Some characters may appear to be a little further apart than others, while some might appear jammed together. Yet, when you print your text, it looks quite good. This is because the resolution of the display is close to the "feature size" of the characters being displayed. Features such as serifs and thin lines may be only 1 pixel wide. The roundoff considerations and hints of the TrueType rendering algorithm work hard to make sure these small features don't disappear to zero-pixel features. This effort may result in a 1-pixel error in the positioning, which on a screen is quite obvious (a 1-pixel error in an 8-pixel-wide character is a significant misplacement). But on a 300 dpi or 600 dpi printer, characters can be more precisely positioned and the features more precisely controlled, so the output looks much better. A 1-pixel error may represent $1/300$th, $1/600$th, or even $1/2400$th of an inch, which is much harder to see. Publication-quality typography, such as this book you are holding, is done on devices capable of 1200 to 2400 dpi resolution. For devices like these, precise pair kerning is not only possible but highly desirable in order to maintain a quality appearance. Pair kerning can be seen using the Font Explorer, as shown in Figure 15.12.

Listing 15.3: GetKerningPairs function

```
LPKERNINGPAIR getpairs(HDC dc)
    {
    int count = GetKerningPairs(dc, 0, NULL);
    LPKERNINGPAIR pairs;

    if(count == 0)
       return NULL;
    // allocate a buffer.  Caller is responsible for
    // freeing it when done
    pairs = (LPKERNINGPAIR)malloc(count * sizeof(KERNINGPAIR));
    if(pairs == NULL)
       return NULL;
    GetKerningPairs(dc, count, pairs);
    return pairs;
    }
```

Track Kerning

Another form of kerning occasionally used is *track kerning*. This form of kerning introduces a constant amount of space between each letter, very similar to the hot-lead LinoType machine we described earlier. It is most often used when formatting narrow columns, where long words that don't hyphenate would result in huge gaps if the only justification algorithm were to expand interword spacing. Figure 15.11 illustrates the effects of no track kerning, positive track kerning (expanded spacing), and negative track kerning (compressed spacing) on such text. As you can see, even very small amounts of negative kerning usually result in very difficult-to-read text, while relatively large amounts of positive kerning are still acceptable. You can set the intercharacter spacing before writing text by calling the `SetTextCharacterExtra` function before writing the string in the DC. The text output functions will automatically add the specified amount of intercharacter spacing between each character, so you don't need to do it for every character. However, this works well only when the logical units are fairly small. You might use it directly on a printer in `MM_TEXT` mapping mode, but for a display, you need a higher resolution than `MM_TEXT`, such as `MM_TWIPS`, `MM_HIENGLISH`, `MM_HIMETRIC`, or `MM_ISOTROPIC` with a large magnification factor. The ultimate rendering, however, will be constrained by your display resolution and consequently may produce irregularities when the logical units are mapped to pixels.

Kerning Type	Effect
With interword justification only	Using the `GetAmazingInformation` function, ambitious programmers can do wondrous things.
With positive track kerning of letters	Using the `GetAmazingInformation` func- tion, ambitious programmers can do wondrous things.
With negative track kerning of letters	Using the `GetAmazingInformation` function, ambitious programmers can do wondrous things.

Figure 15.11: Illustration of track kerning

In the Font Explorer, we implement track kerning manually; you may want to read the `OnPaint` handler in the file `FontDisp.cpp`. Like most of the explorers, Font Explorer is written using C++ and the MFC class library. The key computations, however, are the same in C or C++.

The Font Explorer

The Font Explorer is a sample application that lets you see many parameters of fonts and strings. It has several components, such as the Font Explorer, the `LOGFONT` Explorer, the Kerning Explorer, and the Raster Font Explorer.

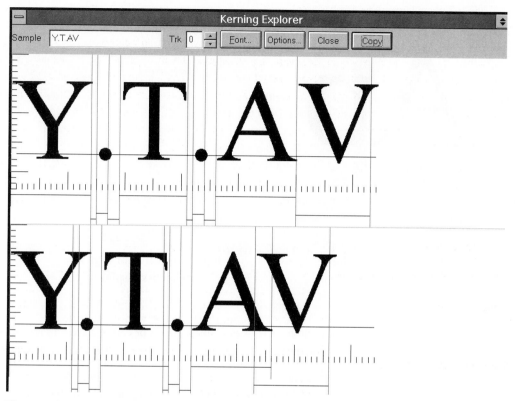

Figure 15.12: Unkerned (upper) and pair-kerned (lower) text

Reading the Font Explorer Display

When the Font Explorer application displays magnified text, as shown in Figure 15.13, it uses a notation under the character cells to display the "character ruler". This lets you graphically see the A, B, and C widths. We do not actually display the letters A, B, and C, but you can quickly interpret the diagrams once you understand the encoding. The B width is always a positive value, so the only variations are positive A and C widths, which extend beyond the B width, or negative A and C widths, which overlap the B width. Figure 15.15 shows how to interpret these rulers (for clarity, the rulers of alternate characters are displayed on one of two "levels" below the character, so you can clearly see which ruler applies to which character). For example, we see that a character with both A and C values of 0 shows only the B width line. The upper line is always the B width. The A and C widths, if nonzero, appear below the B line. If the B line is separate from A or C, such as shown in the A > 0, C = 0, the A > 0, C > 0, and the A = 0, C > 0 cases, then we know that A or

**Figure 15.13: Font Explorer
character display**

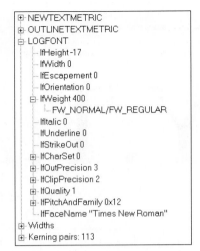

**Figure 15.14: Font Explorer
properties display**

C is positive. If the B line overlaps either or both of the A or C lines, then A or C is negative. To remove clutter, you can also turn this ruler off using the option selection from whatever Font Explorer component you are using.

Various parameters of the font can be viewed in the Info display. This display appears in both the Font Explorer and LOGFONT Explorer components; the LOGFONT Explorer is shown in Figure 15.14. The various properties are stored in a "tree view" that can be expanded by clicking the expansion box associated with each node that contains a subtree.

Some Font Explorer Application Tips

Clicking the right mouse button over one of the magnified font displays will produce an overlaid display of ABC and kerning information. The options selectable under both Font Explorer and Kerning Explorer let you choose whether kerning is used in the display. Kerning Explorer lets you display a string in the "kerned" display using only a single TextOut operation, thus letting the underlying font rendering machinery place the characters, instead of using the ABC widths and kerning data to position the characters.

A	C	Representation		
= 0	= 0		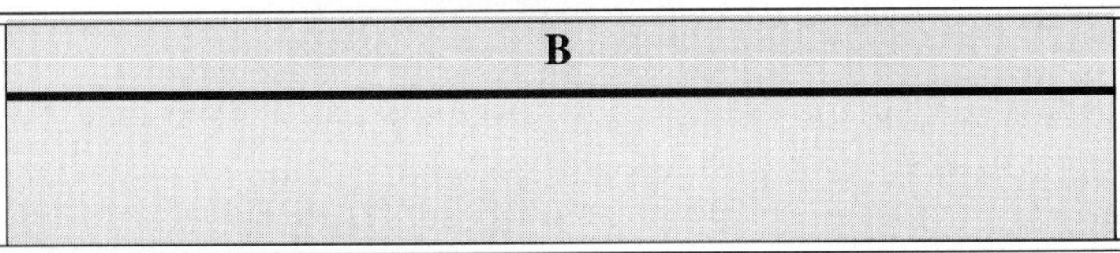 B	

Figure 15.15: Reading Font Explorer ABC notation

A	C	Representation
> 0	= 0	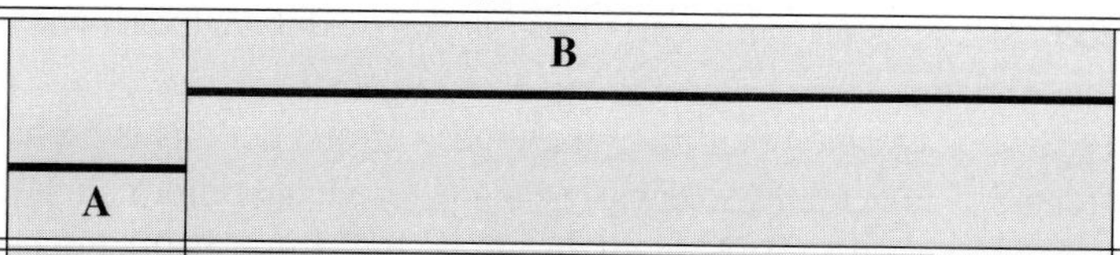 B above, A below (left offset)
< 0	= 0	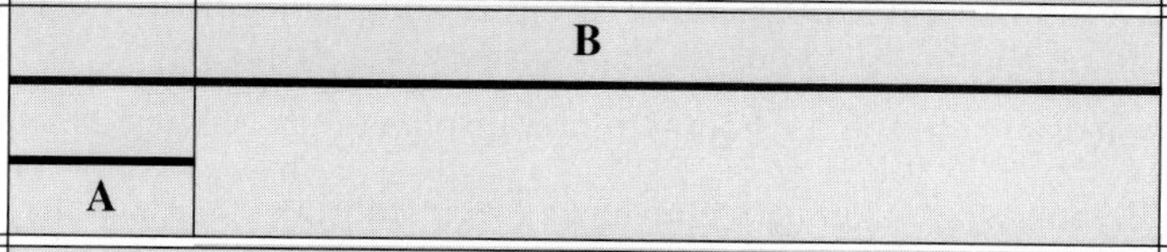 B above, A below (left offset)
= 0	> 0	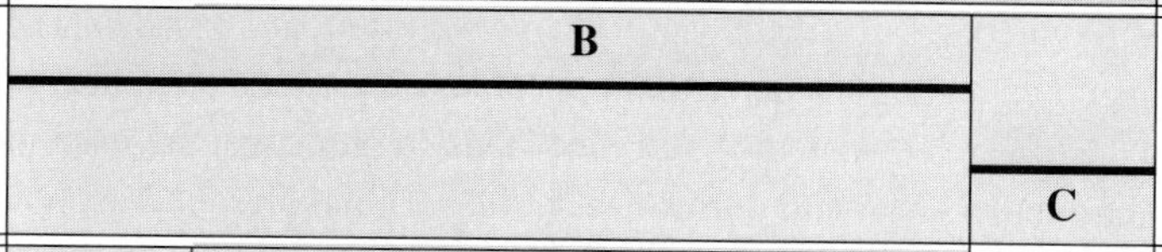 B above, C below (right)
> 0	> 0	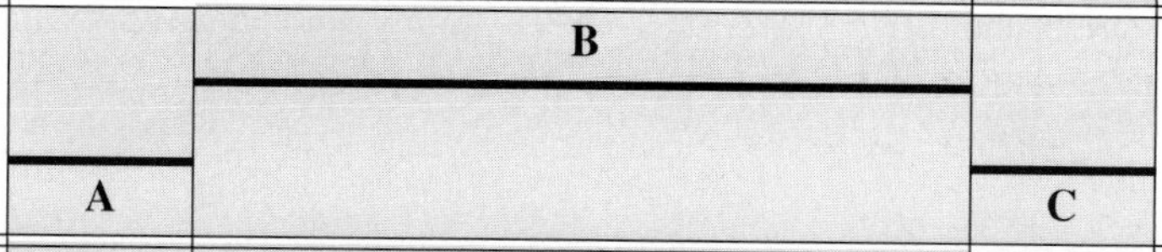 B above, A below left, C below right
< 0	> 0	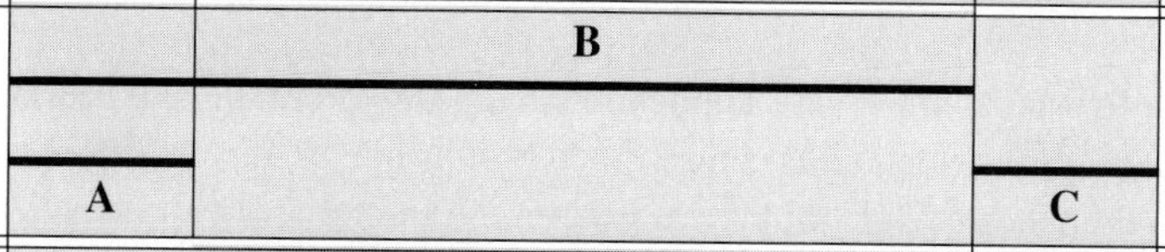 B above, A below left, C below right
= 0	< 0	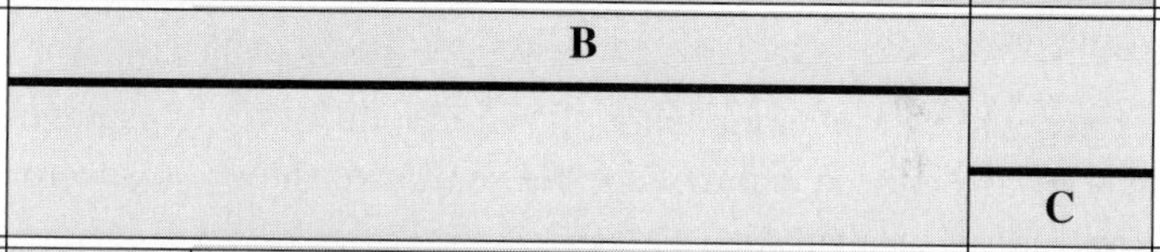 B above, C below right
> 0	< 0	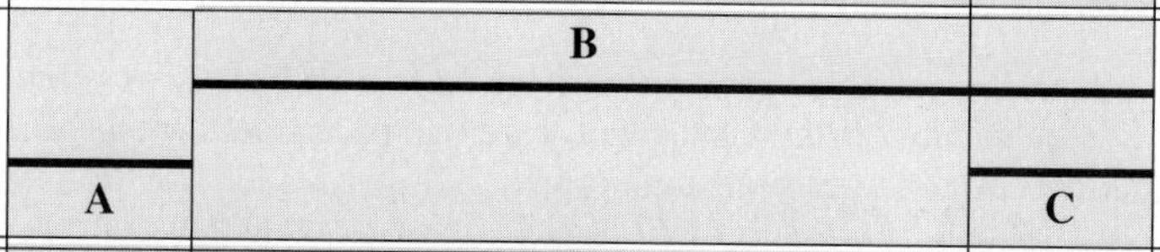 B above, A below left, C below right
< 0	< 0	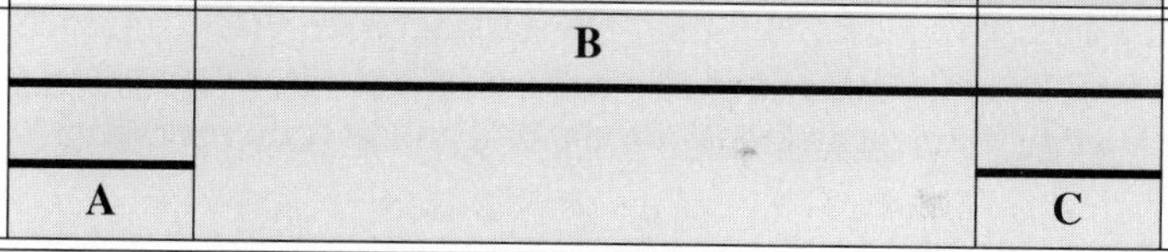 B above, A below left, C below right

Figure 15.15: Reading Font Explorer ABC notation (Continued)

Kerning Explorer Anomalies

The magnified views of Font Explorer and Kerning Explorer are subject to certain errors in the display. This is because we are working with scaled displays, and, as we've indicated, the nonlinear scaling of the True-Type fonts introduces some errors. In particular, characters with negative A widths show this off well. One option is to use the `TextOut` operation to write the entire string for the "kerned display". An 8-point font, when magnified, will gradually exhibit a cumulative error that moves later characters to the *right* of their computed positions; a 32-point font seems to consistently exhibit a (somewhat smaller) cumulative error that moves later characters to the *left* of their computed positions. We have found for many fonts that a 16-point font example scales in a fashion that minimizes these errors, but this is probably not true for all fonts. Because of how fonts scale internally, we simply cannot get enough information from the font rendering engine to precisely place the fiducial lines to represent the actual correct placements. Even the GetCharABCWidthsFloat operation returns only integers expressed as floating-point numbers. (If you are running NT, you can see this in the Font Explorer display of the ABC widths in the Info window.)

We originally hypothesized that the scaling errors were entirely due to our use of MM_ISOTROPIC mode with magnifications from 10X to 20X. However, when we chose font sizes such as 128-point that gave us approximately 1:1 magnification, errors were still noticeable between the computed positions based on ABC widths and the actual positions as rendered by TextOut. This suggests that there is more detail going on in TextOut than we, as programmers, can find out. However, these anomalies tend to show up only in the more unusual fonts in italic mode, and they still seem to correlate highly with negative A width values. This suggests that a certain amount of caution may be appropriate in using these values.

Well-behaved Fonts

Fonts are part of what defines your application's appearance to the end user. If you think of the GUI as the face of your application, then fonts can be thought of as one of the "makeup" techniques for that face. Therefore, you should be tasteful in how you use them. Too much makeup (as any theater person can attest) can produce grotesque results.

Once you start using fonts as a component of your application's appearance, you have moved out of the realm of technology and into the realm of art. We've tried to show you how to use the technology, but the art is up to you! Here are some suggestions:

- Whenever possible, give the user as much control as possible over font selection. Screen resolution and visual acuity are two parameters you have no control over; some users require larger fonts than others. Allow for font selection for key components of your system. Nothing is more frustrating than trying to use an application with unreadably tiny[2] fonts.

- Don't use too many kinds of fonts or too many different sizes.[3]

---

[2] "Unreadably tiny" is a function of age and visual acuity. Just because *you* can read it doesn't mean *I* can. A lot of software seems to be designed according to the "20/20 rule": programmers in their 20s using 20-inch displays. This does not work well when the users fall into the "50/15" category.

[3] There is no simple answer to what constitutes "too many". This book heavily uses two fonts (Times New Roman and Lucida Sans TypeX) and the occasional fonts to indicate keystrokes or menu selections. We felt this was the smallest set we could get away with, and in any case much of the information carried in the font is readily distinguished by context. Encoding *too* much information in fonts means that the reader quickly forgets what a word in each font represents, greatly interfering with the act of reading.

- Unless you deliver application-specific fonts with your product or require them as part of the product specification, avoid using characters from fonts other than the stock Windows fonts. In particular, avoid fancy script fonts, symbol fonts, and the like that are not part of the default Windows set. (If you must use fancy glyphs, restrict yourself to the Symbol and WingDings fonts.) Not every user will necessarily have the fancy fonts.

- Sans serif fonts often look better and are more easily read than serif fonts.[4] In larger sizes, serif fonts are often more attractive. You'll have to experiment. Remember that no matter what font you choose, you should still allow font selection to be your user's choice.

- Whenever possible, obtain font names from the registry, using a different key for each purpose, such as "Title", "Data Entry Field", "Main Sequence Number", and similar names you invent. If an entry does not appear in the registry, default to a "reasonable" (whatever that means!) font. User customization should then update the registry to hold the user-selected values. You should use only the stock fonts delivered with Windows as default values. For TrueType fonts, the best choices are Arial and Times New Roman.

- Beware of localization issues, which could change the default fonts from Latin fonts to other international glyphs. However, fully supporting Middle East and Far East alphabets is more complex than supporting Latin or near-Latin alphabets.

- Think Unicode, even for Windows 95 applications. This means using data types like LPTSTR, not LPSTR. If at all possible, have at least one Windows NT machine you can use to check out the Unicode version of the code. You'll find the initial effort pays off when you have to support other nationalities.

- If you allow the user to change fonts in dialogs and controls, be sure the controls are large enough to accommodate the largest "reasonable" font you allow the user to select. Or be prepared to resize them (and this *is* a lot of tedious programming!).

- You may also wish to limit the point sizes in the `ChooseFont` dialog when allowing the user to select fonts for controls and captions in dialogs and elsewhere.

- Never write any code that "knows" properties of the font that is being used. All font-related parameters should be computed "on the fly" by using the various API functions.

There is a lot more we could say about fonts. We haven't even touched on non-Latin fonts and their support. However, the font fundamentals given in this chapter will go a long way towards satisfying the text display needs of most Windows applications.

---

[4] On a typical display. This violates typographical tradition, which says that serif fonts are easier to read. The basis is that in smaller sizes, displays often distort the character outlines of serif fonts and create harder-to-read fonts. This is not a property of the abstract appearance of serif and sans serif fonts, but an unfortunate feature of using what are fundamentally "low-resolution" renderings. A "low-resolution" rendering means that the feature size of the font is very close to the pixel size of the display. You must be sensitive to issues like these; abstract principles are fine, but you must always re-evaluate them in the context of the actual application.

Wi..ther Reading

Don Knuth was one of the pioneers of computer typesetting and typography. Many of the issues of font realization are discussed in his books.

Knuth, Donald A., *TEX and METAFONT: New Directions in Typesetting*, Digital Press, 1979. ISBN 0-932376-02-9.

> This is one of the seminal publications in computer typesetting and typography. While there were many other simultaneous efforts in font description technology, they were largely proprietary. Knuth has also published a number of papers on typographic design.

If you want to learn more about Adobe technology, the current best references are:

Adobe Systems Incorporated, *PostScript Language Reference Manual*, Addison-Wesley, 1990. ISBN 0-201-18127-4.

> The definitive reference for all PostScript programmers. It contains a lot of high-level detail about fonts. Because of the device-independence of Windows, much of this has little relevance to a Windows programmer, unless you're trying to decrypt a piece of PostScript produced by your application.

Adobe Systems Incorporated, *Adobe Type 1 Font Format*, 1990.

> This short book tells you more than you could ever want to know about the internals of the Adobe Type 1 font format, including descriptions of the drawing operations for font outlines, hinting techniques, and the like. While it carefully documents all of the various fields of a font description, it gives no hints whatsoever on how they should be used ("All the facts and none of the truth"). A book for hard-core font wizards, it gives a lot of detail on low-level font technology; very little of this has much relevance to the average Windows programmer. However, it does give the background and rationale of hinting techniques and font rendering requirements.

Our copy editor, Laura Michaels, has a background in the publishing industry and took exception to the terminology as explained here (since Microsoft uses a slightly different interpretation of the terms than the printing industry uses). Unfortunately, as much as we agree with her, we have to document Microsoft's view of the font world. But for those who would like accurate definitions relative to the printing industry, and typography in general, she recommends these books:

Craig, James, *Designing with Type*, Watson-Guptill Publications, 1980. ISBN 0-8230-1321-9.

Brady, Philip, *Type Right*, North Light, an imprint of F&W Publications, 1988. ISBN 0-89134-255-9.

> *Type Right* gives a typographer's definition of the various terms used to describe type. For example, it defines *typeface* as "a particular style of type design including the full range of characters in all sizes", and a *type family* as "all the variations of typical typeface design, such as italic, bold, extra bold, condensed, etc." It gives variations of a font such as Helvetica: condensed, light, extra light, light condensed, light italic, etc. And finally, *font* is "complete assortment of type of one face and *one size*, [emphasis added–jmn] including upper- and lowercase letters, punctuation, and numerals". It's that size reference that makes the difference. Computer and desktop publishing software don't seem to consider size as significant.

Chapter

16 Dynamic Link Libraries

Dynamic link libraries (DLLs) are central to the design of Windows. Windows places most of its code, data, and resources in a number of interacting DLLs. Many programmers are not familiar with the concept of DLLs, so we begin this chapter by answering the question, "What is a dynamic link library?"

It shouldn't be a surprise that an application dynamically links to functions in a dynamic link library. Dynamic linking is a feature that quite often is new to programmers who are new to Windows programming. We explain dynamic linking and compare it to static linking, the form of linking used by DOS applications.

A DLL runs in the environment of its caller. A DLL is basically a collection of subroutines that can be called by a running program. When an application calls a function in a DLL, the DLL uses the stack of the calling application.

Some functions *must* be placed in a DLL. Windows guarantees that *fixed code segments* of a DLL will always be present in memory. You need to place code that must be available at all times (such as interrupt routines) into fixed code segments of a DLL. Thus, device drivers in Win32 are a form of DLL that can have fixed code segments (Win32 device drivers, particularly Windows NT device drivers, are a deep and complex topic that we don't cover here). Note, however, that in Windows NT the only way you can access a device's registers or its onboard memory is by using a device driver. Windows 95 has no such restriction, but this situation may change in future releases of non-Windows NT 32-bit operating systems. For most programming you will do, fixed code segments will never be used.

Another type of function that must be placed in a DLL is a *system hook function*. Windows provides a way for you to register a hook function for various events. When such an event occurs, Windows passes the notification or message signaling the event to the hook function before distributing the notification or message to its original destination. Because a hooked event can occur at any time, not necessarily when the hooking application is running, the hook function must be placed in a DLL.

In this chapter, we discuss the philosophy and techniques of DLLs. In particular, a DLL should be written as *thread safe*. This means it will implement its specification correctly even when called by multiple threads. Even when one of the threads that is preempted is executing in the DLL at the time it is preempted and, while it is preempted, another thread calls the same or a related function of the DLL, the DLL must exhibit the correct behavior. This is often a new paradigm for thinking of software design. But it is one that is becoming increasingly important in developing Win32 applications.

32 allows many different styles of DLL construction. We explore several of these with a small example ows each style.

'e the Wineyes example program to further demonstrate the use of DLLs. This is a neat little use-program that is a Windows version of a popular Unix X Windows program called xeyes. It draws a little face with two beady little eyes. The eyes track the mouse cursor no matter which application is active or where the cursor moves.

The Wineyes program serves another purpose, other than being neat and useless. You can't write such a Windows program without using a DLL. To track the mouse cursor, we register a hook function and monitor all mouse move messages. The hook function resides in the Wineyes DLL (as it must) and posts a notification message to the Wineyes application program each time the mouse moves. The application redraws the eyes looking toward the new location of the mouse cursor. So the example serves as a complete demonstration of how to build a DLL, how to write an application that calls functions in a DLL, and how to write a hook function.

A Special Note to Win16 Programmers

It is better to know nothing than to know what ain't so.

– Josh Billings[1]

Read this chapter. DLLs in Win32 are very different from DLLs in Win16. Critical differences you will want to take note of include these:

- Static data declared in the DLL is private to each process. In Win16, it was implicitly shared among all processes.

- You can get a shared data segment in Win32, but you have to ask for it. This leads to other problems (see the next two points).

- Private data segments are in private address spaces, and information cannot be shared by passing pointers to these private data segments via messages or shared data segments.

- Shared data segments are not necessarily in the same logical address in every process that shares them. Thus pointers to absolute addresses, even those addresses that are in the shared data segment, cannot be stored in the shared data segment.

- The LibMain functionality is now found in DllEntryPoint and is quite different–different parameters and different actions you must take.

- There is no WEP function. Instead, DllEntryPoint handles the equivalent functionality, but on a per-process basis.

---

[1] From *Josh Billings' Encyclopedia of Wit & Wisdom*, 1874, p. 286.

- DLLs are loaded based on a full path name. Thus the filenames \windows\sys-tem\mystuff.dll and \projects\mystuff\debug\mystuff.dll are considered different DLLs. This matters if you have a shared data segment. In Win16, only the filename portion was used (and in fact it was the internal *module name* that was the real test), so distinctly named files would not necessarily act correctly.

- Memory allocation takes place in the context of the calling executable and is not local to the DLL's heap.

- You must be preemptible-multitasking aware if you are using a shared data segment. Techniques of using DLL static data that worked perfectly in Win16 can fail complete-ly when the same DLL is executing in Win32.

- You also must be thread-aware. Techniques of using DLL static data even within a sin-gle application without a shared data segment that worked perfectly in Win16 can fail completely when the same DLL can be called from multiple threads of a Win32 application.

- Global hook functions don't need to have FIXED code and data segments.

What Is a Dynamic Link Library?

Fundamentally, a dynamic link library is a special form of executable program (.exe) file, although it will often have a different file extension such as .fon, .dll, .drv, or .sys that indicates the type of resource provided by the DLL. A .fon file contains font resources. A .drv file is a device driver. A .sys file is a system file typically used by Windows. The .sys files generally contain device drivers as well. Some DLLs use the .exe file extension. A DLL can contain code, data, and resources just as a normal Windows applica-tions can. But if you look at the internals of a DLL, you'll see that, except for a few flags and some special values that indicate it is a DLL, it is simply a normal Windows executable file in the standard executable for-mat (the format referred to as "Portable Executable", or "PE", format).

The biggest difference between a DLL and a Windows application is that you do not "run" a DLL. You exe-cute a Windows application, and that application might call a function in a DLL, retrieve data from the DLL, and use resources compiled into the DLL by the resource compiler. When an application calls a function in a DLL, the DLL can, in turn, call another function contained in a different DLL, retrieve its data, and use its resources as well. Those readers whose interests include ecology, life sciences, or science fiction will recog-nize the analogy that a DLL is a *symbiont* and the executable file is its *host*. For example, a DLL relies on its host to provide a stack, without which it cannot live.

A DLL function can even call a function in the calling application if it has been given the address of the ap-propriate application callback function. This is actually what happens when Windows calls one of your ap-plication's callback functions. "Windows" typically means, in this case, one of the main Windows DLLs–gdi32, kernel32, or user32–and some typical application callback functions called by routines in Windows' DLLs are your window and dialog functions as well as others such as enumeration and timer call-back functions.

A DLL doesn't execute as a task itself, however. It is called, directly or indirectly, from a Windows application (process). A DLL is simply a repository for resources (in the general sense, code, data, and resource script resources) you make available to Windows and all Windows applications. These resources are shared resources. All Windows applications using a DLL share the same DLL code and resources, and under special conditions can even share data.

We call functions in DLLs in every example program in this book. For example, the `GetMessage` function you call in the message loop actually resides in the `user32.dll` DLL. The `Rectangle` GDI output function resides in the `gdi32.dll` DLL, and the `GlobalAlloc` function resides in the `kernel32.dll` DLL.

Many of the device drivers Windows uses are actually DLLs. The `keyboard.drv`, `mouse.drv`, `system.drv`, `lanman.drv`, and other `.drv` files are DLLs. The `coure.fon`, `roman.fon`, and other `.fon` and `.fot` (TrueType font) files are DLLs that contain font resources but no code or data.

Static and Dynamic Linking

You're probably familiar with the normal process of *static linking*. Static linking is one method of resolving an external reference to a function not present in a program being linked. The linker searches one or more library (`.lib`) files until it locates an object module in a library that contains the requested function or data name. The linker then adds a copy of the object module to the resulting executable (`.exe`) file. The linker fixes up all references to the function to point to the place in the program that now contains the copy of the function.

The `atoi` function, for example, is located in the standard C runtime library. The linker normally includes a copy of the `atoi` function in the executable file of each application that calls it. When you run these applications concurrently, multiple copies of the `atoi` function are resident in memory. However, this memory is almost always at a different physical address in each application and represents a tiny piece of the overall application. It would be impossible to share all these little pieces in any meaningful way.[2]

Dynamic linking works somewhat differently. Again the linker finds a reference to a function not present in an application. The linker again searches one or more library (`.lib`) files, looking for the requested function. When the linker finds an *import record* naming the function, it treats this as the definition of the function. Instead of inserting the code for the function, it creates a dynamic link to the requested function.

An import record doesn't contain code or data for the function. Instead, an import record names the DLL that contains the function and either the *name* of the corresponding function in the specified DLL or its *ordinal number* or both. For example, when you call the `GetMessage` function, the linker finds an import record that states that the `GetMessage` function is the name that corresponds to the function with the ordinal

---

[2] Microsoft's later C compiler releases actually use a single, large DLL to hold much of the C runtime library so it, too, can be shared. The filename has changed several times, on each new release of the compiler, but the current release uses the filenames `msvcrt.dll` (*MicroSoft Visual C RunTime*) and `msvcrtd.dll` (the debugging version). These names may change with a new release.

number 270 (`GetMessageA`) or 274 (`GetMessageW`)[3] in the `user32` DLL. An import record also can provide a different *visible* name for a function than the name stored in the DLL.[4]

The linker copies the information in the import record to the resulting executable file, creating a dynamic link to the function. When you run the executable file, Windows loads the program and looks for any dynamic links present in the file. For each dynamic link it finds, Windows loads the specified DLL (if it isn't already present in memory) and resolves the external reference to the proper location in the DLL. This is the source of the term *dynamic linking*. The actual linkage between the call and the target function isn't resolved once (statically) when you link an application. Rather, it is resolved by Windows each time (dynamically) the user runs the application.

For example, an application can call the Windows `lstrcpy` function, which is similar to the standard C runtime library `strcpy` function. The linker resolves this call to the function with ordinal number 632 in the `kernel32.dll` DLL. When multiple applications that all use the `lstrcpy` function run concurrently, they all call the same function, which exists once in memory. Multiple copies of the function aren't resident as they would be if you used the C runtime and had a statically linked `strcpy`.[5]

This new process has introduced new terminology, so you should know some new terms. Libraries that contain program object modules are often called *object libraries*. Libraries that contain import records are called *import libraries*. However, these are not mutually exclusive in a library file. A library (`.lib`) file can contain both object modules and import records. The linker does not concern itself with which is which until it actually has to use the information it obtains after name resolution has completed.

It's often convenient to maintain object libraries and import libraries independently. The Windows library `libc.lib` is an object library that contains Windows application start-up code and Windows-compatible C runtime statically linked functions. The Windows SDK library `user32.lib` is an import library containing import records for the functions in the `user32.dll` DLL. You will find that most development environments provide you by default with a list of "standard" libraries, which can be as few as five or as many as fifteen; you usually add to these lists. Almost all Windows (nonconsole) applications require the three most important import libraries: `user32.lib`, `kernel32.lib`, and `gdi32.lib`. By the time you add common dialogs, common controls, OLE support, multimedia, and custom libraries, you can have 20 or 30 libraries you use for your link.

Windows uses the term *module* to refer to both executable programs and DLLs. As mentioned earlier in the chapter, both a program module and a DLL module can call functions in other DLL modules. A module can *export* a function, thereby making the function available to other modules.

---

[3] `GetMessageA` is the ANSI version of `GetMessage`, and `GetMessageW` is the Unicode ("wide character") version of `GetMessage`. See the discussion in Chapter 7.

[4] This alternative form of an import record could describe the function name P as a synonym for the function Q, which is contained in a DLL called `proof.dll`. (We leave it to the philosopher in you to decide whether the proposition IF P() THEN Q() is true without calling the function.)

[5] There are other reasons you don't want to use `strcpy`, dealing with localization issues; see Chapter 7 and Chapter 12. Note also that Windows supports `lstrcpy`, `lstrcpyA`, and `lstrcpyW`.

An exported function is in many ways a superset of an extern (global) C function. An extern function can be called from any function in any source file comprising the module. However, an extern function isn't visible to other applications or DLLs. An *exported* function can be called by a completely separate program or DLL module. You export a function by naming it in the EXPORTS section of the module's module definition file, using the /EXPORT linker option or, when the default options of the EXPORTS statement are acceptable, using the __declspec(dllexport) modifier when defining the function.

The notion of "exports" had additional meaning in Win16. For example, all callback functions, including dialog handlers and window handlers, enumeration callbacks, hook functions, and the like, had to be "exported", even from the main module. This was because "export" in Win16 had additional semantics, dealing with how the linker, the compiler, and the Windows system dealt with the 16-bit "data segment addressibility" problem. In Win32, these problems do not exist. The "callback" functions do not need to be exported, not even the dialog handlers or window handlers. They do not need to be mentioned in the EXPORTS section of a module-definition file. They can even be declared static. The __export keyword, so important in Win16, will generate warning messages if it is encountered by the compiler in a Win32 program. Even the module definition file is optional in Win32 and in practice is seldom used.

A module definition file or the linker options provide power beyond the simple exporting of a name. For example, you can make the *external name* of an exported function (the name by which other applications call it) different from the *internal name* of the function as used in the module. You do this by *aliasing* the name on its EXPORTS statement or using the /EXPORT linker option. You can't provide an alias when using only the __declspec(dllexport) modifier. Here is an example of how a module definition file exports three functions:

```
EXPORTS
        MyWndProc
        TimerFunc                @11
        DrawRect = MyRectangle   @17
```

and here is the equivalent set of linker options:

```
/EXPORT:MyWndProc /EXPORT:TimerFunc,@11
/EXPORT:DrawRect=MyRectangle,@17
```

The first exported function has no ordinal number assigned, so the linker automatically assigns it one. This means the ordinal number for the MyWndProc function could change each time the module is relinked. This causes severe anxiety to the functions that call "the function with ordinal number X in DLL Y" because the function could have ordinal number N+1, N, N-1, or a completely unrelated ordinal number the next time you link the module. For all practical purposes, a function exported this way *must* be called by name, not by ordinal number. Calling an exported function by name is not as efficient as calling an exported function by ordinal number.

The second exported function's ordinal number is specified. Because an explicit ordinal number has been assigned, the function will keep the same ordinal number each time the DLL is linked. The third exported function is called by the name DrawRect by other modules and has the ordinal number 17. The actual function that receives control is the function internal to the module called MyRectangle. This form of exported function establishes an alias by which the exported function is called.

Conversely, when a module wants to call a function in a different module, the calling function must *import* the function. When the linker sees that an external reference is imported, it defers resolving the reference until runtime. You import called functions that reside in other modules and export functions in your module that other modules can call.

We've been importing a tremendous number of functions all along–and you probably didn't realize it. Practically all the Windows functions used by an application program reside in one of Windows' DLLs. When you link an application with `user32.lib`, `kernel32.lib`, `gdi32.lib`, and others, the import records provide the information necessary to import the function.

The linker can create an import library when it is creating a DLL. It looks at only the exported names–as determined by the `EXPORTS` of the module definition file–the `/EXPORT` linker option and the information attached to a function by the `__declspec(dllexport)` modifiers, and creates an import library with an import record for each exported function. Applications can link with the created import library to dynamically link to the exported function.

In Win16, a separate program, `implib`, was used to create import libraries. In Win32, this functionality is now part of the linker and the library manager and there is no separate program.

After you've linked and exported functions, the functions can be called by other modules. When you call exported functions, the calling module must import each function. This is normally done automatically by the import records found in the import library. However, you can also use an explicit `__declspec(dllimport)` modifier in the calling module's source files. Windows does the rest of the work of resolving the dynamic link.

In the previous examples, all imported functions must be known at link time. However, what if an application wants to call a routine in a DLL that is not actually linked with the application? This is often done as a custom extension DLL, such as national language support, enhanced feature libraries (as a vendor may sell as "add-on" libraries), or for some other reason.

You can call the `LoadLibrary` function to load any DLL. The function loads the DLL (if it isn't already loaded), increments its usage count, and returns a module handle. The following statement loads the `extends.dll` library, which is a library you might have written:

```
hExtensions = LoadLibrary (_T("extends.dll")) ;
```

Calling the `LoadLibrary` function is the only way to load a DLL that doesn't have the `.dll` file extension. Windows always assumes a `.dll` file extension for DLLs implicitly required by an application. When you want to use a DLL that doesn't have such an extension, you *must* load the DLL explicitly by using the `LoadLibrary` function. Of course, you can always use the `LoadLibrary` function to explicitly load any DLL, including one *with* a `.dll` file extension.

After you have a module handle to a DLL, you must obtain the address of the function you want to call, exported by the DLL. But there is no "linker" to resolve this for you. You must obtain the address yourself by calling the `GetProcAddress` function. You specify the module handle of the DLL containing the function and the name of the function.

We use the following code to retrieve the address of the `getLocalName` function in a previously loaded DLL that we're using for localization. In this example, `getLocalName` is some function that we give two `INT` values as parameters. It returns a string pointer to us that is some useful local version of the name of something. This local name is decoded differently for different international languages. Note that once we load the pointer-to-function value, which we can do in the initialization of our application or when we choose to load the library, we can use it as long as the library remains loaded. If we unload the library, however, the pointer becomes invalid and we must not use it.

The C language syntax lets us make the indirect call look syntactically just like a direct call to a function. To simplify the declaration, we first define a **typedef** for the function type. You must make sure that the *linkage type* of your function and the declaration of the variable used to hold its address are consistent. GetProcAddress is defined to return a FARPROC pointer, but this type is virtually useless for doing any real function calls. You should always expect to cast the result of a GetProcAddress to a function type of your own devising. We prefer to use a **typedef** for these declarations because otherwise the syntactic clutter rapidly becomes unreadable. Also, it is often difficult to maintain and update a call when its specifications change. In the following example, we have chosen to implement our function using the WINAPI linkage type, so we must give it explicitly in the declaration:

```
typedef LPCTSTR (WINAPI * GETLOCALNAMEFUNC)(INT, INT) ;

GETLOCALNAMEFUNC getLocalName ;

getLocalName = (GETLOCALNAMEFUNC)GetProcAddress(hLanguage, "getLocalName") ;
```

Note that the spelling of the function name parameter must match that used in the exported function, the .def file used to create the DLL, or the linker command line, depending on which method you choose. Note also that the name is specified as an ANSI (8-bit) string, *even in a Unicode application.* You can also specify the entry point by ordinal value. For example, if you know the getLocalName function has ordinal number 13, this statement would return the same address:

```
getLocalName = (GETLOCALNAMEFUNC)
    GetProcAddress (hLanguage, MAKEINTRESOURCE (13)) ;
```

After you have the address of the function, you can call the function indirectly through a pointer. The function call syntax to call the getLocalName function looks like this:

```
LPCTSTR name = getLocalName( n1, n2 ) ;
```

Note that the older, pre-ANSI, C syntax *required* that you write

```
LPCTSTR name = (*getLocalName)( n1, n2 );
```

but the ANSI C standard allows the compiler to determine that a pointer to a procedure is implicitly dereferenced. Both forms work; they produce identical code. But the first one is simpler to write and understand. When you no longer need a DLL, you must free it explicitly by calling the FreeLibrary function and passing it the module handle of the DLL, as follows:

```
FreeLibrary (hLanguage) ;
```

Freeing a DLL decrements its usage count. When the usage count is 0, the DLL is no longer being used by any module in the system, so Windows discards it. After you free a DLL, the pointers you obtained using

`GetProcAddress` are no longer valid; using them will most likely generate an access fault. A library is implicitly freed when the process using it terminates.

Benefits of Using DLLs

Large applications in particular gain several significant advantages when they use DLLs rather than statically linked functions:

- Less disk space is used by the application. This is often more important if a suite of application programs can share one or more DLLs.

- Less system memory is required to run the application.

    - This is often more important if a suite of application programs that execute simultaneously can share one or more DLLs.

    - Components that are not needed do not need to be loaded.

- Application components are more easily updated.

- Components do not need to be delivered if they are not needed. This is particularly convenient for packaging optional features with a product.

- You may deliver functionally equivalent but differently-implemented versions of the library. Typical use is for localization in the international market.

- You can provide new, specialized, or enhanced functionality by developing components that use the same logical interface.[6]

Typically, a large application suite has a number of basic, commonly used functions that are used by all components of the suite. For example, an accounting package may share several common functions between components such as order entry, accounts receivable ledger, accounts payable ledger, invoicing, and the like. Placing such functions in one or more DLLs avoids having to link the functions into each program that requires them. Each function is present only once in the DLL rather than in each executable program. Hence, the entire application has less redundancy and uses less disk space.

For the same reason, less system memory is used by an application that consists of multiple, concurrently executing programs that call common functions resident in a DLL. Because memory generally is a scarcer resource than disk space, the space savings can result in a noticeable performance improvement on memory-scarce systems. Perhaps the best instance of this is the shared runtime library used by the Microsoft Foundation Classes (MFC), which is well over 500K. Only one instance of the code is required to support all concurrently running MFC-based applications written for that version of the library.

---

[6] For example, the "graphics filters" or "document filters" provided with most graphics and document applications that allow you to import existing files in a multiplicity of formats are done with DLLs. If a new file format emerges, a new DLL can be written that is just added to the suite of existing filters.

Applications using DLLs also are more easily updated. When you copy a DLL containing one or more updated functions onto a system, all applications that call those functions are updated automatically. The next time the application runs, Windows loads the new DLL and the application uses the updated function(s).[7] Updating a statically linked function requires that the function be replaced in an object library and all applications that link with the library be relinked. This changes the notion of an update distribution from being a single DLL that can be downloaded by the end users over a modem or Internet connection to one that requires a complete new CD-ROM to hold the tens of megabytes of relinked executables. It is this ease of update that enables Windows to be enhanced easily. When a user adds a new display or printer to the system, for example, after the appropriate device driver DLL is installed, all Windows applications use the new device without any changes to the application.

Using a DLL in an application has one disadvantage. At least two files–the application and the DLL–must be distributed. For a small application, this is sometimes inconvenient. In addition, Microsoft provides as part of the Windows, C, and MFC environments a collection of what are called *redistributable DLLs*. When you buy a third-party library, one of its key components is often a DLL (or several DLLs) that you must ship with your product. In many cases, you must ensure the installation procedure does not replace a newer version of the DLL on the end user's machine with an older copy that you shipped. If you do this, some application you never heard of could stop working because it relied on new features or bug fixes of the newer library. This is particularly critical with the Microsoft redistributable DLLs, which include significant support DLLs for MFC and OLE/ActiveX.[8]

At other times you *must* use a DLL. For example, all functions that Windows must be able to call at any time–particularly when the application has released control of the processor–must be placed in a DLL. Functions called by hardware interrupts and *system hook functions* are two examples. The `Wineyes` example program discussed later in this chapter contains a system hook function and does not operate properly without some of its code being placed in a DLL.

Constraints Unique to a DLL

The Stack

A DLL module does not have a stack. Local variables for functions in DLLs reside on the stack of the application that called the DLL. This means that you, the creator of the DLL, have no control over the amount of stack space that will actually be available to you. You should be careful about allocating large blocks of stack data; for example, a potentially deeply recursive function that declares a large array on the stack may cause

---

[7] The corollary is also true, of course. That is, if you introduce a bug into a shared library, you introduce it into all components. Problems like these give your QA staff members ulcers worrying about how to test new DLL versions because they impact every component of the system.

[8] You must get many details right in doing an installation: version checking for your own and shared DLLs, handling the registry database issues, detecting older versions, and the like. These details are much more complex under Win32, and you should consider using a third-party installer generator to deliver a product.

your callers problems. While stack space is generally not a serious problem in Win32 (as it was in Win16), remember that a large stack also can increase the working set size and impact system performance. While you don't need to treat the stack as a scarce resource, you should not be profligate in its usage either.

Static Data

A DLL can have zero or more data segments. Data segments can be private or shared. If data segments are private (the default situation), every executing application gets its own private copy of the data segment when it loads the library (either explicitly or implicitly). Each private data segment starts as a fresh copy of the original data segment from the .dll file. If a data segment is shared, only one copy of the data segment exists for all applications that are using the library. Each new process sees the current state of the shared data segment.

 This multiple segment behavior is quite different from the behavior of Win16 DLLs. In Win16, there was one data segment for a DLL, and it was shared among all concurrent users of the DLL. Elaborate schemes were developed for tracking individual clients of the DLL. These are all irrelevant in Win32, as you will get notification of each time a process, or even a thread, attaches or detaches from the library.

 DLLs in Win32s inherit the behavior of the underlying Win16 system and have a single shared data segment. This will produce very surprising results and can even cause serious malfunctions of your Win32 application. This is why many Win32 applications are not certified to run under Win32s.

The DllEntryPoint Function

Unlike Windows applications, which begin executing at the WinMain function (at least from the perspective of an application programmer), a DLL "begins" executing at the DllEntryPoint function. (The name of this function can be set by a linker option, but we will always call DllEntryPoint.) As mentioned earlier in the chapter, a DLL isn't executable as a task. It doesn't begin executing in the sense of an application program. However, when a module (application or other DLL) causes a DLL to be loaded, Windows calls the entry point function in the DLL to give it a chance to initialize. This function is also called for other events in the life of the DLL, as we discuss shortly. You must make sure that you set the entry point name, for example, by adding the linker option /entry:DllEntryPoint (which you usually do from the development environment by selecting an option that lets you set the entry point name).

 There is no WEP function in Win32 DLLs. WEP was the name of the "Windows Exit Procedure" that was called for a Win16 DLL when it was unloaded. Instead the notifications of process detach and thread detach provide notification of such events when you may want to free up resources.

The function prototype for the DllEntryPoint function is

```
BOOL WINAPI DllEntryPoint(
    HINSTANCE hinstDLL, // handle to DLL module
    DWORD Reason,       // reason for calling function
    LPVOID Reserved     // reserved
    );
```

The actual name does not need to be DllEntryPoint and can be changed by using the linker option /entry:*entryname*.

The DLL entry point is called for four important events, as shown in Table 16.1. This value is passed in as the Reason parameter to the DllEntryPoint. The hInstDLL parameter contains, in all cases, the instance handle of the DLL in the process or thread that is calling it; this is the same as the handle that will be returned to the LoadLibrary function that causes the DLL to load. Normally, you will want to save this in a static variable because it gives you convenient access to the resources stored in the DLL. The Reserved parameter is not really reserved; it provides, in the words of Microsoft, "further aspects of the DLL initialization and cleanup." These are summarized in Table 16.2.

The DllEntryPoint function should return TRUE if the DLL_PROCESS_ATTACH operation is successful. It should return FALSE if there is some error (such as in initializing some state); you may want to call SetLastError to indicate the reason for the failure. If the return value is FALSE, then LoadLibrary will return NULL and an implicit load that fails during process start-up will terminate the process. If DllEntryPoint is called with any other event, the return value is ignored by the caller.

Table 16.1: DllEntryPoint events

Event	Description
DLL_PROCESS_ATTACH	Called on the first LoadLibrary call for the process. This is either an explicit LoadLibrary call or the implicit one executed during process initialization. Return TRUE for success and FALSE for failure.
DLL_THREAD_ATTACH	Called whenever a new thread is created by the attached process. This call is made in the context of the new thread.
DLL_THREAD_DETACH	Called whenever a thread "cleanly" terminates. Gives the DLL a chance to free up any thread-specific resources allocated in DLL_THREAD_ATTACH. This code may be passed in even if there was no corresponding DLL_THREAD_ATTACH call performed. Note that a DLL_PROCESS_DETACH will *not* generate a DLL_THREAD_DETACH for any active threads.
DLL_PROCESS_DETACH	Indicates that the DLL is detaching cleanly from the process. This is a chance to free up any process-specific resources that may have been allocated. This is called when the process terminates or on the last FreeLibrary call that decrements the process's reference count of the library to 0. (The library's reference count may still be greater than 0, but you cannot tell anything about this.)

Table 16.2: Interpretation of the Reserved parameter for `DllEntryPoint` ·

Event	Value	Meaning
`DLL_PROCESS_ATTACH`	NULL	Load is from an explicit `LoadLibrary` call.
	non-NULL	Load is from an implicit load at process startup.
`DLL_PROCESS_DETACH`	NULL	The result of an explicit `FreeLibrary` call reducing the reference count to 0.
	non-NULL	The result of process termination.

Although the model appears reasonably clean, it has several lurking "gotchas" that you have to be aware of. The most important one is that the calls are not necessarily "balanced" calls. That is, you do *not* get a process attach followed by a thread attach, followed by some sequence of thread attach events and their matching thread detach events, and finally the matching process detach. In fact, under conditions of failure of the calling thread or process, you may not get detach events at all! Since this can lead to much confusion, we study it closely.

The `DLL_PROCESS_ATTACH` event comes in when a new process attaches to the DLL for the first time. Once this has been called for a process, it will not be called again–no matter how many `LoadLibrary` calls may be executed by that process–until the process finally sends a `DLL_PROCESS_DETACH` as a consequence of having `FreeLibrary` reduce the process's reference count to 0. After a `DLL_PROCESS_DETACH` operation has occurred, the library is no longer associated with the process and a subsequent `LoadLibrary` call for the same DLL from that same process will again send `DLL_PROCESS_ATTACH`, thereby starting the event sequence all over again.

The `DLL_PROCESS_ATTACH` is executed in the context of the calling thread that executed the first `LoadLibrary` call. If this occurs during process startup, because of implicit linking, it is executed in the context of the process's primary thread (which is the only one active at that point).

When `DLL_PROCESS_ATTACH` occurs, it always occurs in the context of the first thread to attach to the DLL. This thread does *not* generate a separate `DLL_THREAD_ATTACH` event; it generates only a `DLL_PROCESS_ATTACH` event. So if you have any thread-specific initialization to do in the DLL, you must explicitly cause this initialization to occur for the `DLL_PROCESS_ATTACH` event. This is commonly done by having the `case` for `DLL_PROCESS_ATTACH` simply "fall through" to the `DLL_THREAD_ATTACH` case after having completed the per-process initialization, although this may vary depending on what you need to do.

Typically, if you are supporting a multithreaded application, you will use the `DLL_PROCESS_ATTACH` to perform thread-local storage allocation for the attaching thread (see `TlsAlloc`, in Chapter 14, starting on page 1065, and the example we give starting on page 1145 and show in Listing 16.13).

If you are writing a DLL, *you should always write it as a thread-safe library.* You cannot predict exactly how your clients will be built. Building a DLL that assumes a single thread in a process is risky; later changes in the client application can lead to extremely difficult-to-find bugs. If you need static storage that is other than the equivalent of `const` storage (initialized once at the `DLL_PROCESS_ATTACH` event and thereafter only read, until the DLL_PROCESS_DETACH event), you must either allocate it as thread-local storage or use critical sections to control access to it. We describe synchronization in more detail in Chapter 18.

Once you have handled the DLL_PROCESS_ATTACH event, you may get any number of DLL_THREAD_ATTACH events. Whenever a new thread is created in the process (for example, with CreateThread), all DLLs currently associated with the process will receive this event notification via their DllEntryPoint. Note that you will *not* get a DLL_THREAD_ATTACH event for the primary thread, as we just pointed out. You also will not get one for any threads that already exist when the DLL is loaded. Only threads created *after* the DLL is attached to your process will generate DLL_THREAD_ATTACH events. So you must exert a certain amount of care to ensure a thread that is going to access the DLL is not created before the DLL is loaded if the thread will have any local state in the DLL. In general, without reading the code of the DLL, you can't tell if a thread accessing a DLL actually requires local state in the DLL. And even if you know today that your DLL doesn't require local state, this situation can change as the DLL implementation evolves. As a user of a DLL, you should generally assume that any DLL you load will require thread-local state and thus load it (implicitly or explicitly) before any of its client threads are created. As a creator of a DLL, you also should be aware that a programmer who violates this specification may call your DLL from a thread that existed before the DLL was loaded. You should explicitly check that any thread-local storage is properly initialized before attempting to use it.

When a thread cleanly terminates, it will generate a DLL_THREAD_DETACH event. You can get a DLL_THREAD_DETACH even if you've had no corresponding DLL_THREAD_ATTACH event! This can occur under two conditions:

1. You have cleanly terminated the primary thread (other threads may still be executing, so terminating the primary thread does not imply that the process is terminating). You will get the DLL_THREAD_DETACH event even though the primary thread did not generate a DLL_THREAD_ATTACH event.

2. A pre-existing thread terminates. This is a thread that had started before the library was loaded. If it terminates before the library is finally freed, it will generate a DLL_THREAD_DETACH event.

The second case is particularly interesting because you must be prepared to deal with it. Consider that you've started up a number of threads that don't use the DLL at all. Then you load the DLL. Windows doesn't know that a thread doesn't use a DLL, so whenever any existing thread terminates, all attached DLLs are notified that the thread has terminated. Thus your DLL will be called in the context of the terminating thread. You must be prepared to deal with uninitialized thread-local storage and other thread-related state because they were never initialized by a DLL_THREAD_ATTACH event.

You also may not get *any* DLL_THREAD_DETACH events! This occurs when you get a DLL_PROCESS_DETACH event. When the process terminates or the library is freed, the DLLs do *not* get DLL_THREAD_DETACH events for every thread that is being terminated; instead, there is exactly one DLL_PROCESS_DETACH for the entire process. Since much of the static state you maintain is thread-local storage, this storage is implicitly freed as the process terminates. But if you are maintaining either shared state (using a shared data segment or memory-mapped file) or system resources (sockets, communication ports, and the like) on a per-thread basis and you must explicitly free up this state, you must be prepared to store all this state in such a way that you can find it all on a DLL_PROCESS_DETACH. Doing this almost certainly means you will need to deal with at least *critical section* synchronization if not full *mutex* synchronization in order to safely create the shared information.

A DLL Module Definition File

The module definition file for a DLL, if you choose to write one, is somewhat different from that for an application. Module definition files are not required for Win32 applications or DLLs.

> In Win16, a module definition file was mandatory. As Win16 evolved, less and less material of interest appeared in most module definition files. In Win32, all of the functionality of the module definition file is realizable by other mechanisms, such as linker options. Hence, the module definition file is now entirely optional, and in most projects supported by many development environments, it is not normally used.

A module definition file for an application has a NAME statement, which names the application module. A module definition file for a DLL does not have a NAME statement, but it does have a LIBRARY statement, which names the DLL module and identifies the module as a DLL. All letters used in the module name must be in uppercase. You can also use the linker option /DLL to indicate that a DLL is being created.

If the DLL has a shared segment, you name the shared segment by using either the SHARED keyword:

```
SECTION 'sectionname' SHARED
```

or the /SECTION link option:

```
/SECTION:sectionname,S
```

For more details on shared segments, see the discussion starting on page 1148.

Importing Symbols

If a symbol is unresolved during a link, it is implicitly resolved by its being looked up in the library files. If the library file defining a name contains object code or data, the code and/or data is statically linked into your application. If the library file is an export library, a *link* is created to the DLL. When the application starts up, one of the tasks of **CreateProcess** is to "fix" all of these links by finding the DLL, loading it, looking up the unresolved name in the DLL, and resolving the symbolic link to an actual address in the process address space.

It is possible to get a slightly smaller and more efficient linkage if you give the compiler and linker some hints. You can do this by adding the __declspec(dllimport) declaration to the declaration of the function.[9] For example, if you write this declaration in your header file:

---

[9] For more details on this, check out Matt Pietrek's *Under the Hood* column in *Microsoft Systems Journal* 1995:11; see the "Further Reading" section on page 1163.

```
__declspec(dllimport) void someFunction(...);
```

then the call someFunction(...) will be slightly smaller and slightly faster than if the declaration were simply

```
void someFunction(...);
```

Importing Data

Functions are not the only names you can import from a DLL. You can also import data declarations. In this case, however, you *must* use the __declspec(dllimport) modifier on the data value.

 The ability to import data values from a DLL did not exist in Win16. You could import only function names. This was because the data in a DLL was always shared among all clients of the DLL. In Win32, unless you have explicitly created a shared segment, all data is private to the process.

A variable in a DLL can be imported by a declaration of the form

```
__declspec(dllimport) int X;
```

The declaration should appear in the DLL source as

```
__declspec(dllexport) int X;
```

There is a fundamental conflict here. The variable cannot be declared dllimport and dllexport in the same module. Hence, the module cannot include its own .h file without generating a compilation error. However, you can take advantage of some preprocessor symbols that most development environments define for you (they do this because the major libraries, such as windows.h and afxwin.h (MFC) require these symbols be defined). The DLL-related symbols are shown in Table 16.3.

Table 16.3: Preprocessor symbols of interest to DLL writers

Symbol	Meaning
_WINDOWS	Code is being compiled for a Windows application. This symbol is not defined for console applications.
_WINDLL	Code is being compiled for a Windows DLL.
_USRDLL	The DLL contains MFC code but does not export any MFC classes. It contains the MFC library, statically linked.
_AFXDLL	The DLL contains MFC code and links to the shared MFC runtime. The main application is an MFC application.

You can use the presence of the _WINDLL symbol to decide that you are compiling the DLL, in which case you *don't* want the dllimport declaration to appear in the module. Or you can use its absence to decide that you are compiling the main application.

For a dynamically loaded DLL, you can use `GetProcAddress` to get the address of a data item. If the data item is declared in the DLL as

```
__declspec(dllexport) int value;
```

then you can access it in the application after the application has done a dynamic load by doing this:

```
int * val;
val = (int *)GetProcAddress(hDLLinst, "value");
```

Summary of Export Techniques

There are three methods for exporting a definition, listed in the order that Microsoft recommends you use. All three can be used in the same program.

1. The `__declspec(dllexport)` modifier in the source code

2. An `/EXPORT` specification in a linker command

3. An `EXPORTS` statement in a `.def` file

When the linker builds a program that contains exports, it also creates an import library, unless an `.exp` file is used in the build.

Exploring DLL Techniques

We explore several uses of DLLs in the following examples we develop, including these:

- A simple DLL that provides some utility functions, implicitly loaded

- A simple DLL that requires per-process initialization (and finalization)

- A DLL that provides localization support in code, explicitly loaded

- A DLL that provides localization support as a resource-only DLL, explicitly loaded

- A DLL that uses the C runtime system

- A DLL that can support multiple threads using thread-local storage

- A DLL that uses a shared data segment

- A DLL that provides support for a "hook" function to intercept messages, implicitly loaded

One of the most important–and more traditional–uses of DLLs, not in the list above, is to provide custom controls. However, it is being supplanted in modern Win32 applications by the use of OLE Control Extensions (OCX/ActiveX controls).

A DLL Requiring No Initialization

The simplest DLL is one that requires no initialization or termination processing. It doesn't have a DllEntryPoint function, and it looks like a simple collection of library functions. There is no static state in any global variables (this allows us to defer the discussion of threads to a later example). All state of a function is in its parameters or on the stack. We show here how simple it is to use a DLL to encapsulate simple library functions.

We are going to write a simple utility function, formatMessageBox, that can accept either string IDs or string pointers for a caption and a message string plus a variable number of arguments that are formatted according to the message string. The source file for this simple formatting function is shown in Listing 16.1. The header file the client includes is shown in Listing 16.2. An example of how to call it is shown in Listing 16.3, and finally, the STRINGTABLE resource from the resource file used by the DLL is shown in Listing 16.4.

Listing 16.1: formatMessageBox DLL source file msgbox.c

```
#define STRICT
#include <windows.h>
#include <windowsx.h>
#include <winerror.h>


/*************************************************************
*                    formatMessageBox
* Inputs:
*        HWND hWnd: Parent window handle; may be NULL
*        HINSTANCE hInst: Instance handle for string
*                         resources, or NULL if no
*                         resources used, or hWnd
*                         provides instance
*        LPCTSTR body: Body string, or
*                      MAKEINTRESOURCE(id) for string ID
*        LPCTSTR caption: Caption string, or
*                         MAKEINTRESOURCE(id) for string
*                         ID
*        DWORD flags: MessageBox flags
*        ...: Additional parameters used for formatting
*             the message
* Result: int
*        Result of MessageBox call, or 0 if any failure
* Effect:
*        Uses the body string as a formatting string for
*        the variable argument list; formats the
*        arguments and pops up a messagebox
*        If return value is 0, GetLastError will give
*        the reason
* Notes:
*        If the instance handle is NULL and a
*        MAKEINTRESOURCE parameter is passed in, the
*        instance associated with the parent window
*        will be used to locate the string resource.
*        If the parent handle is NULL, the function
*        will return 0 with
*             GetLastError() == ERROR_INVALID_HANDLE.
*        Uses FormatMessage to format the message, so
```

```
 *         the message string must be in terms of
 *         FormatMessage formatting escapes
 **********************************************************/

__declspec(dllexport) int __cdecl
formatMessageBox(HWND hWnd,
                          HINSTANCE hInst,
                          LPCTSTR body,
                          LPCTSTR caption,
                          DWORD flags,
                          ...)
    {
    TCHAR fmt[256];
    TCHAR cap[256];
    LPCTSTR pfmt;
    LPCTSTR pcap;
    HINSTANCE rinst = NULL;
    LPCTSTR pbody = NULL;
    int result;
    va_list args;

    __try
        { /* try */
        va_start(args, flags);

        if (hInst == NULL && hWnd != NULL)
            rinst = GetWindowInstance(hWnd);
        else
            rinst = hInst;

        if(HIWORD(caption) == 0)
            { /* load caption */
            if(rinst == NULL)
                { /* bad handle */
                SetLastError(ERROR_INVALID_HANDLE);
                return 0;
                } /* bad handle */

            LoadString(rinst, LOWORD(caption), cap, DIM(cap));
            pcap = cap;
            } /* load caption */
        else
            { /* string pointer */
            pcap = caption;
            } /* string pointer */

        if(HIWORD(body) == 0)
            { /* load format string */
            if(rinst == NULL)
                { /* bad handle */
                SetLastError(ERROR_INVALID_HANDLE);
                return 0;
                } /* bad handle */

            LoadString(rinst, LOWORD(body), fmt, DIM(fmt));
            pfmt = fmt;
            } /* load format string */
```

```
        else
            { /* fmt pointer */
             pfmt = body;
            } /* fmt pointer */

        if(FormatMessage(FORMAT_MESSAGE_FROM_STRING |

              pfmt,
              0,     // no message ID when FROM_STRING
              0,     // no language ID when FROM_STRING
              (LPTSTR)&pbody,
              0,
              &args) == 0)
            { /* FormatMessage failed */
             // Note: GetLastError already set by
             // FormatMessage
             return 0;
            } /* FormatMessage failed */

        return MessageBox(hWnd, pbody, pcap, flags);
        } /* try */
    __finally
        { /* finally */
         va_end(args);
         if(pbody != NULL)
            LocalFree((LPVOID)pbody);
        } /* finally */
  }
```

Listing 16.2: header file **msgbox.h**

```
#ifdef __cplusplus
extern "C" {
#endif
int __cdecl
formatMessageBox(HWND hWnd, HINSTANCE hInst,
                 LPCTSTR body,
                 LPCTSTR caption,
                 DWORD flags,
                 ...);
#ifdef __cplusplus
          }
#endif
```

Listing 16.3: Calling **formatMessageBox**

```
    TCHAR name[256];
    GetModuleFileName(NULL, name, DIM(name));
    formatMessageBox(hWnd,
                NULL,
                MAKEINTRESOURCE(IDS_MODULE_BODY),
                MAKEINTRESOURCE(IDS_MODULE_CAPTION),
                MB_OK | MB_ICONINFORMATION,
                name);
```

Listing 16.4: The **STRINGTABLE** resource

```
STRINGTABLE PRELOAD DISCARDABLE
BEGIN
```

```
        IDS_MODULE_BODY              "The module name is %1"
        IDS_MODULE_CAPTION           "Module Name"
END
```

You should, if you have not already, read the discussions of the FormatMessage function (Chapter 12, page 927) and structured exception handling, in particular, termination handling (Chapter 7, page 510).

The most important feature of the source code that makes it different from a statically linked function of the same type is the presence of the __declspec(dllexport) attribute. We have written this in directly because this function is always linked as a DLL function. However, if you want to support both a static and dynamic library, you might want to add these declarations:

```
#ifdef _WINDLL
#define DLL_EXPORT __declspec(dllexport)
#else
#define DLL_EXPORT
#endif
```

and replace the __declspec(dllexport) with the new linkage type DLL_EXPORT. In a development environment other than Microsoft's, you may also need to define this symbol differently, depending on your compiler's syntax for exports.

Note the special use of the __cplusplus conditional in Listing 16.2. This allows the header file to be included in both a C and a C++ compilation. Because the code is implemented in a C file and the C compiler does not practice "name mangling", the encoding used to support function overloading in C++. If you don't use this conditional to force a "C" linkage type, you won't be able to call this DLL from a C++ application.

A DLL Requiring Initialization/Finalization

A more common case of a DLL is a DLL that requires per-process initialization and finalization. A custom control, a common use of a DLL prior to OCX and ActiveX controls, is implemented by a window class, so we have to register the window class when the DLL first connects to the process. We do this by responding to the DLL_PROCESS_ATTACH event:

```
BOOL WINAPI DllEntryPoint(HINSTANCE hInst, DWORD Reason, LPVOID reserved)
    {
      switch (Reason)
        { /* reason */
          case DLL_PROCESS_ATTACH:
              return registerMyClass( );
          case DLL_PROCESS_DETACH:
              unregisterMyClass( );
              break;
        } /* reason */
      return TRUE;   // ignore other cases
    }
```

The registerMyClass function is called to handle the DLL_PROCESS_ATTACH event. It registers a class using the RegisterClass function. The result of registerMyClass is a Boolean value indicating whether the class successfully registered. The class is registered in the process that attaches the DLL.

The `unregisterMyClass` calls the `UnregisterClass` function to remove the class from the process. When we get the `DLL_PROCESS_DETACH` event, we know that we aren't going to be able to do anything with the window class because all the code that would act on it is in the DLL that is being detached. But we have to consider the consequences if this was the result of a `FreeLibrary`. When the user selects some other menu item or action, the library might again be loaded with `LoadLibrary` and a new `DLL_PROCESS_ATTACH` event would then occur. If we have not unregistered the class, then the second time we attempt to register the class with the `RegisterClass` function it will fail because the class is already defined and we will return FALSE; this will cause the `LoadLibrary` function to return NULL. So we have to be careful to ensure that whatever state is created in the process on a `DLL_PROCESS_ATTACH` event is cleaned up on a `DLL_PROCESS_DETACH` event, in the expectation that another `DLL_PROCESS_ATTACH` event will occur for this DLL in the context of the same process.

A Simple Localization Function Library

One important use of DLLs is to allow for localization. This support can be as simple as a collection of strings in a specific language or as elaborate as a collection of locale-specific functions, string resources, and dialogs. We look at how to handle resources in the next section. Here we give a very simple example of how you might provide localization support for a railroad timetable. We choose this example because railroad timetables often do *not* use the normal time format of the country. As an example, although the standard in Norway is to express times using a 12-hour clock, railroad timetables in Norway are always expressed in a 24-hour clock.[10]

Listing 16.5 shows the time formatting function from the source file `nortime.c`, which will become part of the code of the DLL `norrail.dll`. This DLL will provide the necessary functions for supporting reports about rail travel for an application running in Norway. Listing 16.6 shows the time formatting function from the source file `ustime.c`. This function will become part of the code of the DLL `usrail.dll`, which provides the same functionality for a U.S.-based application.

Listing 16.7 illustrates a client application that uses these DLLs. The correct implementation of this program would be to search its launch directory for all DLLs and for each DLL that provides localization support. (You can determine the latter with the `VerQueryValue` function, using a private attribute you set to separate language support DLLs from other kinds of DLLs.) We show a much simpler approach here: We assume a fixed number of languages encoded in the menu. This is done solely to simplify the exposition.

Note our use of the `WM_INITMENUPOPUP` message to enable or disable the report menu item, depending on how successful the last language load operation was. This is one way to ensure that we won't ever call

---

[10] For trivia buffs, the reason was that in the early days of railroads in Norway, one train was scheduled to make a high-speed run between two cities at a certain time of day. Another train was scheduled to make a high-speed run in the opposite direction 12 hours later. Due to an error in interpreting the times, the two trains left at the same time and met head-on on the single track between the cities in one of the worst railroad accidents in Norway's history. The rules for railroad schedules were immediately changed to ensure that this particular error would never again occur; railroad timetables in Norway are legislated to use 24-hour time designations. Complexities like this mean that using the locale-specific information provided by Windows is *not* always sufficient to guarantee you will meet the national standards, since there may be more than one standard and the choice of standard may be application-specific.

through a NULL function pointer; we simply don't allow any actions that would require using the uninitialized pointer.

Listing 16.5: Excerpt from `nortime.c`

```
// Format time for Norwegian railway schedule
__declspec(dllexport) void railTime(struct tm * time, LPTSTR dst)
    {
    wsprintf(dst, _T("%02d:%02d"), time->tm_hour, time->tm_min);
    }
```

Listing 16.6: Excerpt from `ustime.c`

```
// Format time for U.S. railway schedule
__declspec(dllexport) void railTime(struct tm * time, LPTSTR dst)
    {
    wsprintf(dst, _T("%02d:%02d%c"),
            (time->tm_hour < 1
                    ? 12
                    : (time->tm_hour > 12
                                ? time->tm_hour - 12
                                : time->tm_hour)),
            time->tm_min,
            (time->tm_hour < 12 ? _T('a') : _T('p')));
    }
```

Listing 16.7: Using the `railTime` function

```
static HMODULE railLib = NULL;
typedef void (*RAILTIME)(struct tm * time, LPTSTR dst);
RAILTIME railTime;

static void loadRail(LPCTSTR libname)
    {
    if(railLib != NULL)
        FreeLibrary(railLib);
    railLib = LoadLibrary(libname);
    if(railLib == NULL)
        { /* error */
        railTime = (RAILTIME) NULL;
        return; // railLib is NULL
        } /* error */
    railTime = (RAILTIME) GetProcAddress(railLib, "railTime");
    }

static void onCommand(HWND hwnd, int id, HWND ctl, UINT codeNotify)
    {
    switch(id)
        { /* id */
        case IDM_NORWAY:
            loadRail(_T("NORRAIL.dll"));
            return;
        case IDM_US:
            loadRail(_T("USRAIL.dll"));
            return;
        // ... other countries here
        } /* id */
    }
```

```
static void onInitMenuPopup(HWND hwnd, HMENU menu)
    {
      BOOL state;
      state = (railLib == NULL || railTime == NULL
                  ? MF_GRAYED
                  : MF_ENABLED);
      EnableMenuItem(IDM_SHOWSCHEDULE, state);
    }

LRESULT CALLBACK mainWndProc(HWND hwnd, UINT msg,
                            WPARAM wParam,
                            LPARAM lParam)
    {
    switch(msg)
        { /* msg */
          HANDLE_MESSAGE(hwnd, WM_COMMAND, onCommand);
          // ...
          HANDLE_MESSAGE(hwnd, WM_INITMENUPOPUP, onInitMenuPopup);
        } /* msg */
    }
```

A DLL Containing Dialog Resources

You can include dialog resources in a DLL. A common use is to provide localization. The longer labels and edit controls required by some languages may necessitate a different layout, Also, for right-to-left languages such as Arabic and Hebrew the labels should be on the right, not the left, of the input boxes. Another use is to provide different implementations of an abstract interface. Since we've already covered localization, we next look at a customization example.

When we include a dialog resource in a DLL, we can take one of two approaches. One is to build a resource-only DLL that contains the dialog resource (among other resources). Another is to place the dialog resource and its handler in the DLL. A good example of the latter is the "common dialog"; the dialog templates for the common dialogs and their handler functions are all in the `comdlg32.dll` library. You invoke a common dialog by calling a function in the DLL. A sample of this is shown in Listing 16.8.

Listing 16.8: A dialog and its code in a DLL

```
#include <windows.h>

HINSTANCE hInst;

BOOL WINAPI DllEntryPoint(HINSTANCE hInstDll, DWORD reason, LPVOID reserved)
    {
    switch(reason)
        { /* reason */
          case DLL_PROCESS_ATTACH:
              hInst = hInstDll;
              // .. other initialization here
              return TRUE;
          // .. other events as required
        } /* reason */
    }

BOOL CALLBACK myDialogWndProc(HWND hDlg,
                UINT msg, WPARAM wParam, LPARAM lParam)
```

```
    {
    // .. handler for dialog
    }

__declspec(dllexport) int doMyDialog(HWND parent, MyDialogData * mdd)
    {
    return DialogBoxParam(hInst,
                    MAKEINTRESOURCE(IDD_MYDIALOG),
                    parent,
                    myDialogWndProc,
                    (LPARAM) mdd);
    }
```

The specification of this DLL is that the use fills in a `MyDialogData` structure according to whatever rules you provide and then passes a pointer to this structure and a reference to a parent window to the visible interface you've provided, the `doMyDialog` function. Upon completion, the dialog will have modified the structure and the return result will indicate the status you care to return to the caller: success, failure, cancellation, or other.

The important points here are that you must save the DLL's instance handle in a statically allocated variable during the `DLL_PROCESS_ATTACH` event so that it can be used later when the `DialogBoxParam` function needs it to specify the source of the dialog resource. When `DialogBoxParam` is called, it specifies this instance handle and the name (in this case, the integer ID) of the resource. A resource is always designated by giving its module (instance) handle.

 According to Matt Pietrek, in *Windows 95 System Programming Secrets* (page 50, to be precise), in Win32 an `HINSTANCE` and an `HMODULE` are exactly the same thing.

There is no particular reason both the handler code and the resource need to be in the same DLL. You could have the handler code in your main application and deliver the dialog resources in a resource-only DLL (see the next section). Or you could put both the code and the handler in the same DLL, as we did here. You could even deliver the code in one DLL and the (localized) resources in another! Windows imposes no limits on how you arrange your system components.

A Resource-only DLL Containing Strings and Other Resources

Another very common usage of a DLL is to construct a *resource-only* DLL. A resource-only DLL has only resources; it has no executable code or program data. The simplest resource you might use is a STRINGTABLE resource; however, icons, accelerator tables, menus, and dialogs are also candidates. In addition, you can define your own kinds of resources (a resource, after all, is just a "bunch of bits" you can access by name or integer ID).

A resource-only DLL can be used for localization, but it can also be used for other kinds of customization. For example, you might use a collection of DLLs to define different keyboard shortcuts by including different accelerator resources in each. You could provide different end-user menu configurations by having different DLLs have different menu resources (these can either be complete menus or simply submenus).

Table 16.4: Resource file functions

Function	Resources
FindResource	Locates a resource in a module.
FindResourceEx	Locates a resource in a module.
LoadAccelerators	Loads an accelerator table resource.
LoadBitmap	Loads a bitmap resource.
LoadCursor	Loads a cursor resource.
LoadIcon	Loads an icon resource.
LoadImage	Loads an icon, cursor, or bitmap resource.
LoadMenu	Loads a menu resource.
LoadResource	Loads a resource from a module, given a resource handle.
LoadString	Loads a string resource.
LockResource	Locks a resource in memory.

```
USA.rc          IDS_GOOD_DAY "Have a nice day"

Australia.rc    IDS_GOOD_DAY "G'day, mate"

Germany.rc      IDS_GOOD_DAY "Guten Tag"

France.rc       IDS_GOOD_DAY "Bonjour"

Spain.rc        IDS_GOOD_DAY "Buenos dias"
```

Figure 16.1: Sample STRINGTABLE entries for various languages

To access resources, you use LoadLibrary just as in the previous example. However, instead of using GetProcAddress to get procedure pointers, you use various resource functions to load the resources. These are summarized in Table 16.4. The simplest form for a resource-only DLL is one with just a STRINGTABLE. Consider a declaration file, such as one called resource.h, that contains the declaration

```
#define IDS_GOOD_DAY 242
```

We can then define, in a variety of .rc files, implementations of this string, such as shown in Figure 16.1. We can then implement an appropriate regional greeting with the function

```
void greet( )
   {
   TCHAR greeting[256];
   if(LoadString(hLanguage, IDS_GOOD_DAY, greeting, DIM(greeting)) == 0)
      return;
   MessageBox(NULL, greeting, _T(""), MB_TASKMODAL | MB_OK);
   }
```

DLLs with User-defined Resources

In Win32, you have two approaches to sharing read-only data with other instances of applications. You can use resources in DLLs, or you can use memory-mapped files (you can also use memory-mapped files for sharing read/write data). Because this is the chapter on DLLs, we show the DLL resource technique here.

Why would you want to use a resource, instead of a file? This is an engineering decision based on several considerations. These include

- a desire to minimize the number of files delivered (the data could be part of a more general resource-only DLL)

- a desire to minimize interaction with localization or component architecture

- a desire to utilize good abstraction techniques

Different implementations of the data layout could be packaged with different implementations of the accessing algorithms in the same DLL, thus allowing you to architect "object-oriented" data. Old data contained its accessing code and new data contains its own accessing code, which could be implemented quite differently.

A simple example of an application that could utilize user-defined resources is a "catalog" application. What we want is a fairly small database that encodes a part number, a description, and pricing data. The goal is to have a database that can be easily downloaded (perhaps daily or weekly) via modem. This is a classic "publication from database" problem. Using tokenization gives substantial compression for certain classes of data. This example is a very brief summary of the article "Tokenized Databases", cited in "Further Reading".

Consider the data shown in Figure 16.2. The numbers in parentheses are the number of bytes in the field shown. We ignore pricing data to simplify the exposition and drawings. The catalog data from Industrial Bolt Manufacturers is stored in a desktop database. Implemented as a file, this data requires 60 bytes per record, so the eight records shown in Figure 16.2 take 480 bytes of data.

Part # (5)	Category (20)	Style (20)	Size (15)
74321	Lockwasher	External star	6
87412	Lockwasher	Internal star	6
71547	Lockwasher	Split	6
78932	Nut	Hex	6-32 × 1/4
78933	Nut	Hex	6-32 × 3/16
12694	Screw	Flat head	6-32 × 1/2
12874	Screw	Flat head	6-32 × 1/2
12345	Screw	Round head	6-32 × 1/2

Figure 16.2: Sample catalog data

Figure 16.3: Sample catalog data, compressed

Part # (4)	Category (2)	Style (2)	Size (2)
74321	9	5	1
87412	9	5	1
71547	9	13	1
78932	10	7	3
78933	10	7	4
12694	12	6	2
12874	12	6	2
12345	12	11	2

String Table Data:

ID (4)	Text	(Length)
1	"6"	1
2	"6-32 × 1/2"	10
3	"6-32 × 1/4"	10
4	"6-32 × 3/16"	11
5	"External star"	13
6	"Flat head"	9
7	"Hex"	3
8	"Internal star"	13
9	"Lockwasher"	10
10	"Nut"	3
11	"Round head"	10
12	"Screw"	5
13	"Split"	5
52	Total	103

If, however, you run a tokenization algorithm, the data can be re-encoded in a fashion similar to that shown in Figure 16.3. Here we observe that the numeric part number can be encoded in 4 bytes. By collecting all the strings, sorting them, and removing duplicates and then adding an integer encoding, we can represent any string in 2 bytes (provided there are fewer than 65,536 unique strings) and thus reduce the actual records to their string references. Now each record takes only 10 bytes, so the eight records shown take only 80 bytes, plus the string data. Counting the 4 bytes required to encode the string ID and the actual strings, there are 155 bytes of "dictionary" data, for a total of 235 bytes of data. The tokenized database for this trivial example is less than *half* the size of the original. For realistic databases, the compression ratio can be even higher.[11]

We can use user-defined resources to prepare this database. Realistically, several resources and perhaps several resource files might be required to encode a large database, due to limitations on resource sizes. For this example, however, we use a simple encoding. In Listing 16.9, we encode the 32-bit part number as two 16-bit integers; the resource values for user-defined data are 16-bit values, even in Win32. The resource ID is 1, and the resource type is 1,000 (user-defined resource types are values greater than 255).

---

[11] For an example of how to use resource-only DLLs for this purpose, see the article by Joseph M. Newcomer, "Tokenized Databases", cited in "Further Reading". The compression ratio for the database in that article, compared to the original database and its indices, is 25:1.

Listing 16.9: Resource script for database

```
1 1000
BEGIN
    0x1,      0x2251,      9,       5,      1,
    0x1,      0x5574,      9,       5,      1,
    0x1,      0x177B,      9,      13,      1,
    0x1,      0x3454,     10,       7,      3,
    0x1,      0x3455,     10,       7,      4,
    0x0,      0x3196,     12,       6,      2,
    0x0,      0x324A,     12,       6,      2,
    0x0,      0x3039,     12,      11,      2,
      0,           0,      0,       0,      0
END

STRINGTABLE
BEGIN
         1,    "6",
         2,    "6-32 x 1/2",
         3,    "6-32 x 1/4",
         4,    "6-32 x 3/16",
         5,    "External star",
         6,    "Flat head",
         7,    "Hex",
         8,    "Internal star",
         9,    "Lockwasher",
        10,    "Nut",
        11,    "Round head",
        12,    "Screw",
        13,    "Split"
END
```

Using `FindResource`, `LoadResource`, and `LockResource`, we can bring in this resource, as shown in Listing 16.10.

Listing 16.10: Using a user-defined resource

```
typedef struct {
    DWORD part;
    WORD category;
    WORD style;
    WORD size; } inventory;

HMODULE hdb;
HRSRC res;

inventory * loadDatabase( )
```

pointer will be returned. When there are no more characters to return as tokens, the result is NULL. For example, if you call `strtoken` using the code shown in Listing 16.12 you should get the results shown in Figure 16.4.

If the list box does not have the LBS_SORT style, it should be a list of the words of the input string, in the order they were parsed.

Listing 16.11 shows a simple–and incorrect–implementation of `strtokenW`, which should be equivalent to a simple implementation of the `wcstok` function. Listing 16.13 shows the example rewritten to be thread-safe.

Listing 16.11: A thread-*un*safe implementation of a DLL function

```
LPWSTR strtokenW(LPSTR string, LPSTR delims)
    {
     static LPWSTR str = NULL;   // Thread-unsafe!
     LPWSTR result = NULL;

     if(string != NULL)
         str = string;
     if(str == NULL)
         return NULL;
     if(string != NULL)
         while(*str && wcschr(delims, *str))
             str++;   // skip leading delimiters
      result = str;
      while(*str && wcschr(delims, *str) == NULL)
          str++;   // skip over non-delimiters
      if(*str)
          *str = L'\0';
      else
          str = NULL;
      return result;
    }
```

Listing 16.12: Calling `strtoken`

```
TCHAR string[] = _T(" This is a sample\nmultiline\tstring\n with spaces");
TCHAR seps[] = _T(" \t\n");

void StringsToList(HWND hListBox, LPSTR string, LPCSTR delims)
    {
     LPSTR result;
     int index;

     for(result = strtoken(string, delims);
             result = strtoken(NULL, delims);)
         { /* scan string */
          index = ListBox_AddString(hListBox, result);
          // ... other processing here
         } /* scan string */
    }
```

Note that this simple implementation has a serious defect in a multithreaded environment. If, in the middle of one thread, control is preempted and some other thread (perhaps a serial line handler worker thread) wants to parse its input, the static pointer `str` will be corrupted. When control returns to the GUI thread, the pointer will now be pointing somewhere other than where we expect it to. We will get, at the very least, non-sensical results and, at the worst, an invalid memory access fault.

To make this thread-safe, we have to use not a static variable, but a thread-local variable. Our complete `strtokenW` function is shown in Listing 16.13. Note our use of a termination handler to ensure that the thread-local value is always correctly updated.

Listing 16.13: Thread-safe DLL with thread-local state

```c
static int threadtoken;

BOOL WINAPI DllEntryPoint(HINSTANCE hInstDLL,DWORD reason, LPVOID reserved)
    {
      switch(reason)
          { /* reason */
          case DLL_PROCESS_ATTACH:
              if(!_CRT_INIT(hInstDLL, reason, reserved))
                  return FALSE;
              threadtoken = TlsAlloc( );
              if(threadtoken == TLS_OUT_OF_INDEXES)
                  return FALSE;
              TlsSetValue(threadtoken, NULL);
              return TRUE;

          case DLL_THREAD_ATTACH:
              _CRT_INIT(hInstDLL, reason, reserved);
              TlsSetValue(threadtoken, NULL);
              return TRUE;
          case DLL_THREAD_DETACH:
              _CRT_INIT(hInstDLL, reason, reserved);
              return TRUE;
          case DLL_PROCESS_DETACH:
              _CRT_INIT(hInstDLL, reason, reserved);
              TlsFree(threadtoken);
              return TRUE;
          } /* reason */
    }


LPWSTR strtokenW(LPSTR string, LPSTR delims)
    {
      LPWSTR str = (LPWSTR)TlsGetValue(threadtoken);
      LPWSTR result = NULL;

      _try {
            if(string != NULL)
                str = string;
            if(str == NULL)
                return NULL;
            if(string != NULL)
                while(*str && wcschr(delims, *str))
                    str++;   // skip leading delimiters
            result = str;
            while(*str && wcschr(delims, *str) == NULL)
                str++;   // skip over non-delimiters
            if(*str)
                *str = L'\0';
```

```
        else
            str = NULL;
        }
    _finally
        {
            TlsSetValue(threadtoken, (DWORD)str);
        }
    return result;
    }
```

A DLL That Uses a Shared Data Segment

There are two ways to share data using a DLL: use a shared data segment or use a memory-mapped file. A common reason to share information across applications is when the applications utilize a pool of resources, usually system resources. For example, several applications might manage a network connection or set of network connections. Or several applications are, without knowing it, using "virtual" resources, such as virtual connections to a remote server using a single dial-up connection. An example of this might be an Internet application that runs FTP, Telnet, Mail, and similar simultaneous logical connections over a single dialup SLIP (Serial Line Internet Protocol) line. While each application thinks it has a unique socket connection, all the sockets are realized by a multiplexing scheme implemented by a DLL managing a single shared connection.

Not all data in a DLL is necessarily shared; some might be private to each process. So we recommend that you place the shared data explicitly in a shareable data segment, rather than simply sharing the entire data segment. This requires that you first create a data segment into which you put the shared data. Do this with a #pragma declaration and then specify that this data segment will be shared (do this either in the module definition file or via a linker option).

Creating Named Segments

To create a data segment using the Microsoft compiler, use the following #pragma data_seg declaration. (A different compiler may have its own #pragma or other means of designating a data segment name.)

```
#pragma data_seg(segmentname)
```

The *segmentname* is the name you wish to use to designate the shared segment. For example, we could use a nice mnemonic name like ".SHARED" or we could use something less descriptive, such as "STUFF"; the actual text of the name doesn't matter. An example of a shared data segment also appears in the Wineyes program in Listing 16.19.

Having established a data segment name, you can now declare the variables for it:

```
#pragma data_seg(".SHARED")
HWND hwndMonitor;
int UseCount;
#pragma data_seg( )
int LocalCount;
```

In the Microsoft compilers, the #pragma with no segment name specified returns to the default data segment name for the compilation. Thus the variable LocalCount is in the default data segment for the compilation, which in our case will not be shared.

Dangers of Shared Segments

In the previous example, the variables hwndMonitor and UseCount will be in the data segment called ".SHARED", but the variable LocalCount will be in the default data segment. If you do the obvious and make the data segment called ".SHARED" actually *be* shared and the default data segment not be shared, then all clients of the DLL will see the identical memory location (but not necessarily the identical *address*!) that holds the shared variables. Hence, a change made by any DLL will be immediately seen by all the other DLLs. However, the variable LocalCount will be private to each client; changes made to LocalCount on behalf of one client will not be visible to the other clients of the DLL. Note that you *can't* write

```
#pragma data_seg(".SHARED")
int * pLocalCount;
#pragma data_seg( )
```

and assign the pointer &LocalCount to the variable pLocalCount. This will not work in Win32 because LocalCount really is a private variable *in a private address space*. This address space cannot be shared simply by assigning a pointer to it. Refer to the diagram shown in Figure 16.5. Each process has a separate address space. Depending on how a DLL is loaded, when it is mapped to an address space it may or may not appear in the same logical address. For example, if you are running two instances of your debugger and look at the addresses of a function, say, for example, DllEntryPoint, in each process, you may or may not see the same address. The *code* is shared in the global memory heap. At any given instance, the same copy of the code, located at physical memory address *phys.code*, is referenced by the two processes. However, the *logical* location of that code in each process is not guaranteed to be the same. (For efficiency reasons, Windows tries very hard to actually put the code in the same logical address in all processes that use the DLL, but that is a performance optimization issue that deals with how Windows manages address spaces.)

Now look at the private data segments. When process 1 is created, a copy of the private data segment is created and placed in physical memory at the location *phys.data1*. Like the code, this location may change from time to time due to paging activity, but you, the programmer, never see this. Instead, you see that for a private data variable, for example, LocalCount, there is a logical address in the area of your address space *p1.data*. Process 2 will also see a data value in *its* private data segment, which is stored in *phys.data2*. Because Windows tries to assign the same addresses when it can, if you display the address &LocalCount in each debugger, you might actually see the same logical address, even though the underlying physical addresses are always separate (or, of course, you might see different logical addresses).

Now consider the case of the shared data segment. Like the shared code segment, there is only one copy, at *phys.shared*. All processes that share the data segment have a reference to this same physical address (ignoring the tendency of paging to change it around at any time, of course). As with all other addresses, if you go into the debugger and ask for &UseCount, you may get the same address or different addresses, but the addresses will always refer to the same physical location in memory. So if you use the debugger to change the value of UseCount to 10 in process 1, switch to process 2 (also stopped in the debugger), and then look at the value, it will indeed be 10.

Now look what happens if we have a shared variable, pLocalCount, and we store &LocalCount into it. Because LocalCount could be at different logical addresses in process 1 and process 2, this is a fundamentally meaningless activity anyway. But even if the address were the same in both, note that you can't actually *do* anything with the address from the other process because the private data pages are not accessible outside their own process. If &LocalCount is the same address in both processes, then writing (*pLocalCount)++ in process 1 will simply increment the variable LocalCount in process 1; it cannot possibly increment the value in process 2. But if &LocalCount is *different* in each process, the expression will either increment a datum in your process that you never heard of or (more likely) give you an access fault because the address may not even be in your address space!

You should never store ordinary pointers in any shared memory objects. You also must be exceedingly careful about how you use such values as handles because handles are often meaningful only within the process that created them. There are also problems about *synchronization* that come into consideration, which we talk about in Chapter 18.

In Win16, this technique not only would have worked; it also would even have been recommended as a means of sharing data across processes. It will not work in Win32.

Sharing Named Segments

Having created a named segment and put a carefully selected collection of data in it, you now have to instruct Windows that this data segment will be a shared data segment. You can do this either by creating a module definition file (or adding to one you already have) and including the SECTIONS declaration:

```
SECTIONS
    sectionname attributes
```

for example,

```
SECTIONS
    .SHARED read write shared
```

or by using the linker option:

```
/SECTION:name[=newname][,attributes][,alignment]
```

where, for our example, we would write

```
/SECTION:.SHARED,rws
```

The complete set of attributes that can be specified is given in Table 16.5. When you are using the linker option switch, you can negate an attribute by placing an ! in front of it. So, for example, a segment that is normally read/write can be made read-only by giving it the attribute: "!w". The command-line option characters and the module definition keywords are not case-sensitive. Note that the module definition file limits you to only a subset of the attributes.

Figure 16.5: DLL shared segments

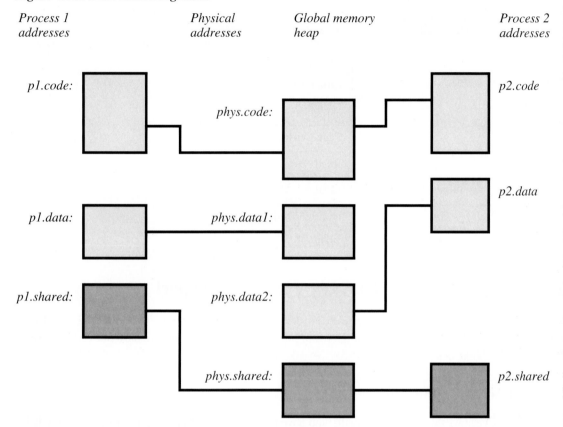

Table 16.5: Section attributes

/SECTION Attribute	SECTION Keyword	Meaning
c		Code.
d		Discardable.
e	execute	Executable.
i		Initialized data.

Table 16.5: Section attributes

/SECTION Attribute	SECTION Keyword	Meaning
k		Cached virtual memory.
m		Link remove.
o		Link info.
p		Paged virtual memory.
r	read	Read.
s	shared	Shared.
u		Uninitialized data.
w	write	Write.

The `Wineyes` Example DLL Module: Hook Support

Now we take all this and put it together into a system-wide "server" application–`Wineyes`–that uses a shared DLL. This DLL illustrates several interesting features of Windows that we have not yet discussed, so we look at it in some detail.

System Hook Function Types

If you've been reading this book sequentially and have read all of this chapter up to this point, there is little in our example DLL that you've not already seen. The `SetWineyesHook` function is meant to be called by the `Wineyes` application program, which passes the handle of its main application window. The function saves the window handle and establishes a system message hook with the following statement:

```
HHOOK hhook ;

hhook = SetWindowsHookEx (WH_GETMESSAGE,
                          (HOOKPROC) WineyesMsgHook,
                          hModule, NULL) ;
```

The `SetWindowsHookEx` function installs a *filter function* for one of several different types of message hooks. Windows calls the filter function whenever one of the selected events occurs, and the filter function can process events before they are sent to an application. More than one filter function may be established for a single hook type by multiple applications. Windows calls each filter function and passes it a message (which a hook function earlier on the hook chain might already have modified) before giving the message to an application. The `hModule` variable is a global variable that contains the value that Windows passes to the DLL's `DllEntryPoint` function.

The types of system hooks are listed in Table 16.6. A hook may be system-wide, thread-local, or process-local. Hooks that can be system-wide have a check mark in the **Sys** column, and hooks that can be thread-local or process-local have a check mark in the **Thr** column.

Table 16.6: System hook types

Symbolic Name	Sys	Thr	Description
WH_CALLWNDPROC	✓	✓	Windows calls the filter whenever the SendMessage function is called.
WH_CALLWNDPROCRET	✓	✓	Windows calls the filter whenever the SendMessage function returns.
WH_CBT	✓	✓	Windows calls the filter before activating, creating, destroying, minimizing, maximizing, moving, or sizing a window; before removing a mouse or keyboard event from the system message queue; before setting the input focus; or before synchronizing with the system message queue.
WH_DEBUG	✓	✓	Windows calls the filter before calling any other filter installed by the SetWindowsHookEx function.
WH_FOREGROUNDIDLE	✓	✓	Allows an application to perform low-priority tasks when its foreground thread is idle. This is called whenever the foreground thread is about to become idle.
WH_GETMESSAGE	✓	✓	Windows calls the filter whenever the GetMessage function is called.
WH_HARDWARE	✓	✓	Windows calls the filter whenever the application calls the GetMessage or PeekMessage function and there is a nonstandard hardware event in the queue. Mouse and keyboard events are standard hardware events and are not processed by this hook.
WH_JOURNALPLAYBACK	✓		Windows calls the filter whenever a request for an event record is made.
WH_JOURNALRECORD	✓		Windows calls the filter whenever it processes a message from the event queue.
WH_KEYBOARD	✓	✓	Windows calls the filter whenever the GetMessage or PeekMessage functions are about to return a WM_KEYUP or WM_KEYDOWN message.
WH_MOUSE	✓	✓	Windows calls the filter whenever the application calls the GetMessage or PeekMessage function and there is a mouse message to be processed.

Table 16.6: System hook types

Symbolic Name	Sys	Thr	Description
WH_MSGFILTER	✓	✓	Windows calls the filter whenever a dialog box, message box, or menu retrieves a message before processing the message. This intercepts such messages for the task.
WH_SHELL	✓	✓	Windows calls a shell application's callback function to notify it of system events of possible interest.
WH_SYSMSGFILTER	✓		Windows calls the filter whenever a dialog box, message box, or menu retrieves a message before processing the message. This intercepts such messages for all applications in the system.

All filter functions except a WH_MSGFILTER filter function must be resident in a DLL. The filter function for a WH_MSGFILTER can reside in an application only if it is thread-local or process-local. The complete source for the Wineyes message hook handler DLL is shown in Listing 16.19 on page 1161.

When the Wineyes application is about to terminate, it calls the unsetWineyesHook function in the DLL. This function removes the hook function from the filter chain with the following statement:

```
Unhooked = UnhookWindowsHookEx (hhook) ;
```

Windows stops passing messages to the filter function after the UnhookWindowsHookEx function removes the filter function from the chain of hook functions.

The setWineyesHook and unsetWineyesHook functions must be exported because they are called from outside the DLL.

The wineyesMsgHook function is a callback function. This is the filter function specified in the call to the SetWindowsHookEx function. Because we're hooking the WH_GETMESSAGE hook, Windows calls the wineyesMsgHook function whenever any application calls the GetMessage function immediately after the GetMessage function has retrieved a message from the application message queue. Windows passes the message to the filter function before giving the message to the requesting application. The filter function can examine or modify the message.

The wineyesMsgHook function examines each message, looking for WM_MOUSEMOVE and WM_NCMOUSEMOVE messages. Whenever it finds such a message, it posts a UWM_WINEYESHOOK message to the application message queue for the Wineyes application program. The UWM_WINEYESHOOK message is a private message understood only by the Wineyes application program and the Wineyes DLL. It is defined in the wineyes.h header file included by all application source files and all DLL source files. The entire purpose of the DLL is to notify the application any time the mouse moves. The Wineyes application handler for this message is shown in Listing 16.17.

You must be extremely careful what you do in a hook function. Windows calls your function on the stack of the currently executing application. You have no control over how much space is available on that stack. So you must not do anything that might result in a number of nested function calls or that uses a considerable amount of stack (like defining a large buffer as a local variable). We simply post a message to the `Wineyes` application and return. When the `Wineyes` application retrieves the message, it is running on its own stack and can do whatever it likes.

Because the `wineyesMsgHook` function must post the message back to a specific application window, it must have the window handle. So the window handle must be in a shared data segment, since every application that uses this DLL will get a private data segment. And because this application sets a system-wide hook, every application will implicitly link to it! We use the techniques we discussed earlier in the chapter to create a shared data segment to hold the window handle. (One way to tell if you've done this wrong, for example, is to notice that `Wineyes` will not move the eyes unless the mouse is moving over its own window. That's because, without a shared data segment, all the other applications see a window handle of 0.)

The `Wineyes` Application Module

The `Wineyes` application is a version of the X Windows xeyes program. It's a little face whose eyes constantly follow the cursor no matter which application is currently active. Figure 16.6 shows the beady little eyes. It is based on the standard template program we developed. We eliminated the toolbar and menu and their associated code.

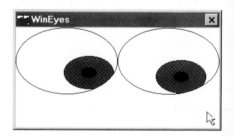

Because we don't have a menu, we placed the menu item that displays the **About...** dialog box on the application's system menu. We also implemented a pop-up menu on the right mouse button that allows us either to show the **About...** dialog box or to exit the application. To create the pop-up menu, we use a menu that contains a popup menu and use `LoadMenu` to get a handle for that menu.

Figure 16.6: The `Wineyes` application at work

Every mouse movement results in the `Wineyes` application's drawing to the screen. The version presented has quite a bit of flicker as the eyes are redrawn. This could be avoided by drawing into a memory device context and calling `BitBlt` to transfer the updated image to the screen.

One added feature is the command-line processing performed in the application. We happen to be quite attached to brown eyes[12] so we made that the default eye color. You can change the eye color by specifying three integer RGB values on the command line. For example, run the application from either the Program Manager's **File|Run** menu (Windows NT 3.*x*) or the Start button's **Run** menu item (Windows 95 and Windows NT 4.*x*) and enter `WINEYES 0 0 255`. You'll have a pair of beady blue eyes following the cursor.

The full set of code is on the CD-ROM that accompanies this book. We show some of the more interesting excerpts here.

---

[12] Historical note: The program was originally written by Brent Rector, who has brown eyes. Since he was the original author, his selection has precedence. My eyes are blue.– *jmn*

Here are some useful techniques you won't find elsewhere in this book. For example, we handle parsing the command line by using the special variables __argc and __argv, which are set up by the Windows initialization and serve the same role as argc and argv in conventional Unix or DOS C applications. You have to explicitly declare them in your program. After that, you can use them just like argc and argv:

```
extern int __argc;
extern char * __argv[];
```

Note that __argv is declared as char, not TCHAR. If you need the Unicode versions of the command line, you can use the functions GetCommandLineW and CommandLineToArgvW to parse the Unicode version of the command line.

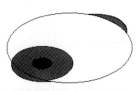

Figure 16.7: Result of failure to clip properly

In the drawEye function in Listing 16.18, we compute a position for the iris of the eye. The actual computation is quite complex, and we approximate it. The effect of this approximation is that without special care the iris is drawn such that it falls partly outside the ellipse defining the border of the eye. This means that although it is drawn, it will not be erased when the ellipse is redrawn, so it leaves a residual trace outside the ellipse. This is shown in Figure 16.7. The obvious solution would be to create a clipping region the same size as the ellipse and use it to clip the area. We also could call FrameRgn and FillRgn to draw the outline. There are some problems with this, however, as outlined in the Knowledge Base article Q83807. The ellipse computed by CreateEllipticRgn is, unfortunately, not the same as that computed by the Ellipse function. If we use FillRgn and FrameRgn to avoid this, as suggested by the article, we find that region outlining and region filling is *much* slower than the Ellipse function. The result is a very annoying flicker.

Our solution is shown in Listing 16.18. We first draw the ellipse using the normal Ellipse function and then create and establish an elliptical clipping region. When we draw the iris, it is clipped by the ellipse, and nothing is drawn outside the eye. This produces the correct output, and the clipping is designed to be very fast. There is a very, very slight error in the region, which works in our favor (if we needed really precise alignment, we would have to tolerate the flicker). One point you should note here is that getting the desired output is often more subtle than the simple solutions would suggest. Also, it turns out that we could have also computed the iris position much more carefully, but that would involve far more complex computations. Note also that it is often easier to approximate than to be precise. It is a matter of taste and engineering decisions to decide what should prevail: precision and complexity or approximation and simplicity. Sometimes you need the precision; sometimes it doesn't matter. Finally, note our use of the SaveDC and RestoreDC functions to preserve the DC state.

Listing 16.14: Excerpts from `initialization.c`

```
BOOL initInstance (HINSTANCE hinst, int CmdShow)
{
    hbrushBlack = GetStockBrush (BLACK_BRUSH) ;
    hbrushWhite = GetStockBrush (WHITE_BRUSH) ;

    if (__argc == 4)
        hbrushIris = CreateSolidBrush (
                RGB (atoi (__argv [1]),
```

```
                    atoi (__argv [2]),
                    atoi (__argv [3]))) ;
        else
            hbrushIris = CreateSolidBrush (RGB(128, 64, 0)) ;// brown

    // Create the application's main frame window
    if (!createMainFrameWindow (hinst, CmdShow))
        return FALSE ;

    return TRUE ;
}

static HWND
createMainFrameWindow (HINSTANCE hinst, int CmdShow)
    {
    HWND   hwnd ;
    TCHAR ClassName [MAX_RESOURCESTRING + 1] ;
    TCHAR Title [MAX_RESOURCESTRING + 1] ;

    // Create the main frame window
    VERIFY (LoadString (hinst, IDR_MAINFRAME,
                ClassName,
                sizeof(ClassName)/sizeof(TCHAR))) ;
    VERIFY (LoadString (hinst, IDS_APP_TITLE, Title,
                sizeof(Title)/sizeof(TCHAR))) ;

    hwnd =
        CreateWindowEx (
                0,          // Extended window styles
                ClassName, // Registered class name
                Title,      // Window caption
                WS_THICKFRAME |
                WS_OVERLAPPED |
                WS_SYSMENU,     // Window style
                CW_USEDEFAULT,  // Horizontal position
                0,              // Vertical position
                GetSystemMetrics(SM_CXSCREEN)/5,// Width
                GetSystemMetrics(SM_CYSCREEN)/5,// Height
                NULL,       // Handle of parent
                            // or owner window
                NULL,       // Handle of menu
                hinst,      // Application instance
                NULL) ;     // Window-creation data

    ASSERT (NULL != hwnd) ;
    if (hwnd == NULL)
        return NULL ;

    ShowWindow (hwnd, CmdShow) ;
    UpdateWindow (hwnd) ;

    return hwnd ;
}
```

After we create the window, we call SetWindowPos to change its Z-order relationship. You can see this in the OnCreate handler in Listing 16.15. By specifying SWP_NOMOVE and SWP_NOSIZE, we cause the position and size parameters to be ignored. This means that only the Z-order will be changed, and it will be positioned to be just before the window whose handle is specified. We specify the special "handle", HWND_TOPMOST, which forces the window to always remain on top of all other windows.

We use the GetSystemMenu function to get a handle to a (copy of) the system menu. Then we extract from its pop-up menu the string for the **About...** box and use it to create a new menu item in the system menu. We have to add a WM_SYSCOMMAND handler to process this menu item, which is also shown in Listing 16.15. We also add the additional cases to our window procedure, shown in Listing 16.16.

Listing 16.15: Excerpts from `MainFrame.c`

```
static BOOL
mainFrame_OnCreate (HWND hwnd, LPCREATESTRUCT cs)
{
 HMENU popupMenu;
 popupMenu = LoadMenu(GetWindowInstance(hwnd), MAKEINTRESOURCE(IDR_POPUP));
 if(popupMenu != NULL)
    { /* add to system menu */
     HMENU menu = GetSystemMenu(hwnd, FALSE);
     TCHAR buffer[40];

     GetMenuString(popupMenu, ID_APP_ABOUT, buffer, DIM(buffer), MF_BYCOMMAND);
     AppendMenu(menu, MF_SEPARATOR, 0, NULL);
     AppendMenu(menu, MF_STRING, ID_APP_ABOUT, buffer);
     DestroyMenu(popupMenu);
    } /* add to system menu */

    setWineyesHook(hwnd);

    SetWindowPos(hwnd, HWND_TOPMOST, 0, 0, 0, 0, SWP_NOMOVE | SWP_NOSIZE);

    return TRUE ;
}

static void mainFrame_OnSysCommand(HWND hwnd, UINT cmd, int x, int y)
    {
     switch(cmd)
        { /* cmd */
        case ID_APP_ABOUT:
                doAbout (hwnd) ;
                return ;
        } /* cmd */
     FORWARD_WM_SYSCOMMAND(hwnd, cmd, x, y, DefWindowProc) ;
    }
```

Listing 16.16: Additional window messages for `Wineyes`

```
LRESULT CALLBACK
mainFrameWndProc (HWND hwnd, UINT message, WPARAM wParam, LPARAM lParam)
{

    switch (message) {
        HANDLE_MSG(hwnd, WM_SYSCOMMAND, mainFrame_OnSysCommand);
        case UWM_WINEYESHOOK:
                return mainFrame_OnWinEyes(hwnd);
```

Listing 16.17: Eye-drawing calls

```
static int mainFrame_OnWinEyes(HWND hwnd)
```

```
      {
      HDC hdc = GetDC (hwnd) ;
      drawEyes (hwnd, hdc) ;
      ReleaseDC (hwnd, hdc) ;
      return 0 ;
      }

static void
mainFrame_OnPaint (HWND hwnd)
      {
      HDC            hdc ;
      PAINTSTRUCT    ps ;

      hdc = BeginPaint (hwnd, &ps) ;

      drawEyes(hwnd, hdc);

      EndPaint (hwnd, &ps) ;
      }
```

Listing 16.18: Eye-drawing functions

```
HBRUSH hbrushIris ;
HBRUSH hbrushBlack;
HBRUSH hbrushWhite;
static POINT ptOldCursorPos ;

static void
drawEye (HWND hwnd, HDC hdc, RECT rectEye, POINT Cursor)
{
      HBRUSH     hbrushOrig ;
      int        RiseSign = 1;
      int        RunSign = 1 ;
      int        Height;
      int        Width;
      int        xDist;
      int        yDist ;
      int        xDelta;
      int        yDelta;
      int        OldROP ;
      LONG       Rise;
      int        Run ;
      POINT      BoundingCenter;
      POINT      IrisCenter ;
      RECT       rectBounding ;
      HRGN       ellipse;

      int        saved = SaveDC(hdc);

      /* Draw the sclera for one eye. */
      hbrushOrig = SelectBrush (hdc, hbrushWhite) ;
      Ellipse (hdc, rectEye.left,  rectEye.top,
                    rectEye.right, rectEye.bottom) ;
      ellipse = CreateEllipticRgn(rectEye.left, rectEye.top,
                            rectEye.right, rectEye.bottom);
      SelectClipRgn(hdc, ellipse);
      /* Calculate the rectangle in which the iris can move. */
      Height = rectEye.bottom - rectEye.top ;
```

```
Width   = rectEye.right  - rectEye.left ;
rectBounding = rectEye ;
InflateRect (&rectBounding, -29 * Width / 100, -27 * Height / 100) ;
ScreenToClient (hwnd, &Cursor) ;
BoundingCenter.x = rectBounding.left +
                (rectBounding.right - rectBounding.left) / 2 ;
BoundingCenter.y = rectBounding.top +
                (rectBounding.bottom - rectBounding.top) / 2 ;
xDelta = Cursor.x - BoundingCenter.x ;
yDelta = Cursor.y - BoundingCenter.y ;
if (!PtInRect (&rectBounding, Cursor)) {
    // Can't center the iris around the cursor point.
    // Use the line from the center of the iris's area of
    // movement to the cursor.  Place the iris at the
    // intersection of this line and the iris movement
    // bounding rectangle.
    Rise = Cursor.y - BoundingCenter.y ;
    RiseSign = (Rise < 0) ? Rise = labs (Rise), -1 : 1 ;
    Run  = Cursor.x - BoundingCenter.x ;
    RunSign = (Run < 0) ? Run = labs (Run), -1 : 1 ;
    xDist = rectBounding.right  - BoundingCenter.x ;
    yDistyDist = rectBounding.bottom - BoundingCenter.y ;
    if (Run != 0 && Rise != 0) {
        yDelta = (int) ((Rise * xDist) / Run) ;
        xDelta = xDist ;
        if (yDelta > yDist) {
            yDelta = yDist ;
            xDelta = (int) ((Run * yDist) / Rise) ;
        }
    }
    else if (Run == 0) {
        yDelta = yDist ;
        xDelta = 0 ;
    }
    else {
        yDelta = 0 ;
        xDelta = xDist ;
    }
}
IrisCenter.x = BoundingCenter.x + xDelta * RunSign ;
IrisCenter.y = BoundingCenter.y + yDelta * RiseSign ;
/* Draw the iris. */
hbrushOrig = SelectBrush (hdc, hbrushIris) ;
Width /= 4 ;
Height /= 4 ;
OldROP = SetROP2 (hdc, R2_MASKPEN) ;
Ellipse (hdc, IrisCenter.x - Width,
            IrisCenter.y - Height,
            IrisCenter.x + Width,
            IrisCenter.y + Height) ;
SetROP2 (hdc, OldROP) ;
SelectBrush (hdc, hbrushBlack) ;
Ellipse (hdc, IrisCenter.x - Width / 3,
            IrisCenter.y - Height / 3,
            IrisCenter.x + Width / 3,
            IrisCenter.y + Height / 3) ;
RestoreDC (hdc, saved) ;
```

```
    DeleteObject(ellipse);
}

void drawEyes (HWND hwnd, HDC hdc)
    {
     POINT  Cursor ;
     RECT   rectEye ;
     RECT   rectClient;

     GetClientRect (hwnd, &rectClient) ;
     GetCursorPos (&Cursor) ;
     if (Cursor.x == ptOldCursorPos.x &&
         Cursor.y == ptOldCursorPos.y)
        return ;
     ptOldCursorPos = Cursor ;
     rectEye.left   = rectClient.left ;
     rectEye.right  = rectClient.right / 2 ;
     rectEye.top    = rectClient.top ;
     rectEye.bottom = 2 * rectClient.bottom / 3 ;
     drawEye (hwnd, hdc, rectEye, Cursor) ;
     rectEye.left   = rectEye.right ;
     rectEye.right  = rectClient.right ;
     drawEye (hwnd, hdc, rectEye, Cursor) ;
    }
```

Listing 16.19: `sethook.c`: The `wineyes.dll` source

```
#define STRICT
#define NOCOMM
#include <windows.h>
#include <windowsx.h>
#include "wineyes.h"

#pragma data_seg(".SHARED")
static HWND hwndWineyes = NULL ;
#pragma data_seg()

static HHOOK       hhook = NULL ;
static HINSTANCE hModule = NULL ;

LRESULT CALLBACK WineyesMsgHook (int nCode, WPARAM wParam, LPARAM lParam) ;

/**********************************************************
*                    DllEntryPoint
* Inputs:
*       HINSTANCE hInstDll: DLL instance
*       DWORD reason: Code for event
*       LPVOID reserved: ignored
* Result: BOOL
*       TRUE for process attach
*       FALSE for all other cases
* Effect:
*       Process attach: Stores the instance handle.
*       Process detach: Unhooks the function
**********************************************************/

BOOL WINAPI DllEntryPoint(HINSTANCE hInstDll, DWORD reason, LPVOID reserved)
    {
```

```
    switch(reason)
        { /* reason */
        case DLL_PROCESS_ATTACH:
            hModule = hInstDll;
            return TRUE;
        case DLL_PROCESS_DETACH:
            if(hwndWineyes != NULL)
                unsetWineyesHook(hwndWineyes);
        } /* reason */
    return FALSE;
    }

/***********************************************************
*                     setWineyesHook
* Inputs:
*       HWND hwnd: Window that will receive notification
*                      messages
* Result: BOOL
*       TRUE if successful
*       FALSE if error, or already hooked
* Effect:
*       Sets a hook to the WineyesMsgHook function for
*       all GetMessage events.
***********************************************************/

__declspec(dllexport)
BOOL WINAPI
setWineyesHook (HWND hwnd)
    {
    /* If already hooked, don't do it again. */
    if (hwndWineyes != NULL)
        return FALSE ;
    hhook =
        SetWindowsHookEx (WH_GETMESSAGE,
                          (HOOKPROC) WineyesMsgHook,
                          hModule,
                          0) ;
    if (hhook != NULL)
        { /* hook set */
        hwndWineyes = hwnd ;
        setter = TRUE;
        return TRUE ;
        } /* hook set */
    return FALSE ;
    }

/***********************************************************
*                     unsetWineyesHook
* Inputs:
*       HWND hwnd: Window reference
* Result: BOOL
*       TRUE if successful
*       FALSE if error
* Effect:
*       Unhooks the hook function
***********************************************************/
```

```
__declspec(dllexport) BOOL WINAPI
unsetWineyesHook (HWND hwnd)
    {
    BOOL Unhooked ;
    if (hwnd != hwndWineyes)
        return FALSE ;
    Unhooked  = FALSE ;
    Unhooked = UnhookWindowsHookEx (hhook) ;
    if (Unhooked)
        hwndWineyes = NULL ;
    return Unhooked ;
    }

/*********************************************************
 *                    WineyesMsgHook
 * Inputs:
 *        int nCode:
 *        WPARAM wParam: not used except as passed on
 *        LPARAM lParam: a reference to the MSG structure
 * Result: LRESULT
 *        0, always
 * Effect:
 *        Intercepts the messages; if it is a mouse move
 *        it redraws the eyes.
 *********************************************************/

LRESULT CALLBACK WineyesMsgHook (int nCode, WPARAM wParam, LPARAM lParam)
    {
    LPMSG lpmsg ;
    if (nCode < 0)
        { /* just pass it on */
        CallNextHookEx (hhook, nCode, wParam, lParam) ;
        return 0 ;
        } /* just pass it on */

    lpmsg = (LPMSG) lParam ;
    if (lpmsg->message == WM_MOUSEMOVE ||
        lpmsg->message == WM_NCMOUSEMOVE)
        PostMessage (hwndWineyes, UWM_WINEYESHOOK, 0, 0) ;

    CallNextHookEx (hhook, nCode, wParam, lParam) ;
    return 0 ;
}
```

Further Reading

The details of DLLs are far too extensive to explore all of them in depth in one chapter. There is a collection of articles on the MSDN CD-ROM that cover highly specialized aspects of DLLs. Particularly interesting ones are included in the list below.

Pietrek, Matt, "Under the Hood" column, *Microsoft Systems Journal,* 1995:11 (November). Also on the MSDN CD-ROM.

Explains in detail the optimization that can be done when __declspec(dllimport) is used, down to the level of the actual instructions in the executable.

Pietrek, Matt, "Windows Q&A" column, *Microsoft Systems Journal,* 1995:8 (August). Also on the MSDN CD-ROM.

> Describes in detail how early binding of DLL addresses can be done so as to improve the performance of a DLL load.

Newcomer, J. M., "Tokenized Databases", *Dr. Dobb's Journal*, November, 1994.

> This article describes how to use token-compression techniques to fit a very large (40MB) database into a very small space (4MB). The database is implemented as a set of resource-only DLLs that are replaceable, so the database can be updated by downloading new DLLs.

Microsoft Corporation, "Dynamic Loading of Win32 DLLs", KB article Q90745.

> A discussion of *preferred base addresses* (also addressed by Matt Pietrek in the cited *Q&A, MSJ* 1995:8) and how Win32 DLLs load.

Richter, Jeffrey, "Load Your 32-bit DLL in Another Process's Address Space Using INJLIB", *Microsoft Systems Journal,* 1994:5 (May). Also on the MSDN CD-ROM.

> Describes how to force a DLL to load in another process's address space. This is a very long and arcane article (40 pages), but it goes into great depth in a number of interesting features you might not otherwise encounter.

17 The Multiple Document Interface

The *multiple document interface* (MDI) is a user interface specification. In particular, the MDI describes how to implement a user interface that permits the user to view and work with several objects within a single application. These objects might be all of the same type or of different types. A word processor that allows the user to open and edit more than one document at a time is an example of multiple objects (documents, in this case) of the same type. A desktop accessory application might display different objects at the same time; for example, a calendar, an appointment book, and a telephone directory.

In many ways, an application following the MDI specification manages its objects similarly to the way Windows manages the application windows on the screen. Windows allows the user to minimize windows and displays them as icons along the bottom of the screen. An MDI application allows the user to minimize an application object, such as a document, which it then displays as an icon along the bottom of the application window's client area.

The code required to coordinate multiple, possibly independent, child windows within an application's main window can become quite complex. For example, when a user switches from one object, such as a document, to a different one, such as a chart, the application might want to provide a completely different menu to the user. As new objects are created within the application, menus need to be changed to allow the user to easily switch between the various windows.

Without MDI support, you would have to write quite a bit of relatively complex code to provide an interface following the MDI specification. Windows has support for MDI applications that you can use to let Windows do much of the messy work while you concentrate on the application itself.

In the first half of this chapter, we explain the three basic steps to creating a MDI application. First, you create the application's main window–the frame window. Next, you create the MDI client window. This window provides most of the window and menu processing logic that is required by MDI applications. Last, you create one or more child (document) windows as required by the application.

In the second half of the chapter, we list and explain a skeletal MDI application. This application uses two types of child (document) windows to illustrate that the child windows are completely independent of each other. You can use this skeletal program as the preliminary structure for your own MDI applications.

The Behavior of an MDI Application

The Microsoft publication *The Windows Interface Guidelines for Software Design* (see "Further Reading") describes the multiple document interface behavior. Following are some of the requirements for a conforming MDI application:

- Minimizing an object (document) window causes an icon representing the object to be displayed in the lower part of the application's window. Minimizing the application window itself hides all the document windows, and Windows displays an icon representing the application in the lower part of the screen (Windows NT 3.*x*) or task bar (Windows 95 or Windows NT 4.*x*), as it does normally.

- MDI applications use additional system keyboard accelerators. Typically, accelerators that apply to the document windows use the **Ctrl** key, whereas a corresponding accelerator for the main application window uses the **Alt** key. For example, **Ctrl+F6** key cycles from one document window to the next. **Ctrl+F4** closes a document window, whereas **Alt+F4** closes the application window. One exception to this pattern is the **Alt+space** and **Alt+minus** accelerators. **Alt+space** pops up the application window's system menu, whereas **Alt+minus** pops up the system menu for the current active document window.

- Document windows do not contain menu bars. The menu bar on the main application window contains the menu for the currently active document window. You might have to change the application menu bar as the user switches from one document window to another. The menu bar should not contain items that do not apply to the currently active document window. When no document window exists, the application menu bar should contain only those items that always apply. Typically, this set-up includes only an item to create a new document window and possibly a **Help** menu item.

- All menu bars should contain the *Window* pop-up menu. Selecting this menu item produces a pop-up window that typically contains, at minimum, the **Tile** and **Cascade** selections, a separator line, and a variable number of following menu items. The **Tile** menu item rearranges all nonminimized document windows and displays them adjacent to each other like floor tiles. The active document window is placed at the top left of the client area of the application window. The **Cascade** menu item rearranges all nonminimized document windows and displays them overlapping from the upper-left corner like stacked index cards. The active document window is placed on top of the stack. A numbered list of all document windows, with a check mark next to the item corresponding to the active document, follows the separator line. Windows maintains this list for you. Selecting a document from the list activates that window.

- When a user maximizes an MDI document window, the title bar for the document window vanishes. Windows appends the text from the document window's title bar to the text in the application's main window's title bar. It inserts the document window's system menu icon as the left-most item on the application window's menu bar. Windows also appends an icon to restore the document window to the far right end of the application window's menu bar.

- The active document window is highlighted to indicate that it is the active document. When the user changes to a different document window, the highlighting is removed. This situation is similar to the way Windows indicates the active window on the screen.

- Creating a new document window in no way affects previously created document windows. For example, when you open a new document window in an MDI-compliant word processor you don't need to close a previously opened document. A new document window is created and coexists with the previously opened document window. You do not display confirmation messages when opening a new document because you don't close the previous one and cannot lose unsaved changes.

Some of these requirements of an MDI application are implemented by code in Windows. Others require you to design your application to operate in a certain fashion. All in all, Windows alleviates much of the work involved in writing an MDI application.

Windows expects an MDI application to handle a few new messages and interact with it in a prescribed manner. The basic structure of the application still follows the fundamental message-loop-based paradigm used by all Windows applications, but it is different in a number of important areas. Next, we look step-by-step at how to create a Window MDI application.

The Basic Steps to Creating an MDI Application

An MDI application needs a window in order to interact with the user. You create the main application window for an MDI application in the same way that you create the main application window for a conventional Windows application. After you've created the main application window, things begin changing.

The sample application, the MDI Explorer, is shown in Figure 17.1. The main application window for an MDI application is called the *frame window*. Normally, you don't display anything within the client area of the frame window. Instead, you create a child window based on the predefined "`MDICLIENT`" window class. This child window is called the *MDI client window* or simply the *client window*. The client window resizes itself to fill the client area of its parent window–the frame window–and provides much of the MDI support for the application.

The client area of the MDI client window is called the *application workspace* and is typically, although not necessarily, the same size as the frame window's client area. Don't mistake the application workspace for the client area of the frame window.

Finally, you create a document window whenever necessary. These windows represent the documents or objects manipulated by the user. A document window is a child window, and its parent window is the MDI client window. In fact, the document windows are called *MDI child windows* in MDI terminology or often just *child windows*. Child windows are displayed within the application workspace and are clipped to its boundaries.

Creating the Frame Window

The frame window for an MDI application is no different from the main application window for a conventional Windows application. You call the `CreateWindow` function to create an overlapped window. The window typically has a caption with a system menu icon to the left of the caption and a minimize icon and a maximize icon to the right. It also generally has a menu bar and a sizing border. The frame window is the main window shown in Figure 17.1. As with most windows, the caption area and menu area are part of the nonclient area. There is a frame client area in which we can do whatever we want our application to do.

You have to register a window class for the frame window and provide a window function to process its messages; however, the message function itself is slightly different. A frame window function calls the `DefFrameProc` function rather than the `DefWindowProc` function to process messages not handled by the window function. In addition, some messages must always be passed to the `DefFrameProc` function even when the frame window function processes the message. The `DefFrameProc` function processes the following messages in addition to those normally processed by a default window function: `WM_COMMAND`, `WM_MENUCHAR`, `WM_NEXTMENU`, `WM_SETFOCUS`, and `WM_SIZE`. The actions are summarized in Table 17.1.

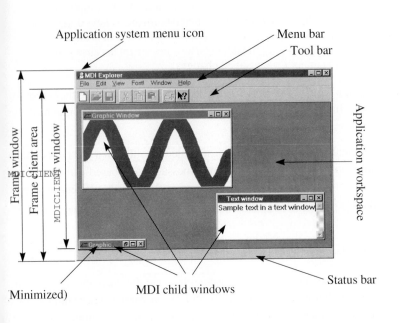

Figure 17.1: Frame and MDI client window layout

Table 17.1: Messages processed by the `DefFrameProc` function

Message	Default Action
WM_COMMAND	If the control ID is one of the child window IDs from the **Window** menu, brings that window to the top, sets focus to it, and makes it the checked window in the menu.
WM_MENUCHAR	If the user selects the **Alt+-** (minus key) combination, activates the system menu of the current MDI child window.
WM_SETFOCUS	Passes the focus message to the MDI client window, which in turn passes it to the active MDI child.
WM_SIZE	Resizes the MDI client window to fit within the client area of the frame. You must override this message if you have other windows that share the client area, such as toolbars or status bars.

Creating the Client Window

You create the MDI client window by calling the CreateWindow function to create a window based on the predefined MDICLIENT window class and the WS_CHILD style. You pass a pointer to a CLIENTCREATESTRUCT structure as the last parameter to the CreateWindow function call. The structure looks like this:

```
typedef struct tagCLIENTCREATESTRUCT {
    HMENU        hWindowMenu;
    UINT         idFirstChild ;
} CLIENTCREATESTRUCT ;
```

The hWindowMenu field contains the handle for the **Window** pop-up menu item on the frame window's menu bar. The MDICLIENT class window function adds the title of each MDI child window to the bottom of this pop-up menu when the child window is created.

The idFirstChild field contains the child window ID, which is assigned to the first MDI child window created. Windows assigns consecutive ascending IDs to each additional MDI child window you create. It reassigns child window IDs, however, when you destroy a child window. The child window IDs for MDI child windows always range from idFirstChild to idFirstChild + n - 1, where n is the current number of MDI child windows.

When the user selects one of the numbered child-window-title menu items on the *Window* pop-up menu on the frame window's menu bar, Windows sends a WM_COMMAND message to the frame window function. The menu ID accompanying this message is a value in the range idFirstChild to idFirstChild + n - 1 and indicates the particular MDI child window that should be activated. Normally, the frame window function passes these WM_COMMAND messages to the active MDI child window, which passes the messages to its default message-handling function, the DefMDIChildProc function. It activates the chosen child window. However, you shouldn't assign any other menu item an ID in the range idFirstChild to idFirstChild + n - 1. If you do, you cannot distinguish between the user's selecting that menu item and an entry on the **Window** pop-up menu. Because you don't usually impose a maximum limit on the number of MDI child windows that the user can create, you don't know the value of n and, therefore, the upper boundary. It probably is best to set idFirstChild to a value greater than all other menu IDs in use.

The MDICLIENT window typically fills the client area of the frame window. However, if your application has windows such as toolbar windows and status windows, these are usually done as sibling windows of the MDICLIENT window. The area available to the MDICLIENT window is what is left over after you have displayed the toolbar, status window, or whatever else you wish to display. This is shown in Figure 17.1, where the toolbar uses part of the top of the client area of the frame window, and the status window uses part of the bottom of the client area of the frame window. The actual window hierarchy is shown in Figure 17.2.

You often will choose to make these additional windows visible or invisible. Typically, when hiding one of these windows, you will resize the MDICLIENT window to cover the space formerly occupied by the window you are hiding, and when making them visible, you will resize the MDICLIENT window to create a space for the now-visible window to display.

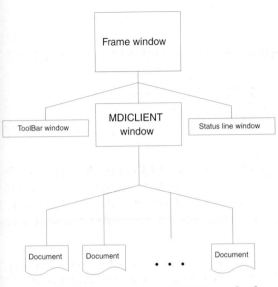

Figure 17.2: Window parent/child hierarchy for MDI applications

Creating a Child Window

You don't create an MDI child window by calling the CreateWindow function. Instead, you use one of two methods. The older method, for compatibility with Win16, calls for you to send a WM_MDICREATE message to the MDI client window, asking it to create an MDI child window for you. You initialize an MDICREATESTRUCT structure and pass a pointer to the structure as part of the WM_MDICREATE message. The contents of this structure inform the MDI client window how you want the child window to appear. The fields of the MDICREATESTRUCT structure contain the same parameters as the ones you would use when you call the CreateWindow function. The structure looks like this:

```
typedef struct tagMDICREATESTRUCT {
        LPCSTR      szClass ;
        LPCSTR      szTitle ;
        HINSTANCE   hOwner ;
        int         x ;
        int         y ;
        int         cx ;
        int         cy ;
        DWORD       style ;
        LPARAM      lParam ;
} MDICREATESTRUCT ;
```

You must register a window class and provide a window function for each distinct child window class. The szClass field of the MDICREATESTRUCT structure specifies the child window class. The MDI client window uses this field and the other fields of the structure when the MDI client window calls the CreateWindow function to create the window.

Under the second method, you use the CreateMDIWindow function:

```
HWND CreateMDIWindow(
    LPTSTR szClass,         // registered child class name
    LPTSTR szTitle,         // window title
    DWORD style,            // window style flags
    int x,                  // horizontal position of window
    int y,                  // vertical position of window
    int cx,                 // width of window
    int cy,                 // height of window
    HWND hOwner,            // handle to owner window (MDI client)
    HINSTANCE hInstance,    // handle to application instance
    LPARAM lParam           // application-defined value
    );;
```

The `CreateMDIWindow` function is not available in Win32s.

Even though the `szClass` and `szTitle` strings are not modified, the formal specification is that they are `LPTSTR`, not the expected `LPCTSTR`, parameters. This appears to be a mistake in the header file. Unfortunately, this requires that you explicitly cast an `LPCTSTR` value to an `LPSTR` to avoid a compiler error message:

```
HWND createMyMDIWindow(LPCTSTR caption)
    {
    return CreateMDIWindow((LPTSTR)mdiClass, (LPTSTR)caption, ...);
    }
```

The frame window function, which, in a sense, is the application itself, never communicates directly with an MDI child window. Instead, it sends messages about an MDI child window to the MDI client window. These messages either elicit information about the child window or request that the MDI client window change a child window in some manner. The MDI client window is the one that actually creates, minimizes, maximizes, restores, and destroys an MDI child window. You can think of the `CreateMDIWindow` as a convenient wrapper around the `WM_MDICREATE` message.

Similarly, an MDI child window doesn't typically communicate directly with the frame window; it communicates with the MDI client window, which acts as an intermediary. For example, when an MDI child window receives notice that it is being activated, it often needs to change the menu on the frame window. The MDI child window sends a message to the MDI client window asking it to change the menu on the frame window. There's isn't quite as much separation of functionality as there should be in this communication path, however. MDI child windows will often directly change the top-level menu on the frame window as menu items need to be checked and unchecked. (Note that as we've explained, we don't believe that this is a robust paradigm for structuring a Windows program. However, it is still popular.)

MDI Client Window Messages

Generally, if you want to affect an MDI child window in a way that affects its relationship to its MDI client window or inquire about the status of an MDI child window as viewed by its MDI client window, you must send a message to the MDI client window. Table 17.2 lists all the MDI-related messages. There is one unusual message in this table: `WM_MDIACTIVATE`. When you send this message to the MDI client window, you are requesting that it activate a specific MDI child window. The currently active MDI child window receives a `WM_MDIACTIVATE` message with `hwnd == wParam`, indicating that it is being deactivated, and the newly activated MDI child window receives a `WM_MDIACTIVATE` message with `hwnd == lParam`, indicating that it is being activated. This is discussed in more detail on page 1206. The distinction between activation and deactivation is determined for you by the `HANDLE_WM_MDIACTIVATE` message cracker and is described on page 1207.

Table 17.2: MDI-related messages

Result	Message	Parameters	
0	WM_MDIACTIVATE *(sent to the MDI client window)*	wParam	Handle of the child window to activate.
		lParam	Unused; must be 0.
BOOL	WM_MDIACTIVATE *(received by the MDI child window)*	wParam	Handle of the child window being de-activated.
		lParam	Handle of the child window being acti-vated.

If a child window handler processes this message, it should return FALSE.

Result	Message	Parameters		
BOOL	WM_MDIACTIVATE	wParam	Cascade flag; one of the following:	
			0	Cascades all windows.
			MDITILE_SKIPDISABLED	
				Skips disabled MDI child windows.
		lParam	Unused; must be 0.	

TRUE if success; FALSE if failure.

Result	Message	Parameters	
HWND	WM_MDICREATE	wParam	Unused; must be 0.
		lParam	LPMDICREATESTRUCT

If successful, returns the window handle of the new child window; otherwise, returns NULL.

Result	Message	Parameters	
0	WM_MDIDESTROY	wParam	Handle of the child window being de-stroyed.
		lParam	Unused; must be 0.
HWND	WM_MDIGETACTIVE	wParam	Unused; must be 0.
		lParam	NULL, or a pointer to the BOOL value that will be set to TRUE if the window is maxi-mized or to FALSE if the window is not maximized.

Handle of the currently active MDI child window; NULL if no child window is active.

Result	Message	Parameters	
void	WM_MDIICONARRANGE	wParam	Unused; must be 0.
		lParam	Unused; must be 0.

Table 17.2: MDI-related messages

Result	Message	Parameters	
0	WM_MDIMAXIMIZE	wParam	Handle of the child window being maximized.
		lParam	Unused; must be 0.
0	WM_MDINEXT	wParam	Handle of the current child window.
		lParam	BOOL value; FALSE to activate the next window and TRUE to activate the previous window.
HMENU	WM_MDIREFRESHMENU [4]	wParam	Unused; must be 0.
		lParam	Unused; must be 0.

If successful, the handle of the frame **Window** menu; otherwise NULL.

Result	Message	Parameters	
0	WM_MDIRESTORE	wParam	Handle of the child window to be restored.
		lParam	Unused; must be 0.
HMENU	WM_MDISETMENU	wParam	Handle of the new frame window menu. If NULL, the frame window menu is unchanged.
		lParam	Handle of the new **Window** menu. If NULL, the **Window** menu is unchanged.

If successful, the handle of the old frame **Window** menu; otherwise NULL.

Result	Message	Parameters	
BOOL	WM_MDITILE	wParam	Tiling flag; one of the following:
			MDITILE_HORIZONTAL
			MDITILE_VERTICAL
			MDITILE_SKIPDISABLED
		lParam	Unused; must be 0.

If successful, TRUE; otherwise FALSE.

[4]Available only at API level 4.

The MDI Example Program

The best way to understand the interactions of the various components to an MDI application is to see how they're used. In the example MDI application, we show one way to structure an MDI application. The application allows the user to create "document" windows of three different types: text, customizable text, and graph. Each child window type has a different menu that is used as the frame window's menu when the child window is active. We also reserve a status line at the bottom of the frame window to show how it's done. Most MDI applications don't do this. You can use this same technique to reserve space for a button/ribbon control panel across the top of the frame window. Figure 17.1 shows the frame window for the MDI example program after we created a few document windows.

The highlights of the various files comprising the MDI example program are shown in Listing 17.1 through Listing 17.9.

Listing 17.1: The MDI Explorer `frame.c` source file

```c
#define STRICT
#define NOCOMM
#include <windows.h>
#include <windowsx.h>
#include "mdi.h"

BOOL CALLBACK closeEnumFunc (HWND hwnd, LPARAM lParam) ;

HMENU hmenuInit ;
HMENU hmenuInitWindow ;
static int cyStatusLine ;

LRESULT CALLBACK
FrameWndProc (HWND hwnd, UINT msg, WPARAM wParam, LPARAM lParam)
{
    switch (msg)
        { /* msg */
         HANDLE_MSG(hwnd, WM_CREATE, mainframe_OnCreate) ;
         HANDLE_MSG(hwnd, WM_COMMAND, mainframe_OnCommand) ;
         HANDLE_MSG(hwnd, WM_SIZE, mainframe_OnSize) ;
         HANDLE_MSG(hwnd, WM_PAINT, mainframe_OnPaint) ;
         HANDLE_MSG(hwnd, WM_DESTROY, mainframe_OnDestroy);
         HANDLE_MSG(hwnd, WM_CLOSE, mainframe_OnClose);
         HANDLE_MSG(hwnd, WM_QUERYENDSESSION, mainframe_OnQueryEndSession);
        } /* msg */

    //****************************************************************
    // All unprocessed messages must be passed to DefFrameProc *
    //****************************************************************

    return DefFrameProc (hwnd, hwndMDIClient, msg, wParam, lParam) ;
}

//================================================================
// closeEnumFunc
//
// Inputs:
//      HWND hwnd: Handle of currently-enumerated child window
//      LPARAM lParam: 32-bit value passed to iterator function
//            (not used)
// Result: BOOL
//      TRUE, always
// Effect:
//      Closes the window as long as it is not the title window of
//      an iconized window
```

```
// Notes:
//      The way to tell an iconized child window is that it has no
//      owner; a title window for an iconized window has an owner.
BOOL CALLBACK
closeEnumFunc (HWND hwnd, LPARAM lParam)
{
  /* Leave out the icon title windows. */
  if (GetWindowOwner (hwnd) == NULL)
      { /* real window */
       /* Restore this child window. */
       FORWARD_WM_MDIRESTORE (hwndMDIClient, hwnd, SendMessage) ;

       /* Ask it politely if it wishes to terminate. */

       if (FORWARD_WM_QUERYENDSESSION (hwnd, SendMessage))
          { /* termination OK */
           FORWARD_WM_MDIDESTROY(hwndMDIClient, hwnd, SendMessage);
          } /* termination OK */
      } /* real window */
  return TRUE ;
}

//================================================================
// mainframe_closeAll
//

static BOOL
mainframe_closeAll(HWND hwnd)
{
  /* First, check this out with all child windows. */
  /* Try to close all child windows.              */
  FORWARD_WM_COMMAND (hwnd, IDM_CLOSEALL, 0, 0, SendMessage) ;

  /* If all child windows agreed to close, */
  /* they are destroyed by now.            */

  if (GetFirstChild (hwndMDIClient))
      { /* not all destroyed */
        /* Don't permit the session to end or the   */
        /* application to close.                     */

        return FALSE ; /* Don't pass to DefFrameProc. */
      } /* not all destroyed */
  return TRUE;
}

//================================================================
// mainframe_OnPaint
static void
mainframe_OnPaint(HWND hwnd)
    {
      PAINTSTRUCT ps;
      HDC hdc = BeginPaint (hwnd, &ps) ;
      RECT rect;
      COLORREF Color;

      GetClientRect (hwnd, &rect) ;
```

```
    rect.top = rect.bottom - cyStatusLine ;

    Color = GetSysColor (COLOR_3DFACE) ;
    SetBkColor (hdc, Color) ;

    hbrush = CreateSolidBrush (Color) ;
    FillRect (hdc, &rect, hbrush) ;


    MoveToEx (hdc, rect.left, rect.top, NULL) ;
    LineTo (hdc, rect.right, rect.top) ;

    hInstance = GetWindowInstance (hwnd) ;
    LoadString (hInstance, IDS_STATUSMSG, Buffer, DIM(Buffer)) ;
    DrawText (hdc, Buffer, -1, &rect,
                        DT_SINGLELINE | DT_CENTER | DT_VCENTER) ;

      EndPaint (hwnd, &ps) ;
    }
//================================================================
// mainframe_OnSize
//
static void
mainframe_OnSize(HWND hwnd, UINT state, int cx, int cy)
    {
    HWND hwndToolbar ;

    hwndToolbar = GetDlgItem (hwnd, IDC_TOOLBAR) ;
    ASSERT (NULL != hwndToolbar) ;

    FORWARD_WM_SIZE (hwndToolbar, state, cx, cy, SendMessage) ;

    if(state != SIZE_MINIMIZED)
      { /* adjust size */
      RECT toolrect;
      RECT client;

      // Get client rectangle
      GetClientRect(hwnd, &client);

      // Compute size of toolbar
      GetWindowRect(hwndToolbar, &toolrect);
      ScreenToClient(hwnd, (LPPOINT)&toolrect.right);

      client.top = toolrect.bottom;

      if(hwndMDIClient != NULL)
         MoveWindow(hwnd
               client.left,
               client.top,
               client.right - client.left,
               client.bottom - client.top,
               TRUE);
      } /* adjust size */

    }
```

```
//====================================================================
// mainframe_OnDestroy
//
static void
mainframe_OnDestroy(HWND hwnd)
    {
    /********************************************************/
    /* Windows is destroying the main application window. */
    /* Post a WM_QUIT message to the application queue     */
    /* to terminate the message loop and the application. */
    /********************************************************/

    SetMenu (hwnd, NULL) ;
    DestroyMenu (hmenuInit) ;
    PostQuitMessage (0) ;
    }

//====================================================================
// mainframe_OnCreate
static BOOL
mainframe_OnCreate(HWND hwnd, LPCREATESTRUCT cs)
    {
    HINSTANCE           hInstance ;
    HDC                 hdc ;
    int                 WindowPos ;
    TEXTMETRIC          tm ;
    CLIENTCREATESTRUCT  ccs;

    hInstance = GetWindowInstance (hwnd) ;

    //==================
    // Create the MDI client window.
    //==================

    ccs.hWindowMenu = hmenuInitWindow ;
    ccs.idFirstChild = IDM_FIRSTDOCUMENT ;

    hwndMDIClient =
            CreateWindow (_T("MDICLIENT"),
                          NULL,
                          WS_CHILD | WS_CLIPCHILDREN | WS_VISIBLE,
                          0, 0, 0, 0,
                          hwnd,
                          (HMENU) 1,
                          hInstance,
                          (LPSTR) &ccs) ;

    hdc = GetDC (hwnd) ;
    GetTextMetrics (hdc, &tm) ;
    ReleaseDC (hwnd, hdc) ;

    cyStatusLine = 5 * (tm.tmHeight + tm.tmExternalLeading) / 4;

    return TRUE;

    }
```

```
//===================================================================
// mainframe_OnCommand
//
// Inputs:
//     HWND hwnd: Window handle of frame window
//     int id: id of control sending message
//     HWND hctl: Control handle
//     UINT codeNotify: Notification code

static void
mainframe_OnCommand(HWND hwnd, int id, HWND hctl, UINT codeNotify)
    {
    switch (id)
        { /* id */
        case IDM_ABOUT:
            mainframe_OnAbout(hwnd);
            return;
        case IDM_ARRANGE:
            FORWARD_WM_MDIICONARRANGE (hwndMDIClient, SendMessage) ;
            return ;

        case IDM_CASCADE:
            FORWARD_WM_MDICASCADE (hwndMDIClient, 0, SendMessage) ;
            return ;

        case IDM_CLOSEALL:
            EnumChildWindows (hwndMDIClient, (WNDENUMPROC)closeEnumFunc, NULL);
            return ;

         case IDM_EXIT:
            FORWARD_WM_CLOSE (hwnd, SendMessage) ;
            return ;

        case IDM_NEW:
            mainframe_OnNew (hwnd);
            return;

        case IDM_TILE:
            FORWARD_WM_MDITILE (hwndMDIClient, 0, SendMessage) ;
            return ;

        default:
            /* Pass all other WM_COMMAND messages to the  */
            /* currently active child window.  It may     */
            /* have changed the menu bar on the frame and */
            /* have selections that it processes.         */

            hwndChild = FORWARD_WM_MDIGETACTIVE (hwndMDIClient, SendMessage) ;
            if (hwndChild)
                SendMessage (hwndChild, msg, wParam, lParam) ;
            break ;
        } /* id */

    }    //Must forward command. See source code for method used . . .
```

Listing 17.2: The MDI Explorer `findwnd.c` file

```
//=================================================================
// findWindowMenu
//
// Inputs:
//      HMENU hmenu: Menu handle of top-level menu
// Result: HMENU
//      The handle of the submenu that is the Window menu, or NULL
//      if one is not found
// Notes:
//      The Window menu is determined as being that menu which
//      contains the IDM_TILE menu item.
//-------
static HMENU
findWindowMenu(HMENU hmenu)
    {
     int i;

     for(i = 0; i < GetMenuItemCount(hmenu); i++)
        { /* find Window menu */
         HMENU tmenu = GetSubMenu(hmenu, i);
         if(GetMenuState(tmenu, IDM_TILE, MF_BYCOMMAND) != (UINT)-1)
            { /* found it */
             return tmenu;
            } /* found it */
        } /* find Window menu */

     return NULL;
    }
```

Listing 17.3: The MDI Explorer `graph.c` source file

```
#define STRICT
#define NOCOMM
#include <windows.h>
#include <windowsx.h>
#include <math.h>
#include "mdi.h"

LRESULT CALLBACK
graphWndProc (HWND hwnd, UINT msg, WPARAM wParam, LPARAM lParam)
    {
     switch (msg)
        { /* msg */
         case WM_CREATE:
             SetWindowWord (hwnd, 0, IDM_RED) ;
             break ;
         HANDLE_MSG(hwnd, WM_COMMAND, graph_OnCommand);
         HANDLE_MSG(hwnd, WM_MDIACTIVATE, graph_OnMDIActivate);
         HANDLE_MSG(hwnd, WM_PAINT, graph_OnPaint) ;
        } /* msg */


/*****************************************************************/
/* All unprocessed messages must be passed to                    */
/* DefMDIChildProc().                                            */
/*****************************************************************/
```

```
        return DefMDIChildProc (hwnd, msg, wParam, lParam) ;
    }

static void
graph_OnCommand(HWND hwnd, int id, HWND hctl, UINT codeNotify)
    {
    switch (id)
        { /* id */
        case IDM_RED:
        case IDM_GREEN:
        case IDM_BLUE:
        case IDM_YELLOW:
                CheckMenuItem (hmenuGraph,
                                SetWindowWord (hwnd, 0, (WORD)id), MF_UNCHECKED) ;
                CheckMenuItem (hmenuGraph, id, MF_CHECKED) ;
                InvalidateRect (hwnd, NULL, TRUE) ;
                return ;
        } /* id */
    }

static void
graph_OnPaint(HWND hwnd)
    {
    COLORREF     Color ;
    double       PI ;
    HDC          hdc ;
    PAINTSTRUCT  ps ;
    RECT         rect ;
    WORD         ColorID ;
    HPEN         hpen ;
    HPEN         hpenPrev ;
    int          xPos ;
    int          yPos ;

    /* Get PI to the maximum precision supported by the RTL. */

    PI = 4.0 * atan (1.0) ;

    hdc = BeginPaint (hwnd, &ps) ;
    GetClientRect (hwnd, &rect) ;

    SetMapMode (hdc, MM_ANISOTROPIC) ;
    SetWindowOrgEx (hdc, 0, 0, NULL) ;
    SetViewportOrgEx (hdc, 0, rect.bottom / 2, NULL) ;
    SetWindowExtEx (hdc, 100, 100, NULL) ;
    SetViewportExtEx (hdc, rect.right, -rect.bottom, NULL) ;

    MoveToEx (hdc, 0, 0, NULL) ;
    LineTo (hdc, 100, 0) ;
    MoveToEx (hdc, 0, 0, NULL) ;

    /* Create a pen of the appropriate color. */

    ColorID = GetWindowWord (hwnd, 0) ;
    switch (ColorID)
        { /* ColorID */
```

```
       case IDM_RED:
           Color = RGB (255, 0, 0) ;
           break ;

       case IDM_GREEN:
           Color = RGB (0, 255, 0) ;
           break ;

       case IDM_BLUE:
           Color = RGB (0, 0, 255) ;
           break ;

       case IDM_YELLOW:
           Color = RGB (255, 255, 0) ;
           break ;

       default:
           Color = RGB (0, 0, 0) ;
           break ;
       } /* wColor */

   hpen = CreatePen (PS_SOLID, 10, Color) ;

   for (xPos = 0; xPos < 100; xPos++)
      { /* loop */
      yPos = (int) (50.0 * sin (((double) xPos * PI) / 25.0));
      LineTo (hdc, xPos, yPos) ;
      } /* loop */

   SelectPen (hdc, hpenPrev) ;
   DeletePen (hpen) ;
   EndPaint (hwnd, &ps) ;
   }

static void
graph_OnMDIActivate(HWND hwnd, BOOL activate, HWND hactivate, HWND hdeactivate)
   {

   /* Either gaining or losing the input focus. */
   if (activate)
      { /* activate */
      /* Gaining the input focus.           */
      /* Check the menu item correspond to the  */
      /* current color for this window's graph. */
      CheckMenuItem (hmenuGraph, GetWindowWord (hwnd, 0), MF_CHECKED) ;
      /* Change the menu to the graph menu.    */
      FORWARD_WM_MDISETMENU (GetParent (hwnd),
                             FALSE,
                             hmenuGraph,
                             hmenuGraphWindow,
                             SendMessage) ;
      } /* activate */
    else
      { /* deactivate */
      /* Losing the input focus.                */
```

```
                  /* Remove the check mark for this window's color. */
                  CheckMenuItem (hmenuGraph, GetWindowWord (hwnd, 0),  MF_UNCHECKED) ;
                  /* Change the menu to the init menu.    */
                  FORWARD_WM_MDISETMENU (GetParent (hwnd),
                                         FALSE,
                                         hmenuInit,
                                         hmenuInitWindow,
                                         SendMessage) ;
          } /* deactivate */

     /* Anytime you change the menu bar, you must redraw it. */

     DrawMenuBar (hwndFrame) ;
    }
```

Listing 17.4: The MDI Explorer `init.c` source file

```
#define STRICT
#define NOCOMM
#include <windows.h>
#include <windowsx.h>
#include "mdi.h"
#include "resource.h"

/***********************************/
/* Allocate some global variables. */
/***********************************/

HACCEL  haccel ;
HWND    hwndMDIClient ;
HWND    hwndFrame ;

BOOL
registerClasses (HINSTANCE hInstance)
{
    ATOM       aWndClass ;
    TCHAR      ClassName [SZCLASSNAME] ;
    WNDCLASS   wc ;

/****************************************************************/
/* Fetch the class name for the application's MDI frame window.*/
/* An MDI frame window corresponds to the main application     */
/* window in a non-MDI application.                            */
/****************************************************************/

    if (LoadString (hInstance, IDS_FRAMECLASS,
                ClassName,
                sizeof(ClassName)/sizeof(TCHAR) == 0)
        return FALSE ;

    /****************************************/
    /* Register the MDI frame window class. */
    /****************************************/

    wc.style          = CS_HREDRAW | CS_VREDRAW ;
    wc.lpfnWndProc    = (WNDPROC) FrameWndProc ;
    wc.cbClsExtra     = 0 ;
    wc.cbWndExtra     = 0 ;
```

```
    wc.hInstance      = hInstance ;
    wc.hIcon          = LoadIcon (NULL, IDI_APPLICATION) ;
    wc.hCursor        = LoadCursor (NULL, IDC_ARROW) ;
    wc.hbrBackground  = (HBRUSH) (COLOR_APPWORKSPACE + 1) ;
    wc.lpszMenuName   = NULL ;
    wc.lpszClassName  = ClassName ;

    /* Register the window class. */

    aWndClass = RegisterClass (&wc) ;
    if (aWndClass == 0)
        return FALSE ;

    return aWndClass != NULL ;
}


/*********************************************************************/
/* Perform all initialization that should be done for the          */
/* application.  In this case, create the main application          */
/* window for this instance and make it visible.                   */
/*********************************************************************/
BOOL
initInstance (HINSTANCE hInstance, int nCmdShow)
{
    if (!registerClasses(hInstance))
        return FALSE;

    // Initialize the Common Controls DLL
    // You must call this function before using
    // any Common Control
    InitCommonControls () ;

    // Create the application's main frame window
    hMainFrame = createMainFrameWindow (hInstance, nCmdShow);

    if (hMainFrame == NULL)
        return FALSE ;

    hMainMenu = GetMenu(hMainFrame);   // restore to this when
                                       // all MDI children gone
    hMainAccel = LoadAccelerators(hInstance, MAKEINTRESOURCE(IDR_MAINFRAME));

    haccel = hMainAccel;    // current accelerators are main
                            // accelerators

// Initialize the child window modules

    if (!graph_InitInstance(hInstance))
        return FALSE;
    if (!text_InitInstance(hInstance))
        return FALSE;
    if (!custom_InitInstance(hInstance))
        return FALSE;

    return TRUE ;
}
```

Listing 17.5: The MDI Explorer `text.c` source file

```c
#define STRICT
#define NOCOMM
#include <windows.h>
#include <windowsx.h>
#include "mdi.h"

//===============================================================

static LRESULT CALLBACK
textWndProc (HWND hwnd, UINT msg, WPARAM wParam, LPARAM lParam)
    {
    switch (msg)
        { /* msg */
        HANDLE_MSG(hwnd, WM_CLOSE, text_OnClose) ;
        HANDLE_MSG(hwnd, WM_COMMAND, text_OnCommand) ;
        HANDLE_MSG(hwnd, WM_CONTEXTMENU, text_OnContextMenu);
        HANDLE_MSG(hwnd, WM_CTLCOLOREDIT, text_OnCtlColorEdit);
        HANDLE_MSG(hwnd, WM_DESTROY, text_OnDestroy);
        HANDLE_MSG(hwnd, WM_INITMENUPOPUP, text_OnInitMenuPopup);
        HANDLE_MSG(hwnd, WM_MDIACTIVATE, text_OnMDIActivate) ;
        HANDLE_MSG(hwnd, WM_QUERYENDSESSION, text_QueryEndSession) ;
        HANDLE_MSG(hwnd, WM_SIZE, text_OnSize);
        case UWM_UPDATE_MENU:
                 text_OnUpdateMenu(hwnd, GetMenu(hMainFrame));
                 return 0;
          case UWM_CONTEXTMENU:
                 return HANDLE_WM_CONTEXTMENU(hwnd, wParam,
                                  lParam, text_OnContextMenu);
        } /* msg */
/****************************************************************/
/* All unprocessed messages must be passed to DefMDIChildProc()*/
/****************************************************************/

    return DefMDIChildProc (hwnd, msg, wParam, lParam) ;
    }

//===============================================================

static void
text_OnMDIActivate(HWND hwnd, BOOL activate, HWND hactivate, HWND hdeactivate)
    {
    /* Either gaining or losing the input focus. */
    CheckMenuItem(textMenu, GetWindowWord(hwnd, 0),
                     (active ? MF_CHECKED : MF_UNCHECKED));
    if(active)
        { /* activating */
        FORWARD_WM_MDISETMENU(MDIClientWnd, TRUE, textMenu,
                                 textWindowMenu,
                                 SendMessage);
        SendMessage(hMainFrame, UWM_SET_ACCELERATOR, 0, (LPARAM)textAccel);
        DrawMenuBar(hMainFrame);
        PostMessage(hMainFrame, UWM_UPDATE_TOOLBAR, 0, 0);
        } /* activating */
```

```
//================================================================

static void
text_OnClose(HWND hwnd)
    {
     if(!text_QueryClose(hwnd))
        return;
     FORWARD_WM_CLOSE(hwnd, DefMDIChildProc);
    }

//================================================================

static void
text_OnCommand(HWND hwnd, int id, HWND hctl, UINT codeNotify)
    {
     switch (id)
        { /* id */
        case IDM_RED:
        case IDM_GREEN:
        case IDM_BLUE:
        case IDM_YELLOW:
                CheckMenuItem (hmenuText,
                                SetWindowWord (hwnd, 0, (WORD)id), MF_UNCHECKED);
                CheckMenuItem (hmenuText, id, MF_CHECKED) ;
                InvalidateRect (hwnd, NULL, TRUE) ;
                return ;
        } /* id */
    }

//================================================================

static void
text_OnDestroy(HWND hwnd)
    {
     FORWARD_WM_DESTROY(hwnd, DefMDIChildProc);
     PostMessage(hMainFrame, UWM_MDI_DESTROY, 0, 0);
    }

//================================================================

static void
text_OnEdit(HWND hwnd, int id, HWND hctl, UINT codeNotify)
    {
     switch(codeNotify)
        { /* codeNotify */
        case EN_CHANGE:
                PostMessage(hwnd, UWM_UPDATE_MENU, 0, 0);
                return;
        } /* codeNotify */
    }

//================================================================

static void
text_OnFont(HWND hwnd)
```

```
      {
      edit_ChooseFont(GetDlgItem(hwnd, ID_EDIT_CONTROL));
      }

//===============================================================

static BOOL
text_queryClose(HWND hwnd)
      {
      BOOL modified = Edit_GetModify(GetDlgItem (hwnd, ID_EDIT_CONTROL));
      TCHAR caption[256];
      TCHAR changed[256];

      if(!modified)
         return TRUE;
      VERIFY(LoadString(GetWindowInstance(hwnd),
                              IDS_SAVE_CHANGES_CAPTION,
                              caption, DIM(caption)));
      VERIFY(LoadString(GetWindowInstance(hwnd), IDS_SAVE_CHANGES,
                              changed, DIM(changed)));

      // We use a more general structure here so that in the
      // future, we could issue a box that said
      // "Save changes [Yes][No][Cancel]" and do a multiway
      // branch based on the three possible return values.

      switch(MessageBox(hwnd, changed, caption, MB_ICONSTOP | MB_OKCANCEL))
         { /* MessageBox */
          case IDOK:
                  return TRUE;
          case IDCANCEL:
                  return FALSE;
         } /* MessageBox */

      return FALSE; // should never get here, but just in case... }

//===============================================================

static void
text_OnCommand(HWND hwnd, int id, HWND hctl, UINT codeNotify)
      {
      switch (id)
          { /* id */
          case IDM_FONT:
                  text_OnFont(hwnd);
                  return ;
          case ID_EDIT_UNDO:
                  FORWARD_WM_UNDO(GetDlgItem(hwnd, ID_EDIT_CONTROL), SendMessage);
                  return;
          case ID_EDIT_REDO:
                  return;
          case ID_EDIT_CUT:
                  FORWARD_WM_CUT(GetDlgItem(hwnd, ID_EDIT_CONTROL), SendMessage);
                  return;
          case ID_EDIT_COPY:
                  FORWARD_WM_COPY(GetDlgItem(hwnd, ID_EDIT_CONTROL), SendMessage);
                  return;
```

```
             case ID_EDIT_PASTE:
                     FORWARD_WM_PASTE(GetDlgItem(hwnd, ID_EDIT_CONTROL),
                                                     SendMessage);
                     return;
             case ID_EDIT_CLEAR:
                     FORWARD_WM_CLEAR(GetDlgItem(hwnd, ID_EDIT_CONTROL), SendMessage);
                     return;
             case ID_EDIT_SELECT_ALL:
                     Edit_SetSel(GetDlgItem(hwnd, ID_EDIT_CONTROL), 0, -1);
                     return;
             case ID_EDIT_PROPERTIES:
                     return;
             case ID_EDIT_CONTROL:
                     text_OnEdit(hwnd, id, hctl, codeNotify);
                     return;
         } /* id */ /* id */
      FORWARD_WM_COMMAND(hwnd, id, hctl, codeNotify, DefMDIChildProc);
      }

//================================================================

HBRUSH text_OnCtlColorEdit(HWND hwnd, HDC hdc, HWND hchild, int type)
    {
     return FORWARD_WM_CTLCOLOREDIT(hchild, hdc, hchild, SendMessage);
    }

//================================================================

static void
text_OnInitMenuPopup(HWND hwnd, HMENU hmenu, UINT item, BOOL sysmenu)
    {
     PostMessage(hwnd, UWM_UPDATE_MENU, 0, 0);
    }

//================================================================

void text_OnSetFocus(HWND hwnd, HWND oldfocus)
    {
     SetFocus(GetDlgItem(hwnd, ID_EDIT_CONTROL));
    }
//================================================================

static void
text_OnSize(HWND hwnd, UINT state, int cx, int cy)
    {
     if(state != SIZEICONIC)
        MoveWindow(GetDlgItem(hwnd, ID_EDIT_CONTROL), 0, 0, cx, cy, TRUE);
     FORWARD_WM_SIZE(hwnd, state, cx, cy, DefMDIChildProc);
    }

//================================================================

static BOOL
text_OnQueryEndSession(HWND hwnd)
    {
     if (text_queryClose(hwnd))
        return FALSE ;
```

```
        return FORWARD_WM_QUERYENDSESSION(hwnd, DefMDIChildProc) ;
    }
```

//===

```
static void
text_OnUpdateMenu(HWND hwnd, HMENU hmenu)
    {
      HWND hedit = GetDlgItem(hwnd, ID_EDIT_CONTROL);

      edit_UpdateMenu(hedit, hmenu);

      PostMessage(hMainFrame, UWM_UPDATE_TOOLBAR, 0, 0);
    }
```

Listing 17.6: The MDI Explorer winmain.c source file

```
#include "StdSDK.h"      // Standard application includes
#include "Init.h"        // For non-static function prototypes
#include "Frame.h"       // For non-static function prototypes
#include "resource.h"    // For resource identifiers
#include "mdi.h"

int
WINAPI WinMain (HINSTANCE hInstance, HINSTANCE hPrevInstance,
                LPSTR lpCmdLine, int nCmdShow)
{
    MSG  msg ;

    // Instance initialization
    if (!initInstance (hInstance, nCmdShow)) {
        return FALSE ;
    }

    // Main message loop:
    while (GetMessage (&msg, NULL, 0, 0))
        {
          if (!TranslateMDISysAccel(hwndMDIClient, &msg))
              if (!TranslateAccelerator (msg.hwnd, haccel, &msg)) {
                  TranslateMessage (&msg) ;
                  DispatchMessage (&msg) ;
          }
        }

    return exitInstance (&msg) ;

}
```

Listing 17.7: Excerpts from the MDI Explorer text.c source file

```
//===================================================================
BOOL text_New(HWND hwnd)
    {
      HINSTANCE hinst = GetWindowInstance(hwnd);
      HWND hwndChild ;
      TCHAR Buffer[80] ;
      TCHAR Title[80] ;
      HWND hwndChild ;
```

```
      hwndChild = mdi_Create(MDIClientWnd, 0, IDR_TEXT, IDS_TEXT);

      if(hwndChild != NULL)
          { /* success */
          HWND hedit;

          hedit = edit_New(hwndChild, WS_CHILD |
                                      WS_VISIBLE |
                                      ES_MULTILINE |
                                      ES_WANTRETURN |
                                      ES_AUTOVSCROLL |
                                      WS_VSCROLL, TRUE);
          if(hedit == NULL)
              { /* no edit window */
              DestroyWindow(hwndChild);
              return FALSE;
              } /* no edit window */
          PostMessage(hwnd, UWM_UPDATE_MENU, 0, 0);

          } /* success */
      return (hwndChild != NULL);
      }


//================================================================

static void
text_OnUpdateMenu(HWND hwnd, HMENU hmenu)
      {
      int first;
      int last;
      BOOL hassel;
      HWND hedit = GetDlgItem(hwnd, ID_EDIT_CONTROL);

      SendMessage(hedit, EM_GETSEL, (WPARAM)&first, (LPARAM)&last);
      hassel = (first != last);

      EnableMenuItem(hmenu, ID_EDIT_CUT,
                  MF_BYCOMMAND |
                      ((!(GetWindowStyle(hwnd) & ES_READONLY) && hassel)
                                              ? MF_ENABLED
                                              : MF_GRAYED));
      EnableMenuItem(hmenu, ID_EDIT_COPY,
                  MF_BYCOMMAND | (hassel
                                              ? MF_ENABLED
                                              : MF_GRAYED));
      EnableMenuItem(hmenu, ID_EDIT_PASTE,
                  MF_BYCOMMAND |
                      (IsClipboardFormatAvailable(CF_TEXT)
                                              ? MF_ENABLED
                                              : MF_GRAYED));
      EnableMenuItem(hmenu, ID_EDIT_UNDO,
                  MF_BYCOMMAND |
                      (Edit_CanUndo(hedit)
                                              ? MF_ENABLED
                                              : MF_GRAYED));
```

```
EnableMenuItem(hmenu, ID_EDIT_SELECT_ALL,
               (Edit_GetTextLength(hedit) > 0
                                    ? MF_ENABLED
                                    : MF_GRAYED));
EnableMenuItem(hmenu, ID_EDIT_CLEAR,
               MF_BYCOMMAND | (hassel ? MF_ENABLED : MF_GRAYED));
PostMessage(hMainFrame, UWM_UPDATE_TOOLBAR, 0, 0);

   }

}
```

Listing 17.8: Excerpts from the MDI Explorer `edit.c` source file showing toolbar update logic

```
//==============================================================

static LRESULT
editsubclass_OnSetSel(HWND hwnd, int message, WPARAM wParam, LPARAM lParam)
    {
     LRESULT result;

     PostMessage(GetParent(hwnd), UWM_UPDATE_MENU, 0, 0);
     result = CallWindowProc(getProc(hwnd), hwnd, message, wParam, lParam);
     SetProp(hwnd, MAKEINTATOM(ATOM_LASTSEL), (HANDLE)Edit_GetSel(hwnd));
     return result;
    }

//==============================================================

static void
editsubclass_CheckSelChange(HWND hwnd)
    {
     DWORD lastsel;
     DWORD newsel;

     // check to see if we changed the selection
     newsel  = Edit_GetSel(hwnd);
     lastsel = (DWORD)GetProp(hwnd, MAKEINTATOM(ATOM_LASTSEL));
     if(lastsel != newsel)
        { /* selection changed */
         SetProp(hwnd, MAKEINTATOM(ATOM_LASTSEL), (HANDLE)newsel);
         PostMessage(GetParent(hwnd), UWM_UPDATE_MENU, 0, 0);
        } /* selection changed */


    }
//==============================================================

static LRESULT CALLBACK
editSubclassProc(HWND hwnd, int message, WPARAM wParam, LPARAM lParam)
    {
     switch(message)
        { /* message */
         HANDLE_MSG(hwnd, WM_RBUTTONDOWN, editsubclass_OnRButtonDown);
         HANDLE_MSG(hwnd, WM_DESTROY, editsubclass_OnDestroy);

         case EM_SETSEL:
                 return editsubclass_OnSetSel(hwnd, message, wParam, lParam);
```

```
            // We intercept these messages, any one of which could
            // have caused a change in the selection status.
            case WM_KEYUP:
            case WM_SYSKEYUP:
            case WM_LBUTTONUP:
                    editsubclass_CheckSelChange(hwnd);
                    break;
        } /* message */

    return CallWindowProc(getProc(hwnd), hwnd, message, wParam, lParam);
    }

//================================================================

HWND edit_New(HWND parent, DWORD styles, BOOL subclassing)
    {
    RECT r;
    HWND hedit;

    GetClientRect(parent, &r);

    hedit = CreateWindow("EDIT", NULL,
                        styles,
                        r.left, r.top,
                        r.right - r.left,
                        r.bottom - r.top,
                        parent,
                        (HMENU) ID_EDIT_CONTROL,
                        GetWindowInstance(parent),
                        (LPVOID)NULL);

    if(hedit != NULL)
        { /* have edit control */
        SetFocus(hedit);

        if(subclassing)
            setProc(hedit, SubclassWindow(hedit, editSubclassProc));

        SetProp(hedit, MAKEINTATOM(ATOM_BKG),
                CreateSolidBrush(GetSysColor(COLOR_WINDOW)));

        if(styles & ES_READONLY)
            { /* read-only */
            TCHAR rodata[256];
            LoadString(GetWindowInstance(parent), IDS_RO_TEXT,
                                rodata, DIM(rodata));
            SetWindowText(hedit, rodata);
            } /* read-only */
        } /* have edit control */

    return hedit;
    }

//================================================================

void edit_ChooseFont(HWND hwnd)
```

```
    {
     LOGFONT lf;
     HFONT hf;
     CHOOSEFONT cf;

     hf = GetWindowFont(hwnd);G

     cf.lStructSize = sizeof(cf);
     cf.hwndOwner = hwnd;
     cf.lpLogFont = &lf;
     cf.Flags = CF_NOVECTORFONTS | CF_SCREENFONTS | CF_EFFECTS;
     cf.rgbColors = getRGB(hwnd);

     if(hf != NULL)
        { /* has font */
         GetObject(hf, sizeof(lf), &lf);
         cf.Flags |= CF_INITTOLOGFONTSTRUCT;
        } /* has font */

     if(ChooseFont(&cf) != 0)
        { /* successful choosefont */
         HFONT nf = CreateFontIndirect(&lf);C
         if(nf != NULL)
            { /* created successfully */
             DeleteFont(hf);
             SetWindowFont(hwnd, nf, TRUE);
             setRGB(hwnd, cf.rgbColors);
            } /* created successfully */
        } /* successful choosefont */

    }
//===================================================================

void edit_UpdateMenu(HWND hedit, HMENU hmenu)
    {
     int first;
     int last;
     BOOL hassel;

     SendMessage(hedit, EM_GETSEL, (WPARAM)&first, (LPARAM)&last);
     hassel = (first != last);

     EnableMenuItem(hmenu, ID_EDIT_CUT,
                    MF_BYCOMMAND |
                        (!(GetWindowStyle(hedit) & ES_READONLY)
                                    && hassel
                                        ? MF_ENABLED
                                        : MF_GRAYED));
     EnableMenuItem(hmenu, ID_EDIT_COPY,
                    MF_BYCOMMAND | (hassel ? MF_ENABLED
                                        : MF_GRAYED));
     EnableMenuItem(hmenu, ID_EDIT_PASTE,
                    MF_BYCOMMAND |
                        (IsClipboardFormatAvailable(CF_TEXT)
                                        ? MF_ENABLED
                                        : MF_GRAYED));
```

```
      EnableMenuItem(hmenu, ID_EDIT_UNDO,
                  MF_BYCOMMAND | (Edit_CanUndo(hedit)
                                        ? MF_ENABLED
                                        : MF_GRAYED));
      EnableMenuItem(hmenu, ID_EDIT_SELECT_ALL,
                      (Edit_GetTextLength(hedit) > 0
                                        ? MF_ENABLED
                                        : MF_GRAYED));
      EnableMenuItem(hmenu, ID_EDIT_CLEAR,
                  MF_BYCOMMAND | (hassel    ? MF_ENABLED
                                        : MF_GRAYED));

    }
```

Listing 17.9: Excerpts from the MDI Explorer `mdi.c` source file

```
HWND mdi_Create(HWND hwnd, DWORD styles, int classid, int titleid)
    {
    HINSTANCE hinst = GetWindowInstance(hwnd);
    HWND hwndChild ;
    TCHAR Class[80] ;
    TCHAR Title[80] ;
#ifdef WIN32S
    MDICREATESTRUCT mcs;
#endif

    LoadString(hinst, classid, Class, DIM(Class));
    LoadString(hinst, titleid, Title, DIM(Title));

#ifdef WIN32S
    mcs.szClass = Class;
    mcs.szTitle = Title;
    mcs.hOwner  = hinst;
    mcs.x       = 0;
    mcs.y       = 0;
    mcs.cx      = CW_USEDEFAULT;
    mcs.cy      = CW_USEDEFAULT;
    mcs.style   = styles;
    mcs.lParam  = 0;

    hwndChild = FORWARD_WM_MDICREATE(hwnd, &mcs, SendMessage);

#else
    hwndChild = CreateMDIWindow(Class, Title, 0,
                                CW_USEDEFAULT, 0,
                                CW_USEDEFAULT, 0,
                                hwnd,
                                hinst,
                                0);
#endif

    if(hwndChild == NULL)
      { /* failed */
      reportError(GetLastError());
      } /* failed */

    return hwndChild;
    }
```

Program Initialization

The MDI example program begins like all the previous examples: It registers the window classes it uses. It registers three window classes in the `init.c` source file, one each for the frame window, the MDI child windows that display text, and the MDI child windows that display graphs.

The frame window class specifies a background color of `COLOR_APPWORKSPACE`, which is the system color for the application workspace. Used by the MDI client window, this color is the same one that covers most of the frame window's client area. In this example, we prevented the MDI client window from occupying the entire client area of the frame window. Room for a status line is reserved at the bottom of the frame window's client area. We don't actually need to specify this color because we paint all of the status line area.

Both the text window class and the graph window class specify that one `WORD` of window extra area is used by text and graph windows. Both windows store the menu ID of the menu item that specifies the color in which to draw the text or graph. We could have just stored the color, but the menu ID takes less space.

The text window class specifies a class icon that is displayed at the bottom of the application work space when the user minimizes a text window. The graph window class doesn't specify a class icon. When the user minimizes a graph window, the window function draws the graph in the selected color scaled to fit the iconic window. Text and graph windows are child (document) windows.

The per-instance initialization code loads an accelerator table and creates the frame window. The frame window is a standard `WS_OVERLAPPEDWINDOW` and `WS_CLIPCHILDREN` style window.

When the `FrameWndProc` function processes the `WM_CREATE` message for the frame window, it loads the three menus used by the MDI example application. The `hmenuInit` menu is the initial menu used by the frame window. It contains only the menu items that pertain to the application when no document windows exist. We call the `SetMenu` function during this time to set the initial menu for the frame window. The `hmenuText` and `hmenuGraph` global variables hold handles to the menus used by the text and graph windows.

We also determine the position of the **Window** pop-up menu item in each of the three menus. This menu item is typically the next-to-last (next-to-right-most) menu item on the menu bar, with the **Help** menu typically being the right-most. As we indicated in Chapter 12, page 835, depending on incidentals such as the physical position of the menu item is risky. So we don't depend on the arrangement of the menu. Instead, we depend on the fairly solid specification that the **Window** menu contains menu items such as **Cascade** and **Tile** and search for the menu that has the **Tile** item. These menu handles are used later in the program so that Windows can append the titles of newly created document windows to the pop-up menu.

Next, we fill out a `CLIENTCREATESTRUCT` structure in preparation for creating the MDI client window. We set the `hmenuItemWindow` field to the handle of the `Window` pop-up submenu in the initial menu. The `idFirstChild` field is set to `IDM_FIRSTDOCUMENT`. Selecting a numbered window title from the Window pop-up menu sends a `WM_COMMAND` message to the frame window function with a menu ID ranging from `IDM_FIRSTDOCUMENT` to `IDM_FIRSTDOCUMENT + n - 1`, where n is the current number of document windows. We never process these `WM_COMMAND` messages but rather pass them on to the active MDI child window. It in turn passes them on to the `DefMDIChildProc` function, which uses them to activate the specified child window.

We create the MDI client window. This window does much of the work in managing the MDI child windows with this ordinary call to the `CreateWindow` function:

```
hwndMDIClient = CreateWindow (_T("MDICLIENT"),
                             NULL,
                             WS_CHILD | WS_CLIPCHILDREN | WS_VISIBLE,
                             0, 0, 0, 0,
                             hwnd,
                             (HMENU) 1,
                             hInstance,
                             (LPSTR) &ccs) ;
```

This procedure is actually not much different from creating a control window. In fact, the MDI client window is really nothing more than a control that manages its various child windows, which are the MDI child or document windows. The MDI client window must have the `MDICLIENT` window class and must have the `WS_CHILD` window style. We set the child window ID arbitrarily to 1 because we don't need to refer to the window by ID. We pass a pointer to the `CLIENTCREATESTRUCT` as the last parameter to the `CreateWindow` function.

We call the `GetTextMetrics` function to obtain the height of characters in the current font and use the information to calculate how much room we need to reserve for the status line at the bottom of the frame window's client area. We save this size for future use.

Now that the `WM_CREATE` message processing is complete, control returns to the `InitInstance` function. This function displays the frame window and returns to the `WinMain` function. Next, the message loop executes.

The MDI Application Message Loop

The message loop for an MDI application looks a bit different than normal. Here is the message loop from the example program:[1]

```
while (GetMessage (&msg, 0, 0, 0))
  { /* message loop */
    if (!TranslateMDISysAccel (hwndMDIClient, &msg) &&
        !TranslateAccelerator (hwndFrame, haccel, &msg))
      {
      TranslateMessage (&msg) ;
      DispatchMessage (&msg) ;
      }
  } /* message loop */
```

After an MDI application retrieves a message from the message queue, it passes the message to the `TranslateMDISysAccel` function. This function translates `WM_KEYDOWN` and `WM_KEYUP` messages for keys corresponding to the MDI system menu accelerators to `WM_SYSCOMMAND` messages. These translated messages are sent to the MDI client window, so that's the window handle you specify when you call the

---

[1] We do not have a modeless dialog handler in our MDI example. If we did, we would have to add the `IsDialogMessage` test (page 755) as well. A full-featured message loop is not as simple as our very first example (Chapter 2, page 72).

`TranslateMDISysAccel` function. A return of TRUE means the message was translated and has been completely processed. You must not pass the message to any other function in this case.

When the message isn't translated (a return of FALSE), the message loop calls the `TranslateAccelerator` function. This function translates WM_KEYDOWN and WM_KEYUP messages for keys corresponding to menu commands to WM_COMMAND or WM_SYSCOMMAND messages. It translates messages that are sent to the frame window, so you specify its window handle here. It also returns TRUE when the message is translated and processed. When neither function translates the message, the message loop translates and dispatches the message normally.

The Frame Window Function

Most of the processing by the frame window function involves passing the message along or converting a message into a different message. Nothing much interesting happens until the user creates a document window, so we look at that first.

Receiving a WM_COMMAND message with a menu ID of IDM_NEWGRAPH or IDM_NEWTEXT creates a new graph or text document window. After we load the class name for either the text or graph window class, we initialize the fields of an MDICREATESTRUCT structure describing the document window to be created. Here is one form of code that creates a text document window:

```
mcs.szClass = Buffer ;
mcs.szTitle = _T("Text Title") ;
mcs.hOwner  = hInstance ;
mcs.x       = CW_USEDEFAULT ;
mcs.y       = 0 ;
mcs.cx      = CW_USEDEFAULT ;
mcs.cy      = 0 ;
mcs.style   = 0 ;
mcs.lParam  = 0 ;

hwndChild = FORWARD_WM_MDICREATE (hwndMDIClient,
                                 (LPMDICREATESTRUCT) &mcs,
                                 SendMessage) ;
```

The fields of the MDICREATESTRUCT structure correspond to parameters used by the CreateWindow function. When the structure is initialized, we send a WM_MDICREATE message to the MDI client window.

In this example, we use the message forwarding macros defined in the windowsx.h header file. The FORWARD_WM_MDICREATE macro assembles the parameters to a WM_MDICREATE message by placing them in the appropriate words of the wParam and lParam parameters. When you use the message cracker functions, you do not need to code into your application any assumptions as to the size and location of the arguments to a message. The macro can be changed to place the arguments in a different location, and your code will remain unchanged. In the previous example, calling the FORWARD_WM_MDICREATE macro produces the same code as writing this, but using the macro conveys the purpose of the statement much more clearly:

```
hwndChild = (HWND) SendMessage(hwndMDIClient, WM_MDICREATE, 0,
                               (LPARAM)(LPMDICREATESTRUCT) &mcs))
```

The 1Param parameter of the message contains a pointer to the initialized structure. The MDI client window creates the specified MDI child window when it receives this message.

The CreateMDIWindow function can be used, as we showed in Listing 17.9:

```
hwndChild = CreateMDIWindow(Buffer, Title, 0,
                            CW_USEDEFAULT, 0,
                            CW_USEDEFAULT, 0,
                            hwndMDIClient,
                            hinst,
                            0);

if(hwndChild == NULL)
    { /* failed */
      reportError(GetLastError());
    } /* failed */
else
    { /* success */
    // whatever is required for initialization here . . .
    // (application-specific)
    } /*success*/
```

The CreateMDIWindow function is not available in Win32s. We have therefore provided in the source listing two implementations, one that runs in full Win32 and one that is required if you plan to run on Win32s.

When the MDI client window creates the MDI child window, it assigns it a child window ID (as described earlier in the chapter, this ID can be reassigned). It also appends the title for the child window to the bottom of the pop-up menu specified in the MDICLIENTSTRUCT used when creating the MDI client window.

Creating the MDI child window sends the window function for the child window a WM_CREATE message. The 1Param of the WM_CREATE message contains a pointer to a CREATESTRUCT structure as it normally does. For an MDI child window, the 1pCreateParams field of the CREATESTRUCT structure contains a pointer to the MDICREATESTRUCT structure that was specified when the window was created.

There is a bug in Windows NT 3.x. The contents of the CREATESTRUCT are incorrect. The class pointer member, 1pszClass, points to a copy of the title string instead of to the class name string.

The graph child window function initializes a field in its window extra area when it receives a WM_CREATE message. The function uses one WORD of window extra area. The WORD of window extra area holds the menu ID for the color last selected by the user for the window. We set the default color to red.

Most of the remaining frame window message processing is straightforward. When a WM_COMMAND message arrives indicating that the user selected the IDM_ARRANGE menu item, we have to arrange the MDI child window icons. Arranging the icons places them neatly side-by-side at the bottom of the application workspace. MDI child windows that are not iconic are not affected. You don't really arrange them, however. You send the WM_MDIICONARRANGE message to the MDI client window, and it arranges them. We do that in the exam-

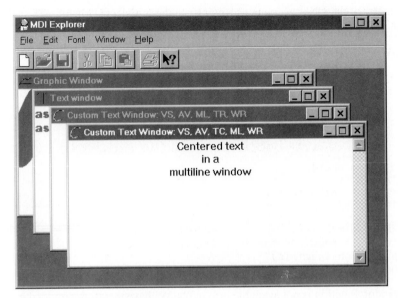

Figure 17.3: Cascaded Windows

ple program by using the FORWARD_WM_MDIICONARRANGE macro. The following two statements both send a WM_MDIICONARRANGE message and are equivalent:

```
FORWARD_WM_MDIICONARRANGE (hwndMDIClient, SendMessage) ;
SendMessage (hwndMDIClient, WM_MDIICONARRANGE, 0, 0) ;
```

Similarly, when a WM_COMMAND message arrives indicating that the user selected the IDM_CASCADE menu item, the noniconic MDI child windows should be displayed overlapping and cascading starting in the upper-left corner of the application work space, as shown in Figure 17.3. To do this, you send a WM_MDICASCADE message to the MDI client window. Again, we use the macro API, but the SendMessage function call is equivalent:

```
FORWARD_WM_MDICASCADE (hwndMDIClient,
                       MDITILE_SKIPDISABLED,
                       SendMessage) ;
SendMessage (hwndMDIClient, WM_MDICASCADE, MDITILE_SKIPDISABLED, 0) ;
```

When a WM_COMMAND message arrives indicating that the user selected the IDM_TILE menu item, the noniconic MDI child windows should be displayed tiled in the application work space. There are two preferences for tiling: horizontal and vertical. Horizontally tiled windows are shown in Figure 17.4 and vertically tiled windows are shown in Figure 17.5 (page 1201). To do this, you send a WM_MDITILE message to the MDI client window like this:

```
FORWARD_WM_MDITILE(hwndMDIClient, MDITILE_VERTICAL, SendMessage);
SendMessage (hwndMDIClient, WM_MDITILE, MDITILE_VERTICAL, 0) ;
```

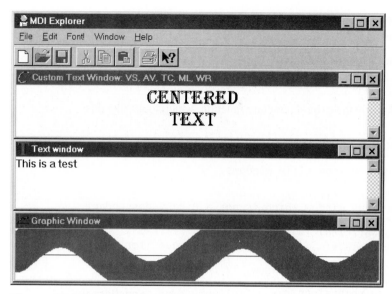

Figure 17.4: Horizontally tiled windows

You can specify any of the options shown in Table 17.3. As you examine Figure 17.5 and Figure 17.6 (page 1202), note that along the bottom of the window there is a small window shape that represents an iconic window. There are actually *four* windows shown in each of these figures. One is iconic. You can see that when there are any iconic windows, the tiling leaves space to show the icons. These iconic windows will stack up at the bottom of the window. However, it

Table 17.3: Codes for WM_MDITILE message

Tile Code	Effect
MDITILE_HORIZONTAL	Tiles MDI child windows so that they show a preference for being wide rather than tall.
MDITILE_SKIPDISABLED	Prevents disabled MDI child windows from being tiled.
MDITILE_VERTICAL	Tiles MDI child windows so that they show a preference for being tall rather than wide.

appears that tiling will leave only one row visible, as we show in Figure 17.6. To get this illustration, we tiled the two remaining windows and then resized them manually to decrease their width, thereby leaving the height as tiled. You can see that the additional iconic windows were left covered.

These iconic windows are *not* like the task bar; they are just little representatives of the windows. You can grab them and drag them around. For example, the arrangement shown in Figure 17.7 (page 1204) was created this way. To cause all the icons to drop down and line up along the bottom again, use the **Arrange Icons** menu item.

We added a **Close All** menu item to the **Window** pop-up menu. When the user selects this menu item, all MDI child windows should be closed. We do that with this code:

```
EnumChildWindows (hwndMDIClient,
                  (WNDENUMPROC) closeEnumFunc,
                  (LPARAM)hwndMDIClient) ;
```

The real work is done by the closeEnumFunc function, which looks like this:

```
BOOL CALLBACK
closeEnumFunc (HWND hwnd, LPARAM lParam)
{
    /* Leave out the icon title windows. */

        { /* not iconic title */
        // Ignore any window which is not a direct descendant
        // of the frame window
        if(GetParent(hwnd) != (HWND)lParam)
             return TRUE;  // ignore, but continue iteration

        /* Restore this child window. */

        FORWARD_WM_MDIRESTORE (hwndMDIClient, hwnd, SendMessage);
        /* Ask it politely if it wishes to terminate. */
        /* If it doesn't mind, destroy it. */
        if (FORWARD_WM_QUERYENDSESSION (hwnd, SendMessage))
            FORWARD_WM_MDIDESTROY (hwndMDIClient, hwnd, SendMessage) ;
        } /* not iconic title */
    return TRUE ;
}
```

An MDI child window has the MDI client window as its parent window. We call the EnumChildWindows function to enumerate all child windows of the hwndMDIClient window. Windows calls our closeEnumFunc function once for each child window in the hwndMDIClient window. The problem with EnumChildWindows is that it enumerates *all* child windows, unto the nth generation. As a result, the child windows that are the immediate descendants of the frame window are enumerated, as well as all of *their* child windows, and so on. If the child window contains controls (such as the edit control we use to get text child windows), the controls are also enumerated. Therefore we need to make sure that we forward only the WM_QUERYENDSESSION message and consequently send the WM_MDIDESTROY message only to the *immediate* child windows. We do this by passing in the handle of the MDI client window as the last parameter of the enumeration call. We use this value to detect if the window we have been given is a direct descendant of the MDI client window.

You also can enumerate the child windows by calling the GetWindow function. However, while doing this we are also potentially destroying some, if not all, of the windows. In this situation, it is possible for code using GetWindow to loop forever, miss a window, or reference a destroyed window. The EnumChildWindows function properly handles the case in which windows being enumerated may also be destroyed during the enumeration.

When an MDI child window is iconic in Windows NT 3.x, it is represented by *two* windows: the title of the icon and the icon itself. Both the icon title window and the icon window are child windows of the MDI client window. The icon window owns the icon title window, but the icon window itself has no owner. (They both have a parent window–the MDI client window–but that's a different relationship.) You must use this distinction and avoid sending messages to an icon title window. We have to deal with this because we want our code to run under both the API level 3 (Windows NT 3.*x*), and API level 4 (Windows 95 and Windows NT 4.*x*) platforms.

Windows passes our `close-EnumFunc` the handle of a child window. We call the `GetWindowOwner` macro API and retrieve the handle

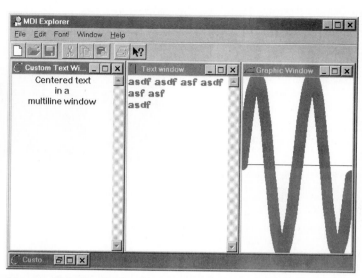

Figure 17.5: Vertically tiled windows

of the child window's owner. When this handle is not NULL, the specified window has an owner and therefore is a title window for an iconic MDI child window on a level 3 platform. We ignore such windows and continue the enumeration. When the handle is NULL, the specified window has no owner and is an MDI client window. (The MDI client window may or may not be iconic at the time.)

We restore each MDI child window just in case it is iconic at the time. You restore an MDI child window by sending a WM_MDIRESTORE message to the MDI client window. The wParam parameter of the message contains the handle of the MDI child window to restore. We use the FORWARD_WM_MDIRESTORE message forwarding API to restore each child window. Here is the statement we use plus the equivalent SendMessage function call:

```
SendMessage (hwndMDIClient, WM_MDIRESTORE, hwnd, 0) ;
```

We send a WM_QUERYENDSESSION message directly to the child window to inquire whether it agrees to be destroyed. Typically, a child window asks the user whether the window should be closed if it contains unsaved data. The window responds with a nonzero value if it agrees to be destroyed. When the window doesn't process this message, the DefMDIChildProc function passes this message to the DefWindowProc function, which returns a nonzero value. The default action is therefore to permit the window to be destroyed.

We send a WM_MDIDESTROY message to the MDI client window to destroy an MDI child window. The wParam parameter specifies the handle of the MDI child window to destroy. We use the FORWARD_WM_MDIDESTROY macro as shown here. We also give the equivalent SendMessage call:

```
FORWARD_WM_MDIDESTROY (hwndMDIClient, hwnd, SendMessage) ;
SendMessage (hwndMDIClient, WM_MDIDESTROY, hwnd, 0) ;
```

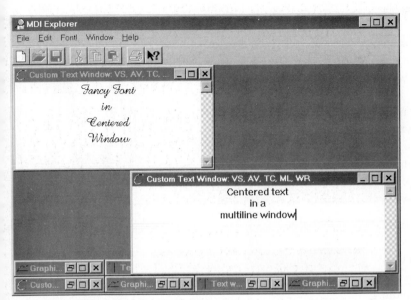

Figure 17.6: Multiple rows of iconic windows

We don't process every possible WM_COMMAND message that may be sent to the frame window function. Specifically, we don't process WM_COMMAND messages from menu items corresponding to selections processed by the active MDI child window. Nor do we process such messages from the child-window title menu items appended to the Window pop-up menu by the MDI client window. Instead, we pass all unprocessed WM_COMMAND messages along to the active MDI child window using the following code:

```
hwndChild = FORWARD_WM_MDIGETACTIVE(hwndMDIClient, SendMessage) ;
if (hwndChild != NULL)
    SendMessage (hwndChild, msg, wParam, lParam) ;
```

When you send the WM_MDIGETACTIVE message to the MDI client window, it returns an LRESULT value. The low-order word contains the window handle of the active MDI child window. The high-order word contains a 1 if the child window is maximized and 0 if it is not. The FORWARD_WM_MDIGETACTIVE macro discards the high-order word of the WM_MDIGETACTIVE message return value. If you want to know if the active MDI child window is maximized, you have to use the SendMessage function to send the message rather than the FORWARD_WM_MDIGETACTIVE macro. When there is an active MDI child window, we send it the unprocessed WM_COMMAND message by calling the SendMessage function.

We handle the WM_SIZE message in a special manner to allow the frame window to have a status line at the bottom of its client window and a toolbar window above it. Suppose the window isn't iconic and the MDI client window has been created. Then, whenever the frame window changes size, we explicitly resize the MDI client window to the new size of the frame window less the area reserved for the status line and toolbar. Here is the code:

```
static void mainframe_OnSize (HWND hwnd, UINT state, int cx, int cy)
{
    HWND hwndToolbar ;
    HWND status;
    RECT r;
    int height;

    hwndToolbar = GetDlgItem (hwnd, IDC_TOOLBAR) ;
    ASSERT (NULL != hwndToolbar) ;
```

```
      FORWARD_WM_SIZE (hwndToolbar, state, cx, cy, SendMessage) ;

      status = GetDlgItem(hwnd, IDC_STATUS);
      ASSERT( NULL != status);
      GetWindowRect(status, &r);
      height = (r.bottom - r.top);
      SetWindowPos(status, NULL, 0, cy - height, cx, height, SWP_NOZORDER);

      if(state != SIZE_MINIMIZED)
          { /* adjust size */
            resize_Frame(hwnd);
          } /* adjust size */
}

static void resize_Frame(HWND hwnd)
      {
        RECT toolrect;
        RECT client;
        HWND hwndToolbar ;

        hwndToolbar = GetDlgItem (hwnd, IDC_TOOLBAR) ;
        ASSERT (NULL != hwndToolbar) ;

        // Get client rectangle
        GetClientRect(hwnd, &client);


        // Compute size of toolbar
        GetWindowRect(hwndToolbar, &toolrect);
        ScreenToClient(hwnd, (LPPOINT)&toolrect.right);

        // Compute the size of the status line (which is drawn on
        // the main frame itself).


        if(view_status_line)
            {
              RECT sr;
              GetWindowRect(GetDlgItem(IDC_STATUS), &sr);
              client.bottom -= (sr.bottom - sr.top);
            }

        client.top = toolrect.bottom;

        if(hwndMDIClient != NULL)
            MoveWindow(hwndMDIClient,
                  client.left,
                  client.top,
                  client.right - client.left,
                  client.bottom - client.top,
                  TRUE);
      }
```

We do not pass the WM_SIZE to the DefFrameProc function. The DefFrameProc function processes a WM_SIZE message by resizing the MDI client window to fit the new size of the frame window's client area.

We've already resized the MDI client window and don't want the DefFrameProc function to resize it again to cover all of the client area.

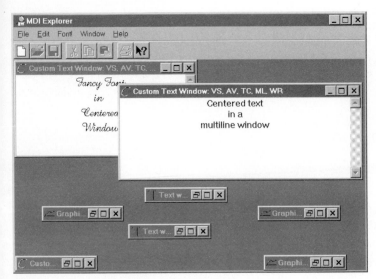

Figure 17.7: Iconic windows rearranged

The WM_DESTROY message indicates that the frame window is being destroyed. We use this notification to destroy the menus loaded during the WM_CREATE message processing. Windows automatically destroys a window's current menu when it destroys the window. You are responsible for destroying all explicitly loaded menus not in use by a window, in particular, all context (floating popup) menus.

Menus that are not destroyed occupy storage within Windows that is not reclaimed until the process terminates. In this respect, a menu that is not destroyed is similar to a GDI object that is not deleted. Repeated LoadMenu calls for a particular menu resource will generate multiple copies of a menu created from that resource. If you fail to call DestroyMenu when you are done with a menu you have explicitly loaded, but lose its handle, you will not be able to delete it. Only process termination will destroy the (probably at this point many) instances of the menu.

In the example program, however, any one of various child window menus may be the current menu for the frame window when it is destroyed. Windows destroys the current menu for a window when it destroys the window. To properly destroy all menus, you must know which menu Windows will destroy and which menus you need to destroy. You could retrieve the handle for the current menu on the frame window using the GetMenu function. After you know which menu the window is using, you can delete the other two menus and let Windows delete the current menu when it destroys the window.

However, this means that the frame window must know all the menus. Yet, we want to maintain as much modularity as possible so that our frame window knows as little as possible about how each child window class is implemented. So we find it simpler to remove the frame window's current menu by calling the SetMenu function and specifying a NULL menu handle. Then we can destroy the menus in their respective modules without worrying which menu Windows will destroy when it destroys the window. Here is the WM_DESTROY logic for the frame window:

```
static void frame_OnDestroy(HWND hwnd)
    {
    SetMenu (hwnd, NULL) ;
    DestroyMenu (hmenuInit) ;
```

```
    PostQuitMessage (0) ;
    }
```

The MDI Child Window Functions

An MDI child window function is in some ways much simpler than the frame window function. For the most part, it works just like a normal window function. Generally, it needs to process the WM_MDIACTIVATE message in addition to the normal messages processed by a window function. It also must pass all unprocessed messages to the DefMDIChildProc function. You should also pass the following messages to the DefMDI-ChildProc function even if you process them:

- WM_CHILDACTIVATE
- WM_GETMINMAXINFO
- WM_MENUCHAR
- WM_MOVE
- WM_NEXTMENU
- WM_SETFOCUS
- WM_SIZE
- WM_SYSCOMMAND

Table 17.4: Messages processed by the DefMDIChildProc function

Message	Default Action
WM_CHILDACTIVATE	Performs activation processing when MDI child windows are sized, moved, or displayed. This message must be passed to DefMDIChildProc.
WM_CONTEXTMENU	Passes the WM_CONTEXTMENU message to the main frame.
WM_GETMINMAXINFO	Calculates the size of a maximized MDI child window, using the current size of the MDI client window as the maximum size.
WM_MENUCHAR	Passes the message to the MDI frame window.
WM_MOVE	Recalculates MDI client scroll bars if they are present. This handles the case of when you move a child window partially off the MDI client window.
WM_SETFOCUS	Activates the child window if it is not the active MDI child window.
WM_SIZE	Performs operations necessary for changing the size of a window, especially for maximizing or restoring an MDI child window.
WM_SYSCOMMAND	Handles the system menu commands: SC_NEXTWINDOW, SC_PREVWINDOW, SC_MOVE, SC_SIZE, and SC_MAXIMIZE.

The graphWndProc function handles messages for the MDI child windows that are displaying a graph. The textWndProc function handles messages for the MDI child windows that are displaying the text string. The functions are actually quite similar, so we concentrate on examining the `graphWndProc` function and point out only the unique aspects in the `textWndProc` function.

When a graph MDI child window receives a `WM_CREATE` message, it initializes a word of the window extra area to the menu ID `IDM_RED`. This step effectively sets the default color for the graph to red.

An MDI child window receives a `WM_MDIACTIVATE` message when it gains or loses the input focus. (Note that this is a second, different use of the `WM_MDIACTIVATE` message. One form is sent to the MDI client window to effect activation, and the other is received by the child window as notification of activation.) The value of the `wParam` parameter is the window handle of the child window being deactivated. The value of `lParam` is the window handle of the child window being activated. When you use the message cracker, you get an additional Boolean parameter that tells you if your window is being activated or deactivated. If you don't use the message cracker, you have to determine which event is occurring by comparing the activated or deactivated window handle to the hwnd parameter of the message.

Each MDI child window class typically requires a unique menu. Even windows within a specific class might use different menus as the state for the window changes. When an MDI child window gains the input focus, the menu present on the frame window may not be the appropriate menu for the activated window. The child window typically changes the frame window's menu while processing a `WM_MDIACTIVATE` message. We use this code to process the `WM_MDIACTIVATE` message in the window function for the graph MDI child windows:

```
case WM_MDIACTIVATE:
    HANDLE_WM_MDIACTIVATE(hwnd, wParam, lParam, graph_OnMDIActivate);
    return;
```

where the `OnMDIActivate` handler is defined as

```
static void graph_OnMDIActivate(HWND hwnd, BOOL active,
                                HWND hactivate, HWND hdeactivate)
{
    CheckMenuItem(graphMenu, GetWindowWord(hwnd, 0),
                  (active ? MF_CHECKED : MF_UNCHECKED));
    if(active)
      { /* activate */
        FORWARD_WM_MDISETMENU(hwndMDIClient, TRUE, graphMenu,
                              graphWindowMenu, SendMessage);
        SendMessage(hMainFrame, UWM_SET_ACCELERATOR, 0,
                                (LPARAM)graphAccel);
        DrawMenuBar(hMainFrame);
        PostMessage(hMainFrame, UWM_UPDATE_TOOLBAR, 0, 0);
      } /* activate */
```

When a graph window gains the input focus, we change the frame menu to the `hmenuGraph` menu. Just as a frame window notifies the MDI client window when it wants something done to an MDI child window, an MDI child window notifies the MDI client window when it wants to change the menu on the frame window.

You send a `WM_MDISETMENU` message to the MDI client window to change the frame window's menu. The `wParam` parameter specifies the menu handle of the new frame window menu. The `lParam` contains the menu handle of the **Window** pop-up menu on the new menu. Either parameter can be NULL, in which case

WM_MDIACTIVATE Message Cracker Handler

void cls_OnMDIActivate(HWND hwnd, BOOL active, HWND hactivate, HWND hdeactivate);					
	wParam		lParam		
Parameter	lo	hi	lo	hi	**Meaning**
hwnd					Window handle of the window.
active					Computed as (hwnd == hactivate).
hactivate			■	■	The handle of the window being activated.
hdeactivate	■	■			The handle of the window being deactivated.

the corresponding frame window menu doesn't change. We use the FORWARD_WM_MDISETMENU macro, which accepts the required parameters and places them in the correct arguments of the WM_MDISETMENU message.

When you change the menu on the frame window while an MDI child window is maximized, the MDI client window function removes the system menu and restores controls from the previous frame window menu. These controls then are added to the new menu. When you change the **Window** pop-up menu, the MDI client window function removes the appended MDI child window titles from the previous **Window** pop-up menu and appends the titles to the new **Window** pop-up menu.

Before changing the menu, we check the menu item corresponding to the color the user last selected for this graph. The last selected color is saved in the window extra area for the window.

The graph menu is shared by all graph MDI child windows. A graph MDI child window cannot simply check its color and leave it checked until the user selects a new color. Because the menu is shared, two graph windows–one in green and one in red–would result in simultaneous checking of both the green and red menu items.

We want only one item on the color pop-up menu to be checked at any time–the color for the graph on the active graph window. It is necessary, therefore, for each graph child window to uncheck its color menu item when the window loses the input focus. This leaves all menu items unchecked (temporarily). When a different graph window gains the input focus, it checks the menu item corresponding to its last selected color.

A graph window also can lose the input focus when it is being destroyed and there is no other graph window and, possibly, no other MDI child window of any class. You don't want to leave a menu on the frame window with selections corresponding to a window that no longer exists.

The example program takes a simplistic approach to handling this situation. When an MDI child window loses the input focus, it sets the frame window's menu to the initial menu that is used when no child windows exist. When an MDI child window gains the input focus, it changes the frame window's menu from whatever it is to the menu used by the child window.

WM_MDISETMENU Message Cracker Handler

HMENU cls_OnMDISetMenu(HWND hwnd, BOOL Refresh, HMENU hmFrame, HMENU hmWindow);					

Result	Menu handle of previously set menu; NULL if no menu was set.				
	wParam		**lParam**		
Parameter	**lo**	**hi**	**lo**	**hi**	**Meaning**
hwnd					Window handle of the window.
Refresh	■				FALSE if frame menu is not being redefined; nonzero if the frame menu is being redefined. For the FORWARD_WM_MDISETMENU, this value should be set to TRUE to replace the frame menu and FALSE to leave the frame menu alone.
hmFrame	■				Handle of the new frame window menu; NULL if not being updated.
hmWindow			■		Handle of the **Window** menu; NULL if not being changed.

Note that both Refresh and hmFrame are derived from wParam.

For proper menu handling, we also must change the corresponding accelerator table. We could do this by posting a message to the main window to do so or by setting a global variable. We have chosen to use a user-defined message to set the accelerator handle. This is because different child windows may use different accelerator tables, and we want to always have the correct accelerator table for the menu.

When we receive a WM_COMMAND message with a menu ID of IDM_RED, IDM_GREEN, IDM_BLUE, or IDM_YELLOW, we uncheck the menu item corresponding to the previously selected color and check the newly selected menu item. (We chose to not list yellow as a color on the text menu, simply to emphasize that it is a different menu from the graph menu.) We invalidate the entire window so that the graph is redrawn in the new color.

When the graphWndProc function receives a WM_PAINT message, it draws two cycles of the sine function scaled to fit the size of the child window. We use a very wide pen and calculate a number of points on the curve so that this paint routine is noticeably sluggish. The only statement whose function may not be obvious is this one:

```
double PI ;

PI = 4.0 * atan (1.0) ;
```

We never can remember more than nine digits of π. This statement generates π to the maximum precision supported by the floating-point runtime library.

All unprocessed messages are passed to the `DefMDIChildProc` function:

```
return DefMDIChildProc (hwnd, message, wParam, lParam) ;
```

The `graphWndProc` function doesn't process the WM_QUERYENDSESSION message, which the frame window function sends before destroying an MDI child window. The `DefMDIChildProc` function returns a nonzero value for this message, which allows a graph window to be destroyed.

The `textWndProc` function processes the WM_QUERYENDSESSION message. The text window represents a document that the user might want to save, so the window function displays a message box asking the user to confirm that the window can be destroyed. Because the frame window function restores each window before sending it a WM_QUERYENDSESSION message, the user can see the window to which the message box pertains even if the window had been previously minimized.

Embedding an Edit Control

For our example program, we want to demonstrate the ability to modify the properties used to display text. We could implement all of the details of how to enter, select, cut, copy, and paste text and the seemingly unending details required to accomplish this in the presence of proportional fonts. This seems to be a lot of unnecessary work, since there is already a control that does this, so instead we use the existing edit control.

There is a problem with using the edit control, particularly in the context we wish to use it. It implements, for example, its own response to a right-button event. This response does not include all of what we wish to do to a "text window". We therefore must subclass the window. We can do this by using the SubclassWindow macro from `windowsx.h`. This sets the GWL_WNDPROC field to point to our own subclassing function. Since we need to call the original function, we need to store its pointer somewhere, in this case, the GWL_USERDATA field. This field exists for all window classes, including built-in classes.

```
SetWindowLong(hedit, GWL_USERDATA,
        (LPARAM)SubclassWindow(hedit, editSubclassProc));
```

We want to attach some other properties to the window. For example, we would like to attach the brush that we will use to paint the background of the control. We could have placed a pointer to a structure in GWL_USERDATA and in that structure put the pointer to the original function and any other attributes we wanted. However, we're going to take this as an opportunity to show another technique, that is, using Set-Prop and GetProp as a means of storing the information. We store the brush handle as the property whose atom code is ATOM_BKG, using the MAKEINTATOM macro to convert the constant atom code to a value that defines an atom.

```
SetProp(hwndChild, MAKEINTATOM(ATOM_BKG),
        CreateSolidBrush(GetSysColor(COLOR_WINDOW)));
```

When we need the value for painting, we can retrieve it using GetProp:

```
HBRUSH EditBackgroundBrush = (HBRUSH)GetProp(hwnd, MAKEINTATOM(ATOM_BKG));
```

We use this same technique to keep the text color and to remember the current selection.

Updating Toolbars

The introduction of toolbars changes somewhat how we have to deal with enabling of controls. Normally, we would get a notification that a menu is dropping down via the WM_INITMENUPOPUP message. However, this is sent only when the menu is about to drop down. Without a toolbar, this is adequate for determining when to enable options such as **Cut**, **Copy**, or **Paste**. But toolbars complicate our life, particularly for MDI-type applications where we can have multiple kinds of windows. The subclassing we use are the functions shown in Listing 17.7 as the editsubclass_ functions. Our application doesn't know how to update the toolbars, but it *can* determine the events when the toolbars should be updated. These are events that would change the state of the toolbar items. (Note that as you add new items to the toolbar, you may have to add new functionality to the child windows.)

For example, suppose we want to enable only **Copy** and **Cut** if there is a selection and enable only **Cut** if the window is not read-only. Only the child window knows what these mean. So we define a message we can send to a child window that will instruct it to update the menu items. We call a common function for WM_INITMENUPOPUP and our own UWM_UPDATE_MENU message. This function checks to see if there is a selection. If there is, it enables **Cut** and **Copy**. The **Cut** menu is, for example, enabled by this code:

```
SendMessage(hedit, EM_GETSEL, (WPARAM)&first, (LPARAM)&last);

EnableMenuItem(hmenu, ID_EDIT_CUT,
                MF_BYCOMMAND |
                    (!(GetWindowStyle(hwnd) & ES_READONLY)
                    && hassel
                                ? MF_ENABLED
                                : MF_GRAYED));
```

We use the SendMessage call rather than the macro Edit_GetSel because the macro does not support the new Win32 functionality that returns the selection in two 32-bit int values. If we have a selection, the start and end values will be different. For the **Copy** menu item, the presence of a selection is sufficient to enable the menu item; for the **Cut** menu item, we must also check to see if the window is not a read-only window. We use the GetWindowStyle macro and check for the ES_READONLY style bit. The read-only property of a window can be set for a dialog control in the dialog resource editor or when the CreateWindow call is made. However, it can be changed dynamically only via an EM_SETREADONLY message to the window (which can be done by using the Edit_SetReadOnly macro). The read-only property can be turned on or off by this message. You cannot change the read-only property dynamically by modifying the ES_READONLY style bit directly.

But there are other events that can change whether menu items and their corresponding toolbar icons should be enabled. For example, the act of typing a character may change the buffer size from zero to nonzero or from nonzero to zero. It may replace a selection, or it may create a selection of nonzero length. A mouse button-up event may signal a change in the current selection. So if any of these events occur, we need to respond to them to determine the potentially new toolbar state. We can do this only if we have subclassed the window. We do this in the EditSubclassWndProc shown in Listing 17.7:

```
        case WM_KEYUP:
        case WM_SYSKEYUP:
        case WM_LBUTTONUP:
```

```
            editsubclass_CheckSelChange(hwnd);
            break;
    } /* message */
```

The `editsubclass_CheckSelChange` looks at the previous selection in the window and looks at the current selection. If the selection changed, it then generates the event that eventually updates the menu items and then the toolbar. We record the current selection as an optimization so as to reduce the effort of doing too-frequent updates. We use another property to store the previous selection. If there is a change in the selection, we post a message to our parent to update the menu. After calling `editsubclass_CheckSelChange`, we do a break. The break then calls the normal handler for the event:

```
return CallWindowProc(getProc(hwnd), hwnd, message, wParam, lParam);
```

where `getProc` is defined as

```
#define getProc(hwnd) (WNDPROC)GetWindowLong(hwnd, GWL_USERDATA)
```

WM_CTLCOLORxxx Messages

Our example program also demonstrates another use of the `ChooseFont` common dialog, this time regarding the use of color. We want to be able to change the color of the text, but the text is in an existing control. We can't set the text color attribute in the `WM_PAINT` handler because we can't see the `WM_PAINT` handler, which is hidden inside the low-level code inside Windows. This could imply that if we needed to change any tiny parameter of a control, we would have to reimplement the entire control, or at least do a full owner-draw version of the control. Fortunately, for the cases that are less ambitious than full owner-draw, Windows is designed with a "hook" that gives us access to the `WM_PAINT` handler of built-in controls: the family of `WM_CTLCOLOR` messages.

The `WM_CTLCOLORxxx` messages allow you to change attributes used to draw a control without having to resort to doing a full owner-drawn control. The set of control-color messages is shown in Table 17.5. Generally, these messages are sent to the parent of a control, except for the `WM_CTLCOLORDLG` message, which is sent to the dialog itself. The `wParam` contains the handle of a DC. You can change certain parameters of the DC to affect how the control is painted; the most common functions are shown in Table 17.7. You must also return the handle of a brush that is used to paint the background of the control. Even if you don't want to explicitly specify a brush for the background, if you want any of the changes you make in the DC to be recognized, you must return the handle of a brush that will be used to paint the background. For example, if you want to change the color of text displayed in a control and you call the `SetTextColor` function, this call will have no effect if you return a `NULL` brush handle.[2]

The behavior of the `WM_CTLCOLORxxx` messages changed between the Win32 level 3 API (Windows NT 3.*x*) and the Win32 level 4 API (Windows 95 and Windows NT 4.*x*). These differences are summarized in Table

---

[2] The implementation is erratic. For some controls, the changes are honored even if you return a `NULL` brush handle. For others, or even for certain styles, the changes are not honored unless you return a non-`NULL` brush handle. For example, single-line edit controls will honor `SetTextColor` even when a `NULL` brush handle is returned, but multiline edit controls require a non-`NULL` handle; otherwise, text color changes will be ignored.

17.5. If you plan to use these messages, be careful to take these differences into consideration. Note that in some cases, a WM_CTLCOLORxxx message is not sent, such as for a disabled scroll bar at API level 3. (But the message *is* sent for a disabled scroll bar at API level 4.)

Table 17.5: WM_CTLCOLORxxx messages

Message	Recipient and Effect
WM_CTLCOLORBTN	Push buttons and default push buttons. The text color, background color, and background mode can be set. The brush that is returned is ignored.
WM_CTLCOLORDLG	Sent to a dialog box before it is painted. The text and background colors can be set.
WM_CTLCOLOREDIT	API 3: Sent to the parent of an edit control. The results are used to paint the edit control. The settings do not affect the edit control of a combo box.
	API 4: Sent to the parent of an enabled, non–read-only edit control or the parent of a combo box. The results are used to paint either the edit control or the edit control of an enabled combo box.
WM_CTLCOLORLISTBOX	API 3: Sent to the parent of a list box or combo box. The results are used to paint the text and background of the list box or the static component of a CBS_DROPDOWNLIST combo box. The color specifications do not affect the drop-down list box component of a combo box or the edit control of a CBS_DROPDOWN style combo box.
	API 4: Sent to the parent of a list box or combo box. The results are used to paint the text and background of the list box or the static control or list box component of a combo box.
WM_CTLCOLORMSGBOX	Sent to the parent of a message box before the message box is painted. Note: In spite of the specification of this message, we have been unable to detect its being sent to any window of the process when a message box is created or redrawn. See the bug inset on page 1215 for additional information.
WM_CTLCOLORSCROLLBAR	Sent to the parent of a scroll bar. The brush returned is used to paint the background of the scroll bar. This does not affect the background of scroll bars that are standard scroll bars associated with a window, the scroll bars of a list box, or the list box component of a combo box.
WM_CTLCOLORSTATIC	API 3: A static text control.
	API 4: Any control that should be displayed using the default dialog or window background color. This includes check boxes, radio buttons, group boxes, static text, read-only edit controls, disabled edit controls, and all variants of disabled combo boxes.

Table 17.6: Controls and their `WM_CTLCOLORxxx` messages

Control Type	Operation				Message to Use						
Button	Text and text background.	3	3	3		3						
	Font.					3						
	Button color.				cp							
Check box	Enabled.	Ω	Ω	Ω	Ω	3						4
	Disabled.	cp	Ω	Ω	Ω	3						4
Combo box	Static control:	3	3	3	3			3				
	enabled.	4	4	4	4		4					
	Static control:	cp	3	3	3			3				
	disabled.	cp	4	4	4		4					
	Edit control: enabled.	4	4	4	4		4					
	Edit control: disabled.	cp4	4	4	4							4
	List box: enabled.	4	4	4	4							4
	List box: disabled.	cp	4	4	4							4
	Static control:	3	3	3	3			3				
	enabled.	4	4	4	4		4					
	Static control:	cp	3	3	3			3				
	disabled.	cp	4	4	4							4
Dialog box: all properties		Ω	Ω	Ω	Ω		Ω					

Legend:

3 indicates the messages and functions that apply only for API level 3.

4 indicates the messages and functions that apply only for API level 4.

Ω indicates the messages and functions that are identical for API level 3 and 4. Note that in some cases, the message differs between API levels, while the API functions work in the same way.

cp3 means the value must be set by the control panel for API level 3.

cp4 means the value must be set by the control panel for API level 4.

cp means the value must be set by the control panel for API levels 3 and 4.

Table 17.6: Controls and their WM_CTLCOLORxxx messages

Control Type	Operation						Message to Use					
Edit control:	Enabled.	Ω	Ω	Ω	Ω			Ω				
	Disabled.	3	3	3	3			3				
			4	4	4						4	
	Read-only.	3	3	3	3			3				
			4	4	4						4	
Group box	Enabled.	3	3	3	3	3						
	Disabled.	cp										4
List box	Enabled.	Ω	Ω	Ω	Ω				Ω			
	Disabled.	cp							4			
Message box												
Radio button		Ω	Ω	Ω	Ω	3						4
Scroll bar	Enabled.	Ω	Ω	Ω	Ω					Ω		
	Disabled.	cp 3										
		4	4	4	4						4	
	In window (WS_HSCROLL/ WS_VSCROLL).											
	In list box or combo box.											
Static text control	Enabled.	Ω	Ω	Ω	Ω							Ω
	Disabled.	cp	Ω	Ω	Ω							Ω

Legend:

3 indicates the messages and functions that apply only for API level 3.

4 indicates the messages and functions that apply only for API level 4.

Ω indicates the messages and functions that are identical for API level 3 and 4. Note that in some cases, the message differs between API levels, while the API functions work in the same way.

cp3 means the value must be set by the control panel for API level 3.

cp4 means the value must be set by the control panel for API level 4.

cp means the value must be set by the control panel for API levels 3 and 4.

In Win16, there was only one message, WM_CTLCOLOR, which took three 16-bit values: the control handle, the DC handle, and a code that indicated the control type. In Win32, the two handles take up the entire 64 bits available between wParam and lParam, leaving no space to supply the control type. So instead the single message became the set of messages shown in Table 17.5.

In Windows NT 3.x and Win16, radio buttons, check boxes, and group boxes would send WM_CTLCOLORBTN messages to paint the background and establish other attributes. In Windows 95 and Windows NT 4.x and later, these controls send WM_CTLCOLORSTATIC messages instead. This change is based on the premise that the background of these controls is more like the background of static controls. If you are porting a Win16 application that uses these messages, you will find that the results are not at all what you expect. If you expect that your program will run on Windows NT 3.x and on API level 4 platforms, you must make your own explicit tests to handle the two different behaviors, or you will find that the users of one or the other platform are going to be unhappy at what they see.

Win16
Win/NT 3.x

The WM_CTLCOLORMSGBOX is specified as being sent to the parent of the message box. We were unable to detect *any* WM_CTLCOLORMSGBOX messages being sent in our application. Microsoft is apparently aware of this problem. The Knowledge Base article Q99808 describes how to obtain an example that intercepts window creation with a hook function and colors the MessageBox. See page 1218.

There are some additional subtleties to handling these messages. Push buttons and default push buttons are *always* drawn in the color selected by the Control Panel. You cannot change the background color of a push button by using the WM_CTLCOLORBTN message. To create a push button that can change color, you must do a full owner-drawn push button.

For controls that are supposed to be drawn in the same color as the window or dialog on which they are placed, the WM_CTLCOLORSTATIC message is sent. In particular, at API level 4 this message is sent for radio buttons, check boxes, and group boxes, all of which normally have the same background as the window on which they are placed. In addition, disabled or read-only edit controls and disabled combo boxes will send a WM_CTLCOLORSTATIC message to their parent to determine the color of their background.

If you want to change the text on either a straight edit control or the edit control of a combo box, you must also send the WM_SETFONT message (for example, by using the SetWindowFont macro from windowsx.h). It is not sufficient to just change the font when the text is drawn. This is because the font that is set as the font handle for the control with the WM_SETFONT message is also used when the text is highlighted or selected for editing. If you don't set your chosen font, the selection operation will highlight using the default font. This will produce very unusual effects. Generally, you should use WM_SETFONT to modify the font of a control instead of using SelectObject to select the font into the DC.

A list box, whether a normal list box or the list box of a combo box, will send a WM_CTLCOLORLISTBOX message to the parent of the control. (Although the "official" parent window of the list box of a drop-down list is the desktop window, the message is sent where expected–to the parent of the combo box itself.) This can be used if you want to set the same color for the entire list box or its text. If you need individual control of an entry, you must use owner-draw list boxes or combo boxes. Note that you cannot create an "owner draw" combo box without the CBS_HASSTRINGS style that has an edit control (CBS_DROPDOWN or CBS_SIMPLE style) because there is no way to have an "owner-draw" edit control. Note that at API level 3, you have no control over the painting of the background, text background, or text color of the edit control of a combo box. See Table 17.6 for the details.

The level 3 API also treats the fonts for combo boxes in an unusual fashion. To set the font for a combo box– either a CBS_DROPDOWN or CBS_DROPDOWNLIST style–you must use WM_SETFONT to set the font in the window whose handle is passed in to a WM_CTLCOLORDLG message. If you use the CtlColor Explorer application, you can see that if you set a font for the dialog, the font for the static control and edit control of the combo boxes, and the list boxes associated with them, will change. This is not true for the level 4 API. Furthermore, this technique (in the level 3 API) does not affect combo boxes that have the CBS_SIMPLE style.

Setting TRANSPARENT background mode for a multiline edit control does not work. As you type in new text, the old text is not erased. It works correctly for single-line edit controls, however.

You cannot use a custom palette to paint the background of a control. Although the SelectPalette and RealizePalette functions do not return error codes, their effects are ignored. If you specify a custom color for SetTextColor or SetBkColor or via CreateSolidBrush that is not in the stock palette, the "nearest" pure color will be used.

Table 17.7: Functions most commonly used in WM_CTLCOLORxxx handlers

Function	Effect	
SetBkColor(HDC, COLORREF)	Sets the color that is used to paint the background of the text. Ignored if the background mode is TRANSPARENT. The nearest pure color of the default palette is used.	
SetBkMode(HDC, int)	Sets the background mode for text drawing. The argument is one of the following:	
	OPAQUE	Text is drawn and the bounding box of each character is filled with the color established by SetBkColor.
	TRANSPARENT	Text is drawn, but only the pixels defining the characters are drawn. The background established by the returned brush shows through.
SetTextColor(HDC, COLORREF)	Sets the color that is used to paint the text. The nearest pure color of the default palette is used.	

WM_CTLCOLORxxx **Message Cracker Handler**

`HBRUSH cls_OnCtlColor(HWND hwnd, HDC hdc, HWND hchild, int type);`					
Result					HBRUSH. The handle of a brush to be used to paint the control background.

	wParam		**lParam**		
Parameter	lo	hi	lo	hi	**Meaning**
hwnd					Window handle of the window.
hdc	■	■			Handle of a DC to be modified.
hchild			■	■	Handle of the child control.
type					Computed based on the type of message. See Table 17.8.

For compatibility with earlier Win16 code, the message crackers (and for MFC users, the `Cwnd::OnCtlColor` method!) use the older Win16 codes. These codes, shown in Table 17.8, are passed into the handler to indicate which message was received. For example, in straight C programming, the `HANDLE_WM_CTLCOLOREDIT` message cracker calls the handler function passing in the `CTLCOLOR_EDIT` code as the `type` parameter. You can use this code to distinguish several different calls to the same handler. Or, if you have separate handlers for each type of message, you can ignore the `type` code. For example, if you write

Table 17.8: `WM_CTLCOLORxxx` codes

Code	Represents Message
CTLCOLOR_BTN	WM_CTLCOLORBTN
CTLCOLOR_DLG	WM_CTLCOLORDLG
CTLCOLOR_EDIT	WM_CTLCOLOREDIT
CTLCOLOR_LISTBOX	WM_CTLCOLORLISTBOX
CTLCOLOR_MSGBOX	WM_CTLCOLORMSGBOX
CTLCOLOR_SCROLLBAR	WM_CTLCOLORSCROLLBAR
CTLCOLOR_STATIC	WM_CTLCOLORSTATIC

```
HANDLE_MSG(hwnd, WM_CTLCOLOREDIT, OnCtlColorEdit);
HANDLE_MSG(hwnd, WM_CTLCOLORSTATIC, OnCtlColorStatic);
```

then the individual handlers can ignore their `type` parameter because the type is implicit in the dispatch. But you can also write the following handler calls, which share a handler; In which case, you must use the `type` parameter to determine the message that was received.

```
HANDLE_MSG(hwnd, WM_CTLCOLOREDIT, OnCtlColor);
HANDLE_MSG(hwnd, WM_CTLCOLORSTATIC, OnCtlColor);
```

If when using this handler you want to pass on the message, you must call the appropriate FORWARD handler. That is, you must put a `switch` statement in that selects, based on the `type`, to which handler to forward. Thus you could write either

```
HBRUSH OnCtlColorEdit(HWND hwnd, HDC hdc, HWND hchild, int type)
    {
    // ... do what you want here
    return FORWARD_WM_CTLCOLOREDIT(hwnd, hdc, hchild, handlerfn);
    }
```

or the more complicated

```
HBRUSH OnCtlColor (HWND hwnd, HDC hdc, HWND hchild, int type)
    {
    // ... do what you want here
    switch(type)
        { /* type */
        case CTLCOLOR_EDIT:
            return FORWARD_WM_CTLCOLOREDIT(hwnd, hdc, hchild, handlerfn);
        case CTLCOLOR_STATIC:
            return FORWARD_WM_CTLCOLORSTATIC(hwnd, hdc, hchild, handlerfn);
        } /* type */
     return NULL;
    }
```

Note that you must use the individual FORWARD_ macros even if they are all calling the same handler function. If you are using MFC, you need to call only the OnCtlColor method of your base class; this method understands how to forward correctly.

Non-solid Brushes

If you use a brush other than a solid color, be prepared to deal with some problems. For example, if you want a patterned background for the window background and for text controls written on it, you have to use TRANSPARENT mode so that the pattern is visible after the text is written. It is not sufficient to set the "background color" of the text, because that background color will be a solid color. In Windows 95, you are still limited to 8 × 8 bitmaps. But if the text box is not aligned to a multiple of the brush width, which is the most common case, you will have to use SetBrushOrgEx to force the brush to be properly aligned. However, there appear to be several problems with this technique. For example, on Windows NT 3.51 you can set the brush origin successfully for a static text control, but not for an icon control. On Windows NT 3.51, you can return a stock HOLLOW_BRUSH; you will get correct behavior for a text control, but not for an icon. Because of the many problems we have encountered in using nonsolid brushes, we suggest that you approach their use with extreme caution. We have included a nonsolid background as an example in the MsgColor example. The nonsolid background works only for certain controls.

Handling MessageBox Color Changes

Despite the claims about the WM_CTLCOLORMSGBOX message, we have been unable to detect that this message is ever sent. There is a vastly more complex method that you can use if you need to change the background, text, or brush colors of a MessageBox; it involves using a "hook function" to intercept the messages being sent to a window. Microsoft documents this method quite thoroughly in the example program that accompanies Knowledge Base article #Q99808; unfortunately, it is Win16-based. When strictly rewritten for Win32, the example is not thread-safe. Our rewrite of the key module is shown in Listing 17.10. The two calls are generated by the code shown in Listing 17.11.

Listing 17.10: Excerpts from `msgcolor.c`

```c
typedef struct {
                HWND hwndMsgBox;
                FARPROC lpMsgBoxSubClassProc;
                BOOL SubClass;

                HHOOK      hhookCBT;     // CBT hook identifier
                HBRUSH     hbrushBkgnd;  // Brush to paint bkg
                COLORREF   clrText;      // Color of text
                FARPROC    MsgBoxProc;   // Message box window proc
                HINSTANCE  hinst;        // HINSTANCE of module
                } CBTvalues;

static __declspec(thread) CBTvalues cbt;

//****************************************************************
// Function: colorMessageBox
//
// Purpose: Creates a message box with a specified background
//          and text color.
//
// Parameters:
//    hwndOwner    == Owner of message box. Can be NULL.
//    Text         == Text in message box.
//    Title        == Title of message box.
//    uFlags       == MessageBox flags.
// The above four parameters are standard MessageBox parameters.
//    hbrushBkgnd  == Brush to paint the background.
//    clrText      == Text color of text in message box.
//    hinst        == Module instance for the message box.
//
// Returns: return value of MessageBox
//
// Comments: The standard message box is subclassed to change the
// color of the text and background. To obtain the handle of
// the message box in order to subclass, a CBT hook is installed
// before MessageBox is called. The CBT hook is called when the
// message box is created and provides access to the window
// handle of the message box.
//
//****************************************************************

int colorMessageBox(HWND hwndOwner, LPCSTR Text, LPCSTR Title,
                UINT uFlags,
                HBRUSH hbrushBkgnd, COLORREF clrText,
                HINSTANCE hinst)
{
    int nResult;

    cbt.hbrushBkgnd = hbrushBkgnd;
    cbt.hinst = hinst;
    cbt.clrText = clrText;

    // Set a thread-specific CBT hook before calling MessageBox.

    cbt.hhookCBT = SetWindowsHookEx(WH_CBT, cbtProc, hinst,
                                GetCurrentThreadId());
```

```
        nResult = MessageBox(hwndOwner, Text, Title, uFlags);

        UnhookWindowsHookEx(cbt.hhookCBT);

        return nResult;
}
//**************************************************************
// Function: cbtProc
//
// Purpose: Callback function of WH_CBT hook
//
// Parameters and return value:
//      See documentation for cbtProc.
//
// Comments: The message box is subclassed on creation and the
// original window procedure is restored on destruction
//
//**************************************************************
static LRESULT CALLBACK
cbtProc(int nCode, WPARAM wParam, LPARAM lParam)
{
    LPCBT_CREATEWND lpcbtcreate;

    if (nCode < 0)
        return CallNextHookEx(cbt.hhookCBT, nCode, wParam, lParam);

    // Window owned by our task is being created. Since the hook
    // is installed just before the MessageBox call and removed
    // after the MessageBox call, the window being created is
    // either the message box or one of its controls.
    if (nCode == HCBT_CREATEWND)
        { /* creation event */
        lpcbtcreate = (LPCBT_CREATEWND)lParam;

        // Check if the window being created is a message box. The
        // class name of a message box is WC_DIALOG since message
        // boxes are just special dialogs. We can't subclass the
        // message box right away because the window procedure of
        // the message box is not set when this hook is called. So
        // we wait till the hook is called again when one of the
        // message box controls is created and then we subclass.
        // This will happen because the message box has at least
        // one control.

        if (WC_DIALOG == lpcbtcreate->lpcs->lpszClass)
            { /* dialog class */
            cbt.hwndMsgBox = (HWND)wParam;
            cbt.SubClass = TRUE;        // Remember to subclass when
                                        // the hook is called next
            } /* dialog class */
        else
        if (cbt.SubClass)
            { /* do subclass now */
            // Subclass the dialog to change the color of the
            // background and text
```

```
                cbt.MsgBoxProc = (FARPROC)SetWindowLong(
                                   cbt.hwndMsgBox, GWL_WNDPROC,
                                   (LONG)msgBoxSubClassProc);
                cbt.SubClass = FALSE;
              } /* do subclass now */
        } /* creation event */
      else
      if (nCode == HCBT_DESTROYWND
          && (HWND)wParam == cbt.hwndMsgBox)
        { /* destroying */
          // Reset the original window procedure when the message
          // box is about to be destroyed.
          SetWindowLong(cbt.hwndMsgBox, GWL_WNDPROC, (LONG)cbt.MsgBoxProc);
          cbt.hwndMsgBox = NULL;
        } /* destroying */
      return 0;
}

//***************************************************************
// Function: msgBoxSubClassProc
//
// Purpose: Subclass procedure for message box to change text and
//          background color
//
// Parameters & return value:
//     Standard. See documentation for WindowProc
//
//***************************************************************
static LRESULT CALLBACK
msgBoxSubClassProc(HWND hwnd, UINT msg, WPARAM wParam,
                                              LPARAM lParam)
    {
    // Change the background and text color of the message box.

    switch(msg)
        { /* msg */
          case WM_CTLCOLORDLG:
          case WM_CTLCOLORSTATIC:
                SetBkMode((HDC)wParam, TRANSPARENT);
                SetTextColor((HDC)wParam, cbt.clrText);
                return (LRESULT)cbt.hbrushBkgnd;
        } /* msg */
      return  CallWindowProc(cbt.MsgBoxProc, hwnd, msg, wParam, lParam);
}
```

Listing 17.11: Calling `msgcolor.c`
from the WM_COMMAND dispatching code:

```
case IDM_GRAYMSGBOX:
        colorMessageBox(hwnd,                        // Owner
                   _T("Gray Background"),// Text
                   _T("Message Box"),    // Title
                   MB_OK,                // Styles
                   GetStockObject(LTGRAY_BRUSH),
                                         // Background brush
                   RGB(0, 0, 0),         // Text color
```

```
                    g_hinst);                    // module inst.
        return 0;

case IDM_REDMSGBOX:
        {
          HBRUSH hbrush = CreateSolidBrush(RGB(255, 0, 0));
          colorMessageBox(hwnd,
                    _T("Red Background"),
                    _T("Message Box"),
                    MB_ICONQUESTION | MB_ABORTRETRYIGNORE,
                    hbrush, RGB(0, 0, 255), g_hinst);
          DeleteObject(hbrush);
          return 0;
        }
```

The subtleties of how you subclass a message box involve some rather obscure and esoteric Windows lore. It's not easy to discover on your own. This is why we are taking time to show it here.

We started with the Win16 version of the code written originally by Microsoft and made substantial changes to achieve a thread-safe Win32 version. First, we stored all of the values that affect the message box in a per-thread variable by using __declspec(thread) to declare it. Each thread that uses this module will be given its own private copy of this object. You must not use static variables to hold any of this information if you want a thread-safe implementation.

To invoke a MessageBox call whereby we can specify colors, we call the colorMessageBox function, passing in three additional parameters: the background brush handle, the text color, and an instance handle for the module. We store these in the per-thread structure that controls the message box.

We next set a "CBT" (Computer-Based Training) hook by calling SetWindowsHookEx. The resulting hook handle is also stored in the per-thread information block. The effects of setting the hook are that certain events will send "hook notifications" to the function we specify. By giving the thread ID, we make this a per-thread hook. We could also give it a process ID to hook all events in all threads, but we want events only for the current thread.

We then call MessageBox, which creates the message box. When we return, we use UnhookWindowsHookEx to remove the hook and return the result from MessageBox. All the rest of the hard work is done in the hook handler.

The hook handler is a subtle piece of code. The simple case is if a negative value is passed in as the code; we just call the next hook in the "hook chain" using CallNextHookEx. If we do not do this, *other* hooks that may have been set (perhaps by other libraries) will not be notified of the events and we may discover that we have broken existing behavior. We get a creation event for *every* window that is being created, whether it is the message box itself or one of its child windows. We want to subclass only if it is the message box itself. But we can query the LPCBT_CREATEWND structure and discover the ID of the class being created. The special class WC_DIALOG represents all dialog classes and is a MAKEINTRESOURCE value, so we can do a direct equality check with the class value in the CREATESTRUCT. If we have a WC_DIALOG class, then it is the creation of the message box itself. In this case, we store the handle of the message box in the set of values that control our subclassing, but we don't actually subclass the window at this point. This is because the GWL_WNDPROC value has not yet been set up. If we did the subclassing now, we would be storing an invalid function pointer for the parent class. Instead, we know that there is at least one other window in the message box (at least the **OK** button!) we get on the next event, so we can use the handle we stored to do the subclassing. When the second creation event comes in, we route the messages through our own handler and then subclass the dialog using standard subclassing techniques. If the event is a window destruction event for the message box window itself, we remove the subclassing.

The subclass handler function responds by setting the text color and background color for both WM_CTLCOLORDLG and WM_CTLCOLORSTATIC events. You must set the colors for both events to get a seamless match. Note that we set the background mode to TRANSPARENT so that we can use background brushes other than those of solid colors.

Object-oriented WM_CTLCOLOR

One problem in handling WM_CTLCOLOR messages is that the *parent* window is supposed to set the parameters for the drawing and return the correct brush. This violates basic design principles in that only the child window should know how to draw itself. In fact, for a child window implemented in a DLL, the parent window *can't* know how to draw the child! So we need a way to indicate to the child that it should specify its own parameters. Fortunately, there is a convenient way to do this: Use the WM_CTLCOLOR messages. The usual technique is to simply "reflect" the WM_CTLCOLORxxx message down to the child that sent it. Since the child window normally does not contain a child window that would be sending a WM_CTLCOLORxxx message, there is basically no confusion. But to handle the case in which there might be an embedded control that we know nothing about, we carefully pass in the window as the child window. The handler can then detect that if the message has itself as a child; if so, it is a reflected message; if not, it is a message from its own embedded child. This is illustrated by the following code from text.c:

```
static HBRUSH
text_OnCtlColorEdit(HWND hwnd, HDC hdc, HWND hchild, int type)
    {
     return FORWARD_WM_CTLCOLOREDIT(hchild, hdc, hchild, SendMessage);
    }
```

which simply shows that the parent needs to know nothing about how to set the parameters. It just delegates that task to the child window. The child window handler, located in edit.c, implements this by having the following function called from its subclass handler procedure:

```
static HBRUSH
editsubclass_OnCtlColor(HWND hwnd, HDC hdc, HWND hchild, int type)
    {
     HBRUSH EditBackgroundBrush = GetProp(hwnd, MAKEINTATOM(ATOM_BKG));
     LOGBRUSH lbr;

     if(type != CTLCOLOR_EDIT)
        return NULL;

     if(EditBackgroundBrush != NULL)
        { /* get color */
         GetObject(EditBackgroundBrush, sizeof(lbr), &lbr);
        } /* get color */

     SetTextColor(hdc, getRGB(hwnd));
```

```
    SetBkColor(hdc, lbr.lbColor);
    return EditBackgroundBrush;

}
```

Since we know that we have no embedded child controls, we don't bother doing any test for that situation. Note that we want the text background to be the same color as the brush used to paint the rest of the control. Normally, we would provide for this by using SetBkMode(hdc, TRANSPARENT). However, for multiline edit controls, this does not work. For such controls, the background mode affects how updating is done when you type new characters. The result is that the old text is not erased before the new text is drawn. So we cannot set TRANSPARENT mode. Rather than store a separate color code, we use the GetObject call with a LOGBRUSH structure to get the parameters of the brush, including the color. We then set this color as the background color.

The result of this technique is to convert an "owner-draw" object, which is drawn (or in this case, has its parameters specified) by its parent window, to a "self-draw" object, which is drawn (or has its parameters specified) by its own private code.

The CtlColor Explorer

We have included on the CD-ROM the CtlColor Explorer program. This is the program that we ran on Windows NT 3.51, Windows 95, and Windows NT 4.0 to produce Table 17.6. It allows you to set the text color, background color, background brush, background mode, and font for each class of controls shown in a control sampler page. For those of you using MFC, you may want to study how we implemented the WM_CTLCOLORMSGBOX handler using a blend of pure C and MFC code.

The CtlColor Explorer demonstrates the techniques in a fairly broad fashion. For example, if you select a "Static" color, that color will apply to *all* the static controls in the sampler window. In practice, of course, you will apply the styles selectively to the controls that you wish to modify. Our simple approach was designed to be illustrative rather than to give you point-by-point control over each individual child control in the window. Nonetheless, you can use this Explorer on various platforms to check the effects your code will have so that you can tune your code to be platform-independent. The differences between the three native Win32 platforms are significant.

Summary

Creating an MDI program looks like a more complex task than it actually is. Basically, you need to structure an MDI application as an independent frame window and independent MDI child windows. The amount of extra code required to implement the MDI is considerably less than what would be necessary if you had to write the MDI client window function yourself. What is important here is the number of cases you must handle correctly to give the correct GUI-standard-compliant behavior. This MDI example application can serve as a skeleton MDI application much as the Skeleton program does for a regular Windows application.

Further Reading

Microsoft Corporation, *The Windows Interface Guidelines for Software Design*, Microsoft Press, 1995. ISBN 1-55615-679-0.

> Reading this book is *not* optional. You must familiarize yourself with the Microsoft specifications, even if you want to ignore them. See the review on page 151.

Further Reading

Chapter

18 Synchronization

Synchronization Basics

What Is Synchronization?

Synchronization is best expressed as the need to have two or more threads of control operate on shared information in such a way that the correctness of the code and the integrity of the data structure are preserved. You hit this problem any time you have a multithreaded process, or you have the need to have two or more processes interact. The most common cases you will have to deal with are those where your program uses "worker threads", when you are writing DLLs, and when you write server applications of any sort. You may have to synchronize accesses to a file (using *record locking* is one such technique you may already be familiar with), but in general you have to deal with synchronization of other shared resources. Most of these resources do not implement sharing operations as part of their primitive functionality. In the case of multithreaded applications, you may need to synchronize access to shared memory locations. All of these involve decisions about what mechanism to use and how to use it.

Simple Synchronization Problems

The simplest synchronization problem comes up when you have two threads working on a common data structure–a key example being a storage allocator. Win32 is a *preemptible multitasking system;* you have no control over when the system will suspend your current thread and transfer control to another thread. This can happen at any time, between the execution of any two instructions, anywhere in your execution: in your code, in the C runtime, or in the middle of executing a shared DLL. When control resumes in the suspended thread, your program will continue where it left off.

But what if you have two (or more) threads running in your process? And what if one of the other threads in your own process is the one that next gets control? Unlike normal "multitasking", in which your Word document is suspended while the print spooler runs, or Solitaire is suspended while the network download runs, when you have multiple threads in one process, you have several threads that have access *to the same address space.*

This points out an important difference between Win32 and other "multitasking" systems. Win32 does *not* have a "process scheduler". Win32 has a *thread* scheduler, and this scheduler makes little distinction between threads which represent different processes and threads in the same process.

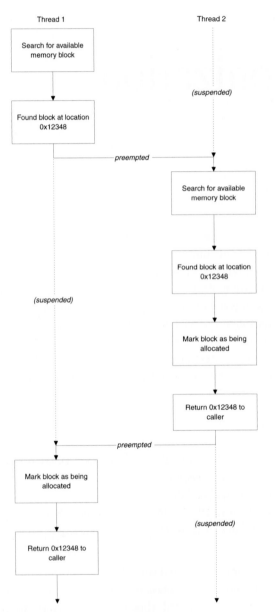

Figure 18.1: Conflict in synchronization

Here's a typical scenario, one which is very likely to occur in some applications that use a storage allocator. To show the problem that can occur, we will first examine a thread-*unsafe* allocator. Look at the execution threads shown in Figure 18.1. Two threads are executing in the same process. The first one calls the storage allocator, which searches for a block of storage and finds it. Just as it finds the address of a block it can return, it is preempted. Before this thread can resume, some other threads will be scheduled, based on the whim of the scheduler. What happens if, before the first thread resumes, the *second* thread in the same process gets to run? Control returns to the process, but now executing the second thread. Suppose that it, too, needs to allocate storage, so it calls the storage allocator. It finds a block large enough to allocate at–unfortunately–the same address, since thread 1 didn't get to mark the block as being in use. Thread 2 happily marks the block as being in use and returns the address to its caller. Shortly thereafter, the processor is preempted again, and thread 1 gets to continue running. Since it has already checked that the storage block is not in use, *and doesn't know (and can't know) that it has been preempted*, it goes on to mark the block as being in use, and returns the address to its caller. Now two threads "own" the same piece of storage and are using it for different purposes, which will almost certainly conflict.

The result of this is that the two threads "step on each other" in ways that will very likely produce, at the very least, incorrect results, and at the worst will actually cause access faults (for example, if one thread thinks it is storing integers in the allocated space while the other is storing pointers, somebody is going to get a very wrong result!). The Good News is that the C and C++ runtimes recognize this problem and, as we discussed in Chapter 14, *serialize* the access to the heap by using synchronization primitives. The problem we have just described cannot occur in the default allocator.

Contrast Figure 18.1 with Figure 18.2, which shows correct synchronization (as done by the default allocator, or any allocator for which serialization is enabled). Thread 1 first attempts to lock the allocator structure, and succeeds in doing so. After it finds a suitable block, it is preempted, just as in our previous example. Thread 2 gains control. But when it calls the allocator, an attempt is made to lock the allocator structure. Since the allocator structure is already locked, thread 2 blocks. Eventually, thread 1 will be scheduled again, and it resumes execution where it left off; it marks the block as allocated and then unlocks the allocator structure. At this point, thread 2, which has been waiting on the lock, becomes feasible for execution, and at some point the scheduler will preempt thread 1 and allow thread 2 to run. Since the block at 0x12348 has already been allocated safely, this block cannot be found when thread 2 executes, and so thread 2 will find a different block. Thus the correctness and integrity of the allocator structures are maintained even in the presence of multithreaded access.

Synchronization Mechanisms

Synchronization is maintained through a family of mechanisms variously referred to in the literature as *locks, semaphores, signals, event queues, monitors*, and *rendezvous mechanisms*. The literature in synchronization goes back many years; see the "Further Reading" section on page 1264 for some selected references (a complete set of references would probably be as long as this entire chapter). All of these mechanisms, however, have one goal: to limit access to resources such that the integrity of the information is preserved, and thus the correctness of the program using the resources. We usually refer to resources whose access is controlled by a synchronization mechanism as resources that are "protected by a lock". Which implementation you choose then depends upon several engineering considerations. As we examine each of the synchronization mechanisms, we show the criteria you can use to determine which one is appropriate.

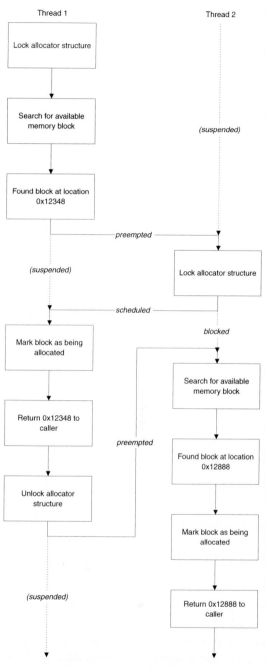

Figure 18.2: Correct synchronization

Once you can exclude a thread of execution from getting to a resource, you end up having to deal with a new class of problems that arise. These problems include:

- *deadlock*, in which two threads permanently block because thread 1 needs a resource held by thread 2 in order to complete a transaction, and thread 2 needs a resource held by thread 1 in order to complete a (possibly different) transaction (and thereby release the resource needed by thread 1 to complete *its* transaction),

- *starvation*, in which contention for resources is such that some thread actually never gets a chance to run. This is often caused by having threads running at different priority levels; higher-priority threads will always get the processor, and a lower-priority thread "politely waits its turn", and consequently never gets to run.

- *priority inversion*, a problem related to starvation, in which a lower-priority thread of a set of threads blocks execution of higher-priority threads. This comes about under the following conditions: first, all higher-priority threads have blocked; the lower-priority thread can run, and locks a resource. Next, some higher-priority threads become available, and because they are higher-priority their execution preempts the lower-priority thread that has the resource locked. Finally, one or more of these higher-priority threads needs the locked resource. Unfortunately, the resource is already locked by the lower-priority thread, and each higher-priority thread that needs the resource blocks. As long as there are any higher-priority threads that can run, the lower-priority thread cannot, and therefore locks out all higher-priority threads that *do* need the resource.

These have a significant impact on overall system performance. Solutions to deadlock avoidance, formal proofs of deadlock-free algorithms, discussion of scheduling to avoid starvation, and the like occupied much of the operating system literature for well over a decade and a half, from 1965 to 1981. However, by 1981, most of the problems had been addressed and many of the key papers had been published. If you want a deeper background in these problems than we can present here, that's the best era to look for papers. Problems like the priority inversion problem continue to be active in the contemporary literature, particularly the literature on real-time embedded systems.

Most standard operating systems architecture books also address these problems; what was once a serious deep research problem is now nicely packaged into quite readable chapters in any modern book on operating system architecture.

Correctness Doesn't Just Happen

We gave this paragraph its own heading because it is very important to understand: a correct multithreaded system (by which we also include multitasking processes, including client/server systems) requires careful design. In particular, you must pay extremely close attention to how shared resources are locked and unlocked and how to deal with all the aspects of multithreaded processes sharing an address space. Most of the assumptions you can make about the correctness of a program are invalidated by multithreading–if any thread can access any memory location at any time, unless you carefully control that access you will get a system that crashes with essentially unreproducible failures. Such systems are virtually impossible to debug using "normal" debugging techniques. It is also *extremely* difficult to take a system that was designed as a single-threaded system and make it a multithreaded system "after the fact". If you have the slightest suspicion that you will want to execute in a multithreaded context, you must design for multithreading–even if the initial release is single-threaded. Otherwise the multithreaded release will probably never come out because you will spend all of your time trying to debug it. Don't try to shortcut the design phase for multithreading–you will only regret it.[1] An example of the careful analysis required is given in the MSDN article by Ruediger Asche, "Synchronization on the Fly", cited in "Further Reading". This painstaking analysis is often necessary.

Win32 Synchronization Primitives

There are several distinct mechanisms you can use for synchronization in Win32: *events*, and the three implementations of mutual-exclusion primitives: *critical sections*, *mutexes*, and *semaphores*.

Win32 synchronization objects are in one of two states: *signaled* or *nonsignaled*. If a synchronization object is signaled, an attempt to pass it will be successful. If it is nonsignaled, an attempt to pass it will be blocked. When you "pass" a synchronization object, it means that your program has tested the synchronization object and has continued execution. If you fail to pass the object, in the simplest case, your thread simply sits there and waits until it can pass. This testing is done by calling an API function appropriate for the type of object. Generally, when the function returns, you have passed the object and can use the resource it is protecting; if the object was nonsignaled, Win32 suspends the thread until the thread that last passed the synchronization object releases the object by marking it as signaled, at which point one of the threads waiting on the object will resume, and return control from the API function that was suspended. (As we get into more detail, you will see that this explanation is somewhat simplified–there are "conditional" wait operations and "time out" conditions that make life a bit more complicated).

The designation of "signaled" and "unsignaled" may cause some confusion if you are coming from a Unix background, where `signal` is a specific operation in the operating system. In Unix, a `signal` causes an interrupt in the target process, changing the flow of control to begin execution at a designated function. The term "signaled" used for Win32 synchronization primitives has nothing to do with the mechanism used in Unix for the `signal` function.

Unix

Many of the techniques, strategies, and hazards of the three major synchronization objects, *semaphores*, *mutexes* and *critical sections*,[2] are the same. We will discuss synchronization strategies in more detail after we

---

[1] I spent several years on the C.mmp/Hydra multiprocessor operating system project–a system most carefully designed to be multithreaded. Our experience confirmed that only by careful design could a multithreaded system be made reliable. Several Hydra papers and a book are cited under "Further Reading" *–jmn*.

[2] Strictly speaking, in Microsoft's terminology a critical section is not a "synchronization object" because that term refers only to events, semaphores, and mutexes. We couldn't come up with a better term that included critical sections, so decided to use a more liberal interpretation of the term "synchronization object". When we need to make the distinction, we will refer to events, semaphores, and critical sections as *kernel synchronization objects*.

present the core synchronization primitives. Synchronization strategy and issues are also discussed in Chapter 14 for storage allocation, and in Chapter 16 for DLLs.

Semaphores

Semaphores are the most general (and the most costly in terms of performance) synchronization mechanism in Win32. A semaphore can be used to synchronize two or more cooperating processes, or to be precise, two or more cooperating threads (whether or not they are in the same process). We will always cast our discussion in terms of thread accesses, but keep in mind that for semaphores the threads can be in different processes.

A semaphore operates by "gating" access. When a thread requests permission to pass a semaphore, either the permission is granted (if the semaphore is *signaled*), and the thread is permitted to continue execution, or permission is denied (if the semaphore is *nonsignaled*), in which case the thread is blocked. The simplest usage of a semaphore is to deny permission when some other thread has already been granted access. The synchronization literature says that this thread is executing a *critical section* of code.[3] However, a semaphore is quite general. A semaphore will allow some limited *number* of threads access to a resource–and is often used to limit usage of some resource to a specified limit. A semaphore may be used to grant access to a server process, allowing no more than (for example) nine clients to pass the semaphore. The tenth client process that attempts to pass the semaphore is blocked until one of the threads of execution already in the critical section exits the critical section. By using semaphores you can impose limits on the resources a thread can gain–whether it is a count of buffers, or a count of network connections, or any other resource you choose to limit.

Semaphores in Win32 are kernel-managed objects, so you can refer to them only by their handles. The set of semaphore operations is given in Table 18.1.

Table 18.1: Semaphore operations

Return	Function	Description
BOOL	CloseHandle	(HANDLE semhandle)
		Closes the semaphore handle. When the last handle to the semaphore is closed, the semaphore is destroyed.
HANDLE	CreateSemaphore	(LPSECURITY_ATTRIBUTES attr, LONG initialcount, LONG maximumcount, LPCTSTR name)
		Creates or locates a semaphore object. If it does not already exist, it is created with the specified parameters.

---

[3] As we will see, Win32 uses the term "critical section" in a very specific technical sense, causing some confusion with the published literature.

Table 18.1: Semaphore operations

Return	Function	Description
BOOL	DuplicateHandle	(HANDLE sourceprocess, HANDLE toduplicate, HANDLE targetprocess, LPHANDLE resulthandle, DWORD access, BOOL inherit, DWORD options)
		Creates a duplicate handle. The options may be one or more of the following flags:
		DUPLICATE_CLOSE_SOURCE–the source handle is closed after the duplicate is created.
		DUPLICATE_SAME_ACCESS–The created handle has the same access rights as the source handle.
DWORD	MsgWaitForMultipleObjects	*see page 1243*
HANDLE	OpenSemaphore	(DWORD access, BOOL inherit, LPCTSTR name)
		Opens a handle to an existing semaphore. The flags can be any of the following values:
		SEMAPHORE_ALL_ACCESS–permits all accesses.
		SEMAPHORE_MODIFY_STATE–permits the Release-Semaphore operation
		SYNCHRONIZE[NT]–permits semaphore to be used by all wait functions.
BOOL	ReleaseSemaphore	(HANDLE semaphore, LONG releasecount, LPLONG prevcount)
DWORD	WaitForMultipleObjects	
DWORD	WaitForMultipleObjectsEx	*see page 1243*
DWORD	WaitForSingleObject	
DWORD	WaitForSingleObjectEx	

[NT]Windows NT only

You use CreateSemaphore to create or access a semaphore. If the semaphore does not already exist, it is created with the initialcount and maximumcount values, and its security is determined by the attr parameter. If the attr parameter is NULL, the object has default security attributes and is not inheritable. The initialcount must be in the range $0 \leq$ initialcount $\leq$ maximumcount. The maximumcount must be greater than 0. The name is the name of the semaphore to create. If the semaphore already exists, and is accessible to the process attempting the creation, its handle is returned, but the count values are ignored. The `attr` values are also ignored, except for the `flag` permitting inheritability. If you call `GetLastError` after a successful return, it will return either 0, meaning the semaphore was newly-created, or the value `ERROR_ALREADY_EXISTS`, indicating that you have a reference to an existing semaphore. If the call fails, you will get a `NULL` handle, and `GetLastError` will return a code indicating the reason the call failed. To simply obtain a semaphore handle without creating one if it does not already exist, you can use the `OpenSemaphore` function. The name of the semaphore is case-sensitive, and must be distinct. Note that events, semaphores, mutexes, and file-mapping objects all share the same name space, so they all must be unique.

If you specify `NULL` for the name, the semaphore is created without a name, and cannot be shared with any other process. If you specify a name, the naming convention you use should be robust, because the name is visible system-wide. You probably shouldn't choose a name like `"DataLock"` for a semaphore–some application you've never heard of might well choose the same name, and you will both end up sharing the same semaphore, with possibly disastrous consequences (for example, you might assume that the semaphore only allows one thread to pass, while the other program assumes that it is gating ten threads–and if the other program runs first, the semaphore it creates will be the one you get!). We suggest either using a name like `"application.Semaphore.name"` where `application` is the application name, the addition of the string "`.Semaphore`" prevents conflict with other objects that share the name space, and "`.name`" represents the name of the semaphore; or using a global unique ID string, as we describe on page 55. In addition, if you need to support development versions running in parallel with production versions on a debug copy of the shared information, you might want to include additional information, such as a major version number, "`.Debug`" qualifier, or the like to permit this. The name may not include the backslash character, so if you use some qualification such as the launch directory name or database filename, you must replace the backslashes in the name with some permitted character.

When you are done with a semaphore, that is, when you no longer need any synchronization based on it, you can call `CloseHandle` to close the handle you obtained from `CreateSemaphore`. Once you close the handle, you cannot use the handle in any synchronization operation. When your process terminates, the system implicitly calls `CloseHandle` for any semaphore handles the process has opened. When the last handle to the semaphore is closed, the semaphore object is destroyed. You may have more than one handle to a semaphore. *Be careful!* You get a new handle to a semaphore each time you call `CreateSemaphore` or `OpenSemaphore`. You can, of course, store an arbitrary number of copies of this handle in your application. Each call on `CreateSemaphore` or `OpenSemaphore` increments the handle count by one; each call on `CloseHandle` decrements the handle count by one. These calls do not know that you have made copies of the handle in your application; they keep track only of the "reference count" to the semaphore. So if you do one `CreateSemaphore` call in your program, store twenty copies in twenty C objects, and then delete one of the C objects, you had better not do a `CloseHandle` when you do the release of one of the C objects. This will release your only "known" copy of the handle, and an attempt to use one of your other copies of the handle will give you an error, because the handle, from the viewpoint of Win32, is no longer valid. You must either do your own reference counting (thus duplicating the work Win32 is already doing for you) or call `CreateSemaphore` or `OpenSemaphore` each time you want to store a copy of the semaphore handle. Then you can safely `CloseHandle` on each copy because it is a copy known to the Win32 operating system. Of course, this means that you *must* do a `CloseHandle` for each handle, or the reference count will never go to 0 and the semaphore will not be released.

You can create a semaphore with an initial count of 0. In this case, the first process that attempts to pass the semaphore will find it nonsignaled, and block. After you have completed whatever initialization you wish to do, you can explicitly call ReleaseSemaphore to set the desired initial count.

To attempt to pass a semaphore, you use its handle in one of the *wait functions* (since both semaphores and mutexes use the same wait functions, we will discuss them all at once; see page 1243). If the thread passes the semaphore successfully, the semaphore's count is decremented by one. If the count reaches zero, the semaphore becomes *nonsignaled*, and the next thread that attempts to wait on the semaphore will be blocked.

When you have finished using a resource controlled by a semaphore, you must release the semaphore so other processes that are blocked waiting for the resource can now execute. You do this by calling the ReleaseSemaphore function, specifying a releasecount of (usually) 1. This adds 1 to the semaphore count, causing the semaphore to enter the signaled state. Any pending threads waiting on the semaphore will become feasible to execute, and (for a release count of 1) one of them will successfully obtain the semaphore while the rest remain blocked.

You can use any of the "wait" primitives to wait for a semaphore. See page 1243.

Mutexes

A common use of semaphores is to permit no more than *one* thread at a time to pass the semaphore. Referred to in the literature as *binary semaphores*, these semaphores can have only two values, 0 (nonsignaled) and 1 (signaled). Because this case is so common, it can be optimized internally by the operating system by using a special-case implementation of a semaphore, the *MUTual EXclusion* object, the "mutex". In addition to the optimization, a mutex behaves slightly differently in the case where the same thread tries to acquire it more than once, a subtle but often very important distinction between a Win32 mutex and a Win32 semaphore. (We add the specific "Win32" qualification here because the general synchronization literature makes no distinction between binary semaphores and general semaphores and treats them exactly the same way, independent of which thread of execution is involved. Win32 definitions are therefore not consistent with much of the general literature, which can lead to confusion if you are accustomed to the traditional specifications of behavior).

A mutex is an operating-system-managed object that provides for simple synchronization. Like a semaphore, a mutex can be used to synchronize two processes, or two threads within the same process. The mutex functions are shown in Table 18.2.

You use CreateMutex to create or access a mutex. If the mutex does not already exist, it is created; its security is determined by the attr parameter. If the attr parameter is NULL, the object has default security attributes and is not inheritable. The initialowner flag indicates whether the mutex is "owned". If set to TRUE, the mutex is created in the nonsignaled state; otherwise, the mutex is created in the signaled state. The name is the name of the mutex to create. If the mutex already exists, and is accessible to the process attempting the creation, its handle is returned, but the initialowner value is ignored. The attr values are also ignored, except for the flag permitting inheritability. If you call GetLastError after a successful return, it will return either 0, indicating that the mutex has been newly created, or the value ERROR_ALREADY_EXISTS,

Table 18.2: Mutex operations

Return	Function	Description
BOOL	CloseHandle	(HANDLE mutexhandle)
		Closes the mutex handle. When the last handle to the mutex is closed, the mutex is destroyed.
HANDLE	CreateMutex	(LPSECURITY_ATTRIBUTES attr, BOOL initialowner, LPCTSTR name)
		Creates or locates a mutex object. If it does not already exist, it is created with the specified parameters.
BOOL	DuplicateHandle	(HANDLE sourceprocess,HANDLE toduplicate, HANDLE targetprocess, LPHANDLE resulthandle, DWORD access, BOOL inherit, DWORD options)
		Creates a duplicate handle. The options may be one or more of the following flags:
		DUPLICATE_CLOSE_SOURCE–the source handle is closed after the duplicate is created.
		DUPLICATE_SAME_ACCESS–The created handle has the same access rights as the source handle.
DWORD	MsgWaitForMultipleObjects	*see page 1243*
HANDLE	OpenMutex	(DWORD access, BOOL inherit, LPCTSTR name)
		Opens a handle to an existing mutex. The flags can be any of the following values:
		MUTEX_ALL_ACCESS–permits all accesses.
		SYNCHRONIZE[NT]–permits mutex to be used by all wait functions.
BOOL	ReleaseMutex	(HANDLE mutex, LONG releasecount, LPLONG prevcount)
DWORD	WaitForMultipleObjects	
DWORD	WaitForMultipleObjectsEx	*see page 1243*
DWORD	WaitForSingleObject	
DWORD	WaitForSingleObjectEx	

[NT]Windows NT only

indicating that you have a reference to an existing mutex. If the call fails, you will get a NULL handle, and GetLastError will return a code indicating the reason the call failed. To simply obtain a mutex handle without creating one if it does not already exist, you can use the OpenMutex function. The name of the mutex is case-sensitive, and must be distinct. Note that events, semaphores, mutexes, and file-mapping objects all share the same name space, so they must all be unique. See the discussion on page 1234 about naming conventions; for a mutex, a name like "*application*.Mutex.*name*" would be our suggestion.

When a mutex is in the nonsignaled state, it is said to be *owned* by the thread that passed the wait function. When a mutex is in the signaled state, it is said to be *not owned*. Unlike a semaphore, in which every wait operation decrements the semaphore count and must be matched by a ReleaseSemaphore, a mutex has special behavior. A wait operation on a mutex from the thread that already owns it does *not* block (since the concept of ownership does not exist for semaphores, a thread that issues a wait on a semaphore can block, even if it has passed the same semaphore one or more times already). Instead of blocking, a second wait on an owned mutex increments a reference count in the mutex but otherwise continues. You must match each wait operation the thread issues on the mutex with a ReleaseMutex. When the number of ReleaseMutex operations issued by a thread matches the number of wait operations it has performed, the ownership of the mutex is relinquished and the mutex becomes signaled. This permits any other threads waiting on the mutex to attempt to obtain ownership; one will, the rest will remain blocked. Only one thread at a time can pass the mutex.

When you are finished using a mutex, you should call CloseHandle to release it. Once you have called CloseHandle on a mutex, you may no longer use that handle for any operation. When the last handle to a mutex is released, the mutex will be destroyed. You should also read the discussion about obtaining multiple semaphore handles on page 1234; the same techniques apply to mutexes.

You can use any of the "wait" primitives to wait for a mutex. See page 1243.

Critical Sections

Because of the significant overhead of semaphores and mutexes, your application could be subject to serious performance degradation if it used them extensively. One situation in which performance has been optimized is in the synchronization of separate threads within a single process. Threads are a high-performance, low-overhead mechanism to allow multitasking to take place within a single process. But because all threads share the same address space in a process, the opportunity for catastrophe due to synchronization problems is substantial (see Figure 18.1 and its discussion). But a heavy-duty synchronization mechanism such as a semaphore or a mutex would defeat much of the performance gain that threads give. So Win32 provides a special intraprocess synchronization mechanism, the *critical section*. A critical section requires that all threads have access to the address of the critical section object. The critical section operations are shown in Table 18.3.

Unlike a semaphore or mutex, a critical section object is part of the process's address space. You create a critical section simply by declaring a variable of type CRITICAL_SECTION. This can be a statically-allocated variable or part of a dynamically-allocated structure, including a member variable of a C++ class or part of a structure allocated by any of the dynamic storage allocation primitives (see Chapter 14). Before you use a critical section variable, you *must* initialize it with the InitializeCriticalSection function (if you're

Table 18.3: Critical Section operations

Return	Function	Description
VOID	DeleteCriticalSection	(LPCRITICAL_SECTION critsec)
		Deletes all the system resources used by the critical section. The critical section may no longer be used.
VOID	EnterCriticalSection	(LPCRITICAL_SECTION critsec)
		Attempts to gain ownership of the critical section. If it is able to gain ownership (or already has ownership), the function returns and the critical section becomes nonsignaled and the thread's ownership reference count is incremented; otherwise the thread blocks.
VOID	InitializeCriticalSection	(LPCRITICAL_SECTION critsec)
		Initializes a critical section.
VOID	LeaveCriticalSection	(LPCRITICAL_SECTION critsec)
		Decrements the thread's reference count for critical section ownership. If the reference count goes to zero, ownership of the critical section is released and the critical section becomes signaled.

using C++, you could do this in the constructor of the class, or you can use the MFC-defined class CCriticalSection whose constructor calls InitializeCriticalSection). When you free the space used by a critical section, you must call DeleteCriticalSection to free up the resources that were allocated by InitializeCriticalSection (if you're using C++, you could do this in the destructor of the class; the MFC CCriticalSection class already does this in its destructor).

Sample code for handling a critical section is illustrated below. Note that in these examples, we can increment or read the value of a "locked integer" and be guaranteed that we get a correct value. However, these do not hold the lock, and reading the value twice in succession could produce different results.

```
typedef struct {
            CRITICAL_SECTION lock;
            int value;
            } locked_integer;

    locked_integer * count;

    count = (locked_integer *)malloc(sizeof(locked_integer));
    // ... handle allocation failure...
    InitializeCriticalSection(&count->lock);
```

```
int incrlock(locked_integer * LI)
    {
     int result;
     EnterCriticalSection(&LI->lock);
     result = ++LI->val;
     LeaveCriticalSection(&LI->lock);
     return result;
    }

int getVal(locked_integer * LI)
    {
     int result;
     EnterCriticalSection(&LI->lock);
     result = LI->val;
     LeaveCriticalSection(&LI->lock);
     return result;
    }
```

In the case where we have to use the value and be guaranteed that it is stable over the entire time we are manipulating it, we must explicitly lock the value:

```
__inline void lockInt(locked_integer * LI)
    {
     EnterCriticalSection(&LI->lock);
    }

__inline void unlockInt(locked_integer * LI)
    {
     LeaveCriticalSection(&LI->lock);
    }
```

We could then write code of the following example safely. Remember that the `min` function is a macro which uses its argument values more than once, and therefore the values must remain stable across all accesses.

```
int setminlocked(locked_integer * LI, int newval)
    {
     lockInt(LI);
     LI->val = min(LI->val, newval);
     unlockInt(LI);
    }
```

Critical sections, since they are not objects managed by the operating system, cannot be used in any of the wait functions. The only way to gain access to a critical section is by using the `EnterCriticalSection` function. This works very much like a mutex; once a thread does a successful `EnterCriticalSection` and owns the critical section, it can do additional `EnterCriticalSection` calls on the same critical section without blocking. These increment the critical section reference count for the thread, and each must have a matching `LeaveCriticalSection` for the thread. When all of the `EnterCriticalSection` calls have been matched by `LeaveCriticalSection` calls, the thread reference count goes to zero and the thread relinquishes ownership of the critical section. The critical section enters the signaled state. Any threads waiting for an `EnterCriticalSection` to complete become feasible, and one of the threads will be scheduled; this thread will gain ownership of the critical section while the other threads remain blocked.

Unlike kernel synchronization objects (semaphores, mutexes, and events), a critical section is referenced by its address, not by its handle, and consequently a critical section cannot, as we indicated, be used in any of the wait functions. You can't set time-outs on critical sections; if you need time-outs, you must use one of the kernel synchronization objects.

Events

An *event* is a special kind of synchronization object. You can get an event by using the CreateEvent function to create an event and return its handle. In addition, you can use the handle of a process or a thread as an event. Like the other kernel objects, events have two states, signaled and nonsignaled. Some events become signaled by external operations; for example, an event that is coupled to doing asynchronous I/O will become signaled when the I/O operation completes (a topic we don't go into in this book). A common usage of events is to synchronize thread start-up with the GUI. When a thread starts up, it may have to do some amount of initialization before it achieves its "steady state". If the thread were created with a lower priority than the GUI thread (a common technique to ensure the GUI remains responsive), then the GUI may have to know when the thread is "stable", that is, when the GUI can safely interact with it because all of the assumptions of their mutual interface are now valid. For example, there may be a GUI command to query the status of the thread ("How much of the image is processed?" or "Did you make the connection?"), and an attempt to query the status before the thread has initialized could return a meaningless result or, worse still, return a value that causes a memory access fault. So a common way to effect this synchronization is to create an event object which is owned by the GUI and which the thread signals as part of its initialization sequence. For a much more detailed discussion of these techniques, we recommend Jeffrey Richter's excellent article "Coordinate Win32 Threads Using Manual-Reset and Auto-Reset Events" (see the Further Reading section at the end of this chapter). The event API functions are shown in Table 18.4.

Table 18.4: Event operations

Return	Function	Description
BOOL	CloseHandle	(HANDLE eventhandle)
		Closes the event handle. When the last handle to the event is closed, the event is destroyed.
HANDLE	CreateEvent	(LPSECURITY_ATTRIBUTES attr, BOOL manualreset, BOOL initialstate, LPCTSTR name)
		Creates or locates a event object. If it does not already exist, it is created with the specified parameters.

Table 18.4: Event operations

Return	Function	Description
BOOL	DuplicateHandle	(HANDLE sourceprocess, HANDLE toduplicate, HANDLE targetprocess, LPHANDLE resulthandle, DWORD access, BOOL inherit, DWORD options)
		Creates a duplicate handle. The options may be one or more of the following flags:
		DUPLICATE_CLOSE_SOURCE–the source handle is closed after the duplicate is created.
		DUPLICATE_SAME_ACCESS–The created handle has the same access rights as the source handle.
DWORD	MsgWaitForMultipleObjects	*see page 1243*
HANDLE	OpenEvent	(DWORD access, BOOL inherit, LPCTSTR name)
		Opens a handle to an existing event. The flags can be any of the following values:
		EVENT_ALL_ACCESS–permits all accesses.
		SYNCHRONIZE[NT]–permits event to be used by all wait functions.
BOOL	PulseEvent	(HANDLE event)
		Manual-reset event: Sets the status of the event to signaled. When all threads waiting on the event are released, the event is reset to the nonsignaled state. Auto-reset event: Sets the status of the event to signaled. Releases exactly one thread, and sets the status to nonsignaled.
BOOL	ResetEvent	(HANDLE event)
		Sets the status of the event to nonsignaled.
BOOL	SetEvent	(HANDLE event)
		Sets the status of the event to signaled. For manual reset events, all waiting threads are released; for auto-reset events, one of the waiting threads is released and the status is reset to nonsignaled.

Table 18.4: Event operations

Return	Function	Description
DWORD	WaitForMultipleObjects	
DWORD	WaitForMultipleObjectsEx	*see page 1243*
DWORD	WaitForSingleObject	
DWORD	WaitForSingleObjectEx	

[NT]Windows NT only

You use CreateEvent to create or access an event. If the event does not already exist, it is created; its security is determined by the attr parameter. If the attr parameter is NULL, the object has default security attributes and is not inheritable. The manualreset parameter is TRUE to get a manual-reset event and FALSE to get an auto-reset event (more on this shortly!). The initialstate parameter is TRUE to create an event which is initially in the signaled state and FALSE to create an event initially in the nonsignaled state. The name is the name of the event to create. If the event already exists, and is accessible to the process attempting the creation, its handle is returned, but the manualreset and initialstate parameters are ignored. The attr values are also ignored, *except* for the flag permitting inheritability. If you call GetLastError after a successful return, it will return either 0, indicating that the event has been newly created, or the value ERROR_ALREADY_EXISTS, indicating that you have a reference to an existing event. If the call fails, you will get a NULL handle, and GetLastError will return a code indicating the reason the call failed. To simply obtain an event handle without creating one if it does not already exist, you can use the OpenEvent function. The name of the event is case-sensitive, and must be distinct. Note that events, semaphores, mutexes, and file-mapping objects all share the same name space, so they must all be unique. See the discussion on page 1234 about naming conventions; for an event, a name like "application.Event.name" would be our suggestion.

When an event is in the signaled state, an attempt to wait on the event is not blocked and execution proceeds. When an event is in the nonsignaled state, an attempt to wait on the event will block.

You can change the state of an event by using the SetEvent and ResetEvent functions. To set the state to signaled, you call SetEvent. This has different effects depending on whether the event is a manual-reset or auto-reset event. For an auto-reset event, the SetEvent function sets the state to signaled. If there are threads already waiting, exactly one of the threads will be released, and the state will be immediately set to nonsignaled. If no thread is waiting, the state remains signaled until a thread issues a wait function, at which point that thread is permitted to pass but the state is reset to nonsignaled, blocking any further threads. For a manual-reset event, *all* threads which are waiting for the event are released. The event remains signaled, and any further threads that issue a wait function on the event are permitted to pass. The ResetEvent function is used for manual-reset events; it changes the state to nonsignaled. It is not needed for auto-reset events.

The special function PulseEvent handles one of the common event usage styles. The PulseEvent function sets the status of the event to signaled. For manual-reset events, this releases all waiting threads, and then sets the status of the event to nonsignaled. For auto-reset events, this releases exactly one of the waiting threads and then sets the status of the event to nonsignaled. If no threads are waiting on the event, or no thread can be released immediately (because of other kernel synchronization objects in a multiple wait), the event object is set to nonsignaled.

Waiting for Synchronization

To synchronize with an event, a semaphore, or a mutex, you can use one of the wait operations shown in Table 18.5. A wait operation waits for the object it references, or for all of the objects it references, to become signaled. When all the objects are signaled, the wait function returns control and the thread continues execution. However, you must always check the return value because it might indicate an error condition, and you must not proceed unless you are proceeding via a valid set of signaled objects.

The wait functions, in addition to waiting for semaphores and mutexes, can wait for other events, including change notifications on directories, console input, events, and processes. Asynchronous I/O and file system notifications are beyond the scope of what we're trying to cover in this book.

You cannot specify a critical section in a wait function, because a critical section is managed in the address space of a process, and is not a kernel synchronization object.

Table 18.5: Wait operations on kernel synchronization objects

Result	Function	Parameters/Description	
DWORD	`MsgWaitForMultipleObjects`	`(DWORD count, CONST LPHANDLE handles, BOOL waitAll, DWORD timeoutms, DWORD wakeMask)`	
DWORD	`WaitForMultipleObjects`	`(DWORD count, CONST LPHANDLE handles, BOOL waitAll, DWORD timeoutms)`	
DWORD	`WaitForMultipleObjectsEx`	`(DWORD count, CONST LPHANDLE handles, BOOL waitAll, DWORD timeoutms, BOOL alertable)`	
		`count`	the number of handles in the array.
		`handles`	pointer to an array of `count` handles of kernel synchronization objects.
		`waitAll`	TRUE to wait for all handles to become signaled; FALSE to accept one or more handles becoming signaled.
		`timeoutms`	A time-out interval expressed in milliseconds. Use 0 for no delay (returns immediately) and INFINITE for no time-out.

Table 18.5: Wait operations on kernel synchronization objects

Result	Function	Parameters/Description	
		alertable	Specifies whether the function returns when the system queues an I/O completion routine for execution by the calling thread. If TRUE, the function returns and the completion routine is executed. If FALSE, the function does not return and the completion routine is not executed.
		waitMask	One or more of the flag values from Table 18.7.
DWORD	WaitForSingleObject	(HANDLE handle, DWORD timeoutms)	
DWORD	WaitForSingleObjectEx	(HANDLE handle, DWORD timeoutms, BOOL alertable)	
		handle	A handle to a kernel synchronization object.
		timeoutms	A time-out interval expressed in milliseconds. Use 0 for no delay (returns immediately) and INFINITE for no time-out.
		alertable	Specifies whether the function returns when the system queues an I/O completion routine for execution by the calling thread. If TRUE, the function returns and the completion routine is executed. If FALSE, the function does not return and the completion routine is not executed.

A wait operation can be used to synchronize with one or more kernel-managed objects. You can wait on a process handle and receive notifications of process completion, a thread handle and receive notifications of thread completion, or wait on a file system notification. We will be concerned only with waiting on an event, semaphore, or mutex.

The simplest wait function is either WaitForSingleObject or WaitForSingleObjectEx. These differ only in the fact that WaitForSingleObjectEx can also unblock if an asynchronous I/O operation completes. When you call the WaitForSingleObject(Ex) function, you provide a handle of a synchronization object and a time-out value. The time-out value is expressed in milliseconds. If you use the special value INFINITE for the time delay, the wait will not time out, but will wait for the object to become signaled. If you use the special value 0, the function will not block on an unsignaled object, but return immediately with the return value `WAIT_TIMEOUT`. This is the way to test if a wait operation would block, without actually blocking.

The `WaitForMultipleObjects(Ex)` function can wait for several objects at once. You will get control back when any one, or all, objects become signaled. You specify this by using the `waitAll` parameter: if you use `TRUE`, you will not get control back until all objects become signaled; if you use `FALSE`, any one object becoming signaled will terminate the wait. You can tell (approximately) which one terminated the wait if you get a result in the range `WAIT_OBJECT_0` to `WAIT_OBJECT_0 + (count - 1)`, which indicates the (lowest-numbered) object that signaled. If multiple objects signal and you are not waiting for all objects, you can't actually tell *which* objects signaled; only one of the objects will be indicated by the return result. If you care about which set of (possibly multiple) objects, that is, threads, processes, or events, released the wait, you can check each handle independently after you get control back from the wait. If you are doing shared-resource protection it is rare to use a wait *other* than for all objects, since you can't tell which objects you have safely passed and which are not safe to use.

As with the `WaitForSingleObject(Ex)` functions, there is a time-out value specified, which behaves the same way: a 0 value does not block and the value `INFINITE` does not time out. The return value `WAIT_TIMEOUT` indicates that the time-out interval has passed without any or all (depending on the `waitAll` parameter) of the objects becoming signaled.

The wait functions return one of the codes shown in Table 18.6. Note that if you specify a time-out, or a mutex is abandoned, you will get a special code that indicates this condition. If this occurs, you have *not* obtained the semaphore or mutex, and you must not proceed into the code that accesses the shared information.

Table 18.6: Return values from wait functions

Value	Meaning
`WAIT_OBJECT_0` to `(WAIT_OBJECT_0 + count - 1)`	`MsgWaitForMultipleObjects`, `WaitForMultiple-Objects` and `WaitForMultipleObjectsEx`: If `waitAll` is TRUE, the return value indicates that the state of all specified objects is signaled. If `waitAll` is FALSE, the return value minus `WAIT_OBJECT_0` indicates the `handles` array index of the object that satisfied the wait. If more than one object became signaled during the call, this is the array index of the signaled object with the smallest index value of all the signaled objects.
	`WaitForSingleObject` and `WaitForSingleObjectEx`: The value `WAIT_OBJECT_0` indicates that the object has become signaled.
`WAIT_OBJECT_0 + count`	`MsgWaitForMultipleObjects`: One of the conditions specified for the `wakeMask` was satisfied.

Table 18.6: Return values from wait functions

Value	Meaning
WAIT_ABANDONED_0 to (WAIT_ABANDONED_0 + count - 1)	MsgWaitForMultipleObjects, WaitForMultipleObjects and WaitForMultipleObjectsEx: If waitAll is TRUE, the return value indicates that the state of all specified objects is signaled and at least one of the objects is an abandoned mutex object. If waitAll is FALSE, the return value minus WAIT_ABANDONED_0 indicates the handles array index of an abandoned mutex object that satisfied the wait.
WAIT_ABANDONED	WaitForSingleObject and WaitForSingleObjectEx: Indicates that the state of the object is signaled and the object is an abandoned mutex object.
WAIT_IO_COMPLETION	WaitForMultipleObjectsEx and WaitForSingleObjectEx: One or more I/O completion routines are queued for execution.
WAIT_TIMEOUT	The time-out interval elapsed and the conditions specified by the waitAll parameter are not satisfied.

A special synchronization function, MsgWaitForMultipleObjects, allows you to respond to other conditions. You might consider using this if you have a single-threaded process working on a semaphore or mutex shared with another process. This allows you to "break out" of a wait in order to process user input or respond to a paint message. Note that you must know the count of objects in order to test the return value; if the special value WAIT_OBJECT_0 + count is returned, it indicates the wake condition has been satisfied. You must check for this special return value and realize that no synchronization object has been signaled. An example of this is shown in Listing 18.1.

Table 18.7: Flags for MsgWaitForMultipleObjects

Code	Condition
QS_ALLINPUT	Any message is in the queue.
QS_HOTKEY	A WM_HOTKEY message is in the queue.
QS_INPUT	Any input message is in the queue.
QS_KEY	A WM_KEYUP, WM_μKEYDOWN, WM_SYSKEYUP, or WM_SYSKEYDOWN message is in the queue.
QS_MOUSE	A WM_MOUSEMOVE message or mouse-button message (WM_LBUTTONUP, WM_RBUTTONDOWN, and so on) is in the queue.
QS_MOUSEBUTTON	A mouse-button message (WM_LBUTTONUP, WM_RBUTTONDOWN, and so on) is in the queue.

Table 18.7: Flags for `MsgWaitForMultipleObjects`

Code	Condition
QS_MOUSEMOVE	A WM_MOUSEMOVE message is in the queue.
QS_PAINT	A WM_PAINT message is in the queue.
QS_POSTMESSAGE	A posted message (other than those just listed) is in the queue.
QS_SENDMESSAGE	A message sent by another thread or application is in the queue.
QS_TIMER	A WM_TIMER message is in the queue.

The code shown in Listing 18.1 demonstrates how to implement a single thread that waits to pass a set of kernel synchronization objects while still maintaining the user interface functionality. It is important in this example to note the use of `PeekMessage`, which is a non-blocking message call. Note that all messages are removed from the queue, after which the loop returns to the wait condition. If the synchronization objects are all signaled, the function returns the value WAIT_OBJECT_0 + n, for $0 \leq n < count$; if a WM_QUIT message is received, the function returns 0. If any of the objects was an abandoned mutex, the value WAIT_ABANDONED_0 + n is returned.

Listing 18.1: Sample `MsgWaitForMultipleObjects`

```
DWORD WaitForObjects(int count, LPHANDLE objects)
{
DWORD result;

while(TRUE)
    { /* message loop */
     result = MsgWaitForMultipleObjects(count, objects,
                 FALSE, INFINITE, QS_ALLINPUT);
     if(result == (WAIT_OBJECT_0 + count))
        { /* PeekMessage */
         MSG msg;
         while(PeekMessage(&msg, NULL, 0, 0, PM_REMOVE))
             { /* handle message */
              if(msg.message == WM_QUIT)
                  return 0;  // end of message loop
              DispatchMessage(&msg);
             } /* handle message */
        } /* PeekMessage */
     else
        { /* handle signaled */
         return result;
        } /* handle signaled */
    } /* message loop */
}
```

Waiting for Threads

As we indicated earlier, you may need to know when a thread has actually successfully started up. We can use an event for this, as shown in Listing 18.2. We create an event and store its handle in a `threadstructure` object, which is something we've defined for our application. After we do a `CreateThread`, passing in a pointer to this structure, we simply do a wait on the event. When the thread has completed its initialization and is ready to go to work (and is therefore, by whatever criteria we've decided, now "stable"), it signals this by calling `SetEvent` on the event. This allows the parent thread, which has blocked on this event, to now resume.

This is, of course, very naïve code. It assumes that the start-up initialization cannot fail, by generating an exception, generating a return, or going into an infinite loop. We'll address those concerns momentarily.

You should never use `TerminateThread` to terminate a thread. This operation *instantly* kills the thread. The thread has no chance to respond to the kill; this means that any locks it has set are not freed; mutexes are abandoned (see page 1250), and DLLs are not notified of the thread's termination (see page 1128). This can be disastrous. Data structures (including some process-local kernel data structures, if the thread was executing in the kernel) can be left in inconsistent states. DLLs you've never heard about can find themselves with inconsistent data. This is Not A Good Thing To Do.

What you usually do if you have a worker thread is to have a shared variable that the GUI sets and the worker thread checks to determine if it should quit, either by returning from its top-level function (the one named in the `CreateThread` call) or by calling `ExitThread`. But you would probably like to know when the thread *actually* terminates so you know that you can safely proceed–for example, by knowing that certain values in your `threadstructure` are now consistent and additionally will not be changed again by the (ideally defunct) thread. In this case, you can use the thread handle as an event handle to a wait function. A running thread is nonsignaled; a terminated thread is signaled.

In the example shown in Listing 18.2, we have our user-defined structure `threadstructure` that contains information local to the thread. We create one of these objects for each thread we want to run; a pointer to an object of this structure is passed as the `param` to the `CreateThread` function so each thread has its own private state. One value in this structure is the `shutdown` flag, a `BOOL` value. This is tested by the loop in the worker thread to determine if the thread should exit. We show a very conservative approach here: we actually *lock* the access to the `shutdown` flag. This is *probably* not necessary, since it is only *read* by the thread and only *written* by the GUI, but since it is, officially, both read and written, the lock is the absolutely safest approach to handling it.

When the thread starts up, the first thing it does is some (perhaps lengthy) initialization. Until this initialization completes, some of its interface may exhibit undefined behavior (for example, reading some value from the `threadstructure` that has not yet been initialized would be a problem). So the thread uses `SetEvent` to signal its readiness, via the `ts->running` event, which is what the parent thread is waiting for.

When we wish to shut down the thread, we can use code like that shown in Listing 18.3. We set the termination flag and wait for the thread to complete. By using the thread handle as the target for the `WaitFor-SingleObject`, we will block until the thread actually terminates. If the thread refuses to honor our request to shut down, we will be blocked permanently, and the GUI will be dead. But if it does shut down, we eventually will need to free up all the resources we allocated to the thread, such as the critical section, the event, and the `threadstructure` object.

Listing 18.2: Starting up a thread

```
    {
    threadstructure * ts = (threadstructure *)malloc(sizeof(threadstructure));

    InitializeCriticalSection(&ts->shutdownlock);
    ts->shutdown = FALSE;
    ts->running = CreateEvent(NULL, FALSE, FALSE, NULL);
    hthread = CreateThread(NULL, 0,
                        (LPTHREAD_START_ROUTINE)worker,
                        (LPVOID)ts,
                        0, &ts->threadID);

    WaitForSingleObject(ts->running, INFINITE);
    // do useful stuff here, like save the threadstructure
    // pointer in a useful place for later use
```

Listing 18.3: Shutting down a thread

```
void killThread(HANDLE hthread, threadstructure * ts)
    {
    EnterCriticalSection(&ts->shutdownlock);
    ts->shutdown = TRUE;
    LeaveCriticalSection(&ts->shutdownlock);

    WaitForSingleObject(hthread, INFINITE);

    // eventually, you will want to do a CloseHandle on the
    // ts->running event, DeleteCriticalSection on the
    // shutdownlock, and ultimately free the threadstructure
    // but you may need the threadstructure until you've
    // extracted all the useful information from it.
    }
```

Listing 18.4: A thread code example

```
long worker(LPVOID tsp)
    {
    threadstructure * ts = (threadstructure *)tsp;

    // . . . initialize the thread here

    SetEvent(ts->running);

    while(TRUE)
        { /* worker loop */
        BOOL quit;
        EnterCriticalSection(&ts->shutdownlock);
        quit = shutdown;
        LeaveCriticalSection(&ts->shutdownlock);
        if(quit)
            break;
        // . . . do the hard work of the loop
        } /* worker loop */
    // . . . do cleanup here
    }
```

As we said, the code is rather naïve in its confidence that everything will go right. We may need to create more robust code that handles more complex situations. Such code is shown in Listing 18.5.

Listing 18.5: Robust thread start-up

```
    HANDLE objects[2];
    int code;

    // much the same as Listing 18.2, except for declarations
    // above; and we replace the WaitForSingleObject with:

#define OFFSET_OF_THREAD 0
#define OFFSET_OF_EVENT  1
    objects[OFFSET_OF_THREAD] = hthread;
    objects[OFFSET_OF_EVENT] = ts->running;

#define TIME_LIMIT 10000 // wait ten seconds...

    code = WaitForMultipleObjects(2, objects, FALSE, TIME_LIMIT);

    switch(code)
        { /* code */
         case WAIT_OBJECT_0 + OFFSET_OF_THREAD:
             // process terminated without initializing
             // handle situation of termination during init.
             break;
         case WAIT_OBJECT_0 + OFFSET_OF_EVENT;
             // successfully running
             break;
         case WAIT_TIMEOUT:
             // something is wrong!  Taking too long!
             // Deal with it
             break;
        } /* code */
```

Abandoned Mutexes

When a thread that owns a mutex is terminated, the mutex is considered to be *abandoned*. The mutex appears to be signaled, and can be acquired by another thread. However, the return code from the multiple-object wait functions will be WAIT_ABANDONED_0 plus an index offset to indicate which of a multiple set of handles represents the abandoned mutex; from the single-object wait functions it will be WAIT_ABANDONED. You should assume that if you get this code that the data being protected by the mutex is in an inconsistent state. This may necessitate aborting the operation, or entering a recovery mode in which you have to validate the consistency of the data and recover from the problem.

Why You Must Use Synchronization Primitives

There is no other way to synchronize threads other than using one of the synchronization objects, or by using messages. Other than these mechanisms, there is no practical way you can write a guaranteed reliable synchronization mechanism on your own. Internally, the operating system uses synchronization primitives to control access to shared structures such as the message queues used by SendMessage and PostMessage, so that using messages ultimately uses one of the synchronization primitives.

The problems arise because of the way hardware works. To guarantee at the simplest level that synchronization works, you must be able to execute an instruction that tests a value in memory *and changes it* without any possibility of being interrupted or overridden. These instructions, historically, have been called "read-pause-write", "test-and-set", or "memory-interlocked" instructions. The problem is that these instructions impose serious performance penalties on a computer, and therefore are no longer "built in" to most systems. Each platform, such as the Intel family, PowerPC, and DEC Alpha, implements memory access in a slightly different fashion. Because of the pervasive use of caches and pipelines, the completion of an instruction does *not* guarantee that the value has actually reached memory. RISC machines such as the Alpha and PowerPC can actually store to memory in a sequence completely different from what you might expect by looking only at the control flow of the instruction set. In some cases, a "write-back" cache will not actually transfer values to memory until the cache line is needed for some other value, which might be hundreds or thousands of instructions after the change. Therefore, you can't execute an "increment" instruction and be guaranteed that upon completion the contents of memory have actually been incremented. This has particularly nasty implications in symmetric-multiprocessor systems (SMP), which Windows NT runs on. Guaranteeing that a semaphore, mutex, or critical section actually works correctly can be quite challenging. Windows NT (currently the only multiplatform implementation of Win32) addresses this problem via its *Hardware Abstraction Layer* (HAL). This implements whatever hardware-specific mechanism (possibly requiring privileged instructions) is required to support proper synchronization. Internally, Win32 guarantees that synchronization objects *will* be properly implemented.

A fully-implemented dual-processor system with massive amounts of RAM and disk space sells, in modern dollars, for a fraction of the price of the original dual-floppy 128K IBM PC. This trend will only continue; quad, hex, and octal multiprocessors are already running Windows NT. You should assume that your application *will* be run on a multiprocessor system, or your DLL *will* be run by multiple threads that may all be simultaneously executing on a multiprocessor. And it will almost certainly be desirable to compile your Win32 application on a variety of platforms; for commercial products, this will be essential to maximize your market. Therefore, you *must* think "thread-safe" and "synchronization".

Using Synchronization Primitives

Semaphores, mutexes, and critical sections all are used in approximately the same fashion. We are not going to discuss how to use semaphores in their most general sense; that is a topic for a different book, such as one on how to write client/server applications. And critical sections, although limited to synchronizing threads of a single process, are otherwise very similar to mutexes. What is more important is to understand synchronization *architecture* in a system; you will then be able to choose the best synchronization means.

The most important consideration in using any synchronization object is that you must always lock *data*, not *code*. This is a subtle distinction, but it is absolutely essential for performance reasons. If you lock *code*, then two threads that are acting on different objects are interlocked because they can't execute the code. If you lock the *data*, then multiple threads can execute the same code.

To execute the code safely, it must not write any shared areas not protected by a synchronization lock. This means that your code cannot write just any global variable because the same code might be writing the same variable via a different thread. If a global variable is modified, that represents *data* which must be locked.

But if you have to lock a global variable, you have in effect locked the code. For performance reasons, you have to carefully think about what your code is going to need to modify.

You might say, "Do I really need to protect a single variable? Isn't memory assignment a single instruction?" The answer is, yes, you must protect even a single integer variable, and no, you can't *depend* on memory assignment being a single instruction. Consider the case where you have a DWORD variable to hold a value, such as a file position. You have cleverly decided that you can simplify your code by "knowing" that the file position is a 32-bit value, is assigned by a single instruction, and consequently needs no critical section to protect it. Six months from now, you get the first "live" datafile from the user, and it is ten gigabytes in length.[4] So you convert your file pointers to __int64 values. On some Win32 platforms, the compiler implements the 64-bit store as two 32-bit store instructions. Now consider: if your thread is preempted after the first 32-bit store, then one half of the file position information will be correct and the other half will not be. *Which* half may depend upon the compiler. So if you don't protect the "simple scalar" with a synchronization primitive, your code will suddenly exhibit sporadically bizarre and unreproducible behavior. Listing 18.6 shows three sample functions and Listing 18.7 shows the generated assembly code for an Intel platform. Some boring detail has been elided (such as the prolog code for the last two functions) and comments have been added to show where a thread preemption would definitely demonstrate that "scalar assignment" is *not* an atomic operation.[5]

---

[4] It happens. One of the major pushes for 64-bit platforms came from a number of sites, such as those that process geophysical data, which cannot live with the 4GB file size restriction that Unix imposes. Windows NT, with its 64-bit file position pointers, makes these sites *very* happy. Geophysical data collection uses many high-bandwidth sensors distributed over a large geographic region. I was once told by one sensor manufacturer, "*You* may call 10GB a whopping lot of data. *We* call it three minutes". These people buy multi-gigabyte drives the way most of us buy floppy disks. It is not uncommon at these sites to find RAID systems in large cabinets filled with hundreds of these multi-gigabyte drives.

Geophysical data processing produces many interesting side effects besides oil and natural gas. For example, many years ago, the world's largest independent geophysical survey company needed a new computer to process their massive geophysical information databases. They went to all the supercomputer companies then extant and gave them the specifications of their computer. They were uniformly turned away; the computer was far too ambitious for the available technology. The geophysical survey company, in desperation, decided to build one themselves. It was quite impressive; it had a backplane wired with coaxial cable and used 15-layer printed circuit boards. The company wanted to have a nice, uniform set of chips from which they could easily construct the computer. Coincidentally, this company had a small subdivision that had been dabbling in the then-new silicon chip business. A fair amount of effort went into designing a very uniform set of chips, where (unlike previous manufacturers' chip designs) each pin had exactly the same input loading and output drive, simplifying the "design rules", and had a regularized layout of power and ground pins. They called this series of chips by a single serial number designation, the "7400" series. The world's largest independent geophysical survey company was called Texas Instruments; the computer was the TI ASC (Advanced Scientific Computer). TI sold the geophysical survey division some years ago; it was no longer their significant business. TI became one of the most significant computer chip manufacturers in the country. . . all because they needed their own computer to support their then-primary business–which had nothing at all to do with computer component manufacture! Somehow, though, "Geophysical Survey Company Discovers Silicon" is not terribly surprising. *–jmn*

[5] Many years ago, I worked on a large operating system. It crashed about once a week for no reason we could explain. While modifying one part of the system, I discovered that a two-pointer assignment, two instructions in a row, was not protected by the equivalent of a critical section. About once a week, a thread got preempted in the middle of the two assignments and the result was a pair of inconsistent pointers. I put in a critical section lock and that bug was fixed. Today's typical desktop is over 50 times faster than this old mainframe was, and if we assume linear probabilities based on instruction speed, the chances of this error would cause a crash once every 3Ω hours. *–jmn*

Listing 18.6: Source for __int64 code

```
__int64 BigInt;

void incFunc()
{
    BigInt++;
}

void myfunc()
{
    BigInt = 27;
}

void setFunc(__int64 newval)
{
    BigInt = newval;
}
```

Listing 18.7: Generated code for __int64 example

```
; 3      : void incFunc()
; 4      : {
        push    ebp             ; prolog code
        mov     ebp, esp
        push    ebx
        push    esi
        push    edi             ; end of prolog code
; 5      :     BigInt++;
        add     DWORD PTR _BigInt, 1
; - - - - - - - - - - - - - - - - - - - - - - - -COULD BE PREEMPTED HERE!
        adc     DWORD PTR _BigInt+4, 0
; 6      : }
        pop     edi             ; epilog code
        pop     esi
        pop     ebx
        leave                   ; end of epilog code
        ret     0

; 8      : void myfunc()
; 9      : {
; same prolog code as above
; 10     :     BigInt = 27;
        mov     DWORD PTR _BigInt, 27                    ; 0000001bH
; - - - - - - - - - - - - - - - - - - - - - - -COULD BE PREEMPTED HERE!
        mov     DWORD PTR _BigInt+4, 0
; 11     : }
; same epilog code as above
        ret     0

; 13     : void setFunc(__int64 newval)
; 14     : {
; same prolog code as above
; 15     :     BigInt = newval;
        mov     eax, DWORD PTR _newval$[ebp]
        mov     ecx, DWORD PTR _newval$[ebp+4]
        mov     DWORD PTR _BigInt, eax
```

```
;  -  -  -  -  -  -  -  -  -  -  -  -  -  -  -  -  -  -  -COULD BE PREEMPTED HERE!
          mov        DWORD PTR _BigInt+4, ecx
; 16  : }
; same epilog code as above
          ret        0
```

To avoid the problems of global state, you can often use *thread-local storage*, which is described in great detail in Chapter 14 (page 1065). This allows you to modify values that are local only to your thread, but that are not stack-allocated.

If you must modify a global variable, you might want to lock it separately, and make your critical section contain as few instructions as possible. Although you have to spend time checking the critical section lock, if the interval of locking is small, you will have a very low probability of actually blocking. You must also be careful about when you actually read the value. For example, in the Synchronization Explorer, we need to read the current state of the locking flag. We use this value to determine if the algorithm should first lock the counter, and then we use it later to determine if we need to unlock the counter. Clearly, the user could change the state of the check box during some other step of the algorithm. Thus, if we actually read the global state each time, we could get inconsistent results. You must make sure that under conditions like this you use a consistent value. We could have locked the locking flag, to keep the GUI from changing it while we were using it, but this would mean that the variable would be locked for the entire duration of the loop. Furthermore, because *all* we are doing in the threads is this loop, the GUI would effectively be locked out entirely, and we would have no guarantee as to when it could actually get in–the GUI thread could be "starved". Instead, we lock the variable, copy the locking flag, and unlock the variable at the start of each loop and use the copy at the end of the loop.

The use of synchronization introduces another hazard: deadlocks. Here is the most important principle you can apply for deadlock avoidance. No, let's be more specific: here is the principle you *must* apply, and is the *only* strategy that guarantees deadlock-free code: every path of execution through your program that locks multiple objects using separate wait functions must lock the objects in the same order, always. No exceptions. It doesn't matter if the objects are the same kind or different kinds; you must always lock them in the same order. If your algorithm doesn't support this, redesign it. *Any* algorithm that guarantees the same order will work; even ones as simple-minded as always locking objects in address-order or alphabetical order by type name (if they're all different types, of course). Otherwise, expect that deadlock *will* occur. This is one reason that it is often desirable, in Win32, to use one of the multiple-wait functions with the waitAll parameter set to TRUE. You acquire all of the synchronization objects at once, and Win32 will guarantee that, for two wait functions that wait on the same set of handles, a deadlock cannot occur.

Deadlock can often be detected by using time-out intervals on the wait functions (this doesn't work for critical sections, which don't have a time-out option; you can't use critical sections for this). But if you do, you now have the problem of how to get out of where you are. This may involve setting up structured exception handlers to undo partial computations. But be warned: it is *extremely* difficult to properly back out of a deadlock situation, and even if you get it right when the program is created, it is even more difficult to maintain the correctness of code this complex as the system evolves over time. This is so fragile that it is considered dangerous to use as a technique. Generally, you should try to acquire a set of synchronization objects using one of the WaitForMultipleObjects functions. The time-out will tell you either that you have hit a deadlock situation or that you are in a potential starvation situation. The difference between starvation and deadlock is that in deadlock, you can never acquire the objects because you are already holding one that must be released before the acquisition becomes feasible; in starvation, you would eventually acquire all the objects, but due to scheduling, contention for the objects by other processes, and system load, you haven't acquired it within the time-out limit you set. Unfortunately, you can't tell which situation you are actually dealing with, and there is no general algorithm that can tell you.

But this raises another issue: whenever you lock an object, you *must* assume that somewhere in an inner call an exception will be raised. Therefore, you *must* have a structured exception handler to properly restore state and unlock the object in case of a failure. Remember, on many platforms, many problems are reported by the hardware via interrupts, and exceptions are generated by the Win32 operating system to reflect these conditions to your program. So you may not have any control over the raising of an exception, such as illegal access or divide-by-zero. Building a system that is robust under synchronization and exceptions is a nontrivial undertaking![6] If you terminate a thread that has a mutex locked, the mutex is *abandoned*. You must check the return value from a wait function to be certain that the reason you are passing the wait function does not involve an abandoned mutex; if it does, you run the risk of working on data that is in an inconsistent state.

Avoiding Synchronization

The fastest synchronization code, however, is the code that is never executed. If you can avoid the need for synchronization, your application will run faster and with less chance of an error.

The simplest way to handle this is to have exactly one thread manage a resource. For example, we discussed thread-local storage in Chapter 14 on page 1065 as one means to avoid the need for synchronization. If the information is not shared, this is a reasonably efficient method to grant each thread its private space. If each thread does a lot of storage allocation, you can avoid the bottleneck of synchronizing the allocator by creating a private heap for each thread, which only that thread manages. This also is discussed in great detail in Chapter 14, starting on page 1057.

You could also use messages, events, unnamed pipes, or named pipes as means of synchronization. By sending information on a named pipe, you can pass information into a thread that manages a resource. If a thread waits for an event, and only that thread accesses the resources it controls, there is no need to block on a semaphore or mutex.

Synchronization via Messages

You can also synchronize using messages. If a process manages a resource, sending a message to its top-level window using SendMessage guarantees that until the message returns, you will not resume execution in the

---

[6] Many years ago we had a multiprocessor-based multithreaded program which was a key part of an operating system but which had an MTBF of approximately 45 minutes. I reworked it to be reliable under exceptions. The original listing was approximately Ω inches thick. After a year of work, it was 4 inches thick, had an MTBF measured in weeks (limited by the reliability of our power utility service), and was able to recover successfully from parity errors. This was a serious engineering effort. Retrofitting reliability is *hard*. *–jmn*

thread that sent the message. If another thread (in your process or another process) does a SendMessage while the first SendMessage is being processed, it will not be seen until the receiving process returns to its main message loop, which it will not do until it has completed the first message. This implicit serialization was the only way to synchronize multiple processes in earlier versions of Windows. It is also possible to synchronize transactions within your own process's threads by sending messages to the windows managed by each thread. Given the availability of semaphores and mutexes, however, this technique is generally less common for inter-process synchronization, and CRITICAL_SECTION is usually used for intraprocess synchronization.

Releases of Win32 at API level 4.0 or lower do not support distributed semaphores or mutexes; to use these for interprocess synchronization, the two processes must be running on the same physical machine (although not necessarily on the same processor in a symmetric-multiprocessor (SMP) configuration). At this level of Win32, in order to synchronize between two processes running on (possibly) different machines, you must use network messages. Discussions of this sort of architecture are beyond the scope of this book, but we recommend the book by Quinn and Shute, listed under "Further Reading".

Threads

Synchronization isn't necessary unless you have threads. Each process, when created, has exactly one thread of execution. We have to deal with interprocess synchronization with events, mutexes, and semaphores. But we can also create *additional* threads of control in a process. The thread functions are shown in Table 18.8.

Table 18.8: Thread primitives

Function	Description	
HANDLE CreateThread	(LPSECURITY_ATTRIBUTES security, DWORD stacksize, LPTHREAD_START_ROUTINE function, LPVOID param, DWORD flags, LPDWORD threadID)	
HANDLE CreateRemoteThread	(HANDLE process, LPSECURITY_ATTRIBUTES security, DWORD stacksize, LPTHREAD_START_ROUTINE function, LPVOID param, DWORD flags, LPDWORD threadID)	
	process	Handle to another process in which the thread is to be run.
	security	Reference to security attributes of thread, or NULL to use the same security as the creating thread.
	stacksize	Size of stack to initially allocate; 0 for default stack.
	function	The top-level function of the thread.
	param	Arbitrary 32-bit value passed to function.

Table 18.8: Thread primitives

Function	Description		
	`flags`	Indicates initial state	
		0	
			Thread starts running immediately upon creation.
		CREATE_SUSPENDED	
			Thread is created suspended and must be explicitly released for execution.
	Creates a new thread. For the `CreateRemoteThread`, the thread is created in a different address space. Execution starts with the specified function and the thread terminates when this function returns, or when an `ExitThread` function call is executed.		
`BOOL CloseHandle`	`(HANDLE hthread)`		
	`hthread`	Thread handle. See page 1260.	
	Closes the thread handle. When the last handle is closed, the thread object is deleted.		
`VOID ExitThread`	`(DWORD exitcode)`		
	`exitcode`	Thread exit code. This is the value that will be returned by `GetExitCodeThread` after the thread terminates.	
	Terminates the thread "cleanly". Attached DLLs receive thread detach notifications.		
`BOOL GetExitCodeThread`	`(HANDLE hthread, LPDWORD exitcode)`		
	`hthread`	Thread handle. See page 1260.	
	`exitcode`	Place where exit code will be stored.	
	Retrieves a thread's exit code. This is the value passed to `Exit-Thread` or the value returned from the thread's top-level function.		
`BOOL GetThreadContext`	`(HANDLE hthread, LPCONTEXT pcontext)`		
	`hthread`	Thread handle. See page 1260.	
	`pcontext`	Pointer to thread context.	

Table 18.8: Thread primitives

Function	Description	
HDESK GetThreadDesktop	(HANDLE hthread)	
	hthread	Thread handle. See page 1260.
	Returns desktop being used by the thread for desktop operations.	
LCID GetThreadLocale	( )	
	Returns calling thread's locale ID.	
int GetThreadPriority	(HANDLE hthread)	
	hthread	Thread handle. See page 1260.
	Retrieves the thread's priority. See SetThreadPriority for the values that can be returned.	
int GetThreadTimes	(HANDLE hthread, LPFILETIME create, LPFILETIME exit, LPFILETIME kernel, LPFILETIME user)	
	hthread	Thread handle. See page 1260.
	create	Time when thread was created.
	exit	Time when thread was destroyed.
	kernel	Time spent in the kernel.
	user	Time spent at user level.
	Retrieves the thread's times.	
DWORD ResumeThread	(HANDLE hthread)	
	hthread	Thread handle. See page 1260.
	Resumes the thread. If the suspend count is greater than 0, it is decremented and the original suspend count is returned. If the suspend count goes to 0, the thread will become schedulable. If there is an error, the return value will be negative. The return values are:	
	0xFFFFFFFF	Error occurred.
	0	Thread was not suspended.
	1	Thread was suspended, but is now executing.
	> 1	Thread is still suspended.

Table 18.8: Thread primitives

Function	Description	
DWORD SetThreadAffinityMask	(HANDLE hthread, DWORD mask)	
	hthread	Thread handle. See page 1260.
	mask	Processor affinity mask.
	Contains a bit mask specifying which processors in a multiprocessor system can run this thread.	
DWORD SetThreadContext	(HANDLE hthread, const CONTEXT * context)	
	hthread	Thread handle. See page 1260.
	context	Thread context.
BOOL SetThreadDesktop	(HANDLE hthread, HDESK desktop)	
	hthread	Thread handle. See page 1260.
	desktop	Desktop which will be used by the thread for desktop operations.
BOOL SetThreadLocale	(LCID locale)	
	locale	Locale to be used for all locale-sensitive operations. Created by MAKELCID macro, or one of the following values:
		LOCALE_SYSTEM_DEFAULT
		LOCAL_USER_DEFAULT
	Sets the locale for the calling thread.	
BOOL SetThreadPriority	(HANDLE hthread, int priority)	
	hthread	Thread handle. See page 1260.
	priority	One of the following codes:
		THREAD_PRIORITY_ABOVE_NORMAL
		THREAD_PRIORITY_BELOW_NORMAL
		THREAD_PRIORITY_HIGHEST
		THREAD_PRIORITY_IDLE
		THREAD_PRIORITY_LOWEST

Table 18.8: Thread primitives

Function	Description	
	THREAD_PRIORITY_NORMAL	
	THREAD_PRIORITY_TIME_CRITICAL	
	Sets the thread priority. The priority value is a boost (positive or negative) relative to the process priority.	
DWORD SetThreadToken	(PHANDLE phthread, HANDLE token)	
	phthread	Pointer to thread handle. See "Thread Creation."
	token	Impersonation token.
HANDLE SuspendThread	(HANDLE hthread)	
	hthread	Thread handle. See "Thread Creation."
	Suspends the thread. The suspend count is incremented. There must be a ResumeThread executed for each SuspendThread; when the suspend count goes to zero, the thread is schedulable.	
VOID TerminateThread	(HANDLE hthread, DWORD exitcode)	
	hthread	Thread handle. See "Thread Creation."
	exitcode	Thread exit code. This is the value that will be returned by GetExitCodeThread after the thread terminates.
	Terminates the thread "dirty". Attached DLLs will not receive thread detach notifications. Locks will not become unlocked.	

Thread Creation

In its simplest form, thread creation is easy. In C, you call the function CreateThread with a default set of parameters:

```
DWORD   threadID;
HANDLE hthread = CreateThread(
               NULL, // no special security attrs
               0,    // default stack
               (LPTHREAD_START_ROUTINE)fcn, // function
               (LPVOID)expression,          // parameter
               0,    // or CREATE_SUSPENDED
               &threadID);
```

The security attributes control features like the inheritability of handles. So if you specify NULL, as we did, the thread will not be able to create a process and pass any handles to it.

The *fcn* parameter represents the name of a function to call, which has the form:

```
long WINAPI fcn(LPVOID param)
```

The 32-bit parameter is passed directly to the function specified. When the function returns, the thread will be terminated. The thread can also be terminated by calling the ExitThread function. The return value from the function, or the argument passed to ExitThread, becomes the *exit code* for the thread. You can get the exit code value by calling GetExitCodeThread.

Many of the functions listed in Table 18.8 are primarily of interest to you only if you're writing client/server applications where you must have threads that "impersonate" (that is, have the same privileges) as a specified user. Generally this is in the context of a server where the thread must execute with privileges far below those of the server itself. We don't cover those here because the design of good client/server applications is worthy of a book itself. You might want to check out the book by Quinn and Shute, or the article by Martin Heller, cited in the Further Reading section at the end of this chapter.

Inter-thread Control

A thread can perform several operations on itself. For example, it can suspend itself. Thread operations require a *thread handle*. However, the function which returns a thread handle, GetCurrentThread, does not really return a useful handle for cross-thread manipulation. Instead, it returns a *pseudo-handle*, a handle which refers to the thread that executed GetCurrentThread. If two threads issue the GetCurrentThread call, they will each get the *same* value, which we can think of as "self". When this pseudo-handle is passed in to one of the thread functions, it says "do this operation to the calling thread". So if you store this "handle" in a place where another thread can access it, and the other thread performs a SuspendThread operation, it will suspend, not the thread whose handle it believes it has, but *itself*, because the handle is the pseudo-handle meaning "do it to the calling thread". If you need to manipulate one thread from another (particularly a child thread from the main thread), you must use the DuplicateHandle call to create a *real* handle to the thread. You can use this handle to control the thread from another thread, or you can use it with a wait function (from Table 18.5) to wait for the thread termination. The DuplicateHandle call we used in the Synchronization Explorer looks like this:

```
DuplicateHandle(
            GetCurrentProcess(),    // source process
            GetCurrentThread(),     // handle to duplicate
            GetCurrentProcess(),    // target process
            &thisThread->hthread,   // place to put result
            0,                      // access: ignored
            FALSE,                  // no need to inherit
            DUPLICATE_SAME_ACCESS); // no change in access
```

When we finally wait for the thread to terminate, we can use this handle:

```
WaitForSingleObject(thisThread->hthread, INFINITE);
```

The thread handle becomes signaled when the thread terminates, terminating the wait. You must remember to close this handle when you are finished with it.

The Synchronization Explorer

The Synchronization Explorer is an application that demonstrates a number of features of multithreading. When started, it displays a "control panel" and a single thread of control. This thread of control locks a critical section, fetches a value from a shared variable, increments it, stores it back, and releases the lock. You can use the **File New** menu item or toolbar icon to create more instances of these threads. This is shown in Figure 18.3. The active thread, #2, has incremented the counter value to 187 and is about to store it. It has not yet unlocked the counter, and hence has not yet completed a full loop, so the "Loops" value shown in the Controller panel is one less than the current counter value. The other threads are locked, and have not yet updated their counter displays.

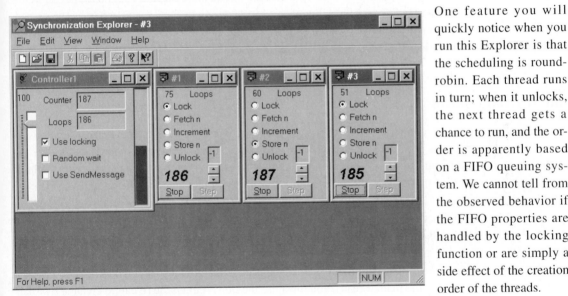

Figure 18.3: Synchronized threads

One feature you will quickly notice when you run this Explorer is that the scheduling is round-robin. Each thread runs in turn; when it unlocks, the next thread gets a chance to run, and the order is apparently based on a FIFO queuing system. We cannot tell from the observed behavior if the FIFO properties are handled by the locking function or are simply a side effect of the creation order of the threads.

Note that all the threads but one sit in the "lock" state except for one that is actually running and incrementing the counter. If you have only one thread, the loop count and counter value will be in sync. If you add a second thread, the sum of the loops of both threads will equal the counter value (or at worst be off by one, because we use PostMessage to update the displays, so it could be off by one until the update occurs). See Figure 18.3 for an example.

The statement about the algorithm running in a separate thread is almost correct. The *computational* algorithm of lock, fetch, increment, store, unlock runs in a separate thread. The *display* of the algorithm state is actually part of the GUI thread. The worker thread posts messages back to the GUI thread to keep the display part, which is what you are seeing, updated. You can observe that when you grab a window and drag it, you've stopped the GUI thread from processing messages, so the display "freezes" for all the displays. But as soon as you release the window, there is an intense flurry of updates as all the pending messages in the queue are processed. Hold and drag the window long enough and you will either get a queue overflow or discover that for a *very* long time the GUI is "non-responsive" as it plays catch-up with all the enqueued messages. Solving *this* problem requires a multithreaded GUI or the use of the synchronous SendMessage call to avoid queue backup. We wanted to avoid the problems of a multithreaded GUI, so instead we allow you to use the SendMessage option. You can adjust the speed of the simulation down to 0 in units of 20 ms. This is the amount of actual time that the process sleeps before executing the next step of the simulation. When the simulation delay goes to 0, the algorithm is running at full speed and we actually force the use of SendMessage to avoid generating a massive input queue to each display window.

We use radio buttons to show the simulation steps because they were a quick-and-easy display mechanism; they aren't really "radio buttons" in that you can't affect the program by clicking on one.

If we disable the use of locking, we immediately get into trouble. To see the importance of synchronization, you can uncheck the "Use locking" option. What will happen now is that several threads can load the value of the counter, increment it, and put it back. The result is that although nominally some number of increments, say five, have happened, the actual value, because it was unprotected by a synchronization primi-

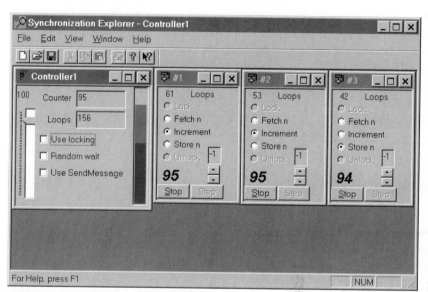

Figure 18.4: Unsynchronized threads

tive, is incremented only once. So the number of iterations and the actual counter value begin to diverge. This is shown graphically by a two-color progress gauge on the right of the controller, where the red portion shows the error caused by lack of synchronization. This can be seen in Figure 18.4. You can see that two threads, #1 and #2, have both fetched the value 95 and are incrementing it to 96. Meanwhile, thread #3 is about to store the value 94 back into the counter. The result you see is that within a small number of iterations we see a large error developing. This is not the sort of error you would like to see in, say, a financial package recording sales, or in an inventory management system tracking how many items were left in stock.

Internally, we use events to synchronize the worker thread with the GUI during initialization and termination. We use critical sections that are invisible to the viewer to synchronize the use of internal variables.

You can use the spin control to modify the priority of each thread. The priority values can be adjusted by what is called the *boost* priority relative to the *process* priority. The *boost* priority is that priority which, when added to the process priority, determines the absolute thread priority. Boost values range from -2 to +2, with 0 being the default. We allow you to modify the priority boost from -2 to 0 (we found that allowing the higher priority boost had a severe impact on the GUI thread. . .it became very non-responsive because it was lower priority than the worker threads). When you have locking disabled, you can see some of the effects of the priority boost. To emphasize them, you can choose the "Random Wait" option, which adjusts the simulated time period by choosing each sleep time not as the value selected by the speed control but as a value randomly chosen in the interval $0.5 \times$ speed..$1.5 \times$ speed. This introduces a random amount of "noise" into the lockstep scheduling and you will begin to see the effects as the "FIFO" order now drifts.

You can also stop a thread and single-step it. This lets you see the effects of locking, or non-locking, in more detail.

We do one really evil thing in the Synchronization Explorer: we use TerminateThread. This pulls out a gigantic sledgehammer and smashes the thread flat without any warning. TerminateThread is generally a disastrous call to use, because it terminates the thread instantly, with no chance for the thread to notify any attached DLLs; it can also leave parts of the kernel in a potentially inconsistent state if the thread was executing in the kernel. If the thread had any synchronization objects locked, they will not be unlocked or abandoned, so any other thread blocked on the synchronization objects will either time out or simply remain locked indefinitely. We only do this in the special case where we are shutting down the application and we really *need* to terminate the thread, which is locked. In looking at the alternative solutions, we decided that it would require at least another lengthy chapter to describe how to do synchronization reliably in the face of events such as shutdown or time-out, and this was getting well beyond the scope of what we wanted to cover in this book.

Except for the TerminateThread, the implementation of the Synchronization Explorer is reasonably clean. We use critical sections for internal locking, and events to synchronize thread start-up and termination (in the case of termination, the event is the process object itself becoming signaled, indicating that it has terminated).

MFC

Although the Synchronization Explorer, like most of the Explorers, is written in C++, we did not use all of the C++/MFC library to implement certain synchronization events. In particular, we discovered a serious race-condition bug in the CSingleLock class that made it impossible to use. In Win32, you can signal an event *before* you execute the wait event that would block on it; if the signaling occurs before the wait, the wait encounters a signaled event and proceeds as you might expect. If, however, you use CSingleLock in the way Microsoft apparently intends, the attempt to signal an event before it is locked will cause the signal request to be ignored, because the event is not in a wait. This is simply incorrect, and renders this class unusable. This bug is so deep and fundamental (it isn't a simple coding error) that the class cannot possibly work; even if it made sense, it is incorrectly implemented. It uses a simple Boolean value to detect if there is a wait pending. This Boolean value is set and tested without any interlock, and is hence thread-unsafe and multiprocessor-unsafe. Ideally, by the time you read this, Microsoft will have fixed the problem, but you cannot trust this code unless you read it carefully to be sure that it has been corrected. This bug is present in MFC 4.*x* and you should be cautious of future implementations.

Further Reading

The following readings are worth investigating. Some of them are deeply mathematical and require a serious background in computer science; others are quite accessible to the experienced programmer. Unfortunately, many of the early classic works are out of print and available only in libraries. They do convey one important message we stated earlier: correct multithreaded behavior is not arrived at except by design.

Note that articles from *Dr. Dobb's Journal* and *Microsoft Systems Journal* are also found on the Microsoft Developer Network CD-ROM (MSDN CD-ROM).

Andres, G. R. and Schneider, F. B., "Concepts and Notations for Concurrent Programming", *Computing Surveys* (15), March 1983.

Asche, Ruediger, "Synchronization on the Fly". MSDN CD-ROM. Article written September 1993.

Atkinson, R. and Hewitt, C., "Synchronization and Proof Techniques for Serializers", *IEEE Transactions on Software Engineering* (SE-5), January 1979.

Brinch-Hansen, Per, "The Programming Language Concurrent Pascal", *IEEE Transactions on Software Engineering* (SE-1), June 1975.

Brinch-Hansen, Per, *Operating System Principles*, Prentice-Hall, 1973.

Campbell, H. and Habermann, A. Nico, "The Specification of Process Synchronization by Path Expressions", in *Operating Systems*, Kaiser, C., (ed.), Springer-Verlag, 1974.

Coffman, E. G., Elphick, M. J., and Shoshani, A., "System Deadlocks", *Computing Surveys*, June 1971.

Courtois, P. J., Heymans, F., and Parnas, D. L., "Concurrent Control with Readers and Writers", *Communications of the ACM* (10), October 1971.

Dijkstra, Edsgar W., "Co-operating Sequential Processes", reprinted in *Programming Languages*, Genuys, F., (ed.), Academic Press, 1965.

Glasser, Daniel, "Efficient Synchronization Techniques for Multithreaded Win32-based Applications", *Microsoft Systems Journal*, February 1995. Source code for the examples is found on the MSDN CD-ROM.

Havender, J. W., "Avoiding Deadlock in Multitasking Systems", *IBM Systems Journal* (7), 1968.

Heller, Martin, "Tips and Tricks on Developing Killer Server Applications for Windows NT", *Microsoft Systems Journal*, August, 1995.

Hoare, C. A. R., "Monitors, An Operating System Structuring Concept", *Communications of the ACM* (17), October 1974.

Holt, R. C., "Some Deadlock Properties of Computer Systems", *Computing Surveys* (4), September 1972.

Lampson, Butler W. and Redell, D. D., "Experience with Processes and Monitors in Mesa", *Communications of the ACM* (23), February 1980.

Newton, G., "Deadlock Prevention, Detection, and Resolution: An Annotated Bibliography", *Operating Systems Review* (13), April 1979.

Pietrek, Matt, "Stepping up to 32 bits: Chicago's[7] Process, Thread, and Memory Management", *Microsoft Systems Journal*, August 1994.

Peterson, G. L., "Myths About the Mutual Exclusion Problem", *Information Processing Letters* (12), June 1981.

Quinn, Bob and Shute, Dave, *Windows Sockets Network Programming*, Addison-Wesley, 1996. ISBN 0-201-63372-8.

Richter, Jeffrey, "Coordinate Win32 Threads Using Manual-Reset and Auto-Reset Events", *Microsoft Systems Journal*, October 1993.

Tanenbaum, Andrew S., *Operating Systems: Design and Implementation*, Prentice-Hall, 1987.

Vaidyanathan, Shankar, "Multitasking Fortran and Windows NT", *Dr. Dobb's Journal* (no citation given, but reprinted on the MSDN CD-ROM).

Wulf, William A., Cohen, Ellis S., Corwin, William M., Jones, Anita K., Levin, Roy, Pierson, Charles, and Pollack, F. J., "Hydra: The Kernel of a Multiprocessor Operating System", *Communications of the ACM* (17), June 1974.[8]

Wulf, William A., Levin, Roy, and Harbison, Samuel P., *C.mmp/Hydra: An Experimental Computer System*, McGraw-Hill, 1981.

---

[7] "Chicago" was the internal release code name of the system which was released as Windows 95. Much of the "Chicago" material is actually generic Win32 material and applies to NT 3.*x* and NT 4.*x* as well.

[8] I highly recommend the series of publications on the Hydra operating system, but that reflects a distinct personal prejudice–I spent several years, just after receiving my Ph.D., working on the Hydra system. *–jmn.*

A Ternary Raster-Operation Codes

This appendix lists the ternary raster-operation codes used by the `BitBlt`, `PatBlt`, `StretchBlt`, and `StretchDIBits` functions. These codes define the 256 possible combinations of the bits in a brush, the bits in a source bitmap, and the bits in a destination bitmap.

The first column lists the hexadecimal raster-operation code for each combination of bits. Table 6.12 on page 349 demonstrates how to calculate the desired raster-operation code. Once you've calculated the desired code, you can find the corresponding ROP code in the second column of the table.

The third column gives a `Boolean` function that describes the raster-operation in terms of `Boolean` operators and the operands used by the ROP code. The abbreviations used for the operands are as follows:

- **P**   Pattern (also called the brush)

- **S**   Source bitmap

- **D**   Destination bitmap

We use the bitwise C operators to describe the `Boolean` functions. The operators are as follows:

- **&**   Bitwise AND

- **~**   Bitwise NOT (complement)

- **|**   Bitwise OR

- **^**   Bitwise XOR (Exclusive OR)

The fourth column gives the symbolic name for the ROP code. Only the 15 most frequently used ROP codes have a symbolic name defined by Windows. You must use one of the hexadecimal ROP codes when using the other raster-operations; for your convenience, we have defined `extrop_` symbolic names for each of these in the file on the CD-ROM `extrops.h`. You can use the GDI Explorer application to study the effects of the various ROP codes. The raster operations defined by `extrops.h` are interpreted as a Polish (postfix) notation for a stack machine. The codes used are as follows:

- S: Represents the source operand.

- D: Represents the destination operand.

- P: Represents the pattern operand.

The appearance of one of these operands pushes the specified value onto the evaluation stack. If you have an HP calculator, the stack push operation is the **Enter** button. The following operations are then defined:

- a: Applies a bitwise AND to the top two operands of the stack, removes them, and replaces them with the result.

- o: Applies a bitwise OR to the top two operands of the stack, removes them, and replaces them with the result.

- x: Applies a bitwise XOR to the top two operands of the stack, removes them, and replaces them with the result.

- n: Applies a bitwise NOT to the top operand of the stack, removes it, and replaces it with the result.

Table A.1: Ternary ROP codes

Hexadecimal Operation Code	Hexadecimal ROP Code	Boolean Function	Symbolic Name
00	00000042	0	BLACKNESS extrop_0
01	00010289	~(P | S | D)	extrop_DPSoon
02	00020C89	~(P | S) & D	extrop_DPSona
03	000300AA	~(P | S)	extrop_PSon
04	00040C88	~(P | D) & S	extrop_SDPona
05	000500A9	~(P | D)	extrop_DPon
06	00060865	~(P | ~(S ∧ D))	extrop_PDSxnon
07	000702C5	~(P | (S & D))	extrop_PDSaon
08	00080F08	~P & S& D	extrop_SDPnaa
09	00090245	~(P | (S ∧ D))	extrop_PDSxon
0A	000A0329	~P & D	extrop_DPna
0B	000B0B2A	~(P | (S & ~D))	extrop_PSDnaon
0C	000C0324	~P & S	extrop_SPna
0D	000D0B25	~(P | (~S & D))	extrop_PDSnaon
0E	000E08A5	~(P | ~(S | D))	extrop_PDSonon
0F	000F0001	~P	extrop_Pn
10	00100C85	P & ~(S | D)	extrop_PDSona

Table A.1: Ternary ROP codes

Hexadecimal Operation Code	Hexadecimal ROP Code	Boolean Function	Symbolic Name
11	001100A6	~(S | D)	NOTSRCERASE extrop_DSon
12	00120868	~(S | ~(P ∧ D))	extrop_SDPxnon
13	001302C8	~(S | (P & D))	extrop_SDPaon
14	00140869	~(D | ~(P ∧ S))	extrop_DPSxnon
15	001502C9	~(D | (P & S))	extrop_DPSaon
16	00165CCA	P ∧ (S ∧ (D & ~(P & S)))	extrop_PSDPSanaxx
17	00171D54	~(S ∧ ((S ∧ P) & (S ∧ D)))	extrop_SSPxDSxaxn
18	00180D59	(P ∧ S) & (P ∧ D)	extrop_SPxPDxa
19	00191CC8	~(S ∧ (D & ~(P & S)))	extrop_SDPSanaxn
1A	001A06C5	P ∧ (D | (S & P))	extrop_PDSPaox
1B	001B0768	~(S ∧ (D & (P ∧ S)))	extrop_SDPSxaxn
1C	001C06CA	P ∧ (S | (P & D))	extrop_PSDPaox
1D	001D0766	~(D ∧ (S & (P ∧ D)))	extrop_DSPDxaxn
1E	001E01A5	P ∧ (S | D)	extrop_PDSox
1F	001F0385	~(P & (S | D))	extrop_PDSoan
20	00200F09	P & ~S & D	extrop_DPSnaa
21	00210248	~(S | (P ∧ D))	extrop_SDPxon
22	00220326	~S& D	extrop_DSna
23	00230B24	~(S| (P & ~D))	extrop_SPDnaon
24	00240D55	(S ∧ P) & (S ∧ D)	extrop_SPxDSxa
25	00251CC5	~(P ∧ (D & ~(S & P)))	extrop_PDSPanaxn
26	002606C8	S ∧ (D | (P & S))	extrop_SDPSaox
27	00271868	S ∧ (D | ~(P ∧ S))	extrop_SDPSxnox
28	00280369	D & (P ∧ S)	extrop_DPSxa
29	002916CA	~(P ∧ (S ∧ (D | (P & S))))	extrop_PSDPSaoxxn
2A	002A0CC9	D & ~(P & S)	extrop_DPSana
2B	002B1D58	~(S ∧ ((S ∧ P) & (P & D)))	extrop_SSPxPDxaxn
2C	002C0784	S ∧ (P & (S | D))	extrop_SPDSoax
2D	002D060A	P ∧ (S | ~D)	extrop_PSDnox
2E	002E064A	P ∧ (S | (P ∧ D))	extrop_PSDPxox
2F	002F0E2A	~(P & (S | ~D))	extrop_PSDnoan

Table A.1: Ternary ROP codes

Hexadecimal Operation Code	Hexadecimal ROP Code	Boolean Function	Symbolic Name
30	0030032A	P & ~S	extrop_PSna
31	00310B28	~(S | (~P & D))	extrop_SDPnaon
32	00320688	S ^ (P | S| D)	extrop_SDPSoox
33	00330008	~S	NOTSRCCOPY extrop_Sn
34	003406C4	S ^ (P | (S & D))	extrop_SPDSaox
35	00351864	S ^ (P | ~(S ^ D))	extrop_SPDSxnox
36	003601A8	S ^ (P | D)	extrop_SDPox
37	00370388	~(S & (P | D))	extrop_SDPoan
38	0038078A	P ^ (S & (P | D))	extrop_PSDPoax
39	00390604	S ^ (P | ~D)	extrop_SPDnox
3A	003A0644	S ^ (P ^ (S ^ D))	extrop_SPDSxox
3B	003B0E24	~(S & (P | ~D))	extrop_SPDnoan
3C	003C004A	P ^ S	extrop_PSx
3D	003D18A4	S ^ (P | ~(S | D))	extrop_SPDSonox
3E	003E1B24	S ^ (P | (~S & D))	extrop_SPDSnaox
3F	003F00EA	~(P & S)	extrop_PSan
40	00400F0A	P & S & ~D	extrop_PSDnaa
41	00410249	~(D | (P ^ S))	extrop_DPSxon
42	00420D5D	(S ^ D) & (P ^ D)	extrop_SDxPDxa
43	00431CC4	~(S ^ (P & ~(S & D)))	extrop_SPDSanaxn
44	00440328	S & ~D	SRCERASE extrop_SDna
45	00450B29	~(D | (P & ~S))	extrop_DPSnaon
46	004606C6	D ^ (S | (P & D))	extrop_DSPDaox
47	0047076A	~(P ^ (S & (P ^ D)))	extrop_PSDPxaxn
48	00480368	S & (P ^ D)	extrop_SDPxa
49	004916C5	~(P ^ (D ^ (S | (P & D))))	extrop_PDSPDaoxxn
4A	004A0789	D ^ (P & (S | D))	extrop_DPSDoax
4B	004B0605	P ^ (~S | D)	extrop_PDSnox
4C	004C0CC8	S & ~(P & D)	extrop_SDPana
4D	004D1954	~(S^ ((P ^ S) | (S^ D)))	extrop_SSPxDSxoxn
4E	004E0645	P ^ (D | (P ^ S))	extrop_PDSPxox

Table A.1: Ternary ROP codes

Hexadecimal Operation Code	Hexadecimal ROP Code	Boolean Function	Symbolic Name
4F	004F0E25	~(P & (~S | D))	extrop_PDSnoan
50	00500325	P & ~D	extrop_PDna
51	00510B26	~(D | (~P & S))	extrop_DSPnaon
52	005206C9	D ∧ (P | (S & D))	extrop_DPSDaox
53	00530764	~(S ∧ (P & (S ∧ D)))	extrop_SPDSxaxn
54	005408A9	~(D | ~(P | S))	extrop_DPSonon
55	00550009	~D	DSTINVERT extrop_Dn
56	005601A9	D ∧ (P | S)	extrop_DPSox
57	00570389	~(D & (P | S))	extrop_DPSoan
58	00580785	P ∧ (D & (P | S))	extrop_PDSPoax
59	00590609	D ∧ (P | ~S)	extrop_DPSnox
5A	005A0049	P ∧ D	PATINVERT extrop_DPx
5B	005B18A9	D ∧ (P | ~(S | D))	extrop_DPSDonox
5C	005C0649	D ∧ (P | (S ∧ D))	extrop_DPSDxox
5D	005D0E29	~(D & (P | ~S))	extrop_DPSnoan
5E	005E1B29	D ∧ (P | (S & ~D))	extrop_DPSDnaox
5F	005F00E9	~(P & D)	extrop_DPan
60	00600365	P & (S ∧ D)	extrop_PDSxa
61	006116C6	~(D ∧ (S ∧ (P | (S & D))))	extrop_DSPDSaoxxn
62	00620786	D ∧ (S & (P | D))	extrop_DSPDoax
63	00630608	S ∧ (~P | D)	extrop_SDPnox
64	00640788	S ∧ (D & (P | S))	extrop_SDPSoax
65	00650606	D ∧ (~P | S)	extrop_DSPnox
66	00660046	S ∧ D	SRCINVERT extrop_DSx
67	006718A8	S ∧ (D | ~(P | S))	extrop_SDPSonox
68	006858A6	~(D ∧ (S ∧ (P | ~(S | D))))	extrop_DSPDSonoxxn
69	00690145	~(P ∧ (S ∧ D))	extrop_PDSxxn
6A	006A01E9	D ∧ (P & S)	extrop_DPSax
6B	006B178A	~(P ∧ (S ∧ (D & (S | P))))	extrop_PSDPSoaxxn
6C	006C01E8	S ∧ (P & D)	extrop_SDPax
6D	006D1785	~(P ∧ (D ∧ (S & (P | D))))	extrop_PDSPDoaxxn

Table A.1: Ternary ROP codes

Hexadecimal Operation Code	Hexadecimal ROP Code	Boolean Function	Symbolic Name
6E	006E1E28	S ∧ (D & (P | ~S))	extrop_SDPSnoax
6F	006F0C65	~(P & ~(S ∧ D))	extrop_PDSxnan
70	00700CC5	P & ~(S& D)	extrop_PDSana
71	00711D5C	~(S ∧ ((S ∧ D) & (P ∧ D)))	extrop_SSDxPDxaxn
72	00720648	S ∧ (D | (P ∧ S))	extrop_SDPSxox
73	00730E28	~(S& (~P | D))	extrop_SDPnoan
74	00740646	D ∧ (S| (P ∧ D))	extrop_DSPDxox
75	00750E26	~(D & (~P | S))	extrop_DSPnoan
76	00761B28	S ∧ (D | (P & ~S))	extrop_SDPSnaox
77	007700E6	~(S & D)	extrop_DSan
78	007801E5	P ∧ (S & D)	extrop_PDSax
79	00791786	~(D ∧ (S ∧ (P & (S | D))))	extrop_DSPDSoaxxn
7A	007A1E29	D ∧ (P & (S | ~D))	extrop_DPSDnoax
7B	007B0C68	~(S & ~(P ∧ D))	extrop_SDPxnan
7C	007C1E24	S ∧ (P & (~S | D))	extrop_SPDSnoax
7D	007D0C69	~(D & ~(S ∧ P))	extrop_DPSxnan
7E	007E0955	(P ∧ S) | (S ∧ D)	extrop_SPxDSxo
7F	007F03C9	~(P & S & D)	extrop_DPSaan
80	008003E9	P & S & D	extrop_DPSaa
81	00810975	~((P ∧ S) | (S ∧ D))	extrop_SPxDSxon
82	00820C49	~(P ∧ S) & D	extrop_DPSxna
83	00831E04	~(S ∧ (P & (~S | D)))	extrop_SPDSnoaxn
84	00840C48	S & ~(P ∧ D)	extrop_SDPxna
85	00851E05	~(P ∧ (D & (~P | S)))	extrop_PDSPnoaxn
86	008617A6	D ∧ (S ∧ (P & (S | D)))	extrop_DSPDSoaxx
87	008701C5	~(P ∧ (S & D))	extrop_PDSaxn
88	008800C6	S & D	SRCAND extrop_DSa
89	00891B08	~(S ∧ (D | (P & ~S)))	extrop_SDPSnaoxn
8A	008A0E06	(~P | S) & D	extrop_DSPnoa
8B	008B0666	~(D ∧ (S | (P ∧ D)))	extrop_DSPDxoxn
8C	008C0E08	S & (~P | D)	extrop_SDPnoa
8D	008D0668	~(S ∧ (D | (P ∧ S)))	extrop_SDPSxoxn

Table A.1: Ternary ROP codes

Hexadecimal Operation Code	Hexadecimal ROP Code	Boolean Function	Symbolic Name
8E	008E1D7C	S ∧ ((S ∧ D) & (P ∧ D))	extrop_SSDxPDxax
8F	008F0CE5	~(P & ~(S & D))	extrop_PDSanan
90	00900C45	P & ~(S ∧ D)	extrop_PDSxna
91	00911E08	~(S ∧ (D & (P | ~S)))	extrop_SDPSnoaxn
92	009217A9	D ∧ (P ∧ (S & (P | D)))	extrop_DPSDPoaxx
93	009301C4	~(S ∧ (P & D))	extrop_SPDaxn
94	009417AA	P ∧ (S ∧ (D & (P | S)))	extrop_PSDPSoaxx
95	009501C9	~(D ∧ (P & S))	extrop_DPSaxn
96	00960169	P ∧ S ∧ D	extrop_DPSxx
97	0097588A	P ∧ (S ∧ (D | ~(P | S)))	extrop_PSDPSonoxx
98	00981888	~(S ∧ (D | ~(P | S)))	extrop_SDPSonoxn
99	00990066	~(S ∧ D)	extrop_DSxn
9A	009A0709	(P & ~S) ∧ D	extrop_DPSnax
9B	009B07A8	~(S ∧ (D & (P | S)))	extrop_SDPSoaxn
9C	009C0704	S ∧ (P & ~D)	extrop_SPDnax
9D	009D07A6	~(D ∧ (S & (P | D)))	extrop_DSPDoaxn
9E	009E16E6	(S ∧ (P | (S & D))) ∧ D	extrop_DSPDSaoxx
9F	009F0345	~(P & (S ∧ D))	extrop_PDSxan
A0	00A000C9	P & D	extrop_DPa
A1	00A11B05	~(P ∧ (D | (~P & S)))	extrop_PDSPnaoxn
A2	00A20E09	(P | ~S) & D	extrop_DPSnoa
A3	00A30669	~(D ∧ (P | (S ∧ D)))	extrop_DPSDxoxn
A4	00A41885	~(P ∧ (D | ~(P | S)))	extrop_PDSPonoxn
A5	00A50065	~(P ∧ D)	extrop_PDxn
A6	00A60706	(~P & S) ∧ D	extrop_DSPnax
A7	00A707A5	~(P ∧ (D & (P | S)))	extrop_PDSPoaxn
A8	00A803A9	(P | S) & D	extrop_DPSoa
A9	00A90189	~((P | S) ∧ D)	extrop_DPSoxn
AA	00AA0029	D	extrop_D
AB	00AB0889	~(P | S) | D	extrop_DPSono
AC	00AC0744	S ∧ (P & (S ∧ D))	extrop_SPDSxax
AD	00AD06E9	~(D ∧ (P | (S & D)))	extrop_DPSDaoxn

Table A.1: Ternary ROP codes

Hexadecimal Operation Code	Hexadecimal ROP Code	Boolean Function	Symbolic Name
AE	00AE0B06	(~P & S) | D	extrop_DSPnao
AF	00AF0229	~P | D	extrop_DPno
B0	00B00E05	P & (~S | D)	extrop_PDSnoa
B1	00B10665	~(P ∧ (D | (P ∧ S)))	extrop_PDSPxoxn
B2	00B21974	S ∧ ((P ∧ S) | (S ∧ D))	extrop_SSPxDSxox
B3	00B30CE8	~(S & ~(P & D))	extrop_SDPanan
B4	00B4070A	P ∧ (S & ~D)	extrop_PSDnax
B5	00B507A9	~(D ∧ (P & (S | D)))	extrop_DPSDoaxn
B6	00B616E9	D ∧ (P ∧ (S | (P & D)))	extrop_DPSDPaoxx
B7	00B70348	~(S & (P ∧ D))	extrop_SDPxan
B8	00B8074A	P ∧ (S & (P ∧ D))	extrop_PSDPxax
B9	00B906E6	~(D ∧ (S | (P & D)))	extrop_DSPDaoxn
BA	00BA0B09	(P & ~S) | D	extrop_DPSnao
BB	00BB0226	~S | D	MERGEPAINT extrop_DSno
BC	00BC1CE4	S ∧ (P & ~(S & D))	extrop_SPDSanax
BD	00BD0D7D	~((P ∧ D) & (S ∧ D))	extrop_SDxPDxan
BE	00BE0269	(P ∧ S) | D	extrop_DPSxo
BF	00BF08C9	~(P & S) | D	extrop_DPSano
C0	00C000CA	P & S	MERGECOPY extrop_PSa
C1	00C11B04	~(S ∧ (P | (~S & D)))	extrop_SPDSnaoxn
C2	00C21884	~(S ∧ (P | ~(S | D)))	extrop_SPDSonoxn
C3	00C3006A	~(P ∧ S)	extrop_PSxn
C4	00C40E04	S & (P | ~D)	extrop_SPDnoa
C5	00C50664	~(S ∧ (P | (S ∧ D)))	extrop_SPDSxoxn
C6	00C60708	S ∧ (~P & D)	extrop_SDPnax
C7	00C707AA	~(P ∧ (S & (P | D)))	extrop_PSDPoaxn
C8	00C803A8	S & (P | D)	extrop_SDPoa
C9	00C90184	~(S ∧ (P | D))	extrop_SPDoxn
CA	00CA0749	D ∧ (P & (S ∧ D))	extrop_DPSDxax
CB	00CB06E4	~(S ∧ (P | (S & D)))	extrop_SPDSaoxn
CC	00CC0020	S	SRCCOPY extrop_S

Table A.1: Ternary ROP codes

Hexadecimal Operation Code	Hexadecimal ROP Code	Boolean Function	Symbolic Name
CD	00CD0888	S | ~(P | D)	extrop_SDPono
CE	00CE0B08	S | (~P & D)	extrop_SDPnao
CF	00CF0224	S | ~P	extrop_SPno
D0	00D00E0A	~(P ∧ (S | (P ∧ D)))	extrop_PSDnoa
D1	00D1066A	P ∧ (~S & D)	extrop_PSDPxoxn
D2	00D20705	~(S ∧ (P & (S | D)))	extrop_PDSnax
D3	00D307A4	S ∧ ((P ∧ S) & (P ∧ D))	extrop_SPDSoaxn
D4	00D41D78	~(D & ~(P & S))	extrop_SSPxPDxax
D5	00D50CE9	P ∧ (S ∧ (D | (P & S)))	extrop_DPSanan
D6	00D616EA	~(D & (P ∧ S))	extrop_PSDPSaoxx
D7	00D70349	~(D & (P ∧ S))	extrop_DPSxan
D8	00D80745	P ∧ (D & (P ∧ S)	extrop_PDSPxax
D9	00D906E8	~(S ∧ (D | (P & S)))	extrop_SDPSaoxn
DA	00DA1CE9	D ∧ (P & ~(S & D))	extrop_DPSDanax
DB	00DB0D75	~((P ∧ S) & (S ∧ D))	extrop_SPxDSxan
DC	00DC0B04	S | (P & ~D)	extrop_SPDnao
DD	00DD0228	S | ~D	extrop_SDno
DE	00DE0268	S | (P ∧ D)	extrop_SDPxo
DF	00DF08C8	S | ~(P & D)	extrop_SDPano
E0	00E003A5	P & (D | S)	extrop_PDSoa
E1	00E10185	~(P ∧ (S | D))	extrop_PDSoxn
E2	00E20746	D ∧ (S & (P ∧ D))	extrop_DSPDxax
E3	00E306EA	~(P ∧ (S | (P & D)))	extrop_PSDPaoxn
E4	00E40748	S ∧ (D & (P ∧ S))	extrop_SDPSxax
E5	00E506E5	~(P ∧ (D | (P & S)))	extrop_PDSPaoxn
E6	00E61CE8	S ∧ (D & ~(P & S))	extrop_SDPSanax
E7	00E70D79	~((P ∧ S) & (P ∧ D))	extrop_SPxPDxan
E8	00E81D74	S ∧ ((P ∧ S) & (S ∧ D))	extrop_SSPxDSxax
E9	00E95CE6	~(D ∧ (S ∧ (P & ~(S & D))))	extrop_DSPDSanaxxn
EA	00EA02E9	(P & S) | D	extrop_DPSao
EB	00EB0849	~(P ∧ S) | D	extrop_DPSxno
EC	00EC02E8	S | (P & D)	extrop_SDPao

Table A.1: Ternary ROP codes

Hexadecimal Operation Code	Hexadecimal ROP Code	Boolean Function	Symbolic Name
ED	00ED0848	S | ~(P ∧ D)	extrop_SDPxno
EE	00EE0086	S | D	SRCPAINT extrop_DSo
EF	00EF0A08	~P | S | D	extrop_SDPnoo
F0	00F00021	P	PATCOPY extrop_P
F1	00F10885	P | ~(S | D)	extrop_PDSono
F2	00F20B05	P | (~S & D)	extrop_PDSnao
F3	00F3022A	P | ~S	extrop_PSno
F4	00F40B0A	P | (S & ~D)	extrop_PSDnao
F5	00F50225	P | ~D	extrop_PDno
F6	00F60265	P | (S ∧ D)	extrop_PDSxo
F7	00F708C5	P | ~(S & D)	extrop_PDSano
F8	00F802E5	P | (S & D)	extrop_PDSao
F9	00F90845	P | ~(S ∧ D)	extrop_PDSxno
FA	00FA0089	P | D	extrop_DPo
FB	00FB0A09	P | ~S | D	PATPAINT extrop_DPSnoo
FC	00FC008A	P | S	extrop_PSo
FD	00FD0A0A	P | S | ~D	extrop_PSDnoo
FE	00FE02A9	P | S | D	extrop_DPSoo
FF	00FF0062	1	WHITENESS extrop_1

B Message Cracker Summary

Table B.1: Message Cracker summary

A
void cls_OnActivate(HWND hwnd, UINT activateState, HWND hwndActDeact, BOOL minimized);
void cls_OnActivateApp(HWND hwnd, BOOL activating, DWORD threadId);
void cls_OnAskCBFormatName(HWND hwnd, int cchMax, LPTSTR fmtName);
C
void cls_OnCancelMode(HWND hwnd);
void cls_OnCaptureChanged(HWND hwnd)[e]
void cls_OnChangeCBChain(HWND hwnd, HWND hwndRemove, HWND hwndNext)
void cls_OnChar(HWND hwnd, TCHAR ch, int repeat);
void cls_OnCharToItem(HWND hwnd, UINT ch, HWND hwndList, int caretPos);
void cls_OnChildActivate(HWND hwnd);
void cls_OnClear(HWND hwnd);
void cls_OnClose(HWND hwnd);
void cls_OnCommand(HWND hwnd, int id, HWND hctl, UINT codeNotify);
void cls_OnCommNotify(HWND hwnd, int cid, UINT commFlags); *(obsolete)*
void cls_OnCompacting(HWND hwnd, UINT compactRatio); *(obsolete)*
int cls_OnCompareItem(HWND hwnd, const COMPAREITEMSTRUCT * cis);

---

[1]This does not support the logoff parameter (lParam) used at API level 4.*x*.

[e]Defined in the file extensions.h, included on the CD-ROM.

Table B.1: Message Cracker summary

BOOL cls_OnContextMenu(HWND hwnd, HWND hwndctl, int x, int y)[e]

void cls_OnCopy(HWND hwnd);

BOOL cls_OnCreate(HWND hwnd, LPCREATESTRUCT cs);

HBRUSH cls_OnCtlColor(HWND hwnd, HDC hdc, HWND hwndChild, int ctlType);

void cls_OnCut(HWND hwnd)

D

void cls_OnDeadChar(HWND hwnd, TCHAR ch, int repeat);

void cls_OnDeleteItem(HWND hwnd, const DELETEITEMSTRUCT * dis);

void cls_OnDestroy(HWND hwnd);

void cls_OnDestroyClipboard(HWND hwnd);

void cls_OnDevModeChange(HWND hwnd, LPCTSTR deviceName);

void cls_OnDisplayChange(HWND hwnd, UINT bitsperpixel, UINT csx, UINT csy);[e]

void cls_OnDrawItem(HWND hwnd, const DRAWITEMSTRUCT * drw);

void cls_OnDrawClipboard(HWND hwnd);

void cls_OnDropFiles(HWND hwnd, HDROP hdrop);

E

void cls_OnEnable(HWND hwnd, BOOL enableFlag);

void cls_OnEndSession(HWND hwnd, BOOL ending);[1]

void cls_OnEnterIdle(HWND hwnd, UINT idleSource, HWND hwndSource);

void cls_OnEnterMenuLoop(HWND hwnd, BOOL isTracking);[e]

void cls_OnEnterSizeMove(HWND hwnd);[e]

void cls_OnExitMenuLoop(HWND hwnd, BOOL isTracking);[e]

void cls_OnExitSizeMove(HWND hwnd);[e]

BOOL cls_OnEraseBkgnd(HWND hwnd, HDC hdc);

F

void cls_OnFontChange(HWND hwnd);

[1]This does not support the logoff parameter (1Param) used at API level 4.*x*.
[e]Defined in the file extensions.h, included on the CD-ROM.

Table B.1: Message Cracker summary

G
UINT cls_OnGetDlgCode(HWND hwnd, LPMSG msg);
HFONT cls_OnGetFont(HWND hwnd);
void cls_OnGetMinMaxInfo(HWND hwnd, LPMINMAXINFO MinMaxInfo);
int cls_OnGetText(HWND hwnd, int cchMax, LPTSTR text);
int cls_OnGetTextLength(HWND hwnd);

H
void cls_OnHelp(HWND hwnd, LPHELPINFO lphi);[e]
void cls_OnHScroll(HWND hwnd, HWND hctl, UINT sbcode, int sbpos);
void cls_OnHScrollClipboard(HWND hwnd, HWND hwndCBViewer, int sbpos);

I
BOOL cls_OnIconEraseBkgnd(HWND hwnd, HDC hdc);
BOOL cls_OnInitDialog(HWND hwnd, HWND hwndFocus, LPARAM lParam);
void cls_OnInitMenu(HWND hwnd, HMENU hmenu);
void cls_OnInitMenuPopup(HWND hwnd, HMENU hMenu, UINT menuPos, BOOL isSystemMenu);

K
void cls_OnKey(HWND hwnd, UINT vk, BOOL down, int repeat, UINT flags);
void cls_OnKillFocus(HWND hwnd, HWND hwndFocus);

L
void cls_OnLButtonDown(HWND hwnd, BOOL dblclk, int xClient, int yClient, UINT keyFlags);
void cls_OnLButtonUp(HWND hwnd, int xClient, int yClient, UINT keyFlags);

M
void cls_OnMButtonDown(HWND hwnd, BOOL dblclk, int xClient, int yClient, UINT keyFlags);
void cls_OnMButtonUp(HWND hwnd, int xClient, int yClient, UINT keyFlags);
void cls_OnMDIActivate(HWND hwnd, BOOL active, HWND hwndActivate, HWND hwndDeactivate);

[l]This does not support the logoff parameter (lParam) used at API level 4.*x*.

[e]Defined in the file extensions.h, included on the CD-ROM.

Table B.1: Message Cracker summary

```
BOOL cls_OnMDICascade(HWND hwndClient, UINT cmd);
```

```
HWND cls_OnMDICreate(HWND hwnd, const LPMDICREATESTRUCT mcs);
```

```
void cls_OnMDIDestroy(HWND hwndClient, HWND hwndDestroy);
```

```
HWND cls_OnMDIGetActive(HWND hwndClient);
```

```
void cls_OnMDIIconArrange(HWND hwndClient);
```

```
void cls_OnMDIMaximize(HWND hwndClient, HWND hwndMaximize);
```

```
HWND cls_OnMDINext(HWND hwndClient, HWND hwndCur, BOOL goPrev);
```

```
void cls_OnMDIRestore(HWND hwndClient, HWND hwndRestore);
```

```
HMENU cls_OnMDISetMenu(HWND hwnd, BOOL Refresh, HMENU hmenuFrame,
HMENU hmenuWindow);
```

```
BOOL cls_OnMDITile(HWND hwndClient, UINT tileOption);
```

```
void cls_OnMeasureItem(HWND hwnd, MEASUREITEMSTRUCT * mis);
```

```
DWORD cls_OnMenuChar(HWND hwnd, UINT ch, UINT flags, HMENU hmenu);
```

```
void cls_OnMenuSelect(HWND hwnd, HMENU hmenu, int menuItem, HMENU hmenuPopup,
UINT flags);
```

```
int  cls_OnMouseActivate(HWND hwnd, HWND topWnd, UINT hitCode, UINT msgno);
```

```
void cls_OnMouseMove(HWND hwnd, int xClient, int yClient, UINT keyFlags);
```

```
void cls_OnMove(HWND hwnd, int px, int py);
```

N

```
BOOL cls_OnNCActivate(HWND hwnd, BOOL Active, HWND hwndActDeact, BOOL Minimized);
```

```
UINT cls_OnNCCalcSize(HWND hwnd, BOOL calcValidRects, NCCALCSIZE_PARAMS * csp);
```

```
BOOL cls_OnNCCreate(HWND hwnd, LPCREATESTRUCT cs);
```

```
void cls_OnNCDestroy(HWND hwnd);
```

```
UINT cls_OnNCHitTest(HWND hwnd, int xScreen, int yScreen);
```

```
void cls_OnNCLButtonDown(HWND hwnd, BOOL dblclk, int xScreen, int yScreen,
UINT hitCode);
```

```
void cls_OnNCLButtonUp(HWND hwnd, int xScreen, int yScreen, UINT hitCode);
```

```
void cls_OnNCMButtonDown(HWND hwnd, BOOL dblclk, int xScreen, int yScreen,
UINT hitCode);
```

[1]This does not support the logoff parameter (lParam) used at API level 4.*x*.

[e]Defined in the file extensions.h, included on the CD-ROM.

Table B.1: Message Cracker summary

```
void cls_OnNCMButtonUp(HWND hwnd, int xScreen, int yScreen, UINT hitCode);
```

```
void cls_OnNCMouseMove(HWND hwnd, int xScreen, int yScreen, UINT hitCode);
```

```
void cls_OnNCPaint(HWND hwnd, HRGN hrgn);
```

```
void cls_OnNCRButtonDown(HWND hwnd, BOOL dblclk, int xScreen, int yScreen,
UINT hitCode);
```

```
void cls_OnNCRButtonUp(HWND hwnd, int xScreen, int yScreen, UINT hitCode);
```

```
HWND cls_OnNextDlgCtl(HWND hwnd, HWND hwndSetFocus, BOOL goNext);
```

P

```
void cls_OnPaint(HWND hwnd)
```

```
void cls_OnPaintClipboard(HWND hwnd, HWND hwndCBViewer, const LPPAINTSTRUCT ps);
```

```
void cls_OnPaletteChanged(HWND hwnd, HWND hwndPaletteChange);
```

```
void cls_OnPaletteIsChanging(HWND hwnd, HWND hwndPaletteChange);
```

```
void cls_OnParentNotify(HWND hwnd, UINT msgno, HWND hwndChild, int idChild);
```

```
void cls_OnPaste(HWND hwnd);
```

```
void cls_OnPower(HWND hwnd, int powerCode);
```

```
void cls_OnPrintClient(HWND hwnd, HDC hdc, UINT prFlags);e
```

Q

```
HICON cls_OnQueryDragIcon(HWND hwnd);
```

```
BOOL cls_OnQueryEndSession(HWND hwnd);
```

```
BOOL cls_OnQueryNewPalette(HWND hwnd);
```

```
BOOL cls_OnQueryOpen(HWND hwnd);
```

```
void cls_OnQueueSync(HWND hwnd);
```

```
void cls_OnQuit(HWND hwnd, int exitCode)
```

R

```
void cls_OnRButtonDown(HWND hwnd, BOOL dblclk, int xClient, int yClient,
UINT keyFlags);
```

```
void cls_OnRButtonUp(HWND hwnd, int xClient, int yClient, UINT keyFlags);
```

```
void cls_OnRenderAllFormats(HWND hwnd);
```

[1]This does not support the logoff parameter (lParam) used at API level 4.x.

[e]Defined in the file extensions.h, included on the CD-ROM.

Table B.1: Message Cracker summary

```
HANDLE cls_OnRenderFormat(HWND hwnd, UINT clipFmt);
```

S

```
BOOL cls_OnSetCursor(HWND hwnd, HWND hwndCursor, UINT hitCode, UINT msgno);
```

```
void cls_OnSetFocus(HWND hwnd, HWND oldwnd);
```

```
void cls_OnSetFont(HWND hwnd, HFONT hfont, BOOL redraw);
```

```
void cls_OnSetRedraw(HWND hwnd, BOOL redraw);
```

```
void cls_OnSetText(HWND hwnd, LPCTSTR Text);
```

```
void cls_OnSettingChange(HWND hwnd, UINT setFlags, LPCTSTR keyname);[e]
```

```
void cls_OnShowWindow(HWND hwnd, BOOL Show, UINT showStatus);[e]
```

```
void cls_OnSize(HWND hwnd, UINT sizeState, int cx, int cy);
```

```
void cls_OnSizeClipboard(HWND hwnd, HWND hwndCBViewer, const LPRECT rect);
```

```
void cls_OnSpoolerStatus(HWND hwnd, UINT spoolStatus, int jobsInQueue);
```

```
void cls_OnSysChar(HWND hwnd, TCHAR ch, int repeat);
```

```
void cls_OnSysColorChange(HWND hwnd);
```

```
void cls_OnSysCommand(HWND hwnd, UINT cmd, int x, int y);
```

```
void cls_OnSysDeadChar(HWND hwnd, TCHAR ch, int repeat);
```

```
void cls_OnSysKey(HWND hwnd, UINT vk, BOOL down, int repeat, UINT flags);
```

T

```
void cls_OnTimeChange(HWND hwnd);
```

```
void cls_OnTimer(HWND hwnd, UINT timerid);
```

U

```
void cls_OnUndo(HWND hwnd)
```

```
void cls_OnUserChanged(HWND hwnd);[e]
```

V

```
void cls_OnVKeyToItem(HWND hwnd, UINT vk, HWND hwndList, int caretPos);
```

```
void cls_OnVScroll(HWND hwnd, HWND hctl, UINT sbcode, int sbpos);
```

[1]This does not support the logoff parameter (1Param) used at API level 4.*x*.

[e]Defined in the file extensions.h, included on the CD-ROM.

Table B.1: Message Cracker summary

void cls_OnVScrollClipboard(HWND hwnd, HWND hwndCBViewer, int sbpos);
W
void cls_OnWindowPosChanged(HWND hwnd, const LPWINDOWPOS wpos);
BOOL cls_OnWindowPosChanging(HWND hwnd, LPWINDOWPOS wpos);
void cls_OnWinIniChange(HWND hwnd, LPCTSTR sectionName);

[1]This does not support the logoff parameter (lParam) used at API level 4.*x*.
[e]Defined in the file extensions.h, included on the CD-ROM.

Table B.2: Parameter descriptions

Parameter		
Type	**Name**	**Meaning**
UINT	activateState	WA_* value indicating the type of activation or deactivation.
BOOL	activating	TRUE if the application is activated; FALSE if deactivated.
BOOL	active	TRUE if the window is being activated.
UINT	bitsperpixel	New screen resolution, in bits per pixel.
BOOL	calcValidRects	TRUE to calculate valid rectangles.
int	caretPos	Current caret position in the list box.
int	cchMax	Maximum number of characters free in the buffer.
TCHAR	ch	ANSI or Unicode character code.
int	cid	Comm connection ID.
COMPAREITEMSTRUCT	cis	Provides information about the two items being compared.
UINT	clipFmt	Clipboard format ID.
UINT	codeNotify	Control notification code from child control.
UINT	commFlags	Comm event status flags.
LPCREATESTRUCT	cs	Creation parameters.

Table B.2: Parameter descriptions

Type	Name	Meaning
NCCALCSIZE_PARAMS *	csp	Parameter to be filled in for size.
UINT	csx	New screen size, in horizontal pixels.
UINT	csy	New screen size, in vertical pixels.
int	ctlType	CTLCOLOR_* symbol for the type of control.
int	cx	Size, in units. Unit type depends on call.
int	cy	Size, in units. Unit type depends on call.
BOOL	dblclk	Mouse: TRUE for double-click message.
LPCTSTR	deviceName	Name of the device whose parameters changed.
DELETEITEMSTRUCT *	dis	Contains information about the item deleted.
BOOL	down	OnKey handlers: key-down transition flag.
DRAWITEMSTRUCT *	drw	Contains information about the item to draw.
BOOL	enableFlag	TRUE if the window is being enabled; FALSE if being disabled.
BOOL	ending	TRUE if the session is ending.
int	exitCode	Value passed to PostQuitMessage.
UINT	flags	OnKey handlers: lParam flags.
LPTSTR	fmtName	Clipboard format name buffer.
BOOL	goNext	Controls interpretation of hwndSetFocus parameter: TRUE, hwndSetFocus is the handle of the window to receive focus; FALSE, hwndSetFocus is a flag value cast as an HWND. A FALSE value moves the focus to the next WS_TABSTOP control; otherwise, the focus moves to the previous WS_TABSTOP control.
BOOL	goPrev	TRUE to move to previous; FALSE to move to next.
HWND	hctl	Handle of the control that is generating the notification.

Table B.2: Parameter descriptions

Type	Name	Meaning
	Parameter	
HDC	hdc	Display context.
HDROP	hdrop	Handle to the DROP structure.
HFONT	hfont	Font handle of the font being set.
UINT	hitCode	HT_ hit-test result code.
HMENU	hmenu	Menu handle.
HMENU	hmenuPopup	Handle of the pop-up menu.
HRGN	hrgn	Region handle of the clipping region.
HWND	hwnd	Window receiving the message.
HWND	hwndActDeact	Window being activated or deactivated.
HWND	hwndActivate	Window being activated.
HWND	hwndCBViewer	Clipboard viewer window.
HWND	hwndChild	Child control handle.
HWND	hwndClient	MDI client window.
HWND	hwndCur	Handle of current MDI window.
HWND	hwndCursor	Window over which cursor is moving.
HWND	hwndDeactivate	Window being deactivated.
HWND	hwndDestroy	Window being destroyed.
HWND	hwndFocus	Handle of the control receiving the focus.
HWND	hwndList	Handle of the list box control.
HWND	hwndMaximize	Handle of the window being maximized.
HWND	hwndNext	Handle of the next window to move to.
HWND	hwndPalette-Change	Handle of the window that caused the palette change.
HWND	hwndRemove	Window being removed from the Clipboard chain.

Table B.2: Parameter descriptions

Parameter		
Type	**Name**	**Meaning**
HWND	hwndRestore	Handle of the window being restored.
HWND	hwndSetFocus	Handle of the window to receive the focus, or the flag indicating the direction of the focus shift. See goNext description.
HWND	hwndSource	Window handle of the source of the idle message when message is from dialog.
int	id	Control ID of the child control.
int	idChild	ID of the child window.
UINT	idleSource	Indicates the source of the idle message.
BOOL	isSystemMenu	TRUE if the menu is the system menu.
int	jobsInQueue	Queue count.
UINT	keyFlags	Mouse: MK_ status flags.
LPHELPINFO	lphi	Help information context.
LPMDICREATESTRUCT	mcs	Creation parameters.
UINT	menuPos	Index of the menu in the top-level menu bar.
UINT	menuItem	Command ID, or the position of the menu item.
BOOL	minimized	TRUE if the window is minimized.
LPMINMAXINFO	MinMaxInfo	Pointer to the structure to the control size and position.
MEASUREITEMSTRUCT *	mis	Structure to be filled in with measurement information.
LPMSG	msg	Pointer to the MSG structure.
UINT	msgno	Message number of the relevant message.
HWND	newwnd	Window receiving the focus.
HWND	oldwnd	Window losing the focus.
int	powerCode	Indicates the type of power notification.

Table B.2: Parameter descriptions

Parameter		Meaning
Type	**Name**	
LPPAINTSTRUCT	ps	PAINTSTRUCT containing information about the area to paint the Clipboard into.
UINT	prFlags	PRF_* flags indicating the nature of the print request.
int	px	Left position of the window: screen coordinates for overlapped and pop-up windows; client coordinates for child windows.
int	py	Top position of the window: screen coordinates for overlapped and pop-up windows; client coordinates for child windows.
LPRECT	rect	Rectangle defining the size of the Clipboard display that has resized.
int	repeat	Keyboard messages repeat count.
UINT	sbcode	Scroll bar code.
int	sbpos	Scroll bar position.
LPCTSTR	sectionName	ID of the section of the configuration that changed.
UINT	showStatus	SW_* codes.
UINT	sizeState	SIZE_ code.
UINT	spoolStatus	Spooler status.
LPTSTR	text	Pointer to the destination buffer for the text.
LPCTSTR	text	Pointer to the source buffer for the text.
DWORD	threadID	ID of the thread being activated.
UINT	tileOption	Indicates horizontal or vertical tiling, or skipping disabled windows.
UINT	timerid	ID of the timer.
HWND	topwnd	Top-most parent window on activation.
UINT	vk	Virtual-key code.

Table B.2: Parameter descriptions

Parameter		Meaning
Type	**Name**	**Meaning**
LPWINDOWPOS	wpos	Window position information.
int	xClient	Horizontal position, in client coordinates.
int	xScreen	Horizontal position, in screen coordinates.
int	yClient	Vertical position, in client coordinates.
int	yScreen	Vertical position, in screen coordinates.

Appendix

C windowsx.h, commctrl.h, extensions.h, and tchar.h

The files `windowsx.h` and `commctrl.h` contain several very useful macros that make interfacing to the API much easier. In particular, having to know how to interpret the values of `wParam` and `lParam` is nicely avoided. However, these files are both undocumented and incomplete. We have taken a step in the completion by supplying an additional file, `extensions.h`, as part of the `Template` application. We have documented many of these macros in the rest of this book, but our documentation is by no means complete. All of these macros are summarized in Table C.1. (This table was created by extracting the contents of the files and running editor scripts over them to format them for the tables, so they should contain everything that is in the files.) The file `tchar.h` contains definitions that support Unicode. In particular, it defines macros that extend string operations in a platform-independent manner, allowing the use of the same source code for both ANSI and Unicode applications. The description of `tchar.h` starts on page 1325.

windowsx.h, commctrl.h, and extensions.h

Table C.1: Summary of **windowsx.h**, **commctrl.h**, and **extensions.h** API interface

.h	Return Type	Function Name and Parameters
c w e	commctrl.h windowsx.h extensions.h	
c	BOOL	Animate_Close(HWND hani)
c	HWND	Animate_Create(HWND parent, int id, DWORD style, HINSTANCE hinstance)
c	BOOL	Animate_Open(HWND hani, LPCTSTR name)

Table C.1: Summary of `windowsx.h`, `commctrl.h`, and `extensions.h` API interface

.h	Return Type	Function Name and Parameters

c
w
e
	`commctrl.h`
	`windowsx.h`
	`extensions.h`	

c	BOOL	`Animate_Play(HWND hani, int from, int to, UINT rep)`
c	BOOL	`Animate_Seek(HWND hani, int frame)`
c	BOOL	`Animate_Stop(HWND hani)`
e	void	`Button_Click(HWND hCtl)`
w	BOOL	`Button_Enable(HWND hCtl, BOOL Enable)`
w	int	`Button_GetCheck(HWND hCtl)`
w	int	`Button_GetState(HWND hCtl)`
w	int	`Button_GetText(HWND hCtl, LPTSTR Buffer, UINT cchMax)`
w	int	`Button_GetTextLength(HWND hCtl)`
w	void	`Button_SetCheck(HWND hCtl, int check)`
w	UINT	`Button_SetState(HWND hCtl, int state)`
w	void	`Button_SetStyle(HWND hCtl, DWORD style, BOOL Redraw)`
w	BOOL	`Button_SetText(HWND hCtl, LPTSTR Text)`
w	void	`CheckDefDlgRecursion(BOOL * pfRecursion)`
w	int	`ComboBox_AddItemData(HWND hCtl, LPARAM data)`
w	int	`ComboBox_AddString(HWND hCtl, LPCTSTR String)`
w	int	`ComboBox_DeleteString(HWND hCtl, int index)`
w	int	`ComboBox_Dir(HWND hCtl, UINT attrs, LPCTSTR FileSpec)`
w	BOOL	`ComboBox_Enable(HWND hCtl, BOOL Enable)`
w	int	`ComboBox_FindItemData(HWND hCtl, int indexStart, LPARAM data)`
w	int	`ComboBox_FindString(HWND hCtl, int indexStart, LPCTSTR FindString)`
w	int	`ComboBox_FindStringExact(HWND hCtl, int indexStart, LPCTSTR FindString)`
w	int	`ComboBox_GetCount(HWND hCtl)`

Table C.1: Summary of `windowsx.h`, `commctrl.h`, and `extensions.h` API interface

.h	Return Type	Function Name and Parameters

c
w
e
	`commctrl.h`
	`windowsx.h`
	`extensions.h`	

w	`int`	`ComboBox_GetCurSel(HWND hCtl)`
w	`void`	`ComboBox_GetDroppedControlRect(HWND hCtl, LPRECT lprect)`
w	`BOOL`	`ComboBox_GetDroppedState(HWND hCtl)`
e	`int`	`ComboBox_GetDroppedWidth(HWND hCtl)`
w	`DWORD`	`ComboBox_GetEditSel(HWND hCtl)`
w	`UINT`	`ComboBox_GetExtendedUI(HWND hCtl)`
w	`LRESULT`	`ComboBox_GetItemData(HWND hCtl, int index)`
w	`int`	`ComboBox_GetItemHeight(HWND hCtl)`
w	`int`	`ComboBox_GetLBText(HWND hCtl, int index, LPTSTR Buffer)`
w	`int`	`ComboBox_GetLBTextLen(HWND hCtl, int index)`
e	`LCID`	`ComboBox_GetLocale(HWND hCtl)`
w	`int`	`ComboBox_GetText(HWND hCtl, LPTSTR Buffer, int BufferLength)`
w	`int`	`ComboBox_GetTextLength(HWND hCtl)`
e	`int`	`ComboBox_GetTopIndex(HWND hCtl)`
w	`int`	`ComboBox_InsertItemData(HWND hCtl, int index, LPARAM data)`
w	`int`	`ComboBox_InsertString(HWND hCtl, int index, LPCTSTR Text)`
w	`int`	`ComboBox_LimitText(HWND hCtl, int Limit)`
w	`int`	`ComboBox_ResetContent(HWND hCtl)`
w	`int`	`ComboBox_SelectItemData(HWND hCtl, int indexStart, LPARAM data)`
w	`int`	`ComboBox_SelectString(HWND hCtl, int indexStart, LPCTSTR SelectString)`
w	`int`	`ComboBox_SetCurSel(HWND hCtl, int index)`
e	`int`	`ComboBox_SetDroppedWidth(HWND hCtl)`
w	`int`	`ComboBox_SetEditSel(HWND hCtl, WORD StartPos, WORD EndPos)`

Table C.1: Summary of `windowsx.h`, `commctrl.h`, and `extensions.h` API interface

.h	Return Type	Function Name and Parameters

c
w
e
	`commctrl.h`
	`windowsx.h`
	`extensions.h`	

w	int	`ComboBox_SetExtendedUI(HWND hCtl, UINT flags)`
w	void	`ComboBox_SetHorizontalExtent(HWND hCtl, int cxExtent)`
w	int	`ComboBox_SetItemData(HWND hCtl, int index, LPARAM data)`
w	int	`ComboBox_SetItemHeight(HWND hCtl, int index, int height)`
e	LCID	`ComboBox_SetLocale(HWND hCtl, LCID locale)`
w	int	`ComboBox_SetText(HWND hCtl, LPCTSTR Text)`
e	int	`ComboBox_SetTopIndex(HWND hCtl, int index)`
w	BOOL	`ComboBox_ShowDropdown(HWND hCtl, BOOL Show)`
w	int	`CopyRgn(HRGN Dst, HRGN Src)`
c	HBITMAP	`CreateMappedBitmap(HINSTANCE hinst, int idbm, UINT flags, LPCOLORMAP map, int numMaps)`
c	void	`CreateStatusWindow(LONG style, LPCTSTR text, HWND parent, UINT id)`
c	HWND	`CreateToolbarEx(HWND hparent, DWORD style, UINT id, int bitmapcount, HINSTANCE hbminst, UINT hbmid, LPCTBBUTTON lpbuttons, int dxbm, int dybm, UINT structsize)`
c	HWND	`CreateUpDownControl(DWORD style, int x, int y, int cx, int cy, HWND hparent, int id, HINSTANCE hinst, HWND hbuddy, int upper, int lower, int pos)`
w	LRESULT	`DefDlgProcEx(HWND hwnd, UINT msg, WPARAM wParam, LPARAM lParam, BOOL * pfRecursion)`
w	BOOL	`DeleteBitmap(HBITMAP hbm)`
w	BOOL	`DeleteBrush(HBRUSH hbr)`
w	BOOL	`DeleteFont(HFONT hfont)`
w	BOOL	`DeletePalette(HPALETTE hpal)`
w	BOOL	`DeletePen(HPEN hpen)`
w	BOOL	`DeleteRgn(HRGN hrgn)`
c	void	`DrawInsert(HWND hparent, HWND hlb, int nitem)`

Table C.1: Summary of **windowsx.h**, **commctrl.h**, and **extensions.h** API interface

.h	Return Type	Function Name and Parameters
c w e	**commctrl.h** **windowsx.h** **extensions.h**	
c	void	DrawStatusText(HDC hdc, LPRECT lprect, LPCTSTR text, UINT flags)
w	BOOL	Edit_CanUndo(HWND hCtl)
e	int	Edit_CharFromPos(HWND hwnd, int x, int y)
w	void	Edit_EmptyUndoBuffer(HWND hCtl)
w	BOOL	Edit_Enable(HWND hCtl, BOOL Enable)
w	BOOL	Edit_FmtLines(HWND hCtl, BOOL AddEOL)
w	int	Edit_GetFirstVisibleLine(HWND hCtl)
w	HLOCAL	Edit_GetHandle(HWND hCtl) *(obsolete)*
w	int	Edit_GetLine(HWND hCtl, UINT line LPTSTR Buffer, int BufferLength)
w	int	Edit_GetLineCount(HWND hCtl)
w	BOOL	Edit_GetModify(HWND hCtl)
w	TCHAR	Edit_GetPasswordChar(HWND hCtl)
w	void	Edit_GetRect(HWND hCtl, LPRECT lprc)
w	DWORD	Edit_GetSel(HWND hCtl)
w	int	Edit_GetText(HWND hCtl, LPCTSTR Buffer, int BufferLength)
w	int	Edit_GetTextLength(HWND hCtl)
e	int	Edit_GetThumb(HWND hCtl)
w	EDITWORD- BREAKPROC	Edit_GetWordBreakProc(HWND hCtl)
w	void	Edit_LimitText(HWND hCtl, UINT Limit)
w	int	Edit_LineFromChar(HWND hCtl, int CharPos)
w	int	Edit_LineIndex(HWND hCtl, int line)
w	int	Edit_LineLength(HWND hCtl, int line)
e	BOOL	Edit_LineScroll(HWND hCtl, int hScroll, int vScroll)

Table C.1: Summary of `windowsx.h`, `commctrl.h`, and `extensions.h` API interface

.h	Return Type	Function Name and Parameters

c
w
e
	`commctrl.h`
	`windowsx.h`
	`extensions.h`	

e	void	`Edit_PosFromChar(HWND hCtl, LPPOINT pt, int pos)`
w	void	`Edit_ReplaceSel(HWND hCtl, LPCTSTR Replacement)`
w	void	`Edit_Scroll(HWND hCtl, int dv, int dh)`
w	BOOL	`Edit_ScrollCaret(HWND hCtl)`
w	void	`Edit_SetHandle(HWND hCtl, HLOCAL h)` *(obsolete)*
e	void	`Edit_SetMargins(HWND hCtl, int whichMargin, int left, int right)`
w	void	`Edit_SetModify(HWND hCtl, BOOL Modified)`
w	void	`Edit_SetPasswordChar(HWND hCtl, TCHAR ch)`
w	BOOL	`Edit_SetReadOnly(HWND hCtl, BOOL ReadOnly)`
w	void	`Edit_SetRect(HWND hCtl, LPRECT lprc)`
w	void	`Edit_SetRectNoPaint(HWND hCtl, LPRECT lprc)`
w	void	`Edit_SetSel(HWND hCtl, UINT StartPos, UINT EndPos)`
w	void	`Edit_SetTabStops(HWND hCtl, int cTabs, LPINT lpTabs)`
w	BOOL	`Edit_SetText(HWND hCtl, LPCTSTR text)`
w	void	`Edit_SetWordBreakProc(HWND hCtl, EDITWORDBREAKPROC WordBreakProc)`
e	void	`Edit_SetWordBreakProcEx(HWND hCtl, EDITWORDBREAKPROCEX WordBreakProc)`
w	BOOL	`Edit_Undo(HWND hCtl)`
w	void	`FORWARD_WM_ACTIVATE(HWND hwnd, UINT state, HWND hwndActDeact, BOOL minimized, MSGFN)`
w	void	`FORWARD_WM_ACTIVATEAPP(HWND hwnd, BOOL Activate, DWORD threadId, MSGFN)`
w	void	`FORWARD_WM_ASKCBFORMATNAME(HWND hwnd, int NameLength, LPTSTR Name, MSGFN)`
w	void	`FORWARD_WM_CANCELMODE(HWND hwnd, MSGFN)`

Table C.1: Summary of `windowsx.h`, `commctrl.h`, and `extensions.h` API interface

.h	Return Type	Function Name and Parameters

c
w
e
	`commctrl.h`
	`windowsx.h`
	`extensions.h`	

e	int	FORWARD_WM_CAPTURECHANGED(HWND hwnd)
w	void	FORWARD_WM_CHANGECBCHAIN(HWND hwnd, HWND hwndRemove, HWND hwndNext, MSGFN)
w	void	FORWARD_WM_CHAR(HWND hwnd, TCHAR ch, int Repeat, MSGFN)
w	int	FORWARD_WM_CHARTOITEM(HWND hwnd, UINT ch, HWND hList, int iCaret, MSGFN)
w	void	FORWARD_WM_CHILDACTIVATE(HWND hwnd, MSGFN)
w	void	FORWARD_WM_CLEAR(HWND hwnd, MSGFN)
w	void	FORWARD_WM_CLOSE(HWND hwnd, MSGFN)
w	void	FORWARD_WM_COMMAND(HWND hwnd, int id, HWND hCtl, UINT codeNotify, MSGFN)
w	void	FORWARD_WM_COMMNOTIFY(HWND hwnd, int cid, UINT flags, MSGFN)
w	void	FORWARD_WM_COMPACTING(HWND hwnd, UINT compactRatio, MSGFN) *(obsolete)*
w	int	FORWARD_WM_COMPAREITEM(HWND hwnd, const COMPAREITEMSTRUCT * lpCompareItem, MSGFN)
e	BOOL	FORWARD_WM_CONTEXTMENU(HWND hwnd, HWND hwndCtl, int xPos, int yPos, MSGFN)
w	void	FORWARD_WM_COPY(HWND hwnd, MSGFN)
w	BOOL	FORWARD_WM_CREATE(HWND hwnd, LPCREATESTRUCT lpCreateStruct, MSGFN)
w	HBRUSH	FORWARD_WM_CTLCOLORBTN(HWND hwnd, HDC hdc, HWND hChild, MSGFN)
w	HBRUSH	FORWARD_WM_CTLCOLORDLG(HWND hwnd, HDC hdc, HWND hChild, MSGFN)
w	HBRUSH	FORWARD_WM_CTLCOLOREDIT(HWND hwnd, HDC hdc, HWND hChild, MSGFN)
w	HBRUSH	FORWARD_WM_CTLCOLORLISTBOX(HWND hwnd, HDC hdc, HWND hChild, MSGFN)
w	HBRUSH	FORWARD_WM_CTLCOLORMSGBOX(HWND hwnd, HDC hdc, HWND hChild, MSGFN) *(See Chapter 17).*

Table C.1: Summary of `windowsx.h`, `commctrl.h`, and `extensions.h` API interface

.h	Return Type	Function Name and Parameters

c
w
e
	`commctrl.h`
	`windowsx.h`
	`extensions.h`	

w	HBRUSH	FORWARD_WM_CTLCOLORSCROLLBAR(HWND hwnd, HDC hdc, HWND hChild, MSGFN)
w	HBRUSH	FORWARD_WM_CTLCOLORSTATIC(HWND hwnd, HDC hdc, HWND hChild, MSGFN)
w	void	FORWARD_WM_CUT(HWND hwnd, MSGFN)
w	void	FORWARD_WM_DEADCHAR(HWND hwnd, TCHAR ch, int RepeatCount, MSGFN)
w	void	FORWARD_WM_DELETEITEM(HWND hwnd, const DELETEITEMSTRUCT * lpDeleteItem, MSGFN)
w	void	FORWARD_WM_DESTROY(HWND hwnd, MSGFN)
w	void	FORWARD_WM_DESTROYCLIPBOARD(HWND hwnd, MSGFN)
w	void	FORWARD_WM_DEVMODECHANGE(HWND hwnd, LPCTSTR DeviceName, MSGFN)
e	void	FORWARD_WM_DISPLAYCHANGE(HWND hwnd, UINT BitsPerPixel, UINT cxScreen, UINT cyScreen, MSGFN)
w	void	FORWARD_WM_DRAWCLIPBOARD(HWND hwnd, MSGFN)
w	void	FORWARD_WM_DRAWITEM(HWND hwnd, const DRAWITEMSTRUCT * lpDrawItem, MSGFN)
w	void	FORWARD_WM_DROPFILES(HWND hwnd, HDROP hdrop, MSGFN)
w	void	FORWARD_WM_ENABLE(HWND hwnd, BOOL Enable, MSGFN)
w	void	FORWARD_WM_ENDSESSION(HWND hwnd, BOOL Ending, MSGFN)
w	void	FORWARD_WM_ENTERIDLE(HWND hwnd, UINT source, HWND hwndSource, MSGFN)
e	void	FORWARD_WM_ENTERMENULOOP(HWND hwnd, BOOL isTrackPopup, MSGFN)
e	void	FORWARD_WM_ENTERSIZEMOVE(HWND hwnd, MSGFN)
e	void	FORWARD_WM_EXITMENULOOP(HWND hwnd, BOOL isTrackPopup, MSGFN)
e	void	FORWARD_WM_EXITSIZEMOVE(HWND hwnd, MSGFN)
w	BOOL	FORWARD_WM_ERASEBKGND(HWND hwnd, HDC hdc, MSGFN)

Table C.1: Summary of `windowsx.h`, `commctrl.h`, and `extensions.h` API interface

.h	Return Type	Function Name and Parameters

c
w
e
	`commctrl.h`
	`windowsx.h`
	`extensions.h`	

w	`void`	`FORWARD_WM_FONTCHANGE(HWND hwnd, MSGFN)`
w	`UINT`	`FORWARD_WM_GETDLGCODE(HWND hwnd, LPMSG lpmsg, MSGFN)`
w	`HFONT`	`FORWARD_WM_GETFONT(HWND hwnd, MSGFN)`
w	`void`	`FORWARD_WM_GETMINMAXINFO(HWND hwnd, lpMinMaxInfo, MSGFN)`
w	`int`	`FORWARD_WM_GETTEXT(HWND hwnd, int BufferLength, LPTSTR Buffer, MSGFN)`
w	`int`	`FORWARD_WM_GETTEXTLENGTH(HWND hwnd, MSGFN)`
e	`void`	`FORWARD_WM_HELP(HWND hwnd, LPHELPINFO lphi, MSGFN)`
w	`void`	`FORWARD_WM_HSCROLL(HWND hwnd, HWND hCtl, UINT code, int pos, MSGFN)`
w	`void`	`FORWARD_WM_HSCROLLCLIPBOARD(HWND hwnd, HWND hwndCBViewer, UINT code, int pos, MSGFN)`
w	`BOOL`	`FORWARD_WM_ICONERASEBKGND(HWND hwnd, HDC hdc, MSGFN)`
w	`BOOL`	`FORWARD_WM_INITDIALOG(HWND hwnd, HWND hwndFocus, LPARAM lParam, MSGFN)`
w	`void`	`FORWARD_WM_INITMENU(HWND hwnd, HMENU hMenu, MSGFN)`
w	`void`	`FORWARD_WM_INITMENUPOPUP(HWND hwnd, HMENU hMenu, UINT item, BOOL SystemMenu, MSGFN)`
w	`void`	`FORWARD_WM_KEYDOWN(HWND hwnd, UINT vk, int RepeatCount, UINT flags, MSGFN)`
w	`void`	`FORWARD_WM_KEYUP(HWND hwnd, UINT vk, int RepeatCount, UINT flags, MSGFN)`
w	`void`	`FORWARD_WM_KILLFOCUS(HWND hwnd, HWND NewFocus, MSGFN)`
w	`void`	`FORWARD_WM_LBUTTONDOWN(HWND hwnd, BOOL DoubleClick, int x, int y, UINT keyFlags, MSGFN)`
w	`void`	`FORWARD_WM_LBUTTONUP(HWND hwnd, short x, short y, UINT keyFlags, MSGFN)`
w	`void`	`FORWARD_WM_MBUTTONDOWN(HWND hwnd, BOOL DoubleClick, int x, int y, UINT keyFlags, MSGFN)`

Table C.1: Summary of `windowsx.h`, `commctrl.h`, and `extensions.h` API interface

.h	Return Type	Function Name and Parameters

c
w
e
	`commctrl.h`
	`windowsx.h`
	`extensions.h`	

w	void	`FORWARD_WM_MBUTTONUP(HWND hwnd, int x, int y, UINT keyFlags, MSGFN)`
w	void	`FORWARD_WM_MDIACTIVATE(HWND hwnd, BOOL Active, HWND hwndActivate, HWND hwndDeactivate, MSGFN)`
w	BOOL	`FORWARD_WM_MDICASCADE(HWND hwnd, UINT cmd, MSGFN)`
w	HWND	`FORWARD_WM_MDICREATE(HWND hwnd, const LPMDICREATESTRUCT lpmcs, MSGFN)`
w	void	`FORWARD_WM_MDIDESTROY(HWND hwnd, HWND hwndDestroy, MSGFN)`
w	HWND	`FORWARD_WM_MDIGETACTIVE(HWND hwnd, MSGFN)`
w	void	`FORWARD_WM_MDIICONARRANGE(HWND hwnd, MSGFN)`
w	void	`FORWARD_WM_MDIMAXIMIZE(HWND hwnd, HWND hwndMaximize, MSGFN)`
w	HWND	`FORWARD_WM_MDINEXT(HWND hwnd, HWND hwndCur, BOOL Prev, MSGFN)`
w	void	`FORWARD_WM_MDIRESTORE(HWND hwnd, HWND hwndRestore, MSGFN)`
w	HMENU	`FORWARD_WM_MDISETMENU(HWND hwnd, BOOL Refresh, HMENU hmenuFrame, HMENU hmenuWindow, MSGFN)`
w	BOOL	`FORWARD_WM_MDITILE(HWND hwnd, UINT cmd, MSGFN)`
w	void	`FORWARD_WM_MEASUREITEM(HWND hwnd, MEASUREITEMSTRUCT * lpMeasureItem, MSGFN)`
w	DWORD	`FORWARD_WM_MENUCHAR(HWND hwnd, UINT ch, UINT flags, HMENU hmenu, MSGFN)`
w	void	`FORWARD_WM_MENUSELECT(HWND hwnd, HMENU hmenu, int item, HMENU hmenuPopup, UINT flags, MSGFN)`
w	int	`FORWARD_WM_MOUSEACTIVATE(HWND hwnd, HWND hwndTopLevel, UINT codeHitTest, UINT msg, MSGFN)`
w	void	`FORWARD_WM_MOUSEMOVE(HWND hwnd, int x, int y, UINT keyFlags, MSGFN)`
w	void	`FORWARD_WM_MOVE(HWND hwnd, int x, int y, MSGFN)`
w	BOOL	`FORWARD_WM_NCACTIVATE(HWND hwnd, BOOL Active, HWND hwndActDeact, BOOL Minimized, MSGFN)`

Table C.1: Summary of `windowsx.h`, `commctrl.h`, and `extensions.h` API interface

.h	Return Type	Function Name and Parameters

c
w
e
	`commctrl.h`
	`windowsx.h`
	`extensions.h`	

w	UINT	FORWARD_WM_NCCALCSIZE(HWND hwnd, BOOL CalcValidRects, NCCALCSIZE_PARAMS * lpcsp, MSGFN)
w	BOOL	FORWARD_WM_NCCREATE(HWND hwnd, LPCREATESTRUCT lpCreateStruct, MSGFN)
w	void	FORWARD_WM_NCDESTROY(HWND hwnd, MSGFN)
w	UINT	FORWARD_WM_NCHITTEST(HWND hwnd, short x, short y, MSGFN)
w	void	FORWARD_WM_NCLBUTTONDOWN(HWND hwnd, BOOL DoubleClick, int x, int y, UINT codeHitTest, MSGFN)
w	void	FORWARD_WM_NCLBUTTONUP(HWND hwnd, int x, int y, UINT codeHitTest, MSGFN)
w	void	FORWARD_WM_NCMBUTTONDOWN(HWND hwnd, BOOL DoubleClick, int x, int y, UINT codeHitTest, MSGFN)
w	void	FORWARD_WM_NCMBUTTONUP(HWND hwnd, int x, int y, UINT codeHitTest, MSGFN)
w	void	FORWARD_WM_NCMOUSEMOVE(HWND hwnd, int x, int y, UINT codeHitTest, MSGFN)
w	void	FORWARD_WM_NCPAINT(HWND hwnd, HRGN hrgn, MSGFN)
w	void	FORWARD_WM_NCRBUTTONDOWN(HWND hwnd, BOOL DoubleClick, int x, int y, UINT codeHitTest, MSGFN)
w	void	FORWARD_WM_NCRBUTTONUP(HWND hwnd, int x, int y, UINT codeHitTest, MSGFN)
w	HWND	FORWARD_WM_NEXTDLGCTL(HWND hwnd, HWND hwndSetFocus, BOOL Next, MSGFN)
c	LRESULT	FORWARD_WM_NOTIFY(HWND hwnd, int id, NMHDR * hdr, MSGFN)
w	void	FORWARD_WM_PAINT(HWND hwnd, MSGFN)
w	void	FORWARD_WM_PAINTCLIPBOARD(HWND hwnd, HWND hwndCBViewer, LPPAINTSTRUCT lpPaintStruct, MSGFN)
w	void	FORWARD_WM_PALETTECHANGED(HWND hwnd, HWND hwndPaletteChange, MSGFN)
w	void	FORWARD_WM_PALETTEISCHANGING(HWND hwnd, HWND PaletteChange, MSGFN)

Table C.1: Summary of windowsx.h, commctrl.h, and extensions.h API interface

.h	Return Type	Function Name and Parameters
c w e	commctrl.h windowsx.h extensions.h	
w	void	FORWARD_WM_PARENTNOTIFY(HWND hwnd, UINT msg, HWND hChild, int idChild, MSGFN)
w	void	FORWARD_WM_PASTE(HWND hwnd, MSGFN)
w	void	FORWARD_WM_POWER(HWND hwnd, int code, MSGFN)
e	void	FORWARD_WM_PRINTCLIENT(HWND hwnd, HDC hdc, UINT Flags, MSGFN)
w	HICON	FORWARD_WM_QUERYDRAGICON(HWND hwnd, MSGFN)
w	BOOL	FORWARD_WM_QUERYENDSESSION(HWND hwnd, MSGFN)
w	BOOL	FORWARD_WM_QUERYNEWPALETTE(HWND hwnd, MSGFN)
w	BOOL	FORWARD_WM_QUERYOPEN(HWND hwnd, MSGFN)
w	void	FORWARD_WM_QUEUESYNC(HWND hwnd, MSGFN)
w	void	FORWARD_WM_QUIT(HWND hwnd, int exitCode, MSGFN)
w	void	FORWARD_WM_RBUTTONDOWN(HWND hwnd, BOOL DoubleClick, int x, int y, UINT keyFlags, MSGFN)
w	void	FORWARD_WM_RBUTTONUP(HWND hwnd, int x, int y, UINT keyFlags, MSGFN)
w	void	FORWARD_WM_RENDERALLFORMATS(HWND hwnd, MSGFN)
w	HANDLE	FORWARD_WM_RENDERFORMAT(HWND hwnd, UINT fmt, MSGFN)
w	BOOL	FORWARD_WM_SETCURSOR(HWND hwnd, HWND hwndCursor, UINT codeHitTest, UINT msg, MSGFN)
w	void	FORWARD_WM_SETFOCUS(HWND hwnd, HWND OldFocus, MSGFN)
w	void	FORWARD_WM_SETFONT(HWND hwnd, HFONT hfont, BOOL Redraw, MSGFN)
w	void	FORWARD_WM_SETREDRAW(HWND hwnd, BOOL Redraw, MSGFN)
w	void	FORWARD_WM_SETTEXT(HWND hwnd, LPCTSTR text, MSGFN)
e	void	FORWARD_WM_SETTINGCHANGE(HWND hwnd, UINT Flag, LPCTSTR key, MSGFN)
w	void	FORWARD_WM_SHOWWINDOW(HWND hwnd, BOOL Show, UINT status, MSGFN)

Table C.1: Summary of `windowsx.h`, `commctrl.h`, and `extensions.h` API interface

.h	Return Type	Function Name and Parameters

c
w
e
	`commctrl.h`
	`windowsx.h`
	`extensions.h`	

w	`void`	`FORWARD_WM_SIZE(HWND hwnd, UINT state, int cx, int cy, MSGFN)`
w	`void`	`FORWARD_WM_SIZECLIPBOARD(HWND hwnd, HWND hwndCBViewer,` `const LPRECT lprc, MSGFN)`
w	`void`	`FORWARD_WM_SPOOLERSTATUS(HWND hwnd, UINT status,` `int cJobInQueue, MSGFN)`
w	`void`	`FORWARD_WM_SYSCHAR(HWND hwnd, TCHAR ch, int RepeatCount,` `MSGFN)`
w	`void`	`FORWARD_WM_SYSCOLORCHANGE(HWND hwnd, MSGFN)`
w	`void`	`FORWARD_WM_SYSCOMMAND(HWND hwnd, UINT cmd, int x, int y,` `MSGFN)`
w	`void`	`FORWARD_WM_SYSDEADCHAR(HWND hwnd, TCHAR ch, int RepeatCount,` `MSGFN)`
w	`void`	`FORWARD_WM_SYSKEYDOWN(HWND hwnd, UINT vk, int RepeatCount,` `UINT flags, MSGFN)`
w	`void`	`FORWARD_WM_SYSKEYUP(HWND hwnd, UINT vk, int RepeatCount,` `UINT flags, MSGFN)`
w	`void`	`FORWARD_WM_TIMECHANGE(HWND hwnd, MSGFN)`
w	`void`	`FORWARD_WM_TIMER(HWND hwnd, UINT id, MSGFN)`
w	`void`	`FORWARD_WM_UNDO(HWND hwnd, MSGFN)`
e	`void`	`FORWARD_WM_USERCHANGED(HWND hwnd, MSGFN)`
w	`int`	`FORWARD_WM_VKEYTOITEM(HWND hwnd, UINT vk, HWND hList,` `int iCaret, MSGFN)`
w	`void`	`FORWARD_WM_VSCROLL(HWND hwnd, HWND hCtl, UINT code, int pos,` `MSGFN)`
w	`void`	`FORWARD_WM_VSCROLLCLIPBOARD(HWND hwnd, HWND hwndCBViewer,` `UINT code, int pos, MSGFN)`
w	`void`	`FORWARD_WM_WINDOWPOSCHANGED(HWND hwnd, lpwpos, MSGFN)`
w	`BOOL`	`FORWARD_WM_WINDOWPOSCHANGING(HWND hwnd, LPWINDOWPOS lpwpos,` `MSGFN)`
w	`void`	`FORWARD_WM_WININICHANGE(HWND hwnd, LPCTSTR SectionName,` `MSGFN)`

Table C.1: Summary of `windowsx.h`, `commctrl.h`, and `extensions.h` API interface

.h	Return Type	Function Name and Parameters

c
w
e
	`commctrl.h`
	`windowsx.h`
	`extensions.h`	

c	void	`GetEffectiveClientRect(HWND hwnd, LPRECT lprect,` `LPINT lpinfo)`
w	HWND	`GetFirstChild(HWND hwnd)`
w	HWND	`GetFirstSibling(HWND hwnd)`
w	HMODULE	`GetInstanceModule(HINSTANCE hinstance)`
w	HWND	`GetLastSibling(HWND hwnd)`
w	HWND	`GetNextSibling(HWND hwnd)`
w	HWND	`GetPrevSibling(HWND hwnd)`
w	HBRUSH	`GetStockBrush(int brushid)`
w	HFONT	`GetStockFont(int fontid)`
w	HPEN	`GetStockPen(int penid)`
w	DWORD	`GetWindowExStyle(HWND hwnd)`
w	HFONT	`GetWindowFont(HWND hwnd)`
w ――― e	int	`GetWindowID(HWND hwnd)` (*incorrect in* `windowsx.h`)
w	HMODULE	`GetWindowInstance(HWND hwnd)`
w	HWND	`GetWindowOwner(HWND hwnd)`
w	DWORD	`GetWindowStyle(HWND hwnd)`
w	LPVOID	`GlobalAllocPtr(UINT flags, UINT cb)`
w	BOOL	`GlobalFreePtr(LPVOID lp)`
w	BOOL	`GlobalLockPtr(LPVOID lp)`
w	HGLOBAL	`GlobalPtrHandle(LPVOID lp)`
w	LPVOID	`GlobalReAllocPtr(LPVOID lp, UINT cbNew, UINT flags)`
w	BOOL	`GlobalUnlockPtr(lp)`

Table C.1: Summary of `windowsx.h`, `commctrl.h`, and `extensions.h` API interface

.h	Return Type	Function Name and Parameters

c
w
e
	`commctrl.h`
	`windowsx.h`
	`extensions.h`	

w	LRESULT	`HANDLE_MSG(HWND hwnd, UINT message, result (*fn)())`
w	0	`HANDLE_WM_ACTIVATE(HWND hwnd, WPARAM wParam, LPARAM lParam, void (*OnActivate)(HWND hwnd, UINT state, HWND hwndActDeact, BOOL minimized))`
w	0	`HANDLE_WM_ACTIVATEAPP(HWND hwnd, WPARAM wParam, LPARAM lParam, void (*OnActivateApp)(HWND hwnd, BOOL activate, DWORD threadid))`
w	0	`HANDLE_WM_ASKCBFORMATNAME(HWND hwnd, WPARAM wParam, LPARAM lParam, void (*OnAskCBFormatName)(HWND hwnd, int cchMax, LPTSTR rgchName))`
w	0	`HANDLE_WM_CANCELMODE(HWND hwnd, WPARAM wParam, LPARAM lParam, void (*OnCancelMode)(HWND hwnd))`
e	int	`HANDLE_WM_CAPTURECHANGED(HWND hwnd, WPARAM wParam, LPARAM lParam, void (*OnCaptureChanged)(HWND hwnd))`
w	0	`HANDLE_WM_CHANGECBCHAIN(HWND hwnd, WPARAM wParam, LPARAM lParam, void (*OnChangeCBChain)(HWND hwnd, HWND hwndRemove, HWND hwndNext))`
w	0	`HANDLE_WM_CHAR(HWND hwnd, WPARAM wParam, LPARAM lParam, void (*OnChar)(HWND hwnd, TCHAR ch, int RepeatCount))`
w	LRESULT	`HANDLE_WM_CHARTOITEM(HWND hwnd, WPARAM wParam, LPARAM lParam, int (*OnCharToItem)(HWND hwnd, UINT ch, HWND hList, int iCaret))`
w	0	`HANDLE_WM_CHILDACTIVATE(HWND hwnd, WPARAM wParam, LPARAM lParam, void (*OnChildActivate)(HWND hwnd))`
w	0	`HANDLE_WM_CLEAR(HWND hwnd, WPARAM wParam, LPARAM lParam, void (*OnClear)(HWND hwnd))`
w	0	`HANDLE_WM_CLOSE(HWND hwnd, WPARAM wParam, LPARAM lParam, void (*OnClose)(HWND hwnd))`
w	0	`HANDLE_WM_COMMAND(HWND hwnd, WPARAM wParam, LPARAM lParam, void (*OnCommand)(HWND hwnd, int id, HWND hCtl, UINT codeNotify))`
w	0	`HANDLE_WM_COMMNOTIFY(HWND hwnd, WPARAM wParam, LPARAM lParam, void (*OnCommNotify)(HWND hwnd, int cid, UINT flags))`

Table C.1: Summary of `windowsx.h`, `commctrl.h`, and `extensions.h` API interface

.h	Return Type	Function Name and Parameters

c
w
e
	`commctrl.h`
	`windowsx.h`
	`extensions.h`	

w	0	HANDLE_WM_COMPACTING(HWND hwnd, WPARAM wParam, LPARAM lParam, void (*OnCompacting)(HWND hwnd, UINT compactratio)) *(obsolete)*
w	LRESULT	HANDLE_WM_COMPAREITEM(HWND hwnd, WPARAM wParam, LPARAM lParam, int (*OnCompareItem)(HWND hwnd, const COMPAREITEMSTRUCT * lpCompareItem))
e	BOOL	HANDLE_WM_CONTEXTMENU(HWND hwnd, WPARAM wParam, LPARAM lParam, BOOL (*OnContextMenu)(HWND hwnd, HWND hwndCtl, int xPos, int yPos))
w	0	HANDLE_WM_COPY(HWND hwnd, WPARAM wParam, LPARAM lParam, void (*OnCopy)(HWND hwnd))
w	LRESULT	HANDLE_WM_CREATE(HWND hwnd, WPARAM wParam, LPARAM lParam, BOOL (*OnCreate)(HWND hwnd, LPCREATESTRUCT lpCreateStruct))
w	LRESULT	HANDLE_WM_CTLCOLORBTN(HWND hwnd, WPARAM wParam, LPARAM lParam, HBRUSH (*OnCtlColor)(HWND hwnd, HDC hdc, HWND hChild, int type))
w	LRESULT	HANDLE_WM_CTLCOLORDLG(HWND hwnd, WPARAM wParam, LPARAM lParam, HBRUSH (*OnCtlColor)(HWND hwnd, HDC hdc, HWND hChild, int type))
w	LRESULT	HANDLE_WM_CTLCOLOREDIT(HWND hwnd, WPARAM wParam, LPARAM lParam, HBRUSH (*OnCtlColor)(HWND hwnd, HDC hdc, HWND hChild, int type))
w	LRESULT	HANDLE_WM_CTLCOLORLISTBOX(HWND hwnd, WPARAM wParam, LPARAM lParam, HBRUSH (*OnCtlColor)(HWND hwnd, HDC hdc, HWND hChild, int type))
w	LRESULT	HANDLE_WM_CTLCOLORMSGBOX(HWND hwnd, WPARAM wParam, LPARAM lParam, HBRUSH (*OnCtlColor)(HWND hwnd, HDC hdc, HWND hChild, int type)) *(See Chapter 17)*.
w	LRESULT	HANDLE_WM_CTLCOLORSCROLLBAR(HWND hwnd, WPARAM wParam, LPARAM lParam, HBRUSH (*OnCtlColor)(HWND hwnd, HDC hdc, HWND hChild, int type))
w	LRESULT	HANDLE_WM_CTLCOLORSTATIC(HWND hwnd, WPARAM wParam, LPARAM lParam, HBRUSH (*OnCtlColor)(HWND hwnd, HDC hdc, HWND hChild, int type))
w	0	HANDLE_WM_CUT(HWND hwnd, WPARAM wParam, LPARAM lParam, void (*OnCut)(HWND hwnd))

Table C.1: Summary of `windowsx.h`, `commctrl.h`, and `extensions.h` API interface

.h	Return Type	Function Name and Parameters
c w e	commctrl.h windowsx.h extensions.h	
w	0	HANDLE_WM_DEADCHAR(HWND hwnd, WPARAM wParam, LPARAM lParam, void (*OnDeadChar)(HWND hwnd, TCHAR ch, int RepeatCount))
w	0	HANDLE_WM_DELETEITEM(HWND hwnd, WPARAM wParam, LPARAM lParam, void (*OnDeleteItem)(HWND hwnd, const DELETEITEMSTRUCT * lpDeleteItem))
w	0	HANDLE_WM_DESTROY(HWND hwnd, WPARAM wParam, LPARAM lParam, void (*OnDestroy)(HWND hwnd))
w	0	HANDLE_WM_DESTROYCLIPBOARD(HWND hwnd, WPARAM wParam, LPARAM lParam, void (*OnDestroyClipboard)(HWND hwnd))
w	0	HANDLE_WM_DEVMODECHANGE(HWND hwnd, WPARAM wParam, LPARAM lParam, void (*OnDevModeChange)(HWND hwnd, LPCTSTR DeviceName))
e	0	HANDLE_WM_DISPLAYCHANGE(HWND hwnd, WPARAM wParam, LPARAM lParam, void (*OnDisplayChange)(HWND hwnd, UINT BitsPerPixel, UINT cx, UINT cy)
w	0	HANDLE_WM_DRAWCLIPBOARD(HWND hwnd, WPARAM wParam, LPARAM lParam, void (*OnDrawClipboard)(HWND hwnd))
w	0	HANDLE_WM_DRAWITEM(HWND hwnd, WPARAM wParam, LPARAM lParam, void (*OnDrawItem)(HWND hwnd, const DRAWITEMSTRUCT * lpDrawItem))
w	0	HANDLE_WM_DROPFILES(HWND hwnd, WPARAM wParam, LPARAM lParam, void (*OnDropFiles)(HWND hwnd, HDROP hdrop))
w	0	HANDLE_WM_ENABLE(HWND hwnd, WPARAM wParam, LPARAM lParam, void (*OnEnable)(HWND hwnd, BOOL Enable))
w	0	HANDLE_WM_ENDSESSION(HWND hwnd, WPARAM wParam, LPARAM lParam, void (*OnEndSession)(HWND hwnd, BOOL Ending))
w	0	HANDLE_WM_ENTERIDLE(HWND hwnd, WPARAM wParam, LPARAM lParam, void (*OnEnterIdle)(HWND hwnd, UINT source, HWND hwndSource))
e	0	HANDLE_WM_ENTERMENULOOP(HWND hwnd, WPARAM wParam, LPARAM lParam, void (*OnEnterMenuLoop)(HWND hwnd, BOOL isTrackPopup))
e	void	HANDLE_WM_ENTERSIZEMOVE(HWND hwnd, WPARAM wParam, LPARAM lParam, void (*OnEnterSizeMove)(HWND hwnd))
w	LRESULT	HANDLE_WM_ERASEBKGND(HWND hwnd, WPARAM wParam, LPARAM lParam, BOOL (*OnEraseBkgnd)(HWND hwnd, HDC hdc))

Table C.1: Summary of `windowsx.h`, `commctrl.h`, and `extensions.h` API interface

.h	Return Type	Function Name and Parameters

c
w
e
	`commctrl.h`
	`windowsx.h`
	`extensions.h`	

e	0	`HANDLE_WM_EXITMENULOOP(HWND hwnd, WPARAM wParam,`
		`LPARAM lParam, void (*OnExitMenuLoop)(HWND hwnd,`
		`BOOL isTrackPopup))`

e	void	`HANDLE_WM_EXITSIZEMOVE(HWND hwnd, WPARAM wParam,` `LPARAM lParam, void (*OnEnterSizeMove)(HWND hwnd))`
w	0	`HANDLE_WM_FONTCHANGE(HWND hwnd, WPARAM wParam,` `LPARAM lParam, void (*OnFontChange)(HWND hwnd))`
w	LRESULT	`HANDLE_WM_GETDLGCODE(HWND hwnd, WPARAM wParam,` `LPARAM lParam, UINT (*OnGetDlgCode)(HWND hwnd, LPMSG lpmsg))`
w	LRESULT	`HANDLE_WM_GETFONT(HWND hwnd, WPARAM wParam, LPARAM lParam,` `HFONT (*OnGetFont)(HWND hwnd))`

w	0	`HANDLE_WM_GETMINMAXINFO(HWND hwnd, WPARAM wParam,`
		`LPARAM lParam, void (*OnGetMinMaxInfo)(HWND hwnd,`
		`LPMINMAXINFO lpMinMaxInfo))`

w	int	`HANDLE_WM_GETTEXT(HWND hwnd, WPARAM wParam, LPARAM lParam,` `int (*OnGetText)(HWND hwnd, int cchMax, LPTSTR text))`
w	int	`HANDLE_WM_GETTEXTLENGTH(HWND hwnd, WPARAM wParam,` `LPARAM lParam, int (*OnGetTextLength)(HWND hwnd))`
e	0	`HANDLE_WM_HELP(HWND hwnd, WPARAM wParam, LPARAM lParam,` `void (*OnHelp)(HWND hwnd, LPHELPINFO lphi))`
w	0	`HANDLE_WM_HSCROLL(HWND hwnd, WPARAM wParam, LPARAM lParam,` `void (*OnHScroll)(HWND hwnd, HWND hCtl, UINT code, int pos))`

w	0	`HANDLE_WM_HSCROLLCLIPBOARD(HWND hwnd, WPARAM wParam,`
		`LPARAM lParam, void (*OnHScrollClipboard)(HWND hwnd,`
		`HWND hwndCBViewer, UINT code, int pos))`

w	LRESULT	`HANDLE_WM_ICONERASEBKGND(HWND hwnd, WPARAM wParam,` `LPARAM lParam, BOOL (*OnIconEraseBkgnd)(HWND hwnd, HDC hdc))`

w	LRESULT	`HANDLE_WM_INITDIALOG(HWND hwnd, WPARAM wParam,`
		`LPARAM lParam, BOOL (*OnInitDialog)(HWND hwnd,`
		`HWND hwndFocus, LPARAM lParam))`

w	0	`HANDLE_WM_INITMENU(HWND hwnd, WPARAM wParam, LPARAM lParam,` `void (*OnInitMenu)(HWND hwnd, HMENU hMenu))`

w	0	`HANDLE_WM_INITMENUPOPUP(HWND hwnd, WPARAM wParam,`
		`LPARAM lParam, void (*OnInitMenuPopup)(HWND hwnd,`
		`HMENU hMenu, UINT item, BOOL SystemMenu))`

Table C.1: Summary of `windowsx.h`, `commctrl.h`, and `extensions.h` API interface

.h	Return Type	Function Name and Parameters

c
w
e
	`commctrl.h`
	`windowsx.h`
	`extensions.h`	

w	0	`HANDLE_WM_KEYDOWN(HWND hwnd, WPARAM wParam, LPARAM lParam,`
		`void (*OnKey)(HWND hwnd, UINT vk, BOOL Down,`
		`int RepeatCount, UINT flags))`

w	0	`HANDLE_WM_KEYUP(HWND hwnd, WPARAM wParam, LPARAM lParam,`
		`void (*OnKey)(HWND hwnd, UINT vk, BOOL Down,`
		`int RepeatCount, UINT flags))`

w	0	`HANDLE_WM_KILLFOCUS(HWND hwnd, WPARAM wParam, LPARAM lParam,` `void (*OnKillFocus)(HWND hwnd, HWND NewFocus))`

w	void	`HANDLE_WM_LBUTTONDBLCLK(HWND hwnd, WPARAM wParam,`
		`LPARAM lParam, void (*OnLButtonDown)(HWND hwnd,`
		`BOOL DoubleClick, int x, int y, UINT keyFlags))`

w	0	`HANDLE_WM_LBUTTONDOWN(HWND hwnd, WPARAM wParam,`
		`LPARAM lParam, void (*OnLButtonDown)(HWND hwnd,`
		`BOOL DoubleClick, int x, int y, UINT keyFlags))`

w	0	`HANDLE_WM_LBUTTONUP(HWND hwnd, WPARAM wParam, LPARAM lParam,`
		`void (*OnLButtonUp)(HWND hwnd, BOOL DoubleClick, int x,`
		`int y, UINT keyFlags))`

w	0	`HANDLE_WM_MBUTTONDBLCLK(HWND hwnd, WPARAM wParam,`
		`LPARAM lParam, void (*OnMButtonDown)(HWND hwnd,`
		`BOOL DoubleClick, int x, int y, UINT keyFlags))`

w	0	`HANDLE_WM_MBUTTONDOWN(HWND hwnd, WPARAM wParam,`
		`LPARAM lParam, void(*OnMButtonDown)(HWND hwnd,`
		`BOOL DoubleClick, int x, int y, UINT keyFlags))`

w	0	`HANDLE_WM_MBUTTONUP(HWND hwnd, WPARAM wParam, LPARAM lParam,` `void (*OnMButtonUp)(HWND hwnd, int x, int y, UINT flags))`

w	0	`HANDLE_WM_MDIACTIVATE(HWND hwnd, WPARAM wParam,`
		`LPARAM lParam, void (*OnMDIActivate)(HWND hwnd, BOOL Active,`
		`HWND hwndActivate, HWND hwndDeactivate))`

w	LRESULT	`HANDLE_WM_MDICASCADE(HWND hwnd, WPARAM wParam,` `LPARAM lParam, OnMDICascade(HWND hwnd, UINT cmd))`

w	LRESULT	`HANDLE_WM_MDICREATE(HWND hwnd, WPARAM wParam, LPARAM lParam,`
		`HWND (*OnMDICreate)(HWND hwnd,`
		`const LPMDICREATESTRUCT lpmcs))`

w	0	`HANDLE_WM_MDIDESTROY(HWND hwnd, WPARAM wParam,`
		`LPARAM lParam, void (*OnMDIDestroy)(HWND hwnd,`
		`HWND hwndDestroy))`

Table C.1: Summary of `windowsx.h`, `commctrl.h`, and `extensions.h` API interface

.h	Return Type	Function Name and Parameters

c
w
e
	`commctrl.h`
	`windowsx.h`
	`extensions.h`	

w	LRESULT	`HANDLE_WM_MDIGETACTIVE(HWND hwnd, WPARAM wParam,` `LPARAM lParam, HWND (*OnMDIGetActive)(HWND hwnd))`
w	0	`HANDLE_WM_MDIICONARRANGE(HWND hwnd, WPARAM wParam,` `LPARAM lParam, void (*OnMDIIconArrange)(HWND hwnd)`

w	0	`HANDLE_WM_MDIMAXIMIZE(HWND hwnd, WPARAM wParam,`
		`LPARAM lParam, void (*OnMDIMaximize)(HWND hwnd,`
		`HWND hwndMaximize))`

w	LRESULT	`HANDLE_WM_MDINEXT(HWND hwnd, WPARAM wParam, LPARAM lParam,` `HWND (*OnMDINext)(HWND hwnd, HWND hwndCur, BOOL Prev))`

w	0	`HANDLE_WM_MDIRESTORE(HWND hwnd, WPARAM wParam,`
		`LPARAM lParam, void (*OnMDIRestore)(HWND hwnd,`
		`HWND hwndRestore))`

w	LRESULT	`HANDLE_WM_MDISETMENU(HWND hwnd, WPARAM wParam,`
		`LPARAM lParam, HMENU (*OnMDISetMenu)(HWND hwnd,`
		`BOOL Refresh, HMENU hmenuFrame, HMENU hmenuWindow)`

w	LRESULT	`HANDLE_WM_MDITILE(HWND hwnd, WPARAM wParam, LPARAM lParam,` `BOOL (*OnMDITile)(HWND hwnd, UINT cmd))`

w	0	`HANDLE_WM_MEASUREITEM(HWND hwnd, WPARAM wParam,`
		`LPARAM lParam, void (*OnMeasureItem)(HWND hwnd,`
		`MEASUREITEMSTRUCT * lpMeasureItem))`

w	DWORD	`HANDLE_WM_MENUCHAR(HWND hwnd, WPARAM wParam, LPARAM lParam,`
		`void (*OnMenuChar)(HWND hwnd, UINT ch, UINT flags,`
		`HMENU hmenu))`

w	0	`HANDLE_WM_MENUSELECT(HWND hwnd, WPARAM wParam,`
		`LPARAM lParam, void (*OnMenuSelect)(HWND hwnd, HMENU hmenu,`
		`int item, HMENU hmenuPopup, UINT flags))`

w	LRESULT	`HANDLE_WM_MOUSEACTIVATE(HWND hwnd, WPARAM wParam,`
		`LPARAM lParam, int (*OnMouseActivate)(HWND hwnd,`
		`HWND hwndTopLevel, UINT codeHitTest, UINT msg))`

w	0	`HANDLE_WM_MOUSEMOVE(HWND hwnd, WPARAM wParam, LPARAM lParam,`
		`void (*OnMouseMove) (HWND hwnd, int x, int y,`
		`UINT keyFlags))`

w	0	`HANDLE_WM_MOVE(HWND hwnd, WPARAM wParam, LPARAM lParam,` `void (*OnMove)(HWND hwnd, int x, int y))`

w	LRESULT	`HANDLE_WM_NCACTIVATE(HWND hwnd, WPARAM wParam,`
		`LPARAM lParam, BOOL (*OnNCActivate)(HWND hwnd, BOOL Active,`
		`HWND hwndActDeact, BOOL Minimized))`

Table C.1: Summary of windowsx.h, commctrl.h, and extensions.h API interface

.h	Return Type	Function Name and Parameters
c w e	commctrl.h windowsx.h extensions.h	
w	LRESULT	HANDLE_WM_NCCALCSIZE(HWND hwnd, WPARAM wParam, LPARAM lParam, UINT (*OnNCCalcSize)(HWND hwnd, BOOL CalcValidRects, NCCALCSIZE_PARAMS * lpcsp))
w	LRESULT	HANDLE_WM_NCCREATE(HWND hwnd, WPARAM wParam, LPARAM lParam, BOOL (*OnNCCreate)(HWND hwnd, LPCREATESTRUCT lpCreateStruct))
w	0	HANDLE_WM_NCDESTROY(HWND hwnd, WPARAM wParam, LPARAM lParam, void (*OnNCDestroy)(HWND hwnd))
w	LRESULT	HANDLE_WM_NCHITTEST(HWND hwnd, WPARAM wParam, LPARAM lParam, UINT (*OnNCHitTest)(HWND hwnd, int x, int y))
w	0	HANDLE_WM_NCLBUTTONDBLCLK(HWND hwnd, WPARAM wParam, LPARAM lParam, void (*OnNCLButtonDown)(HWND hwnd, BOOL DoubleClick, int x, int y, UINT codeHitTest))
w	0	HANDLE_WM_NCLBUTTONDOWN(HWND hwnd, WPARAM wParam, LPARAM lParam, void (*OnNCLButtonDown) (HWND hwnd, BOOL DoubleClick, int x, int y, UINT codeHitTest))
w	0	HANDLE_WM_NCLBUTTONUP(HWND hwnd, WPARAM wParam, LPARAM lParam, void (*OnNCLButtonUp)(HWND hwnd, int x, int y, UINT codeHitTest))
w	0	HANDLE_WM_NCMBUTTONDBLCLK(HWND hwnd, WPARAM wParam, LPARAM lParam, void (*OnNCMButtonDown)(HWND hwnd, BOOL DoubleClick, int x, int y, UINT codeHitTest))
w	0	HANDLE_WM_NCMBUTTONDOWN(HWND hwnd, WPARAM wParam, LPARAM lParam, void (*OnNCMButtonDown)(HWND hwnd, BOOL DoubleClick, int x, int y, UINT codeHitTest))
w	0	HANDLE_WM_NCMBUTTONUP(HWND hwnd, WPARAM wParam, LPARAM lParam, void (*OnNCMButtonUp(HWND hwnd, int x, int y, UINT codeHitTest))
w	0	HANDLE_WM_NCMOUSEMOVE(HWND hwnd, WPARAM wParam, LPARAM lParam, void (*OnMouseMove)(HWND hwnd, int x, int y, UINT codeHitTest))
w	0	HANDLE_WM_NCPAINT(HWND hwnd, WPARAM wParam, LPARAM lParam, void (*OnNCPaint)(HWND hwnd, HRGN hrgn))
w	0	HANDLE_WM_NCRBUTTONDBLCLK(HWND hwnd, WPARAM wParam, LPARAM lParam, void (*OnNCRButtonDown)(HWND hwnd, BOOL DoubleClick, int x, int y, UINT codeHitTest))

Table C.1: Summary of `windowsx.h`, `commctrl.h`, and `extensions.h` API interface

.h	Return Type	Function Name and Parameters

c
w
e
	`commctrl.h`
	`windowsx.h`
	`extensions.h`	

w	0	`HANDLE_WM_NCRBUTTONDOWN(HWND hwnd, WPARAM wParam, LPARAM lParam, void (*OnNCRButtonDown)(HWND hwnd, BOOL DoubleClick, int x, int y, UINT codeHitTest))`
w	0	`HANDLE_WM_NCRBUTTONUP(HWND hwnd, WPARAM wParam, LPARAM lParam, void (*OnNCRButtonUp) (HWND hwnd, int x, int y, UINT codeHitTest))`
w	LRESULT	`HANDLE_WM_NEXTDLGCTL(HWND hwnd, WPARAM wParam, LPARAM lParam, HWND (*OnNextDlgCtl)(HWND hwnd, HWND hwndSetFocus, BOOL Next))`
c	LRESULT	`HANDLE_WM_NOTIFY(HWND hwnd, WPARAM wParam, LPARAM lParam, LRESULT (*OnNotify)(HWND hwnd, int id, NMHDR * hdr)`
w	0	`HANDLE_WM_PAINT(HWND hwnd, WPARAM wParam, LPARAM lParam, void (*OnPaint)(HWND hwnd))`
w	0	`HANDLE_WM_PAINTCLIPBOARD(HWND hwnd, WPARAM wParam, LPARAM lParam, void (*OnPaintClipboard)(HWND hwnd, HWND hwndCBViewer, const LPPAINTSTRUCT lpPaintStruct))`
w	0	`HANDLE_WM_PALETTECHANGED(HWND hwnd, WPARAM wParam, LPARAM lParam, void (*OnPaletteChanged)(HWND hwnd, HWND hwndPaletteChange))`
w	0	`HANDLE_WM_PALETTEISCHANGING(HWND hwnd, WPARAM wParam, LPARAM lParam, void (*OnPaletteIsChanging)(HWND hwnd, HWND paletteChange))`
w	0	`HANDLE_WM_PARENTNOTIFY(HWND hwnd, WPARAM wParam, LPARAM lParam, void (*OnParentNotify)(HWND hwnd, UINT msg, HWND hChild, int idChild))`
w	0	`HANDLE_WM_PASTE(HWND hwnd, WPARAM wParam, LPARAM lParam, void(*OnPaste)(HWND hwnd))`
w	0	`HANDLE_WM_POWER(HWND hwnd, WPARAM wParam, LPARAM lParam, void (*OnPower)(HWND hwnd))`
e	0	`HANDLE_WM_PRINTCLIENT(HWND hwnd, WPARAM wParam, LPARAM lParam, void (*OnPrintClient)(HWND hwnd, HDC hdc, UINT Flags))`
w	HICON	`HANDLE_WM_QUERYDRAGICON(HWND hwnd, WPARAM wParam, LPARAM lParam, HICON (*OnQueryDragIcon)(HWND hwnd))`
w	LRESULT	`HANDLE_WM_QUERYENDSESSION(HWND hwnd, WPARAM wParam, LPARAM lParam, BOOL (*OnQueryEndSession)(HWND hwnd))`

Table C.1: Summary of windowsx.h, commctrl.h, and extensions.h API interface

.h	Return Type	Function Name and Parameters
c w e	commctrl.h windowsx.h extensions.h	
w	LRESULT	HANDLE_WM_QUERYNEWPALETTE(HWND hwnd, WPARAM wParam, LPARAM lParam, BOOL (*OnQueryNewPalette)(HWND hwnd))
w	LRESULT	HANDLE_WM_QUERYOPEN(HWND hwnd, WPARAM wParam, LPARAM lParam, BOOL (*OnQueryOpen)(HWND hwnd))
w	0	HANDLE_WM_QUEUESYNC(HWND hwnd, WPARAM wParam, LPARAM lParam, void (*OnQueueSync)(HWND hwnd))
w	0	HANDLE_WM_QUIT(HWND hwnd, WPARAM wParam, LPARAM lParam, void (*OnQuit)(HWND hwnd, int exitcode))
w	0	HANDLE_WM_RBUTTONDBLCLK(HWND hwnd, WPARAM wParam, LPARAM lParam, void (*OnRButtonDown)(HWND hwnd, BOOL DoubleClick, int x, int y, UINT keyFlags))
w	0	HANDLE_WM_RBUTTONDOWN(HWND hwnd, WPARAM wParam, LPARAM lParam, void (*OnRButtonDown)(HWND hwnd, BOOL DoubleClick, int x, int y, UINT keyFlags))
w	0	HANDLE_WM_RBUTTONUP(HWND hwnd, WPARAM wParam, LPARAM lParam, void (*OnRButtonUp)(HWND hwnd, int x, int y, UINT flags))
w	0	HANDLE_WM_RENDERALLFORMATS(HWND hwnd, WPARAM wParam, LPARAM lParam, void (*OnRenderAllFormats)(HWND hwnd))
w	HANDLE	HANDLE_WM_RENDERFORMAT(HWND hwnd, WPARAM wParam, LPARAM lParam, HANDLE (*OnRenderFormat)(HWND hwnd, UINT fmt))
w	LRESULT	HANDLE_WM_SETCURSOR(HWND hwnd, WPARAM wParam, LPARAM lParam, BOOL (*OnSetCursor)(HWND hwnd, HWND hwndCursor, UINT codeHitTest, UINT msg))
w	0	HANDLE_WM_SETFOCUS(HWND hwnd, WPARAM wParam, LPARAM lParam, void (*OnSetFocus)(HWND hwnd, HWND oldFocus))
w	0	HANDLE_WM_SETFONT(HWND hwnd, WPARAM wParam, LPARAM lParam, void (*OnSetFont)(HWND hCtl, HFONT hfont, BOOL Redraw))
w	0	HANDLE_WM_SETREDRAW(HWND hwnd, WPARAM wParam, LPARAM lParam, void (*OnSetRedraw)(HWND hwnd, BOOL Redraw))
w	0	HANDLE_WM_SETTEXT(HWND hwnd, WPARAM wParam, LPARAM lParam, void (*OnSetText)(HWND hwnd, LPCTSTR text))
e	0	HANDLE_WM_SETTINGCHANGE(HWND hwnd, WPARAM wParam, LPARAM lParam, void (*OnSettingChange)(HWND hwnd, UINT Flags, LPCTSTR key))

Table C.1: Summary of `windowsx.h`, `commctrl.h`, and `extensions.h` API interface

.h	Return Type	Function Name and Parameters

c
w
e
	`commctrl.h`
	`windowsx.h`
	`extensions.h`	

w	0	`HANDLE_WM_SHOWWINDOW(HWND hwnd, WPARAM wParam,`
		`LPARAM lParam, void (*OnShowWindow)(HWND hwnd, BOOL Show,`
		`UINT status))`

w	0	`HANDLE_WM_SIZE(HWND hwnd, WPARAM wParam, LPARAM lParam,` `void (*OnSize)(HWND hwnd, UINT state, int cx, int cy))`

w	0	`HANDLE_WM_SIZECLIPBOARD(HWND hwnd, WPARAM wParam,`
		`LPARAM lParam, void (*OnSizeClipboard)(HWND hwnd,`
		`HWND hwndCBViewer, const LPRECT lprc))`

w	0	`HANDLE_WM_SPOOLERSTATUS(HWND hwnd, WPARAM wParam,`
		`LPARAM lParam, void (*OnSpoolerStatus)(HWND hwnd,`
		`UINT status, int cJobInQueue))`

w	0	`HANDLE_WM_SYSCHAR(HWND hwnd, WPARAM wParam, LPARAM lParam,` `void (*OnSysChar)(HWND hwnd, TCHAR ch, int RepeatCount))`
w	0	`HANDLE_WM_SYSCOLORCHANGE(HWND hwnd, WPARAM wParam,` `LPARAM lParam, void (*OnSysColorChange)(HWND hwnd))`

w	0	`HANDLE_WM_SYSCOMMAND(HWND hwnd, WPARAM wParam,`
		`LPARAM lParam, void (*OnSysCommand)(HWND hwnd, UINT cmd,`
		`int x, int y))`

w	0	`HANDLE_WM_SYSDEADCHAR(HWND hwnd, WPARAM wParam,`
		`LPARAM lParam, void (*OnSysDeadChar)(HWND hwnd, TCHAR ch,`
		`int RepeatCount))`

w	0	`HANDLE_WM_SYSKEYDOWN(HWND hwnd, WPARAM wParam,`
		`LPARAM lParam, void (*OnSysKey)(HWND hwnd, UINT vk,`
		`BOOL Down, int RepeatCount, UINT flags))`

w	0	`HANDLE_WM_SYSKEYUP(HWND hwnd, WPARAM wParam, LPARAM lParam,`
		`void (*OnSysKey)(HWND hwnd, UINT vk, BOOL Down,`
		`int RepeatCount, UINT flags))`

w	0	`HANDLE_WM_TIMECHANGE(HWND hwnd, WPARAM wParam,` `LPARAM lParam, void (*OnTimeChange)(HWND hwnd))`
w	0	`HANDLE_WM_TIMER(HWND hwnd, WPARAM wParam, LPARAM lParam,` `void (*OnTimer)(HWND hwnd, UINT id))`
w	0	`HANDLE_WM_UNDO(HWND hwnd, WPARAM wParam, LPARAM lParam,` `void (*OnUndo)(HWND hwnd))`
e	0	`HANDLE_WM_USERCHANGED(HWND hwnd, WPARAM wParam,` `LPARAM lParam, void (*OnUserChanged)(HWND hwnd))`

Table C.1: Summary of `windowsx.h`, `commctrl.h`, and `extensions.h` API interface

.h	Return Type	Function Name and Parameters

c
w
e
	`commctrl.h`
	`windowsx.h`
	`extensions.h`	

w	LRESULT	`HANDLE_WM_VKEYTOITEM(HWND hwnd, WPARAM wParam, LPARAM lParam, int (*OnVkeyToItem)(HWND hwnd, UINT vk, HWND hList, int iCaret))`
w	0	`HANDLE_WM_VSCROLL(HWND hwnd, WPARAM wParam, LPARAM lParam, void (*OnVScroll)(HWND hwnd, HWND hCtl, UINT code, int pos))`
w	0	`HANDLE_WM_VSCROLLCLIPBOARD(HWND hwnd, WPARAM wParam, LPARAM lParam, void (*OnVScrollClipboard)(HWND hwnd, HWND hwndCBViewer, UINT code, int pos))`
w	0	`HANDLE_WM_WINDOWPOSCHANGED(HWND hwnd, WPARAM wParam, LPARAM lParam, void (*OnWindowPosChanged)(HWND hwnd, const LPWINDOWPOS lpwpos))`
w	BOOL	`HANDLE_WM_WINDOWPOSCHANGING(HWND hwnd, WPARAM wParam, LPARAM lParam, BOOL (*OnWindowPosChanging)(HWND hwnd, LPWINDOWPOS lpwpos))`
w	0	`HANDLE_WM_WININICHANGE(HWND hwnd, WPARAM wParam, LPARAM lParam, void (*OnWinIniChange)(HWND hwnd, LPCTSTR sectionName))`
c	BOOL	`Header_DeleteItem(HWND hhdr, int i)`
c	BOOL	`Header_GetItem(HWND hhdr, int i, HD_ITEM * pinfo)`
c	int	`Header_GetItemCount(HWND hhdr)`
c	int	`Header_InsertItem(HWND hhdr, int i, const HD_ITEM * pinfo)`
c	BOOL	`Header_Layout(HWND hhdr, HD_LAYOUT * layout)`
c	BOOL	`Header_SetItem(HWND hhdr, int i, const HD_ITEM * pinfo)`
c	int	`ImageList_Add(HIMAGELIST himl, HBITMAP hbm, HBITMAP hmask)`
c	int	`ImageList_AddIcon(HIMAGELIST himl, HICON hicon)`
c	int	`ImageList_AddMasked(HIMAGELIST himl, HBITMAP himage, COLORREF maskColor)`
c	BOOL	`ImageList_BeginDrag(HIMAGELIST himl, int track, int hotx, int hoty)`
c	HIMAGELIST	`ImageList_Create(int cx, int cy, UINT flags, int initial, int grow)`
c	BOOL	`ImageList_Destroy(HIMAGELIST himl)`

Table C.1: Summary of `windowsx.h`, `commctrl.h`, and `extensions.h` API interface

.h	Return Type	Function Name and Parameters
c w e	commctrl.h windowsx.h extensions.h	
c	BOOL	ImageList_DragEnter(HWND hlock, int x, int y)
c	BOOL	ImageList_DragLeave(HWND hlock)
c	BOOL	ImageList_DragMove(int x, int y)
c	BOOL	ImageList_DragShowNolock(BOOL show)
c	BOOL	ImageList_Draw(HIMAGELIST himl, int i, hDC hdc, int x, int y, UINT style)
c	BOOL	ImageList_DrawEx(HIMAGELIST himl, int i, HDC hdc, int x, int y, int dx, int dy, COLORREF bkColor, COLORREF fgColor, UINT style)
c	void	ImageList_EndDrag()
c	HICON	ImageList_ExtractIcon(HINSTANCE hinst, HIMAGELIST himl, int i)
c	COLORREF	ImageList_GetBkColor(HIMAGELIST himl)
c	HIMAGELIST	ImageList_GetDragImage(LPPOINT pt, LPPOINT hotspot)
c	HICON	ImageList_GetIcon(HIMAGELIST himl, int i, UINT flags)
c	BOOL	ImageList_GetIconSize(HIMAGELIST himl, LPINT cx, LPINT cy)
c	int	ImageList_GetImageCount(HIMAGELIST himl)
c	BOOL	ImageList_GetImageInfo(HIMAGELIST himl, int i, IMAGEINFO * pinfo)
c	HIMAGELIST	ImageList_LoadBitmap(HINSTANCE hinst, LPCTSTR lpbmp, int cx, int grow, COLORREF maskColor)
c	HIMAGELIST	ImageList_LoadImage(HINSTANCE hinst, LPCTSTR lpbmp, int cx, int cgrow, COLORREF maskColor, UINT type, UINT flags)
c	HIMAGELIST	ImageList_Merge(HIMAGELIST himl1, int i1, HIMAGELIST himl2, int i2, int dx, int dy)
c	HIMAGELIST	ImageList_Read(LPSTREAM stream)
c	BOOL	ImageList_Remove(HIMAGELIST himl, int i)
c	BOOL	ImageList_RemoveAll(HIMAGELIST himl)

Table C.1: Summary of windowsx.h, commctrl.h, and extensions.h API interface

.h	Return Type	Function Name and Parameters
c w e	commctrl.h windowsx.h extensions.h	
c	BOOL	ImageList_Replace(HIMAGELIST himl, int i, HBITMAP himage, HBITMAP hmask)
c	int	ImageList_ReplaceIcon(HIMAGELIST himl, int i, HICON hicon)
c	COLORREF	ImageList_SetBkColor(HIMAGELIST himl, COLORREF bkColor)
c	BOOL	ImageList_SetDragCursorImage(HIMAGELIST himl, int idrag, int hotx, int hoty)
c	BOOL	ImageList_SetIconSize(HIMAGELIST himl, int cx, int cy)
c	BOOL	ImageList_SetOverlayImage(HIMAGELIST himl, int image, int overlay)
c	BOOL	ImageList_Write(HIMAGELIST himl, LPSTREAM stream)
w	BOOL	InsetRect(LPRECT lprc, int dx, int dy)
w	int	IntersectRgn(HRGN Result, HRGN hrgnA, HRGN hrgnB)
w	BOOL	IsLButtonDown()
w	BOOL	IsMaximized(HWND hwnd)
w	BOOL	IsMButtonDown()
w	BOOL	IsMinimized(HWND hwnd)
w	BOOL	IsRButtonDown()
w	BOOL	IsRestored(HWND hwnd)
c	int	LBItemFromPt(HWND hlb, POINT pt, BOOL autoscroll)
e	int	ListBox_AddFile(HWND hCtl, LPCTSTR filename)
w	int	ListBox_AddItemData(HWND hCtl, LPARAM data)
w	int	ListBox_AddString(HWND hCtl, LPCTSTR String)
w	int	ListBox_DeleteString(HWND hCtl, int index)
w	int	ListBox_Dir(HWND hCtl, UINT attrs, LPCTSTR FileSpec)
w	BOOL	ListBox_Enable(HWND hCtl, BOOL Enable)
w	int	ListBox_FindItemData(HWND hCtl, int indexStart, LPARAM data)

Table C.1: Summary of `windowsx.h`, `commctrl.h`, and `extensions.h` API interface

.h	Return Type	Function Name and Parameters

c
w
e
	`commctrl.h`
	`windowsx.h`
	`extensions.h`	

w	int	`ListBox_FindString(HWND hCtl, int indexStart,` `LPCTSTR String)`
w	int	`ListBox_FindStringExact(HWND hCtl, int indexStart,` `LPCTSTR String)`
e	int	`ListBox_GetAnchorIndex(HWND hCtl)`
w	int	`ListBox_GetCaretIndex(HWND hCtl)`
w	int	`ListBox_GetCount(HWND hCtl)`
w	int	`ListBox_GetCurSel(HWND hCtl)`
w	int	`ListBox_GetHorizontalExtent(HWND hCtl)`
w	LRESULT	`ListBox_GetItemData(HWND hCtl, int index)`
w	int	`ListBox_GetItemHeight(HWND hCtl, int index)`
w	int	`ListBox_GetItemRect(HWND hCtl, int index, LPRECT lprc)`
e	LCID	`ListBox_GetLocale(HWND hCtl)`
w	int	`ListBox_GetSel(HWND hCtl, int index)`
w	int	`ListBox_GetSelCount(HWND hCtl)`
w	int	`ListBox_GetSelItems(HWND hCtl, int cItems, LPINT lpItems)`
w	int	`ListBox_GetText(HWND hCtl, int index, LPTSTR Buffer)`
w	int	`ListBox_GetTextLen(HWND hCtl, int index)`
w	int	`ListBox_GetTopIndex(HWND hCtl)`
e	int	`ListBox_InitStorage(HWND hCtl, int itemCount, int bytes)`
w	int	`ListBox_InsertItemData(HWND hCtl, int index, LPARAM data)`
w	int	`ListBox_InsertString(HWND hCtl, int index, LPCTSTR String)`
e	int	`ListBox_ItemFromPoint(HWND hCtl, int x, int y)`
w	BOOL	`ListBox_ResetContent(HWND hCtl)`
w	int	`ListBox_SelectItemData(HWND hCtl, int indexStart,` `LPARAM data)`

Table C.1: Summary of `windowsx.h`, `commctrl.h`, and `extensions.h` API interface

.h	Return Type	Function Name and Parameters

c
w
e
	`commctrl.h`
	`windowsx.h`
	`extensions.h`	

w	int	`ListBox_SelectString(HWND hCtl, int indexStart, LPCTSTR String)`
w	int	`ListBox_SelItemRange(HWND hCtl, BOOL Select, WORD first, WORD last)`
w	int	`ListBox_SelItemRangeEx(HWND hCtl, WORD first, WORD last)`
e	int	`ListBox_SetAnchorIndex(HWND hCtl, int index)`
w	int	`ListBox_SetCaretIndex(HWND hCtl, int index)`
w	void	`ListBox_SetColumnWidth(HWND hCtl, int cxColumn)`
w	int	`ListBox_SetCurSel(HWND hCtl, int index)`
w	void	`ListBox_SetHorizontalExtent(HWND hCtl, int cxExtent)`
w	int	`ListBox_SetItemData(HWND hCtl, int index, LPARAM data)`
w	int	`ListBox_SetItemHeight(HWND hCtl, int index, int cy)`
e	LCID	`ListBox_SetLocale(HWND hCtl, LCID locale)`
w	int	`ListBox_SetSel(HWND hCtl, BOOL Select, int index)`
w	BOOL	`ListBox_SetTabStops(HWND hCtl, int cTabs, LPINT lpTabs)`
w	int	`ListBox_SetTopIndex(HWND hCtl, int indexTop)`
c	BOOL	`ListView_Arrange(HWND hlistv, UINT code)`
c	HIMAGELIST	`ListView_CreateDragImage(HWND hlistv, int i, LPPOINT topleft)`
c	BOOL	`ListView_DeleteAllItems(HWND hlistv)`
c	BOOL	`ListView_DeleteColumn(HWND hlistv, int col)`
c	BOOL	`ListView_DeleteItem(HWND hlistv, int i)`
c	HWND	`ListView_EditLabel(HWND hlistv, UINT i)`
c	BOOL	`ListView_EnsureVisible(HWND hlistv, int i, BOOL PartialOK)`
c	int	`ListView_FindItem(HWND hlistv, int Start, LV_FINDINFO * FindInfo)`

Table C.1: Summary of `windowsx.h`, `commctrl.h`, and `extensions.h` API interface

.h	Return Type	Function Name and Parameters

c
w
e
	`commctrl.h`
	`windowsx.h`
	`extensions.h`	

c	COLORREF	`ListView_GetBkColor(HWND hlistv)`
c	BOOL	`ListView_GetCallbackMask(HWND hlistv)`
c	BOOL	`ListView_GetColumn(HWND hlistv, int col, LV_COLUMN * pcol)`
c	int	`ListView_GetColumnWidth(HWND hlistv, int col)`
c	int	`ListView_GetCountPerPage(HWND hlistv)`
c	HWND	`ListView_GetEditControl(HWND hlistv)`
c	HIMAGELIST	`ListView_GetImageList(HWND hlistv, int iImageList)`
c	BOOL	`ListView_GetISearchString(HWND hlistv, LPTSTR Buffer)`
c	BOOL	`ListView_GetItem(HWND hlistv, LV_ITEM * pitem)`
c	BOOL	`ListView_GetItemPosition(HWND hlistv, int i, LPPOINT pt)`
c	BOOL	`ListView_GetItemRect(HWND hlistv, int i, LPRECT lprect, int code)`
c	DWORD	`ListView_GetItemSpacing(HWND hlistv, BOOL Small)`
c	UINT	`ListView_GetItemState(HWND hlistv, int i, UINT mask)`
c	void	`ListView_GetItemText(HWND hlistv, int i, int subitem, LPTSTR Buffer, int BufferLength)`
c	int	`ListView_GetNextItem(HWND hlistv, int i, WORD flags)`
c	BOOL	`ListView_GetOrigin(HWND hlistv, LPPOINT pt)`
c	UINT	`ListView_GetSelectedCount(HWND hlistv)`
c	int	`ListView_GetStringWidth(HWND hlistv, LPCTSTR String)`
c	COLORREF	`ListView_GetTextBkColor(HWND hlistv)`
c	COLORREF	`ListView_GetTextColor(HWND hlistv)`
c	int	`ListView_GetTopIndex(HWND hlistv)`
c	BOOL	`ListView_GetViewRect(HWND hlistv, LPRECT rect)`
c	int	`ListView_HitTest(HWND hlistv, LV_HITTESTINFO * info)`

Table C.1: Summary of `windowsx.h`, `commctrl.h`, and `extensions.h` API interface

.h	Return Type	Function Name and Parameters

c
w
e
	`commctrl.h`
	`windowsx.h`
	`extensions.h`	

c	int	`ListView_InsertColumn(HWND hlistv, int col, LV_COLUMN * Pcol)`
c	int	`ListView_InsertItem(HWND hlistv, LV_ITEM * pitem)`
c	BOOL	`ListView_RedrawItems(HWND hlistv, int first, int last)`
c	BOOL	`ListView_Scroll(HWND hlistv, int dx, int dy)`
c	BOOL	`ListView_SetBkColor(HWND hlistv, COLORREF bkColor)`
c	BOOL	`ListView_SetCallbackMask(HWND hlistv, UINT mask)`
c	BOOL	`ListView_SetColumn(HWND hlistv, int col, LV_COLUMN * pcol)`
c	BOOL	`ListView_SetColumnWidth(HWND hlistv, int col, WORD cx)`
c	BOOL	`ListView_SetItem(HWND hlistv, LV_ITEM * pitem)`
c	LRESULT	`ListView_SetItemCount(HWND hlistv, int ItemCount)`
c	BOOL	`ListView_SetItemPosition(HWND hlistv, int i, int x, int y)`
c	void	`ListView_SetItemPosition32(HWND hlistv, int i, int x, int y)`
c	void	`ListView_SetItemState(HWND hlistv, int i, UINT data, UINT mask)`
c	void	`ListView_SetItemText(HWND hlistv, int i, int subitem, LPCTSTR Text)`
c	BOOL	`ListView_SetTextBkColor(HWND hlistv, COLORREF bkColor)`
c	BOOL	`ListView_SetTextColor(HWND hlistv, COLORREF textColor)`
c	BOOL	`ListView_SortItems(HWND hlistv, PFNLVCOMPARE pfncompare, DWORD parm)`
c	BOOL	`ListView_Update(HWND hlistv, int i)`
c	BOOL	`MakeDragList(HWND hlb)`
w	int	`MapWindowRect(HWND hwndFrom, HWND hwndTo, LPRECT lprc)`
c	void	`MenuHelp(UINT msg, WPARAM wParam, LPARAM lParam, HMENU hmain, HINSTANCE hinst, HWND hstatus, UINT * ids)`
w	BOOL	`ScrollBar_Enable(HWND hCtl, UINT sbflags)`

Table C.1: Summary of `windowsx.h`, `commctrl.h`, and `extensions.h` API interface

.h	Return Type	Function Name and Parameters

c
w
e
	`commctrl.h`
	`windowsx.h`
	`extensions.h`	

w	int	`ScrollBar_GetPos(HWND hCtl)`
w	BOOL	`ScrollBar_GetRange(HWND hCtl, LPINT lpposMin,` `LPINT lpposMax)`
w	int	`ScrollBar_SetPos(HWND hCtl, int pos, BOOL Redraw)`
w	BOOL	`ScrollBar_SetRange(HWND hCtl, int posMin, int posMax,` `BOOL Redraw)`
w	BOOL	`ScrollBar_Show(HWND hCtl, BOOL Show)`
w	HBITMAP	`SelectBitmap(HDC hdc, HBITMAP hbm)`
w	HBRUSH	`SelectBrush(HDC hdc, HBRUSH hbr)`
w	HFONT	`SelectFont(HDC hdc, HFONT hfont)`
w	HPEN	`SelectPen(HDC hdc, HPEN hpen)`
w	BOOL	`SetDlgMsgResult(HWND hwnd, UINT msg, LRESULT result)`
w	void	`SetWindowFont(HWND hwnd, HFONT hfont, BOOL Redraw)`
w	void	`SetWindowRedraw(HWND hwnd, BOOL Redraw)`
w	BOOL	`Static_Enable(HWND hCtl, BOOL Enable)`
w	HICON	`Static_GetIcon(HWND hCtl, LPVOID unused)`
e	HANDLE	`Static_GetImage(HWND hCtl, int imageType)`
w	int	`Static_GetText(HWND hCtl, LPTSTR lpch, UINT cchMax)`
w	int	`Static_GetTextLength(HWND hCtl)`
w	HICON	`Static_SetIcon(HWND hCtl, HICON hIcon)`
e	HANDLE	`Static_SetImage(HWND hCtl, int imageType, HANDLE hImage)`
w	BOOL	`Static_SetText(HWND hCtl, LPCTSTR Text)`
w	DLGPROC	`SubclassDialog(HWND hDlg, DLGPROC proc)`
w	WNDPROC	`SubclassWindow(HWND hwnd, WNDPROC proc)`
w	int	`SubtractRgn(HRGN Result, HRGN hrgnA, HRGN hrgnB)`

Table C.1: Summary of windowsx.h, commctrl.h, and extensions.h API interface

.h	Return Type	Function Name and Parameters
c w e	commctrl.h windowsx.h extensions.h	
c	int	TabCtrl_AdjustRect(HWND htab, BOOL larger, LPRECT lprect)
c	BOOL	TabCtrl_DeleteAllItems(HWND htab)
c	BOOL	TabCtrl_DeleteItem(HWND htab, int item)
c	int	TabCtrl_GetCurFocus(HWND htab)
c	int	TabCtrl_GetCurSel(HWND htab)
c	HIMAGELIST	TabCtrl_GetImageList(HWND htab)
c	BOOL	TabCtrl_GetItem(HWND htab, int item, TC_ITEM * pitem)
c	int	TabCtrl_GetItemCount(HWND htab)
c	BOOL	TabCtrl_GetItemRect(HWND htab, int item, LPRECT lprect)
c	int	TabCtrl_GetRowCount(HWND htab)
c	HWND	TabCtrl_GetToolTips(HWND htab)
c	int	TabCtrl_HitTest(HWND htab, TC_HITTESTINFO * pinfo)
c	int	TabCtrl_InsertItem(HWND htab, int item, const TC_ITEM * pitem)
c	void	TabCtrl_RemoveImage(HWND htab, int i)
c	void	TabCtrl_SetCurFocus(HWND htab, int i)
c	int	TabCtrl_SetCurSel(HWND htab, int item)
c	HIMAGELIST	TabCtrl_SetImageList(HWND htab, HIMAGELIST list)
c	BOOL	TabCtrl_SetItem(HWND htab, int item, TC_ITEM * pitem)
c	BOOL	TabCtrl_SetItemExtra(HWND htab, DWORD cb)
c	DWORD	TabCtrl_SetItemSize(HWND htab, int x, int y)
c	void	TabCtrl_SetPadding(HWND htab, int cx, int cy)
c	void	TabCtrl_SetToolTips(HWND htab, HWND tips)TabCtrl_SetToolTips
e	int	Toolbar_AddBitmap(HWND hwnd, UINT nButtons, LPTBADDBITMAP lptbab)

Table C.1: Summary of `windowsx.h`, `commctrl.h`, and `extensions.h` API interface

.h	Return Type	Function Name and Parameters

c
w
e
	`commctrl.h`
	`windowsx.h`
	`extensions.h`	

e	BOOL	`Toolbar_AddButtons(HWND hwnd, UINT nButtons, LPTBBUTTON lpButtons)`
e	int	`Toolbar_AddString(HWND hwnd, HINSTANCE hinst, LPCTSTR idString)`
e	void	`Toolbar_AutoSize(HWND hwnd)`
e	UINT	`Toolbar_ButtonCount(HWND hwnd)`
e	void	`Toolbar_ButtonStructSize(hwnd)`
e	BOOL	`Toolbar_ChangeBitmap(HWND hwnd, int idButton, UINT BitmapIndex)`
e	BOOL	`Toolbar_CheckButton(HWND hwnd, int idButton, BOOL Checked)`
e	UINT	`Toolbar_CommandToIndex(HWND hwnd, int idButton)`
e	void	`Toolbar_Customize(HWND hwnd)`
e	BOOL	`Toolbar_DeleteButton(HWND hwnd, UINT ButtonIndex)`
e	BOOL	`Toolbar_EnableButton(HWND hwnd, int idButton, BOOL Enable)`
e	UINT	`Toolbar_GetBitmap(HWND hwnd, int idButton)`
e	UINT	`Toolbar_GetBitmapFlags(HWND hwnd)`
e	BOOL	`Toolbar_GetButton(HWND hwnd, UINT ButtonIndex, LPTBBUTTON lpButton)`
e	BOOL	`Toolbar_GetButtonText(HWND hwnd, int idButton, LPTSTR Text)`
e	BOOL	`Toolbar_GetItemRect(HWND hwnd, UINT ButtonIndex, LPRECT r)`
e	UINT	`Toolbar_GetRows(HWND hwnd)`
e	int	`Toolbar_GetState(HWND hwnd, int idButton)`
e	HANDLE	`Toolbar_GetToolTips(HWND hwnd)`
e	BOOL	`Toolbar_HideButton(HWND hwnd, int idButton, BOOL Show)`
e	BOOL	`Toolbar_Indeterminate(HWND hwnd, int idButton, BOOL Indeterminate)`

Table C.1: Summary of `windowsx.h`, `commctrl.h`, and `extensions.h` API interface

.h	Return Type	Function Name and Parameters

c
w
e
	`commctrl.h`
	`windowsx.h`
	`extensions.h`	

e	BOOL	`Toolbar_InsertButton(HWND hwnd, UINT ButtonIndex, LPCTBBBUTTON lpButton)`
e	int	`Toolbar_IsButtonChecked(HWND hwnd, int idButton)`
e	int	`Toolbar_IsButtonEnabled(HWND hwnd, int idButton)`
e	int	`Toolbar_IsButtonHidden(HWND hwnd, int idButton)`
e	int	`Toolbar_IsButtonIndeterminate(HWND hwnd, int idButton)`
e	int	`Toolbar_IsButtonPressed(HWND hwnd, int idButton)`
e	BOOL	`Toolbar_PressButton(HWND hwnd, int idButton, BOOL Press)`
e	void	`Toolbar_SaveRestore(HWND hwnd, BOOL Save, const TBSAVEPARAMS * ptbsp)`
e	BOOL	`Toolbar_SetBitmapSize(HWND hwnd, int cx, int cy)`
e	BOOL	`Toolbar_SetButtonSize(HWND hwnd, int cx, int cy)`
e	BOOL	`Toolbar_SetCmdID(HWND hwnd, UINT ButtonIndex, int idButton)`
e	void	`Toolbar_SetParent(HWND hwnd, HWND hwndParent)`
e	void	`Toolbar_SetRows(HWND hwnd, UINT Rows, BOOL Larger, LPRECT lprc)`
e	BOOL	`Toolbar_SetState(HWND hwnd, int idButton, UINT State)`
e	void	`Toolbar_SetToolTips(HWND hwnd, HWND hwndToolTip)`
c	HIMAGELIST	`TreeView_CreateDragImage(HWND htree, HTREEITEM hitem)`
c	BOOL	`TreeView_DeleteAllItems(HWND htree)`
c	BOOL	`TreeView_DeleteItem(HWND htree, HTREEITEM hitem)`
c	HWND	`TreeView_EditLabel(HWND htree, HTREEITEM hitem)`
c	BOOL	`TreeView_EndEditLabelNow(HWND htree, BOOL cancel)`
c	BOOL	`TreeView_EnsureVisible(HWND htree, HTREEITEM hitem)`
c	BOOL	`TreeView_Expand(HWND htree, HTREEITEM hitem, UINT code)`
c	HTREEITEM	`TreeView_GetChild(HWND htree, HTREEITEM hitem)`

Table C.1: Summary of `windowsx.h`, `commctrl.h`, and `extensions.h` API interface

.h	Return Type	Function Name and Parameters

c
w
e
	`commctrl.h`
	`windowsx.h`
	`extensions.h`	

c	UINT	`TreeView_GetCount(HWND htree)`
c	HTREEITEM	`TreeView_GetDropHilight(HWND htree)`
c	HWND	`TreeView_GetEditControl(HWND htree)`
c	HTREEITEM	`TreeView_GetFirstVisible(HWND htree)`
c	HIMAGELIST	`TreeView_GetImageList(HWND htree, int image)`
c	UINT	`TreeView_GetIndent(HWND htree)`
c	BOOL	`TreeView_GetISearchString(HWND htree, LPTSTR Buffer)`
c	HTREEITEM	`TreeView_GetItem(HWND htree, TV_ITEM * item)`
c	BOOL	`TreeView_GetItemRect(HWND htree, HTREEITEM hitem,` `LPRECT lprect, UINT code)`
c	HTREEITEM	`TreeView_GetNextItem(HWND htree, HTREEITEM hitem, UINT code)`
c	HTREEITEM	`TreeView_GetNextSibling(HWND htree, HTREEITEM hitem)`
c	HTREEITEM	`TreeView_GetNextVisible(HWND htree, HTREEITEM hitem)`
c	HTREEITEM	`TreeView_GetParent(HWND htree, HTREEITEM hitem)`
c	HTREEITEM	`TreeView_GetPrevSibling(HWND htree, HTREEITEM hitem)`
c	HTREEITEM	`TreeView_GetPrevVisible(HWND htree, HTREEITEM hitem)`
c	HTREEITEM	`TreeView_GetRoot(HWND htree)`
c	HTREEITEM	`TreeView_GetSelection(HWND htree)`
c	UINT	`TreeView_GetVisibleCount(HWND htree)`
c	HTREEITEM	`TreeView_HitTest(HWND htree, LPTV_HITTESTINFO htinfo)`
c	HTREEITEM	`TreeView_InsertItem(HWND htree, LPTV_INSERTSTRUCTURE instr)`
c	HTREEITEM	`TreeView_Select(HWND htree, HTREEITEM hitem, UINT code)`
c	HTREEITEM	`TreeView_SelectDropTarget(HWND htree, HTREEITEM hitem)`
c	HTREEITEM	`TreeView_SelectItem(HWND htree, HTREEITEM hitem)`

Table C.1: Summary of `windowsx.h`, `commctrl.h`, and `extensions.h` API interface

.h	Return Type	Function Name and Parameters

c
w
e
	`commctrl.h`
	`windowsx.h`
	`extensions.h`	

c	HTREEITEM	`TreeView_SelectSetFirstVisible(HWND htree, HTREEITEM hitem)`
c	HIMAGELIST	`TreeView_SetImageList(HWND htree, HIMAGELIST imagelist, int image)`
c	BOOL	`TreeView_SetIndent(HWND Htree, int indent)`
c	BOOL	`TreeView_SetItem(HWND htree, TV_ITEM * item)`
c	BOOL	`TreeView_SortChildren(HWND htree, HTREEITEM hitem, BOOL recurse)`
c	BOOL	`TreeView_SortChildrenCB(HWND htree, LPTV_SORTCB posrt, BOOL recurse)`
w	int	`UnionRgn(HRGN Result, HRGN hrgnA, HRGN hrgnB)`
w	int	`XorRgn(HRGN Result, HRGN hrgnA, HRGN hrgnB)`

The `tchar.h` File

The file `tchar.h` contains a set of definitions that makes it possible to compile a common source file for both Unicode (if the _UNICODE symbol is defined) or ANSI (if the _UNICODE symbol is not defined). In Table C.2, the column labeled "Unicode/ANSI version" lists symbols defined in `tchar.h`. The function generates an ANSI version if the _UNICODE symbol is not defined and a wide-character version if the _UNICODE symbol is defined. Table C.3, which starts on page 1332, was created by copying the definitions from `tchar.h` and sorting them.

Microsoft has not been consistent in its naming convention. To get the Unicode version of the Windows API, you must define the UNICODE symbol before including `windows.h`. To get the Unicode version of `tchar.h`, you must define the _UNICODE symbol before including `tchar.h`. Generally, for Unicode support, you should define both the UNICODE and _UNICODE symbols.

Table C.2: Win16-to-Win32 mappings

Win16 C Function	Win32 C Function	Wide-character Version	Unicode/ANSI Version	Win32 API Function
access	access	_waccess	_taccess	
asctime	asctime	_wasctime	_tasctime	
atoi	atoi	_wtoi	_ttoi	
atol	atol	_wtol	_ttol	
char	char	wchar_t	TCHAR	
_chdir	_chdir	_wchdir	_tchdir	SetCurrentDirectory[U]
_chmod	_chmod	_wchmod	_tchmod	
_creat	_creat	_wcreat	_tcreat	CreateFile[U]
_environ	_environ	_wenviron	_tenviron	
EOF	EOF	WEOF	TEOF	
_execl	_execl	_wexecl	_texecl	
_execle	_execle	_wexecle	_texecle	
_execlp	_execlp	_wexeclp	_texeclp	
_execlpe	_execlpe	_wexeclpe	_texeclpe	
_execv	_execv	_wexecv	_texecv	CreateProcess[U]
_execve	_execve	_wexecve	_texecve	
_execvp	_execvp	_wexecvp	_texecvp	
_execvpe	_execvpe	_wexecvpe	_texecvpe	
fdopen	fdopen	_wfdopen	_tfdopen	
_ffree	free			HeapFree
fgetc	fgetc	fgetwc	_fgettc	
_fgetchar	_fgetchar	_fgetwchar	_fgettchar	
fgets	fgets	fgetws	_fgetts	
_finddata_t	_finddata_t	_wfinddata_t	_tfinddata_t	
_findfirst	_findfirst	_wfindfirst	_tfindfirst	
_findnext	_findnext	_wfindnext	_tfindnext	
_fmalloc	malloc			HeapAlloc GlobalAlloc
_fmemccpy	_memccpy			CopyMemory MoveMemory
_fmemchr	memchr			
_fmemcmp	memcmp			

[U]Function properly handles Unicode strings when the application is compiled for Unicode. Locale is dynamic based on user-selected locale.

[1]lstrcpyn is not quite like strncpy or wcsncpy in that lstrcpyn always appends a NUL character to the destination.

[2]These functions can use only the locale for which they were compiled. Do not take advantage of dynamic locale of Windows.

[3]These names are not typographical errors; they really are _wctime (not _wcstime) and _tctime (not _tcstime).

[4]Allows addition specification of security attributes.

Table C.2: Win16-to-Win32 mappings

Win16 C Function	Win32 C Function	Wide-character Version	Unicode/ANSI Version	Win32 API Function
_fmemcpy	memcpy			CopyMemory
_fmemicmp	_memicmp			
_fmemmove	memmove			MoveMemory
_fmemset	memset			FillMemory ZeroMemory
_fmsize	_msize			
fopen	fopen	_wfopen	_tfopen	OpenFile
fputc	fputc	fputwc	_fputtc	
_fputchar	_fputchar	_fputwchar	_fputtchar	Write
fputs	fputs	_fputws	_fputts	
_frealloc	realloc			HeapRealloc GlobalReAlloc
freopen	freopen	_wfreopen	_tfreopen	
_fsopen	_fsopen	_wfsopen	_tfsopen	
_fstrcat	strcat	wcscat	_tcscat	lstrcat[U]
_fstrchr	strchr	wcschr	_tcschr	
_fstrcmp[2]	strcmp[2]	wcscmp[2]	_tcscmp[2]	lstrcmp[U]
		wcscoll	_tcscoll	
_fstrcpy	strcpy	wcscpy	_tcscpy	lstrcpy[U]
_fstrcspn	strcspn	wcscspn	_tcscspn	
_fstrdup	_strdup	_wcsdup	_tcsdup	
_fstricmp[2]	_stricmp[2]	_wcsicmp[2]	_tcsicmp[2]	lstrcmpi[U]
		_wcsicoll	_tcsicoll	
_fstrlen	strlen	wcslen	_tcslen	lstrlen[U]
_fstrlwr[2]	_strlwr[2]	_wcslwr[2]	_tcslwr[2]	CharLowerBuff[U]
_fstrncat	strncat	wcsncat	_tcsncat	
_fstrncmp	strncmp	wcsncmp	_tcsncmp	
	_strnicmp	_wcsnicmp	_tcsncicmp	
_fstrncpy	strncpy	wcsncpy	_tcsncpy	lstrcpyn[U,1]
_fstrnicmp	_strnicmp	_wcsnicmp	_tcsnicmp	

[U]Function properly handles Unicode strings when the application is compiled for Unicode. Locale is dynamic based on user-selected locale.

[1]lstrcpyn is not quite like strncpy or wcsncpy in that lstrcpyn always appends a NUL character to the destination.

[2]These functions can use only the locale for which they were compiled. Do not take advantage of dynamic locale of Windows.

[3]These names are not typographical errors; they really are _wctime (not _wcstime) and _tctime (not _tcstime).

[4]Allows addition specification of security attributes.

Table C.2: Win16-to-Win32 mappings

Win16 C Function	Win32 C Function	Wide-character Version	Unicode/ANSI Version	Win32 API Function
_fstrnset	_strnset	wcsnset	_tcsnset	
_fstrpbrk	strpbrk	wcspbrk	_tcspbrk	
_fstrrchr	strrchr	wcsrchr	_tcsrchr	
_fstrrev	_strrev	_wcsrev	_tcsrev	
_fstrset	_strset	_wcsset	_tcsset	
_fstrspn	strspn	wcsspn	_tcsspn	
_fstrstr	strstr	wcsstr	_tcsstr	
_fstrtok	strtok	wcstok	_tcstok	
_fstrupr[2]	_strupr[2]	_wcsupr[2]	_tcsupr[2]	CharUpperBuf[U]
fprintf	fprintf	fwprintf	_ftprintf	
fscanf	fscanf	fwscanf	_ftscanf	
_fullpath	_fullpath	_wfullpath	_tfullpath	
getc	getc	getwc	_gettc	Read
getchar	getchar	getwchar	_gettchar	
_getcwd	_getcwd	_wgetcwd	_tgetcwd	GetCurrentDirectory[U]
_getdcwd	_getdcwd	_getdcwd	_tgetdcwd	GetCurrentDirectory[U]
getenv	getenv	_wgetenv	_tgetenv	
gets	gets	_getws	_getts	Read
hmemcpy	memcpy			CopyMemory MoveMemory
isalnum[2]	isalnum[2]	iswalnum[2]	_istalnum[2]	IsCharAlphaNumeric[U]
isalpha[2]	isalpha[2]	iswalpha[2]	_istalpha[2]	IsCharAlpha[U]
isascii[2]	isascii[2]	iswascii[2]	_istascii[2]	
iscntrl	iscntrl	iswcntrl	_istcntrl	
isdigit[2]	isdigit[2]	iswdigit[2]	_istdigit[2]	
isgraph[2]	isgraph[2]	iswgraph[2]	_istgraph	
islower[2]	islower[2]	iswlower[2]	_istlower[2]	IsCharLower[U]
isprint	isprint	iswprint	_istprint	
ispunct[2]	ispunct[2]	iswpunct[2]	_istpunct[2]	
isspace	isspace	iswspace	_istspace	

[U]Function properly handles Unicode strings when the application is compiled for Unicode. Locale is dynamic based on user-selected locale.

[1]lstrcpyn is not quite like strncpy or wcsncpy in that lstrcpyn always appends a NUL character to the destination.

[2]These functions can use only the locale for which they were compiled. Do not take advantage of dynamic locale of Windows.

[3]These names are not typographical errors; they really are _wctime (not _wcstime) and _tctime (not _tcstime).

[4]Allows addition specification of security attributes.

Table C.2: Win16-to-Win32 mappings

Win16 C Function	Win32 C Function	Wide-character Version	Unicode/ANSI Version	Win32 API Function
isupper[2]	isupper[2]	iswupper[2]	_istupper[2]	IsCharUpper[U]
isxdigit[2]	isxdigit[2]	iswxdigit[2]	_istxdigit[2]	
_itoa	_itoa	_itow	_itot	
_ltoa	_ltoa	_ltow	_ltot	
main	main	wmain	_tmain	
_makepath	_makepath	_wmakepath	_tmakepath	
_mkdir	_mkdir	_wmkdir	_tmkdir	CreateDirectory[4]
_ncalloc	calloc			HeapAlloc GlobalAlloc
_nexpand	_expand			
_nfree	free			HeapFree GlobalFree
_nmalloc	malloc			HeapAlloc GlobalAlloc
_nmsize	_msize			
_nrealloc	realloc			HeapRealloc GlobalReAlloc
_nstrdup	_strdup	_wcsdup	_tcsdup	
open	open	_wopen	_topen	OpenFile[U] CreateFile[U]
perror	perror	_wperror	_tperror	FormatMessage[U]
printf	printf	wprintf	_tprintf	
putc	putc	putwc	_puttc	Write
_putchar	_putchar	putwchar	_puttchar	
_putenv	_putenv	_wputenv	_tputenv	
puts	puts	_putws	_putts	Write
remove	remove	_wremove	_tremove	DeleteFile[U]
rename	rename	_wrename	_trename	MoveFile[U] MoveFileEx[U]
_rmdir	_rmdir	_wrmdir	_trmdir	DeleteFile[U]
scanf	scanf	wscanf	_tscanf	
setlocale	setlocale	_wsetlocale	_tsetlocale	

[U]Function properly handles Unicode strings when the application is compiled for Unicode. Locale is dynamic based on user-selected locale.

[1]lstrcpyn is not quite like strncpy or wcsncpy in that lstrcpyn always appends a NUL character to the destination.

[2]These functions can use only the locale for which they were compiled. Do not take advantage of dynamic locale of Windows.

[3]These names are not typographical errors; they really are _wctime (not _wcstime) and _tctime (not _tcstime).

[4]Allows addition specification of security attributes.

Table C.2: Win16-to-Win32 mappings

Win16 C Function	Win32 C Function	Wide-charac-ter Version	Unicode/ANSI Version	Win32 API Function
_snprintf	_snprintf	_snwprintf	_sntprintf	
_sopen	_sopen	_wsopen	_tsopen	OpenFile[U] CreateFile[U]
_spawnl	_spawnl	_wspawnl	_tspawnl	
_spawnle	_spawnle	_wspawnle	_tspawnle	
_spawnlp	_spawnlp	_wspawnlp	_tspawnlp	
_spawnlpe	_spawnlpe	_wspawnlpe	_tspawnlpe	CreateProcess
_spawnv	_spawnv	_wspawnv	_tspawnv	
_spawnve	_spawnve	_wspawnve	_tspawnve	
_spawnvp	_spawnvp	_wspawnvp	_tspawnvp	
_spawnvpe	_spawnvpe	_wspawnvpe	_tspawnvpe	
_splitpath	_splitpath	_wsplitpath	_tsplitpath	
sprintf	sprintf	swprintf	_stprintf	
sscanf	sscanf	swscanf	_stscanf	
_stat	_stat	_wstat	_tstat	
_stati64	_stati64	_wstati64	_tstati64	
strcat	strcat	wcscat	_tcscat	lstrcat[U]
strchr	strchr	wcschr	_tcschr	
strcmp[2]	strcmp[2]	wcscmp[2]	_tcscmp[2]	lstrcmp[U]
strcoll	strcoll	wcscoll	_tcscoll	
strcpy	strcpy	wcscpy	_tcscpy	lstrcpy[U]
strcspn	strcspn	wcscspn	_tcscspn	
_strdate	_strdate	_wstrdate	_tstrdate	
_strdec	_strdec	_wcsdec	_tcsdec	
_strdup	_strdup	_wcsdup	_tcsdup	
strftime	strftime	wcsftime	_tcsftime	
_stricmp	_stricmp	_wcsicmp	_tcsicmp	lstrcmpi[U]
_stricoll	_stricoll	_wcsicoll	_tcsicoll	
_strinc	_strinc	_wcsinc	_tcsinc	
strlen	strlen	wcslen	_tcslen	lstrlen[U]
_strlwr	_strlwr	_wcslwr	_tcslwr	CharLowerBuff[U]

[U]Function properly handles Unicode strings when the application is compiled for Unicode. Locale is dynamic based on user-selected locale.

[1]lstrcpyn is not quite like strncpy or wcsncpy in that lstrcpyn always appends a NUL character to the destination.

[2]These functions can use only the locale for which they were compiled. Do not take advantage of dynamic locale of Windows.

[3]These names are not typographical errors; they really are _wctime (not _wcstime) and _tctime (not _tcstime).

[4]Allows addition specification of security attributes.

Table C.2: Win16-to-Win32 mappings

Win16 C Function	Win32 C Function	Wide-character Version	Unicode/ANSI Version	Win32 API Function
_strncnt	_strncnt	_wcsncnt	_tcsbcnt	
strncat	strncat	wcsncat	_tcsncat	
strncmp	strncmp	wcsncmp	_tcsncmp	
_strncoll	_strncoll	_wcsncoll	_tcsncoll	
strncpy	strncpy	wcsncpy	_tcsncpy	
_strnicmp	_strnicmp	_wcsnicmp	_tcsnicmp	
_strnicoll	_strnicoll	_wcsnicoll	_tcsnicoll	
_strninc	_strnicn	_wcsninc	_tcsninc	
_strnset	_strnset	_wcsnset	_tcsnset	
_strpbrk	_strpbrk	_wcspbrk	_tcspbrk	
strrchr	strrchr	wcsrchr	_tcsrchr	
_strrev	_strrev	_wcsrev	_tcsrev	
_strset	_strset	_wcsset	_tcsset	
strspn	strspn	wcsspn	_tcsspn	
strstr	strstr	wcsstr	_tcsstr	
_strtime	_strtime	_wctime[3]	_tctime[3]	
strtod	strtod	wcstod	_tcstod	
strtok	strtok	wcstok	_tcstok	
strtol	strtol	wcstol	_tcstol	
strtoul	strtoul	wcstoul	_tcstoul	
_strupr[2]	_strupr[2]	_wcsupr[2]	_tcsupr[2]	CharUpperBuff[U]
strxfrm	strxfrm	wcsxfrm	_tcsxfrm	
system	system	_wsystem	_tsystem	CreateProcess[U] WinExec[U]
_tempnam	_tempnam	_wtempnam	_ttempnam	GetTempFileName[U]
tolower[2]	tolower[2]	towlower[2]	_totlower[2]	CharLower[U]
toupper[2]	toupper[2]	towupper[2]	_totupper[2]	CharUpper[U]
_ultoa	_ultoa	_ultow	_ultot	
ungetc	ungetc	ungetwc	_ungettc	
_unlink	_unlink	_wunlink	_tunlink	DeleteFile[U] OpenFile[U] *using* OF_DELETE

[U]Function properly handles Unicode strings when the application is compiled for Unicode. Locale is dynamic based on user-selected locale.

[1]lstrcpyn is not quite like strncpy or wcsncpy in that lstrcpyn always appends a NUL character to the destination.

[2]These functions can use only the locale for which they were compiled. Do not take advantage of dynamic locale of Windows.

[3]These names are not typographical errors; they really are _wctime (not _wcstime) and _tctime (not _tcstime).

[4]Allows addition specification of security attributes.

Table C.2: Win16-to-Win32 mappings

Win16 C Function	Win32 C Function	Wide-character Version	Unicode/ANSI Version	Win32 API Function
_utime	_utime	_wutime	_tutime	
vfprintf	vfprintf	vfwprintf	_vftprintf	
_vsnprintf	_vsnprintf	_vsnwprintf	_vsntprintf	
vsprintf	vsprintf	vswprintf	_vstprintf	
vprintf	vprintf	vwprintf	_vtprintf	
WinMain	WinMain	wWinMain	_tWinMain	

[U]Function properly handles Unicode strings when the application is compiled for Unicode. Locale is dynamic based on user-selected locale.

[1]lstrcpyn is not quite like strncpy or wcsncpy in that lstrcpyn always appends a NUL character to the destination.

[2]These functions can use only the locale for which they were compiled. Do not take advantage of dynamic locale of Windows.

[3]These names are not typographical errors; they really are _wctime (not _wcstime) and _tctime (not _tcstime).

[4]Allows addition specification of security attributes.

Table C.3: Definitions from `tchar.h`

Macro or Typedef	UNICODE Definition	ANSI Definition
__T(x)	L ## x	x
__targv	__wargv	__argv
_fgettc	fgetwc	fgetc
_fgettchar	_fgetwchar	_fgetchar
_fgetts	fgetws	fgets
_fputtc	fputwc	fputc
_fputtchar	_fputwchar	_fputchar
_fputts	fputws	fputs
_ftccmp	_tccmp	_tcsncmp
_ftcscat	_tcscat	strcat
_ftcschr	_tcschr	strchr
_ftcsclen	_tcsclen	strlen
_ftcscmp	_tcscmp	strcmp
_ftcscoll	_tcscoll	strcoll
_ftcscpy	_tcscpy	strcpy
_ftcscspn	_tcscspn	strcspn

Table C.3: Definitions from `tchar.h`

Macro or Typedef	UNICODE Definition	ANSI Definition
_ftcsdec	_tcsdec	_strdec
_ftcsdup	_tcsdup	_strdup
_ftcsicmp	_tcsicmp	_stricmp
_ftcsicoll	_tcsicoll	_stricoll
_ftcsinc	_tcsinc	_strinc
_ftcslen	_tcslen	strlen
_ftcslwr	_tcslwr	_strlwr
_ftcsnbcnt	_tcsnbcnt	_strncnt
_ftcsncat	_tcsncat	strncat
_ftcsnccat	_tcsnccat	strncat
_ftcsnccmp	_tcsnccmp	strncmp
_ftcsnccnt	_tcsnccnt	_strncnt
_ftcsnccoll	_tcsnccoll	_strncoll
_ftcsnccpy	_tcsnccpy	strncpy
_ftcsncicmp	_tcsncicmp	_strnicmp
_ftcsncicoll	_tcsncicoll	_strnicoll
_ftcsncmp	_tcsncmp	strncmp
_ftcsncoll	_tcsncoll	_strncoll
_ftcsncpy	_tcsncpy	strncpy
_ftcsncset	_tcsncset	_strnset
_ftcsnextc	_tcsnextc	_strnextc
_ftcsnicmp	_tcsnicmp	_strnicmp
_ftcsnicoll	_tcsnicoll	_strnicoll
_ftcsninc	_tcsninc	_strninc
_ftcsnset	_tcsnset	_strnset
_ftcspbrk	_tcspbrk	strpbrk
_ftcsrchr	_tcsrchr	strrchr
_ftcsrev	_tcsrev	_strrev

Table C.3: Definitions from `tchar.h`

Macro or Typedef	UNICODE Definition	ANSI Definition
_ftcsset	_tcsset	_strset
_ftcsspn	_tcsspn	strspn
_ftcsspnp	_tcsspnp	_strspnp
_ftcsstr	_tcsstr	strstr
_ftcstok	_tcstok	strtok
_ftcsupr	_tcsupr	_strupr
_ftprintf	fwprintf	fprintf
_ftscanf	fwscanf	fscanf
_gettc	getwc	getc
_gettchar	getwchar	getchar
_getts	_getws	gets
_istalnum	iswalnum	isalnum
_istalpha	iswalpha	isalpha
_istascii	iswascii	isascii
_istcntrl	iswcntrl	iscntrl
_istdigit	iswdigit	isdigit
_istgraph	iswgraph	isgraph
_istlead(_c)	(0)	(0)
_istleadbyte(_c)	(0)	(0)
_istlegal(_c)	(1)	(1)
_istlower	iswlower	islower
_istprint	iswprint	isprint
_istpunct	iswpunct	ispunct
_istspace	iswspace	isspace
_istupper	iswupper	isupper
_istxdigit	iswxdigit	isxdigit
_itot	_itow	_itoa
_ltot	_ltow	_ltoa

Table C.3: Definitions from `tchar.h`

Macro or Typedef	UNICODE Definition	ANSI Definition
_puttc	putwc	putc
_puttchar	putwchar	_putchar
_putts	_putws	puts
_sntprintf	_snwprintf	_snprintf
_stprintf	swprintf	sprintf
_stscanf	swscanf	sscanf
_T(x)	__T(x)	__T(x)
_taccess	_waccess	access
_tasctime	_wasctime	asctime
_TCHAR	wchar_t	char
TCHAR	wchar_t	char
_tchdir	_wchdir	_chdir
_tchmod	_wchmod	_chmod
_tcreat	_wcreat	_creat
_tcscat	wcscat	strcat
_tcschr	wcschr	strchr
_tcsclen	wcslen	strlen
_tcscmp	wcscmp	strcmp
_tcscoll	wcscoll	strcoll
_tcscpy	wcscpy	strcpy
_tcscspn	wcscspn	strcspn
_tcsdec	_wcsdec	_strdec
_tcsdup	_wcsdup	_strdup
_tcsftime	wcsftime	strftime
_tcsicmp	_wcsicmp	_stricmp
_tcsicoll	_wcsicoll	_stricoll
_tcsinc	_wcsinc	_strinc
_tcslen	wcslen	strlen

Table C.3: Definitions from `tchar.h`

Macro or Typedef	UNICODE Definition	ANSI Definition
_tcslwr	_wcslwr	_strlwr
_tcsnbcnt	_wcsncnt	_strncnt
_tcsncat	wcsncat	strncat
_tcsnccat	wcsncat	strncat
_tcsnccmp	wcsncmp	strncmp
_tcsnccnt	_wcsncnt	_strncnt
_tcsnccoll	_wcsncoll	_strncoll
_tcsnccpy	wcsncpy	strncpy
_tcsncicmp	_wcsnicmp	_strnicmp
_tcsncicoll	_wcsnicoll	_strnicoll
_tcsncmp	wcsncmp	strncmp
_tcsncoll	_wcsncoll	_strncoll
_tcsncpy	wcsncpy	strncpy
_tcsncset	_wcsnset	_strnset
_tcsnextc	_wcsnextc	_strnextc
_tcsnicmp	_wcsnicmp	_strnicmp
_tcsnicoll	_wcsnicoll	_strnicoll
_tcsninc	_wcsninc	_strninc
_tcsnset	_wcsnset	_strnset
_tcspbrk	wcspbrk	_strpbrk
_tcsrchr	wcsrchr	strrchr
_tcsrev	_wcsrev	_strrev
_tcsset	_wcsset	_strset
_tcsspn	wcsspn	strspn
_tcsspnp	_wcsspnp	_strspnp
_tcsstr	wcsstr	strstr
_tcstod	wcstod	strtod
_tcstok	wcstok	strtok

Table C.3: Definitions from `tchar.h`

Macro or Typedef	UNICODE Definition	ANSI Definition
_tcstol	wcstol	strtol
_tcstoul	wcstoul	strtoul
_tcsupr	_wcsupr	_strupr
_tcsxfrm	wcsxfrm	strxfrm
_tctime	_wctime	_strtime
_tenviron	_wenviron	_environ
_TEOF	WEOF	EOF
_texecl	_wexecl	_execl
_texecle	_wexecle	_execle
_texeclp	_wexeclp	_execlp
_texeclpe	_wexeclpe	_execlpe
_texecv	_wexecv	_execv
_texecve	_wexecve	_execve
_texecvp	_wexecvp	_execvp
_texecvpe	_wexecvpe	_execvpe
_TEXT(x)	__T(x)	__T(x)
_tfdopen	_wfdopen	fdopen
_tfinddata_t	_wfinddata_t	_finddata_t
_tfinddatai64_t	_wfinddatai64_t	_finddatai64_t
_tfindfirst	_wfindfirst	_findfirst
_tfindfirsti64	_wfindfirsti64	_findfirsti64
_tfindnext	_wfindnext	_findnext
_tfindnexti64	_wfindnexti64	_findnexti64
_tfopen	_wfopen	fopen
_tfreopen	_wfreopen	freopen
_tfsopen	_wfsopen	_fsopen
_tfullpath	_wfullpath	_fullpath
_tgetcwd	_wgetcwd	_getcwd

Table C.3: Definitions from `tchar.h`

Macro or Typedef	UNICODE Definition	ANSI Definition
_tgetdcwd	_wgetdcwd	_getdcwd
_tgetenv	_wgetenv	getenv
_TINT	wint_t	wint_t
_TINT	wint_t	wint_t
_tmain	wmain	main
_tmakepath	_wmakepath	_makepath
_tmkdir	_wmkdir	_mkdir
_tmktemp	_wmktemp	_mktemp
_topen	_wopen	open
_totlower	towlower	tolower
_totupper	towupper	toupper
_tperror	_wperror	perror
_tpopen	_wpopen	_popen
_tprintf	wprintf	printf
_tputenv	_wputenv	_putenv
_tremove	_wremove	remove
_trename	_wrename	rename
_trmdir	_wrmdir	_rmdir
_tscanf	wscanf	scanf
_TSCHAR	wchar_t	signed char
_tsearchenv	_wsearchenv	_searchenv
_tsetlocale	_wsetlocale	setlocale
_tsopen	_wsopen	_sopen
_tspawnl	_wspawnl	_spawnl
_tspawnle	_wspawnle	_spawnle
_tspawnlp	_wspawnlp	_spawnlp
_tspawnlpe	_wspawnlpe	_spawnlpe
_tspawnv	_wspawnv	_spawnv

Table C.3: Definitions from `tchar.h`

Macro or Typedef	UNICODE Definition	ANSI Definition
_tspawnve	_wspawnve	_spawnve
_tspawnvp	_wspawnvp	_spawnvp
_tspawnvpe	_wspawnvpe	_spawnvpe
_tsplitpath	_wsplitpath	_splitpath
_tstat	_wstat	_stat
_tstati64	_wstati64	_stati64
_tstrdate	_wstrdate	_strdate
_tstrtime	_wstrtime	_strtime
_tsystem	_wsystem	system
_ttempnam	_wtempnam	_tempnam
_ttmpnam	_wtmpnam	tmpnam
_ttoi	_wtoi	atoi
_ttol	_wtol	atol
_TUCHAR	wchar_t	unsigned char
_tunlink	_wunlink	_unlink
_tutime	_wutime	_utime
_tWinMain	wWinMain	WinMain
_TXCHAR	wchar_t	unsigned char
_ultot	_ultow	_ultoa
_ungettc	ungetwc	ungetc
_vftprintf	vfwprintf	vfprintf
_vsntprintf	_vsnwprintf	_vsnprintf
_vstprintf	vswprintf	vsprintf
_vtprintf	vwprintf	vprintf
wctype_t	wchar_t	wchar_t
wint_t	wchar_t	wchar_t

D Using #pragma(warning)

This collection of #pragma statements represents a nice collection of declarations that make the C and C++ languages quite conservative. These work with the Microsoft C compilers. They represent one programmer's opinion (*jmn*) of a more suitable level of warning and error levels than the default set.

```
//{{NO_DEPENDENCIES}}
/* Custom error level stuff */
#pragma warning(error:4002) /* too many actual parameters to macro */
#pragma warning(error:4003) /* too few actual parameters to macro */
#pragma warning(1:4010)     /* single-line comment ends with \ */
#pragma warning(error:4013) /* missing prototype */
#pragma warning(1:4016)     /* no function return type */
#pragma warning(error:4020) /* too many actual parameters */
#pragma warning(error:4021) /* too few actual parameters */
#pragma warning(error:4027) /* function declared w/o formal parameter list*/
#pragma warning(error:4029) /* declared formal list different from defn */
#pragma warning(error:4035) /* no return value */
#pragma warning(error:4033) /* 'return;' in value-returning proc */
#pragma warning(error:4045) /* array bounds overflow */
#pragma warning(error:4047) /* different levels of indirection */
#pragma warning(error:4049) /* indirection to different types */
#pragma warning(error:4053) /* one void operand for ?: */
#pragma warning(error:4071) /* no function prototype given */
#pragma warning(disable:4101) /* unreferenced local variable */
#pragma warning(error:4150) /*   deletion of pointer to incomplete type '...';
                                 no destructor called */
#pragma warning(error:4211)   /* nonstandard extension used : redefined extern
                                 to static */
#pragma warning(1:4306)       /* conversion from <integer type> to <pointer type>
                                 of greater size */
```

The //{{NO_DEPENDENCIES}} line at the start is Microsoft-specific and tells the development environment that changes in this file should not force a recompilation of the files that include it.

Index

It's not often you run across an index with instructions on how to use it. But this index is exceptional, if for no other reason than its thickness. To make an index this large useful, some conventions had to be established. The basic conventions are:

- Any name which is a Windows API name and appears with a page number at the top level represents the description of this name in a summary table.

- The key phrase "discussion" as a sub-topic indicates a discussion in the text which explains something about the name.

- The key phrase "example" as a sub-topic indicates a code example, either in-line in the text or as part of one of the example programs.

- The key phrase "illustrated" as a sub-topic indicates an illustration, usually a screen snapshot.

- The key phrase "defined" as a sub-topic indicates an actual definition. This could be a `typedef` declaration, a `#define`, a function prototype, or other suitable form of definition.

The running head at the top of each page tells the first and last entry on the page.